SAHIH AL-BUKHARI,
ENGLISH TRANSLATION AND
EXPLANATORY NOTES

Sahih al-Bukhari

English Translation and Explanatory Notes

Based on

Faḍl al-Bārī

by Maulana Muhammad Ali

Volume 1:

Books 1 – 33 of Sahih al-Bukhari

Covering the fundamentals of Islam

Rendered into English by

Maulana Aftab-ud-Din Ahmad

and

Dr Zahid Aziz

Ahmadiyya Anjuman Lahore Publications, U.K.

2019

A Lahore Ahmadiyya Publication

Part 1 (Books 1–4), 1956
Part 2 (Books 5–8), 1962
Part 3 (Books 9–10), 1973
Parts 4–7 (Books 11–33), *online only,* 2016–2018
Parts 1–3 (Books 1–10) revised, *online only,* June 2019
First print edition of Parts 1–7 (Books 1–33), October 2019

This printing, July 2022

Copyright © 2019 by Ahmadiyya Anjuman Lahore Foundation

Darus Salaam, 15 Stanley Avenue, Wembley, U.K., HA0 4JQ

Websites: www.aaiil.org
            www.ahmadiyya.org

e-mails: aaiil.uk@gmail.com
            info@ahmadiyya.org

This book is available on the Internet at:
www.ahmadiyya.org/islam/bukhari

ISBN: 978-1-906109-67-7

Preface

The work *Faḍl al-Bārī* is an Urdu translation of *Ṣaḥīḥ al-Bukhārī* with extensive explanatory notes by Maulana Muhammad Ali (d. 1951). Its first volume, consisting of nearly the first half of Bukhari, was published in 1932. The same contents had been appearing in the form of instalments of about 100 pages long, starting in 1926. The remainder was published all together as the second volume in 1937. A newly-typeset edition of the entire Urdu work was published in 2012, again in two volumes, by the Ahmadiyya Anjuman Isha'at Islam Lahore, based in Dublin, Ohio, U.S.A.

Maulana Muhammad Ali started an English translation of this enormous work near the end of his life. He had only reached as far as Book 2, ch. 21, when he passed the manuscript to Maulana Aftab-ud-Din Ahmad, then editor of *The Light*,[1] to continue the translation. He took it up with great devotion, but after completing the first three Parts and some of the fourth Part,[2] he died in 1956. Parts 1 to 3 were published in 1956, 1962 and 1973 respectively.

In the mid-1970s Mr Iqbal Ahmad, elder son of Maulana Aftab-ud-Din Ahmad, who had served in the Woking Muslim Mission in the 1950s, revised the partial translation of Part 4 done by his father. This was serialised in *The Light* of Lahore, the organ of the Ahmadiyya Anjuman Lahore, from its issue dated June 8, 1983 to its issue dated February 8, 1985.

In 2015 Mr Nasir Ahmad, also son of Maulana Aftab-ud-Din Ahmad, and a veteran of the Ahmadiyya Anjuman Lahore in its propagation and literary work, proposed that the translation should be continued. The first step was to complete the remaining translation of Part 4. This was done by me in collaboration with Mr Nasir Ahmad. The portion of Part 4 that was previously translated was also revised for consistency with the new translation.

Following that, Parts 5, 6 and 7 were completed by the collaborative work of myself, Mr Nasir Ahmad, and others. He and his helpers prepared the draft, which I then thoroughly checked, revised and finalised. In fact, we have

---

[1] For more about Maulana Aftab-ud-Din Ahmad, see *Editor's Note* on p. xi.

[2] This is up to the end of Book 13, *The Two Eid Festivals.* For the meaning of 'Parts' of Bukhari, see the footnote under 'General Contents' on p. v.

included the first two short books of Part 8, so that our translation covers Sahih Bukhari up to the point where it finishes dealing with the five fundamentals of Islam.

Then we took up the revision of the existing published translations of Parts 1 to 3. The introductory material within Part 1 of that edition was also revised for our new edition. Some extracts from Maulana Muhammad Ali's preface to the original Urdu work have also been added in this new edition.

As Parts 4 to 7 and then Parts 1 to 3 were completed, these were published online between January 2016 and June 2019, but revisions still continued to be made in these Parts. Now that the entire work is considered as finalized in October 2019, it is being printed all together in the proper order.

Principles of work, sources and acknowledgements

It is essential to mention here briefly the nature of our work in this translation and the sources used. The 2012 newly-typeset edition of *Faḍl al-Bārī* greatly facilitated our translation because of its clear layout, modern formatting and easy readability. It also uses the system of numbering the reports in Bukhari that is in commonly accepted use now, and we have adopted the same in this translation.

In translating the text of Bukhari, we have not merely relied on Maulana Muhammad Ali's Urdu work, but also kept in view other published translations of Bukhari in Urdu as well as the well-known English translation by Dr Muhammad Muhsin Khan. Of course, for Parts 1 to 3, and some of Part 4, we already had the great advantage of our own English translation by Maulana Aftab-ud-Din Ahmad. I must pay tribute here to his excellent, accurate and idiomatic translation. The revisions we made to his translation are mainly for reasons of consistency, and not due to any shortcoming in his work.

We have also carefully checked our translation, word for word, with the original Arabic text of Bukhari.

An Urdu translation and commentary of Bukhari which we found most useful in clarifying many points of interpretation is that of Maulana Muhammad Dawud Raz.[3] Occasionally, we consulted other Urdu translations and commentaries of Bukhari for clarifying particular points. We must also express our gratitude to the maintainers of the *www.sunnah.com* website which provides the English translation of Bukhari by Dr Muhsin Khan, as well as English translations of several other Hadith collections, in a conveniently

---

[3] Published in 2004 by the *Markazi Jami'at Ahl Hadith* of India.

accessible form. Its search feature to find Hadith reports by the text they contain, in the original Arabic or in English translation, has been a vital tool for us.

Sahih Bukhari contains 7563 hadith reports, but of these some 2450 may be considered as distinct, while the others may be called their repetitions in one form or another. Repetitions of the same report very often occur in different books and chapters because Bukhari applies them to different situations, and he also makes inferences based on the variations between the repetitions of the same hadith.

The repetitions, indispensable though they are, make Sahih Bukhari a very voluminous tome. Facing this difficulty, Maulana Muhammad Ali, as he himself explains in the preface to his Urdu translation, did not reproduce the repetitions in the main translation, but instead he added a footnote at such points in which he quoted either the entire or just the differing parts of the repetition, commented on the differences, and referred the reader to the hadith whose repetition this was. In the English translation of the Parts done by Maulana Aftab-ud-Din Ahmad, naturally the same scheme is followed.[4] However, in most cases this makes it quite burdensome for the reader to visualise the repetition as a complete hadith.

Therefore, we decided that in most cases a repetition should be given in the main translation like any other report, and its points of difference with the original hadith be highlighted in footnotes as Maulana Muhammad Ali had done. Still there were some cases in which it was easier for readability to give only a part of a repetition in the main text and omit the rest. At such places, ellipses (…) is used to indicate omission and a footnote is provided which refers the reader to another report in which the omitted translation can be found. It may be added that in our times, with the rise of digital documents and online publishing, we do not face the same restrictions of space that Maulana Muhammad Ali did in the days when paper itself was not always easy to obtain.

As regards the explanatory footnotes of Maulana Muhammad Ali, we have made a few small additions in them, here and there, and in a few instances we have summarised a lengthy discussion. In the Parts translated by Maulana Aftab-ud-Din Ahmad, he had already added useful brief comments

---

[4] In the original Urdu edition the texts from the repetitions, given in the footnotes, are generally quoted only in Arabic, without translation. In the 2012 edition of *Faḍl al-Bārī*, mentioned earlier, the Urdu translations have been added. In Maulana Aftab-ud-Din Ahmad's translation these texts had been rendered into English.

of his own in some places while translating the footnotes, and we have mostly retained these.

The original footnotes of Maulana Muhammad Ali contain references to other collections of Hadith, citing only the name of the collection, such as Sahih Muslim, without providing the location within the book. In the 2012 edition of the Urdu work, the compilers have in many cases added the chapter name and hadith number, or volume and page, of the reference concerned. In this translation I have filled in many more such references, so that these are now complete except in a few cases.

Before closing this Preface, I must acknowledge that the drive and impetus for continuing the English translation of Sahih Bukhari came from Mr Nasir Ahmad. He continuously urged the completion of this work and provided all necessary help and support, without which this new translation would not have been possible.

Zahid Aziz, Dr.
October 2019

General Contents

---

* (1) The collection of Bukhārī has, like the Holy Qur'ān, been divided into 30 roughly equal parts, irrespective of subject-matter. In terms of subject-matter, it is divided into books, each book being known as a *kitāb*, which are of greatly varying lengths, and each book is divided into chapters, each chapter known as a *bāb*.

(2) In the numbering of the books and chapters of Bukhārī, small variations are to be found in different publications. This arises because, in certain cases, what some consider to be one book, others divide the same into two books. For example, Book 8 of this translation is divided into Books 8 and 9 in some other publications. This can occur with chapters within a book as well. In book 10, for example, ch. 162 of this translation is divided into chs. 162 and 163 by some others.

From the Preface to *Faḍl al-Bārī*

Among the works of the service of Islām which I had in mind, after completing the translations of the Holy Qur'ān and its commentary in English and Urdu, was the translation of *Ṣaḥīḥ al-Bukhārī* with explanatory notes. A most substantial amount of material relating to the religion of Islām, the life of the Holy Prophet Muḥammad, and the history of early Islām, is to be found in books of Ḥadīth, and Bukhārī holds the highest rank of all among these collections. Due to my various other engagements this work kept being postponed. However, in the meantime, I had the opportunity to write a booklet on the compilation of Ḥadīth, with the object of removing misconceptions about this literature as well as clarifying the true position of Ḥadīth. It therefore refutes the extreme views held by some Islamic groups which either give Ḥadīth a place even above the Qur'ān or reject it altogether. This book was published under the title *Maqām-i Ḥadīth* and can serve as an introduction for a translation of Bukhārī, or indeed any other Ḥadīth collection. Topics discussed in it include the position of Ḥadīth in Islām, reliability of its reports, and the status of Bukhārī among the collections of Ḥadīth.

In this translation I have included also those reports from Bukhārī which have a break or missing link in the line of narrators (reports known as *maqṭū'* or *mu'allaq*) as well as the sayings and comments of the Companions of the Holy Prophet and authorities of the next generation. These are omitted by some translators, but their inclusion gives access to the reader to all reports that Bukhārī has presented in his collection. However, as regards the *isnād,* the lists of names of the narrators in the chain which appear preceding each report, I have omitted these, except for the name of the first narrator, most often a Companions of the Holy Prophet, as the full lists are of no benefit to the ordinary reader.

As to the footnotes, the explanations I have provided in them are based on the principles which I have set down in my booklet *Maqām-i Ḥadīth.* If I found a report to contradict the Holy Qur'ān, I have tried to interpret it in a sense which makes it accord with the Qur'ān. Where it proved impossible to find such an interpretation, I have rejected the report in whole or in part, as necessary. If a report could be interpreted in more than one way, I have given preference to the sense which makes it accord with human experience or

accepted history. In case of reports which clash with each other, I have accepted that view which is supported by the majority of reports or by the stronger evidence. In writing these notes I have borne in mind allegations of the critics of Islam as well as the doubts and objections raised in our present times due to modern thought.

I have to confess my handicap that I lack a sufficiently broad knowledge of the field of Ḥadīth. Most of all, I regret that, for the translation of Bukhārī, I could not benefit from the vast and detailed knowledge of the learned Maulana Nur-ud-Din, as I had done in case of translating the Holy Qur'ān. This regret was expressed by the Maulana himself in the last days of his life when he said to me: "The Qur'ān has been done, but Bukhārī remains." I must also mention here that this shortcoming of mine has to some extent been removed by the participation of Maulana Ahmad in this work, who shared with me the task of writing the footnotes. I also received much help from Maulana Abdus Sattar.

Muhammad Ali
Dalhousie (India)
8 June 1926

Introduction to the
First English Edition

In presenting this translation of the great work of Ḥadīth, the *Ṣaḥīḥ al-Bukhārī*, to the English-speaking world, I am doing no more service than fulfilling practically a dying wish of the late Maulana Muhammad Ali, to whom I owe so much in my humble knowledge of Islām. Not only the instructions for the work as a whole, but also the bulk of knowledge contained in these pages is the gift of the Maulana. The translation of the text here presented is mostly my own responsibility, but the commentary is mainly from the Urdu work of the Maulana, *Faḍl al-Bārī*.

The necessity of a work like the present one arises from the fact that being more or less conversant now with the contents of the Qur'ān, as a result of a number of translations having seen the light of day, inquisitive minds are eager to know the authentic history of the person who gave this wonderful Book to the world. This consideration aside, there is also the fact that Islām is pre-eminently a religion of practice, not a religion of principles and ideas alone, and practice requires demonstration. None could be a better demonstrator than the man who received this religion from on High, and whose heart was illumined by a direct impact of the Source of all knowledge. Rightly, therefore, Muslim saints, savants, theologians and jurists united in regarding the *Sunnah*, i.e., the practice of the Prophet Muḥammad, as the secondary source of the teachings and the law of Islām, after the Qur'ān.

Unlike other religions, Islām is a religion of one authoritative man, responsible for the whole code of the law and its application to all the various aspects of life. Every word, deed and hint of the Holy Prophet was taken, and instructed to be taken, as interpreting, explaining or demonstrating these laws. No corner of his life was in that way private. Any other human would have been offended in a few days at being observed so closely. Even his wives viewed him in their most private moments as not merely a marital partner but a moral exemplar, and they saw all his deeds and actions in the light of Quranic principles.

The need for the *Sunnah* having been established, the questions that now arises are: where can it be found, and why was it not, as with the Qur'ān, recorded contemporaneously? The fact is that the *Sunnah* was a way of life, meant to be copied in action, not on paper. The *Sunnah* of the Holy Prophet was naturally to be found in the lives of those thousands of disciples who would avidly copy his example, even in the smallest matters. This is why no systematic effort was made to codify these actions of the Holy Prophet during his life and even for some time after his death. The case of the Qur'ān was different. It was a body of arguments, enunciations, precepts and laws of life. Its best place was on paper or the memories of men, and it was preserved accordingly. The *Sunnah,* on the other hand, was preserved in the lives and habits of the believers. Some of the Holy Prophet's exhortations were recorded in writing at the time but this was rather infrequent.

It may be noted that historicity is the very starting point of the truth of a religion. To investigate its truth, the life and personality of the man to whom it was revealed must necessarily form the basis of the enquiry. The historical tests and documentary evidences about the existence of the Prophet Muḥammad and his everyday life are numerous and in abundance, more so than any other human being. For this unique documentary evidence, we are indebted to the Collectors of Ḥadīth. They have achieved a historical accuracy which is unparalleled among all records of the life story of the Founder of a religion, and beyond which human resources cannot go. These saintly chroniclers have given the names of the links in the chain of narrators of each report. They have retained certain inaccuracies because of their unapproachable sincerity. *Ṣaḥīḥ al-Bukhārī,* the most careful of these illustrious collections, has been called "the most correct of books after the Book of Allāh." This is a statement without the least exaggeration in it.

In view of the various doubts that have been aroused in the minds of many people by numerous adverse criticisms of Ḥadīth, the present publication has become all the more necessary. Instead of speculative criticism that has been going on, it will be more useful to read the Ḥadīth itself and then see how much truth there is in the criticism. Let the world know what this much-discussed literature contains before it can be in a position to rightly evaluate the observations, adverse or favourable, about Ḥadīth.

AFTAB-UD-DIN AHMAD
Ahmadiyya Buildings,
Lahore-7, Pakistan
January 12, 1956.

Editor's Note:

The above Introduction by Maulana Aftab-ud-Din Ahmad has been revised from the original which appeared in the 1956 edition. The Maulana died on 13 January 1956 in Lahore.

Born in Burdwan, West Bengal in 1901, Maulana Aftab-ud-Din Ahmad obtained a degree, with distinction in English, from Presidency College, Calcutta in 1923. He followed this up by studying Islam and Arabic at the famous religious seminary of Deoband near Delhi for almost two years. Shortly after this, being attracted towards the Lahore Ahmadiyya Movement, he became a missionary, author and scholar of the Movement for the rest of his life.

During the 1930s he served in England, first as deputy Imam and then as Imam of the world-famous Shah Jahan Mosque at Woking, Surrey, and the Woking Muslim Mission. Later in Lahore in 1939 he became editor of *The Islamic Review,* the monthly journal of the Woking Muslim mission.

In 1950 he was appointed as editor of *The Light,* the English weekly organ of the Lahore Ahmadiyya Movement published from Lahore, and served in this capacity till his death, while also engaged in translating Sahih Bukhari into English during this time. He also translated the well-known Sufi work *Futūh al-Ghaib,* by Hazrat Shaikh Abdul Qadir Jilani, into English.

The Qur'ān and Ḥadīth

As is well known, there are two sources from which all the principles and precepts of Islām are derived: the Holy Qur'ān and the Ḥadīth. The Qur'ān is a collection of revelations vouchsafed by God to the Prophet Muḥammad (may peace and the blessings of God be upon him) and it is the Book of God. The Ḥadīth, using the word in its broader sense, is a collection of the Sayings of the Holy Prophet and of reports about his actions and behaviour. Strictly speaking, it is the former, i.e. the Sayings, which is Ḥadīth, while the term for the latter is *Sunnah.*

Of the two sources, the Qur'ān is obviously more important. The Ḥadīth is subordinate to the Qur'ān, and no reported saying or action of the Holy Prophet in the Ḥadīth is to be accepted as authentic and authoritative which is not in conformity with the letter and spirit of the Qur'ān. However, the importance of the Ḥadīth as the secondary source of Islām is emphasized by the Qur'ān itself. It is written:

> "Certainly Allāh conferred a favour on the believers when He raised among them a Messenger from among themselves, reciting to them His messages and purifying them, and teaching them the Book and the Wisdom, although before that they were surely in manifest error." (3:164)

From this verse of the Holy Qur'ān it is clear that the Holy Prophet Muḥammad had come to this world as God's Messenger with a threefold mission: (1) to convey to mankind the messages that were revealed to him by God, to adopt measures to preserve them intact, and to spread them to all the corners of the world; (2) to explain the various doctrines and injunctions of the Qur'ān and to apply them to the concrete and particular situations of life; and (3) to set a perfect example for others to follow by practising in their true sense the teachings of the Qur'ān in his own daily life and in his dealings with other people.

All prophets, whenever they were raised by God, had come with the same threefold mission. But the Prophet Muḥammad is the last and greatest of the prophets. The Qur'ān revealed to him is the Book of complete and all-

embracing Divine guidance for all mankind; and he himself is the perfect exemplar for people in all walks of life and for all times to come. Hence, the importance of both the Qur'ān and the Ḥadīth.

The Qur'ān says: "Obey Allāh and obey the Messenger" (24:54), where to obey Allāh obviously means to follow the Holy Qur'ān (the Book of Allāh), and to obey the Messenger means to follow the precepts and examples of the Holy Prophet (i.e., Ḥadīth and *Sunnah*). The Holy Prophet has been described in the Qur'ān as "an excellent exemplar" (33:21) and "a mercy to all the nations" (21:107), and it is proclaimed: "O Prophet, surely We have sent you as a witness and a bearer of good news and a warner, and as an inviter to Allāh by His permission, and as a light-giving sun" (33:45–46).

The Qur'ān enjoins upon those who love God and long to win His grace and attain nearness to Him, to follow in the footsteps of the Holy Prophet:

> "Say: If you love Allāh, follow me. Allāh will love you, and grant you protection from your sins, and Allāh is Forgiving, Merciful." (3:31)

Thus, the importance of the Ḥadīth as a collection of the sayings of the Holy Prophet and reports of eye-witnesses about his life and actions cannot be denied by anyone. The Holy Qur'ān, as is well recognized, lays down broad principles of life. It was the Holy Prophet who provided the explanations and details and showed how they were to be translated into practice.

The Qur'ān, as is well known, was written down in the lifetime of the Holy Prophet. As soon as any revelation came to him, he would have it written down, and several of his followers would also learn it by heart. Immediately after his passing away, the revelations thus recorded and preserved were collected in the form of a book in the order of sequence that the Holy Prophet had himself determined under Divine guidance.

Why were the Sayings and the *Sunnah* of the Prophet not reduced to writing in the same manner in his lifetime? The answer to this is that the Holy Prophet was anxious that his own sayings should not get mixed up with the verses of the Qur'ān. It was for this reason that the sayings and *Sunnah* of the Holy Prophet were not, generally speaking, committed to writing in his lifetime. Nevertheless, it is an undoubted fact that hundreds of his followers who saw him and heard his conversations, discourses and speeches memorized them and conveyed them to others who were not present. Thus the reports of the sayings and actions of the Holy Prophet passed from mouth to mouth, and from one generation to another, and were preserved in the memories of his devoted disciples before they were finally written down. The Arabs

were famous for their vast and retentive memories, and whatever had been recorded on their minds was as good as recorded with pen and ink on paper.

But with the passage of time, as the early followers of the Holy Prophet began to pass away, the danger was felt that the knowledge of the Ḥadīth and *Sunnah* would die with them. So the need was felt to write them down and collect them in the form of books. The collectors of Ḥadīth observed certain definite principles and rules in accepting a report about the life and sayings of the Holy Prophet for inclusion in their collections. The first and the most important of these principles was that the Ḥadīth must be in conformity with the letter and spirit of the Qur'ān. Secondly, that it must be in keeping with the highest moral principles. Thirdly, that it must not be in flagrant opposition to reason and common sense. Fourthly, that it must have come down to the collector through an unbroken chain of narrators from an eye-witness or from the first one who had heard it from the Holy Prophet himself. If the chain of narrators was not complete or if it was broken at any point, then the report was not considered of the highest authenticity.

Moreover, the collectors of Ḥadīth made inquiries about and studied the characters of the narrators through whom the report had come to them. If any-one of the narrators was known to have told a lie or was prone to exaggeration or was not otherwise a man of perfect moral integrity, then the report which had come through him was not regarded as reliable. If it was found that a particular report was serving and advancing the worldly ambitions of the narrator or of the faction to which he belonged, then also it was not considered above suspicion. The collectors of Ḥadīth also made sure that the narrators had good memories and had enough intelligence to understand what they were reporting. If the report passed all these tests, then alone was it declared to be absolutely authentic. Otherwise the collectors either totally rejected it or if they included it in their works they took good care to point out in what way and how far it fell short of the required test.

No report of any historical event or statement of any historical personage has ever been so thoroughly scrutinized and tested as the reports about the life and sayings of the Holy Prophet were tested by the collectors of Ḥadīth. We can safely speak of the collections of Ḥadīth as the most authentic and reliable works of history.

Six collections of Ḥadīth are regarded as reliable by the vast majority of the Sunni Muslims. They are the collections of Bukhārī, Muslim, Abū Dāwūd, Ibn Mājah, Nasā'i and Tirmidhī. Of these the *Ṣaḥīḥ al-Bukhārī* is considered the most careful and trustworthy. Firstly, Bukhārī has the unquestioned dis-tinction of being first, all the others modelling their writings on his. Secondly,

he is the most critical of all. He did not accept any report unless all its transmitters were reliable and until there was proof that the later transmitter had actually met the first; the mere fact that the two were contemporaries, which is the test adopted by the compiler of Ṣaḥīḥ Muslim, did not satisfy him. Thirdly, in his acumen he surpasses all. Fourthly, he heads the more important of his chapters with text from the Quran, and thus shows that Hadith is only an explanation of the Quran, and as such a secondary source of the teachings of Islām.

Note about Imām Bukhārī

Abū ʿAbdullāh Muḥammad ibn Ismāʿīl al-Bukhārī was born in the city of Bukhara (now in Uzbekistan) in 810 C.E. (194 A.H.). His father was a leading scholar of Ḥadīth. Completing his early education at the age of ten years, he started memorising sayings of the Holy Prophet. Even before he was sixteen, senior scholars of Ḥadīth were astonished by his ability to remember tens of thousands of reports along with the names of their narrators. At sixteen he accompanied his mother and a brother to the Pilgrimage at Makkah. While the mother and brother returned home, he remained in Makkah for two years to acquire more knowledge of Ḥadīth from the great scholars he met there. He then went to Madīnah to study under the teachers of that city. He wrote two books while in Arabia and then travelled to Iraq where several times he visited Baghdad, the centre of Islamic learning and civilisation at the time.

It was at the suggestion of one of his teachers that Bukhārī became convinced that he should compile a book of the most authentic Ḥadīth reports. Over a period of sixteen years he produced his compilation by selecting out of some 600,000 reports those which met his standards. (This large number were not all different reports but included reports repeated with variations in wording or in lines of narrators.) After selecting a report for inclusion, he would say two *rak'ahs* of prayer before writing it down in his manuscript.

In Bukhara, the ruler became angry with him after Bukhārī refused his request to teach his sons Ṣaḥīḥ Bukhārī privately at the royal palace. The ruler exiled him and Bukhārī went to Nishapur. Here too he had a disagreement with the ruler and he moved to settle in Khartung, near Samarkand. His opponents had made life impossible for him and he prayed to God to call him back as "this earth has become narrow for me". There he died on the night before *Eid-ul-Fitr* at the age of just over 60 years in the year 870 C.E. (256 A.H.).

List of Chapters of the Books

Book 17: *Sujūd al-Qur'ān* — Prostrations (during the recitation) of the Qur'ān 411

PART 1

Book 1: *Bad' al-Waḥy*
The Beginning of Revelation

In the name of Allāh, the Beneficent, the Merciful

*Ash-Shaikh al-Imām al-Ḥāfiẓ Abū 'Abdullāh Muḥammad ibn Ismā'īl ibn Ibrāhīm ibn al-Mughīrah **al-Bukhārī**,* may Allāh, the Most High, have mercy on him, said:

Ch. 1: **How did revelation begin to the Messenger of Allāh? ﷺ** [1]

The Word of Allāh, may His name be glorified, "Surely We have revealed to you (O Muḥammad) as We revealed to Noah and the prophets after him" (the Qur'ān, 4:163).[2]

1 'Umar ibn al-Khaṭṭāb said[3] while he was on the pulpit: I heard the Messenger of Allāh ﷺ say: "Actions shall be judged only by the intentions

---

[1] Bukhārī opens his collection with a chapter on Revelation because revelation is the basis of religion. Man is gifted with power to make all kinds of discoveries in nature, but the scope of his discovery is limited to creation and does not extend to the Creator. So out of mercy, the Infinite and Living God reveals Himself to man.

[2] It is a characteristic of Bukhārī that he very often quotes the Holy Qur'ān to throw light on what the Ḥadīth says, and thus shows that the basic source of all religious doctrines of Islām is the Holy Book, and the Ḥadīth is really an explanation of the Qur'ān. As the report in this chapter explains how revelation (*waḥy*) came to the Prophet Muḥammad, a verse is quoted here to show that his revelation was of the same nature as the revelation which was granted to previous prophets. As revelation granted to non-prophets is also sometimes called *waḥy*, such as revelation to the mother of Moses (the Qur'ān, 20:38, 28:7) and to the disciples of Jesus (5:111), this verse 4:163 is quoted to distinguish the revelation to the Holy Prophet Muḥammad as being that received only by prophets. For revelation received by the saintly persons among the Muslims, the term *ilhām* is used in general parlance. The verse quoted here also shows that revelation to prophets was the universal experience of humanity.

[3] Each ḥadīth in Bukhārī begins with its chain of reporters, starting with his direct informant and going up, in most cases, to a Companion of the Holy Prophet who reports some words or actions of the Holy Prophet. In translations, it is usual for brevity to omit this line of names up to the name of the reporting Companion. To illustrate, this ḥadīth begins as follows: "Al-Ḥumaidī related to us, saying that Sufyān related to us, saying that Yaḥyā ibn Sa'īd al-Anṣārī related to us, saying that Muḥammad ibn Ibrāhīm informed me that he heard 'Alqamah ibn Waqqāṣ al-Laithī saying: I heard 'Umar ibn al-Khaṭṭāb, while he was on the pulpit, say…".

1

and every person shall have only what he intends.[4] So whoever flies from his home for the sake of worldly gain which he aims to attain or for a woman whom he wants to marry, his flight shall be accounted for that for which he flies." [5]

2 'Ā'ishah, mother of the faithful, reported that al-Ḥārith ibn Hishām[6] asked the Messenger of Allah ﷺ: "O Messenger of Allah! How does revelation

---

[4] The word for "intentions" is *niyyāt*, singular *niyyah*. It is from *nawā*, meaning 'intention', but also includes 'making effort' as in a ḥadīth: "Whoever makes all effort (only) for the world, it brings him failure" (*Al-Muṣannaf* of Ibn Abū Shaibah, v. 7, p. 106).

By "actions" (*a'māl*) are meant not all kinds of deeds, good or bad, but the good and noble deeds to which the Holy Prophet invited, as the later mention of *hijrah* (Flight) shows, which under the circumstances, was the noblest of deeds, being the only means which enabled a man to practise freely good deeds. The hadith shows that the best of deeds would be worthless if the motive was not sincere. Sincerity thus occupies the first place in the moral development of a Muslim. The man who teaches that good deeds are not sufficient unless done with good intentions cannot himself be insincere and an imposter.

Bukhārī himself undertook much travel to collect ḥadīth reports, thus showing that service to Islām requires a kind of *hijrah,* or leaving one's home.

[5] The word *hijrah* literally means forsaking someone, or flying from a place, or giving up low desires or evil tendencies or bad morals, and specially refers to the historic Flight of the Holy Prophet from Makkah to Madīnah, the starting point of the Muslim era. The Muslims had to fly from Makkah because they did not enjoy freedom of conscience there and were persecuted on account of their religious convictions. Many people migrate from their homes for material prosperity and a better life. Few are those who migrate for the sake of religion and the cause of propagating Islām. These are the ones valued by God.

This ḥadīth is narrated six times again in Bukhārī (h. 54, h. 2529, h. 3898, h. 5070, h. 6689, and h. 6953), and h. 1 here is the only occasion on which the following words are omitted: *fa-man kānat hijratu-hu ila Allāhi wa Rasūli-hi fa-hijratu-hu ila Allāhi wa-Rasūli-hi* — "So whoever flies from his home for the sake of Allāh and His Messenger, his flight shall be (counted as) for Allāh and His Messenger." Other variations are of a very minor nature. This ḥadīth also occurs in the collections of Muslim (book: *Al-Amārah* — 'Government', ch. 45), Abū Dāwūd (book: 'Divorce', h. 2201), Tirmidhī (book: 'Virtues of *Jihād*', h. 1647), Nasā'ī (book: 'Oaths and Vows', h. 3794), and Ibn Mājah (book: *Zuhd* — 'Righteousness', h. 4367).

This ḥadīth, h. 1, is like an introduction to the whole collection. As its subject-matter shows, it is not related to this chapter in particular. It is an appropriate introduction indeed, for it shows not only the sincerity of purpose and the good intention of the author Bukhārī but also warns the reader that the good and noble deeds to which he is guided by the sayings and doings of the Holy Prophet will bear fruit only if there is sincerity of purpose and good intentions beneath them.

[6] Al-Ḥārith ibn Hishām embraced Islām after the conquest of Makkah in the year 8 A.H. 'Ā'ishah was the daughter of Abū Bakr and wife of the Holy Prophet who married her in 2 A.H. Apparently the question and the answer were heard by 'Ā'ishah. If al-Ḥārith mentioned it to her later, then this ḥadīth is of the *mursal* type. (This term is applied to a report by a Companion who was not present in person at the occasion which he or she is reporting, and also to a report whose channel of narrators only goes as far as a person who never met the Holy Prophet.)

come to you?" [7] The Messenger of Allāh ﷺ said: "Sometimes it comes to me like the ringing of a bell, and that is the hardest on me, then he (the Angel) departs from me and I retain in memory from him what he had said. Sometimes the Angel comes to me in the likeness of a man and he speaks to me and I retain in memory what he says." [8]

'Ā'ishah said: I saw him when revelation descended on him on a severely cold day; when it departed from him his forehead dripped with sweat.[9]

3 'Ā'ishah, mother of the faithful, reported: The first revelation that was granted to the Messenger of Allāh ﷺ was the true dream in sleep,[10] so that

---

[7] The question seems to relate to the severity of the Holy Prophet's experience of receiving revelation. See next footnote.

[8] The severity or intensity of the experience was of two kinds. In both cases it was the angel who spoke to the Holy Prophet, as shown by the Holy Prophet's two statements that he retains in memory what the angel says. In the second case it is expressly stated that the angel assumed the likeness of a man and spoke to the Holy Prophet as one man speaks to another. In the first case, which was the more severe experience, it is not stated what likeness the angel assumed; it was an angelic form beyond description, and the words of the angel came forth with the clear resonant sound of vibrating metal. The version of this ḥadīth in h. 3215 makes it clearer.

[9] 'Ā'ishah adds to the ḥadīth her own experience of the change that came over the Holy Prophet, or its severity, when revelation came to him. She states that she saw perspiration running down his brow on a severely cold day. It is also reported that on some such occasion, Zaid's thigh was under the thigh of the Holy Prophet and the Prophet's thigh became so heavy that Zaid thought that it would be crushed (h. 2832, h. 4592). According to h. 1536, Ya'lā saw the Prophet when revelation came to him and he saw that the Prophet's face was red. 'Ubādah stated that when revelation was sent to the Prophet, he (the Prophet) felt like one in grief and a change came over his face (Muslim, book: *Ḥudūd*, ch. 3). All these reports show that whenever revelation came down upon the Prophet, whether he was in public or in private, a real change came over him which he could not have brought about by pretence. The state of physical change was due to translation from the physical environment to a spiritual sphere in which the Holy Prophet received the revelation.

[10] Here 'Ā'ishah has mentioned the form of Divine communication which started coming down upon the Holy Prophet in the early part of his life, called "true dreams" (*al-ru'yā aṣ-ṣāliḥah*). Her account cannot be questioned on the grounds that this took place before her birth. The fact is that she was the closest to the Holy Prophet in his later life and was very inquisitive about his life. She was no doubt told about this by the Holy Prophet himself. A true dream, according to 'Ā'ishah, is thus a kind of Divine revelation, and is expressly called here as *waḥy* (revelation). According to another ḥadīth, a true dream is a part of prophethood: "Nothing has remained of prophethood except *mubashshirāt* (lit.,"good news")", said the Holy Prophet, and on being asked what is meant by *mubashshirāt*, he said: *"al-ru'yā aṣ-ṣāliḥah"*, i.e., a true dream (h. 6990). The true dream of a believer is expressly called as part of prophethood in h. 7017, and it is stated in h. 3689 that God also speaks to those of His servants who are not prophets. Thus every Divine communication to a righteous servant is a kind of revelation, and it continues after the ending of prophethood with the Prophet Muḥammad, but does not make its recipient a prophet. In the Qur'ān, *al-bushrā* or true visions are promised to the believers (10:64). The

he never saw a dream but the truth of it shone forth like the dawn at morning.[11] Then solitude became dear to him and he used to seclude himself in the cave of Ḥirā',[12] where he would devote himself to Divine worship[13] for several nights before coming back to his family. He would take provisions for this purpose, and again he would return to Khadījah[14] and take more provisions for a similar (period), until the Truth came to him[15] while he was in the cave of Ḥirā'. So the angel (of revelation) came to him[16] and said: "Read." He (the Holy Prophet) related:

Qur'ān has mentioned three kinds of revelation to human beings, the second of which is called "from behind a veil" (42:51). This includes dreams since these are seen, as it were, from behind a veil and require interpretation. It also includes the state in which the recipient, while awake, sees some kind of light or hear sounds. Similarly, the offering of greetings by stones to the Holy Prophet, mentioned in Ṣaḥīḥ Muslim (book: *Faḍā'il* — 'Virtues', ch. 1), is in the same kind of state. The third, or the highest, form of revelation is that which only came to prophets through angels, and is described in 42:51 as being sent by Allāh through a messenger, i.e., the angel who recites words to a prophet. In Islamic terminology this highest form of revelation, exclusive to prophets, is called *waḥy matluww* or *waḥy nubuwwat*. This form of revelation will be discussed later.

[11] These dreams used to be true and moreover they were fulfilled clearly like the light of dawn. Thus the Holy Prophet's conviction grew ever stronger that these were from Allāh. This was meant to prepare him for that grand message which was to come to him in the form of the Holy Qur'ān.

[12] From his early youth the Holy Prophet loved solitude. However, as his connection with the spiritual world became stronger through his true dreams, he became increasingly engrossed in worship in solitude. It is the Divine law that prophets, before their appointment, spent time in worship cut off from the world. Their natural inclination towards solitude grew more and more, until they attained full closeness to Allāh. Then, after their appointment as prophet, they were made to turn to the world for preaching and bringing about reform. This is why the words "solitude became dear to him" (*ḥubbiba ilai-hi*) are in the passive tense, without a subject.

The cave of Ḥirā' is located about three miles north-east of Makkah. It is said that it was 6 ft. long by 2 ft. wide.

[13] The word used here, *taḥannatha,* means worship. Although its root, *ḥinth,* means 'sin', this form of the verb means *to repel sin* (by worship). Other such examples are that the root *athima* means to sin, but its form *ta'ath-thama* means to avoid sin, and the root *hajada* means to sleep, but its form *tahajjada* means to repel sleep.

[14] Khadījah was the Holy Prophet's wife whom he married when he was 25 years old while she was a widow of forty years of age. She remained his only wife till her death when he was fifty years old. All his children were by Khadījah, except a son Ibrāhīm who died in infancy by his Coptic wife Mary.

[15] By "the Truth" (*al-Ḥaqq*) is meant the Spirit of Truth or the Holy Spirit, i.e. the angel Gabriel. It also refers to the prophecy of the advent of the Holy Prophet made by Jesus: "However, when he, the Spirit of Truth, has come, he will guide you into all truth…" (John, 16:13).

[16] *Al-Malak* refers to the angel Gabriel. Previously the Holy Prophet's revelation was of the lower forms as mentioned earlier in footnote 10. This was the first time that the word of Allāh

I said: "I am not one who can read." [17] Then he (the angel) took hold of me and pressed me so hard that I could not bear it any more. Then he let me go and said: "Read." I said: "I am not one who can read." So he took hold of me and pressed me a second time so hard that I could not bear it any more. Then he let me go again and said: "Read." I said: "I am not one who can read." [18] So he took hold of me and pressed me hard for a third time. Then he let me go, and said:

"Read in the name of your Lord Who creates,[19] creates man from a clot. Read and your Lord is most Generous" (the Qur'ān, 96:1–3).[20]

The Messenger of Allāh ﷺ returned with this (revelation), his heart trembling,[21] and he went to Khadījah, daughter of Khuwailid, and said: "Wrap

---

was brought down to the Holy Prophet in the form of *waḥy matluww* by the angel Gabriel. Some have given the date of this event as 17th of Ramaḍān, but Ibn Jarīr has a report placing it on the 25th of Ramaḍān. Either that report is correct, or 17th has been recorded by error and it should be 27th. This is because the Qur'ān (97:1) places it on the Night of Majesty (*Lailat al-Qadr*) and according to Ḥadīth this night was the 25th, 27th, or the 29th night of Ramaḍān. Ibn ʿAbbās says that the Holy Prophet had then attained the age of forty (h. 3851).

[17] This is the clearest evidence by the Holy Prophet himself that he did not know reading up to this time; he had never learned it. It is also clear from the minutest details of his history after prophethood, which are on record, that he never acquired the knowledge of reading or writing even after this.

[18] The command to read (*Iqra'*) has been repeated three times, and the fourth time the Holy Prophet was made to read the first five verses of chapter *al-ʿAlaq* (ch. 96, The Clot). Some say that Gabriel showed him a writing and said about it: "Read." In reply to this the Holy Prophet three times said: "I am not one who can read." The first time he meant it was impossible for him, the second time it was a statement of fact that he was unable to read, and the third time it was as an enquiry: "What should I read?" On every reply, Gabriel would press him towards him hard. The word *ghaṭṭa* used here means 'to embrace or hug' (*ḍamma*) and then 'to press or squeeze' (*ʿaṣara*).

[19] This command to "read in the name of your Lord" is carried out by the recitation of the well-known expression "In the name of Allāh, the Beneficent, the Merciful".

[20] These are the first three verses of chapter 96 of the Holy Qur'ān, but according to one report in Bukhārī ('Commentary on the Qur'ān,' h. 4953), it was the first five verses of chapter 96 and this is confirmed by consensus of opinion. The 4th and 5th verses run thus: "Who taught by the pen, taught man what he knew not." It is one of the most amazing facts of history that the very first message to a man who knew neither reading nor writing was that he should seek the bounties of the Lord through reading and through the use of the pen.

[21] The "heart trembling" was due to the intensity that the Holy Prophet experienced during this first Divine revelation. Although the Holy Prophet had been receiving Divine communication in the form of visions and true dreams, the experience of receiving prophetic revelation (*waḥy nubuwwat*) through the angel was of an entirely different kind. Hence when he received the revelation the second time: "O you who wrap yourself up! arise and warn" (74:1–2), he experienced the same intensity. Even later on, the intensity of the experience continued, so much

me up, wrap me up." So they wrapped him up until the state of awe had left him. Then he spoke to Khadījah and informed her of what had happened (saying): "I fear for myself." [22] Thereupon Khadījah said: "No, by Allāh, Allāh will never bring you to disgrace; for you unite the ties of relationship and bear the burdens of the weak and earn for the destitute and honour the guest and help those in real distress." [23]

Then Khadījah took him to Waraqah ibn Naufal ibn Asad ibn 'Abdul 'Uzzā, her uncle's son, and he was one of those who had become Christian in the time of Ignorance[24] and used to write the Hebrew script, and he wrote from the Gospel in Hebrew what it pleased Allāh that he should write. He was a very old man who had turned blind. Khadījah said to him: "O son of my uncle! Listen to your nephew." Waraqah said to him: "My nephew, what have you seen?" So the Messenger of Allāh ﷺ related to him what he had seen. Waraqah said to him: "This is the *Nāmūs*[25] whom Allāh sent down

---

so that even in the cold days of winter he would get perspiration, as has just been mentioned in h. 2.

[22] The fear to which the Holy Prophet gave expression was lest he should be unable to achieve the great task of reformation of humanity entrusted to him. Moses expressed a similar fear about his being unequal for his mission and asked for his brother to be made his helper: "...so send him with me as a helper to confirm me. Surely I fear that they would reject me" (28 : 34). Khadījah's comforting words show this to be the import. "If anyone was equal to the great task", she comforted him, "it was he who had already devoted his life to the service of humanity." This also shows how the Holy Prophet's life was spent before prophethood: a life of devotion to the service of humanity. Neither in this ḥadīth, nor in any other, is there anything to show that the Holy Prophet feared that he would be killed by Jinn or that he was insane. He knew for sure at the very first experience of revelation from on High that he had been raised to the dignity of prophethood and entrusted with the great task of reforming humanity and he knew also that it was a stupendous task for a human being.

[23] In another ḥadīth in Bukhārī, Khadījah mentions a sixth quality of the Holy Prophet in addition to these five: "you speak the truth" (h. 4953). There is a report in the *Muṣannaf* of Ibn Abū Shaibah (v. 7, p. 329) mentioning a seventh quality: "you are faithful", meaning faithful to whatever he is entrusted with. This quality was so well known that the Holy Prophet was given the title *al-amīn* by the people before he started his mission of prophethood.

[24] Pre-Islamic days are called *al-jāhiliyyah* or *ayyām al-jāhiliyyah* (days of Ignorance), as compared with the learning and light which followed in the wake of Islām. Waraqah, becoming disgusted with idol-worship, had gone to Syria where he embraced Christianity. Khadījah took the Holy Prophet to him because he had knowledge of the prophecies in the Bible about the coming Prophet, and because she knew from his past that he would accept the truth when he saw it.

[25] The following explanation of this word is given in the *Nihāyah: Nāmūs* is the person to whom the king entrusts his secrets. Here it refers to the angel Gabriel whom Allāh has chosen to communicate His revelations. This meaning has also been given by Bukhārī himself when

upon Moses. I wish I were a young man now. I wish I were alive when your people expel you." The Messenger of Allāh ﷺ said: "Would they expel me?" He said: "Yes. Never has a man appeared with the like of what you have brought but he had been held in enmity,[26] and if I live to see your day, I shall help you with the fullest help." After that it was not long that Waraqah died and there was a temporary break in the revelation.[27]

4 Jābir ibn 'Abdullāh al-Anṣārī, while speaking of the temporary break in revelation, said that he (the Prophet) said in his account: "While I was walking along, I heard a voice from heaven and I looked up, and lo! the angel that had appeared to me in Ḥirā was sitting on a throne between heaven and earth, and I was struck with awe because of him, so I returned (home) and said: "Wrap me up, wrap me up." Then Allāh revealed: O you who wrap yourself up! Arise and warn, and your Lord do magnify, and your garments do purify, and uncleanness do shun" (the Qur'ān, 74 : 1–5). Then revelation became abundant and came one after another.[28]

5 Ibn 'Abbās, in regard to the word of Allāh "Do not move your tongue therewith to make haste with it" (the Qur'ān, 75 : 16), reported: The Messenger of Allāh ﷺ used to exert himself hard in receiving Divine revelation and would on this account move his lips (quickly). Ibn 'Abbās said: I move them

---

repeating this ḥadīth: *ṣāḥib al-sirr* or the keeper of secrets (h. 3392). Waraqah, in fact, bore testimony to the truth of what the Holy Prophet had stated, viz., that the Holy Spirit (Gabriel) had come to him with such and such a message. Waraqah added that it was the same angel that had come to Moses, and this was probably a reference to the Biblical prophecy that a prophet "like unto Moses" would be raised. Waraqah has been counted among the Companions of the Holy Prophet, as he believed in him. It is absurd to suggest that the Holy Prophet was unsure that Divine revelation had come to him and he only believed this after Waraqah assured him that it was revelation.

[26] Waraqah inferred this from the histories of previous prophets. He may also have known from Biblical prophecies that the Promised Prophet would have to migrate.

[27] The temporary break was not very long; certainly not longer than six months, as stated by Baihaqī. Ibn Isḥāq's report that it was three years is belied by historical facts, as a large part of the Holy Qur'ān had been revealed before the expiry of three years.

H. 3 is repeated nearly in the same words in Bukhārī's book on Commentary of the Qur'ān in h. 4953, and also later in h. 6982; and parts of it are repeated briefly in h. 4954, 4955 and 4956. While repeating it in h. 6982, Zuhrī, who was not a Companion of the Prophet, adds on his own authority that during the break the Holy Prophet used to go to the tops of the mountains to throw himself down on account of his great grief and was only dissuaded from doing so by Gabriel comforting him. This is belied by what is stated in the next hadith, h. 4.

[28] This ḥadīth speaks of the Holy Prophet's second experience of Divine revelation. On this occasion the first five verses of ch. 74 were revealed to him. The ḥadīth makes it clear that Gabriel was never seen by the Holy Prophet during the break, and that when he saw him on the second occasion he was struck with awe as on the first occasion. The Holy Prophet, therefore, never saw Gabriel during the break. This ḥadīth is repeated in h. 3238, 4925, 4926, 4954 and 6214.

for you in the same way as the Messenger of Allāh ﷺ used to move them. And Saʿīd ibn Jubair (who reported from Ibn ʿAbbās) said: I move them as I saw Ibn ʿAbbās moving them, so he moved his lips.[29]

(Ibn ʿAbbās continued:) So Allāh revealed: "Do not move your tongue therewith to make haste with it. Surely on Us rests the collecting of it and the reciting of it" (the Qurʾān, 75:16–17). He (Ibn ʿAbbās) said (this means): Your heart has gathered it for you and you will recite it. "So when We recite it, follow its recitation" (75:18). He (Ibn ʿAbbās) said (this means): Listen you to it and remain silent. "Again on Us rests the explaining of it" (75:19) means it also rests on Us that you shall recite it.[30]

So the Messenger of Allāh ﷺ, after this, whenever Gabriel came to him, would listen and when Gabriel departed, the Prophet ﷺ would recite it as he (Gabriel) recited it.

6 Ibn ʿAbbās reported: The Messenger of Allāh ﷺ was the most generous of all people and he would be at his most generous in Ramaḍān when Gabriel met him, and he met him in every night of Ramaḍān and read with him the

---

[29] This ḥadīth shows that all revelations to the Holy Prophet were delivered by the angel Gabriel, and that the method of their delivery was the same: Gabriel first recited the revelation and the Holy Prophet listened to it and remembered it and when Gabriel departed, the Holy Prophet recited the words. The chapter *Al-Qiyāmah*, ch. 75, some of whose verses are referred to in this ḥadīth, is one of the earliest revelations, and only short revelations were received before it. On the first two occasions only five short verses of ch. 96 and ch. 74 were revealed. In the beginning, we are told here, the Holy Prophet made haste to follow Gabriel's recitation, lest any word might be lost. He was, therefore, told not to make haste and to wait until Gabriel delivered the whole message, being assured that it was a Divine arrangement and that nothing would be lost. In another very early chapter, he was even more plainly told: "We will make you recite, so that you shall not forget" (87:6). He was promised that he would never forget what was revealed to him, even though as a mortal he forgot things as any other human being does. Many short chapters and some of the longer ones were revealed to the Holy Prophet in their entirety on a single occasion, one of these, ch. 6, being a chapter of 165 verses, yet so miraculous was the impress of the angel's recital on the Holy Prophet's mind that he repeated them without omission of a word and ordered them to be written down at once. It would further appear from this ḥadīth that other people saw the Holy Prophet's lips move when he received the revelation, which shows that revelation was not a subjective but a real and external experience.

[30] In the verses, of which one explanation in this ḥadīth is given by Ibn ʿAbbās, three distinct points are mentioned: (1) The reciting of the Qurʾān, (2) the collection of the Qurʾān, and (3) the explanation of the Qurʾān. While the first of these was brought about by *waḥy matluww*, the angel reciting the words and the Holy Prophet retaining them in memory, the second and third were brought about by what is known as *waḥy khafī* or inner revelation, in which an idea is impressed into the heart, so that it was by Divine guidance that the Holy Prophet arranged the verses in different chapters and the chapters themselves in their present order. This ḥadīth is repeated with minor variations in h. 4927–4929, 5044 and 7524.

Qur'ān, so the Messenger of Allāh ﷺ was more generous in the doing of good than the wind which is sent forth (on everyone).[31]

7 'Abdullāh ibn 'Abbās reported that Abū Sufyān ibn Ḥarb[32] informed him: Heraclius[33] sent for him with a party of the Quraish, when they had gone for trading to Syria during the truce which the Messenger of Allāh ﷺ had arranged with Abū Sufyān and the unbelievers of the Quraish. [34] They came to him and they were then in Jerusalem. So he invited them to his court, and around him were gathered the chiefs of the Romans. Then he called them and called his interpreter, and said: "Who among you is nearest in relation to this man who claims to be a Prophet?" I (Abū Sufyān) said: "I am the nearest to him in relationship." Then he (Heraclius) said: "Bring him nearer to me and bring his companions nearer (to him) and keep them behind his back." Then he said to his interpreter: "Tell them that I am going to put some questions to him (Abū Sufyān) about the man (who claims to be a Prophet), so if what he tells me a lie, they should belie him." (Abū Sufyān said in his report:) By Allāh, if it were not a matter of shame that my companions would call me a liar, I would have lied against him (the Prophet).[35]

Then the first question that he put to me about him was: "What is his family standing among you?" I said: "He is a man of noble descent among us."

He said: "Did anyone from among you ever advance such a claim before him?" I said: "No."

---

[31] The reading of the Qur'ān by the Holy Prophet with Gabriel during every night of the Ramaḍān means the repeating of the whole of the Qur'ān that had been revealed up to that time. In other versions the words are that the Prophet repeated the Qur'ān in the presence of Gabriel. Ramaḍān is the Muslim month of fasting. This ḥadīth shows that the quality of generosity was found in its utmost perfection in the Holy Prophet, and his generosity extended to all, without distinction, just like the air. He never turned away anyone who asked him for something. This ḥadīth is repeated in h. 1902, 3220, 3554 and 4997.

[32] Abū Sufyān was the leader of the Quraish opposition to the Holy Prophet till the conquest of Makkah when he embraced Islām of his own free will. At the time spoken of in this ḥadīth, 6 A.H., he was still an opponent.

[33] Heraclius was the Emperor of the Byzantine (Eastern Roman) Empire from 610 to 641 C.E. At the time of this incident he was in Jerusalem, to which place he had come for thanksgiving for the victory which he had achieved over the Sassanid Persian Empire, for which see h. 2940–2941. It is made clear there that he called for Abū Sufyān after he had received the Holy Prophet's letter from Diḥyah al-Kalbī.

[34] The truce of Ḥudaibiyah is meant. During that time, the Holy Prophet sent letters to kings of neighbouring countries inviting them to Islām. When Heraclius received his letter in Syria, he called for someone from Arabia to be found who would know the Holy Prophet.

[35] He feared not that if he lied any of his companions would contradict him in front of Heraclius, but that they would later call him a liar.

He said: "Was anyone of his forefathers a king?" I said: "No."

He said: "Do the men of high class follow him or the poor ones?" I said: "Rather the poorer among them."

He said: "Are they increasing or decreasing in number?" I said: "No, they are increasing."

He said: "Does anyone of them become an apostate, having become displeased with his religion after having embraced it?" I said: "No."

He said: "Did you ever accuse him of telling lies before he said what he says?" I said: "No."

He said: "Is he unfaithful (to his agreements)?" I said: "No, but we have made a truce with him and we do not know what he will do with it" — and I could find no opportunity to say something (against the Prophet) except this remark.[36]

He said: "Have you fought battles with him?" I said: "Yes." He said: "How were your battles with him?" I said: "War between us and him has had different turns — sometimes he causes us loss and at other times we cause him loss."

He said: "What is it that he enjoins you?" I said: "He says, Serve Allāh alone and do not set up any partners with Him, and give up what your forefathers believed, and he enjoins on us prayer and truthfulness and chastity and regard for the ties of relationship." [37]

Then he said to the interpreter: "Tell him this."

"I questioned you about his family standing and you said that he was a man of noble descent among you. And such are messengers (of God), raised from among the noblest of their people.

I questioned you whether any of you had ever advanced such a claim, and you said, No. I thought if anyone had advanced such a claim before him, I could have said that this man imitates what has been said before him.

I questioned you whether anyone of his forefathers was a king, and you

---

[36] The Holy Prophet's opponents were entirely convinced of his truthfulness to his agreements and Abū Sufyān could only make this hypothetical remark against him.

[37] Such was the gist of the Holy Prophet's message as known even to his bitterest enemies. In similar words did Jaʿfar, a Companion of the Holy Prophet, relate the Holy Prophet's message before the Negus of Abyssinia.

said, No. I thought if there been a king among his forefathers, I could have said that this man wants the kingdom of his forefathers.

I questioned you whether you had ever accused him of telling lies before he said what he says, and you said, No. So I knew that it could not be that a man who had abstained from telling lies about people should tell lies about Allāh.

I questioned you whether it was the men of high class who follow him or the poor ones, and you said that it is the poor people who followed him; and such are the followers of the messengers (of God).

I questioned you whether they are increasing or decreasing in number, and you said that they were increasing. This is the case of the (true) faith until it attains completion.[38]

I questioned you whether any of them becomes an apostate, having become displeased with his religion after having embraced it, and you said, No. Such is the faith when its cheerfulness is infused into the hearts.[39]

I questioned you whether he is unfaithful (to his agreements) and you said, No. Such are the messengers (of God), they are never unfaithful.

I questioned you about what he enjoins you, and you said that he enjoins you that you should serve Allāh and not set up any partners with Him, and he forbids you the worship of idols, and he enjoins on you prayer and truthfulness and chastity.

If what you say is true, he shall soon be master of the place where I stand. I knew that he would appear[40] but I never thought that he would be from among you. If I knew that I could get to him, I would have made a hard endeavour to meet him, and if I were with him, I would indeed wash his feet." [41]

---

[38] He means that the true religion cannot be destroyed by its opposition, no matter how severe, and eventually overcomes it.

[39] This refers to the believer attaining full conviction of his belief in his heart.

[40] Both the Jews and the Christians knew that there was a prophecy of the appearance of a Prophet like unto Moses, and many of them were awaiting his advent at that time. This is clear both from what Waraqah ibn Naufal said to the Prophet (h. 3) and from what Heraclius admits here, and from what his friend wrote to him as stated later on.

[41] Instead of asking Abu Sufyān to give his views of the Prophet, he put to him pointed questions, which shows that Heraclius was not only a great ruler but also a man of religious learning. The answer to the two questions regarding the Prophet's character, that he never told

Then he called for the letter of the Messenger of Allāh ﷺ with which he had sent Diḥyah al-Kalbī to the governor of Baṣrah and the governor of Baṣrah had sent it to Heraclius.[42] He read it and it contained the following:

"In the name of Allāh, the Beneficent, the Merciful. From Muḥammad, the servant of Allāh and His Messenger, to Heraclius, the Chief of the (Byzantine) Romans. Peace be on him who is rightly guided. After this (preamble), I invite you to the faith of Islām: Be a Muslim and you will be in peace. Allāh will give you double reward, but if you turn away, on you will be the sins of your peasants.[43] And: 'O People of the Book, come to an equitable word between us and you, that we shall serve none but Allāh and that we shall not set up any partner with Him, and that some of us shall not take others for lords besides Allāh. But if they turn away, then say: Bear witness, we are Muslims' (the Qur'ān, 3:64)."[44]

Abū Sufyān said: When he ended what he was saying and finished the reading of the letter, there was a great uproar in his presence and voices became loud and we were turned out. I said to my companions, when we were turned out, that the cause of the son of Abū Kabshah (the Holy Prophet) has become so great[45] that even the king of the Byzantine is afraid of him. Then

---

lie and that he was never unfaithful to his agreements, and the answer to the question regarding his teaching — that he taught the doctrine of Divine unity and enjoined prayers, truthfulness and chastity — convinced Heraclius that he was a true Prophet, but he knew that if he confessed faith in the Prophet's truth he would be killed by his own subjects and would not be able to reach Madīnah and this kept him back from an open avowal of the truth of Islām.

Later on, when the Holy Prophet had to lead an expedition to Tabūk, on hearing the news that the Byzantines were about to attack Arabia, he found no army of the enemy there. Heraclius may have failed to appear against him because he believed him in his heart to be a true prophet.

[42] The governor of Baṣrah was the same King of Ghassān who is mentioned later.

[43] The reward is double because his acceptance of Islām would open the door to his subjects accepting Islām. On the other hand, by rejecting Islām he would be guilty of depriving his subjects of the opportunity of accepting Islām.

[44] Letters in similar words were addressed to other potentates: to Muqauqis, the King of Egypt, to the Negus of Abyssinia, to Chosroes of Persia and certain Arab chiefs. Muqauqis placed the letter in a precious casket and in reply sent some presents to the Prophet. The facsimile of this letter has now been published and reads exactly as in this ḥadīth. Muqauqis embraced Islām, and Heraclius was convinced of the Prophet's truth and of his ultimate triumph, while Chosroes tore the letter to pieces. All these letters were written in the year 6 A.H. after the Prophet's return from Ḥudaibiyah. This was the beginning of the victories of Islām as declared in chapter 48 of the Qur'ān, 'Victory', revealed to the Prophet during this journey.

[45] The reference in these words is to the Holy Prophet. Abū Kabshah was the *kunya* of the Prophet's foster-father Ḥārith, Kabshah being the name of one of his daughters. The Quraish used this name in a disparaging sense because Ḥārith, who was the husband of Ḥalīmah, the Prophet's wet-nurse, belonged to a Bedouin tribe.

I began to be certain that he (the Prophet) would prevail, until Allāh caused me to embrace Islām.[46]

Ibn al-Nāṭūr,[47] the Governor of Jerusalem and friend of Heraclius, head of the Syrian Christians, related: Heraclius, when he came to Jerusalem, was one day most unhappy. Some of his priests said: We notice a change in your appearance.

Ibn al-Nāṭūr added: Heraclius was an astrologer and used to observe the stars.[48] When they asked him (about his worry), he said: "I saw, when I observed the stars last night, that the King of those who circumcise has prevailed.[49] Who are they who circumcise among these people?" They said: "No one circumcises except the Jews and their case need not cause you any anxiety. Write to the cities of your kingdom that they kill the Jews in them."

While they were thus occupied, a man was brought to Heraclius whom the King of Ghassān had sent bearing news about the Messenger of Allāh ﷺ.[50] When Heraclius had the news from him, he said: "Go and see whether he is circumcised or not." So they saw him and told him that he was circumcised. He then asked him about the Arabs and he said that they circumcise. So Heraclius said: It is this people's King who will surely prevail. Then Heraclius wrote to a friend of his who was in Rūmiyyah and who was knowledgeable like him. And Heraclius started for Ḥimṣ, and he had not left Ḥimṣ when a letter came to him from his friend agreeing with the opinion of Heraclius in the matter of the appearance of the Prophet ﷺ, and that he was a prophet.[51]

---

[46] The account given by Abū Sufyān ends here.

[47] Ibn al-Nāṭūr was, as stated in the ḥadīth, the governor of Jerusalem. This part of h. 7 was related to Zuhrī by Ibn al-Nāṭūr whom he met at Damascus in the time of the Caliph 'Abdul Malik ibn Marwān, and does not belong to Abu Sufyān's narrative.

[48] Although Islām does not recognize astrological predictions of events, this is brought in by Bukhārī to show how various people, in line with their own customs, were awaiting the appearance of the Promised Prophet.

[49] It is remarkable that, at about the time when ch. 48 of the Qur'ān entitled 'Victory' was revealed, containing the prophecy of a great victory for the Holy Prophet, a Christian King discovers by his own methods that the King of the circumcised has become victorious.

[50] This king is the governor of Baṣrah mentioned earlier. This incident seems to have taken place before the arrival of Diḥyah al-Kalbī with the Holy Prophet's letter. Heraclius was already almost convinced of the truth of the Holy Prophet's claim.

[51] The name of this friend in some reports is given as Ḍaghāṭar. It is said that he embraced Islām and was murdered by his people because of this. Heraclius wrote this letter after he was fully convinced of the Holy Prophet's truth.

Then Heraclius invited the Chiefs of the Byzantines to a palace of his in Ḥimṣ, and gave an order regarding its doors to be closed. Then he appeared and said: "You people of Byzantine! do you want success and right guidance and that your empire may continue? Then swear allegiance to this Prophet." Thereupon they fled to the doors like wild asses but they found them closed. So when Heraclius saw their hatred and despaired of their faith (in the Prophet), he said: "Bring them back to me." He said (to them): "I said what I just said to test your firmness in your religion, and indeed I have seen (it)." So they prostrated themselves before him and were pleased with him. And this was the last condition of Heraclius.[52]

---

[52] The meaning is that Heraclius never accepted Islām. This long ḥadīth does not state how revelation came to the Holy Prophet, but it contains evidence of his truth, and hence it is included in this chapter.

The first part of h. 7, the narrative of Abū Sufyān, is repeated in h. 2940–41 and h. 4553 with slight variations. The part containing the narrative by Ibn al-Nāṭūr is mentioned very briefly only in h. 4553. Small portions of h. 7 are found in many reports; see h. 51, 2681, 2804, 2936, 2978, 3174, 5980, 6260, and 7196.

In h. 7541 it is mentioned briefly that "Heraclius called his interpreter" and then called for the Holy Prophet's letter which he read. Obviously, it was the interpreter who translated the Holy Prophet's letter for Heraclius, including the verse of the Qur'ān which is quoted in it (3 : 64). This shows that the Qur'ān can be translated into other languages for those who do not know Arabic, and in fact the Holy Prophet must have been aware that when his letters reached the kings to whom he sent them, they would be translated so that the recipients could understand them. The chapter heading given by Bukhārī to h. 7541 shows that he infers from that report that it is permissible to translate the Word of Allāh into languages other than the one in which it was revealed.

Book 2: *Al-Īmān*

Faith[1]

In the name of Allāh, the Beneficent, the Merciful

Ch. 1: **The saying of the Prophet ﷺ: "Islām is based on five (fundamentals)"**

It (faith) consists of word and deed,[2] and it increases and decreases, as Allāh, the Most High, says (in the Qur'ān):

"…that they might add faith to their faith" (48:4).

"And We increased them in guidance" (18:13).

"And Allāh increases in guidance those who go aright" (19:76).

"And those who follow guidance, He increases them in guidance and grants them their observance of duty" (47:17).

"Which of you has it strengthened in faith? So as for those who believe, it strengthens them in faith" (9:124).

"Surely men have gathered against you, so fear them; but this increased their faith" (3:173).

"And it only added to their faith and submission" (33:22).[3]

And love for the sake of Allāh and hatred for the sake of Allāh are a part of the faith.

---

[1] *Īmān* is derived from *amn*, meaning 'security'; and *āmana* as transitive means 'he granted him security', hence God is *al-Mu'min*, the Granter of security, and as intransitive it means 'he came into peace or security', and hence the *mu'min* or believer is one who has come into peace or security. To enable man to enter peace or security is thus the essence of the religion of Islām.

[2] See h. 8 below. Bukhārī uses the words *Īmān* (faith), *Islām* (submission) and *Hudā* (guidance), interchangeably. He regards faith as including actions, and therefore says here that faith increases and decreases and in support of this he quotes the Holy Qur'ān. In Islām, faith is not the acceptance of a certain religious doctrine but of a religious principle which must be translated into practice. Hence he says, it is *qaul* (word) and *fi'l* (deed). A distinction, however, does exist between *Īmān* and *Islām*, for which see ch. 37 in this Book of Faith and h. 50 under it.

[3] All these verses explicitly speak of increase in faith, but it is implied that faith can decrease as well, which would happen by failure to perform good deeds.

'Umar ibn 'Abdul al-'Azīz[4] wrote to 'Adiyy ibn 'Adiyy: "Faith has its duties and laws and limits and ways. So whoever accomplishes them, he completes the faith, and he who does not accomplish them does not complete the faith. If I live, I will explain them to you so that you may act upon them.[5] But if I die, know that I am not very desirous of remaining in your company." And Abraham, peace be on him, said: "But that my heart may be at ease" (the Qur'ān, 2:260).[6]

Mu'ādh said: Sit down with us, we may have (increased) faith for some time.[7] Ibn Mas'ūd said: Certainty is the sum total of faith (*al-īmān kullu-hu*).[8] Ibn 'Umar said: A believer does not attain true righteousness until he gives up what perturbs his conscience.[9] Mujāhid said, in regard to (the verse) "He has made plain to you that religion which He enjoined upon Noah" (42:13): We enjoined on you, O Muḥammad, and on him, the same religion.[10] Ibn 'Abbās said: The meaning of "a law and a way" (*shir'at-an wa minhāj-an*, the Qur'ān, 5:48) is a path and a tradition (*sabīl-an wa sunnat-an*), and the meaning of "your prayer" (the Qur'ān, 25:77) is your faith.[11]

8 Ibn 'Umar reported that the Messenger of Allāh ﷺ said: "Islām is based on five (fundamentals): the testimony that there is no god but Allāh and that

---

[4] 'Umar ibn 'Abdul 'Azīz, also called 'Umar the second on account of his righteousness, ruled the empire of Islām from 99 to 101 A.H. 'Adiyy was one of his governors.

[5] It appears from this that 'Umar the second contemplated to have a collection of Ḥadīth prepared for the guidance of the Muslims. In fact, he issued directions to his governors to this effect, but his reign was very short and the task does not seem to have been accomplished.

[6] This verse is quoted separately from the earlier ones because it does not explicitly speak of increase in faith. It implies increase in conviction of the heart.

[7] The word in the original is *nu'min* (lit. "we may believe"), but Mu'ādh was already a believer. The addition of the word *sā'at-an* ("for some time") shows that it meant talking about matters of faith.

[8] The addition of "its total" (*kullu-hu*) to "faith" (*al-īmān*) here indicates that faith can increase or decrease, and "certainty" (*yaqīn*) is the full manifestation of faith.

[9] In Ṣaḥīḥ Muslim a similar statement is attributed to the Holy Prophet: "…and sin is what rankles in your heart…" (book: 'Virtue, ties of relationship, and good manners', ch. 5).

[10] Here it is made clear that the essence of the religion of all the Prophets of God was the same. The Holy Prophet Muḥammad did not bring a new religion in that sense, but he perfected religion. If religion could be perfected, faith also could be perfected.

[11] The words of the Qur'ān referred to here are: "Say: My Lord would not care for you, if it were not for *your prayer*" (25:77).

Muḥammad is the Messenger of Allāh, the keeping up of prayer, the giving of *Zakāt,* the Pilgrimage, and the fasting during Ramaḍān." [12]

Ch. 2:   Matters relating to Faith

The word of Allāh: "It is not righteousness that you turn your faces towards the East and the West, but righteous is the one who believes in Allāh… and these are they who keep their duty" (2:177), and His word: "Successful indeed are the believers…" (23:1). [13]

9 Abū Hurairah reported from the Prophet ﷺ that he said: "Faith has more than sixty branches and modesty (*ḥayā'*) is a branch of faith." [14]

Ch. 3:   The Muslim is one from whose tongue and hand Muslims are safe

10 'Abdullāh ibn 'Amr reported from the Prophet ﷺ that he said: "The Muslim[15] is one from whose tongue and hand Muslims are safe, and the *Muhājir* (one who flees from his home) is one who abandons (*hajara*) what Allāh has prohibited." [16]

---

[12] It is a well-established fact that a person enters the religion of Islām by bearing testimony to the Unity of God and the Messengership of Muḥammad, through declaring his faith in the *Kalimah Shahādah*: "I bear witness that there is no god but Allāh and that Muḥammad is the Messenger of Allāh." With it are here coupled the four fundamental institutions of prayer, *Zakāt,* Fasting and Pilgrimage on account of their importance. See h. 26 which mentions *Jihād* after faith in Allāh and His Messenger. These words of Ibn 'Umar occur again within h. 4514.

[13] Both the verses referred to here bear on the subject of the chapter heading. They show how wide is the conception of righteousness or faith in Islām, including not only principles of faith but also all kinds of good and charitable deeds, relating to the service of humanity and rights of fellow-beings, and even such high moral qualities as fortitude under the most adverse circumstances are included in faith.

[14] The word for "more than" (*biḍ'-un*) indicates exceeding sixty by between three and nine. In other reports in Ḥadīth collections, "more than seventy" is also mentioned (as in Ṣaḥīḥ Muslim, book: 'Faith', ch. 12). What is meant is a large number, since the numbers seven, seventy and seven hundred are used in Arabic to indicate an indefinitely large number. Here *Īmān* is represented as a big tree, with branches extending in all directions. Thus, faith in its wider significance is not only the conviction that certain principles are true but also extends to the carrying out of those into action, nor is it limited to religious acts or devotions but covers all good qualities and actions that benefit humanity, as shown further on in this chapter. In Ṣaḥīḥ Muslim this ḥadīth is as follows: "Faith has more than seventy or more than sixty branches, the highest of which is to say 'There is no god but Allāh', and the lowest of which is to remove from the road things that may cause harm. And modesty (*ḥayā'*) is a branch of faith" (book: 'Faith', ch. 12). The wider meaning of *ḥayā'* is the quality which makes one refrain from all kinds of evil.

[15] The definite article *al* ("the") here indicates that a perfect Muslim is meant, i.e., it is not meant that a Muslim who fails in this respect actually ceases to be a Muslim.

[16] Ibn Ḥibbān reports the same ḥadīth in the following words: "The *Muhājir* is one who

Ch. 4:   What Islām[17] is the most excellent?

11 Abū Mūsā reported: People asked, "O Messenger of Allāh! What Islām is the most excellent?" He said: "The one from whose tongue and hand Muslims are safe."

Ch. 5:   The giving of food is a part of Islām

12 'Abdullāh ibn 'Amr reported that a man asked the Messenger of Allāh ﷺ: "What Islām is the best?" He said: "That you give food (to the needy) and greet those you know and those you do not know." [18]

Ch. 6:   It is part of faith that a person loves for his brother what he loves for himself

13 Anas reported from the Prophet ﷺ that he said: "None of you has faith until he loves for his brother what he loves for himself." [19]

Ch. 7:   The love of the Messenger ﷺ is a part of faith

14 Abū Hurairah reported that the Messenger of Allāh ﷺ said: "By Him in Whose hand is my life! None of you believes until I am dearer to him than his father and his son."

15 Anas reported that the Prophet ﷺ said: "None of you believes until I am dearer to him than his father and his son and all the people." [20]

---

abandons evil, and the Muslim is one from whose tongue and hand people are safe." See also Nasā'ī, 47:8, h. 4995. It is undoubtedly true that a Muslim has to deal more frequently with his own brethren but in principle the Qur'ān recognized all human beings as one nation (2:213) and therefore the word "people" is more appropriate than "Muslims". After describing what a real Muslim is, it is stated that a real *muhājir* is not merely one who is forced to flee his homeland but anyone who flees from all forbidden acts. This ḥadīth is repeated in h. 6484.

[17] Commentators of Ḥadīth say that by "what Islām" is meant "which follower of Islām", or "which quality of Islām" may be meant.

[18] This is repeated in h. 28 and h. 6236.

[19] By having faith is meant fulfilling all the requirements of faith. It is not meant that a Muslim has no faith whatsoever unless he has this quality. In a version in Nasā'ī, the closing words are: "what he loves for himself of good (things)" (book: 'Faith and its Signs', ch. 19).

[20] Love of the Holy Prophet is not an empty word. It signifies that a person should be willing to suffer the hardest trials and make the greatest sacrifices for his cause. The Holy Prophet is the greatest benefactor of humanity, a greater benefactor than even one's father. Once when the Holy Prophet was performing *Wuḍū'*, the Companions started rubbing upon themselves the water pouring down from him. He asked them why they were doing this and they replied: "Because of love for Allāh and His Messenger." The Holy Prophet told them: "He who wishes to love Allāh and His Messenger, or wishes that Allāh and His Messenger love him, should speak the truth

Ch. 8:   The sweetness of faith

16 Anas reported from the Prophet 👑 that he said: "There are three qualities which are such that if anyone possesses them he tastes the sweetness of faith: that Allāh and His Messenger are dearer to him than anything besides these two, that (when) he loves a man he loves him only for the sake of Allāh, and that he hates going back to unbelief as he hates being thrown into fire." [21]

Ch. 9:   A sign of faith is love of the *Anṣār*

17 Anas reported from the Prophet 👑 that he said: "A sign of faith is love of the *Anṣār* and a sign of hypocrisy is to bear malice towards the *Anṣār*." [22]

Ch. 10:   (Without a heading)[23]

18 ʿUbādah ibn aṣ-Ṣāmit, who was present in (the battle of) Badr and was appointed one of the leaders on the night of al-ʿAqabah, reported that the Messenger of Allāh 👑, while there was around him a group of his Companions, said:

> "Give me a pledge that you will not set up anything as partner with Allāh, will not steal, will not commit illicit sexual acts, will not kill your children, will not bring a calumny which you have forged yourselves, will not disobey in that which is good.[24] So whoever of you fulfils it, he shall have his reward from Allāh, but whoever commits any of these sins and is then punished in this world, it will be an expiation for him, and

---

when he talks, faithfully return anything that he is entrusted with, and fulfil the rights of his neighbour" (*Mishkāt*, book: *Ādāb*, ch. 'Affection and Mercy for the Creation', sec. 3). Love for the Holy Prophet, or for Allāh and the Holy Prophet, means to place obedience to them above all else and to emulate the qualities and character of the Holy Prophet.

[21] Tasting of the sweetness of faith indicates feeling happiness in doing acts of obedience to God and His Prophet. See h. 21. It also occurs in h. 6041 and h. 6941.

[22] *Al-Anṣār* means literally *the Helpers*. The tribes of Aus and Khazraj of Madīnah were so called because they gave asylum to the Holy Prophet and his Companions when they had to flee from Makkah owing to the severe persecutions of the Quraish. By this act of self-sacrifice, they incurred the enmity of the whole of Arabia and particularly of the Quraish who attacked them repeatedly. It was on account of their great sacrifices in the cause of Islām that they were given the name *Anṣār* and love for them was declared to be a sign of faith, and hatred for them a sign of hypocrisy. This shows that everyone who loves the cause of Islām, and makes sacrifices for it, should have the same place of honour in the hearts of the Muslims. This ḥadīth is repeated in h. 3784.

[23] This chapter has no heading because it relates to the same subject of the *Anṣār* as the last one.

[24] This condition is stipulated to indicate that obedience to human beings is only obligatory when it does not conflict with obedience to Allāh.

whoever commits any of these sins and then Allāh covers it, it is up to Allāh to forgive him if He pleases or to punish him if He pleases."

And we pledged to him thus.[25]

Ch. 11: Fleeing from trials is a part of religion

19 Abū Saʿīd al-Khudrī reported that the Messenger of Allāh ﷺ said: "It will soon happen that the best property of a Muslim will be goats with which he will repair to the tops of mountains and to places where rain falls, fleeing with his religion from trials." [26]

Ch. 12:   The saying of the Prophet ﷺ: "I have more knowledge of Allāh than you." [27]

> And knowledge is an action of the heart,[28] as Allāh says: "But He will call you to account for what your hearts have earned" (2:225).

20 ʿĀʾishah reported: Whenever the Messenger of Allāh ﷺ commanded them (the Companions), he commanded them doing of (good) deeds which they had the power to do. They said: "We are not like you, O Messenger of Allāh! He has given you protection (*ghafara la-ka*) against all your faults which have preceded and those which are to come." So he became displeased until the displeasure could be seen on his face. Then he said: "I am the one

---

[25] ʿAqabah is the name of a place near Makkah. Here the Holy Prophet used to go to preach Islām to the pilgrims who stayed in Minā for three days after the Pilgrimage. Six people from Madīnah responded to his call and embraced Islām. Through them Islām began to gain ground in Madīnah and next year twelve of them, who had come to perform the pilgrimage swore allegiance to the Holy Prophet at ʿAqabah. This is known as the first pledge of ʿAqabah. Muṣʿab Ibn ʿUmair was then sent by the Holy Prophet to preach Islām at Madīnah. The following year, which was the Holy Prophet's last year at Makkah, seventy-three people of Madīnah came to perform a pilgrimage and gave a pledge in the words of the ḥadīth. Twelve of these were chosen as leaders, ʿUbādah being one of them. On this occasion they also swore allegiance to the Holy Prophet on behalf of the people of Madīnah that they would defend him against his enemies as they defended their wives and children.

Repetitions of this ḥadīth, with variations, are in: h. 3892, 3893, 4894, 6784, 6801, 7055–7056, 7199–7200, and 7468. A very brief version is in h. 3999.

[26] This ḥadīth aims at teaching contentment to the Muslims at a time when people would run after wealth and become morally degenerate. A little wealth, even a few goats, with a clear conscience is preferable to heaps of wealth bringing about moral degradation. This ḥadīth is repeated in h. 3300, 3600, 6495 and 7088.

[27] This shows that there are degrees of man's knowledge of God, and accordingly people's faith is of different degrees, high and low.

[28] Just as there are actions of the body for which a person is accountable, knowledge is also an action, although of the heart, for which a person is accountable.

who has more regard for duty than you and more knowledge of Allāh than you." [29]

Ch. 13: It is a part of faith that one should hate going back to unbelief as one hates being thrown into fire

21 Anas reported from the Prophet 🕌 that he said: "There are three qualities which are such that if anyone possesses them he tastes the sweetness of faith: The one to whom Allāh and His Messenger are dearer than anything besides these two, the one who (when) he loves a man loves him only for the sake of Allāh, and the one who hates going back to unbelief after Allāh has saved him as he hates being thrown into fire." [30]

Ch. 14: Excelling of those who believe over one another in deeds

22 Abū Saʿīd al-Khudrī reported from the Prophet 🕌 that he said: "Those deserving the Garden (*ahl al-Jannah*) will enter the Garden and those deserving the Fire (*ahl an-nār*) will enter the Fire; then Allāh will say: "Take out (of the fire) those in whose heart there is faith equal to the grain of a mustard seed. So they will be taken out of it, quite blackened and they will be thrown into the river of rain (*al-ḥayā*) — or the river of life (*al-ḥayāt*), for Mālik (a reporter in the chain) was not sure (which of the two was the original

---

[29] There exists a misunderstanding in many minds regarding the significance of this ḥadīth due to the wrong interpretation given to the word *ghafr* (protection or forgiveness). As Qastalānī puts it by quoting Barmāwī: *ghafara la-ka Allāhu,* means *ḥāla baina-ka wa baina adh-dhunūb* i.e., Allāh has intervened between you and sins. And he adds: "*Ghafr* is covering, and it is either in respect of the servant and the commission of the sin or between the sin committed and its punishment." In other words, *ghafr* conveys a two-fold meaning. It means the granting of protection to a person against the commission of sin as also the granting of protection against the punishment of a sin if he has committed it. It is the first meaning that applies here, as the sinlessness of the Holy Prophet is an admitted fact, based on the clear words of the Holy Qur'ān about prophets: "They do not speak before He speaks, and according to His command they act" (21 : 27). And of the Holy Prophet himself, it is stated that even before prophethood he was sinless: "Your companion is not in error, nor does he deviate. Nor does he speak out of desire" (53 : 2–3).

The meaning of the ḥadīth is clear. The Holy Prophet commanded them to do deeds of devotion which were easy; in fact, he forbade them hard devotions. They thought that as the protection was granted to the Prophet against the commission of sins and not to them, they needed harder devotions as a counterpoise against, or as an atonement for, the sins which they committed. This idea was basically wrong and the Holy Prophet told them that it was through regard for duty and through a right knowledge of God that a person found protection against commission of sins.

[30] This is a repetition of h. 16 with slight variations. The words "after Allāh has saved him" are an addition here. For other versions, see h. 6041 and h. 6941.

word).[31] So they will grow as grows the grain along the bank of the river. Do you not see that it becomes yellow and folded?"

Wuhaib said:[32] ʿAmr related to us "life (*al-ḥayāt*)" and said "good equal to the grain of a mustard seed." [33]

23 Abū Saʿīd al-Khudrī reported that the Messenger of Allāh ﷺ said: "While I was sleeping I saw (in a dream) people being brought before me who were wearing shirts, some of which reached down to the breast and some were shorter than this. And ʿUmar ibn al-Khaṭṭāb was brought before me and he was wearing a shirt which (was so long that it) trailed behind him." They said: "How do you interpret this, O Messenger of Allāh?" He said: "Religion." [34]

Ch. 15:   Modesty is a part of faith

24 ʿAbdullāh ibn ʿUmar reported that the Messenger of Allāh ﷺ passed by a man of the *Anṣār* who was admonishing his brother in the matter of modesty. So the Messenger of Allāh ﷺ said: "Leave him (alone), for modesty is a part of faith." [35]

---

[31] This uncertainty is due to the similarity of the words *al-ḥayā* and *al-ḥayāt*. The reporter mentioned here is Imām Mālik.

[32] The statement by Wuhaib from ʿAmr supports that the word in this ḥadīth was "life", and it reports this ḥadīth as using the word "good" (*khair*) instead of "faith".

[33] This ḥadīth shows that all those people who have in their hearts any faith at all will be ultimately taken out of the Fire and they will then grow into a new life. *Faith* is here taken as meaning a confession of Divine Unity, but Bukhārī has throughout this chapter taken *Faith* as including all kinds of good deeds and according to the variation reported by Wuhaib the words are "those in whose heart there is good (*khair*) equal to the grain of a mustard seed", which has *khair* (good) instead of *īmān* (faith). The plain significance of this ḥadīth is, therefore, that whoever has done the least good will be ultimately taken out of hell and granted a new life, life spiritual.

This broad conception of the life spiritual which includes the whole of humanity is peculiar to Islām. It is true that the Holy Qurʾān states that Allāh will not pardon the act of *shirk* or the associating of other gods with Him, but it means only this that the one guilty of it, the *mushrik*, will be punished. So when the sentence of punishment has been executed he will be granted the life spiritual, as this ḥadīth shows. Its version as given in h. 7439 (book: *Tauḥīd*) supports this view, for there it is stated that after the prophets and the angels and the believers will have interceded for the sinners: "Allāh will say: 'My intercession yet remains,' and He will take out a handful from the Fire who will have been entirely burned and they will be thrown into a river at the entrance of Paradise called the water of life (*al-ḥayāt*)." The handful of God cannot leave anything behind. According to the Qurʾān, "the whole earth will be in His grip on the day of Resurrection and the heavens rolled up in His right hand" (39:67). This ḥadīth is also repeated in h. 6560. See also h. 44.

[34] *Dīn* or religion here stands for faith, and the ḥadīth shows that some people perfected their faith or religion to a greater extent than others. This ḥadīth is repeated in h. 3691, 7008 and 7009.

[35] This ḥadīth is repeated in h. 6118 (book: 'Good Manners'), where it is detailed that the man was telling his brother that his modesty was causing him worldly loss.

Ch. 16:   **"But if they repent and keep up prayer and pay the *Zakāt*, leave their way free" (the Qur'ān, 9:5)**

25 Ibn 'Umar reported that the Messenger of Allāh ﷺ said: "I have been commanded that I should fight the people till they bear witness that there is no god but Allāh and that Muḥammad is the Messenger of Allāh and keep up prayer and pay the *Zakāt*. When they do this, their blood and their property will be safe with me except as Islām requires, and their reckoning is with Allāh." [36]

Ch. 17:   **He who says that faith is a deed**

For Allāh says: "And this is the Garden which you are made to inherit because of what you did" (43:72). Many men of learning have said regarding the word of Allāh, "So, by your Lord, We shall question them all, as to what they did" (15:92–93), that the reference is to the declaration: "There is no god but Allāh". And He (Allāh) says: "For the like of this, then, let the workers work" (37:61).[37]

26 Abū Hurairah reported that the Messenger of Allāh ﷺ was asked: "What deed is the most excellent?" He said: "Faith in Allāh and His Messenger." It was asked: "What after that?" He said: "*Jihād* in the way of Allāh." It

---

[36] This is another much misunderstood ḥadīth. In the first place, it speaks of fighting with people, not killing them. It does not and cannot mean that a man could be killed if he did not make the declaration to accept Islām. It states clearly that the Prophet had been *commanded* to fight with certain people under certain conditions. What was that *command,* who were the people and what were the conditions, is stated plainly in the Qur'ān: "And fight in the way of Allāh against those who fight against you but do not be aggressive" (2:190), and again: "Permission (to fight) is given to those upon whom war is made, because they are oppressed. ... Those who have been driven from their homes without a just cause" (22:39–40).

The ḥadīth does not state when war against certain people was to begin, it only says when it was to cease. It says that war begun under the conditions stated in 2:190 was to cease if the people against whom war was justly begun accepted Islām and entered the brotherhood of Islām. Within the brotherhood of Islām there was to be no fighting and the most hostile of former enemies were to be forgiven their past attacks on Muslims if they repented and embraced Islām. Bukhārī himself makes this clear by the heading of his chapter in the words of the Qur'ān: "But if they repent and keep up prayer and pay the *Zakāt,* leave their way free" (9:5), i.e., cease fighting with them. The verse itself, as a reference to the context would show, related to certain idolatrous Arabian tribes who broke their agreements again and again, as stated elsewhere: "those with whom you make an agreement, then they break their agreement every time" (8:56). It is these people that are spoken of in the beginning of ch. 9 of the Qur'ān, where the clear exception is added: "Except those of the idolaters with whom you made an agreement, then they have not failed you in anything" (9:4).

[37] The purpose of this chapter is to show that faith is included as a part of deeds.

was asked: "What after that?" He said: "A Pilgrimage of righteousness (*Ḥajj Mabrūr*)." [38]

Ch. 18: **When (someone's acceptance of) Islām is not in the real sense and is merely outward submission or due to fear of being killed**

As Allāh says: "The dwellers of the desert say: We believe. Say (to them): You do not believe, but (you should) say, 'We submit'." (49:14). But when it is in the real sense, it is according to His word: "Surely the religion with Allāh is Islām" (3:19).[39]

27 Saʿd ibn Abī Waqqāṣ reported that the Messenger of Allāh ﷺ gave some gifts to a party (*rahṭ*) of men, while he was sitting there. (Saʿd added:) But he omitted the one whom I admired the most. So I said: "Messenger of Allāh, what is your reason in his case, for, by Allāh, I consider him to be a believer?" He replied: "No, a Muslim." I was silent for a while, but I was overcome by what I knew of him, so I repeated my question: "What is your reason in his case, for, by Allāh, I consider him to be a believer?" He replied: "No, a Muslim." Again I was silent for a while, but I was overcome by what I knew of him, so I repeated my question, and the Messenger of Allāh ﷺ repeated (his reply), then he said: "Saʿd, I give to a man while another is dearer to me than him, out of fear that Allāh may throw him on his face into the fire (of hell)." [40]

---

[38] Faith in Allāh and his Messenger is the basis of all good deeds and undoubtedly occupies the first place among good deeds. *Jihād* means to exert oneself in repelling one's inclinations to sin and the promptings of the devil, and when necessary to fight an external enemy in the defence of Islām. It also includes striving hard to take the message of Islām to the world. Pilgrimage (*Ḥajj*) involves the suffering of the hardship of journey, but here the condition is added that it must be *mabrūr* (from *birr* meaning righteousness) or free from every sin and insincerity, and only such a Pilgrimage is acceptable to God. This ḥadīth is repeated in h. 1519.

[39] Here Bukhārī shows the breadth of application of the word *Islām*. Having mentioned before what is Islām at its best and most perfect, here it is said that merely to acknowledge its acceptance is also Islām, and a person indicating by word that he is a Muslim is to be treated as a Muslim, however little or much he acts on Islām, but he cannot be called a believer (*mu'min*). The first verse quoted shows the difference between Islām and *īmān* (faith), according to which those without faith are also called followers of Islām.

[40] The man referred to in this ḥadīth whom the Holy Prophet did not give a gift was Juʿail ibn Surāqah, a *Muhājir* who had already undergone hardships for the sake of faith and could undergo more, while the party (*rahṭ* means a party of three to ten) to whom he gave were newly converted Bedouins. It was *Zakāt* money as its repetition in the Book of *Zakāt* shows (see h. 1478). They were all from among the needy, but the Holy Prophet preferred, on this occasion, the new converts for they had not as yet known the beauties of Islām, and he feared that if their needs were not fulfilled they might entertain doubts about Islām itself as being unable to do anything to ameliorate their worldly condition. The word "Muslim" in the ḥadīth is used in the sense of

Ch. 19:   Offering of greeting is a part of Islām

ʿAmmār said: There are three things such that whoever combines them perfects his faith[41] — To be just to oneself,[42] offering greeting to all people, and spending (in Allāh's way) despite lack of means.

28 ʿAbdullāh ibn ʿAmr reported that a man asked the Messenger of Allāh ﷺ: "What Islām is the best?" He said: "That you give food (to the needy) and greet those you know and those you do not know." [43]

Ch. 20:   Ungratefulness to the husband, and (one) *kufr* being less in degree than (another) *kufr* [44]

29 Ibn ʿAbbās reported that the Prophet ﷺ said: "I was shown the fire, and most of its inmates were women who were ungrateful." It was said: "Were they ungrateful to Allāh?" He said: "They were ungrateful to their husbands and ungrateful for goodness (done to them). If you do good to one of them all life and she sees something from you (which she does not like), she says: I have never seen any good from you." [45]

---

perfect submission. The Holy Prophet knew the man and told Saʿd that he knew him to be not only an ordinary believer, but to be one who could undergo all hardships for the sake of faith. In the repetition of this ḥadīth in h. 1478, the meaning of the word "thrown", as in "Allāh may throw him", is also discussed by Bukhārī.

[41] The word translated here as "combines" and "perfects" is the same in Arabic, *jamaʿa.* Although a person joins Islām by declaring the *Kalimah Shahādah,* or the testimony of faith, he needs to acquire certain qualities to perfect his faith.

[42] To be just to oneself means fulfilling one's responsibilities while availing of one's rights.

[43] This is a repetition of h. 12.

[44] *Kufr* means denial as well as ungratefulness, in the latter case being often indicated by *kufrān.* Denial of God and His Prophet is *kufr* but there are lesser degrees of *kufr* as shown in the next chapter. So every *kufr,* or act of unbelief, does not mean a denial of Islām and becoming a non-Muslim. To encourage the doing of good, many good actions are called *īmān* (faith), and similarly to warn against wrongdoing bad actions are called *kufr* (unbelief).

[45] Before the advent of Islām women were kept ignorant and morally and spiritually backward and this was the reason that the Holy Prophet was shown that most of the inmates of the Fire were women. While they suffered many hardships, they were not given an occasion to better their moral condition. Islām came to better their condition and to deliver them from hardships of this life and Fire in the next. Ungratefulness to the husband was one defect of women which Islām aimed at uprooting. Islām deals with all questions of life in a realistic manner and therefore it raised the dignity of women on the one hand by granting them all the rights which the males had, temporally as well as spiritually, and on the other, it pointed out their distinctive defects so that they might be better able to remove them.

H. 29 is repeated in h. 1052 and in h. 5197, at the end of a long ḥadīth relating to an eclipse of the sun.

Ch. 21:   Sins are a part of *Jāhiliyyah*

But the man who commits them cannot be called *kāfir* on account of committing them, except in the case of *shirk*. This is because of the statement of the Prophet ﷺ: "Surely you are a man in whom is ignorance (*jāhiliyyah*)", and Allāh said: "Surely Allāh does not forgive that a partner should be set up with Him, and He forgives all besides that to whom He pleases" (the Qur'ān, 4:48).[46]

30 Al-Ma'rūr reported: I met Abū Dharr at Ar-Rabadhah.[47] He wore a garment and his slave was wearing a (similar) garment. I asked him about it (i.e., the reason for wearing similar garments). He said: "I abused a man, calling him by a bad name because of his mother." [48] The Prophet ﷺ said to me: "Abū Dharr! You called him by a bad name because of his mother. Surely you are a man in whom is ignorance (*jāhiliyyah*).[49] Your slaves are your brothers. Allāh has placed them in your charge. So whoever has his brother in his charge, he should feed him with what he himself eats, clothe him with what he himself wears. And do not burden them with work which overwhelms them. If you burden them (with such work), then help them in doing it." [50]

Ch. 22:   Relating to the previous chapter

"And if two groups of the believers quarrel, make peace between them" (the Qur'ān, 49:9). Allāh has called them both believers.[51]

---

[46] The term *jāhiliyyah,* or 'ignorance', is applied to the times before Islām. To commit a sin is to revert to the pre-Islamic stage. However, the sinner cannot be called an unbeliever. See footnote 51 on the heading of the next chapter, ch. 22.

[47] This was a village about three stages of journey from Madīnah. Abū Dharr, a Companion of the Holy Prophet, was interned here by 'Uthmān, the 3rd Caliph, as he was too severe in denouncing the possession of wealth and public peace was being disturbed on this account.

[48] It appears from another ḥadīth that the man who was abused was Bilāl and Abū Dharr addressed him as: "O son of a black woman."

[49] By ignorance (*jāhiliyyah*) is here meant a trait of the days of Ignorance or pre-Islamic times.

[50] Islām aimed at abolishing slavery gradually and therefore it enjoined that people who were still in the condition of slavery should be treated most leniently and should be more or less on a footing of equality with their masters in matters relating to basic human needs. This ḥadīth is repeated in h. 2545 and h. 6050.

[51] The heading of this chapter is a continuation of the heading of the previous chapter, ch. 21. The verses quoted in these headings make it clear that a Muslim as a believer who commits a sin, or disobeys God and His Prophet in any one matter, cannot be called a *kāfir* (unbeliever), as is the tendency among the modern Muslim religious leaders, but he must still be called a Muslim or a believer. Bukhārī condemns the attitude of calling a Muslim as *kāfir*. No one can be declared outside the pale of Islām until he denies Allāh and His Prophet.

31 Al-Aḥnaf ibn Qais reported: I went out to help this man (ʿAli, the fourth Caliph),[52] and Abū Bakrah met me. He said: Where do you intend to go? I said: To help this man. He said:

> Go back, for I heard the Messenger of Allāh ﷺ say: "When two Muslims meet with their swords (drawn against each other), the murderer and the one murdered will (both) be in the fire (of hell)." I said: "Messenger of Allāh! This is (for) the murderer, but why for the one who was murdered?" He said: "He desired to murder his companion." [53]

Ch. 23: One wrongdoing (*ẓulm*) being less in degree than (another) wrongdoing

32 ʿAbdullāh (ibn Masʿūd) reported: When it was revealed, "Those who believe and do not mix up their faith with wrongdoing (*ẓulm*)" (the Qurʾān, 6:82), the Companions of the Messenger of Allāh ﷺ said: "Who among us has not committed wrong?" So Allāh revealed: "Surely *shirk* (setting up partners with Allāh) is a grievous wrong (*ẓulm*)" (the Qurʾān, 31:13).[54]

Ch. 24: The sign of a hypocrite

33 Abū Hurairah reported from the Prophet ﷺ that he said: "The signs of a hypocrite are three: when he speaks he lies, and when he makes a promise

---

[52] The reference is to the battle known as Battle of the Camel (*Jamal*) fought in 36 A.H. between the forces of the fourth Caliph ʿAlī on the one hand and those of ʿĀʾishah, Ṭalḥah and Zubair on the other. The person referred to as *this man* is ʿAlī. This ḥadīth is repeated in h. 6875 and h. 7083, and in the latter instead of "this man" it says: "son of the uncle of the Messenger of Allāh", meaning ʿAlī.

[53] Although al-Aḥnaf took Abū Bakrah's advice at this point, later he joined the forces of ʿAlī. Abū Bakrah's argument was not correct, and to show its error Bukhārī has quoted the Qurʾān, 49:9, in which both parties of Muslims fighting each other are called believers. The war between the Companions was not out of the desire to murder the other side but due to a difference on a national matter.

In spite of the punishment with which Muslims are threatened if they fight against each other, they were still called Muslims by the Holy Prophet, not *kāfirs*. Nothing has weakened the cause of Islām so much as the tendency of Muslims to call their brethren *kāfir* on the slightest pretext. Such people are themselves clearly going against the Holy Prophet's plain teachings.

[54] The words, "so Allāh revealed", do not mean that this verse was actually revealed at that very moment. On the contrary, another report in Bukhārī shows that the Holy Prophet remarked in reply to the question of the Companions: "It is not like this" or "It is not as you think." And then he read this particular verse of the chapter *Luqmān* (see h. 6937). The meaning of "occasion of revelation" (*shān nuzūl*) had this wide significance in the minds of the Companions. Any incident to which a particular verse was applicable, and was actually applied by the Holy Prophet, was called the occasion of revelation in those days. The meaning of the ḥadīth is that there are grades of injustice and the greatest injustice is that of polytheism (*shirk*), which robs man of inner and outer security.

he goes against it, and when he is entrusted with anything, he betrays the trust."

34 'Abdullāh ibn 'Amr reported that the Prophet ﷺ said: "There are four (characteristics) such that if they are found in anyone he is a complete hypocrite, and if one of these is found in anyone he has a characteristic of hypocrisy in him till he abandons it: when he is entrusted with anything he betrays the trust, and when he speaks he lies, and when he makes a covenant he acts treacherously, and when he quarrels he behaves immorally." [55]

Ch. 25: Prayer on the Night of Majesty (*Lailat-ul-Qadr*) is a part of faith[56]

35 Abū Hurairah reported that the Messenger of Allāh ﷺ said: "Whoever keeps up (the optional night) prayers in *Lailat-ul-Qadr* with faith and seeking the pleasure of Allāh, he is forgiven the sins he committed before." [57]

Ch. 26: *Jihād* is a part of faith

36 Abū Hurairah reported from the Prophet ﷺ that he said: "Allāh takes the responsibility for whosoever goes forth in His way, (saying) 'if nothing causes him to go forth except faith in Me and affirmation of the truth of My messengers,[58] that I will bring him back with what he may gain as a reward or as a booty or make him enter the paradise.' And had it not been hard for my followers, I would not have remained behind an army, and it has always been

---

[55] The signs of a hypocrite are given in these two reports. In one, the signs given are three and in the other these are four. The implication is that if any of these traits are found in a believer he may be said to be somewhat tainted with hypocrisy; and if all these traits are found in a person he may be said to be living a wholly hypocritical life. But this is hypocrisy of deeds, not belief, and even such a person cannot be called a hypocrite in the legal sense of Islām. The traits of hypocrisy recounted in different reports are three, four and five. This is not a conflict among these reports. All it shows is that the traits mentioned do not exhaust the list.

[56] *Laital-ul-Qadr* or The Night of Majesty is one of the odd nights towards the end of the month of Fasting, Ramaḍān, more generally believed to be the 25th, 27th or 29th night. It is the night which saw the beginning of the revelation of the Qur'ān.

[57] Prayer on the Night of Majesty is also stated to be an act of faith, meaning that it leads to the perfection of faith. The word for "seeking the pleasure of Allāh" is *iḥtisāb* which indicates the doing of good for its own sake; see further note 94 under ch. 41. To derive the spiritual benefit, however, the prayer must be accompanied by complete faith in God and the desire to secure His approval, because it is only such a frame of mind that can enable a man to free himself from the tentacles of the habits of sin. When there is true repentance, and a complete change in life, the sins of the past are forgiven. See also h. 1901.

[58] *Jihād* in the sense mentioned here is fighting in defence of the freedom of faith for one's own self or for others. In its full sense *Jihād* means striving in the cause of truth, whatever form such a striving may take. The aim must always be purely for the sake of faith and truth.

my passionate desire that I should be killed in the way of Allāh, then be given life again, and killed again, and given life again and killed again." [59]

Ch. 27:   Optional (nightly) prayers in Ramaḍān is a part of faith

37 Abū Hurairah reported that the Messenger of Allāh ﷺ said: "Whoever keeps up (the optional night) prayers in Ramaḍān with faith and seeking the pleasure of Allāh, he is forgiven the sins he committed before." [60]

Ch. 28:   Fasting in Ramaḍān to seek the pleasure of Allāh is a part of faith

38 Abū Hurairah reported that the Messenger of Allāh ﷺ said: "Whoever fasts in Ramaḍān with faith and seeking the pleasure of Allāh, he is forgiven the sins he committed before." [61]

Ch. 29:   Religion is easy (in its observance)

The Prophet ﷺ said: "The religion that is most liked by Allāh is that which is moderate and is easy (in its observance)." [62]

39 Abū Hurairah reported from the Prophet ﷺ that he said: "Religion is easy, and no one exerts himself too much in religion but it overpowers him; so act aright and keep to the mean and be of good cheer and ask for (Divine) help in the morning and in the evening and during a part of the night."

Ch. 30:   Prayer is a part of faith

And the word of Allāh, the Most High: "Nor was Allāh going to make your faith to be fruitless" (2:143), meaning "Your prayer near the Ka'bah." [63]

---

[59] The Holy Prophet's making it a rule for himself to accompany every army on the march would have made it necessary, a *Sunnah,* for every Muslim ruler to accompany his army; this would make a ruler's position difficult. This ḥadīth also shows the Holy Prophet's unfathomable devotion to God — he would love to be killed for His sake again and again.

[60] See h. 2008 and h. 2009 for a repetition of this ḥadīth.

[61] The object in recounting the different acts of devotion, one after another, is to impress upon the believers the necessity of attending to all of them. Each of prayers, *Jihād,* and fasting being called "part of faith" shows that all of these are essential, and the pursuance of one of these should not lead to the neglect of any other. Hence the exhortation in the next ḥadīth for moderation. See also h. 1901.

[62] Moderation means avoidance of the opposite extremes of falling short of duty or being excessive in it, and it applies to both deeds and faith. Some religious codes leave their followers absolutely free to behave as they like, while there are others that have regulations for the minutest details of life. Islām takes the middle course.

[63] The question is the change of *Qiblah* or direction in prayers. The verse quoted affirms the

40 Al-Barā' reported that the Prophet ﷺ, when he first arrived at Madīnah, alighted at the place of his paternal grandparents — or he (the reporter) said, at his maternal grandparents — from among the *Anṣār*,[64] and that he said his prayers facing Jerusalem for sixteen or seventeen months. He longed that the Ka'bah would become his *Qiblah* (direction of prayer), and the first prayer which he offered (in this latter direction) was the *'Aṣr* prayer, and a group of people prayed with him. Then a man from among those who prayed with him came out and passed by some people in a mosque who were in the posture of *rukū'* (bowing down) and he said: "I call Allāh to witness that I have indeed prayed with the Messenger of Allāh ﷺ facing Makkah." So they turned to face the Ka'bah in the state in which they were (in prayer).[65] And the Jews, the People of the Book,[66] used to be pleased as long as he (the Prophet) prayed facing towards Jerusalem, but when he turned his face towards the Ka'bah they disapproved.

Zuhair said: Abū Isḥāq related to us from al-Barā' (the following) in this ḥadīth of his. Some people had died or had been killed before the *Qiblah* which they followed was changed, so we did not know what we to say about them. Then Allāh revealed: "Nor was Allāh going to make your faith to be fruitless." [67]

---

validity of prayers offered by the Holy Prophet and his followers with their face towards Jerusalem before they were commanded by an express revelation to face the Ka'bah in their prayers. The remarks by Bukhārī here consider only those prayers that were offered in Makkah, but the fact is that prayers facing Jerusalem continued for sixteen or seventeen months after the Holy Prophet and other believers had migrated to Madīnah. The reason for his remark may be that for most of the time that Jerusalem was faced in prayer Muslims were at Makkah. Another view is that the words "Your prayer near the Ka'bah (*'ind al-bait*)" contain an error and they should actually be: "Your prayer not facing (*li-ghair al-bait*) the Ka'bah".

[64] Those with whom the Holy Prophet stayed on his arrival at Madīnah were Banū Mālik ibn an-Najjār. Salmā, the mother of the Holy Prophet's paternal grandfather 'Abdul Muṭṭalib, belonged to the tribe of Ibn an-Najjār; hence the alternate terms have been used to indicate the relation. The clan can be called both paternal and maternal relations of the Holy Prophet.

[65] This Mosque was in Banū Ḥārithah, which is now known as *Masjid al-Qiblatain* ('the Mosque of two Qiblahs') because a particular prayer started there with the congregation facing one *Qiblah* and during it they turned towards another *Qiblah*. See also the version of this ḥadīth in h. 399.

[66] Although the words are literally "the Jews *and* the People of the Book", it is a case of merely indicating the general category (People of the Book) to which the particular class mentioned (the Jews) belongs. The word "and" here does not indicate addition but has this significance: Jews "who are from among" the People of the Book.

[67] The meaning is that the change of *Qiblah* did not render null and void the earlier prayers. The prayers were the same before it as after it. The change did not in any way enhance the nature of the prayers or their acceptance by Allāh. It was merely a direction that was faced in prayer, and this was changed.

Ch. 31:   Admirable Islām of a man

41 Abū Saʿīd al-Khudrī reported that he heard the Messenger of Allāh ﷺ say: "When a servant of Allāh embraces Islām and his Islām becomes admirable, Allāh will remove from him all the evils which he may have committed, and requital will come after that. For a good deed it is from ten to seven hundred times like the deed, and for an evil deed it is like the deed, unless Allāh overlooks it." [68]

42 Abū Hurairah reported that the Messenger of Allāh ﷺ said: "When anyone of you makes his Islām admirable, for every good deed that he does, it is written for him as being ten to seven hundred times like the deed, and for every evil deed that he does, it is written for him as being like the deed."

Ch. 32:   The religion dearest to Allāh is that which is observed with constancy

43 ʿĀʾishah reported that the Prophet ﷺ came to her while there was a woman with her. He said: "Who is she?" She said: "She is so-and-so," and began to speak (highly) of her prayers. He said: "Enough! Only that is binding on you which you are able to do. By Allāh, Allāh does not get tired (of accepting your prayers), but you get tired (of saying them); and the religion dearest to Him is that in which its follower is constant." [69]

Ch. 33:   Increase and decrease in faith

And the word of Allāh: "And We increased them in guidance" (18:13), "And those who believe may increase in faith" (74:31). And Allāh says: "This day have I perfected for you your religion" (5:3). Whenever one misses anything of perfection, he is deficient.[70]

---

[68] The evil effects of past sins are removed only when his submission to the law of God is not nominal but a real one, deserving to be called admirable. In such a case, as there is a complete change in life from evil to good, the past evils are removed. Thus, Islām believes in personal atonement of sins through a changed course of life and without any kind of mediation. The reward for a good deed depends on the person's sincerity and on how much that deed leads him to do other good deeds.

[69] Religion (*dīn*) here means the practice of religion. Allāh best approves of those deeds which are done with regularity, even if they are small. The woman referred to here is said to be one named Ḥawlah, who prayed all night without sleeping. The word here for the act of "getting tired" (*milāl*) means to dislike a thing after liking it. See also h. 1970.

[70] The verse 5:3, quoted last, is cited here as an evidence of increase and decrease in faith, because any stage below perfection is imperfection in comparison. But this does not mean that believers that had died before the revelation of this verse died with imperfect faith. In fact, they

44 Anas reported from the Prophet ﷺ that he said: "He who says 'There is no god but Allāh' (*Lā ilāha ill-Allāh*), and in his heart there is goodness of the weight of a grain of barley, will come out of the fire. He who says 'There is no god but Allāh' (*Lā ilāha ill-Allāh*), and in his heart there is goodness of the weight of a grain of wheat, will come out of the fire. He who says 'There is no god but Allāh' (*Lā ilāha ill-Allāh*), and in his heart there is goodness of the weight of an atom, will come out of the fire."

In another report from Anas, the words are "there is faith" instead of "there is goodness".[71]

45 'Umar ibn al-Khaṭṭāb reported that a man from among the Jews said to him: "Chief of the faithful! There is a verse in your Book which you read, and had it been revealed to us of the Jewish community, we would have observed that day (when it was revealed) as a festival (Eid)." He asked: "Which verse?" He said: "This day have I perfected for you your religion and completed My favour on you and chosen for you Islām as a religion" (the Qur'ān, 5:3). 'Umar said: "We know the day and the place it was, that it was revealed to the Prophet ﷺ. He was standing at 'Arafāt on a Friday." [72]

Ch. 34:   *Zakāt* is a part of Islām

> And word of Allāh: "And they are enjoined nothing but to serve Allāh, being sincere to Him in obedience, upright, and to keep up prayer and give the *Zakāt,* and that is the right religion" (the Qur'ān, 98:5).

46 Ṭalḥah ibn 'Ubaidullāh reported: A man of the people of Najd came to the Messenger of Allāh ﷺ, the hair of his head disheveled. We could hear the sound of his voice but could not understand what he was saying till he came

---

had carried out all the commandments that had been given to them, and it was the commandments which were revealed gradually.

[71] By the saying of 'There is no god but Allāh' could be meant that acceptance of the oneness of God which is a part of human nature, or acceptance of Islām could be meant. In the latter case, being taken out of the fire refers to Muslims who had done the least good. This ḥadīth does not show that non-Muslims will not be taken out of the fire ultimately; see h. 22 and note 33. All it says is that believers in the Divine unity will be taken out of the fire, whatever be their other sins, and this is a warning for those Muslim religious leaders who declare Muslims to be unbelievers and destined for eternal hell even though they recite the confession of the Unity of God.

[72] The man referred to here was Ka'b al-Aḥbār who later became a Muslim. While he said that they would have declared the day of the revelation of such a verse as a festival, 'Umar replied that the revelation itself came at a solemn festival, at a blessed place, because it was the day of *'Arafah* and a Friday, a day of two Eids.

near, and he was asking about Islām.[73] The Messenger of Allāh ﷺ said: "Five prayers in (every) day and night." He (the man) asked: "Is anything else (of prayer) incumbent on me?" He (the Prophet) said: "No, unless you do it of your own accord." The Messenger of Allāh ﷺ then said: "And fasting during Ramaḍān." He asked: "Is anything else (of fasting) incumbent on me?" He said: "No, unless you do it of your own accord." The Messenger of Allāh ﷺ then mentioned *Zakāt* to him. He (the man) asked: "Is anything else (of it) incumbent on me?" He (the Prophet) replied: "No, unless you do it of your own accord." Then the man departed, saying: "By Allāh, I shall not add anything to this nor fall short of it." The Messenger of Allāh ﷺ said: "He will be successful if he has spoken the truth."

Ch. 35: To accompany funerals is a part of faith

47 Abū Hurairah reported that the Messenger of Allāh ﷺ said: "Whoever accompanies the funeral of a Muslim with faith and seeking the pleasure of Allāh, and remains with it till the (funeral) prayer is said over it (the body) and the burial is completed, he will surely return with reward equal to two *qīrāṭs,* each *qīrāṭ* being like (the Mount) Uḥud. And whoever says prayer over it (the body) and returns before it is buried, he will surely return with the reward equal to one *qīrāṭ.*"[74]

Ch. 36: The fear of a believer that his deed may become void without his knowing

Ibrāhīm al-Taimī said: Whenever I compared my words with my deeds I feared that I would become a denier (of faith). Ibn Abī Mulaikah said: I met thirty persons from among the Companions of the Prophet ﷺ, every one of whom was afraid of committing hypocrisy on their own part; not one of them said that he had the faith of (the angels) Gabriel or Michael. It is related of Ḥasan (al-Baṣrī): No one is afraid of it but a believer, and no one feels secure from it but a hypocrite.[75]

---

[73] As the Holy Prophet's reply shows, the man's question was about the practices of Islām, and not Islām itself, and this is why the Holy Prophet did not mention the *Kalimah* in his reply.

[74] *Qī'rāṭ,* or a carat, is a measure of weight for precious articles, about four grains, but slightly different in different countries, mostly being a twentieth part of a Dinār, a gold coin weighing about 71 barely corns or 69 grain of wheat. But the use of the word in literature indicates both a small quantity as well as large one (Qasṭalānī). Here it has been compared to a huge mass like the mount of Uḥud near Madīnah.

[75] This chapter has been devoted to the beliefs of a sect called the Murji'ah, according to whom deeds have nothing to do with faith, committing sins does not affect faith, and evil-doers are as perfect in faith as the angels. From what has gone before, it is clear that Bukhārī holds a

A warning has been issued against persistence in mutual fighting and sin (*'iṣyān*) without repentance, as Allāh has said: "And they do not persist knowingly in what they do" (3:135).[76]

48 Zubaid reported: I asked Abū Wā'il about the Murji'ah (sect), and he said 'Abdullāh (ibn Mas'ūd) related to me that the Prophet 🕮 said: "To abuse a Muslim is transgression (*fusūq*) and to fight him is unbelief (*kufr*)." [77]

49 'Ubādah ibn aṣ-Ṣāmit reported that the Messenger of Allāh 🕮 came out to inform (people) about *Lailat-ul-Qadr,* but two men from among the Muslims were quarrelling with one another. So he said: "I came out to inform you about *Lailat-ul-Qadr* but so-and-so were quarrelling with one another, and it (i.e., news about it) was taken away. It may be that this is better for you. So seek it on the 27th, 29th, and the 25th." [78]

---

different view, the correct view of the increase and decrease of faith. Here he produces evidence that to be afraid of the nullification of deeds is also a requirement of faith. Ibrāhīm al-Taimī was a preacher (d. 92 A.H.), by whose time this sect had already come into existence. As a preacher he always feared not practising what he was preaching, i.e. hypocrisy. Ibn Abū Mulaikah (d. 117 A.H.) used to say that the Companions of the Holy Prophet always feared lest they should be guilty of hypocrisy, being cautious in the highest degree. The fact is that whoever is indifferent to the guiles of the devil becomes a victim to them. This is why Ḥasan, the great saint of Baṣrah, says that a man of faith must be afraid of any element of hypocrisy, and one not afraid of it becomes a hypocrite.

[76] This constitutes the second part of this chapter, and the first ḥadīth, h. 48, relates to it. The unbelief spoken of in h. 48 is not real unbelief, but an expression of strong disapproval, as is evident from Bukhārī using the word "warning" in the heading.

[77] The word for "abuse" here (*sibāb*) is the same as the one used by Abū Dharr in h. 30. The word *fusūq* indicates worse disobedience than "sin" (*'iṣyān*), the word used in the chapter heading. Fighting with a Muslim is called unbelief and this accords with the Qur'ān which says: "a believer would not kill a believer except by mistake" (4:92). As only an unbeliever could fight a Muslim, the word "unbelief" is applied metaphorically to this act if committed by a Muslim, but real unbelief is not meant here. The "mistake" referred to in 4:92 covers all kinds of unintentional killing. In Ṣaḥīḥ Muslim there is a ḥadīth that to curse a Muslim is like killing him (Book of Faith, ch. 47), but obviously it is not meant literally.

[78] This shows that too much quarrelling causes spiritual damage and the fighting of two Muslims among themselves made the Holy Prophet forget the exact date. It appears that the exact date was specific to that year. Had it been the same date for every year, the Holy Prophet would have disclosed it after he experienced the night itself. The 27th is mentioned first because that is most often the date. The words used here for the dates are literally 7th, 9th and 5th, their application being from the 20th or the start of the last ten nights. A repetition of this ḥadīth is in h. 2023.

Ch. 37: **Gabriel asking the Prophet ﷺ about faith (*īmān*), Islām, and *iḥsān* (doing good) and the knowledge of the hour**[79]

And the explanation of the Prophet ﷺ to him. Then he (the Prophet) said: "Gabriel, on whom be peace, came to teach you your religion." So he affirmed the whole of it as religion, and what the Prophet ﷺ explained to the deputation of ʿAbdul Qais about faith, and the Word of Allāh: "And whoever seeks a religion other than Islām, it will not be accepted from him" (the Qurʾān, 3:85).

50 Abū Hurairah reported: One day the Prophet ﷺ was sitting out among the people when a man came to him and asked: "What is faith (*īmān*)?" He (the Prophet) replied: "Faith is that you should believe in Allāh and His angels and in meeting with Him and His messengers and that you should believe in the life after death." [80] He then asked: "What is Islām?" He (the Prophet) replied: "Islām is that you should serve Allāh and not set up partners with Him, and keep up prayer, and pay the *Zakāt* as obligatory, and fast in Ramaḍān." [81] He then asked: "What is *iḥsān*?" He (the Prophet) replied: "It is that you should serve Allāh as though you are seeing Him, and if you do not see Him then (bear in mind that) He is surely seeing you." [82]

---

[79] A difference has been made here between *īmān* and *Islām*, making the former to comprise the articles of faith and the latter to concern the practice of the religion. But this distinction is only according to the apparent meanings of these terms. In fact, the religion of Islām consists of both *īmān* and *Islām* described in this ḥadīth.

[80] By the question, "what is faith?" it is meant to ask: what things are included in faith. Five are stated in answer: belief in Allāh, His angels, meeting with Him, His messengers and the Resurrection. Belief in meeting the Lord has been taken to mean presence before Him on the Day of Judgment, while some have taken this expression to mean man's leaving this world for the next. Some devoted servants of Allāh are privileged to meet Him even while they are in this world, but the perfect expression of this phenomenon is only in the life after death. In some reports outside Bukhārī belief in *Qadr* has been added in this list, which is construed as pre-destination. The word *qadr* in fact means 'measurement' and, of course, Allāh knows for each and every thing the measure according to which He has created it, but there is no mention of belief in it as a separate article of faith in the Qurʾān or Bukhārī. Belief in it is a part of belief in all the attributes of Allāh.

[81] Among the practices of Islām, mention is made here of prayers, fasting and *Zakāt*. No mention is made of pilgrimage to Makkah (*Ḥajj*). This seems to be an error in the memory of the reporter, because in some other reports its mention is found.

[82] The word *iḥsān*, from the root *ḥ-s-n*, means making beautiful. Here it means 'to beautify worship of Allāh', and this consists of serving Him in such a way that the worshipper feels he is seeing Him or at least feels that Allāh is seeing him. In such a frame of mind, service of Allāh becomes a source of unspeakable joy and comfort, because the awe and majesty of Allāh dominates over the heart, and to attain that state is the object of worship.

He asked: "When is the Hour (to come)?" He (the Prophet) replied: "The one who is questioned about it has no better knowledge than the one who has asked the question, but I will tell you its signs — when the female slave will give birth to her own master, and when the graziers of black camels will raise huge buildings[83] —among five things which no one knows except Allāh. Then the Prophet ﷺ recited the verse: "Surely Allāh is He with Whom is the knowledge of the Hour" (the Qur'ān, 31:34).

Then the man left and he (the Prophet) said: "Call him back." But they did not find anyone, so he said: "That was Gabriel who came to teach the people their religion." [84]

Abū 'Abdullāh (Bukhārī) said: He (the Prophet) characterized the whole of it as part of Faith.

Ch. 38:   Relating to the above[85]

51 'Abdullāh ibn 'Abbās reported that Abū Sufyān told him that Heraclius said to him: "I questioned you whether they (Muslims) are increasing or decreasing in number, and you said that they were increasing. This is (the case of the true) faith until it attains completion. I questioned you whether any of them becomes an apostate, having become displeased with his religion after having embraced it, and you said, No. Such is the faith when its cheerfulness is infused into the hearts, no one becomes displeased with it." [86]

---

[83] The *Hour* may mean the Day of Judgment or some particular time. As the word *ba'th* or rising after death is not used here, the hour seems to mean the downfall of the Muslim nation. Rāghib in his *Mufradāt* says that there are three of these hours of doom: the great (*kubrā*) which is the final Doomsday of all humanity, the intermediate (*wusṭā*) which is the doom of a nation, and the lesser (*ṣughrā*) which is the death of an individual. As to the female slave giving birth to its master, many interpretations of this have been given. In *Fatḥ al-Bārī* it is written that in the early days of Islām the leading and prominent men refrained from marrying slave girls and were inclined to marry free women, but it became the opposite later on, as they turned more to physical attractions and pleasure. The other sign is that even the humblest man will be anxious to erect imposing buildings. Black camels are the cheapest and their graziers the most ordinary of people. The two signs taken together may mean that the progress of Muslims will cease when their leading men become pleasure seeking and the ordinary people indulge in worldly show. The signs could also mean that those who were like slaves of other nations at the time of this prophecy would become masters of the world, and those who at this time were poor would be so enriched as to build huge buildings. See also h. 59 and h. 1039.

[84] The meaning may be that the man was the angel Gabriel appearing in human form or that the answers given by the Holy Prophet was the teaching imparted to him by revelation through the angel Gabriel. In the first case, it would be a spiritual vision of the Holy Prophet in which the others present also shared.

[85] No title for the chapter is given here, as if it is a continuation of the previous chapter.

[86] This ḥadīth is only a repetition of a small part of h. 7.

Ch. 39:   The excellence of one who guards his (practice of) religion

52 An-Nuʿmān ibn Bashīr said, I heard the Messenger of Allāh ﷺ say: "What is lawful is clear and what is unlawful is clear, but between the two are (some) doubtful things which many people do not know. So whoever guards himself against the doubtful things, guards his religion and honour, and whoever falls into the doubtful things is like a herdsman who grazes his cattle on the border of a reserve — he is likely to enter it. Beware! every king has a reserve. Beware! the reserve of Allāh in His land consists of the things He has forbidden. Beware! in the body there is a piece of flesh; when it is sound the whole body is sound, and when it is corrupt the whole body is corrupt — it is the heart." [87]

Ch. 40:   Paying the one-fifth is a part of Faith

53 Abū Jamrah reported: I was sitting with Ibn ʿAbbās, and he used to make me sit on his couch, and he said: Stay with me till I allot a part of my wealth to you. So I stayed with him for two months. Once he said:

When the deputation of ʿAbdul Qais[88] came to the Prophet ﷺ, he (the Prophet) said: "Who are these people?" or "What deputation is this?" They said: "It is (the tribe of) Rabīʿah." He said: "Welcome to this tribe — or this deputation — (let you) be not disgraced nor put to shame." They said: "O Messenger of Allāh, we are unable to come to you except in the sacred month, as between you and us is this tribe of unbelievers called Muḍar, so give us a categorical instruction which we may convey to those whom we have left behind, and by (acting on) which we may enter Paradise." They asked him about drinks, so he enjoined upon them four things and forbade them four things. He enjoined upon them faith in Allāh Who is one. He said: "Do you know what constitutes faith in Allāh Who is one?" They said: "Allāh and His Messenger know best." He said: "To bear witness that there is no god but Allāh (*Lā ilāha ill-Allāh*) and that Muḥammad is the Messenger of Allāh

---

[87] A space should be created between oneself and the unlawful things, and that space which must be avoided consists of the doubtful things. This prevents one from trespassing into the prohibited territory. Then it is added that just as the condition of the physical body of man is determined by the condition of his heart, similarly there is a spiritual heart which must be kept pure and sound if all our deeds are to be pure. The Qur'ān refers to this spiritual heart in the words: "Surely there is a reminder in this for him who has a heart" (50:37).

[88] The tribe of ʿAbdul Qais lived in Baḥrain, and the narrator of this ḥadīth Abū Jamrah belonged to this tribe. They embraced Islām at a very early date when Madīnah itself was still surrounded by unbelieving tribes. The incident mentioned here occurred before 6 A.H., but sometime after the battle of Badr because it mentions the rule relating to one-fifth of war acquisitions.

(*Muḥammad-ar rasūlu-Allāh*),[89] to keep up prayer, and pay the *Zakāt,* and fast in Ramaḍān, and that you pay (in Allāh's way) one-fifth of the war acquisitions." [90] He forbade them four things: *ḥantam, dubbā', naqīr* and *muzaffat.*[91] And he said: "Remember these and convey these to those whom you have left behind."

Ch. 41:   Regarding actions being judged by intentions and devotion (*ḥisbah*) and every person having only what he intends

This includes faith, ablution (*Wuḍū'*), prayer, *Zakāt,* pilgrimage, fasting and all (his) dealings.[92] Allāh has said: "Say: Everyone acts according to his manner" (the Qur'ān, 17:84), that is, according to his intention.[93] A man's spending on his family, seeking thereby the pleasure of Allāh (*iḥtisāb*), is a charity; and the Prophet ﷺ said: "But *Jihād* and intention." [94]

54 'Umar reported that the Messenger of Allāh ﷺ said: "Actions shall be judged by intention and every person shall have what he intends. So whoever flies from his home for the sake of Allāh and His Messenger, his flight shall be (counted as) for Allāh and His Messenger, and whoever flies from his home for the sake of worldly gain which he aims to attain or a woman whom he wants to marry, his flight shall be accounted for that for which he flies." [95]

---

[89] Here belief in the oneness of God is further explained as belief in the whole formula of faith which includes belief in the Prophethood of Muḥammad. This shows that no one can attain to true belief in the oneness of God without believing in the Prophet Muḥammad and following his guidance.

[90] After stating that four things were enjoined, here five are mentioned. One opinion is that *Zakāt* and the one-fifth of war acquisitions, being similar, count as one. However, in the repetition of this ḥadīth in h. 523, four are mentioned by omitting fasting from the five mentioned here.

[91] These are names of utensils used in those days for preparing alcoholic drinks, being respectively: green jars, vessels made of gourd, troughs of hollowed palm-trunk, and vessels smeared with pitch. See also h. 1398. Eradicating the evil of drinking at that time required that even the utensils with which drinking was associated should not be used.

[92] If any act, including *Wuḍū',* is done for show, it brings no benefit to the doer.

[93] The meaning of "manner" in this verse of the Qur'ān is "intention" according to Ḥasan of Baṣrah, but it also means the way in which someone does something.

[94] The words for devotion (*ḥisbah*) and seeking the pleasure of Allāh (*iḥtisāb*) are both from the root *ḥ-s-b* which conveys the significance of sufficiency. Thus both words mean the doing of good for its own sake without having any other intention. Doing good because it is a good act and doing good for the sake of Allāh are the same. The words "But *Jihād* and intention" are from the ḥadīth from Ibn 'Abbās beginning with the words: "There is no migration (*hijrah*) after the conquest (of Makkah) but *Jihād* and intention (remain)" (Bukhārī, book: *Jihād,* h. 2783).

[95] This is a repetition of h. 1, with the addition relating to "whoever flies from his home for

55 Abū Masʿūd reported from the Prophet ﷺ that he said: "When a man spends upon his family seeking thereby the pleasure of Allāh, it is an act of charity from him."

56 Saʿd ibn Abī Waqqāṣ reported that the Messenger of Allāh ﷺ said: "You do not spend anything seeking thereby the pleasure of Allāh, but you are rewarded for it, even for that (morsel of food) which you put in your wife's mouth." [96]

Ch. 42: **The saying of the Prophet ﷺ that religion is sincere obedience (*naṣīḥah*) to Allāh and His Messenger, and showing goodwill (*naṣīḥah*) to the leaders of the Muslims and to their ordinary people**

And the Word of Allāh: "…if they are sincere to Allāh and His Messenger" (9:91).[97]

57 Jarīr ibn ʿAbdullāh al-Bajalī reported: I swore allegiance to the Messenger of Allāh ﷺ to keep up prayer, pay the *Zakāt* and have goodwill for every Muslim.[98]

58 Ziyād ibn ʿIlāqah reported: I heard Jarīr ibn ʿAbdullāh, on the day al-Mughīrah ibn Shuʿbah died, he stood up, praised Allāh and eulogized him, and said: "It is incumbent on you to be careful of your duty to Allāh, Who is One without any partner, and to have forbearance and remain calm till a leader

---

the sake of Allāh and His Messenger". Also, the word for "intention" here is singular (*niyyah*), while in h. 1 it is the plural "intentions" (*niyyāt*).

[96] Islām introduces a new meaning in the conception of religion. In these two ḥadīth reports it is taught that every work done seeking the pleasure of Allāh is a good deed, even if it is a mundane or self-satisfying act done for the benefit of the person himself or those close to him. It is counted as an act of charity done by him, provided that it was done to earn the pleasure of Allāh.

[97] The word translated as "sincere obedience" and "showing goodwill" in the chapter heading is *naṣīḥah,* which means to purify. Then a verse of the Qurʾān is quoted in which it is used for sincere obedience on the part of those who were unable to take part in war due to their disability or infirmity, despite their deep desire to fulfil this duty. Used in connection with Allāh, *naṣīḥah* means to place duties to Him above all other duties. In connection with His Messenger, *naṣīḥah* means to honour, love and help him. *Naṣīḥah* towards the leaders of the Muslims means to help them in the conduct of the offices assigned to them, to warn them when they are negligent or fall short, to convey the truth to them, and to obey them in the matters required. In connection with Muslims in general, *naṣīḥah* towards them means to give them their rights, as you ask of your rights from them, to teach them what is good for them, and to remove whatever would be harmful to them.

[98] See h. 1401. The word for allegiance here is *baiʿat.*

(*amīr*) comes to you, and he will come to you presently." Then he said: "Ask forgiveness for your (deceased) leader, for surely he liked forgiveness."

Then he added: "To continue, I went to the Prophet ﷺ and said: I swear allegiance to you to follow Islām. So he imposed the condition on me that I should be a well-wisher of every Muslim, and I swore allegiance to him on this. And I swear by the Lord of this mosque, I am your well-wisher." Then he asked Allāh for forgiveness and came down (from the pulpit).[99]

---

[99] Al-Mughīrah ibn Shuʿbah (d. 50 A.H.) was appointed governor of Kūfah by Muʿāwiyah. Jarīr acted as his deputy. The people of Kūfah were generally troublesome and rebellious; hence he explained to them that the new leader would come to them soon. In the statement, "I swear by the Lord of this mosque", the Kaʿbah is meant, and accordingly in the report in Ṭabrānī the words are *Rabbi-l-Kaʿbah* (Lord of the Kaʿbah).

Book 3: *Al-ʿIlm*

Knowledge

In the name of Allāh, the Beneficent, the Merciful

Ch. 1: Excellence of knowledge

The Word of Allāh: "Allāh will exalt those of you who believe, and those who are given knowledge, to high ranks. And Allāh is Aware of what you do" (58:11), and His Word: "My Lord, increase me in knowledge" (20:114).[1]

Ch. 2: One who is asked to impart knowledge while he is engaged in his own talk, so he finishes the talk and then replies to the inquirer

59 Abū Hurairah reported: Once when the Prophet ﷺ was sitting in a company talking to people, a Bedouin came and said: "When will the (Last) Hour come?" The Messenger of Allāh ﷺ, however, continued his talk. Some of the people said that he (the Prophet) heard what the man had said and he disliked it. Some others said that he did not hear it. When he had finished his talk, he (the Holy Prophet) said: "Where is the inquirer who asked about the Hour?" [2] He said: "I am here, O Messenger of Allāh." He (the Holy Prophet) said: "When trust will be lost, then wait for the Hour." He (the man) asked: "How will it be lost?" He (the Holy Prophet) replied: "When government is entrusted to people unworthy of it, then wait for the Hour." [3]

---

[1] Bukhārī does not seem to have found any ḥadīth in support of this subject which met his standards. So he has contented himself with quoting verses from the Qurʾān. This shows his caution in regard to including reports in his collection. Unless he could find a ḥadīth meeting his standards of authenticity, he would not cite a ḥadīth.

[2] This is a lesson in good manners. The Holy Prophet did not rebuke the man who interrupted his talk with his question, nor show any indignation. He avoided doing what the Qurʾān had referred to in the verse: "He frowned and turned away" (80:1). He indicated by his response that the enquirer should ask his question, not by interrupting, but at the end of the speaker's talk.

[3] The vesting of authority in unworthy hands may be an appropriate sign of the end of the world but it may also indicate the doom of a particular nation. The fall of the Muslim nation is due to this bane of misplacement of authority. See also the last part of h. 50.

Ch. 3: One who raises his voice with knowledge

60 'Abdullāh ibn 'Amr reported: The Prophet ﷺ remained behind us on one of the journeys we had undertaken (together). Then he joined us while we were getting late for prayer and performing *Wuḍū'*.[4] We were not fully washing our feet, so he called out to us at the top of his voice, "Woe to the heels because of the fire", two or three times.[5]

Ch. 4: The narrator of a ḥadīth saying *haddatha-nā* ("he narrated to us"), and *akhbara-nā* ("he informed us"), and *anba'a-nā* ("he gave us the news")

Al-Ḥumaidī said: In the opinion of Ibn 'Uyainah the words *haddatha-nā, akhbara-nā* and *anba'-nā,* I heard that they had the same meaning.[6] Ibn Mas'ūd said: The Messenger of Allāh ﷺ narrated (*haddatha-nā*) to us and he was truthful, and whatever is told from him was also true. Shaqīq reported from (*'an*) 'Abdullāh (ibn Mas'ūd): I heard (*sami'tu*) from the Prophet ﷺ such a word. Ḥudhai-fah said: The Messenger of Allāh ﷺ narrated (*haddatha-nā*) to us two ḥadīth. Abul 'Āliyah reported from Ibn 'Abbās who reported from the Prophet ﷺ about what he used to report from his Lord. Anas reported from the Prophet ﷺ who reported it from his Lord. Abū Hurairah reported from the Prophet ﷺ who reported it from your Lord, the Blessed and Most High.[7]

61 Ibn 'Umar reported that the Messenger of Allāh ﷺ said: "Surely among the trees there is one which does not shed its leaves, and it may be likened to the Muslim; so tell me which is it?" People began to think of (and mention) the trees of the wilderness. 'Abdullāh (ibn 'Umar) said: The thought occurred to me that it was the date tree but I felt shy (to speak). Then they asked: "Tell us which it is, O Messenger of Allāh?" He replied: "It is the date tree." [8]

---

[4] In its repetition in h. 96, the prayer is said to be *'Aṣr*.

[5] It seems that some people did not wash their feet properly due to shortage of water. The word *mash* used in the text for "not fully washing" is not meant here in its technical sense of passing wet fingers over socks when wearing them, which is allowed. Here it indicates insufficient washing, to which the Holy Prophet drew attention.

[6] In narrating Ḥadīth reports, different words have been used by the narrators to signify the act of narration (so-and-so "narrated to us", "informed us" or "gave us news"), but all of them mean the same thing.

[7] The Holy Prophet's reporting from his Lord means that in whatever he said in matters religious he was inspired by Allāh to do so, whether or not he directly attributed it to Allāh in a ḥadīth. The word for "reported from" in this passage is *'an*.

[8] No part of the date tree ever goes to waste, but it is of some use in one way or another.

Ch. 5: The Imām referring a question to his companions to test their knowledge

62 Ibn 'Umar reported from the Prophet ﷺ that he said: ...[9]

Ch. 6: Reciting (a ḥadīth) to a narrator and putting it to him[10]

Al-Ḥasan and al-Thaurī and Mālik consider such reciting permissible, and some of them have deduced (the sanction for) reciting (a ḥadīth) before the teacher from the ḥadīth of Ḍimām ibn Tha'labah who said to the Prophet ﷺ: "Has Allāh commanded you that we should say prayers?" He (the Prophet) said: "Yes." He (Ḍimām) said: "So this was reciting before the Prophet ﷺ." Ḍimām reported this to his people, so they considered it permissible. And Mālik deduced it from documents which were read to the people, so they used to say: "So and so have made us witness (to this document)." And it is read out before the teacher, so that the reader will say: "So and so has made me to read it." [11]

Al-Ḥasan (al-Baṣrī) reported: "There is no harm in reciting (a ḥadīth) before the teacher." 'Ubaidullāh ibn Mūsā narrated to us from Sufyān: "When one recites (a ḥadīth) before a narrator of ḥadīth there is no harm if he says that 'he (the latter) narrated it to me'." He (al-Ḥasan) said: "And I heard Abū 'Āṣim reporting from Mālik and Sufyān: 'Reciting before the teacher is the same as the latter reciting it'."

63 Anas ibn Mālik reported: Once we were sitting with the Prophet ﷺ in the mosque, when a man came riding on a camel, and he made it sit in the mosque and then tied it.[12] Then he said to the people: "Which one of you is Muḥammad?" The Prophet ﷺ was reclining among them, so we said: "This

---

A Muslim should be as a date tree, so that every aspect of his life is beneficial to the people of the world, and that should be his aim in every action. See also h. 72.

[9] This is a repetition of the previous h. 61, with the difference that the words "but I felt shy" do not occur here. To teach people by asking them questions improves their understanding and is a most effective way of imparting education.

[10] The discussion in this chapter is on the stating of a fact of religion before an authority who confirms it, by his silence or otherwise, which is as good as that authority stating the same himself.

[11] A document is authoritative if it was read out before the original authority in the presence of witnesses who can later confirm that the authority had verified it. Similarly, if a book is read before an authority who confirms it, then the reader can propagate it to others as authenticated.

[12] The camel was brought to the door or the outer courtyard of the mosque and tied there.

man of white complexion[13] whom you see reclining (is Muḥammad)". So the man said to him: "O son of ʿAbdul Muṭṭalib!" and the Prophet ﷺ said to him: "I am listening to you". Then the man said: "I am going to ask you some questions and I am going to be hard on you in asking them, so be not offended with me." He (the Holy Prophet) said: "Ask whatever occurs to you." So he said: "I ask you by your Lord and the Lord of all those before you, has Allāh sent you to all mankind?" He (the Holy Prophet) said: "I call Allāh to witness, it is so." Then he said: "I adjure you by Allāh, has Allāh commanded you that you should say five prayers during day and night?" He (the Holy Prophet) said: "I call Allāh to witness, it is so." He said: "I adjure you by Allāh, has Allāh commanded you that you should fast during this month (Ramaḍān) every year?" He (the Holy Prophet) said: "I call Allāh to witness, it is so. He said: "I adjure you by Allāh, has Allāh commanded you that you should take charity from the rich amongst us so that you may distribute it to the poor amongst us?" And the Prophet ﷺ said: "I call Allāh to witness, it is so." Then the man said: "I believe in what you have brought and I am a messenger of those whom I have left behind me from among my people and I am Ḍimām ibn Thaʿlabah, a member of (the tribe of) Banū Saʿd ibn Bakr." [14]

Anas reported: We had been forbidden in the Qur'ān to put (too many) questions to the Prophet ﷺ, and (yet) we used to love that some intelligent man from among the people of rural areas should come and ask him questions and that we should hear. So a man from among the people of rural areas came and said: "Your messenger came to us and informed us that you claim that Allāh, the Mighty, the Glorious, had sent you." He (the Prophet) said: "He has spoken the truth." Then he (the man) asked: "Who has created the heaven?" He (the Holy Prophet) replied: "Allāh, the Mighty, the Glorious." He asked: "And Who created the earth and the mountains?" He replied: "Allāh, the Mighty, the Glorious." He asked: "And Who made in it the things of benefit?" He replied: "Allāh, the Mighty, the Glorious." He asked: "So (I adjure you) by Him Who created the heaven and created the earth and installed the mountains and made in it things of benefit, has Allāh sent you?" He replied: "Yes."

---

[13] The word "white" here only denotes fairer in colour than the other people. As other ḥadīth show, he was not too white nor too brown. He was bright in complexion, a mixture of redness and whiteness.

[14] In this ḥadīth Ḍimām ibn Thaʿlabah puts detailed questions to the Holy Prophet who replies by saying *Allāhumma, naʿam,* literally "By Allāh, yes", thus affirming it more strongly by citing Allāh as witness. This incident took place in 9 A.H. The question of *Ḥajj* is not raised here because it was a universal practice even in pre-Islamic days. Incidentally, this incident shows that the Holy Prophet sat so informally in the midst of his Companions that he could not be distinguished from them, and a visitor had to enquire: "Which one of you is Muḥammad?"

He (the man) said: "Your messenger said that five prayers are obligatory on us, as also *Zakāt* out of our wealth." He (the Holy Prophet) said: "He has spoken the truth." He said: "So (I adjure you) by Him Who has sent you, has Allāh given you this commandment?" He replied: "Yes." He said: "And your messenger said that it is obligatory on us to fast for a month every year." He replied: "He has spoken the truth." He said: "So (I adjure you) by Him Who has sent you, has Allāh given you this commandment?" He replied: "Yes." He said: "And your messenger said that the pilgrimage to the House (of Ka'bah) is obligatory on us for him who has the means for it." He replied: "He has spoken the truth." He said: "So (I adjure you) by Him Who has sent you, has Allāh given you this commandment?" He replied: "Yes." He (the man) said: "By Him Who has sent you with the truth, I will not add anything to these (requirements) nor shall I fall short." So the Prophet ﷺ said: "If he has spoken the truth, he will certainly enter Paradise."

Ch. 7: **What has been stated about *munāwalah* (letter of authority) and the writing (*kitāb*) of learned ones about knowledge (sent) to the cities**[15]

Anas said: 'Uthmān had copies of the Qur'ān written down and sent out to outlying parts of the country, and 'Abdullāh ibn 'Umar and Yaḥyā ibn Sa'īd and Mālik have regarded this as permissible, and some people of Ḥijāz have derived authority for *munāwalah* in a ḥadīth of the Prophet ﷺ wherein he wrote a letter to the commander of a detachment of an army and said: "Do not read it till you reach such and such place." So when he reached that place he read it out to the people and communicated to them the order of the Prophet ﷺ.[16]

64 'Abdullāh ibn 'Abbās reported that the Messenger of Allāh ﷺ sent a man with a letter and instructed him to deliver it to the Governor of Baḥrain.[17]

---

[15] *Munāwalah* is a writing given by a master to his pupil to the effect that it is his own writing and that the pupil carrying it has the permission to narrate reports on his authority. *Kitāb* or *mukātabah* is a writing in his own hand by a teacher of Ḥadīth, or by another on his dictation, which he sends to some other person with due care. The difference is that in *munāwalah* the pupil takes delivery of the writing from the master himself.

[16] The officer commanding the division to whom the letter referred to in this ḥadīth was given was 'Abdullāh ibn Jaḥsh. The Holy Prophet's instruction in the letter was to report about the Quraish at Nakhlah, a place between Ṭā'if and Makkah. The incident of 'Uthmān having copies of the Qur'ān written down and sent to various places is cited here as an evidence in support of this practice.

[17] Baḥrain is a city between 'Amān and Baṣrah, whose Governor of the time was Mundhir ibn Sāwī. The Chosroes (*Kisrā*) of Persia was Pervaiz (d. 628 C.E.), grandson of Nawshirwān.

The Governor of Baḥrain sent it on to the Chosroes, but when he (the Chosroes) read it he tore it into pieces. I understand that Ibn al-Musayyab said: "So the Messenger of Allāh ﷺ prayed against them that they might be torn to pieces."[18]

65 Anas ibn Mālik reported: The Prophet ﷺ had a letter written, or he intended that a letter should be written, and he was told that they (to whom it was to be sent) did not read a letter unless it was sealed.[19] So he had a ring made of silver on which was inscribed: *Muḥammad Rasūl Allāh*. It is as if I am looking (even now) at the whiteness of it in his hand. So I said to Qatādah: "Who said that the inscription was *Muḥammad Rasūl Allāh*?" He said: "Anas."[20]

Ch. 8:   One who sits at the furthest place in the assembly and one who finds space in the circle and sits there

66 Abū Wāqid al-Laithī reported that the Messenger of Allāh ﷺ was once sitting in the mosque and people were with him, when three persons arrived, two of whom proceeded towards the Messenger of Allāh ﷺ and one went away. He added: Then the two kept standing before the Messenger of Allāh ﷺ and one of the two found an empty space in the circle and sat down there; as for the second, he sat behind the people, and as for the third he turned and went away. So when the Messenger of Allāh ﷺ became free, he said: "Shall

---

Letters of this kind by the Holy Prophet were sent also to other neighbouring monarchs. These were invitations to Islām and were written and dispatched immediately after the truce of Ḥudaibiyah. The letter addressed to the Chosroes was delivered by ʿAbdullāh ibn Ḥudhāfah al-Sahmī.

[18] The Chosroes treated this letter with great contempt and tore it into pieces, or had it burnt. "I understand…" is a statement by Ibn Shihāb, a narrator in the line of the reporting of this ḥadīth. Therefore, the words of the prayer of the Holy Prophet are *mursal*, i.e., reported by someone who was not present to hear them from the Holy Prophet. However, it is a historical fact that after the Holy Prophet uttered these words of curse, Pervaiz, who had also sent men to arrest the Prophet, was murdered the same night by his own son and the Persian Empire soon broke up into pieces.

[19] The Holy Prophet could not himself read or write, and by the words *kataba an-nabī kitāb-an* (lit., "the Prophet wrote a letter"), with which this ḥadīth begins, is meant that he dictated a letter. The letter referred to in this ḥadīth was sent to the monarchs of the neighbouring countries; see footnote 44 under h. 7.

[20] "So I said to Qatādah" is a statement by Shuʿbah, who was reporting from Qatādah, who in turn was reporting from Anas. The seal can be seen on the letter to Maqauqis which has been discovered and whose image has been published. It is round in shape, bearing the words *Allāh, Rasūl* and *Muḥammad* placed one above the other in this order. The discovery of this document provides a most strong evidence of the authenticity of Ḥadīth reports. Qatādah was not a very reliable reporter, so the authenticity of the statement about the words of the inscription had to be confirmed with reference to a Companion of the Holy Prophet, Anas.

I tell you about these three persons? As for the first of them, he took the shelter of Allāh and Allāh gave him shelter; as for the second he felt shy and Allāh (also) was shy of him (i.e., showed him consideration);[21] and as for the third, he turned away, so Allāh turned away from him." [22]

Ch. 9:   The saying of the Prophet ﷺ that perhaps the one to whom a thing is communicated (by someone) remembers it better than the one who heard it (directly)[23]

67 Abū Bakrah reported, mentioning the Prophet ﷺ, that while he was sitting on his camel and a man was holding its string or its rein, he said: "Which day is this?" At this we kept silent, for we thought that he was going to give it a name besides the one it had. He said: "Is not this the Day of Sacrifices?" We said: "Yes." He said: "Which month is this?" At this also we kept silent, for we thought that he was going to give it a name other than the one it had. He said: "Is not this Dhul Ḥijjah?" We said: "Yes." He said: "Surely your blood and your wealth and your honour are sacred to one another as this day of yours is sacred, in this (sacred) month of yours, in this (sacred) city of yours. Those who are present must convey it to those who are absent. It is possible that he who is present might convey it to one who will remember it better than himself." [24]

---

[21] The meaning of "Allāh was shy of him" (*fa-staḥyā Allāh min-hu*) is given in *Fatḥ al-Bārī* as "Allāh had mercy on him and overlooked his other faults". The words which are applied to human beings are also used when speaking of the attributes of Allāh (in this case, being "shy"), but in a different sense.

[22] The idea is that a person is rewarded and guided according to his efforts in search of truth. The first man, who left the place at the very sight of the crowd surrounding the Holy Prophet, was not at all enterprising in his search for truth, so he remained deprived of the blessing of the Holy Prophet's guidance. The man who did not make any attempt to find a room for himself in the assembly, but chose to sit at the furthest place in it, had still the desire to find out the truth, and about him Allāh is spoken of as being considerate and merciful. The man who had courage, and found an empty space in the middle of the assembly itself, showed vigour and zeal for learning and he proved to be the best.

[23] The possibility is mentioned here that the man, the original hearer (*sāmi'*), who communicates a certain ḥadīth to another (called here *muballagh* or receiver) does not preserve it in his memory as well as the one to whom he communicated it. This makes the transmission or communication of truth not only a duty of a man of knowledge but a necessary procedure for the preservation of knowledge.

[24] See also h. 1739, h. 1741 and h. 1742. The emphasis laid in this ḥadīth on the sanctity of the blood, wealth and honour of the believer, in the eyes of another believer, has unfortunately been ignored by Muslims, particularly in this age when many preachers make it the means of their livelihood to ridicule a religious leader and to arouse the Muslim public against him by declaring him as an unbeliever, thereby causing friction between Muslims. To impugn one another's honour has become a common practice among Muslims.

Ch. 10: **Having knowledge before word and action (i.e., before saying or doing something)**

Because of the Word of Allāh, the Mighty, the Glorious: "So know that there is no god but Allāh" (47:19).[25] So He has begun with knowledge; and because the learned ones (*'ulamā'*) are the heirs of the prophets who have left knowledge as their heritage. Whoever takes it, takes a full share and whoever walks on a certain path seeking knowledge thereby, Allāh makes the path to Paradise easy for him.[26]

And Allāh says: "Those of His servants only who are possessed of knowledge (*'ulamā'*) fear Allāh" (35:28), and: "And none understand them but the knowledgeable" (29:43), and: "And they say: If only we had listened or pondered, we should not have been among the inmates of the burning fire" (67:10), and: "Are those who know and those who do not know alike"? (39:9)[27]

The Prophet ﷺ said: "For whom Allāh intends good, He gives him understanding of religion" [28] and "knowledge comes through learning." Abū Dharr said: "If you place the sword on this" — and he pointed towards his neck — "and I feel that I must transmit a word which I have heard from the Prophet ﷺ before you finish me off, I will certainly convey it." [29] And the word of the Prophet ﷺ:

---

[25] In this chapter, knowledge is made a pre-requisite for belief and action because knowledge is the basis of these. The verse quoted, which begins with the command "know" (*fa'lam*), shows that the most fundamental belief, that there is but One God, should be based on knowledge.

[26] This is a part of a ḥadīth in Abū Dāwūd (book: 'Knowledge', ch. 1), Tirmidhī (book: 'Knowledge', ch. 19) and Ibn Mājah (book: '*Sunnah*', h. 228). The knowledge which the prophets brought to the world was left by them as a heritage for those that are competent to understand it thoroughly and teach it to others. The *'ulamā'* spoken of here are not those to whom this title is generally applied; those are in fact *fuqahā'* or scholars who interpret the external law. The *'ulamā'* here are the Godly ones who possess spiritual insight and the subtle knowledge of reality, not merely the superficial knowledge taught in religious schools. This inheriting is mentioned in the Qur'ān as follows: "Then We have given the Book as inheritance to those whom We have chosen from among Our servants" (35:32). It is added here that by seeking knowledge the path to Paradise becomes easier.

[27] The verses of the Qur'ān quoted here tell us that only knowledge leads man to fear the majesty and power of God, only those having knowledge can understand the teachings of the Qur'ān in depth, and that by means of knowledge one can avoid wrongdoing and thus be saved from the fire of hell. Accordingly, there can be no comparison between those who possess knowledge and those who are devoid of it.

[28] This occurs as a ḥadīth in h. 71.

[29] Abū Dharr al-Ghifārī was a Companion of the Holy Prophet who had a disagreement with

"Those who are present must convey it to those who are absent."

Ibn 'Abbās said: " 'Be worshippers of the Lord (*rabbāniyyūn*)' (the Qur'ān, 3:79)[30] means those who are forbearing,[31] possessing knowledge and having understanding"; and it has been said that *Rabbāniy* (a man of God) is one who teaches people easy knowledge before the advanced kind."[32]

Ch. 11:   **That the Prophet ﷺ used to have consideration for people while preaching and imparting knowledge, that they might not become averse to it**

68 Ibn Mas'ūd reported: The Prophet ﷺ used to have consideration for us while preaching, by selecting suitable (times and) days, as he did not like that we should get bored.[33]

69 Anas reported from the Prophet ﷺ that he said: "Make it (i.e., preaching) easy and do not make it difficult (for people), and give them happy news and do not make them averse (to religion)."[34]

Mu'āwiyah in Syria in regard to the verse "those who heard up gold and silver" (the Qur'ān, 9:34). Abū Dharr believed that Muslims were totally prohibited from possessing gold and silver. This extreme position was disturbing public peace in Syria, so the Caliph 'Uthmān asked him to settle down in Madīnah, but he preferred retirement to a nearby village called ar-Rabadhah. See h. 1406. The incident referred to here seems to relate to this period of his life, when someone said to him that he had been forbidden to preach such an interpretation. He replied that he would not stop transmitting the words of the Holy Prophet even if his life was threatened. Bukhārī mentions this to show his undaunted spirit of narrating ḥadīth.

[30] The words of the Qur'ān quoted here say that people should become *rabbāniyyūn*, worshippers of the Lord or Godly people.

[31] Some editions of the text of Ṣaḥīḥ Bukhārī have here the word *ḥulamā'*, meaning forbearing or gentle, while other editions have instead the word *ḥukamā'*, meaning wise ones.

[32] *Rabbāniy* is the singular of *rabbāniyyūn*. That status is only attained by possessing a high level of knowledge. The "easy knowledge" (*ṣighār,* lit. "small matters of knowledge") refers to the broad and basic matters which can be readily understood, and should be taught first. The "advanced" knowledge (*kibār,* lit. "great matters") refers to deep and subtle truths, which should only be taught later.

[33] This is a repetition of the last statement of h. 70 in different words. It is taught in this chapter that imparting of education should be done in a considerate manner which does not burden or inconvenience people and has due regard for their time.

[34] The meaning is that in giving religious training to people the teacher should put a liberal interpretation on the rules of religion and not make its practice hard for them. Severity in this matter will defeat its own object. Mild and loving persuasion and some amount of leniency will be more effective, especially when instructing new converts to Islām. This is also a warning to the preachers of our times who adopt a blunt approach, present religion as very strict and rigid, cannot tolerate a question or objection, and denounce people as unbelievers for asking questions.

Ch. 12: One who fixes days for the learners of knowledge

70 Abū Wā'il reported: 'Abdullāh (ibn Mas'ūd) used to preach to people every Thursday. Once a man said to him: "O Abū 'Abdur Raḥmān! I wish that you could preach every day." He said: "What prevents me from doing so is that I do not like to bore you, and I have consideration for you in preaching, as the Prophet ﷺ used to have consideration for us for fear that we should get bored." [35]

Ch. 13: For whom Allāh intends good, He gives him understanding of religion

71 Ḥumaid ibn 'Abdur Raḥmān said: I heard Mu'āwiyah delivering a sermon, saying: I heard the Prophet ﷺ say: "For whom Allāh intends good, He gives him understanding of religion. I am only a distributor; it is Allāh Who gives.[36] So long as this religious community (*ummah*) continues to act upon the commandments of Allāh, no harm will come to them from their adversaries, till the command of Allāh comes." [37]

Ch. 14: Understanding in knowledge

72 Mujāhid reported: I accompanied Ibn 'Umar to Madīnah and I did not hear him narrating any ḥadīth from the Messenger of Allāh ﷺ except a single one. He said:

We were with the Prophet ﷺ when a spathe (of date-tree) was brought to him. He said: "Surely among the trees there is one which may be likened to the Muslim." I intended to say that it was the date-tree but I was then the youngest of all the people, so I kept silent. Then the Prophet ﷺ said: "It is the date-tree." [38]

---

[35] This is a warning to the average preacher of our times who, once he gets possession of a platform, takes pleasure in tiring his audience out. Tactless preaching, we are reminded, drives people away from religion rather than bringing them nearer.

[36] This is the highest teaching of the oneness of God: that the Holy Prophet is only the distributor (*qāsim*) while the real source and giver (*mu'ṭī*) is Allāh.

[37] The Holy Prophet's calling himself a "distributor" seems to have reference to the distribution of the knowledge of religion. The concluding words also refer to the same thing, *viz.*, that no amount of hostility from outside will cause any harm to the Muslims as long as they remain established in the correct knowledge of religion. The command of Allāh means Divine punishment. The implication is that it is when the true understanding of religion disappears from the Muslims Allāh will punish them by allowing the enemy forces to prevail upon them.

[38] The last part of this ḥadīth has already occurred in h. 61.

Ch. 15:   Envy in knowledge ('*ilm*) and wisdom (*ḥikmah*)[39]

'Umar said: Acquire understanding (of religion) before you become leaders.[40] Abū 'Abdullāh (Bukhārī) says: Even after you become leaders, and the Companions of the Prophet ﷺ acquired knowledge after they had attained old age.

73 'Abdullāh ibn Mas'ūd said that the Prophet ﷺ said: "There shall be no envy except in (case of) two:[41] a man to whom Allāh has given wealth and the power to spend it in the way of truth, and a man to whom Allāh has given wisdom[42] and he judges according to it and teaches it." [43]

Ch. 16:   What has been said about Moses going along the river towards al-Khaḍir[44]

The Word of Allāh, the Blessed and the Most High: "… May I follow you that you may teach me…" (18:66).

---

[39] In the heading of this chapter the word used for "envy" is *ghabṭ*, while in the ḥadīth, which follows, the word *ḥasad* has been used. The former means the desire of a person to attain the same position which another possesses, so as to rise to his level, while the latter indicates the desire of a person to see another deprived of what he possesses and his downfall. Bukhārī has used *ghabṭ* in the heading to clarify that the "envy" spoken of in the ḥadīth is meant not in the sense of *ḥasad* but of *ghabṭ*. The English word "envy" correctly represents what is meant.

[40] The statement of 'Umar means that if a man becomes a leader or senior figure before acquiring knowledge and understanding, he considers it beneath his dignity to acquire these. Bukhārī comments that if a man has not acquired knowledge before attaining high rank, seniority or old age, he can do it afterwards, showing that 'Umar did not mean that you cannot acquire knowledge afterwards.

[41] Some take *ḥasad* ("envy") here in its real sense of wishing to see another deprived of what he possesses and consider "except" as referring to something separate, so that the words mean: "There shall be no envy at all; but two are to be emulated."

[42] The word *ḥikmah* here may be rendered as "wisdom" or "knowledge".

[43] Acquiring knowledge and wisdom is as important as acquiring wealth. They are not only to be possessed but also must be put to good use, as stated here.

[44] The purpose of relating the journey of Moses here is to show that one must undergo any amount of hardship to acquire knowledge, and even persons of the highest status, such as Moses, should still continue to seek more knowledge. There is a divergence of opinion as regards the identity of Khaḍir. Some hold that the story in this ḥadīth is not the same as the one related in ch. 18 of the Qur'ān, and that the Moses mentioned here is not the Israelite prophet Moses. However, the words of the Qur'ān as quoted in this ḥadīth and the mention of the Israelites show that this view is not correct. The common conception that Khaḍir is still alive and will remain so till the Day of Judgment, because he drank the elixir of life, is not supported by any authentic source. Thus Qasṭalānī says: "A body of authorities have denied his being alive", and he has named some of them.

74 Ibn ʿAbbās reported that he quarreled with al-Ḥurr ibn Qais ibn Ḥiṣn al-Fazārī about the companion of Moses. Ibn ʿAbbās said that it was Khaḍir. Ubayy ibn Kaʿb was passing by them and Ibn ʿAbbās called him and said: "I have quarreled with this friend of mine on the question of the companion of Moses to meet whom Moses asked for the way; have you heard the Prophet ﷺ say anything about this matter?" He said: "Yes, I have heard the Messenger of Allāh ﷺ say:

"Once when Moses was sitting in the midst of the chiefs of the Israelites, a man came to him and asked: 'Do you know anyone greater in knowledge than yourself?' Moses said: 'No.' So Allāh revealed to Moses: 'Yes (there is), Our servant Khaḍir.' Moses asked for the way to meet him. So Allāh made the fish a sign for him, and he was told: 'When the fish is lost, return (to where you have lost it); you will meet him there.' So he followed the signs of the fish in the river. The servant of Moses said to him: 'Did you see when we took refuge on the rock, I forgot the fish, and none but the devil made me forget to speak of it'. He (Moses) said: 'This is what we sought for.' So they returned retracing their footsteps and found Khaḍir (the Qurʾān, 18:63–64). Their story is related by Allāh in His Book." [45]

Ch. 17: The saying of the Prophet ﷺ: "O Allāh, grant him the knowledge of the Book."

75 Ibn ʿAbbās reported: The Messenger of Allāh ﷺ embraced me and said: "O Allāh, grant him the knowledge of the Book." [46]

Ch. 18: When is it right to listen to a youngster?

76 ʿAbdullāh ibn ʿAbbās reported: I came riding on a she-ass, and at that time I was approaching the age of maturity, and the Messenger of Allāh ﷺ

---

[45] This is a briefer repetition of h. 122 with differences. Here the quarrel of Ibn ʿAbbās is with al-Ḥurr ibn Qais regarding who was the companion of Moses; in h. 122 the quarrel of Ibn ʿAbbās is with Nauf al-Bakālī who said that the Moses of this story is not the Israelite prophet Moses. The significant difference is that here the question asked is: "Do you know anyone greater in knowledge than yourself?", to which Moses replies: "No." But according to h. 122 the question was, "Which of the people was the greatest in knowledge," and in reply Moses said: "I am the greatest in knowledge." This shows that the statements of the Holy Prophet found in Ḥadīth reports, especially those in which stories are related, have not been transmitted word for word in their exact original forms, despite the best efforts of the reporters, and it is not known with full certainty, as in this case, what words he actually uttered.

[46] The word *Book* here refers to the Qurʾān. It was because of this prayer of the Holy Prophet that the Caliph ʿUmar had a great regard for the opinion of Ibn ʿAbbās in the interpretation of the Qurʾān even though he was so young, far younger than ʿUmar.

was saying prayers at Minā without facing any wall. So I passed in front of some of the rows (in the congregation) and I sent away the she-ass to graze and joined in the row. This was not made an objection against me by anyone.[47]

77 Maḥmūd ibn al-Rabī' reported: I remember the Prophet ﷺ once drawing a mouthful of water from a bucket (to rinse his mouth) and splashing it on my face and I was a boy of five years.[48]

Ch. 19:   Undertaking journey to acquire knowledge

> Jābir ibn 'Abdullāh undertook a journey of a month to hear one ḥadīth from 'Abdullāh ibn Unais.[49]

78 Ibn 'Abbās reported that he quarreled with al-Ḥurr ibn Qais ibn Ḥiṣn al-Fazārī about the companion of Moses. ...[50]

Ch. 20:   The excellence of one who learns and of one who teaches

79 Abū Mūsā reported from the Prophet ﷺ that he said: The guidance and knowledge with which Allāh has sent me are like abundant rain which fell on some ground. Some of it was fertile ground which absorbed the water and

---

[47] Ibn 'Abbās has been considered competent to narrate this ḥadīth which relates to a principle of religion even though at the time of the incident he was a minor. This shows that adulthood is not a qualification for the narrator of such a ḥadīth but his understanding and intellect, and this is indicated in the heading of this chapter. As to the question of prayers not being invalidated by someone passing in front, this is further discussed in the book of Prayer; see h. 376, h. 495, h. 510 and h. 511. Prayer remains valid even with the passing of someone across the front, but to disturb the attention of the person praying by passing in front of him is a most reprehensible act.

[48] This ḥadīth proves only that a boy of five can clearly retain in memory impressionable events witnessed by him even at that tender age. This does not mean that as a general rule a boy of such an age can understand the religious significance of such events and convey it to people.

[49] This chapter furnishes an unimpeachable evidence on the reliability of Ḥadīth literature. Jābir ibn 'Abdullāh was himself a Companion of the Holy Prophet, but he felt so anxious about the authenticity of a particular ḥadīth, which he had heard from another Companion, that he undertook a journey of one month to have it verified by the original narrator who had himself heard it from the Holy Prophet. This happened in the year 54 A.H. during the rule of Mu'āwiyah. This was not an isolated incident. It is related that Abū Ayyūb al-Anṣārī undertook a journey to ascertain a ḥadīth from 'Uqbah ibn 'Āmir. Imām Mālik has related from Sa'īd ibn al-Musayyab the statement: "I used to travel for days and nights in search of a ḥadīth." Sha'bī said that it was an ordinary matter for a man to go to Madīnah in those days for the investigation of a religious matter. Abul 'Āliyah said: "Whenever we heard any narration attributed to a Companion of the Holy Prophet we would not rest satisfied until we heard it narrated by that Companion himself." All this clearly shows the great eagerness of the Companions of the Holy Prophet and their next generation, the *Tābi'īn*, for acquiring knowledge of Ḥadīth and its preservation.

[50] This is a repetition of h. 122 in words almost the same as h. 74.

brought forth herbage and vegetation in abundance.[51] Some of it was rocky soil, which retained the water by which Allāh gave benefit to people, so they drank it, gave it (to their beasts) to drink and used it to water the land.[52] Some of it (the rain) fell on another part which was barren (*qī'ān*), which could neither retain the water nor produce any herbage.[53] So that is the likeness of one who acquires understanding of the religion of Allāh and benefits from what Allāh has sent me with; so he learns it and teaches it. But the likeness of the man who does not pay any attention to it, and does not accept the guidance of Allāh with which I have been sent —[54] is that of the part of the ground which takes in water, it is *qā'*, meaning water rises to it and flows away. And *ṣafṣaf* is a level ground.[55]

Ch. 21: The removal of knowledge (from the world) and the advent of ignorance

> Rabī'ah said: It is not befitting anyone who may have some knowledge that he should waste himself.[56]

80 Anas reported that the Messenger of Allāh ﷺ said: "Surely among the signs of the Hour will be the removal of knowledge, the abundance of ignorance, drinking of alcoholic liquor, and the prevalence of illicit sexual relations." [57]

---

[51] Three kinds of people are described in this ḥadīth. One kind is of those who themselves benefit by the light of knowledge and make others benefit from it. These are likened to the fertile soil quick to bring forth vegetation at the first touch of rain.

[52] The second kind is of those who benefit little themselves but preserve it for others. These are likened to rocky land which acts as a reservoir for rain water.

[53] The third kind are those who neither benefit from knowledge nor have the capacity to preserve it or convey it to others. These are likened to the barren soil which has no use for rain-water. This ḥadīth emphasizes the importance of acquiring and teaching knowledge.

[54] Here Bukhārī has inserted a comment saying that the following words are from another report which Isḥāq narrated from Abū Usāmah.

[55] In this ḥadīth the Holy Prophet had used the word *qī'ān* to indicate barren land which is level, and which neither retains the water nor produces vegetation from it. In this other report added here by Bukhārī, the meaning of *qā'*, which is the singular of *qī'ān*, is explained by referring to its occurrence in a verse of the Qur'ān (20:106) which contains the words *qā'-an ṣafṣaf-an*, meaning "a plain, smooth level".

[56] The removal, lit. "the lifting up", of knowledge means the disappearance of the true, sincere and Godly persons who are learned in religion, and the world being left with self-seeking, worldly-minded theologians who are concerned only with the letter of the law. See also h. 100. The saying of Rabī'ah that anyone having anything of knowledge should not waste himself may mean that he should not lose it by doing nothing with it but he must continue to study it and propagate it. It may also mean that he should not waste his life in less important matters as knowledge is most valuable.

[57] Prevalence of ignorance, consumption of intoxicating liquors and laxity of sexual morality

81 Anas reported: I am narrating a ḥadīth which no one will narrate to you after me. I heard the Messenger of Allāh ﷺ say: "Among the signs of the Hour will be that knowledge will dwindle, ignorance will be widespread, illicit sexual relations will be prevalent, and women will be numerous and men will be few, so much so that for fifty women there will be one (man) to support them." [58]

Ch. 22:   Excellence of Knowledge

82 'Abdullāh ibn 'Umar said: I heard the Messenger of Allāh ﷺ say: "Once, when I was sleeping, I was given a cup of milk (in a dream); so I drank till I felt freshness coming out from my nails. Then I gave what was left over to 'Umar ibn al-Khaṭṭāb." People asked: "So what interpretation do you put on this, O Messenger of Allāh?" He said: "Knowledge." [59]

Ch. 23:   Giving decision on religious questions (*fatwā*) while seated on the back of an animal or on anything else

83 'Abdullāh ibn 'Amr ibn al-'Āṣ reported that the Messenger of Allāh ﷺ stopped during the Farewell Pilgrimage at Minā for people who had something to ask him. A man came to him and said: "I did not know, and I got my head shaved before I slaughtered (the sacrificial animal)." He said: "Slaughter (now), and there is no harm." Another man came and said: "I did not know, and I made the sacrifice before throwing pebbles." He said: "Throw (the pebbles now), and there is no harm." So whenever the Prophet ﷺ was asked about an act which had been done sooner and not later (than another act

---

are causes for the downfall of any society, and the "Hour" here may mean the doom of a nation. Certainly, these were the factors responsible for the downfall of the Muslims from being the leaders of light, knowledge and morality in the world to lying in the depths of ignorance and degradation. If the Day of Judgment is meant, then these vices may be even more widespread at the time, but the first meaning is more suitable.

[58] This is similar to the last ḥadīth. Relating to the downfall of the Muslims, it was indeed the case that many of their kings, sultans and chiefs had not just fifty but hundreds of women as their concubines, and these leaders fell into the pursuit of sensual pleasures. The reference here may also be to wars which reduce the number of males as compared to females, as in the First World War in particular. The statement of Anas that no one will narrate this ḥadīth after him means narrate directly from the Holy Prophet. This refers to the fact that he was aged at this time and very few Companions were left alive to narrate directly from the Holy Prophet.

[59] This shows the exalted position of 'Umar in respect of possessing knowledge, in which he surpassed all other Companions. Abū Bakr represented the perfection of faith among the Companions. Hence, Abū Bakr is at the head of those having the quality of *ṣiddīq* or true to the faith, and 'Umar is at the head of those known as *shahīd* who bear witness to the truth through knowledge. The Qur'ān speaks of the prophets, the *ṣiddīq,* the *shahīd,* and the *ṣāliḥ* (righteous) as being "a goodly company" (4:69).

which should have been done before it), he said (about the other act): "Do it (now), and there is no harm." [60]

Ch. 24: One who replies to religious questions by the sign of the hand or the head

84 Ibn 'Abbās reported that the Prophet ﷺ was asked during his pilgrimage by one who said: "I slaughtered (the sacrificial animal) before throwing pebbles." He (the Holy Prophet) indicated with his hand and said: "There is no harm." One said: "I got my head shaved before I slaughtered (the sacrificial animal)." He (the Holy Prophet) indicated with his hand (to say): "There is no harm." [61]

85 Abū Hurairah reported from the Prophet ﷺ that he said: "Knowledge will be withheld, and ignorance and tribulations will prevail, and there will be great *harj*." It was said: "O Messenger of Allāh, what is *harj*?" He said: "Like this", with his hand which he moved to indicate killing. [62]

86 Asmā' reported: [63] I came to 'Ā'ishah and she was praying. I said (to her): "What has happened to the people?" She pointed towards (the eclipse in) the sky, and people were standing (for prayer). Then she said: "*Subḥān Allāh* (glory be to God)." I said: "A sign?" She indicated with her head to say "Yes." I (also) stood up (for prayer) until I began to faint, so I poured water on my head. [64] The Prophet ﷺ praised Allāh and eulogized Him and then said:

---

[60] This ḥadīth shows that mistakes in the performance of rituals are not very serious matters, and they can be amended very easily. See also h. 84, h. 124, h. 1721–1723 and h. 1734–1738.

[61] This is a repetition of the previous h. 83. Here it is mentioned that the Holy Prophet indicated with his hand to answer, which gives rise to the chapter heading.

[62] The word *harj* originally means prevalence of harm, evil and mischief. In the language of the Habesha (who live in the South of Arabia), it means killing or slaughter. It seems that ignorance and evil lead to killings on a large scale since people become devoid of love for fellow human beings and are filled with hatred for one another. See also h. 1036.

[63] See also h. 184, h. 922, h. 1053 and h. 1061. The narrator is Asmā', daughter of Abū Bakr, the first Caliph and the sister of 'Ā'ishah, wife of the Prophet. She died in 73 A.H. at the age of a hundred years, but showed no physical signs of old age such as losing of teeth. Equally strong was her mind and determination. When 'Abdullāh ibn Zubair, her son, came to seek advice from her whether to accept the authority of Ḥajjāj the despot, she told him that it would be unbecoming of him, and to die fighting him would be preferable.

[64] The occasion of this ḥadīth was an eclipse of the sun. People had gathered in the mosque for prayers connected with this incident, and 'Ā'ishah was saying the same prayer in her own room. Making sign towards the sky was to indicate that the prayer was due to this eclipse.

"There is nothing which I was not shown before that I did not see on this spot, even Paradise and Hell.[65] Then it was revealed to me: Surely you will be tried in your graves like or near — I (a narrator) do not know which of these Asmā' said[66] — the trial of Dajjāl (the Anti-Christ), and it will be said: 'What is your knowledge about this man?'[67] So one who is a believer or has certainty — I (a narrator) do not know which of these two Asmā' said — will say: 'He is Muḥammad, the Messenger of Allāh, who has come to us with clear signs and guidance, so we have accepted him and followed him; he is Muḥammad'. Three times (this will be said). So it will be said: 'Sleep well, we had known that you had certainty of it.' And as for the hypocrite or the doubter — I (a narrator) do not know which of these Asmā' said — he will say: 'I do not know. I heard people saying something, so I said the same'."

Ch. 25: **The Prophet ﷺ persuading the deputation of 'Abdul Qais to preserve the faith and the knowledge and to convey the same to those left behind them**

> Mālik ibn al-Ḥuwairith said: The Prophet ﷺ said to us: "Return to your people and teach them." [68]

87 Abū Jamrah reported: I used to interpret between Ibn 'Abbās and the people. Once he (Ibn 'Abbās) said:

> When the deputation of 'Abdul Qais came to the Prophet ﷺ, he (the Prophet) said: "What deputation is this?" or "Who are these people?" They said: "It is (the tribe of) Rabī'ah." …[69]

---

[65] The words which the Holy Prophet spoke indicate that he fell into a spiritual trance during the prayer and actually saw the heavenly things in that condition without his body travelling to the heavens. Since he was shown Paradise and Hell while leading his Companions in prayer here on earth, it proves that during what is known as his *Mi'rāj* or Ascension he did not need to be taken physically from this earth to be shown the heavenly sights.

[66] The narrator's parenthesis indicating his doubt about the actual word used by Asmā', which he expresses on three occasions while narrating this ḥadīth, shows his anxiety for absolute accuracy.

[67] By "this man" is meant the Holy Prophet. The word *qabr* or grave is a condition of every human being immediately after death, even if his body is not buried in a grave, and the trial spoken of here takes place in this condition known as *barzakh*. An individual's awareness of this condition depends on his spiritual development during his life. The reference to the *Dajjāl* or Anti-Christ is made to show that his function will be to cast doubts on the faith in the hearts.

[68] This shows that the Holy Prophet used to exhort his Companions to preserve whatever he taught them. This was one of the measures taken in the earliest times for the preservation of Ḥadīth.

[69] This is a repetition of h. 53, and from this point onwards its wording differs only slightly

Ch. 26:   Undertaking a journey in connection with a problem that may arise

88 'Uqbah ibn al-Ḥārith reported that he married the daughter of Abū Ihāb ibn 'Azīz. Later a woman came to him and said: "I have suckled 'Uqbah and the girl whom he has married." 'Uqbah said to her: "I do not know that you have suckled me, nor have you ever told me." So he rode to the Messenger of Allāh ﷺ at Madīnah and asked him about it. The Messenger of Allāh ﷺ said: "How (can this marriage remain valid) when this has been said?" So 'Uqbah divorced her and she married another husband.

Ch. 27:   Fixing turns for acquiring knowledge

89 'Umar reported: I and a neighbour of mine from among the *Anṣār* were (living) in Banū Umayyah ibn Zaid, which was among the uplands of Madīnah, and we used to attend upon the Messenger of Allāh ﷺ by turns. He used to attend one day and I used to attend another day. When I was there I would bring him news of that day about the revelation and other matters, and when he was there he did similarly.[70] One day, when it was his turn, my *Anṣārī* friend came and knocked at my door violently and asked if I was there. I got frightened and came out to him. He said: "A great event has taken place." I then went to Ḥafṣah and she was weeping. So I said: "Has the Messenger of Allāh ﷺ divorced you?" She replied: "I do not know." Then I went to the Prophet ﷺ and while standing said: "Have you divorced your wives?" He said: "No." So I said: "Allāh is Great."[71]

---

and insignificantly from the same point in h. 53. The initial words of Abū Jamrah about Ibn 'Abbās as found in h. 53 are not present here.

[70] This ḥadīth will come again in greater detail in h. 2468. Its part which is relevant here is that which speaks of 'Umar having entered into an arrangement with an *Anṣārī*, whose name was 'Utbān ibn Mālik, to go in turn to the Holy Prophet and keep each other informed of what he said or did. This shows the eagerness of the Companions to acquire knowledge and not to miss anything. While they used to conduct their worldly work, they did not allow it to be an obstacle in the way of acquiring knowledge. 'Umar lived some three or four miles away from Madīnah. It may be noted that here the word *nuzūl* (lit. 'descent') is repeatedly used for their going to Madīnah. This shows that the word *nuzūl* does not mean descending from heaven, which it is mistakenly taken to mean in the prophecy of the coming of Jesus.

[71] Ḥafṣah was the daughter 'Umar and was a wife of the Holy Prophet. A reference to this incident is also found in the Qur'ān, 33 : 28–29. It belongs to 9 A.H. when the wives of the Holy Prophet were given a choice between living with him in marriage a life of simplicity or living a comfortable life divorced from him. It was natural that when the Muslim community became more prosperous the wives of the Holy Prophet also desired to share in this more comfortable life. But the Qur'ān and the Holy Prophet wanted them to act as models of simplicity and austerity for Muslim women. He accordingly retired from them for a whole month to allow them a chance for a thorough heart-searching and to make their choice between him and the world.

Ch. 28:   Anger during preaching and teaching on seeing what one dislikes

90 Abū Masʿūd al-Anṣārī reported: A man said: "O Messenger of Allāh, I may fail to attend prayer on account of so-and-so because he makes it very long." I never saw the Prophet ﷺ more angry in preaching than he was on that day. He said: "O people, surely you will make them dislike it; so whoever leads the people in prayer should make it light, for surely among them are the sick, the weak and those with needs to attend to." [72]

91 Zaid ibn Khālid al-Juhanī reported that a man asked the Prophet ﷺ about (finding) a fallen thing (lost by someone). He said: "Take note of what it is tied with — or he said "its pot" — and its bag, and keep trying to have it identified for a year. Then use it for your own purpose. Then if its owner comes hand it over to him." He asked: "(What about) a strayed camel?" He (the Holy Prophet) became angry, so much so that his cheeks turned red — or the narrator said, his face turned red — and he said: "What is that to do with you? It has its water-bag and its feet. It can go to the water and graze on trees, so leave it till its owner finds it." He asked: "(What about) a lost goat? He (the Holy Prophet) replied: "It is for you or for your brother (i.e., another person) or for the wolf!"

92 Abū Mūsā reported: The Prophet ﷺ was questioned about (certain) things which he disliked. When he was asked too much he became displeased. Then he said to the people: "Ask me whatever you like." A man asked: "Who is my father?" He (the Holy Prophet) replied: "Your father is Ḥudhāfah." Another man stood up and asked: "Who is my father, O Messenger of Allāh?" He said: "Your father is Sālim, the slave of Shaibah." So when ʿUmar saw what (displeasure) was on his face, he said: "O Messenger of Allāh! Surely we turn towards Allāh, the Mighty, the Glorious." [73]

---

[72] The Holy Prophet was very anxious to make the observance of religion easy and convenient to people. So at times he would be angry with those who would make such observance difficult for people. However, even his anger would not go beyond a mild rebuke such as the one mentioned here. The appearance of anger on his face was a natural reaction, which is not in human control. This shows that a Muslim must restrain his anger, keeping it within due, civilized bounds.

[73] In pre-Islamic Arab society, people used to taunt one another on the basis of their parentage and to ascribe a man's parentage to someone other than his father. It seems that this custom continued among Muslims and some people had taunted ʿAbdullāh ibn Ḥudhāfah Sahmī (who was sent as an envoy to the court of the Chosroes of Persia) and Saʿd ibn Sālim in this way. This displeased the Holy Prophet, so he said, "Ask me whatever you like", meaning that anyone who wished to may ask him to clear the aspersion cast against him. On the other hand, ʿUmar felt that such low matters should not be brought to the notice of the Holy Prophet. He, therefore, assured

Ch. 29:   He who sits with his knees folded before the Imām or the teacher of Ḥadīth (*muḥaddith*)

93 Anas ibn Mālik informed that the Messenger of Allāh ﷺ came out and ʿAbdullāh ibn Ḥudhāfah stood up and asked: "Who is my father?" He (the Holy Prophet) replied: "Your father is Ḥudhāfah." Then he said repeatedly: "Ask me." ʿUmar, who was sitting with his knees folded, said: "We are pleased with Allāh as our Lord, Islām as our religion, and Muḥammad ﷺ as our Prophet" three times. Then he became silent.[74]

Ch. 30:   He who repeats a talk three times so that it may be understood

The Prophet ﷺ said: "Beware of telling lies." He went on repeating it, and Ibn ʿUmar said that the Prophet ﷺ said, "Have I conveyed the message?", three times."

94 Anas reported, regarding the Prophet ﷺ, that when he used to greet (with *Salām*) he would greet three times and when he said anything he would say it three times so that it was understood.

95 Anas reported, regarding the Prophet ﷺ, that when he said anything he would say it three times so that it was understood, and when he came to a people and greeted them (with *Salām*) he would greet them three times.[75]

96 ʿAbdullāh ibn ʿAmr reported: The Messenger of Allāh ﷺ remained behind on one of the journeys we had undertaken (together). Then he joined us while we were getting late for *ʿAṣr* prayers and performing *Wuḍū'*. We were not fully washing our feet, so he called out to us at the top of his voice, "Woe to the heels because of the fire", two or three times.[76]

---

the Holy Prophet that Muslims would not continue this practice in future. ʿUmar himself was not indulging in this practice and by saying "we turn towards Allāh" he was only representing the people.

[74] H. 92 is repeated here with differences. The chapter heading is derived from the mention that ʿUmar was sitting with his knees folded. By his statement in this version of the ḥadīth, ʿUmar assured the Holy Prophet that Muslims would adhere to the principles of Islām and this evil practice would be stopped for good. See also h. 540.

[75] In h. 94 and h. 95 it is not meant that the Holy Prophet used to repeat every statement that he made. He did it only in the case of important statements which had to be conveyed clearly, as shown by the words: "so that it was understood." The repetition of the greetings was done when the Holy Prophet went to houses whose occupants he wanted to visit. If there was no response to the first greeting he would repeat it, and again a third time if necessary. Also, when meeting a group of people, one often repeats a greeting.

[76] This is a repetition of h. 60. The prayer mentioned there is stated here to be *ʿAṣr*.

Ch. 31:   A man's imparting education to his female slave and his family

97 Abū Burdah reported from his father (Abū Mūsā al-Ash'arī) that the Messenger of Allāh ﷺ said: "There are three persons for whom there is double reward: (firstly) a man from among the People of the Book who believes in his own Prophet and believes in Muḥammad,[77] (secondly) a slave owned by another man when he fulfills his obligations to Allāh and his obligations to his master, and (thirdly) a man who has a female slave and he teaches her good manners, making her manners the best, and he educates her, making her education the best, then he sets her free and marries her, so for him there is a double reward." [78]

Then 'Āmir (a narrator) said: We gave this (ḥadīth) to you free; there was a time when for lesser things people used to ride to Madīnah." [79]

Ch. 32:   The preaching of the Imām to women and giving them education

98 Ibn 'Abbās said: I was witness of the Prophet ﷺ that he, the Prophet ﷺ, came out and with him was Bilāl and he thought that women did not hear (his sermon), so he preached to them and exhorted them to give in charity. The women began to throw ear-rings and rings, and Bilāl collected them in a part of his garment.[80]

---

[77] This seems to relate to such People of the Book as were faithful to their previous guidance and yet did not hesitate to accept the claims of the Holy Prophet when he advanced them. Through their example others were guided to the right path.

[78] The fact that the necessity of imparting good upbringing to a female-slave has been so much emphasized by the Holy Prophet shows that is even more necessary to look after the intellectual and moral education of wives and daughters in Muslim households. Bukhārī has realized this importance himself by adding "and his family" at the end of this chapter heading, even though the ḥadīth itself only mentions a female-slave (*ama-tun*). By the words "and marries her", the Holy Prophet has indicated that he wanted to see all Muslim wives to be well-educated and cultured, but Muslims have been greatly neglectful in this respect.

This ḥadīth also removes the misconception that concubinage is allowed in Islām, i.e., the practice of a master having sexual relations with his female slave without marrying her. In certain manuscripts of Bukhārī, after "a female slave" are added the words "with whom he has sexual relations". However, in the authentic manuscripts of Bukhārī, such as that used by the author of *Fatḥ al-Bārī*, this addition does not occur. Even in the manuscripts containing this addition, it occurs only in this version of the ḥadīth and not in its repetitions, for example h. 2547 and h. 3011, thus showing that it is an erroneous addition in some manuscripts.

[79] These concluding words are from one of the narrators of this ḥadīth addressed to another narrator in the chain of narration. The speaker of these words wants to convey to his listeners the importance of the knowledge of Ḥadīth.

[80] According to Bukhārī exhortations on charity are a part of education. The ḥadīth shows

Ch. 33: Yearning for ḥadīth

99 Abū Hurairah reported that he asked: "O Messenger of Allāh! Who will be the most fortunate of people in securing your intercession on the Day of Resurrection"? The Messenger of Allāh ﷺ replied: "Abū Hurairah, I know that no one would ask me about this matter before you, for I have seen in you a yearning for ḥadīth. The most fortunate of people to secure my intercession on the Day of Resurrection will be the one who says 'There is no god but Allāh (*Lā ilāha ill-Allāh*)' sincerely from his heart or his soul." [81]

Ch. 34: How knowledge will be withheld?

'Umar ibn 'Abdul 'Azīz wrote to Abū Bakr ibn Ḥazm: "Look out for any ḥadīth of the Messenger of Allāh ﷺ and write it down, as I fear that knowledge may vanish and the learned ones may disappear. Do not accept anything but the ḥadīth of the Prophet ﷺ and people should disseminate knowledge and establish gatherings until those who have no knowledge have been taught, for surely knowledge does not disappear unless it is kept secret." [82]

100 'Abdullāh ibn 'Amr ibn al-'Āṣ reported: I heard the Messenger of Allāh ﷺ saying: "Allāh will not take away knowledge by snatching it from people, but He will take away knowledge by taking away the learned ones till no learned one will remain. People will take ignorant ones as their leaders,

---

how the Holy Prophet was anxious to include women in the recipients of preaching and education like men, and to ensure that they too participated in community work. See also h. 863, h. 964, h. 975, h. 1431 and h. 1449.

[81] The words "There is no god but Allāh" are a common way in Ḥadīth of referring to the full formula of the Islamic faith: "There is no god but Allāh, Muḥammad is the Messenger of Allāh." This is just as in the Qur'ān belief in "Allāh and the Last Day" is a shorthand way of referring to all the fundamental beliefs of Islām, i.e., in Allāh, His angels, Books, Prophets and the Last Day. The description "sincerely from his heart" means that there should be no hypocrisy and there must be full determination in the heart to follow the principles of Islām in actual life.

[82] Abū Bakr ibn Ḥazm belonged to the generation after the generation of the Companions of the Holy Prophet, known as the *Tābi'īn*, and was appointed by 'Umar ibn 'Abdul 'Azīz as the Qāḍī of Madīnah. Just as 'Umar, the second Caliph, was anxious for a written collection of the Holy Qur'ān to be made, this "second 'Umar" evinced his anxiety for a written collection of the Ḥadīth. He feared the disappearance of this knowledge or its corruption due to it being only in the memories of people. He ordered the writing down of Ḥadīth reports and gave the instruction that this compilation should contain only the words and actions of the Holy Prophet, and not statements and deeds of others. This incident belongs to the end of the first century A.H. 'Umar ibn 'Abdul 'Azīz, who was a saintly figure, ruled from 99 A.H. to 101 A.H. and died at the age of 40. Abū Na'īm al-Aṣbahānī writes in his history that 'Umar ibn 'Abdul 'Azīz sent such instructions for the collection of Ḥadīth to all important parts of the dominion of Islām.

who will be asked questions and they will give religious verdicts without knowledge, going astray themselves and leading others astray." [83]

Ch. 35:   Should a (separate) day be fixed for women to teach (them) knowledge?

101 Abū Saʿīd al-Khudrī reported: Women said to the Prophet ﷺ: "Men have an advantage over us in approaching you, so appoint for us a day that you can (to teach women only)." So he promised them a day to meet them on it. He preached to them and gave them instructions. Among what he said to them was: "There is none among you women before whom three of her children die but these will serve as a screen for her from the fire (of Hell)." A woman said: "And (what about) two?" He replied: "Two also." [84]

102 And Abū Hurairah reported (about h. 101) to say: Three that have not attained maturity. [85]

Ch. 36:   Whoever hears anything and does not understand it, he should ask again and again till he understands it

103 Ibn Abū Mulaikah related that ʿĀ'ishah, wife of the Prophet ﷺ, whenever she heard a thing which she did not understand, she would ask about it again and again, till she understood it. [86] Once the Prophet ﷺ said: "Whoever is taken to account (on the Day of Resurrection), he will be punished." ʿĀ'ishah said:

I asked, Does not Allāh, the Mighty, the Glorious, say: "his account will be taken by an easy reckoning" (84:8), and he (the Holy Prophet) replied:

---

[83] Knowledge vanishes when learned persons no longer remain. This ḥadīth gives great encouragement to the acquisition of knowledge. These exhortations led to the foundation of various seats of learning that sprung up all over the Muslim world immediately after the Holy Prophet's demise. Unless each and every person considers it his duty to acquire knowledge, learned persons cannot be produced.

[84] The fixing of a particular day exclusively for women's education shows the Holy Prophet's emphasis on their education. As he knew that the greater part of women's time was taken up by their duties to their children, he informed them that bringing up their children was also a work which earns heavenly reward. If a woman suffers the bereavement of three, or even two, young children (some ḥadīth speak of one child as well) she will be entitled to heavenly life as their death causes her anguish and makes her turn to God.

[85] In h. 101 those children are meant who die while still under the care of the mother.

[86] This ḥadīth shows that the Holy Prophet was an example of a perfect teacher who encouraged questions on himself. A real teacher should ensure that his teachings are fully comprehended by those taught. He should not mind even being repeatedly asked a certain question, nor are such questions to be taken as showing disrespect for the teacher.

"This is only about presenting (the account), but whoever is called upon to explain the account, he will perish." [87]

Ch. 37: Those who are present must convey knowledge to those who are absent

Ibn ʿAbbās reported this from the Prophet ﷺ.[88]

104 Abū Shuraiḥ reported that he said to ʿAmr ibn Saʿīd when he was sending armies to Makkah (to fight ʿAbdullāh ibn Zubair): "Permit me, O chief, I will relate to you a saying which came from the Messenger of Allāh ﷺ the day after the conquest of Makkah. My ears heard it, my heart preserved it and my eyes saw him when he said it. He praised Allāh and eulogised Him, and then said:

'Surely it is Allāh Who has made Makkah sacred, it is not people who have made it sacred.[89] So it is not lawful for a man who believes in Allāh and the Last Day to shed blood in it, nor to cut down any tree. If anyone wants leave (to fight in it) on the basis of the Messenger of Allāh ﷺ fighting in it, say (to him): Allāh has certainly permitted His Messenger ﷺ and not permitted you. He permitted me only for a few hours of one day, and today its sacredness has returned as it was sacred yesterday. So those who are present must convey this to those who are absent.' "

Abū Shuraiḥ was asked: "What did ʿAmr say (in reply)?" He said: "(ʿAmr replied) O Abū Shuraiḥ, I know better (about it) than you. It does not give protection to a sinner, nor to a fugitive who has murdered or committed a crime (*kharbah*)." [90]

---

[87] ʿĀ'ishah pointed out to the Holy Prophet that his statement seemed to contradict the Qur'ān. This shows also that the Qur'ān holds a higher status than his statements. The Holy Prophet did not resent this objection or take it ill. He explained that by "taken to account" he meant "called upon to explain the account", i.e., held to account. What the Qur'ān is referring to is the person who is presented with his account of deeds, but these are not such that he can be held to account for them.

[88] This chapter is meant to emphasize the necessity and the duty of one possessing knowledge to communicate it to others.

[89] These words are decisive in showing that the sanctity attached to the Kaʿbah was ordained by the Divine revelation of a prophet. This is why the whole Arab nation recognized this tradition.

[90] This ḥadīth is repeated in h. 1832. Abū Shuraiḥ was a Companion of the Holy Prophet, and ʿAmr ibn Saʿīd was appointed by Yazīd as governor of Madīnah. When Yazīd proclaimed himself as Caliph, Ḥusain, son of ʿAlī, who lived in Madīnah and ʿAbdullāh ibn Zubair who lived in Makkah refused to recognize his caliphate. Hence the expedition sent against Makkah spoken of here. Ḥusain's defiance led to his martyrdom at Karbala. Abū Shuraiḥ tried to stop ʿAmr by reminding him of the inviolable sanctity of the Kaʿbah ordained by the Holy Prophet. But ʿAmr

105 Abū Bakrah reported, mentioning the Prophet ﷺ, that he said: "Surely your blood and your wealth" — Muḥammad (a narrator) said, I think he added "and your honour" — "are sacred to one another as this day of yours is sacred, in this (sacred) month of yours. Beware! Those of you who are present must convey it to those who are absent."

Muḥammad (a narrator in the line of reporting) used to say: The Messenger of Allāh ﷺ told the truth. He (the Holy Prophet) added twice: "Beware! Have I not conveyed the message?" [91]

Ch. 38: The sin of one who ascribes anything falsely to the Prophet ﷺ

106 'Alī said that the Prophet ﷺ said: "Do not ascribe anything to me falsely, for whoever ascribes anything to me falsely will surely enter the fire (of hell)." [92]

107 'Abdullāh ibn Zubair reported: I said to Zubair (i.e., his father), "I do not hear you narrating from the Messenger of Allāh ﷺ as such-and-such other people narrate." He said: "I never remained away from him,[93] but I heard him say: 'Whoever ascribes anything to me falsely, let him make his place in the fire'." [94]

108 Anas said: What prevents me from narrating ḥadīth in large numbers is that the Prophet ﷺ said: "Whoever intentionally ascribes anything to me falsely, let him make his place in the fire." [95]

---

rejected this plea, saying that this sanctity should not stand in the way of apprehending a murderer and a rebel. The words of the Holy Prophet show that his own entry into this Sacred city with drawn swords as a conqueror was by a special permission of God for one day, and anyone else who invades it is disobeying the Holy Prophet.

[91] This is a repetition of h. 67 with some differences.

[92] According to Islām, telling any kind of lie leads to hell, but this refers to the practice in previous religions of falsely attributing sayings and acts to prophets and holy persons with the pious intention of exhorting people to follow religion. Among Christians there was the practice of the use of falsehood in the promotion of truth and religion. The Companions of the Holy Prophet, and the highly-regarded narrators of Ḥadīth, are acknowledged as telling only the truth. If a narrator is proved to have fabricated a ḥadīth, all reports narrated by him are treated as doubtful.

[93] Zubair had to migrate to Abyssinia during the early part of the mission of the Holy Prophet. Therefore, by never remaining away he means that he lived most of the time in close companionship of the Holy Prophet.

[94] The Companions were scrupulous to the highest degree in narrating ḥadīth accurately. They even feared misreporting them unintentionally and by mistake. Hence Zubair's caution in narrating ḥadīth. This particular ḥadīth has been narrated by so many Companions through such a variety of channels that it is regarded by the authorities as of undoubted authenticity.

[95] Anas means that anyone who is anxious to relate many things of the Holy Prophet's time will lower the standard of accuracy in order to include more details, and this amounts to lying, which is a sin.

109 Salamah ibn al-Akwaʿ reported: I heard the Prophet ﷺ say: "Whoever ascribes to me what I have not said, let him make his place in the fire."

110 Abū Hurairah reported from the Prophet ﷺ that he said: "Name yourselves with my name but do not give my lineage (*kunya*) to yourselves.[96] And whoever sees me in a dream, surely he has indeed seen me, for surely the Devil cannot assume my form.[97] And whoever intentionally ascribes anything to me falsely, let him make his place in the fire."

Ch. 39:   Writing down (matters of) knowledge[98]

111 Abū Juḥaifah reported: I said to ʿAlī: "Do you have a book?" He said: "No, except the Book of Allāh, or the (power of) understanding which has been given to every Muslim,[99] or whatever is on this paper." I said: "What is on this paper?" He replied: "(It is about) Blood-money, the setting free of prisoners, and that a Muslim should not be killed for (killing) an unbeliever." [100]

112 Abū Hurairah reported that people of the Khuzāʿah tribe killed a man of Banū Laith in the year of the Conquest of Makkah in retaliation for one of their own whom they had murdered. This news was conveyed to the Prophet ﷺ. So he mounted his she-camel and delivered an address, saying: "Surely

---

[96] In some Ḥadīth reports the opposite has been stated, that you can name yourselves with the lineage (*kunya*) of the Holy Prophet but not with his name. The Holy Prophet's *kunya* was Abul Qāsim. The idea seems to be that both the name and the lineage should not be used together to avoid confusion about the identity. But even this prohibition should be regarded as confined to the Holy Prophet's own time.

[97] This is a particular distinction of the Holy Prophet granted to him by Allāh, but dreams require interpretation. A person cannot take words of the Holy Prophet spoken to him in a dream literally if they conflict with Islamic law, but he must interpret them to accord with the teachings of Islām.

[98] In this chapter Bukhārī has shown that sometimes the Companions of the Holy Prophet wrote down Ḥadīth reports and he himself also had them written.

[99] Abū Juḥaifah asked ʿAlī whether the people of the Holy Prophet's household had any written work other than the Qur'ān. His reply by ʿAlī was that the Qur'ān was the only book with them and also the same gift of understanding as any other Muslim. This dispels the wrong idea that ʿAlī was given some secret knowledge of the Qur'ān by the Holy Prophet which was then passed down confidentially from one generation to the next through selected persons. By mentioning "understanding given to every Muslim" this ḥadīth allows every Muslim to interpret the Holy Qur'ān and draw conclusions from its verses, and also to differ from other interpreters, however great they may be. In Qasṭalānī, the commentary of Ṣaḥīḥ Bukhārī, it is stated that a scholar may deduce some point from the Qur'ān which is not found in earlier commentaries of the Qur'ān.

[100] This paper contained certain instructions applicable at the time in the state of war between Muslims and the unbelievers. According to Abū Ḥanīfah, if an unbeliever living under Muslim rule is killed by a Muslim, the Muslim will be punished for committing murder.

Allāh has restrained from Makkah murder" — or he said "the elephant", the narrator is in doubt[101] — "and has given the Messenger of Allāh and the believers power over them. Beware, surely it (fighting) was not lawful for anyone before me, nor will it be lawful for anyone after me. Beware, it was made lawful for me only for a few hours one day. Beware, surely this time of mine is sacred; not a thorn of it should be uprooted, nor a tree cut down, nor any fallen thing therein should be picked up except by one who wants to have it identified. Whoever is killed (therein), in his case there is one of two alternatives: either blood-money be paid for him or he (the murderer) be handed over to the heirs of the murdered."

Then came a man from among the people of Yaman and said: "Write this for me, O Messenger of Allāh". So he (Holy Prophet) said: "Write it for the father of so-and-so". Then a man from the Quraish said: "O Messenger of Allāh, make an exception for *al-idhkhir* (*idh-khir,* a kind of grass) for we put it in our houses and in our graves." Then the Prophet ﷺ said: "Except *al-idhkhir,* except *al-idhkhir.*" [102]

113 Abū Hurairah said: No one from among the Companions of the Prophet ﷺ narrated more reports from him than myself, except the case of ʿAbdullāh ibn ʿAmr, for he used to write (them down) but I did not write.[103]

114 Ibn ʿAbbās reported: When the illness of the Prophet ﷺ became serious, he said: "Bring me writing material and I will write for you a document after which you will not go astray." ʿUmar said: "The Prophet ﷺ has been overwhelmed by illness, and we have the Book of Allāh with us which is sufficient for us." Then people disagreed and the noise increased. He (the Holy Prophet) said: "Go away from me, for it is not proper that there should be any dispute near me."

---

[101] The word here for "murder" is *al-qatl* (القتل) and for "elephant" is *al-fīl* (الفيل). The narrator is unsure which of these two words it was, perhaps because of their similarity when written in Arabic script. If murder is meant, it shows that killing is forbidden in the Sacred City, except in case of punishing a murderer in order to maintain law and order. More likely, the word is "the elephant" and the reference is to the attack on Makkah by the forces of Abrahah from Yaman who had elephants with them. This happened in the year of the birth of the Holy Prophet. Allāh protected His House from destruction by this army, even though idolators were custodians of this House at the time, and they had little humanly available resources to defend it. Now that Muslims were custodians of this House, they should respect its sanctity even more.

[102] See h. 1834, which is a repetition of this ḥadīth.

[103] Abū Hurairah does not mean that no one narrated more reports than him *except* ʿAbdullāh ibn ʿAmr ibn al-ʿĀṣ. In fact, more than 5000 reports are narrated from Abū Hurairah, while some 700 are narrated from ʿAbdullāh ibn ʿAmr. He means that ʿAbdullāh ibn ʿAmr had the distinction over him of writing them down. However, it appears that, after the death of the Holy Prophet, Abū Hurairah also resorted to writing as it is reported in *Fatḥ al-Bārī* that he showed someone papers on which Ḥadīth reports were written down.

So Ibn 'Abbās went out saying: "It was the most terrible tragedy which intervened between the Messenger of Allāh ﷺ and his writing." [104]

Ch. 40:   Knowledge and its preaching at night

115 Umm Salamah reported: One night the Prophet ﷺ woke up and said: "Glory be to Allāh! What trials have descended tonight, and what treasures have been opened! Awaken the occupants of the (female) chambers, for many

---

[104] This ḥadīth occurs several times in Bukhārī; see h. 3053 and h. 4431. It is stated there that this incident happened on Thursday and that on the same day later on he made a will for three things, first being that the idolaters should be turned out of the Arabian Peninsula, the second that deputations that come from elsewhere must be entertained with due honour as they were treated by the Holy Prophet himself, and the third item was forgotten by Ibn 'Abbās. It would appear from this ḥadīth that the Holy Prophet wanted to leave some written instructions but 'Umar prevented this, and Ibn 'Abbās regarded this as a great tragedy. But facts and reason are against this conclusion. 'Umar could not have prevented the Holy Prophet from speaking out those instructions, and it was by speaking, and not writing, that the Holy Prophet used to give his teachings and instructions to his followers. In h. 3053 and h. 4431 Ibn 'Abbās says that at about the same time the Holy Prophet spoke out three instructions, one of which must have been very unimportant because he forgot it! Moreover, this happened on Thursday and he died on Monday. He could have asked for writing material during these four days, especially as his condition had improved in this time.

It is clear from this ḥadīth that either it is misattributed to Ibn 'Abbās or he is under a misunderstanding. It begins by saying: "When the illness of the Prophet became serious". It was this which prompted 'Umar to say that in that condition he should not be subjected to dictating a document. He did not tell people not to listen to the Holy Prophet. Ibn 'Abbās himself admits that when 'Umar said: "we have the Book of Allāh with us which is sufficient for us", the Holy Prophet became silent. What was it which the Holy Prophet wanted to convey to Muslims to prevent them from going astray that? It could not be that 'Alī should be made Caliph because eventually he did become Caliph and could then have saved the Muslims from going astray. Nor did Abū Bakr, the first Caliph, fail to do something to save the Muslims which 'Alī would have done. The only thing which could prevent Muslims from going astray was adherence to the Qur'ān. That was exactly what 'Umar said, because he realized that this was the will that the Holy Prophet wanted to leave. The Holy Prophet's statement "go away from me" shows that he approved of what 'Umar said. There are many instances in the life of the Holy Prophet in which he accepted the advice of 'Umar in religious issues as being the most sound.

If there is anything else we find in Ḥadīth reports that the Holy Prophet wanted to leave as his will, it is that Abū Bakr should be his successor. There is a report from 'Ā'ishah in Ṣaḥīḥ Muslim that the Holy Prophet said to her during his illness: "Send for Abū Bakr and your brother that I may give them a writing for I fear that a desirous one might say, 'I have a better claim to it', whereas Allāh and the believers deny anyone but Abū Bakr" (see book: 'Merits of the Companions', ch. 1). This report as well as the events that followed the Holy Prophet's death show that Abū Bakr's becoming Caliph was part of the Divine plan to save the Muslim nation in a moment of grave crisis and revive Islām anew. To conclude, this ḥadīth shows that the Holy Prophet wanted to tell Muslims to adhere firmly to the Qur'ān, and 'Umar expressed the same in words. The people's disputing on this occasion foreshadowed the disagreements that would arise among Muslims later.

women who are clothed in this world (physically) will be naked in the hereafter (spiritually)!" [105]

Ch. 41:   To talk at night (*samar*) about knowledge

116 'Abdullāh Ibn 'Umar said: Once when the Prophet ﷺ led us in *'Ishā'* prayer towards the last part of his life, after (concluding the prayer with) *Salām,* he stood up and said: "Keep this night in your mind, for surely after a hundred years from it no one will have remained from among those who are (now living) on the surface of the earth." [106]

117 Ibn 'Abbās reported: I spent a night in the house of my maternal aunt Maimūnah, daughter of al-Ḥārith, wife of the Prophet ﷺ, and the Prophet ﷺ was with her that night. The Prophet ﷺ said the *'Ishā'* prayer (in the mosque) and then came to his house and said four *rak'ahs* of prayer and went to sleep. Later he woke up (at night) and asked: "Is the young boy asleep?" or something like this. Then he stood up for prayer and I stood at his left side but he made me stand on his right. He said five *rak'ahs* of prayer, and then two more *rak'ahs* of prayer. Then he went to sleep again, so much so that I could hear his snoring. Then (in the morning) he went out for prayer (of *Fajr* in the mosque).[107]

Ch. 42:   Remembering things of Knowledge

118 Abū Hurairah reported: People surely say, "Abū Hurairah narrates plenty (of ḥadīth reports)", but if it were not for two verses in the Book of

---

[105] This is repeated in h. 1126. This shows that it is quite in order to learn and teach at night. The "occupants of the chambers" were the Holy Prophet's wives. He asked them to leave their beds at night and ask for the mercy of the Lord because he knew that no human connection could bring such mercy and that even his wives could not be saved but by their own efforts. The trials or the treasures which he was shown on this night must be connected with the future of his followers.

[106] The word *samar* means talking at night. In a report in Ṣaḥīḥ Muslim (book: 'Merits of the Companions', ch. 53), it has been stated that this incident took place just a month before his death. The Holy Prophet's saying that none of those that were living at that moment would be alive after one hundred years was a mighty prophecy that saw literal fulfilment later on, because his last Companion to die was Abū al-Ṭufail 'Amr ibn Wā'il who died in 110 A.H. See also h. 564 and h. 601.

[107] In another version of this ḥadīth, h. 4569, the Holy Prophet is reported to have talked to his wife before going to sleep. This shows that talking after the *'Ishā'* prayer is not altogether forbidden, and the reports which mention it as being not allowed mean only that unnecessary talk should be avoided. Here it is mentioned that the Holy Prophet said altogether nine *rak'ahs* in his *Tahajjud* prayer. This ḥadīth occurs in more detail in h. 138 and h. 183 in the Book of Ablution. (See also the Book of *Adhān,* h. 697 to h. 699, and the Book of *Tafsīr* — 'Commentary on the Qur'ān', h. 4569 to h. 4572.)

Allāh I would not have narrated any ḥadīth. Then he recited: "Surely those who conceal the clear proofs and the guidance that We revealed after We have made it clear in the Book for people, these it is whom Allāh curses, and those who curse, curse them (too). Except those who repent and amend and make manifest (the truth), these it is to whom I turn (mercifully); and I am the Oft-returning (to mercy), the Merciful" (2:159–160).

(He added:) Surely as for our brothers from among the Refugees (*Muhā-jirīn*), business transactions used to keep them busy in the markets, and as for our brothers from among the Helpers (*Anṣār*), their financial affairs used to keep them engaged, but Abū Hurairah used to stick with the Messenger of Allāh ﷺ for the (spiritual) filling of his stomach (with his sayings) and he used to be present (with him) when they would not be present and used to preserve what they could not preserve (of his sayings).[108]

119 Abū Hurairah reported: I said: "O Messenger of Allāh, surely I hear from you a large number of ḥadīth which I forget." He said: "Spread your cloak." So I spread it and he made a gesture, with his two hands cupped, of putting something (in it). Then he said: "Draw it to yourself." So I drew it to myself and I did not forget anything after that."[109]

Ibn Abū Fudaik reported the same, or with the words: "he made a gesture, with his hand cupped, of putting something in it."

120 Abū Hurairah reported: I preserved (in my memory) two kinds of knowledge (*wi'ā'ain*) from the Messenger of Allāh ﷺ: one of these I have

---

[108] Abū Hurairah is generally acknowledged by authorities on Ḥadīth as the one who, more than anyone else, preserved reports from the Holy Prophet. Among those who acknowledge this are Imām Shāfi'ī, Ibn 'Umar, Bukhārī in his history *Al-Tārīkh*, and Baihaqī. There is a report in Tirmidhī that Ibn 'Umar said to Abū Hurairah: "You used to be with the Messenger of Allāh more than any of us and you know his ḥadīth better than any of us" (book: *Al-Manāqib* — Virtues, h. 4207). Abū Hurairah was from the beginning keen to remember whatever the Holy Prophet said and to relate it. So he preserved many sayings which others could not. He was one of the *Aṣḥāb aṣ-Ṣuffah*, the students which chose to live in the vicinity of the Holy Prophet's house, devoting themselves to religious study away from all worldly occupations. He says in this ḥadīth that if he holds back any knowledge regarding the Holy Prophet that he possesses, this is disobedience to the injunctions of Allāh not to conceal guidance.

[109] The Holy Prophet prayed for increased strength in the memory of Abū Hurairah. Although the exact meaning of the Holy Prophet's act described here is not very clear, it appears that when he felt, while praying with his raised hands joined together, that the prayer had been granted he lowered the same hands so as to touch Abū Hurairah's cloak spread on the ground. It was a symbolic act expressing the Holy Prophet's transmitting the acceptance of prayer to the physical body of Abū Hurairah, which included his memory.

spread, but as to the other, if I were to disclose it, this gullet-pipe (*bul'ūm*) of mine would be cut." [110]

Abū 'Abdullāh (Bukhārī) said: *Bul'ūm* is the food tract.

Ch. 43:   To keep silence for the learned ones

121 Jarīr reported that the Prophet ﷺ said to him at the Farewell Pilgrimage: "Silence the people." Then he said (addressing them): "Do not return to unbelief after me by striking off necks of one another." [111]

Ch. 44:   It is proper for a learned one when he is asked, who among the people is the greatest in knowledge, he should attribute knowledge to Allāh, the Most High

122 Sa'īd ibn Jubair informed: I said to Ibn 'Abbās that Nauf al-Bakālī claims that Moses is not the Moses of the Israelites; he is another Moses. He said: "The enemy of Allāh has told a lie." [112] Ubaiy ibn Ka'b has reported from the Prophet ﷺ that he said:[113]

Moses the Prophet once stood to deliver a sermon to the Israelites. He was asked who among the people was the greatest in knowledge, and he said: "I am the greatest in knowledge." So Allāh reproved him, because he did not

---

[110] The word *wi'ā'-un,* originally meaning 'a vessel', occurs here in the dual form meaning two items of knowledge pregnant with deep significance. The first has been mentioned in h. 118, and it relates to matters of guidance, regarding which Abū Hurairah fears punishment from God if he fails to spread it. The other relates to prophecies of the trials and tribulations to befall the Muslims due to misconduct by their leaders. These have no bearing on the beliefs and practices of Islām, so there is no obligation to propagate them; moreover, there are difficulties in propagating them as they can be seen as a condemnation of the government of the time. Abū Hurairah used to pray: "I seek refuge in Allāh from the opening of the year 60 and rule by young men" (*Fath al-Bārī*). Yazīd became ruler in 60 A.H. and Abū Hurairah died a year before this.

[111] See also h. 1739. This is again a reference to minor unbelief or *kufr* within the fold of Islām; see footnote 44 to Ch. 20 of Book 2. A Muslim has been forbidden to shed the blood of another Muslim. If he commits this sin, he is acting like an unbeliever and "returning to unbelief", but he still remains within the fold of Islām.

[112] For the story of Moses referred to in this ḥadīth, see the Qur'ān, 18:60–82. Nauf al-Bakālī was a scholar and Imām in the generation after the Companions. Ibn 'Abbās lost his temper and uttered these words unworthy of him. Our exemplar is the Holy Prophet, and not Ibn 'Abbās, and the Prophet would not have uttered such words against a believer even under the greatest provocation.

[113] This incident has been mentioned previously in h. 74 and h. 78; see footnotes 44 and 45 under those reports. The question asked of Moses and his answer are different there from what they are here in h. 122. This shows that in relating stories the narrators introduced their own words. In general too, Ḥadīth reports cannot always be taken as being word for word what the Holy Prophet said, nor can they be elevated in authenticity and authority to the Qur'ān.

ascribe the (source of) knowledge to Him. Then Allāh revealed to him: "A servant from among My servants who lives at the confluence of two rivers, is greater in knowledge than yourself." He said: "My Lord, how am I to get to him"? He was told: "Carry a fish in a basket, so when it is lost, that is the place where he will be."

So he set out and with him went his servant Joshua, son of Nūn, and they carried a fish in the basket till they came to a rock. They placed their heads (on the ground) and slept. Meanwhile, the fish slipped out of the basket. And it took its way into the river, being free (the Qur'ān, 18:61). It was a surprise for Moses and his servant. Then they went on for the rest of that night and day. When it was morning time, Moses said to his servant: "Bring us our breakfast, we have certainly found this journey of ours tiring" (18:62); and Moses had not a touch of tiredness till they had gone past the place, about which he was commanded. His servant said to him: "Did you see, when we took refuge on the rock, I forgot the fish?" (18:63). Moses said: "This is what we sought for", so they returned retracing their footsteps (18:64).

When they ended the journey to the rock, a man wrapped in a cloth, or wrapping himself with his cloth, was there. Moses greeted him with salutation. Al-Khaḍir said: "How could there be salutation in your land?" He (Moses) said: "I am Moses." He asked: "Moses of the Israelites?" He (Moses) said: "Yes" and (added): "May I follow you that you may teach me some of the good you have been taught?" (18:66). He said: "You will not be able to have patience with me" (18:67), (adding) "Moses I possess sure knowledge from the knowledge of Allāh which He has taught me and which you do not know, and you have sure knowledge which Allāh has taught you and which I do not know." He (Moses) said: "If Allāh please, you will find me patient, nor I shall disobey you in anything" (18:69).

So they set out walking along the bank of the river and they had no boat. A boat happened to pass by them, and they asked them (i.e., the people of the boat) to take them on board. Al-Khaḍir was recognized, so they took them on without any fare. Then a sparrow came and sat on the edge of the boat and dipped her beak in the river once or twice. Al-Khaḍir said: "Moses, my knowledge and your knowledge does not take away from the knowledge of Allāh but to the extent of this sparrow's dipping her beak in the river." [114] Then Al-Khaḍir went towards a plank from among the planks of the boat and pulled it out. Upon this, Moses said: "These people took us without any fare

---

[114] The analogy of the sparrow's dipping its beak in the river is meant to convey that man with all his knowledge does not touch even the fringe of the ocean of Divine knowledge. It is not even a drop from an ocean.

and you damaged their boat, boring a hole in it so that you may drown its people?" He said: "Did I not say that you will not be able to have patience with me?" (18:72). He (Moses) said: "Do not blame me for what I forgot, and do not be hard upon me for what I did" (18:73). This was the first occasion on which Moses forgot (to remain patience).

So they went on, and there was a boy playing with other boys. Al-Khaḍir took hold of his head from above and severed his head with his hands.[115] At this Moses said: "Have you killed an innocent person, not guilty of killing another?" (18:74). He said: "Did I not say to you that you will not be able to have patience with me?" (18:75).

So they went on, until, when they came to the people of a town, they asked its people for food, but they refused to entertain them as guests; then they found in it a wall which was on the point of falling (18:77). Al-Khaḍir made a sign with his hand and then put it right. So Moses said to him: "If you had wished, you could have taken a recompense for it" (18:77). He said: "This is the parting between me and you" (18:78).[116]

The Prophet ﷺ said: "May Allāh have mercy on Moses! We wish he could have had patience so that we could be told (more) about the story of the two of them."

Ch. 45: One who asks questions while standing to a learned one who is sitting

123 Abū Mūsā reported: A man came to the Prophet ﷺ and said: "O Messenger of Allāh, what is fighting in the way of Allāh? For, one of us fights in a state of anger and another fights out of pride." At this he (the Prophet) raised his head towards him. He (the narrator) said that he raised his head because the man was standing. He (the Prophet then) said: "The one who fights so that Allāh's word may be raised high, he is (fighting) in the way of Allāh, the Mighty, the Glorious." [117]

---

[115] The killing of the boy has been described by the word *iqtala'a* which literally means 'snatching away' (his head). It indicates 'cutting off' as is stated in the version in h. 4727: "Al-Khaḍir took hold of his head and cut it off (*qaṭa'a-hu*)".

[116] In such lengthy reports, the exact words cannot be relied upon, and it is the general sense which should be taken. Anything in the report which is not justifiable from the Qur'ān cannot be accepted. Moses' experience with Al-Khaḍir taught him that underneath what appears to man to be the injustice of certain decrees of God, there lies wisdom and mercy. It is also indicated that prophets of God do not possess knowledge of matters unseen, like God does.

[117] This ḥadīth makes it perfectly clear that fighting in the way of Allāh (*fī sabīli-llāh*) is only that of which the sole object is the exaltation of God; in other words, fighting in the cause of truth

Ch. 46: Asking questions and giving of religious verdicts at the time of throwing pebbles (during the Pilgrimage)

124 'Abdullāh ibn 'Amr reported: I saw the Prophet ﷺ near the Jamrah and he was being asked questions. A man said: "O Messenger of Allāh, I made the sacrifice before throwing pebbles." He said: "Throw (the pebbles now), and there is no harm." Another man said: "I got my head shaved before I sacrificed (the animal)." He said: "Sacrifice (now), and there is no harm." So whenever he was asked about an act which had been done sooner and not later (than another act which should have been done before it), he said (about the other act): "Do it (now), and there is no harm." [118]

Ch. 47: The word of Allāh, the Most High: "And you are not given knowledge but a little" (the Qur'an, 17:85)

125 'Abdullāh (ibn Mas'ūd) reported: Once I was walking with the Prophet ﷺ in the uninhabited quarters of Madīnah and he was leaning against a stick which he had with him. A party of Jews was passing by, and some of them told others: "Ask him about the *Rūḥ* (the spirit)." Some of them said: "Do not ask him, lest he should say something which you will dislike." Some of them said: "We must ask him." So a man from among them stood up and said: "O Abul Qāsim! What is the *Rūḥ*?" He (the Prophet) kept silent. I then thought: "Surely revelation is coming to him." Then I stopped; so when that state passed away from him, he said: "And they ask you about the *Rūḥ*. Say: The *Rūḥ* is by the commandment of my Lord, and you are not given knowledge (about it) but a little" (17:85).[119]

---

and justice. If it is prompted by anger or pride, it is not fighting in the way of Allāh. Again, if its object is spoils of war or conquest of land, it is not fighting in the way of Allāh. Of course, if the purpose is to save Muslims from persecution or to remove obstructions from the path of preaching of Islām, it can be called fighting in the way of Allāh because its ultimate object is the exaltation of the word of Allāh.

[118] H. 83 has been repeated here with slightly different wording. *Jamrah* means small pieces of stone, its plural being *Jimār*. The plain of Minā is the place where small pieces of stone are thrown and Jamrah is the name especially given to 'Aqabah. There are two other Jamrahs besides this one. Because throwing of stones is a ritual of the Pilgrimage and an act of devotion, it might appear that no kind of talk is allowed in this state. This ḥadīth, however, makes an exception of such talks in this state as are connected with religion.

[119] In the Qur'ān the word *Rūḥ* has been used in several senses: as meaning the Qur'ān itself as in "We have revealed to you a *Rūḥ*" (42:52), as meaning the word of God as in "He casts the *Rūḥ* by His command..." (40:15), and as meaning human soul and consciousness as in "And He breathed into him from His *Rūḥ*" (32:9). The angel Gabriel has also been called *al-rūḥ al-amīn* (26:193) or the "Faithful Spirit". It is not clear from this ḥadīth in which sense the Jews asked about the *Rūḥ*. Bukhārī has only included this ḥadīth to show that man's knowledge is nothing

Ch. 48:   One who discards some of the optional things fearing that some of the people do not possess sufficient understanding and they may fall into worse sins

126 Al-Aswad reported: Ibn Zubair said to me: 'Ā'ishah used to disclose to you many secrets; what did she relate to you about the Ka'bah? I said: She told me that the Prophet ﷺ said: "O 'Ā'ishah! if your tribe had not come out of the era of unbelief so newly,[120] I would have demolished the Ka'bah and made for it two doors, one by which people would enter and the other by which they would leave." So Ibn Zubair accomplished that (wish of the Prophet)." [121]

---

as compared to that of God. The incident narrated here is of a doubtful nature since the revelation of the verse of the Qur'ān mentioned here took place in Makkah in the early period whereas this incident took place in Madīnah. Of course, it is possible that the Holy Prophet was merely quoting this verse which had been revealed to him years earlier, not that it was revealed to him in the state of receiving revelation into which he had just entered.

[120] Similar words occur in h. 1583 to h. 1586.

[121] The House of Ka'bah is reported to have been built seven times in history. The first building was raised by Adam (see the Qur'ān, 3:96). Its second building took place at the hands of Abraham and Ishmael (the Qur'ān, 2:127), the third by the Amalekites, the fourth by the Jurham, the fifth re-construction was by the Quraish when the Holy Prophet, aged 35 years, was asked to place the Black Stone. 'Abdullāh ibn Zubair rebuilt it for the sixth time and the seventh rebuilding was done by al-Ḥajjāj ibn Yūsuf. Some do not include the building by the Amalekites and the Jurham and say that it was built five times. This ḥadīth states that the Holy Prophet wanted to make two doors in the House, one for entrance and the other for exit. This was intended for the convenience of the pilgrims. From h. 1585 and h. 1586 it is seen that the Holy Prophet said that he wanted to rebuild the Ka'bah "on the foundations of Abraham because the Quraish had decreased (the area of) its building," and that he would have "brought its door to the level of the ground" and "inserted two doors, one eastern and one western." When 'Abdullāh ibn Zubair captured Makkah, he found the house damaged by fire and he rebuilt it in the way that he had heard from 'Ā'ishah that the Holy Prophet wanted it rebuilt.

When, however, he was killed and Ḥajjāj came to power, he reconstructed the house with the permission of 'Abdul Malik ibn Marwān as the Quraish had it built. There is a ḥadīth in Ṣaḥīḥ Muslim that 'Abdul Malik, while circumambulating the Ka'bah, had remarked that Ibn Zubair falsely ascribed to 'Ā'ishah that the Holy Prophet had said to her: "If your people had not come out of disbelief so newly, I would have demolished the House and added the *Hijr* because your people had decreased its building." Hearing this, Ḥārith ibn 'Abdullāh ibn Abū Rabī'ah, said: "O Chief of the faithful, do not say so, for I have myself heard the Mother of the Faithful narrating this ḥadīth." At this 'Abdul Malik said: "If I had heard this before the rebuilding it I would have left it as Ibn Zubair had built it." (Muslim, book: Pilgrimage, ch. 'Demolishing the Ka'bah and rebuilding it', h. 1333i). However, because it is neither any principle nor any part of the faith of Islām as to whether the Ka'ba has one door or two, the Holy Prophet did not make any change in the building due to the exigencies of the time.

Ch. 49: **One who selects a particular people for (communication of) knowledge, to the exclusion of others, lest these others should not understand it**

'Alī said: "Speak to people what they can understand; do you want them to belie Allāh and His Messenger ﷺ?"

127 'Alī reported as above.

128 Anas ibn Mālik related that the Prophet ﷺ was riding, and sitting behind him was Mu'ādh on the saddle, when he said: "O Mu'ādh ibn Jabal!" He replied: "Here I am, O Messenger of Allāh." [122] He (the Holy Prophet again) said: "O Mu'ādh!" He replied: "Here I am, O Messenger of Allāh." He (the Holy Prophet again) said: "O Mu'ādh!" He replied: "Here I am, O Messenger of Allāh." This happened three times. He (the Holy Prophet) said: "There is none who bears witness that there is no god but Allāh and that Muḥammad is the Messenger of Allāh, with the sincerity of his heart, but Allāh has made him forbidden to the fire (of hell)." [123] He (Mu'ādh) said: "O Messenger of Allāh, should I not convey this news to the people so that they may be pleased?" He replied: "In that case they will depend on this (solely)." And Mu'ādh (only) informed about this (incident) near the time of his death for fear of sin (of keeping back a ḥadīth). [124]

---

[122] The words used by Mu'ādh are: *Labbai-ka wa sa'dai-ka.* From their roots (*labb* and *sa'd*), the significance of these expressions is, respectively, "I am established on your obedience" and "I respond to you".

[123] This statement only means that he must perform deeds in accordance with this belief. The condition "with the sincerity of his heart" indicates that one who believes sincerely in God and the Holy Prophet Muḥammad cannot ignore acting on the teachings of Islām. As long as there is sincere determination, minor shortcomings and unmindful lapses will surely be forgiven and the fire of hell will be forbidden. By ignoring the words "sincerity of his heart" many people have blundered in the interpretation of this ḥadīth and taken it to mean that a person may commit any amount of sin, he is safe from the fire of hell provided he has assented to belief in the Oneness of God and the Prophethood of Muḥammad even in a merely formal manner. This is mocking at Islām and negating the principle declared in the Qur'ān that the basis of salvation is good deeds: "So whoever does an atom's weight of good deeds will see it and whoever does an atom's weight of evil will see it" (99 : 7–8). In h. 425 similar words occur: "Surely Allāh has forbidden to the fire one who says, 'There is no god but Allāh,' seeking thereby the pleasure of Allāh." It is evident that one who seeks the pleasure of Allāh must strive to walk along the path taught in the Book of God.

[124] The Holy Prophet communicated this news to Mu'ādh and instructed him not to spread it among the people. They would draw a wrong conclusion from it and discard the struggle for good deeds. This shows that every item of knowledge is not comprehensible by all kinds of people. In h. 127 the statement of 'Alī has been quoted: "Speak to people what they can under-stand..." It was for this reason that Mu'ādh kept this ḥadīth secret. But as it was a sin to conceal

129 Anas said: It was mentioned to me that the Prophet ﷺ said to Mu'ādh: "Whoever meets Allāh without having set up any partner with Him will enter Paradise." He (Mu'ādh) said: "Should I not give this good news to the people?" He said: "No, for I fear they will depend on this (solely)." [125]

Ch. 50:   Shyness in the matter of knowledge

> Mujāhid said: One who is shy about knowledge or feels proud cannot learn knowledge. And 'Ā'ishah said: The best of the women are the women of the *Anṣār*, for shyness does not prevent them from acquiring knowledge of religion.

130 Umm Salamah reported: Umm Sulaim came to the Messenger of Allāh ﷺ and said: "O Messenger of Allāh, Allāh does not feel shy of truth; so, is bath obligatory upon a woman when she has nocturnal sexual discharge?" The Prophet ﷺ said: "When she sees signs of discharge." At this Umm Salamah covered her face and said: "O Messenger of Allāh, does a woman have a nocturnal sexual discharge?" He said: "Yes, may your right hand get covered with dust![126] That is why her child resembles her."

131 'Abdullāh ibn 'Umar reported that the Messenger of Allāh ﷺ said: "Surely among the trees there is a one which does not shed its leaves, and it may be likened to the Muslim; so, tell me which is it?" People began to think of (and mention) the trees of the wilderness. The thought occurred to me that it was the date tree. 'Abdullāh added: But I felt shy (to speak). Then they said: "O Messenger of Allāh, inform us about it." The Messenger of Allāh ﷺ said: "It is the date tree."

---

a saying of the Holy Prophet, he narrated it close to his death. According to a ḥadīth in Ṣaḥīḥ Muslim (book: Faith, ch. 10), the Holy Prophet told Abū Hurairah to give the good news to anyone whom he meets, who testifies that there is no god but Allāh with certainty of heart, that he would enter into Paradise. When 'Umar saw Abū Hurairah doing this, he said to the Holy Prophet that people hearing this would give up doing good deeds. So the Holy Prophet stopped the dissemination of this news.

[125] This ḥadīth repeats the significance of the previous ḥadīth in different words. Instead of the testimony required in h. 128, that "there is no god but Allāh and that Muḥammad is the Messenger of Allāh, with the sincerity of his heart", this ḥadīth speaks of one who does not set up any partner with Allāh. The two are equivalent. Their equivalence shows that it is only through Islām that a person does not set up any partner with Allāh. He who does not believe that "Muḥammad is the Messenger of Allāh" is not a true believer in the Oneness of God since all other religions have some polytheistic element in them.

[126] This expression is not meant literally but is a mild form of rebuke.

'Abdullāh said: I related to my father the thought that had occurred to me. He said: "If you had said it, it would have been dearer to me than so much wealth." [127]

Ch. 51:   One who feels shy and tells another to ask a question

132 'Alī reported: I was a man who used to have frequent urethral discharge,[128] so I told al-Miqdād ibn al-Aswad to ask the Prophet ﷺ about it. He asked him, and he (the Holy Prophet) said: "It requires *Wuḍū'*."

Ch. 52:   Discussion of knowledge and giving of religious verdicts in the mosque[129]

133 'Abdullāh ibn 'Umar reported that a man was standing in the mosque when he said: "O Messenger of Allāh, from where do you order us to enter into the state of *Iḥrām?*" So the Messenger of Allāh ﷺ said: "The people of Madīnah should enter into *Iḥrām* from Dhul Ḥulaifah, the people of Syria should enter into it from al-Juḥfah, and the people of Najd should enter into it from Qarn." And Ibn 'Umar said: They claim that the Messenger of Allāh ﷺ also said: "The people of Yaman should enter into *Iḥrām* from Yalamlam." And Ibn 'Umar used to say: I did not have this knowledge from the Messenger of Allāh ﷺ." [130]

Ch. 53:   He who replies to an enquirer with more than what he asked from him

134 Ibn 'Umar reported from the Prophet ﷺ that a man asked him: "What should a person in *Iḥrām* wear?" He said: "He should not wear a shirt, or a turban, or trousers, or headgear, or clothes perfumed with *wars* (a kind of scent) or saffron. And if he cannot find shoes, he should wear socks, cutting them off so they are below the ankles." [131]

---

[127] This is a repeat of h. 61, with the addition of this last part.

[128] This is different from discharge of semen. When this happens, it is enough to perform ablution (*Wuḍū'*) to be pure in body.

[129] This is intended to mean that the mosque can be used for other religious purposes than prayers. In the time of the Holy Prophet, religious preaching, moral instruction, lessons on various aspects of religious life, and even discussions on national affairs used to be held in the Mosque. Deputations of foreign nations, including those of Christians and idolators, alighted in the Mosque and were lodged there. For a long time, mosques were the only centres of education in the Muslim world.

[130] See also h. 1525 and h. 1528.

[131] See also h. 1542, h. 1838, and h. 1841 to h. 1843.

Book 4: *Al-Wuḍū'*

Ablution

In the name of Allāh, the Beneficent, the Merciful

Ch. 1: Concerning *Wuḍū'*

The Word of Allāh, the Most High: "O you who believe, when you rise up for prayer, wash your faces, and your hands up to the elbows, and wipe your heads, and (wash) your feet up to the ankles" (The Qur'ān, 5:6).[1]

Abū 'Abdullāh (Bukhārī) said: The Prophet ﷺ has explained that the obligatory part of the ablution is (washing) once (of each part); and he has also washed twice and three times as well, and has not gone beyond three times, and the learned ones have disliked wastage in it by people going beyond the practice of the Prophet ﷺ.[2]

Ch. 2: Prayer without ablution is not accepted

135 Abū Hurairah said that the Messenger of Allāh ﷺ said: "The prayer of one who does *ḥadath* will not be accepted until he performs ablution." A man from Ḥaḍramaut asked: "What is *ḥadath*, O Abū Hurairah?" He replied: "It is the voiding of wind." [3]

---

[1] The verse of the Qur'ān which Bukhārī quotes as an introduction to the chapter was revealed at Madīnah, and not even in the earlier period there. But prayers used to be said at Makkah as well, preceded by ablution. So the description of the ablution as given here must be in confirmation of what the Holy Prophet practised before this revelation came. There is a report in Ibn Mājah and Musnad Aḥmad that the angel Gabriel taught the Holy Prophet the manner of ablution at the commencement of his revelation. The confirmation in this verse of what the Holy Prophet already practised shows that the details of prayer, *Wuḍū'*, or other matters that the Holy Prophet taught to Muslims were given to him by Allāh's command and this was by means of the "inner revelation" (*waḥy khafī*) that the Holy Prophet received.

[2] To wash the limbs more than three times in ablution has been disapproved but as Imām Shāfi'ī holds, it is not altogether forbidden. One can wash more times than is prescribed under some special necessity or for the sake of cleanliness. It has been reported about Ibn 'Umar that he used to wash his feet seven times on occasions. But wastage of water is not allowed, and to continue washing by merely imagining that full purity has not been attained is to put oneself to needless hardship.

[3] *Ḥadath* means the coming out of anything from either of the two outlets of the body from where waste is discharged. It includes the breaking of wind, which is its lightest form. Ablution

Ch. 3:   The excellence of ablution and the brightening of the limbs (*al-ghurr al-muḥajjalūn*) from the effects of ablution

136 Nu'aim al-Mujmir reported: I ascended with Abū Hurairah to the roof of the Mosque; he then performed ablution and said: I have indeed heard the Messenger of Allāh ﷺ say: "Surely my followers will be called on the day of Resurrection by the brightness of their appearance from the effects of ablution." So whoever among you is able to augment his brightness, he should do it.[4]

Ch. 4:   Not to perform ablution on mere doubt unless sure

137 'Abdullāh ibn Zaid al-Anṣārī reported that he complained to the Messenger of Allāh ﷺ of a man who thinks while in prayer that he has broken wind. He (the Holy Prophet) said: "He should not turn — or (he said) should not go away — unless he hears a sound or smells it." [5]

Ch. 5:   Making the ablution light

138 Ibn 'Abbās reported that the Prophet ﷺ slept, so much so that he snored, then he said his prayer; and sometimes he (the reporter) said: He (the Holy Prophet) lay down, so much so that he snored, then he stood up and said his prayer.

---

only becomes necessary in case of such voiding. The Qur'ān has used the words "when one of you has come from the toilet (*ghā'iṭ*)" (4:43). The Arabic word *ghā'iṭ* means 'a low land' and applies to a place where one goes to answer the call of nature. Many reports say that the state of *Wuḍū'* remains in force as long as there is no *ḥadath,* so that a person does not need to perform ablution before a prayer if his *Wuḍū'* is still holding since the last prayer. The command in the Qur'ān to perform *Wuḍū'* before prayer, "O you who believe, when you rise up for prayer, wash your faces, (etc.)" (5:6), is not contradicted by these Ḥadīth reports, but is in fact explained by them, because "when you rise up" means here when you rise up after an instance of *ḥadath* has taken place. The later words of this verse about *tayammum* — "or one of you has come from the toilet … and you cannot find water" — also show that purification for prayer is only necessary if the state of *Wuḍū'* has been annulled by *ḥadath.*

[4] *Ghurr* is the whiteness or the brightness of the forehead of the horse. Here it means the spiritual brightness of the forehead of the person who prostrates frequently in prayers because the forehead touches the ground in prostration. *Muḥajjal* is the whiteness to be found on the knees and ankles of the horse. In prayer the knees and the ankles of a person also touch the ground in a special manner. It is understandable that in the spiritual body there will be a corresponding luminosity in these parts because of their frequent use in prayers. This ḥadīth is also related by ten other Companions, but the words "So whoever is able to augment his brightness, he should do it" do not occur in any of them. This shows that they are not the words spoken by the Holy Prophet, but Abū Hurairah himself.

[5] Some people wrongly imagine on minor things that their *Wuḍū'* has been invalidated. Mere doubt does not nullify the ablution.

He (Ibn ‘Abbās further) reported: I spent a night at my maternal aunt Maimūnah’s place, and the Prophet ﷺ slept during the night. When part of the night had passed, the Messenger of Allāh ﷺ got up and performed ablution from a water skin which was hanging there, performing a light *Wuḍū’* — ‘Amr described it as light and little. And he stood up to pray. So I also performed ablution in the manner he had done, then I came and stood on his left. He pulled me round and made me (stand) on his right. Then he said the prayer as Allāh willed, then he lay down and slept, so much so that he snored. Then the caller to prayer came to him and called him for prayer; so he went with him for prayer and said the prayer and did not perform ablution.[6]

We said to ‘Amr: People say that the eyes of the Messenger of Allāh ﷺ used to sleep but his heart would not sleep. ‘Amr said: I have heard ‘Ubaid ibn ‘Umair say: “The dreams of the Prophets are revelation,” then he recited: “Surely I see in a dream that I am slaughtering you” (the Qur’ān, 37:102).[7]

Ch. 6:　The perfection (i.e., thoroughness) of ablution

> Ibn ‘Umar said: The perfection of ablution (*isbāgh-ul-Wuḍū’*) is to clean the limbs well.[8]

139 Usāmah ibn Zaid reported: The Messenger of Allāh ﷺ returned from ‘Arafāt till he came to the valley wherein he descended, urinated and then performed ablution but not a thorough *Wuḍū’*. Then I asked: “Prayer, O Messenger of Allāh?” He said: “Prayer will be further on from where you are.” So he rode, and when he came to Muzdalifah he alighted and performed

---

[6] This ḥadīth has already occurred in h. 117 and comes again in h. 183. It also occurs several other times (see h. 697–699, 726, 859, 4569–4572, 5919, 6215, 7452). In h. 117 there is no mention of the Holy Prophet’s having performed ablution. Here Bukhārī records this ḥadīth only to point out the validity of light or short ablution. This does not mean that a complete *Wuḍū’* was not performed, but that it was done quickly, perhaps using a small quantity of water. In h.183 it is reported that he well-performed his *Wuḍū’*.

The later part of this report shows that sleep as such does not nullify ablution but a person in deep sleep loses awareness as to whether his ablution has been invalidated. Therefore, light sleep, during which awareness remains, does not by itself require a *Wuḍū’* after it. Even in light sleep a person may snore.

[7] The statement that the Holy Prophet’s eyes slept but not his heart show that a prophet is always conscious of Allāh even during sleep or while having a dream, and his connection with Allāh is permanently clear and vivid, unlike other people. It is to express this that the words of ‘Ubaid ibn ‘Umair are mentioned. The verse of the Qur’ān quoted is the statement of prophet Abraham to his son Ishmael.

[8] *Isbāgh-ul-Wuḍū’* means that all parts should be cleaned thoroughly. See next note.

ablution, and made it a thorough *Wuḍū'* (*asbagha al-Wuḍū'*).[9] Then the prayer was called and he said the *Maghrib* prayer. Then everyone made his camel sit in his own alighting place. Then the *'Ishā'* prayer was called and he prayed, and no prayer was said between these.[10]

Ch. 7:   Washing the face with both hands from one handful (of water)

140 'Aṭā' ibn Yasār reported regarding Ibn 'Abbās that he once performed ablution and washed his face by taking one handful of water, rinsing with it his mouth and nostrils. Then he took another handful of water and did this with it that he joined this hand with the other one and washed his face therewith. Then he took a handful of water and washed with it his right hand, then he took a handful of water and washed with it his left hand, then he wiped his head, then he took a handful of water and poured it on his right foot until he had washed it, then he took another handful (of water) and washed with it his left foot. Then he said: "I saw the Messenger of Allāh ﷺ performing ablution like this." [11]

Ch. 8:   Taking the name of Allāh (*Bismillāh*) in every condition and at the time of sexual intercourse

141 Ibn 'Abbās reported, tracing it to the Prophet ﷺ, that he said: "If any of you, when he approaches his wife sexually, should say, 'In the name of Allāh, O Allāh! Protect us from the devil and keep the devil away from what

---

[9] The light or little *Wuḍū'* mentioned in h. 138 means performing ablution quickly, but still including all its actions. That is also what is meant in this ḥadīth by the words "but not a thorough *Wuḍū'*." Had it not been a proper ablution, 'Usāmah ibn Zaid would not have asked the Holy Prophet if they were going to pray. The Holy Prophet never remained without ablution and would perform it again before a prayer even if his previous *Wuḍū'* was still valid. The second ablution, described here as "thorough" (lit. "complete", was an additional ablution. This description is intended to convey that ablution is not merely a religious rite of pouring water on the limbs but it has also the physical purpose of bodily cleanliness.

[10] See also h. 1667, h. 1669 and h. 1672.

[11] It is allowed to use the same handful of water both for rinsing the mouth and washing the nostrils, but it is wrong to infer that it is necessary. It depends on the circumstances at a particular moment, and it may be done due to shortage of water. The previous reports make it perfectly clear that the Holy Prophet performed "light" ablution as well as "thorough" ablution, and this would be according to the exigency of the time. Whoever saw him doing whichever kind of ablution, reported it accordingly. It is a mistake to lay down strict rules in this regard. The second point worth noting is that taking water in one hand and then using both the hands in putting that water on the face is quite admissible. It seems that by the time of Bukhārī people had started quibbling over minor points, and he wants to show that the Holy Prophet's practice sanctions a wide range in such matters.

You give us', then if a child is decreed for them, he (the devil) will not cause any harm to it." [12]

Ch. 9:   What is to be said while in the toilet

142 Anas said that the Prophet ﷺ used to say, when entering the lavatory: "O Allāh! I seek Your protection from impurities (*khubuth*) and immoralities (*khabā'ith*)." [13]

Ch. 10:   Keeping water in the toilet

143 Ibn ʿAbbās reported that the Prophet ﷺ once entered the toilet and I placed for him water for ablution. He asked, "Who placed this?", and he was informed. He said: "O Allāh, give him the understanding of the faith." [14]

Ch. 11:   Not to face the *Qiblah* (Kaʿbah) while passing stool or urine, except from behind a building such as a wall or something like it

144 Abū Ayyūb al-Anṣārī reported that the Messenger of Allāh ﷺ said: "When any of you goes to the toilet, he should not face the *Qiblah* nor turn his back towards it; he should face either towards the east or the west." [15]

---

[12] The conclusion drawn from this ḥadīth is that the name of God should be invoked in ablution by saying *Bismillāh* ('In the name of Allāh'). Since invoking it is required at the height of sexual excitement, it shows that it must be invoked before undertaking any task, particularly one connected with religious practice such as ablution.

[13] The word *khubuth* is the plural of *khabīth* (a masculine), and the word *khabā'ith* is the plural of *khabīthah* (which is the feminine of *khabīth*). These are generally taken to mean evil spirits. But the word *khubuth* has also been read as *khubth*, meaning something undesirable or disliked, which would refer to physical impurity. The latter word (*khabā'ith*) refers to impure morals or sins. Even if evil spirits were meant, seeking protection against them in the physical sense would mean protection against the germs that lurk in the unclean places to which a person goes for passing urine and stools.

[14] Seeing the intelligence shown by Ibn ʿAbbās, the Holy Prophet prayed for him to be granted understanding of religion. Hence Ibn ʿAbbās is held in high esteem among the Companions of the Holy Prophet. The water brought by Ibn ʿAbbas for the Holy Prophet is reported to be for his ablution (*Wuḍu'*) in the ḥadīth, but the chapter heading indicates that it was meant both for washing private parts as well as for the religious ablution. Although the cleaning in those days used to be done by clods of earth and stones, water was also used in addition. In modern life, the place of clods of earth etc. has been taken by the toilet paper. The use of water should, however, be considered as indispensable unless there is scarcity or even unavailability of water.

[15] The ḥadīth does not mention the exception which Bukhārī has added in his chapter heading. This shows that by "toilet" in the ḥadīth is meant a piece of open, low land, the kind of location to which people used to go for urinating or defecating. In built-up areas, the location and direction

Ch. 12:   One who answers the call of nature (sitting) on two bricks

145 ʿAbdullāh ibn ʿUmar used to say: People say that when you sit to answer the call of nature, you should not face the *Qiblah* or the *Bait al-Maqdis* (Jerusalem)." He added: One day I climbed to the roof of our house, and I found the Messenger of Allāh ﷺ answering the call of nature, (while sitting) on two bricks facing *Bait al-Maqdis* (Jerusalem). And he said: "Perhaps you are among those who say their prayers reclining on their thighs (during prostration)." So I said: "By Allāh! I do not know." [16]

Ch. 13:   The going out of women to answer the call of nature

146 ʿĀʾishah reported that the wives of the Prophet ﷺ used to go out during the night towards al-Manāṣiʿ for answering the call of nature, and this is an open ground. ʿUmar used to say to the Prophet ﷺ: "Keep your women in seclusion." But the Prophet ﷺ would not do so. One night at *ʿIshāʾ* time Saudah bint Zamʿah, wife of the Prophet ﷺ, went out and she was a tall woman. So ʿUmar called out to her: "O Saudah! I have recognized you", desiring that an ordinance be revealed for seclusion. So Allāh revealed the verse of seclusion.[17]

---

of a toilet is determined by housing space, building regulations as well as the rights of the neighbours. The rule has, therefore, been relaxed for such places. As the next ḥadīth shows, the Holy Prophet was found to answer the call of nature on the roof of his house with his face towards Jerusalem, and hence his back towards the Kaʿbah. The instruction for facing east or west is obviously due to the location of Madīnah relative to Makkah, and cannot be applied literally in most places elsewhere. This formal regard for the Holy Kaʿbah is a psychological necessity, as this is the place from which flowed the spiritual fountain of guidance for the whole world. External respect draws attention to real respect. Islām neither goes to the extreme of making the Kaʿbah an object of worship and reverence nor to the opposite extreme of treating it as an ordinary building. See h. 394.

[16] The words *yuṣallūna ʿalā aurāki-him* mean 'people who repose their bellies on their thighs while going in prostration for prayer'. It is difficult to see what connection this has with the earlier part of the ḥadīth, unless these words are intended to hint at the general ignorance of the people so addressed in matters of religious practice. It appears that Ibn ʿUmar was attempting to remove the misconception from the minds of certain Companions of the Holy Prophet, such as Abū Ayyūb al-Anṣārī and Abū Hurairah, who believed that one cannot turn the face or the back towards the Kaʿbah under any circumstances while sitting to answer a call of nature. He explained that this instruction does not apply to toilets which are built as rooms, for it would cause great difficulty in the construction of houses and their division into rooms.

[17] This ḥadīth occurs again in the Book of *Tafsīr* (the commentary of the Qurʾān) as h. 4795. There it is clearly stated that this incident took place after the revelation of the verse on the seclusion of women. It appears that ʿUmar objected that the wives of the Holy Prophet should even go out for their needs. According to h. 4795, after ʿUmar said this to Saudah, she went to the Holy Prophet and said that she had gone out for her need. Then Allāh sent him revelation and he said: "You women are permitted to go out for your needs." As there is no such revelation in

147 'Ā'ishah reported from the Prophet ﷺ that he said: "You are permitted to go out for your needs." Hishām said: "This means answering the call of nature." [18]

Ch. 14:   Toilet arrangements in houses

148 'Abdullāh ibn 'Umar reported: I climbed to the roof of the house of Ḥafṣah to attend to a certain need of mine, and I found the Messenger of Allāh ﷺ answering the call of nature, with his back towards the *Qiblah* and facing Syria.[19]

149 'Abdullāh ibn 'Umar informed, saying: One day I went up to the roof of our house, and I found the Messenger of Allāh ﷺ sitting on two bricks facing *Bait al-Maqdis* (Jerusalem).[20]

Ch. 15:   Cleaning with water after answering the call of nature

150 Anas ibn Mālik said: When the Prophet ﷺ used to go out to answer a call of nature, I and a boy used to go with him, (taking) with us a pot of water. He meant that he (the Holy Prophet) would clean with it.[21]

---

the Qur'ān, either this was *waḥy khafī* ('inner revelation') or the Holy Prophet's inference based on some verse of the Qur'ān revealed just then. The statement in this ḥadīth that the verse of seclusion was revealed after this incident either refers to the Holy Prophet's clarification that women were allowed to go out for their needs or it is confusion on the part of a narrator. This incident also shows that it is not forbidden for men and women to talk to each other as 'Umar spoke to Saudah.

Thus the Holy Prophet has made clear the limits of seclusion himself and said on the basis of Divine revelation that women are allowed to go out of their houses for their needs. What was forbidden was going out for displaying feminine beauty which is a precursor of widespread sexual corruption. It was never intended by the Qur'ān to restrict women from performing any necessary activity of life.

[18] This shows that this statement was not like a Quranic revelation but an inference made by the Holy Prophet from the Qur'ān through his 'inner revelation'. It clarifies that a woman can go out to attend her needs inspite of the fact that 'Umar would not like any woman going out of her own house.

[19] This is a repetition of a part of h. 145.

[20] As with h. 148, this is also repetition of a part of h. 145. Ibn 'Umar was a child at the time. The toilet was on the roof of the house.

[21] This shows that the Holy Prophet used to go out to answer the call of nature and even there he would take water for cleaning and washing, so meticulous was he about physical cleanliness. The details mentioned in these reports may appear to relate to small matters, but they are historically important in providing a glimpse into the personal habits of the Holy Prophet who is to be a model for human conduct in all aspects of life.

Ch. 16:   One with whom water is carried for cleaning him

> Abū ad-Dardā' said: Is there not among you one who used to carry the shoes and the washing water and the pillow (of the Holy Prophet)?[22]

151 Anas ibn Mālik said: When the Messenger of Allāh ﷺ used to go out to answer a call of nature, I and a boy from among us used to follow him, (taking) with us a vessel of water.[23]

Ch. 17:   Carrying a stick having a blade along with water for cleaning

152 Anas ibn Mālik said: When the Messenger of Allāh ﷺ used to enter into isolation,[24] I and a boy used to carry a vessel of water and a stick having a blade (*'anazah*). He would clean himself with the water. *'Anazah* is a stick tipped with a blade.[25]

Ch. 18:   Prohibition against cleaning with the right hand

153 Abū Qatādah reported that the Messenger of Allāh ﷺ said: "When any of you drink anything, he should not breathe into the drinking pot, and when he goes to the toilet he should not touch his private organ with his right hand nor wash it with his right hand." [26]

Ch. 19:   Not to hold the private organ with the right hand while urinating

154 Abū Qatādah reported from the Prophet ﷺ that he said: "When any of you urinates, he should not hold his private organ with his right hand nor clean it with his right hand. And he should not breathe into the drinking pot." [27]

---

[22] The man referred to is 'Abdullāh ibn Mas'ūd. Abū ad-Dardā' was telling this to the people of Iraq because 'Abdullāh ibn Mas'ūd was going to Kūfah. He meant that there were still people present who used to follow the Holy Prophet day and night in his ordinary activities. The chapter heading relates to water being carried for him for washing after he answered the call of nature.

[23] This is a repetition of h. 150 with minor differences and omission of the last words.

[24] In this repetition of h. 150 the words "enter into isolation" are used, which mean being away from people in the ground where he answered the call of nature.

[25] There must have been some purpose for such a stick, for example, breaking clumps of earth or making a screen by poking it in the ground and putting a cloth over it.

[26] The necessity of keeping the right hand away from either touching the private parts or from using it in washing these parts is because the same hand is used for picking up food to eat. Although the hand has to be washed after using it for cleaning the private parts, this instruction is for extra cleanliness. This ḥadīth also draws attention to the fact that it is unclean to breathe in the pot out of which you are drinking, for example to cool a hot drink. It is only recently that modern hygiene has discouraged this on scientific grounds. But the revelation of God had informed the Holy Prophet Muḥammad of its harm when no one knew about it.

[27] This is a repetition of h. 153 with minor difference of wording.

Ch. 20:   To clean (private parts) with stones

155 Abū Hurairah reported: I followed the Prophet ﷺ once when he went out to answer a call of nature and he was not turning to look back, so I approached him and he said: "Find for me stones with which I can clean myself" or he said something like this, and "Do not bring for me bone or dung". Then I brought him some stones in a corner of my cloth and placed them by his side and went away from him. When he finished, he used them (for cleaning).[28]

Ch. 21:   Not to clean (private parts) with dung

156 'Abdullāh ibn Mas'ūd used to say: The Prophet ﷺ went to the toilet and asked me to bring him three stones. I found two stones and searched for a third one but I could not find it, so I took a piece of dung and brought it to him. He took the two stones and threw away the piece of dung and said: "This is unclean."

Ch. 22:   Washing (each limb) only once in ablution

157 Ibn 'Abbās reported: The Prophet ﷺ performed ablution, washing (each limb) only once.

Ch. 23:   Washing (each limb) twice in ablution

158 'Abdullāh ibn Zaid reported that the Prophet ﷺ performed ablution, washing (each limb) twice.

Ch. 24:   Washing (each limb) three times in ablution

159 Ḥumrān, the freed slave of 'Uthmān, informed that he saw 'Uthmān ibn 'Affān asking for a pot and pouring water (from it) on his hands three

---

[28] This shows that after the call of nature some dry article, such as earth, paper, tissue or cloth, may be used for cleaning. For extra cleanliness this should be followed by using water. Use of some dry articles for cleaning keeps the hand clean when one takes to washing. Those things are not allowed which are themselves unclean, such as dung or bone. Also, an object such as a bone is non-absorbent.

In the next ḥadīth, h. 156, the Holy Prophet says that dung is unclean. In the repetition of h. 155 in h. 3860 he says regarding bone and dung that "these two are the food of the *jinn*". What is meant is that they carry germs of diseases which cannot be seen; hence they are called unclean. It is absurd to suggest that ethereal beings, such as the devil, eat something physical. Anything which cannot be seen by the naked eye is called *jinn* in Arabic. It may also be noted that in itself bone is not impure and unclean. Bones may be used for any purpose. The Qur'ān used to be written on bones. Those bones are meant here which may have been left exposed in fields or have some decayed flesh sticking to them.

times and washing them, and then dipping his right hand in the pot and rinsing his mouth (with water) and cleaning out his nostrils. Then he washed his face three times and also his arms up to the elbows three times. Then he wiped his head, then he washed his feet three times up to the ankles. [29]

Then he said: The Messenger of Allāh ﷺ said: "Whoever performs ablution like this *Wuḍū'* of mine,[30] and then says two *rak'ahs* of prayer during which no (other) thought enters his mind, all his past sins are forgiven." [31]

160 'Urwah reported from Ḥumrān (adding to the above report, h. 159): So when 'Uthmān performed ablution, he said: "I will narrate to you a ḥadīth which I would not have narrated to you but for a verse (of the Qur'ān). I heard the Prophet ﷺ saying: "If a man performs his ablution, doing the *Wuḍū'* well, and says his prayer, he is forgiven all that is between that and the (next) prayer until he prays it."

'Urwah said: That verse (referred to) is: "Those who conceal what we have revealed…" (the Qur'ān, 2:159).

---

[29] The recording of reports that speak differently about the number of times one should wash the limbs in ablution (h. 157–159) is to show the flexibility of the regulations in this connection. The number of times washing is done can be varied according to the circumstances. If the face and hands had been washed shortly before a *Wuḍū'*, or it was not long since a previous *Wuḍū'*, or there is shortage of water, in such cases washing each limb once is enough. If there is need for thorough washing, each limb can be washed three times, and if necessary even more than three times.

[30] In the Qur'ān *Wuḍū'* is described as follows: "O you who believe, when you rise up to prayer, wash your faces, and your hands as far as the elbows, and wipe your heads, and (wash) your feet up to the ankles" (5 : 6). In the Qur'ān the washing of the face comes first, while in the Holy Prophet's ablution mentioned here the washing of the hands comes first, followed by rinsing the mouth and cleaning out the nostrils. To wash the face, it is obviously necessary first to wash the hands, and rinsing the mouth and cleaning out the nostrils are a part of washing the face. So there is no difference between the sequence in the Qur'ān (face, arms, head, feet) and the sequence described here (hands, face, arms, head, feet).

[31] In the next ḥadīth, h. 160, it is stated that he is forgiven the sins he commits between that prayer and the next prayer when he says it. This does not mean that a person should consider himself free to commit any amount of sin between one prayer and the next. The Qur'ān makes clear what is meant by forgiveness through prayer: "Surely prayer keeps (one) away from indecency and evil" (29 : 45). If a person says his prayers properly, not merely as a mechanical ritual, and does not let his mind drift to any other thought except prayer, as stated in this ḥadīth, he would never deliberately disobey the Divine commands. When a person walks along this path, Allāh out of His boundless mercy forgives him the sins he committed before he changed the course of his life. The common conception, that Allāh keeps an account of good and bad deeds, and the good deeds cancel out the bad deeds, and therefore a person who says prayers may still constantly commit sins because he will be forgiven due to his prayers, is an idea entirely against the Qur'ān and Ḥadīth.

Ch. 25:   The washing of nostrils in *Wuḍū'*

'Uthmān, 'Abdullāh ibn Zaid and Ibn 'Abbās reported it from the Prophet ﷺ.

161 Abū Hurairah reported from the Prophet ﷺ that he said: "Whoever performs ablution should clean his nostrils and whoever uses stones to clean (his private parts after answering the call of nature) should use an odd number (of stones)."

Ch. 26:   To clean (private parts) with an odd number of stones

162 Abū Hurairah reported that the Messenger of Allāh ﷺ said: "When any of you performs ablution he should put water inside his nose and clean the nostrils, and whoever uses stones to clean (his private parts after answering the call of nature) should use an odd number (of stones), and when any of you awakes from his sleep he should wash his hands before he dips it in water meant for *Wuḍū'*, for surely none of you knows where the hand rested during the night."

Ch. 27:   Washing both feet and not (just) wiping them

163 'Abdullāh ibn 'Amr reported: The Prophet ﷺ remained behind us on one of the journeys we had undertaken (together). Then he joined us while we were getting late for *'Aṣr* and performing *Wuḍū'*. We were not fully washing our feet, so he called out to us at the top of his voice, "Woe to the heels because of the fire", two or three times.[32]

Ch. 28:   Rinsing the mouth in ablution

Ibn 'Abbās and 'Abdullāh ibn Zaid reported it from the Prophet ﷺ.

164 Ḥumrān, the freed slave of 'Uthmān, reported that he saw 'Uthmān ibn 'Affān asking to perform *Wuḍū'* and pouring water on his hands from the pot and washing them three times, and then dipping his right hand (in the pot) for *Wuḍū'* and rinsing his mouth (with water), drawing water into the nose and cleaning out his nostrils. Then he washed his face three times and also his arms up to the elbows three times. Then he wiped his head, then he washed his feet three times.

---

[32] This is a repetition of h. 60 and h. 96. The chapter heading makes it clear that *mash* or mere wiping of the feet is not right, and they must be washed. The command to wash the feet is in the Qur'ān: "O you who believe, when you rise up for prayer, wash your faces, and your hands up to the elbows, and wipe your heads, and (wash) your feet up to the ankles" (5:6), where the command "wash" for face and hands applies also to the feet. This was also the practice of the Holy Prophet.

Then he ('Uthmān) said: I saw the Prophet ﷺ performing ablution like this, and he (the Holy Prophet) said: "Whoever performs ablution like this *Wuḍū'* of mine, and then says two *rak'ahs* of prayer during which no (other) thought enters his mind, Allāh will forgive him all his past sins." [33]

Ch. 29:   Washing of the heels

Ibn Sīrīn used to wash the places of the ring (over which it was worn) when he performed ablution.

165 Muḥammad ibn Ziyād related: I heard Abū Hurairah, and he used to pass by us when people used to perform ablution from a pot of water, saying: "Make your *Wuḍū'* complete, for surely Abul Qāsim ﷺ (the Holy Prophet) said: "Woe to the heels because of the fire." [34]

Ch. 30:   Washing the feet when shoes (*na'lain*) are worn and not (merely) wiping the shoes[35]

166 'Ubaid ibn Juraij reported that he said to 'Abdullāh ibn 'Umar: "O 'Abdur Raḥmān! I have seen you doing four things which I have not seen any one from among your Companions doing." He said: "Which are those, O Ibn Juraij?" He said: "I have seen you not touching any corner (of the Ka'bah) except the two Yamani (corners of the Ka'bah),[36] and I have seen you wearing shoes of tanned leather, and I have seen you dyeing yourself with yellow colour, and I have seen that you were in Makkah while people entered into the state of *Iḥrām* when they saw the new moon, but you would not enter into *Iḥrām* until the eighth day (*yaum al-tarwiyah*)." 'Abdullāh said: "Regarding the corners, I did not see the Messenger of Allāh ﷺ touching any but the Yamani corners. As for the shoes made of tanned leather, I have indeed seen the Messenger of Allāh ﷺ wearing shoes on which there would be no hair and he used to perform ablution while wearing them,[37] so I like to wear them.

---

[33] This is a repetition of h. 159, and the chapter heading here relates to the mention of rinsing of the mouth.

[34] See h. 60, h. 96 and h. 163 and notes under them.

[35] The shoes spoken of here, *na'lain,* are those that do not cover the whole of the feet up to the ankles. Wiping (*mash*) with wet hands is not sufficient for *Wuḍū'* in such cases, but is only allowed on shoes which cover the feet up to the ankles and on socks. Some authorities do consider wiping sufficient when shoes cover the feet only below the ankles, and there is a report in Abū Dāwūd supporting this but it has been called weak.

[36] The Ka'bah has four corners. The two Yamani corners (*al-yamāniyain*) are the one in which lies the Black Stone, called the Iraqi corner because it lies towards Iraq, and the one which lies towards Yaman. It appears that other people used to touch all the four corners.

[37] Bukhārī infers from this that the Holy Prophet washed his feet even though he was wearing

As for the yellow colour, I have indeed seen the Messenger of Allāh ﷺ dyeing himself with it, so I like to dye with it. As for entering into the state of *Iḥrām,* I did not see the Messenger of Allāh ﷺ entering into *Iḥrām* until his she-camel got up with him." [38]

Ch. 31: Starting with the right side in *Wuḍū'* and bath

167 Umm 'Atiyyah reported that the Prophet ﷺ said to them regarding the washing of (the body of) his (deceased) daughter (Zainab): "Start from the right side and with the parts washed in *Wuḍū'*."

168 'Ā'ishah reported: The Prophet ﷺ loved to start with the right side in his wearing of shoes, his combing of hair, his washing, and (in fact) in every affair of his.

Ch. 32: Seeking water for *Wuḍū'* when the time for prayer is very close

'Ā'ishah said: Once the time of morning prayer arrived and water was sought but was not available. So the injunction for *Tayammum* was revealed

169 Anas ibn Mālik reported: I saw the Prophet ﷺ when once the time of the *'Aṣr* prayer was very close. People started looking for water for *Wuḍū'* but did not find it. Meanwhile some water for *Wuḍū'* was brought to the Messenger of Allāh ﷺ. He put his hand into that pot and told people to perform ablution from it. I saw water gushing forth from underneath his fingers till the last of them had performed ablution.[39]

Ch. 33: Water with which man's hair are to be washed

'Aṭā' did not find anything wrong in using them (i.e., human hair) to make threads and strings; and the remaining water after dogs have drunk from it, and their going about in the mosque. Az-Zuhrī said: When it (i.e., a dog) puts his mouth in a pot and one has no

---

these shoes. Hence his chapter heading about washing the feet, and not just wiping the shoes. Ibn 'Umar means to say that shoes of leather were considered by the Holy Prophet as quite clean because he used to put them on after ablution.

[38] The rising up of the she-camel indicates the start of the rites of the Pilgrimage, and this is on the 8th of Dhul Ḥijjah. This whole ḥadīth shows that the Companions differed among themselves on many points, but instead of condemning one another they still respected one another.

[39] This appears to have been a miracle of the Holy Prophet. It is reported that the water sufficed for seventy or eighty persons, while according to some reports it was hundreds of people. See also h. 195. Such miracles are to be found in large numbers in the life of the Holy Prophet, but Muslims do not advance them as proof of the truth of his claim of being a Prophet of God when presenting Islām to non-Muslims.

water for *Wuḍū'* except this (water), he can perform ablution with it. Sufyān said: This is understood from the word of Allāh, the Most High: "… and you cannot find water, then resort to pure earth" (the Qur'ān, 4:43). And here is water (after being drunk by a dog), but even though a (bad) thought occurs about it in the mind, still one should perform *Wuḍū'* with it and do also *Tayammum*.[40]

170 Ibn Sīrīn reported: I said to 'Abīdah, We have got some hair of the Prophet ﷺ we obtained from Anas or from the family of Anas. At this he said: If I could get even one hair out of these, it would be dearer to me than all the world and all that is in it.

171 Anas reported that when the Messenger of Allāh ﷺ once shaved his head, Abū Ṭalḥah was the first to take some of his hair.

Ch. 34:   When a dog drinks from a pot

172 Abū Hurairah reported that the Messenger of Allāh ﷺ said: "When the dog drinks from a pot belonging to any one of you, he must wash it seven times."

173 Abū Hurairah reported from the Prophet ﷺ: "A man saw a dog eating moist earth because of thirst, so the man took his stocking and kept on filling it with water for it to drink till he quenched its thirst. So Allāh appreciated his deed[41] and made him enter Paradise." [42]

---

[40] Bukhārī brings in some reports which show that the dog is not impure. Some of these speak directly of dogs going about in mosques but the mosque floors not being required to be washed, and of the allowability of eating the meat of an animal which has been hunted by dogs. Therefore, it cannot be that a dog is so impure that its very touch can make a person or his dress impure. However, in h. 172 further on, it is said that if a dog drinks from a vessel you must wash it seven times, and according to reports in other Ḥadīth collections the same must be done if a dog licks a vessel (for example, Ṣaḥīḥ Muslim, book: 'Purification', ch. 27). These appear, on the face of it, to show that the dog is impure. Bukhārī's argument is that such washing is made necessary not because of the dog's impurity but because of poisonous matter which comes out of the mouth of the dog. Hence water remaining in a vessel after a dog has drunk from it has been considered as good enough for performing ablution. However, if a person feels a natural revulsion for using such water for ablution, he can perform *Tayammum* or rubbing the limbs with pure dust.

[41] These words are literally "So Allāh thanked him" (*fa shakara-Allāh la-hu*).

[42] This hadith also occurs at other places (see h. 2363, h. 2466 and h. 6009), and this incident is from the history of the Israelites. Having mercy for dumb animals and caring for them is a part of the teachings of Islām. It has been rightly observed by Bosworth Smith: "There is no religion which has taken a higher view in its authoritative documents of animal life" and that there was no need for any administrative laws for the protection of the animals against the cruelties of man in the society created by the Holy Prophet (see his *Mohammed and Mohammedanism*, London,

174 Ḥamzah ibn 'Abdullāh reported from his father ('Abdullāh ibn 'Umar): Dogs used to come in and go out from the mosque[43] in the time of the Messenger of Allāh ﷺ and people would not sprinkle any water on account of that.

175 'Adiyy ibn Ḥātim reported: I asked the Prophet ﷺ (a question) and in reply he said: "When you send forth your trained dog and he kills (a game), eat (it) and when he eats (out of it) do not eat (that meat), because he caught (the game) for itself." I said: "If I send forth my own dog and I find with him another dog?" He said: "Then do not eat it because you invoked the name of Allāh on your own dog but you did not invoke it on the other dog." [44]

Ch. 35: **One who does not see the necessity of *Wuḍū'* except when something comes out of the two exits from the front and the back (i.e., wind, urine or stools)**

Because of the word of Allāh, the Most High: "…or one of you has come from the toilet" (the Qur'ān, 5:6).[45]

'Aṭā' said of one from whose anus worms come out or from his male organ something resembling lice: He must renew his *Wuḍū'*. Jābir ibn 'Abdullāh said: When anyone laughs in prayer he must repeat his prayer but need not renew the *Wuḍū'*. Ḥasan (al-Baṣrī) said: When anyone has his hair or nails removed, or takes off his socks, there is no need for a fresh *Wuḍū'* for him.[46] Abū Hurairah

---

1874, p. 178–180). If a man can be promised Paradise for having mercy on a dog, how much higher will his rank be with Allāh for doing good to mankind!

[43] In some versions of Bukhārī, before the words "come in and go out" it is added that they used to urinate, and the words are: "*tabūlu* (urinate) *wa tuqbilu* (and come in) *wa tudbiru* (and go out)".

[44] If a game caught by a trained dog is eaten by it, such a game is forbidden, but in a ḥadīth in Abū Dāwūd (book: 'Game', h. 2857) it is permitted. This apparent conflict between these two injunctions has been reconciled by some who observe that the prohibition in this ḥadīth is not absolute but is a discouragement. The name of Allāh must be mentioned at the time of setting the dog on the chase, and it is also necessary when shooting an arrow or firing a gun. According to Imām Abū Ḥanīfah, if one forgets to invoke the name of Allāh at this time the game is still allowed as food. However, the verse "and do not eat of that on which Allāh's name has not been mentioned, and that is surely a transgression" (the Qur'ān, 6:121) does not appear to support this view.

[45] According to the Qur'ān, coming from the toilet, meaning passing stools, urine or wind, is regarded as nullifying the *Wuḍū'*. These are called minor impurities. The major impurity occurs after sexual intercourse which necessitates a complete bath from head to foot, as mentioned in the Qur'ān in the words: "… or you have had contact with women" (5:6). Here "contact" or touching is not meant literally, but indicates sexual intercourse.

[46] In *Wuḍū'* the head has to be wiped. The same has to be done on socks or shoes when the

said: No *Wuḍū'* is required except after *ḥadath* (discharge from the anus or the organ of urination). It is reported by Jābir that the Prophet ﷺ was engaged in the battle of Dhat ar-Riqā' when a man was wounded with an arrow and blood flowing in abundance made him weak, (yet) he bowed in *rukū'* and went in prostration and continued in his prayers. Ḥasan said Muslims would continue to say prayers when they were wounded. Ṭāwus and Muḥammad ibn 'Alī and 'Aṭā' and the people of Ḥijāz said: There is no need for *Wuḍū'* in the case of oozing of blood. Ibn 'Umar once pressed his boil and blood came out of it and he did not perform ablution. Ibn Abū Aufā once spat blood and he continued in his prayers. Ibn 'Umar and Ḥasan said of one who takes to cupping: There is no need for him to do anything except washing the spots where the cupping is done.⁴⁷

176 Abū Hurairah reported that the Messenger of Allāh ﷺ said: "The servant of Allāh remains in a state of prayers so long as he is in the mosque waiting for the prayer and does not void anything (*ḥadath*)." A non-Arab said: "What is voiding (*ḥadath*), O Abū Hurairah?" He said: "It is the sound, that is to say, the wind (which comes out of anus)."

177 'Abbād ibn Tamīm reported from his uncle that the Prophet ﷺ said: "He should not go away unless he hears a sound or smells it." ⁴⁸

178 Muḥammad ibn al-Ḥanafiyyah reported that 'Alī said: I was a man who used to have frequent urethral discharge and I felt shy of asking the Messenger of Allāh ﷺ about it. So I asked al-Miqdād ibn al-Aswad (to ask the Prophet about it). He asked him, and he (the Holy Prophet) said: "It requires *Wuḍū'*." ⁴⁹

179 Zaid ibn Khālid informed that he asked 'Uthmān ibn 'Affān: "What do you think about a man who had sexual intercourse but did not discharge

---

feet are covered by them. If, after *Wuḍū'* has been performed, one has a hair-cut or has shaved the head or taken off the socks or the boots while in the state of *Wuḍū'*, it does not void the *Wuḍū'*. Some authorities are of the opinion that the parts of the body thus laid bare should be washed, but Ḥasan al-Baṣrī says clearly that this is not necessary and Bukhārī agrees with him.

⁴⁷ There is no need for fresh ablution if there is any oozing of blood from any part of the body. Caliph 'Umar, when he was mortally wounded during *Fajr* prayers, completed his prayer while bleeding. This was the injury which brought about his death.

⁴⁸ This is a repetition of h. 137, consisting of only the last part.

⁴⁹ This is a repetition of h. 132, with the addition of the mention of 'Alī being shy to asking the Holy Prophet. His shyness about such a question was natural as he was of the Holy Prophet's son-in-law.

any semen?" 'Uthmān said: "He should perform the ablution as he does for prayer and wash his male organ." 'Uthmān added: "I have heard this from the Messenger of Allāh ﷺ." Then I (Zaid) asked 'Alī and Zubair and Ṭalḥah and Ubayy ibn Ka'b about it, and they commanded the same." [50]

180 Abū Sa'īd al-Khudrī reported that the Messenger of Allāh ﷺ sent for a man from among the Anṣār, and when he came his head was dripping with water. At this, the Prophet ﷺ said: "Perhaps we have made you hurry up." He said: "Yes." So the Messenger of Allāh ﷺ said: "When you are made to hurry up or the discharge is withheld, (only) *Wuḍū'* is required for you." [51]

Ch. 36: A man helping his companion to perform ablution

181 Usāmah ibn Zaid reported that the Messenger of Allāh ﷺ departed from 'Arafāt till he came to the valley where he answered the call of nature. Usāmah ibn Zaid added: I poured water on him and he performed ablution. I said: "O Messenger of Allāh, will you say prayer?" He said: "The place of prayer is further on from where you are." [52]

182 Al-Mughīrah ibn Shu'bah reported that he was with the Messenger of Allāh ﷺ on a journey and that he (the Holy Prophet) went to answer the call of nature, and that Mughīrah poured water on him while he was performing ablution. So he washed his face and his hands and wiped his head and wiped over his socks (with wet hands).

---

[50] There is a difference of opinion as to whether a full bath is obligatory if no discharge of semen had taken place. The four leaders of Fiqh hold that bath in such a case is required. However, this ḥadīth, in which 'Uthmān reports from the Holy Prophet, says clearly that a bath is not required, and the next ḥadīth contains a statement by the Holy Prophet making the same clear. Some regard these reports as abrogated by later commands that a bath is required in such a case, but given that for the expiration of *Wuḍū'* it is necessary that something must emerge from one of the two well-known outlets of the body, it would seem to follow that only the discharge of semen requires a full bath. Only requiring *Wuḍū'* if there was no discharge of semen during sexual intercourse makes it rather like the case of passing of urine, stools or wind. It must also be noted that the words of the Qur'ān, "or you have had contact with women" (5:6), are a euphemism for complete sexual intercourse ending in discharge, and do not mean mere touching or caressing.

[51] By making him "hurry up", what is meant is that the Holy Prophet's message obliged the man to leave his wife before the completion of intercourse. That is why the Holy Prophet says that only *Wuḍū'* is required and the man need not have taken a full bath as there was no discharge.

[52] This is a repetition of h. 139 with some variations. The addition here of pouring water for the Holy Prophet gives rise to the chapter heading.

Ch. 37:   **Reciting the Quran after *ḥadath* (passing wind, urine or stools)**

Manṣūr reported from Ibrāhīm: There is no harm in reciting (the Qur'ān) in the bathroom,[53] or in writing a letter while a *Wuḍū'* is required. Ḥammād reported from Ibrāhīm: If there is a lower garment (*izār*) on them (while bathing) then greet them, otherwise do not greet.

183 'Abdullāh ibn 'Abbās informed that he spent a night at the place of Maimūnah, wife of the Prophet ﷺ, who was his maternal aunt. (He said:) Then I lay down across the width of the bed, and the Messenger of Allāh ﷺ and his wife lay down along its length. Then the Messenger of Allāh ﷺ slept until half of the night had passed, or a little before it or a little after it, when the Messenger of Allāh ﷺ woke up and sat up rubbing his face with his hands to drive away the sleep, and then read the ten verses with which the *Sūrah Āl-i 'Imrān* (ch. 3 of the Qur'ān) ends. Then he stood up and went to a water-skin which was hanging and performed ablution therefrom, making his *Wuḍū'* very well. Then he stood up to pray.

Ibn 'Abbās (further) said: So I stood up and did as he did, then I went and stood by his side. He placed his right hand on my head and caught me by my right ear and turned it. Then he said two *rak'ahs* of prayer, and then two more *rak'ahs,* then two more, then two more, then two more, then two more. Then he said his *Witr* prayer. Then he lay down until the caller to prayer came to him and he stood up and said two *rak'ahs* of short prayer. Then he went out and said the morning prayer.[54]

Ch. 38:   **One who does not consider ablution necessary except if he falls in a deep stupor[55]**

---

[53] It is permissible to recite the Qur'ān in the bathroom, although opinion differs as to whether it is disapproved. To recite it without wearing any clothes is certainly disapproved.

[54] This ḥadīth has occurred before in h. 117 and h. 138. See the footnotes there. Bukhārī has brought it again here to show that reciting the Qur'ān while one is not in the state of *Wuḍū'* is permissible because the Holy Prophet is reported here to have recited it immediately after waking up from sleep and before he had performed *Wuḍū'*. Ibn 'Abbās was very young and therefore he could sleep in the same bed, but lying separately across its width. The Holy Prophet's catching the boy by his ear and turning it means pulling him to make him pass behind the Holy Prophet so that he moves from the Holy Prophet's left side to his right side, as stated in h. 138: "Then he pulled me round and made me (stand) on his right." That is the place for the second man who joins a man already praying on his own.

[55] The meaning is that light unconsciousness, like light sleep, does not necessitate fresh ablution, because in both these states a person would be aware of anything happening which nullified his *Wuḍū'*.

184 Asmā’, daughter of Abū Bakr, reported: I came to ‘Ā’ishah, wife of the Prophet ﷺ, when the sun was eclipsed and (saw that) people were standing praying, and she was also standing praying. I said (to her): "What has happened to the people?" She pointed with her hand to the sky and said: "*Subḥān Allāh* (glory be to God)." I said: "A sign?" She indicated to say Yes. I (also) stood up (for prayer) until I began to faint, so I poured water on my head. When Messenger of Allāh ﷺ finished (the prayer) he praised Allāh and eulogized Him and then said: …[56]

Ch. 39:   Wiping the whole head

Because of the word of Allāh, the Most High: "And wipe your heads" (the Qur’ān, 5:6). Ibn al-Musayyab said: The woman is in the same position as the man and she should wipe her head. Mālik was asked: Is it enough to wipe a part of one's head? So he derived the argument from the ḥadīth of ‘Abdullāh ibn Zaid.

185 Yaḥyā al-Māzinī reported that a man said to ‘Abdullāh ibn Zaid, the grandfather of ‘Amr ibn Yaḥyā: "Can you show me how the Messenger of Allāh ﷺ used to perform ablution?" ‘Abdullāh ibn Zaid said: "Yes." So he sent for some water and poured it over his hands and washed them twice. Then he rinsed his mouth and cleaned out his nostrils, doing so three times. Then he washed his face three times. Then he washed his hands up to the elbows twice each. Then he wiped his head with his (wet) hands, taking them from the front and bringing them from the back, beginning from the front part of the head, such that he took them both up to the nape of the neck and then brought them back to the place where he had begun. Then he washed his feet.

Ch. 40:   Washing both feet up to the ankles

186 Yaḥyā al-Māzinī reported: I saw ‘Amr ibn Abī Ḥasan asking ‘Abdullāh ibn Zaid about the *Wuḍū’* of the Prophet ﷺ. He sent for a pot of water and performed ablution for them like the *Wuḍū’* of the Prophet ﷺ. He poured water from the pot over his hands and washed his hands three times. Then he put his hands in the pot and rinsed his mouth and drew water into his nose and cleaned out his nostrils, with three handfuls (of water). Then he put his hands (in the water) and washed his face three times. Then he put his hands (in the water) and washed his hands up to the elbows twice each. Then he put

---

[56] This is a repetition of h. 86, with some differences in the opening part which we have given here. H. 86 does not mention that this took place at the eclipse of the sun, but it is mentioned here. The remainder of this ḥadīth from this point on, consisting of the statement made by the Holy Prophet, is the same as h. 86 with very minor differences. Hence it is omitted here. See also the footnotes under h. 86. See also h. 1053 where h. 184 is repeated.

his hands (in the water) and wiped his head, taking them from the front (to the back) and bringing them from the back, once. Then he washed his feet up to the ankles.[57]

Ch. 41:   Using the remaining water after people's *Wuḍū'*

Jarīr ibn 'Abdullāh enjoined the people of his house that they should perform ablution with the water left after his cleaning of teeth.[58]

187 Abū Juḥaifah said: The Prophet came out to us one day at noon time and water was brought to him for *Wuḍū'*. He performed ablution, and people began to take from the water remaining after his *Wuḍū'* and started to smear it on their bodies.[59] Then the Prophet said two *rak'ahs* of *Ẓuhr* prayer and two *rak'ahs* of *'Aṣr* prayer, and he had (placed) in front of him a spear (to mark off the boundary of his prayer place).

---

[57] This is a repetition of h. 185 with minor differences in wording. In h. 185 it is stated that the washing of the hands was done twice, but here it is three times. This seems to be an error of a narrator. In h. 185 only the cleaning of the nose is mentioned, while here it is added before it that he drew water into his nose. At the end here, after "he washed his feet", the words "up to the ankles" have been added.

[58] Some people regarded any water left over in a pot, after any such washing had been done using water from it, as unfit to be used for *Wuḍū'*.

[59] All this report says is that the remainder of the water used for ablution by the Holy Prophet was rubbed by people over their bodies, which is taken to mean that it was a way of seeking blessing. In its repetition in h. 376, it is also stated that anyone who could not get such spare water would take the moisture from his companion's hand. This ḥadīth occurs twice under 'The Description of the Prophet', in h. 3553 and h. 3566, the former only mentioning that people took the hands of the Holy Prophet and touched their faces therewith. In the Book of 'Conditions' (*ash-shurūṭ*), in h. 2731–2732, instead of the spare water from the *Wuḍū'* the Holy Prophet's spit is mentioned as being rubbed by people on their faces, but this is evidently a mistake on the part of some narrator. See also the heading of ch. 73 further on, above h. 241.

It should be noted that the word *yatamassaḥūna bi-hī* does not only mean smearing the water on the body but can equally mean performing ablution. What the four reports agree on is that people took the remainder of the water from the ablution of the Holy Prophet and performed *Wuḍū'* with it. Even if they actually rubbed this water on their bodies, it must be remembered that Islām was yet in its infancy and new entrants still acted on much of their wrong traditions when they accepted Islām. In any case the Holy Prophet was not responsible for this behaviour of some initiates and discouraged such expression of religious love. There is a ḥadīth that the Holy Prophet asked some people who were using the dripping water from his *Wuḍū'* to rub on their bodies why they did so. They replied: "Because of love for Allāh and His Messenger." The Holy Prophet told them: "He who wishes to love Allāh and His Messenger, or wishes that Allāh and His Messenger love him, should speak the truth when he talks, faithfully return anything that he is entrusted with, and fulfil the rights of his neighbour" (*Mishkāt al-Maṣābiḥ,* book: *Adab —* Good Manners, ch. Love and mercy for the creation). Thus the Holy Prophet did not approve of such acts for seeking blessings, and instructed them instead to do their duties.

188 Abū Mūsā said: The Prophet ﷺ asked for a bowl containing water and he washed both his hands and his face with it (*fī-hi*) and rinsed his mouth with it (*fī-hi*). Then he said to these two: "Drink of this and pour it over your faces and chests." [60]

189 Maḥmūd ibn ar-Rabīʿ informed — and he was the one on whose face the Messenger of Allāh ﷺ had thrown a mouthful of water from one of their wells when he was a child — and ʿUrwah reported from al-Miswar etc., each of the two confirming his companion: And when the Prophet ﷺ performed his ablution, the people (present there) almost fought over the water left by him. [61]

Ch. 42:   Relating to the above[62]

190 As-Sāʾib ibn Yazīd used to say: My maternal aunt took me to the Prophet ﷺ and said: "O Messenger of Allāh, my sister's son is ill." At this he passed his hands on my head and prayed for me for blessings. Then he performed ablution and I drank out of the water left after his *Wuḍū'*. Then I stood behind his back and looked at the seal of prophethood between his two shoulders which was like *zirr al-ḥajalah*. [63]

---

[60] The word *fī-hi* usually means "in it", and this has given rise to the misunderstanding that the Holy Prophet washed his hands and his face and rinsed his mouth in the bowl itself. But *fī-hi* here has the meaning of "from it", so that the Holy Prophet took water from the bowl to wash his hands and face and rinse his mouth, and then gave the remaining water to two of his Companions for drinking. In any ablution the water that passes over the body or is thrown out of the mouth must be allowed to pass out of the vessel or reservoir, otherwise it would be no ablution.

[61] There appears to have been a scramble for the spare water of the Holy Prophet's ablution. This is one sentence from the lengthy narrative in h. 2731–2732 about the truce of Ḥudaibiyah. This incident is reported to have been witnessed by the representatives of the Makkan unbelievers on that occasion. When they questioned the loyalty of the Companions of the Holy Prophet towards him, the Companions did this, and some other things mentioned in that narrative, just to demonstrate their love, devotion and reverence for the Holy Prophet.

[62] This chapter carries no heading because it continues the subject of the previous one.

[63] *Zirr* means 'button' and *ḥajalah* means 'a curtained canopy' which is carried by camels and serves as a covered sitting place for the women particularly. So *zirr al-ḥajalah* would mean the button of such a canopy. *Ḥajalah* is also the name of a bird like a partridge and if this meaning is taken then *zirr* would mean egg, and the expression would mean the egg of a partridge. There are reports in which this seal is likened to the egg of a pigeon; for example, Ṣaḥīḥ Muslim, Book of Virtues (*Faḍā'il*), ch. 30. The simile is meant to indicate the size of what is regarded as the Seal of Prophethood on the body of the Holy Prophet. There are many reports about this seal, in some of which it is said that this seal had inscribed in it the name of the Holy Prophet. Some of these reports have been described as having weak and unreliable narrators and as contradicting reliable reports. There seems no doubt that there was some sort of a mark between the shoulders

Ch. 43:   One who rinses his mouth and draws water into his nose from the same handful of water

191 Yaḥyā al-Māzinī reported from ʿAbdullāh ibn Zaid that he poured water from a pot over his hands and washed them. Then he rinsed his mouth and drew water into his nose from the same handful of water. He did this three times. Then he washed his hands up to the elbows twice each, and wiped his head from front (to back) and from back (to front). Then he washed his feet up to the ankles. Then he said: "This is like the *Wuḍū'* of the Messenger of Allāh ﷺ." [64]

Ch. 44:   Wiping the head only once

192 Yaḥyā al-Māzinī reported: I saw ʿAmr ibn Abī Ḥasan asking ʿAbdullāh ibn Zaid about the *Wuḍū'* of the Prophet ﷺ. So he sent for a pot of water … [65]

Wuhaib said: He wiped his head once only. [66]

Ch. 45:   The (performing of) *Wuḍū'* of a man in the company of his wife, and using the remainder of the water after the *Wuḍū'* of a woman

ʿUmar performed ablution with hot water and from the (water from) house of a Christian woman. [67]

193 ʿAbdullāh ibn ʿUmar is reported as saying: Men and women used to

---

of the Holy Prophet and some who saw it called it the seal of prophethood. However, it does not mean that it was a sign or proof of his prophethood. As to the shapes of some letters being discernable in this mark, it is not entirely implausible.

[64] This is a repetition of h. 185 with minor difference in wording. The question asked at the start of h. 185 is not found here, and the statement at the end here is not found in h. 185.

[65] This again is a repetition of h. 185 with minor difference in wording, which may be read here from this point onwards. It has some similarities to h. 186, such as giving the name of the man who asked ʿAbdullāh ibn Zaid the question.

[66] This is an extra statement here. Wiping the head "once" is not mentioned in the main body of h. 192 here, nor in h. 185. It is, however, mentioned in h. 186.

[67] This shows that water from the homes of non-Muslims does not become impure thereby. The Qur'ān has given the clear ruling that food cooked in the house of, and by, a non-Muslim is pure enough for a Muslim to eat: "And the food of those who have been given the Book is lawful for you" (5:5). All this shows that there is no concept of "untouchability" in Islām of food and water etc. Merely the fact that a non-Muslim has provided food, drink or water does not make it unfit or unlawful for a Muslim to make use of. Of course, if the food or drink itself was unlawful for a Muslim to consume, he cannot consume it no matter who provides it.

perform ablution together (*jamī'-an*) in the time of the Messenger of Allāh
ﷺ.[68]

Ch. 46: The Prophet ﷺ pouring the water left from his *Wuḍū'* on an unconscious man

194 Jābir said: The Messenger of Allāh ﷺ came to see me in my illness, and I was sick and unconscious. He performed ablution and poured on me some water left from his *Wuḍū'*. I regained my consciousness and said: "O Messenger of Allāh! To whom is my heritage to go, as I have no heirs but *kalālah*?" So the verse on inheritance was revealed.[69]

Ch. 47: Taking bath and performing *Wuḍū'* in a trough and cup and in vessels of wood and stone

195 Anas reported: The time of prayer arrived, so those whose houses were near went to the people of their household and some remained. Then a trough (*mikhḍab*) made of stone containing water was brought to the Messenger of Allāh ﷺ. The trough was so small that he could not spread his hand in it, yet all the people performed ablution. We asked (Anas): "How many of you was it?" He said: "Eighty and even more." [70]

196 Abū Mūsā reported that the Prophet ﷺ asked for a bowl containing water and he washed his hands and his face from it and rinsed his mouth out of it.

---

[68] The word *jamī'-an* in this ḥadīth shows that there were occasions when men and women performed *Wuḍū'* from the same water. This may mean that men and women of the same household performed ablution together in the house, or that the husband and the wife shared the same vessel of water as indicated by Bukhārī in the chapter heading. There is a report by Ibn 'Umar in Ṣaḥīḥ Ibn Khuzaimah that he found the Holy Prophet and his Companions performing ablution along with women from the same vessel of water, which would mean that each husband and wife were sharing one vessel. However, it is possible that on a journey all the men and women had no option but to perform ablution from one vessel.

[69] The object of including this ḥadīth here is only to show that the remaining water from *Wuḍū'* can be used, even though drops of water from performing the ablution might have fallen into it. The word *kalālah* means one who has neither ascendants nor descendants, or one who has no children, or one who has heirs other than his father or children. In this ḥadīth *kalālah* is used to mean the heirs themselves, other than these.

[70] This ḥadīth also occurs in the Book 'Virtues' (*Manāqib*) under 'Signs of Prophethood in Islām' (see h. 3572–3575). According to h. 3572, the number of people was three hundred. This was evidently a miracle, either on the physical or the psychological plane. Without such invisible power of control, God will be reduced to a helpless observer of the affairs of the universe. See also h. 169.

197 'Abdullāh ibn Zaid reported: The Messenger of Allāh ﷺ came (to us) and we brought him water in a bronze bowl. He performed ablution (thus): he washed his face three times, and his hands each twice, he wiped his head from front (to back) and from back (to front), and he washed his feet.[71]

198 'Ā'ishah said: When the Prophet ﷺ became ill and his ailment became severe, he asked permission from his wives to be nursed in my house. They gave him the permission, and the Prophet ﷺ came out between two men, with his feet dragging on the ground, between 'Abbās and another man.

'Ubaidullāh (who reported the above from 'Ā'ishah) said: I informed 'Abdullāh ibn 'Abbās (of this) and he said: "Do you know who the other man was?" I said: "No." He said: "He was 'Alī, son of Abū Ṭālib."

'Ā'ishah used to narrate: The Prophet ﷺ, after he had entered his house, and his illness became severe, said: "Pour on me seven skins full of water whose mouths have not been opened, so that I may speak to the people." He was made to sit in a trough of Ḥafṣah, wife of the Prophet ﷺ, and we began to pour on him from these water-skins, until he began to beckon to us as if to say, "You have done it". Then he went out to the people.[72]

Ch. 48:   Performing *Wuḍū'* from a pot (*taur*)

199 Yaḥyā al-Māzinī reported: My paternal uncle used to perform *Wuḍū'* using much water. Once he asked 'Abdullāh ibn Zaid: "Tell me how you saw the Prophet performing ablution?" He sent for a pot of water (*taur*) and poured water from it over his hands and washed them three times. Then he put his hands in the pot and rinsed his mouth and cleaned out his nostrils, three times with one handful (of water). Then he put his hands (in the water), took a handful of it and washed his face three times. Then he washed his hands up to the

---

[71] This is a brief repetition of h. 185. Here the addition is that the water was brought in a bronze bowl.

[72] This report occurs seven times in Bukhārī (see also h. 665, 687, 2588, 3628, 4442 and 5714) and is also recorded in Muslim, Nasā'ī and Tirmidhī. It relates to the last illness of the Holy Prophet that led to his death. When he proceeded towards the chamber of 'Ā'ishah, he felt so weak that he could not raise his feet from the ground. 'Ā'ishah does not mention the name of 'Alī as one of the two men who helped the Holy Prophet and it has been suggested that this was due to some ill-feeling between her and 'Alī. However, one report gives the name of Faḍl ibn 'Abbās and another mentions Usāmah. It appears that while 'Abbās remained a constant support of the Holy Prophet on one side, the other side was attended by several men one after another. The purpose of having water poured on his head was obviously to reduce the temperature of the body so that he could address the people before he died. All his anxiety even in the extreme condition of his illness was for people's welfare, and not for his own condition. As soon as he felt temporary relief he made for the mosque for prayer and delivered a sermon (see h. 3628).

elbows twice each. Then he took some water with his hand and wiped his head, taking his hands back (from the front) and bringing them to the front. Then he washed his feet. Then he said: "This is how I saw the Prophet ﷺ performing ablution." [73]

200 Anas reported that the Prophet ﷺ sent for a vessel of water. So a bowl having a broad brim containing a little water was brought and he put his fingers in it. Anas (also) said: I looked at the water which began to gush out from his fingers. Anas (further) said: I estimated that those who performed ablution (from that water) numbered between seventy and eighty. [74]

Ch. 49: *Wuḍū'* **with one *mudd* of water**

201 Anas said: The Prophet ﷺ used to take a bath with between one *ṣā'* to five *mudds* of water, and he used to perform ablution with one *mudd*. [75]

Ch. 50: **Wiping over socks**

202 Saʻd ibn Abū Waqqāṣ reported from the Prophet ﷺ that he wiped over the socks, and that ʻAbdullāh ibn ʻUmar asked ʻUmar about this. ʻUmar said: "Yes. And when Saʻd reports anything from the Prophet ﷺ, do not ask anyone else about it." [76]

---

[73] This is a repetition of h. 185, with some words from the versions in h. 186 and h. 191.

[74] This is very similar to what is stated in h. 195, which is also reported by Anas. However, these appear to be two different incidents because h. 195 speaks of a container (*mikhḍab*) which was so small that the Holy Prophet could not spread his hand in it, while this report speaks of a wide open-top bowl (*qadaḥ-in raḥrāḥ-in*).

[75] One *ṣā'*, a measure of weight, is equivalent to about 3 kgs, and is four *mudd*. In terms of volume, one *mudd* of water would be about 750 mls. This report is not intended to impose a limit on the quantity of water to be used in bath or ablution, but indicates that there should be no wastage of water. In hot countries like Arabia water might be scarce.

[76] Wiping the socks with wet hands is reported so frequently that this repetition makes those reports highly authentic. There are more than eighty reports confirming this, and Ḥasan of Baṣrah has said that more than seventy Companions narrated to him about wiping over the socks. This does not contravene the injunction of the Qur'ān to wash the feet because wiping is only allowable if the feet have been washed at least once in twenty-four hours and socks were put on after the washing of the feet. As it is inconvenient to remove socks for every ablution, they may be wiped with wet hands as a token of obedience to the injunction for washing. The Qur'ān has issued broad orders and not added details of how to follow them under difficult circumstances. These details are supplied by the Holy Prophet. Even before the injunction to perform *Wuḍū'* was revealed in the Qur'ān, the Holy Prophet and his Companions used to perform it in the same manner as they did afterwards. It was mentioned in the Qur'ān later in order to show that the details of religion taught by the Holy Prophet were also intimated to him from Allāh. The permission to wipe over the socks neither contradicts the Qur'ān nor abrogates the command in the

203 Al-Mughīrah ibn Shuʻbah reported from the Messenger of Allāh ﷺ that he went out to answer the call of nature and Al-Mughīrah followed him with a vessel containing water. He poured it over him when he finished answering the call of nature, and he performed ablution and wiped over his socks (with wet hands).[77]

204 Jaʻfar ibn ʻAmr ibn Umayyah al-Ḍamrī reported that his father informed him that he saw the Messenger of Allāh ﷺ wiping over his socks.

205 Jaʻfar ibn ʻAmr ibn Umayyah reported from his father that he said: I saw the Prophet ﷺ wiping over his turban and his socks.

Ch. 51:   Putting the feet (in the socks) when they are clean[78]

206 Al-Mughīrah reported: I was with the Prophet ﷺ on a journey and I bent down to remove his socks (from his feet) but he said: "Leave them, for I put them on when they (the feet) were clean." So he wiped over them.

Ch. 52:   One who does not perform ablution after eating goat's meat and gruel

Abū Bakr and ʻUmar and ʻUthmān, may Allāh be pleased with them, ate meat and did not perform ablution.[79]

207 ʻAbdullāh ibn ʻAbbās reported that the Messenger of Allāh ﷺ ate (the meat of) the shoulder of a goat and then said his prayer without performing ablution.

208 Jaʻfar ibn ʻAmr ibn Umayyah said that his father informed him that he saw the Messenger of Allāh ﷺ cutting pieces from the shoulder of a

---

Qurʼān, as the Holy Prophet and his Companions continued to do the same after the command was revealed in the Qurʼān.

[77] This is a repetition of h. 182. There more details of the *Wuḍūʼ* are given. The wiping of the socks is mentioned in both reports.

[78] The mention, in the chapter heading and in the ḥadīth itself, of the feet being clean when the socks were put on does not only mean that the feet themselves should be clean but that the person should be in the state of the cleanliness as required by *Wuḍūʼ*. If not on a journey, the wiping over the feet can be done for up to a whole day and night, and if on a journey wiping is allowed for up to three days and nights.

[79] That is to say, eating of cooked food does not nullify *Wuḍūʼ*. Some reports indicate that in the beginning eating of cooked food was considered as requiring *Wuḍūʼ* after it but that this order was repealed later on. It is possible that the earlier order was by way of precaution because even some cooked food leaves a bad smell in the mouth. Later on, just rinsing the mouth was considered sufficient. According to some authorities the use of camel flesh is excluded and does nullify *Wuḍūʼ*, and there is a report in Ṣaḥīḥ Muslim (book: Menstruation, ch. 25) to this effect, but this also may be regarded as a desirable recommendation and not a strict rule.

(cooked) goat (and eating them). Then he was called for prayer and he left the knife and said his prayer without performing ablution.[80]

Ch. 53: One who rinses his mouth after taking gruel and does not perform ablution

209 Suwaid ibn al-Nuʿmān informed that he went out with the Messenger of Allāh ﷺ in the year of (the battle of) Khaibar, till they were at aṣ-Ṣahbā', and it was a place very near to Khaibar. He (the Holy Prophet) said the *'Aṣr* prayer, then he asked for some food but he was not brought anything except some gruel (*as-sawīq*), so he ordered it to be soaked in water. The Messenger of Allāh ﷺ ate it and we too ate. Then he stood up for the *Maghrib* prayer, rinsed his mouth and we too rinsed our mouths. He then said his prayer without performing ablution.[81]

210 Maimūnah reported that the Prophet ﷺ ate meat of the shoulder, then said his prayer without performing ablution.

Ch. 54: Should the mouth be rinsed after drinking milk?

211 Ibn ʿAbbās reported that the Messenger of Allāh ﷺ drank milk, then rinsed his mouth and said: "Surely there is fat in it." [82]

Ch. 55: *Wuḍū'* after sleep, and one who does not see the necessity of *Wuḍū'* after dozing once or twice or nodding in sleep

212 ʿĀ'ishah reported that the Messenger of Allāh ﷺ said: "When any of you dozes in prayer he should sleep till the sleep leaves him, because when someone dozes while he is praying he might perhaps not know whether he is asking forgiveness (from Allāh) or cursing himself." [83]

---

[80] The Holy Prophet's leaving aside the knife shows that he was cutting the meat with it as he was eating. It may be concluded from this that the use of knife, fork and spoon in eating is allowed.

[81] This incident belongs to the year 6 A.H. when the Holy Prophet was the undisputed ruler of a state. It shows the simplicity of the life of the Holy Prophet and his Companions, as they were subsisting on the ordinary and coarse food available to the poor.

[82] This shows the refinement of the Holy Prophet. Even after drinking milk he rinsed his mouth in case it left any smell in the mouth. If he was extremely anxious for moral purity, equally anxious was he for physical purity. To keep the mouth clean is essential for good health, and in our times modern knowledge has revealed this fact.

[83] This shows that dozing in prayer does not make the ablution void nor does it necessitate repetition of the prayer.

213 Anas reported from the Prophet ﷺ that he said: "When any of you dozes in prayer, he should sleep till he understands what he is reciting." [84]

Ch. 56: To perform *Wuḍū'* even if there was no *ḥadath* (passing of wind, urine or stools)

214 Anas reported that the Prophet ﷺ used to perform (a fresh) ablution for every prayer. I said: "What did you used to do?" [85] He said: "For any of us, a *Wuḍū'* was enough which was not voided by *ḥadath*."

215 Suwaid ibn al-Nuʿmān informed: We went out with the Messenger of Allāh ﷺ in the year of (the battle of) Khaibar, till we were at aṣ-Ṣahbā'. The Messenger of Allāh ﷺ led us in *'Aṣr* prayer. When he had prayed, he asked for some food but he was not brought anything except some gruel (*as-sawīq*). So we ate and drank. Then the Prophet ﷺ stood up for the *Maghrib* prayer and rinsed his mouth. He then led us in the *Maghrib* prayer without performing ablution.[86]

Ch. 57: It is one of the major sins not to protect oneself from one's urine

216 Ibn ʿAbbās reported: The Prophet ﷺ passed by one of the gardens of Madīnah or Makkah and he heard the voices of two men who were being punished in their graves.[87] The Prophet ﷺ said: "These two are being punished, but they are not being punished for a major sin." Then he said: "Yes (these are also major), one of these two did not protect himself from his own urine and the other one used to go about spreading falsehood about others." [88]

---

[84] The real benefit of prayer accrues to a person when he understands what he is saying in his prayer. For this it is essential that he should have education enough to be able to understand the meanings of the Arabic words used in prayer. It also means that whatever one says in prayer, it should have an effect on the heart. For this purpose, stray thoughts that come to mind during prayers should be repelled and full concentration should be towards Allāh. Prayer also teaches the lesson that to achieve any aim one must not let attention be diverted towards other matters but focus only on the objective.

[85] The person asking the question was ʿAmr ibn ʿĀmir, who was reporting from Anas.

[86] This is a repetition of h. 209 with slight difference of wording. It shows that the statement from Anas in h. 214, that the Holy Prophet used to make a fresh ablution for every prayer, refers to his general practice, and that it also used to happen occasionally that he said a prayer without a fresh ablution while his *Wuḍū'* was still in effect from the previous prayer.

[87] The Holy Prophet's hearing the sounds of the two men was in a vision, and not physically.

[88] To protect oneself from urine (*istitār baul*) may mean to hide oneself while urinating and it may also mean to prevent the urine or drops of it from contaminating the body or the clothes. Islām wants both cleanliness as well as modesty while answering the call of nature. Violation of minor regulations, when committed persistently, assumes the form of a major sin. Hence their

Then he asked for a branch of a date-tree and broke it into two pieces and placed one piece on each grave. He was asked: "O Messenger of Allāh, Why did you do this?" He said: "May be their punishment will be lightened until these two (pieces of date branch) dry up." [89]

Ch. 58: What has been said about the washing of urine

The Prophet ﷺ said about the person in the grave: "He did not protect himself from his own urine", and he mentioned only the urine of human beings.

217 Anas ibn Mālik reported: When the Messenger of Allāh ﷺ would go out to answer a call of nature I would bring to him water and he would wash with it.

Ch. 59: Related to the above

218 Ibn 'Abbās reported: The Prophet ﷺ passed by a grave and said: "Surely these two are being punished, and they are not being punished for any major sin. As for one of these two, he did not protect himself from (his own) urine, and as for the other, he used to go about spreading falsehood about others." Then he took a green branch of a date-tree and split it into two halves and fixed one on each grave. People asked: "O Messenger of Allāh, Why did

---

violations are first called by the Holy Prophet as *not* being major sins, but then he says they *are* major sins.

[89] The relief in the spiritual torture of the men buried in these graves was not because of the branches of tree but on account of the Holy Prophet's prayer for them. The planting of the branches was only an outward symbol of the acceptance of the Holy Prophet's prayer for these men. Otherwise, if such things as the planting of a branch of a tree could lighten the spiritual torment of the major sins, all rules of moral conduct as given in the religion would become meaningless.

Various kinds of questions have been discussed in connection with this ḥadīth, such as: if these men were disbelievers, how could the Holy Prophet pray for them, and if they were Muslims, why was the punishment lightened only for a certain time. But it must be remembered that it is unwarranted to derive any principles of religious law from reports that relate stories, and there is no injunction or ruling issued by the Holy Prophet on this occasion. It is also difficult to say how far the narrators have preserved in their memory all the facts connected with this incident or the words uttered by the Holy Prophet. Planting fresh branches of trees on graves has no bearing on the punishment suffered in the life after death by those buried there, but it is their deeds which count. As for the acceptance of prayer, it is true that the prayers of prophets and other righteous persons are accepted even for sinners and unbelievers, and prayers can be accepted for the dead as for the living. As to punishment in the grave, it is not derived from this ḥadīth but from the Qur'ān which clearly mentions the state of *barzakh,* the state after death which is the real "grave". The receiving of reward and punishment, to some extent, in this state is established from the Qur'ān. As to physical graves, many people do not have graves in which their bodies are buried, but they still experience the state of *barzakh* after death.

you do this?" He said: "May be their punishment will be lightened until these two (pieces of date branch) dry up." [90]

Ch. 60: The Prophet ﷺ and the people (around him) leaving a desert Arab (alone) until he finished urinating in the mosque

219 Anas ibn Mālik reported that the Prophet ﷺ saw a desert Arab urinating in the mosque. He said: "Leave him." When he finished, he called for water and poured it over it. [91]

Ch. 61 Pouring water over urine in the mosque

220 Abū Hurairah said: A desert Arab stood in the mosque and urinated. People were about to take hold of him but the Prophet ﷺ said to them: "Leave him alone and throw a bucket of water, or pot of water, over his urine, for you have been raised to make things easy (for people), not raised to make things difficult." [92]

221 Anas ibn Mālik said: A desert Arab came and started urinating in a corner of the mosque. People tried to prevent him but the Prophet ﷺ stopped them. When he finished urinating, the Prophet ﷺ ordered a pot of water to be thrown over it. [93]

Ch. 62: Urine of children

222 'Ā'ishah, mother of the believers, reported saying: A child was brought to the Messenger of Allāh ﷺ and it urinated on his garment, so he called for water and let it flow over it. [94]

---

[90] This is a repetition of h. 216 with a different opening and other minor differences.

[91] This ḥadīth is repeated in more detail in h. 220

[92] Here is a great lesson for the intolerant and rigid among Muslims. Muslims are instructed here to be mild in correcting the errors of their fellow-believers, without causing them inconvenience. The Qur'ān had taught even in regard to the opponents of the Muslims: "Call to the way of your Lord with wisdom and goodly exhortation, and argue with them in the best manner" (16:125). Yet today Muslim religious leaders, while failing to condemn the great evils taking place in front of their eyes, are so harsh and strict in requiring observance of small details that they have alienated the people from the religion.

[93] This is the third version of the report in h. 219 and h. 220.

[94] An extraordinary leniency has been observed here in the matter of the urine of babies to avoid inconvenience to the parents. Islām is a practical religion and as such it does not lay down rules which are a trouble to act upon. On the basis of some reports, a distinction is made between the urine of a male baby and that of a female, in that for a boy the pouring or sprinkling of water is sufficient, but for a girl full washing is necessary. But some authorities hold that both the cases

223 Umm Qais bint Miḥṣan reported that she took her small boy, who had not started eating food, to the Messenger of Allāh ﷺ. He made him sit on his lap, and the boy urinated on the garment of the Messenger of Allāh ﷺ. So he called for water and sprinkled it on it and did not wash it (i.e., the soiled garment).

Ch. 63:   To urinate standing and sitting

224 Ḥudhaifah reported: The Prophet ﷺ came to the dung-heap of a community and urinated while standing. Then he called for water. I brought him water and he performed ablution.[95]

Ch. 64:   To urinate near one's companion while screened by a wall

225 Ḥudhaifah reported: Once I and the Prophet ﷺ were walking together and he came to the dung-heap of a community which was behind a wall. He stood just as any of you would stand and he urinated. I withdrew from him, so he beckoned to me. I came to him and stood behind him till he finished.[96]

Ch. 65:   To urinate near the dung-heap of a community

226 Abū Wā’il reported: Abū Mūsā al-Ashʿarī was very strict in the matter of urine and used to say that among the Israelites when anyone's garment was soiled by urine he used to tear off that portion. So Ḥudhaifah said: "I wish he (Abū Mūsā) would refrain (from this strictness), for the Messenger of Allāh ﷺ came to the dung-heap of a community and urinated while standing." [97]

---

should be treated the same. The word for "child" in this ḥadīth is only *ṣabbiyy-an,* meaning boy, but in the next ḥadīth the adjective "small" (*ṣaghīr*) has been added and it is further added: "who had not started eating food", showing that the baby was still on breast milk.

These reports give a glimpse into the humanity of the Holy Prophet, showing how fond he was of small children. An ordinary woman brings a child to him and he makes it sit on his lap lovingly and cuddles it. When that baby passes urine on his lap he does not get annoyed, nor make it look as if he would never again hold a baby. Those Muslim religious leaders today who claim to be his successors, with few exceptions, are so far removed from treating people with the Holy Prophet's humanity that they appear to have no connection with him.

[95] This ḥadīth covers the same subject as h. 225.

[96] According to one report the Holy Prophet said to Ḥudhaifah: "Act as a screen for me" (*Fatḥ al-Bārī*). His asking Ḥudhaifah to come to him and stand behind him may have been for this purpose. This ḥadīth and the previous one show that urinating while standing is allowed.

[97] Abū Mūsā used to be very hard on those whom he saw urinating while standing. Ḥudhaifah regretted this strictness since he had seen the Holy Prophet urinating while standing. It appears that, because of this, the Companions of the Holy Prophet also urinated while standing, when necessary. There is no report showing that the Holy Prophet had ever forbidden anyone to urinate while standing; on the contrary, he himself had done so. Of course, care must be taken to protect the body and the clothes from being soiled by drops from the urine.

Ch. 66:   Washing off blood

227 Asmā' reported: A woman came to the Prophet ﷺ and said: "What do you say about one of us who starts menstruating in her garment, what she should do?" He said: "She should rub it off (the garment), then put water on it and rub it, and wash it with water. Then she can pray in it."

228 'Ā'ishah reported: Fāṭimah bint Abū Ḥubaish went to the Prophet ﷺ and said: "O Messenger of Allāh! I am a woman who suffers from bleeding outside periods (*istiḥāḍah,* or metrorrhagia),[98] and I can never be clean, should I then give up prayer?" The Messenger of Allāh ﷺ said: "No, it is nothing but (bleeding from) a vein, and it is not menstruation. So when your menstruation period arrives, give up prayer, and when it passes, wash yourself clean of the blood and then say your prayers."

Ḥishām said: And my father said[99] (that the Holy Prophet further said): "Then perform ablution for every prayer until that period comes again." [100]

Ch. 67:   Washing of semen and rubbing it off and washing that which touches (the man) from the woman

229 'Ā'ishah reported: I used to wash off (traces of) semen from the clothes of the Prophet ﷺ, and he would go out to prayer while the marks (*buqa'a*) of water would (still) be on his clothes.[101]

230 Sulaimān ibn Yasār reported: I asked 'Ā'ishah about semen sticking to clothes. She said: "I used to wash it off from the clothes of the Messenger of Allāh ﷺ, and he would go out to prayer while, due to the traces of washing, the marks (*buqa'a*) of water would (still) be on his clothes." [102]

Ch. 68:   When semen etc. is washed but its traces do not disappear

231 'Amr ibn Maimūn related: I asked Sulaimān ibn Yasār about the clothes to which semen is sticking. He replied that 'Ā'ishah said: ... (see h. 230).[103]

---

[98] For *Istiḥāḍah,* or metrorrhagia, see h. 306, 309–311 and h. 327 in the next Book.

[99] Ḥishām was reporting from his father 'Urwah, who in turn was reporting from 'Ā'ishah.

[100] It may also be concluded from this that people who suffer from some condition in which urine drips persistently or there is incessant breaking of wind are not required to interrupt their prayer to repeat their *Wuḍū'* if this happens during prayer. The *Wuḍū'* performed before the prayer is sufficient in the case of such people to complete the prayer.

[101] *Buqa'a* (plural of *buqa'ah*) means difference between two colours. A spot that is lightly washed must show some kind of stain, but this does not matter.

[102] This is a repetition of h. 229 with an addition at the beginning.

[103] In this repetition of h. 229 and h. 230, the report from this point onwards, consisting of the statement by 'Ā'ishah, is as in h. 230 with very minor differences.

232 'Ā'ishah reported that she used to wash off semen from the clothes of the Prophet ﷺ. (She added:) Then I (still) used to notice one or more marks (of water) on them.

Ch. 69:   The urine of camels and cattle and sheep and their enclosures

Abū Mūsā said his prayer in Dārul Barīd where there was dung, and the woods were near him. He said: Here and there is the same.[104]

233 Anas reported: Some people from the tribe of 'Ukl or 'Urainah came but (the climate of) Madīnah did not suit them.[105] So the Prophet ﷺ ordered them to go to the milch-camels (*liqāḥ*),[106] so that they could drink the urine and the milk thereof.[107] They proceeded (there) and when they regained their health, they killed the herdsman of the Prophet ﷺ and took away the she-camels. When the news reached (the Holy Prophet) early in the morning, he sent (a party) after them, and as the day advanced, they were brought (before him). So by his order their hands and their feet were cut off. Their eyes were pricked and they were put on stony ground. They were asking for water but they were not given any water to drink.

Abū Qilābah said: These people had committed theft and murder, and disbelieved after their belief, and waged war against Allāh and his Messenger.[108]

---

[104] Dārul Barīd is a place in Kūfah in Iraq where the ambassadors of the Caliph used to stay. The coming and going of camels made the place strewn with dung. Of course, only a part of the whole place was like that, where Abū Mūsā wanted to say his prayer. By saying "same" (*sawā'*) he meant that one need not search for a cleaner spot for prayer, and that even if there were camel dung lying about a place, that place was clean enough for prayer. Dung was not something the proximity of which made a place unfit for prayers.

[105] The words here *fa-jtawawu al-madīnah* mean "they disliked staying in the city", or that "the place proved harmful to their health", i.e., the climate there did not suit them. The word *jawā* means a form of epidemic.

[106] *Liqāḥ* is the plural of *liqḥah*, and means camels that give milk. From some reports it appears that they themselves asked the Holy Prophet's permission to go to this place and he allowed them. Milch-camels were the property of the state from *Zakāt* and were kept at a pasture six miles away from Madīnah.

[107] The giving of the urine of camel to these people was only by way of medicine. It is an accepted principle that the use of things ordinarily forbidden is permissible as a remedy for diseases.

[108] The punishment meted out to these barbarous people, though apparently harsh, was appropriate to the occasion. These people were treated kindly by the Holy Prophet who ordered their stay in a healthier place with plenty of milk to drink. Instead of being grateful for this kind treatment they ran away with the camels of the state, and, as is found in reliable reports, when Yasār, the herdsman appointed by the Holy Prophet, followed them to get the camels back, they

234 Anas reported: The Prophet ﷺ used to say his prayer in the enclosure of the sheep (*marābiḍ al-ghanam*) before the mosque was built.[109]

Ch. 70:   Anything of filth falling in melted butter or water

Az-Zuhrī said: There is no harm in (using) the water of which the taste and the smell and the colour have not changed.[110] Ḥammād said: There is no harm if the feather of an animal that dies of itself (falls in the liquid). Az-Zuhrī said about the bones of an animal dying of itself such as the elephant etc.: I have seen people from among the learned men of the previous generations combing their hair with such things and keeping oil in them without seeing any harm in it. Ibn Sīrīn and Ibrāhīm said: There is no harm in trading in ivory.

235 Maimūnah reported that the Messenger of Allāh ﷺ was asked about the mouse that had fallen in melted butter and he said: "Throw it (the mouse) away and what is around it, and eat (the rest of) the butter." [111]

236 Maimūnah reported that the Prophet ﷺ was asked about the mouse that had fallen in melted butter and he said: "Take it out and what is around it, and throw that away."

237 Abū Hurairah reported from the Prophet ﷺ that he said: "Every wound which a Muslim receives in the way of Allāh will, on the Day of Resurrection, appear in the form it was when it was inflicted, with blood flowing from it, its colour being the colour of blood and its smell being the smell of musk." [112]

---

amputated his hands and feet, and pricked his tongue and his eyes with thorns, and killed him after severe torture. The law of retaliation used to be applied in Arabia at the time and the Holy Prophet punished them accordingly, as they had treated the herdsman. He never applied such punishments in any other case. Later on, Muslims were forbidden from retaliating in kind with the same acts that the criminals perpetrated.

[109] *Marābiḍ al-ghanam* means a place where sheep are kept. The report means that when a better place is not available, it is not forbidden to use such places for prayer. Of course, the place of prayer must always be cleaned as Muslims are required to keep such places and mosques clean. Here the purpose is also to show that the whole of the earth is holy enough for holding prayers, whatever it may have been used for before.

[110] The subject of the chapter is that, as long as the colour, taste or smell of water does not alter due to something falling into it, it can be used. However, this does not mean that water is only polluted if a change is observed in its colour, smell or taste, but not by an impurity which does not cause such a change. For this reason, the next chapter says that it is forbidden to urinate in standing water because people take bath in it.

[111] Some authorities have restricted the butter spoken of here to butter solidified by cooling. They are of the opinion that if it is in liquid form it should be heated and then cleaned by straining.

[112] Some authorities hold that this ḥadīth is not relevant to the subject of this chapter. Others

Ch. 71:   Passing urine in standing water

238 Abū Hurairah heard the Messenger of Allāh ﷺ say: "We, the last ones to come (in this life), will be the foremost (on the Day of Resurrection)."

239 According to the same chain of narration (as above in h. 238), he said: "None of you should urinate in standing water which does not flow, (as you may) then (need to) take bath in it."

Ch. 72:   When any filth or carcass is thrown on the back of a person who is praying, his prayer does not become void thereby

> Ibn 'Umar, when he could see blood on his clothes while praying, would keep it aside and continue in his prayer.[113] Ibn al-Musayyab and ash-Sha'bī said: When someone says his prayer and there is blood or semen on his clothes, or he is not facing the *Qiblah,* or he performs *Tayammum* and says his prayer and then he finds water within the prayer time, he is not to repeat the prayers (in any of these cases).

240 'Abdullāh ibn Mas'ūd reported: While the Messenger of Allāh ﷺ was prostrating — and (through other narrators) he related that the Prophet ﷺ was praying near the Sacred House — and Abū Jahl and his companions were sitting there, some of them said to others: "Which of you will bring the stomach contents (*salā jazūr*)[114] of a she-camel of such and such tribe, and then place it on the back of Muḥammad when he goes in prostration?" Then the most unfortunate one among them got up and brought it. He looked on till the Prophet ﷺ went in prostration, and then placed it on his back between his shoulders. I was watching and could not do anything, and I wished I had power to prevent it.

He ('Abdullāh) continued: So they began to laugh and fall upon one another, and the Messenger of Allāh ﷺ continued his prostration, not raising his head until Fāṭimah came to him and threw it away from his back. Then he

---

give various explanations of its inclusion here. Bukhārī may be citing it as an example where the state of a liquid becomes altered and this is indicated by its smell. The bad odour from the water indicates that it has gone bad, while the spiritual fragrance from the blood of the martyr indicates its high spiritual value.

[113] The cloth which Ibn 'Umar could lay aside while praying must be one that could be easily dropped during prayer, such as an over-garment draped over a person.

[114] *Jazūr* means the she-camels that have been slaughtered, and *salā* is the bag in which the baby lives while still in the womb. After an animal is slaughtered it is sometimes found to be pregnant. The slaughterers naturally have to take out the uterus and with it the young one in the bag.

raised his head and said: "O Allāh seize the Quraish!", three times. This proved hard for them when he prayed against them.

He ('Abdullāh) continued: And these people were aware that prayer in that city was accepted (by Allāh). Then he took their names: "O Allāh seize Abū Jahl, seize 'Utbah ibn Rabī'ah, and Shaibah ibn Rabī'ah and al-Walīd ibn 'Utbah and Umayyah ibn Khalaf and 'Uqbah ibn Abū Mu'aiṭ." He also mentioned a seventh name but we do not remember it. By Him in Whose hand lies my life! I saw them whom the Messenger of Allāh ﷺ counted (by names) lying dead in the well of Badr.[115]

Ch. 73:   **The spittle and the discharge of the nose and such like on the cloth**

'Urwah reported from al-Miswar and Marwān: The Messenger of Allāh ﷺ came out during the time of Ḥudaibiyah. Then he narrated the whole ḥadīth (and said): Whenever (on that occasion) the Prophet ﷺ spitted any spittle which happened to fall on the hands of any man among them, he would rub it on his face and his skin.[116]

241 Anas reported: The Prophet ﷺ spat on his cloth.

Ch. 74:   ***Wuḍū' is not permissible with nabīdh or any intoxicating drink***[117]

Ḥasan and 'Abul 'Āliyah disapproved it, and 'Aṭā' said: To me *Tayammum* is preferable to *Wuḍū'* with *nabīdh* and milk.

242 'Ā'ishah reported from the Prophet ﷺ that he said: "Every drink that intoxicates is forbidden."

---

[115] This ḥadīth shows the lengths to which the unbelievers of Makkah had gone to inflict distress and trouble upon the Holy Prophet, and how much they delighted in doing so. Of the persons mentioned here, the six who are named were killed in the battle of Badr. The seventh, whose name is not mentioned here but is in h. 520, was 'Umārah ibn al-Walīd who died insane in Abyssinia. These seven were the most bitter and inveterate enemies of Islām and the Holy Prophet.

[116] This incident belongs to the time of the Truce of Ḥudaibiyah. See footnote 59 on h. 187 where it is shown that the word *nukhāmah*, i.e., spittle, seems to have been mentioned by mistake. This word is only found in the version of this story in h. 2731–2732, from which this short extract is quoted here. That version is so lengthy that errors in it are probable. The other versions of this story mention only the water from the *Wuḍū'* of the Holy Prophet being sought after by the Companions. It is also to be noted that Marwān was not a Companion and it is known that al-Miswar was not present at the Truce of Ḥudaibiyah. Thus neither of them could have witnessed the incident of the spit of the Holy Prophet.

[117] *Nabīdh* is water in which dates or grapes are soaked but has not fermented. It is permissible to drink it but not to perform *Wuḍū'* with it because, instead of cleaning the hands and face, it would spoil them.

Ch. 75:   A woman's washing of blood from the face of her father

> 'Abul 'Āliyah said: Massage my foot because it is ailing.

243 Abū Ḥāzim reported that he heard Sahl ibn Sa'd as-Sā'idī saying, when there was no one other than the two of them, that people asked him: By what were the wounds of the Prophet ﷺ treated? He (Sahl) replied: "There is no one alive who knows better about it than me. 'Alī used to bring water in his shield and Fāṭimah used to wash the blood from his face. Then a (straw) mat was burnt and with it were filled his wounds." [118]

Ch. 76:   *As-siwāk* (the tooth-brush or tooth-stick)

> Ibn 'Abbās said: I spent a night with the Prophet ﷺ and he brushed his teeth.

244 Abū Burdah reported from his father (Abū Mūsā al-Ash'arī) that he said: I went to the Prophet ﷺ and found him cleaning his teeth with the tooth-stick in his hand and making the sound "O", "O", while the tooth-stick was in his mouth, as if he was vomiting.[119]

245 Ḥudhaifah reported: The Prophet ﷺ, when he used to get up at night, would clean his mouth with the tooth-stick.

Ch. 77:   Passing on a tooth-stick to the older ones

246 Ibn 'Umar reported that the Prophet ﷺ said: "I found myself (in a dream) cleaning my teeth with the tooth-stick, and two men came to me, one of them older than the other. I gave the tooth-stick to the younger one of the two, but I was told: Show regard to the older one. So I passed it on to the older one of the two."

---

[118] It is thus permissible for one person to clean another.

[119] This ḥadīth stresses the importance of brushing the teeth. The Holy Prophet used to clean his teeth with a tooth-stick frequently. Keeping the teeth clean is important in preventing many diseases. It not only keeps the mouth clean and free from bad smell but prevents diseases of the gums and the stomach. The Holy Prophet laid the utmost emphasis on keeping the teeth clean. He is reported to have cleaned his teeth at night and when rising for prayer in the morning. The necessity of keeping the teeth clean when going to bed has become a matter of common knowledge. The Holy Prophet's emphasis on this shows that he regarded cleaning and protecting the body as important as the purification of the soul. A report from 'Ā'ishah shows that the Holy Prophet used to wash his teeth up and down, that is, from the gum downwards to the edge of the teeth and vice versa, and this is the method also recommended by modern dentistry.

Ch. 78:   The excellence of one who spends the night in a state of *Wuḍū'*

247 Al-Barā' ibn 'Āzib reported that the Prophet ﷺ said: "When you go to your bed, make ablution like your *Wuḍū'* for prayer, then lie on your right side, and then say:

> 'O Allāh, I submit myself to You entirely, and I entrust all my affairs to You, and place all reliance in You through love and fear (of You). There is no refuge nor rescue but with You. O Allāh! I believe in Your Book which You have revealed and in Your Prophet (*nabī*) whom You have sent.'

Then if you die in that night, you die in (the religion of) human nature (Islām). So make these the last thing that you say."

He (al-Barā') said: Then I repeated it to the Prophet ﷺ and when I reached the words, "O Allāh! I believe in Your Book which You have revealed", and I then said, "And in Your Messenger (*rasūl*)", he said: "No, (say) 'Your Prophet (*nabī*)'." [120]

---

[120] The Holy Prophet was not only particular about the cleanliness of the body when going to bed but he also secures the purity of the spirit by resigning himself completely to the will of God. While awake too, he keeps the body and the soul both clean to perfection. This ḥadīth also shows that the narrators took the utmost care to preserve the actual words of the Holy Prophet in matters relating to the ordinances of religion and to words of prayer. Here even the substitution of the word "Messenger" for "Prophet" is not approved of, even though the meaning remains the same, for the reason that the Holy Prophet had used the word *nabī* and not *rasūl* when teaching this prayer. The narrators did not take the same care to preserve his words when conveying reports that do not impose any commands or prohibitions to be observed by a Muslim.

The summary of the Book on Ablution shows that, as Bukhārī sees it, a necessary preparation for attaining purity of the soul is to attend to keeping one's body and person clean.

PART 2

Book 5: *Al-Ghusl*

Bath

In the name of Allāh, the Beneficent, the Merciful

The word of Allāh, the Most High: "And if you are under obligation (to take a bath),[1] then wash (your body). And if you are sick, or on a journey, or one of you has come from the toilet, or you have had (sexual) contact with women, and you cannot find water, then resort to pure earth and wipe your faces and your hands with it. Allāh does not desire to place a burden on you but He wishes to purify you, and that He may complete His favour on you, so that you may give thanks" (the Qur'ān, 5:6), and His word: "O you who believe, do not go near prayer when you are intoxicated till you know what you say, nor after sexual intercourse — except you are merely passing by — until you have bathed. And if you are sick, or on a journey, or one of you has come from the toilet, or you have had (sexual) contact with women, and you cannot find water, then resort to pure earth and wipe your faces and your hands (with it). Surely Allah is ever Pardoning, Forgiving." (4:43).[2]

Ch. 1: *Wuḍū'* before bath

248 'Ā'ishah, wife of the Prophet ﷺ, reported that the Prophet ﷺ, when taking a bath under obligation,[3] used to begin by washing his hands, then he

---

[1] The word here, for a person under obligation to take a bath, is *junub*. See note 3.

[2] The citation by Bukhārī of a relevant passage from the Qur'ān at the beginning of every book shows that the principles of religion are to be found in the Qur'ān and that the Holy Prophet Muḥammad's practice and utterances are a mere exposition of those principles. In this case, the command to have a bath is in the Qur'ān, and details regarding the bath are explained in Ḥadīth. It may also be noted that under this rule, as accepted by Bukhārī himself, a ḥadīth or any part of it may be rejected as spurious if it militates against any clear ordinance of the Qur'ān.

[3] The word translated here as "obligation" is *janābah*. This term refers to the state of a person when he or she is under obligation to take a full bath after sexual intercourse or nocturnal discharge. Such a person is called a *junub*.

would perform ablution as he would perform ablution for prayer. Then he would put his fingers in the water and rub the roots of his hair with them, then he would pour water on his head three times by handfuls, and then he would pour water all over his body.[4]

249 Maimūnah, wife of the Prophet ﷺ, reported: The Messenger of Allāh ﷺ performed ablution, (like) his *Wuḍū'* for prayer except for (washing) his feet. He washed his private parts, washing off any impurity on them, and then poured water over himself. Then he withdrew his feet from there (where he took the bath) and washed them. This was his bath under obligation.[5]

Ch. 2:   A man taking bath with his wife

250 'Ā'ishah reported: I used to take bath, both I and the Prophet ﷺ, from the same vessel which was a bowl called *al-faraq*.[6]

Ch. 3:   Taking bath with one *ṣā'* (of water) or something like it

251 Abū Salamah said: I and the brother of 'Ā'ishah went to her, and her brother asked her about the bath of the Messenger of Allāh ﷺ. She asked for a vessel with about one *ṣā'* (of water) and took a bath, pouring it over her head; and there was a screen between her and ourselves." [7]

---

[4] This description of a bath, namely that it includes the act of wetting and cleaning even the roots of the hair, shows that it is no mere ceremonial affair but a serious effort to clean the body, the whole of it, physically. In some religions bath is taken only as a religious ritual, without properly and thoroughly cleaning the body.

[5] Ḥadīth 257 describes his *Wuḍū'* preceding the bath. Here it is stated that the Holy Prophet performed an ablution before the bath in all its particulars except for washing his feet.

[6] *Al-Faraq* is a vessel which could contain water of quantity three *ṣā'* which is about nine litres. The ḥadīth only intends to show that the Holy Prophet and his wife 'Ā'ishah could both together finish their bath with this amount of water, but the chapter heading refers to a man taking bath with his wife. There is nothing wrong in that, provided, as other reports show, the private parts are covered. That the Holy Prophet and his wife used to have their bath from same water and at the same spot is shown by h. 261 where it is said: "Our hands used to go into the water alternately."

[7] Abū Salamah also belonged to the circle of permissible male relatives of 'Ā'ishah, being the son of her foster-sister. The words "the brother of 'Ā'ishah" have been taken by some to mean 'Abdur Raḥmān, son of Abū Bakr. Others have taken them to mean her brother Ṭufail from her mother's side, and still others consider that her foster-brother is meant. Bukhārī deduces from this ḥadīth the quantity of water that is to be used in a bath. The words of the ḥadīth also show that the question was about the quantity of water to be used for having a bath, and not about how to have the bath. The next ḥadīth also shows, from the answer given therein, that "asking about the bath" was a question about the quantity of water to be used. Here 'Ā'ishah, in reply to the question, called for a vessel containing about one *ṣā'* of water (about three litres). She could not

Abū 'Abdullāh (Bukhārī) said: Yazīd ibn Hārūn and Bahz and al-Juddī reported from Shu'bah: "(vessel) of measure one *ṣā'*".

252 Abū Ja'far related that he and his father were with Jābir ibn 'Abdullāh, and there also were present some people who asked him about taking a bath. He said: "One *ṣā'* (of water) should be enough for you." A man said: "It is not enough for me." At this Jābir said: "It was enough for one who had more hair than you have and was better than you." [8] Then he (Jābir) led us in prayer wearing one piece of cloth.[9]

253 Ibn 'Abbās reported that the Prophet ﷺ and Maimūnah used to take bath from the same vessel.[10]

Ch. 4: One who pours water on his own head three times

254 Jubair ibn Muṭ'im said that the Messenger of Allāh ﷺ said: "As for myself, I pour (water) on my head three times," and he made a sign with both his hands.[11]

255 Jābir ibn 'Abdullāh reported that the Prophet ﷺ used to pour (water) on his own head three times.

256 Abū Ja'far related that Jābir said to him: Your paternal uncle's son, meaning al-Ḥasan ibn Muḥammad ibn al-Ḥanafiyyah, came to me and said: "How is the bath under obligation (to be taken)?" I said (to him): "The Prophet ﷺ used to take three handfuls (of water) and pour them over his head and then he used to pour (water) over his whole body."

Then al-Ḥasan said to me: "I am a man with much hair." I said: "The Prophet ﷺ had more hair than you." [12]

---

have taken the bath in the presence of two men, however closely they might be related to her. That she was taking the bath in privacy is shown by the words: "and there was a screen between her and ourselves."

[8] The Holy Prophet Muḥammad is meant.

[9] This is a lesson in the economic use of water in a country where it is scarce.

[10] This seems to refer to the vessel which is spoken of in h. 250 and has been termed *al-faraq*. The sense is the same in both, namely, that two persons can have full bath using a total of six to nine litres of water.

[11] This means joining of two palms to form a cup with which to take water from the vessel and pour it on the head. The simple habits of the Holy Prophet had, it seems, no room for a jug or any other pot with which to pour water on his body. In the absence of such a pot the hands, when they are washed, can be used for this purpose. This ḥadīth also shows that the Holy Prophet washed his head thoroughly.

[12] This appears to be the same incident as in h. 252. But whereas there the question was about the quantity of water to be used for the bath, here it is about the manner of taking the bath.

Ch. 5:   Taking bath (by pouring water) all at one time

257 Ibn ʿAbbās reported that Maimūnah said: I placed water for the Prophet ﷺ for his bath. He washed his hands two or three times, then he poured (water) on his left hand and washed his private parts (with his left hand), then he rubbed his (left) hand on the earth, then he rinsed his mouth and drew water into his nose and washed his face and his hands, then he poured (water) on his body, then he moved from his place and washed his feet.

Ch. 6:   One who starts with *ḥilāb*[13] or scent at the time of bath

258 ʿĀʾishah reported: The Prophet ﷺ, when taking a bath under obligation, used to ask for something like *ḥilāb*. He would take (water) with his hand, begin with the right side of his head and then the left (in pouring water over it) and then pour (water) with both his hands in the middle of his head.

Ch. 7:   Rinsing of the mouth and drawing water into the nose in the bath under obligation

259 Ibn ʿAbbās reported that Maimūnah related, saying: I placed water for the Prophet ﷺ for his bath. He poured (water) with his right hand on his left hand and washed them. Then he washed his private parts (with his left hand), then with his (left) hand on the earth he rubbed it with dust and washed it, then he rinsed his mouth and drew water into his nose and washed his face and poured (water) on his head. Then he withdrew from there (where he took the bath) and washed his feet. Then he was given a bath-towel but he did not use it to wipe his body with.[14]

---

[13] *Ḥilāb* is the pot in which a cow is milched. It must be deep enough to be used as a vessel to keep water for bath. The adding of *ṭīb* (scent) after the word *ḥilāb* has given rise to the impression that Bukhārī takes this word to mean some kind of scent or perfume and that he made an error in this regard. Some authorities have suggested that the original word was not *ḥilāb* but *julāb* which is an Arabicized form of the word Persian word *gulāb*, i.e., rose, and it is a well-known fact that rose-water is widely used as perfume. The general sense of the ḥadīth seems to point in this direction, that the Holy Prophet used to apply some sort of scent to his head after his bath, whether the word be *ḥilāb* or *julāb*. Other reports show that he applied scent.

[14] This is a repetition of h. 257 with slight difference of wording, omission of his washing of the hands (up to the elbows), and addition at the end about being given a bath-towel. These last words, however, should not be taken as a prohibition against wiping the body after a bath. There may be many reasons why he did not dry his body with the towel. It may not have been clean enough or he may have wanted his body to remain wet because of severe heat. In the repetition of this ḥadīth in h. 266 it is stated: "I handed him a cloth (i.e., towel) and he indicated with his hand like this (to take it away), and did not take it."

Ch. 8:   Wiping the hand with earth for better cleaning

260 Maimūnah reported that the Prophet ﷺ took a bath under obligation. He washed his private parts with his (left) hand, then rubbed it on the wall and washed it. Then he performed ablution, (like) his *Wuḍū'* for prayer. When he finished his bath, he washed his feet.[15]

Ch. 9:   Should one who is under obligation of bath (a *junub*) dip his hand in a vessel before he washes it when there is no impurity on his hand except that he is under obligation to have a bath?

Ibn 'Umar and al-Barā' ibn 'Āzib dipped their hands in the water meant for ablution and did not wash them. Then they performed ablution. And Ibn 'Umar and Ibn 'Abbās did not see anything wrong in the splattering of water from a bath that was under obligation.

261 'Ā'ishah reported: I used to take bath, both I and the Prophet ﷺ, from the same vessel. Our hands used to go into the water alternately.[16]

262 'Ā'ishah reported: Whenever the Messenger of Allāh ﷺ took a bath under obligation he washed his hands first.[17]

263 'Ā'ishah reported: I used to take bath, both I and the Prophet ﷺ, from the same vessel when under obligation of bath.[18]

264 Anas ibn Mālik said: The Prophet ﷺ and one of his wives used to take bath both from the same vessel. Shu'bah added: the bath under obligation.[19]

---

[15] In h. 257 it is stated: "and (he) washed his private parts, then he rubbed his (left) hand on the earth", in h. 259 it is stated: "with his hand on the earth he rubbed it with dust", and here it is stated that he rubbed his hand "on the wall". The meaning in all these cases is the same. The Holy Prophet was thus in the habit of cleaning his hands with earth after washing the private parts with water. The dust of the earth was available everywhere in past times. Soap is now the substitute for it. In any case, these reports show the high sense of physical cleanliness that the Holy Prophet had.

[16] See the note on h. 250. It has been deduced from this report that the state of the body when under obligation of a bath after sexual intercourse is not one of impurity, because, had it been so, the hand of such a person touching the water must have made the water impure.

[17] Here only the beginning of h. 248 has been repeated. It has been deduced from this that he used to pour water on his hands to wash them before he dipped them in the water to have the bath. But from other reports, this deduction does not seem justified. There is no necessity for a person in this state to wash his hands before dipping them in water.

[18] This is a repetition of h. 250, but the words about the bath being the one under obligation do not occur in h. 250 or in its repetition in h. 261.

[19] This is a repetition of h. 253, that ḥadīth being reported by Ibn 'Abbās.

Ch. 10:   Interval during bath and *Wuḍū'*

It is related of Ibn 'Umar that he washed his feet after the moisture of his *Wuḍū'* had dried.[20]

265 Ibn 'Abbās reported that Maimūnah said: I placed water for the Messenger of Allāh ﷺ for him to have bath with it. He poured (water) on his hands and washed them two or three times each, then he poured (water) with his right hand on his left hand and washed his private parts, then he rubbed his hand on the earth, then he rinsed his mouth and drew water into his nose, then he washed his face and his hands, then he washed his head three times, then he poured (water) on his body, then he withdrew from his place and washed his feet.[21]

Ch. 11:   One who pours (water) with his right hand on his left one in the course of bath

266 Maimūnah, daughter of al-Ḥārith, reported: I placed (water) for the Messenger of Allāh ﷺ for a bath and put a screen for him. He poured (water) on his hands and washed them once or twice — a narrator said he did not know if she mentioned three times or not — then he poured (water) with his right hand on his left hand and washed his private parts (with his left hand), then he rubbed his (left) hand on the earth or the wall, then he rinsed his mouth and drew water into his nose, and washed his face and his hands, and washed his head, then he poured (water) on his body, then he withdrew (from his place) and washed his feet. I handed him a cloth (i.e., towel) and he indicated with his hand like this (to take it away), and did not take it.[22]

Ch. 12:   One who has sexual intercourse, then repeats it. And one who goes round his wives and takes only one bath

---

[20] This shows that there is no harm if a little time elapses between the washing of one organ of the body and another in *Wuḍū'*, so much so that the first organ has dried. Of course, the whole washing should be a continuous and serial process, done in one and the same sitting in as quick succession as possible.

[21] In this repetition of h. 257 it is stated that the Holy Prophet in his preliminary ablution washed all the organs except the feet, and that he washed the feet after he had taken his bath. This also shows that to leave an interval between the washing of one part of the body and another in *Wuḍū'* is permissible.

[22] In this repetition of h. 257 it is stated that "he poured (water) *with his right hand* on his left hand and washed his private parts", while h. 257 does not mention pouring with the right hand. This shows that the Holy Prophet always used his left hand for cleaning the private parts, as the right was used for eating. Despite the fact that the right hand was to be washed later on, he did not use it to clean impurities from the private parts.

267 Muḥammad ibn al-Muntashir reported: I mentioned it (i.e., the view of Ibn ʿUmar) to ʿĀʾishah and she said: "May Allāh have mercy on Abū ʿAbdur Raḥmān.[23] I used to apply perfume to the Messenger of Allāh ﷺ and he used to go round his wives, then in the morning he used to enter into the state of *Iḥrām,* diffusing the scent." [24]

268 Qatādah reported: Anas ibn Mālik related to us, saying: "The Prophet ﷺ used to go round his wives at one time during the night and the day, and they were eleven in number".[25] I (Qatādah) said to Anas: "Had he the strength for it?" He said: "We used to talk about it and say that he was given the strength of thirty men".[26]

Saʿīd reported from Qatādah that Anas had related to them: Nine wives.

Ch. 13: The washing of prostatic fluid (*madhī*) and performing *Wuḍūʾ* on account of that[27]

269 ʿAlī reported: I was a man who used to have frequent urethral discharge, so I told a man to ask the Prophet ﷺ about it, as I was his son-in-

---

[23] Abū ʿAbdur Raḥmān is Ibn ʿUmar. It appears that he did not like the trace of any perfume that had been used before entering into the state of *Iḥrām,* and the words "I mentioned it to ʿĀʾishah" refer to this opinion of Ibn ʿUmar.

[24] The words used for the Holy Prophet's going round his wives (*dāra* in this chapter heading and in h. 268, and *yaṭūfu* in h. 267) have been taken by Anas in h. 268 to mean having sexual intercourse with them. It is not, however, necessary to draw such a conclusion. He may only have met them and talked to them one after another. From the fact that the fragrance of the perfume was still apparent the following morning, it has been concluded that he must have had only one obligatory bath after visiting several wives (as more would have removed the fragrance). This conclusion is also unwarranted because there is no mention of any bath at all in the ḥadīth.

[25] In some reports it is nine instead of eleven and this is the correct number because at no time did he have eleven wives together. See also h. 284.

[26] These are all conjectures of the reporters. It is nowhere stated in the ḥadīth that the Holy Prophet actually had sexual intercourse with all his wives at a stretch. All that is stated is that he went to his wives one by one in one round. As for the Holy Prophet having physical power equivalent to that of thirty men, that is true because he conserved his energy. Had he been profligate, as alleged by evil-minded critics, he would have lost his power and strength. As a mortal he had sexual desire, but he had complete mastery over it. He had lived the purest form of life as a single man up to the age of 25 years, after which he married a woman fifteen years his senior and lived with her with devotion and faithfulness for another 25 years. No one could raise the least objection to his character or morals during this entire period. It must be remembered that the more a man of sound and wholesome nature guards his natural powers, keeping them in his control and remaining moderate and balanced, the stronger his powers become.

[27] *Madhī* is the thin transparent fluid secreted by the male sexual organ and is different from semen. Its emission nullifies *Wuḍūʾ* and it should also be washed from the cloth being worn. The ḥadīth that follows is a repetition of h. 132 and makes the point clear: "Perform ablution and wash your private parts."

law. He asked him, and he (the Holy Prophet) said: "Perform ablution and wash your private parts."

Ch. 14: One who perfumes himself, then takes his bath and the effect of the perfume still remains

270 Muḥammad ibn al-Muntashir reported: I asked ʿĀ'ishah, mentioning to her the statement of Ibn ʿUmar, "I do not like to enter into the state of *Iḥrām* while I am diffusing scent." ʿĀ'ishah said: "I applied perfume to the Messenger of Allāh ﷺ, then he went round his wives, then in the morning he entered into the state of *Iḥrām*." [28]

271 ʿĀ'ishah reported: I seem to see the sparkling of perfume in the parting of the hair of the Prophet ﷺ while he would be in the state of *Iḥrām*." [29]

Ch. 15: Combing the hair (with hand) till one feels that water has reached the skin (of the head), and then pouring water on oneself

272 ʿĀ'ishah reported: The Messenger of Allāh ﷺ, when taking a bath under obligation, used to wash his hands and perform ablution, (like) his *Wuḍū'* for prayer, then he would take his bath, then comb with his hand his hair until he felt that he had made water to reach his skin.[30] Then he would pour water on himself three times, then he would wash the whole of his body.

273 And ʿĀ'ishah (further) said: I used to take bath, both I and the Messenger of Allāh ﷺ, from the same vessel, and we took water from it together.

Ch. 16: One who performs ablution when under obligation of bath, then washes his whole body but does not repeat washing the parts (of the body) to be washed in *Wuḍū'*

274 Maimūnah reported: The Messenger of Allāh ﷺ placed water for *Wuḍū'* when under obligation of bath. He poured (water) with his right hand on his left hand twice or three times. Then he washed his private parts (with his left hand), then he struck his (left) hand on the earth, or the wall, twice or three times, then he rinsed his mouth and drew water into his nose and washed

---

[28] In this repetition of h. 267, the opening is clearer and mentions the statement of Ibn ʿUmar.

[29] Since this ḥadīth and h. 267 relate the same incident, and since the Holy Prophet used to take a bath before entering into the state of *Iḥrām*, which is even now continued as his *Sunnah*, this ḥadīth fits under the heading of this chapter.

[30] This ḥadīth shows that the Holy Prophet was very anxious to clean every part of his body including the head thoroughly.

his face and forearms. Then he poured water on his head, then washed his body. Then he withdrew from there (where he took the bath) and washed his feet.

She said: Then I brought to him a cloth but he did not want it, and he began to remove the water (on his body) with his hand.[31]

Ch. 17: When a person remembers in the mosque that he is under obligation of bath (*junub*), he should leave and not perform *Tayammum*

275 Abū Hurairah reported: The prayer had been announced by *Iqāmah* for and the rows were made correct in standing. The Messenger of Allāh ﷺ came out to us, and when he stood in the place of prayer, he remembered that he was under obligation of bath. So he said to us, "Remain where you are", then he went back and took a bath and then came out to us while drops of water were falling from his head. He said *Allāhu Akbar,* and we said our prayer with him.[32]

Ch. 18: Shaking one's hands (to dry) after taking a bath under obligation

276 Ibn 'Abbās reported that Maimūnah said: I placed (water) for the Prophet ﷺ for a bath and screened him with a garment. He poured (water) on his hands and washed them both. Then he poured (water) with his right hand on his left hand and washed his private parts (with his left hand). He struck his (left) hand on the earth and rubbed it (with dust) and washed it. He rinsed his mouth and drew water into his nose and washed his face and forearms. Then he poured (water) on his head and his body. Then he withdrew from there (where he took the bath) and washed his feet. I gave him a cloth but he did not take it, and he came out shaking his hands (to remove the water).[33]

---

[31] This is as in h. 249, h. 257, h. 259 and h. 266 with difference in wording.

[32] In this ḥadīth there is no mention of *Tayammum,* i.e., rubbing earth on hands and face in the absence of water for ablution. All that is intended is that if one gets a wet dream while sleeping in the mosque, or by mistake enters the mosque while under an obligation for a bath, a *Tayam-mum* is not required; one should just leave the mosque and take a bath. Some think that since, in such a case, the man had entered the mosque while under obligation of a bath, which is prohibited, he must out of respect for the prohibition immediately perform *Tayammum* before leaving the mosque to have a bath. This ḥadīth seems intended to remove this misconception. Another inter-pretation is that while placed in such circumstances a person should not take to the short process of *Tayammum* to be qualified for prayer but leave the mosque and take a full bath. See also h. 639 and h. 640.

[33] H. 257 is repeated here, but at the end occurs the mention of the towel or cloth as in h. 259 and h. 266. As stated in the note under h. 259, this refusal to use a towel does not mean that it is

Ch. 19: Starting with the right side of the head in taking bath

277 'Ā'ishah reported: Whenever any of us (wives of the Holy Prophet) was under obligation of a bath, she would take water with both her hands three times and pour it over her head, then she would take water with her hand and pour it on her right side, and with her other hand and pour it on her left side.[34]

Ch. 20: To take bath naked and alone in seclusion, and to screen oneself is better

Bahz ibn Ḥakīm reported from his father and the latter reported from his grandfather (i.e., of Bahz) who reported from the Prophet ﷺ: "Allāh is more entitled than people are, that a man should feel shy of Him." [35]

278 Abū Hurairah reported from the Prophet ﷺ that he said: "The Israelites used to take bath naked, looking at each other, whereas Moses used to take bath alone. At this they said: 'By Allāh, what prevents Moses from taking bath with us is that he has got enlarged testicles.' So once when he (Moses) went out to have a bath and he placed his clothes on a stone, the stone fled with his clothes, and Moses ran after it saying, 'My clothes, O stone, my clothes, O stone,' until the Israelites looked at Moses and said: 'By Allāh, there is no defect in Moses.' And he took his clothes and began to beat the stone."

Abū Hurairah added: By Allāh, his beating the stone caused six or seven scars on it.[36]

---

prohibited to use it to wipe the water on the body after the bath. There must be some other reason for his refusal on this occasion.

[34] The left and right sides of the head are implied here; see h. 258.

[35] The complete report from Bahz ibn Ḥakīm, which has been recorded by Tirmidhī and others, runs as follows in Tirmidhī:

I asked: "O Prophet of Allāh, regarding our private parts, when should we cover them and when should we expose them?" He replied: "Guard your private parts except from your wife or those whom your right hands possess." I said: "O Messenger of Allāh, what about when people are together?" He replied: "If you are able to not let anyone see them, then do not let them see them." I said: "O Prophet of Allāh, what about when one of us is by himself?" He replied: "Allāh is more entitled than people are, that a man should feel shy of Him" (Tirmidhī, book: 'Manners', h. 3024).

This shows that one should cover one's private parts even when alone. This is the most refined form of modesty for which Islām stands. However, this does not mean that private parts cannot be exposed under necessity, such as for answering calls of nature or having a bath, or for showing to others for medical purposes.

[36] This is obviously a narration of a story of the past ages intended to support the chapter heading relating to taking bath naked. As is admitted by all authorities, there has been so much

279 Abū Hurairah reported from the Prophet 鷺 that he said: "Once when Prophet Job was taking bath naked, some golden locusts fell on him. He started to gather them in his clothes. So his Lord called out to him: 'O Job, have I not made you above the need of what you see?' He said: 'Indeed, by Your honour, but I am not above the need of Your blessings'." [37]

Ch. 21: Screening oneself while taking bath near people

280 Umm Hānī, daughter of Abū Ṭālib, said: I went to the Messenger of Allāh 鷺 in the year of the conquest of Makkah and I found him taking a bath and Fāṭimah screening him. He said: "Who is it?" And I said: "It is Umm Hānī." [38]

281 Maimūnah reported: I screened the Prophet 鷺 while he took a bath under obligation. He washed his hands, then he poured (water) with his right hand on his left hand and washed his private parts and what (impurity) was on them (with his left hand). Then he rubbed his (left) hand on the wall or the earth, then he performed ablution, (like) his *Wuḍū'* for prayer except for (washing) his feet, then he poured water on his body. Then he withdrew from there (where he took the bath) and washed his feet. [39]

---

interference with the narration of such stories that these accounts cannot be taken as accurate in all details, nor do they contain any religious teachings to be acted upon by Muslims. All this story shows is that the Israelites were in the habit of taking bath together naked and that Prophet Moses, in his modesty, used to take his bath alone. The grotesque part of the story, of the stone running away with his clothes and Moses running after it and beating it, must be regarded as spurious. All that the Holy Prophet might have said was that Moses had placed his clothes on a stone and that on one occasion some Israelite ran away with these clothes as a jest. It is also possible that that person's name might be *Ḥajar* (Stone). The statement about scars on the stone is an addition by Abū Hurairah, who could not have had actual knowledge of it.

[37] This is a story of the same kind as the previous one and as such cannot be relied upon for its literal accuracy. Golden locusts may be an idiom to indicate the favours of God. The remonstrance of God seems to be with regard to Job's using his clothes for gathering something instead of keeping them on his body. The topic of this chapter would suggest that Job was alone and he had one piece of cloth to cover his body and that he found no harm in using that cloth for the time being for other purposes than covering his private parts.

[38] In the last chapter Bukhārī has proved that it is permissible to take bath naked and that to cover the private parts is more commendable. In this chapter he wants to show that when taking bath in the presence of people there should be a screen behind which it should be taken. That is why Fāṭimah is reported to have stood as a screen between him and the people while he was taking a bath. See also h. 357.

[39] Although this is a repetition of h. 257 and its various versions, its opening words "I screened the Prophet" are not present there. This shows the extreme modesty of the Holy Prophet, who did not show his bare body even to his wife while having a bath. According to one report, he was more bashful than a virgin girl.

Abū 'Awānah and Ibn Fuḍail also followed this version in mentioning the screening.

Ch. 22:   When a woman has nocturnal sexual discharge

282 Umm Salamah, mother of the believers, reported: Umm Sulaim, wife of Abū Ṭalḥah, came to the Messenger of Allāh ﷺ and said: "O Messenger of Allāh, Allāh does not feel shy of truth; is bath obligatory upon a woman when she has nocturnal sexual discharge?" The Messenger of Allāh ﷺ said: "Yes, when she sees signs of discharge." [40]

Ch. 23:   The sweat of one under obligation of bath (*junub*), and that a Muslim does not become impure (*najs*)

283 Abū Hurairah reported that the Prophet ﷺ met him in a street of Madīnah while he was under obligation of bath. (Abū Hurairah added:) Considering myself to be impure (*najs*), I kept away from him, and went and took a bath and came again. So he said: "Where were you, Abū Hurairah?" I said: "I was under obligation of bath (*junub*), so I did not like to sit by you while I was not in a state of purity." He said: "Glory be to Allāh, surely a believer does not become impure." [41]

Ch. 24:   A person under obligation of bath going out and walking about in the market and other places

'Aṭā' said: A man under obligation of bath may have cupping and may pare his nails and shave his head even if he has not performed ablution.

---

[40] This is a repetition of the first part of h. 130.

[41] The meaning of "a believer does not become impure" is that a believer does not become unclean by sexual intercourse, or by breaking wind, urinating or passing excrement, i.e., actions which require him to perform *Wuḍū'* or take a bath before he can say prayers. It is a quite different matter if some external dirt or filth sticks to the body or the clothes of a person and makes him unclean thereby. It has been concluded from this that the sweat of a believer under obligation of bath, i.e., one who is *junub*, is not unclean. It was a Jewish belief that a woman becomes unclean during her menstruation and this led to her being completely isolated by society during her period of menstruation. Islām rejected this concept. The Holy Prophet used to lie on the same bed with his wife when she was menstruating and did not hesitate to touch her body with his own (see, for example, h. 298 and h. 1929). Even an unbeliever does not become physically unclean by being an unbeliever. As for the polytheists who have been declared unclean by the Holy Qur'ān (9:29), this is not in the physical sense. It is the unclean beliefs and acts that are condemned and for which they were debarred from entering the Sacred Mosque, because of the practices they would indulge in while there.

284 Qatādah reported that Anas ibn Mālik related to them that the Prophet ﷺ used to go round his wives in one night, and he had nine (wives) at the time.[42]

285 Abū Hurairah reported: The Messenger of Allāh ﷺ met me while I was under obligation of bath. He took my hand and I walked with him until he sat down. I slipped away, came to my house and took a bath. Then I came back and he was (still) sitting there. He said: "Where were you, Abū Hurairah?" I told him. He said: "Glory be to Allāh, Abū Hurairah, surely a believer does not become impure." [43]

Ch. 25:   A person under obligation of bath remaining in the house when he has performed ablution before he has taken bath

286 Abū Salamah reported: I asked ʿĀʾishah, "Did the Prophet ﷺ sleep while he was under obligation of bath?" She said: "Yes, after he had performed ablution." [44]

Ch. 26:   The sleeping of one under obligation of bath

287 Ibn ʿUmar reported that ʿUmar ibn al-Khaṭṭāb asked the Messenger of Allāh ﷺ: "Should any of us sleep while he is under obligation of bath?" He replied: "Yes, when any of you has performed ablution he may sleep while he is under obligation of bath."

---

[42] This is a repetition of h. 268 wherein it was stated that the Holy Prophet used to go round to all his wives on certain occasions. The connection of the ḥadīth with the chapter heading may be that on some such occasion the Holy Prophet might have had sexual relations with one of his wives and then gone on to see other wives and talked to them without taking a bath. There was a belief in those days, which persists even now, that a man in a state of being under obligation of a bath is not allowed to eat or drink, talk to anyone, or conduct any business with others unless he has taken his bath. Bukhārī has concluded here that a man in such a state can do anything.

[43] This is a repetition of h. 283 wherein it is related that Abū Hurairah, being under an obligation of bath, kept away from the Holy Prophet, considering himself to be impure. Here a few more details are given.

[44] There is a ḥadīth in Abū Dāwūd reported by ʿAlī that angels do not enter a house in which there is a person under the obligation of bath (book: ʿPurificationʾ, h. 227). Bukhārī seems to indicate the weakness of this report in Abū Dāwūd by the heading he has given to this chapter, and the ḥadīth here shows that the Holy Prophet himself used to sleep while under the obligation of bath with just a *Wuḍū*'. Had the report in Abū Dāwūd been correct, he could not have slept without taking a bath.

Ch. 27:   One under obligation of bath should perform ablution, then sleep

288 'Ā'ishah reported: Whenever the Prophet ﷺ wanted to sleep while he would be under obligation of bath, he would wash his private parts and perform ablution as that for prayer.[45]

289 'Abdullāh (Ibn 'Umar) reported that 'Umar ibn al-Khaṭṭāb enquired of the Prophet ﷺ: "Should any of us sleep while he is under obligation of bath?" He replied: "Yes, when he has performed ablution."

290 'Abdullāh ibn 'Umar reported: 'Umar ibn al-Khaṭṭāb mentioned to the Messenger of Allāh ﷺ that one night he was under obligation of bath, at which the Messenger of Allāh ﷺ said to him: "Perform ablution and wash your private parts, then sleep." [46]

Ch. 28:   When the two sex organs (male and female) meet

291 Abū Hurairah reported from the Prophet ﷺ that he said: "When a man has sexual intercourse with a woman and struggles with her, the bath becomes obligatory for him."

Abū 'Abdullāh (Bukhārī) said: This is better and necessary and we have narrated the latter ḥadīth because of divergence of opinion, and bath is a greater precaution.[47]

---

[45] This is a repetition of the substance of h. 286 with a few more details.

[46] Both h. 289 and h. 290 are repetitions of h. 287. In the first case, the words are almost the same but in the second case the wording is different.

[47] There is a divergence of opinion, as we have already noted, as to the obligation of bath if there is no discharge during sexual intercourse (see h. 179 and h. 180 and the notes on them). Ḥadīth reports both for and against this proposition are found. Ibn Mājah, Bukhārī and Imām Aḥmad have recorded reports from the Holy Prophet that bath becomes obligatory only when there is discharge of semen. This rule is stated in the words *Al-mā' min al-mā'*, "water (i.e., bath) is only needed in case of water (i.e., seminal discharge)". It is also in Muslim and Bukhārī that the Holy Prophet told this to a man of the *Anṣār*. Reports from 'Uthmān and Ubayy ibn Ka'b are to the same effect. However, h. 291 narrated by Abū Hurairah goes against all these reports. As on a previous occasion, here Bukhārī gives his own view, that preference should be given to a bath as a precautionary step. Ibn 'Abbās has confined the application of the principle *Al-mā' min al-mā'* to wet dreams, as reported in Tirmidhī. It is also reported that the exemption from bath in case of non-discharge was given in the early days of Islām and that later on the Holy Prophet issued the injunction of a bath in such cases as well. However, the practice of the Companions of the Holy Prophet was both ways. If there was a later change, it is improbable that Companions of the position of 'Uthmān and 'Alī, whose opinions are reported in h. 179 and h. 292, would have been unaware of it. Also, there seems no reason why at first only one case, that of seminal discharge, placed a person in the state in which a bath became obligatory, but later on another case, that of non-discharge, should be added to it.

Ch. 29:   The washing of what is discharged from the private parts of the woman (and touches man)

292 Zaid ibn Khālid al-Juhanī informed that he asked ʿUthmān ibn ʿAffān: "What do you think about a man who had sexual intercourse with his wife but did not discharge any semen?" ʿUthmān said: "He should perform the ablution as he does for prayer and wash his male organ." ʿUthmān added: "I have heard this from the Messenger of Allāh ﷺ." Then I (Zaid) asked ʿAlī ibn Abū Ṭālib and Zubair ibn al-ʿAwwām and Ṭalḥah ibn ʿUbaidullāh and Ubayy ibn Kaʿb about it, and they commanded the same." [48]

293 Ubayy ibn Kaʿb informed that he asked: "O Messenger of Allāh, when a man has sexual intercourse with a woman and he does not discharge (what is he to do)?" He replied: "He should wash what touches the woman from him and then perform ablution and say his prayer."

Abū ʿAbdullāh (Bukhārī) said: Bath is a greater precaution, and this latter (ḥadīth) we have narrated because of divergence of opinion; and water is better for cleaning.

---

[48] This is a repetition of h. 179 in almost the same words.

Book 6: *Al-Ḥaiḍ*
Menstruation

In the name of Allāh, the Beneficent, the Merciful

The word of Allāh, the Most High: "And they ask you about menstruation.[1] Say: It is harmful;[2] so keep aloof from women during the menstrual discharge and do not approach them (for sexual intercourse) until they are clean. But when they have cleansed themselves, go to them as Allāh has commanded you. Surely Allāh loves those who turn much (to Him), and He loves those who purify themselves" (the Qur'ān, 2:222).

Ch. 1: How was the beginning of menstruation?

The saying of the Prophet ﷺ: "This is a thing which Allāh has ordained for the daughters of Adam." And some people say: Menstruation was first sent to the Israelites. Abū ʿAbdullāh (Bukhārī) says: The ḥadīth of the Prophet ﷺ covers (all).[3]

294 ʿĀʾishah said: We set out for nothing but *Hajj* and when we were at Sarif I had menstruation.[4] The Messenger of Allāh ﷺ came to me while I was weeping. He said: "What has happened to you? Have you started menstruating?" I said: "Yes." He said: "Indeed this is a matter which Allāh has

---

[1] The word *ḥaiḍ* is used for the discharge of blood which a woman experiences for a period of days every month from the age of puberty till the age of menopause.

[2] In the Qur'ān here, it has been called "harmful", the word used being *adh-an*, which signifies a slight harm. However, it is not the discharge that is called harmful but having sexual intercourse during menstruation. That is why the Holy Book has required the cessation of sexual intercourse during this time.

[3] The word *aktharu* here, with which the chapter head note ends, means *ashmalu*, that is to say "comprises all". In other words, it is not the Israelites with whom menstruation began, but women of all humanity have the same experience which they have always had. The words "Menstruation was first sent to the Israelites" have either been misreported or contain some omission. They may, however, mean that the injunction relating to restraints in sexual relations during menstruation was first given to the Israelites.

[4] *Sarif* is a place at a distance of some ten miles from Makkah.

ordained for the daughters of Adam,[5] so perform what the pilgrims perform except do not make circuits of the Ka'bah (*Ṭawāf*)." [6] She further reported: And the Messenger of Allāh ﷺ sacrificed cows on behalf of his wives.

Ch. 2: A menstruating woman washing the head of her husband and combing it

295 'Ā'ishah reported: I used to comb the head of the Messenger of Allāh ﷺ while I would be menstruating.

296 'Urwah reported that he was asked (by someone): "Should a menstruating woman serve me or should a woman approach me while she is under obligation of bath?" 'Urwah replied: "All this is easy for me and every one of these can serve me and there is no harm in this for anyone (to do the same). 'Ā'ishah informed me that she used to comb the hair of the Messenger of Allāh ﷺ while she would be menstruating, and the Messenger of Allāh ﷺ used to be in devotional retirement in the mosque and he used to take his head close to her while she would be in her own chamber, so she used to comb it while she would be menstruating.[7]

Ch. 3: A man reciting the Qur'ān in the lap of his wife while she is menstruating

Abū Wā'il used to send his maid-servant, while she would be menstruating, to Abū Razīn and she used to bring the Qur'ān to him holding it by its tape.[8]

297 'Ā'ishah related: The Prophet ﷺ used to recline on my lap while I would be menstruating and he used to recite the Qur'ān (in that state).[9]

---

[5] God's ordaining menstruation for the daughters of Adam means that it is the nature of women to have this experience and that no healthy woman is an exception.

[6] See also h. 1560, 1561, 1650, 1651, 1733, 1757–1759, and 1771–1772. The Holy Prophet thus permitted women in menstruation to perform all the rites of the pilgrimage (*Hajj*) except for making the circuits of the Ka'bah (*Ṭawāf*). But women in menstruation are not to perform prayers (*ṣalāt*) or to fast. Of course, there are reports that the Holy Prophet asked women in menstruation to attend the sermon part of the Eid congregation.

[7] See h. 2028 in the book of *I'tikāf.*

[8] Abū Wā'il and Abū Razīn belonged to the next generation after that of the Companions of the Holy Prophet, members of which are known as the *Tabi'ūn*. As the ḥadīth under this shows, a woman in menstruation does not become unclean in the sense that one should not recite the Qur'ān while touching her body. Similarly, there is nothing wrong in her handling the Holy Book or touching it with her hand. This is also view of Imām Abū Ḥanīfah.

[9] This incident shows the deep attachment of the Holy Prophet to the Book of God. Even

Ch. 4:   One who calls menstruation as lochia (*nifās*)[10]

298 Umm Salamah related: Once I was lying with the Prophet ﷺ under a sheet when I started menstruating, so I moved away and took my cloth of menstruation (to put it on). He said: "Have you got menstruation?" I said: "Yes." He called me, so I lay with him under the sheet (again).[11]

Ch. 5:   Touching of (the body of) a woman in menstruation (by a man with his own body)[12]

299–301 'Ā'ishah reported: I used to take bath, both I and the Prophet ﷺ, from the same vessel when the two of us were under obligation of bath. [300] And he used to tell me to put on a lower garment and (then) he would touch my body with his own while I would be having menstruation. [301] And he (also) used to extend his head towards me while observing *I'tikāf* and I would wash it while I would be having menstruation.

302 'Ā'ishah reported: When any of us would be having menstruation and the Messenger of Allāh ﷺ wanted to touch her body with his own, he would tell her to put on a lower garment during the paroxysm (*faur*) of her menstruation.[13] Then he would touch her body with his own. She further said: And who among you has got so much control over his needs as had the Prophet ﷺ over his own needs?"[14]

---

when he was sitting with his wife, at times of love and affection, he was overcome by devotion to the Word of God.

[10] Properly speaking, the word *nifās* refers to lochia or the bleeding after childbirth. In h. 298 the Holy Prophet has used this word when asking: "'Have you got menstruation (*a-nufisti*)?'" It is indicated here that the words *nifās* and *ḥaiḍ* (menstruation) may be applied interchangeably.

[11] See also h. 322 and h. 1929.

[12] *Mubāsharah*, according to *Lisān al-'Arab*, originally means 'a man lying with his wife under one sheet'. It is added in it: "*Mubāsharah* with a woman means touching." So this ḥadīth will mean that there is no harm in a man lying in the same bed with his wife in the days of her menstruation or in his touching her body with his own. This has been explained because different nations have gone to opposite extremes in this matter. Among some nations, there is no prohibition on sexual intercourse during menstruation while among others the menstruating woman has been declared so unclean that she is made to eat, drink and sleep separately, and even food touched by her is regarded as impure. Islām takes the middle course and forbids only the act of sexual intercourse with a menstruating woman during these days while regarding all her other activities and social contacts to be just as allowable as they are outside these days. The word *mubasharah* is also used to imply sexual intercourse in a euphemistic sense, but that cannot be meant here.

[13] *Faur* means 'the raging stage' or paroxysm. This would be at the beginning when blood flows copiously. The extra precaution was to prevent the man's clothes being stained by the discharge.

[14] 'Ā'ishah was the youngest and most intelligent of all the wives of the Holy Prophet. She

303 Maimūnah said: Whenever the Messenger of Allāh ﷺ wanted to touch the body of one of his wives with his own and she was having menstruation, he would tell her to put on a lower garment.[15]

Ch. 6:   A menstruating woman's discontinuing fasting

304 Abū Saʿīd al-Khudrī reported: The Messenger of Allāh ﷺ went out on the day of *('Īd al-) Aḍḥā* or *('Īd al-) Fiṭr* towards the place of prayer. He passed by the women and said: "You women! Give in charity because I have been shown you as being most of the people of Hell." At this they said: "And why, O Messenger of Allāh?" He said: "You curse too much and are ungrateful to your husbands and I have not seen anyone more defective in understanding and in religion who take away the wisdom of a resolute man more than you." They said: "And what is the defect in our religion and our understanding, O Messenger of Allāh?" He said: "Is not evidence of a woman equivalent to half the evidence of a man?" They said: "Yes." He said: "Then this is among the defects in her understanding. Is it not the case that when she is having menstruation, she neither prays nor fasts?" They said: "Yes." He said: "Then this is among the defects in her religion."[16]

---

uttered these words at a time when the Holy Prophet had a number of wives. As to before that time also, there is clear evidence of the mastery he had over his sexual desires. Note that these words were uttered, not to make a special point, but quite incidentally by one who was privy to the secrets of the house, and thus refer to a well-known fact. This shows the deep impression which the Holy Prophet's self-restraint made on the minds of his wives including ʿĀ'ishah, who was quite young even when she became a widow. It was one of his missions to redeem womanhood by a special demonstration of the fact of his God-realisation, and it was for that purpose that he married several women polygamously. To those evil-minded critics who attribute his marriages to unrestrained sexual desire, this testimony of ʿĀ'ishah is comprehensive reply.

[15] Just as the statement of ʿĀ'ishah in h. 302, here another wife of the Holy Prophet has made the same statement about tying a waist-wrapper during menstruation.

[16] This is repeated in h. 1462; see also h. 29. According to the clear teachings of the Qur'ān, women can attain the same moral qualities and spiritual ranks as men; see 33:35, 3:195, 4:124, 16:97 and 40:40. There is not the least indication in the Qur'ān that women are, due to their nature, in any way prevented from reaching the highest spiritual status. It would thus appear that the Holy Prophet's censure here is directed at certain women whom he knew were too inclined towards material wealth and ungrateful to their husbands for the necessities of life that they had provided them with. Hence he exhorted them to give in charity, which would save them from the hell of the next life. He is informing them of what deeds they can perform to avoid entry into hell, not telling them that they are doomed to hell by Divine decree regardless. As to the "defect in understanding and in religion", if there be such defects, women cannot be held responsible for them, or punished on account of them, because they would be due to God's ordinance and not to any misdeeds committed by women. According to the teachings of Islām, any human beings can only be punished, or sent to hell, for actions committed by them, and not because of how God has created them.   *(Footnote continued)*

Ch. 7: A menstruating woman should complete all the rites of the *Ḥajj* except making circuits of the Ka‘bah

Ibrāhīm said: There is no harm that she should read verses of the Qur'ān, and Ibn 'Abbās did not see any harm in a person under obligation of a bath reciting the Qur'ān. The Prophet ﷺ used to remember Allāh during all his time. Umm 'Aṭiyyah said: We were instructed that we should take out the menstruating women and they should call out *Allāhu Akbar* along with the men calling out the same; and that they should call upon Allāh.[17] Ibn 'Abbās said: Abū Sufyān informed me that Heraclius sent for the letter of the Prophet ﷺ and read it, and in it was: "In the name of Allāh, the Beneficent, the Merciful" and: "O People of the Book, come to an equitable word between us and you, that we shall not serve none but Allāh and that we shall not set up any partner with Him" till the end of the verse (the Qur'ān, 3:64).[18] 'Aṭā' reported from Jābir that 'Ā'ishah started menstruating

---

In *the very repetition of this ḥadīth* in h. 1462, an incident is added at the end relating that a woman came to ask the Holy Prophet if what she intended to give in charity could be given by her to her husband and his children (from his former wife), and the Holy Prophet replied in the affirmative; see also h. 1466 for this. This shows that, despite mentioning the "defect in understanding and in religion" of women, it is accepted in the very same ḥadīth that a woman was entitled to possess property and dispose of any part of it in charity at her discretion; in fact she could even give it to her husband to support him financially, which would in a sense give her the upper hand over him.

It may be added that in the Holy Prophet's time, and with his full knowledge, Muslim women conducted business and acquired education. In the various collections of Ḥadīth, in their chapters on the high qualities of individual Companions of the Holy Prophet, women are also included. Regarding 'Ā'ishah it is related by a Companion of the renown of Abū Mūsā: "Whenever there was any ḥadīth that was difficult for us, the (male) Companions of the Messenger of Allāh, (to understand) and we asked 'Ā'ishah, we always found that she had knowledge about it" (Tirmidhī, ch. 'Virtues', h. 4257). Note also that the compilers of Ḥadīth themselves, when determining which reports met their tests of authenticity for inclusion in their collections, made no distinction between a male and a female reporter of a ḥadīth, and did not regard female reporters as being inferior to men in terms of the mental capability of remembering and transmitting a ḥadīth or having the faculty of judgment in interpreting it.

[17] This means that, except those particular rites that are clearly mentioned in Ḥadīth, a menstruating woman, or a man or woman under obligation of a bath, can attend all other affairs of religion. Thus, a person can recite the Qur'ān even without being in the state of purity required for saying the prescribed prayers, and from the opinion of Ibn 'Abbās it has been concluded here that this also applies to a woman in menstruation. Such women are particularly to be present in the Eid congregation and call out *Allāhu Akbar*.

[18] As for reading from the Qur'ān, the Holy Prophet did not consider even the unbelievers, who are not in the state of purity for the observance of any rite of Islām, to be unworthy of reading

and she performed all the rites of *Ḥajj* except making circuits of the Ka‘bah, and she did not observe the prayer. Al-Ḥakam said: I used to slaughter (animals) while I would be under obligation of a bath, while Allāh the Mighty and Glorious has said: "And do not eat of that on which Allāh's name has not been mentioned" (6 : 121).[19]

305 ‘Ā’ishah reported: We set out with the Prophet ﷺ for nothing but *Ḥajj* and when we reached Sarif I had menstruation. The Messenger of Allāh ﷺ came to me while I was weeping. He said: "Why are you weeping?" I said: "I wish I was not performing *Ḥajj* this year." He said: "Perhaps you have started menstruating." I said: "Yes." He said: "Indeed this is something which Allāh has ordained for the daughters of Adam,[20] so do what the pilgrims do except do not make circuits of the Ka‘bah (*Ṭawāf*) until you are clean." [21]

Ch. 8: Metrorrhagia[22]

306 ‘Ā’ishah reported: Fāṭimah, daughter of Abū Ḥubaish, said to the Messenger of Allāh ﷺ: "O Messenger of Allāh! I can never be clean, should I then give up prayer?" The Messenger of Allāh ﷺ said: "It is nothing but (bleeding from) a vein, and it is not menstruation. So when the menstruation period arrives refrain from prayer, and when its determined time has gone, wash yourself clean of the blood and say your prayers." [23]

---

it. In his letters to the various rulers of unbelieving people of the time, he quoted verses of the Qur’ān which were obviously intended to be read by the recipients of the letters. Hence it cannot be impermissible for a Muslim woman in menstruation or a Muslim under obligation of bath to read the Qur’ān.

[19] As it is allowed for a man under obligation of bath to slaughter an animal for meat, for which act one has to mention the name of God, it is concluded that the reciting of the Qur’ān in this state is permissible.

[20] See note 5 under h. 294.

[21] This ḥadīth is a repetition of h. 294 with slight variation of wording and omission of the mention of the Holy Prophet sacrificing cows on behalf of his wives.

[22] *Istiḥāḍah* i.e., metrorrhagia, is the bleeding which some women experience outside the period of their menstruation. If there is no interval between the normal period of menstruation and metrorrhagia, a woman should not observe prayer and fasting during the days which she knows to be of normal menstruation, but at the end of this period she should take her bath and resume praying and fasting despite the bleeding. According to a version of this report, she is required to perform *Wuḍū’* before every prayer while the bleeding continues. The Ḥanafī school accepts this view, but according to the followers of Imām Mālik *Wuḍū’* before every prayer is not required, but only recommended.

[23] This is a repetition of h. 228. While in h. 228 the words were *wa idhā adbarat*, "when it passes", here it is: *fa idhā dhahaba qadru-hā*, "when its determined time has gone". The meaning is the same.

Ch. 9:   Washing of the blood of menstruation

307 Asmā', daughter of Abū Bakr, reported: A woman asked the Messenger of Allāh ﷺ: "O Messenger of Allāh! What do you say about one of us if the blood of menstruation soils her garment, what she should do?" The Messenger of Allāh ﷺ said: "When the blood of menstruation soils the garment of anyone of you, she should rub it off, then wash it with water. Then she can pray in it." [24]

308 'Ā'ishah reported: When anyone of us was having menstruation, she would rub off the blood from her garment when she was clean, wash it (i.e., the spot), and let water flow over the rest of it (i.e., the garment). Then she would pray wearing it.[25]

Ch. 10:   Retirement to mosque *(I'tikāf)* of a woman suffering from metrorrhagia (bleeding outside of periods)

309 'Ā'ishah reported that the Prophet ﷺ observed *I'tikāf* and one of his wives was with him while she was suffering from metrorrhagia, discharging blood.[26] So sometimes she would keep a bowl underneath her on account of blood. 'Ikrimah (who reported from 'Ā'ishah) said that 'Ā'ishah experienced discharge of water that was the colour of safflower (i.e., yellow) and she said: "This thing is what such and such woman had experienced."

310 'Ā'ishah reported: One of the wives of the Messenger of Allāh ﷺ observed *I'tikāf* with him. She experienced bleeding and yellow discharge. A bowl was (placed by her) beneath her (for this reason), and she said prayers.

311 'Ā'ishah reported: One of the Mothers of the Faithful (i.e., wives of the Holy Prophet) observed *I'tikāf* while suffering from metrorrhagia (bleeding outside of periods).[27]

---

[24] This is a repetition of h. 227 with slight difference in wording.

[25] The garment referred to here is the one worn as a dress, not the cloth or pad which is placed underneath to absorb the blood of the menstrual flow. Sometimes the clothes being worn may be stained by the menstrual flow inspite of the pad for absorbing the blood.

[26] In the month of Ramaḍān the Holy Prophet generally used to retire to the Mosque for exclusive devotion during the last ten days. This is called *I'tikāf* in the terminology of Islām. It is a *Sunnah* for striving for purification of the soul, but it is much neglected today by Muslims. This ḥadīth shows the anxiety even of women of those days for spiritual upliftment, in as much as a wife of the Holy Prophet observed this retirement with him while she was bleeding outside her periods. It also shows that it is quite in order for a woman suffering from metrorrhagia to be present in a mosque for such spiritual exercise. Of course, the mosque must be kept clean of the discharge. See also h. 2037.

[27] Both h. 310 and h. 311 are repetitions of h. 309. See also h. 2037.

Ch. 11:   Should a woman say her prayer in the same clothes in which she has had menstruation?

312 Mujāhid reported that ʿĀʾishah said: None of us had more than one garment and we used to have menstruation while wearing it. Whenever anything of blood soiled it, she would moisten it with her spittle and scratch it off with her nail.[28]

Ch. 12:   A woman using perfume at the time of taking bath after menstruation

313 Umm ʿAṭiyya reported: We were forbidden to mourn over a deceased person for more than three days, except over the husband for four months and ten days;[29] and that we should not use apply *kuḥl* (eye cosmetic) or use perfume or wear dyed clothes except a cloth of which the yarn itself is coloured. It was permitted for us, when any of us at the time of cleaning took a bath after her menstruation, to use a little of *Kust Azfār*.[30] And we were prohibited from accompanying a funeral procession.[31]

Ch. 13:   A woman's rubbing her own body when cleansing after menstruation, and how she is to have her bath, and that she should take a piece of perfumed cotton and touch with it marks of blood[32]

314 ʿĀʾishah reported that a woman asked the Prophet ﷺ about her bath at the end of menstruation, so he instructed her how she should take her bath,

---

[28] This shows the extent of the austerity to which the Holy Prophet and his wives subjected themselves in the cause of Truth. His wives had no separate clothes for the period of menstruation. Inspite of this, their standard of cleanliness was very high. Affluence is not a requirement of cleanliness. One can be clean even in poverty.

[29] See also h. 1281 and h. 1282 where these periods of mourning are mentioned.

[30] *Kust* is aloe's wood, a fragrant plant, and *azfār* is the name of a city on the coast of Yaman. *Kust Azfār* is a black colour perfume. According to Imām Nawawī the permission for the use of this perfume is for cleanliness and not as scent, but this ḥadīth and h. 315 are against his view. There is a ḥadīth according to which applying perfume is forbidden but this prohibition is against women going out for the sake of display and using perfume as attraction for men.

[31] In h. 1278, also from Umm ʿAṭiyya, it is stated: "We (women) were prohibited from accompanying a funeral procession, but it was not an absolute prohibition." The prohibition was only because women tended to wail and cry excessively over the dead body. As such there is no harm in their accompanying the funeral.

[32] This chapter undertakes to prove three things: rubbing of body, the manner of bath and the use of perfume; but whereas the last item is clearly stated in the following ḥadīth, the other two items are missing. In version of this ḥadīth in Ṣaḥīḥ Muslim (book: Menstruation, ch. 13) the rubbing of the body and the manner of bath have been clearly stated. Bukhārī has alluded to this version in his chapter heading but not included it as a ḥadīth because it did not meet his test.

saying: "Take a piece of cotton perfumed by musk, and clean yourself with it." She said: "How should I clean myself with it?" He said: "Clean yourself with it." She said: "How?" He said: "Glory be to Allāh, clean yourself!" ('Ā'ishah added): So I drew her towards myself and said: "Follow the marks of blood with it." [33]

Ch. 14: The bath of menstruation

315 'Ā'ishah reported that a woman from among the Anṣār said to the Prophet 🕌: "How should I take bath after menstruation?" He said: "Take a piece of musk-perfumed cotton and wash yourself three times." Then the Prophet 🕌 felt shy and turned his face away, or he said: "Wash yourself with it." Then I ('Ā'ishah) took hold of her and drew her (towards myself) and told her what the Prophet 🕌 meant.[34]

Ch. 15: A woman combing her hair at the time of her bath at the end of menstruation

316 'Ā'ishah said: I entered into the state of *Ihrām* with the Messenger of Allāh 🕌 in the Farewell Pilgrimage and I was one of those who intended *Tamattu'* and who were not taking any sacrificial animals. She (further) said that she started having menstruation and did not become clean till the night of *'Arafah*.[35] She said: "O Messenger of Allāh, this is the night of *'Arafah* and indeed I have entered into *Ihrām* for *'Umrah* (previous to the *Hajj*)." So the Messenger of Allāh 🕌 said to her: "Loosen the hair of your head and comb it and refrain from your *'Umrah*." (She continued): I did accordingly and when I finished the *Hajj* he (the Holy Prophet) ordered 'Abdur Raḥmān on

---

[33] In answering all such questions, the Holy Prophet spoke with shyness and indirectly, using emphemisms. As this woman failed to understand his allusion, 'Ā'ishah took her aside to explain it. This incidentally throws light on the purpose of the Holy Prophet's marriages during the closing years of his life. Islām provides directions for the most private aspects of the life of a man and a woman, and those particularly meant for women could not be discussed frankly by the Holy Prophet himself with any woman except his own wife. He conveyed such directions to his wives, whose duty it was then to impart them to women in general. His wives, therefore, were in this way both a band of disciples and preachers.

[34] This is a repetition of h. 314. The word used for cleaning in h. 314 is from *tahārah*, while in h. 315 the word used for washing comes from *Wuḍū'*. Both convey the same significance here.

[35] *Tamattu'* means that a person enters into the state of *Ihrām* on reaching the place prescribed for it with the intention of *'Umrah* (minor pilgrimage) and on his arrival at Makkah he performs *'Umrah* previous to the *Hajj*, leaves the state of *Ihrām*, and enters into it again for the *Hajj* at its appointed time. See also Book 25: *Al-Manāsik (Hajj)*, ch. 34. 'Ā'ishah followed this course but she experienced menstruation during the *'Umrah*, so she could not complete it until the time of *Hajj* came.

the night of al-Ḥasbah so that he took me to perform *'Umrah* from Tan'īm in place of the *'Umrah* for which I had entered into *Iḥrām*.[36]

Ch. 16: A woman loosening her hair at the time of taking bath after menstruation

317 'Ā'ishah reported: We set out, as the new moon of Dhul Ḥajjah was about to appear, and the Messenger of Allāh ﷺ said: "Whoever wishes to enter into the state of *Iḥrām* for *'Umrah* may do so, and whoever wishes to enter into the state of *Iḥrām* for *Ḥajj* may do so. As for me, if I had not brought the sacrificial animal with me, I would have entered into the state of *Iḥrām* for *'Umrah*." So some of them entered into *Iḥrām* for *'Umrah* and others entered into it for *Ḥajj*. I myself was among those who entered into it for *'Umrah*. When the day of *'Arafah* came, I was having menstruation. So I complained to the Prophet ﷺ and he said: "Leave your *'Umrah,* undo your hair, comb it and enter into *Iḥrām* for *Ḥajj*." So I did that. When it was the night of (stopping at) al-Ḥasbah he sent with me my brother 'Abdur Raḥmān ibn Abū Bakr and I went to Tan'īm and entered into the state of *Iḥrām* for *'Umrah* in place of my (earlier missed) *'Umrah*.

Hishām said: And in none of these was there was any sacrifice, fasting or charity.[37]

Ch. 17: The word of Allāh, the Mighty, the Glorious: "Complete in make and incomplete" (the Qur'ān, 22:5)[38]

---

[36] She then performed the *Ḥajj* and thereafter prepared herself for the rites of *'Umrah* by entering into *Iḥrām* at a place called Tan'īm, at a distance of three miles from Makkah. See also h. 1556, h. 1561 and h. 1651. Al-Ḥasbah or al-Muḥaṣṣab is a place outside Makkah where pilgrims stay on their way back from Minā on the 14th or 15th of *Dhul Ḥajjah*. The mention of combing here is to show its connection with the bath after menstruation ends.

[37] H. 316 is repeated here with difference in wording. See also h. 1783 and h. 1786.

[38] The verse from which these words are quoted mentions the stages in the creation of a human being and its development in the womb. From that verse the following text is relevant here: "...surely We created you from dust, then from a drop of semen (*nuṭfah*), then from a clot (*'alaqah*), then from a lump of flesh (*muḍghah*), complete in make (*mukhallaqah*) and incomplete (*ghair mukhallaqah*), that We may make clear to you. And We cause what We please to remain in the wombs till an appointed time, then We bring you forth as babies..." (22:5). The terms used in this verse, as indicated, occur in this ḥadīth.

This chapter is related to menstruation and the permissibility of the observance of *Ḥajj* rites by a woman in that state. The inclusion of this ḥadīth here is to suggest that the clot of blood which leads to the formation of the human body in the womb is only another form of the blood of menstruation, and that its growth and development take place under the direction of an angel because angels are the agents of God in the conduct of the affairs of the universe. Or, it is meant

318 Anas ibn Mālik reported from the Prophet ﷺ that he said: "Surely Allāh, the Blessed and the Most High, has appointed an angel over the womb who says: 'My Lord! a drop of semen (*nuṭfah*); My Lord! a clot (*'alaqah*); My Lord! a lump of flesh (*muḍghah*).' Then when Allāh wills that He should complete His creation, he (the same angel) says: 'Is it a male or a female, is it (spiritually) unfortunate or auspicious, what will be its sustenance, and what will be its life span?' So this is written (while the child is) in the womb of its mother." [39]

Ch. 18:   How is a menstruating woman to enter into the state of *Iḥrām* for *Ḥajj* and *'Umrah?*

319 'Ā'ishah reported: We set out with the Prophet ﷺ in the Farewell Pilgrimage. Some of us entered into the state of *Iḥrām* for *'Umrah,* and some of us for *Ḥajj.* When we reached Makkah the Messenger of Allāh ﷺ said: "Whoever entered into *Iḥrām* for *'Umrah* and he does not have a sacrificial animal, he should leave the state of *Iḥrām,* whoever entered into *Iḥrām* for *'Umrah* and he has a sacrificial animal, he should not leave the state of *Iḥrām* until he has sacrificed his animal, and whoever entered into *Iḥrām* for *Ḥajj,* he should complete his *Ḥajj.*

She added: I started menstruating and continued to menstruate until the day of *'Arafah.* I had entered into *Iḥrām* only for *'Umrah.* So the Prophet ﷺ ordered me to undo my hair, comb it, enter into *Iḥrām* for *Ḥajj* and leave the *'Umrah.* So I did that until I completed my *Ḥajj.* Then he sent with me (my

---

to suggest that the coming of the angel shows that a pregnant woman is not a woman having menstruation.

[39] The cries of the angel at different stages of the creation of man are only indications of the end of one stage and the beginning of the next. In another ḥadīth, narrated by Ibn Mas'ūd, the time intervening between one cry and the next is forty days (see h. 3332 and h. 6594), so that each stage takes forty days and it is after this that the human body starts taking its shape and the sex is determined. *Mukhallaqah* ("complete in make" or created) means the completed form of the lump of flesh which is to become a baby while *ghair mukhallaqah* ("incomplete" or un-created) means un-formed lump which is not meant to be a foetus and as such not to attain a ripeness for a birth as a human being.

A person's becoming spiritually "unfortunate or auspicious" must depend upon his or her own actions, as the Qur'ān so clearly states at so many places. The Qur'ān also states that man is created in the purity of true human nature or *fiṭrah* (30:30) and in a ḥadīth the Holy Prophet has said that every child is born conforming to *fiṭrah* or true human nature of submission to God, and that it is his parents who make it Jew or Christian or Magian (h. 1385). In the light of these principles the present ḥadīth can only mean that, even at the time of the first creation, the knowledge of God comprehends all that is going to happen to the human being up to the end of its life; it does not mean that being wicked or righteous has been pre-destined at birth.

brother) ʿAbdur Raḥmān ibn Abū Bakr and ordered me to perform *'Umrah* from Tanʿīm in place of my (earlier missed) *'Umrah*.[40]

Ch. 19: Coming and receding of menstruation

Women used to send to ʿĀ'ishah bags containing cotton that was yellow so she used to say: "Do not hurry until you see white gypsum"[41] meaning thereby purity of the body after menstruation. The news reached the daughter of Zaid ibn Thābit that women sent for lamps in the middle of the night to look at the purification of their bodies, so she said: "Women (of the days of the Holy Prophet) did not do this" and she disliked this conduct of theirs.[42]

320 ʿĀ'ishah reported that Fāṭimah bint Abū Ḥubaish used to suffer from bleeding outside periods (*istiḥāḍah,* or metrorrhagia), so she asked the Prophet ﷺ. He said: "It is (bleeding from) a vein, and it is not menstruation. So when menstruation arrives give up prayer, and when it passes, wash yourself and say your prayers."[43]

Ch. 20: The menstruating woman is not to make up the missed prayers (after the period)

Jābir ibn ʿAbdullāh and Abū Saʿīd reported from the Prophet ﷺ: "Give up prayer."

321 Muʿadhah related that a woman said to ʿĀ'ishah: "Is one of us to perform the (missed) prayers when she has become clean (after menstruation)? She said: "Are you a *Harūriyyah*?[44] We used to have menstruation when we

---

[40] This is a repetition of h. 316 and h. 317. See later h. 1560, h. 1561, h. 1638, etc.

[41] *Qassah* is the Arabic for gypsum or lime. The meaning is that the cotton used on such occasions should be as white as gypsum, i.e., it should not be in any way stained from blood flow.

[42] It seems that women in the early days of Islām used to be overcautious, worrying in case they miss a prayer if they did not realize that their period had ended before that prayer. So they used to get up repeatedly during the night to check if the menstruation had ended. The daughter of Zaid disliked it because she was aware that it is stated in the Qur'ān that God "has not laid upon you any hardship in religion" (22:78) and that God "desires ease for you, and He does not desire hardship for you" (2:185). Islām is not intended to be unnecessarily difficult and burdensome to its followers and accordingly if there be slight inaccuracies in the observance of religious duties on account of confusion, it is not a very serious matter.

[43] This is a repetition of h. 228.

[44] *Harūriyyah* refers to being from Ḥarūrā', a place two miles away from Kūfah, from which sprang the Kharijite movement, and thus means a Khariji. They believe that the prayers missed during the time of menstruation have to be performed afterwards in arrears. They are an extremist

were with the Prophet ﷺ and he did not command us to do so." Or she said: "And we did not do it."

Ch. 21:   Sleeping with a menstruating woman while she is in her clothes (of menstruation)

322 Umm Salamah related: I started menstruating while I was (lying) with the Prophet ﷺ under a sheet, so I moved away, went out from under it and took my cloth of menstruation and put it on. The Messenger of Allāh ﷺ said to me: "Have you got menstruation?" I said: "Yes." He called me, then took me with him under the sheet (again).

She further said that the Prophet ﷺ used to kiss her while he would be fasting, and: "I used to take bath, both I and the Prophet ﷺ, from the same vessel when under obligation of bath." [45]

Ch. 22:   One who keeps clothes for the time of menstruation other than the clothes of the time of purity

323 Umm Salamah reported: Once I was lying with the Prophet ﷺ under a sheet and I started menstruating, so I moved away and took my cloth of menstruation (to put it on). He said: "Have you got menstruation?" I said: "Yes." He called me, so I lay with him under the sheet (again).[46]

Ch. 23:   Presence of a menstruating woman in the two Eid (*'Īd*) congregations and at the prayers of Muslims while keeping apart from the place of prayer

324 Ḥafṣah reported: We used to prohibit our virgin girls from going out for the two Eid gatherings. Then a woman came and stayed at the palace of Banū Khalaf and she narrated from her sister, whose husband had fought alongside the Prophet ﷺ in twelve battles, and (she said) "my sister was with him six times". She said:

> "We used to treat the wounded and look after the sick. My sister asked the Prophet ﷺ: 'Is it a sin for any of us not to go out when she does not

---

sect who do not accept from Ḥadīth any teaching not mentioned in the Qur'ān. Not performing missed prayers is found only in Ḥadīth, and therefore they do not accept this.

[45] This is a repetition of h. 298, with an addition at the end. A man should keep company with his wife during her menstruation in the same manner as he does otherwise, so as not to make her feel embarrassed or estranged from him. The Holy Prophet used to sleep in bed with his wife during her menstruation and his relationship with her was as it was before or after menstruation.

[46] This is a repetition of h. 298. It occurs in this chapter because of the words, "and (I) took my cloth of menstruation", showing that women kept separate clothes to wear during menstruation. This all depends on the circumstances. See also h. 1929.

possess any over-garment?' He said: 'Her companion should cover her with her own over-garment as well, and she should be present at the doing of good works and at the prayers of the believers'."

So when Umm 'Aṭiyyah came, I asked her: "Did you hear the Prophet ﷺ (saying this)?" She said: "May my father be sacrificed (for him), Yes — and she never used to mention him (the Holy Prophet) but by saying: May my father be sacrificed (for him) — I did hear him say: 'Virgins and those in seclusion and menstruating women should come out and be present at the doing of good works and at the prayers of the believers, and the menstruating women should keep apart from the place of prayer'."

Ḥafṣah said: Then I said, "The menstruating women (are they to go out)?" She said: "Did they not remain present at 'Arafah and at such and such places?" [47]

Ch. 24: **When a woman has three menstrual periods in one month**

And women should be believed in the matter of menstruation and pregnancy as to what can happen with menstruation, because of the word of Allāh, the Most High: "And it is not lawful for them to conceal what Allāh has created in their wombs" (the Qur'ān, 2:228).

It is reported from 'Alī and Shuraiḥ: If a woman brings a clear witness from among her close relatives who follow religion well that she had menstruated three times in the course of a month she should be believed. 'Aṭā' said: Her days of menstruation will remain as they were before. Ibrāhīm said the same thing. And 'Aṭā' said: Menstruation lasts from one day to fifteen days. Mu'tamir reported from his father: I asked Ibn Sīrīn about the woman who experiences bleeding five days after her period, and he said, "Women know it better".[48]

---

[47] See also h. 1652, in which the words are almost the same. See also h. 971 and h. 974. This shows that women in the early days of Islām were active participants in all kinds of affairs of the Muslim community, particularly in collective religious affairs. As Muslim men at that time presented a perfect example of acting upon the teachings of Islām, they had also given women freedom to do the same. In later days this participation came to be considered as against the seclusion and modesty of women. The critics of Islām ascribe these restrictive practices to Islām itself, and thus Muslims are themselves providing the critics of Islām with ammunition to attack it. Recently Muslim women have started to exercise freedom in worldly matters, but they are still not generally taking an active part in religious affairs. Fortunately, Muslim women continue to perform the *Hajj* side by side with men. This practice can be extended to revive the whole tradition of the time of the Holy Prophet.

[48] This chapter is really concerned with the question of divorce although it has a bearing on

325 ʿĀʾishah reported that Fāṭimah bint Abū Ḥubaish asked the Prophet ﷺ: "I suffer from bleeding outside periods (*istiḥāḍah*, or metrorrhagia), and I can never be clean, should I then give up prayer?" He said: "No, it is (bleeding from) a vein. But give up prayer for the days on which you usually have menstruation. Then wash yourself and say your prayers." [49]

Ch. 25: The appearance of yellow and discoloured matter in days outside the menstrual period.

326 Umm ʿAṭiyyah reported: We took no account of the discoloured and yellow matter as being anything (to do with menstruation).

Ch. 26: The vein of metrorrhagia

327 ʿĀʾishah, wife of the Prophet ﷺ, reported that Umm Ḥabībah suffered from metrorrhagia for seven years. She asked the Messenger of Allāh ﷺ about it and he commanded her to take a bath. He also said: "This is (bleeding from) a vein". So she used to take a bath for every prayer.[50]

Ch. 27: A woman menstruating after *al-Ifāḍah* (making those circuits of the Kaʿbah known as *Ṭawāf al-ifāḍah*)[51]

---

prayer and purification as well. The period of waiting after divorce consists of three periods of menstruation, and although generally these occur monthly there is sometimes a variation. The evidence of women on the question of menstruation and pregnancy is mentioned here as accepted. This shows that the reason why, in matters relating to debt, two women witnesses are required in place of one man by the Qurʾān (2:282), is not because the evidence of a woman is less reliable than that of a man but because women in general have less experience in such matters.

[49] This is a repetition of h. 228, speaking of a woman suffering from metrorrhagia, but with somewhat different wording. It means that in case of such a condition the days of menstruation will be estimated, for instance with reference to past experience when this condition had not arisen. However, if there is a normal variation in the number of days of menstruation, then the period of bleeding determines the length of menstruation, whether it is more or less than the usual.

[50] The Holy Prophet told her to take a bath at the time when, according to her reckoning, her menstruation would have ended under normal circumstances. After that bath, she would say her prayers as if there were no bleeding of menstruation. However, either through some misunderstanding or over-caution on her part, she used to take a bath before every prayer.

[51] *Ṭawāf al-ifāḍah* is made on the tenth day of the month of Dhul Ḥajjah and is obligatory. There is another *Ṭawāf*, or making circuits of the Kaʿbah, which is called *Ṭawāf al-widāʿ* which the pilgrims are to make on the eve of their departure from Makkah. If a woman menstruates after the *Ṭawāf al-ifāḍah* she need not remain to perform the other *Ṭawāf*. Ṣafiyyah had performed the first-mentioned *Ṭawāf*, which is what the Holy Prophet's question relates to. The Holy Prophet accordingly asked people not to wait for her periods to end to perform the last *Ṭawāf*. See also h. 1733, 1757, 1771 and 1772.

328 ʿĀ'ishah, wife of the Prophet ﷺ, reported that she said to the Messenger of Allāh ﷺ: "O Messenger of Allāh, surely Ṣafiyyah bint Ḥuyayy is having menstruation." The Messenger of Allāh ﷺ said: "Perhaps she will delay us; has she not made circuits with you women?" And they said: "Yes." He said: "Then proceed."

329–330 Ibn ʿAbbās reported: A menstruating woman is permitted to go when she has menstruation. [330] Ibn ʿUmar used to say at first that she should not go, then I heard him saying: "She should go. Surely the Messenger of Allāh ﷺ has permitted them."

Ch. 28: When a woman suffering from metrorrhagia sees purity

> Ibn ʿAbbās said: She should take a bath and say prayers even if it (purity) be for a short while in the day; and her husband can approach her (sexually) as she can say her prayers, and prayer is a great thing.[52]

331 ʿĀ'ishah reported that the Prophet ﷺ said: "When the menstruation period arrives, give up prayer, and when it passes, wash yourself clean of the blood and say your prayers." [53]

Ch. 29: Funeral Prayer over a woman (dying) during or after delivery[54] and its *Sunnah*

332 Samurah ibn Jundub reported that a woman died as a result of child-birth.[55] So the Prophet ﷺ said (the funeral) prayer over her and he stood by the central part of her body.

---

[52] Distinction must be made between the blood of menstruation and the bleeding outside the normal time of menstruation due to a woman suffering from metrorrhagia. The purity here means purity from the blood of menstruation and not from that of metrorrhagia. Bukhārī argues that as prayer, which is "a great thing" due to its spiritual blessings, is allowed for the woman in metrorrhagia, sexual intercourse should also be allowed. This is his opinion. According to other authorities, it is not allowed to have any sexual intercourse during metrorrhagia.

[53] This is a brief repetition of h. 228.

[54] The word used here refers to *nifās* which means lochia or the bleeding after childbirth (see note 10 under ch. 4 of this book).

[55] The words *fī baṭn-in* (lit. "in the stomach") mean "as a result of childbirth". In the repetition of this ḥadīth in the Book of Funerals in h. 1331, instead of this, the words used are *fī nifāsi-hā*, meaning "in her *nifās*" or the course of lochia discharge, which clarifies the meaning. The word *fī* ("in") means here "as a result of".

Ch. 30: (Related to the above)

333 'Abdullāh ibn Shaddād reported that he heard from his aunt Maimūnah, wife of the Prophet ﷺ, that when she had menstruation she would not say her prayers and used to lie on the floor in front of the place of prostration of the Messenger of Allāh ﷺ, while he prayed on his small mat. (She said:) "When he went in prostration, some of his clothes used to touch me." [56]

---

[56] This chapter has no heading as it is related to the previous chapter because a woman in menstruation, mentioned in this ḥadīth, is subject to the same rules as a woman bleeding after childbirth. As the Holy Prophet's clothes during his prayers used to touch Maimūnah's body while she would be in menstruation, it means that her body was not impure, nor would the body of a woman suffering bleeding after childbirth be impure. Abstention from observance of prayer and fasting, etc., has other grounds than impurity as it is generally understood. See also h. 379.

Book 7: *At-Tayammum*
Dry Ablution

In the name of Allāh, the Beneficent, the Merciful

Ch. 1:   Continuation of the previous one

The word of Allāh, the Mighty, the Glorious: "And (if) you cannot find water, then resort to pure earth (*fa-tayammamū*)[1] and wipe your faces and your hands with it" (the Qur'ān, 5:6; see also 4:43).

334 'Ā'ishah, wife of the Prophet ﷺ reported: We set out with the Messenger of Allāh ﷺ in one of his journeys till we reached al-Baidā', or Dhāt al-Jaish,[2] when my necklace broke. The Messenger of Allāh ﷺ stopped for a search of it, and the people (also) stopped with him and they were not within reach of water. So people came to Abū Bakr aṣ-Ṣiddīq and said: "Do you not see what 'Ā'ishah has done? She has made the Messenger of Allāh ﷺ and the people stay where they are neither within reach of water nor do they have any water with them." So Abū Bakr came and found the Messenger of Allāh ﷺ sleeping, resting his head on my thigh. He said (to me): "You have detained the Messenger of Allāh ﷺ and the people where they are neither within reach of water nor do they have any water with them."

'Ā'ishah said: Abū Bakr remonstrated with me and said whatever Allāh wished him to say, and he jabbed me with his hand in my side, but what prevented me from moving was the placement of (the head of) the Messenger of Allāh ﷺ on my thigh. Then when the Messenger of Allāh ﷺ woke up in the morning and there was no water, Allāh, the Mighty, the Glorious, revealed the verse about *Tayammum*; so they all performed *Tayammum*. Usaid ibn al-Ḥuḍair said: "This is not the first blessing of you, O progeny of Abū Bakr."

She ('Ā'ishah) said: Then we made the camel on which I was sitting to get up and we found the necklace under it.[3]

---

[1] The noun *tayammum* literally means 'to intend anything'. In the terminology of the Sharī'ah it means to have recourse to earth in order to clean oneself thereby for the purpose of prayer, etc.

[2] Al-Baidā' and Dhāt al-Jaish are two places close to Madīnah on the way to Makkah.

[3] 'Ā'ishah had borrowed this necklace from her sister Asmā' and it was worth twelve dirhams.

335 Jābir ibn ʿAbdullāh informed that the Prophet ﷺ said: "I have been given five things which were not given to anyone before me. I have been helped with an awe of the extent of a month's distance; and the earth has been made a mosque for me, as also a means of purification, so any man from among my followers for whom the prayer time comes he should say prayers; and war gains have been made lawful for me and were not made lawful for anyone before me; and I have been given the (power of) intercession; and a prophet used to be sent to his own people only, whereas I have been sent to mankind in general." [4]

Ch. 2:　When neither water nor earth is available

336 ʿĀʾishah reported that she borrowed a necklace from Asmāʾ and it was lost. So the Messenger of Allāh ﷺ sent a man (to search for it) and he found it. Then the time for prayer came for people and they had no water with them. They said their prayers and complained about it to the Messenger of Allāh ﷺ. So Allāh revealed the verse about *Tayammum*. Usaid ibn al-Ḥuḍair said to ʿĀʾishah: "May Allāh reward you with the best, for by Allāh whatever befalls you that you dislike, Allāh makes it for you and for the Muslims a means of good." [5]

This shows the consideration which the Holy Prophet had for his wives. It was not for the article lost but on account of his regard for ʿĀʾishah's feelings. The words of Usaid mean that on a similar occasion previously when ʿĀʾishah was distressed because of being left alone in the wilderness, known as the incident of *ifk* or "the slander" (see the Qurʾān, 24 : 11 onwards), some guidance was revealed from Allāh, which was the first blessing. This was the second occasion when a valuable guidance from God came in the wake of ʿĀʾishah's embarrassment. The report in Ṭabarānī states explicitly that this incident occurred after the incident of *ifk*.

[4] Among the special distinctions of the Holy Prophet, one is the awe his name inspires in the minds of people. The distance of a month means a long distance. His name has always inspired awe in people living even a long way from Muslims. The Holy Prophet's intercession, mentioned here, means his ability to redeem the whole community of believers and the followers of all other religions. Lastly, his universal mission is mentioned and the Holy Prophet very clearly states here that all prophets who preceded him were sent only to their respective nations. This means, for instance, that as Noah was not sent for the whole world the punishment for his people that came in the form of the Deluge could not have submerged the whole of the world. Similarly, Jesus, as he himself says in the Gospels (Matthew, 15 : 24), and as the Qurʾān also says of him (3 : 49, 61 : 6), was sent only for the Israelites. Accordingly, he can have no mission for the whole world, and this refutes the popular idea that he will return to make Islām victorious in the world.

The connection of this ḥadīth with the chapter is only as regards the whole of the earth being made a means of purification, meaning the means of *Tayammum*.

[5] This is a repetition briefly of h. 334. The Qurʾān is clear that, in the absence of water, *Tayammum* is a substitute for *Wuḍūʾ*, but when neither water nor earth is available what should be done? H. 334 shows that the Companions of the Holy Prophet said their prayer without *Wuḍūʾ* and the injunction for *Tayammum* had not yet been revealed. The Holy Prophet did not ask them

Ch. 3: **_Tayammum_ when one is at home and cannot get water and fears the expiry of the prayer time**

'Aṭā' says the same. Al-Ḥasan said about an ill person who had water near him, but found no one who could give it to him, that he could perform *Tayammum.* Ibn 'Umar came from his land at al-Juruf and the time for *'Aṣr* prayer came when he was at Marbad an-Na'am.[6] So he said his prayer and then entered the city while the sun was high and he did not repeat (the prayer).[7]

337 'Umair, the freed slave of Ibn 'Abbās, said: I and 'Abdullāh ibn Yasār, the freed slave of Maimūnah, wife of the Prophet ﷺ, set out till we reached Abū Juhaim ibn al-Ḥārith ibn aṣ-Ṣimmah al-Anṣārī. Abū Juhaim said: "The Prophet ﷺ came from the direction of Bi'r Jamal and a man met him and greeted him with *salām,* but the Prophet ﷺ did not return his greeting till he made for a wall and wiped his face and his hands (with earth), then he returned to him the greeting." [8]

Ch. 4: **Should a person blow on his hands after they have been made to strike on earth for *Tayammum***

338 'Abdur Raḥmān ibn Abzā reported: A man came to 'Umar ibn al-Khaṭṭāb and said: "I was under obligation of bath but water was not available".[9] Then 'Ammār ibn Yāsir said to 'Umar ibn al-Khaṭṭāb: "Do you not remember that we were on a journey, you and I, and we were under obligation of bath? You did not say your prayers, but I rolled on the earth and

---

to repeat their prayers, thus showing that those prayers were quite in order. Thus when there is neither water nor earth available, prayers can be said without *Wuḍū'* or *Tayammum.*

[6] Juruf is at a distance of three miles from Madīnah. Soldiers used to gather there in preparation for any expedition. *Marbad an-Na'am,* meaning 'fold for camels' was another place which was one mile from Madīnah.

[7] Because coming from, and going to, Juruf and Marbad does not come under the category of a "journey", the *Tayammum* made in these places cannot be regarded as being due to a journey. So Ibn 'Umar must have regarded *Tayammum* as quite in order even while not on a journey, if no water is available and the time of prayer is at the point of ending. If for any reason water cannot be used due to ill-health, *Tayammum* can be performed instead of *Wuḍū'* even at home.

[8] This *Tayammum* was not for prayer, but from this it has been deduced that recourse can be had to *Tayammum* even at home when no water is ready at hand or when its use is not possible. It should not be concluded from this ḥadīth that replying to the greeting of peace is not permitted by one who is not in a state of ablution. It was the Holy Prophet's habit in any case to remain in a state of ablution at any time.

[9] In the report in Bukhārī the reply of 'Umar is not mentioned. In this report as given in Ṣaḥīḥ Muslim and Nasā'ī, 'Umar replied: "Do not pray" (Muslim, book: 'Menstruation', ch. 28; Nasā'ī, book: 'Purification', h. 314), i.e., until water is available. It was because of this reply that 'Ammār had to remind 'Umar of this past incident.

said my prayer. I mentioned this to the Prophet ﷺ and he said: 'It was sufficient for you to have done like this', and the Prophet ﷺ struck the earth with both his hands and blew on them, then he wiped his face and his hands with them." [10]

Ch. 5: *Tayammum* is for the face and the hands (*kaffain*)[11]

339 'Abdur Raḥmān ibn Abzā reported: 'Ammār said as above (in h. 338). And Shu'bah struck the ground with his hands, then he drew them towards his mouth, then he rubbed his face and his hands (with them).

340 'Abdur Raḥmān ibn Abzā reported that he was present with 'Umar when 'Ammār said to him: "We were on an expedition and became under obligation of bath," and he said, "Blow hard on them" (i.e., remove the extra dust on the hands before wiping the face with them).

341 'Abdur Raḥmān ibn Abzā reported: 'Ammār said to 'Umar, "I rolled on the earth and came to the Prophet ﷺ who said: "It was sufficient for you to have wiped the face and hands."

342 'Abdur Raḥmān ibn Abzā reported: I was present with 'Umar when 'Ammār said to him. And he related the (above) ḥadīth.

343 'Abdur Raḥmān ibn Abzā reported: 'Ammār said the Prophet ﷺ struck the ground with his hands and wiped his face and his hands.[12]

Ch. 6: Pure earth is (as water) for *Wuḍū'* of a Muslim, sufficing him in place of water

Al-Ḥasan said: *Tayammum* suffices for him so long as he does not void anything. Ibn 'Abbās acted as Imām while in a state of *Tayammum*. Yaḥyā ibn Sa'īd said: There is nothing wrong in saying prayers on a saline ground and to use it for *Tayammum*.[13]

---

[10] When a person is under obligation of bath and cannot get any water, it is not necessary to rub earth over the whole body. It is sufficient to rub earth on the hands and the face in the same way as performing *Tayammum* in place of *Wuḍū'*.

[11] There are varying reports about how to perform *Tayammum*. According to some, the hands have to be rubbed with earth up to the wrists (*kaffain*), others mention only hands (*yadain*), while still others require rubbing up to the elbows. Bukhārī has accepted the first kind of reports, which is why he has used the word *kaffain* in the heading of this chapter. Imām Mālik as well as the Ahl-i Ḥadīth sect hold the same view and they interpret *yadain* used by Abū Juhaim in h. 337 as meaning *kaffain*.

[12] H. 339–343 are brief repetitions of h. 338.

[13] The heading of the chapter is taken from a report by Bazzār, regarded as authentic by Ibn

344 'Imrān reported: We were on a journey with the Prophet ﷺ, and we started at night till when it was the last part of the night we went to rest for a while; and there can be no sleep sweeter to the traveller than this. It was only the heat of the sun which woke us up. The first to wake was so and so, then so and so, then so and so —Abū Rajā' named them but 'Auf forgot.[14] 'Umar ibn al-Khaṭṭāb was the fourth (to wake up). When the Prophet ﷺ used to sleep we would not wake him until he himself got up, because we did not know what took place on him in his sleep (i.e., some spiritual experience). So when 'Umar got up and saw what had happened to the people, and he was a robust man, he said *Allāhu Akbar* and he raised his voice, and he continued to say *Allāhu Akbar* and raise his voice with *Takbīr* till the Prophet ﷺ woke up by his voice.[15]

So when he woke up, people complained to him about what had happened to them. He said: "There is no harm — or it will cause no harm — march on", so they marched.[16] He went on for a short while, then alighted and called for (water for) *Wuḍū'* and performed ablution. The call was sounded for prayer, and he led the people in prayer.[17] When he was free from his prayer, he came to notice a man who was keeping away and did not say his prayer with the people. He said: "What prevented you, O so and so, from saying prayer with the people?" He said: "I am under obligation of bath and there is no water."

Qaṭān. A report to the same effect has been recorded by Imām Aḥmad and is found in the *Sunan* books of Ḥadīth, the words of which are: "Surely, pure earth is a means of cleaning for a Muslim even if he does not find water for ten years" (Tirmidhī, book: 'Purification', ch. 92, h. 124). This ḥadīth has been considered as authentic by Ibn Ḥibbān and Dār Quṭnī. The object of this chapter is to show that *Tayammum* is a perfect substitute for *Wuḍū'*. Anything for which *Wuḍū'* is required may be done with *Tayammum* if water is not available, and whatever nullifies *Wuḍū'* nullifies *Tayammum*. A man can act as an Imām of prayer with *Tayammum*.

[14] 'Auf reported this ḥadīth from Abū Rajā' who reported from 'Imrān.

[15] There is much difference of opinion about this journey. Some say it was on the way back from Khaibar and this is reported in Muslim. According to a report in Abū Dāwūd it was on the return from Ḥudaibiyah. Others report it as on the way to Makkah or on the occasion of the Tabūk expedition. According to some reports the Holy Prophet was the first man to wake up. In an attempt to reconcile this divergence, it is suggested in *Fatḥ al-Bārī* that it might have happened several times. The night on which this incident took place is called *Lailat al-Ta'rīs* in the books of Ḥadīth and Fiqh, meaning 'the night of rest'.

[16] According to the report in Ṣaḥīḥ Muslim the Holy Prophet said: "This is a place where the devil appeared before us" (book: 'Mosques', ch. 55). In the report in Abū Dāwūd, he said: "Go away from this place in which you were overcome by carelessness" (book: 'Prayer', h. 436). In other words, the carelessness caused by overpowering sleep is attributed to the beguiling of the devil.

[17] This shows the validity of holding congregational prayers after the prayer time has expired.

He (the Holy Prophet) said: "You should resort to (*Tayammum* with) earth, for it is sufficient for you." [18]

Then the Prophet ﷺ went on and the people complained to him about thirst. So he alighted and sent for so and so —Abū Rajā' used to name him but 'Auf forgot it — and he (also) sent for 'Alī and said: "You two go and search for water." So they set out and met a woman who was sitting between two water-skins full of water (laden) on her camel. They asked her: "Where is water?" She said: "I left (the place of) water yesterday at this time and our party is behind (me)." They said to her: "Then come along with us." She said: "Where to?" They said: "To the Messenger of Allāh ﷺ." She said: "To him who is called the *Ṣābī*?' They said: "It is he whom you mean, so come along." So they brought her to the Messenger of Allāh ﷺ and related to him the story. They dismounted her from her camel, and the Prophet ﷺ asked for a pot and poured in it from the mouths of the two water skins and closed their mouths and opened the bottom-holes and it was announced to the people: "Give drink (to your animals) and drink yourselves." So he who wanted gave drink and he who wanted drank. At the end he (the Holy Prophet) gave a pot of water to the man who was under obligation of bath and said: "Go and pour it on yourself." And she was standing, looking at what was being done with her water. And by Allāh, when the pouring of water from them (the water skins) was stopped, we thought they were fuller than when he began with them.

Then the Prophet ﷺ said: "Collect (something) for her." So they collected for her dates and flour and powdered parched barley till they collected for her (a big quantity of) food and they put all this in a cloth, and helped her to get on her camel and placed the cloth in front of her.[19] He (the Prophet) said to her: "Do you know that we have not taken your water at all, but it is Allāh Who gave us drink?" [20]

Then she went to her people and she kept herself away from them. They said: "What kept you back, so and so?" She said: "A strange thing (happened to me). Two men met me and took me to that man who is called the *Ṣābī* and he did such and such things. By Allāh, he is the greatest magician among the

---

[18] These words indicate the connection of this ḥadīth with the chapter heading.

[19] They compensated the woman for the small quantity of water they had taken from her water-skins and for the delay caused by this transaction. But this was not all. As stated in this ḥadīth, when Muslims later needed to attack in that direction, they made it a point to spare the tribe to which this particular woman belonged. It was this display of morals that ultimately led her whole tribe to embrace Islām.

[20] This was a miracle of the Holy Prophet and seems to have taken place several times at his hands when a little water was sufficient for a large number of people.

people between this and this" — and she made a sign (while saying this) with her middle and index fingers and raised them towards the sky meaning (between) the heaven and the earth — "or he is the Messenger of Allāh truly."

After this, the Muslims began to attack the idolaters that were living around her, but they did not cause any harm to the tribe to which she belonged. Then one day she said to her people: "These people (Muslims) are leaving you (alone) knowingly; so are you inclined towards Islām?" They accepted her advice and became Muslims.

Abū 'Abdullāh (Bukhārī) says: *Saba'a* means 'one who has left his religion for another.' And Abul 'Āliyah says: The *Ṣābī* are a sect of the People of the Book[21] who read the *Zabūr* (i.e., the scripture of David or the Psalms). *Aṣb* means 'I would incline'.[22]

Ch. 7:   **When a person under obligation of bath fears for himself illness or death or thirst, he should perform *Tayammum***

It has been mentioned that one cold night 'Amr ibn al-'Āṣ was under obligation of bath, so he made *Tayammum* and recited: "And do not kill yourselves. Surely Allāh is ever Merciful to you" (the Qur'ān, 4:29).[23] This was mentioned to the Prophet ﷺ and he did not take it ill.

345 Abū Wā'il reported: Abū Mūsā said to 'Abdullāh ibn Mas'ūd: "When no water is available, should a person not pray?" 'Abdullāh said: "Yes. If I do not find water for a month, I would not say my prayers, and if I give people exemption in this matter, whenever any of them found it cold he will do like this, meaning *Tayammum,* and say prayers." Abū Mūsā said: "Then what of the words which 'Ammār spoke to 'Umar?" He said: "I do not think 'Umar was satisfied with what 'Ammār said."

346 Shaqīq ibn Salamah said: I was with 'Abdullāh (ibn Mas'ūd) and Abū Mūsā, and Abū Mūsā said to him: "What is your opinion, Abū 'Abdur

---

[21] Sabians (*aṣ-Ṣābi'īn*) are mentioned in the Qur'ān, 2:62, 5:69 and 22:17.

[22] This refers to the statement of Joseph in the Qur'ān expressing his fear that "I shall incline (*aṣb*) towards them" (12:33). It is brought in to explain the meaning of *Ṣābī*.

[23] This ḥadīth has been recorded in Abū Dāwūd as a report from 'Amr ibn al-'Āṣ who said: "I had a wet dream one night when it was very cold during the battle of Dhāt as-Salāsil. I feared that if I took bath I would die. So I performed *Tayammum,* then led my companions in the morning prayer. People mentioned this to the Prophet ﷺ and he said: 'Amr, you led your companions in prayer while you were under obligation of bath? I informed him of the reason which prevented me from having a bath and I said that I had heard Allāh say: 'And do not kill yourselves. Surely Allāh is ever Merciful to you.' The Messenger of Allāh ﷺ laughed and did not say anything" (book: 'Purification', ch. 128, h. 334)

Raḥmān, if someone who becomes under obligation of bath cannot find water, what should he do?" 'Abdullāh said: "He should not pray until he finds water." Abū Mūsā said: "What do you make of the statement of 'Ammār when the Prophet ﷺ said to him: 'It (the usual *Tayammum*) was sufficient for you'?" He said: "Do you not see that 'Umar was not satisfied by that (statement)?" Abū Mūsā said: "Leave aside the statement of 'Ammār, what do you make of this verse (of *Tayammum*)?" 'Abdullāh (ibn Mas'ūd) could not reply to this, but said: "If we give people exemption in this matter, whenever any of them felt water to be cold he would probably leave it and perform *Tayammum*." I (Al-A'mash, who was reporting from Shaqīq) said to Shaqīq: "Then 'Abdullāh disliked it because of this?" He said: "Yes." [24]

Ch. 8: *Tayammum* consists of once striking (the earth with hands)

347 Shaqīq reported: I was sitting with 'Abdullāh (ibn Mas'ūd) and Abū Mūsā al-Ash'arī, and Abū Mūsā said to him: "If a man becomes under obligation of bath and he cannot find water for (even) a whole month, should he not perform *Tayammum* and say prayers?" 'Abdullāh said: "He should not perform *Tayammum* even if he cannot find it for a month." So Abū Mūsā said to him: "Then what will you make of this verse in *Sūrah al-Mā'idah:* 'And if you cannot find water, then resort to pure earth' (5:6)?" 'Abdullāh said: "If they are given exemption in this matter it is probable that whenever they felt water to be cold they would perform *Tayammum* with pure earth." I said: "You dislike it because of this?" He said: "Yes." Then Abū Mūsā said: "Have you not heard the statement of 'Ammār to 'Umar ibn al-Khaṭṭāb (as follows):

> The Messenger of Allāh ﷺ sent me on some task and I became under obligation of bath. I did not find water, so I rolled on the earth just as the animals roll (to perform *Tayammum* over the whole body). I mentioned

---

[24] The incident mentioned in h. 345 and h. 346 is described in detail in h. 347. This is a disagreement between 'Abdullāh ibn Mas'ūd and Abū Mūsā al-Ash'arī on the question of *Tayammum*. Ibn Mas'ūd is definitely wrong in contending that if a man under obligation of bath cannot find water even for a whole month, he should rather not say prayers than perform *Tayammum* for saying prayers. Abū Mūsā presents a verse of the Qur'ān in support of his own view and no reply is forthcoming from Ibn Mas'ūd except to say that such a concession would open the door for people to perform *Tayammum* instead of bath on the plea even of water being slightly cold. It is possible that the report has not recorded all that actually happened, and perhaps Ibn Mas'ūd meant that the mere apprehension of illness should not be made a reason for doing *Tayammum* instead of a full bath. The Qur'ān allows this concession only in cases of actual illness. The apprehension of illness makes it a disputed matter.

Reports like this quite incidentally give a glimpse into the relationship among the Companions of the Holy Prophet. As we see here, they did not consider such differences as disturbing the fraternal relationship that existed among them. In spite of such differences they respected one another's personal views.

this to the Prophet ﷺ and he said: "It was sufficient for you to have done like this." Then he struck his hand once on the earth, then he shook it off, then he wiped with it the back of his (right) hand with his left hand or the back of his left hand with his (right) hand. Then he wiped his face with both (hands).[25]

On this, 'Abdullāh said: "Do you not see that 'Umar was not satisfied by the statement of 'Ammār?"

In another narration, Shaqīq reported: I was with 'Abdullāh (ibn Mas'ūd) and Abū Mūsā, and Abū Mūsā said to him: "Have you not heard the statement of 'Ammār to 'Umar: 'The Messenger of Allāh ﷺ sent me and you, and I became under obligation of bath, so I rolled on the earth. Then we came to the Messenger of Allāh ﷺ and informed him about it, and he said: 'It was sufficient for you to have done like this', and he wiped his face and his hands once (with earth)?"

Ch. 9:   Relating to the above

348 'Imrān ibn Ḥusain al-Khuzā'ī related that the Messenger of Allāh ﷺ found a man standing aside and not saying his prayer with the people. The Prophet ﷺ said (to him): "O so and so, what prevented you from saying prayer with the people?" He said: "O Messenger of Allāh, I am under obligation of bath and there is no water." He (the Holy Prophet) said: "You should resort to (*Tayammum* with) earth, for it is sufficient for you." [26]

---

[25] Some reports speak of striking the hands twice on earth and rubbing the hands with dust up to the elbows. But preference has been given to the report that speaks of striking only once and rubbing the backs of the hands with dust only up to wrists.

[26] This is a repetition of a small part of h. 344.

Book 8: *Aṣ-Ṣalāt*

Prayer

In the name of Allāh, the Beneficent, the Merciful

Ch. 1: How the prayer was made obligatory on the occasion of the *Isrā'* (the Holy Prophet's Night Journey)[1]

Ibn ʿAbbās said: Abū Sufyān ibn Ḥarb related to me in the course of the ḥadīth about Heraclius: "he — meaning the Prophet ﷺ — enjoins on us prayers and truthfulness and chastity".[2]

---

[1] Three views are mentioned in *Fatḥ al-Bārī* in connection with the journey of the Holy Prophet: (1) that the journey which is described in the Quran as the *Isrā'* (17:1) and the event which is known as *Miʿrāj* or Ascension both took place in the same night and in a state of wakefulness; (2) that both took place in the same night in a state of sleep as a dream; (3) that the journey took place in a state of wakefulness and the Ascension in a state of sleep whether in the same night or not. Bukhārī, by placing a report about the *Miʿrāj* in a chapter headed with the word *Isrā'*, has considered these incidents to be the same. The reports being divergent, some people have taken the view that there have been several incidents of this kind.

As to when this journey took place, it is evident that it took place while the Holy Prophet was still at Makkah because the prayers were made obligatory in Makkah. It is also evident that *Sūrah al-Najm* also speaks of the Ascension: "Then he drew near, drew nearer yet, so he was the measure of two bows or closer still" (53:8–9). This chapter belongs to the fifth year of the Holy Prophet's mission. Moreover, the *Sidrat al-Muntahā*, or "the farthest lote-tree", is spoken of in the same manner in this ḥadīth h. 349 near the end as it is in this chapter of the Qur'ān. In the Qur'ān the words are: "At the farthest lote-tree, near which is the Garden of Abode. When that which covers covered the lote-tree" (53:14–16). In this ḥadīth it is related that the Holy Prophet, with the angel Gabriel, reached the *Sidrat al-Muntahā* which was "covered by several colours which I did not know what they were" and then he was admitted into Paradise. All this clearly shows that the chapter *al-Najm* is speaking of the Ascension of the Holy Prophet. Now, the injunction of prayer is found in very early chapters of the Qur'ān. Hence, without specifying any particular date, it can be said that the Ascension of the Holy Prophet belongs to the very early days of his mission and that the prayer was made obligatory about this time. It is an established fact that the Holy Prophet used to say his prayers in the house of Arqam in the fourth year of his mission and that his Companions used to gather there for the same purpose. Similarly, chapter 17 of the Qur'ān, 'The Israelites', which starts with the mention of this journey, belongs to the early days of the Holy Prophet's mission.

As for the nature of this experience, it can neither be considered as a dream in a state of sleep nor to have happened in wakefulness. It was a *kashf* or grand spiritual vision, a state in which the physical senses are suspended and spiritual senses completely overshadow consciousness.

[2] This statement is found in h. 7.

349 Anas ibn Mālik reported that Abū Dharr used to relate that the Messenger of Allāh ﷺ said:

The roof of my house was opened while I was at Makkah and Gabriel descended. He opened my breast, then washed it with the water of Zamzam. Then he brought a golden trough filled with wisdom and faith and poured it in my breast,[3] and then closed it. Then he took hold of my hand and ascended with me to the heaven. When I reached the nearest heaven, Gabriel said to the gatekeeper of the heaven: "Open." He said: "Who is it?" He replied: "This is Gabriel." He said: "Is there anyone with you?" He said: "Yes, with me is Muḥammad." Then he said: "Has he been sent for?" He said: "Yes." Then when he opened (the door) we rose to the nearest heaven, and saw a man sitting there. On his right side there were some people and on his left there were some people.[4] When he looked towards his right he laughed, and when he looked towards his left he wept. He said: "Welcome, O righteous Prophet and righteous son." I said to Gabriel: "Who is this?" He said: "This is Adam and these people on his right and on his left are the souls of his progeny, and those of them on the right are the people of Paradise and the those on the left are the people of Hell, so when he looks towards his right he laughs and when he looks towards his left he weeps." [5] Then he (Gabriel) ascended with me to the second heaven and said to its gatekeeper: "Open." Its gatekeeper said to him like what the first one had said, and it was opened.

Anas said that he (Abū Dharr) related (further) that he (the Holy Prophet) found in the heavens Adam and Idrīs and Moses and Jesus and Abraham, and he did not describe what places they were in, except that he mentioned that he found Adam in the nearest heaven and Abraham in the sixth heaven.[6] Anas (further) said: So when Gabriel moved on with the Prophet ﷺ to Idrīs, he

---

[3] The mention of the trough filled with knowledge and wisdom indicates very clearly that the experience was of a spiritual vision, since knowledge and wisdom are not physical things that can be contained in a vessel. It is to be noted that the opening of the breast of the Holy Prophet took place on this occasion of his Ascension. See also h. 1636.

[4] *Aswidah* ("people") is plural of *sawād*.

[5] The Holy Prophet's seeing all the souls in the first heaven is another clear indication that he was having this experience in a vision. Otherwise, according to the Qur'ān, the souls of the unbelievers should be in what is called *sijjīn* or prison (83:7) and those of the righteous should be in what is called *'illiyyīn* or the highest places (83:18). The explanations that have been offered by the commentators of Ḥadīth are all baseless. For example, some have said that at times these souls are taken out of their respective stations and presented before Adam, and that this was quite incidentally the time when these souls were being presented before him. But the very idea of these souls being presented before Adam is itself absurd.

[6] This shows that the heaven spoken of here has nothing to do with physical height but is only a way of describing the spiritual ranks of the persons concerned.

(Idrīs) said: "Welcome, O righteous Prophet and righteous brother." So I (i.e., the Holy Prophet) said:

"Who is this?" He (Gabriel) said: "This is Idrīs." Then I passed by Moses and he said: "Welcome, O righteous Prophet and righteous brother." I said: "Who is this?" He said: "This is Moses." Then I passed by Jesus and he said: "Welcome, O righteous brother and righteous Prophet." I said: "Who is this?" He said: "This is Jesus".[7] Then I passed by Abraham and he said: "Welcome, O righteous Prophet and righteous son." I said: "Who is this?" He said: "This is Abraham."

Ibn Shihāb said: Ibn Ḥazm informed me that Ibn ʿAbbās and Abū Ḥabbah al-Anṣārī used to say that the Prophet ﷺ said: Then he (Gabriel) ascended with me till I reached a plain in which I began to hear the sound of pens (in writing).

Ibn Ḥazm and Anas ibn Mālik said that the Prophet ﷺ said:

Then Allāh, the Mighty, the Glorious made fifty prayers obligatory on my followers. So I returned with this (commandment) till I passed by Moses and he said: "What has Allāh made obligatory for you on your followers?" I said: "He has made fifty prayers as obligatory." He said: "Return to your Lord, for surely your followers will not have the power for (observing) it." So I returned (to Allāh with this plea) and He set aside a part of it. So I returned to Moses and said: "He has set aside a part of it." He said: "Return to your Lord, for surely your followers will not have the power for (observing) it." So I returned (to Allāh with this plea) and He said: "These are five and these are (equal to) fifty — My word cannot be changed." So I returned to Moses and he said: "Return to your Lord." But I said: "I feel shy of my Lord (to ask again)."

Then he (Gabriel) led me on till I was taken to the farthest lote-tree (*Sidrat al-Muntahā*) and it was covered by several colours which I did not know what they were. Then I was made to enter Paradise, and there were in it necklaces of pearls and its earth was of musk.[8]

---

[7] The Holy Prophet's seeing Jesus is, according to all reports, of the same nature as his seeing other prophets. There is no mention that Jesus was seen in his physical body but other prophets were seen in a spiritual form. This incidentally proves that Jesus at the time was dead in the same way as other prophets were dead. The Holy Prophet saw only the soul of Jesus in the spiritual world as he saw the souls of other prophets. A full discussion on the *Miʿrāj* will take place at the proper occasion.

[8] All that is narrated in this ḥadīth makes it evident that it was purely a vision. The Holy Prophet enters Paradise and after having seen it thoroughly comes back, but the Qurʾān says of Paradise: "nor will they be ejected from there" (15 : 48). This sight of heaven was a spiritual sight

350 ʿĀʾishah, Mother of the Faithful, reported: Allāh made the prayer obligatory, and when He did so it was (to consist of) two *rak'ahs* every time, while at home as well as while on a journey. Then the prayer on a journey remained as it was, and the prayer while at home was increased.[9]

Ch. 2:   The necessity of prayer in clothes

The word of Allāh, the Most High: "Attend to your adornment at every time of prayer" (7:31). And whoever prays covering himself in one piece of cloth,[10] it has been reported from Salamah ibn al-Akwaʿ that the Prophet ﷺ said: "Stitch it, even if with a thorn", though there is some defect in the chain of narration.[11] Whoever prays in the cloth which he was wearing during sexual intercourse,

---

and is of the same kind as his having seen Paradise while he was engaged in prayer at the time of the solar eclipse; see h. 86 and also h. 1386, last footnote to that ḥadīth. The prayer being reduced from fifty times also points to the same direction. It amounts to saying that these five prayers should prepare the mind for a continuous state of prayerfulness. In the same way, the sound of pens as mentioned here confirms the view that it was a spiritual experience. The affairs that are written down in the presence of God are not written down in the same manner as people do in this world with pens and ink.

[9] In h. 3935 ʿĀʾishah says that the prayers were made to consist of four *rak'ahs* only after *Hijrah,* the migration to Madīnah. But as against this the Qurʾān says: "And when you journey in the earth, there is no blame on you if you shorten the prayer" (4:101), showing that from the very beginning the prayer consisted of four *rak'ahs* and that shortening was permitted only in the case of journey. A saying of the Holy Prophet accords with this which describes this shortening as "a charity which Allāh has given you, so accept His charity" (Ṣaḥīḥ Muslim, book: 'Prayer of Travellers and its shortening', ch. 1). In the same chapter of Ṣaḥīḥ Muslim there is report of Ibn ʿAbbās that the prayer made obligatory by Allāh through the tongue of the Holy Prophet consists of four *rak'ahs* at home and two *rak'ahs* on a journey. So the statement by ʿĀʾishah here does not seem to be correct, and when prayer was made obligatory it was as it is today. That the prayer consists of four *rak'ahs* while at home is further proved by the words of Allāh in h. 349: "My word cannot be changed." (This is similar to an expression in the Qurʾān, 50:29.) If prayer even at home were originally two *rak'ahs* and was then changed to four *rak'ahs,* the word of God is evidently changed. The state of journey being temporary, the reduction of prayer to two *rak'ahs* in this condition does not amount to a change in the word of God.

[10] The Holy Prophet and his Companions said their prayers wearing one sheet of cloth and stressed on the necessity of covering the part of the body which cannot be exposed. That part is termed *ʿaurah* in the terminology of the Sharīʿah, and for men it extends from the navel to the knees, and for women it extends to much higher up and much further down. Ibn Ḥazm says it is agreed on all hands that in the words of the Qurʾān, "attend to your adornment at every time of prayer" (7:31), attending to your adornment (lit. "take your adornment" — *khudhū zīnata-kum*) means to cover the unexposable parts of the body. Wrapping the body in one cloth in prayer was an indication that these parts of the body must be covered properly.

[11] Some authorities regard it as authentic. Even if the chain of narrators is not reliable, its content finds support from others reports which forbid the uncovering of the *'Aurah.* These reports will occur shortly further on.

so long as he does not find any pollution in it, and the Prophet ﷺ ordered that no one should make circuits of the House of Ka'bah (*Ṭawāf*) while naked.[12]

351 Umm 'Aṭiyyah reported: We were ordered to bring out menstruating women on Eid days, and also those in seclusion, so that they may be present at the congregation of the Muslims and their prayers, and the menstruating women should keep apart from the place of prayer. A woman asked: "O Messenger of Allāh, what if one of us does not have an over-garment?" He said: "Her companion should cover her with her own over-garment as well." [13]

Ch. 3: Tying the lower garment (*izār*) on the shoulder while at prayer

Abū Ḥāzim reported from Sahl ibn Sa'd: People said their prayers with the Prophet ﷺ, tying their lower garments on their shoulders.[14]

352 Muḥammad ibn al-Munkadir reported: Jābir said his prayer in a lower garment which he tied from the side of his shoulder, while his (upper) garment was placed on a cloth-stand. Someone asked him: "Do you say your prayer in one lower garment?" He replied: "I have done this only to make a fool like you see me, and which of us had two pieces of cloth in the time of the Prophet ﷺ?"[15]

---

[12] The Holy Prophet had this injunction proclaimed by 'Alī in Makkah at the time of the pilgrimage, viz., no nude person should be allowed to make circuits of the House of God. What applies to making circuits of the Ka'bah applies also to prayer, and as the latter requires more caution to avoid exposure than the *Ṭawāf*, the covering of the *'aurah* must be considered as essential. Before Islām some Arabs made circuits of the Ka'bah while naked, and among some other nations it is considered a more excellent form of worship to perform it while wholly or partly naked.

[13] This is a repetition of h. 324 with some brevity. As the covering of the body is necessary when not praying, it is all the more necessary when praying. This is what links this ḥadīth to the chapter heading. Incidentally this ḥadīth shows the utmost necessity of women's presence in Muslim religious gatherings. Today, Muslims have drifted so far from this teaching of Islām that it is considered, if not prohibited, then certainly undesirable for women to attend a meeting or lecture.

[14] According to *Fatḥ al-Bārī* these were the persons known as the *Aṣḥāb aṣ-Ṣuffah*, who spent all their time in the company of the Holy Prophet and in the mosque. The waist cloth or lower garment (*izār*) used to be tied on the shoulder to prevent the unexposable part of the body from being exposed during bowing and prostration.

[15] In the earlier days of Islām, people were so poor that most of them had but one piece of cloth to wear, and in that they said their prayers as well. Jābir said his prayer in one piece of cloth not only to draw attention to a point of Islamic teachings, but also to show people the economic conditions of the earlier days. He did this at a time of comfort and plenty when people had forgotten the earlier days.

353 Muḥammad ibn al-Munkadir reported: I saw Jābir ibn ʿAbdullāh saying his prayers in one piece of cloth and he said: "I saw the Prophet ﷺ saying his prayers in one piece of cloth".[16]

Ch. 4: Prayer in one piece of cloth wrapped around the body

Az-Zuhrī said in his report: *Al-Multaḥif* means *al-Mutawashshiḥ*;[17] and it is the turning of its two ends oppositely (*al-mukhālif baina ṭarafai-hi*) over the shoulders and this is called *al-Ishtimāl* of a cloth over the shoulders. He said that Umm Hānī said: The Prophet ﷺ covered himself with his piece of cloth and turned its two ends oppositely over his shoulders.

354 ʿUmar ibn Abū Salamah reported that the Prophet ﷺ prayed in one piece of cloth, having turned its two ends oppositely (over his shoulders).

355 ʿUmar ibn Abū Salamah reported that he saw the Prophet ﷺ saying his prayers in one piece of cloth in the house of Umm Salamah, having thrown its two ends over his shoulders.

356 ʿUmar ibn Abū Salamah informed: I saw the Messenger of Allāh ﷺ saying his prayers in one piece of cloth, wrapped in it, in the house of Umm Salamah, placing its ends over his shoulders.[18]

357 Umm Hānī, daughter of Abū Ṭālib, said: I went to the Messenger of Allāh ﷺ in the year of the conquest of Makkah and I found him taking a bath and Fāṭimah, his daughter, screening him. I greeted him. He said: "Who is it?" I said: "It is Umm Hānī, daughter of Abū Ṭālib", and he said: "Welcome to Umm Hānī."

So when he had finished his bath he stood and said eight *rakʿahs* of prayer, wrapping himself in one piece of cloth. When he had finished, I said:

---

[16] This is a repetition of h. 352 in a shortened form with the addition quoting Jābir about the Holy Prophet. Jābir means that he saw the Holy Prophet saying his prayers wearing only one piece of cloth as he himself had been doing with the corners of the cloth tied to the shoulders. In the repetition in h. 370 Jābir, in reply to the question about how he was praying, says that he saw the Holy Prophet "saying his prayers like this".

[17] Saying of prayer in one piece of cloth has been described in different reports by different words as *multaḥif* (wrapped), *mutawashshiḥ* (wearing), *mukhālif baina ṭarafai-hi* (crossing of its opposite ends), and *mushtamil-an bi-hi* (having wrapped himself). They mean the same thing, viz., a man's so wrapping himself in a piece of cloth that each of its upper corners is placed on the opposite shoulder and then both the corners are tied together. The object is to cover the whole body and to prevent the corners of the cloth from slipping away in bowing and prostration.

[18] H. 355 and 356 are repetitions of h. 354 with the additional words: "in the house of Umm Salamah."

"O Messenger of Allāh, the son of my mother is determined to kill a man whom I have given refuge, and who is so and so, son of Hubairah." The Messenger of Allāh ﷺ said: "We have given protection to whom you have given protection, O Umm Hānī." Umm Hānī said: And this was forenoon prayer (*Ḍuḥā*).[19]

358 Abū Hurairah reported that a man asked the Messenger of Allāh ﷺ about saying prayers in one piece of cloth, and the Messenger of Allāh ﷺ said: "Has every one of you got two pieces of cloth?"

Ch. 5:   When anyone says his prayers in one piece of cloth, he should place (corners of) it over his shoulders

359 Abū Hurairah reported: The Messenger of Allāh ﷺ said: "None of you should say his prayers in one piece of cloth if he has not anything over his shoulders." [20]

360 Abū Hurairah said: I bear witness that I heard the Messenger of Allāh ﷺ say: "Whoever says his prayers in one piece of cloth, he should turn its two ends oppositely (over his shoulders)."

Ch. 6:   When the cloth is narrow

361 Saʿīd ibn al-Ḥārith reported that they asked Jābir ibn ʿAbdullāh about prayer in one piece of cloth, and he said: I went out with the Prophet ﷺ in one of his journeys and I came one night on some business of mine and I found him saying prayers. I had only one piece of cloth, so I wrapped it round me and prayed by his side. When he finished, he said: "What brought you during the night, O Jābir?" I told him about my business and when I finished he said: "What is this wrapping which I see?" I said: "It is one piece of cloth." He said: "If it is wide enough, wrap it round yourself, and if it is narrow, wrap it on the waist."

362 Sahl (ibn Saʿd) reported: Men used to say their prayers with the Prophet ﷺ, tying their waist-wrappers around their necks in the manner of

---

[19] Up to her statement, "It is Umm Hānī", this ḥadīth is a repetition of h. 280. See also h. 1103. This ḥadīth shows that Islām has given women the highest of rights. Umm Hānī was a sister of ʿAlī and she gave protection to a man whom ʿAlī wanted to kill, but the Holy Prophet honours the word given by this woman to the man, saying that her word was binding over the whole nation.

[20] This is provided that his cloth is wide enough as explained in h. 361. If it is a narrow piece of cloth, he should only tie it on the waist and let it hang downwards.

children, and the women were told: Do not raise your heads until the men are sitting upright." [21]

Ch. 7: Saying prayer in Syrian upper gown

Al-Ḥasan said with regard to the clothes woven by the Magians that he found nothing wrong in them. Maʻmar said: I have seen az-Zuhrī wearing Yemenite cloth that was dyed in urine. ʻAlī ibn Abū Ṭālib said his prayers in a piece of cloth which was not bleached.[22]

363 Mughīrah ibn Shuʻbah reported: I was with the Prophet ﷺ on a certain journey and he said: "O Mughīrah, take a water-skin", so I took it. Then the Messenger of Allāh ﷺ went on till he disappeared from me. He answered the call of nature and on him was an upper gown made in Syria. He began to push his hands out of its sleeves but they were narrow, so he put out his hand from underneath it and I poured water on it, and he performed ablution, his *Wuḍū',* for prayer and wiped over his socks and said his prayer.

Ch. 8: Disapproval of nudity in prayer and otherwise

364 Jābir ibn ʻAbdullāh related that the Messenger of Allāh ﷺ was carrying with him stones with the people for (the construction of) the Kaʻbah and he had his waist-wrapper (*izār*) on him. ʻAbbās, his uncle, said to him: "O son of my brother, if you would take off your waist-wrapper and place it on your shoulder underneath the stone (it would be better)." So he (the Holy Prophet) took it off and placed it on his shoulders, but he fell down unconscious and he was never seen exposed after that.[23]

---

[21] This was to prevent the women seeing the exposed coverable part of the men's body. Muslims were at that time in the most straitened circumstances. They had left behind all their possessions in Makkah, so much so that many of them had not sufficient cloth to wear. All this hardship meant nothing to them as compared with the great spiritual wealth which they received from the Holy Prophet. The word for "waist-wrappers" is *uzr,* plural of *izār.* See repetition of this in h. 814 and h. 1215.

[22] Syria in those days was in the hands of non-Muslims, and the cloth that came from that country was made by those people. By narrating such incidents Bukhārī wants to convey that no rigidity should be observed in the matter of cloth used by Muslims, so long as there is no tangible impurity found in it. The urine used for the dying of this particular cloth seems to be urine of some animal lawful for food, and is not impure in the opinion of Zuhrī. The real purity in prayer is that of the mind and heart, while external purity is a matter of good form and presentation.

[23] This incident evidently belongs to a time when the Holy Prophet was a very small boy. It cannot be that famous incident of the reconstruction of the Kaʻbah in which the Holy Prophet took part when he was 35 years of age. Or it could mean that he raised his waist-wrapper so that his thighs became bare. Being entirely naked cannot be meant because it is known from reliable Ḥadīth reports that the Holy Prophet was as modest and shy as a virgin girl.

Ch. 9:   Prayer in shirt and trousers and shorts and full-sleeved gowns

365 Abū Hurairah reported: A man went to the Prophet ﷺ and asked him about prayer in one piece of cloth. He said: "Has every one of you got two pieces of cloth?" Then (later on) a man asked 'Umar (about the same) and he said: "When Allāh has bestowed abundance (of means), spend abundantly (on yourselves). A man should put on all his clothes. A man can say his prayers in a waist-wrapper (*izār*) and cloak, in a waist-wrapper and shirt, in a waist-wrapper and full-sleeved gown, in trousers and a cloak, in trousers and a shirt, in trousers and a full-sleeved gown, in shorts and a full-sleeved gown, in shorts and a shirt." The narrator said: And I think 'Umar said: "In shorts and a cloak." [24]

366 Ibn 'Umar reported: A man asked the Messenger of Allāh ﷺ: "What should a person in *Iḥrām* wear?" He said: "He should not wear a shirt, or trousers, or headgear, or clothes perfumed with saffron or *wars* (a kind of scent). And whoever cannot find shoes, he should wear socks, cutting them off so they are lower than the ankles." [25]

Ch. 10:   What is to be covered is private parts

367 Abū Sa'īd al-Khudrī reported that the Messenger of Allāh ﷺ forbade wrapping one's body with a cloth so that the hands are shut up within (*ishtimāl aṣ-ṣammā'*), and a man's sitting on his buttocks with his knees raised up (*iḥtibā'*) while wearing only one piece of cloth so that none of it is covering his private parts.[26]

368 Abū Hurairah reported: The Prophet ﷺ forbade two kinds of sale —

---

[24] *Tubbān* means shorts or knicker, the length of which is reported to be one span of hand. Naturally this cannot go beneath the knees. But even this much covering of the body is accepted for prayers, provided it is supplemented by a shirt; but this permission should not be allowed to be an excuse for laziness in not dressing well for prayers.

[25] This is a repetition of h. 134. That ḥadīth contains the additional words "or turban" after "He should not wear a shirt" which do not occur here. Since a man in the state of *Iḥrām* can say prayers while he does not wear a shirt or trousers, it follows that in normal conditions also prayers can be said without wearing a shirt or trousers, provided the unexposable parts of the body are covered.

[26] *Ishtimāl aṣ-ṣammā'* means to so wrap a cloth round the body that even the hands etc. are closed inside. If it is just one piece of cloth it is forbidden in prayer because while rising the hands for *Takbīr* or in taking other postures the private parts are likely to be exposed. Similarly, it is forbidden to sit with buttocks on the ground and the knees raised high, called *iḥtibā'*, because such a posture taken in one piece of cloth has the same risk of exposing the private parts. See also h. 1991–1992.

through touch (*al-limās*) and through throwing (*an-nibādh*)[27] — and wrapping one's body with a cloth so that the hands are shut up within, and a man's sitting on his buttocks with his knees raised up while wearing only one piece of cloth.

369 Abū Hurairah said: Abū Bakr sent me to that pilgrimage as one of the announcers on the day of Sacrifice, so that we may announce at Minā that no idolater may perform the pilgrimage after this year, nor make circuits of the House of Kaʿbah naked.[28]

Ḥumaid ibn ʿAbdur Raḥmān said:[29] Then the Messenger of Allāh ﷺ sent after this ʿAlī and ordered him to announce the freedom from obligation (of the Muslims to the unbelievers).[30]

Abū Hurairah said: So ʿAlī announced with us among the people gathered at Minā on the day of Sacrifice: "After this year no idolater may perform the pilgrimage nor make circuits of the House of Kaʿbah naked." [31]

Ch. 11:   Saying prayer without any cloak (*ridā'*)

370 Muḥammad ibn al-Munkadir reported: I came upon Jābir ibn ʿAbdullāh and he was saying his prayer wrapped in a garment while his cloak was lying beside him. When he finished, we asked: "O Abū ʿAbdullāh, you are saying your prayer while your cloak is lying beside you?" He replied: "Yes, I wanted to make ignorant ones like you people see me. I saw the Prophet ﷺ saying his prayers like this." [32]

---

[27] The term *bai' al-limās* (purchase by touch) is used for a bargain in which the buyer's touching the goods indicated finalisation of the deal. Similarly, sometimes the throwing of articles by the seller towards the buyer (*an-nibādh*) was regarded as a sign of finalisation of the deal. See also h. 584 and h. 1993 and its footnote.

[28] This pilgrimage was the one previous to the Farewell Pilgrimage performed in the year before. It was announced in this pilgrimage that no one should be allowed to visit the House of God naked. This is also a proof that covering the private parts is necessary in any act of devotion. See also h. 1622.

[29] Ḥumaid ibn ʿAbdur Raḥmān ibn ʿAuf is the reporter of the earlier and the later part of this ḥadīth from Abū Hurairah.

[30] The word for "freedom from obligation" is *barā'at*, one of the titles of ch. 9 of the Qur'ān. Its first thirteen verses were publicly proclaimed by ʿAlī at the pilgrimage in 9 A.H. See also h. 4656 and h. 4657 in the book on Commentary of the Qur'ān.

[31] This pilgrimage was the one previous to the Farewell Pilgrimage, performed in the year before. It was announced at this Pilgrimage that no one would be allowed to visit the House of God naked. This is also a proof that covering the private parts is necessary in any act of devotion.

[32] In this repetition of h. 352 the word *ridā'* ("cloak") has been used in place of *thiyāb*, translated in h. 352 as "(upper) garment", so that it was a cloak that was found beside him. There are some other minor differences in wording as well.

Ch. 12:   **What has been said regarding the thigh?**

Abū ʿAbdullāh (Bukhārī) said: It has been reported by Ibn ʿAbbās and Jarhad and Muḥammad ibn Jaḥsh from the Prophet ﷺ that the thigh is among the unexposable parts. Anas said: The Prophet ﷺ uncovered his thigh. Abū ʿAbdullāh (Bukhārī) said: The ḥadīth of Anas is more reliable in its chain of narration while the ḥadīth of Jarhad is more cautious, so that we can resolve their difference. Abū Mūsā said: The Prophet ﷺ covered his knees when ʿUthmān entered. Zaid ibn Thābit said: Allāh revealed to his Messenger ﷺ while his thigh was on my thigh and it proved so heavy that I feared lest my thigh should be broken.

371 Anas (ibn Mālik) reported that the Messenger of Allāh ﷺ went to the Battle of Khaibar, and we said our morning prayer near that place when it was still dark. Then the Prophet of Allāh ﷺ rode on his horse, and Abū Ṭalḥah also rode, and I rode behind Abū Ṭalḥah. The Prophet of Allāh ﷺ made it (i.e., his beast) run in the streets of Khaibar and my knee was touching the thigh of the Prophet of Allāh ﷺ. Then he (the Holy Prophet) raised his waist-wrapper (*izār*) from his thigh so much so that I could see the whiteness of the thigh of the Prophet of Allāh ﷺ.[33] When he entered the town, he said: "*Allāhu Akbar,* Khaibar is ruined. When we alight in the fields of a nation, the morning of these people, who had been warned, turns evil." He said this three times.

Anas added: The people (i.e., the Jews of Khaibar) went out for their affairs and said: "It is Muḥammad" — ʿAbdul ʿAzīz said: And some of our Companions said: "And (Muḥammad with) the *khamīs,* meaning army."[34] So we took it (the city) by force and prisoners were collected. Then came Diḥyah, and said: "O Prophet of Allāh, give me a female slave from among the prisoners." He (the Holy Prophet) said: "Go and take a female slave", and he (Diḥyah) took Ṣafiyyah, daughter of Ḥuyayy. Then a man came to the Prophet ﷺ and said: "O Prophet of Allāh, you have given Ṣafiyyah, daughter of Ḥuyayy to Diḥyah, and she is the chief of the tribe of Quraiẓah and an-Naḍīr. She is suitable to none but yourself." He (the Holy Prophet) said: "Send for him together with her." So he (Diḥyah) came with her, and when the Prophet ﷺ looked at her he said: "Take a female from the prisoners other than her."

---

[33] It is this part of the ḥadīth which has a bearing on the heading of this chapter. Evidently, there is some difference on the question of keeping the thighs bare. The report shows the Holy Prophet himself having once exposed his thighs. Other reports indicate prohibition against exposing the thighs. These two divergent reports can be reconciled as follows: the upper part of the thighs next to the private parts must not be exposed, but the lower parts just above the knees may be exposed under some necessity.

[34] ʿAbdul ʿAzīz is the reporter of this ḥadīth next in the chain from Anas.

He (the narrator) added: Then the Prophet ﷺ set her free and took her in marriage. Then Thābit said to him (Anas): "O father of Ḥamzah! What nuptial gift did he give her?" He said: "Her own self, for he set her free and took her in marriage." When he was still on the way (back), Umm Sulaim adorned her and led her to him at night time. As the Prophet was a bridegroom he said: "Whoever has with him anything (of food), he should bring it." He spread a sheet and one man brought dates and another brought melted butter — he (the narrator) said: I think he (Anas) mentioned gruel (*as-sawīq*). They made a mixture (of these) and this was the marriage feast (*walīmah*) of the Prophet ﷺ.[35]

Ch. 13: In how many pieces of cloth should a woman say prayers?

'Ikrimah said: If she covers her body in one piece of cloth, it is permissible.

372 'Ā'ishah said: The Messenger of Allāh ﷺ used to say the morning prayer (*Fajr*) and with him (many) believing women used to attend, wrapped in their cloaks. Then they would return to their houses and no one would recognize them.[36]

---

[35] Incidents such as these show the simplicity of the Holy Prophet's life and the scantiness of his economic means. The Jews are proverbially rich in all ages, and throughout history Christian rulers are known to have extorted fabulous wealth from their Jewish subjects. Here the Holy Prophet is returning after a victory over the Jews, but he is so empty-handed that he has no means to entertain his friends in a marriage feast. So he asks his friends to bring their own meals to constitute the marriage feast. The Holy Prophet's marriage with Ṣafiyyah was an attempt to win over Jewish tribes. He could have married her as a female slave but the emancipator of the slaves must set an example of how to abolish this inhumane system. He accordingly gave this lady her freedom, married her as a free woman and conferred on her rights similar to those enjoyed by the proud Quraish, and this generosity towards a Jew came very shortly after a Jew had poisoned him in Khaibar.

Once one of the Holy Prophet's wives, Ḥafṣah, daughter of 'Umar, derogatorily called Ṣafiyyah as "daughter of a Jew". When the Prophet heard of this, he said to Ṣafiyyah: "You are the daughter of a Prophet, your uncle was a Prophet, and you are living under a Prophet. So what is she proud of over you?" In another ḥadīth the Holy Prophet said to her: "Why did you not say: How can you be better than me when my husband is Muḥammad, my father is Aaron, and my uncle is Moses?" (Tirmidhī, book: *Manāqib* — 'Virtues', h. 4268 and 4266). Thus the Holy Prophet did not regard a Jewish captive whom he had married as any the lesser than those of his wives who belonged to the most honoured of the Arab tribes of Quraish.

[36] This shows that women in those days used to attend the congregational prayers in the mosque equally with men, so much so that they attended the early morning *Fajr* prayer. In h. 578, h. 867 and h. 872 it is reported that the women could not be recognized owing to the darkness. Unfortunately, this wholesome practice of the Holy Prophet has been discarded by Muslims and women are conspicuous by their absence from the mosque. And yet in modern times Muslim women attend all sorts of other public functions, some of which are not at all spiritually elevating.

Ch. 14:　When anyone says prayers in a cloth on which there are borders and he looks at its border

373 'Ā'ishah reported that the Prophet ﷺ said his prayer in a shawl in which there were borders, and he looked at its borders once and when he had finished (his prayer) he said: "Take this shawl of mine to Abū Jahm and bring me the *anbijāniyyah* of Abū Jahm, because this one has diverted my attention from my prayer."

'Ā'ishah (also) reported that the Prophet ﷺ said: "I was looking at its border while I was in prayer and I fear that it may put me in trouble." [37]

Ch. 15:　If someone prays in a cloth marked with crosses or having pictures, does his prayer become annulled (thereby), and what is prohibited in regard to it

374 Anas reported: There was a curtain belonging to 'Ā'ishah with which she used to screen a side of her house. The Prophet ﷺ said: "Remove this curtain of yours from us because its pictures continue to present themselves (before me) during my prayer." [38]

---

[37] Anbajān is the name of a place which was known for its shawls and *anbijāniyyah* was a thick shawl which was made there. It appears that the border on the cloth consisted of some kind of picture or pattern because of which the Holy Prophet's attention was diverted. Mere borders could not have caused this diversion. It is known that the Holy Prophet used to wear striped clothes, and borders are also a kind of stripes. This ḥadīth incidentally shows the concentration of the Holy Prophet's devotion at the time of prayer. Anything that was likely to cause the slightest diversion was considered by him as an obstruction.

[38] The Holy Prophet disliked curtains with pictures on them because they were likely to divert attention during prayer. But he did not order anything beyond their removal. If pictures were entirely forbidden he would have said so in clear words. Cloth being marked with the cross, as mentioned in the chapter heading, is not to be found in this ḥadīth. Bukhārī has deduced this because it was a common practice in those days to have such pictures on the cloth, particularly that which came from Christian lands. Bukhārī has recorded a ḥadīth in the Book on Dress from 'Ā'ishah as follows: "The Messenger of Allāh would not leave in his house anything on which there would be the picture of the cross but he would break it" (h. 5952) and some have added the words "curtain or cloth" to this ḥadīth. The words in the chapter heading about the cross may refer to this ḥadīth. The Holy Prophet's anxiety to discard the picture of the cross points to his mission to demolish the doctrine of the crucifixion of Jesus. This ḥadīth also shows the desirability of keeping mosques free from unnecessary paintings and decorations. However, this does not mean that prayers cannot be said in a room with pictures on its walls or in front of pictures. All that it means is that pictures should not be so suspended before a person in prayer as to divert his attention. Anything causing such diversion should be removed.

Ch. 16:   One who says his prayers in a silk shirt with a slit (*farrāj ḥarīr*) and then takes it off

375 ʿUqbah ibn ʿĀmir reported: A silk shirt with a slit was brought to the Prophet ﷺ as a present and he put it on. Then he said prayers in it. When he finished, he took it off vehemently as if he disliked it and said: "It does not befit the righteous." [39]

Ch. 17:   Saying prayers in a red cloth

376 Abū Juḥaifah reported: I saw the Messenger of Allāh ﷺ in a red cloak made of leather, and I saw Bilāl taking the (remaining) water of the *Wuḍū'* of the Messenger of Allāh ﷺ, and I saw people in haste to take some of that water. So whoever got some of it, he rubbed it (on his own body) and whoever could not get anything of it, he took some of the moisture of the hand of his Companion. Then I saw Bilāl taking his javelin and fixing it (on the ground), and the Prophet ﷺ came out in a red cloak tucked up, and led the people in two *rak'ahs* of prayer with the javelin in front of him. I saw people and cattle moving about in front of the javelin.[40]

Ch.18:   Saying prayers on the roofs, pulpit and timber

    Abū ʿAbdullāh (Bukhārī) said: Al-Ḥasan did not see anything wrong in prayers being said on frozen water and bridges even if urine flowed underneath it or above it or in front of it, if there is a screen between them. Abū Hurairah said prayers on the roof of a mosque, following an Imām in prayer and Ibn ʿUmar said his prayers on ice.

377 Abū Ḥāzim related: People asked Sahl ibn Saʿd of what thing was the pulpit (of the Holy Prophet) made? He said: "No one among the surviving people is better aware of it than myself. It was of tamarisk tree of *al-Ghābah*

---

[39] This shows the Holy Prophet's disapproval of silk cloth. But it is also well known that the wearing of silk clothes by women is not forbidden, even to the most highly spiritual women. This shows that there is a difference in the external indicators of righteousness of a man and a woman. Nature has itself allotted different kinds of tasks to the two sexes to some extent. It also shows that the prohibition against wearing of silk cloth by men is not based on any spiritual impurity of this material, but it is for other reasons, chiefly that men are expected to be simpler in dress and bodily adornment than women, and to wear clothes in which they can do hard work.

[40] According to Ibn al-Qayyim, the cloth worn by the Holy Prophet on this occasion had red stripes on it. In any case, it means that the colour and design of the cloth being worn make no difference to the prayers. The incident of the people hastening for the remaining water from the *Wuḍū'* of the Holy Prophet took place at the time of the Truce of Ḥudaibiyah; see h. 187 and h. 189 and the footnotes there.

and it was made by so-and-so, the freed slave of so-and-so woman, for the Messenger of Allāh ﷺ.[41] When it was made and installed in its place, the Messenger of Allāh ﷺ stood upon it and faced the *Qiblah* and called out *Allāhu Akbar,* and the people stood behind him. Then he recited (the prayer) and went into *Rukū'* and people went into *Rukū'* behind him. Then he raised his head, then stepped back and prostrated on the ground. Then he returned to the pulpit, (recited the prayer), went into *Rukū',* raised his head, then stepped back and prostrated on the ground. So this is the story of it.[42]

Abū 'Abdullāh (Bukhārī) said that 'Alī ibn 'Abdullāh said: Aḥmad ibn Ḥanbal, may the mercy of Allāh be upon him, asked me about this ḥadīth, saying: "Do you mean that the Prophet ﷺ was on a higher level than the people, so there is no harm that the Imām should be in a higher place than the people according to this ḥadīth?" He said, so I said: "Sufyān ibn 'Uyainah used to be asked about this very often, did you not hear it from him?" He said: "No."

378 Anas ibn Mālik reported that the Messenger of Allāh ﷺ once fell down from his horse and his calf muscle or his shoulder was bruised. He took a vow to be away from his wives for a month, so he sat in the upper room (of his house),[43] the stairs of which were made of trunks of the date tree. His Companions came to visit him in his illness and he led them in prayer in a sitting posture while they were standing (in prayer). So when he invoked *Salām* (at the end of the prayer), he said: "The Imām is appointed to be followed: so when he says *Allāhu Akbar*, you must say *Allāhu Akbar,* and when he bows (in *Rukū'*), you must bow, and when he prostrates (in *Sajdah*), you must prostrate, and if he says his prayer standing, you must say your prayer standing." He came down (from the upper room) after twenty-nine days and people said: "O Messenger of Allāh, you vowed to keep aloof for a month." He said: "A month is also twenty-nine days." [44]

---

[41] *Ghābah*, literally meaning 'wood' or 'forest', is the name of a place near Madīnah. The wood, of which the Holy Prophet's pulpit was made, was brought from this particular place which seems to be famous for its wood.

[42] Bukhārī has deduced from this ḥadīth the permissibility of saying prayers on the roof of a house or a bridge etc. According to its repetition in h. 917, after finishing the prayer the Holy Prophet said to the people: "I have done this only so that you may follow me and learn my prayer." While it is possible that he kept himself on a higher level just for the people to see him clearly while in the act of prayer, the real object of this ḥadīth is that the Imām and the followers can, if required, be at different levels; for example, the Imām on a roof and the followers down below.

[43] The Holy Prophet was in the upper storey. This fact justifies the chapter heading that prayers can be said on the roof of a house.

[44] See h. 688, 689, 1910 and 1991 and the footnotes there. See also h. 5289.

Ch. 19: When the cloth of a man praying touches his wife while he is in prostration,

379 'Abdullāh ibn Shaddād reported from Maimūnah that she said: The Messenger of Allāh ﷺ would be saying his prayers and I would be in front of him while I had menstruation, and sometimes his clothes would touch me when he went into prostration. She said: He used to pray on a small mat.[45]

Ch. 20: Saying prayers on a mat (*ḥaṣīr*)

> Jābir ibn 'Abdullāh and Abū Sa'īd said their prayers in a boat while they were standing. Al-Ḥasan said: Say your prayers standing so long as it does not prove hard on your companions, turn with the boat or else say it sitting.[46]

380 Anas ibn Mālik reported that his grandmother Mulaikah invited the Messenger of Allāh ﷺ to a meal which she had prepared for him. He ate of it and then said: "Stand up so I may lead you in prayer." Anas said: So I stood up to get hold of a mat (*ḥaṣīr*) of ours which had become black by long use, and I washed it with water. The Messenger of Allāh ﷺ stood up and I made myself and an orphan into a line behind him and the old lady was behind us. So the Messenger of Allāh ﷺ led us in two *rak'ahs* of prayer, then he departed.

Ch. 21: Saying prayers on a small palm-leaf mat (*khumrah*)

381 'Abdullāh ibn Shaddād reported from Maimūnah that she said: The Prophet ﷺ used to pray on a small mat.[47]

Ch. 22: Saying prayers on the bed

> Anas ibn Mālik said his prayers on his bed, and he said: We used

---

[45] H. 333 has been repeated here with some difference of wording.

[46] What is applicable to the boat is also applicable to a moving carriage, either drawn by an animal or driven by power, whether on land or in the air. Of course, in a moving carriage there is the chance of falling down if standing to pray, and this very thought of falling down may distract attention from prayer. So it is better to say prayers sitting in such journeys. In those circumstances, a person should turn his face towards the *Qiblah* when starting the prayer, if it is possible to do so, and then maintain the same direction in the carriage regardless of any change in its direction as it travels during the prayer. If facing the *Qiblah* is not possible, it does not affect the validity of the prayers. In modern journeys prayers can be performed while sitting in a seat without the normal form of bowing or prostration. Prayers should be said in whatever posture a person can physically adopt, whether travelling in a carriage or if suffering from some bodily disability.

[47] This is a brief repetition of h. 333.

to say our prayers with the Prophet ﷺ and one of us used to prostrate on his own cloak.

382 ʿĀ'ishah, wife of the Prophet ﷺ, reported: I used to sleep in front of the Messenger of Allāh ﷺ and my two legs used to be in front of him. When he would go into prostration, he would press me and I would withdraw my legs, and when he would stand up, I would stretch them. She (further) said: There used to be no lamps in houses in those days.[48]

383 ʿĀ'ishah informed that the Messenger of Allāh ﷺ used to say his prayers on the bed of the people of his house, and she used to be lying between him and the *Qiblah* in the manner of a dead body at a funeral.[49]

384 ʿUrwah reported that the Prophet ﷺ used to say his prayers on the bed on which he and ʿĀ'ishah used to sleep, and she used to be lying between him and the *Qiblah*.

Ch. 23:   **Going in prostration on some cloth in excessive heat**

Al-Ḥasan said: People used to go into prostration on a turban and a cap, and their hands would be within their sleeves.[50]

385 Anas ibn Mālik reported: We used to say our prayers with the Prophet ﷺ and there would be one among us who would keep the end of his cloth at the place of prostration on account of excessive heat.

Ch. 24:   **Saying prayers with shoes on**

386 Abū Maslamah Saʿīd ibn Yazīd al-Azdiyy informed: I asked Anas ibn Mālik, "Did the Prophet ﷺ say his prayers with his shoes on?" He said: "Yes." [51]

---

[48] In other words, there being no light in the room the only way ʿĀ'ishah could know about the Holy Prophet's prostration was that his hands would touch her legs and she would have to withdraw them to make room for his prostration. This shows the simplicity of the living conditions of the Holy Prophet and the extreme sparseness of the environment in which Muslim prayers can be said. See also h. 513.

[49] The meaning of the previous ḥadīth, h. 382, and this ḥadīth appears to be the same, although h. 382 speaks of just the legs near the place of prostration while this speaks of the whole body of ʿĀ'ishah lying in front of the Holy Prophet like a dead body during a funeral prayer. Again, whereas this ḥadīth has the words "the bed of the people of his house", h. 384 which follows has the words: "on the bed on which the two of them (i.e., he and ʿĀ'ishah) used to sleep."

[50] In those early days there were no mats to cover the floor of a mosque which would thus naturally be extremely hot in summer. Hence it is that people used to keep something on the floor before they would go in prostration to prevent the skin of the forehead from being scorched by the heat of the floor.

[51] As stated in the previous footnote there were no mats in the mosques and people had to

Ch. 25:   Saying prayers with socks on

387 Hammām ibn al-Ḥārith related: I saw Jarīr ibn ʿAbdullāh passing urine, then performing ablution and wiping over his socks, then standing up and praying. He said on being asked: "I saw the Prophet ﷺ doing like this."

Ibrāhīm said: And this ḥadīth was to their liking because Jarīr was one of those who embraced Islām at the end.[52]

388 Al-Mughīrah ibn Shuʿbah reported: I helped the Prophet ﷺ to perform ablution and he wiped over his socks and said his prayers.

Ch. 26:   When prostrations are not completed (properly)

389 Ḥudhaifah reported that he saw a man not completing his *Rukūʿ* nor his prostrations (*Sujūd*). When he finished his prayer, Ḥudhaifah said to him: "You have not said your prayer." He (Abū Wāʾil, reporting from Ḥudhaifah) said: I think he also said: "If you were to die, you would die in a state of acting contrarily to the *Sunnah* of Muḥammad ﷺ."

---

pray on their rocky and sandy floors which would be very hot on a hot day. It was as a protection against this heat that the Holy Prophet would sometimes pray with his shoes on. Some have inferred from a report in Abū Dāwūd that Muslims should pray wearing shoes in order to "act differently from the Jews" (book: 'Prayer', h. 652). But such an inference is unwarranted because in that case the wearing of shoes in prayer would be for a particular need which no longer exists. In this age the floors of mosques are generally covered with mats or carpets. This being so, it is not only unnecessary to say one's prayers with shoes on but is also contrary to the rules of cleanliness unless it is too cold to take of the shoes, as is the case in the extremely cold climates in winter. In tropical countries, to enter the mosque with shoes on should be avoided. In a journey, of course, where no clean floor or ground is available for prayers, and one is wearing boots or full shoes, such footwear need not be removed. The circumstances should be taken into consideration in a particular case and one should not go to either extreme in this matter. It should neither be done as a matter of course nor regarded as entirely impermissible.

[52] The report of Jarīr was agreeable to the people because he was a person who had accepted Islām after the revelation of the rules of ablution as given in ch. 5 of the Qurʾān, *al-Māʾidah*. The meaning is that some people used to think that, although the wiping over the socks was permissible in the beginning, it was abrogated by this rule of ablution as given in this chapter. Jarīr, however, having embraced Islām after the revelation of these rules, his evidence about the Holy Prophet refuted their notion of abrogation and established that wiping over the socks continued to be permissible even after the revelation of the rules about ablution. This is explained in more detail in a report in Tirmidhī in his book of 'Purification' (ch. 70, h. 94), in which Jarīr says: "I did not accept Islām until after *al-Māʾidah*", when he saw the Holy Prophet wiping over his socks. It may be noted that *Wuḍūʾ* as performed and taught by the Holy Prophet even before the revelation in the Qurʾān was the same as that described in this revelation, which came only to confirm that he had been already acting under Divine guidance as received by him through his "inner" form of revelation.

Ch. 27:   Keeping the arms open and away from the sides in prostration

390 ʿAbdullāh ibn Mālik ibn Buḥainah reported that the Prophet ﷺ, when he said his prayers, used to keep his hands so far apart from the body that the whiteness of his armpits was visible.

Ch. 28:   The excellence of facing the *Qiblah*

His toes should face the *Qiblah,* reported Abū Ḥumaid from the Prophet ﷺ.

391 Anas ibn Mālik reported that the Messenger of Allāh ﷺ said: "Whoever says prayers as we pray, and faces our *Qiblah,* and eats the meat as slaughtered by us, that is a Muslim who has the security of Allāh and the security of the Messenger of Allāh ﷺ. So do not be unfaithful to Allāh as regards the security granted by Him." [53]

392 Anas ibn Mālik reported that the Messenger of Allāh ﷺ said: "I have been commanded that I should fight the people till they say 'There is no god but Allāh'. If they say so, and say prayers as we pray, and face our *Qiblah,* and eat the meat as slaughtered by us, it has been forbidden to us to violate their blood or their property except in the course of justice, and their accounting (of their beliefs and deeds) will be with Allāh." [54]

---

[53] That is to say, no detailed investigation should be set up in determining if a person is a Muslim. It should be a broad measure as laid down here. If someone is seen to be praying as Muslims are required to do, facing the *Qiblah* they face, and to eat meat as slaughtered by Muslims, he is entitled to all the rights and privileges of the brotherhood of Islām. It is unknown on what basis Muslim clerics have adopted the practice of declaring Muslims as *kāfir* (unbelievers) and outside the fold of Islām on all kinds of issues. To do so is to be "unfaithful to Allāh as regards the security granted by Him". A disregard of this broad principle and the pernicious habit of declaring Muslims as heretic on minor differences of belief and practice has brought about disintegration in the Muslim fraternity. The words of this ḥadīth are a standing prohibition against the issuing of *fatwas* of unbelief against fellow Muslims.

[54] H. 25 has been repeated here with some differences. There the whole formula of faith has been mentioned, "there is no god but Allāh and that Muḥammad is the Messenger of Allāh", while here only the first part is given. There *Zakāt* is mentioned after prayer but not here; and here *Qiblah* and slaughtering is mentioned but not in h. 25. This ḥadīth should not be taken to mean that a Muslim who is not found to say his prayers regularly or who does not eat the meat as slaughtered by Muslims should be considered as outside the pale of Islām. All that it means is that a believer should adhere to these teachings. Nor does this ḥadīth mean that those who are outside the pale of Islām shall have no security of life, property or honour at the hands of the Muslims. See the footnote under h. 25 for fuller explanation. Such a distorted meaning is belied by the actions of the Holy Prophet Muḥammad himself. He signed the peace treaty of Ḥudaibiyah with the unbelievers, and at the conquest of Makkah he granted pardon to the unbelievers who had been bitter enemies of the Muslims. These actions would be directly contrary to his statement in this ḥadīth if he had meant that he has been commanded by Allāh to fight people till they accept Islām.

393 Ḥumaid related that Maimūn ibn Siyāh asked Anas ibn Mālik: "O Abū Ḥamzah, What makes the blood of a person and his property inviolable?" He replied: "Whoever bears witness that 'There is no god but Allāh', and faces our *Qiblah,* and says prayers as we pray, and eats the meat as slaughtered by us, he is a Muslim. For him are the rights of a Muslim, and upon him are the obligations of a Muslim." [55]

Ch. 29:   The *Qiblah* of the people of Madīnah and of the people of Syria and the East

> *Qiblah* does not lie in the east or in the west[56] because of the saying of the Prophet ﷺ: "Turn not your faces towards the *Qiblah* while you are in the toilet or while passing urine but turn your faces towards the east or towards the west."

394 Abū Ayyūb al-Anṣārī reported that the Prophet ﷺ said: "When you go to the toilet, you should not face the *Qiblah* nor turn your back towards it; but you should face either towards the east or the west." Abū Ayyūb said: "We arrived in Syria and we found toilets constructed facing the *Qiblah*, so we turned round (when using them) and asked the forgiveness of Allāh, the Most High." [57]

Ch. 30:   The word of Allāh, the Most High: "And take the place of Abraham as a place of prayer" (2:125) [58]

395–396 ʿAmr ibn Dīnār related: We asked Ibn ʿUmar whether a man who has made circuits of the Kaʿbah for *ʿUmrah* but has not gone between the Ṣafā and the Marwah, can have intercourse with his wife. He said: "The Prophet ﷺ came (to Makkah) and made circuits of the Kaʿbah seven times, then

---

[55] This is a repetition of h. 391 with different wording.

[56] In other words, the *Qiblah* of the people of Madīnah and those of Syria is not east or west, as they live north of the Kaʿbah. Only for those people who live to the east or the west of the Kaʿbah is the *Qiblah* to the west and east respectively.

[57] This is a repetition of h. 144 with the additional words of Abī Ayyūb at the end.

[58] The object of citing these words of the Qurʾān is to show that it contains the commandment of turning the face towards the Kaʿbah in prayer. Thus Mujāhid is of the view that *Maqām Ibrāhīm* or the place of Abraham means the House of Kaʿbah and not merely the particular spot which goes by this name. Although the first ḥadīth of this chapter does not clearly indicate this but those that follow make this point clear, because these latter two, h. 397 and h. 398, make no mention of *Maqām Ibrāhīm* but rather say that the Holy Prophet came out of the Kaʿbah and said two *rakʿahs* of prayer in front of it. The last words of h. 398 about the Kaʿbah, "This is the *Qiblah*", make clear that the verse in this chapter heading contains the command to make the Kaʿbah the *Qiblah.*

he said two *rak'ahs* of prayer behind the place (of Abraham) and went between the Ṣafā and the Marwah" and (he added:) "Certainly you have in the Messenger of Allāh an excellent exemplar" (the Qur'ān, 33:21). [396] And we asked Jābir ibn 'Abdullāh and he said: "He should not approach his wife (for intercourse) before going between the Ṣafā and the Marwah." [59]

397 Mujāhid said: Someone came to Ibn 'Umar and told him: "This is the Messenger of Allāh ﷺ who has entered the Ka'bah." Ibn 'Umar said: So I reached there and the Prophet ﷺ had gone out. I found Bilāl standing between the two doors and I asked Bilāl, saying to him: "Did the Prophet ﷺ say his prayer inside the Ka'bah?" He said: "Yes, two *rak'ahs* between the two pillars that stand on the left as you enter, then he came out and said two *rak'ahs* of prayer in front of the Ka'bah."

398 'Aṭā' reported: I heard Ibn 'Abbās say: "When the Prophet ﷺ entered the House of Ka'bah he called (on Allāh) in all its sides and did not say prayers until he came out of it. When he came out, he said two *rak'ahs* of prayer in front of the Ka'bah and said: "This is the *Qiblah*." [60]

Ch. 31: To face the *Qiblah* wherever one may be

Abū Hurairah said that the Prophet ﷺ said: "Turn your faces towards the *Qibla* and call out *Allāhu Akbar*." [61]

399 Al-Barā' ibn 'Āzib reported: The Messenger of Allāh ﷺ said his prayers facing towards the *Bait al-Maqdis* for sixteen months or seventeen months; and the Messenger of Allāh ﷺ was desirous of turning his face towards the Ka'bah. So Allāh revealed: "Indeed, We see the turning of your face to heaven" (2:144). So he turned towards the Ka'bah. "The fools among the people" — and they were the Jews — said: "What has turned them from

---

[59] See also h. 1623–1624, 1645–1646 and 1793–1794.

[60] According to the previous report the Holy Prophet said his prayer inside the Ka'bah and the report comes from Bilāl who accompanied him, so this should be accepted. Ibn 'Abbās had not gone in with the Holy Prophet, so he could only say what the Holy Prophet did after he had come out of the Sacred House. The previous reports show that according to Bukhārī, *Maqām Ibrāhīm* or the place of Abraham means the Ka'bah itself, and not just the spot known by that name. In h. 395 it is stated by Ibn 'Umar that the Holy Prophet said his prayer "behind the place (of Abraham)". This respect was due evidently not particularly to the spot going under this name but to the whole area of the Ka'bah.

[61] It is not of the fundamentals of religion to turn the face towards the *Qiblah* in prayer. Had it been so, all religions should have had only one *Qiblah*. The last and universal religion given to man in the form of Islām appointed the Ka'bah as the *Qiblah* because this happens to be the earliest house of worship and also happens to be in the centre of the inhabited world. This was to bring about the unity of mankind. The House of Ka'bah may or may not be there, but the direction is an essential need. The House in itself as a building has nothing to do with the worship.

their *Qiblah* which they had? Say: The East and the West belong only to Allāh. He guides whom He pleases to the right path?" (2 : 142).

A man said his prayer with the Prophet ﷺ and went out after he had said the prayer. He passed by a group of the *Anṣār* who were saying their *'Aṣr* prayer facing towards the *Bait al-Maqdis.* So he said that he bore witness that he had said his prayers with the Messenger of Allāh ﷺ who had turned his face towards the Kaʿbah. Then those people turned round till they faced towards the Kaʿbah.[62]

400 Jābir ibn ʿAbdullāh reported: The Messenger of Allāh ﷺ used to say his prayers on his mount, in whichever direction it was facing; and when he intended to say the obligatory prayer he would alight and turn his face towards the *Qiblah.*[63]

401 ʿAbdullāh (ibn Masʿūd) reported that the Prophet ﷺ said his prayer — Ibrāhīm said: I do not know whether he (the Holy Prophet) said more of it or less (than he should have) — so when he finished it with *Salām* he was asked: "O Messenger of Allāh, has anything new happened to the prayer?" He said: "And what is that?" They said: "You said this much of prayer." At this he turned on his feet, faced the *Qiblah* and performed two prostrations,[64] and then finished it with *Salām.* When he turned his face towards us, he said:

---

[62] See also h. 40. Some people have held the view that when the Holy Prophet was in Makkah he used to turn towards the Kaʿbah for his *Qiblah* and that when he went over to Madīnah he began to turn his face towards the *Bait al-Maqdis* at Jerusalem and this continued for sixteen or seventeen months after which he was commanded by Allāh to make the Kaʿbah his *Qiblah,* and that thus there were two changes of the *Qiblah.* In fact, there was no change of commandment even once because there had never been a command to face the *Bait al-Maqdis.* Even when at Makkah he would at times face the Kaʿbah when he would not have to turn his back towards the *Bait al-Maqdis.* It was the *Qiblah* of the People of the Book, and he as a Prophet could not have disregarded it without some clear ordinance of God. And this ordinance to turn towards the Sacred Mosque at Makkah came only once and it was for good. All his actions before this ordinance were based on his personal judgment.

[63] That is to say, the Holy Prophet used to say his optional prayers on the camel and the direction would, therefore, change as the camel changed its course, but so far as the obligatory prayers were concerned he would alight on the ground for their performance, to turn his face towards the *Qiblah.* This shows that the Quranic ordinance for turning towards the Kaʿbah for prayers applies to obligatory prayers. But even in this case it applies when it is possible. It has already been seen that even in obligatory prayers, when travelling in a moving vehicle, any direction may be faced. See also h. 1094 and h. 1099.

[64] According to the last ḥadīth of the next chapter (h. 404), the Holy Prophet said five *rakʿahs* in his *Ẓuhr* prayer instead of four, and that he turned his face towards the Kaʿbah to perform the two additional prostrations that are required in case a mistake is made in the prayer. This shows that in prostrations and similar devout postures, a person should turn his face towards the *Qiblah,* if he is able to do so.

"If anything new had happened in the matter of prayer, I would have told you about it, but I am only a mortal like you, I forget as you forget. So when I forget remind me, and when anyone of you is in doubt about his prayer, he should seek what appears to be correct, and complete it (from that point). Then he should finish with *Salām,* and then perform prostration twice." [65]

Ch. 32: What has been enjoined about the Qiblah?

And one who does not consider it necessary to repeat (prayers) after he forgetfully says his prayer in a direction other than the *Qiblah.* The Prophet ﷺ finished with *Salām* after saying two *rak'ahs* in the *Ẓuhr* prayer and turned his face towards the people and completed what he had missed of it.

402 Anas ibn Mālik reported that 'Umar said: My view turned out to be in accord with that of my Lord in three things. I said: "O Messenger of Allāh, I wish we had taken the place of Abraham as our place of prayer", so it was revealed: "Take the Place of Abraham (*Maqām Ibrāhīm*) for a place of prayer" (the Qur'ān, 2:125).[66] And the verse on seclusion, I said: "O Messenger of Allāh, I wish you had told your wives that they should be in seclusion, for

---

[65] That is to say, one should decide upon what should have been the right thing to do in the prayer in question and should rectify the mistake of omission or addition and then go in for two extra prostrations as an atonement for the mistake committed. See further Book 22 of Bukhārī, 'Forgetting during Prayer'.

[66] The description *Maqām Ibrāhīm* has been given three different meanings: (1) the particular spot known by this name, (2) the Ka'bah itself, and (3) the whole of the sacred area known as the *Ḥaram.* Evidently 'Umar did not mean that the Holy Prophet said the two *rak'ahs* of prayer at the exact place known as *Maqām Ibrāhīm* as the Holy Prophet was in Madīnah. His object was to indicate the desirability of making the Sacred House of Ka'bah as the direction of prayer. Bukhārī brings this verse in his chapter the heading of which refers to the *Qiblah,* thus showing that he does not take *Maqām Ibrāhīm* to mean just that particular spot. The words of the Qur'ān, "turn then your face towards the Sacred Mosque" (2:144), prove conclusively that by *Maqām Ibrāhīm* the Sacred Mosque is meant.

In *Fatḥ al-Bārī* it is stated that it was on fifteen occasions on which the suggestions of 'Umar turned out to accord with what Allāh later revealed. In Bukhārī itself, apart from the three incidents mentioned here, there are other such cases recorded; for example, on the question of whether or not to say funeral prayers over the bodies of the hypocrites. It is reported from Ibn 'Umar in Tirmidhī (book: *Manāqib* — 'Virtues', h. 4046) that, during the life of the Holy Prophet, whenever any matter came before the people and they gave different opinions, it would be the opinion of 'Umar which would later be confirmed by a revelation in the Qur'ān. The fact is that the very nature of some believers closely resembles that of the Holy Prophet, and such a person is called a *muḥaddath.* 'Umar was one of the persons of this rank as declared by the Holy Prophet (see Bukhārī, h. 3689 in the book: 'Virtues of the Companions'), and hence it is that the Holy Prophet also said of him: "If there were to be a prophet after me, it would have been 'Umar" (Tirmidhī, book: 'Virtues', h. 4050).

surely the good as well as the bad people talk to them." So came the verse on seclusion. And the wives of the Prophet ﷺ united in making demands on him, and I said to them: "Maybe, his Lord, if he divorce you, will give him in your place wives better than you, submitting (to Allāh)" (65:5)," so this verse was revealed.[67]

403 ʿAbdullāh ibn ʿUmar reported: Once when the people were at morning prayer at Qubā', suddenly a man came to them and said: "The Messenger of Allāh ﷺ has received revelation of the Qur'ān at night and he has been commanded to face towards the Kaʿbah (in prayer)." So they faced towards it. Their faces were towards Syria, so they turned towards the Kaʿbah.[68]

404 ʿAbdullāh (ibn Masʿūd) reported that the Prophet ﷺ said the *Ẓuhr* prayer with five *rak'ahs*. People asked: "Has there been an increase in the prayer?" He said: "And what is that?" They said: "You prayed five *rak'ahs*." At this he turned on his feet and performed two prostrations.[69]

Ch. 33: Scraping off the spittle with hand from the mosque

405 Anas ibn Mālik reported that the Prophet ﷺ saw some phlegm before him (on the wall). It made him annoyed, so much so that this (feeling) was visible on his face. So he stood up and scraped it off with his hand and said: "When anyone of you stands for his prayer, he is privately communicating with his Lord — or surely his Lord is between him and the *Qiblah* — so none of you should spit towards his *Qiblah*[70] but towards his left or underneath his

---

[67] The explanation of these two issues, seclusion and the united action of the wives of the Holy Prophet, will be given later in the book: 'Commentary on the Qur'ān', on chapters 33 and 66 respectively.

[68] This incidentally shows the highest degree of obedience of the Companions to the Holy Prophet. No command produced reluctance in their hearts in obeying it.

[69] This is a repetition of h. 401 in which it was not clearly stated whether the Holy Prophet increased or decreased the prayers from the prescribed amount. Here it is made clear that he said five *rak'ahs* for the *Ẓuhr* prayer instead of four.

[70] It is in the interest of good manners that spitting is forbidden towards the *Qiblah* because in the state of prayer a man is like one who is standing in the court of a king and submitting his petition. This is the meaning of the words: "Surely his Lord is between him and the *Qiblah*." As for spitting under the left foot, it was suggested in view of the fact that in those days the floor of the mosque was made of loose bricks and stone pieces, which would cover the spit. Of course, in a cemented or paved floor such spitting is out of place. The best method is, therefore, the one shown by the Holy Prophet himself, namely, to spit on a corner of one's cloak or, to speak in terms of modern life, on a handkerchief and clean it later on outside the mosque. The Holy Prophet's scraping the phlegm with his own hands means he did it himself. As stated in h. 408 and

foot." Then he took an end of his cloak, and spat on it, then folded it over, and said: "Or he can do like this."

406 'Abdullāh ibn 'Umar reported that the Messenger of Allāh ﷺ saw spittle on the wall of the *Qiblah,* so he scraped it off. Then he faced the people and said: "Whenever any of you is saying prayers, he should not spit in front of him, for Allāh is surely in front of him when he prays." [71]

407 'Ā'ishah reported that the Messenger of Allāh ﷺ saw on the wall of the *Qiblah* nasal discharge or spittle or phlegm, so he scraped it off.[72]

Ch. 34:   Scraping off nasal discharge from the mosque with a pebble

> Ibn 'Abbās said: If you tread upon wet filth, then wash it and if it is dry then there is no need.[73]

408–409 Ḥumaid ibn 'Abdur Raḥmān reported that Abū Hurairah and Abū Sa'īd related to him that the Messenger of Allāh ﷺ saw phlegm on the wall of the mosque, so he took a pebble and scraped it off. He said: "If any of you want to spit, he should neither spit in front of him nor towards his right. Let him spit towards his left or underneath his left foot." [74]

Ch. 35:   A person should not spit on his right during his prayer

410-411 Ḥumaid ibn 'Abdur Raḥmān reported that Abū Hurairah and Abū Sa'īd informed him that the Messenger of Allāh ﷺ saw phlegm on the wall of the mosque, so the Messenger of Allāh ﷺ took a pebble and scraped it off. Then he said: "If any of you want to spit, he should neither spit in front of him nor towards his right. Let him spit towards his left or underneath his left foot."

409, he did this scraping using a stone-piece. This incident shows that the Holy Prophet, inspite of his exalted position, both as the religious head and the king of the nation, did not, in any way, feel it beneath his dignity to do such trivial things as the removing of a filthy matter from the walls of a mosque. This is indeed an example worthy to be emulated by men in high position, particularly those of religious circles. This also shows his anxiety for the maintenance of a high standard of cleanliness in the mosques. Another report bearing on this subject tells us further that not satisfied with the cleaning, he also sent for some saffron and had it rubbed on the spot that was cleaned (Abū Dāwūd, book: 'Prayer', h. 479).

[71] This is a repetition of h. 405 in brief with difference in wording.

[72] This again is a repetition of h. 405 in brief with difference in wording. The words used in h. 405 to 407 are, respectively, *nukhāmah* (phlegm), *buṣāq* (spittle) and *mukhāṭ* (nasal discharge, such as mucus).

[73] Apparently, the comment by Ibn 'Abbās has no connection with the chapter heading. It is possible that the connection is that since there is nothing wrong in walking over dry filth, there can be no harm in scraping dried phlegm by hand.

[74] This is a repetition of h. 405 with some additional words.

412 Anas (ibn Mālik) said that the Prophet ﷺ said: "None of you should spit in front of him or towards his right, but (he could spit) towards his left or underneath his foot.[75]

Ch. 36:   A person should spit towards his left or under his left foot

413 Anas ibn Mālik said that the Prophet ﷺ said: "A believer, when he is praying, is privately communicating with his Lord. He should neither spit in front of him nor towards his right, but (he could spit) towards his left or underneath his foot." [76]

414 Abū Saʻīd reported that the Prophet ﷺ saw some phlegm on the wall of the mosque. So he scraped it off with a pebble. Then he forbade that a man should spit in front of himself or towards his right, but (he could spit) towards his left or underneath his left foot.[77]

Ch. 37:   The penance for spitting in the mosque

415 Anas ibn Mālik said that the Prophet ﷺ said: "It is a sin to spit in the mosque and the penance for it is to bury it." [78]

Ch. 38:   The burying of phlegm in the mosque

416 Abū Hurairah reported from the Prophet ﷺ that he said: "When anyone of you stands for prayer, he should not spit in front of him, for he is privately communicating with Allāh so long as he is in the place of his prayer, nor towards his right, for on his right is an angel. Let him spit towards his left or underneath his foot, and bury it." [79]

---

[75] H. 410–411, 412 are repetitions of h. 405. H. 412 is in the form of an injunction.

[76] This repetition of h. 405 is abbreviated.

[77] This repetition of h. 405 is similar to h. 408–409.

[78] The word "bury" shows that the floor of the mosque in those days used to be of loose materials. The aim was to keep the mosque clean whatever the method adopted. Apart from the respect due to a place of worship, a mosque is also a place where people gather and as diseases may spread through spitting it is inappropriate to do so in such places. Such a sense of cleanliness is a feature of modern scientific civilization. That a teacher of religion and spiritual guide should be so particular about this in the seventh century C.E. is truly amazing and one of the many proofs of the perfection of religion at the hands of the Holy Prophet Muḥammad.

[79] This is a repetition of h. 405 in different words. Its last words "bury it" give rise to the chapter heading.

Ch. 39: When the spittle comes irresistibly, one should take it in a side of one's cloth

417 Anas (ibn Mālik) reported that the Prophet ﷺ saw some phlegm before him, so he scraped it off with his hand. He showed dislike — or (the narrator said) because of it his severe dislike appeared on him. He said: "When anyone of you stands for his prayer, he is privately communicating with his Lord — or his Lord is between him and the *Qiblah* — so he should not spit towards his *Qiblah* but towards his left or underneath his foot." Then he took an end of his cloak, and spat on it, folded it over, and said: "Or he can do like this." [80]

Ch. 40: The Imām admonishing the people for the completion of the prayer and a mention of the *Qiblah*

418 Abū Hurairah reported that the Messenger of Allāh ﷺ said: "Do you think my *Qiblah* to be here (i.e., I am looking ahead)? By Allāh, neither your submissiveness (to God) nor your bowing is hidden from me, for surely I see you from behind my back." [81]

419 Anas ibn Mālik reported: The Prophet ﷺ led us in prayer and then he mounted the pulpit and said as regards the people's prayer and the bowing: "I can surely see you behind me as I see you (now)." [82]

Ch. 41: Can it be said: "It is the mosque of such and such a clan"?

420 ʿAbdullāh ibn ʿUmar reported that the Messenger of Allāh ﷺ held a race between horses that were trained for the purpose from al-Ḥafyā' ending at Thaniyyah al-Wadāʿ, and he (also) held a race of horses that were not trained from Thaniyyah to the mosque of Banū Zuraiq, and that ʿAbdullāh ibn ʿUmar was among those who competed in the race.[83]

---

[80] This is a repetition of h. 405 with only a slight difference of wording. Although there is no specific mention in it of the urgent need for spitting as in the chapter heading, it is evident that spitting during prayer is not allowed unless it is absolutely unavoidable.

[81] This should not be taken to mean that the Holy Prophet could actually see things happening behind his back, because in the Qur'ān he is instructed to tell people: "I am only a mortal like you" (18:110). It was rather through spiritual vision that he could perceive the spiritual devotion or otherwise of those who followed him in prayer. Also in a general way, the relationship between the Imām and the congregation is so close that the humility and concentration of the one has an effect on that of the other. With the sensitive mind that the Holy Prophet had, he could perceive the spiritual state of those praying behind him. See also h. 718, 719, 741 and 742.

[82] This is a repetition of h. 418.

[83] The object of the chapter is to show that there is no harm is calling a mosque by the name

Ch. 42: **Distribution (of goods and wealth) and hanging of bunches of dates (*qinw*) in the mosque**

Abū 'Abdullāh (Bukhārī) said: *Qinw* means bunch and its dual form is *qinwān*, and its plural is also *qinwān,* as with the words *ṣinw* (singular) and *ṣinwān* (dual and plural).

421 Anas (ibn Mālik) reported: Riches from Baḥrain were brought to the Prophet ﷺ and he said: "Place it in the Mosque"; and it was the largest quantity of riches that was ever brought to the Messenger of Allāh ﷺ. Then the Messenger of Allāh ﷺ came out for prayer and he took no notice of it. When he finished the prayer he came and sat by it, and he gave out of it to anyone he saw.[84] At that moment 'Abbās came to him and said: "O Messenger of Allāh, give me (something too), for surely I paid the ransom for myself and also for 'Aqīl.[85] The Messenger of Allāh ﷺ said to him, "Take." So he put

---

of some clan or community, as "the mosque of Banū Zuraiq" is mentioned. However, there is the danger of such mosques being regarded as the property of the persons or communities to whom they are ascribed, excluding other Muslims from praying in them. A mosque should be treated as the common property of all the believers of the world, and no one should be barred from saying his prayer in it, whatever sect or school of thought he may belong to. The Qur'ān issues the following warning against this: "And who is more unjust than he who prevents (people) from the mosques of Allah, from His name being remembered in them..." (2:114). To name a mosque after a person or a society for the sake of identifying it is, of course, not objectionable.

The places mentioned are situated near Madīnah, the distance between the first two being six miles and between the next two being one mile. The holding of the race shows that the Holy Prophet wanted to keep Muslims prepared for confrontation with their enemies.

[84] This money was taxes given by the people in Baḥrain and amounted to one hundred thousand Dirhams. The Holy Prophet distributed it so liberally among the believers that by the evening nothing was left there. This does not mean that nothing at all should be kept in the public exchequer. This was the first money coming from a foreign land, Muslims were hard up and the Holy Prophet distributed it among those who had made great sacrifices of their possessions at the time of dire need for Islām. The Holy Prophet also set an example of equality by making no distinction between the great and the small in this connection. It can also be seen that the Holy Prophet himself was absolutely indifferent towards this heap of money. Then the Muslims are shown here to be so strictly honest and devoid of greed that all this cash money needed no guard or locked room to protect it and it was lying in a heap in the courtyard of the Mosque. The critics of Islām who accuse the Muslims of fighting for material gain and booty should cast a glance at these incidents. Far from these being inspired by any greed for pelf, they were a band of saints, so to speak, who had no attraction for anything material or worldly. Like their illustrious leader they lived and died for values purely spiritual.

[85] 'Abbās was an uncle of the Holy Prophet and was deeply attached to him from the very beginning of his life. Although he did not become a Muslim when the Holy Prophet was called to the office, yet he had great sympathy for his nephew and was anxious for his safety when he and his followers came under the severe persecution of the Makkans. When the people of Madīnah swore their protection to the Holy Prophet, it was 'Abbās who negotiated this solemn contract. In the battle of Badr, he being from among the unbelieving Quraish, came with the

(the riches) on his cloth with his joined hands and started lifting it but was not able to do so. He said: "O Messenger of Allāh, order some people to lift it on to me," but he (the Prophet) said: "No". He said: "Then lift it yourself on to me." He (the Prophet) said: "No." So he took something out of it and then started lifting it. He (again) said: 'O Messenger of Allāh, order some people to lift it on to me." He (the Prophet) said: "No." He said: "Then lift it yourself on to me." He (the Prophet) said: "No." So he took something out of it, and then lifted it and placed it on his shoulders and left. The Messenger of Allāh ﷺ continued to gaze at him till he disappeared from our sight, wondering at his greed. And the Messenger of Allāh ﷺ did not rise from his seat so long as there remained even one Dirham of it.

Ch. 43:   One who is invited to a meal when he is in the mosque and he accepts the invitation[86]

422 Anas (ibn Mālik) said: I found the Prophet ﷺ in the Mosque and with him were some people. I stood and he said to me: "Has Abū Ṭalḥah sent you?" I said: "Yes." He said: For a meal?" I said: "Yes." Then he said to those around him: "Get up (let us all go)." So he departed and I went ahead of him.[87]

---

enemy army and when it was defeated by the Holy Prophet he was taken prisoner and had accordingly to pay his ransom as well as that of 'Aqīl, the brother of 'Alī. He was treated just like the other prisoners of war. It is this ransom that this ḥadīth refers to. Later on, however, he proved a very dashing soldier of Islām and was one of the most trusted of the Holy Prophet's Companions. Despite this, he seems to have had some weakness for wealth. The Holy Prophet was naturally surprised because this kind of weakness was evidently rare among the Companions.

[86] The heading of this chapter and the ḥadīth recorded under it show that Bukhārī is anxious to prove that mosques are not devoted exclusively to prayers but can equally be the venue of many kinds of communal assemblies and affairs of the Muslims. The Holy Prophet himself had lodged foreign deputations in his Mosque at Madīnah. The distribution of public money is also reported in h. 421 to have taken place in this Mosque, and here it is mentioned that people who were in the Mosque were invited to go to someone's house for a meal. The fact is that from the very beginning mosques were intended to be centres of Muslim national activities and have been used for the welfare of the believers, not only spiritual but also educational, social, cultural and of all other kinds. In the Holy Prophet's own time and even after him the consultations for national affairs used to be held in the mosque and it was also a centre for religious education. Libraries used to be attached to these mosques. This tradition should be revived and kept up.

[87] H. 422 has been repeated later on in detail in h. 3578 in the book 'Virtues' (*Manāqib*) under its chapter on 'Signs of Prophethood in Islām'. According to those details, Anas had been sent by Abū Ṭalḥah with food for the Holy Prophet at a time when Muslims were very short of food. But instead of taking it himself, the Holy Prophet who was in the Mosque got up and took the people with him to the house of Abū Ṭalḥah and his wife Umm Sulaim (who was also Anas's mother). There was only a little food in their house but due to a miracle of the Holy Prophet it increased so much that some seventy or eighty people were fed.

Ch. 44:   Giving judgments and invoking mutual curse (*al-liʿān*) between husband and wife in the mosque

423 Sahl ibn Saʿd reported that a man said: "O Messenger of Allāh, what do you think of a man who finds another man with his wife, should he (the husband) kill him?" Then they (the husband and the wife) both invoked curses on one another in the mosque and I was present.[88]

Ch. 45:   When a person enters a house, should he pray wherever he wants, or wherever he is asked to pray and should not indulge in investigation (of the house)?

424 ʿItbān ibn Mālik reported that the Prophet ﷺ came to his house and said: "Where do you like me to say my prayer in your house?" He added (in his report): So I pointed to him a place. The Prophet ﷺ proclaimed *Allāhu Akbar* and we lined up behind him and said two *rakʿahs* of prayer.[89]

Ch. 46:   Mosques in houses

Al-Barāʾ ibn ʿĀzib said his prayers in the mosque of his house in congregation

425 Maḥmūd ibn ar-Rabīʿ al-Anṣārī informed[90] that ʿItbān ibn Mālik, who was one of the Companions of the Messenger of Allāh ﷺ and among those who were in the Battle of Badr from among the *Anṣar,* went to the Messenger of Allāh ﷺ and said: "O Messenger of Allāh, my eyesight has become weakened and I lead my people in prayer, so when it rains and water flows in the low ground that lies between me and them, I am unable to go to their mosque to lead them in prayer, and I would like you, O Messenger of Allāh, to come here and say your prayer in my house and I make it a place of prayer." The Messenger of Allāh ﷺ said to him: "I shall do so, if Allāh wills."

ʿItbān said: So the next day the Messenger of Allāh ﷺ and Abū Bakr came to me when the sun had risen high, and the Messenger of Allāh ﷺ asked permission (to enter) and I gave him permission. He did not sit when he

---

[88] H. 423 occurs in more detail in h. 5259, h. 5308 and h. 5309 in the book 'Divorce'. *Liʿān* or the procedure of mutual cursing between husband and wife, mentioned in the Qurʾān in 24 : 6–9, takes place when the husband accuses his wife of adultery, of which he is an eye-witness, and the wife denies the charge. Both are required to swear on oath that their respective statements are true and each invokes the curse of God on whoever is the liar. After this procedure, the marriage tie is terminated.

[89] This is a very brief version of the next ḥadīth, h. 425. The Holy Prophet prayed in the place that he was asked to, without enquiring further.

[90] For a longer version of this ḥadīth, see h. 1185–1186. See also h. 839–840.

entered the house but said: "Where do you like me to say my prayer in your house?" I pointed to him a side of the house and the Messenger of Allāh ﷺ stood up and proclaimed *Allāhu Akbar*. We stood and lined up and he said two *rak'ahs* of prayer, and then finished with *Salām*.[91] We detained him for some *khazīrah* (a meat pie) which we had prepared for him.[92] Then some men from the neighbourhood came in the house and gathered there. One of them said: "Where is Mālik ibn ad-Dukhaishin or ibn ad-Dukhshun?"[93] Some of them said: "He is a hypocrite who does not love Allāh and His Messenger." The Messenger of Allāh ﷺ said: "Do not say that. Have you not seen that he says 'There is no god but Allāh' (*Lā ilāha ill-Allāh*), desiring thereby the pleasure of Allāh?" He (that man) said: "Allāh and His Messenger know best. We surely see his attention and well wishes for the hypocrites." The Messenger of Allāh ﷺ said: "Surely Allāh has forbidden the fire for the one who says: 'There is no god but Allāh', seeking thereby the pleasure of Allāh."[94]

Ch. 47:   To begin with the right step in entering the mosque etc.

Ibn 'Umar used to begin with his right foot and when he would come out he would begin with his left foot.[95]

---

[91] This shows that there are occasions when optional (*nafl*) prayers can be said in congregation, although usually the Holy Prophet used to say such prayers by himself without any congregation behind him.

[92] *Khazīrah*, according to *Fatḥ al-Bārī*, is prepared in the following manner: The meat is made into very small pieces and boiled in a large quantity of water. When the meat has thoroughly softened, flour is sprinkled on it.

[93] Mālik ibn ad-Dukhaishin (or Mālik ibn ad-Dukhshun) is reported to be one who had taken part in the Battle of Badr. Ibn Isḥāq has written in his *Maghāzī* that he was one of the two men whom the Holy Prophet had sent to burn the mosque erected by the intriguers in the outskirts of Madīnah known as *masjid-an ḍirār-an* in the Qur'ān, 9:107. In the meeting referred to in this ḥadīth, there was someone who had become suspicious about him just because he had seen him mixing with some known hypocrites. But even this suspicion was distasteful to the Holy Prophet and he gave the ruling that no one who testified to the Muslim formula of faith should be suspected in this way.

[94] There is much food for thought here for the Muslim religious leaders who dub any Muslim a *kāfir* or unbeliever if he happens to differ from the popular interpretation of some aspect of Islām. Although the Holy Prophet has attached the condition of a person's believing in the *Kalimah* with the object of winning God's pleasure, yet anyone who has not been converted to Islām through coercion and professes Islām without any compulsion must be regarded as doing so only for the sake of God's pleasure. And when he is thus a *bona fide* Muslim, according to the interpretation of the Holy Prophet nothing can turn him out of the fold of Islām, whatever the differences in his interpretation of the faith, and however short he falls of acting on its teachings.

[95] This is a requirement of good manners and the Holy Prophet himself and his Companions were never amiss even in these small details. It is polished behaviour carried to perfection. It has

426 'Ā'ishah reported: The Prophet ﷺ loved to start with the right side, if he could, in every affair of his, in his washing, his combing of hair, his wearing of shoes.[96]

Ch. 48:   **Should the graves of the idolaters of the time of Ignorance be dug up and mosques constructed in their place?**

Because of the saying of the Prophet ﷺ: "Allāh cursed the Jews taking the graves of their prophets as places of prayer" and what is disliked about prayers at the graves. And 'Umar ibn al-Khaṭṭāb found Anas ibn Mālik praying by a grave and he said: "Beware of the grave! beware of the grave!", and he did not tell him to repeat the prayer.[97]

427 'Ā'ishah reported that Umm Ḥabībah and Umm Salamah mentioned a church which they had seen in Abyssinia in which there were pictures. So they mentioned them to the Prophet ﷺ and he said: "Those are a people who, when a righteous man among them dies, build a place of worship over his grave and make these pictures in it. So they are the worst of creatures in the sight of Allāh on the Day of Resurrection." [98]

---

the underlying meaning of associating the mosque with the purity of mind and body, rather than with their impure side.

[96] This is a repetition of h. 168 with the addition of the words: "if he could". That is to say, in everything that a person is inclined towards doing, the Holy Prophet began from the right side. Entrance into a mosque is among such actions. But cleaning the nose or washing the private parts after voiding of any manner are acts of a different kind and the Holy Prophet used to do them with his left hand.

[97] Idolatry had become second nature with the Arabs and the Holy Prophet was commissioned to root out this habit from his nation. Hence it is that he would not allow anything that smacked of polytheism of any kind. His prohibition against saying prayers in burial grounds and on a cloak having pictures are acts inspired by his anxiety for the eradication of polytheistic tendencies from the minds of the Arabs. This, however, should not be taken to mean absolute prohibition but mere discouragement. If, under unavoidable necessity, prayer is said in some burial ground or on a prayer-mat with pictures on it, the prayer does not become null and void.

[98] This implies that those ḥadīth reports which speak of angels refraining from entering a house in which there are pictures (see h. 3226, 3227, 3322, 3351, 5957, etc.) refer to pictures that are kept as objects of veneration and worship, as for example among Christians. The reference to angels in those reports means the agencies or forces that inspire man with noble thoughts. People who are given to undue veneration or worship of deities other than God cannot have visions of higher objects of life. Umm Ḥabībah and Umm Salamah were both wives of the Holy Prophet and had migrated to Abyssinia in the early days of Islām before they were married to the Holy Prophet. They mentioned seeing churches with pictures to the Holy Prophet during his last illness, and he issued a warning in these words to his followers against making his own tomb a place of veneration and worship. See the repetition of this ḥadīth in h. 1341 where his illness is mentioned.

428 Anas (ibn Mālik) reported: The Prophet ﷺ came to Madīnah and alighted at the higher quarters of Madīnah in a tribe known as Banī ʿAmr ibn ʿAuf. The Prophet ﷺ stayed with them for twenty-four nights, then he sent a message to Banī an-Najjār, so they came with the swords hanging from their necks. It is as if I can (still) see the Prophet ﷺ on his she-camel and Abū Bakr riding behind him and the members of Banī an-Najjār around him, till he halted at the courtyard of Abū Ayyūb. He liked to pray wherever the time for prayer arrived, and he (even) used to say his prayers in the pens of sheep. He ordered the construction of a mosque and sent a message to the members of Banī an-Najjār saying: "O Banī an-Najjar! Agree a price with me for this plot of land of yours." They said: "No, by Allāh, we ask its price only from Allāh."

Anas said: There was in it what I am going to tell you, namely, the graves of the idolaters, and in it were ruins,[99] and in it also were date trees. So the Prophet ﷺ gave an order regarding the graves of the idolaters and they were dug up,[100] then (he gave an order) regarding the ruins and they were levelled, and (he gave an order) regarding the date trees, they were cut down. The date trees were laid in lines in the direction of the *qiblah* of the mosque, and the stones were placed at the two sides of it. People were bringing the stones while reciting poetic verses, and the Prophet ﷺ was with them and he was reciting (the poetic verse): "O Allāh! There is no good but the good of the Hereafter, so grant protection (against sin) to the *Anṣār* and the *Muhājira*." [101]

Ch. 49:   Saying prayers in the pens of sheep

429 Anas (ibn Malik) reported: The Prophet ﷺ used to say his prayers in the pens of sheep. Later on, I (one of the narrators) heard him (Anas) say: He used to say his prayers in the pens of sheep before the Mosque was constructed.[102]

---

[99] This shows that the graves were extremely old and in a dilapidated condition, looking like ruins. Incidentally, this report shows that in the construction of the Mosque the Holy Prophet joined his Companions in doing manual labour. Thus the most humble of labour, such as the carrying of loads, has come to be regarded as a practice of the Holy Prophet, so that no shame whatsoever is attached by Islām to doing such work.

[100] The meaning of this ḥadīth is that when the graves of a particular place are dug up and the ground is made smooth and level, leaving no sign of these graves, it can no longer be regarded as a burial ground and prayers can be said in it.

[101] This ḥadīth is repeated briefly in h. 1868.

[102] Only a part of h. 428 is repeated here with some additional words. The Holy Prophet began to say his prayers in this mosque when it was constructed, but prior to that he used to say prayers even in the enclosures of sheep. This means that if no other place is available one can say prayers even in places strewn with the dung of these animals. Considering his maintenance of

Ch. 50:   Saying prayers at places where camels are kept

430 Nāfiʿ reported: I saw Ibn ʿUmar saying his prayers towards his camel and he said: "I have seen the Prophet ﷺ doing so." [103]

Ch. 51:   He who says prayers while in front of him is an oven or a fire or something which is worshipped, but he intends to seek the pleasure of Allāh

Az-Zuhrī said: Anas ibn Mālik has informed me that the Prophet ﷺ said: "Fire was brought before me while I was saying prayers."

431 ʿAbdullāh ibn ʿAbbās reported: The sun eclipsed and the Messenger of Allāh ﷺ said prayers and then he said: "I have been shown the fire (of hell), and I have never seen a sight more horrible than what I have seen today." [104]

Ch. 52:   Disapproval of saying prayers in burial places

432 Ibn ʿUmar reported from the Prophet ﷺ that he said: "Say some of your prayers in your houses and do not make them graves."[105]

Ch. 53:   Saying prayers in sunken places and in those visited with punishment from Allāh

It is related that ʿAlī disliked saying his prayers in the sunken ground of Babylonia.

433 ʿAbdullāh ibn ʿUmar reported that the Messenger of Allāh ﷺ said: "Do not go to these people visited with Divine wrath[106] unless you are weeping, and if you are not weeping then do not go to them so that what befell them may not befall you."

---

cleanliness, the Holy Prophet even in such places must have chosen a clean spot for prayer or he cleaned a spot before praying there.

[103] There would seem to be no distinction between a place where sheep are kept and where camels are kept. But some reports speak of the place used for keeping camels as forbidden for prayers. This may be due to the great amount of filth in such a place, making it difficult to clean.

[104] H. 86 has been repeated here with brevity.

[105] That is to say, some of our prayers should be said at home, such as the optional prayers (*nafl*) and the midnight prayers (*Tahajjud*). The obligatory prayers must be said with the congregation in the mosque. See also h. 1187.

[106] This incident took place during the Holy Prophet's expedition to Tabūk when he had to pass by the ruined habitations of the ancient tribe of Thamūd. It is taught here that Muslims should learn a lesson from the fate of the earlier nations which were destroyed because of their wrongdoing.

Ch. 54: Saying prayers in church

'Umar said: We do not enter your churches because of the statues in which there are pictures. Ibn 'Abbās used to say his prayers in the church except for any in which there were statues.

434 'Ā'ishah reported that Umm Salamah mentioned to the Messenger of Allāh ﷺ a church she had seen in the land of Abyssinia which was called Māriya. She mentioned to him the pictures she had seen in it. The Messenger of Allāh ﷺ said: "Those are a people who, when a righteous servant (of God) — or a righteous man — among them dies, build a place of worship over his grave and make these pictures in it. They are the worst of creatures in the sight of Allāh." [107]

Ch. 55: Relating to the previous chapter

435–436 'Ā'ishah and 'Abdullāh ibn 'Abbās both said: When the condition of the Messenger of Allāh ﷺ became serious (during his last illness), he began to draw his sheet of cloth over his face, and when he would feel suffocated thereby, he would remove it from his face. In that condition he said: "May the curse of Allāh be upon the Jews and Christians who took the graves of their prophets as places of worship." He was warning (Muslims) against what those people did. [108]

---

[107] In this repetition of h. 427 only the name of Umm Salamah is mentioned, while h. 427 mentions both her and Umm Ḥabībah. Also, here the name of the church is given which is not given in h. 427. Roman Catholics install statues of their religious personalities in their churches and it was this which the Holy Prophet disliked. From this it is concluded that saying of prayers is forbidden in a place where pictures or statues are installed. The purpose is to prevent the infiltration of idolatry into Islām. See also the footnote on h. 427.

[108] What an anxiety the Holy Prophet bore for the spiritual welfare of his followers and concern for the doctrine of the oneness of God! Even when death was before him, he was found admonishing people not to raise him from the level of a mortal to that of God and not to worship his grave after his death as had been done by the Jews and Christians in case of their prophets. The Jews, of course, revered many prophets that appeared among them, but the only prophet whom the Christians have a real regard for, and was raised by them even to divinity, was Jesus. As for the other prophets of the Jewish tradition, the Christians have very scant regard for them because according to the Christian beliefs they were all guilty of heinous sins and as such incapable of saving their own souls, not to speak of saving others. The Holy Prophet's reference to the Christians paying worshipful homage to the grave of their prophet must, therefore, be taken to mean what is regarded by the Christians as the tomb of Jesus in Jerusalem where his body was kept for a while after the event known as Crucifixion. This ḥadīth proves categorically and absolutely that the Holy Prophet Muḥammad considered that Jesus lies buried in his grave somewhere on this earth. This is thus a repudiation of the notion that this great Prophet is still alive with his physical body in heaven. See also h. 1330.

437 Abū Hurairah reported that the Messenger of Allāh ﷺ said: "May the curse of Allāh be upon the Jews for their taking the graves of their prophets for places of worship." [109]

Ch. 56: The saying of the Prophet ﷺ: "The earth has been made a mosque for me, as also a means of purification" [110]

438 Jābir ibn ʿAbdullāh related that the Messenger of Allāh ﷺ said: "I have been given five things which were not given to anyone of the prophets before me. I have been helped with an awe of the extent of a month's distance; and the earth has been made a mosque for me, as also a means of purification, and any man from among my followers for whom the prayer time comes he should say prayers; and war gains have been made lawful for me; and a prophet used to be sent to his own people only, whereas I have been sent to all mankind; and I have been given the (power of) intercession." [111]

Ch. 57: Woman sleeping in the mosque

438 ʿĀ'ishah reported that a certain Arab tribe had a black female slave and they set her free and she continued to be with them. She said (to ʿĀ'ishah):

"A girl of this tribe came to her wearing a necklace of red laces. She (this girl) either placed it (somewhere) or it fell down (from her hand). A kite happened to pass by it while it was lying dropped, and she thought it to be some piece of meat and she carried it away. People searched for it and did not find it, and they accused me on account of it. They began to search me, even searching my frontal private parts. And by Allāh, I was still standing with them, when the kite flew by and dropped the necklace, and it fell in their midst. I said: 'This is the thing on account of which you were making an accusation against me; you suspected (me) and I was innocent, and here is the thing'."

ʿĀ'ishah added: Then she (that girl) came to the Messenger of Allāh ﷺ and embraced Islam. She had a tent in the mosque, or say a booth.[112] She used to come to me and talk to me about various things. Whenever she sat in my

---

[109] This is a repetition in brief of h. 435–436.

[110] This is to say, any spot on the surface of this earth, can be used as a place of worship by Muslims and needs no consecration for that purpose. Of course, if a place is rendered filthy by tangible impurity one should not use it for the purpose of prayer unless it is first cleaned.

[111] This is a repetition of h. 335. The only significant difference is the addition of the words "of the prophets" in the sentence: "I have been given five things which were not given to anyone *of the prophets* before me." It means that no other prophet before our Holy Prophet had the privilege of these five things.

[112] This shows that a person can stay in the mosque with a tent pitched for the purpose, and it can even be a woman. The present-day seclusion of Muslim women would not allow this.

company she used to recite (the poetic verse): "And the day of the necklace is among the wonders of our Lord. Know that it is this which rescued me from the city of unbelief." 'Ā'ishah said: So I said to her, "What is the matter with you that whenever you sit with me for a while you say this?" On that, she told me this story.

Ch. 58:   Men sleeping in the mosque

Abū Qilābah reported from Anas ibn Mālik: Some people belonging to the tribe of 'Ukl came to the Prophet ﷺ and they stayed in the Ṣuffah.[113] 'Abdur Raḥmān ibn Abū Bakr said: The people of the Ṣuffah were poor.

440 'Abdullāh ibn 'Umar informed that he used to sleep in the Mosque of the Prophet ﷺ when he was a youth who had no wife.[114]

441 Sahl ibn Sa'd reported: The Messenger of Allāh ﷺ went to the house of Fāṭimah and did not find 'Alī in the house. So he said: "Where is the son of your uncle?" She said: "Something has happened between me and him and he is angry with me. So he went out and did not have the midday sleep with at my place." So the Messenger of Allāh ﷺ said to a person: "Look to find where he is." When he came back he said: "O Messenger of Allāh, he is sleeping in the Mosque." So the Messenger of Allāh ﷺ went there and he was lying with his cover having fallen to one side of his body and dust was over him. The Messenger of Allāh ﷺ began to remove the dust from him and say: "Get up, *Abū Turāb* (one covered with dust)! Get up, *Abū Turāb!*"[115]

---

[113] These are the same people mentioned in h. 233 who had become ill and were sent to the public enclosure for the camels to help them recover their health, but who, on regaining their health, turned apostates and killed the keepers of the place and carried away the camels. This incident is repeated in Bukhārī's book on 'Those who wage war (on Muslims) from among the unbelievers and the apostates' in h. 6802, 6804 and 6805. The Ṣuffah was a part of the Holy Prophet's Mosque in Madīnah especially covered to serve the purpose of residence for homeless believers.

[114] This shows that the Companions of the Holy Prophet did not see anything wrong if anyone slept in the mosque. Unmarried people were often found to sleep in the mosque. It is true that persons like 'Abdullāh ibn Mas'ūd and 'Abdullāh ibn 'Abbās did not like this. This may be because they feared that such sleepers might take up too much space in the mosque, or what they disliked was people taking up permanent residence in the mosque.

[115] This shows the frank and unassuming manners and love of the Holy Prophet. He takes interest even in the small domestic quarrels of a married couple and himself goes to the mosque and tries to appease the angry husband by shaking the dust from his body, even resorting to good humour. *Abū Turāb* literally means 'father of dust'.

442 Abū Hurairah reported: I saw seventy people from among the people of the Ṣuffah and not one man among them had a sheet of cloth (to cover the whole body). They had either a waist-wrapper (*izār*) or a blanket which they tied on their necks. Some of these would reach only up to the middle of their calf-muscles and some of them would reach up to the ankles, and a man would hold the sheet with his hand for fear of exposing his private parts.

Ch. 59: Saying prayers on returning from a journey

Ka'b ibn Mālik said: The Prophet ﷺ, when he returned from a journey, used first to come to the mosque and say prayers therein.

443 Jābir ibn 'Abdullāh reported: I went to the Prophet ﷺ while he was in the Mosque — Mis'ar (a narrator in the chain) said: I think he said "in the forenoon" — and he (the Holy Prophet) said: "Say two *rak'ahs* of prayer." He owed me some money, so he paid it back and gave me more (than the amount due).[116]

Ch. 60: When any of you enters a mosque, he should say two *rak'ahs* of prayer before he sits down

444 Abū Qatādah as-Salamiyy reported that the Messenger of Allāh ﷺ said: "When any of you enters a mosque, he should say two *rak'ahs* of prayer before he sits down."

Ch. 61: Nullification of ablution (*ḥadath*) in the mosque

445 Abū Hurairah reported that the Messenger of Allāh ﷺ said: "The angels pray for one of you so long as he is in his place of prayer in which he has said his prayer until he does something which nullifies ablution.[117] They say: O Allāh, forgive him! O Allāh, have mercy on him!"

Ch. 62: The building of the mosque

Abū Sa'īd said: The roof of the (Prophet's) Mosque was of branches of the date-tree. 'Umar ordered the building of a mosque

---

[116] This report is found in greater details in the Book of 'Terms' (*Ash-Shurūṭ*) in h. 2718, and in even more detail in the Book of 'Sales' (*Al-Buyū'*) in h. 2097. There it is stated that during a journey Jābir agreed to sell his camel to the Holy Prophet on condition that he could ride it back to his house. When they reached Madīnah, he gave the camel to the Holy Prophet as stipulated and he gave him the agreed price. This is the money owed mentioned in the above ḥadīth. After Jābir returned home the Holy Prophet sent for him and gave him his camel back and told him to keep what he had been paid for it as well.

[117] The word for nullification of ablution is *ḥadath,* meaning the coming out of wind, or passing of urine or stools. For a further discussion see the footnote to h. 135.

and said: I protect the people from rain, and beware of making it (mosque) red or making it yellow as you may put people in trial. Anas said: People will show their pride for it, then they will not frequent it but a little. Ibn ʿAbbās said: You will certainly adorn it as the Jews and Christians adorn (their houses of worship).[118]

446 ʿAbdullāh ibn ʿUmar informed that the mosque in the time of the Messenger of Allāh ﷺ was built of raw bricks, its roof was of branches (of date-trees) and its pillars were of the wood of date-trees. Abū Bakr did not add anything to it. ʿUmar added to it and built it in the manner of the time of the Messenger of Allāh ﷺ with raw bricks and branches of date-trees and he built again its pillars with wood. Then ʿUthmān changed it, adding much to it and he built its walls with sculptured slabs of stone and lime, and made its pillars (also) of sculptured slabs of stone and its roof of teak wood.[119]

Ch. 63:   Helping the building of the mosque

The word of Allāh, the Mighty, the Glorious: "The idolaters have no right to maintain the mosques of Allāh" (the Qur'ān, 9:17).

447 ʿIkrimah reported: Ibn ʿAbbās said to me and to his son ʿAlī: "Go to Abū Saʿīd (al-Khudrī) and listen to his talk." So we went and he was in a garden, putting it right. He took his cloak and sat on his heels, then he began to talk to us, until he came to the discussion about the construction of the mosque. He said:

We were carrying one raw brick per person at a time, and ʿAmmār was carrying two bricks at a time and the Prophet ﷺ saw him and began to shake the dust from him and he was saying: "Pity on ʿAmmār, the rebellious party

---

[118] This does not mean that to make a beautiful mosque is forbidden. What is forbidden is the lavishness of decoration. As prayer in Islām is simple, it is also required that there should be simplicity in the surrounding of the place of worship. Such places are meant for drawing the worshippers' attention towards God, and this object would be defeated by adornment which attracts worshippers to itself. Anas and Ibn ʿAbbās have pointed out here that people would gradually be very anxious for the adornment of mosques but would neglect the very object of the mosque, i.e., their being frequented by people with devout minds for spiritual elevation, and it is this which is happening today. Mosques are being constructed not because of need but for vanity and show. The reference to the Jews and Christians is intended to point out the dangers of mere ceremonialism, diminishing the spirit of the faith.

[119] As will be seen later in h. 450, some Companions disliked this action of ʿUthmān, although he did not have any pictures engraved or painted in the walls. It seems the Caliph did not like the mosque building to be so plain at a time when people were making very fine buildings for their homes. This reconstruction by ʿUthmān took place in 30 A.H.

will kill him. He will invite them towards Paradise and they will invite him to the Fire." 'Ammār used to say: "I seek refuge in Allāh from the trials." [120]

Ch. 64:   Seeking assistance from carpenters and artisans in connection with the wood of the pulpit and with (building) the mosque

448 Sahl reported: The Messenger of Allāh ﷺ sent (a message) to a woman saying: "Order your slave carpenter to make for me a wooden pulpit on which I will sit."

449 Jābir ibn 'Abdullāh reported that a woman said: "O Messenger of Allāh, should I not make for you a thing on which you can sit, for surely I have a slave who is a carpenter?" He said: "If you like you may make a pulpit." [121]

---

[120] 'Alī ibn 'Abdullāh ibn 'Abbās, who is said here to have accompanied 'Ikrimah, was born during the closing days of the rule of the fourth Caliph 'Alī. Abū Sa'īd al-Khudrī was one of the most distinguished Companions of the Holy Prophet, from whom a large number of ḥadīth reports are related. It is remarkable that even at the time of the incident referred to in this ḥadīth, when Muslims had acquired an empire, these leading figures of early Islām are found to do the work of a manual labourer without feeling any humiliation. In fact, it was this austerity of life that made Muslims deserving of the great position of ruling over much of the world. On the other hand, these stalwarts of early Islām kept their love and eagerness for knowledge and learning undimmed by the material prosperity of their nation. Thus we see a man like Ibn 'Abbās, renowned for his own learning and knowledge of religion, sending his own son and a disciple to this great Companion of the Holy Prophet.

The words of the Holy Prophet, "the rebellious party will kill him," are regarded as constituting a prophecy about the battle of Ṣiffīn between 'Alī and Mu'āwiyah, in which 'Ammār was killed fighting on the side of 'Alī. If the Holy Prophet uttered these words, it would mean that Mu'āwiyah was a rebel against the constituted authority. It is true 'Alī was reluctant to punish the murderers of 'Uthmān as the party of Mu'āwiyah wanted him to do and it was this hesitation on the part of 'Ali that created a misunderstanding in the minds of many Companions, even those as great as 'Ā'ishah, Ṭalḥah and Zubair, and it was this which caused the internecine warfare among the Companions. On the other hand, the difficulties faced by 'Alī cannot be denied, and coming to know of these Ṭalḥah and Zubair withdrew from fighting against him. The fact that Mu'āwiyah continued to fight 'Alī means that he had become rebellious. The words "he will invite them towards Paradise and they will invite him to the Fire" should not be taken to mean the heaven and hell of the life after death, but the heaven of peace by obeying the ruler of the time and the hell of internecine war by rebelling against him. It has, however, been suggested, as in *Fatḥ al-Bārī*, that these words ascribed to the Holy Prophet are not to be found in the original report of Bukhārī and that Bazzār has reported from Abū Sa'īd al-Khudrī that the latter did not hear these words from the Holy Prophet himself but only from other people. This accords with another explanation which is that these words refer to the past and those inviting him to the fire were the unbelieving Quraish who had persecuted 'Ammār and tortured his father and mother to death, whereas he on his part was arguing with them all the time on behalf of the truth of Islam, which promised a passage to Paradise. This ḥadīth is repeated in h. 2812.

[121] Between this version and the one given in h. 448 there is no contradiction. In h. 448 the

Ch. 65: He who constructs a mosque

450 'Ubaidullāh al-Khaulāniyy said that he heard 'Uthmān ibn 'Affān say, when people were talking against him, on his having reconstructed the mosque of the Messenger of Allāh ﷺ: Surely you are talking too much and I have heard the Messenger of Allāh ﷺ say: "Whoever constructs a mosque" — Bukair said: I think that he said, "seeking thereby the pleasure of Allāh — "Allāh will construct for him the like of it in Paradise." [122]

Ch. 66: Not to hold (in hand) the blades of the arrows (one may be carrying) when passing through the mosque

451 Sufyān related that he said to 'Amr: Have you heard Jābir ibn 'Abdullāh say: A man passed through the mosque carrying arrows, so the Messenger of Allāh ﷺ said to him: "Hold the blades in your hand"? [123]

Ch. 67: Passing through the mosque

452 Abū Burdah reported from his father who reported that the Prophet ﷺ said: "Whoever passes through any part of our mosques or our markets with arrows, he should hold the bare blades so that he does not injure a Muslim with his hand." [124]

Ch. 68: Reciting poetry in the mosque

453 Abū Salamah ibn 'Abdur Raḥmān ibn 'Auf informed that he heard Ḥassān ibn Thābit al-Anṣārī calling to witness Abū Hurairah, saying (to him): "I adjure you in the name of Allāh, Did you hear the Prophet ﷺ say:

Holy Prophet himself is reported to have asked her to have the pulpit made for him. This could have happened after she made the offer mentioned here in h. 449. One reporter has reported only one part of the story and the other the other part.

[122] The meaning is that there is no sin in making a good mosque so long as the object is to make the place fit for devoted prayers. The explanation was occasioned by some people observing that the mosque of the Holy Prophet should continue to be as plain and simple in structure as it was at the time of the Holy Prophet himself. 'Uthmān told them that this was not forbidden. These are matters determined by the needs of the times.

[123] The reply of 'Amr is not stated here but we read it in the Book of 'Trials' (*Fitn*) in h. 7073 and it was that he said: "Yes." In other words, one is not permitted to pass through the mosque with exposed arrows unless these are covered as not to prove a means of causing injuries to others. The act of passing through the mosque as such is not disallowed.

[124] A very useful principle is enunciated here, that one can exercise a right freely up to the extent that it does not clash with the similar freedom of other people or harm the interests and safety of others. The civilized existence of man has always been based on this fundamental rule.

'O Ḥassān, reply on behalf of the Messenger of Allāh. O Allāh, help him with the Holy Spirit'?" Abū Hurairah said: "Yes." [125]

Ch. 69: People with javelins in the mosque

454–455 'Ā'ishah said: I saw the Messenger of Allāh ﷺ one day at the door of my chamber and some Abyssinians were sporting in the mosque. The Messenger of Allāh ﷺ was screening me with his cloak, and I was watching their sport. [455] (And in another narration) 'Ā'ishah reported: I saw the Prophet ﷺ, and some Abyssinians were sporting with their javelins. [126]

Ch. 70: Mentioning buying and selling from the pulpit in the mosque[127]

456 'Ā'ishah reported that Barīrah came to her and asked (for her help) in respect of her *kitābah*. [128] Upon this she said: "If you like I will give (the remaining amount) to your master and the *walā'* will be mine." [129] Her

---

[125] 'Umar, a great champion of austerity, tried to prevent Ḥassān, the poet-laureate so to speak of early Islām, from reciting poems in the mosque. In response Ḥassān called on Abū Hurairah to bear witness that he, Ḥassān, used to recite poems in the presence of the Holy Prophet himself and that the Holy Prophet used to pray for a successful composition and recitation. The Holy Prophet's prayer also shows that ordinary believers can also receive assistance from the Holy Spirit (*Rūḥ al-Qudus*). However, poetry which is of a romantic or immoral nature cannot be recited in the mosque, as shown by other reports. Some versions of this report, instead of referring to the Holy Spirit, have the words: "And the angel Gabriel is with you" (h. 3213, h. 4123, h. 6153), showing by the Holy Spirit is meant Gabriel. In a report from 'Ā'ishah it is stated that the Holy Prophet kept a pulpit in the mosque for Ḥassān, on which he stood to recite his replies in verse form to the scurrilous attacks of the unbelievers against the Holy Prophet (Tirmidhī, book: *Al-Adab* — 'Manners', h. 3082; Abū Dāwūd, book: *Al-Adab* — 'Manners', h. 5015).

[126] This shows that women are allowed to watch games and sports from behind screens, and also how much the Holy Prophet cared for his wives. This report does not conflict with h. 451, according to which the blades of arrows should be held in the hand while passing through a mosque. When there is a game, spectators are kept at a safe distance and separated from those participating in it, and there is no danger of injury to the people in the mosque. This incident also shows that the mosque can be used for all kinds of purposes for the benefit of the Muslims. See also h. 988.

[127] That is to say, it is not only permissible but even necessary to give guidance relating to what is allowed and what is prohibited in business transactions from the pulpit of the mosque because the very object of the mosque is to bring about reform. However, a mosque cannot be made a place of conducting business. If a business transaction is discussed casually and by chance in a mosque, that is not forbidden.

[128] *Kitābah* is a technical term connoting a contract between a slave and the slave-owner according to which the slave can purchase his or her freedom. The slave who makes such a contract is called a *mukātib*.

[129] *Walā'* was a form of guardianship which the former owner of a freed slave could still retain over the freed slave, even after the slave's freedom. It included the right to inherit the freed slave's property on his or her death. According to Islām, any such rights pass to the person who

masters said: "If you like you can give her the remaining amount (due from her to them)." And Sufyān (a narrator in the chain) once said (that her masters had said): "If you like you can set her free but the *walā'* will be ours."

('Ā'ishah added:) So when the Messenger of Allāh ﷺ came, I mentioned it to him and he said: "Buy her and set her free, for surely the *walā'* is with the one who frees (the slave)." Then the Messenger of Allāh ﷺ stood on the pulpit — and Sufyān once said, So the Messenger of Allāh ﷺ ascended the pulpit — and said: "What is the state of those people who impose conditions that are not in the Book of Allāh? Whoever imposes a condition that is not in the Book of Allāh, he is not entitled to it, even if he imposes the condition a hundred times.[130]

Ch. 71: Demanding return of debt and following (the debtor) into the mosque

457 Ka'b (ibn Mālik) reported that he demanded from Ibn Abū Ḥadrad the repayment of a debt which the latter owed to him in the mosque. Their voices grew louder so much so that the Messenger of Allāh ﷺ heard this while he was in his house. So he came out to them, raising the curtain of his chamber, and called out: "O Ka'b!" He said: "Here am I, O Messenger of Allāh." He (the Prophet) said: "Leave this much from the debt owed to you", and he made a sign to him meaning "half". He said: "I have done so, O Messenger of Allāh." He (the Prophet) said (to the debtor): "Get up and pay it off." [131]

Ch. 72: Sweeping the mosque and removing the rags and sticks and pieces of wood

458 Abū Hurairah reported that there was a black man or a black woman who used to sweep the mosque and that person died. So the Prophet ﷺ asked

---

paid to free the slave and who might need to act as guardian as if in a kinship relationship. The only sense in which it seems to apply is that if the freed slave dies leaving no relatives to inherit from him, then the person who paid to free the slave, who had the *walā'*, would be the heir.

[130] Barīrah had a contract to purchase her freedom (*kitābah*) but had not paid all the price to her masters. She asked for this money from 'Ā'ishah, who told them that in case she paid this balance she would also take the *walā'*. They, however, contended that even if the female slave were thus freed, the *walā'* would remain with them. It was when the Holy Prophet was apprised of this that he preached his sermon in the mosque to say that it does not lie within the rights of a person to impose conditions on a contract that are not sanctioned by Islām. See also h. 1493.

[131] It is a noble form of charity that is recommended here. Not only is money lent without interest, but afterwards if it is found that the debtor is unable to repay it all, the creditor is advised to forego a part of the debt. It is such treatment of others which creates a cohesive community in which love and harmony prevail. See also the footnote under the repetition of this ḥadīth in h. 471.

about him and people said: "He (or she) has died." He said: "Why did you not inform me about it? Show me his grave" — or he said "her grave". So he (the Holy Prophet) went to the grave and said prayers over it.[132]

Ch. 73:   Prohibition against trade in intoxicants (announced) in the mosque

459 ʿĀʾishah reported: When the verses in the *Sūrah al-Baqarah* dealing with usury were revealed, the Prophet ﷺ came out to the mosque and recited them before the people. Then he prohibited trade in intoxicants.[133]

Ch. 74:   Servant for the mosque

Ibn ʿAbbās said: "I vow to You (God) what is in my womb, to be devoted (to Your service)" (the prayer of Mary's mother in the Qurʾān, 3:35), it means to the service of the mosque.[134]

460 Abū Hurairah reported that there was a woman — or a man — who used to sweep the mosque. (Abū Rāfiʿ, reporting from Abū Hurairah said:) I think it was a woman. Then he mentioned the ḥadīth of the Prophet ﷺ, that he said prayers over her grave.[135]

Ch. 75:   Tying the prisoner or the debtor in the Mosque

461 Abū Hurairah reported from the Prophet ﷺ that he said: "Surely an audacious one from among the Jinn[136] suddenly came upon me last night" — or words similar to this —"with the object of interrupting my prayers, but

---

[132] The Holy Prophet was very attentive towards all those persons, high or low, male or female, whom he dealt with. In this case he honoured this man or woman because of that person's services to the mosque. See also its repetition in h. 1337 in which it is reported that people told the Holy Prophet that they did not inform him of the death because they considered the deceased unworthy of mention.

[133] In the verses dealing with usury, referred to in this ḥadīth, it is stated: "And Allāh has allowed trading and forbidden usury" (2:275). Because the allowing of trade in general is mentioned here, the Holy Prophet clarified that trading in intoxicants is prohibited, as their use is prohibited.

[134] The word *muḥarrar* used in this verse 3:35, and translated as "to be devoted", literally means 'one who is freed'. This ḥadīth explains the underlying meaning of this word as used in the Qurʾān. It is that Mary was freed from all other obligations to be solely devoted to the service of the house of God.

[135] In this repetition of h. 458 the additional words, "I think it was a woman", show that the caretaker of the mosque who thus died was a woman.

[136] The words here, "an audacious one from among the Jinn" (*ʿifrīt min al-jinn*), occur in the Qurʾān in 27:39 in connection with the story of Solomon.

Allāh gave me power over him. I intended to tie him to one of the pillars of the mosque, so that you may all have a look at him in the morning. Then I remembered the words of my brother Solomon: 'My Lord, … grant me a kingdom which is not fit for anyone after me' (the Qur'ān, 38:35)." Rauḥ (a narrator in the chain) said: So he turned him back, humiliated.[137]

Ch. 76: Taking bath when embracing Islām and tying the prisoner in the mosque

Shuraiḥ used to enjoin people to tie the debtor to a pillar of the mosque.

462 Abū Hurairah said: The Prophet ﷺ sent some men on horseback towards Najd and they brought a man of Banī Ḥanīfah called Thumāmah ibn Uthāl, and they tied him to one of the pillars of the mosque. The Prophet ﷺ came out to him and said: "Release Thumāmah." He (Thumāmah) went towards the date-trees near the mosque, took a bath, entered the mosque (again) and said: "I bear witness that there is no god but Allāh and that Muḥammad is the Messenger of Allāh." [138]

Ch. 77: Tent in the mosque for the sick and others

463 'Ā'ishah reported: Sa'd received a wound on the day of the Battle of the Ditch in the middle vein of his arm. So the Prophet ﷺ pitched a tent in the mosque to look after him from near. In the mosque there was a tent of Banī

---

[137] If the Jinn spoken of here was one of the invisible beings, as jinn are commonly conceived of, the Holy Prophet could not have thought of tying him to a pillar of the mosque for all the people to see him. It must be a human being of a rebellious nature, as Bukhārī himself has characterised him as a prisoner in the chapter heading. It seems this unruly man had attacked the Holy Prophet and that the Holy Prophet overpowered him and out of mercy let him go. It is possible it is the same person who is spoken of in the next ḥadīth whose name is given there as Thumāmah. The Holy Prophet's generosity in setting this man free had a very wholesome effect on this man's mind and he became a Muslim, as stated in h. 462.

The Holy Prophet's reciting the prayer of Solomon to God as given in the Qur'ān, "grant me a kingdom which is not fit for anyone after me", shows that like his predecessor Solomon, he was anxious to carve out not an earthly empire but a spiritual one in which he would rule over people's hearts and minds with his spiritual influence and not through political power. It was this view of his whole rulership that prompted him to set this man free.

[138] This incident is reported in much greater detail in h. 4372 in a chapter headed: 'The delegation of Banī Ḥanīfah and the ḥadīth of Thumāmah'. He was kept tied in the mosque not for any punishment but to make him realise his vanquishment and appreciate the generosity of the Holy Prophet. Thus when, on the third day, the Holy Prophet felt that this lesson had gone into the prisoner's heart, he ordered his release and the man embraced Islām of his own accord. This shows whatever punishment the Holy Prophet meted out to people, it was for correction and not revenge.

Ghifār, and what frightened them was the blood which flowed towards them. They called out: "O people of the tent, what is this coming to us from your side?" It was Saʻd whose wound was bleeding and he died of it.[139]

Ch. 78:   Taking a camel inside the mosque for some need

Ibn ʻAbbās said: The Prophet ﷺ made circuits of the Kaʻbah on his camel.[140]

464 Umm Salamah reported: I complained to the Messenger of Allāh ﷺ that I was ill. He said: "Make circuits behind the people riding (on an animal)." So I made circuits (in that way), and the Messenger of Allāh ﷺ was saying his prayers at the side of the House (of Kaʻbah), reciting: "By the Mountain, and a Book written" (the Qurʼān 52:1–2).[141]

Ch. 79:   Going to a mosque in a dark night

465 Anas related: Two men from among the Companions of the Prophet ﷺ departed from him on a dark night, one of them was ʻAbbād ibn Bishr and I think the second one was Usaid ibn Ḥuḍair, and with them was something like two lamps lighting (the way) in front of them. When they parted from one another, each of them had one (lamp) continuing to be with him till he reached his house.[142]

Ch. 80:   Entry window (*khaukhah*) and passage in the mosque

466 Abū Saʻīd al-Khudrī reported: The Prophet ﷺ delivered a sermon and said: "Surely Allāh, glory be to Him, gave a choice to a servant between this

---

[139] This was Saʻd ibn Muʻādh. He was wounded in the Battle of the Ditch (*Khandaq*), known also as the Battle of the Allies (*Aḥzāb*). He was lodged in the mosque at Madīnah for nursing and attention, and also so that the Holy Prophet could be near him. Thus the mosque was used by the Holy Prophet as a sort of hospital. At that time it was not possible to have separate buildings for different purposes.

[140] In Abū Dāwūd there is a report from Ibn ʻAbbās that the Holy Prophet on his arrival at Makkah felt indisposed and had to make circuits of the Kaʻbah riding on an animal, and that Jābir said that he rode on an animal in order that he might be properly seen by people who could approach him with questions on religious matters (book: 'Rites of the *Ḥajj*', h. 1881 and 1880). In making the circuits one has to pass through the Sacred Mosque and the Holy Prophet's passing through it riding an animal shows that at a time of necessity even animals can be led through a mosque.

[141] This is repeated in h. 1633. See also h. 1619.

[142] These two Companions of the Holy Prophet were sitting in the mosque with the Holy Prophet waiting for the *'Ishā'* (night) prayer. It was a very dark night, which connects this ḥadīth with the chapter heading. The light that guided their path was evidently a miraculous phenomenon. Many instances of such miraculous signs are found in the lives of the Companions of the Holy Prophet.

world and what is with Himself, and he chose what is with Allāh." At this Abū Bakr wept, and I said to myself: What makes this old man weep if Allāh gave a choice to a servant between this world and what is with Himself, and he chose what is with Allāh, the Mighty, the Glorious? But it was the Messenger of Allāh ﷺ who was the servant, and Abū Bakr knew more than us. So he (the Holy Prophet) said: "Abū Bakr! Do not weep. Surely from among the people the one who has done me the most favour by his companionship and his property is Abū Bakr, and if I were to take as friend anyone from among my followers, I would certainly have taken Abū Bakr, but (there remains) the brotherhood of Islām and its love. No door to the mosque should be left unclosed except the door of Abū Bakr." [143]

467 Ibn ʿAbbās reported: The Messenger of Allāh ﷺ came out during his illness that led to his death, having tied a cloth round his head. He sat on the pulpit and praised Allāh and extolled him and then said: "There is no one among the people who has done me more favour by his life and his property than Abū Bakr, son of Abī Quḥāfah, and if I were to take as friend anyone

---

[143] Abū Bakr was gifted with a very high order of knowledge which secured for him the title of *Ṣiddīq*. It was this extraordinary insight into reality that enabled him to recognize the prophethood of the Holy Prophet at the first announcement of his claim. All the other Companions of the Holy Prophet acknowledged this superiority of Abū Bakr's knowledge. On the occasion of the truce of Ḥudaibiyah, a Companion of the stature of ʿUmar began to have doubts and asked the Holy Prophet how Muslims could accept such humiliating terms when they were on the side of truth and the enemy on the side of falsehood. He further said to the Holy Prophet that he had promised that they would perform circuits of the Kaʿbah, to which the Holy Prophet replied that he did not say that it would be this year. Then ʿUmar went to Abū Bakr and raised the same questions but Abū Bakr gave exactly the same replies as the Holy Prophet, and considered the treaty to be good for Islām and the Muslims, just like the Holy Prophet, showing the same perfect faith in the help of Allāh as the Holy Prophet. According to authorities on *Taṣawwuf* (mysticism) the *Ṣiddīq* are very close to the position of the Holy Prophet in respect of their insight into reality, and for this reason Abū Bakr was considered as the personality next only to the Holy Prophet. His perfect, unwavering faith in the decisions and views of the Holy Prophet made him the first person among the believers.

The ḥadīth provides another illustration of the unrivalled understanding of Abū Bakr in discerning the true meaning of the Holy Prophet's expressions. He at once understood that the person to whom the choice between the life on this earth and the life with God was given was no other than the Holy Prophet himself and that it was a prediction of his death. It was due to this knowledge, insight and foresight that he was made Imām of the prayer by order of the Holy Prophet before his death, and made the leader of the Muslims and the first *Khalīfah* of Islām after his death. Whatever emanated from the blessed hands of this man of faith was blessed with auspicious results for the Muslims. The Holy Prophet's instruction to leave the window of Abū Bakr open to his Mosque indicated not only the highest position of this great believer but also that he should succeed the Holy Prophet as Head of the Muslims. This ḥadīth incidentally shows that it is permissible to have the doors or windows of residential houses opening into a mosque, but also that due care should be exercised to prevent any dangers that may arise from such entrances. This may be why the Holy Prophet ordered the closing of all other doors.

from among the people, I would certainly have taken Abū Bakr as friend, but the friendship of Islām is superior. Close every entry window (*khaukhah*) into this mosque except that of Abū Bakr." [144]

Ch. 81:   Doors and locks for the Ka'bah and the mosques

> Abū 'Abdullāh (Bukhārī) said: 'Abdullāh ibn Muḥammad said to me that Sufyān narrated to us from Ibn Juraij that Ibn Abū Mulaikah said to him: "O 'Abdul Mālik, if only you had seen the mosques of Ibn 'Abbās and their doors."

468 Ibn 'Umar reported that the Prophet ﷺ on his arrival in Makkah sent for 'Uthmān ibn Ṭalḥah, who then opened the door (of the Ka'bah), and the Prophet ﷺ, Bilāl, Usāmah ibn Zaid and 'Uthmān ibn Ṭalḥah entered (the Ka'bah) and then the door was closed. He stayed within it for some time and then they came out. Ibn 'Umar said: I hurried and asked Bilāl who said: "He (the Holy Prophet) prayed within it." I asked: "Where?" He said: "Between the two pillars." Ibn 'Umar added: I forgot to ask him how much he prayed? [145]

Ch. 82:   An idolater entering the mosque[146]

469 Abū Hurairah said: The Messenger of Allāh ﷺ sent some men on horseback towards Najd and they brought a man of Banī Ḥanīfah called Thumāmah ibn Uthāl, and they tied him to one of the pillars of the mosque.[147]

Ch. 83:   Raising of voice in the mosques

470 As-Sā'ib ibn Yazīd reported: I was standing in the mosque and a man threw a pebble at me. I looked and it was 'Umar ibn al-Khaṭṭāb. He said: "Go

---

[144] This is partly a repetition of h. 466.

[145] This repetition of h. 397 has many differences with h. 397. The concluding words evidently clash with what has been said in h. 397 where the reply given by Bilāl begins: "Yes, two *rak'ahs* between the two columns". We have either to assume that this reply of Bilāl in h. 397 does not form a part of the original report, or that Ibn 'Umar later on inquired of Bilāl about this and got the information about the two *rak'ahs,* or that Ibn 'Umar has himself added these words. Note that in all such reports the narrators have not been very particular to maintain the accuracy of their narrations because these were not concerned with any religious principle.

[146] The permissibility of idolaters entering the mosques is evident from the practice of the Holy Prophet, except, of course, the Sacred House of Ka'bah, in case of which there is the clear prohibition in the Qur'ān: "they shall not approach the Sacred Mosque after this year of theirs" (9:28). This is indicated in this chapter heading, for Thumāmah was an idolater. Another example is the Holy Prophet's lodging the deputation of Thaqīf in the mosque. Of course, such staying in the mosque must be by the permission of the Imām, but a mere visit does not require any such permission. The "uncleanliness" of the idolaters, spoken of at the beginning of 9:28 in the Qur'ān, is not a bar because it is of the mind and heart which has nothing to do with their body as they come to the mosque.

[147] This is a repetition of the opening of h. 462.

and bring these two (men) to me." So I took them to him and he said "Who are you?" or "From where are you?" They said: "(We are) from the people of Ṭā'if." He said: "Had you been from among the people of this city, I would have punished you. You are raising your voices in the Mosque of the Messenger of Allāh ﷺ."

471 Ka'b ibn Mālik informed that he demanded from Ibn Abū Ḥadrad the repayment of a debt which the latter owed to him, in the time of the Messenger of Allāh ﷺ in the mosque. Their voices grew louder so much so that the Messenger of Allāh ﷺ heard this while he was in his house. So the Messenger of Allāh ﷺ came out to them, raising the curtain of his chamber, and called out: "O Ka'b ibn Mālik! O Ka'b!" He said: "Here am I, O Messenger of Allāh." He (the Prophet) indicated with his hand to leave a half from his debt. Ka'b said: "I have done so, O Messenger of Allāh." The Messenger of Allāh ﷺ said (to the debtor): "Get up and pay it off." [148]

Ch. 84:   Forming into circles and sitting in the mosque[149]

---

[148] H. 457 has been repeated here practically in the same words. Ka'b ibn Mālik and Ibn Abū Ḥadrad had a dispute between themselves on the question of some loan in the Mosque of the Holy Prophet, and the voices of both became so loud that the Holy Prophet heard them. He did not show any harshness to them but according to the previous ḥadīth, h. 470, 'Umar told two men who had raised their voices in the Mosque that if they had not been strangers to the place, he would have punished them. There is no clash between the two reports. In both, they were told to stop raising their voices. It was as a result of the Holy Prophet stopping the noise-making by Ka'b and his debtor that 'Umar warned the two men in h. 470 not to raise their voices. The mosque is a place of prayer and devotion and nothing should be allowed in it that may disturb the solemnity and serenity of its atmosphere or distract the attention of the worshippers. It is for this reason that, in h. 451 and h. 452, people were told that if they carried sharp-edged weapons in the mosque the blades must be covered so that they do not cause injury to worshippers. It is true that the mosque can be used for many kinds of national and community affairs, as is clear from the foregoing reports, but at the same time this should not stand in the way of the devotees pursuing their spiritual aims in the mosque. Not only loud voices, but also the sound of many people talking softly among themselves can disturb the concentration of those praying. Particular care should be taken at prayer times. In short, Islām takes its usual middle course and requires an atmosphere in the mosque which is neither so sacrosanct that no worldly activity is allowed, nor is it so secular as to be profane and distracting from spirituality.

[149] The chapter heading is intended to show that it is permissible to sit in the mosque in a circle when there is any religious talk in it. Although in the first two reports of this chapter there is no mention of this sitting in a circle, but such a mention is found in the third report, h. 474, in which it is related that the Holy Prophet was preaching to people when a man came in and sat down in a space which was vacant in the circle. It is evident from this event that people used to sit around the Holy Prophet on such occasions because the speaker can keep the entire gathering in view and the people find it convenient to hear him. There is, of course, a report found in Ṣaḥīḥ Muslim that once when the Holy Prophet, on entering the mosque, found the people sitting in circles, he said: "What is the matter that I see you divided into groups?" (book: 'Prayer', ch. 27).

472 Ibn 'Umar reported: A man asked the Prophet 鷺 while the latter was on the pulpit: "What do you think about (how to say) the prayer of the night?" He said: "Say two *rak'ahs* followed by two *rak'ahs* (and so on), and when any of you fears (the approach of) dawn, he should say one *rak'ah* and it will make the prayer which he has said as *Witr*." He (Ibn 'Umar) used to say: "Make your last prayer at night as *Witr*, for the Prophet 鷺 has enjoined it."

473 Ibn 'Umar reported that a man came to the Prophet 鷺 while the latter was delivering the sermon and said: "How is the prayer of the night (to be said)?" He said: "Say two *rak'ahs* followed by two *rak'ahs* (and so on), and when you fear (the approach of) dawn, say one *rak'ah* to make it *Witr*, so it will make the prayer which you have said as *Witr*." Ibn 'Umar related (according to another narration) that a man called out to the Prophet 鷺 while the latter was in the mosque.[150]

474 Abū Wāqid al-Laithī reported that the Messenger of Allāh 鷺 was once in the mosque when three persons arrived, two of whom proceeded towards the Messenger of Allāh 鷺 and one went away. One of the two found an empty space (in the circle) and sat down (there); as for the second, he sat behind the people. When the Messenger of Allāh 鷺 became free, he said: "Shall I tell you about these three persons? As for the first of them, he took the shelter of Allāh and Allāh gave him shelter; as for the second he felt shy and Allāh (also) was shy of him (i.e., showed him consideration); and as for the third, he turned away, so Allāh turned away from him." [151]

Ch. 85:   Lying flat on one's back in the mosque

475 'Abbād ibn Tamīm reported from his paternal uncle that he saw the Messenger of Allāh 鷺 lying on his back in the mosque placing one of his legs on the other. Ibn Shihāb reported from Sa'īd ibn al-Musayyab that 'Umar and 'Uthmān used to do the same.[152]

Ch. 86:   A mosque situated on a thoroughfare without causing difficulty to the people

Al-Ḥasan, Ayyūb and Mālik held the same view.

What is prohibited here is for people to sit in separate circles, each group talking among themselves, creating noise and giving the appearance of a disorganised community. Sitting around one person, such as the Imām, to listen to his talk is quite different.

[150] This is a repetition of h. 472 with slight differences.

[151] This is a repetition of h. 66 with slight differences. See the footnotes under h. 66.

[152] Some ḥadīth reports contain a prohibition of lying like this. The reason may be that there is a risk of exposing the private parts in case the clothes being worn are too short, particularly if the lower garment is an unsewn piece of cloth.

476 'Ā'ishah, wife of the Prophet ﷺ, said: I have found my parents following the path of Islām ever since I have been able to understand things. Not a day passed on us but the Messenger of Allāh ﷺ came to us at the two ends of the day, morning and evening. Then it occurred to Abū Bakr to construct a mosque in the courtyard (*finā'*) of his house. He used to say his prayers in it and recite the Qur'ān. The women of the idolaters and their sons would stand by him, wondering and looking at him. Abū Bakr was a man easily moved to tears and he had no control over his weeping when he recited the Qur'ān. This perturbed the leaders of the Quraish idolaters.[153]

Ch. 87:   Saying prayers in the mosque of a market

> Ibn 'Aun said his prayers in a mosque situated in a house the doors of which were closed to people.

477 Abū Hurairah reported from the Prophet ﷺ that he said: "The prayer in congregation excels prayers said alone in one's house and prayers said in a market[154] by twenty-five degrees. So surely when any of you performs ablution, doing the *Wuḍū'* well, and comes to the mosque for the sole purpose of prayer, he does not take a step but Allāh raises him a degree because of it, and removes from him a sin, till he enters the mosque. When he enters the mosque, he is in a state of prayer as long as it keeps him there; and the angels pray for him as long as he is in his sitting-place in which he prays, saying

---

[153] Roads and thoroughfares are for the public who have every right to pass through them and to use them. They are the property of the road users and no one is entitled to appropriate any part of a road for his private use without permission from the public or the rightful authorities. As clearly stated in this ḥadīth, Abū Bakr built the mosque in the courtyard of his own house, not in the street. The word *finā'* is applied to an open space in front of a person's house. The idolaters of Makkah, who did not allow him even to say his prayers and to recite the Qur'ān openly, could not have allowed him to construct a mosque on the road. They complained to Ibn ad-Daghinah, under whose protection Abū Bakr returned to Makkah after he had resolved to leave the city to be away from the persistent annoyance caused by these people, that Abū Bakr had violated the terms of the agreement by saying his prayers and reciting the Qur'ān openly. When they could not tolerate this, they could not have allowed him to construct a mosque on the road. So if by the chapter heading Bukhārī means constructing on a ground that is one's private property by the side of a road, but not obstructing the traffic, the heading is correct; otherwise this heading would be inappropriate. This ḥadīth occurs in much greater detail in h. 2297 and h. 3905.

[154] Saying prayers in the market may mean either at the place where a person works or in a mosque situated in the market area. If the first meaning is accepted, it can also imply the second meaning because when it is permissible to say prayers at the place of business or work it must be permissible to construct something there to serve as a mosque. However, the "mosque of a market" cannot be in the middle of the street obstructing people and traffic. It means a mosque whose entrance is in the market place. Regarding the excelling of the prayer in congregation by so many degrees, see the footnote under h. 646.

'O Allāh, grant him protection against sin, O Allāh, have mercy on him', so long as he does not harm anyone and does not void wind."

Ch. 88: *Tashbīk* (dovetailing the fingers of one hand into those of the other) in the mosque and other places[155]

478–479 'Āṣim related that Wāqid reported from his father that ('Abdullāh) Ibn 'Umar or Ibn 'Amr (ibn al-'Āṣ) said: The Prophet ﷺ dovetailed the fingers of his one hand into those of the other.

480 'Āṣim ibn 'Alī said that 'Āṣim ibn Muḥammad related to us: I heard this ḥadīth from my father but I could not preserve it in my memory, so Wāqid corrected me in this from his father and said: I heard it from my father who used to say that 'Abdullāh ibn 'Amr (ibn al-'Āṣ) said that the Messenger of Allāh ﷺ said to him: "O 'Abdullāh ibn 'Amr, what will be your condition when you will be left in the midst of unworthy people?"

481 Abū Musa reported from the Prophet ﷺ that he said: "Surely a believer is to another believer like parts of a solid wall, imparting strength to each other." And he dovetailed the fingers of his one hand into those of the other.[156]

482 Abū Hurairah reported: The Messenger of Allāh ﷺ led us in prayer, being one of the two prayers after the sun declines — Ibn Sīrīn said: Abū Hurairah told the name of this prayer but I have forgotten. Abū Hurairah added: So he led us in two *rak'ahs* of prayer, then finished it with *Salām*. He stood up near a piece of wood which was lying across the mosque and reclined on it as if he was angry. He placed his right hand over his left hand and dovetailed the fingers of the one hand into those of the other and placed his right cheek on the back of his left hand. People who were in a hurry went out by the doors of the mosque and said: "The prayers have been shortened." Among the people were Abū Bakr and 'Umar and these two were hesitant of talking to him. And among the people there was a man whose hands were long, and

---

[155] The word *tashbīk* means that the fingers of one hand are dovetailed or interlaced into those of the other. There are ḥadīth to the effect that *tashbīk* is forbidden but either they should be considered unreliable or taken as meaning that it is forbidden while a person is performing his prayers. Otherwise, as seen in the ḥadīth here, the Holy Prophet himself used to do this to illustrate some point.

[156] By interlocking the fingers of the two hands into each other, the Holy Prophet illustrated the strength which can resist and foil all attempts to separate them. Similarly, when Muslims are united in the manner of interlocked fingers, this will protect them from any harm from an enemy. It is to be regretted that the Muslims of today fail to understand this instruction of the Holy Prophet. Instead of being like an impregnable edifice, they resemble a heap of stray, disorderly bricks.

who used to be called "the man with two hands" (*Dhul-Yadain*). He said: "O Messenger of Allāh, have you forgotten or has the prayer been shortened?" He (the Holy Prophet) said: "Neither have I forgotten nor has it been shortened." Then he asked: "Is it as Dhul-Yadain is saying?" People said: "Yes."[157] So he (the Holy Prophet) went forward and said what he had left out (of the prayer) and then finished it with *Salām*. Then he called out *Allāhu Akbar* and prostrated like his (usual) prostrations or for longer. Then he raised his head and called out *Allāhu Akbar,* and again called out *Allāhu Akbar* and prostrated like his (usual) prostrations or for longer. Then he raised his head and called out *Allāhu Akbar.*

People asked him (Ibn Sīrīn) several times: "Then he finished it with *Salām*?" He would say: "I have been informed that 'Imrān ibn Ḥusain said: 'Then he finished it with *Salām*'."[158]

Ch. 89: Mosques that are situated on the ways to Madīnah and in places in which the Prophet ﷺ said his prayer

483 Mūsā ibn 'Uqbah related: I saw Sālim ibn 'Abdullāh (ibn 'Umar) searching for certain spots on the road and saying his prayers at those places. He narrated that his father ('Abdullāh ibn 'Umar) used to say his prayers at these places and that he (the father) had seen the Prophet ﷺ saying prayers at those places.

He added: Nāfi' reported to me from Ibn 'Umar that he used to say prayers at these places, and I asked Sālim and as far as I know he agreed with Nāfi' about all these places but they disagreed only as regards the mosque at Sharaf al-Rauhā'.[159]

---

[157] In h. 401 it is reported that the Holy Prophet said: "I am only a mortal like you, I forget as you forget." In the Qur'ān, he is told: "We shall make you recite so you shall not forget, except what Allāh please" (87:6–7). This means that the Holy Prophet could forget things except what came to him through revelation. There is a ḥadīth: "Adam forgot and his offspring also forget" (Tirmidhī, 'Commentary on the Qur'ān, h. 3356). Allāh is the being Who "neither makes error nor forgets" (the Qur'ān, 20:52). Prophets are mortal with the attributes of mortals, so that people should not take them as God.

[158] In this incident the Holy Prophet only said two *rak'ahs* instead of four. After being reminded of this mistake, he led a two *rak'ah* prayer, closing it with *Salām*. After performing the prostrations of forgetfulness and sitting down, he again did the *Salām*. See h. 1227 where this ḥadīth is repeated briefly. Further details of these issues are discussed in Bukhārī's book: 'Forgetting during Prayer'.

[159] 'Abdullāh ibn 'Umar was so fond of imitating the practice of the Holy Prophet that he would do every kind of act which the Holy Prophet did. This included stopping off to say prayers

484 ʿAbdullāh ibn ʿUmar informed (Nāfiʿ)[160] that the Messenger of Allāh ﷺ used to alight at Dhul Ḥulaifah, when he used to go for *ʿUmrah* and also in his *Ḥajj* when he would make the *Ḥajj,* under a tree on the spot of the mosque which is in Dhul Ḥulaifah. When he used to return from an expedition and would be on this road, or (when returning) from *Ḥajj* or *ʿUmrah,* he would alight in the midst of the valley. When he would ascend from the bottom of the valley he would make his she-camel to sit down on the stony ground which is at the eastern border of the valley and take rest there during the later part of the night at this place till it would be morning. This place is not near the mosque which is on the rocks, nor on the hillock on which the mosque is situated. There is a stream near which ʿAbdullāh (ibn ʿUmar) used to say his prayers; in the bed of the stream there were mounds where the Messenger of Allāh ﷺ used to say his prayers. Torrents of water had filled it with pebbles so much so that the spot wherein ʿAbdullāh used to pray is buried.

485 And ʿAbdullāh ibn ʿUmar related to him that the Prophet ﷺ said his prayers where lies the small mosque which is near the mosque that is in Sharaf al-Rauḥāʾ. ʿAbdullāh used to know this place at which the Prophet ﷺ used to say his prayers. He used to say: "This place would be on your right as you stand to pray in the mosque, and this mosque is on the right edge of the road when you start going towards Makkah, and between it and the big mosque is the distance of a stone's throw or like it."

486 And that Ibn ʿUmar used to pray towards the hillock which is near the end of Rauḥāʾ and this hillock has its side ending at the edge of the road near

---

at all those places on the way to Makkah for *Ḥajj* and *ʿUmrah* where the Holy Prophet stopped off to say his prayers. Such imitation is only an expression of love and devotion but it is not required by the religion as it causes undue hardship when people in general try to do the same. It carries the risk of becoming a form of man-worship. Caliph ʿUmar took a different view of such imitation. Finding people rushing towards a place to reach it before others, he asked what it was for, and on being told that it was a place where the Holy Prophet had once said his prayers, he stopped them and said that they should say their prayer wherever they were at the time of prayer. If the enthusiasm for such imitation is kept within proper bounds there is, of course, no harm in such imitations. It is a good thing to perpetuate the memory of a great event of the past which happened in a certain place, but not to the extent of revering and worshipping such places. Sharaf al-Rauḥāʾ is a place 36 miles away from Madīnah.

[160] In reports from h. 484 to h. 492 those places are mentioned at which the Holy Prophet stopped on his way and said his prayers, and ʿAbdullāh ibn ʿUmar did the same in imitation. Eight stages are mentioned on the way from Madīnah to Makkah but, except the mosque at Dhul Ḥulaifah, here is no sign of these stages left now. The distance between Makkah and Madīnah is 270 miles and if there were eight stages it means that the Holy Prophet covered a distance of more than 30 miles per day. It seems that ordinary caravans completed the journey in twelve stages. Each of h. 485 to h. 492, except h. 486, begins with the words: "And ʿAbdullāh ibn ʿUmar related to him (i.e., to Nāfiʿ)"; these indicate the beginning of the next stage, the first being in h. 484. See also h. 1532 and h. 1533.

the mosque which lies between it and the end (of Rauhā') as you go towards Makkah, and a mosque has been built there. 'Abdullāh ibn 'Umar did not pray in this mosque and he used to leave it on his left and behind himself and he used to pray in front of it towards the hillock itself. 'Abdullāh used to start from Rauhā' and would not say the *Ẓuhr* prayer till he came to this place and said his *Ẓuhr* prayer in it. When he proceeded from Makkah, if he happened to pass by it an hour before the morning or towards the end of dawn, he would alight till he would say his morning prayer here.

487 And 'Abdullāh Ibn 'Umar related to him that the Prophet ﷺ used to alight under a massive tree near ar-Ruwaithah on the right side of the road, and opposite the road, at a place that was open and soft, so that he would depart from the hillock which was at a distance of two miles from ar-Ruwaithah.[161] The top of the tree has broken and hangs down, bent in the middle, and it stands on a trunk and in its trunk there are mounds many in number.

488 And 'Abdullāh ibn 'Umar related to him that the Prophet ﷺ said his prayers on the edge of the mound behind al-'Arj, and as you go towards Haḍbah.[162] Near this mosque there are two or three graves and on the graves are huge stones. On the right side of the road near the stones of the road.[163] Between these stones 'Abdullāh used to depart from al-'Arj after the sun had declined at mid-day and he used to say the *Ẓuhr* prayer in this mosque.

489 And 'Abdullāh ibn 'Umar related to him that the Messenger of Allāh ﷺ alighted near the trees (*saraḥāt*) on the left side of the road in the stream near Harshai.[164] This stream touches the outskirts of Harshai and between it and the road is a distance of about a bow-shot. 'Abdullāh ibn 'Umar used to

---

[161] Ruwaithah is the name of a village situated at a distance of some 60 miles from Madīnah. The word *barīd* commonly means distance, as translated here. However, some consider *barīd ar-Ruwaithah* to means the road leading to Ruwaithah, and others take it to mean a stage in the journey of those travellers.

[162] *Tal'at-in* means mound and 'Arj is the name of a big village which is at a distance of 14 miles from Ruwaithah. The Arabic word *haḍbah* means a hill which is spread irregularly over a large area without any sharp peak. In the opinion of some, 'Arj is at a distance of 17 miles from the Mosque of the Holy Prophet at Madīnah as one proceeds towards Haḍbah.

[163] *Salamāt* is plural of *salamah,* and means 'stones'.

[164] *Saraḥāt* is the plural of *sarḥah* meaning a big tree. Harshai is the name of a hill in the region of Tihāmah and is situated at the point where the roads from Madīnah and Syria meet. The tree closest to this point and the biggest of all is the one which 'Abdullāh ibn 'Umar used to face while saying his prayers there because the Holy Prophet in his own days had said his prayers at this point.

say his prayers towards the tree which was the nearest of the trees to the road, and it was the tallest of them all.

490 And ʿAbdullāh ibn ʿUmar related to him that the Prophet ﷺ used to alight in this stream which was below Marr aẓ-Ẓahrān in the direction of Madīnah when you descend from aṣ-Ṣafrāwāt. He (the Holy Prophet) would alight in the bed of this stream on the left side of the road as you go towards Makkah, the distance between the alighting place of the Messenger of Allāh ﷺ and this road being no more than a stone-throw.

491 And ʿAbdullāh ibn ʿUmar related to him that the Prophet ﷺ used to alight at Dhī Ṭuwā and spend the night till it was morning, and he would say his morning prayer when he would arrive at Makkah, and this spot where the Messenger of Allāh ﷺ said his prayer is on a hard rock and it was not in the mosque which has been built there but below that on a hard rock.

492 And ʿAbdullāh ibn ʿUmar related to him that the Prophet ﷺ turned his face towards the two peaks of the mountain which were between him and the high mountain in the direction of the Kaʿbah. So he (ʿAbdullāh ibn ʿUmar) kept the mosque which has been built there on the left of the mosque which is on the edge of the rock. And the place of prayer of the Prophet ﷺ is below this on the black rocks. You leave ten hand-lengths or so from the rocks, then say your prayers facing towards the two peaks of the mountain which lie between you and the Kaʿbah.

Ch. 90:   **The *sutrah* (or screening) in front of the Imām is (also) the *sutrah* for those who are behind him**

493 ʿAbdullāh ibn ʿAbbās reported: I came riding on a she-ass, and at that time I was approaching the age of maturity, and the Messenger of Allāh ﷺ was leading the people in prayer at Minā without facing any wall. So I passed in front of some of the rows (in the congregation), I dismounted and sent away the she-ass to graze and joined in the row. This was not made an objection against me by anyone.[165]

494 Ibn ʿUmar reported that when the Messenger of Allāh ﷺ used to come out on the day of Eid, he would order for a spearhead that would then be placed before him and he would pray towards it, while the people would

---

[165] This is a repetition of h. 76, but here the words *bi-n-nās* (lit. "with the people") have been added after *yuṣallī* ("saying prayers"), showing that the Holy Prophet was leading the people in prayer. In this report there is no mention of any *sutrah* or screen in front. However, it was the Holy Prophet's practice to fix some spear or javelin in front of himself while saying his prayer on a journey, as stated in the next two reports, h. 494 and h. 495. The object of such a screen is to prevent people from passing closely in front of a man in prayer, thereby distracting him.

be behind him. He used to do the same while on a journey. Because of this the leaders (of the Muslims) have adopted this (practice).

495 ʿAun ibn Abū Juḥaifah reported that he heard from his father (Abū Juḥaifah) that the Prophet ﷺ led them in prayer at al-Baṭḥā', while in front of him was a spear (planted), of two *rakʿahs* of *Ẓuhr* and two *rakʿahs* of *ʿAṣr*, and women and donkeys were passing in front of him.[166]

Ch. 91: What should be the distance between the person praying and the *sutrah*?

496 Sahl (ibn Saʿd) reported: There used to be a space sufficient between the prayer place of the Messenger of Allāh ﷺ and the wall for a goat to pass through.[167]

497 Salamah reported: The wall of the mosque was near the pulpit, leaving a space just enough for a goat to pass through.[168]

Ch. 92: Saying prayers towards the spearhead

498 ʿAbdullāh (ibn ʿUmar) reported that the Prophet ﷺ used to have a spear fixed before him and he would pray towards it.[169]

Ch. 93: Saying prayers towards a javelin

499 ʿAun ibn Abū Juḥaifah related that he heard his father (Abū Juḥaifah) say: The Messenger of Allāh ﷺ came out to us at mid-day. Water was brought for *Wuḍū'* and he performed ablution. Then he led us in *Ẓuhr* and *ʿAṣr* prayers, while in front of him was a spear (planted), and women and donkeys were passing behind it.[170]

---

[166] This repetition of h. 376 contains only a small part of it, but in addition it mentions the prayers as being *Ẓuhr* and *ʿAṣr* and the name of the place as being al-Baṭḥā'. The prayers were shortened on account of the journey.

[167] According to a report, Bilāl stated that there was a space of three arm-lengths between the Holy Prophet and the *sutrah* (see h. 506 and h. 1599) which was sufficient for going in prostration. The prayer place or *muṣallā* of the Holy Prophet means the whole space taken by a man to pray up to the state of prostration. Thus the space that intervened between the point of prostration and the wall that acted as a screen was large enough for a goat to pass through.

[168] The Holy Prophet said his prayers to one side of the pulpit and his point of prostration would be aligned with the back of the pulpit. So this is consistent with the previous ḥadīth as to the amount of space between his point of prostration and the wall.

[169] This is a repetition of part of h. 494.

[170] This is a repetition of h. 376 similar to h. 495. It is further stated here that the Holy Prophet came out at noon time and water for ablution was brought to him.

500 Anas ibn Mālik said: When the Prophet ﷺ used to go out to answer a call of nature, I and a boy used to follow him, (taking) with us a spear or staff or javelin, and with us a pot (of water). When he finished from the call of nature, we would hand him that pot.[171]

Ch. 94:   *Sutrah* at Makkah and other places

501 Abū Juḥaifah reported: The Messenger of Allāh ﷺ came out at midday, and he said *Ẓuhr* and *'Aṣr* prayers of two *rak'ahs* at al-Baṭḥā' while in front of him was a spear (planted). He performed ablution and people began to rub on their bodies the water of his *Wuḍū'*.[172]

Ch. 95:   Saying prayers towards pillars

'Umar said: The people in prayer have a better right to the pillars than those who are engaged in talking near it. Ibn 'Umar saw a man saying prayers between two pillars and he brought him near a pillar and said: Pray towards it.[173]

502 Yazīd ibn Abū 'Ubaid related: I used to come with Salamah ibn al-Akwa' and he used to pray by the pillar which was near the scriptures *(muṣḥaf)*. I said: "O Abū Muslim, I have seen you trying to say your prayers near this pillar." He said: "I have surely seen the Prophet ﷺ trying to say his prayers near it." [174]

503 Anas (ibn Mālik) reported: I have seen the greatest of the Companions of the Prophet ﷺ hurrying towards the pillars at the time of the *Maghrib* prayer.

---

[171] This is a repetition of h. 150 with the addition referring to taking "a spear or staff or javelin" and also the last sentence.

[172] This is a repetition of h. 376 which resembles the repetitions in h. 495 and h. 499. The wording of the chapter heading is to indicate that a *sutrah* is required whether the prayer is held in Makkah or elsewhere. Bukhārī thus refutes certain inauthentic reports according to which the Holy Prophet was seen praying in the Sacred Mosque without a *sutrah* between him and the people walking in front (see Abū Dāwūd, book: 'Rites of the *Ḥajj*', h. 2016; Nasā'ī, book: *Qiblah*, h. 758).

[173] All the reports speaking of saying prayers towards some pillar mean that the pillar was used as a *sutrah*, so that other people coming in and going out from the mosque could do so without disturbing people's prayers. This is the object of forbidding people to say prayers between the pillars, and it applies to prayers said alone, for prayers said in congregation would be organized in rows.

[174] The word *muṣḥaf*, meaning the holy text, refers to the manuscript which 'Uthmān, the third Caliph, had got written and sent to various centres of the Islamic kingdom. A copy of this was kept in Madīnah in the Mosque of the Holy Prophet.

Shu'bah added from 'Amr and Anas (to this report): Until the Prophet ﷺ came out.[175]

Ch. 96: Prayer between the pillars other than the congregational prayers

504 Ibn 'Umar reported: The Prophet ﷺ entered the House (of Ka'bah) with Usāmah ibn Zaid, 'Uthmān ibn Ṭalḥah and Bilāl. He remained there for a long time, then he came out. I was the first among the people to follow him, and I asked Bilāl: "Where did he pray?" He said: "Between the two front pillars.[176]

505 'Abdullāh ibn 'Umar reported that the Messenger of Allāh ﷺ entered the Ka'bah with Usāmah ibn Zaid, Bilāl and 'Uthmān ibn Ṭalḥah al-Ḥajabī. He ('Uthmān) locked the door and he (the Holy Prophet) remained in it. I asked Bilāl when he came out: "What did the Prophet ﷺ do?" He said: "He kept one pillar to his left and one pillar to his right and three pillars behind him, and in those days the Ka'bah had six pillars, then he said his prayers." [177]

Ismā'īl told us (i.e., told Bukhārī) that (Imām) Mālik related to me: "two pillars on his right." [178]

Ch. 97:   Related to the above

506 Nāfi' reported that whenever 'Abdullāh (ibn 'Umar) entered the Ka'bah he would walk straight ahead on entering, keeping the door at his back. He would proceed until there were about three arm-lengths between him and the wall in front of him. There he would pray aiming at the place where Bilāl had informed him that the Messenger of Allāh ﷺ prayed. He (Ibn 'Umar) said: There is no harm for anyone to pray at any place where he wishes inside the Ka'bah.[179]

---

[175] In h. 624 in the Book of *Adhān* ('Call to Prayer'), the Holy Prophet is reported as saying: "Between every two *Adhāns* there is a prayer, for whoever wishes." In other words, optional prayers can be said between the *Adhān* and the *Iqāmah*. Accordingly, the Companions of the Holy Prophet used to say some optional prayer before the *Iqāmah* in the *Maghrib* prayer, with the pillars of the mosque as their *sutrah*.

[176] This is a repetition of h. 397, which has also been repeated in h. 468. See also h. 1598.

[177] This is again a repetition of h. 397. Its opening is similar to h. 504. See h. 1598.

[178] The words added by Ismā'īl take account of all the six pillars.

[179] This is repeated in h. 1599. Ibn 'Umar says that one may pray anywhere in the House of God; he prayed where the Holy Prophet did due to his deep love for and attachment to the Holy Prophet. If the Holy Prophet did a certain thing in a certain way for some purpose, and there are

Ch. 98:   Saying prayers towards a she-camel or a he-camel or a tree or towards a saddle

507 Nāfiʿ reported from Ibn ʿUmar who reported from the Prophet ﷺ that he used to make his she-camel sit across and pray towards it. I (a narrator) asked (Nāfiʿ): "What do you think (he did) if the beast moved." He said: "He used to take the saddle off, put it in a right state, and pray towards its back part" or he said "towards its end". And Ibn ʿUmar used to do the same.[180]

Ch. 99:   Saying prayers towards a bedstead

508 ʿĀ'ishah reported: Do you equate us (women) with the dog and the donkey? And actually, I have seen myself lying in bed and the Prophet ﷺ coming in and placing himself by the middle of the bedstead and saying prayers. I disliked remaining in front of him, so I used to slip towards the foot of my bed till I slipped out of my quilt.[181]

Ch. 100: The person praying should repel the one who passes in front of him

Ibn ʿUmar repelled (one such man) when he was reciting the testimony of faith (*Tashahhud*) and (he was) in the Kaʿbah, and he said: "If he refuses unless you fight with him, you should fight with him." [182]

---

other ways of achieving the same purpose, it is not contrary to the *Sunnah* to do it in a different way. For instance, to cover the unexposable parts of his body the Holy Prophet wore a waist-wrapper. This does not mean that wearing it is *Sunnah* and to wear trousers is against the *Sunnah*. People are needlessly strict in these matters and have added all kinds of small requirements into the observance of Islamic teachings as if these were matters of principle.

[180] The meaning is that an animal or an inanimate object can be used as a *sutrah*. The chapter heading also includes "tree", whose permissibility is deduced from the mention of a "saddle" because the latter also contains wood. Using them as *sutrah* does not imply taking them as objects of worship, just as facing the Kaʿbah does not imply that it is being worshipped.

[181] Some people have unwarrantedly taken this ḥadīth to mean that the Holy Prophet stood on the bedstead in prayer. Bukhārī, however, is right that he was standing on the ground near the bedstead lying in front of him. In h. 514 the words are: "…the bed was between him and the *Qiblah*." ʿĀ'ishah was anxious to contradict the wrong view held by some people that there was a saying of the Holy Prophet to the effect that if a woman or a dog or an ass passed in front of a man in prayer, his prayer becomes void. She ridicules the idea. This shows how, even as early as the time of the Companions of the Holy Prophet, certain wrong notions had entered among the Muslims through lack of understanding.

[182] This does not mean that one should start fighting in the midst of the prayer. All it means is that one should be very strict in this matter so that people are careful not to disturb the prayer of others. This remonstration can be done after the prayer.

509 Abū Ṣāliḥ as-Sammān reported: I saw Abū Saʿīd al-Khudrī praying on a Friday towards a thing that screened him from people, and a young man from among the tribe of Banū Abū Muʿaiṭ wanted to pass in front of him. Abū Saʿīd prevented him (from doing so) by pushing him on his chest. The young man looked but did not find any passage except through the space in front of him. So he tried again to pass but Abū Saʿīd prevented him more severely than before. He abused Abū Saʿīd and then went to Marwān and complained about what he had experienced from Abū Saʿīd. Abū Saʿīd went after him to Marwān who asked: "What has happened between you and the son of your brother, O Abū Saʿīd?" He said: "I have heard the Prophet ﷺ say: When any of you says his prayer towards something that screens him from people and someone wants to pass in front of him, he should prevent him and if he refuses he should fight with him, for surely he is a devil." [183]

Ch. 101: The sin of one who passes in front of a person who is praying

510 Busr ibn Saʿīd reported that Zaid ibn Khālid sent him to Abū Juhaim inquiring from him about what he had heard from the Messenger of Allāh ﷺ about one who passes in front of a person who is praying, and Abū Juhaim said that the Messenger of Allāh ﷺ said: "If only the one who passes in front of a person who is praying knew what sin would be upon him! Waiting for forty (years) would have been better for him than passing in front." Abū an-Naḍr said: "I do not know whether he said forty days or months or years." [184]

Ch. 102: A man's standing in front of a man while the latter is in prayer

> ʿUthmān disliked that one should be in front of a man in prayer. This is in cases where it causes any diversion in him. As to cases in which no diversion is caused in him, Zaid ibn Thābit said: I do not mind, for surely a man does not cause distraction to the prayer of a man.

511 ʿĀʾishah, when it was mentioned before her as to what annuls prayer (if it passes in front) and people said: "A dog, a donkey and a woman", she said: "You have made us (women) dogs. I certainly saw the Prophet ﷺ saying

---

[183] A person who thus causes disturbance in prayer has been called a devil (*shaiṭān*). This shows the wide meaning of this term. Some have concluded from this use of the word *shaiṭān* that such a man should be fought in the way that *shaiṭān* is fought, i.e., in a moral sense and not physically. Abū Saʿīd himself only tried to stop the man from passing in front of him twice and did not fight him during prayer. It appears that he resorted to this only because the man was passing very close to him.

[184] In *Musnad al-Bazzār* the words are *arba ʿīna kharīf-an,* meaning forty years (vol. 2, p. 62, h. 3782). All this is meant to prevent anyone from causing diversion in the mind of the person in prayer.

prayers and I would be lying on the bed between him and the *Qiblah*. If I needed anything, as I disliked to pass in front of him, I would slip away quietly." [185]

Ch. 103: Saying prayers while a sleeping person lies in front[186]

512 'Ā'ishah reported: The Prophet ﷺ used to say his prayers while I would be sleeping, lying across (the width of) his bed. When he wanted to say his *Witr* prayer, he would awake me, so I would say my *Witr* prayer.[187]

Ch. 104: Saying optional prayers while a woman is in the front

513 'Ā'ishah, wife of the Prophet ﷺ, reported: I used to sleep in front of the Messenger of Allāh ﷺ and my two legs used to be in front of him. When he would go into prostration, he would press me and I would withdraw my legs, and when he would stand up, I would stretch them. She (further) said: There used to be no lamps in houses in those days.[188]

Ch. 105: One who says that nothing can annul prayer

514 'Ā'ishah, when it was mentioned before her as to what annuls prayer (if it passes in front), a dog, a donkey and a woman, she said: "You have likened us (women) to donkeys and dogs. By Allāh! I certainly saw the Prophet ﷺ saying prayers and I would be lying on the bed between him and the *Qiblah*. If I needed anything, as I disliked to sit and trouble the Prophet ﷺ, I would slip away by the side of his feet." [189]

515 Ibn Akhī ibn Shihāb related that he asked his uncle as to what annuls prayer, and he said: Nothing annuls it.

'Urwah ibn Zubair informed that 'Ā'ishah, wife of the Prophet ﷺ, said: The Messenger of Allāh ﷺ certainly used to get up to say prayers at night,

---

[185] This is a repetition of h. 508 with a different opening and other differences.

[186] According to some authorities such as Mujāhid and Imām Mālik, it is undesirable to say prayers while someone is sleeping in front. Abū Dāwūd, Ibn Mājah and Ṭabarānī have included weak reports to the effect that it is forbidden. Bukhārī shows in this chapter that these views are not correct.

[187] This shows that the wives of the Holy Prophet would also get up towards the end of the night and say their prayers. Thus women were no less keen for worship than men. This ḥadīth is repeated in h. 997.

[188] This is a repetition of h. 382 in the same words. The prayer referred to is *Tahajjud*, which is said after midnight and is optional.

[189] This repetition of h. 508 is like its repetition in h. 511 except that the closing words about slipping away are different.

while I would be lying across between him and the *Qiblah* on the bed of the people of his house.[190]

Ch. 106: When a person carries a small girl on his neck during prayer

516 Abū Qatādah al-Anṣārī reported that the Messenger of Allāh ﷺ used to say his prayers while carrying Umāmah, daughter of Zainab — the daughter of the Messenger of Allāh ﷺ — and of Abū al-ʿĀṣ ibn Rabīʿah ibn ʿAbdush-Shams. When he went in prostration he would lay put down, and when he would stand up he would carry her.[191]

Ch. 107: When a person says prayers towards a bed wherein is a woman in menstruation

517 ʿAbdullāh ibn Shaddād ibn al-Hād reported that his aunt Maimūnah, daughter of al-Ḥārith, informed him: My bed was near the prayer place of the Prophet ﷺ, and sometimes his clothes would fall upon me while I was lying on my bed.[192]

518 ʿAbdullāh ibn Shaddād related that he heard his aunt Maimūnah say: The Prophet ﷺ used to pray while I would be sleeping besides him. When he

---

[190] The second part of h. 515 here is a repetition of h. 383. Some hold that if a dog, donkey or woman passes in front of a man praying, his prayer is rendered null and void. This is contradicted by the statement of ʿĀʾishah in h. 508, h. 511 and h. 514, and by the report from Ibn ʿAbbās in h. 493 to the effect that he passed in front of the rows of congregational prayer riding on his ass. Some have tried to reconcile the two views by explaining that by prayer being annulled is only meant that the person praying is distracted. There is no doubt that prayer cannot become null and void by the mere passing of something, whatever it may be, in front of the person praying.

[191] According to reports in Ṣaḥīḥ Muslim and Abū Dāwūd, the Holy Prophet was leading prayers at that time (Muslim, book: 'Mosques', ch. 9; Abū Dāwūd, book: 'Prayer', h. 917), and Abū Dāwūd also contains a report that it was either the *Ẓuhr* or the *ʿAṣr* prayer (Abū Dāwūd, book: 'Prayer', h. 920). Other reports say that he used to place the baby on the floor while going into *rukūʿ*. The Holy Prophet had great love for children in general and this particular child was the daughter of his daughter. Incidentally this shows that the Holy Prophet had great regard for girls and respect for women, something quite contrary to the attitude of the Arabs of the time who used to hate the very birth of a female child and went to the extent of burying them alive. This regard of the Holy Prophet for the daughter's daughter was a silent protest, in fact, at that deprecable attitude of the Arab mind. Some people have tried to belittle the importance of this report by giving this incident interpretations that are unfounded. Some have declared his action as abrogated. But these attempts are unwarranted. It needs no argument to say that if some action is established from the Holy Prophet's example, it cannot be declared as void by any school of jurisprudence.

[192] This is a repetition of h. 333.

went in prostration, his clothes used to touch me while I would be having menstruation.[193]

Ch. 108: Should a man press his wife at the time of going in prostration so that he may prostrate

519 Al-Qāsim related that ʿĀ'ishah said: How bad that you equate us (women) with the dog and the donkey! I certainly saw the Messenger of Allāh ﷺ saying prayers while I would be lying between him and the *Qiblah*. When he wanted to go in prostration he would press my legs and I would withdraw them.[194]

Ch. 109: A woman removing something dirty from a man praying

520 ʿAbdullāh (ibn Masʿūd) reported: While the Messenger of Allāh ﷺ was standing praying near the Kaʿbah, and the Quraish were in a gathering of theirs (nearby), one of them said: "Do you not see this show (of worship)? Which of you can go and bring the dung, blood and stomach contents of the slaughtered camel of such and such family? Then he should wait till he (the Holy Prophet) goes in prostration and place it between his shoulders."

Then the most unfortunate one among them got up and when the Messenger of Allāh ﷺ went in prostration, he placed it between his shoulders. The Prophet ﷺ remained in prostration. They laughed so much that they fell upon one another because of laughing.

At this, someone went to Fāṭimah who was then a young girl and she came running. The Prophet ﷺ was still in prostration. She removed the filth from him and cursed them to the face. When the Messenger of Allāh ﷺ finished the prayer, he said: "O Allāh, seize the Quraish! O Allāh, seize the Quraish! O Allāh, seize the Quraish!" Then he took their names: "O Allāh, seize ʿAmr ibn Hishām and ʿUtbah ibn Rabīʿah, and Shaibah ibn Rabīʿah and al-Walīd ibn ʿUtbah and Umayyah ibn Khalaf and ʿUqbah ibn Abū Muʿaiṭ and ʿUmārah ibn al-Walīd."

ʿAbdullāh (ibn Masʿūd) added: By Allāh! I certainly saw them lying dead on the day of Badr. Then they were dragged to the well of Badr. Then the Messenger of Allāh ﷺ said: "The people of the well are followed by a curse." [195]

---

[193] This is also a repetition of h. 333, similar to the last ḥadīth.

[194] This is a repetition of h. 508.

[195] This is a repetition of h. 240 with some differences. Here the name of the seventh man, whose name was said in h. 240 to have been forgotten by the narrators, is given as ʿUmārah ibn al-Walīd. In h. 240 the first man in this list is Abū Jahl, but here his real name is given instead, which was ʿAmr ibn Hishām. The connection with the chapter heading is that Fāṭimah, a female, removed filth from the Holy Prophet who was at prayer.

PART 3

Book 9: Mawāqīt aṣ-Ṣalāt
Times of Prayer

In the name of Allāh, the Beneficent, the Merciful

Ch. 1: Times of prayer and their excellence

The word of Allāh, the Most High: "Prayer indeed has been enjoined on the believers at fixed times (*mauqūt-an*)" (the Qur'ān, 4:103), i.e., *muwaqqat-an*, it is an obligation upon them assigned with times.[1]

521 Ibn Shihāb reported that 'Umar ibn 'Abdul 'Azīz one day said his prayer late,[2] so 'Urwah ibn az-Zubair came to him and told him that al-

---

[1] As usual Bukhārī starts this book by citing a verse of the Qur'ān as the authority for the ḥadīth reports that follow. He explains the word *mauqūt* occurring in the verse of the Qur'ān by the word *muwaqqat* which means that a time schedule must be observed in the performance of prayer. The times of prayer were communicated to the Holy Prophet by Allāh through the angel Gabriel, as is shown by the ḥadīth that follows. This communication, however, was through what is called *waḥy khafī*, which is different from *waḥy matluww*, i.e., the kind of revelation through which the Qur'ān came. These times of prayers were also later revealed through the Qur'ān on different occasions. It was in confirmation of what the Holy Prophet was instructed before and what he followed in practice. The Holy Prophet, it must be borne in mind, began these prayers long before the Quranic revelations were received in this connection. Some critics have objected that the appointment of time takes away the spiritual position of the prayers, meaning that it should have been left to the inclinations of a person as to when to pray and that would have been more natural. God, however, Who knows the nature of man has very rightly prescribed a time-table for prayer. He knew that without some such timetable man fails to attend to any regular duty. Indirectly this regularization of prayer points to the necessity of regularity in every other affair of life. It is much to be regretted that Muslims, whose religious life was systematized in this way, need to be taught the lesson of regularity and punctuality as they are today behind other nations in displaying this virtue. To make the habit of prayer an ensured feature of Muslim communal life, and not merely an individual matter, it has further been ordained that it should be said in congregation. But for these rules the Muslim prayer would have fallen into disuse.

[2] In the repetition of this ḥadīth in h. 3221 the words are that he "delayed the *'Aṣr* prayer a little." According to Ṭabarānī, at this time 'Umar ibn 'Abdul 'Azīz (d. 720 C.E./101 A.H.) was Governor of Madīnah under the rule of Walīd ibn 'Abdul Malik. During the rulership of the Umayyads punctuality in the performance of prayers was not strictly observed. However, this was not the reason of 'Umar ibn 'Abdul 'Azīz delaying this particular prayer. As a rule he was

Mughīrah ibn Shu'bah one day said his prayer late while he was in Iraq,[3] and Abū Mas'ūd al-Anṣārī came to him and said: "What is this, O Mughīrah? Do you not know that Gabriel descended and said the prayer, so the Messenger of Allāh ﷺ said the prayer;[4] then he (Gabriel) said the prayer, so the Messenger of Allāh ﷺ said the prayer; then he (Gabriel) said the prayer, so the Messenger of Allāh ﷺ said the prayer; then he (Gabriel) said the prayer, so the Messenger of Allāh ﷺ said the prayer; then he (Gabriel) said the prayer, so the Messenger of Allāh ﷺ said the prayer. Then he (Gabriel) said: This is what you have been enjoined to do."

Then 'Umar (ibn 'Abdul 'Azīz) said to 'Urwah: "Be careful of what you are narrating; was it Gabriel who appointed the time of prayer for the Messenger of Allāh ﷺ?"[5] 'Urwah said: "Bashīr ibn Abū Mas'ūd used to narrate just like this from his father."[6]

522 'Urwah said: 'Ā'ishah related to me that the Messenger of Allāh ﷺ used to say the *'Aṣr* prayer while the sun would be in her chamber before it would go up (on the wall)."[7]

Ch. 2:   (Importance of prayer)

The word of Allāh, the Mighty the Glorious: "(That is the right religion …) turning to Him; and keep your duty to Him, and keep up

---

very strict in this matter and it must have been by chance that he delayed this prayer. 'Urwah ibn az-Zubair accordingly informed him that the Holy Prophet's time of saying this prayer was different.

[3] Al-Mughīrah ibn Shu'bah was Governor of the city of Kūfah under Mu'āwiyah.

[4] It is stated in the *Maghāzī* of Ibn Isḥāq that this was on the morning following the night in which the prayer was made obligatory. The first prayer in which the angel Gabriel led the Holy Prophet in prayer was the *Ẓuhr* prayer. Here the question is dealt with very briefly. Details are found in other reports. This report also shows the commendable courage and boldness of the religious scholars of the time in correcting the rulers in their conduct without fear. Nor did the rulers prevent them from pointing out their mistakes. People had the freedom to approach their rulers, and they were easily accessible in those days.

[5] Evidently 'Umar ibn 'Abdul 'Azīz asked this question because he was unaware that the times of prayer were communicated to the Holy Prophet by Gabriel. This shows that people in those days would not accept any statement without verification.

[6] This shows that the ḥadīth which 'Urwah has narrated before 'Umar ibn 'Abdul 'Azīz was on the authority of Bashīr ibn Abū Mas'ūd and that 'Urwah had not referred to this authority when he first reported this ḥadīth.

[7] Since the question discussed was of the *'Aṣr* prayer, 'Urwah produced the evidence of 'Ā'ishah as well. Her apartment was very small and its height was just enough for a man to stand up without his head touching the ceiling. The fact that the sun's rays could be seen falling at that time inside the room shows that the sun was quite high.

prayer and be not of those who set up partners (with Allāh)" (the Qur'ān, 30:31).[8]

523 Ibn 'Abbās reported: The deputation of 'Abdul Qais came to the Messenger of Allāh ﷺ and said: "We are a tribe belonging to Rabī'ah and we cannot come to you except in the sacred month; so give us a commandment which we may take from you and convey to those (whom we have left) behind us." He (the Holy Prophet) said: "I enjoin you to observe four things and I forbid you to do four things: To believe in Allāh (is the basis)" — then he explained it to them — "To bear witness that there is no god but Allāh and that I am the Messenger of Allāh, to keep up prayer, and pay the *Zakāt*, and that you give one-fifth of the war acquisitions. And I forbid you *dubbā'*, *ḥantam*, *muqayyar* and *naqīr*.[9]

Ch. 3:   Giving a pledge to keep up prayer

524 Jarīr ibn 'Abdullāh reported: I swore allegiance to the Messenger of Allāh ﷺ to keep up prayer, pay the *Zakāt* and have goodwill for every Muslim.[10]

Ch. 4:   Prayer is an expiation (*kaffārah*)[11]

525 Ḥudhaifah said: We were sitting near 'Umar when he said: "Who among you has preserved the word of the Messenger of Allāh ﷺ relating to the Trial (*fitnah*)?" I said: "I (remember it) as he (the Holy Prophet) said it." He said: "You are surely bold about it." I said: "The trial of a man in connection with his family and his property and his children and his neighbour

---

[8] Here Bukhārī starts dealing with the importance of prayer, and again he first quotes a text from the Qur'ān. Evidently it means that submission or turning to God and keeping your duty to Him is only possible through prayer, and that prayer is what distinguishes a Muslim from one who sets up partners with God. Those who abandon prayer are akin to those who worship others alongside the One God.

[9] These are names of utensils used in those days for preparing alcoholic drinks, being respectively: vessels made of gourd, green jars, oily earthen cups and troughs of hollowed palm-trunk. Their use for other purposes is not forbidden. This is a repetition of h. 53 in a briefer form; see also h. 1398. Prayer here is included in believing in God, which emphasises its importance.

[10] H. 57 has been repeated here exactly in the same words. The Holy Prophet's taking of pledge from people to keep up prayer shows the importance of this institution.

[11] The word *kaffārah* is derived from the root *kafara*, meaning 'to cover'. Thus *kaffārah*, considered as an expiation, is something that covers or suppresses the sin. This means the suppression of the tendency to sin. Thus prayer becomes a *kaffārah* for sins in the sense that repeated presence before God, and expression of one's helplessness before Him, and filling the mind with a sense of His greatness and glory, prevents a person from disobedience to Him. The Qur'ān speaks of this as follows: "Surely prayer keeps one away from indecency and evil" (29:45).

is expiated by (his) prayer and fasting and charity and enjoining (what is good) and forbidding (what is evil)." [12] He ('Umar) said: "I do not mean this but the Trial which surges like the surging waves of the ocean." He (Ḥudhaifah) said: "You have nothing to fear from it, O Chief of the Believers, for surely between you and it there is a closed door." He ('Umar) said: "Will it be broken or opened?" He (Ḥudhaifah) said: "It will be broken." He ('Umar) said: "In that case it will never be closed."

We[13] asked: "Did 'Umar know this door?" He (Ḥudhaifah) said: "Yes, just as (he knew that) there is night after the next day. I certainly narrated a ḥadīth which is not wrong." We feared to ask Ḥudhaifah (more about it), so we asked Masrūq and he asked him (Ḥudhaifah) and he said: "The door was 'Umar." [14]

526 Ibn Mas'ūd reported that a man happened to kiss a woman and he came to the Prophet ﷺ and told him about it. So Allāh revealed: "And keep up prayer at the two ends of the day and in the first hours of the night. Surely good deeds take away evil deeds" (the Qur'ān, 11:114). The man asked: "O Messenger of Allāh, Is it (just) for me?" He said: "It is for all my followers." [15]

---

[12] The word *fitnah* originally means 'to put a thing in fire to separate the genuine from the spurious'. It is used also for chastisement, suffering and trouble, as well as unbelief and perfidity. A man is placed in *fitnah* (trial) in respect of his family and property as he is tested if he fulfils his duties and responsibilities in dealing with them. The idea evidently is that prayer enables a man to succeed in this test.

[13] By "we" are meant the narrators to whom Ḥudhaifah was relating this report.

[14] What 'Umar meant was that he did not want to know about the ordinary trials which individuals face personally in their daily lives but that great Trial which Muslims as a people would face. Accordingly, Ḥudhaifah told him that there was a door lying between the reign of 'Umar and that Trial, and that door was none but 'Umar himself. Ḥudhaifah's remark that this door would be broken pointed to the coming event of the martyrdom of 'Umar. History bears witness that, immediately after his martyrdom, troubles of the most serious magnitude befell the Muslims, and continued to befall after that. This ḥadīth is repeated in h. 1435 and h. 1895.

[15] This incident is referred to in Abū Dāwūd (book: *Ḥudūd*, ch. 32, h. 4468) in more detail. According to that account, the man said to the Holy Prophet: "I had sexual contact with a woman at the furthest part of the city, and I did with her everything except sexual intercourse. So here I am; do with me as you wish." A similar incident is reported in Bukhārī, h. 6823. These must have been incidents in which no one else was harmed, and the man, feeling that he had committed a sin against the code of morality of Islām, confessed to the Holy Prophet and asked to be punished. The Holy Prophet regarded his confession as sufficient.

The Holy Prophet also provided him with a remedy for sinful habits. It is to concentrate on doing good deeds and to have recourse to prayers devotedly. This will gradually diminish the inclination towards sin, which is why this prescription is said here to be meant for all Muslims. However, the concept of atonement or expiation for sin in Islām is different from what is generally understood. According to the Qur'ān, atonement consists in removing the very disposition for sin. This is indicated in the verse here: "Surely good deeds take away evil deeds."

Ch. 5:   The excellence of (saying) prayer at its appointed time

527 ʿAbdullāh (ibn Masʿūd) reported: I asked the Prophet ﷺ: "Which action is the dearest to God?" He said: "The prayer at its appointed time." ʿAbdullāh said: "Then which." He said: "Then goodness to the parents." ʿAbdullāh said: "Then which?" He said: "*Jihād* in the way of Allāh."

ʿAbdullāh said: He told me these things, and had I asked him more he would have told me more.[16]

Ch. 6:   The five prayers are an expiation for sins if they are said at their proper time with the congregation or without it

528 Abū Hurairah reported that he heard the Messenger of Allāh ﷺ say: "Tell me if there were a stream running by the door of any of you and he takes bath in it every day five times, what do you say, will it leave anything of the dirt which was on him?" They said: "Nothing of the dirt on him will be left." He said: "So that is the example of the five prayers by which Allāh obliterates the sins."

Ch. 7:   The omission (*taḍyīʿ*) of prayer from its proper time

529 Anas said: "I do not see anything out of what there used to be in the days of the Prophet ﷺ." It was said to him: "The prayer?" He said: "Have you not done with it what you do?"[17]

530 Az-Zuhrī said: I came to Anas ibn Mālik in Damascus and he was weeping. I said: "What makes you weep?" He said: "I do not see anything out of what I had witnessed except this prayer, and even this prayer is being wasted."[18]

---

[16] It is not prayer by itself but its observance at the proper time that has been described as most pleasing to Allāh because punctuality in prayer should lead to punctuality in every other affair of life, making the course of life smooth. The observance of prayer on time has been given the first place in the list of one's duties to God, and good treatment of parents the first place in the list of duties towards fellow beings. Parents on a small scale reflect the attribute *Rabb* of Allāh, Who creates and then fosters the development of His creation. The next item in the list is *Jihād* or striving in the way of Allāh, i.e., making utmost efforts in establishing truth in the world. In the Qurʾān also, duty to God comes before duty to fellow beings, the first in the latter category being the parents; see 17:23 and 31:14.

[17] This ḥadīth speaks of a time when the righteous Caliphate had been replaced by hereditary kingship and laxity and indifference had started to creep in towards the observance of the institutions of the Faith. Naturally those who had seen the days of the Holy Prophet found it difficult to reconcile the previous state with the one prevailing at that time. The delaying of the prayers from their appointed time is called "wasting" (*taḍyīʿ*) the prayers in the chapter heading and in h. 530.

[18] This was the time of Ḥajjāj ibn Yūsuf when prayers were much delayed beyond their proper

Ch. 8: The one who is praying is privately communicating with his Lord[19]

531 Anas reported that the Prophet ﷺ said: "When anyone of you is praying, he is privately communicating with his Lord, so he should not spit towards his right, but underneath his left foot.[20]

532 Anas reported from the Prophet ﷺ that he said: "Keep a balance in your prostrations and one of you should not stretch his two arms like the dog. And if anyone spits, he should neither spit in front of him nor towards his right, for he is privately communicating with his Lord."

Qatādah said: He should not spit ahead of him or in front of him, but towards his left or underneath his foot. Shu'bah said: He should neither spit in front of him nor towards his right, but (he could spit) towards his left or underneath his foot. Ḥumaid reported from Anas who reported from the Prophet ﷺ that he should not spit towards the *Qiblah* nor towards his right, but (he could spit) towards his left or underneath his foot.[21]

Ch. 9: During severity of heat, saying the *Ẓuhr* prayer at a cooler time[22]

times. Nonetheless, the kings and governors still used to join prayer congregations in mosques. Anas appears to mean that the zeal and fervour to spread the faith, and willingness to bear trials and tribulations for its sake and to make sacrifices, which characterised the first generation of the Muslims, was no longer to be found to the same extent.

[19] *Najā'* and *munājāt* mean to talk to someone in complete privacy. Its root means to be alone with a person in an elevated land (*najwah*). By describing prayer as an occasion for a private talk with God, the real object of prayer is conveyed, that is, to submit heartfelt petitions before one's Lord in privacy. Thus a person is expected to present all his troubles and difficulties without reservation to his Master at the time of prayer, observing this institution with complete faith in the power of the Master to grant his petition. This implies praying with full attention of the mind with all its feelings and expressions. Mechanical utterance of prescribed prayers and ritual adoption of certain bodily postures, without any reference to feelings, emotions and thoughts, is thus completely ruled out by Islām as constituting the real prayer. This makes it essential that during the established prayer a person must also, in addition to the prescribed words, present his own heart-felt petitions to God in his own language. Without this, the state of humility required in prayer cannot be created.

[20] This is a repetition of h. 405 with some difference in wording.

[21] Apart from the addition at the beginning regarding the prostrations, the other reports here are repetitions of statements occurring in h. 405–417.

[22] After dealing with the importance and purpose of prayer, Bukhārī now takes us to the question of the times of prayer. A mention is made first of the *Ẓuhr* prayer, thus indicating that this is the first prayer of the day. This may sound strange as many consider the day to begin with the morning, while for the arrangement of worldly affairs in modern times the day begins at midnight. However, in a spiritual sense the real beginning of the day is when the sun starts to decline. The underlying idea is that when the physical means of support start to fail, then the spiritual day begins.

533–534 Abū Hurairah reported and ʿAbdullāh ibn ʿUmar also reported, both relating it from the Messenger of Allāh ﷺ, that he said: "When the heat is very severe, say your prayer at a cooler hour, for surely the severity of heat is from the raging of Hell." [23]

535 Abū Dharr reported: The caller of the *Adhān* of the Prophet ﷺ gave the call to prayer for *Ẓuhr*. But he (the Holy Prophet) said: "Let it get cooler, let it get cooler", or he said: "Wait, wait". Then he said: "The severity of heat is from the raging of Hell. So when the heat is very severe, let it get cooler before the prayer." It was until we saw the shadows of hillocks (that we said the prayer).[24]

536–537 Abū Hurairah reported from the Prophet ﷺ that he said: "When the heat is very severe, let it get cooler before the prayer, for surely the severity of heat is from the raging of Hell. [537] And the fire complained to its Lord, saying: 'My Lord, some parts of mine are devouring other parts.' At this He permitted it to take two breaths, one in winter and the other in summer. These are when you find the severest heat and the severest coldest." [25]

538 Abū Saʿīd reported that the Messenger of Allāh ﷺ said: "Let it get cooler before (saying) the *Ẓuhr* prayer, for surely the severity of heat is from the raging of Hell."

Ch. 10:   Letting it get cooler before (saying) *Ẓuhr* (prayer) during a journey

539 Abū Dharr al-Ghifārī reported: We were with the Prophet ﷺ in a journey and the caller to prayer wanted to sound the call to prayer for *Ẓuhr*.

---

[23] Some people have interpreted cooler hour as meaning that this prayer should be said as soon as it is midday. But this is wrong because this particular hour is the hottest part of the day. The correct observance of this instruction should be to perform this prayer between 2.30 and 3.00 p.m. when the heat of the sun is comparatively less. Note also that while there is stress on the necessity of observing the prayers at their appointed times, the Holy Prophet also recommends varying the times according to climatic conditions. Thus the midday prayer called *Ẓuhr* could be said earlier in winter and later in summer in tropical countries.

[24] This report occurs in greater detail in h. 539, where it is stated that the caller to prayer (*muʾadh-dhin*) twice tried to sound the call to prayer for this prayer and each time he was prevented by the Holy Prophet from doing so. See also footnote 26.

[25] Statements relating the "complaint" of the fire are metaphorical, as Baiḍāwī has said. According to Ibn Ḥajar, its complaint means its blazing, and parts of it devouring each other means the concentration of its heat, and its taking breath means its varying in intensity. The Holy Prophet's mention of the freezing cold belies the unfounded allegation that he could think only in terms of the hot conditions in his part of the world and thus regarded all cold as bringing comfort.

The Prophet ﷺ said: "Let it get cooler." He again (after a while) wanted to sound the call but the Prophet ﷺ said: "Let it get cooler." It was until we saw the shadows of hillocks (that we said the prayer). Then the Prophet ﷺ said: "Surely the severity of heat is from the raging of Hell. So when the heat is very severe, let it get cooler before the prayer."

Ibn 'Abbās said: The word *yatafayya'u* means 'it inclines'.[26]

Ch. 11:   The time of *Ẓuhr* prayer is when the sun declines

Jābir said: The Prophet ﷺ used to say his prayer at midday.[27]

540 Anas ibn Mālik informed that the Messenger of Allāh ﷺ came out (one day) when the sun had begun to decline, and he said the *Ẓuhr* prayer. Then he stood up on the pulpit and talked about the Hour and mentioned in the course of it about the great disasters. Then he said: "Whoever likes to ask about anything, let him ask, for I will inform you regarding whatever you ask me as long as I am at this place of mine." So people wept much and he said repeatedly: "Ask me." So 'Abdullāh ibn Ḥudhāfah as-Sahmī stood up and said: "Who is my father?" He said: "Your father is Ḥudhāfah." Again he said repeatedly: "Ask me." 'Umar, who was sitting with his knees folded, said: "We are pleased with Allāh as our Lord, Islām as our religion, and Muḥammad ﷺ as our Prophet." Then he (the Prophet) became silent.[28] Then he said:

---

[26] The explanation of Ibn 'Abbās is in relation to the words "shadows of hillocks", *fai' at-tulūl*. The word *fai'* is used for the shadow of a thing after the decline of the sun, and *tulūl* is plural of *tal* which means a heap of sand or dust etc., flat in shape and of small height. Ibn 'Abbās refers to the word *yatafayya'u* from the Qur'ān (16:48), which is from the same root as *fai'*, and says it means 'declining'. It is evident that the shadow of such flat heaps is not visible until it is late in the afternoon. This description is meant to show that the Holy Prophet said his *Ẓuhr* prayer quite late in the afternoon. In the repetition of this ḥadīth in h. 629 the words are *ḥatta sāwa aẓ-ẓillu at-tulūl*, "until the shadows of the *tulūl* became equal", meaning until the shadow became of the same length as the height of the heap.

[27] There is no evidence to show that the Holy Prophet ever said his *Ẓuhr* prayer before the decline of the sun. For this reason, it is agreed on all hands that the time for *Ẓuhr* starts with the decline of the sun. In h. 560 from Jābir in the chapter 'Time of the *Maghrib* prayer' it is stated that the Holy Prophet said his *Ẓuhr* prayer at midday (*hājirah*) when the temperature is naturally high. This may be true on some occasion but the Holy Prophet's repeated instruction about the cooler time for the *Ẓuhr* prayer demands delay in this prayer.

[28] Some people are in the habit of asking unnecessary questions. The Holy Prophet disliked such questions as it showed a lack of manners. The people's weeping was due to their realization of their own fault. 'Umar very respectfully and tactfully assuaged the annoyance and anger of the Holy Prophet. The part of this ḥadīth, before the Holy Prophet's statement about being shown Paradise and Hell, has already occurred in h. 92 and h. 93.

"Paradise and Hell were just now presented before me in the direction of this wall and I had never seen such a good and a bad sight." [29]

541 Abū Barzah reported: The Prophet ﷺ used to say the morning prayer when one of us could (just) recognize the person sitting with him and he used to recite in it between sixty and one hundred (verses of the Qur'ān). He used to say the *Ẓuhr* prayer when the sun would be in decline, and the *'Aṣr* prayer when one of us could go to the far end of Madīnah and come back and the sun would be still bright — and I (a sub-narrator) forgot what he said about the *Maghrib* prayer. (And he further said): He (the Holy Prophet) did not mind delaying the *'Ishā'* prayer to one-third of the night, then he said: to the middle of the night.

542 Anas ibn Mālik reported: When we used to say our prayer behind the Messenger of Allāh ﷺ for *Ẓuhr,* we used to prostrate on our clothes as a protection against heat.

Ch. 12:   Delaying the *Ẓuhr* prayer till the *'Aṣr* prayer

543 Ibn 'Abbās reported that the Prophet ﷺ in Madīnah said seven or eight *rak'ahs* of prayer, at *Ẓuhr* and *'Aṣr,* and at *Maghrib* and *'Ishā'*.[30] Ayyūb said: "Perhaps it was a rainy night." Jābir said: "Perhaps." [31]

---

[29] The experience of the Holy Prophet seeing Paradise and Hell is to be found also in h. 86 and h. 184, the ḥadīth speaking of the solar eclipse; see also h. 1052 and h. 1053. But this is a different occasion. The ḥadīth about the *Mi'rāj,* h. 349, also speaks of this experience of the Holy Prophet seeing Paradise and Hell. This shows that the Holy Prophet saw the heaven and the hell at least twice from this earth. So if these things, which consist of the highest of the high and the lowest of the low, could be seen by the Holy Prophet while he was on earth, it follows that what he saw during his *Mi'rāj* was also seen by him while he was physically on this earth. The fact is that the prophets are gifted with faculties by which they can see things of the spiritual world while their bodies are on this earth and there is no need for them to be taken physically to the other world for this purpose.

[30] The meaning is that he combined *Ẓuhr* and *'Aṣr,* saying eight *rak'ahs* in total, and he combined *Maghrib* and *'Ishā',* saying seven *rak'ahs* in total.

[31] Jābir was reporting from Ibn 'Abbās. This shows that it is permissible for a person resident at home to combine two prayers. It was not certain that this was because it was raining; that is only a conjecture. A report in Ṣaḥīḥ Muslim shows that it was not a rainy night nor was there fear of anything. Other reports show that the Holy Prophet said his two prayers together without any reason of journey, rain or fear. (See Muslim, book: 'The prayer of travellers and its shortening', ch. 6; Abū Dāwūd, book: 'Prayer during journey', h. 1211; Nasā'ī, book: 'Times of Prayer', h. 608, 609; Tirmidhī, book: 'Prayer', h. 187.) The *Ẓuhr* and the *'Aṣr* prayers can thus be combined, as can the *Maghrib* and *'Ishā'.* For the traveller and the sick, the combining is always allowed. The combining mentioned here is to delay the first of the prayers till the time of the second. Such a permission is only for the facility of the believers, as has been rightly observed

Ch. 13:   The Time of the *'Aṣr* prayer

544 'Ā'ishah said that the Messenger of Allāh ﷺ used to say the *'Aṣr* prayer while the sun had not gone from her chamber.

545 'Ā'ishah reported that the Messenger of Allāh ﷺ said the *'Aṣr* prayer while the sun was in her chamber and shadow had not appeared in it.

546 'Ā'ishah reported: The Prophet ﷺ used to say the *'Aṣr* prayer while the sun would be shining in my chamber and shadow had not appeared in it.[32]

547 Sayyār ibn Salāmah reported: I and my father went to Abū Barzah al-Aslamī, and my father asked him: "How did the Messenger of Allāh ﷺ say the prescribed prayers?" He said: "He used to say the *Hajīr* (i.e., *Ẓuhr*), which you call the first one, as soon as the sun would decline, and he used to say the *'Aṣr* prayer so that, after it, one of us could return to his own house at the far end of Madīnah and the sun would be still bright." And I forgot what he said about the *Maghrib* prayer. "He liked to delay the *'Ishā'* prayer, which you call *al-'Atamah,* and he disliked sleeping before it and talking after it. And he used to return after the morning prayer (*Fajr*) when a man could (just) recognize the person sitting with him and he used to recite (in *Fajr*) sixty to one hundred (verses of the Qur'ān)." [33]

548 Anas ibn Mālik reported: We used to say the *'Aṣr* prayer, then if a man went out towards Banū 'Amr ibn 'Auf he would find them saying the *'Aṣr* prayer.[34]

549 Abū Umāmah said: We said our *Ẓuhr* prayer with 'Umar ibn 'Abdul 'Azīz, then we went out till we came upon Anas ibn Mālik and we found him saying the *'Aṣr* prayer. I said: "O my uncle, what is this prayer you have said?" He said: "It was *'Aṣr,* and this is the prayer of the Messenger of Allāh ﷺ which we used to say with him." [35]

550 Anas ibn Mālik related: The Messenger of Allāh ﷺ used to say the *'Aṣr* prayer while the sun would be high and bright, so that someone going

---

by Ibn 'Abbās in the above references. There is a report in Ṭabarānī from 'Abdullāh ibn Mas'ūd that the Holy Prophet, on being asked on one such occasion when he combined prayers, as to the reason for it, replied that it was to avoid hardship for his followers. See also h. 562 and h. 1174.

[32] H. 544 to h. 546 are repetitions of h. 522 with different wording.

[33] This is a repetition of h. 541 with some additions and difference of wording.

[34] Banū 'Amr ibn 'Auf used to live in Qubā'. Imām Nawawī writes that their houses were situated at the distance of two miles from Madīnah. The meaning is that the Holy Prophet used to say the *'Aṣr* prayer at its earliest time, while these people used to say the same prayer somewhat later because of their worldly occupations.

[35] That is to say, this was the proper time for the *'Aṣr* prayer.

would go to Al-ʿAwālī and reach the people there while the sun would still be high. Some parts of Al-ʿAwālī were about four miles from Madīnah.[36]

551 Anas ibn Mālik reported: We used to say the *ʿAṣr* prayer, then someone going from among us would go to Qubā' and reach the people there while the sun would still be high.[37]

Ch. 14:   The sin of one who has missed the *ʿAṣr* prayer

552 ʿAbdullāh ibn ʿUmar reported that the Messenger of Allāh ﷺ said: "One who has missed the *ʿAṣr* prayer is as if he has been robbed (*wutira*) of his family and his wealth."[38]

Abū ʿAbdullāh (Bukhārī) said: *Yatira-kum*, the expression *watarta ar-rajula* is used when you have killed a person of a man or taken the property of a man.[39]

Ch. 15:   The sin of one who has given up the *ʿAṣr* prayer

553 Abul Malīḥ reported: We were with Buraidah in a battle on a cloudy day and he said: Say your *ʿAṣr* prayer early, for surely the Prophet ﷺ said: "One who gives up the *ʿAṣr* prayer, his deeds will become useless."[40]

Ch. 16:   Excellence of the *ʿAṣr* prayer

554 Jarīr ibn ʿAbdullāh reported: We were with the Prophet ﷺ and he looked towards the (full) moon one night and said: "Surely you will see your

---

[36] Some suburbs of Madīnah in the direction of Najd were at a height and known as Al-ʿAwālī, while those in the direction of Tihāmah were on a lower level and known as As-Sāfilah. The distance of Al-ʿAwālī from Madīnah ranged from two to six miles. Some authorities say its farthest point was at a distance of eight miles.

[37] This is a repetition of h. 550. Qubā' is in al-ʿAwālī.

[38] The time for *ʿAṣr* is the busiest time for conducting worldly business. The meaning is that one who discards the prayer in favour of the interest of his family and property is, in fact, robbed of them in a spiritual sense.

[39] This is in explanation of the word *wutira* ("has been robbed"). The word *yatira* is based on the same root and hence Bukhārī refers to the occurrence of *yatira-kum* in the Qur'ān (47:35), which means reducing something that you have to nothing.

[40] The words *ḥabiṭa ʿamalu-hu* ("his deeds will become useless") have been taken to mean that this sin obliterates the purifying effects of other good deeds on the soul of man. It means that just as some good deeds overcome the bad effects of sins, similarly some evil deeds overcome and kill off the good effects of many other deeds of virtue. It has also been taken to mean that the work a person does, at the cost of saying his prayer, becomes fruitless and cannot contribute to his salvation. This meaning is in accord with the last ḥadīth, h. 552, and both reports mean the same.

Lord as you see this moon; you will not be hindering each other in looking at Him.[41] So if you are able to not be overcome (by other business) in the matter of prayer before the rising of the sun and before its setting, then do it (*if'alū*)." Then he recited: "and celebrate the praise of your Lord before the rising of the sun and before its setting" (the Qur'ān, 20:130, 50:39).[42]

Ismā'īl said: *If'alu* means 'do not miss them at all'.

555 Abū Hurairah reported that the Messenger of Allāh ﷺ said: "Some angels at night and some angels in the day follow one another in your midst[43] and they come together at the *Fajr* prayer and the *'Aṣr* prayer. Then those (angels) who spend their night in your midst ascend (to heaven) and their Lord asks them, although He knows about them very well:[44] 'In what condition did you leave My servants?' They say: 'We left them while they were praying and we came to them while they were praying'."

---

[41] Here God has not been likened to the moon, as the Qur'ān says: "There is nothing like a likeness of Him" (42:11). The likeness relates to the act of seeing. As to the words "you not be hindering each other" (*lā tuḍāmmūna*), it is stated in the repetition of this ḥadīth in h. 573 that this expression is either this or it is *lā tuḍāhūna* meaning "not doubting". The latter seems more appropriate; see also footnote 248 to h. 806. Needless to say, God is not a physical body that can be seen with the physical eyes. The vision which is used to see God is produced by the purity of the mind and is spiritual in nature. The purer and cleaner the heart, the clearer will be the sight of God, just as the reflection of the sun in a glass is brighter if the glass is cleaner. Just as millions of mirrors can all have in them the reflection of the sun at the same time without hindering each other's light, similarly millions of people can have full sight of God in their hearts at one and the same time without coming in each other's way.

[42] The words "before its (the sun's) setting" refer to the *'Aṣr* prayer while "before the rising of the sun" refer to the *Fajr* prayer. The *Ẓuhr* prayer is implied in the Qur'ān in the words "Keep up prayer from the declining of the sun…" (17:78). In case of the *'Ishā'* prayer, it is mentioned by its very name in the Qur'ān (24:58): "after the prayer of the night (*ṣalāt al-'Ishā'*)." Thus the times of all the prayers are specified in the Qur'ān.

[43] These are the angels that keep a record of the good and evil deeds of the individual man and woman and they are referred to in many places in the Qur'ān, such as: "For him are (angels) guarding the consequences (of his deeds)" (13:11), "He utters not a word but there is by him a watcher at hand" (50:18), and "surely there are keepers over you, honourable recorders; they know what you do" (82:10–12). They are called *mu'aqqibāt* from the word *'aqaba* meaning 'to follow'. This is because they *pursue* the actions of a person and preserve them, and also because they *follow one another* in performing their respective functions. That is why in this ḥadīth the word *yata'āqabūn* has been used for them, as they follow one another.

[44] The purpose of God's question is not the same as that of man who wants to gain knowledge of what he does not know. Whenever God is said to have asked a question, its purpose is to convey a truth to man through the answer. Here the object is to tell man that every action of his is being preserved and that it has consequences.

Ch. 17: He who gets one *rak'ah* of the *'Aṣr* prayer before the setting of the sun

556 Abū Hurairah reported that the Messenger of Allāh ﷺ said: "When any of you gets (only) one prostration in the *'Aṣr* prayer before the setting of the sun, he should complete his prayer, and when he gets (only) one prostration in the morning prayer before the rising of the sun, he should complete his prayer." [45]

557 Sālim ibn 'Abdullāh reported from his father who informed him that he heard the Messenger of Allāh ﷺ say: "Your existence in relation to those that have gone before you from among the religious communities is like that of the period between the *'Aṣr* prayer and the setting of the sun. The followers of the Torah were given the Torah and they acted (on it) till, when half the day passed, they were exhausted and were given a *qīrāṭ* each. Then the followers of the Gospel were given the Gospel and they acted (on it) till the time of the *'Aṣr* prayer. Then they were exhausted and were given a *qīrāṭ* each. Then we were given the Qur'ān and we acted (on it) till the setting of the sun and we were given two *qīrāṭ* each. At this, the followers of the other two books said: 'Our Lord, You have given these people two *qīrāṭ* each and You have given us one *qīrāṭ* each although we have acted more.' Allāh, the Mighty, the Glorious, said: 'Have I been unjust to you in any way in giving you your reward?' They said: 'No.' He said: 'This is My favour, I give it to whomsoever I wish.' " [46]

558 Abū Mūsā reported from the Prophet ﷺ that he said: "The parable of the Muslims and the Jews and the Christians is that of a man who engaged some people on wages to do work for him up to the night. They worked up to midday and said: 'We have no need for your payment.' Then he engaged another people and said (to them): 'Complete the rest of the work this day and you will have what I stipulated (for the first people).' So they worked till it

---

[45] *Sajdah* or prostration here means the whole *rak'ah* beginning from the standing posture and ending in prostration. A person is considered to have completed a *rak'ah* when he joins it before the bowing posture (*Rukū'*) of it has ended. The word *Sajdah* should, therefore, be taken here to mean *Rukū'*. In the repetition of this ḥadīth in h. 579, the word *rak'ah* is used instead of *Sajdah*. According to some reports, the Holy Prophet himself said that if a person is able to join the Imām at the point of *Rukū'* he should consider himself as having completed that *rak'ah* of prayer, but if he joins him in prostration, he should not consider that he completed that *rak'ah*. From this, Bukhārī in this chapter heading has spoken of a person as getting one *rak'ah* of prayer. The sum and substance is that if for some unavoidable reason a person joins the prayer congregation late and performs only the last *rak'ah* within the time of that prayer, he can regard himself as having performed the prayer at the right time.

[46] This ḥadīth is repeated below in h. 558 from Abū Mūsā with some difference in the wording. See the next footnote.

was the time for the *'Aṣr* prayer and said: 'We leave to you what we have done.' So he engaged yet another people and they worked for the rest of the day till the sun disappeared and they received the full wages of the other two sets of people." [47]

Ch. 18:   The time of the *Maghrib* prayer

'Aṭā' said: A sick person should combine the *Maghrib* and the *'Ishā'* prayers.

559 Rāfi' ibn Khudīj said: We used to say the *Maghrib* prayer with the Prophet ﷺ, and one of us would return (to his own place) while he could still see the spot where his arrow would fall.[48]

560 Muḥammad ibn 'Amr ibn al-Ḥasan ibn 'Alī reported: Al-Ḥajjāj arrived and we asked Jābir ibn 'Abdullāh and he said: The Prophet ﷺ used to say the *Ẓuhr* prayer at midday, and the *'Aṣr* prayer when the sun would (still) be clear, and the *Maghrib* prayer when it would set, and the *'Ishā'* prayer sometimes (sooner) and sometimes (later). When he would find people assembled (for *'Ishā'*), he would say it sooner and when he would find them coming late he would delay it. And for the morning prayer, they — or the Prophet ﷺ — would say it when it would still be somewhat dark.[49]

561 Salamah reported: We used to say the *Maghrib* prayer with the Prophet ﷺ when the sun would hide behind the horizon.

---

[47] The differences between this and the previous ḥadīth confirm the general point that those reports that have nothing to do with the ordinances of religion have not been preserved as accurately as those connected with such ordinances. In such cases it is more the sense than the actual words of the Holy Prophet that has been preserved, and we cannot stick literally to the reported words which represent the understanding of the narrators. Taking the two reports together, the meaning is that the duty of spreading guidance and virtue till the end was not properly performed by the previous covenanted peoples. After they refused to continue doing it, it was handed to the Muslims to do this work till the end and receive the promised reward. They were to be given all the reward because they completed the work. No other people or *ummah* would need to be raised after them to finish it. The relevance of these two reports to this chapter is that the topic here is that if a person joins the last *rak'ah* of a prayer he is considered as having joined the whole of it. Similarly, the Muslim community, although it came after other religious communities in history, will be considered as if it were performing the work from the very beginning.

[48] The meaning is that the Holy Prophet used to say the *Maghrib* prayer so early after the setting of the sun that he finished it quite some time before it was dark. The distance which an arrow covers is quite far, and things that far would still be visible.

[49] Ḥajjāj became the ruler of Ḥijāz, appointed in 74 A.H. by 'Abdul Malik ibn Marwān after the killing of 'Abdullāh ibn Zubair. The prayers began to be delayed during his rulership.

562 Ibn ʿAbbās reported: The Prophet ﷺ said prayers in seven *rakʿahs* together and eight *rakʿahs* together.[50]

Ch. 19: One who disliked that the *Maghrib* prayer should be called *'Ishā'*

563 ʿAbdullāh al-Muzanī related that the Prophet ﷺ said: "The desert Arabs should by no means prevail upon you in assigning the name to your *Maghrib* prayer." He (further) said: "The desert Arabs say that it is *'Ishā'*." [51]

Ch. 20: The discussion on *'Ishā'* and *'Atamah* and one who takes it in the wide sense[52]

Abū Hurairah reported from the Prophet ﷺ: "The most difficult prayer for the hypocrites is the *'Ishā'* and the *Fajr*." He (also) said: "If only they knew what (reward) is to be found in the *'Atamah* and *Fajr* (prayers)."

Abū ʿAbdullāh (Bukhārī) said: It is better that one should call it *'Ishā'* because of the words of Allāh, the Most High: "…and after the *'Ishā'* prayer" (the Qurʾān, 24:58).

It has been related of Abū Mūsā that he said: We used to take turns to be with the Prophet ﷺ at *'Ishā'* prayer and he would say it late. Ibn ʿAbbās and ʿĀʾishah said: The Prophet ﷺ delayed the *'Ishā'* prayer. Some reported from ʿĀʾishah that the Prophet ﷺ delayed the *'Atamah* prayer. Jābir said: The Prophet ﷺ used to say the *'Ishā'* prayer. Abū Barzah said: The Prophet ﷺ used to delay the *'Ishā'* prayer. Anas said: The Prophet ﷺ delayed the late *'Ishā'* prayer. Ibn ʿUmar, Abū Ayyūb and Ibn ʿAbbās said: The Prophet ﷺ said the *Maghrib* and the *'Ishā'* prayers.

564 ʿAbdullāh (ibn ʿUmar) informed: One night the Messenger of Allāh ﷺ led us in *'Ishā'* prayer, which is called *'Atamah* by people. Then he finished and turned towards us and said: "Keep this night in your mind, for

---

[50] See h. 543 and its footnote. This shows that he said his *Maghrib* and *'Ishā'* prayers together, seven *rakʿahs*, and similarly the *Ẓuhr* and *'Aṣr* prayers together, eight *rakʿahs*. This was without either being on a journey or due to rainfall. See also h. 1174.

[51] The object was to guard against people confusing the two times of the two prayers and delaying the *Maghrib* prayer till the *'Ishā'* prayer.

[52] The *'Ishā'* prayer was also called *'Atamah* or *A'tam* by the Companions, but as the word *'Ishā'* has been used in the Qurʾān this is preferable.

surely after a hundred years from it no one will have remained from among those who are now (living) on the surface of the earth." [53]

Ch. 21: The time of the *'Ishā'* prayer when people gather (early) or are late

565 Muḥammad ibn 'Amr, who was son of al-Ḥasan ibn 'Alī, reported: We asked Jābir ibn 'Abdullāh about the prayer of the Prophet ﷺ and he said: He used to say the *Ẓuhr* prayer at midday, and the *'Aṣr* prayer while the sun would (still) be hot, and the *Maghrib* prayer when it would set, and the *'Ishā'* prayer he said sooner if people had gathered and he delayed it if there were few, and the morning prayer when it would still be somewhat dark.[54]

Ch. 22: Excellence of the *'Ishā'* prayer

566 'Urwah reported that 'Ā'ishah informed him: The Messenger of Allāh ﷺ delayed the *'Ishā'* prayer one night and it was before Islām had spread. He did not come out until 'Umar said: "The women and the children have fallen asleep." So he came out and said to the people in the mosque: "No one living on the earth is waiting for it (i.e., for the prayer) except you."

567 Abū Mūsā reported: I and my companions who came with me in the boat alighted one day in the plain (*baqī'*) of Buṭḥān. The Prophet ﷺ was in Madīnah and some of these would take turns to come to the Prophet ﷺ at the time of the *'Ishā'* prayer every night. Once we met the Prophet ﷺ, myself and my companions, when he was engaged in some of his affairs, so he delayed the prayer till it was midnight. Then the Prophet ﷺ came out and led them in prayer. When he had finished his prayer, he said to those present: "Stay on! Receive the good news that surely it is a blessing of Allāh on you that no one from among the people is saying prayers at this hour except you", or he said: "…no one has said prayers at this hour except you." The narrator did not know which of these two sentences he uttered. Abū Mūsā said: So we returned rejoicing at what we heard from the Messenger of Allāh ﷺ.[55]

---

[53] This is a repetition of h. 116 with some different wording at the beginning. The words of the Holy Prophet were a very great prophecy which saw literal fulfilment. The incident belongs to the closing days of the Holy Prophet's life.

[54] See h. 560. This shows that, unless it involves a very lengthy delay, the time for a congregational prayer may be put back a little if it is expected that many more people would thereby be able to join the congregation. The consideration of a larger number of people joining the prayer should have priority over observing absolutely rigid punctuality of prayer times.

[55] This was the high regard in which the Holy Prophet and his Companions held the observance of prayer! It was a matter of pride for them that at a particular moment they would be the

Ch. 23:   Sleeping before the *'Ishā'* prayer is disapproved

568 Abū Barzah reported that the Messenger of Allāh ﷺ used to dislike sleeping before the *'Ishā'* prayer and talking after it.[56]

Ch. 24:   Sleeping before *'Ishā'* for one overcome by sleep

569 'Urwah reported that 'Ā'ishah said: The Messenger of Allāh ﷺ delayed the *'Ishā'* prayer until 'Umar called out to him for prayer, saying: "The women and the children have fallen asleep." So he came out and said: "No one living on the earth is waiting for it (i.e., for the prayer) except you."

Prayers were not said in those days (with freedom) except in Madīnah, and they used to say this prayer between the disappearance of twilight and the (end of the) first one-third of the night.[57]

570 'Abdullāh ibn 'Umar related that the Messenger of Allāh ﷺ was kept away from prayer one night by some engagement, so he delayed it till we slept in the mosque. Then we woke up and slept again, and woke up again. Then the Prophet ﷺ came out to us and said: "No one living on the earth is waiting for prayer except you."

Ibn 'Umar did not mind saying it earlier or later when he did not fear that sleep will overcome him at the time of prayer, and he used to sleep before it.

571 Ibn Juraij said: I said (this) to 'Aṭā' and he said: I have heard Ibn 'Abbās say: The Messenger of Allāh ﷺ delayed the *'Ishā'* prayer one night till people fell asleep, and they woke up and they slept (again), and they woke up again. 'Umar ibn al-Khaṭṭāb stood up and said: "Prayer." 'Aṭā' said that

---

only people bowing before God. So they returned home rejoicing after receiving this good news. These friends of Abū Mūsā al-Ash'arī and Abū Hurairah were the inhabitants of Yaman, from where they migrated to Madīnah to join the Holy Prophet. Most probably this migration took place immediately after the fall of Khaibar. *Baqī'* means a wide expanse of plain land with trees on it, and Buṭḥān is the name of a valley in Madīnah. Ṭabarī says that the Holy Prophet made this delay in his prayer because he was busy in the preparation of an army for battle.

[56] H. 541, of which this is a repetition, does not contain these words, but they occur in its repetition in h. 547. It is obvious that sleeping before *'Ishā'* may cause this prayer to be missed. As for talking after it, it is forbidden because it would delay going to bed, making it difficult to rise for the *Tahajjud* or even the morning prayer. Today people in many societies stay up till late, wasting their time in talking and then getting up late the next morning. If they avoid wasting their time in useless talk, they would be able to rise early and take part in activities which are good for their spiritual as well as physical welfare.

[57] This is a repetition of h. 566. The falling asleep of the women and children before the *'Ishā'* prayer was beyond their control and as such forgivable. They remained in the mosque and woke up for prayer. The prohibition of sleeping before *'Ishā'* relates only to intentional sleep as it risks the missing of the prayer. See also h. 864.

Ibn 'Abbās said: The Prophet of Allāh ﷺ came out, and it is as if I can see him even now, water was dripping from his head and he was placing his hands on his head. He said: "If it had not been hard for my followers, I would have ordered them to say prayer at this time."

I wanted to verify from 'Aṭā' how the Prophet ﷺ placed his hands over his head as Ibn 'Abbās told him. So 'Aṭā' parted his fingers for me slightly, then he placed the ends of his fingers on the side of his head, then he joined them and drew them like that over the head till his thumb touched the side of his ear that was adjoining his face on his temple and the border of his beard. He was neither doing it quick nor slow except like this, and he (the Holy Prophet) said: "If it had not been hard for my followers, I would have ordered them to say prayer at this time."

Ch. 25:   The time of the *'Ishā'* prayer extends up to midnight

Abū Barzah said: The Prophet ﷺ liked to delay it.

572 Anas reported: The Prophet ﷺ delayed the *'Ishā'* prayer until midnight,[58] then he said the prayer, and then said: "People have said their prayers and slept. Beware, you are in prayer so long as you wait for it."

In a report from Ḥumaid it is said that he heard Anas saying: "It is as if I am still seeing the sparkling of his ring on that night."

Ch. 26:   Excellence of the *Fajr* prayer and the *Ḥadīth*[59]

573 Qais related that Jarīr ibn 'Abdullāh said to him: We were with the Prophet ﷺ when he looked towards the full moon of the night and said: "Surely you will see your Lord as you see this (moon); you will not be hindering each other in looking at Him — or (he said) you will not be doubting. So if you are able to not be overcome (by other business) in the matter of prayer before the rising of the sun and before its setting, then do it (*if'alū*)." Then he said: "So celebrate the praise of your Lord before the rising of the sun and before its setting." [60]

---

[58] From this it is seen that one should not say the *'Ishā'* prayer after midnight because some time must be given to a person for sleep and also because the time for the optional midnight prayer is to begin at this point. See also h. 847.

[59] The word *ḥadīth* here is either an incorrect addition which somehow found its way into this heading or it should be the word *'Aṣr* since that prayer is referred to in the report which follows along with the *Fajr* prayer. The word *ḥadīth* is found in only one manuscript.

[60] This is a repetition of h. 554. See the footnotes there. This report mentions the full moon night by adding the word *al-badr* which is not found in h. 554. Also, the reporter is uncertain

574 Abū Mūsā reported that the Messenger of Allāh ﷺ said: "One who has said the two cool prayers shall enter Paradise." [61]

Ch. 27: The time of the *Fajr* prayer

575 Anas reported that Zaid ibn Thābit related to him that they took the pre-fast meal (*saḥūr*) with the Prophet of Allāh ﷺ and then stood up for prayer. I asked: "How much (time) was between them?" He said: "As much as fifty or sixty", meaning (reciting) verses.[62]

576 Anas ibn Mālik reported that the Prophet of Allāh ﷺ and Zaid ibn Thābit took their pre-fast meals and when they had finished taking these meals, the Prophet of Allāh ﷺ stood up for prayer and he said the prayer. We said to Anas: "How much (time) was there between their finishing the pre-fast meal and their engaging in the prayer?" He said: "As much as (the time in which) a man can recite fifty verses (of the Qur'ān)." [63]

577 Abū Ḥāzim reported that he heard Sahl ibn Saʿd say: "I used to take my pre-fast meal at home. Then I would hurry to catch the *Fajr* prayer with the Messenger of Allāh ﷺ." [64]

---

whether the Holy Prophet used the words *lā tuḍāmmūna* ("not be hindering each other") or *lā tuḍāhūna*, meaning "not doubting". The latter seems more appropriate. The connection of the sight or vision of God with prayer is quite obvious. It is through prayer that man develops the sight which enables him to see God in the Hereafter. Seeing God in the Hereafter is established from this ḥadīth, but it is, of course, a different phenomenon from our seeing physical objects. It needs other faculties than the physical ones, and these faculties are developed through faith and constant devotion. In this world, this kind of vision of God is the privilege of only a few and that even not in complete form. In the life after death, this will be the experience of many in its full blaze; and the prayer that does not lead one to this developed inner vision is an ineffective one. See also h. 806.

[61] *Bardain* means two cool times of prayers and has been taken to refer to the *Fajr* and *ʿAṣr* prayers, as is indicated in Ṣaḥīḥ Muslim (book: 'Mosques and Places of Prayer', ch. 37). In fact, all good deeds should lead to Paradise, but the stress on these two prayers leading to Paradise seems to be due to the moral struggle against one's desires which they involve. In the *Fajr* prayer the struggle is against the desire to sleep and in the *ʿAṣr* prayer it is against engrossment in worldly activities.

[62] This is repeated next in h. 576. Here Zaid ibn Thābit uses the plural (*tasaḥḥarū*) for the people who took their pre-fast meal, which means there were more than two people, but in h. 576 Anas uses the dual tense (*tasaḥḥarā*) so that the number of persons was two, namely, the Holy Prophet and Zaid ibn Thābit. We learn from other Ḥadīth collections that Anas was also present (see Nasāʾī, book: 'Fasting', h. 2167), but in that case there would be no point in his saying that he heard the report from Zaid. It may be that the other persons besides the Holy Prophet and Zaid did not include Anas or else we have to take the dual form of the word to be the correct one. This also shows that the time for the *Fajr* prayer starts with what is called *ṣubḥ ṣādiq* (the true dawn) because that is the time of the end of the pre-fast meal.

[63] This is repeated in h. 1134 and h. 1921.

[64] This is repeated in h. 1920.

578 'Ā'ishah informed, saying: Believing women used to attend the *Fajr* prayer with the Messenger of Allāh ﷺ, wrapped in their cloaks. Then they would turn back to their houses after finishing the prayer and no one would recognize them on account of darkness.[65]

Ch. 28:   He who gets one *rak'ah* of the *Fajr* prayer

579 Abū Hurairah reported that the Messenger of Allāh ﷺ said: "He who gets only one *rak'ah* in the morning prayer before the rising of the sun has indeed got the (whole) morning prayer, and he who gets only one *rak'ah* of the *'Aṣr* prayer before the setting of the sun has indeed got the (whole) *'Aṣr* prayer." [66]

Ch. 29:   He who gets one *rak'ah* of a prayer

580 Abū Hurairah reported that the Messenger of Allāh ﷺ said: "He who gets one *rak'ah* of a prayer gets the (whole) prayer."

Ch. 30:   Prayer after the *Fajr* prayer until the sun rises high[67]

---

[65] This is a repetition of h. 372. The closing words show that the Holy Prophet used to say the *Fajr* prayer so early at dawn that even after the prayers were finished it would be dark enough for women not to be recognized as they passed by men. In h. 541 and h. 547 it is stated that after the prayers were finished, there was light enough for a man to just about recognize the man next to him. There is no contradiction here because the women would be sitting at a distance behind the men and would be walking off after the prayers. It shows also that if it had not been so dark the women could have been recognized. This would be because their faces were not covered. See also h. 867 and h. 872.

[66] See h. 556.

[67] Some chapters and reports from here onwards contain prohibitions of saying prayers at certain times. One is that prayer should not be said aiming at the rising and the setting of the sun. On the other hand, a foregoing report (h. 556) instructs a man who has already started his prayer before the rising of the sun or just before its setting to finish his prayer. Hence he would be saying his prayer at the actual moment of sunrise or sunset. Thus what is forbidden is that one should not "aim at" starting the prayer at these two meeting points of the day and the night, as shown by the word *taharrī* in h. 582. But if a person is obliged by circumstances to say his prayers at these two points, this is not prohibited. The object of this prohibition is that the believer should not pray in a manner resembling that of a sun-worshipper. While some reports prohibit saying of prayers after the *Fajr* prayer till sunrise and after the *'Aṣr* prayer till sunset, there are other reports, which follow, that speak of prayers said during these intervals. For example, it is reported that the Holy Prophet himself once said his *sunnah* prayers of *Ẓuhr* after his *'Aṣr* prayer, and that he said two *rak'ahs* of optional prayers after his *'Aṣr* prayer. The object in giving some irregularity to these post-*Ẓuhr* and post-*'Aṣr* prayers seems to be to not make them an inseparable part of the prayer appointed for these times so that these may not become burdensome for people. Thus in h. 590 'Ā'ishah reports that the Holy Prophet used to say post-*'Aṣr* prayers not in the mosque but on his return home for this reason.

581 Ibn 'Abbās reported: Some approved men bore witness before me, and the most approved among them in my view was 'Umar, that the Prophet ﷺ forbade saying prayer after the morning prayer until the sun becomes bright, and after the *'Aṣr* prayer until it has set.

582 Ibn 'Umar informed that the Messenger of Allāh ﷺ said: "Do not aim to say your prayers at the rising of the sun or at its setting."

583 Ibn 'Umar related that the Messenger of Allāh ﷺ said: "When the border of the sun makes its appearance, delay the prayer until it becomes high, and when the border of the sun disappears, delay the prayer until it has disappeared (completely)."

584 Abū Hurairah reported that the Messenger of Allāh ﷺ forbade two kinds of sales and two kinds of dresses and two kinds of prayer. He forbade prayer after the *Fajr* prayer until the sun has risen and after the *'Aṣr* prayer until the sun has set, and wrapping one's body with a cloth so that the hands are shut up within (*ishtimāl aṣ-ṣammā'*), and a man's sitting on his buttocks with his knees raised up (*iḥtibā'*),[68] while wearing only one piece of cloth, exposing his private parts to the sky, and also from *munābadhah* and *mulāmasah.*[69]

Ch. 31:   Not to aim at saying prayers immediately before sunset

585 Ibn 'Umar reported that the Messenger of Allāh ﷺ said: "Let not anyone of you aim at saying prayers at about the rising of the sun nor at about its setting." [70]

The substance of the whole question is that if a person misses any optional prayers he can say them in the period between the *Fajr* prayer and sunrise, and the period between the *'Aṣr* prayer and sunset. Similarly, funeral prayers, prostrations recommended at certain points in the recitation of the Qur'ān, prostrations in gratitude, the prayers of solar and lunar eclipses or some prayers that have been missed, can very well be said in these two periods, although certain schools of thought consider it disapproved. A report from Mu'āwiyah in h. 587 says that the Holy Prophet forbade a two-*rak'ah* prayer after *'Aṣr*. This may have been for the convenience of people, and not because such a prayer is forbidden. Still another point of time in which it is reported that prayer has been forbidden is that of midday. This may have been due to the heat at noon, since there are reports recommending the delay of *Ẓuhr* prayer in hot summer days, as in ch. 12 above. Thus, at none of these times mentioned above, is prayer altogether forbidden unconditionally, but there are certain reasons for asking people to refrain from praying at those times.

[68] For *ishtimāl aṣ-ṣammā'* and *iḥtibā'*, see h. 367 and its footnote, and h. 1991–1992.

[69] *Munābadhah* and *mulāmasah* are two types of sales, for which see the footnote to h. 368 and to h. 1993.

[70] This is a repetition of h. 582 with different wording. Sometimes a person is engaged in

586 Abū Sa'īd al-Khudrī said: I heard the Messenger of Allāh ﷺ say: "There is no prayer after the morning prayer until the sun becomes high, and no prayer after the *'Aṣr* prayer until the sun has disappeared (completely)."

587 Mu'āwiyah said: Surely you say a certain prayer but we have indeed been with the Messenger of Allāh ﷺ and we did not see him saying these two (*rak'ahs*); he certainly forbade them, meaning the two *rak'ahs* after the *'Aṣr* prayer.[71]

588 Abū Hurairah reported: The Messenger of Allāh ﷺ forbade two kinds of prayer: after the *Fajr* prayer until the sun has risen and after the *'Aṣr* prayer until the sun has set.[72]

Ch. 32.   **One who does not dislike saying prayers immediately after the *'Aṣr* and *Fajr* prayer**

This was reported by 'Umar, Ibn 'Umar, Abū Sa'īd and Abū Hurairah.

589 Ibn 'Umar reported: I pray as I saw my companions pray. I do not forbid anyone to say prayers at any time of the night or the day that he wishes, except that they should not aim at the rising of the sun or its setting.[73]

Ch. 33:   **The missed prayer, or the like of it, said after the *'Aṣr* prayer**

Kuraib reported from Umm Salamah: The Prophet ﷺ said two *rak'ahs* of prayer after the *'Aṣr* prayer and said: "Some people from (the tribe of) 'Abdul Qais kept me engaged from (being able to say) the two *rak'ahs* after the *Ẓuhr* prayer." [74]

---

some worldly affair or pre-occupation and he delays his *Fajr* or *'Aṣr* prayer through laxity or distraction and all of a sudden he finds that the sun is rising or setting, as the case may be. Such procrastination is disapproved of. However, if it happens by chance or for some unavoidable reason, prayers at these times are not prohibited. As noted earlier, if even one *rak'ah* of prayer has been completed before sunrise or before sunset, the whole prayer is treated as having been said on time.

[71] Further on, in the title of ch. 33, it is stated that the Holy Prophet said two *rak'ahs* of prayer after the *'Aṣr* prayer and 'Ā'ishah says in that chapter that he did so till the end of his life. But since he said these prayers always at home, the people in general did not know this. Mu'āwiyah, who speaks against this prayer, had not been long in the company of the Holy Prophet because he embraced Islām after the conquest of Makkah.

[72] This is a repetition of h. 584, with only the part about prayer.

[73] This is a repetition of h. 582 except that here Ibn 'Umar does not report the words of the Holy Prophet but speaks of himself.

[74] This shows that if for unavoidable reasons one is obliged to say some prayers at such times,

590 'Ā'ishah said: "By Him Who has taken him (i.e., the Holy Prophet) away, he did not discard these two (*rak'ahs*) until he met Allāh, and he did not meet Allāh, the Most High, until (standing for) prayer became difficult for him and he used to say many of his prayer sitting." She meant the two *rak'ahs* after *the 'Aṣr* prayer.[75] "And the Prophet ﷺ used to pray these two *rak'ahs* (at home) but not pray them in the mosque fearing that he would make it a burden on his followers. And he used to like anything that would be easy for them."

591 Hishām related that his father 'Urwah informed him that 'Ā'ishah said (to him): "O son of my sister, the Prophet ﷺ never discarded the two prostrations[76] after the *'Aṣr* prayer at my house."

592 'Ā'ishah reported: There were two *rak'ahs* which the Messenger of Allāh ﷺ never gave up, (saying them) either privately or publicly: two *rak'ahs* before the morning prayer and two *rak'ahs* after *'Aṣr*.

593 Abū Isḥāq reported: I saw al-Aswad and Masrūq bearing witness that 'Ā'ishah said: The Prophet ﷺ never came to me on any day after the *'Aṣr* prayer except after saying two *rak'ahs* of prayer.[77]

Ch. 34:   To say prayer early on a cloudy day

594 Abul Malīḥ related: We were with Buraidah on a cloudy day and he said: Say your prayer early, for surely the Prophet ﷺ said: "One who gives up the *'Aṣr* prayer, his deeds will become useless." [78]

---

it is permissible. It also shows that if some *sunnah* prayers have been missed, these can be said later on at the earliest opportunity. Hence if someone misses the two *sunnah rak'ahs* before the congregational *Fajr* prayer, he can say them till the rising of the sun.

[75] As the Holy Prophet used to recite long chapters of the Qur'ān in his optional prayers, it became hard for him in the closing days of his life to stand for the length of time required for the recitations. So he was obliged to say these prayers sitting.

[76] By the two prostrations, or two *Sajdahs*, are meant the two *rak'ahs* of prayer.

[77] H. 591–593 are repetitions of h. 590 with different wording. See also h. 1631.

[78] This is a repetition of h. 553. Whereas in the chapter heading it is stated that, on a cloudy day, prayers may be said earlier than the usual time, the ḥadīth mentions the *'Aṣr* prayer. The object seems to be to avoid the confusion about the exact time on account of the invisibility of the sun, which may lead to the missing of the *'Aṣr* prayer. There is a report from 'Umar that on a cloudy day the *Ẓuhr* prayer may be delayed and the *'Aṣr* prayer brought forward to combine the two on a cloudy day. It may be that the ḥadīth under consideration suggests the same combining. This shows that when combining two prayers (*Ẓuhr* with *'Aṣr*, or *Maghrib* with *'Ishā'*) the second prayer can be brought forward to join it with the first prayer.

Ch. 35:   To call the *Adhān* after the time has expired

595 'Abdullāh ibn Abū Qatādah reported that his father (Abū Qatādah) said: We set out one night for a journey with the Prophet ﷺ and some of the people said: "We wish you had halted for us to rest in the last part of the night, O Messenger of Allāh." He said: "I fear in case you go to sleep and miss the prayer." Bilāl said: "I will wake you up." So they went to sleep and Bilāl rested his back against his she-camel and his eyes were overpowered and he went to sleep. The Prophet ﷺ woke up when the border of the sun had risen and he said: "O Bilāl, what happened to what you said?" He said: "Never was I over-come by sleep like this." He (the Holy Prophet) said: "Surely Allāh took away your souls (O people) when He willed and returned them to you when he willed. O Bilāl, get up and call the people for prayer (with *Adhān*)." So he (the Holy Prophet) performed ablution and when the sun had become high and it was bright he stood up and said the prayer.

Ch. 36:   Leading the people in prayer after the time has expired

596 Jābir ibn 'Abdullāh reported that 'Umar ibn al-Khaṭṭāb came on the day of the (battle of the) Ditch after the sun had set and began to curse the unbelievers of the Quraish. He said: "O Messenger of Allāh, I could not say the *'Aṣr* prayer until the sun was on the point of setting." The Prophet ﷺ said: "By Allāh, I have not said it (either)." So we went towards Buṭḥān and he (the Prophet) performed ablution for prayer and we also performed ablution for it, and he said the *'Aṣr* prayer after the sun had set. Then after it he said the *Maghrib* prayer.[79]

Ch. 37:   He who forgets a prayer should say it when he remembers, and he does not repeat any but this prayer

Ibrāhīm said: Whoever misses a particular prayer for twenty years, he should not repeat anything but that prayer.

597 Anas ibn Mālik reported from the Prophet ﷺ that he said: "He who forgets to say a (certain) prayer, he should say it when he remembers. There is no expiation for it except that." (Allāh says:) "Keep up prayer for My remembrance" (the Qur'ān, 20:14).[80]

---

[79] Some reports speak of the *Ẓuhr* and *'Aṣr* prayers being missed and some others mention also the *Maghrib* prayer as being missed. But here only the missing of the *'Aṣr* prayer is mentioned and this seems to be the correct version. This is supported by a report in Ṣaḥīḥ Muslim which runs as follows: "They kept us diverted from the middle prayer, namely, the *'Aṣr* prayer" (book: 'Mosques and Places of Prayer', ch. 36). This report also indicates that a missed prayer can be said in congregation. It occurs again in h. 945.

[80] According to Imām Mālik after a person has said any scheduled prayer and he remembers

Ch. 38:   In saying missed prayers, to say the first missed one first

598 Jābir ibn 'Abdullāh reported: 'Umar began to curse the unbelievers (of the Quraish) on the day of the (battle of the) Ditch and said: "I could not say the *'Aṣr* prayer until sunset." Then we went to Buṭḥān and he prayed (*'Aṣr*) after sunset. Then he prayed *Maghrib*.[81]

Ch. 39:   What is disliked about talking (*samar*) after the *'Ishā'* prayer[82]

> *Sāmir* is derived from *samar* and its plural is *summār*. And *sāmir* is here used as a plural.[83]

599 Abul Minhāl related: I and my father went to Abū Barzah al-Aslamī and my father asked him: "Tell us how did the Messenger of Allāh ﷺ say the prescribed prayers?" He said: "He used to say the *Hajīr* (i.e., *Ẓuhr*), which you call the first prayer, as soon as the sun would decline, and he used to say the *'Aṣr* prayer so that, after it, one of us could return to his own house at the far end of Madīnah and the sun would be still bright." And I forgot what he said about the *Maghrib* prayer. He further said: "He liked to delay the *'Ishā'* prayer, and he disliked sleeping before it and talking after it. And he used to return after the morning prayer (*Fajr*) when one of us could (just) recognize the person sitting with him and he used to recite (in *Fajr*) sixty to one hundred (verses of the Qur'ān)." [84]

---

that he has not said the previous prayer, he should say the missed prayer and then repeat the prayer which he has already said at the right time, so that the two prayers are in the correct sequence. According to a report in Abū Dāwūd (book: 'Prayer', h. 437 and 438), the next day, after saying the same prayer for that day, he should say the missed prayer of the day before. Bukhārī has advanced this ḥadīth and quoted a verse of the Qur'ān to refute these two views. The missed prayer can be said at any time when it is remembered, and without requiring the person concerned to repeat a prayer which has been already said at the right time.

[81] This is a repetition of h. 596, with brevity. There is no mention here of the Holy Prophet performing ablution or of his saying prayers. 'Umar said the missed prayers in their order.

[82] *Samar* means the colour of the moonlight. The Arabs were in the habit in those days of sitting for long in the moonlit night, telling and listening to tales. For this reason, talking at night is called *samar*. See also the chapter heading above h. 116.

[83] Bukhārī is here referring to words of the Qur'ān about the unbelievers "passing nights talking (*sāmir*)", talking nonsense about revelation from God (23:67). He notes that the word *sāmir* is derived from *samar*, the word in the chapter heading, and that the Qur'ān is using the singular *sāmir* as a plural.

[84] This is a repetition of h. 541 in the words almost exactly of h. 547. The mention of the Holy Prophet disliking sleeping before the *'Ishā'* prayer and talking after it connects it with the chapter heading. Sleeping before the *'Ishā'* prayer may lead to the prayer in congregation being missed and talking after it may lead to missing the morning prayer and wastes time. But it is not prohibited to conduct some important business or discussion after this prayer.

Ch. 40:   Talking about knowledge and the good after the *'Ishā'* prayer

600 Qurrah ibn Khālid related: We waited for al-Ḥasan (al-Baṣrī) and he took so long (coming) that we began to approach the time of his leaving (the audience). Then he came and said: Those neighbours of ours had sent for us. Then he said, Anas ibn Mālik said:

> One night we waited for the Prophet ﷺ till it was midnight; then he came and led us in prayer and then addressed us saying: "Look, people have said their prayer and then they have gone to sleep, and as for you, you had been in (the state of) prayer so long as you were waiting for the prayer."

Al-Ḥasan said: And surely people are regarded as doing a good deed while they wait to do the good deed. Qurrah said: This is from a ḥadīth reported by Anas from the Prophet ﷺ.[85]

601 'Abdullāh ibn 'Umar said: Once when the Prophet ﷺ said the *'Ishā'* prayer towards the last part of his life, after (concluding the prayer with) *Salām,* the Prophet ﷺ stood up and said: "Keep this night in your mind, for surely after a hundred (years from it) no one will have remained from among those who are today on the surface of the earth."

People have made a mistake in understanding this statement of the Messenger of Allāh ﷺ so much so that they began to make conjectures about the hundred years, and (Ibn 'Umar says that) the Prophet ﷺ had only said: "no one will have remained from among those who are today on the surface of the earth", meaning thereby that it (a hundred years) would bring an end to this generation.[86]

Ch. 41:   Talking at night with the guest and one's wife

602 'Abdur Raḥmān ibn Abū Bakr reported: The people of the Ṣuffah were destitute people and the Prophet ﷺ said: "Whoever has got food for two

---

[85] Ḥasan of Baṣrah used to teach his disciples at night in the mosque. One night, his neighbours having taken him away in an important matter, he was detained there for long and could not be back for the teaching hour in time. This provided him an occasion to narrate this particular ḥadīth, which means that to wait for a good work is a part of doing the work itself. This ḥadīth shows that the Holy Prophet at times talked to his Companions after the *'Ishā'* prayer. There is a report from 'Umar that the Holy Prophet "used to talk at night with Abū Bakr on some affair of the Muslims and I used to be with them" (Tirmidhī, book: 'Prayer', ch. 12, h. 169).

[86] This is a repetition of h. 116 followed by an addition. People began to say that the Day of Judgment would come after a hundred years. When Ibn 'Umar realized that people were misinterpreting this ḥadīth in this way, he clarified its meaning, which was that the Holy Prophet only meant the passing away of the current generation, not the coming of the Day of Judgment. See also the footnote to h. 116.

persons he should take with him a third person, and if (he has got food) for four he should take a fifth or a sixth one." Abū Bakr brought three persons and the Prophet 鷺 took himself ten persons.[87] He (ʿAbdur Raḥmān) said: "It was me and my father and my mother." (A narrator said:) I do not know if he said "and my wife and a servant who was common to our house and the house of Abū Bakr."

Abū Bakr had his evening meal with the Prophet 鷺, then he stayed on there till the *'Ishā'* prayer was said. Then he returned and stayed on till the Prophet 鷺 had his evening meal.[88] Then he came (back home) after such a part of the night had elapsed as Allāh willed. His wife said to him: "What kept you away from your guests?", or she said: "your guest?" He said: "What! Have you not served them with the evening meal?" She said: "They refused (to eat) till you come." Then it was served but (again) they refused. (ʿAbdur Raḥmān added:) So I went away and hid myself. And he (Abū Bakr) said: "O you lazy one", and he called me bad names and reproached me. Then he said (addressing the guests): "Eat, it will not be digestible to you." [89] He (also) said: "By Allāh, I will never eat it." (The reporter said:) And I swear by Allāh, whenever we took a morsel, it increased from underneath. They had their fill and (yet) it (the food) became larger in quantity than it was before this. Abū Bakr looked at it and it was exactly the same (as before) or even more. So he said to his wife: "O sister of Banū Firās, what is this?" She said: "Nay, by the coolness of my eyes! It is certainly now three times more than it was before." Abū Bakr ate of it and said: "It was only from the Satan", meaning his own oath (not to eat), then he ate one morsel out of it.[90] Then he took it to the

---

[87] *Ṣuffah* was a covered platform in the mosque meant for the homeless Companions of the Holy Prophet, who used to spend their whole time in the mosque and would not take to any worldly occupation. Those people who had no food to eat at that time were distributed among several persons who could afford to give them some food so that the entire burden might not fall on one man. A golden principle is laid down here, that where there is food for three, a fourth one can easily be accommodated and so on. This shows the spirit of Islām in the entertainment of guests as opposed to modern civilized society in which even if arrangements have been made for ten guests, no room is found for an eleventh if he happens to come by chance.

[88] The repetition of *ta'ashshā* ("had his evening meal") becomes meaningless. The same ḥadīth in Ṣaḥīḥ Muslim has instead the word *na'asa* meaning that the Holy Prophet felt drowsy (book: 'Drinks', ch. 32). This seems to be the proper word.

[89] Abū Bakr scolded his son ʿAbdur Raḥmān for having kept the guests hungry till so late at night. His suggestion that the food would not be digestible to the guests was because they had taken the meal so late.

[90] Abū Bakr took only one morsel of the food just out of courtesy for the guests, otherwise as the ḥadīth says he had already taken his meal with the Holy Prophet. As he had sworn in anger that he would not eat it, he attributed that anger to the devil. There is a ḥadīth: "Jealousy is a devil and anger is a devil" (الحسد شيطانٌ والغضب شيطانٌ).

Prophet ﷺ and it remained with him (the Prophet) till the morning. There was a treaty between ourselves and a people and its period had expired.[91] So we set apart twelve men, with each man having some of these people with him. And Allāh knows how many people were with each man, and all of them ate of it, or what he (ʿAbdur Raḥmān) said.[92]

[91] A delegation of these people was in Madīnah to discuss the treaty.

[92] Miraculous increase in the quantity of food when feeding people has been recorded in the Gospels as a miracle of Jesus, but here is a similar miracle happening at the hands of a Companion of the Holy Prophet Muḥammad.

Book 10: *Al-Adhān*
The Call to Prayer

In the name of Allāh, the Beneficent, the Merciful[1]

Ch. 1: The beginning of the Call to Prayer

The word of Allāh, the Most High: "And when you call to prayer they take it as a mockery and a sport. That is because they are a people who do not understand" (the Qur'ān, 5:58), and the word of Allāh, the Most High: "When the call is sounded for prayer on Friday" (62:9).[2]

603 Anas reported: People talked about the fire and the gong and they also mentioned the Jews and the Christians. So Bilāl was ordered to use each expression twice in *Adhān* and once in *Iqāmah*.[3]

604 Ibn 'Umar used to say: Muslims when they came to Madīnah used to assemble and appoint times for prayer; no call was sounded for it. Then one day they talked about it and some of them said: "Use a gong like the gong of the Christians", and some of them said: "No, a horn like that of the Jews." Then 'Umar said: "Why do you not send out a man calling for prayer?" So the Messenger of Allāh ﷺ, said: "O Bilāl, get up and call out for prayer." [4]

---

[1] Although the title of this book refers only to the *Adhān* or Call to Prayer, it moves to other topics from ch. 20 and h. 635 onwards, dealing with matters relating to the Imām, congregational prayer, recitations in prayer, postures of prayer, etc.

[2] The first *Adhān* was sounded in Madīnah as is evident from the report of Ibn 'Umar which comes below. The Holy Qur'ān also refers to the *Adhān* only in its chapters revealed in Madīnah. The reason is that in Makkah before the *Hijrah* Muslims could not say their prayers with freedom on account of the violent opposition of the Quraish. Those reports purporting to say that the *Adhān* was taught simultaneously with the injunction for prayer on the night of the *Mi'rāj* in Makkah are not reliable, as the commentary *Fatḥ al-Bārī* has rightly concluded after a full discussion of those reports.

[3] This ḥadīth occurs in greater detail in h. 606. The fire and the gong (or bell) were considered as possible ways of calling Muslims to prayer, being used by Jews and Christians.

[4] Bukhārī has these two ḥadīth, h. 604 and h. 606, about how *Adhān* started. The first says that a consultation was held about the manner of calling people to prayer and when suggestions were made about gong, etc., 'Umar suggested that a man should be appointed to call the people to prayer, at which the Holy Prophet asked Bilāl to do this job. The second says that a consultation was held and some suggested the lighting of fire and others the ringing of bell etc., and Bilāl was ordered to recite the expressions of *Adhān* twice each and the expressions of *Iqāmah* once each.

The order that was issued to Bilāl should have been recorded as the same in both the reports. Accordingly, the conclusions some people have reached, on the basis of a report in Ṣaḥīḥ Ibn Khuzaimah and Ibn Ḥibbān, that the first order to Bilāl was that he should only call out *aṣ-ṣalatu jāmi'at-un* ("Gather for prayer"), and that the words of the present *Adhān* were taught on the basis of a dream of 'Abdullāh ibn Zaid, is not correct. The fact is that the very first call to prayer consisted of the words that are current even now. It is true that some other reports speak of people having dispersed immediately after the consultation and before any decision was taken and that 'Abdullāh ibn Zaid spoke to the Holy Prophet about a vision in which he had seen a man repeating the words of the *Adhān* twice and that the Holy Prophet in his turn instructed Bilāl to recite these words. But there are other reports which speak of 'Umar having related his vision to the Holy Prophet in which he too heard the same words of the *Adhān*. (See Abū Dāwūd, book: 'Prayer', h. 499.) In fact, there is a report to the effect that 'Umar's vision preceded the discussion by twenty days but he did not speak about it to the Holy Prophet until he had heard Bilāl using these words in the *Adhān*.

Apparently, there is divergence between all these reports, but in fact there is no conflict. The true position seems to be that although 'Umar had seen the vision before the consultation, he did not relate it to the Holy Prophet out of humility and respect for his status as Prophet. And when people presented their different views on this subject, all 'Umar said was that a man should be appointed to call people to prayer, without mentioning his own vision. He knew that in all questions bearing on religion, the Holy Prophet was himself guided by the direct revelation of God. So he only made a passing suggestion when other people proposed different ways.

It seems that after this consultation ending in 'Umar's suggestion, the meeting dispersed and that some time later, perhaps on the following night, 'Abdullāh ibn Zaid saw a vision similar to that of 'Umar and he told it to the Holy Prophet. With all this, however, the Holy Prophet himself must have received a commandment in this connection, through what is called *waḥy khafī* (inner revelation), either already before this or in confirmation of 'Abdullāh ibn Zaid's vision, revealing to him the same call to prayer. It was then that he ordered Bilāl to give out the call for prayer in the manner that we know. The Holy Prophet's ordering Bilāl, as in h. 604 and h. 606, should accordingly be considered a separate incident that took place not at the time of this consultation but some time after it. It must be remembered that believers other than the Holy Prophet himself may have received suggestions from on High about the institutions of Islām, but these acquired the status of the law of Islām only after confirmation by the Holy Prophet through his revelation of what the others had seen or heard. Thus it is stated in a ḥadīth in the *Muṣannaf* of 'Abdur Razzāq (h. 1775) that when 'Umar, after hearing the words of the *Adhān*, stated his own dream before the Holy Prophet, the Holy Prophet said to him: "Revelation from Allāh has preceded this (vision) of yours", meaning that the revelation had come to the Holy Prophet before 'Umar related his vision to him.

The words of the *Adhān* are themselves an evidence that its source is revelation and it is not of human devising. No such call existed in the previous religions, whereas human opinion would have copied something from them. This shows that Islām did not copy the existing religions, rather it reformed them. The *Adhān*, to begin with, proclaims the glory of Allāh, the supreme object of a man of religious life. Then comes the proclamation of the unity of Allāh. Next comes the prophethood of Muḥammad. Thus the fundamental principles of Islām are proclaimed five times a day when inviting people to congregational prayer. Then come the actual words calling to prayer and it is added that this is the way to achieve the object of life, an announcement of another principle of religious life. The loud proclamation of these fundamental principles refreshes the memory of the believers and inspires them with the courage of conviction. It also shows that Muslims, wherever they may be, must proclaim the message of Islām.

Ch. 2: The (wording of the) Call to Prayer is (pronounced) twice each[5]

605 Anas reported: Bilāl was ordered to use each expression twice in *Adhān* and once in *Iqāmah,* except for *Iqāmah* (itself).[6]

606 Anas ibn Mālik reported: When people became numerous — and he added — they discussed that the time of prayer should be indicated by something which people may recognize. So they suggested that a fire should be lit or a gong should be rung. So Bilāl was ordered to use each expression twice in *Adhān* and once in *Iqāmah.*[7]

Ch. 3: *Iqāmah* (its clauses to be said) only once, except "Prayer is ready" (*qad qāmati-ṣ-ṣalāt*)

607 Anas reported: Bilāl was ordered to use each expression twice in *Adhān* and once in *Iqāmah.* Ismāʿīl (a sub-narrator) said: I mentioned this to Ayyūb and he added: Except for *Iqāmah* (itself).[8]

Ch. 4: Excellence of sounding the call to prayer

608 Abū Hurairah reported that the Prophet ﷺ said: "When the call is made for prayer Satan turns back fleeing,[9] making sounds of scoffing and denying, so that he may not hear the call to prayer.[10] And when the call is finished,

---

[5] The meaning of "The *Adhān* is twice each" is that each of its clauses should be repeated twice, except that the opening expression *Allāhu Akbar* ("Allāh is the greatest") is repeated four times and the closing expression *Lā ilāha ill-Allāh* ("There is no god but Allāh") is said only once. In the *Iqāmah* these are said only once.

[6] This is a repetition of the last part of h. 606, with the addition "except for *Iqāmah*" (*ill-al-Iqāmah*). This addition refers to the clause of the *Iqāmah* from which its name is derived and which is not in the *Adhān:* "Prayer is ready" (*qad qāmati-ṣ-ṣalāt*). This is said twice. Since in the *Adhān* the expression *Allāhu Akbar* is said four times, in the *Iqāmah* it is said only twice.

[7] As has already been noted, the Holy Prophet's ordering Bilāl, to recite the clauses of the *Adhān* twice each and those of the *Iqāmah* only once, did not take place at the time of the discussion about how to call people to prayer, but later on. The ḥadīth has put the two incidents together only for the sake of brevity.

[8] This is a repetition of h. 605, but the final words are those of Ayyūb who was a narrator in the chain of narrators of h. 605. For their meaning, see footnote to h. 605.

[9] The devil fleeing from the call to prayer is in the spiritual sense. Just as light and heat kill deadly germs, or foul air in a closed room disappears with the fresh air let in, when truth is proclaimed openly the devil flees because he cannot confront it, as he can only work by stealth. Also, the proclamation of the principal clauses of our creed in a loud voice removes the spiritual lethargy which naturally comes upon a believer when he is pre-occupied with his worldly life.

[10] The word *ḍurāṭ* ("making sounds of scoffing and denying") refers to the sound of emission of wind from the anus. But Satan is a non-physical being and this word cannot be applied to him

he advances till when the *Iqāmah* is sounded for prayer, he turns back fleeing till when the call of the *Iqāmah* is finished. He advances again till he casts evil suggestions between man and his self, saying, 'Remember this and remember that', about what he did not remember, till the man is in such a condition that he does not know how much of the prayer he has said." [11]

Ch. 5:   Raising the voice in calling to prayer

> 'Umar ibn 'Abdul 'Azīz said: Call out the *Adhān* in a simple manner or else get away from us.[12]

609 'Abdullāh ibn 'Abdur Raḥmān al-Anṣārī, later (known as) al-Māzinī, reported from his father that he informed him that Abū Sa'īd al-Khudrī said to him: "I see you are fond of goats and forests. So when you are in the midst of your goats or in your forests and you give the call to prayer, make your voice loud in this call, for surely whoever hears the limit of the voice of the caller to prayer, whether Jinn or people or anything else, will bear witness for him on the Day of Resurrection." [13] Abū Sa'īd added: "I have heard this from the Messenger of Allāh ﷺ."

---

in a literal sense. Ibn Athīr explains a ḥadīth, "He was asked about something and he acted with *ḍurāṭ* towards the questioner", as meaning: "He belittled it and disliked it". He writes here that this word is used "when a person, on the speech of another, brings his lips together and makes a sound resembling the passing of wind by way of belittling and scoffing". In *Fatḥ al-Bārī* this word has been described as meaning "fleeing with great speed". In a report in Ṣaḥīḥ Muslim, the Holy Prophet said: "When the caller to prayer gives the Call, Satan flees turning his back, with great speed" (book: 'Prayer', ch. 8), where the description of Satan's action is the same as in the above ḥadīth except that instead of the word *ḍurāṭ* the word used is *ḥuṣāṣ*, meaning "great speed". The Qur'ān itself makes a reference to human beings who behave like Satan on hearing the call to prayer as follows: "And when you call to prayer, they take it as a mockery and a sport. That is because they are a people who do not understand" (5 : 58).

[11] From this it can be inferred that when extraneous thoughts enter the mind during individual prayer said in silence, one could raise the voice slightly, since the reciting aloud of the *Adhān* and the *Iqāmah* makes the devil flee. The real aim is to maintain attention in prayer by uttering the words in a low voice, so that there is full control over one's focus and attention.

[12] The man was sounding the *Adhān* in a singing tone and was stopped by 'Umar ibn 'Abdul 'Azīz. Proclaiming it in the form of singing takes away its solemnity and is calculated to touch other chords of the mind than that of devotion. Followers of some great religions of the world, who say their prayers with singing and music, have ignored the fact that the emotional side of man and his devotional side, while being very close, are still two different things altogether.

[13] The words "or anything else" here are taken by some to mean the angels, but it could be general. Their bearing witness is by their condition, by whatever the different groups do as a result of the *Adhān*. When the Qur'ān says: "And there is not a single thing but glorifies Him with His praise, but you do not understand their glorification" (17 : 44), the glorification is not by uttering words but by condition.

Ch. 6:   Refraining from bloodshed on account of the *Adhān*

610 Anas ibn Mālik reported that the Prophet ﷺ, when he would attack a people along with us, would not direct us to attack till it would be dawn and he would wait and see. If he heard the *Adhān* he would withhold from them and if he did not hear the *Adhān* he would fall on them.[14]

He added:[15] We left for Khaibar and reached there at night. When it was dawn and he (the Holy Prophet) did not hear the *Adhān* he rode and I rode behind Abū Ṭalḥah, and my foot was touching the foot of the Prophet ﷺ. They (the people of Khaibar) came out with their baskets and their spades (for their daily work), and when they saw the Prophet ﷺ they said: "It is Muḥammad, by Allāh, it is Muḥammad and an army." When the Messenger of Allāh ﷺ saw them he said: "*Allāhu Akbar, Allāhu Akbar,* Khaibar is ruined. When we alight in the fields of a nation, the morning of these people, who had been warned, turns evil."

Ch. 7:   What should one say when hearing the call to prayer

611 Abū Saʿīd al-Khudrī reported that the Messenger of Allāh ﷺ said: "When you hear the call to prayer, you should say the like of what the caller to prayer says."

612 ʿĪsā ibn Ṭalḥah reported that he heard Muʿāwiyah one day saying like what he (the caller to prayer) said up to the words: "I bear witness that Muḥammad is the Messenger of Allāh." [16]

613 Yaḥyā said: Some of our brothers related to me that when he (the caller to prayer) said, "Come to prayer" (*ḥayya ʿala-ṣ-ṣalāh*), he (Muʿāwiyah) said:

---

[14] In such reports the causes of the Holy Prophet's expeditions are not mentioned, so it must not be thought that the Holy Prophet ever attacked any people without being threatened by them first. He always acted according to the principle laid down in the Qur'ān: "And fight in the way of Allāh against those who fight against you" (2:190). As for the Battle of Khaibar itself, mentioned in this ḥadīth, the Holy Prophet's attack on the Jews of the place was not unprovoked. These people were busily engaged in preparations for war and in creating trouble for the Holy Prophet. He attacked them before they had made full preparations. The precaution of not attacking a people if the sound of the *Adhān* is heard from their quarters shows that it was a rule with the Holy Prophet not to engage in warfare with a people who allowed religious freedom to Muslims living in that State. This shows that the only object of his wars was the establishment of complete religious freedom in all places.

[15] This addition is a briefer version of the report by Anas in h. 371 of the attack on Khaibar and its conquest. See the footnote to that ḥadīth.

[16] This is completed in the report that follows. See also h. 914 for further details.

"There is no might nor power except with (the help of) Allāh", and added: "Thus have we heard your Prophet ﷺ say." [17]

Ch. 8: Supplication (*du ʿā'*) after the call to prayer is given

614 Jābir ibn ʿAbdullāh reported that the Messenger of Allāh ﷺ said: "He who says, on hearing the call to prayer: 'O Allāh, the Lord of this perfect call[18] and ever-living prayer, grant Muḥammad nearness and excellence and raise him to the position of glory which You have promised him', for him my intercession becomes due on the day of Resurrection." [19]

---

[17] That is to say, the Holy Prophet used to repeat the words of the *Adhān* when he would hear it, except that in response to "Come to prayer" and "Come to success" he would say: "There is no might nor power except with (the help of) Allāh" (*Lā ḥaul wa lā quwwat illā bi-llāh*). This was because the other expressions in the *Adhān* are points of principle, which one accepts by repeating them, but these are calls to action, the response to which is that the power of action must come from God Who is the source of all power. Some have suggested that in response to "Come to success" one should say: "It is as Allāh pleases" (*mā shā'-llāh*).

[18] This ḥadīth gives us the prayer that is to be said on hearing the *Adhān*. It has been described as the "perfect call" which, in fact, it is. It is no mere call to prayer but a re-proclamation and preaching of the fundamental rules of Islām and its religious life, and as such has no parallel and cannot be improved upon nor replaced by any other call that can be delivered for this purpose. An explanation of its phrases has been given under h. 604 in the last paragraph of footnote 4. It may be added that the proclamation of the prophethood of Muḥammad in the call, which is the "perfect call", shows that his prophethood is also perfect and ever-lasting, and only his prophethood need be proclaimed to the world. Hence a Muslim cannot believe in a prophet coming after the Holy Prophet Muḥammad, because it would require either changing the *Adhān* to proclaim the new prophet or to consider the *Adhān* as no longer a perfect call. After the physical departure of the Prophet Muḥammad, there is nothing but a continuation of his prophethood, and he remains the Last Prophet in spite of the appearance of the great reformers and spiritual figures known as *Mujaddids,* with additional titles such as Mahdī and Promised Messiah.

[19] The *Adhān* not only underlines the basic principles of the faith but it also announces that to carry those principles into practice the first essential step is prayer, by means of which man establishes a relationship with God that takes him to his utmost point of development and success. This supplication refers to prayer as *aṣ-ṣalāt al-qā'imah*, the ever-living or the established prayer, and this indicates that the spirit of the prayer must also be maintained, along with the bodily movements and spoken words, with the heart being full of the realization that during prayer one is standing in the Divine presence. The word *Rabb* ("Lord") in this prayer means God is He Who not only creates but He also leads His creation gradually, step by step, towards perfection. This is a hint that the "perfect call" of Islām will attain its goal of reaching all over the world and the Holy Prophet's excellence will be recognized everywhere. Even after God has, out of His own mercy, sent us the perfect Book and perfect example, it is for us to pray earnestly to God for the continuity of this mercy, to the fulfilment of the mission of Prophet Muḥammad.

The prayer for the Holy Prophet to be granted "nearness" (*wasīlah*) to Allāh shows the real meaning of this word. In the Qur'ān the believers are instructed to seek a *wasīlah* to Allāh (5 : 35), and this is mistakenly taken by some to mean seeking a spiritual leader (*shaikh* or *pīr*) to act as an intermediary to reach Allāh. This prayer shows that it means "nearness" because a Muslim

Ch. 9: Drawing lots for giving the *Adhān*

It has been related that people differed in the matter of giving the *Adhān*, so Saʿd drew lots between them.[20]

615 Abū Hurairah reported that the Messenger of Allāh ﷺ said: "If people knew what is (the reward) for (giving) the call to prayer and for (being in) the first row (in the congregational prayer), and they could not find any way (to decide) except that they should draw lots, they would draw lots; and if they knew what is (the reward) for appearing early for the *Ẓuhr* prayer, they would have raced with one another for it; and if they knew what is (the reward) for the *'Ishā'* and the morning prayers, they would come to these two prayers even if they had to crawl on their knees." [21]

Ch. 10: Talking in the course of giving the *Adhān*

Sulaimān ibn Ṣurad talked in the course of his *Adhān*, and al-Ḥasan said: There is no harm if one laughs while one is giving the *Adhān* or calling out the *Iqāmah*.[22]

616 ʿAbdullāh ibn al-Ḥārith reported: Ibn ʿAbbās delivered to us a sermon on a muddy day, and when the caller to prayer reached "Come to prayer" (*Ḥayya 'ala-ṣ-ṣalāh*), he ordered him to call out: "Say your prayer at home" (*Aṣ-Ṣalātu fi-r-riḥāl*). So people looked at one another, at which he said: "One

---

cannot possibly pray that the Holy Prophet be granted a spiritual leader to reach Allāh. While this part of the prayer is asking for the advancement of the spiritual rank of the Holy Prophet, the next part, asking for him to be granted "excellence", relates to his status in this world, i.e., the recognition of his greatness by the people of the world. As there is no limit to "nearness" or to "excellence", the prayer for these will continue to be said by Muslims for all time, and the Holy Prophet will continue, day by day, to rise higher in these terms, and he will be raised to the ultimate "position of glory" (*maqām-an maḥmūd-an*). The Holy Prophet's statement at the end shows that one who prays as described, and accompanies his prayer with action, will thereby be among those who have earned the intercession of the Holy Prophet. But this does not exclude others.

[20] This is about Saʿd ibn Abī Waqqāṣ who led the Muslim army in the Battle of Qādisiyyah against the Persians during the rule of ʿUmar. In this battle the official caller to prayer was wounded, and as there were many candidates for this vacant post, Saʿd decided the case by the drawing of lots. It must be remembered that the appointed caller to prayer in those days did not hold a paid position.

[21] See also h. 653–654, h. 657 and h. 720–721.

[22] It means that whereas talking or laughing during prayer invalidates the prayer, neither of these invalidates the *Adhān* or the *Iqāmah*. Of course, it is not good to talk without necessity, or to laugh, while giving the *Adhān* or the *Iqāmah*. This also shows that, if necessary, talk can take place in these situations.

who was better than him had done this, and surely it (the *Jumu'ah* prayer) is obligatory." [23]

Ch. 11:   The *Adhān* sounded by a blind man when there is someone to inform him

617 Sālim ibn 'Abdullāh reported from his father ('Abdullāh ibn 'Umar) that the Messenger of Allāh ﷺ said: "Surely Bilāl sounds the *Adhān* when it is still night, so eat and drink until Ibn Umm Maktūm sounds the call to prayer." He (Sālim) added: And he was a blind man who would not sound the call to prayer until he was told: "It is morning, it is morning." [24]

Ch. 12:   The *Adhān* after daybreak

618 Ḥafṣah informed that the Messenger of Allāh ﷺ, when the caller to prayer sat down in the morning (after the *Adhān*) and the day broke, prayed two *rak'ahs* briefly before the *Iqāmah* was called for prayer.

619 'Ā'ishah reported: The Prophet ﷺ used to say two *rak'ahs* of short prayer between the call and the *Iqāmah* for the morning prayer.

---

[23] It was a rainy day that Friday when Ibn 'Abbās was to lead the *Jumu'ah* prayer and deliver the sermon. The streets had become muddy and slippery. The Qur'ān contains the injunction for believers: "when the call is sounded for prayer on Friday, hasten to the remembrance of Allāh" (62:9); so if in the *Adhān* the usual expression "Come to prayer" had been called out, it would have become obligatory to come to the mosque, and a sin to ignore this. That is why Ibn 'Abbās issued the order that in the course of *Adhān* people should be asked to stay in their homes and say their prayers there. There is a report in Musnad Aḥmad that once, on a bitterly cold night, the caller to prayer of the Holy Prophet, while sounding the *Adhān* for the *Fajr* prayer, after he had uttered the words "Prayer is better than sleep", added the words: "Whoever stays home, there is no blame on him" (*man qa'ada fa-lā ḥaraja 'alai-hi* — in Urdu translation of Musnad Aḥmad by Maulana Zafar Iqbal see under 'ḥadīth from Nu'aim ibn an-Naḥḥām', h. 18099). Note that the words "one who is better than him" refer to the Holy Prophet. See also h. 668 and h. 901.

[24] Bilāl was the permanent caller to prayer (*mu'adh-dhin*) of the Holy Prophet. It seems he used to sound an extra *Adhān* in the month of Ramaḍān sometime before the *Adhān* for the morning prayer. The purpose of this *Adhān*, as seen from the report by Ibn Mas'ūd in h. 621, was to remind those who were praying *Tahajjud* to return home to eat before *Fajr,* and also to alert those who were asleep of the approaching time of prayer. Ibn Umm Maktūm used to give the *Adhān* for the *Fajr* prayer when people told him that it was dawn, because he was a blind man. It is implied in this ḥadīth that cessation of eating and drinking for the fast is to begin only after the appearance of dawn. In fact, it is stated in the Qur'ān itself that this eating and drinking is to be stopped only when the brightness of the morning is properly visible as is evident from the words: "and eat and drink until the whiteness of the day becomes distinct from the blackness of the night at dawn" (2:187).

620 'Abdullāh ibn 'Umar reported that the Messenger of Allāh ﷺ said: "Surely Bilāl sounds the call to prayer when it is still night, so eat and drink until Ibn Umm Maktūm sounds the call to prayer." [25]

Ch. 13: The *Adhān* before daybreak

621 'Abdullāh ibn Mas'ūd reported from the Prophet ﷺ that he said: "The *Adhān* of Bilāl should by no means prevent any of you — or (he said) anyone among you — from taking the pre-fast meal, for surely he sounds the *Adhān* — or (he said) sounds the call to prayer —while it is still night so that he may induce those of you who are engaged in (*Tahajjud*) prayers to return, and wake up those of you who are sleeping. It is not that *Fajr* or the morning has appeared." [26] And he (the Prophet) indicated with his fingers, raising them upwards and then lowering them downwards, and then said: "Until it becomes like this."

Zuhair (a narrator) gestured with his two forefingers, one of them placed over the other, and then he stretched them towards his right and towards his left. [27]

622–623 'Ā'ishah reported from the Prophet ﷺ that he said: "Surely Bilāl sounds the *Adhān* when it is still night, so eat and drink until Ibn Umm Maktūm sounds the *Adhān*." [28]

Ch. 14: What should be the interval between the *Adhān* and *Iqāmah*?

624 'Abdullāh ibn Mughaffal al-Muzanī reported that the Messenger of Allāh ﷺ said: "Between every two *Adhāns* there is a prayer" — (and he said it) three times — "for whoever wishes." [29]

---

[25] This is a repetition of the first part of h. 617. (See also h. 1918–1919.)

[26] The verb here, applying to *Fajr* and to morning, is *yaqūla*, which literally means "says", and is used here to mean that *Fajr* or the morning has appeared.

[27] While uttering these words, the Holy Prophet appears to have raised and lowered his fingers to indicate that *Fajr* is not when whiteness rises from below towards the middle of the sky in a line. This is known as the "false dawn" or the "zodiacal light" and extends up from the horizon like a hazy pyramid. The true dawn is when whiteness spreads across the sky, as indicated by one of the narrators of this ḥadīth.

[28] This is a repetition of h. 617 in the form of h. 620 with a slight variation.

[29] The two *Adhāns* mean the *Adhān* and the *Iqāmah*. The meaning is that there should be such an interval between the *Adhān* and the *Iqāmah* as to make it possible for someone to say two *rak'ahs* of prayer if he wishes. A further clarification of this report is found in its repetition in h. 627 where the words "for whoever wishes" are added separately.

625 Anas ibn Mālik reported: When the caller to prayer used to sound the *Adhān,* some of the Companions of the Prophet ﷺ would hurry towards the pillars till the Prophet ﷺ came out and they used to pray like this two *rak'ahs* before the *Maghrib* prayer and there would be very little interval between the *Adhān* and the *Iqāmah.*

Shu'bah said: There would be only a little (time) between them.[30]

Ch. 15:   One who waits for the *Iqāmah*

626 'Ā'ishah reported: The Messenger of Allāh ﷺ would get up, when the caller to prayer would be silent after the first call to the *Fajr* prayer, and would say two *rak'ahs* of short prayer before the *Fajr* prayer after dawn would be clear in appearance. Then he would lie down on his right side until the caller to prayer would come to him for the *Iqāmah.*[31]

Ch. 16:   Between any two *Adhāns* there is a prayer for whoever wishes

627 'Abdullāh ibn Mughaffal reported, saying that the Prophet ﷺ said: "Between every two *Adhāns* there is a prayer, between every two *Adhāns* there is a prayer." Then, saying it a third time, he added: "for whoever wishes." [32]

Ch. 17:   He who says: During a journey only one caller to prayer should sound the *Adhān?*[33]

628 Mālik ibn al-Ḥuwairith reported: I came to the Prophet ﷺ with some people of my community and we stayed with him for twenty nights. He was very kind and tender-hearted.[34] So when he realized our attachment to our

---

[30] See h. 503 and its footnote. The closing words by Anas ibn Mālik are literally: "and there would be nothing between the *Adhān* and the *Iqāmah.*" It is an idiomatic expression to indicate that there would be very little time between the two or that only a short two *rak'ah* prayer could somehow be said in this interval. This is made clear by the statement of Shu'bah, in which the word "little" (*qalīl*) is used.

[31] This is a repetition of h. 619 with additional matter. The lying down of the Holy Prophet for a while was both to take a short rest after his lengthy *Tahajjud* prayers and to allow time for people to gather for prayer.

[32] This is a repetition of h. 624. See the footnote to that ḥadīth.

[33] In a journey, therefore, there should be only one caller to prayer (*mu'adh-dhin*). Even at home there is always one man appointed for this purpose generally. The ḥadīth here makes no mention of a journey as the Holy Prophet is reported to have said that this procedure should be adopted when the people have returned to their homes. Perhaps the chapter heading contains the word "journey" to indicate that the same rule applies whether on a journey or not. Anyhow, this issue is not important.

[34] This was the time when the Holy Prophet, threatened by Christian invasion from the north,

families, he said: "Go back and be with them. Teach them, and say your prayers. When the time for prayer comes, one of you should give the call to prayer for you, and the eldest among you should act as your Imām."

Ch. 18: **The *Adhān* and the *Iqāmah* for travellers when they are a group (*jamā'at*),[35] and likewise at 'Arafah and Muzdalifah[36]**

The caller to prayer saying on a cold and rainy night: "Say your prayer at home."

629 Abū Dharr reported: We were with the Prophet ﷺ in a journey and the caller to prayer wanted to sound the call to prayer. He (the Holy Prophet) said to him: "Let it get cooler." He again (after a while) wanted to sound the call but the Prophet ﷺ said: "Let it get cooler." He (yet) again wanted to sound the call but the Prophet ﷺ said: "Let it get cooler." It was until the shadows of hillocks became equal (to their height) that he said: "Surely the severity of heat is from the raging of Hell." [37]

630 Mālik ibn al-Ḥuwairith reported: Two men came to the Prophet ﷺ, intending to go on a journey and the Prophet ﷺ said: "When you two set out, you should sound the call to prayer and then say the *Iqāmah*. Then the elder of you should act as your Imām." [38]

---

was extremely busy in making preparations for the expedition of Tabūk. He was not only bearing the burden of being a ruler but was also anxious and vigilant due to constant warfare. In such circumstances a man is inclined to be irritable and unfriendly. But, as this ḥadīth shows, his genial human sympathy, courtesy and tender-heartedness was there as it was before, when he had no such responsibilities and pressure upon him. Displaying such morals is all the more commendable on the part of a ruler and leader of a nation, engaged in other important duties.

[35] The ḥadīth reports in this chapter establish that in a journey both the *Adhān* and the *Iqāmah* are to be sounded for congregational prayers, but there is no prohibition in them against the *Adhān* in the case of an individual saying his prayer alone while on a journey. There is a saying of Ibn 'Umar in the *Muṣannaf* of 'Abdur Razzāq, with sound transmission, that an individual saying his prayer alone should only say the *Iqāmah*. This, however, is not supported by any ḥadīth of the Holy Prophet. In h. 609 from Abū Sa'īd al-Khudrī, the *Adhān* is recommended for a man saying his prayers alone and this is the view of three of the Imāms of Fiqh, Abū Ḥanīfah, Shāfi'ī and Aḥmad. As for the *Iqāmah*, there is no difference of opinion about it, in that it is both for individual and congregational prayers.

[36] During the *Ḥajj*, at 'Arafat the *Ẓuhr* and the *'Aṣr* prayers are combined, and at Muzdalifah the *Maghrib* and the *'Ishā'* prayers are combined. In both these cases the *Adhān* and the *Iqāmah* have to be sounded.

[37] This is a repetition of h. 539, with the difference that there is no specification of the *Ẓuhr* prayer in this ḥadīth and the last sentence of the Holy Prophet is cut short.

[38] This shows that even two persons can constitute a congregation for prayer. Bukhārī has indicated this conclusion by repeating this ḥadīth in h. 658 under a chapter heading referring to a congregation (*jamā'at*).

631 Mālik (ibn al-Ḥuwairith) related: We went to the Prophet ﷺ, and we were young men of about the same age, and we stayed with him for twenty days and nights. The Messenger of Allāh ﷺ was very kind and tender-hearted. So when he felt that we were desiring to return to our families, or were eager for it, he asked us whom we had left behind. So we told him and he said: "Return to your families and stay with them. Teach them (the religion) and enjoin them (to act upon it)."

(A narrator said:) He (Mālik) mentioned certain things which either I remembered or have not. (The Prophet continued:) "And say your prayers as you have seen me pray. When the time for prayer comes, one of you should give the call to prayer for you, and the eldest among you should act as your Imām." [39]

632 Nāfiʿ related: Ibn ʿUmar called out the *Adhān* on one cold night at Ḍajnān, then he said: "Say your prayer in your homes". He informed us that the Messenger of Allāh ﷺ used to order a caller to prayer to sound the *Adhān* and then say at the end of it, "Beware, say your prayer at home", on a cold or rainy night and a journey." [40]

633 ʿAun ibn Abū Juḥaifah reported from his father (Abū Juḥaifah) that he said: I saw the Messenger of Allāh ﷺ at al-Abṭaḥ. Bilāl came to him and informed him of the prayer. Then Bilāl came out with a spear and planted it in front of the Messenger of Allāh ﷺ at al-Abṭaḥ, and sounded the *Iqāmah* for prayer. [41]

Ch. 19: **Should the caller to prayer turn his face this way and that way, and should he turn his look in other directions during the *Adhān*?**

It is related of Bilāl that he used to put his fingers in his ears, and Ibn ʿUmar would not put his fingers in his ears. Ibrāhīm said: There

---

[39] This is a repetition of h. 628 with some differences in wording.

[40] This shows the words "Beware, say your prayer at home" being announced at the end of the *Adhān*. In the same report in Ṣaḥīḥ Muslim it is also stated that these words were said "at the end of the call to prayer" (book: 'Prayer of travellers and its shortening', ch. 3). However, according to h. 616 above, Ibn ʿAbbās asked the caller to prayer to announce "Say your prayer at home" in place of "Come to prayer". There may be no conflict here because the words "Come to prayer" do occur towards the end of the *Adhān*. The sense of the ḥadīth is that there is no harm if a person fails to join the prayer congregation either due to bad weather or if on a journey. In some versions of this ḥadīth the closing words are *fi-s-safar* (not *wa-s-safar*), which would render the statement as "on a cold or rainy night *during* a journey", thus making being on a journey an additional condition. But see h. 666, where there is no mention at all of a journey.

[41] This is a repetition of h. 376. See also h. 495, h. 499 and h. 501.

is no harm that he sounds the call to prayer without (having per-formed) *Wuḍū'*. 'Aṭā' said: *Wuḍū'* is a required *Sunnah*. 'Ā'ishah said: The Prophet ﷺ used to remember Allāh at all times.

634 'Aun ibn Abū Juḥaifah reported from his father (Abū Juḥaifah) that he saw Bilāl sounding the call to prayer, and (he said:) "so I began to follow him as he turned his face this way and that way in the *Adhān*."

Ch. 20:   A man's saying "Prayer escaped us" (*fātat-nā aṣ-ṣalāt*)

Ibn Sīrīn disliked that someone should say *fātat-nā aṣ-ṣalāt* ("Prayer escaped us"), rather he should say *lam nudrik* ("We did not reach it"). But the saying of the Prophet ﷺ is the most correct.[42]

635 Abū Qatādah reported: Once we were saying our prayers with the Prophet ﷺ when, all of a sudden, he heard the noise of people running. So when he finished the prayer, he said: "What was the matter with you?" They said: "We were hurrying for the prayer." He said: "Do not do so. When you come for prayer you should be calm, and whatever (part of prayer) you reach, pray it (accordingly), and what has escaped you, (you should) complete it (afterwards)." [43]

Ch. 21:   "Whatever (part of prayer) you reach, pray it, and what has escaped you, complete it (afterwards)"

Abū Qatādah reported this from the Prophet ﷺ.

636 Abū Hurairah reported from the Prophet ﷺ that he said: "When you hear the *Iqāmah*, walk to the prayer. You should be calm and dignified, and not make haste. So whatever (part of prayer) you reach, pray it (accordingly), and what has escaped you, (you should) complete it (afterwards)." [44]

---

[42] The word derived from *faut* has been used both in the chapter heading as well as in the ḥadīth under it for a prayer partly or wholly missed. Thus Bukhārī concludes that the opinion of Ibn Sīrīn is not correct since this word has been used by the Holy Prophet. Ibn Sīrīn's objection seems to be that one should not say that the prayer missed us, but rather that we missed the prayer.

[43] This shows that if a man joins the congregation when some part of the prayer has already been said, he should stand up when the Imām has invoked *Salām* at the end of the prayer and, on his own, say the earlier part of the prayer which he missed after the congregation has finished its prayer.

[44] This is a repetition of h. 635. There is no mention here of people running, and it only gives the words of the Holy Prophet. See also h. 908.

Ch. 22: When should people stand (for prayer) when they see the Imām at the time of the *Iqāmah*?

637 Abū Qatādah reported that the Messenger of Allāh ﷺ said: "When the prayer is announced by *Iqāmah*, do not stand up until you see me." [45]

Ch. 23: Not to stand up for prayer in a hurry, but stand up with calmness and dignity[46]

638 Abū Qatādah reported that the Messenger of Allāh ﷺ said: "When the prayer is announced by *Iqāmah*, do not stand up until you see me, and you should be calm." [47]

Ch. 24: Can one go out of the mosque for some need?

639 Abū Hurairah reported that the Messenger of Allāh ﷺ came out when the prayer had been announced by *Iqāmah* and the rows were made correct in standing. When he stood in the place of prayer, we waited for him to say *Allāhu Akbar*. But he left, saying: "Remain where you are". We remained in our positions till he came back out to us, water trickling from his head, as he had taken a bath.[48]

Ch. 25: When the Imām says "Remain where you are," they should wait for him till he returns

640 Abū Hurairah reported: The prayer had been announced by *Iqāmah* and people had straightened their rows. The Messenger of Allāh ﷺ came out and went to the front. But he was under obligation of bath, so he said: "Remain where you are". He returned, took a bath, and then came out while drops of water were falling from his head. Then he led them in prayer.[49]

---

[45] The chambers of the Holy Prophet had their doors opening into the mosque. It seems that sometimes people, thinking that the Holy Prophet was coming out for prayers, would have the *Iqāmah* called. So here the Holy Prophet asks them to wait till he actually comes out and then to stand up for prayer. He might be delayed and they would be inconvenienced by standing waiting for him. See also h. 909.

[46] It is emphasized that one should not rush to reach prayer just to be counted as included in the congregation. The real object is to create a spiritual state in the heart, and this would be impossible to attain by rushing instead of reaching the prayer in a state of calmness. Besides, hurrying in this way disturbs the prayer of other people, distracting them. This shows that silence of surroundings is essential for prayer.

[47] This is a repetition of h. 637 with a small addition at the end.

[48] This is a repetition of h. 275, but does not say that he left because he was under obligation of bath. Even then, since the Holy Prophet had asked people to remain where they were, it means he must have left for some important reason.

[49] This is also a repetition of h. 275, but with less difference than in the above h. 639. The

Ch. 26: A man's saying: "We have not said our prayer."

641 Jābir ibn 'Abdullāh informed that 'Umar ibn al-Khaṭṭāb came to the Prophet ﷺ on the day of the (battle of the) Ditch and said: "O Messenger of Allāh, by Allāh! I could not say the ('Aṣr) prayer until the sun was on the point of setting." And this was (when he said this) after the time when a person would break his fast. The Prophet ﷺ said: "By Allāh, I have not said this prayer (either)." So the Prophet ﷺ alighted at Buṭḥān and I was with him. He performed ablution for prayer, then said the prayer, that is, the 'Aṣr prayer, after the sun had set. Then he said the *Maghrib* prayer after it.[50]

Ch. 27: The Imām confronted with some need after the *Iqāmah*

642 Anas reported: The prayer had been announced by *Iqāmah* and the Prophet ﷺ was talking privately to a man in a side of the mosque and did not stand for prayer until (some) people had gone to sleep.[51]

Ch. 28: Talking when the prayer has been announced by *Iqāmah*

643 Anas ibn Mālik related: The prayer had been announced by *Iqāmah*. But a man appeared before the Prophet ﷺ and detained him after the prayer had been announced by *Iqāmah*.[52]

Ch. 29: The obligatory nature of congregational prayer

Al-Ḥasan said: If anyone's mother prevents him from the *'Ishā'* prayer in congregation out of affection, he should not obey her.

644 Abū Hurairah reported that the Messenger of Allāh ﷺ said: "By Him in Whose hand is my life, I certainly intended that I should order the collecting of firewood, then order prayer so that the *Adhān* is called out for it, then order a man to lead the people in prayer, then I should go out to people (absent from prayer)[53] and set fire to their houses! And by Him in Whose hand is my life,

---

inference is that if an Imām has to leave the mosque for some urgent need, and he tells the congregation to remain in their places, they should wait there for his return.

[50] This is a repetition of h. 596. It would appear that certain chapters of Bukhārī were designed to meet some need of that time, and the need of this chapter arose because Ibrāhīm Nakha'ī disapproved of the expression "We have not said our prayers." Bukhārī wants to discredit this view by quoting 'Umar and the Holy Prophet.

[51] This shows that, if the necessity arises, there is no harm in having some interval between the *Iqāmah* and the prayers.

[52] This is a repetition of h. 642 with some difference of wording.

[53] The expression *ukhālifa ilā rijāl-in* has been interpreted in several ways. The one adopted in this translation is "to go to people who are absent". Another suggested interpretation is: "I will

if any of them knew that he would get a bone with thick flesh (to eat) or two nice games (to play), he would have been present at the *'Ishā'* prayer." [54]

Ch. 30:   Excellence of the congregational prayer

Aswad, when he missed the congregational prayer (in his mosque), would go to another mosque. Anas ibn Mālik went to a mosque in which the prayer had already been said, so he sounded the *Adhān* and pronounced the *Iqāmah* and said his prayer in congregation.[55]

645 'Abdullāh ibn 'Umar reported that the Messenger of Allāh ﷺ said: "The prayer in congregation excels the individual prayer by twenty-seven degrees."

646 Abū Sa'īd reported that he heard the Prophet ﷺ say: "The prayer in congregation excels the individual prayer by twenty-five degrees." [56]

---

act contrary to the call to prayer", meaning that instead of going to the prayer he would go to the houses of those who were absent.

[54] The greatest emphasis has been laid here on the importance of the congregational prayer and those not attending have been severely condemned. Of course, it is not meant that the houses of the absentees should be burned down or their property taken away, for the Holy Prophet himself never did so. He only said that he would have wanted to do so, not that he would actually do so. The ḥadīth ends with the statement that whereas people take all sorts of trouble to go to functions where food or entertainment is provided but they excuse themselves on various pleas from the congregational prayer. The word *mirmāt* ("games") means the arrows used for learning the art of throwing them. According to some authorities, it was a sport in which the players threw arrows at a heap of earth and the winner was the one whose arrows penetrated the heap the most. Here it means any kind of sport. This rebuke of the Holy Prophet is more appropriate to present-day Muslims than to those to whom he was speaking. They attend social functions and entertainment in the evening till midnight, but find it difficult to come to *'Ishā'* prayers at 9 p.m. See also h. 657.

[55] This shows that a second congregation can take place in a mosque after the scheduled one has finished. Baihaqī says that Anas was accompanied by twenty men at that time, and he sounded the *Adhān* to enable any other people who might have missed the first congregation to avail of this second one.

[56] The number of degrees of excellence is given differently in different reports. It is twenty-seven according to some, twenty-five according to others, and "twenty and some more" in some other reports. There is, however, no real divergence, as what is meant is a great excellence. The Holy Prophet might have used different numbers for different situations. According to *Fatḥ al-Bārī*, for congregational prayers in which the recitation from the Qur'ān is aloud, the degrees are twenty-seven, and for those where it is in silence, these are twenty-five. The two additional degrees in the first case are owing to the opportunity of listening to the recitation, and saying *Āmīn* at the end, which is said to coincide with the angels saying the same. *Fatḥ al-Bārī* lists the twenty-five excellences. These start from the listening and responding to the *Adhān,* and step by step go through the whole process of going to the mosque on time, waiting for the prayer to start, saying the prayer, and end with the social benefit of mutual contact with other members of the

647 Abū Hurairah said that the Messenger of Allāh ﷺ said: "The prayer of a man in congregation is greater (in reward) than his prayer (alone) in his house or in the market by twenty-five times. This is because when he performs ablution, doing the *Wuḍū'* well, then goes out to the mosque, going out only for prayer, he does not take a step but he is raised one degree by it, and a sin is removed from him. When he says his prayers, the angels do not cease to pray for him, as long as he is in his place of prayer: 'O Allāh, send blessings on him, O Allāh, have mercy on him.' And everyone of you is in (the state of) prayer when he is waiting for the prayer." [57]

Ch. 31: Excellence of the *Fajr* prayer in congregation

648 Abū Hurairah said that he heard the Messenger of Allāh ﷺ say: "The prayer in congregation excels the prayer of one of you said individually by twenty-five parts, and angels of the night and the angels of the day gather in the *Fajr* prayer."

Then Abū Hurairah added: You can read (in the Qur'ān) if you wish: "Surely the recital of the Qur'ān at *Fajr* time is witnessed" (the Qur'ān, 17:78).[58]

649 'Abdullāh ibn 'Umar reported: It excels it by twenty-seven degrees.

650 Umm ad-Dardā' was heard to have said: "Abū ad-Dardā' came to me and he was in a state of anger. I said: "What makes you angry?" He said: "By Allāh, I do not recognize anything from among the works of the followers of Muḥammad ﷺ except that they pray in congregation." [59]

---

community. There are many other benefits of the congregational prayers, not only moral and spiritual, but also physical and social, which help to build a society adhering to the morals of Islām.

[57] This is a repetition of h. 477 with differences in wording. The closing words of h. 477 about not harming anyone and not voiding his *Wuḍū'* do not occur here.

[58] According to Abū Hurairah, the word *mash-hūd* ("witnessed") in this verse means the presence of the angels in the *Fajr* prayer. This word, meaning 'presence', indicates that presence of mind and consequent depth of devotion is greater in the *Fajr* prayer than the other prayers. The gathering of the angels of the night and of the day points to the same direction, for angels draw a person towards virtue, and virtue can only arise in a heart which is full of humility and attention towards God. Thus the presence of angels indicates the presence and concentration of the minds of people.

[59] This is an incident relating to the final days of the Caliphate of 'Uthmān. The passage of time, and the entry into the fold of Islām of a huge number of new people, and the passing away of many of the Companions, had relaxed the order and discipline in the observation of religion as compared to the earlier days. It appears that Abū ad-Dardā' was referring to the rebels who had besieged the Caliph. They were an evil-minded group, but they did maintain the congregational prayer to convince people that they were good Muslims, so that they might side with them.

651 Abū Mūsā reported that the Prophet ﷺ said: "The greater from among the people in receiving reward in the matter of prayer are those who come to it from a greater distance and then those who come from a still greater distance walking. And he who waits for the prayer till he has said it with the Imām is greater in reward than the one who says the prayer and then goes to sleep." [60]

Ch. 32: Excellence of coming early for the *Ẓuhr* prayer

652 Abū Hurairah reported that the Messenger of Allāh ﷺ said: "Once when a certain man was walking along a road, he came across a twig of thorns on the road, so he removed it. So Allāh appreciated his work and forgave him."

653–654 Then he (the Holy Prophet) said: "Martyrs are five: one who dies of plague, and one who dies of diarrhoea, and one who dies by drowning, and one who dies by being buried under a collapsed thing, and one who dies a martyr in the way of Allāh." And he said:[61] "If people knew what is (the reward) for (giving) the call to prayer and for (being in) the first row (in the congregational prayer), and they could not find any way (to decide) except that they should draw lots, they would draw lots; [654] and if they knew what is (the reward) for appearing early for the *Ẓuhr* prayer, they would have raced with one another for it; and if they knew what is (the reward) for the *'Ishā'* and the morning prayers, they would come to these two prayers even if they had to crawl on their knees."

Ch. 33: The reward for footsteps (for congregational prayers)

655–656 Anas ibn Mālik reported that the Prophet ﷺ said: "O Banū Salimah, do you not want reward for your footsteps (*āthār*)?" [656] It was added (to the above) that Anas related that the Banū Salimah intended that they should change their dwellings and settle down nearer the Prophet ﷺ. The narrator said: The Messenger of Allāh ﷺ did not like that they leave Madīnah exposed, so he said: "Do you not want reward for your footsteps?" [62]

---

[60] The merit of any action and the reform of the soul is enhanced as the amount of sacrifice undertaken increases, be it the sacrifice of comforts, time or money. While h. 648 is directly related to the chapter heading about *Fajr*, the remaining reports of this chapter have no specific connection with *Fajr*. Of course, the report of Abū ad-Dardā' speaks of the congregation in general in which the morning congregation is included. The report from Abū Mūsā applies more to the *Fajr* prayer than to the other prayers as the amount of sacrifice to reach it is greater. It implies that because the attendance for *Fajr* is fraught with most difficulties, it will bring the largest amount of spiritual benefit to the worshipper.

[61] From this point in h. 653 to the end of h. 654, the wording is an exact repetition of h. 615. See also h. 657 and h. 720–721.

[62] Banū Salimah used to live about one mile from the Mosque of the Holy Prophet. They were thinking of moving to settle in some place nearer to the Mosque only for the sake of easy

Mujāhid said: Their paces are the traces (*āthār*) of their feet on the ground as they walk.[63]

Ch. 34: Excellence of the *'Ishā'* prayer in congregation

657 Abū Hurairah reported that the Prophet ﷺ said: "No prayer is more difficult for the hypocrites than the *Fajr* and the *'Ishā'*.[64] If they knew what (reward) is to be found in these two prayers, they would have come to these even if they had to crawl on their knees.[65] I certainly intended to order a caller to prayer to call out the *Iqāmah,* then order a man to lead the people in prayer, then I would take an amber from the fire and set fire (to the houses) over those who do not come to the prayer after this." [66]

Ch. 35: Two and more are a congregation *(jamā'at)*

658 Mālik ibn al-Ḥuwairith reported from the Prophet ﷺ that he said: "When the prayer time comes, you should sound the call to prayer and say the *Iqāmah.* Then the elder of you should act as your Imām." [67]

Ch. 36: One who sits in the mosque waiting for the prayer, and excellence of the mosques[68]

---

attendance of the congregational prayers. The Holy Prophet advised them not to do so, in view of the strategic position of their residence in the outskirts of the city in those days of wars and enemy threats. As for the attendance to congregational prayers, he rightly felt that the difficulties of traversing the distance would add to the merits of their attendance. Those who undertake such trouble would become more inclined to bear hardship in the way of carrying out Divine commandments in general, and it is this feeling of obeying God which prayer seeks to create in the hearts. Incidentally this ḥadīth shows the Holy Prophet's keen insight in matters of defence. See also h. 1887.

[63] Mujāhid is referring to the following words of the Qur'ān: "and We write down what they send on ahead and their footprints (*āthār*)" (36:12). The word used in this ḥadīth, translated as "footsteps", is also *āthār* (lit. footprints). Mujāhid has explained the literal meaning of this word as the impressions of their feet on the ground.

[64] The congregational prayers in the morning and in the late evening are really testing prayers which measure a person's commitment to faith. Those who feel these prayers to be difficult for them are warned that they have something in common with the hypocrites. The Holy Prophet has described prayer as a means of his inner comfort and consolation. So, rather than a burden, the prayer should appear to a believer as pleasant. See h. 644 which mentions only the *'Ishā'* prayer.

[65] A similar sentence is found in h. 615 and h. 654. See also Book 9 ('Times of Prayer'), ch. 20, first paragraph under the chapter heading (above h. 564).

[66] The substance of the last part of this ḥadīth, beginning "I certainly intended", has already occurred in h. 644 in somewhat different wording.

[67] This is a repetition of h. 630 with a different opening. The Holy Prophet was addressing two men who were setting out on a journey.

[68] This shows that all obligatory prayers must be said in the mosque in congregation and this is the real purpose of mosques. To say the obligatory prayers at home is only permissible in case of a valid reason.

659 Abū Hurairah reported that the Messenger of Allāh ﷺ said: "The angels pray for one of you so long as he is in his place of prayer until he does something which nullifies ablution, (saying): 'O Allāh, forgive him! O Allāh, have mercy on him!' Everyone of you is in (the state of) prayer as long as (waiting for) the prayer keeps him there, and nothing prevents him from returning home except prayer." [69]

660 Abū Hurairah reported from the Prophet ﷺ that he said: "There are seven persons whom Allāh will give His protection[70] on the day when there is no protection except His protection: the just Imām, and a young man who has grown up in the service of his Lord, and a man whose heart is attached to the mosque, and two men who love each other for the sake of Allāh, and they meet because of this and they separate because of this, and a man whom a woman of position and beauty invites but who says, 'I fear Allāh', and a man who gives charity in secret so much so that his left hand does not know what his right hand spends, and a man who remembers Allāh in solitude so that his eyes shed tears." [71]

661 Ḥumaid reported: Anas was asked, Had the Messenger of Allāh ﷺ a ring made (for himself)? He said: Yes, one night he delayed the *'Ishā'* prayer until midnight, then he turned his face towards us after he had prayed and said: "People have said their prayers and slept, and you remained in (the state of) prayer from the time you waited for it."

He (Anas) added: "It is as if I am still seeing the sparkling of his ring." [72]

Ch. 37:   Excellence of one who goes out (in the morning) towards the mosque and of one who does so after the decline of the sun

662 Abū Hurairah reported from the Prophet ﷺ that he said: "One who goes out in the morning towards the mosque or does so in the afternoon, Allāh

---

[69] This is a repetition h. 445 with an addition at the end. See also h. 647 and h. 477.

[70] The word translated as "protection" is *ẓill,* meaning "shade".

[71] Statements of the Holy Prophet of this form ("There are seven persons") are not exhaustive, so here it does not mean that the protection of God is only for the seven types of people mentioned here. There are other qualities in a person, and deeds done by him, mentioned in Ḥadīth collections, that lead to him being deserving of God's protection. For example, there is mention of helping needy people, allowing time to a debtor to repay his loan and even to write it off, being an honest trader, and a just judge. Nevertheless, the qualities enumerated here produce other virtues in man, all of which take him to a great spiritual eminence. For instance, taking the last one mentioned, if a person remembers God in solitude with such devotion that his eyes shed tears, all his deeds will be put in a right state. See also h. 1423.

[72] This is a repetition of h. 572 with an addition at the beginning and some difference of wording.

has prepared for him entertainment in Paradise when he goes out in the morning or in the afternoon."

Ch. 38: When prayer has been announced by *Iqāmah*, there is no prayer except the obligatory one

663 Ḥafṣ ibn 'Āṣim reported from 'Abdullāh ibn Mālik ibn Buḥainah: The Prophet ﷺ passed by a man. (In another version) Ḥafṣ ibn 'Āṣim said: I have heard a man from the tribe of al-Azd, who was called Mālik ibn Buḥainah, that the Messenger of Allāh ﷺ saw a man saying two *rak'ahs* of prayer (by himself) when prayer had been announced by *Iqāmah.* So when the Messenger of Allāh ﷺ finished his prayer, people gathered round that man and the Messenger of Allāh ﷺ said to him: "Four *rak'ahs* in the morning prayer? Four *rak'ahs* in the morning prayer?" [73]

Ch. 39: The limit for an ill person to be present in the congregation

664 Ibrāhīm reported that al-Aswad said: We were with 'Ā'ishah and we made a mention of regularity in prayers and respect for them. She said:

When the Prophet ﷺ became ill with the disease of which he died and the prayer time came and the *Adhān* was sounded, he said: "Tell Abū Bakr to lead the people in prayer." He was told that Abū Bakr was a soft-hearted man: "When he stands in your place, he will not be able to lead people in prayer." He repeated (what he said before) and they repeated to him (what they had said), so he repeated it for the third time and said: "Surely you are (like) the women of (the story of) Joseph. Tell Abū Bakr to lead the people in prayer."[74]

---

[73] The *Iqāmah* is the call of God to man inviting him to attend the congregation, and man must respond to this call, leaving aside his individual intention for private prayer. If someone is engaged in any optional prayer he must leave that and attend the congregation. Thus there is a ḥadīth: "When prayer has been announced by *Iqāmah,* there is no prayer except the obligatory one" (Ṣaḥīḥ Muslim, book: 'Prayer of travellers and its shortening', ch. 9; Tirmidhī, book: 'Prayer', h. 421; Ibn Mājah, book: 'Establishing the prayer and the *Sunnah* regarding it', h. 1205; Abū Dāwūd, book: 'Optional prayers', h. 1266; Nasā'ī, book: 'Imāmah', h. 865). This was why the Holy Prophet asked the man who first said two *rak'ahs* of *sunnah* prayer before he joined the congregation, whether he meant to say four *rak'ahs* for his obligatory morning prayer. It was to make him understand that after the *Iqāmah* there could only be the obligatory prayer, which for *Fajr* is only two *rak'ahs*.

[74] In the repetition of this ḥadīth in h. 679 it is stated that it was 'Ā'ishah who made this plea the first time, and probably the second time also, and for the third time she asked Ḥafṣah to say the same. In likening his wives to the women who had conspired against Joseph, he was indicating only a very partial similarity, in as much as these ladies appeared to the Holy Prophet to have united in obstructing a noble desire of the Holy Prophet. He wanted to indicate his appointment of Abū Bakr as his successor, and these ladies were unknowingly creating obstacles in the way

So Abū Bakr came out and began to lead the prayer. When the Prophet ﷺ felt a little better and he came out supported by two men, one on each side, as if I can still see his feet dragging on the ground on account of illness.[75] So Abū Bakr wanted to retreat, but the Prophet ﷺ indicated to him by a sign to stay where he was. Then he (the Holy Prophet) was brought till he sat by his (Abū Bakr's) side.

Al-A'mish (a narrator in the chain) was asked: "Was the Prophet ﷺ saying the prayer and Abū Bakr was praying following his prayer and the people were praying following the prayer of Abū Bakr?" He said "Yes" by the nod of his head.[76]

Abū Mu'āwiyah (in another narration) added: He (the Holy Prophet) sat on the left side of Abū Bakr and Abū Bakr was saying the prayer standing.

665 'Ubaidullāh ibn 'Abdullāh informed that 'Ā'ishah said: When the Prophet ﷺ became seriously ill and his ailment became severe, he asked permission from his wives to be nursed in my house. They gave him the permission, and he came out between two men, with his feet dragging on the ground, and he was between 'Abbās and another man.

'Ubaidullāh said: I mentioned this to Ibn 'Abbās, what 'Ā'ishah had said, and he said to me: "And do you know who the man whom 'Ā'ishah did not name?" I said: "No." He said: "He was 'Alī, son of Abū Ṭālib." [77]

---

of the expression of his will. Otherwise, there is a world of difference between the intentions of the women in the story of Joseph and the wives of the Holy Prophet. Whereas the former were wicked in their intention, the latter were actuated by a noble idea, however mistaken. They wanted to spare Abū Bakr the difficulties of this onerous responsibility of leading the prayers in place of the Holy Prophet. In fact, it shows the selflessness and sincerity of 'Ā'ishah that she would prefer someone other than her father to be given the esteemed position of Imām of the prayer.

[75] The slight improvement in the condition of the Holy Prophet is a later event and not during the same prayer referred to at the start of this ḥadīth. The Holy Prophet took all this trouble to go to the mosque to give some instructions to the people. Evidently, Bukhārī regards this degree of illness as the proper ground for a man to absent himself from congregational prayer. However, this cannot be the limit in all conditions because, although a sick person might be able to walk, his movement or exposure outside may worsen his illness. The Holy Prophet came out for a special purpose. (See also h. 198.)

[76] The real Imām in this prayer was the Holy Prophet himself, but since his voice had become very weak, Abū Bakr was acting as a repeater for him and naturally people were following Abū Bakr and his voice, and not directly the Holy Prophet.

[77] This is a repetition of h. 198 with small differences, as well as omitting the last part of h. 198 where it goes on to report: " 'Ā'ishah used to narrate: …"

Ch. 40: Permission to say prayer in one's house an account of rain or on some other plea

666 Nāfiʿ reported that Ibn ʿUmar called out the *Adhān* for prayer on one cold and windy night, then he said: "Beware! Say your prayer at home." Then he said that the Messenger of Allāh ﷺ used to order the caller to prayer, when it was a cold and rainy night, to say: "Beware! say your prayer at home." [78]

667 Maḥmūd ibn ar-Rabīʿ al-Anṣārī reported that ʿItbān ibn Mālik used to lead his people in prayer and he was a blind man. He said to the Messenger of Allāh ﷺ: "O Messenger of Allāh, it is sometimes dark and torrential rain water flows and I am a blind man. So, O Messenger of Allāh, say prayer at some place in my house and I will take it as a place of prayer." So the Messenger of Allāh ﷺ came to him and said: "Where do you like me to pray?" He pointed towards a place in his house, and the Messenger of Allāh ﷺ said his prayer there.[79]

Ch. 41: Is the Imām to lead in prayer only those who are present, and is he to deliver the sermon on Friday when it is raining?

668 ʿAbdullāh ibn Ḥārith said: Ibn ʿAbbās delivered to us a sermon on a muddy day, and he ordered the caller to prayer, when he reached (the words) "Come to prayer", to say: "Say your prayer at home". They (the people) looked at one another as if they disliked this, so he said: "You seem to dislike this. Surely one who was better than me" — meaning the Prophet ﷺ — "had done this. Surely it (the *Jumuʿah* prayer) is obligatory and I disliked to bring you out."

---

[78] This repetition of h. 632 has certain minor changes in its wording. Also, the words of h. 632 about "a journey" do not occur here, nor is it mentioned that this happened at Ḍajnān, a place twenty-five miles away from Makkah. This is an indication that this ḥadīth does not require journey as a condition. However, because the incident is the same and the original reporter is Ibn ʿUmar, it is plausible that the mention of Ḍajnān and journey have been missed by the further narrators, and the condition of being on a journey does apply. In any case, the concession of saying prayers at home on these grounds, even when not on a journey, is to be found granted in other reports, for example, h. 616 is obviously for this concession to the people while at home. Similarly, h. 668 speaks of the Holy Prophet himself as having acted in this manner. Although this is not a ḥadīth of the Holy Prophet, but there is a ḥadīth report that, in the course of the *Adhān* for the *Fajr* prayer one day, the caller to prayer of the Holy Prophet said at the end of his *Adhān*: "Whoever stays at home, there is no blame on him" (see reference in footnote to h. 616). It is not stated whether this incident took place in a journey or at home.

[79] This report is to be found in greater detail in h. 425. The later part of h. 425, beginning "We detained him for some *khazīrah* (a meat pie)", is omitted here.

In another narration, (instead of "I disliked to bring you out"), Ibn ʿAbbās said: "I disliked to make you commit sin (of not coming) or make you come wading through mud up to your knees." [80]

669 Abū Salamah reported: I asked Abū Saʿīd al-Khudrī and he said: "A cloud appeared and it rained until the roof (of the mosque) started leaking, and it was made of branches of palm trees. Prayer was announced by *Iqāmah* and I saw the Messenger of Allāh ﷺ performing *Sajdah* in mud so much so that I saw patches of mud on his forehead." [81]

670 Anas said: A man from among the Anṣār said: "I am unable to say my prayer with you." He was a fat man and he prepared a meal for the Prophet ﷺ and invited him to his house. He spread a mat for him and cleaned a side of the mat with water, and the Prophet ﷺ said two *rakʿahs* of prayer on it. A man from among the Āl-i al-Jārūd said to Anas: "Did the Prophet ﷺ say the forenoon prayer (*Ḍuḥā*)?" He said: "I did not see him saying it except on that day." [82]

Ch. 42:   **When the meal is ready and prayer is announced**

>Ibn ʿUmar used to begin by taking the meal. Abū ad-Dardā' said: It should be a part of the understanding of a man that he should attend to his (other) need (first) so that he comes to his prayer with a relieved mind.

---

[80] This repetition of h. 616 contains greater detail. See the footnote to that ḥadīth. The meaning of "making you commit sin" is also explained there. It must have been unusually muddy on that day because if it had been a common practice to declare "Say your prayer at home" in the *Adhān* whenever it was raining, people would not have been surprised or disliked it.

[81] The question which Abū Salamah asked Abū Saʿīd is given in h. 2036: "Did you hear the Messenger of Allāh mentioning *Lailat-ul-Qadr*?" This ḥadīth is given in greater details there. See also h. 2016 and h. 813. This shows that even when the floor of the mosque had become muddy by the roof leaking, the Holy Prophet led the congregational prayer in it. This clearly indicates that even in such circumstances congregational prayer should be held in the mosque, but those who cannot come to it due to the weather are excused.

[82] The account given here accords with the ḥadīth about ʿItbān ibn Mālik in h. 425 and h. 667 just above. This is why some suggest that the man spoken of here was ʿItbān. However, this man is described here as fat whereas ʿItbān has been described in those reports as a blind man which was why he excused himself from attending the congregational prayer when it was dark and flooded. Therefore, the two incidents are different and concern two different men. Incidentally, the fact that Anas did not see the Holy Prophet saying his optional forenoon prayer, known as *Ḍuḥā*, except once was because the Holy Prophet said this prayer at home and it seems he said it only occasionally.

671 ʿĀʾishah reported from the Prophet 🅿 that he said: "When the evening meal is served and the prayer is announced by *Iqāmah*, start with the meal."[83]

672 Anas ibn Mālik reported that the Messenger of Allāh 🅿 said: "When the time for the evening meal comes, start with it before you say the *Maghrib* prayer, and do not make haste in your meal."[84]

673 Ibn ʿUmar reported that the Messenger of Allāh 🅿 said: "When the evening meal is served for anyone of you and the prayer is announced by *Iqāmah*, start with the meal, and do not make haste before finishing it."

Ibn ʿUmar, if food was served for him and the prayer was announced by *Iqāmah*, would not come to the prayer until he finished (his meal), and he would be listening to the recitation of the Imām.[85]

674 Ibn ʿUmar reported that the Prophet 🅿 said: "When anyone of you is taking food, he should not make haste until he has satisfied his need of it, even if prayer is announced by *Iqāmah*."

Ch. 43: When the Imām is called to prayer and he has in his hand something that he is eating

675 Jaʿfar ibn ʿAmr ibn Umayyah informed that his father said: I saw the Messenger of Allāh 🅿 eating meat from the foreleg of a (cooked) goat, cutting from it, when he was called for prayer. He stood up, put the knife down and said his prayer without performing ablution.[86]

Ch. 44: One who is attending to some need of the people of his house and the prayer is announced by *Iqāmah* and he comes out

676 Al-Aswad reported: I asked ʿĀʾishah, "What did the Prophet 🅿 do in his house?" She said: "He used to serve the people of his house" — she

---

[83] The object of prayer is that a person presents himself before God with devotion and full presence of mind and heart. Attending prayer when he is distracted by excessive hunger and thirst, or any call of nature, defeats this object. That is why he is asked to give preference to the satisfaction of such needs before going to prayer so that he can concentrate on the prayer. But this is for occasions of necessity. Times of meals must be set so as not to clash with the times of prayer.

[84] This is a repetition of the substance of the previous ḥadīth, h. 671.

[85] This again is a repetition of h. 671 with the addition about Ibn ʿUmar at the end.

[86] This is a repetition of h. 208 with a slight difference in wording. It is possible that he had eaten as much as he wanted, or it may be that the need to eat, and needs of this kind, did not hold him back from prayer. In the latter case, his example in this respect cannot be binding on an ordinary believer.

meant doing work for the people of his house — "and when the prayer time came, he would go out for the prayer." [87]

Ch. 45:   One who leads people in prayer intending only to teach them the prayer of the Prophet ﷺ and his practice

677 Abū Qilābah reported: Mālik ibn al-Ḥuwairith came to us in this our mosque and said: "I am going to lead you in prayer but I do not intend to pray. I will say the prayer as I saw the Prophet ﷺ do it." I said to Abū Qilābah: "How did he use to pray?" He said: "Like this Shaikh of ours." And the Shaikh used to sit when he raised his head from prostration before he stood up in the first *rak'ah*.[88]

Ch. 46:   Those possessing knowledge and excellence have a better title to lead the prayer

678 Abū Mūsā reported: The Prophet ﷺ became ill and his illness became serious. So he said: "Tell Abū Bakr to lead the people in prayer." 'Ā'ishah said: "Surely he is a tender-hearted man. When he stands in your place, he will not be able to lead the people in prayer." He (again) said: "Tell Abū Bakr to lead the people in prayer." She repeated (the same reply) and he said: "Tell Abū Bakr to lead the people in prayer. Surely you are (like) the women of (the story of) Joseph." So the messenger came to him (Abū Bakr), and he led the people in prayer in the lifetime of the Prophet.[89]

---

[87] The Holy Prophet was an example for people in every walk and all conditions of life. A poor man who cannot afford to keep domestic servants and has to do his own housework will feel encouraged by the fact that the Holy Prophet did the same, including performing the most menial of household chores. He is reported to have sewn his own clothes or even mended them, mended his own shoes, milched his own goats and washed the pots. By this he meant to show that manual labour of any kind does not take away the dignity of a man. He also demonstrated that helping the wife in her domestic work was also an act of merit. But going beyond this, he would help to perform the domestic affairs of others as well, such as doing their shopping. Such an example of dignifying ordinary work and labour cannot be found in the life of any other spiritual or temporal leader of a nation.

[88] This was a mosque at Baṣrah. In h. 818–819, where this ḥadīth occurs in greater detail, the name of the Shaikh is given as 'Amr ibn Salimah; see also h. 824. There are reports saying that the Holy Prophet used to sit for a moment before rising to stand after the prostration in the first and third *rak'ahs* of prayer. This, however, should not be taken to be a constant practice of the Holy Prophet, as in such matters variations are found in his practice. See also h. 802.

[89] This is a repetition of h. 664 with differences in wording. For explanation of the comparison with the story of Joseph, here and in h. 679, see first footnote to h. 664.

679 ʿĀʾishah reported: The Messenger of Allāh ﷺ said during his illness: "Tell Abū Bakr to lead the people in prayer." I said: "Surely Abū Bakr, when he stands in your place, will not make people hear because of his weeping (while reciting the Qurʾān), so tell ʿUmar to lead the people in prayer." I said to Ḥafṣah: "Say to him (the Prophet), 'Surely Abū Bakr, when he stands in your place, will not make people hear because of his weeping, so tell ʿUmar to lead the people in prayer'." Ḥafṣah did this, but the Messenger of Allah ﷺ said: "Keep quiet! Surely you are (like) the women of (the story of) Joseph. Tell Abū Bakr to lead the people in prayer."

Ḥafṣah said to ʿĀʾishah: "I have never got any good from you." [90]

680 Az-Zuhrī reported: Anas ibn Mālik al-Anṣārī informed me, and he worked under the Prophet ﷺ and served him and kept company with him, that Abū Bakr used to lead them in prayer during the illness of the Prophet ﷺ, of which he died. This was until it was Monday and they were standing in rows in prayer and the Prophet ﷺ removed the curtain of his chamber and looked at us. He was standing as if his face was a page of the Holy Book. Then he gave a broad smile. We were put to the test whether to break off (from prayer) in our excitement of joy of seeing the Prophet ﷺ, and Abū Bakr began to retreat to join the row as he thought that the Prophet ﷺ was coming out to the prayer. But the Prophet ﷺ made a sign to us as if to say "Complete your prayers", and he pulled down the curtain. He expired on the same day. [91]

681 Anas reported: The Prophet ﷺ did not come out for three days. Then when prayer was announced by *Iqāmah* and Abū Bakr stepped forward (to

---

[90] This again is a repetition of h. 664, with the added mention of Ḥafṣah. This shows that ʿĀʾishah sought her help in supporting her view to the Holy Prophet. But he did not accept it from Ḥafṣah either. By "never getting any good from you", Ḥafṣah means that by acting on the advice from ʿĀʾishah to approach the Holy Prophet with this opinion, Ḥafṣah earned his disapproval. See footnote 74 to h. 664. There is another ḥadīth in this connection in which the Holy Prophet told ʿĀʾishah: "Allāh and the believers want none but Abū Bakr (as his successor)"; see Ṣaḥīḥ Muslim, book: 'Merits of the Companions', ch. 1.

[91] According to the next ḥadīth, h. 681, the Holy Prophet was unable to attend the prayers in the mosque for three successive days. A little while before his death he felt so much better that he removed the curtain from his door to see his Companions and he found them engaged in prayer. This sight aroused high emotions of spiritual satisfaction that were reflected on his face and made him smile. On the other hand, these devoted followers had not seen him for three long days and were deeply anxious for a glimpse of his face. At seeing the smiling face of the Holy Prophet, quite naturally their wistful eyes turned in his direction to see the face which acted as a mirror of the very existence of God to them. They thought he was coming out for his prayer. That is why Abū Bakr wanted to recede from his place to make room for the Holy Prophet to act as Imām, but he made a sign to him to keep to his place. The day was Monday and on the same day he breathed his last.

lead it), the Prophet of Allāh ﷺ held[92] the curtain and raised it. When the face of the Prophet ﷺ appeared, we had never seen a sight more wonderful to us than the face of the Prophet ﷺ when it appeared before us. The Prophet ﷺ made a sign with his hand to Abū Bakr that he should step forward. Then the Prophet ﷺ let the curtain drop and he was not accessible again till he died.[93]

682 Ḥamzah ibn ʿAbdullāh informed from his father (ʿAbdullāh ibn ʿUmar) that he said: When the illness of the Messenger of Allāh ﷺ became severe he was asked about the prayer and he said: "Tell Abū Bakr to lead the people in prayer." ʿĀ'ishah said: "Surely Abū Bakr is a tender-hearted man. When he would recite (the prayer) he will be overcome with weeping." He said: "Tell him to lead the prayer." She repeated it (i.e., her reply). He said: "Tell him to lead the prayer. Surely you are (like) the women of (the story of) Joseph.[94]

Ch. 47:   One who stands by the side of the Imām for a reason

683 ʿĀ'ishah reported: The Messenger of Allāh ﷺ ordered Abū Bakr to lead people in prayer during his illness, so he led them in prayer. ʿUrwah (reporting from ʿĀ'ishah) said: The Messenger of Allāh ﷺ (one day) felt a little better and he came out when Abū Bakr was acting as the Imām of the people. When Abū Bakr saw him, he wanted to retreat but he made a sign to him to say "Remain as you are." The Messenger of Allāh ﷺ sat parallel to Abū Bakr by his side and Abū Bakr was praying following the prayer of the Messenger of Allāh ﷺ and the people were praying following the prayer of Abū Bakr.[95]

Ch. 48:   One who comes to lead the people in prayer and the previous Imām arrives, then whether the former withdraws or does not withdraw, his prayer is valid

On this question, ʿĀ'ishah reports[96] from the Prophet ﷺ.

---

[92] The word for "held" here is *qāla,* usually meaning "said", but it also indicates actions.

[93] This is a repetition of h. 680 in different words. It was three days since he had led them in prayer while sitting.

[94] This is a repetition of h. 664 with differences in wording. The same tender-hearted Abū Bakr could be equally strong when the situation demanded it, as it did on the death of the Holy Prophet. When there was rebellion in Arabia against the central authority of Madīnah, Abū Bakr was not shaken in the least and stood like a rock. Soft heartedness during prayer, which creates love for humanity, and strength of heart, which is needed to overcome difficulties, were both found in Abū Bakr to the highest degree. This was what made him the rightful successor to the Holy Prophet.

[95] This is again a repetition of h. 664, with some details omitted.

[96] In h. 664 and h. 683, reported by ʿĀ'ishah, it is said that Abū Bakr kept standing in his own

684 Sahl ibn Sa'd as-Sā'idī reported that the Messenger of Allāh ﷺ went to the Banī 'Amr ibn 'Auf to effect reconciliation between them, and the time for prayer came, so the caller to prayer came to Abū Bakr and said: "Will you lead the people in prayer and I call the *Iqāmah*?" He said: "Yes." So Abū Bakr began to lead the prayer.[97] Then came the Messenger of Allāh ﷺ while the people were in prayer and he advanced till he stopped in the (first) row. So people clapped,[98] but Abū Bakr would not look around in his prayer. When people clapped more, he turned round and saw the Messenger of Allāh ﷺ and the Messenger of Allāh ﷺ made a sign to him to say: "Stay in your place". Abū Bakr raised both his hands and praised Allāh for what the Messenger of Allāh ﷺ ordered him about it. Then Abū Bakr retreated until he came parallel to the (first) row and the Messenger of Allāh ﷺ stepped forward and led the prayer. When he had finished, he said: "O Abū Bakr, what prevented you from staying (in your place) when I ordered you?" Abū Bakr replied: "It did not befit Ibn Abū Quḥāfah that he should say his prayer ahead of the Messenger of Allāh ﷺ." [99] So the Messenger of Allāh ﷺ said: "What was

---

place and the Holy Prophet was placed in a sitting posture on his left and that the Holy Prophet then acted as Imām. But in h. 684 below it is stated that, in spite of the Holy Prophet asking Abū Bakr to keep to his place the latter retreated and the Holy Prophet stood in his place. From these two divergent reports, rightly does Bukhārī conclude in his chapter heading that it is the same whether the acting Imām makes room for the appointed Imām or not.

[97] In this report in Musnad Aḥmad and some other collections of Ḥadīth further information is given that the Holy Prophet, while leaving, had instructed Bilāl to ask Abū Bakr to lead the prayer if he could not be back in time for the *'Aṣr* prayer (Abū Dāwūd, book: 'Prayer', h. 941; Nasā'ī, book: 'Imāmat', ch. 15, h. 793).

[98] The purpose of the clapping of hands was to draw the attention of the Imām that something had happened. It was in this connection that the Holy Prophet gave the rule that in such cases, instead of clapping hands, one should utter the words *Subḥān Allāh* ("Glory be to Allāh"). The utterance of these words serves a double purpose: it is a prayer inasmuch as it is glorifying God, and indirectly it is an indication that the Imām has made some mistake as the only being which is free from mistakes is God.

[99] In h. 683, it is seen that, in the course of his illness, when the Holy Prophet came to the mosque after prayer had started, he had made a sign to Abū Bakr to keep to his place, which the latter did and the Holy Prophet took his place on his left side and began to act as the Imām while Abū Bakr acted as the Imām for the people and stood between them and the Holy Prophet. But on this particular occasion, Abū Bakr, in spite of the Holy Prophet asking him to stay in his place, left his place and retreated to make room for the Holy Prophet. The difference between the two conducts of Abū Bakr may be explained by assuming that in the first case Abū Bakr was conscious that the Holy Prophet had not the strength to stand up and act as the direct Imām of the whole congregation. In any case, on that occasion also the Holy Prophet did not act as the real Imām as people followed Abū Bakr. Of course, here in the first case we read that the Holy Prophet first stayed in the front row; this may be explained by the assumption that his arrival was not first noticed by Abū Bakr and he did not want to disturb him either. It is also possible that he first intended to create an example for the Muslims as to how an Imām should behave when he

the matter that I found you clapping more? If something happens in one's prayer he should say *Subḥān Allāh,* for when he glorifies Allāh, attention will turn to him; and clapping is only for the women." [100]

Ch. 49: When (several) persons are equal in their recitation of the Qur'ān, the oldest among them should act as their Imām

685 Mālik ibn al-Ḥuwairith reported: We went to the Prophet ﷺ and we were young men. We stayed with him for about twenty nights and the Prophet ﷺ was very kind. He said: "When you return to your own land you should teach the people there (about religion). Tell them that they should say a prayer at such and such a time, and a prayer at such and such a time, and when the time for prayer comes, one of you should give the call to prayer and the eldest of you should act as your Imām." [101]

---

comes late. But Abū Bakr was anxious to demonstrate a higher principle, namely, in the presence of the Holy Prophet, no other man should at all act as an Imām of a congregation and the Holy Prophet's ultimate conduct confirmed this view of the case. As for other Imāms, it should be a rule that if he is late in joining the congregation and someone else has already begun to lead the prayer, he should consider himself just as a member of the congregation and take his place where convenient.

[100] This report and others in this connection appear to show that, if anything untoward happens in the course of prayer, the men are to say *Subḥān Allāh* ("Glory be to Allāh") whereas the women are to clap their hands if need be. This position, however, seems inexplicable. When all the rules connected with prayer are the same for men and women, why should there be a distinction in this particular case? What is the harm in women saying *Subḥān Allāh* like men? Is it to be assumed that women are not to raise their voice in a congregation? There is no indication of this prohibition anywhere. So all that this ḥadīth seems to mean is that the clapping of hands being an expression typically feminine, should not be indulged in the mosque atmosphere and that even if a woman is to make a sign to an erring Imām she is to refrain from clapping. In the time of the Holy Prophet there was no separate section for women, and they used to say prayers standing behind the men, so this differentiation in how to point out an error of the Imām does not seem correct from that point of view either. See also h. 1201, 1203 and 1204.

[101] This is a repetition of h. 628 in an abbreviated form. It mentions that the eldest should act as the Imām but there is no mention of the equality in the ability to recite the Qur'ān, which is suggested in the chapter heading. The heading is part of a ḥadīth in Ṣaḥīḥ Muslim which runs as follows: "He should act as the Imām of the people who is the greatest in knowledge (*aqra'u*) of the Book of God and the best in recitation; if they (i.e., more than one) are equal in the ability to recite it, one who is the earliest of them in *Hijrah* should act as the Imām ; and if they are equal in terms of *Hijrah*, the one who is oldest of them in age should act as the Imām" (book: 'Mosques and Places of Prayer', ch. 53: 'Who is entitled to lead prayer'). In the version of this ḥadīth in Abū Dāwūd it is stated that a Companion said: "At that time we were equal in knowledge" (book: 'Prayer', h. 589). The word *aqra'u* has been taken by some to mean one who recites the Qur'ān the best, but others have taken it to mean *a'lamu* or the one who has the most knowledge and understanding of the Qur'ān, and this is the right view. It was on this basis that the Holy Prophet appointed Abū Bakr as Imām.

Ch. 50: When the Imām visits a people and acts as their Imām (in prayer)

686 'Itbān ibn Mālik said: The Prophet ﷺ asked my permission (to enter my house) and I gave him permission. He said: "Where do you like me to say my prayer in your house?" So I pointed to him a place which I liked and he stood up and we formed into a row behind him. Then (at the end of the prayer) he finished with *Salām* and we also said *Salām*.[102]

Ch. 51: The Imām is appointed to be followed

The Prophet ﷺ, during his illness of which he died, led the people in prayer and he was sitting.[103] Ibn Mas'ūd said: When anyone rises (from a position in prayer) before the Imām, he should resume the posture and stay in it for the length of time that he had risen, and then follow the Imām.[104] Al-Ḥasan said about one who has gone in to *Rukū'* with the Imām for two *rak'ahs* and is unable to go into prostration, he should go into prostration for the last *rak'ah* twice and then complete the first *rak'ah* with its prostrations;[105] and about one who forgets any prostration till he stands up, he should go into prostration.

---

[102] This ḥadīth has occurred in detail in h. 425 and briefly in h. 667. Here Bukhārī aims to show that the recognized Imām of a people, in this case the Holy Prophet as Imām of all Muslims, should act as the Imām even when he is in the locality other than the usual place of congregation. Here the Holy Prophet acted as the Imām in the house of a man whom he visited. As against this, there is a ḥadīth as follows: "Whoever visits a people, he should not lead them in prayer and a man from among themselves should act as the Imām" (Tirmidhī, book: 'Prayer', h. 356; Abū Dāwūd, book: 'Prayer', h. 596). This should be taken to refer to the case where the visitor is not their Imām.

[103] That is to say, a person in congregation should do in his prayer exactly as the Imām does, neither doing anything contrary to the Imām's movement, nor preceding the Imām in anything. This is a lesson in discipline of collective action under one leadership. There must, however, be exceptions for a valid reason, such as in this case. The Holy Prophet was extremely ill and unable to stand up, so he said his prayer sitting, but the reason of illness did not apply to the congregation, so they all stood when one stands in prayer. There is no breach of discipline in this case.

[104] In other words, he should go back into prostration or bowing down (*Sajdah* or *Rukū'*) and stay in it for extra time, as much as the time that he missed, and then follow the Imām.

[105] The elucidation of this point is to be found in Ibn al-Mundhir. It is that in the Friday congregational prayer if the space is so congested as to leave no room for the late comers to be able to stretch themselves in prostration, they may be regarded as joining the prayer if they just keep on standing in the last row and go in prostration when the people in front have finished their prayer and made room for their prostration. Thus, after the other people's prayers, when space for prostration has become available, they should make two prostrations and this is considered as performing the second *rak'ah*, the prostrations of which they had been unable to do. Then they should rise after this and complete the first *rak'ah* with the two necessary prostrations in it.

687 'Ubaidullāh ibn 'Abdullāh ibn 'Utbah reported: I went to 'Ā'ishah and said: Will you not narrate to me the incident of the illness of the Messenger of Allāh ﷺ? She said:

Yes. When the Prophet ﷺ became seriously ill, he said: "Have the people said their prayer?" We said: "No, they are waiting for you, O Messenger of Allāh." He said: "Make ready some water for me in a trough." So we did it and he had a bath and he began to get up with some efforts but he fell in a swoon. Then he regained his consciousness and said: "Have the people said their prayer?" We said: "No, they are waiting for you, O Messenger of Allāh." He said: "Make ready some water for me in a trough." So we did it and he had a bath and then he began to get up with some efforts but he fell in a swoon. Then he regained his consciousness and said: "Have the people said their prayer?" We said: "No, they are waiting for you, O Messenger of Allāh." He said: "Make ready some water for me in trough." Then he sat up and had a bath and then he began to get up with some efforts but he fell in swoon. Then he regained his consciousness and said: "Have the people said their prayer?" We said: "No, they are waiting for you, O Messenger of Allāh." And people were sitting in the mosque waiting for the Prophet ﷺ for the last *'Ishā'* prayer.

So the Prophet ﷺ sent a message to Abū Bakr that he should lead the people in prayer. The messenger went to him and said: "The Messenger of Allāh ﷺ orders you to lead the people in prayer." Abū Bakr was a tender-hearted man and he said: "O 'Umar, lead the people in prayer." 'Umar said to him: "You have a better title to it." So Abū Bakr led the prayer in those days.

Then the Prophet ﷺ felt a little better and he came out between two men, one of whom was 'Abbās, for the *Ẓuhr* prayer while Abū Bakr was leading the people to prayer. So when Abū Bakr saw him, he began to retreat but the Prophet ﷺ made a sign to him to say that he should not retreat and said (to the two men): "Make me sit by his side." So they put him in a sitting position by the side of Abū Bakr. Abū Bakr continued to say the prayer and he was following the prayer of the Prophet ﷺ, and the people were following the prayer of Abū Bakr, and the Prophet ﷺ was sitting.

'Ubaidullāh said: So I went to 'Abdullāh ibn 'Abbās and said to him: "Shall I not state before you what 'Ā'ishah narrated to me about the illness of the Prophet ﷺ?" He said: "Go on." So I stated before him her ḥadīth and he did not deny anything out for it, but he said: "Did she tell you the name of the man who was with 'Abbās?" I said: "No." He said: "It was 'Alī." [106]

---

[106] The subject of this ḥadīth has occurred in h. 198, and again in h. 664 and its repetitions

688 'Ā'ishah, mother of the believers, reported that the Messenger of Allāh ﷺ said his prayers in his house while he was ill. He said his prayers sitting and behind him a party of people said their prayers standing, so he made a sign to them to sit down. When he finished, he said: "The Imām is appointed to be followed: so when he bows (in *Rukū'*), you must bow, and when he rises up, you must rise up, and when he says, *Sami' Allāhu li-man ḥamidah* ('Allāh hears him who praises Him'), say: *Rabba-nā wa la-ka-l-ḥamd* ('Our Lord! And Yours is the praise'), and when he says his prayer sitting, you must say your prayer sitting, all of you." [107]

689 Anas ibn Mālik reported that the Messenger of Allāh ﷺ rode a horse and he fell down from it and his right side got bruised thereby. So he said one of the prayers while he was sitting, and we also said the prayer behind him

---

(h. 678, h. 679, h. 682, h. 683, h. 712, h. 713, h. 716). Here the first part of the incident is given in more detail. For example, we are told that Abū Bakr himself approached 'Umar and requested him to lead the prayer in the absence of the Holy Prophet. This shows that he was most reluctant to undertake this task himself. But the only object of Bukhārī tracing this ḥadīth here is to show that there have been occasions when the Holy Prophet kept sitting in front of the congregation that followed him while they performed their prayers in the usual standing posture.

H. 688 and h. 689 (repetitions of h. 378) that immediately follow this ḥadīth, relating to a much earlier incident, mention that if the Imām is sitting and cannot stand up the congregation also should do likewise. But at the end of h. 689 Bukhārī gives his own view of the case, that the very latest act of the acts of the Holy Prophet should be followed, and the very last act was that while he said the prayer sitting due to illness, the congregation prayed standing as usual. Firstly, the earlier incident, when the Holy Prophet took a temporary separation of one month from his wives, relates to the year 7 A.H. At that time, though he was confined to bed due to injuries on his body, yet he was not so weak as during his last illness towards the end of the year 10 A.H., so it was but natural that he should have asked the followers to sit down. Secondly, a person is allowed to say his prayers sitting when he is unable to stand due to some weakness. But such allowance cannot be extended to the followers of the Imām, if he is unable to stand, just because they are required to copy him. The last act of the Holy Prophet appears more appropriate and this practice is in vogue in almost all Muslim countries. See also h. 378 and the footnotes under it.

[107] In repeating h. 378 here, its first and last part have been omitted. The remaining intermediate part contains the addition, "so he made a sign to them to sit down", and has some difference in wording. In h. 689 occur the words: "so we said our prayer behind him sitting", and it may be meant that they sat down when he indicated to them to do so. However, in h. 378 it is stated: "he led them in prayer in a sitting posture while they were standing". Another difficulty is that if the Holy Prophet, while leading the prayer sitting, had asked the people also to sit down, why did it happen during his final illness that when he led the prayer sitting, people were standing? It is possible that, since the Holy Prophet has here mentioned various *stages* of prayer in which the Imām is to be followed, so his statement "when he says his prayer sitting, you must say your prayer sitting" refers only to following the Imām in that stage of prayer which is said sitting. Anyhow, the view of Bukhārī given at the end of h. 689 seems to be correct, that the Holy Prophet's latest practice must be followed in preference to an earlier one, in case of a clash between the two.

sitting. When he finished, he said:[108] "The Imām is appointed to be followed: so when he says his prayer standing, you must say your prayer standing, and when he bows (in *Rukū'*), you must bow, and when he rises up, you must rise up, and when he says, *Sami' Allāhu li-man ḥamidah* ('Allāh hears him who praises Him'), say: *Rabba-nā wa la-ka-l-ḥamd* ('Our Lord! And Yours is the praise'), and when he says his prayer standing, you must say your prayer standing, and when he says his prayer sitting, you must say your prayer sitting, all of you."

Abū 'Abdullāh (Bukhārī) said that al-Ḥumaidī said: His saying (i.e., of the Holy Prophet), "when he says his prayer sitting, you must say your prayer sitting", was during his previous illness. After that (during his last illness), the Prophet ﷺ said his prayer sitting and the people were (praying) standing behind him, and he did not tell them to sit down. It is the very last act of the acts of the Prophet ﷺ which should be taken as decisive.

Ch. 52: When is one, who is behind the Imām, to go in prostration?

Anas reported from the Prophet ﷺ: "So when he (the Imām) prostrates, you must prostrate."

690 Al-Barā', who never lied, related: When the Messenger of Allāh ﷺ would say *Sami' Allāhu li-man ḥamidah* ("Allāh hears him who praises Him"), none of us would bend his back until the Prophet ﷺ fell in prostration. Then we would fall in prostration after that.

Ch. 53: The sin of one who raises his head before the Imām[109]

691 Abū Hurairah reported from the Prophet ﷺ that he said: "Does not one of you fear when he raises his head before the Imām that Allāh will make his head the head of an ass or make his appearance the appearance of an ass?" [110]

---

[108] The statement of the Holy Prophet in this report from Anas is much the same as in h. 688 from 'Ā'ishah. See also h. 722 from Abū Hurairah.

[109] This shows the standard of discipline and unity to be maintained in the congregational prayer. The conduct of the devotees in prayer should be as disciplined as an army on parade. The slightest laxity in this matter has been disapproved. It is a great lesson in discipline in life.

[110] It is absurd to think that this supports the belief that the soul of a human being, after his death, may come back to this life in the body of an animal. The Qur'ān has used such similes and metaphors, likening people to animals. In one place it likens them to asses: "The likeness of those who were charged with the Torah, then they did not observe it, is as the likeness of the ass carrying books" (62:5). The meaning in this ḥadīth is that those who do not observe discipline in prayer are devoid of all sense and they resemble an ass in understanding. The Holy Prophet

Ch. 54: A slave and a freed slave acting as an Imām[111]

'Ā'ishah used to be led in her prayer by her slave Dhakwān as Imām from (a copy of) the scripture.[112] And the illegitimately born and the rustic and the boy who has not reached maturity[113] (can also be Imām) because of the saying of the Prophet ﷺ: "The one most knowledgeable of the Book of Allāh should act as their Imām." A slave should not be prevented from (leading or being in) the congregation without some reason.

692 'Abdullāh ibn 'Umar reported: When the first emigrants arrived at al-'Uṣbah, a quarter of Qubā', before the arrival of the Messenger of Allāh ﷺ, Sālim, the freed slave of Abū Ḥudhaifah, used to lead them in prayer and he had the most knowledge of the Qur'ān of them all.[114]

693 Anas ibn Mālik reported from the Prophet ﷺ that he said: "Hear and obey even if an Abyssinian is appointed as ruler, whose head seems to be like a raisin." [115]

---

has related a dream in which he saw cows, and he interpreted it as meaning that these "cows" were the innocent believers who were killed at the battle of Uḥud (see h. 7035).

[111] This chapter makes it clear that social status, nobility of family, race or nationality are no considerations in the eye of God. As the Qur'ān says: "Surely the noblest of you with Allah is the most dutiful of you" (49:18). Hence it is that the Holy Prophet has laid down as a principle for the selection of the Imām that he should be "the one most knowledgeable of the Book of Allāh" (see footnote 101 above). Thus, if a slave, or a man of illegitimate birth or of low social status or from an uncultured background, or a minor comes up to the standard of righteousness and knowledge of the Qur'ān, there is nothing to prevent him from acting as Imām. Although some authorities have regarded it as undesirable, even impermissible in certain situations, for such men to be made Imām, the grounds they have cited are not that their being made Imām is prohibited as such, but relate to their qualifications or to the public's aversion for them. However, according to principles of the Qur'ān and Ḥadīth, they are quite capable of being qualified to be Imām.

[112] In Ramaḍān when the whole of the Qur'ān is recited in prayer over this month, this slave of 'Ā'ishah used to lead her in prayer with the Qur'ān open in front of him.

[113] In h. 4302 'Amr ibn Salamah reports that his people made him their Imām when he was a boy six or seven years old. Similar reports by him are found in Abū Dāwūd (book: 'Prayer', h. 585, 587).

[114] Sālim was a slave of a woman of the Anṣār who later on emancipated him. The incident narrated here belonged to the period when he was still a slave.

[115] The likeness is in reference to the black colour of his skin. Islām is the only religion which has made the white and the black stand together on the same level, equally under the law and in society. Here the principle is stated that leadership is as much open to a black African as to a white man of any nationality. By including this ḥadīth in this chapter, the suggestion is that the head of the nation is also expected to lead the people in prayer. Thus the most dark-skinned man in the world may become the spiritual and temporal leader of the believers. This also shows that when appointing someone as Imām, his nationality or race is not a consideration.

Ch. 55:   When the Imām does not complete (the prayer) and he who has joined him completes it

694 Abū Hurairah reported that the Messenger of Allāh ﷺ said: "They will lead you in prayer, so if they act rightly, you shall have the reward, and if they act mistakenly, you shall still have the reward and the responsibility will be upon them." [116]

Ch. 56:   A rebel or an innovator being the Imām

Al-Ḥasan said: Say your prayers (behind him) and the responsibility for innovation will be upon him.

695 'Ubaidullāh ibn 'Adī ibn Khiyār reported that he went to 'Uthmān ibn 'Affān when he was besieged and said: "Surely you are the chief of all the people and you see what has befallen you, and the head of the rebellion is leading us in prayer and we consider it a sin." He said: "Prayer is the best of all the deeds which people do, so when people do a good deed, you should do the good deed with them, and when they do a bad deed you should refrain from their bad deed." [117]

Az-Zubaidī said that az-Zuhrī said: We do not regard it as proper to say prayers behind an effeminate man unless there is a need from which there is no escape.[118]

---

[116] When the heads of the community act also as Imāms for prayers, then even if they are found to be lacking in punctuality, or fall short in some other way in the conduct of prayer, the people should still follow them, as the responsibility before God for the neglect will be upon such Imāms while the followers shall still have the reward for praying behind them.

[117] This refers to the closing days of the Caliphate of the third Caliph 'Uthmān when he was besieged by the rebels in his house. Because the Caliph was not allowed to come out, the head of the rebels was acting as the Imām in the mosque in his absence. This incident and the utterance of 'Uthmān is a testimony to his great generosity and forbearance as he would not allow his personal grievances to interfere with the principles of the faith. It also shows his anxiety for preventing any rift among the Muslims, as he was admonishing people to cooperate with the rebels in any good work that they did. If this spirit returns to the Muslims today, they will emerge once more in this world as a powerful nation in spite of the many sects and sub-sects into which they are unfortunately divided. It is not right for a Muslim to withhold co-operation with another Muslim in any good work prescribed by Islām because of disagreement in some views or beliefs. In spite of all this broadness, it must be remembered that it is not recommended to allow a man of glaring sinful habits or bad character to lead the prayer as is evident from the next part of this report.

[118] The word *mukhannith* means a man who talks and behaves like a woman while the word *mukhannath* means a man who is homosexual. Prayer being a means to the nearness of God, the leadership of it going to such a man must defeat its purpose. If it is unavoidable, prayer may be said behind such a man.

696 Anas ibn Mālik said that the Prophet ﷺ said: "Hear and obey even an Abyssinian (appointed as ruler), whose head seems to be like a raisin." [119]

Ch. 57:   To stand on the right side of the Imām parallel to him when there are two (in the congregation)

697 Ibn 'Abbās reported: I spent a night in the house of my maternal aunt Maimūnah. The Messenger of Allāh ﷺ said the *'Ishā'* prayer (in the mosque) and then came (to his house) and said four *rak'ahs* of prayer and went to sleep. Then he stood up for prayer and I came and stood at his left side but he made me stand on his right. He said five *rak'ahs* of prayer, and then two more *rak'ahs* of prayer. Then he went to sleep again, so much so that I could hear his snoring. Then (in the morning) he went out for prayer (of *Fajr* in the mosque).[120]

Ch. 58:   When a man stands on the left of the Imām and the Imām draws him round to his right, the prayer of the two does not become void

698 Ibn 'Abbās reported: I slept one night at Maimūnah's place and the Prophet ﷺ was with her that night. He performed ablution and then stood up for prayer and I stood at his left side but he caught me and made me stand on his right. He said thirteen *rak'ahs* of prayer, and then went to sleep till he snored, and he used to snore when he slept. Then the caller to prayer came to him and he went out and said his prayer and did not perform any ablution.[121]

---

[119] This is a repetition of h. 693.

[120] H. 117 has been repeated here with slight difference of wording. It is mentioned here that the Holy Prophet made Ibn 'Abbās stand on his right and said the *Tahajjud* prayer. See also h. 138.

[121] This is another repetition of h. 117, but the divergence is greater than in h. 697. Here thirteen *rak'ahs* are mentioned and nothing is said about the two *rak'ahs* of *sunnah* prayer preceding the obligatory *Fajr* prayer. If these two are included in the thirteen, then it gives eleven *rak'ahs* for the *Tahajjud* prayer. In h. 117 and its repetition in h. 697 it is mentioned that he first said four *rak'ahs* and then slept and then said another five *rak'ahs*, which makes nine. Again in h. 183 where this incident is narrated in more details, it speaks of six prayers of two *rak'ahs* followed by the *Witr* (one *rak'ah*), which makes thirteen *rak'ahs* of *Tahajjud,* and adding two *sunnah rak'ahs* of *Fajr* prayer makes fifteen in all. It seems that the narrators have inserted their own conjectures in these reports. The only way to reconcile these reports is to regard the present report, h. 698, as correct: eleven *rak'ahs* including the *Witr* were said in *Tahajjud,* and two *rak'ahs* of *sunnah Fajr* prayer, making a total of thirteen.

Ch. 59: **When the Imām had no intention of leading any prayer, then some people arrive and he leads them in prayer**

699 Ibn ʿAbbās reported: I spent a night at my maternal aunt Maimūnah's place. The Prophet ﷺ stood up for prayer during the night. So I stood at his left side but he caught me by my head and made me stand on his right.[122]

Ch. 60: **When the Imām prolongs (the prayer) and a man is pressed by some need, so he goes out (of the congregation) and then says his prayer (on his own)**

700 Jābir ibn ʿAbdullāh reported that Muʿādh ibn Jabal used to say his prayer with the Prophet ﷺ, then he would return to lead his people in prayer.[123]

701 Jābir ibn ʿAbdullāh said: Muʿādh ibn Jabal used to say his prayer with the Prophet ﷺ, then he would return to lead his people in prayer. He once led the *'Ishā'* prayer and recited the chapter *Al-Baqarah*. So a man left and Muʿādh began to speak ill of him. This (news) reached the Prophet ﷺ, at which he said: "*Fattān-un, Fattān-un, Fattān-un*" three times, or he said: "*Fātin-an, Fātin-an, Fātin-an*",[124] and ordered him (to recite) two chapters from among the middle ones of the *Mufaṣṣal* chapters.[125] ʿAmr said:[126] I do not remember which two.[127]

---

[122] This is another repetition of h. 117, but is brief. The deduction is that the Holy Prophet started the prayer alone but when Ibn ʿAbbās joined him he began to act as Imām. Thus if a man is praying alone, and during his prayer another comes, they can form a congregation.

[123] See next ḥadīth, h. 701.

[124] *Fattān-un* means one who causes great trouble to people or puts them to a great trial. *Fātin-an* means the same but indicates just trouble or trial more mildly.

[125] Chapters of the Qur'ān from ch. 49 (*Al-Ḥujurāt*), or ch. 50 (*Qāf*), to ch. 78 (*An-Nabā'*) are known as the *Mufaṣṣal* chapters. These are also called *Ṭawwāl* or long. After these, the chapters up to ch. 93 (*Aḍ-Ḍuḥā*) are called *Ausaṭ* or medium length.

[126] ʿAmr was reporting from Jābir ibn ʿAbdullāh.

[127] The object of recording this ḥadīth here is that if, on the one hand, it is permissible to join someone praying alone and make it a congregational prayer, it is equally permissible to start prayer behind an Imām and then leave it for some valid reason and finish it alone. In this incident the reason for leaving the congregation is reported to be the length of the recitation from the Qur'ān. But in its repetition in h. 705 it is stated that the man had two camels with him, which he used to water his fields. Thus, on the one hand, he was exhausted, and on the other, the camels had to be given their feed. In his natural attraction for prayer he joined the congregation which was going on, when he was on his way home from work. But due to the Imām's length of recitation he left the congregation, completed his prayer on his own and left. In h. 705 it is also stated that when Muʿādh criticised his action, the man went to the Holy Prophet and complained about it, and on hearing his complaint the Holy Prophet told Muʿādh that he should have recited a shorter chapter such as *Al-Aʿlā* (ch. 87), *Ash-Shams* (ch. 91) or *Al-Lail* (ch. 92).

Ch. 61: The Imām taking shorter time in the standing posture and completing the *Rukū'* and the *Sajdah* in full

702 Abū Mas'ūd informed that a man said: "By Allāh, O Messenger of Allāh, I delay going to the morning prayer because of so-and-so prolonging it for us." I never saw the Messenger of Allāh ﷺ more angry in preaching than he was on that day. Then he said: "Some of you will make them dislike it; so whoever of you is leading people in prayer he should make it shorter, for surely among them are the weak, the old and those with needs to attend to." [128]

Ch. 62: When anyone says his prayer alone, he may prolong it as much as he likes

703 Abū Hurairah reported that the Messenger of Allāh ﷺ said: "When any of you leads the people in prayer, he should make it light, for surely among them are the weak, the sick and the old, and when any of you says his prayer alone he may prolong it as much as he likes."

Ch. 63: One who complains about his Imām when the latter prolongs the prayer

Abū Usaid said: "O my son, you have made the prayer long for us."

704 Abū Mas'ūd reported: A man said: "O Messenger of Allāh, I delay going to the prayer for *Fajr* because of so-and-so prolonging it." The Messenger of Allāh ﷺ was angry, and I had not seen him more angry in that place than he was on that day. Then he said: "O people, some of you will make them dislike it; so who is acting as Imām of the people he should make it shorter, for surely behind him are the weak, the old and those with needs to attend to." [129]

705 Jābir ibn 'Abdullāh al-Anṣārī said: A man came with two camels meant for watering the fields and it was dark after nightfall, and he found Mu'ādh saying prayer. So he made his camel kneel down and proceeded towards Mu'ādh who recited either the chapter *Al-Baqarah* or the chapter *An-Nisā'*. The man left and was (later) informed that Mu'ādh had spoken ill

---

[128] This is a repetition of h. 90 with a slight difference in wording. It is stated here that it was the morning prayer and towards the end it mentions "the old" instead of "the sick". The ḥadīth speaks only of the necessity of the Imām to make the prayer light but the chapter heading refers also to the proper prolongation of the bowing down (*Rukū'*) and the prostration (*Sajdah*). It seems that Bukhārī is suggesting that the Imāms who prolong the recitation in the standing posture do not perform the *Rukū'* and the *Sajdah* for a sufficient duration of time. This is improper because full humility and melting of the heart is found particularly in the postures of bowing and prostration.

[129] This again is a repetition of h. 90 and is much like h. 702. It mentions the *Fajr* prayer explicitly.

of him. So he went to the Prophet ﷺ and complained to him against Muʿādh. The Prophet said: "O Muʿādh, are you putting people to a great trial" or "a trial" three times,[130] adding: "So why did you not say your prayer with *Sabbiḥ isma Rabbi-ka-l-aʿlā* (ch. 87) or *Wa-sh-shamsi wa ḍuḥā-hā* (ch. 91) or *Wa-l-laili idhā yaghshā* (ch. 92), for surely behind you are praying the old, the weak and those with needs to attend to." [131]

Ch. 64:   Shortening of prayer and (yet) making it complete

706 Anas ibn Mālik reported: The Prophet ﷺ used to shorten as well as complete the prayer.[132]

Ch. 65:   One who makes the prayer light at the crying of a child

707 Abū Qatādah reported from the Prophet ﷺ that he said: "I stand up for prayer desiring to make it long, but I hear the crying of a child, so I shorten my prayer as I dislike to put his mother in difficulty." [133]

708 Anas ibn Mālik said: I have never said my prayer behind any Imām who makes the prayer shorter and (yet) more complete than that of the Prophet ﷺ. And if he (the Prophet) would hear the cry of a child, he would make it light, fearing in case he would put the child's mother to difficulty.

709 Anas ibn Mālik related that the Prophet ﷺ said: "I start prayer desiring to make it long, but I hear the crying of a child, so I shorten my prayer because I know the depth of its mother's feelings on its crying."

710 Anas ibn Mālik reported from the Prophet ﷺ that he said: "I start prayer desiring to make it long, but I hear the crying of a child, so I shorten it because I know the depth of its mother's feelings on its crying." [134]

---

[130] See footnote 124 under h. 701 about *Fattānun* and *Fātinan.*

[131] This repetition of h. 701 contains more details. See the footnotes to h. 701.

[132] That is to say, the Holy Prophet used to say his prayers to perfection and yet his prayers would not be very long. In other words, he never recited very long passages from the Qur'ān but used to perform the postures of bowing, prostration, standing, sitting etc. with composure of mind and perfection. He used to recite long passages from the Holy Book in the morning prayers, but even those would be between 60 to 100 verses. This was his rule in congregational prayers. In his own *Tahajjud* prayers he would recite a considerable portion of the Qur'ān.

[133] In such cases the mother feels distressed and also gets diverted from her prayer. It also causes trouble to the baby. So shortening of prayers in such cases is to show sympathy both for the mother and the baby. There is a report in *Muṣannaf* Ibn Abī Shaibah that the Holy Prophet recited a long chapter in the first *rakʿah*, but in the second *rakʿah*, when he heard a baby crying, he finished it with only three verses.

[134] H. 709 and h. 710 are repetitions of h. 707. The manner in which the Holy Prophet combines his devotion to the commandments of God and his love for the creatures of God is unique

Ch. 66:   When a person says his prayer and then he leads people in prayer

711 Jābir reported: Muʿādh used to say his prayer with the Prophet ﷺ, then he would go to his people and lead them in prayer.[135]

Ch. 67:   One who makes people hear the *Takbīr* (calling out of *Allāhu Akbar*) of the Imām

712 ʿĀ'ishah reported: When the Prophet ﷺ became ill with the disease of which he died, Bilāl came to him to inform him of the prayer. He said: "Tell Abū Bakr to lead the prayer." I said: "Abū Bakr is a soft-hearted man. If he stands in your place, he will weep and would not be able to continue the recitation." He said (again): "Tell Abū Bakr to lead the prayer." I repeated what I said before and he repeated what he said. On the third or fourth time (that this happened) he said: "Surely you are (like) the women of (the story of) Joseph. Tell Abū Bakr to lead the prayer."

So he (Abū Bakr) led the prayer and the Prophet ﷺ came out supported by two men, one on each side, as if I can still see him dragging his feet on the ground. When Abū Bakr saw him, he made to retreat, but he (the Holy Prophet) pointed to him to continue in the prayer. So Abū Bakr retreated and the Prophet ﷺ sat by his side, and Abū Bakr was making people hear the *Takbīr* (of the Holy Prophet).[136]

Ch. 68:   A man following the Imām and people following the man who is following the Imām

It is reported of the Prophet ﷺ that he said: "Follow my leadership and those who come after you would follow your leadership." [137]

---

in history. His regard for the commandments of God compels him to persuade mothers with infants to attend the congregational prayers, but his tenderness for human beings was so great that he was quick to share the feelings of a mother disturbed by the cry of her baby and he shortened the prayer.

[135] This is a repetition of h. 701 in the form of h. 700.

[136] This is a repetition of h. 664, which has also occurred in h. 678, 679, 682 and 683. It occurs in detail in h. 687. Here the words are very similar to those in h. 664, but it has the addition at the end to say that Abū Bakr was making the people hear the *Takbīr* of the Holy Prophet, by repeating it loudly; hence the chapter heading.

[137] These words are from a ḥadīth in Ṣaḥīḥ Muslim (book: 'Prayer', ch. 28), Abū Dāwūd (book: 'Prayer', h. 680), Nasā'ī (book: 'Imāmat', h. 795) and Ibn Mājah (book 5, h. 1031). Its obvious meaning is that the rear lines of prayer should follow the movements of those in front of them; hence the chapter heading. There is also a deeper implication, that if his Companions should learn the religion from him, those who were to come later would learn from them and

713 ʿĀʾishah reported: When the Prophet ﷺ became seriously ill, Bilāl came to inform him of the prayer. He said: "Tell Abū Bakr to lead the people in prayer." I said: "O Messenger of Allāh, surely Abū Bakr is a soft-hearted man. When he stands in your place, he will not be able to make the people hear. Would you tell ʿUmar (to lead the prayer)?" He said: "Tell Abū Bakr to lead the people in prayer." I said to Ḥafṣah: "Say to him: Surely Abū Bakr is a soft-hearted man. When he stands in your place, he will not be able to make the people hear. Would you tell ʿUmar (to lead the prayer)?" He said: "Most surely you are (like) the women of (the story of) Joseph. Tell Abū Bakr to lead the people in prayer."

When he (Abū Bakr) started the prayer, the Messenger of Allāh ﷺ felt a little better and he came supported by two men, one on each side, with his feet dragging on the ground, until he entered the mosque. When Abū Bakr heard the sound of his coming, he made to retreat, but the Messenger of Allāh ﷺ indicated to him (by sign to stay where he was). The Messenger of Allāh ﷺ then came until he sat on the left side of Abū Bakr. Abū Bakr was saying the prayer standing while the Messenger of Allāh ﷺ was saying the prayer sitting. Abū Bakr was following the prayer of the Messenger of Allāh ﷺ and the people were following the prayer of Abū Bakr.[138]

Ch. 69:   Should an Imām, when in doubt, accept what people say?

714 Abū Hurairah reported that the Messenger of Allāh ﷺ departed after (saying) two *rakʿahs*. Dhul-Yadain said to him: "Has the prayer been short-ened or have you forgotten, O Messenger of Allāh?" The Messenger of Allāh ﷺ asked (the people): "Is Dhul-Yadain right?" People said: "Yes." So the Messenger of Allāh ﷺ stood up and prayed the remaining two *rakʿahs*, then finished it with *Salām*. Then he called out *Allāhu Akbar* and prostrated like his (usual) prostration or longer.[139]

715 Abū Hurairah reported: The Prophet ﷺ said (only) two *rakʿahs* of *Ẓuhr* prayer, and it was said to him: "You have said two *rakʿahs* of prayer." So he said two (more) *rakʿahs,* then finished it with *Salām* and then made two prostrations.[140]

---

thus the teachings of the faith would be carried from generation to generation and from nation to nation.

[138] This is a repetition of h. 664, having similarity to its repetition in h. 679. The last part here, starting "until he sat on the left side of Abū Bakr", is different.

[139] This is a repetition of h. 482 in brief.

[140] This is an even more brief repetition of h. 482.

Ch. 70: When the Imām weeps in prayer

> ʿAbdullāh ibn Shaddād said: I heard the sobbing of ʿUmar when I was in the last row (in prayer), and he was reciting: "I only complain of my grief and sorrow to Allāh" (the Qur'ān, 12:86).

716 ʿĀ'ishah, mother of the believers, reported that the Messenger of Allāh ﷺ said during his illness: "Tell Abū Bakr to lead the people in prayer." I said: ...[141]

Ch. 71: Making the rows straight at the time of the *Iqāmah* and after it

717 An-Nuʿmān ibn Bashīr said that the Prophet ﷺ said: "You should make your rows straight or else Allāh will turn your faces against each other." [142]

718 Anas reported that the Prophet ﷺ said: "Make the rows straight, for surely I see you behind my back." [143]

Ch. 72: The Imām facing the people at the time of making the rows straight

719 Anas ibn Mālik related: The prayer had been announced by *Iqāmah* and the Messenger of Allāh ﷺ turned his face towards us and said: "Make your rows straight and close your ranks, for surely I see you from behind from my back." [144]

---

[141] See h. 679 for the rest of this report. This is a repetition of h. 664 in almost the same words as h. 679. As in h. 679, it ends with the statement of Ḥafṣah to ʿĀ'ishah: "I have never got any good from you." The point made in the chapter heading is that a prayer does not become void if the Imām weeps in it. It is stated in the Qur'ān: "When the messages of the Beneficent were recited to them, they fell down in submission, weeping" (19:58). Weeping in prayer is thus regarded as a sign of the utmost humility and submission, and it cannot possibly make the prayer void.

[142] This expression should not be taken literally, as some have done, to mean any physical displacement of the face in the body. Nawawī in his commentary on Ṣaḥīḥ Muslim has taken it to mean that "enmity, malice and disagreements in the hearts will arise among you." Al-Qurṭabī interprets it as meaning that "you will be divided so that each will have a different opinion." This is supported by the version of this ḥadīth in Abū Dāwūd (book: 'Prayer', h. 662), in which the word "hearts" is used instead of "faces". It may also be noted that the word for "face", *wajh*, is also applied to one's purpose or to one's entire being. Lack of unity in outward forms creates disunity of purpose in the hearts.

[143] This is the last part of h. 719. See also h. 418 and h. 419.

[144] This shows that it is one of the duties of the Imām to instruct the congregation to set the rows in order. The meaning of the Holy Prophet seeing the congregation behind him has already been discussed in the footnote on h. 418.

Ch. 73: The first row (in a congregation)

720–721 Abū Hurairah reported that the Prophet ﷺ said: "Martyrs are those who die by drowning, and of diarrhea, and of plague, and by being buried under a collapsed thing. [721] And he said: "And if they knew what is (the reward) for appearing early for the *Ẓuhr* prayer, they would have raced with one another for it; and if they knew what is (the reward) for the *'Ishā'* and the morning prayers, they would come to these two prayers even if they had to crawl on their knees; and if they knew what is (the reward) for the first row, they would draw lots for it." [145]

Ch. 74: Making the row straight is a part of the completion of prayer

722 Abū Hurairah reported from the Prophet ﷺ that he said: "The Imām is appointed to be followed, so do not differ from him. When he bows (in *Rukū'*), you must bow, and when he says, *Sami' Allāhu li-man ḥamidah* ('Allāh hears him who praises Him'), say: *Rabba-nā la-ka-l-ḥamd* ('Our Lord! Yours is the praise'), and when he prostrates, you must prostrate, and when he says his prayer sitting, you must say your prayer sitting, all of you, and make the rows straight in prayer, for surely the straightening of rows is among the beauties of the prayer." [146]

723 Anas reported from the Prophet ﷺ that he said: "Make your rows straight, for surely making the rows straight is a part of the performance of prayer."

Ch. 75: The sin of one who does not make the row correct

724 Anas ibn Mālik reported that he came to Madīnah and was asked: "What do you find different in us since you saw the time of the Messenger of Allāh ﷺ?" He said: "I do not find anything different except that you do not make the rows straight." [147]

---

[145] This is a repetition of h. 653–654 with some difference in wording. See also h. 615.

[146] This is a repetition of h. 378, similar to its repetitions in h. 688 and h. 689. Its closing words about straightening the rows are additional and relate to the chapter heading.

[147] In h. 530 it is reported that Anas noticed a change for the worse since the time of the Holy Prophet, in people having become lax in observing the commands of Islām, but that was his experience in Damascus. Here in Madīnah the only thing he disliked was that people attending the prayer were not particular about the straightness in the rows. This shows that at that time the people of Madīnah followed the religious observances of Islām quite well.

Ch. 76:   Joining of shoulder to shoulder and foot to foot in the row[148]

An-Nu'mān ibn Bashīr said: I saw a man among us joining his ankle to the ankle of his companion.

725 Anas reported from the Prophet ﷺ that he said: "Make your rows straight, for surely I see you from behind from my back."

Anas added: And each one of us used to join his shoulder with the shoulder of his companion and his foot with his foot.[149]

Ch. 77:   When a man stands on the left of the Imām and the Imām wheels him round his back to his right, his prayer is complete

726 Ibn 'Abbās reported: I said my prayer with the Prophet ﷺ one night, and I stood at his left side. But the Messenger of Allāh ﷺ caught me by my head from behind me and made me stand on his right. He said his prayers and went to sleep. Then the caller to prayer came to him, so he stood for prayer and did not perform any ablution.[150]

Ch. 78:   A woman constitutes a row by herself

727 Anas ibn Mālik reported: I and an orphan boy prayed behind the Prophet ﷺ in our house and my mother Umm Sulaim was behind us.[151]

Ch. 79:   The right side of the mosque and of the Imām

728 Ibn 'Abbās reported: I got up one night and began to say my prayer on the left of the Prophet ﷺ, but he caught me by my hand or my shoulder till he made me stand on his right and he indicated with his hand as if to say, "(come) from behind me".[152]

---

[148] This should not be taken too literally. In *Fatḥ al-Bārī*, the commentary on Bukhārī, this is explained as follows: "What it means is that the rows should be properly straightened and vacant spaces filled up."

[149] The words of the Holy Prophet in this report are a repetition of those in h. 718 and h. 719. The addition by Anas is extra here.

[150] This repetition of h. 138 is much like its repetition in h. 698, but is briefer.

[151] The last part of h. 380 occurs here in different words. That ḥadīth mentions his grand-mother Mulaikah instead of his mother as here. See also h. 860 and h. 871.

[152] This repetition of h. 183 is even more brief than h. 699. In h. 183 Ibn 'Abbās says that the Holy Prophet "caught me by my right ear and turned it", so there is a slight difference in this version. The chapter heading suggests that there is blessing on the right side.

Ch. 80: **When between the Imām and the people there is a wall or**
**   *sutrah* (screening)**

Al-Ḥasan said: There is no harm in that you say your prayer and
there is a stream between you and him (the Imām). Abū Mijlaz said:
A person should follow the Imām even if between the two (i.e., him
and the Imām) there is a road or a wall, when he hears the calling
out of *Allāhu Akbar* by the Imām.[153]

729 ʿĀ'ishah reported: The Messenger of Allāh ﷺ used to say his prayer
at night in his own chamber. The wall of the chamber was short and people
saw the person of the Prophet ﷺ, so some people stood praying following his
prayer. When it was morning, they talked about it among themselves. So when
he stood for prayer the next night, some people stood with him praying
following his prayer. This they did for two or three nights, until when the
following (night) came the Messenger of Allāh ﷺ kept sitting and did not
come out. When it was morning, people mentioned this and he said: "Surely I
feared the prayer of the night would be made obligatory for you." [154]

Ch. 81: **The night prayer (*Tahajjud*)**

730 ʿĀ'ishah reported that the Prophet ﷺ had a mat that he would spread
during the day and make an enclosure with it at night. So some people
gathered near him and prayed behind him.[155]

731 Zaid ibn Thābit reported that the Messenger of Allāh ﷺ had a
chamber made in the month of Ramaḍān — he (Busr ibn Saʿīd reporting from
Zaid) said: I think that he (Zaid) said it was made of a mat. He said his prayers
in that for several nights and some of his Companions also said their prayers
following his prayer. When he came to know of what they were doing, he
began to keep sitting. Then he came out to them and said: "I know what I have
seen you doing. Say your prayers, O people, in your own houses. For surely
the best of the prayers is the prayer of a man in his own house, except for the
obligatory ones." [156]

---

[153] If necessary, congregational prayers can be held in this way. It does not mean that if the
sound of the Imām saying *Allāhu Akbar* reaches people's homes they can say their prayer at
home following him, and it would be considered as congregational prayer. As the chapter heading
indicates, this relates only to the case where something intervenes between the Imām and the
rows behind him.

[154] The prayer mentioned here was the Holy Prophet's *Tahajjud* prayer during Ramaḍān. See
also h. 924, h. 1129 and h. 2011–2012.

[155] See the next ḥadīth, h. 731.

[156] The subject matter of this ḥadīth is the same as in h. 729. Besides mentioning that people

Ch. 82:   The obligatory nature of *Takbīr* (calling out *Allāhu Akbar*) and the opening of prayer[157]

732 Anas ibn Mālik informed that the Messenger of Allāh ﷺ once rode a horse, (he fell down) and his right side was bruised. Anas added: On that day he led us in one of the prayers while sitting, and we prayed behind him (also) sitting. Then when he invoked *Salām* (at the end of the prayer), he said: "The Imām is appointed to be followed: so when he says his prayer standing, you must say your prayer standing, and when he bows, you must bow, and when he raises (his head), you must raise, and when he prostrates, you must prostrate, and when he says, *Sami' Allāhu li-man ḥamidah* ('Allāh hears him who praises Him'), say: *Rabba-nā wa la-ka-l-ḥamd* ('Our Lord! And Yours is the praise')."

733 Anas reported: The Messenger of Allāh ﷺ fell from a horse and was bruised. So he led us in prayer while sitting, and we prayed with him (also) sitting. When he finished he said: "The Imām is — or (he said) the Imām is appointed — to be followed: so when he says the *Takbīr,* you must say the *Takbīr,* and when he bows, you must bow, and when he raises (his head), you must raise, and when he says, *Sami' Allāhu li-man ḥamidah* ('Allāh hears him who praises Him'), say: *Rabba-nā la-ka-l-ḥamd* ('Our Lord! Yours is the praise'), and when he prostrates, you must prostrate."

734 Abū Hurairah reported that the Prophet ﷺ said: "The Imām is appointed to be followed: so when he says the *Takbīr,* you must say the *Takbīr,* and when he bows, you must bow, and when he says, *Sami' Allāhu li-man ḥamidah* ('Allāh hears him who praises Him'), say: *Rabba-nā wa la-ka-l-ḥamd* ('Our Lord! And Yours is the praise'), and when he says his prayer sitting, you must say your prayer sitting, all of you." [158]

---

prayed with him, this report is either more explanatory than h. 729 or conflicts with it, for instance as regards making an enclosure with his mat and that it was the month of Ramaḍān. As regards the statements of the Holy Prophet to the people in h. 729 and here, perhaps he said both of them. The saying of optional prayers at home is important for the creation of a sacred atmosphere in the house and for the family living there.

[157] It necessary to say *Allāhu Akbar* at the start of the prayer. Bukhārī arrives at this conclusion from the words found in h. 733 and 734. Those words are also in h. 805.

[158] H. 378 is repeated three times in this chapter, but without its middle part about the Holy Prophet taking a vow to be away from his wives for a month and his Companions coming to visit him. The first two reports, h. 732 and 733, are by Anas, and in both of these, as in h. 378, the Holy Prophet's falling down from a horse is mentioned, but in h. 733 the injury is not specified while in h. 732 it is said: "and his right side was bruised." H. 734 is reported by Abū Hurairah and consists only of the Holy Prophet's saying. The end of h. 734 about sitting is not found in h. 378, h. 732 or h. 733, but it is at the end of h. 688 and h. 689.

Ch. 83: The raising of both hands in saying the first *Takbīr* at opening (the prayer)[159]

735 Sālim ibn 'Abdullāh reported from his father ('Abdullāh ibn 'Umar) that the Messenger of Allāh ﷺ used to raise his hands up to the level of his shoulders when opening the prayer, and when he would say *Takbīr* for *Rukū'* and when he would raise his head from *Rukū'* he would raise them in the same way and would say *Sami' Allāhu li-man ḥamidah, Rabba-nā wa la-ka-l-ḥamd* ('Allāh hears him who praises Him, Our Lord! And Yours is the praise'). And he would not do that in prostrations.[160]

Ch. 84: Raising of the hands when saying *Takbīr* and when going into *Rukū'* and when raising (the head from *Rukū'*)

736 Sālim ibn 'Abdullāh informed from 'Abdullāh ibn 'Umar that he said: I saw the Messenger of Allāh ﷺ when he stood for prayer raising his hands until they were up to the level of his shoulders, and he used to do the same at the time of saying *Takbīr* for (going into) *Rukū'*, and he used to do the same when raising his head from *Rukū'* and saying *Sami' Allāhu li-man ḥamidah* ('Allāh hears him who praises Him'). But he did not do this (i.e., raise his hands) in prostrations.[161]

737 Abū Qilābah reported that he saw Mālik ibn al-Ḥuwairith, when he was praying, saying *Takbīr* and raising his hands (to start the prayer), and when he wanted to go into *Rukū'* raising his hands, and when he raised his

---

[159] There are several kinds of reports on this question of saying *Allāhu Akbar* and the raising of hands. In some reports the two actions are said to be simultaneous, while according to others the *Takbīr* is either before or after the raising of the hands. In such small matters, variety is found in the practice of the Holy Prophet, and he seems to have given much latitude. These variations make no difference. The raising of the hands is a sign of being attentive to God with total exclusion of all other thoughts, and the saying of *Allāhu Akbar* means the negation of the greatness of everything else besides God and the affirmation of the same solely in God.

[160] The raising of hands at the start of the prayer is a rule established by universal agreement. There is difference, however, on the question of raising the hands at the time of going into *Rukū'*, rising from *Rukū'*, and again at the time of rising from the sitting posture. The practice of the Companions is found in both ways, some raising the hands and others not. The Holy Prophet's practice is more on the side of raising hands in these intervening postures than not doing it. 'Abdullāh ibn Mas'ūd considered the discarding of the raising of the hands by the Holy Prophet as his last and final practice, cancelling the earlier one. Those who believe in raising the hands do not consider the report from 'Abdullāh ibn Mas'ūd to be authentic, or they say that if it is authentic then it does not cancel the earlier practice but only shows that sometimes, only a minority of times, he did not raise his hands, and thus raising the hands remains the *Sunnah*. However, as stated in the last footnote, these are all matters of judgment and should not be escalated into points of dispute and wrangling.

[161] This is a repetition of h. 735.

head from *Rukū'* raising his hands, and he related that the Messenger of Allāh ﷺ used to do the same.

Ch. 85:   Up to where should a person raise his hands?

Abū Ḥumaid said amongst his companions: The Prophet ﷺ raised (his hands) up to the level of his shoulders.[162]

738 Sālim ibn 'Abdullāh informed that 'Abdullāh ibn 'Umar said: I saw the Messenger of Allāh ﷺ opening with *Takbīr* for the prayer, and he raised his hands at the time of *Takbīr* until he brought them to the level of his shoulders, and when he said *Takbīr* for *Rukū'* he did the same, and when he said *Sami' Allāhu li-man ḥamidah* ('Allāh hears him who praises Him') he did the same and then said *Rabba-nā wa la-ka-l-ḥamd* ('Our Lord! And Yours is the praise'). But he did not do the same when he went into prostration nor when he raised his head from the prostrations.[163]

Ch. 86:   Raising of the hands when standing up after the two *rak'ahs* (for the third *rak'ah*)

739 Nāfi' reported that Ibn 'Umar, when he started his prayer, would say the *Takbīr* and raise his hands and when he went into *Rukū'* he would raise his hands, and when he said *Sami' Allāhu li-man ḥamidah* ('Allāh hears him who praises Him') he would raise his hands, and when he stood after the two *rak'ahs* (for the third *rak'ah*) he would raise his hands. Ibn 'Umar raised them thus, after the example of the Prophet ﷺ.[164]

Ch. 87:   Placing the right hand over the left in prayer

740 Sahl ibn Sa'd reported: People were commanded that a man should place his right hand over his left forearm in prayer.

Abū Ḥāzim said: I only know that he ascribed it to the Prophet ﷺ.[165]

---

[162] The ḥadīth from Abū Ḥumaid containing these words occurs in h. 828. In all such reports it is stated that the Holy Prophet raised his hands up to his shoulders. However, in the version of h. 737 reported by Mālik ibn al-Ḥuwairith in Ṣaḥīḥ Muslim it is stated that the Holy Prophet raised his hands "until he took them to the lobes of his ears" (book: 'Prayer', ch. 9). A similar report in Abū Dāwūd by Wā'il ibn Ḥujr says: "until they were parallel to his ears" (book: 'Prayer', h. 726). This is also a minor point and it makes no difference to the performance of the prayer.

[163] This is a repetition of h. 735 with a small addition at the end.

[164] This is also a repetition of h. 735 with an addition about raising the hands when standing up from the sitting position for the third *rak'ah*. This connects it with the chapter heading.

[165] This says that the right hand should be placed on the left *dhirā'*. This word applies to the part from the fingers to the elbow. Thus there is great latitude given in this requirement. It may

Ch. 88:   Submissiveness in prayer

741 Abū Hurairah reported that the Messenger of Allāh ﷺ said: "Do you think my *Qiblah* to be here (i.e., I am looking ahead)? By Allāh, neither your bowing nor your submissiveness (to God) is hidden from me, for surely I see you behind my back." [166]

742 Anas ibn Mālik reported from the Prophet ﷺ that he said: "Make the bowing (*Rukū'*) and prostrations (*Sajdah*) correct, for, by Allāh, surely I see you from behind me — or perhaps he said: from behind my back — when you go into *Rukū'* or *Sajdah*." [167]

Ch. 89:   What is to be recited after *Takbīr*?

743 Anas reported that the Prophet ﷺ, Abū Bakr and 'Umar used to open the prayer with *Al-ḥamdu li-llāhi Rabbi-l-'ālamīn* ("All praise is due to Allāh, the Lord of the worlds").[168]

744 Abū Hurairah related that the Messenger of Allāh ﷺ used to keep silent between the *Takbīr* (calling out *Allāhu Akbar*) and the recitation (of the Qur'ān). He (the narrator from Abū Hurairah) said: I think he (Abū Hurairah) said: "for a short while (*huniyyat-un*)". So I (Abū Hurairah) said: "May my father and mother be sacrificed for you, O Messenger of Allāh, What do you read during your silence between the *Takbīr* and the recitation?" He said:

"I say: O Allāh! Keep a distance between me and my faults just as you have kept a distance between the east and the west. O Allāh! Purify me

---

be placed at any point between the fingers and the elbow: at the elbow end, or at the fingers, or in between the two. The hands may be at the level of the naval or above it or below it. Such differences have absolutely no effect on the prayer. The concluding words, stating that the tradition reaches up to the Holy Prophet himself, emphasise the importance of the flexibility given in this regard.

[166] This is a repetition of h. 418. See also h. 718 and h. 719.

[167] In this repetition of h. 719 the emphasis, instead of on the straightening of rows, is on the correctness of postures.

[168] In another report the words are that the Holy Prophet, Abū Bakr, 'Umar and 'Uthmān "used to open the recitation with *Al-ḥamdu li-llāhi Rabbi-l-'ālamīn*" (Abū Dāwūd, book: 'Prayer', h. 782). So in this ḥadīth too, the beginning of prayer means the beginning of the recitation of the Qur'ān. In a report in Ṣaḥīḥ Muslim, Anas says that he said prayers with the Holy Prophet, Abū Bakr, 'Umar and 'Uthmān, and "I never heard anyone of them reciting *Bismillāhi-r-Raḥmāni-r-Raḥīm* ('In the name of Allāh, the Beneficent, the Merciful')" (Muslim, book: 'Prayer', ch. 13). That is to say, the words of the *Bismillāh* were not recited aloud. In a report in the collection of Ibn Khuzaimah, it is explicitly said: "They used to keep low the recitation of *Bismillāhi-r-Raḥmāni-r-Raḥīm*" (vol. 1, h. 249). The conclusion from all these reports is that they used to recite the *Bismillāh* but in a low voice to themselves, and started reciting aloud with *Al-ḥamdu li-llāhi Rabbi-l-'ālamīn*.

from faults just as a white cloth is washed clean of its dirt. O Allāh! Wash my faults with water and ice and hail stones." [169]

Ch. 90: Related to the above

745 Asmā', daughter of Abū Bakr, reported that the Prophet ﷺ said the prayer of the (solar) eclipse. He stood up and prolonged his standing, then he went into *Rukū'* and prolonged the *Ruku'*, then he stood and prolonged his standing, then he went into *Rukū'* and prolonged the *Ruku'*, then he raised (his head), then he went into prostration and prolonged the prostration, then he raised (his head), then he went into prostration and prolonged the prostration.

Then he stood up and prolonged his standing, then he went into *Rukū'* and prolonged the *Ruku'*, then he raised (his head) and prolonged his standing, then he went into *Rukū'* and prolonged the *Ruku'*, then he raised (his head) and went into prostration and prolonged the prostration, then he raised (his head), then he went into prostration and prolonged the prostration. Then he finished and said:

"Paradise became very close to me so much so that if I had felt bold I could have brought for you some bunches from its bunches (of fruit); and the fire (of hell) became very close to me so much so that I said: 'My Lord, (are you going to punish them) and I am still with them?' [170] There

---

[169] This shows that before the recitation of the Qur'ān the Holy Prophet used to recite this prayer in a low voice. Some other prayers are also attributed to him at this stage. The most well-known of these is as follows: *Subḥāna-k-Allāhumma wa bi-ḥamdi-ka wa tabāraka-smu-ka wa taʿāla jaddu-ka, wa lā ilāha ghairu-ka* ("Glory be to You, O Allāh, and Yours is the praise, and blessed is Your name, and exalted is Your majesty, and there is no god beside You"). This is in Ṣaḥīḥ Muslim, book: 'Prayer', ch. 13; Tirmidhī, book: 'Prayer', h. 242 and h. 243; Abū Dāwūd, book: 'Prayer', h. 776; Ibn Mājah, book: 'Establishing the prayer and the *Sunnah* about it', h. 804 and h. 806; Nasā'ī, book: 'Opening the Prayer', h. 900). The Holy Prophet's prayer to the effect that the "distance between the east and the west" be maintained between himself and his faults shows that the object of his prayer was to keep him entirely and wholly safe from faults. "My faults" means the faults that he, as a human being, had the potential to commit. The reference to "water and ice and hail stones" is because the result of sin is fire, and the mercy and forgiveness of God is being sought to protect a man from that fire. They indicate solace of the heart which keeps away the fire of sin.

[170] These are visions of the spiritual world experienced by the Holy Prophet, not things seen with his physical eye. The approach of fire made the Holy Prophet fear that it would burn the whole nation. He was surprised at this because God in the Qur'ān had given him the promise: "And Allāh would not punish them while you were among them" (8:33). The prolonged *Rukū'* and *Sajdah* on this occasion shows the extreme sense of humility and submissiveness to Allāh in his mind. In the prayer on the occasion of the eclipse, there are two *Rukū's* and two standing postures in each *rak'ah*. The report from Asmā' has been given in h. 86, but the details here are different from those in that report. The bringing near of paradise and hell is mentioned here and

was a woman — I think that he said[171] — a cat was scratching her. I (the Holy Prophet) said: 'What is the matter with her?' They said: 'She kept the cat confined till it died of hunger, she would neither give it food nor would she let it go out so that it might eat'."

Nāfi' said: I think that (after "it might eat"), he (Ibn Abī Mulaikah) added: "from the worms or insects of the earth." [172]

Ch. 91: Raising one's look towards the Imām during prayer

'Ā'ishah said that the Prophet ﷺ said after the prayer of solar eclipse: "When you saw me stepping backward I surely saw Hell, different parts of which were destroying one another." [173]

746 Abū Ma'mar reported: We said to Khabbāb, "Did the Messenger of Allāh ﷺ recite (from the Qur'ān) in the *Zuhr* and *'Aṣr* prayers?" He said: "Yes." We said: "How did you come to know it?" He said: "By the movement of his beard."

747 Al-Barā', who never lied, related that when they used to pray with the Prophet ﷺ and he would raise his head from *Rukū'*, they would keep standing until they saw him going into prostration.[174]

748 'Abdullāh ibn 'Abbās reported: The sun eclipsed in the time of the Prophet ﷺ, so he said prayers (due to the eclipse). People said: "O Messenger of Allāh, we saw you going forward a little from your place and then we saw you retreating." He said: "I saw Paradise and tried to take a bunch (of fruit),

---

in h. 86, while h. 431 contains only the mention of seeing these. See also Bukhārī's Book of Eclipses and in particular h. 1044 and h. 1046 in that book.

[171] In this parenthetical insertion, the speaker is Nāfi' and in the words "he said" he is referring to Ibn Abī Mulaikah who was relating to Nāfi' from Asmā'.

[172] This shows that Divine punishment can even come down upon those who cause pain or injury to animals. Thus, the first law for the prevention of cruelty to animals was promulgated from a spiritual plain at the hands of the Holy Prophet of Islām.

[173] See h. 1212 for these words of the Holy Prophet. The meaning of the chapter heading is that if something extraordinary happens and the people in the congregation look at the Imām, as did the Companions when they found the Holy Prophet stepping backward, it does not invalidate the prayer. The reference in the next ḥadīth to some people seeing the movements of the Holy Prophet's beard must apply to people who were standing behind him in the first row and whose sight could naturally catch the Holy Prophet's face.

[174] This is a repetition of h. 690 in different words. People could see the Holy Prophet as their eyes were not fully closed.

and if I had taken it you would have eaten from it as long as the world remained." [175]

749 Anas ibn Mālik reported: The Prophet ﷺ led us in prayer, then he ascended the pulpit and pointed with his hands towards the *qiblah* of the mosque, then said: "I surely saw just now, while I was leading you in prayer, Paradise and Hell appearing as it were towards the *qiblah* on this wall, and I had never seen such a good and a bad sight as today." He said it three times. [176]

Ch. 92:　Raising the look towards the sky during prayer

750 Anas ibn Mālik related that the Prophet ﷺ said: "What will be the condition of people who raise their looks towards the sky during their prayer?" His words became more severe about this, so much so that he said: "They must refrain from this or else their eyesight will be snatched away." [177]

Ch. 93:　Looking around during prayer

751 ʿĀʾishah reported: I asked the Messenger of Allāh ﷺ about looking around during prayer, and he said: "It is the carrying away, the devil carrying away a part of the prayer of the servant (of God)." [178]

752 ʿĀʾishah reported that the Prophet ﷺ said his prayer in a shawl in which there were borders. So he said: "These borders have distracted me. Take this (shawl) to Abū Jahm and bring me an *anbijāniyyah*." [179]

---

[175] This, in a way, explains that the rewards of good deeds in paradise will be eternal whereas blessings of this world come to an end. These words are repeated exactly as such within the lengthy ḥadīth h. 1052.

[176] This is a repetition of the last part of h. 540 with some more details. According to h. 540, this incident took place after the *Ẓuhr* prayer. The Holy Prophet's seeing of Paradise and Hell during the prayer at the solar eclipse is a separate incident. It has been inferred from this ḥadīth that when the Imām sees anything in front of him the congregation can also see the same.

[177] It is natural for a person's eyes to see things lying in front during prayer. Seeing such things does not amount to lack of attention in prayer. However, raising the sight to look above does indicate distraction from prayer. The reference to their sight being carried off means that they will remain spiritually blind due to being inattentive in prayer. See the next ḥadīth for looking around during prayer.

[178] Looking here and there will distract attention from prayer, and this amounts to a success for the devil.

[179] This is a repetition of h. 373 in somewhat different words. See the footnote to that ḥadīth for further explanation. This shows that distraction from prayer leads to a failure to achieve the objective of prayer.

Ch. 94: **Should a person look around (during prayer) if something happens to him or if he sees something or some phlegm in front of him?**

Sahl said: Abū Bakr looked around and saw the Prophet ﷺ.[180]

753 Ibn 'Umar reported that the Prophet ﷺ saw some phlegm before him in the mosque (on the wall) while he was leading the people in prayer, so he scraped it off. Then when he finished (the prayer), he said: "When any of you is in prayer, surely Allāh is in front of him. So no one should spit in front of him in prayer." [181]

754 Anas ibn Mālik informed that while the Muslims were engaged in the *Fajr* prayer nothing disturbed them but the Messenger of Allāh ﷺ removing the curtain of the chamber of 'Ā'ishah. He looked at them while they were standing in rows. So he gave a broad smile. Abū Bakr began to retreat to join the line as he thought that he (the Holy Prophet) wanted to come out (for the prayer). The Muslims were put to the test whether to break off from their prayer, but he made a sign to them as if to say "Complete your prayers". Then he pulled down the curtain, and he expired at the end of that day.[182]

Ch. 95: **The reading from the Qur'ān being obligatory both on the Imām and those who follow him, in all prayers whether at home**

---

[180] In accordance with the middle course as taught by Islām, on the one hand nothing must be done in prayer which may cause any diversion from the remembrance of God, and on the other a person may look at something if it is in connection with the prayer itself. An example is provided by Abū Bakr's seeing the Holy Prophet when the latter happened to join the congregation during prayer, which happened on two occasions (for which see h. 683 and h. 684 and footnote 99 under h. 684). Other reports show that Abū Bakr used to be totally absorbed in his prayers and yet he took notice of an event such as the Holy Prophet's arrival while the congregation was engaged in prayer. Turning attention to an unusual occurrence or looking at it cannot be considered as spoiling the prayer if attention then goes back to the prayer.

[181] This is a repetition of h. 405, which has been repeated in h. 407 to h. 411, h. 414 and h. 417. But in none of those reports is it mentioned that the Holy Prophet was praying when he saw the phlegm and scraped it off. This report shows that the Holy Prophet saw the phlegm while he was leading the prayer, but to say that he scraped it off during the prayer seems to be an error in this report. Merely sighting the phlegm is quite natural and beyond human control. Bukhārī himself has not inferred that the Holy Prophet scraped off the phlegm during prayer because in the chapter heading he has only mentioned seeing phlegm.

[182] In this repetition of h. 680 there is the addition: "while the Muslims were engaged in the *Fajr* prayer." So h. 680 must be the report of an event which took place at the time of the morning prayer, and the Holy Prophet felt very much better in the morning of the day on which he breathed his last. He felt strong enough to lift the curtain of his chamber and have a sight of the congregational prayer, which pleased him. Here, however, there is no mention that it was Monday, which is in h. 680.

or in a journey, whether in a prayer in which it is done aloud or in a low voice[183]

755 Jābir ibn Samurah reported: The people of Kūfah complained to 'Umar against Sa'd, so he discharged him from office[184] and appointed 'Ammār as their Governor. They carried the complaint so far that they said that he did not lead prayers well. So he ('Umar) sent for him and said: "O Abū Isḥāq, these people assert that you do not lead prayers well." He said: "Look, by Allāh, I used to lead them in prayer as the prayer of the Messenger of Allāh

---

[183] According to Abū Ḥanīfah, the recital of the Qur'ān by the Imām obviates the necessity of its recital by those following him, whether in prayers in which this recitation is done aloud or those in which it is done in a low voice. He does not consider it obligatory for those in the congregation, and in fact he prohibits it. According to the followers of Imām Mālik, on the other hand, those in the congregation do not need to recite only when the recital is being done aloud by the Imām, but otherwise they must. The Ḥanafīs put forward the following ḥadīth: "Whoever says his prayer behind an Imām, the recital of the Imām is his recital" (*Ad-Dār Quṭnī*, vol. 1, p. 402). But people have differed on the question of its authenticity. As for prayers in which the recital is done aloud, both the followers of Imām Abū Ḥanīfah and Imām Mālik rely on the following ḥadīth: "When he (the Imām) recites, you should be silent" (Ṣaḥīḥ Muslim, book: 'Prayer', ch. 16: 'The *Tashahhud* in prayer'). This is a reliable report but there is nothing in this ḥadīth against those in the congregation reciting from the Qur'ān when the Imām's recital is silent. In the ḥadīth which follows here, h. 755, Sa'd mentions prolonging the first two *rak'ahs* and shortening the last two. Evidently, the lengthening and shortening can take place only when the recital is done of a part of the Qur'ān other than the obligatory *Fātiḥah*. This shows that Sa'd was in the habit of reciting other parts of the Qur'ān besides the *Fātiḥah* in all the four *rak'ahs* and he claims that his prayer was the same as that of the Holy Prophet. Sa'd, however, acted as the Imām, and there is nothing said in this ḥadīth about the rule to be followed by the congregation. However, in h. 756 from 'Ubādah ibn aṣ-Ṣāmit it is stated: "There is no prayer for one who has not recited the Opening (*Fātiḥah*) of the Book", which may apply both to the Imām and the congregation. Again in h. 757, in which the Holy Prophet teaches a man how to pray, there is the clear direction for recital of the Qur'ān in the first *rak'ah*, and at the end the Holy Prophet tells the man to say all his prayer in the same way. This shows that in every prayer and in every *rak'ah* something from the Qur'ān should be read after the *Fātiḥah*. Taking all these views together, it seems that there is no harm in those in the congregation reciting the *Fātiḥah* followed by some portion of the Qur'ān inaudibly while the Imām is not heard to recite anything. But when the Imām is heard to recite, anyone in the congregation is free either to listen to him attentively, which will be as good as his own recital, or repeat quietly what the Imām recites when the latter pauses.

[184] Sa'd ibn Abī Waqqāṣ was a great and venerable Companion of the Holy Prophet, who was counted among the ten Companions to whom the Holy Prophet gave good news of entry into paradise. In 14 A.H. Caliph 'Umar sent him to war against the Persians as the head of the army. The conquest of Iraq took place at his hands. He remained the Governor of Kūfah till 20 or 21 A.H. Some inhabitants of Kūfah made various complaints against him to 'Umar, one being that he did not conduct the prayers properly. 'Umar instituted an enquiry on these complaints and found him absolved of all the charges. He mentioned in his Will that it was not on the grounds of any fault or untrustworthiness in him that he dispensed with his services. The fact is that 'Umar relieved Sa'd of his governorship because of the people's feeling about him, so he did not reinstate him. He appointed 'Ammār in his place, and sent Ibn Mas'ūd to look after the treasury and 'Uthmān ibn Ḥanīf to deal with land matters.

and did not fall short from it. I led the *'Ishā'* prayer[185] and I prolonged the first two *rak'ahs* and shortened the last two." He ('Umar) said: "That is what I thought about you, O Abū Isḥāq." So he sent a man or some men with him to Kūfah enquiring about him from the people of Kūfah.[186] They left no mosque but asked about him, and the people spoke well of him till they came to a mosque belonging to Banī 'Abs, and a man among them stood up, who was called Usāmah ibn Qatādah, and whose surname was Abū Sa'dah. He said: "As you seek testimony from us, so Sa'd did not go out with any body of troops and he did not distribute things with justice and did not observe justice in deciding cases." Sa'd said: "Be it known by Allāh, I will make three prayers: 'O Allāh, if this servant of yours is a liar, and he is standing up for show and to make a name for himself, prolong his life and prolong his destitution and make him a target of trials.'" [187]

Later on, when this man used to be asked, he would say: "I am a very old man, beset with trials; the curse of Sa'd has overtaken me." 'Abdul Malik said: So I found him afterwards with his eye-brows suspended on his eyes on account of old age but still he used to hang about in the roads for girls, pestering them.

756 'Ubādah ibn aṣ-Ṣāmit reported that the Messenger of Allāh said: "There is no prayer for one who has not recited the Opening (*Fātiḥah*) of the Book (in it)." [188]

---

[185] In h. 758 the words used are *ṣalātayi-l-'Ishā'*, lit. the two *'Ishā'* prayers, and mean the *Maghrib* and the *'Ishā'* prayers (as distinct from *ṣalāta-l-'Ishā'* used here, meaning the *'Ishā'* prayer). In most versions of this report the words are *ṣalātayi-l-'ashiyy,* meaning the two prayers of *Ẓuhr* and *'Aṣr*.

[186] This shows that the great Companions of the Holy Prophet never left any complaint against any administrator without proper investigation and their decisions were based on accurate facts and figures.

[187] It is a tragedy of human history that even if some innocent man is absolved by proper authorities of false charges levelled against him, the accusers continue in their malicious propaganda. This is a form of persecution which sometimes proves so unbearable to the man concerned that he cannot help invoking the judgment of God against his persecutors and his prayers in such a moment of agony are readily accepted by God. Thus there is a warning issued by the Holy Prophet regarding the curse invoked by one who has been wronged: "Beware of the curse of the one who has been wronged, for surely there is no barrier between it and God (Ṣaḥīḥ Muslim, book: 'Faith', ch. 7).

[188] This applies both to the Imām and the congregation. The *Sūrah Fātiḥah* must be recited by everyone in all prayers. When the *Fātiḥah* is recited aloud by the Imām, he should leave a short pause after each verse so that those in the congregation may repeat it inaudibly after him. It has, however, been suggested that if a person in a congregation listens attentively to the recitation without missing any word of it, it is as good as reciting it. It must be remembered that the *Fātiḥah* is an essential part of the prayer because it is not only a brief summary of the whole

757 Abū Hurairah reported that the Messenger of Allāh ﷺ entered the mosque and a man also entered who said his prayer and greeted the Prophet ﷺ with *Salām*. He returned the greeting and said: "Go back and say your prayer, for surely you have not said your prayer." So he returned and said his prayer as he had said it before, then came and greeted the Prophet ﷺ with *salām*. He (the Holy Prophet) said: "Go back and say your prayer, for surely you have not said your prayer." This happened three times. So he (the man) said: "By Him Who has sent you with truth, I do not know any better way than this, so teach me." He (the Holy Prophet) said: "When you stand up for prayer, say the *Takbīr* (*Allāhu Akbar*), then recite what is easy for you from the Qur'ān,[189] then go into *Rukū'* until you are restful in *Rukū'*, then rise up until you have stood up quite straight, then perform prostration until you are restful in *Sajdah*, then rise up until you are restful in sitting, and do this in every prayer of yours."

Ch. 96:   Reciting the Qur'ān in the *Ẓuhr* prayer

758 Jābir ibn Samurah reported that Sa'd said: "I used to lead them in prayer as the prayer of the Messenger of Allāh ﷺ in the two *'Ishā'* prayers,[190] not falling short from it. I prolonged the first two *rak'ahs* and shortened the last two." 'Umar said: "That is what I thought about you." [191]

759 Abū Qatādah reported: The Prophet ﷺ used to recite the Opening (*Fātiḥah*) of the Book and two (other) chapters in the first two *rak'ahs* of the *Ẓuhr* prayer, prolonging it in the first and shortening it in the second, and sometimes he would make a verse heard. And in the *Aṣr* prayer he would recite the Opening (*Fātiḥah*) of the Book and two (other) chapters, prolonging

---

Qur'ān but also because the prayer which it teaches has no parallel in the world. If the words of this prayer reflect corresponding feelings in the mind of the person praying, he can acquire all the best qualities for his worldly as well as moral and spiritual benefit.

[189] In Abū Dāwūd, instead of the words "then recite what is easy for you from the Qur'ān", the words are: "Then recite the *Umm-ul-Qur'ān* (i.e., the *Fātiḥah*) and what Allāh wills that you should read" (book: 'Prayer', h. 859). Another report in Abū Dāwūd says that the Holy Prophet commanded that "we should recite the Opening (*Fātiḥah*) of the Book and what is easy for us" (*ibid.*, h. 818). This shows that the words "what is easy for you from the Qur'ān" means passages of the Qur'ān other than the *Fātiḥah*, so that the *Fātiḥah* should be recited in every *rak'ah*, followed by some other passages from any place in the Qur'ān as convenient.

[190] See footnote 185 to h. 755 for this expression.

[191] This is a repetition in brief of h. 755. The mention of "the last two" *rak'ahs* conflicts with calling these as the "two *'Ishā'* prayers" because this expression indicates the *Maghrib* and the *'Ishā'* prayers, and the *Maghrib* prayer has three *rak'ahs*, not four. As stated in footnote 185 to h. 755, the words here may be *ṣalātayi-l-'ashiyy*, meaning the two prayers of *Ẓuhr* and *'Aṣr*. Bukhārī himself suggests the same in the chapter heading by referring to the *Ẓuhr* prayer.

it in the first. In the morning prayer he used to prolong the first *rak'ah* and shorten the second.[192]

760 Abū Ma'mar reported: We asked Khabbāb, "Did the Prophet ﷺ recite (from the Qur'ān) in the *Zuhr* and *'Asr* prayers?" He said: "Yes." We said: "By what did you know it?" He said: "By the movement of his beard." [193]

Ch. 97:   Reciting the Qur'ān in the *'Asr* prayer

761 Abū Ma'mar reported: I said to Khabbāb ibn al-Arat…[194]

762 Abū Qatādah reported: The Prophet ﷺ used to recite the Opening (*Fātihah*) of the Book and a chapter each time in the two *rak'ahs* of the *Zuhr* and *'Asr* prayers, and sometimes he would make us hear a verse.[195]

Ch. 98:   Reciting the Qur'ān in the *Maghrib* prayer

763 Ibn 'Abbās reported that Umm al-Fadl (his mother) heard him reciting *Wa-l-Mursalāti 'urf-an* ("By those sent forth to spread goodness", the Qur'ān, 77:1), and she said: "O my child, your recitation has reminded me of this chapter, for surely it was the last one that I heard the Messenger of Allāh ﷺ reciting in the *Maghrib* prayer." [196]

764 Marwān ibn al-Ḥakam reported: Zaid ibn Thābit asked me: "What is the matter with you that you recite small chapters in the *Maghrib* prayer? I have certainly heard the Prophet ﷺ reciting the longer one of the two long chapters." [197]

---

[192] The prolonging of the first *rak'ah* may have been in order to enable more people to join the congregation.

[193] This is a repetition of h. 746 in almost the same words.

[194] This, like h. 760, is also a repetition of h. 746 with insignificant differences.

[195] This is a repetition of h. 759 in a briefer form.

[196] This report is repeated in h. 4429 (book: 'Military expeditions') where it is stated: "Then he did not lead us in prayer after this until Allāh took him." In h. 687 it is stated that during his last ailment the prayer in which the Holy Prophet led the congregation was *Zuhr*. In Nasā'ī in a report of this incident, Umm al-Fadl says that this *Maghrib* prayer was said in the house of the Holy Prophet (Nasā'ī, book: 'The Opening of Prayer', ch. 64, h. 985). On the other hand, the incident described in h. 687 and speaking of the *Zuhr* prayer refers to congregational prayer in the mosque. Incidentally, it seems to be a proven fact that the Holy Prophet used to recite chapters comprising of two sections from the Holy Qur'ān in the *Maghrib* prayer.

[197] In a version in Nasā'ī, it is stated that Zaid ibn Thābit asked Marwān: "Do you recite *Qul huwa-llāhu ahad* (ch. 112 of the Qur'ān) and *Innā a'tainā-ka-l-kauthar* (ch. 108) in the *Maghrib* prayer?", to which Marwān replied: "Yes" (book: 'The Opening of Prayer', ch. 67, h. 989). This shows that the small chapters referred to here are ch. 112 and ch. 108. The long chapters are those

Ch. 99:   Reciting aloud in the *Maghrib* prayer

765 Jubair ibn Muṭ'im reported from his father that he said: I heard the Messenger of Allāh ﷺ reciting *At-Ṭūr* (ch. 52) in the *Maghrib* prayer.[198]

Ch. 100: Reciting aloud in the *'Ishā'* prayer

766 Abū Rāfi' reported: I said my *'Ishā'* prayer with Abū Hurairah and he recited *Idha-s-samā'u-nshaqqat* (ch. 84 of the Qur'ān) and went into prostration. So I asked him about it. He said: "I went into prostration (while saying prayer) behind Abul Qāsim ﷺ (the Holy Prophet), so I will continue to make this prostration at this (i.e., at 84:21) until I meet him (after death)."

767 'Adī reported: I heard from al-Bara' that once when the Prophet ﷺ was on a journey, he recited in the *'Ishā'* prayer in one of the two *rak'ahs*: *Wa-t-tīni wa-z-zaitūni* (ch. 95 of the Qur'ān).

Ch. 101: Reciting the Qur'ān in the *'Ishā'* prayer where there is prostration

768 Abū Rāfi' reported: I said my *'Ishā'* prayer ...[199]

Ch. 102: Reciting the Qur'ān in the *'Ishā'* prayer

769 'Adī ibn Thābit related that he heard al-Bara' say: I heard the Prophet ﷺ reciting *Wa-t-tīni wa-z-zaitūni* (ch. 95 of the Qur'ān) in the *'Ishā'* prayer, and I did not hear anyone who is sweeter in voice and recitation than he.[200]

Ch. 103: Prolonging (the recitation) in the first two *rak'ahs* and shortening (it) in the last two *rak'ahs*

770 Jābir ibn Samurah said that 'Umar said to Sa'd: "They have complained against you in every matter, even about prayer." He said: "Look,

---

from ch. 2 to ch. 9. It may be that the Holy Prophet used to recite some part of such a long chapter, or on some occasions the whole of it. According to reports in Nasā'ī, the "longer one of the two long chapters" was ch. 7, *Al-A'rāf,* and he completed its recitation in two *rak'ahs* (*ibid.,* ch. 67, h. 990, h. 991). The general reported practice of the Holy Prophet seems to have been to recite the smaller chapters from those entitled the *Mufaṣṣalāt*. See also footnote 125 under h. 701.

[198] In Tirmidhī (book: 'Prayer', ch. 113, h. 308) the opinion of Imam Mālik has been recorded that it is disapproved to recite long chapters in the *Maghrib* prayer such as *At-Ṭūr* (ch. 52) and *Al-Mursalāt* (ch. 77). But it is found in reliable reports that the Holy Prophet himself used to recite long chapters in the *Maghrib* prayer.

[199] This is a repetition of h. 766 in the same words, except that instead of "So I asked him about it", the words are: "So I asked him, What is this?"

[200] This is a repetition of h. 767, without any mention of a journey and with an addition at the end.

I used to prolong the first two *rak'ahs* and shorten the last two, and I did not neglect in following the prayer of the Messenger of Allāh ﷺ." He said: "You have spoken the truth. That is what I thought about you — or (he said) my notion about you."[201]

Ch. 104: Reciting the Qur'ān in the *Fajr* prayer

> Umm Salamah said: The Prophet ﷺ recited *At-Ṭūr* (ch. 52 of the Qur'ān).

771 Sayyār ibn Salāmah related: I and my father went to Abū Barzah al-Aslamī, and we asked him about the times of prayer. He said: "The Prophet ﷺ used to say the *Ẓuhr* prayer as soon as the sun would decline, and the *'Aṣr* prayer so that a man could return to the far end of Madīnah and the sun would be still bright." And I forgot what he said about the *Maghrib* prayer. "He (the Holy Prophet) did not mind delaying the *'Ishā'* prayer to one-third of the night, and he did not like sleeping before it and talking after it. He used to say the morning prayer and finish when a man could (just) recognize the person sitting with him, and he used to recite in both *rak'ahs,* or in one of them, between sixty and one hundred (verses of the Qur'ān)." [202]

772 'Aṭā' informed that he heard Abū Hurairah say: The Qur'ān is to be recited in every prayer, so what the Messenger of Allāh ﷺ made us hear, we have made you hear, and what he did not make us hear we did not make you hear. If you do not add anything to the *'Umm al-Qur'ān* (the *Fātiḥah*), it is enough, and if you add anything it is better.[203]

Ch. 105: Reciting the Qur'ān aloud in the *Fajr* prayer

> Umm Salamah said: I made circuits (of the Ka'bah) from behind the people while the Prophet ﷺ was reciting *At-Ṭūr* (ch. 52 of the Qur'ān).

773 Ibn 'Abbās reported: The Prophet ﷺ set out together with a group of his Companions with the intention of going to the market of 'Ukāẓ.[204] There

---

[201] This is a much briefer repetition of h. 755.

[202] This is a repetition of h. 541 in wording similar to that of h. 547. One difference is that, in case of the *Fajr* prayer, the report is not sure whether the Holy Prophet recited the number of verses mentioned in both *rak'ahs* or in only one of them.

[203] The prayer will be quite in order if the *Fātiḥah* alone is recited without adding any other portion of the Qur'ān, but it cannot be shown that the Holy Prophet ever recited only the *Fātiḥah* in the first two *rak'ahs*.

[204] Abū 'Ubaidah says that 'Ukāẓ was a place lying between Nakhla and Ṭā'if, ten miles from

was (at that time) an interruption between the devils[205] and news from heaven,[206] and flames of fire were sent forth against them. So the devils returned to their people who asked them: "What has happened to you?" They said: "Something has interrupted between us and news from heaven, and flames of fire have been sent forth against us." They said: "What has interrupted between you and news from heaven is only something new that has happened. So go to the eastern and the western ends of the land and find out what it is that has interrupted between you and news from heaven." [207]

Those who had set out towards Tihāmah came across the Prophet ﷺ while he was at Nakhlah intending to go to the market of ʿUkāẓ. He was saying the

---

Ṭāʾif. The market or fair of ʿUkāẓ was held from the morning of the first day of the month of Dhul Qaʿdah, the 11th month of the Muslim calendar, and lasted for twenty days. It was the Holy Prophet's practice to go anywhere where there would be a gathering of people in order to preach to them. His going to ʿUkāẓ had the same object. This particular incident took place when the Holy Prophet was still at Makkah, and Ibn ʿAbbās, the narrator of this ḥadīth, might not yet have been born, and as such could not have personal knowledge of it.

[205] The devils (plural: *shayāṭīn*, singular: *shaiṭān*) here were human beings. Al-Jauharī writes: "Every rebellious one from among humans, the jinn and the cattle is a *shaiṭān*" (*Aṣ-Ṣiḥāḥ fi-l-Lughah*). The Qurʾān also speaks of the leaders of the unbelievers as devils in the verse: "And when they are alone with their devils (*shayāṭīn*), they say: Surely we are with you, we were only mocking" (2:14). There is a ḥadīth that the Holy Prophet, seeing a man running after a pigeon, said: "A devil is pursuing a devil" (Abū Dāwūd, book: 'Behaviour', h. 4240). The ḥadīth here begins with a reference to devils and ends with a reference to jinn and to verses of the Qurʾān that speak of a group of jinn. The word *shaiṭān* connotes practically the same thing as jinn and the Qurʾān says that the devil *Iblīs* belongs to the class of jinn (18:50), and was created of fire (7:12) just as jinn were created of fire (15:27). All this shows that everything that is evil or every man who is engaged in evil-doing can be called in Arabic as *shaiṭān* or devil. In this particular incident, the ignorant leaders of opposition to the truth, who were like devils, were suddenly so impressed by the message of the Qurʾān that they were themselves surprised. This is the import of the verses at beginning of chapter 72 of the Qurʾān, entitled *The Jinn*.

[206] This does not mean that the devils can at any time catch messages from heaven because such an idea is contrary to the teachings of the Qurʾān which says: "And the devils have not brought it, and it is not befitting for them, nor have they the power to do it. Surely they are far removed from hearing it" (26:210–212), and "Or do they have the means by which they listen? Then let their listener bring a clear authority" (52:38). It is clear that the devils have no opportunity to listen to anything that may come from heaven, nor can they do so. As the word *shaiṭān* can be applied to human beings as well, here it may refer to soothsayers and fortune-tellers who claim to know about the future and things unseen through astrology and such like arts but attribute their knowledge to heavenly sources. Thus they make money from the ignorant people. The "interruption" may mean that, with the advent of the Holy Prophet, the hearts of the people were turning towards righteousness, so they had lost confidence in the soothsayers and spurned them, and were turning towards the Holy Prophet's guidance. It is this situation which is described as flames of fire being sent against them.

[207] It appears that they went to different parts of the country to investigate why people were turning away from them.

Fajr prayer with his Companions. When they heard the Qur'ān they listened to it and said: "By Allāh, this is what has interrupted between you and news from heaven." So after this when they returned to their people, they said: "O our people, surely we have heard a wonderful Qur'ān, guiding to the right way, so we believe in it and we shall not set up anyone as partner with our Lord." [208] So Allāh revealed to His Prophet ﷺ: "Say: It has been revealed to me" [209] and the saying of the jinn was revealed to him.

774 Ibn 'Abbās reported: The Prophet ﷺ recited aloud (from the Qur'ān) in whatever (prayer) he was commanded (to do so), and he remained silent in whatever (prayer) he was commanded to do so. "Your Lord is never forgetful" (the Qur'ān, 19:64), and "Certainly you have in the Messenger of Allāh an excellent exemplar" (33:21).[210]

Ch. 106: Combining (the recitation of) two chapters in one *rak'ah*, and reciting the last portions of chapters, and reciting a chapter before the chapter that comes before it, and reciting the beginning of a chapter[211]

---

[208] This statement is in the Qur'ān, 72:1–2, where it is attributed to a group of jinn. Some of them came across the Holy Prophet while he was leading the morning prayer. The fact that they believed in the Qur'ān shows that they were human beings. According to the Qur'ān, only human beings were sent as messengers of Allāh because they had to be teachers and guides for human beings and not for any other creation; see 17:94–95.

[209] These are the opening words of ch. 72 of the Qur'ān in 72:1, which is as follows: "Say: It has been revealed to me that a group of the jinn listened, so they said: Surely we have heard a wonderful Quran." The next verse continues with the rest of the statement of the jinn ("guiding to the right way…"), quoted just above in this ḥadīth.

[210] This shows that in the view of his Companions every religious act of the Holy Prophet was inspired by Divine commandment and his conduct was a practical exposition of the teachings of the Qur'ān. They considered his practice as binding upon them to follow. Thus, although there is no verse in the Holy Qur'ān indicating which parts of the prayer should be said aloud and which ones in silence, the Holy Prophet's practice, as regards when to recite aloud and when to do so silently, was considered to be in obedience to commandments of God.

[211] In this chapter, four questions are dealt with. Firstly, two chapters (*sūrahs*) of the Qur'ān can be recited in the same *rak'ah*. This is shown by the report from Anas in this chapter heading and by h. 775. Secondly, the last part of any chapter can be recited in prayer without reciting the whole of it. This is deduced from the allowability of reciting the beginning of a chapter and is supported by the statement quoted from Qatādah: "All are from the book of Allāh." Thirdly, it is not necessary in recitation that the order in which the chapters are found in the Qur'ān should be followed. This is shown by the report from Anas and the action of al-Aḥnaf and his statement about 'Umar. However, it is preferable that if a portion of the Qur'ān occurs earlier than another portion, the former should be recited before the latter. Fourthly, one may recite only the first part of a chapter. This is evident from the report of 'Abdullāh ibn as-Sā'ib about the Holy Prophet given at the beginning of this chapter head note, which is also found in Ṣaḥīḥ Muslim stating that

It has been reported from 'Abdullāh ibn as-Sā'ib that the Prophet ﷺ recited the chapter *Al-Mu'minūn* (ch. 23) in the morning prayer until he came to the story of Moses and Aaron, or of Jesus, when he began coughing. So he went into *Rukū'*.

'Umar recited one hundred and twenty verses from the chapter *Al-Baqarah* (ch. 2) in the first *rak'ah,* and one of the chapters called *mathānī* in the second.[212]

Al-Aḥnaf recited the chapter *Al-Kahf* (ch. 18) in the first (*rak'ah*), and in the second (*rak'ah*) the chapter *Yūsuf* (ch. 12) or *Yūnus* (ch. 10), and he mentioned that he said his morning prayer with 'Umar wherein these two chapters were recited.

Ibn Mas'ūd recited forty verses from the chapter *Al-Anfāl* (ch. 8) and in the second (*rak'ah*) a chapter from among the *Mufaṣṣal.*

Qatādah said with regard to one who recites one chapter (divided) in two *rak'ahs,* or the same chapter in each of two *rak'ahs,* that all are from the Book of Allāh, the Mighty, the Glorious.

774a 'Ubaidullāh reported from Thābit who reported from Anas: A man from among the *Anṣār* used to lead the people in prayer in the mosque of Qubā' and whenever he would begin to recite any chapter for them in prayer, he used to begin with *Qul huwa-Allāhu aḥad* (ch. 112) until he finished it, then he would recite another chapter along with it. He used to do this in every *rak'ah.* So his companions talked to him about it and said: "You begin the prayer with this chapter and do not consider that it is enough for you, so you recite another. Either recite just this one or leave it and recite some another." He said: "I will not leave it. If you like me to lead you in prayer this way, I will do it, and if you dislike it I will leave you." They were aware that he was the best of them and they did not like that any other person should lead them in prayer. So when the Prophet ﷺ came to them, they told him of this. He said: "O so and so, what prevents you from doing what your friends ask you to do, and what makes it obligatory for you to recite this chapter in every

---

this incident happened in Makkah (book: 'Prayer', ch. 35). There is a report in the *Muṣannaf* of 'Abdur Razzāq, with sound transmission, that Abū Bakr led the morning prayer in which he recited *Al-Baqarah* over two *rak'ahs.* The statement in this chapter head note that Ibn Mas'ūd recited forty verses of *Al-Anfāl* is also reported in the *Muṣannaf* of 'Abdur Razzāq, where it is made clear that it was from the beginning of this *sūrah.*

[212] The word *Mathānī* is used for those chapters that contain hundred verses or thereabouts. According to some, it is the chapters from chapter 8 up to the group of chapters that are known as *Mufaṣṣal,* the latter being from chapter 50 (*Qāf*) to the end of the Qur'ān.

rak'ah?" He said: "I love it." He (the Holy Prophet) said: "Your love for it (i.e., this chapter) will make you enter Paradise." [213]

775 Abū Wā'il said: A man came to Ibn Mas'ūd and said: "I recited the *Mufaṣṣal* chapters tonight in one *rak'ah*." He (Ibn Mas'ūd) said: "This is like rapid recital of poetry. I know similar chapters which the Prophet ﷺ used to recite together." He mentioned twenty chapters from among the *Mufaṣṣal* chapters, two chapters in each *rak'ah*.[214]

Ch. 107: One should read the opening chapter of the Qur'ān in the last two *rak'ahs*

776 Abū Qatādah reported that the Prophet ﷺ used to recite the *Umm-ul-Kitāb* (opening chapter of the Qur'ān) and two (other) chapters in the *Ẓuhr* prayer in the first two *rak'ahs*, and (only) the *Umm-ul-Kitāb* in the last two *rak'ahs,* and he used to make us hear a verse (sometimes). He used to prolong the first *rak'ah* as he did not in the second *rak'ah.* And it was the same in the *'Aṣr* prayer and the same in the morning prayer.[215]

Ch. 108: One who recites the Qur'ān quietly in the *Ẓuhr* and *'Aṣr* prayers

777 Abū Ma'mar reported: I said to Khabbāb, "Did the Messenger of Allāh ﷺ recite (from the Qur'ān) in the *Ẓuhr* and *'Aṣr* prayers?" He said: "Yes." We said: "How did you know?" He said: "By the movement of his beard." [216]

---

[213] This shows that one particular *sūrah* can be recited in every *rak'ah,* whether some other passages or *sūrahs* are added to it or not.

[214] This man was Nahīk ibn Sanān who recited all the *sūrahs* from *Qāf* (ch. 50) to the end of the Qur'ān in one night. The Arabs used to recite their poems fast and rapidly. That is why 'Abdullāh ibn Mas'ūd told him that he was not reciting the Qur'ān at the necessary slow pace (*tartīl,* the "leisurely pace" mentioned in the Qur'ān, 73 : 4), but fast like poetry. Such recitation fails to achieve the very object of recitation. As to Ibn Mas'ūd saying that he knew which *sūrahs* of the Qur'ān the Holy Prophet used to recite together, he meant the *sūrahs* the Holy Prophet recited in his *Tahajjud* prayer. It is a misconception to think that Ibn Mas'ūd followed an arrangement of the chapters of the Qur'ān different from their established order, in what is known as *Tā'līf Ibn Mas'ūd.* That arrangement relates to reciting *sūrahs* in prayers, not to their sequence in the Qur'ān. As seen in the above reports, in recitation during prayer, a different order could be followed than that of the Qur'ān.

[215] This is a repetition of h. 759 with an addition about the last two *rak'ahs* of the *Ẓuhr* prayer. This connects it with the chapter heading. Thus the third and the fourth *rak'ahs* in the prayer may consist only of the *Fātiḥah* and nothing more.

[216] This is a repetition of h. 746 with very slight variations.

Ch. 109: When the Imām makes any verse to be heard

778 Abū Qatādah reported that the Prophet ﷺ used to recite the *Umm-ul-Kitāb* and another chapter with it in the first two *rak'ahs* of the *Ẓuhr* prayer and the *'Aṣr* prayer, and sometimes he would make us hear a verse. And he used to prolong the first *rak'ah.*[217]

Ch. 110: To prolong (the recitation in) the first *rak'ah*

779 Abū Qatādah reported that the Prophet ﷺ used to prolong the first *rak'ah* in the *Ẓuhr* prayer and shorten the second. And he did the same in the morning prayer. [218]

Ch. 111: The Imām saying *Āmīn* in a loud voice

'Aṭā' said: *Āmīn* is a prayer ('Amen', meaning, Be it so). Ibn Zubair and those who were behind him said *Āmīn* until the mosque resounded with it. And Abū Hurairah used to call aloud to the Imām: "Do not make me miss *Āmīn*." [219] Nāfi' said: Ibn 'Umar would never miss it and used to encourage others, and I have heard from him a report to this effect.

780 Abū Hurairah reported that the Messenger of Allāh ﷺ said: "When the Imām says *Āmīn*, you must also say, *Āmīn*. For surely whosoever's saying of *Āmīn* coincides with the saying of *Āmīn* by the angels, he is forgiven the sins he committed before." [220]

---

[217] This is a repetition in brief of h. 759. See also h. 776.

[218] This is a repetition in brief of h. 759.

[219] Abū Hurairah meant that the Imām should not start the prayer early so as to finish reciting the *Fātiḥah* quickly while he would not be in time for saying *Āmīn* at the end.

[220] The Holy Prophet's saying that when the Imām says *Āmīn* the congregation should also say the same, indicates that *Āmīn* used to be said in a loud voice. However, it is a minor question and depends on the feelings of the moment of the person saying the prayers. No rule can be laid down about it. There are also reports of *Āmīn* being said in a low voice. Difference is to be found in the practice of the Companions, which shows that the Holy Prophet must have said it sometimes loudly and at other times in a low voice. In reciting the Qur'ān during the *Ẓuhr* and *'Aṣr* prayers, the Holy Prophet sometimes used to say a verse to people's hearing.

There is no doubt that saying *Āmīn* loudly draws a person's attention towards his prayer. The coinciding with the saying of *Āmīn* by the angels means that a person's saying of *Āmīn* should be done with the utmost sincerity and devoutness since the angels are always in the state of obedience to God. The saying of *Āmīn* by one who is in the state of perfect obedience to God in his heart is the saying which coincides with the saying of *Āmīn* by the angels.

Ch. 112: The excellence of saying *Āmīn*

781 Abū Hurairah reported that the Messenger of Allāh ﷺ said: "When any of you says *Āmīn* and the angels in the heaven say *Āmīn,* and the one coincides with the other, he is forgiven the sins he committed before."

Ch. 113: The congregation saying *Āmīn* in a loud voice

782 Abū Hurairah reported that the Messenger of Allāh ﷺ said: "When the Imām says *Ghairi-l-maghḍūbi 'alai-him wa la-ḍ-ḍālīn* ('Not those upon whom wrath is brought down, nor those who go astray'), you should say: *Āmīn.* For surely whosoever's saying (of *Āmīn*) coincides with the saying by the angels, he is forgiven the sins he committed before." [221]

Ch. 114: When a person goes into *Rukū'* while not in a row

783 Abū Bakrah reported that he came to the Prophet ﷺ (in the mosque) when he (the Holy Prophet) was in *Rukū',* so he went into *Rukū'* before he could join a row. This was mentioned to the Prophet ﷺ who said: "May Allāh increase your eagerness (to do good) but do not repeat it again."

Ch. 115: Completing the *Takbīr* at *Rukū'* [222]

Ibn 'Abbās reported it from the Prophet ﷺ. Mālik ibn al-Ḥuwairith (also) has a report to this effect. [223]

784 'Imrān ibn Ḥusain reported that he said his prayer with 'Alī in Baṣrah. He said: This man has reminded us of the prayer which we used to say with the Messenger of Allāh ﷺ. Then he mentioned that he ('Alī) used to say *Takbīr* every time he raised his head and every time he bent it. [224]

785 Abū Salamah reported of Abū Hurairah that he used to lead them in prayer and he would say *Takbīr* whenever he lowered and raised (his head).

---

[221] This is a repetition of h. 780 with a difference at the beginning. The inference in the chapter heading is that by saying *Āmīn* is meant that it should be said aloud.

[222] Completing the *Takbīr* means that when going into *Rukū'* the words *Allāhu Akbar* should be uttered distinctly so as to be heard by other people. According to *Fatḥ al-Bārī*, this is intended to refute the weak report of 'Abdur Raḥmān ibn Abzā that he said his prayer with the Holy Prophet and the latter did not utter the *Takbīr* on going into prostration or on rising from it (Abū Dāwūd, book: 'Prayer', h. 837).

[223] The statement of Ibn 'Abbās is contained in h. 787. The report of Mālik ibn al-Ḥuwairith is h. 677, but the reference here is to the repetition of h. 677 in h. 818–819 which contains the words: "then he went into *Rukū'* saying *Allāhu Akbar*".

[224] This report is found in greater detail in h. 786.

When he finished, he said: "I am the one who, out of you all, most resembles the Messenger of Allāh ﷺ in prayer."

Ch. 116: Completing the *Takbīr* at prostration

786 Muṭarrif ibn ʿAbdullāh reported: I said my prayer behind ʿAlī ibn Abū Ṭālib together with ʿImrān ibn Ḥusain. When he (ʿAlī) went into prostration, he said *Takbīr* and when he raised his head he (likewise) said *Takbīr* and when he got up from the (first) two *rakʿahs*, he said *Takbīr*. When he finished the prayer, ʿImrān ibn Ḥusain took me by my hand and said: "This has reminded me of the prayer of Muḥammad ﷺ", or he said: "He has certainly led us in prayer like the prayer of Muḥammad ﷺ." 225

787 ʿIkrimah reported: I saw a man near the Maqām (Ibrāhīm) who was saying *Takbīr* with every lowering and raising (of the head), and when he would stand up, and when he would bend down. I told Ibn ʿAbbās (about it) and he said: "May you have no mother! Is this not the prayer of the Prophet ﷺ?" 226

Ch. 117: Saying the *Takbīr* when standing up from prostration

788 ʿIkrimah reported: I said my prayer behind an elderly man in Makkah and he said *Takbīr* twenty-two times. I said to Ibn ʿAbbās: "Surely he is a stupid man." He said: "May your mother lose you! This is the practice of Abul Qāsim ﷺ." 227

789 Abū Hurairah said: The Messenger of Allāh ﷺ, when he stood up for prayer, used to say *Takbīr* at the time of standing up, then he would say *Takbīr* when going into *Rukūʿ*, then he would say *Samiʿ Allāhu li-man ḥamidah* ("Allāh hears him who praises Him") when raising his back from *Rukūʿ*. Then, while standing, he would say: *Rabba-nā la-ka-l-ḥamd* ("Our Lord! Yours is the praise") — ʿAbdullāh ibn Ṣāliḥ reported from al-Laith: *wa la-ka-l-ḥamd* ("Our Lord! And Yours in the praise"). Then he would say *Takbīr* when going down, then he would say *Takbīr* when raising his head, then he would say

---

225 As mentioned in h. 784, this prayer was said in Baṣrah. The report does not mean that it was only the saying of *Takbīr* that reminded him of the prayer of the Holy Prophet. It seems that there was such depth of sincere feeling in the sounding of *Takbīr* that it overwhelmed him, reminding him of prayer with the Holy Prophet.

226 A report in the Musnad of Aḥmad says that this man was Abū Hurairah. It appears that some people in those days were not very particular about the clear utterance of *Takbīr*, so that the congregation behind them would not hear it. The expression, "May you have no mother", is only to indicate pity and is not abuse.

227 This is a repetition of h. 787. In a prayer of four *rakʿahs* there are twenty-two *Takbīrs*, apart from the one with which the prayer begins.

Takbīr when going into prostration, then he would say *Takbīr* when raising his head. Then he would do the same in the whole of the prayer until he finished it. And he would say *Takbīr* when standing up from the two *rak'ahs* after his sitting.

Ch. 118: Placing of hands on the knees in *Rukū'*

> Abū Ḥumaid, while he was among his companions, said: The Prophet ﷺ would place his two hands firmly on his knees.

790 Abū Ya'fūr reported that he heard Muṣ'ab ibn Sa'd saying: I said my prayer by the side of my father and I joined my two hands, then placed them between my two thighs. My father forbade me to do so and said: "We used to do this but we were forbidden it and we were commanded to place our hands on our knees."

Ch. 119: When the *Rukū'* is not completed properly

791 Zaid ibn Wahb said: Ḥudhaifah saw a man not completing *Rukū'* nor prostrations (*Sujūd*). He said (to him): "You have not said your prayer. If you were to die, you would die in a state of acting contrarily to the religion with which Allāh sent Muḥammad ﷺ." [228]

Ch. 120: Making the back level in *Rukū'*

> Abū Ḥumaid, while he was among his companions, said: The Prophet ﷺ would go in *Rukū'*, then he would bend his back straight.[229]

Ch. 121: The extent of the completion of *Rukū'*, and to be moderate (i.e., level) and restful therein

792 Al-Barā' reported: The *Rukū'* of the Prophet ﷺ and his prostrations (*Sujūd*), and (his pause) between the two prostrations and when he rose from *Rukū'* except his standing and sitting postures (*qiyām* and *qu'ūd*), would almost be equal.[230]

---

[228] This is a repetition of h. 389, with a difference at the end. Instead of "acting contrarily to the *Sunnah* of Muḥammad", the words are literally: "acting contrarily to the *fiṭrah* with which Allāh made Muḥammad". The word *fiṭrah* here means religion or faith. See also h. 808.

[229] The actual ḥadīth of Abū Ḥumaid is at h. 828 where speaking of the *Rukū'* it has been said: "then he would bend his back straight".

[230] That is to say, the two intervals, (1) the standing position after rising from *Rukū'*, and (2) the sitting position between the two *Sajdahs*, should be of the same duration of time as the *Rukū'* or the *Sajdah* itself. This is a warning to those who are in a hurry during these intervals to go into

Ch. 122: The Prophet ﷺ ordering the one who would not complete his *Rukū'* to repeat it

793 Abū Hurairah reported that the Prophet ﷺ entered the mosque and a man also entered who said his prayer. Then he came and greeted the Prophet ﷺ with *Salām.* ...[231]

Ch. 123: Praying during *Rukū'*

794 'Ā'ishah reported that the Prophet ﷺ used to say in his *Rukū'* and his prostrations: *Subḥāna-ka-llāhumma, rabba-nā wa bi-ḥamdi-ka, Allāhumma-ghfir-lī* ("Glory be to You, O Allāh, our Lord, and praise be to You; O Allāh, grant me protection"). [232]

Ch. 124: What should the Imām and those behind him say, when he raises his head from *Rukū'*?

795 Abū Hurairah reported: The Prophet ﷺ, when he used to say *Sami' Allāhu li-man ḥamidah* ("Allāh hears him who praises Him"), he would say: *Allāhumma Rabba-nā wa la-ka-l-ḥamd* ("O Allah, our Lord! And Yours is the praise"). When the Prophet ﷺ used to go into *Rukū'* and when he raised his head (from it), he would say *Takbīr.* When he stood after the two prostrations, he would say *Allāhu Akbar.*[233]

Ch. 125: Excellence of (saying): *Allāhumma Rabba-nā la-ka-l-ḥamd* ("O Allāh, Yours is the praise")

796 Abū Hurairah reported that the Messenger of Allāh ﷺ said: "When the Imām says *Sami' Allāhu li-man ḥamidah* ('Allāh hears him who praises

---

prostration without any pause. There are certain prayers to be said during these intervals before going into prostration. See also h. 801 and h. 820.

[231] This is a repetition of h. 757 with minor differences. That ḥadīth ends with the words: "then perform prostration until you are restful in *Sajdah,* then rise up until you are restful in sitting, and do this in every prayer of yours", while here in h. 793 the second prostration is added as follows: "then perform prostration until you are restful in *Sajdah,* then rise up until you are restful in sitting, then perform prostration until you are restful in *Sajdah.* Then do this in every prayer of yours."

[232] Submission of petition (*du'ā'*) to God of any kind of need or desire is allowed in any language at any stage in prayer. Petitions during *Rukū'* and the prostrations are mentioned here, in which the Holy Prophet used to ask Allāh's protection or forgiveness. It is a mistake to think that making petitions of one's own during *Rukū'* is undesirable. There is a report in Ṣaḥīḥ Muslim: "As for *Rukū',* proclaim in it the greatness of the Lord, the Mighty, the Glorious, and as for *Sajdah,* strive to make *du'ā'* so that it is answered" (book: 'Prayer', ch. 41). This does not mean that a supplication or *du'ā'* should not be made during *Rukū'.* Submitting a petition to God is also a way of proclaiming His greatness. See also the repetition of this in h. 817.

[233] This is a repetition of h. 789 in brief.

Him'), you should say *Allāhumma Rabba-nā la-ka-l-ḥamd* ('O Allāh! our Lord! Yours is the praise').[234] For surely whosoever's saying coincides with the saying by the angels, he is forgiven the sins he committed before.[235]

Ch. 126: Related to the last chapter[236]

797 Abū Hurairah reported: I will certainly try to be close to the prayer of the Prophet ﷺ. Abū Hurairah used to say the (prayer known as) *Qunūt* in the last *rak'ah* of the *Ẓuhr* prayer and the *'Ishā'* prayer and the morning prayer after he had said *Sami' Allāhu li-man ḥamidah* ("Allāh hears him who praises Him"). And he used to pray for the believers and curse the unbelievers.[237]

798 Anas reported: The *Qunūt* used to be said in the *Maghrib* and *Fajr* prayers.[238]

799 Rifā'ah ibn Rāfi' az-Zuraqī reported: One day we were saying prayers behind the Prophet ﷺ. When he raised his head from *Rukū'*, he said: *Sami' Allāhu li-man ḥamidah* ("Allāh hears him who praises Him"). A man who was behind him said: *Rabba-nā wa la-ka-l-ḥamd, ḥamd-an kathīr-an ṭayyib-an mubārak-an fīhi* ("Our Lord, and Yours is the praise, a praise in which is abundance, purity and blessing"). When he (the Holy Prophet) finished (the prayer), he asked: "Who said this?" He (the man) said: "I". He (the Holy Prophet) said: "I saw thirty angels, and some more, racing with one another to see who among them would be the first to write it down." [239]

---

[234] Followers of Imām Abū Ḥanīfah and Imām Mālik have inferred from this that the Imām is not to say *Allāhumma Rabba-nā la-ka-l-ḥamd.* But this inference is not correct because, according to h. 795, the Holy Prophet himself said these words.

[235] See this last statement in h. 782.

[236] This chapter speaks of the prayer known as *Qunūt,* which is recited after rising from *Rukū',* hence it has no separate heading.

[237] For a number of days the Holy Prophet, in the *Qunūt* prayer, sent curses on those unbelievers who had murdered his seventy innocent reciters of the Qur'ān by treachery and deceit. But he was stopped by the following verse of the Qur'ān: "You have no concern in the matter whether He turns to them (mercifully) or punishes them; surely they are wrongdoers" (3 : 128). Abū Hurairah is not drawing attention to the curses but to the fact that the Holy Prophet used to address at times a special prayer in the course of the established formal prayer. Otherwise, the fact that the Holy Prophet was stopped by Divine intervention from sending curses shows that it is not allowed in Islām. Of course, in h. 804 it is mentioned that he sent curses on the unbelievers of the Quraish for famine to overtake them, but this again was to bring them to their senses and was prompted by the desire of their spiritual regeneration.

[238] In h. 797 from Abū Hurairah it is stated that the *Qunūt* prayer used to be recited in the *Ẓuhr, 'Ishā'* and *Fajr* prayers. But here Anas says that it was in the *Fajr* and *Maghrib* prayers. Perhaps at one time this was done in particular in the *Fajr* and *Maghrib* prayers, and on certain occasions in the other prayers.

[239] Obviously, the man's exclamation was a natural and spontaneous expression of a deep

Ch. 127: Calm posture when raising the head from *Rukū'*

Abū Ḥumaid said: The Prophet ﷺ raised (his head from *Rukū'*) and stood straight until every joint returned to its place.

800 Thābit reported: Anas used to demonstrate to us the prayer of the Prophet ﷺ. He used to pray, and when he would raise his head from *Rukū'*, he stood for so long that we would say: "He has forgotten." [240]

801 Al-Barā' reported: The *Rukū'* of the Prophet ﷺ, and his prostrations, and (his pause) when he raised his head from *Rukū'* and between the two prostrations, would almost be equal.[241]

802 Abū Qilābah reported: Mālik ibn al-Ḥuwairith used to show us how was the prayer of the Prophet ﷺ, and this was at a time other than the time of prayer. So he stood up and made the standing perfect, then he went into *Rukū'* and made the *Rukū'* perfect, then he raised his head and remained in this position for a while.

He (Abū Qilābah) added: So he led us in prayer like the prayer of this Shaikh of ours, Abū Yazīd. And Abū Yazīd, when he would raise his head from the second *Sajdah,* he would sit up completely and then stand up (for the next *rak'ah*).[242]

Ch. 128: When going in prostration, saying *Takbīr*

Nāfi' said: Ibn 'Umar used to place his hands (on the ground) before his knees.[243]

803 Abū Salamah ibn 'Abdur Raḥmān informed that Abū Hurairah used to say *Takbīr* in every prayer, whether obligatory or otherwise, in the month of Ramaḍān and (also) at other times. He used to say *Takbīr* at the time of standing up, then he would say *Takbīr* when going in *Rukū'*, then he would say, *Sami' Allāhu li-man ḥamidah* ("Allāh hears him who praises Him"), then he would say, *Rabba-nā wa la-ka-l-ḥamd,* before going in prostration. Then

---

feeling and was accordingly readily acceptable to God. It is this acceptability that is described here by the expression of thirty angels, and some more, vying with one another to record the event. This is another way of saying that the event has been preserved forever.

[240] This is a repetition in brief of h. 821. That ḥadīth also mentions the similar time that the Holy Prophet used to spend in the sitting position between two *Sajdahs.*

[241] This is a repetition of h. 792, without the mention of the exception relating to his standing and sitting postures. See also h. 820.

[242] This is a repetition of h. 677 in different words.

[243] This is just an act of Ibn 'Umar, and although this is also permissible, the normal physical sequence is for the knees to touch the ground before the hands.

he would say *Allāhu Akbar* when going in prostration, then he would say *Takbīr* when raising his head from prostration, then he would say *Takbīr* when going in prostration, then he would say *Takbīr* when raising his head from prostration, then he would say *Takbīr* when standing up from sitting after the *two rak'ahs*. He would do this in every *rak'ah* till he would be free from the prayer. Then, when he had finished, he would say: "By Him in Whose hand is my life, I am surely the closest in resemblance to the prayer of the Messenger of Allāh ﷺ." This indeed used to be his prayer till he left the world." [244]

804 Abū Hurairah said: And the Messenger of Allāh ﷺ, when he raised his head (from *Rukū'*), would say: *Sami' Allāhu li-man ḥamidah, Rabba-nā wa la-ka-l-ḥamd,* and pray for certain men whom he would mention by name, and say: "O Allāh, give salvation to al-Walīd ibn al-Walīd and Salamah ibn Hishām and 'Ayyāsh ibn Abū Rabī'ah and the weak from among the believers! O Allāh, make your punishment severe for the Muḍar and bring upon them years (of famine) like the years of (the time of) Joseph!" And the eastern people from among (the tribe of) the Muḍar used to be hostile to him in those days. [245]

805 Anas ibn Mālik said: The Messenger of Allāh ﷺ fell from a horse and his right side got bruised thereby, so we went to him to visit him in his illness. The time for prayer came, and he led us in prayer sitting while we also sat (behind him praying). When he finished the prayer, he said: "The Imām is appointed to be followed: so when he says *Allāhu Akbar*, you must say *Allāhu Akbar,* and when he bows (*Rukū'*), you must bow, and when he rises up, you must rise up, and when he says, *Sami' Allāhu li-man ḥamidah* ('Allāh hears him who praises Him'), say: *Rabba-nā wa la-ka-l-ḥamd* ('Our Lord! And Yours is the praise'), and when he prostrates (*Sajdah*), you must prostrate." [246]

---

[244] This ḥadīth, up to the words "then he would say *Takbīr* when standing up from sitting after the *two rak'ahs*", very much resembles h. 789. However, here it is described as the act of Abū Hurairah whereas in h. 789 he reports it as the act of the Holy Prophet himself.

[245] This report resembles h. 797 in speaking of the prayer known as *Qunūt* with the difference that in h. 797 it is the description of an act of Abū Hurairah whereas here he ascribes it to the Holy Prophet. It can be seen that the reason for the Holy Prophet's curses on the unbelievers was for the deliverance of Muslims from the hands of those persecutors. The other object seems to be that when all other methods have failed, some such calamity might bring them to their senses and make their hearts bow before God. Thus when famine visited the Makkans after the prayer of the Holy Prophet some of these unbelievers approached him for a prayer to God on their behalf to remove their suffering.

[246] This is a repetition of h. 378 with wording closer to the repetition of the same in h. 689. The closing words about prostrating, not found in h. 689, connect this ḥadīth with chapter heading, and this is made clear by the following words in h. 803: "Then he would say *Allāhu Akbar* when going in prostration".

Abū Juraij said that his right calf muscle was bruised.

Ch. 129: The excellence of prostration[247]

806 Abū Hurairah informed that the people said: "O Messenger of Allāh, shall we see our Lord on the day of Resurrection"? He said: "Do you doubt about the moon on the night of the full moon when there is no cloud around it?" They said: "No, O Messenger of Allāh." He said: "Then do you doubt about the sun when there is no cloud around it?" They said: "No." He said: "So, surely you will see Him in like manner.[248] On the day of Resurrection when the people will be gathered and He will say: 'Whosoever used to worship anything (else), let him follow it.' So among them will be those who will follow the sun and among them will be those who follow the moon and among them will be those who follow the devils.[249] This *Ummah* (i.e., the Muslims) will remain, in which will be its hypocrites. So Allāh will come to them and will say: 'I am your Lord.' They will say: 'This is our place till our Lord comes to us, and when our Lord will come, we shall know Him.' So Allāh, the Mighty, the Glorious, will come to them (again) and will say: 'I am your Lord.' They will say: 'You are our Lord.' So He will call them and a way (*sirāt*) will be thrown across Hell,[250] and I shall be the first among the Messengers to cross over it with my community. No one on that day will speak

---

[247] For the connection of the following ḥadīth h. 806 with this chapter heading, see footnote 252 on this ḥadīth further along.

[248] The vision of God has already been discussed in footnote 41 to h. 554. From what has been said here, it is clear that in h. 554 the words "not be hindering each other" (*lā tuḍāmmūna*) mean nothing but that all people will perceive the existence of God as they perceive the existence of the sun and the moon.

[249] This shows that the purpose of worshipping God is to seek contact with Him. Thus a man will see only what he has been worshipping in his life. The worshippers of the sun will see the sun but the worshippers of God will see God. The word *ṭāghūt* (the plural of which, *ṭawāghīt*, is used here) means idol and devil as well as the man who goes beyond all limits in unbelief and evil-doing. Hence the word here may mean the leaders of the unbelievers (see *Nihāyah*).

[250] This is the way known as the *sirāt* bridge. The word *sirāt* means 'a way', and as it is mentioned here that it will be laid above or across hell, it is called the *sirāt* bridge. What will be the nature of this passage, it is difficult to say and is known only to God. The object evidently is to separate the hypocrites from the believers. Believers, those who walk on the right path in this life, will find themselves on the right path on that fearful day, whereas hypocrites who would in this life, to outward appearance, be siding with the believers but would not be really on the right path, will be unable to follow this path on the Judgment day. According to the Qur'ān, the ability to walk over this bridge of the next life is developed by man in this life: "And whoever is blind in this (world), he will be blind in the Hereafter, and further away from the path" (17:72). The straight path of going over and across Hell means that those who walk on this path need all the alertness and vigilance of a man who is always in danger of falling over a precipice at the slightest unmindfulness.

except the Messengers, and the words of the Messengers on that day will be: 'O Allāh! grant peace, grant peace.' In Hell there will be hooks like the thorns of as-Sa'dān. Have you seen the thorns of as-Sa'dān?" They said: "Yes."

He (the Holy Prophet) continued: "So surely it will be like the thorns of as-Sa'dān but no one will know their largeness except Allāh. They will entangle people according to their actions.[251] So among them will be those who will perish on account of their actions, and among them will be those who will be smashed to pieces. Then they will be saved until when Allāh wills to show mercy to whomsoever He wills from among the inmates of the Fire (of Hell). Allāh will command the angels that they should take out those who were worshipping Allāh, so they will be taking them out and will recognize them from the signs of prostration. And Allāh has forbidden it for the Fire that it should expunge the mark of prostration.[252] So they will come out of the Fire and the Fire will consume the whole of the son of Adam except the mark of prostration. So they will come out of the Fire while they will have been burnt black and on them will be poured the water of (eternal) life and they will grow as the grain grows in the silt left by the flood.[253]

Then Allāh will have finished the judgment between His servants, and there will remain one man (suspended) between the Garden (i.e., Heaven or Paradise) and the Fire (of Hell), and he will be the last among the inmates of the Fire who will have entered Heaven[254] and he will have his face turned

---

[251] These thorny shrubs of Hell are in fact the creations of man's evil actions in this life whereas the fruits of righteous deeds in this life will be manifested in happiness and delicious fruits. The obstructions in this life which hindered the spiritual progress of a man will be found manifested in the form of thorns and thorny shrubs preventing him from reaching heaven.

[252] The connection of this ḥadīth with the chapter heading lies in its reference to the marks of prostration. Such marks, it is stated here, cannot be consumed by the fire of Hell. A mark on the body cannot be meant because the real objective of prayer is not to create any impression on the body of man but to mould the soul inside. It is the invisible mark on the soul which is meant. With every real prostration the soul acquires additional humility and submission, and the resulting connection with God is such that nothing in the world or in the Hereafter can remove it. Evidently, it is this effect of prostration that the fire of Hell will be unable to undo and on the basis of this the person will obtain his deliverance from Hell in the long run.

[253] That is to say, man will receive a new life after the fire of Hell has consumed all the germs of spiritual disease that had entered within him due to his own misdeeds and removed all the obstructions that were retarding spiritual progress. The fire being the most powerful of all elements for removing the dross, its spiritual counterpart in the life Hereafter will be used for the purification of all the filth sticking to the soul of a man in consequence of his evil deeds and he will be enabled to live a new and holy life that will be in heaven. See also h. 22 and footnotes under it.

[254] It is obvious that it will not be only one man but many. The number of one has been used

towards the Fire and he will say: 'My Lord, turn my face away from the Fire and its smell has already killed me and its scorching heat already burnt me.' So He will say: 'Is it not possible that if this is done to you, you will ask for more besides this?' He will say: 'No, by Your honour!' And he will give Allāh, the Mighty, the Glorious, a promise and a covenant as he wishes. So Allāh will turn his face from the Fire. When he will turn his face towards Heaven he will see its pleasant appearance and he will remain silent as much as Allāh wills that he should remain silent. Then he will say: 'My Lord, let me advance up to the gate of Heaven', and Allāh will say to him: 'Did you not give promises and covenants that you will not ask for more besides what you had already asked for?' He will say: 'My Lord, let me not be the most wretched of Your creatures.' He (Allāh) will say: Is it not possible that if you are given this, you will ask for more besides this?' He will say: 'No, by Your honour! I will not ask for more besides this.' So he will give his Lord a promise and a covenant as he wishes.

He (Allāh) will let him advance towards the gate of Heaven. When he will reach its gate and see its beauty, and what is in it of freshness and happiness, he will remain silent as much as Allāh wills that he should remain silent. Then he will say: 'My Lord, let me enter Heaven', and Allāh, the Mighty, the Glorious, will say: 'Alas for you, O son of Adam, how unfaithful you are! Did you not give the promise and the covenant that you will not ask for more besides what you have been given?' He will say: 'My Lord! Do not make me the most wretched of Your creatures.' So Allāh will be pleased[255] with him, then allow him to enter Heaven. He will say: 'Express a desire!' So he will express his desire until all his desires will be fulfilled. Allāh, the Mighty, the Glorious, will say: 'Desire more of such and such.' His Lord will go on reminding him until when all his desires will be fulfilled, Allāh, the Most High, will say: 'For you is this and as much again.' "

Abū Saʿīd al-Khudrī told Abū Hurairah that the Messenger of Allāh ﷺ said that Allāh, the Mighty, the Glorious, said: "For you is this and ten times like it." Abū Hurairah said: I remember from the Messenger of Allāh ﷺ

---

here to indicate a typical case. Those who have kept before their eyes nothing but the satisfaction of their low desires will find nothing but a kind of fire burning in their souls. The grace of God, however, will save them from the fire and enable them to raise their eyes to the higher life. Seeing its joy and freshness, he advances towards it till he attains the highest places.

[255] The verb *ḍaḥika,* from the root *ḍ-ḥ-k,* would generally mean 'to laugh' but should not be taken literally here in this sense. It also means 'to be pleased' or 'to wonder' because laughing refers to a certain facial expression. As applied to God the sense cannot be laughter as He does not have a body like a human being.

nothing but his saying: "For you is this and as much again." Abū Saʿīd said: I surely heard him say: "For you is this and ten times like it." [256]

Ch. 130: Keeping the arms open and away from the sides in prostration

807 ʿAbdullāh ibn Mālik ibn Buḥainah reported that the Prophet ﷺ, when he said his prayers, used to keep his hands so far apart (from the body) that the whiteness of his armpits was visible.[257]

Ch. 131: Toes should face the *Qiblah*

Abū Ḥumaid as-Sāʿidiyy reported it from the Prophet ﷺ.[258]

Ch. 132: When prostrations are not completed (properly)

808 Ḥudhaifah reported that he saw a man not completing his *Rukūʿ* nor his prostrations (*Sujūd*). …[259]

Ch. 133: Prostration (resting) upon seven bones

809 Ibn ʿAbbās reported: The Prophet ﷺ was commanded (by Allāh) to prostrate on seven parts, and not tidy up hair or clothes; (the seven are:) the forehead, both hands, both knees and (the toes of) both feet.[260]

810 Ibn ʿAbbās reported from the Prophet ﷺ that he said: "We have been commanded (by Allāh) to prostrate on seven bones and not tidy up hair or clothes." [261]

---

[256] The meaning is that when the wonders of the life Hereafter open out before man, he experiences such great pleasure that it is beyond his wildest imagination and his greatest possible desires. As to whether the Holy Prophet said "as much again" or "ten times like it", in such a long narration all the words are not necessarily exactly what he said. Abū Hurairah may have related the general sense.

[257] This ḥadīth and its chapter heading are repetitions of h. 390 and its chapter heading. The meaning is that a posture should be adopted in prostration that may indicate, not carelessness and laxity, but alertness and awareness.

[258] This chapter heading is a repetition of the statement under the heading of ch. 28 of the Book of Prayer. We find similar words in a detailed ḥadīth by this very narrator Abū Ḥumaid in h. 828: "And he (the Holy Prophet) would turn his toes towards the *Qiblah*."

[259] This chapter heading and ḥadīth have already occurred in the same words in the Book of Prayer as ch. 26 and h. 389. See also h. 791.

[260] This is the best form of prostration, which has both a fine physical appearance and creates the utmost humility in the heart. The instruction not to care for the hair or the clothes is directed against those who attend to their external appearance while going into, and rising from, the postures of *Rukūʿ* and *Sajdah,* and thus become inattentive to their prayer.

[261] This is a briefer repetition of h. 809.

811 Al-Barā' ibn 'Āzib, who never lied, related: We used to say prayers behind the Prophet ﷺ. When he would say *Sami' Allāhu li-man ḥamidah* ("Allāh hears him who praises Him"), none of us would bend his back until the Prophet ﷺ had placed his forehead on the ground. [262]

Ch. 134: Prostration on the nose

812 Ibn 'Abbās reported that the Prophet ﷺ said: "I have been commanded (by Allāh) to prostrate on seven bones: on the forehead" — and he pointed with his hand towards his nose — "and both hands, both knees, and toes of both feet, and not tidy up clothes or hair." [263]

Ch. 135: Prostration on the nose in the mud

813 Abū Salamah reported: I went to Abū Sa'īd al-Khudrī and said: "Are you not coming out with us towards the date trees so that we may talk?" So he came out and I said: "Relate to me what you have heard from the Prophet ﷺ about *Lailat-ul-Qadr* (the Night of Majesty)." He said: "The Messenger of Allāh ﷺ was observing *I'tikāf* (devotional retirement to the mosque) for the first ten days of Ramaḍān and we were also observing *I'tikāf* with him. Gabriel came to him and said: 'Surely what you are seeking is ahead of you.' Then he observed *I'tikāf* for the middle ten days (of Ramaḍān) and we also observed *I'tikāf* with him. Gabriel came to him and said: 'Surely what you are seeking is ahead of you.' Then the Prophet ﷺ stood up, addressing (us) on the morning of the 20th of Ramaḍān and said:

'Whoever has been observing *I'tikāf* with the Prophet ﷺ should return (to observing *I'tikāf*). For surely I have been shown the (date of) *Lailat-ul-Qadr* but I have forgotten it. It is surely in the last ten among the odd ones.[264] And surely I saw (in a dream) as if I am performing *Sajdah* in mud and water.'

---

[262] This is a repetition of h. 690, but with the words referring to the placing of the forehead on the ground, instead of referring to prostrating. While the chapter heading and h. 809 and h. 810 mention seven bones or parts, this mentions only the forehead as it is the noblest of those seven parts of the body.

[263] This is a repetition of h. 809 containing a mention of the Holy Prophet's pointing towards his nose, not found in h. 809. After mentioning the forehead, he placed his hand on it and drew it down towards his nose to indicate that the nose too, along with the forehead, should be placed on the ground. The nose symbolizes the honour of a person more than any other part of his body. While h. 809 refers to "both feet" (*rijlain*), this ḥadīth clarifies it by saying, literally, "the ends of the footsteps (*aṭrāf al-qadamain*)", meaning the toes.

[264] That is to say, the Holy Prophet was told the period of *Lailat-ul-Qadr* before this, namely,

The roof of the Mosque was made of branches of palm trees, and we had not seen anything in the sky. Then a patch of cloud appeared and rain came upon us. The Prophet ﷺ led us in prayer until I saw signs of mud on the forehead and the end of the nose of the Messenger of Allāh ﷺ — the fulfilment of his dream." [265]

Ch. 136: Knotting of garments and wrapping them round

> And he who wraps his garment around him for fear of exposing himself.

814 Sahl ibn Saʿd reported: Men used to say their prayers with the Prophet ﷺ, tying their waist-wrappers, on account of short size, around their necks. So the women were told: Do not raise your heads until the men are sitting upright.[266]

Ch. 137: Not to tidy up one's hair (during prayer)

815 Ibn ʿAbbās reported: The Prophet ﷺ was commanded (by Allāh) to prostrate on seven bones, and not tidy up his clothes or his hair.[267]

Ch. 138: Not to tidy up one's garments during prayer

816 Ibn ʿAbbās reported from the Prophet ﷺ that he said: "I have been

---

it was one of the odd nights of the last ten days of the month of Ramaḍān. He forgot all about it and accordingly sat in the devotional retirement of *I'tikāf* for the first ten days of the month, and after that for the middle ten days, and it was when the morning of the 20th arrived that he remembered that the real time was the last ten days. The Holy Prophet's words instructing a return to observing *I'tikāf* show that his forgetting the information was under a Divine plan to make people sit longer for this devotional retirement.

[265] This ḥadīth is repeated in h. 2016, h. 2018, h. 2027, h. 2036 and h. 2040. In h. 2018 and h. 2027 it is reported that this rain took place on the night of the 21st and the Holy Prophet's prostration in water and mud was during the morning prayers on the 21st. The dream was fulfilled on the morning of the 21st, showing that *Lailat-ul-Qadr* in that particular year had taken place on the preceding night of the 21st. (Note that in the Islamic calendar, the day is considered to begin at sunset, so the night of the 21st would precede the daytime of the 21st.)

[266] This is a repetition of h. 362. Here, after the words, "tying their waist-wrappers (*uzr*, plural of *izār*)", it is added: "on account of short size". So whereas in h. 362 it mentions "tying their waist-wrappers around their necks in the manner of children", here it is made clear that these people were obliged to do so on account of the short size of the clothes on them. Since according to h. 812 it is forbidden to gather or tidy one's clothes or hair in the course of prayer, here it is made clear that in case of fear of exposure of private parts, or for other necessity, this is not forbidden.

[267] This is a repetition of h. 809. Prostrating on "seven bones" means to prostrate in a proper way in which the forehead, the forearms etc. touch the ground.

commanded (by Allāh) to prostrate on seven (bones), and not tidy up hair or clothes." [268]

Ch. 139: Glorification of Allāh and supplication (to Him) during prostration

817 ʿĀʾishah reported: The Prophet ﷺ used to say frequently in his *Rukūʿ* and his prostrations: "Glory be to You, O Allāh, our Lord, and praise be to You; O Allāh, grant me protection," in pursuance of the Qurʾān.[269]

Ch. 140: Waiting between the two prostrations

818–819 Abū Qilābah reported that Mālik ibn al-Ḥawairith said to his companions: "Shall I tell you the manner of prayer of the Messenger of Allāh ﷺ?" And this was done when it was not the time of prayer. So he stood up, then he went into *Rukūʿ* saying *Allāhu Akbar,* then he raised his head. He stood for a while, then he went into prostration, then he raised his head for a while, then he went into prostration (again), then he raised his head for a while. So he said his prayer in the manner of ʿAmr ibn Salimah, this shaikh of ours. Ayyūb said: "He (ʿAmr ibn Salimah) used to do a certain thing which I do not see people doing now. He used to sit (for a while) in the third or fourth *rakʿah.*" [270]

[819] He (Mālik ibn al-Ḥawairith) said: We went to the Prophet ﷺ and stayed with him and he said: "When you return to your people, say such and such prayer at such and such time, and say such and such a prayer at such and such time, and when the time for prayer comes, one of you should give the call to prayer and the eldest among you should act as your Imām." [271]

---

[268] See h. 809. As in h. 812, the first person is used here: "I have been commanded".

[269] This is a repetition of h. 794, with the closing words added: "in pursuance of the Qurʾān". These words mean that he used to recite this prayer in obedience to the commandment of God revealed in the Qurʾān, and that command is: "Celebrate the praise of your Lord and seek His protection (or forgiveness); surely He is ever returning (to mercy)" (110:3). This shows that whatever special prayer the Holy Prophet recited was, in fact, in obedience to some injunction of the Qurʾān.

[270] This is a repetition of h. 677. The connection with the chapter heading is only the words "then he went into prostration, then he raised his head for a while". The repetition of these words is not found in some manuscripts, and this repetition means that after the second *Sajdah* of the first *rakʿah* and of the third *rakʿah* (in a four *rakʿah* prayer) he sat for a while before standing up. This sitting is called *jalsah al-istirāḥah.* The words "He used to sit in the third or fourth *rakʿah*" mean that at the end of the third *rakʿah,* or in other words at the beginning of the fourth, he would sit for a while before getting up.

[271] This is a repetition of h. 628. See also h. 631 and h. 685.

820 Al-Barā' reported: The prostrations (*Sujūd*) of the Prophet ﷺ and his *Rukū'* and his sitting between the two prostrations would almost be equal.[272]

821 Anas reported: I shall not fail in leading you in prayer as I saw the Prophet ﷺ leading us in prayer. Thābit (who reported this from Anas) said: Anas did something which I do not see you doing — when he would raise his head from *Rukū'*, he would stand for so long that someone would say, "he has forgotten", and (he would sit) between the two prostrations until someone would say, "he has forgotten".

Ch. 141: Not to place one's forearms on the floor during prostrations

> Abū Ḥumaid said: The Prophet ﷺ went into prostration and placed his hands (on the ground), neither spreading (his forearms) on the ground nor keeping them close to the body.

822 Anas ibn Mālik reported from the Prophet ﷺ that he said: "Perform your prostrations properly and none of you should stretch his forearms like a dog." [273]

Ch. 142: Sitting (after prostration) in odd *rak'ahs* of prayer, then standing up (for the second or fourth *rak'ah*)

823 Mālik ibn al-Ḥuwairith al-Laithī informed that he saw the Prophet ﷺ while he was praying, and when he was in the odd *rak'ah* of the prayer he would not get up until he had sat fully.[274]

Ch. 143: How to support oneself on the ground when getting up to stand after completion of a *rak'ah*

824 Abū Qilābah reported: Mālik ibn al-Ḥuwairith came to us and led us in prayer in this our mosque. Then he said: "I am going to lead you in prayer but I do not intend to pray; rather, I intend to show you how I saw the Prophet ﷺ saying his prayers."

---

[272] This is a repetition of h. 792, without some of its words. See also h. 801.

[273] That is to say, your forearms should not be spread on the ground while in prostration as a dog spreads its forelegs on the ground while sitting. This prohibition is aimed at removing the inclination to be lax in the course of prayer.

[274] This is a repetition of h. 677 in different words. This sitting before getting up for the second or the fourth *rak'ah* has been regarded as desirable by Imām Shāfi'ī and some other authorities on Ḥadīth. But there are reports which omit the mention of this sitting. According to one report, towards the close of Holy Prophet's life his body had grown heavy, and it is possible that because of this he rested momentarily before standing up for the second and the fourth *rak'ahs*. See the next footnote and the report from Ibn Mas'ūd mentioned in it.

Ayyūb said that he asked Abū Qilābah how was his (i.e., Mālik's) prayer. He said: It was like the prayer of this Shaikh of ours, meaning Amr ibn Salimah. Ayyūb said: And that Shaikh used to complete the *Takbīr* and when he raised his head from the second prostration he would sit and support himself on the ground, and then stand up.[275]

Ch. 144: *Allāhu Akbar* should be said before rising from the two prostrations

Ibn Zubair used to say *Allāhu Akbar* when rising.

825 Sa'īd ibn al-Ḥārith reported: Abū Sa'īd (al-Khudrī) led us in prayer and he uttered *Takbīr* loudly when he raised his head from prostration, and when he went into prostration and when he raised (his head) again and when he stood up from the two *rak'ahs*. He said: "I saw the Prophet ﷺ doing it like this." [276]

826 Muṭarrif (ibn 'Abdullāh) reported: I and 'Imrān (ibn Ḥusain) prayed behind 'Alī ibn Abū Ṭālib. When he went into prostration, he said *Takbīr,* and when he rose he said *Takbīr,* and when he got up from the (first) two *rak'ahs* he said *Takbīr.* When he finished with *Salām,* 'Imrān took me by my hand and said: "He has certainly led us in this prayer like the prayer of Muḥammad ﷺ", or he said: "This has reminded me of the prayer of Muḥammad ﷺ.[277]

Ch. 145: Prophet's manner of sitting for saying *Tashahhud*

Umm ad-Dardā' sat in her prayer as men sat, and she was well-versed in jurisprudence.[278]

827 'Abdullāh ibn 'Abdullāh informed that he saw 'Abdullāh ibn 'Umar sitting cross-legged when he sat in prayer. (He added:) So I did the same, and

---

[275] This is a repetition of h. 677; see also h. 818. It is reported from Ibn Mas'ūd with sound transmission that the Holy Prophet "used to get up on the toes of his feet." In other words, he did not lean on the ground while rising from prostration to take the standing position. It is for this reason that according to the Ḥanafī jurisprudence it is improper to lean on the ground at this stage of prayer. Here, as in h. 818, the name of the Shaikh is given as 'Amr ibn Salimah. The closing statement in this repetition, about what the Shaikh used to do, is different from that in h. 677. Ḥanafī jurisprudence makes this sitting before standing up as conditional on inability.

[276] The *Takbīr* (*Allāhu Akbar*) can be uttered while getting up after performing two *rak'ahs* or when actually reaching the standing position. Bukhārī is in favour of the first view while Imām Mālik supports the second. This is only a minor point.

[277] H. 786 is repeated here in almost the same words.

[278] This lady, Umm ad-Dardā', was not a Companion of the Holy Prophet, but belonged to the next generation after the Companions, known as the *Tābi'īn.*

at that time I was young. ʿAbdullāh ibn ʿUmar forbade me and said: "The way you should sit in prayer is that your right foot is propped up (on its toes) and the left is folded." I said: "But you do it like that (crossing your legs)." He replied: "My two feet are unable to bear my weight." [279]

828 Muḥammad ibn ʿAmr ibn ʿAṭāʾ reported that he was sitting with some of the Companions of the Prophet ﷺ, and (he added) we were discussing how the Prophet ﷺ said his prayers. Abū Ḥumaid as-Saʿidī said: I am one who has preserved in memory more than any of you the (manner of saying) prayers of the Messenger of Allāh ﷺ. I observed that when he said *Allāhu Akbar,* he would raise his hands as high as his shoulders. Then when he went into *Rukūʿ* he would place his hands on his knees, then he would bend his back straight; when he raised his head, he would straighten himself until every joint had returned to its place. He would go into prostration placing his hands (on the ground), neither spreading (his forearms) on the ground nor keeping them close to the body, and he would turn his toes towards the *Qiblah*. When sitting after the two *rakʿahs* he would sit on his left foot and prop up the right one (on its toes). When sitting in the last *rakʿah* he pushed his left foot forward, keeping the other one standing, and sat on his sitting place.[280]

Ch. 146: Is it unnecessary to say the first *Tashahhud,* because the Prophet ﷺ once stood up after the two *rakʿahs* and did not assume a sitting posture?

829 ʿAbdullāh ibn Buḥainah, who belonged to the Azd-i Shanūʾah tribe, which was an ally of Banī ʿAbd-i Manāf, and was a Companion of the Prophet ﷺ, said that the Prophet ﷺ led them in the *Ẓuhr* prayer, and he stood up after the first two *rakʿahs* and did not sit down. The people stood up with him. When the prayer was about to end and people were waiting for his *Taslīm*,[281] he called out *Allāhu Akbar* while he was sitting and performed two prostrations before saying the *Salām* and then he said the *Salām*.[282]

---

[279] The right foot is to be kept perpendicular to the ground, putting the weight of the body on the left foot which is lying on its back on the ground. But in cases of any physical difficulty, any manner can be adopted in this posture.

[280] Here it is mentioned that while sitting after the second *rakʿah* the Holy Prophet used to sit on his left foot, lying its back on the ground, and that while sitting after the last *rakʿah* he used to slip forward his left foot placing the burden of the body directly on the ground. This was done perhaps to make the sitting more comfortable due to the longer length of sitting in the second case.

[281] *Taslīm,* or *Salām,* is the saying of *as-salāmu ʿalai-kum wa raḥmatu-llāh,* turning the face first to the right and then to the left, with which the prayer comes to an end.

[282] Such a *Sajdah* is called *Sajdah Sahw,* that is, a prostration for a mistake committed in the course of prayer. Its details follow later in Book 22.

Ch. 147: *Tashahhud* in the first sitting posture

830 ʿAbdullāh ibn Mālik ibn Buḥainah reported: The Messenger of Allāh ﷺ led us in the *Ẓuhr* prayer, and he stood up when he should have been sitting. So when he was at the end of his prayer he performed two prostrations while he was sitting.[283]

Ch. 148: *Tashahhud* in the last sitting posture

831 ʿAbdullāh (ibn Masʿūd) said: When we prayed behind the Prophet ﷺ we recited: "Peace be on Gabriel and Michael, peace be on so-and-so." Once the Messenger of Allāh ﷺ turned towards us and said: "Surely Allāh Himself is Peace,[284] so if anyone of you prays, he should say: 'All services (*At-taḥiyyāt*) rendered through words, actions and wealth are due to Allāh alone.[285] Peace be on you, O Prophet, and the mercy of Allāh and His blessings.[286]

---

[283] This is a repetition of h. 829.

[284] In a repetition of this report later in h. 835 it is stated that at first people used to say: *as-salamu 'ala-llāhi min 'ibādi-hī*, i.e., "Peace be on Allāh from His servants." So the Holy Prophet said: "Do not say, Peace be on Allāh," and added that *as-Salām* (peace) is itself an attribute of Allāh. He it is Who gives peace to all, hence the prayer of peace for Him makes no sense at all. The question naturally arises whether people used to add some prayers of their own in the prescribed prayer in those days. The correct reply would be that, apart from those set prayers which were taught by the Holy Prophet himself, people were free to make any supplication to God in their own way in the course of the prayer or to glorify His name in any manner they wanted. Thus, though they were taught to utter the words *Rabba-nā wa la-ka-l-ḥamd* ("Our Lord! And Yours is the praise"), someone once added on his own: *ḥamd-an kathīr-an ṭayyib-an mubārak-an fīh* ("a praise in which is abundance, purity and blessing"); see h. 799. Similarly, it appears that someone added the words under reference to those prescribed for the prayer in the sitting posture which begins with the words *At-taḥiyyāt*. It was at this that the Holy Prophet corrected him and said that *'ibādi-llāhi-ṣ-ṣāliḥīn* ("the righteous servants of Allāh") is comprehensive.

[285] *Taḥiyyāt* is the plural of *taḥiyyah*. This word originally means to bless others by saying the words *ḥayya-ka-llāh*, meaning "May Allāh give you life". But in a wider sense it means any kind of prayer (Raghib). It has been said by authorities variously that the blessings intended in the word *taḥiyyah* refer to rule or to permanence. This means that all such prayers that are meant for sovereignty and peace and permanence are meant for Allāh alone. In other words, the words *At-taḥiyyatu li-llāhi wa-ṣ-ṣalawātu wa-ṭ-ṭayyibātu* mean that all kinds of prayers and worship and good deeds which a servant of God can present before his Lord can have nothing as their object but Allāh Himself.

[286] The words evidently are addressed to the Holy Prophet and from some reports we learn that during his lifetime the Companions of the Holy Prophet used to say, *as-salamu 'alai-ka*, meaning "peace be on you", and that it was after his death that the words were changed into *as-salamu 'ala-n-nabiyy*, meaning "peace be on the Prophet". But this cannot be accepted because these words of blessings were never said to the Holy Prophet and it would make no difference whether he was alive or dead at the time of saying these words. To address him in this way is not

Peace be on us and on the righteous servants of Allāh.' [287] If you say this, it will reach every righteous servant of Allāh in heaven and earth. (And then say:) I bear witness that there is no god but Allāh and I bear witness that Muḥammad is His servant and Messenger." [288]

Ch. 149: Prayers (*du'ā'*) before saying *Salām*

832 'Ā'ishah, wife of the Prophet ﷺ, reported that the Messenger of Allāh ﷺ used to make the following supplication during prayer:[289] "O Allāh, I seek refuge in You from the punishment of the grave, and I seek refuge in You from the tribulation of the Anti-Christ (*Al-Masīḥ ad-Dajjāl*), and I seek refuge in You from the trial of life and the trial of death; O Allāh, I seek refuge in You from sin and debt." A person said to him: "You frequently seek refuge from debt." He replied: "When a person is in debt, he tells lies when he speaks, and breaks promises when he makes them."

833 And Muḥammad ibn Yūsuf said: I heard Khalf ibn 'Āmir say: "There is no difference between (the words) *masīḥ* and *missīḥ*, they are the same.[290] One of them is Jesus and the other is Dajjāl." And az-Zuhrī reported: 'Urwah ibn Zubair told me that 'Ā'ishah said: "I heard the Messenger of Allāh ﷺ seeking refuge in his prayer from the evils of Dajjāl (the Anti-Christ)."

834 It is reported from Abū Bakr aṣ-Ṣiddīq that he said to the Messenger of Allāh ﷺ: "Teach me a supplication wherewith I may supplicate before

---

tantamount to associating him with God (*shirk*), but is merely out of love. It may also be that, as this prayer was taught by Allāh through revelation, the words *as-sālamu 'alai-ka* ("peace be on you") are how Allāh Himself addressed the Holy Prophet, and Muslims are only repeating the words of revelation, just as while reading the Qur'ān a Muslim says: *Yā ayyuha-n-nabiyyu,* i.e., "O Prophet" and such expressions.

[287] The words quoted here ('All services … righteous servants of Allāh') are as follows in Arabic: *At-taḥyyātu li-llāhi wa-ṣ-ṣalawātu wa-ṭ-ṭayyibātu. As-salāmu 'alai-ka ayyuh-annabiyyu wa raḥmatu-llāhi wa barakātu-hū. As-salāmu 'alai-nā wa 'ala 'ibādi-llāhi-ṣ-ṣāliḥīn.*

[288] In Arabic this is as follows: *Ashhadu an lā ilāha ill-Allāh wa ashhadu anna Muḥammad-an 'abdu-hū wa rasūlu-h.*

[289] In Ṣaḥīḥ Muslim (book: 'Prayer', ch. 25) it is stated in a report from Abū Hurairah that this prayer should be said in the *Tashahhud,* and in a report in the Ṣaḥīḥ of Ibn Khuzaimah by 'Ā'ishah it is stated that he made this supplication after the *Tashahhud.* This prayer was meant as a lesson for the Muslims, and in fact only he is safe from these trials who comes under the protection of Allāh, as did the Holy Prophet. See also h. 1377.

[290] That is to say, the same word is applied to Jesus and to the Antichrist (Dajjāl). This word is derived from *siyāḥah,* meaning 'to travel'. Jesus travelled extensively to preach his religion and the truth, and the Antichrist or Dajjāl also travels extensively but to suppress the truth and preach his false doctrines. The word has two forms: *masīḥ* and *missīḥ,* the latter being of the measure of *ṣiddīq.*

Allāh in my prayer." He said: "Say: O Allāh, I have been greatly unjust[291] to myself, and no one forgives sins except You, so forgive me with forgiveness from Yourself and have mercy on me. Surely You are the Forgiving, the Merciful'." [292]

Ch. 150: To choose some supplication (*du'ā'*) — and it is not obligatory — after *Tashahhud*

835 'Abdullāh (ibn Mas'ūd) reported: When we used to be with the Prophet ﷺ during prayer, we would say: "Peace be on Allāh from His servants, peace be on so and so". The Prophet ﷺ said: "Do not say, Peace be on Allāh, for surely Allāh Himself is Peace. You should say: 'All services (*At-taḥiyyāt*) rendered through words, actions and wealth are due to Allāh alone. Peace be on you, O Prophet, and the mercy of Allāh and His blessings. Peace be on us and on the righteous servants of Allāh.' If you say this, it will reach every servant (of Allāh) in heaven or between heaven and earth. (And then say:) 'I bear witness that there is no god but Allāh and I bear witness that Muḥammad is His servant and Messenger.' Then he should choose some supplication (*du'ā'*) which he likes and pray accordingly." [293]

---

[291] The word *ẓulm* ('injustice') really means 'placing a thing somewhere other than at its rightful location.' This word is used in quite a wide sense. The least fault, which can be a hindrance in the way to progress of a human being, can be called as *ẓulm*. Thus, *ẓulm* in each case will be of a different nature. Similarly, *ghafar* (forgiveness or protection) in respect of sin can have two meanings: protection against commission of a sin, so that sin is not committed at all, and protection against punishment for a sin that has been committed so that one is forgiven the sin.

[292] This prayer in Arabic is as follows: *Allāhumma, innī ẓalamtu nafsī ẓulm-an kathīr-an, wa lā yaghfiru-dh-dhunūba illā anta, fa-ghfir-lī maghfirat-an min 'indi-ka wa-rḥam-nī. Inna-ka anta-l-Ghafūru-r-raḥīm.*

[293] This is a repetition of h. 831 with some differences and additions. From the words, "he should choose", Bukhārī has drawn two conclusions. Firstly, that a person is at liberty to choose any prayer for himself at this stage according to his desire and preference, and there is no prescribed prayer to be recited as a ritual. Secondly, the choice of prayer has been left to the worshipper and it is not obligatory. The words in the chapter heading, *laisa bi wājib-in* ("is not obligatory"), mean only that no *particular* prayer is to be prescribed for this stage, as it is known that the Holy Prophet used to make some kind of supplication at the end of *Tashahhud*. This ḥadīth shows that the present practice of Muslims in general, to make certain prescribed supplications, is not in accord with the true purpose of the regular prayer. Its main purpose is to attain nearness to God and this is possible only when certain prayers and words of praise emerge from the heart of the worshipper spontaneously. The state of mind and heart would be different for each person, and there is no harm if such prayers and words are said in the language which a person speaks. In fact, it is essential that they should be in the person's own language so that he can express his deepest feelings. This is the middle path, and it avoids the adoption of the extreme, suggested by some at present, to give up the use of Arabic altogether in prayers.

Ch. 151: Not wiping of forehead and nose until completion of prayer

Abū 'Abdullāh (Bukhārī) said: I saw al-Ḥumaidī inferring from this ḥadīth that a person should not wipe his forehead during prayer.

836 Abū Salamah reported: I asked Abū Sa'īd al-Khudrī and he said: "I saw the Messenger of Allāh ﷺ performing *Sajdah* in mud so much so that I saw patches of mud on his forehead." [294]

Ch. 152: *Taslīm* (concluding the prayer)

837 Umm Salamah said: When the Messenger of Allāh ﷺ would conclude the prayer with *Salām,* the women would stand up at the time when he completed it, but he would remain (sitting) for a while before getting up.

Ibn Shihāb said: I presume, and Allāh knows best, that his remaining was to allow the women to leave before the departing people came across them. [295]

Ch. 153: Doing *Salām* when the Imām does *Salām*

Ibn 'Umar liked that when the Imām does *Salām,* those behind him should also do *Salām.*

838 'Itbān ibn Mālik reported: We prayed with the Messenger of Allāh ﷺ and we did our *Salām* when he did *Salām.* [296]

Ch. 154: Not returning the *Salām* of the Imām, but considering the *Taslīm* of the prayer to be sufficient [297]

839–840 Maḥmūd ibn ar-Rabī' informed me (az-Zuhrī), saying that he remembered the Messenger of Allāh ﷺ well and he remembered him drawing a mouthful of water (to rinse his mouth) from a bucket in their house. [298]

---

[294] This is a repetition of the last part of h. 669. Mud was sticking to the Holy Prophet's forehead, yet he did not wipe it off during prayer due to his concentration in worship. Not everyone can attain to such a state of total absorption in prayer, but it is necessary that, so far as possible, one's attention should be towards Allāh at this time, and small matters of inconvenience to the body should not draw the attention of the worshipper.

[295] This shows that, even after the command for women to be in seclusion from men, women came to mosques for prayer and formed rows behind those of the men. See also h. 849, h. 850 and h. 870.

[296] This is a very brief repetition of the long report in h. 425 by 'Itbān ibn Mālik in which he relates inviting the Holy Prophet to his house to lead prayers. The words of this repetition are not in h. 425.

[297] According to Mālikī jurisprudence, those praying behind the Imām should, apart from the two *Salāms* as *Taslīm* at the end of the prayer, also say a third *Salām* in between the two for the Imām. Bukhārī impliedly refuted this view by this chapter.

[298] This has already occurred in h. 77 in the book of Knowledge.

[840] He also said: I heard ʿItbān ibn Mālik al-Anṣārī say, and then someone who was a member of the tribe of Banū Sālim (confirmed it): I used to lead my people, the Banū Sālim in prayer, so I went to the Prophet ﷺ and said: "My eyesight has become weakened and (sometimes) water flows which intervenes between me and the mosque of my people. I wish you would come and say your prayer at some place in my house, so that I could make it a place of prayer." He said: "I shall do so, if Allāh wills."

So the next day the Messenger of Allāh ﷺ and Abū Bakr with him came to me after the sun had become intense. The Prophet ﷺ asked permission (to enter) and I gave him permission. He did not sit until he said: "Where do you like me to say my prayer in your house?" I pointed to him a place in it where I wanted him to say his prayer. So he stood and we lined up behind him. Then he ended the prayer with *Salām* and we did *Salām* at the same time.[299]

Ch. 155: Remembrance of Allāh (*dhikr*) after prayer

841 Ibn ʿAbbās informed that remembrance of Allāh was done aloud when people finished the prescribed prayers in the time of the Prophet ﷺ. Ibn ʿAbbās (further) said: When I heard this (remembrance), I used to know that people had finished (the prayers).[300]

842 Ibn ʿAbbās reported: I used to recognize the end of the prayer of the Prophet ﷺ by the *Takbīr*.[301]

843 Abū Hurairah reported: Some poor people came to the Prophet ﷺ and said: "The wealthy were able to attain high (spiritual) status and abiding happiness; they pray as we pray and fast as we fast, and they have a superiority on account of wealth because they can perform Pilgrimage and *ʿUmra* (minor pilgrimage), take part in *Jihād* and give in charity."[302] He said: "Should I not tell you something which, if you act upon it, will enable you to excel those

---

[299] This is a repetition of h. 425 without its latter part about what happened after the prayer. See also h. 1185–1186.

[300] This report shows the practice of *dhikr* (remembrance of God) in a loud voice after the prescribed prayers. Muslims of the present time, instead of proclaiming the remembrance which is proved from Ḥadīth, raise their hands with the Imām who recites some prayers and the worshippers pass their hands over their faces without themselves uttering any *dhikr* or supplication.

[301] See h. 841 just above this. Here *dhikr* in a loud voice is referred to as *Takbīr*. This, incidentally, shows that Ibn ʿAbbās was very young in those days and did not attend the congregational prayers regularly.

[302] This shows the extent of people's love and readiness for good deeds. As the Qurʾān describes them: "These hasten to good things and they are foremost in attaining them" (23:61). They feel that as they do not possess any wealth to do good with, they must seek nearness to God through other deeds.

who are ahead of you, and those behind you will not be able to catch up with you? Thus you will be the best among people of your time except those who do similar deeds? You should say *Subḥān Allāh* (Glory be to Allāh) and *Al-ḥamdu li-llāh* (all praise be to Allāh) and *Allāhu Akbar* (Allāh is the Greatest) thirty-three times after every prayer." But we differed among ourselves, some saying (that it is) *Subḥān Allāh* thirty-three times, *Al-ḥamdu li-llāh* thirty-three times and *Allāhu Akbar* thirty-four times. So I went back to him[303] and he said: "You should say *Subḥān Allāh* and *Al-ḥamdu li-llāh* and *Allāhu Akbar* so that each one of these expressions would be thirty-three in number." [304]

844 Warrād, the scribe of al-Mughīrah ibn Shuʿbah reported: Al-Mughīrah ibn Shuʿbah dictated to me in the course of a letter addressed to Muʿāwiyah that the Prophet ﷺ, after every prescribed prayer, used to say: "There is no god but Allāh, Who is One without any partner. His is the kingdom and all praise is due to Him and He has power over all things. O Allāh! no one can prevent what You bestow, and no one can grant what You withhold, and no wealth (*jadd*) can avail its possessor except by You." [305]

Ch. 156: The Imām should turn and face the people after saying *Salām*

845 Samrah ibn Jundub reported: The Prophet ﷺ used to turn his face towards us when he finished his prayer.

---

[303] Some take the words "So I went back to him" to mean that this is Abū Hurairah speaking who went back to the Holy Prophet for clarification. Others consider these to be the words of Sumayy, a narrator in the chain of this narration, who went back to the preceding narrator, his own teacher, Abū Ṣāliḥ, being the person reporting from Abū Hurairah. The version of this report in Ṣaḥīḥ Muslim (book: 'Mosques and Places of Prayer', ch. 26) seems to suggest the latter case.

[304] In some reports (see Ṣaḥīḥ Muslim, as in last footnote) it says that the thirty-fourth time it should be the words *Lā ilāha ill-Allāh, waḥdahu lā sharīka lahu*, etc. ("There is no God but Allāh, Who is One without any partner..."), but some others say that *Allāhu Akbar* itself should be recited thirty-four times (see Tirmidhī, book: 'Prayer', h. 410). Bukhārī inserts a report from Sumayy in the Book on 'Supplications', under the chapter headed 'Supplications after Prayer' (h. 6329), saying that *Subḥān Allāh, Al-ḥamdu li-llāh* and *Allāhu Akbar* should be recited ten times each.

The ḥadīth here contains the words "after every prayer", showing that this is a remembrance (*dhikr*) after every regular prayer. The expression *Subḥān Allāh* implies that no defect or imperfection can be attributed to God, *Al-ḥamdu li-llāh* is a reminder that all achievements and favours are from God alone, and *Allāhu Akbar* is the declaration of the unique greatness of God and of the necessity of our bowing before Him in recognition of His greatness.

[305] *Jadd* means both grandfather and wealth. The words translated as "except by You", i.e., by Your will, are *min-ka*, where *min* means "in place of". This expression means that neither high ancestry nor abundance of wealth can avail anything if its possessor leaves his connection with God.

846 Zaid ibn Khālid al-Juhanī reported: The Messenger of Allāh ﷺ led us in the morning prayer at Ḥudaibiyah after it had rained during the night. After finishing his prayers, he turned towards the people and said: "Do you know what it is that your Lord, the Almighty, the Glorious said?" They said: "Allāh and His Messenger know best." He said: "(Allāh said:) Among My servants some get up in the morning believing in Me and (some) as unbelievers. So whoever says, 'It rained on us by the grace of Allāh and His mercy,' he indeed is a believer in Me and an unbeliever in the stars. And whoever says, 'It rained on us because of the rising of such and such (star),' he indeed is an unbeliever in Me and a believer in the stars'." [306]

847 Anas reported: The Messenger of Allāh ﷺ delayed the night prayer (i.e., *'Ishā'*) until midnight, then he came out to us. When he had said the prayer he turned his face towards us and said: "People have said their prayers and slept, but you were in prayer while you were waiting for the prayer." [307]

Ch. 157: The staying of the Imām in his place after *Salām*

848 Nāfi' reported: Ibn 'Umar used to say his (optional) prayers in the same place where he said his obligatory prayers and Qāsim did the same. And it is reported from Abū Hurairah as *marfū'* (traceable to the Holy Prophet): "The Imām should not say optional prayers in the same place (from where he has led the obligatory prayers)." This is not correct.[308]

---

[306] *Nau'* means *rising*. People of Arabia in those days used to think that rain is caused by the movement of stars and this was due to the influence of astrology on their minds. The Holy Prophet obliterated from Arabia all ideas connected with divining by stars. This, however, does not mean that it is wrong to say that the rainfall coincided with the rising of some star or with its being in a certain position. The purpose is to do away with superstition. Thus it is stated in *Nihāyah:* "The Prophet ﷺ has given this strict order as regards the rising (i.e., taking omens from the rising of stars) because the Arabs attributed rain to them. As to him who considers rain to be an act of Allāh, and by the words 'it rained on us because of the rising of such and such (star)" he means 'at such a time', and it is the (time of) the rising of such and such, that is permissible because Allāh has established a rule that rain should come at those times."

[307] H. 572 is repeated here with a slight difference in wording. The turning of the face in this repetition relates it to the chapter heading. The addition from Ḥumaid in h. 572 is not found here.

[308] Bukhārī has declared this report by Abū Hurairah, which is in Abū Dāwūd (book: 'Prayer', h. 616 and see also h. 1006 in same book), as not being correct although it is regarded as a *marfū'* (one whose narration is traceable to the Holy Prophet). It appears that the Holy Prophet generally used to say the optional prayers not at the mosque but in his own house, because at home a person can devote as much time to such a prayer as he likes, and also because in this way there is remembrance of Allāh at home. It is possible that for these reasons the Holy Prophet may have made this statement on some occasion. But this should not be taken to mean total prohibition because the Companions are known to have said these prayers at the mosque, and this is what Bukhārī is indicating. Some people have taken it to mean that optional prayers should not be said at exactly

849 Umm Salamah reported that the Prophet ﷺ, when he concluded his prayer with *Salām,* he would remain in his place for a while. Ibn Shihāb said: We presume, and Allāh knows best, this was to allow the women to leave.[309]

850 Umm Salamah, wife of the Prophet ﷺ, reported: When he concluded his prayer with *Salām,* the women would depart and enter their houses before the Messenger of Allāh ﷺ departed.[310]

Ch. 158: One who led people in prayer, then remembered a necessity and passed over them (to leave)

851 ʿUqbah reported: I said my *ʿAṣr* prayer behind the Prophet ﷺ at Madīnah, and after finishing it with *Salām* he quickly stood up and went over the heads of people towards the chamber of one of his wives. The people were concerned by his haste. Then he came out to them and found that they were wondering at his haste. He said: "I remembered that something of gold was in my house and I did not want it to distract me, so I ordered its distribution." [311]

Ch. 159: To depart (after prayer), turning right or left

Anas ibn Mālik would turn to his right or to his left, and disapproved if someone purposely and deliberately always turned to the right.

852 ʿAbdullāh (ibn Masʿūd) said: None of you should allow the devil to spoil his prayer by thinking that it is incumbent on him to depart (after the prayer) only towards his right. I have often seen the Prophet ﷺ departing towards his left.[312]

---

the same spot as the obligatory prayer but a little distance away. But the fact is that prayer is valid wherever it may be said.

[309] This is a repetition of h. 837. See also h. 870.

[310] In this repetition of h. 837, the entire report, including the part about the women leaving, is attributed to Umm Salamah. This delay by the Holy Prophet served a double purpose: he would find time for the remembrance of Allāh after the prayer was over and the women would get the opportunity of conveniently leaving the mosque.

[311] Whenever any wealth was brought to him, it was the habit of the Holy Prophet to distribute it among the people immediately and he would always feel anxious that it should reach deserving persons. That is why he hurried towards his home as soon as the prayer was over. Only that man can have such supreme indifference towards material things who has the strongest connection with God. It leaves not the least doubt that the Holy Prophet had no inclination whatsoever for worldly wealth and desires. As the head of the state, there would have been nothing wrong if he kept some gold for himself, but no one other than him showed the example of being a monarch without wealth in his possession. It is not as difficult to give up worldly rule and become an ascetic, as it is to be both a ruler and an ascetic at one and the same time. See also h. 1430.

[312] To apply rules in such small matters is really to allow the devil to interfere. Controversies

Ch. 160:　About (eating of) raw garlic, onion and leek

The saying of the Prophet ﷺ: "Whoever eats garlic or onion due to hunger or for some other reason should not come near our mosque." [313]

853 Ibn ʿUmar reported that the Prophet ﷺ said during the Khaibar expedition: "Whoever eats from this plant" — that is to say, garlic — "he should not come near our mosque." [314]

854 ʿAṭāʾ informed that he heard Jābir ibn ʿAbdullāh say that the Prophet ﷺ said: "Whoever eats from this plant" — he meant garlic — "he should not come in our mosques." I said (to Jābir): "What did he mean by it?" He said: "I think he meant only raw garlic." In another version, it is: "only bad smell." [315]

855 Jābir ibn ʿAbdullāh reported that the Prophet ﷺ said: "One who eats garlic or onion should keep away from us — or he said, should keep away from our mosque — and should stay at home." An urn was brought to the Prophet ﷺ which contained green vegetables. He detected some smell in them. On enquiring, he was told that it contained such and such vegetables. He said: "Give it to so and so," that is, to one of his Companions who was present. When he (the Prophet) saw him disliking to eat it, he said: "Eat, for surely I am privy to that to which you are not privy."

(And according to another report:) A dish was brought to him, in which there were green vegetables. [316]

---

of the Muslims of today all relate to such trivial things. Caring little for the real purpose of religion, they fight over these insignificant matters, call each other as misguided and unbelievers, and expend all their energies in such disputes. Hence they are unable to combat the external opponents.

[313] Garlic, onion and other similar things create a bad odour in the mouth which causes unpleasantness to other people. There is nothing special about a mosque except that there is a gathering of people in it, and this instruction is applicable to all assemblies. Such a person should not come to the mosque until the bad smell has disappeared from his mouth, as is clear from h. 855, which contains the words: "and should stay at home." It is not only that hygiene and cleanliness are kept in view. It also shows that the concept has been developed to the highest level that no action of anyone, however trivial, should harm or annoy others. When a person has this much regard for others, that he refrains from offending them by bad odour from his mouth, more general feelings of human sympathy must be deeply embedded in his heart.

[314] H. 853, h. 854 and h. 856 are repetitions of h. 855. In this version it is added that this was said during the Khaibar expedition.

[315] In this repetition of h. 855, a version is mentioned which refers to "bad smell".

[316] What he meant was that this should not be considered forbidden. The more a person develops a sense of the spiritual world, the more he avoids eating things which are difficult to

856 ʿAbdul ʿAzīz reported: A man asked Anas ibn Mālik: "What have you heard the Prophet ﷺ say about garlic?" He said that the Prophet ﷺ said: "Whoever eats from this plant, he should not come near to us nor should he pray with us." [317]

Ch. 161: *Wuḍūʾ* for boys — When does it become obligatory for them to bathe, to be in a state of purity, and their attendance at prayers, Eid services, funeral prayers, and formation of rows?

857 Ash-Shaʿbī said: One who passed along with the Prophet ﷺ by a grave that was separate (from other graves) informed me that he (the Holy Prophet) led people in (the funeral) prayer and they formed rows for it. I said: "O Abū ʿAmr, who related this to you?" He said: "Ibn ʿAbbās." [318]

858 Abū Saʿīd al-Khudrī reported from the Prophet ﷺ that he said: "A bath on Friday is incumbent on every adult." [319]

---

digest. This is the meaning of the words: "I am privy to that to which you are not privy." It was the Holy Prophet's habit in any case to eat very little and to eat simple food. There seems to be something in the vegetables brought before him on this occasion which he considered to be difficult to digest and that was the reason for his refusal to eat it.

[317] This repetition of h. 855 shows that the injunction is not confined to the mosque. The purpose seems to be that a person should not inconvenience others by the bad smell of his mouth. Thus those who do not properly brush their teeth and keep them clean not only cause harm to themselves but also cause discomfort to others by the bad smell of their mouth.

[318] In this chapter there are four reports from Ibn ʿAbbās. This report says that he attended a funeral prayer. H. 859 says that he joined the Holy Prophet in his midnight prayer. H. 861 says that he attended an obligatory prayer during the days of the pilgrimage and stood in the row of congregation. In h. 863 it says that he joined the Eid congregation. In h. 861 and h. 863 it has been clearly stated that he had not attained maturity at the time. See also the repetitions in h. 1319, 1322 and 1336.

[319] This means that bath or *Wuḍūʾ* as a condition of prayer does not apply to non-adults. There is a ḥadīth stating that "the pen has been lifted" (*rufiʿa-l-qalam*) from, among others, a child until he becomes a youth, meaning that rules and punishments cannot be applied to a minor (Abū Dāwūd, book: 'Punishments', h. 4398; Tirmidhī, book: 'Punishments', h. 1423; Nasāʾī, book: 'Divorce', h. 3432; Ibn Mājah, book: 'Divorce', h. 2119). However, another ḥadīth says that a child should be taught to say prayers when he is seven years old, and when he is ten he should be beaten if he does not say prayers (Tirmidhī, book: 'Prayer', h. 407; Abū Dāwūd, book: 'Prayer', h. 494). The first part is undoubtedly right because what is taught at an early age makes a deep, life-long impression. But the second part about beating conflicts with the general practice of the Holy Prophet Muḥammad. He never punished even the adults who did not come to prayer, such as the hypocrites, let alone that a child should be punished, making him resentful of religion. In any case, to force someone to fulfil a religious duty is against the principle taught in the Qurʾān: "There is no compulsion in religion" (2:256). The proper course is to show them one's own example, teach them the benefits of prayer and warn them of the harm of omitting it.

859 Ibn ʿAbbās reported: I spent a night at my maternal aunt Maimūnah's place, and the Prophet ﷺ slept. When part of the night had passed, the Messenger of Allāh ﷺ got up and performed ablution from a water skin which was hanging there, performing a light *Wuḍū'* — ʿAmr described it as light and very little. Then he stood up to pray. So I also got up and performed ablution in the manner he had done, then I came and stood on his left. He pulled me round and made me (stand) on his right. Then he said the prayer as Allāh willed, then he lay down and slept, so much so that he snored. (Later) the caller to prayer came to him, calling him for prayer; so he went with him for prayer and said the prayer and did not perform ablution.

We said to ʿAmr: People say that the eyes of the Prophet ﷺ used to sleep but his heart would not sleep. ʿAmr said: I have heard ʿUbaid ibn ʿUmair say: "Surely the dreams of the Prophets are revelation," then he recited: "Surely I see in a dream that I am slaughtering you" (the Qur'ān, 37:102).[320]

860 Anas ibn Mālik reported that his grandmother Mulaikah invited the Messenger of Allāh ﷺ to a meal which she had prepared. He ate of it and said: "Stand up so I may lead you in prayer." So (said Anas) I stood up to get hold of a mat (*ḥaṣīr*) of ours which had become black by long use, and I washed it with water. The Messenger of Allāh ﷺ stood up, and an orphan was with me (the two making a row behind him) and the old lady was behind us. He led us in two *rakʿahs* of prayer.[321]

861 Ibn ʿAbbās reported: I came riding on a she-ass, and at that time I was approaching the age of maturity, and the Messenger of Allāh ﷺ was leading people in prayer at Minā without facing any wall. So I passed in front of some of the rows (in the congregation) and arriving there I sent away the she-ass to graze and joined in the row. This was not made an objection against me by anyone.[322]

862 ʿĀ'ishah reported: The Messenger of Allāh ﷺ delayed the *ʿIshā'* prayer (one night) until ʿUmar called out to him: "The women and the children have indeed fallen asleep." So the Messenger of Allāh ﷺ came out and said: "No one living on the earth has said this prayer except you." There was no one in those days who said prayers other than the people of Madīnah.[323]

---

[320] This is a repetition of h. 138 with only slight differences in wording.

[321] This is a repetition of h. 380 with the same content and wording, except for a minor difference of wording at the end. See also h. 727 and h. 871.

[322] This is a repetition of h. 76 with very little difference in wording. Ibn ʿAbbās was close to attaining majority but was yet a minor boy and he joined the prayer and no one objected.

[323] This is a repetition of h. 566 with slight variations. In h. 566 it is stated near the beginning:

863 'Abdur Raḥmān ibn 'Ābis reported: I heard from Ibn 'Abbās that a certain person said to him: "Were you present in the company of the Prophet ﷺ at the going out (of women for Eid prayers)?" He said: "Yes, and if I had not been related to him, I could not have been present," that is, because of his young age. He (the Holy Prophet) came to the roadside mark near the house of Kathīr ibn aṣ-Ṣalt, then he delivered a sermon, and then went towards the women and preached to them and reminded them and exhorted them to give in charity. So the women began to take off their rings and throw them into the garment of Bilāl. Then he (the Prophet) and Bilāl returned home.

Ch. 162: Women going out to the mosque at night and in darkness (before dawn)

864 'Ā'ishah reported: The Messenger of Allāh ﷺ delayed the *'Ishā'* prayer (one night) until 'Umar called out: "The women and the children have fallen asleep." So the Messenger of Allāh ﷺ came out and said: "No one living on the earth is waiting for it (i.e., for the prayer) except you." Prayers were not said in those days (with freedom) except in Madīnah, and they used to say the *'Ishā'* prayer between the disappearance of twilight and the (end of the) first one-third of the night.[324]

865 Ibn 'Umar reported from the Prophet ﷺ that he said: "When your women ask permission of you to go to the mosque at night, give them your permission." [325]

866 Umm Salamah, wife of the Prophet ﷺ, informed that in the time of the Messenger of Allāh ﷺ women used to get up after they had finished the obligatory prayers with *Salām* while the Messenger of Allāh ﷺ and those men who said their prayers stayed, as long as Allāh willed. When the Messenger of Allāh ﷺ stood up, the men also stood up.[326]

"And it was before Islām had spread." This repetition puts it differently at the end by saying that prayers in those days were only said by the people of Madīnah, i.e., Islām was yet confined to Madīnah.

[324] This is a repetition of h. 566 in words very much the same as in h. 862, but with the addition at the end, which is not even in h. 566, about the time interval during which the *'Ishā'* prayer was said. This addition also occurs at the end of h. 569.

[325] At night that risk is greater, for the fear of which Muslims today do not allow their women to go to mosques even during the day! This instruction of the Holy Prophet is the very opposite of the present-day practice of Muslims. This saying does not mean that permission must be sought whenever a woman wishes to go to the mosque. Its real purpose is to forbid husbands to prevent their wives from going to mosques, even at night. See also h. 899.

[326] This is a repetition of h. 837 in different words.

867 ʿĀʾishah reported: When the Messenger of Allāh ﷺ had said the morning prayer, the women would depart, wrapped in their cloaks. They were not recognized on account of darkness.[327]

868 Abū Qatādah reported that the Messenger of Allāh ﷺ said: "I stand up for prayer and I desire to make it long, but I hear the crying of a child, so I shorten my prayer as I dislike to put his mother in difficulty." [328]

869 ʿĀʾishah reported: "Had the Messenger of Allāh ﷺ seen what women have now introduced (in their habits), he would have forbidden them from going to the mosque as the women of the Israelites were forbidden." [329] I asked ʿAmrah:[330] "Were they (the women of the Israelites) forbidden?" She said: "Yes."

Ch. 163: The prayer of women behind men

870 Umm Salamah reported: When the Messenger of Allāh ﷺ would conclude the prayer with *Salām,* the women would stand up at the time when he completed it, but he would remain in his place for a while before getting up.

---

[327] This is a repetition of h. 372 with a slight difference of wording. Though, as stated in this report, they covered themselves with sheets, the reason they were not recognized was not because they were covering themselves but because of darkness. Two points are clear from this: firstly, that if it were not dark they would have been recognized despite being covered, and this could only be because their faces were not covered; and secondly, this was the practice after the injunction for women to cover themselves had been revealed.

[328] This is a repetition of h. 707 in almost the same words. The first five reports in this chapter clearly show that women used to join the congregational prayers in the mosque in the days of the Holy Prophet. In Abū Dāwūd and Ṣaḥīḥ Ibn Khuzaimah there is a report from Ibn ʿUmar that the Holy Prophet said: "Do not prevent your women from going to the mosques but their houses are better for them" (Abū Dāwūd, book: 'Prayer', h. 567). However, all the reports in Bukhārī mention that women used to join the congregation in the mosque. In none of them is it mentioned that the Holy Prophet told women that it is better for them to say their prayers at home. In Abū Dāwūd the chapter containing h. 567 has four reports, h. 565 to h. 568, but only h. 567 contains the addition "but their houses are better for them."

[329] This is nothing more than a presumption by ʿĀʾishah. Neither did the Holy Prophet see the women of later times nor did he forbid them, nor can it be proved that it was for such a reason that Israelite women were forbidden to go to their places of worship. The Holy Prophet found both men and women in the most degraded moral condition, and he brought about their reform. Had he found any women behaving in the objectionable manner that ʿĀʾishah alludes to, he would have corrected them instead of forbidding them to go to mosques. A Divinely-raised reformer does not forbid people to perform a good act because of some weakness on their part, thus depriving them of its benefits. Ever since Muslim women have been excluded from national life and activities, and kept uninformed about them, the Muslims have gone into decline. It is to be regretted that they made their women unable to do worldly work as well as rendering them incapable of performing religious duties.

[330] The speaker here is Yaḥyā ibn Saʿīd who narrated this ḥadīth from ʿAmrah, who in her turn was reporting from ʿĀʾishah.

He (az-Zuhrī, a narrator in the chain) said: We presume, and Allāh knows best, that this was to allow the women to leave before any of the men came across them.[331]

871 Anas reported: The Prophet ﷺ prayed in the house of Umm Sulaim, and I and an orphan stood behind him, and Umm Sulaim was behind us.[332]

Ch. 164: Departure of women soon after the morning prayers and their short stay in the mosque

872 'Ā'ishah reported that the Messenger of Allāh ﷺ used to say the morning prayer when it was still dark, and the women of the believers used to depart and they would not be recognized on account of darkness, nor would they recognize one another.[333]

Ch. 165: A woman seeking permission from her husband to go to the mosque

873 'Abdullāh (ibn 'Umar) reported from the Prophet ﷺ that he said: "When the wife of any of you asks permission, do not forbid her." [334]

Ch. 166: The prayer of women behind men[335]

874 Anas reported: The Prophet ﷺ prayed in the house of ...[336]

875 Umm Salamah reported: When the Messenger of Allāh ﷺ would conclude the prayer with *Salām*, ...[337]

---

[331] This is a repetition of h. 837 with only a slight difference in wording. See also h. 849 and h. 850. Women used to leave the mosque when the Holy Prophet completed the prayer with *Salām,* while he kept on sitting with the men. This shows that women formed a row at the rear and this was to keep the two sexes from mixing with one another. Such mixing in Christian churches leads people into temptation.

[332] This is a repetition of a small part of h. 380. See also h. 727 and h. 860.

[333] This is a repetition of h. 372. It shows that because of darkness women did not recognize one another. See also h. 867.

[334] This is a repetition of h. 865. There is no mention here of going to mosques. Since, as this shows, it is not right to forbid women to go out for worldly business, it follows that it cannot be right to forbid them to go to mosques.

[335] This chapter and its two reports are a repetition of chapter 163 and the reports h. 871 and h. 870 respectively under that chapter.

[336] This is a repetition of h. 380, in exactly the same words as h. 871.

[337] This is a repetition of h. 837, in exactly the same words as h. 870.

PART 4

Book 11: *Al-Jumuʿah*
Friday Congregation

In the name of Allāh, the Beneficent, the Merciful

Ch. 1:   Obligation of Friday prayer

On account of the word of Allāh, the Most High: "…when the call is sounded for prayer on Friday, hasten (*fa-sʿau*) to the remembrance of Allāh[1] and leave off business. That is better for you, if you know" (62:9). The word *fa-sʿau* means go forth (*fa-mḍū*).

876 Abū Hurairah said that he heard the Messenger of Allāh ﷺ say: "We are the last (religious community) but we will be the foremost on the day of Resurrection though they (other nations) were given the revealed books before us. And this was their day which was made obligatory for them, but they differed about it. So Allāh gave us guidance in this matter, and all other people

---

[1] Bukhārī, as is his usual practice of first quoting the Qurʾān to substantiate his reports, which is the right principle, quotes a verse of the chapter *Jumuʿah* (meaning 'The Congregation' or 'Friday') of the Qurʾān on the obligation of the Friday prayer. Most authorities have inferred from this that the *Jumuʿah* prayer became obligatory with the revelation of this verse which took place in Madīnah. ʿAbdur Razzāq has reported from Muḥammad ibn Sīrīn that even before the Holy Prophet's migration people in Madīnah held Friday congregational prayer and it was led by Asʿad ibn Zarārah. This is supported by the report from Kaʿb ibn Mālik recorded by Aḥmad ibn Ḥanbal, Ibn Mājah and Ibn Khuzaimah. If this report is correct, it would mean that as soon as a community of Muslims was formed in Madīnah the Holy Prophet sent instructions there for the holding of Friday prayers, and Asʿad followed them. This is borne out by the fact that the Holy Prophet started holding Friday prayers as soon as he arrived in Madīnah. The "call to prayer" mentioned here came later on. Hence there is no objection if this verse was revealed later on. As to how the Friday prayer was ordered before the revelation of this verse, it was just as the Holy Prophet was Divinely taught details of the other prayers by means of inner revelation (*waḥy khafiyy*), the same was the case with Friday prayers. Later, the revelation which came in words (*waḥy matluww*) gave this obligation greater importance as it stresses the necessity of suspension of other affairs of life for its sake. However, h. 892 shows that the first congregational prayer on Friday was conducted by the Holy Prophet himself because it is particularly mentioned in that report that the very next *Jumuʿah* congregation that took place was at Juwāthā in Bahrain. This second *Jumuʿah* would not have had this significance if Friday prayers had been held before the first one led by the Holy Prophet.

are behind us in this respect: the Jews tomorrow and the Christians the day after tomorrow."[2]

Ch. 2:   The excellence of bath on Friday[3] and whether the presence of children and women is obligatory in the Friday congregation[4]

877 'Abdullāh ibn 'Umar reported that the Messenger of Allāh ﷺ said: "Anyone of you coming to the Friday prayer must take a bath."

878 Ibn 'Umar reported that 'Umar ibn al-Khaṭṭāb was standing delivering the Friday sermon, when a man from among the early *muhājirs* (emigrants), from among the Companions of the Prophet ﷺ, came along, and 'Umar called out to him: "What time is this?" He said: "I was busy and was unable

---

[2] In the Qur'ān it is stated: "The Sabbath was ordained only for those who differed about it" (16:124), showing that the Sabbath was made obligatory for the Jews and the Christians. The reference to differing may mean either that these people violated the sanctity of this day or that whereas in the beginning of Christian history the Jews and the Christians both observed the same Sabbath, but later on the Christians changed the Sabbath from Saturday to Sunday in imitation of pagan nations. The words, "this was their day which was made obligatory for them", cannot mean that it was Friday which was appointed for them and God did not tell them it was Friday. This is contrary to the verse quoted earlier (16:124) and is also absurd. These words mean nothing more than that just as one day has been specially appointed for Muslims for religious congregation, a day was particularly reserved for this purpose for previous communities as well, and such a day can literally be described by the word *Jumu'ah* since this word means 'congregation.' The words "Allāh gave us guidance in this matter" mean that Muslims in their history will have no difference regarding this, unlike the Jews and the Christians whose difference is described in the words "the Jews tomorrow and the Christians the day after tomorrow".

[3] Islam has laid great stress on physical purity as a preparation for worship since it is an aid to attaining spiritual purity. This is particularly required at gatherings, such as Friday and Eid prayers, so that the close mixing may not cause discomfort and inconvenience to others, but increase mutual love and harmony. This is why the Holy Prophet gave the instruction to have a bath before Friday prayers.

[4] The report of Abu Sa'īd al-Khudrī, which is the third report of this chapter and has already occurred as h. 858, and is a part of h. 880, is as follows: "A bath on Friday is incumbent on every adult." This implies that children are not required to have a bath on Friday because *Jumu'ah* prayer is not obligatory on them. Still, the elders should see that children attend congregational prayers in their young age to accustom them to it, even though it is not obligatory. As to whether *Jumu'ah* prayer is obligatory or not on women, no report has been recorded here, nor has Bukhārī decided this question. There is a report in Abū Dāwūd, regarded as authentic, which says that *Jumu'ah* prayer is not obligatory on women and children. However, according to Abū Dāwūd, the narrator of this report is Ibn Shahāb, a man who only saw the Holy Prophet and did not report anything from him. This fact apart, the words of the Qur'ān, "hasten to the remembrance of God" (62:9), apply to both men and women. Though it uses the masculine form, this is the case generally with injunctions of the Qur'ān. However, in accordance with the verse "He has not laid upon you any hardship in the matter of religion" (22:78), there can be an exemption for women if, for example, a long distance has to be travelled to the place of prayer or there is some other hardship which women cannot bear.

to get home and I heard the call to prayer, and I was only able to perform ablution (*Wuḍū*)." He ('Umar) said: "Just ablution![5] You know that the Messenger of Allāh ﷺ enjoined the taking of a bath."

879 Abū Sa'īd al-Khudrī reported that the Messenger of Allāh, ﷺ said: "A bath on Friday is incumbent on every adult." [6]

Ch. 3: Using perfume for Friday prayer

880 'Amr ibn Sulaim al-Anṣārī related: I bear witness that Abū Sa'īd (al-Khudrī) said: I bear witness that the Messenger of Allāh, ﷺ said: "A bath on Friday is incumbent on every adult as also is the cleaning of teeth and use of perfume if he can get hold of it."

'Amr said: As for bath, I bear witness that it is incumbent, and as for cleaning of teeth and the use of perfume, Allāh knows best whether these are incumbent or not, but this is how it occurs in the ḥadīth.[7]

Ch. 4: Virtues of (attending) the Friday congregation

881 Abū Hurairah reported that the Messenger of Allāh ﷺ said: "Whosoever takes a bath on Friday, like the bath which is required (after sexual intercourse), and proceeds (for congregational prayers), it is as if he has sacrificed a camel; and whoever proceeds a little later, it is as if he has sacrificed a cow; and whoever proceeds later still, it is as if he has sacrificed a ram; and whoever proceeds even later, it is as if he has sacrificed a chicken; and whoever proceeds last of all, it is as if he has given away an egg (in the way of Allāh). Then when the Imām comes out (for the sermon) the angels make their presence to listen to the sermon." [8]

---

[5] Two defaults were pointed out: firstly, coming late, and secondly, not having taken a bath. The man referred to here was 'Uthmān.

[6] This is a repetition of h. 858 in the same words. See also h. 895.

[7] The use of a toothbrush and perfume on Friday is necessary to make the atmosphere pleasant in the congregation. It is the Holy Prophet's instruction and he himself used perfume on such occasions. The part of this report, "A bath on Friday is incumbent on every adult", has already occurred in h. 858.

[8] This is an illustration of being foremost and prompt in responding to the call of God. The quicker a person goes towards God, the closer to Him he becomes. Similarly, the greater time he can devote in the service of God, the more he gains spiritually. The reference to angels is meant to convey that as their function is to inspire the hearts of people with goodness they are present at the sermon and whoever listens to it attentively they inspire noble thoughts within him. The listening by the angels indicates that the audience too must listen with full attention.

Ch. 5:   Chapter concerning the above

882 Abū Hurairah reported that 'Umar was delivering the Friday sermon when a man entered. 'Umar said: "Why are you late for the prayer?" The man said: "It was only when I heard the call to prayer that I performed ablution." He ('Umar) said: "Have you not heard that the Prophet ﷺ said: 'When anyone of you goes to the Friday prayer he must take a bath' ?" [9]

Ch. 6:   Applying oil to the hair for Friday prayers

883 Salmān al-Fārisī reported that the Prophet ﷺ said: "Any person who takes bath on Friday, and cleanses himself as much as he can, and applies oil (to his hair) or uses some perfume of his own, then goes out and (enters the mosque) without pushing people apart,[10] then says the prayer prescribed for him, then remains silent when the Imām delivers the sermon, his sins from then to the following Friday will be forgiven." [11]

884 Ṭāwus said that he said to Ibn 'Abbās: "People mention that the Prophet ﷺ said: 'Take bath on Friday and wash your heads (i.e., hair) even if you are not under an obligation of bath (due to sexual intercourse), and apply some perfume.' Ibn 'Abbās said: "As for bath, Yes, and as for perfume, I do not know." [12]

---

[9] This is a repetition of h. 878 with some brevity and difference of wording. Its closing words make it even clearer that a bath must be taken for the Friday prayer.

[10] In other words, one should not disturb people who are sitting close to each other by passing between them.

[11] There is no atonement in Islām. So the words here cannot at all mean that a person who acts in the manner described here on Friday can behave as he likes throughout the next week and his sins will be forgiven. For this reason, commentators of Ḥadīth have taken it to mean forgiveness of minor sins, and in one report this has been added: "so long as he does not indulge in major sins" (Ṣaḥīḥ Muslim, book: 'Purification' — *Ṭahārah*, ch. 5). In other words, such a man will receive the forgiveness of God in minor omissions provided he does not knowingly violate any clear commandment of God. What is meant are unintentional faults. However, the word *ghafara* means not only 'forgiveness' but also 'protection'. Thus, what may be meant is that if a man becomes so devout on Friday as is suggested here, he will receive the protection of God from all kinds of sins during the rest of the week. The next Friday is mentioned because he has the same opportunity to renew this a week later. The fact is that the Friday sermon is an excellent arrangement for Muslims, and if they took care to benefit from it, it would be the best way for strengthening their communal life. If every week they were told of the needs of the community and made aware of their obligations, they would not be like the dead nation that they are today. Unfortunately, there is no true spirit left in Friday sermons generally. They are usually delivered in Arabic, which people do not understand, and those delivering the sermons have no spiritual connection with God as they have made their prayer leadership and delivery of sermons a mere job and occupation for earning their livelihood.

[12] In the Ḥadīth collection of Ibn Mājah there is another report from Ibn 'Abbās, traceable to

885 Ṭāwus reported regarding Ibn ʿAbbās: He mentioned the saying of the Prophet ﷺ on the question of bath on Friday, and I said to Ibn ʿAbbās: "Should one use perfume or oil if he has it in his house?" He said: "I do not know".[13]

Ch. 7:   Wearing the best clothes one can find

886 ʿAbdullāh ibn ʿUmar reported that ʿUmar ibn al-Khaṭṭāb saw a silk garment (being sold) near the entrance of the mosque and said: "O Messenger of Allāh, I wish you would buy this to wear on Fridays and for (meeting) the envoys when they call on you." The Messenger of Allāh ﷺ said: "Only such people wear it who have no share in the Hereafter." Then garments of that cloth came to the Messenger of Allāh ﷺ and he gave one of those garments to ʿUmar ibn al-Khaṭṭāb, and ʿUmar said: "O Messenger of Allāh, you give it to me to wear it in spite of what you said about this garment of *'Uṭārid*?" The Messenger of Allāh said: "Surely I have not given it to you to wear it." So ʿUmar ibn al-Khaṭṭāb gave it to his brother who was in Makkah and was an idolater.[14]

Ch. 8:   Brushing teeth on Friday

> Abū Sāʿīd reported from the Prophet ﷺ: "One should brush one's teeth."

887 Abū Hurairah reported that the Messenger of Allāh ﷺ said: "Had it not been hard upon my followers" — or people — "I would have enjoined upon them the brushing of teeth for every prayer." [15]

888 Anas related that the Messenger of Allāh ﷺ said: "I have repeatedly told you about brushing your teeth."

---

the Holy Prophet, which speaks of bath and the using of perfume (book: 'Establishing the Prayer', h. 1152). If that report is authentic, the mention here of not knowing about perfume must be due to forgetfulness on the part of Ibn ʿAbbās.

[13] This is a repetition of h. 884 with the difference of wording.

[14] Best clothing is not the same as silk clothing, and silk clothing is discouraged for men to avoid leading a life of luxury. Bukhārī seems to imply here that ʿUmar suggested the wearing of good clothes to the Holy Prophet, and he declined only because it was made of silk. ʿUmar loved the Holy Prophet and wished to see him wearing best clothes. ʿUmar himself had no desire for silk clothing. Even as a ruler of an extensive empire he felt pleasure in wearing clothes with patches. On his arrival at Jerusalem after its conquest by the Muslims, ʿUmar was offered some precious costumes, but he refused the offer. See also h. 948.

[15] Since he regarded it as almost necessary to brush the teeth at every time of daily prayer, it would be really necessary in the case of the *Jumuʿah* prayer. The cleaning of teeth not only keeps the mouth clean but is also a remedy and a preventative for many diseases of the gums and teeth. Not brushing the teeth also leads to many ailments of the digestive system.

889 Hudhaifah reported: The Prophet ﷺ, when he used to get up at night, would clean his mouth.[16]

Ch. 9:   Using tooth-stick (*as-siwāk*) other than one's own

890 ʿĀʾishah reported: ʿAbdur Raḥmān, son of Abū Bakr, came with a tooth-stick which he was using. The Messenger of Allāh ﷺ looked at him, so I said to him: " ʿAbdur Raḥmān, Give me this tooth-stick." So he gave it to me and I broke it, chewed it a little and gave it to the Messenger of Allāh ﷺ. He cleaned his teeth with it and he was resting against my chest.[17]

Ch. 10:   What should be recited in the *Fajr* prayer on Friday

891 Abū Hurairah reported: The Prophet ﷺ used to recite in the *Fajr* prayer on Friday *Alif, Lām, Mīm, Tanzīl* (ch. 32 of the Holy Qurʾān) and *Hal atā ʾala-l-insān* (ch. 76).[18]

Ch. 11:   Friday prayers in villages and towns[19]

892 Ibn ʿAbbās reported: The first Friday prayer that was held after a Friday prayer in the mosque of the Messenger of Allāh ﷺ was in the mosque of ʿAbdul Qais in Juwāthā in Bahrain.[20]

893 Ibn ʿUmar reported that the Messenger of Allāh ﷺ said: "Each one of you is a guardian." Al-Laith added: Yūnus said that Ruzaiq ibn Ḥukaim wrote to Ibn Shihāb, and I was with him on that day at the valley of Qurā:

---

[16] This is a repetition of h. 245, omitting the closing words "with the tooth-stick".

[17] This was during the last illness of the Holy Prophet before his death.

[18] See also h. 1068.

[19] According to the Ḥanafīs and some Companions such as Ḥudhaifah and ʿAlī, the *Jumu'ah* congregation can be held only in towns, not in villages and small hamlets. Then there is such a wide divergence of opinion in the books of Ḥanafī jurisprudence as to the definition of a town that according to some a small village can be regarded as a town for this purpose. For places where there is a doubt as to it being a town, some people have invented a prayer known as *iḥtiyāṭī* ("by way of caution"). It is absolutely unjustified to limit the command to hold the Friday prayer to so-called towns and then define towns in different ways. Bukhārī rejects all these views by the very title of this chapter. Friday congregation can be held anywhere, whether it is a town or a village or even a place without any habitation. To confine the *Jumu'ah* congregation to certain places reserved for this purpose is to copy Christians whose prayers can be held only in churches. The Holy Prophet has said that the whole of the earth has been made a mosque for him and considered it a special characteristic of his religion. Other religions may require the holding of their services within their appointed places of worship, but prayer in Islām can be held anywhere.

[20] In some reports we read the word *qaryah*, meaning town, with Juwāthā, and this links it with the title of the chapter. The deputation of ʿAbdul Qais visited the Holy Prophet and after learning the teachings of Islam went back to their own home.

"Do you think I should hold Friday congregational prayers?" Ruzaiq was supervising the land which was being brought under cultivation by some Abyssinian and other (labourers) and he was at that time was governor of Aylah.[21] Ibn Shihāb wrote, and I heard him, ordering him that the Friday congregational prayer should be held, and also informed him that Sālim reported to him that 'Abdullāh ibn 'Umar used to say: I heard the Messenger of Allāh ﷺ say: "Each one of you is a guardian and will be questioned (by Allāh) about those in his care. A Muslim ruler is a guardian and will be questioned about his subjects; a man is a guardian of his own family and he will be questioned about those for whom he is responsible; a woman is a guardian of her husband's house, and will be questioned about those dependent on her; and a servant is a guardian of his master's property and will be questioned about that for which he is responsible." He (also) said: And I think that he (the Prophet) said: "A man is a guardian over the property of his father and will be questioned about what is under his care. Thus each one of you is a guardian and will be questioned about his responsibilities."

Ch. 12:   Is bath obligatory for those women and children, etc., who do not attend Friday prayers?

Ibn 'Umar said: Bath is obligatory only for those on whom Friday congregational prayers are incumbent.

894 'Abdullāh ibn 'Umar said: I heard the Messenger of Allāh ﷺ say: "Whoever of you is coming to the Friday prayer must take a bath." [22]

895 Abū Sa'īd al-Khudrī reported that the Messenger of Allāh, ﷺ said: "A bath on Friday is incumbent on every adult." [23]

896–898 Abū Hurairah reported that the Messenger of Allāh ﷺ said: "We are the last (religious community) but we will be the foremost on the day of Resurrection though they (other nations) were given the revealed books

---

[21] Aylah was a famous city lying on the route between Syria and Madīnah. Ruzaiq was its governor, appointed by 'Umar ibn 'Abdul 'Azīz. At the time of the incident referred to here, Ruzaiq was away from the city engaged in supervising the cultivation of fields. Ibn Shihāb wrote to him in reply that he should hold the *Jumu'ah* prayer at the place he was staying, because as the governor it was his responsibility to make arrangements for such prayers and that his negligence in the matter will be a dereliction of duty. In support of his view, he cited a report of Ibn 'Umar saying that everyone is in a way a ruler on whom devolves the duty of looking after those under his rulership, both in respect of their religious and their social needs. According to Ḥanafīs, a Friday congregation can be held only where the ruler is a Muslim. The ḥadīth under discussion rejects this idea as well because, according to it, every person, in a domain where he has authority, is a kind of king and ruler. So Friday prayer can be held at any place under any circumstances.

[22] This is a repetition of h. 877.

[23] This is a repetition of h. 858.

before us and we were given it after them. And this was the day about which they differed. So Allāh gave us guidance (in this matter). Tomorrow is (the day) for the Jews and the day after tomorrow is (the day) for the Christians." Then he became silent.[24] [897] Then he said: "It is obligatory upon every Muslim to have a bath once in seven days, in which he should wash his head and body." [898] Abū Hurairah reported that the Prophet ﷺ said: "From Allāh, the Most High, it is obligatory upon every Muslim to have a bath once in seven days." [25]

Ch. 13:   Chapter concerning the above

899 Ibn 'Umar reported from the Prophet ﷺ that he said: "Permit women to go to mosques at night." [26]

900 Ibn 'Umar reported: A wife of 'Umar used to attend the *Fajr* and *'Ishā'* congregational prayers in the mosque and someone said to her: "Why do you come when you know that 'Umar does not like it and has a strong sense of honour?" She said: "What prevents him from forbidding me?" He said: "What prevents him is the saying of the Messenger of Allāh ﷺ: 'Do not forbid the women dedicated to Allāh from coming to the mosques of Allāh'." [27]

---

[24] H. 896 in this group is a repetition of h. 876 with slight differences and a small addition at the end. See the footnote to h. 876. It is then followed in this group by h. 897 and h. 898.

[25] Having a bath is not limited to those attending Friday prayers, as it says "every Muslim." Thus, whoever attends the *Jumu'ah* prayer should have a bath before he comes to the mosque, and as for those who do not attend, they also should have a bath whether before the prayer or after it, whether on Friday or on some other day. In any case, everyone should have a bath at least once in a week, even including children. Cleanliness is among the teachings of Islām and one bath at least in a week is essential to physical cleanliness. Of course, a person may have a bath as many times as he needs or wishes or is able to do it.

[26] This is a repetition of h. 865. It has been inferred from it that women should not be allowed to go to mosques during the day and hence they are not required to attend the *Jumu'ah* prayers or to have the bath recommended for Friday. This conclusion is absolutely opposed to the reasoning of this ḥadīth and illogical. The meaning is clear: since women cannot be disallowed to attend the mosque prayers at night, they certainly cannot be prohibited from doing so during the daytime. So they should be expected to attend the Friday congregation. The importance of the Friday prayer has been made clear by the Qur'ān, and for women to attend it is even more necessary than their attendance at the daily prayers. And when woman are to attend the *Jumu'ah* prayers, the bath becomes necessary. The exclusion of women from the education and instruction given in the Friday sermon is among the major causes of the decline of the Muslims. This has led to the spread of ignorant and idolatrous customs within the home, and women who can make the home free of these un-Islamic practices are not given the knowledge of the teachings of Allāh and His Messenger.

[27] 'Umar used to live in the suburb of Madīnah at a distance at least of two miles. From this distance his wife 'Ātikah used to come to the Prophet's mosque for her morning and *'Ishā'*

Ch. 14: Exemption from attending Friday prayers on account of rain

901 ʿAbdullāh ibn al-Ḥārith, son of uncle of Muḥammad ibn Sīrīn, related that Ibn ʿAbbās said to his caller to prayer on a rainy day: When you say *Ash-hadu anna Muḥammad-ar Rasūl-ullāh* ("I bear witness that Muḥammad is the Messenger of Allāh"), do not say *Ḥayya ʿala-ṣ-ṣalāh* ("Come to prayer") but say: *Ṣallū fī buyūti-kum* ("Say your prayers in your own houses"). At this, the people were surprised. So he said: "One who was better than me had done this; surely the *Jumuʿah* prayer is obligatory and I did not like that I bring you out so that you walk in mud and slush." [28]

Ch. 15: From how far should one come to Friday prayers, and on whom is it obligatory?

Due to the word of Allāh, the Most High: "When the call is sounded for prayer on Friday" (62:9).[29]

ʿAṭāʾ said: "When you are in a locality where there are arrangements for Friday prayers and the call for prayer on Friday is given, it is your duty to attend it whether you hear the call or not." Anas sometimes used to say his Friday prayers at home, and sometimes would miss saying them, and he lived in al-Zawia, at a distance of six miles.[30]

902 ʿĀʾishah, wife of the Prophet ﷺ, reported: People came for Friday congregational prayers from their settlements and from ʿAwālī in turns.[31] They would come in the midst of dust which would cover them, and drenched in sweat which would drip from them. A man from among them once came to

---

prayers. Another report adds that she used to accompany ʿUmar and that although he did not approve of her coming he could not prevent her because of the clear injunction of the Holy Prophet.

[28] This is a repetition of h. 616 with some difference in the wording. Here it is clear that it was a Friday and the prayer concerned was the *Jumuʿah* prayer. So in spite of its obligatory nature and importance, when it was found that it would be hard and difficult for people to some out due to mud and rain, they were allowed not to come and join the congregation.

[29] In the words *nūdiya li-ṣ-ṣalāti* ("the call is sounded for prayer"), it is not the necessity of hearing the call which is mentioned but that of sounding the call. Even if the call is not actually heard, the time for prayer can be known by other means such as a clock.

[30] Anas' house was situated at a place which was at a distance of six miles from the city of Baṣrah. He was not regular in attending Friday congregations at Baṣrah. It has been inferred from this that those who would have to travel six miles should be excused from attending the congregational prayers.

[31] ʿAwālī was at a distance of two to three miles from Madīnah. People coming from there by turns shows that some used to be absent. This indicates exemption from attendance to *Jumuʿah* prayers from a distance of three miles as well.

the Messenger of Allāh ﷺ while he (the Prophet) was with me. The Prophet ﷺ said: "Would it not be better if you cleanse your bodies on this (special) day?"

Ch. 16:   Time for Friday prayers (is) when the sun declines

This is reported on the authority of 'Umar, 'Alī, Nu'mān ibn Bashīr and 'Amr ibn Ḥuraith.[32]

903 Yaḥya ibn Sa'īd informed that he asked 'Amrah about taking a bath on Friday and she said: " 'Ā'ishah said: People used to work themselves and when they came for Friday prayers they came in the same condition.[33] They were told: (It would be better) if you took a bath (before coming)."

904 Anas ibn Mālik reported that the Prophet ﷺ used to say Friday congregational prayers when the sun was on the decline.

905 Anas ibn Mālik reported: We used to say Friday prayers earliest possible and would have our midday nap after the Friday prayers.[34]

Ch. 17:   When it is extremely hot on Friday

906 Anas ibn Mālik said: The Prophet ﷺ said prayers earlier if it was very cold, and when it was extremely hot he would delay the prayers (till the heat lessened), that is, the Friday prayer.

(And according to another report:) He (Anas) did not mention the Friday prayers.[35]

---

[32] Because the *Jumu'ah* prayers take the place of *Zuhr* prayers, the time for which, according to the Holy Qur'ān (17:78), begins from the declining of the sun, the same is also the time for the *Jumu'ah* prayers. As the report from Anas in this chapter shows, it was the practice of the Holy Prophet to hold the Friday prayers after the sun began to decline. Certain reports show a different action on the part of the Companions, but the correct time for *Jumu'ah* is the time of the declining of the sun.

[33] The inference has been drawn from the words "when they came (*rāḥū*) for Friday prayers" that the time for Friday prayers is after the sun starts to decline. *Rāḥū* is derived from the word *rawāḥ* which means walking after the decline of the sun has set in. This applied to the majority. People coming from long distances would have started before noon.

[34] In other words, people used to have a little rest immediately after the *Jumu'ah* prayers held shortly after the decline of the sun. The word *qailūlah*, used for midday nap here, means sleep after midday. This rest could not be taken before the *Jumu'ah* prayers because they would miss the prayers.

[35] Since the *Jumu'ah* prayers take the place of *Zuhr* prayers, the time for *Jumu'ah* prayer should be set according to the time for the *Zuhr* prayers.

(And according to another report:) The *Amīr* (ruler) led us in Friday congregational prayers and then asked Anas: At what time did the Prophet ﷺ say *Zuhr* prayers?[36]

Ch. 18:   Walking to the Friday prayers

The word of Allāh, the Mighty, the Glorious: "Hasten (*fa-s'au*) to the remembrance of Allāh" (the Qur'ān, 62:9). *Sa'y* means to make an effort or exert one's self by walking, as the Most High has said: "He strives (*sa'ā*) for it as he ought to strive (*sa'ya*)" (the Qur'ān, 17:19). Ibn 'Abbās said: During that time (of Friday prayers), buying and selling is forbidden. 'Aṭā' said: All work is forbidden. Ibrāhīm ibn Sa'd said on the authority of az-Zuhrī: When the *mu'adhdhin* gives the call for prayers on Friday, it is incumbent on one who is travelling to attend the prayers. [37]

907 'Abāyah ibn Rifā'ah related: Abū 'Abas came and met me when I was going for *Jumu'ah* prayers and he said to me: I heard the Messenger of Allāh ﷺ say: "He whose feet are covered with dust in the way of Allāh, Allāh protects him from hell-fire."

908 Abū Hurairah said that he heard the Messenger of Allāh ﷺ say: "When the prayer is announced by *Iqāmah*, do not come to it running, but come to it walking and you should be calm. So whatever (part of prayer) you reach, pray it (accordingly), and what has escaped you, (you should) complete it (afterwards)." [38]

909 Abū Qatādah reported from the Prophet ﷺ that he said: "Do not stand up (for prayer) until you see me and you should be calm." [39]

Ch. 19:   One should not push apart two persons on Friday (i.e., pass between people)

910 Salmān al-Fārisī reported that the Messenger of Allāh ﷺ said:

---

[36] This *Amīr* was Hakam ibn Abū 'Aqīl who was representing his cousin Ḥajjāj ibn Yūsuf. He used to deliver such long sermons that the time for *'Aṣr* prayer would approach. One Yazīd al-Ḍabī objected to this. The *Amīr* asked Anas about the time at which the Holy Prophet used to say the *Zuhr* prayer, implying that the same time should be observed for the *Jumu'ah* prayer. Anas' reply was that in hot weather the Holy Prophet used to say the *Zuhr* prayer when it had cooled down, implying that the *Jumu'ah* prayer should also be said when the weather had cooled down.

[37] Az-Zuhrī has also reported that *Jumu'ah* prayer is not obligatory on a traveller. He may have expressed these different opinions according to the circumstances of the traveller.

[38] This is a repetition of h. 636 with differences in the first half.

[39] This is a repetition of h. 637. See the footnote there.

"Whoever takes a bath on Friday ... ... his sins from then to the following Friday will be forgiven." [40]

Ch. 20: A man should not make his brother get up in the Friday congregation and take his place

911 Ibn 'Umar said: The Prophet ﷺ forbade any man from making his brother get up from his place to sit there himself. I (the reporter narrating from Nāfi') said to Nāfi': "Was it for the Friday congregation?" He said: "It is irrespective of whether it is the Friday congregation or not."

Ch. 21: The Call to Prayer (*Adhān*) for Friday

912 As-Sā'ib ibn Yazīd reported: The first call to prayer on Friday in the days of the Prophet ﷺ, Abū Bakr and 'Umar used to be when the Imām sat on the pulpit. When 'Uthmān's time came, and the number of people (coming for prayer) increased, he added a third call to be given from az-Zaurā'.[41]

Abū 'Abdullāh (Bukhārī) said: Az-Zaurā' is a place in the market of Madīnah.

Ch. 22: Only one caller to prayer (*mu'adh-dhin*) giving the call for Friday prayers

913 As-Sā'ib ibn Yazīd reported that the one who added the third *Adhān* for Friday was 'Uthmān ibn 'Affān when the number of people of Madīnah increased. The Prophet ﷺ had only one caller to prayer (*mu'adh-dhin*) and *Adhān* on Friday used to be given only when the Imām would take his seat on the pulpit.[42]

Ch. 23: The *Imām* should repeat the words of the *Adhān* from the pulpit when he hears the call to prayer

914 Abū Umāmah ibn Sahl ibn Ḥunaif reported: I heard Mu'āwiyah ibn Abū Sufyān while he was sitting on the pulpit. The caller to prayer (*mu'adh-dhin*) gave the call to prayer, saying *Allāhu Akbar, Allāhu Akbar* ("Allāh is the Greatest, Allāh is the Greatest"), Mu'āwiyah said: *Allāhu Akbar, Allāhu Akbar.* Then he (the caller) said *Ashhadu an lā ilāha ill-Allāh* ("I bear witness

---

[40] This is a repetition of h. 883 with little change. See that ḥadīth for the full text, which is omitted here, and see also the footnote there.

[41] What is now the first call to prayer for *Jumu'ah* has been called the third one here because it came into vogue after the *Adhān* for the sermon and the *Iqāmah* for it.

[42] This is a repetition of h. 912. It would be the same *mu'adh-dhin* who gave the call to prayer as well as calling out the *Iqāmah.*

that there is no god but Allāh") and Muʿāwiyah said: "And (so do) I." Then he (the caller) said *As̲h̲hadu anna Muḥammad-ar Rasūl-ullāh* ("I bear witness that Muḥammad is Messenger of Allāh") and Muʿāwiyah said: "And (so do) I." Then, when the *Adhān* was finished, he (Muʿāwiyah) said: "O people, I heard the Messenger of Allāh ﷺ, while sitting at this place, when the caller to prayer gave the call to prayer, saying what you have heard me saying." [43]

Ch. 24:   Sitting on the pulpit at the time of the *Adhān*

915 As-Sā'ib ibn Yazīd informed that the second call for prayer on Friday was ordered by ʿUthmān when the number of people coming to the mosque increased. *Adhān* on Friday used to be given only when the Imām would take his seat (on the pulpit).[44]

Ch. 25:   *Adhān* for commencement of Friday sermon

916 As-Sā'ib ibn Yazīd said that the first *Adhān* on Friday in the days of the Messenger of Allāh ﷺ, Abū Bakr and ʿUmar used to be when the Imām sat on the pulpit. When the Caliphate of ʿUthmān came, and they (the number of people coming for prayer) increased, ʿUthmān ordered a third *Adhān* on Friday, and the *Adhān* was given from az-Zaurā'. So the practice was established accordingly.[45]

Ch. 26:   Sermon from the pulpit

Anas said: The Prophet ﷺ delivered sermons from the pulpit.

917 Abū Ḥāzim ibn Dīnār related: Some people came to Sahl ibn Saʿd al-Sāʿidī and they were differing about the pulpit (of the Holy Prophet), as to the tree of which it was made; so they asked him about it. So he said: By Allāh! I know of which wood it was made and I saw it on the first day it was installed and the first day the Messenger of Allāh ﷺ sat on it; the Messenger of Allāh ﷺ sent for such and such a woman — Sahl mentioned her name — and said to her: "Tell your slave, who is a carpenter, that he should make for me a seat made of wood on which I would sit when I speak to the people." So she ordered him (her slave) and he made it of the tamarisk wood taken from the forest, then brought it to her. She sent it on to the Messenger of Allāh ﷺ who ordered it to be placed there. Then I saw the Messenger of Allāh ﷺ praying

---

[43] This is a repetition of h. 612. Whereas h. 612 is very brief, here it is given in some detail.

[44] This is a repetition of h. 912 with the closing words from h. 913. Here this *Adhān* ordered by ʿUthmān has been called the second *Adhān*, not counting the *Takbīr* which signifies the start of congregational prayer.

[45] This is a repetition of h. 912 in very similar words with an addition at the end.

on it. He called out *Allāhu Akbar* while he was on it, then he went into *Rukū'* while he was still on it, then he came down from it, stepping back. He then prostrated at the base of the pulpit, then went back (to the top of the pulpit and said the second *rak'ah* in the same way). When he finished his prayers, he turned his face towards the people and said: "O people, I have done this only so that you may follow me and learn my prayer." [46]

918 Jābir ibn 'Abdullāh said: There was a stump of a palm-tree on which the Prophet ﷺ used to stand (to deliver his sermons). When a pulpit was installed for him, we heard from the stump sounds like that of a pregnant she-camel in her tenth month, so much so that the Prophet ﷺ came down (from the pulpit) and placed his hand on it (i.e., on the stump).[47]

919 Sālim's father ('Abdullāh ibn 'Umar) reported: I heard the Prophet ﷺ delivering the sermon from the pulpit and he said: "Whoever is coming to the Friday prayer must take a bath." [48]

Ch. 27: Delivering the sermon (*khuṭbah*) while standing

Anas said: The Prophet ﷺ delivered sermons while standing.[49]

920 Ibn 'Umar reported: The Prophet ﷺ delivered sermons while standing, then he would sit down and stand up again in the same way as you do it now.[50]

Ch. 28: People should face the Imām when he delivers the sermon

And Ibn 'Umar and Anas faced the Imām.[51]

---

[46] This is a repetition of h. 377 with some difference in the wording. In the last words, the Holy Prophet explained the reason for standing higher up in prayer and then stepping back for prostration. The statement in h. 377 beginning with "Abū 'Abdullāh said", to the end, is not found here.

[47] Rumi has well written: "The rationalist may deny the (incident of the) *ḥanānah*, but he is a stranger to the spiritual senses of the prophets." Ḥanānah was the name of the tree. The Holy Prophet heard the sound of weeping from the wood by means of his spiritual senses not possessed by most people. The vision was so powerful that people around him were granted the sense with which to hear this sound.

[48] This is a repetition of h. 877. The addition, "I heard the Prophet ﷺ delivering the sermon from the pulpit", relates it to the chapter heading.

[49] Bukhārī has taken the mention of "standing" from h. 1013 and h. 1014.

[50] The purpose in sitting after the first sermon seems to be to allow the preacher to take some rest and also to complete the sermon if something has been missed in the first address. It is not a mere ritual.

[51] In speaking of people turning their faces towards the Imām, it is emphasized that the

921 Abū Saʿīd al-Khudrī said that the Prophet ﷺ one day sat down on the pulpit and we sat around it (facing him).

Ch. 29: Saying the words *Ammā baʿd* ("After this") after praising Allāh in the sermon

ʿIkrimah reported it from Ibn ʿAbbās, from the Prophet ﷺ.[52]

922 Asmāʾ, daughter of Abū Bakr, reported: I went to see ʿĀʾishah and people were saying their prayer. I said: "What has happened to the people?" So she indicated with her head towards the sky and I said: "A sign?" She indicated with her head to say "Yes." She (Asmāʾ) said: And the Messenger of Allāh ﷺ prolonged (the prayer) so much so that fainting began to over-power me and there was a water-skin by my side in which there was water and I opened it and began to pour water from it on my head. When the Messenger of Allāh ﷺ finished, the sun became clear, and he addressed the people and praised Allāh as befits Him, and then he said: *Ammā baʿd.* She (Asmāʾ) said: And some women of the Anṣār began to make noise and I turned towards them to silence them, and I said to ʿĀʾishah: "What did he (the Prophet) say?" She said, he said: "There is nothing which I was not shown before that I did not see on this spot, even Paradise and Hell. ..."[53]

Hishām said: I have preserved what Fāṭimah (daughter of al-Mundhir) said to me except what she said about severity (of the punishment in the grave) on the hypocrites.

923 ʿAmr ibn Taghlib related that the Messenger of Allāh ﷺ received some wealth or goods which he distributed among some people and left out some. When the news reached him that those left out were unhappy, he recited

---

congregation should not take the sermon to be a meaningless ritual but listen to it with all attention. The importance of the *Jumuʿah* prayer lies in the sermon. Some take the words of the Qurʾān, "Hasten to the remembrance of Allāh" (62:9), to mean the Friday sermon. Abū Ḥanīfah says that the Imām in the Friday congregation should turn his face towards the right and the left in order to be seen addressing all the people. If the sermon consists of mere repetition of custom-ary words and formulae as a ritual, the listeners do not benefit at all, nor does it fulfil the purpose of the Friday service. To deliver the entire sermon in Arabic to a non-Arab congregation is sense-less.

[52] Under this heading, Bukhārī has placed together all those reports wherein it is stated that the Holy Prophet, at the start of his sermons and discourses, said the words *ammā baʿd* (literally "after this", meaning "to continue" or "now").

[53] After this beginning, h. 922 continues with the statement of the Holy Prophet as it occurs in h. 86. See the footnote under h. 86. This shows that at the time of the Holy Prophet women attended not only the daily obligatory prayers in the mosque, but also the supererogatory prayers that used to be held on extraordinary occasions. The addition by Hishām at the end here is not in h. 86.

the praise of Allāh and then said: "*Ammā ba'd,* by Allāh, I give (something) to one man and leave out another man. The one whom I leave out is dearer to me than the one to whom I give, but I give it to some people because I see impatience and restlessness in their hearts,[54] and I entrust some people to what Allāh has implanted in their hearts, a sense of sufficiency and goodness, and among them is 'Amr ibn Taghlib." ('Amr ibn Taghlib added:) By Allāh, I attach more value to this utterance of the Messenger of Allāh ﷺ than to a herd of red camels.

924 'Urwah reported that 'Ā'ishah informed him that the Messenger of Allāh ﷺ came out one night in the middle of the night (from his apartment) and said his prayer (i.e., *Tahajjud*) in the mosque and some people said the same prayer with him. Then in the morning people talked about it and (the next night) more of them gathered (in the mosque) and said their prayer with him. Then again in the morning people talked about it and the people in the mosque increased in number on the third night. So the Messenger of Allāh ﷺ came out and they said their prayer with him. And when it was the fourth night the mosque proved too small for the people who were there (but the Holy Prophet did not come out) till he came out for his morning prayer. When he had finished the *Fajr* prayer, he turned his face towards the people and after reciting the *shahādah* he said: "*Ammā ba'du,* surely it was not that I feared your attendance but I feared that it (the *Tahajjud* prayer) would be made compulsory for you and you are unable to observe it." [55]

925 Abū Ḥumaid as-Sā'idī reported that the Messenger of Allāh ﷺ rose one evening after the (*'Ishā'*) prayer and said *Tashahhud* and eulogised Allāh as befits Him, then said: "*Ammā ba'd.*" [56]

---

[54] These are the people called *mu'allafat-ul-qulūb,* literally meaning 'those whose hearts are made to incline (to truth)' and for whom the Holy Qur'ān sets apart a portion of the *zakāt* fund (see 9:60). The idea behind it was to afford relief to those who had been deprived of their livelihood on account of their change of faith, so that the hardships may not compel them to leave the faith before they have learnt about it and appreciated its qualities. This wise teaching of the Holy Prophet led to these people in time becoming confirmed believers who were able to withstand financial hardship. Compared to them was that noble band called Companions of the Holy Prophet Muḥammad whose faith was unshakeable by any trial and who are mentioned in the Qur'ān in the words: "they prefer others before themselves (to receive help) even though poverty may afflict them" (59:9). To say that the Holy Prophet offered people financial inducements to remain in Islām is against historical facts. He possessed no treasure to offer people to become Muslims; on the contrary, as soon as they became Muslims they had to make every kind of sacrifice, give their properties, leave their homes, and bear persecution. Later on, such people joined Islām who could not bear these hardships and they are the ones mentioned here.

[55] This is a repetition of h. 729 in different words. See also h. 1129 and h. 2011–2012.

[56] This ḥadīth has occurred in detail in the Book of Faith.

926 Al-Miswar ibn Makhramah reported: The Messenger of Allāh ﷺ stood up and I heard him saying *Ammā ba'd* after the *Tashahhud.*[57]

927 Ibn 'Abbās reported: The Prophet ﷺ ascended the pulpit on the occasion of the last time he was seen sitting (in the mosque), with a sheet thrown over his shoulders and a black headband tied on his head, he praised and glorified Allāh and then said: "O people, come nearer to me." People drew closer and he proceeded to say: "*Ammā ba'd.* Surely those alive from among the Helpers (*Anṣār*) will grow smaller in number and other people will increase in number, so whoever from among the followers of Muḥammad acquires any rule and the power to harm or benefit a person, he should appreciate the good ones among them (the Helpers) and overlook their wrong-doers."[58]

Ch. 30:   Sitting between the two sermons on Friday

928 'Abdullāh (ibn 'Umar) reported: The Prophet ﷺ used to deliver two sermons and he used to sit down between the two.[59]

Ch. 31:   Listening attentively to the sermon

929 Abū Hurairah reported that the Prophet ﷺ said: "When it is Friday, angels stand at the gate of the mosque and write down the names of those coming in, the first as the first (and so on). And the likeness of one who comes earliest is that of one who has sacrificed a camel, then the next as one who has sacrificed a cow, then the next as one who has sacrificed a ram, then the next as one who has sacrificed a chicken, then the next as one who has offered an egg. When the Imām comes out (for the sermon) they roll up their scrolls and listen to the sermon."[60]

---

[57] This ḥadīth occurs in detail later in the Book of Qualities.

[58] The proportion of the *Anṣār* among the Muslims was obviously decreasing as Islām was spreading in the world and the number of Muslims was increasing. The admonition of the Holy Prophet regarding the *Anṣār,* to the effect that their good works should be valued and their weaknesses should be ignored, was in view of their services to the cause of Islam at a time when it was hard pressed by the enemies from all sides. They undertook to stand up against Arabs and non-Arabs to defend Islām in practice, provided refuge to Muslims and were prepared to make every kind of sacrifice. Allāh stated the same about them in words similar to those used in this ḥadīth: "These are they from whom We accept the best of what they do and overlook their evil deeds — among the owners of the Garden" (46:16).

[59] This is a repetition of h. 920 in different words. See note on h. 920.

[60] This is a repetition of h. 881 with brevity and a change in the wording. Its last words are related to the chapter heading. The angels listening to the sermon means only that they get ready to cast the influence of the sermon into the hearts of those among the audience who take care to

Ch. 32: **When the Imām, seeing a man coming while he is delivering his sermon, asks him to say two *rak'ahs* of prayer**

930 Jābir ibn 'Abdullāh reported: A man came while the Prophet ﷺ was giving the sermon to the people on Friday. He (the Prophet) said: "So-and-so, have you said your prayers?" He said: "No." He (the Prophet) said: "Stand up and say your prayers."

Ch. 33: **He who arrives when the Imām is delivering his sermon should say two *rak'ahs* of prayer briefly**

931 Jābir (ibn 'Abdullāh) said: A man entered on Friday while the Prophet ﷺ was giving the sermon. He (the Prophet) said: "Have you said your prayers?" He said: "No." He (the Prophet) said: "Say two *rak'ahs* (of prayer)." [61]

Ch. 34: **Raising of hands (in prayer) during the sermon**

932 Anas reported: Once when the Prophet ﷺ was delivering the sermon on Friday, a man got up and said: "O Messenger of Allāh, the horses have perished and so have the goats, so pray to Allāh that He give us rain!" So he (the Prophet) stretched out his hands and prayed.[62]

Ch. 35: **Praying for rain during the Friday sermon**

933 Anas ibn Mālik reported: A famine visited the people in the time of the Prophet ﷺ. When the Prophet ﷺ was delivering his sermon on a Friday, a Bedouin got up and said: "O Messenger of Allāh, our wealth has perished and our families are starving, so pray to Allāh for us." He (the Holy Prophet) raised his hands and we could not see a patch of cloud in the sky. By Him in Whose hand is my life, he had not lowered them (his hands) when billows of clouds appeared, and he had hardly left the pulpit when I saw rain dripping from his beard. We had rainfall on that day, the next day, the day after that and so on till the following Friday. That same Bedouin — or he (the narrator) said, someone else — got up and said: "O Messenger of Allāh, buildings have collapsed and property has been submerged in water, so pray to Allāh for us."

---

listen. This shows that those who do not appear in the *Jumu'ah* congregation before the sermon starts miss the real purpose of their participation.

[61] The previous chapter heading requires the Imām to ask the newcomer to the mosque to say two *rak'ahs* of prayer before he sits down to listen to the sermon, and this if he does not say them himself. This chapter heading requires the newcomer himself to say these two *rak'ahs*. This ḥadīth is a repetition of h. 930. According to h. 930 the Holy Prophet asked him to "say your prayers", whereas in this report two *rak'ahs* of prayer are explicitly mentioned.

[62] This report is given in detail in h. 933 that follows. This report shows that to raise hands for prayer in the course of sermon is allowed.

He (the Prophet) raised his hands and said: "O Allāh, (let it rain) around us and not on us," and any cloud he pointed towards, it cleared away and Madīnah became like a pool of water and the stream of Qanāt flowed with water for a month. Anyone who came from anywhere talked of nothing else but heavy rainfall.[63]

Ch. 36: Keeping silent on Friday while the Imām is delivering the sermon, and to say to one's companion "Be quiet" is senseless

Salmān reported from the Prophet ﷺ: "Be quiet once the Imām starts speaking."

934 Abū Hurairah informed that the Messenger of Allāh ﷺ said: "When you say to your companion on Friday, 'Keep quiet,' while the Imām is delivering the sermon, you have certainly acted senselessly." [64]

Ch. 37: A special moment during on Friday

935 Abū Hurairah reported that the Messenger of Allāh ﷺ was speaking about Friday and he said: "There is a moment during it (Friday) when, if a dutiful Muslim standing in prayer, asks of Allāh something, Allāh grants him that very thing," and he indicated with his hand that it (the moment) is very short.[65]

---

[63] This is one of the miracles of the acceptance of the Holy Prophet's prayer. He has also taught the holding of prayer for rain, showing that such acceptance of prayer would be granted to his followers as well. There are persons among his followers whose prayers are granted such miraculous acceptance by Allāh that through them He shows extraordinary occurrences even now which appear as miraculous to the people. In the chapter after the next, there is mention of a particular moment during Friday congregational prayer in which such acceptance of prayer takes place. See also h. 1013 – h. 1019, h. 1021, h. 1029 – h. 1030, h. 1033 and footnote to h. 1020.

[64] A person who speaks, if only to ask another to keep quiet, becomes a source of noise himself. It is quite a different thing if the Imām asks people to keep silent.

[65] There is such a divergence of opinion on the identification of this particular moment that in *Fatḥ al-Bārī* there are as many as thirty-eight different opinions quoted, each one of which has been attributed to the Holy Prophet or some Companions or someone from the next generation after the Companions. It has also been said that this particular moment existed in earlier times but is no longer in existence. Some have suggested that this moment comes on a Friday only once in a year. It is stated in *Fatḥ al-Bārī* that, out of these divergent reports, two appear to be the most reliable of all: (1) it is between the time the Imām takes his seat on the pulpit and when he finishes the prayer, and (2) it comes between the *'Aṣr* prayer and sunset. But in this ḥadīth there are the words "standing for prayer," which show that it is to be found in the course of some prayer. But, as we know, no prayer is said in the course of the sermon nor between the hours of *'Aṣr* prayer and sunset. The fact is that this moment of acceptance is connected with the inner condition of the heart which exerts itself in the way of God to try to reach Him. A person may pray constantly

Ch. 38: When some people leave while the Imām is engaged in Friday prayers, the prayer of the Imām and those who remain is valid[66]

936 Jābir ibn 'Abdullāh related: Once when we were saying our prayers with the Prophet ﷺ a caravan arrived carrying food grains and people became attentive towards it so much that no more than twelve people remained with the Prophet ﷺ, so this verse was revealed: "And when they see merchandise or sport, they break away to it and leave you standing" (the Qur'ān, 62:11).[67]

---

all day and he may not find this moment. To find it depends on the inner humility and melting of the heart that commends the soul to the mercy of Allāh. We can reach this state by the special efforts we make on Friday to cleanse ourselves physically and spiritually. These efforts make an impression on our soul, which then attains nearness to God. Moreover, the gathering of people seeking the same object intensifies the feeling of nearness to God. On such a day, the collective prayers of these pure souls are welcomed at the Divine threshold and the blessings of God descend on them. This effect, be it during the sermon, or during the Friday prayer, or at the time of the next *'Aṣr* prayer, does not go to waste and Allāh hears the prayer. There can be no objection to this interpretation, i.e., that the moment of acceptance can be at different times. It is impossible to fix one and the same time for everyone since people live in different time zones and do not say Friday prayers at the same time. As for granting whatever one asks for at that moment of acceptance, it should be remembered that only such prayers are granted that do not run counter to any promise or law of Allāh. Thus, in one ḥadīth we read that the father of Jābir, who died a martyr's death, was told by Allāh that He was so pleased with him that he will be given whatever he asked for, at which he prayed that he might be sent back alive to the world and enjoy death by martyrdom as before. Allāh told him in reply that this prayer could not be granted because it was contrary to the promise of Allāh.

[66] The purpose of this chapter seems to be to indicate that no particular number is required for the validity of *Jumu'ah* congregation. In *Fatḥ al-Bārī* fifteen opinions have been quoted on the question of the minimum number to form a Friday congregation. According to Imām Abū Ḥanīfah, there should be at least three people besides the Imām to form the congregation.

[67] Opinions differ in respect of the number of people referred to here. In al-Dār Quṭnī the report gives the number to be forty. The report mentioning twelve has been regarded as authentic, and while it may be authentic according to the principles of Ḥadīth narrations, it does not seem to be true according to knowledge and reason. At that time the number of Helpers and the number of Emigrants were both considerable, and all used to attend the Friday prayers. According to the verse "hasten to the remembrance of Allāh and leave off business" (62:9), listening to the sermon is obligatory and conducting business is disallowed. These were people who had made great sacrifices of giving up their properties and loved ones for the sake of Allāh, and included those who had helped their fellow Muslims of Makkah to settle, preferring their needs over their own while themselves being in need (the Qur'ān, 59:9), only for the love of Islām. It is unthinkable that they would leave during the sermon to run after mere worldly gain and not return even for the prayer. Besides, if the verses relating to the Friday prayer (62:9–11) are considered together, it will be seen that the first two verses address the believers, "*O you who believe,* when the call is sounded for prayer on Friday, ... that *you* may be successful", while the third verse uses the third person, "And when *they* see trading or entertainment, *they* break away to it...", to refer to a different group of people, i.e., the hypocrites. It was the worldly-minded hypocrites who did not obey God, did not listen to the sermon, went after mundane attractions, and did not listen to the mention of God. Just as the hypocrites did not attend the sermon, they also separated themselves when required to fight in the way of Allāh.

Ch. 39: Prayers before and after the Friday congregational prayer[68]

937 ʿAbdullāh ibn ʿUmar reported that the Messenger of Allāh ﷺ used to say two *rak'ahs* of prayer before *Ẓuhr* and two *rak'ahs* after it, and two *rak'ahs* in his house after *Maghrib* prayers and two *rak'ahs* after the *'Ishā'* prayers. He would not say any prayers after the Friday congregational prayers until he returned home and then he would say two *rak'ahs* of prayer.

Ch. 40: The word of Allāh, the Mighty, the Glorious: "But when the prayer is ended, disperse in the land and seek of Allāh's grace" (62:11)[69]

938 Sahl reported: A woman among us sowed beetroot in her cultivated fields. On Friday she used to pull out the roots of the beet and put them in a cooking pot and add to it a handful of ground barley, and cook it. The roots of the beet would appear like pieces of meat in it. On our return from Friday prayers we would greet her with *salām* and she would bring this food to us, and we would devour it. We looked forward to Friday for this food of hers.[70]

939 It is added (in another report) from Sahl that he said: We would not have our mid-day nap or lunch till after the Friday congregational prayers.

Ch. 41: Having a nap after the Friday congregational prayers

940 Anas said: We used to say the *Jumu'ah* prayer rather early and then have our mid-day nap.

941 Sahl reported: We used to say the *Jumu'ah* prayer with the Prophet ﷺ and then have the mid-day nap.[71]

---

[68] There is no mention of any prayer preceding the *Jumu'ah* congregation in the report in this chapter. Bukhārī has either regarded *Jumu'ah* as analogous to *Ẓuhr* prayers, and before *Ẓuhr* the Holy Prophet used to say two *rak'ahs* of prayer, or he is referring to h. 930 reported by Jābir, in which the Holy Prophet asked a certain man, who arrived as he was delivering the sermon, to say two *rak'ahs* of prayer before he sat down to listen to the sermon.

[69] There are three verses in connection with the *Jumu'ah* prayer (62:9–11), all three of which speak of business transactions and affairs of the world, showing that attending to worldly affairs on Friday is quite lawful. The Muslim Friday is accordingly not like the Jewish or Christian Sabbath. It is not a day for wholesale asceticism, or giving up all business entirely and engaging in the remembrance of God in seclusion. It is only from the time of hearing the call to prayer till the end of the prayer that all other work is abandoned. Both before and after the prayers all kinds of worldly affairs can be attended to as usual. The Jews and Christians tried observing the seventh day when no work was allowed, but they could not maintain it.

[70] This shows that in those days women engaged in shop-keeping and there was nothing wrong in their selling to men or men buying from them.

[71] H. 940 and h. 941 consist of the additional part of h. 938 which is given as h. 939.

Book 12: *Ṣalāt al-Khauf*
Prayer when facing fear

In the name of Allāh, the Beneficent, the Merciful

Ch. 1:   Prayer when facing fear

Allāh, the Most High, said: "And when you journey in the earth, there is no blame on you if you shorten the prayer, if you fear that those who disbelieve will give you trouble. Surely the disbelievers are an open enemy to you. … Surely Allāh has prepared a humiliating punishment for the disbelievers." (4 : 101–102).[1]

Ch. 2:   Chapter concerning the above

942 'Abdullāh ibn 'Umar said: I set off with the Messenger of Allāh ﷺ for a battle at Najd. When we were faced with the enemy and arrayed in rows against them, the Messenger of Allāh ﷺ got up to lead us in prayer and a

---

[1] The Qur'ān twice deals with the question of prayer in a state of fear. In 4 : 101 it is stated: "And when you journey in the earth, there is no blame on you if you shorten the prayer, if you fear that those who disbelieve will give you trouble", which is referred to here. The other occasion is in 2 : 239: "But if you are in danger, then (say your prayers) on foot or on horseback", which is referred to in the heading of the next chapter. This again shows that Bukhārī treats the Qur'ān as the primary source of Islām and adds ḥadīth in further explanation of it. The first passage is intended for a situation in which congregational prayer is possible inspite of the state of fear, whereas the second regulation is meant for a situation in which congregation is not possible due to combat with the enemy. In this latter condition prayer can be said by each one on his own, whether on foot or riding, as stated in the next chapter. In case of an ordinary journey, in which there is no fear, prayer can similarly be shortened. This is proved by the practice and the sayings of the Holy Prophet. Thus we read in Abū Dāwūd, Nasā'i and Muslim a report of Ibn 'Abbās saying: "Allāh has ordained prayers by the tongue of your Prophet: four *rak'ahs* when resident (i.e., not travelling), two *rak'ahs* in journey and one *rak'ah* in a state of fear." Accordingly, the rule of prayer is that those which are ordinarily four *rak'ahs* become two *rak'ahs* in a journey. The Holy Qur'ān confirms this view in 4 : 102 in which, while in the battlefield, the congregation is to say just one *rak'ah* and the Imām says only two *rak'ahs* in prayers that normally consists of four *rak'ahs*. This shows that reduction from four to two *rak'ahs* is on account of journey and that the further concession of one *rak'ah* to the congregation is only on account of fear. Thus this verse also speaks of two conditions: one, that of journey, and the second, that of fear. As for fear, there are divergent reports about concessions allowed, showing that the *rak'ahs* vary according to the situation and the Holy Prophet led prayers in whatever way was possible according to the circumstances. Today too, if such a situation arises, prayers can be said in whatever way is suitable.

group of people stood with him and the other group faced the enemy. The Messenger of Allāh ﷺ performed *Rukū'* with those who were with him and performed *Sajdah* twice. Then they (who had prayed with the Holy Prophet) went to take the place of the group who had not said their prayers. When they came, the Messenger of Allāh ﷺ performed *Rukū'* and two *Sajdahs* with them as well and then (he concluded the prayers with) *Taslīm*. Then everyone stood up in prayer, and individually performed *Rukū'* once and *Sajdah* twice.[2]

Ch. 3:   Prayer when facing fear while on foot (*rijāl*) or riding

Rājil means standing.

943 Ibn 'Umar reported, like the saying of Mujāhid, that when people are mixed up (in a battle with the enemy), they should pray while standing. Ibn 'Umar has added on the authority of the Prophet ﷺ: "And when they (the enemy) are more numerous, they (the Muslims) should say their prayers while standing or riding.[3]

Ch. 4:   In the prayer when facing fear, one group guards another and vice versa

944 Ibn 'Abbās reported: The Prophet ﷺ stood up for prayers and people

---

[2] The word *najd* means *an elevated place*. It is the name of that plateau which lies in the middle of the Arabian Peninsula and is a verdant region. The battle to which these words refer is the battle known as *Dhāt al-Riqā'*. The manner of prayer herein described is that the whole army should be divided into two sections, one of which should stand ready to fight the enemy and the second is to say one *rak'ah* of prayer with the Holy Prophet. The second section, after finishing the first *rak'ah*, should go and replace the first section in facing the enemy, thus releasing the first one to join the Holy Prophet in the second *rak'ah* of the prayer. At the end, this report adds that each section completed its prayer by saying the missing one *rak'ah*, in which every man prayed on his own. The manner of this completion, as reported by Ibn Mas'ūd in Abū Dāwūd, is that the section that came last to join the Holy Prophet in prayer, completed its missing *rak'ah* on the spot and when they had finished it, they took the place of the other section to face the enemy, releasing them to complete their missing *rak'ah* (Abū Dāwūd, book: 'Prayer during journey', h. 1238).

[3] The statement of Mujāhid has been reported by Ismā'īlī and runs thus: "When they are mixed up (i.e., Muslims are mixed up with the enemies in fighting), it is sufficient (to say the prayer) by indicating with the head." A report from Ibn 'Umar by Nāfi' is similar to this statement of Mujāhid and runs as follows: "When they are mixed up, there can be only remembrance of (Allāh) at heart and by indicating with the head." But these reports are not traceable in their lines of transmission to the Holy Prophet. The word "standing", occurring after "mixed up" in h. 943, is missing in the reports just referred to. It seems that this word is employed to summarize the manner of prayer described by the expression "indicating with the head". The addition by Ibn 'Umar in h. 943 means that when the enemy is so numerous that one part of the Muslim army is not enough to confront it, no division should be made in the army and prayer should be said in whichever position in battle any individual believer finds himself. It is evident that such a prayer is possible only by making indications.

stood likewise with him. He said *Takbīr* and the people said the same with him. He performed *Rukū'* and some people from among them went into *Rukū'* with him. Then he performed *Sajdah* and people performed *Sajdah* with him. Then he stood up for the second *rak'ah* and those who had already performed *Sajdah* stood up to guard their brothers. The others (who had previously been guarding) performed *Rukū'* and *Sajdah* with him. Everyone prayed but some had to guard others (while these others prayed).[4]

Ch. 5: Prayers when there is hope of gaining fortresses and when in combat with the enemy

Al-Auzāʿī said: When victory is imminent and people are unable to perform prayers, everyone should say prayers individually by gesture. If they are unable to (pray) even by gesture, they should defer prayers until the end of the battle or till peace is established, when they should pray two *rak'ahs*. If they are unable to do this, they should say one *rak'ah* and perform two *Sajdahs*. If they are unable to do (even this), then *Takbīr* alone is not sufficient for them and they should defer (prayers) until they are in peace (conditions).

Makhūl said the same.

Anas ibn Mālik said: I was present when the fort of Tustar was attacked at the break of dawn. The fury of the battle intensified and people were unable to say their prayers. We did not say prayers till it was well into the morning and then we prayed, and (on this occasion) we were with Abū Mūsā. Thus (ultimately) we captured the fort.

---

[4] The manner of saying the prayer in fear as given here by Ibn ʿAbbās differs from the one given by Ibn ʿUmar in h. 942. Here the whole army stood up in the prayer position behind the Holy Prophet, but as he went into *Rukū'* only the first row followed him in *Rukū'* while the rear row kept guard. Then when the Holy Prophet finished the first *rak'ah* together with the first row, this batch kept standing in readiness for the enemy while the rear row followed him in *Rukū'* and *Sajdah*. Thus every row said only one *rak'ah* of prayer with the Holy Prophet. This is when the enemy is close at hand. In this report there is no mention as to whether people completed their missing *rak'ah* of prayer or not. But there is a report by Ibn ʿAbbās in Nasā'ī (h. 1533) in which it is added at the end: "And did not complete the missing *rak'ah*." In Abū Dāwūd (h. 1247), Nasā'ī (h. 1532) and Muslim (book: 'Prayer of travellers', ch. 1) there is a report from Ibn ʿAbbās saying: "Allāh has ordained prayers by the tongue of your Prophet: four *rak'ahs* when resident (i.e., not travelling), two *rak'ahs* in journey and one *rak'ah* in a state of fear." Companions like Abū Hurairah and Abū Mūsā Ashʿarī and many of those from the next generation, and Isḥāq and Thaurī, are of the same view. The majority holds that prayer in the state of fear consists of two *rak'ahs,* and say that even the report under discussion does not negate it but says nothing about it. The report from Ibn ʿUmar also mentions two *rak'ahs*. It seems that the second *rak'ah* in such a condition was said by the congregation only by gesture or indication.

Anas ibn Mālik said: And the world and whatever is in it could not have pleased me so much as prayers (did at that time).[5]

945 Jābir ibn ʿAbdullāh reported: ʿUmar came on the day of the (battle of the) Ditch and began to curse the unbelievers of the Quraish, saying: "O Messenger of Allāh, I have not said the *ʿAṣr* prayer and the sun is setting." The Prophet ﷺ said: "I too, by Allāh, have not said it (either)." So he went towards Buṭḥān and performed ablution, and he said the *ʿAṣr* prayer after the sun had disappeared. Then he said the *Maghrib* prayer after it.[6]

Ch. 6: Prayer of the pursuer (*ṭālib*) and the pursued (*maṭlūb*) while riding and by gesture

Walīd said: I spoke to al-Auzāʿī about Shuraḥbīl ibn al-Simṭ and his companions praying while mounted on the back of their animals and he said: "In our view, this is the rule when there is fear of missing (prayers)." Walīd reasoned the same from the saying of the Prophet ﷺ: "None should say his *ʿAṣr* prayers until he reaches Banī Quraiẓah." [7]

946 Ibn ʿUmar reported: The Prophet ﷺ said to us on his return from the battle of al-Aḥzāb: "No one should say his *ʿAṣr* prayers until he reaches Banī Quraiẓah." Some of them were on the way when it was time for *ʿAṣr* prayer, and some of them said: "We shall not say our prayer until we reach there." But some of them said: "We will say our prayers as this has not been required of us." This was mentioned to the Prophet ﷺ but he did not reproach anyone.[8]

---

[5] Tustar is a famous city in Ahwāz. It was conquered by the Muslims in 20 A.H. during the Caliphate of ʿUmar. Abū Mūsā Ashʿarī was the commander of the Muslim army, and Anas was the officer commanding the vanguard. On this occasion, the battle that ensued took precedence over saying the prayer at the appointed time. In the same way the Holy Prophet himself, on the day of the battle of the Ditch (known also as battle of al-Aḥzāb), deferred the prayer in consideration of the seriousness of the battle, as reported in h. 596. In both these cases, if the prayers were not deferred there was every likelihood of the army being routed by the enemies.

[6] H. 596 is repeated here with a slight change in the wording. The Holy Prophet and his Companions could not say their *ʿAṣr* prayer in time on account of their engagement with the enemy.

[7] The word *ṭālib* refers to the person who chases the enemy either to capture him or to kill him, and *maṭlūb* is the man so chased. Walīd sought justification for the action of Shuraḥbīl from the orders of the Holy Prophet on the day of the battle of the Ditch to his Companions saying that they should say their *Aṣr* prayer only after they had reached the tribe of Banī Quraiẓah, and some of the Companions acted on it by putting off their *ʿAṣr* prayer at the appointed time.

[8] Immediately after the battle of al-Aḥzāb, the Holy Prophet ordered an attack on Banī Quraiẓah due to their breach of covenant and treachery. He had it announced in Madīnah that the

Ch. 7:   Saying of morning prayers at the earliest time and in the dark when an attack is taking place or during fighting

947 Anas ibn Mālik reported that the Messenger of Allāh ﷺ led the morning prayers in the dark, then he rode and said: "*Allāhu Akbar,* Khaibar is ruined. When we alight in the fields of a nation, the morning of these people, who had been warned, turns evil." People came out into the streets running and saying: "Muḥammad and the *khamīs*" — he (the reporter of the ḥadīth) said: *khamīs* means army. The Messenger of Allāh ﷺ defeated them, the fighting men were killed, and the women and children taken captive. And Ṣafiyyah fell to the lot of Diḥyah al-Kalbī and then she came to the Messenger of Allāh ﷺ who married her and freed her by way of her dowry.

'Abdul 'Azīz said to Thābit: "O Abū Muḥammad, did you ask Anas what was the dowry he (the Holy Prophet) gave to her?" And he (Thābit) said: "He gave herself to her by way of dowry." And he smiled.[9]

'Aṣr prayer should be said only when the Muslim forces had reached the colony of Banī Quraiẓah. When it was found on the way that the sun was about to set, the Companions of the Holy Prophet differed in their opinion on the question of prayer. Some held the view that real sense of the Holy Prophet's order was that the Muslim forces should be quick in their march, not that the prayer should be deferred. Others held that the Holy Prophet had said that they should not say their prayer before they had arrived at the colony of Banī Quraiẓah even if they missed the prayer time. Each acted upon his own understanding, some praying on time on the way there, and others delaying the prayer until they reached the destination. When this difference of opinion and action was communicated to the Holy Prophet he did not disapprove of anyone's conduct. This shows that a particular prayer can be delayed from its proper time if the gravity of the situation calls for it.

[9] H. 371 has been repeated here with much brevity.

Book 13: *Al-'Īdain*
The Two Eid Festivals

In the name of Allāh, the Beneficent, the Merciful

Ch. 1: Concerning the two Eid festivals and dressing up for them[1]

948 'Abdullāh ibn 'Umar said: 'Umar bought a thick silk cloak which was on sale in the market and came with it to the Messenger of Allāh ﷺ and said: "O Messenger of Allāh, buy this to adorn yourself for Eid and for (meeting) the envoys." The Messenger of Allāh ﷺ said to him: "This garment is only for those who have no share (in the Hereafter)." So the matter remained as it was for 'Umar, for as long as Allāh willed. Then the Messenger of Allāh ﷺ sent him a silk cloak. 'Umar came with it to the Messenger of Allāh ﷺ and said: "O Messenger of Allāh, you said, 'This garment is only for those who have no share (in the Hereafter)', and you have sent this cloak to me." The Messenger of Allāh ﷺ said to him: "Sell it or fulfil some other need by it." [2]

Ch. 2: Lances and shields on Eid day[3]

949–950 'Ā'ishah reported: The Prophet ﷺ came to me when there were

---

[1] We have used the common spelling of Eid in English, while its transliteration is *'Īd*. Bukhārī starts this book on the two Eids with reports referring to external embellishment and sport and play, because generally the Eid or a festival is considered to consist of such activities. After this, Bukhārī proceeds to tell us the Holy Prophet's practice in celebrating Eid and its inner significance. The reports also tell us that there should be no extravagance in physical embellishment. That is why wearing silk has not been approved for men. It is, however, permissible for women. The significance of Eid in Islām involves three principal points: a collective devotional service to God which impresses the greatness of God upon the heart, developing loving relationships within the community, and showing concern for the poor.

[2] This is a repetition of h. 886 with some difference in the wording. Where h. 886 uses the words "to wear on Fridays and for (meeting) the envoys", this mentions Eid instead of Friday. At the end, the Holy Prophet's utterance is more explicit, "Sell it or fulfil some other need by it", than in h. 886. There is no mention here of 'Umar sending it to his idolater brother, as in h. 886.

[3] Javelins and shields were the weapons of war in those days. These Abyssinians were having a game with these weapons on Eid day. However, it was no mere recreation but was also an exercise for the development of physical strength, courage and skill in the use of these weapons.

two girls with me singing the song of (the battle of) Bu'āth.[4] He lay down on the bed and turned his face the other way. Abū Bakr came and scolded me and said: "Satan's music near the Prophet ﷺ!" So the Messenger of Allāh turned his face towards him (Abū Bakr) and said: "Leave them alone."[5] So when his attention was diverted I signalled the two girls and they left.

[950] It was the day of Eid and the Abyssinians were sporting with lances and leather shields. I asked the Messenger of Allāh ﷺ, or (perhaps) he said (himself): "Do you want to see (the sport)?" I said: "Yes." So he made me stand behind him and my cheek was touching his and he was saying: "Carry on, O Banī Arfadah", until such time as I became tired. He asked me: "Is that enough for you?" I said: "Yes." He said: "Then you may go."[6]

Ch. 3: *Sunnah* on the two Eids to be followed by Muslims

951 Al-Barā' reported: I heard the Prophet ﷺ delivering a sermon and he said: "The first thing with which we begin this day of ours is that we say our prayers,[7] then we return (home) and make sacrifice (on the Eid of Sacrifice). So whosoever does this, he follows our practice."

952 'Ā'ishah reported: Abū Bakr came in and with me were two girls from among the girls of the *Anṣār* singing what the *Anṣār* used to say on the day of (the battle of) Bu'āth. She further said: And these two were no professional singers. Abū Bakr said: "Satan's music in the house of the Messenger of Allāh

---

In the report in this chapter, mention is made of two girls singing and the Holy Prophet not stopping them. This shows that ordinary singing is not forbidden in Islām.

[4] Bu'āth is the name of the fort belonging to the Madinite tribe of 'Aus and was situated at a distance of two days journey from Madīnah. According to some, the battle of Bu'āth took place between the tribes of 'Aus and Khazraj and lasted for one hundred and twenty years. According to others, this battle took place three or five years before the *Hijrah*.

[5] "Leave them alone" obviously means that the girls should not be stopped from singing the particular songs. In h. 952 reported by Hishām there are the additional words: "Surely every nation has an Eid, and this is our Eid." H. 987 also contains the words: "These are the days of Eid." In that ḥadīth it also says: "Those days were the days of Minā," showing that the days following Eid are included in Eid since the days of Minā are the 10th, 11th, 12th and 13th of the month of Dhul Ḥijjah. All this goes to prove that there is no harm in singing in chorus on occasions of happiness. H. 987 states that they were also beating the tambourine.

[6] The Holy Prophet helped 'Ā'ishah to watch the game. His making her stand behind him as a spectator shows that the incident belongs to a period following the ordinance of seclusion. Thus it is not forbidden for women to watch any entertainment, provided that they are not exposed.

[7] The Muslim festival is to begin with a humble bow of the believers before God and a remembrance of His greatness. The sacrifice of animals should come after that, as it is involved with eating and drinking. This order of procedure is also hinted at in the Holy Qur'ān itself: "So pray to your Lord and sacrifice" (108:2).

﷽?" And this was on an Eid day. So the Messenger of Allāh ﷺ said: "O Abū Bakr, surely every nation has an Eid, and this is our Eid." [8]

Ch. 4: Eating on the day of Fiṭr (i.e., Eid-ul-Fiṭr) before leaving for prayer

953 Anas reported: The Messenger of Allāh ﷺ would not leave his home (for prayer) on the day of Fiṭr until he had eaten some dates. (Another report further says:) And he would eat them in odd numbers.

Ch. 5: Eating on the day of Sacrifices (i.e., Eid-ul-Aḍḥā)

954 Anas ibn Mālik reported that the Prophet ﷺ said: "Whosoever slaughters his animal before the prayer, he should do it (the slaughtering) again." A man got up and said: "This is a day wherein meat is desired (by people)", and he mentioned the condition of his neighbours. The Prophet ﷺ seemed to accept it (what he said). He (the man) said: "I have with me a she-kid (*jadha'ah*) which is dearer to me than two goats of meat." So the Prophet ﷺ gave him permission and I do not know if this permission extends to anyone else or not.[9]

955 Al-Barā' ibn 'Āzib reported: The Prophet ﷺ delivered to us a sermon on the Day of Sacrifices after the (Eid) prayers and he said: "Whoever says his prayers as we do and makes sacrifices as we do, he indeed has correctly sacrificed. Whoever makes sacrifice before the (congregational) prayers, his sacrifice is not proper." Abū Burdah ibn Niyār, the maternal uncle of al-Barā', said: "O Messenger of Allāh, I have sacrificed my goat before the prayers because I thought that today is the day for eating and drinking and I wanted that my goat should be the first one to be slaughtered in my house. So I slaughtered my goat and took my morning meal before setting out for prayers." [10] He (the Holy Prophet) said: "Your goat is (merely) a goat for meat

---

[8] This is a repetition of h. 949 with different wording.

[9] In the next ḥadīth, h. 955, this report occurs in greater detail. The Arabic word for she-kid in this report is *jadha'ah,* which means a camel which has entered its fifth year, or a calf which is in its second or third year, or a kid which is one year old, as also a lamb which is nearly one year old. In h. 955 it has been called *'anāq,* and according to the *Nihāyah* this is a kid which has not completed its first year. Whatever the age of the animal was, it was a well grown one and this is why the Holy Prophet admitted it as an animal for sacrifice. According to h. 955 this exemption was only for this man and not general. However, in similar circumstances such permission can be given following the precedent of the Holy Prophet. See also h. 965.

[10] There is a report in Tirmidhī (book: 'The Two Eids', h. 542) and Ḥākim that the Holy Prophet would not eat anything on the day of Eid-ul-Aḍḥā before the prayers. It has, therefore,

(not a sacrifice)." He said: "O Messenger of Allāh, I have a young she-goat (*'anāq*) less than a year old which is dearer to me than two she-goats. Will that do on my behalf (as sacrifice)?" He said: "Yes, but it will never be considered sufficient for anyone else after you." [11]

Ch. 6:   Going to the prayer ground where there is no pulpit

956 Abū Sa'īd al-Khudrī reported: The Messenger of Allāh ﷺ used to come out on the day of Eid-ul-Fiṭr and Eid-ul-Aḍḥā and proceed towards the prayer-ground. He would start the day with Eid prayers. After that, he would stand facing the people while the people would be sitting in rows. He would exhort them and preach to them and would give them instructions. If he wanted to send an army he would give his decision about it, or if he wanted to give an order in some matter he would do it. He would then return (home). Abū Sa'īd said: People continued to follow this practice until when I (once) went out with Marwān, who was then Governor of Madīnah, on Eid-ul-Aḍḥā or Eid-ul-Fiṭr. When we reached the prayer ground, there was a pulpit which had been made by Kathīr ibn aṣ-Ṣalt.[12] When Marwān wanted to ascend it before the prayers, I pulled him by his garment and he pulled (back his garment from) me, and he ascended the pulpit and delivered the sermon before the congregational prayers. I said to him: "You people, by Allāh, have changed (the *Sunnah*)." [13] He said: "O Abu Sa'īd, the times you knew have gone now." I retorted: "By Allāh, what I know is better than that which I do not know." He answered: "People do not stay behind for us after prayers, that is why I did it (i.e., delivered the sermon) before the prayers." [14]

---

been regarded as necessary not to eat anything on the morning of this day till the prayer is over. However, that report is weak. Bukhārī has indicated that it is weak and shown that sacrifice should not take place before prayer but there is no proof that one should not eat before prayer.

[11] See note on h. 954.

[12] The prayer-ground was at a distance of about five hundred yards from the city of Madīnah. Kathīr ibn aṣ-Ṣalt built his house there after the death of the Holy Prophet which was very close to the ground. This pulpit was made of unbaked bricks.

[13] Abu Sa'īd, it appears, did not object to the use of the pulpit but to the sermon being delivered before the prayer. The excuse presented by Marwān also contains no reference to the pulpit. In the time of the Holy Prophet and the first four rightly-guided Caliphs the Eid sermon was not delivered from a pulpit, but this was not prohibited either. As it seems that the Friday sermons were delivered from a pulpit, there would be nothing wrong in doing the same for Eid sermons. In fact, it would be preferable because of the larger gathering for Eid than for Friday prayers. Imām Shāfi'ī has recorded a report to the effect that Mu'āwiyah was the first man who delivered an Eid sermon before the prayers. As Marwān was governor of Madīnah appointed by Mu'āwiyah, it is possible that he did this under his orders.

[14] According to some reports, Marwān in his sermons used to speak ill of 'Alī and his companions and praise the Banī Umayya excessively, and that was the reason why people were reluctant to listen to his sermons.

Ch. 7:   Going to Eid prayers on foot and riding,[15] without *Adhān* or *Iqāmah*

957 'Abdullāh ibn 'Umar reported that the Messenger of Allāh ﷺ used to say prayers for Eid-ul-Aḍḥā and Eid-ul-Fiṭr, and then deliver the sermon after the prayers.

958 Jābir ibn 'Abdullāh reported[16] that the Prophet ﷺ set out on the day of Eid-ul-Fiṭr and started with prayers before the sermon.

959 He (Ibn Juraij) said: 'Aṭā' told me that Ibn 'Abbās sent a message to Ibn Zubair, soon after he had given his pledge of allegiance, that *Adhān* should not be given for (Eid) prayers on the day of Eid-ul-Fiṭr and that the sermon should follow the prayers.

960 'Aṭā' reported from Ibn 'Abbās and from Jābir ibn 'Abdullāh that they both said: There was no *Adhān* on Eid-ul-Fiṭr or on Eid-ul-Aḍḥā (for Eid prayers).

961 Jābir ibn 'Abdullāh reported that the Prophet ﷺ stood up and started with the prayers and then delivered the sermon to the people after that. After the Prophet of Allāh ﷺ finished, he descended (from the pulpit) and came to the women and preached to them. He was leaning on Bilāl's hand, who spread his garment on which women placed their charity. I said to 'Aṭā': "Do you think it is incumbent on the Imām even now to go to women and preach to them after he has finished?" He said: "Surely that is incumbent on them and why should they not do it?"[17]

Ch. 8:   The sermon to be after the Eid prayers

962 Ibn 'Abbās reported: I attended Eid prayers with the Messenger of Allāh ﷺ and Abū Bakr and 'Umar and 'Uthmān (i.e., during the times of these Caliphs) and all of them used to say prayers before the sermon.[18]

---

[15] Some reports indicate that it is against the *Sunnah* to go to the place of Eid riding. Bukhārī has, quite rightly, not considered these reports to be reliable. Even supposing that the Holy Prophet did not ride to the Eid prayer ground, it could not make it prohibited for other people to do so, especially if they came from longer distances.

[16] 'Aṭā' narrated this from Jābir ibn 'Abdullāh, and Ibn Juraij narrated from 'Aṭā'. See h. 959.

[17] Today in the Muslim world, how many Eid congregations are there where women are to be found and the Imām goes to address them! This neglect of women's education is one of the reasons which has made Muslims indifferent to the needs of the nation. The Holy Prophet used to instruct and teach women just as he used to instruct and teach men, and he used to make them aware of community works and the need to take part in them. Unfortunately, Muslims treat this half of their community, which is responsible for training the next generation, as if it were dead. The part about preaching to women in this report has already occurred in h. 98.

[18] Certain reports speak of 'Umar and 'Uthmān as delivering their Eid sermons before the prayer. H. 962 and h. 963 show those reports to be wrong. See also h. 979.

963 Ibn 'Umar reported: The Prophet ﷺ and Abū Bakr and 'Umar used to say the prayers before the sermon on both Eids.

964 Ibn 'Abbās reported that the Prophet ﷺ said two *rak'ahs* of prayer on the day of Eid-ul-Fiṭr and he did not say any prayer before or after it. Then he came to the women and with him was Bilāl. He exhorted them to give in charity and they began to throw (their ornaments), some throwing their earrings and others their necklaces.[19]

965 Al-Barā' ibn 'Āzib reported that the Prophet ﷺ said: "The first thing with which we begin this day of ours is that we say our prayer and then come back (home) and make sacrifices; so whoever does like this follows the *Sunnah* and one who makes sacrifice before the prayer is only providing meat for his people and it has nothing to do with sacrifices." At this, a man from among the *Anṣār* named Abū Burdah ibn Niyār said: "O Messenger of Allāh, I have slaughtered already but I have a she-kid (*jadha'ah*) with me which is better than a two year old goat." He (the Holy Prophet) said: "Sacrifice it in the place of the one required, but it will not be sufficient (as a sacrifice) for anyone after you." [20]

Ch. 9: The carrying of weapons to an Eid congregation and to the Sacred Precincts (of the Ka'bah) is disapproved

Al-Ḥasan said: It is prohibited to carry weapons on Eid day unless there is fear of the enemy.[21]

966 Sa'īd ibn Jubair reported: I was in the company of Ibn 'Umar when he was injured in the sole of his foot by the blade of a spear and his foot stuck to the stirrup. So I got down (from my animal) and pulled it (the blade) out. This happened at Minā. The news reached Ḥajjāj who came to enquire about his health. Ḥajjāj said: "I wish I knew who caused you the injury." Ibn 'Umar said: "You caused me (the injury)." He (Ḥajjāj) said: "How is that?" He said: "You carried weapons on a day on which they should not be carried. You

---

[19] This is a repetition of h. 98. There ring is mentioned instead of necklace. It appears that necklaces as well as rings were both contributed by these women. It is not mentioned in h. 98 that he said two *rak'ahs* of Eid prayer, the opening words here, ending with "after it", being an addition to h. 98.

[20] This is a repetition of h. 955. See also h. 954.

[21] That is to say, one should not carry weapons when attending the Eid congregation. The reason obviously is that there is the danger of causing injury to someone in the crowd. Similarly, one should not carry weapons in the Sacred Precincts of the Ka'bah (*al-Ḥaram*) because that is a place of security for all, and people also gather there in larger numbers. In chapter 2 of this book, it is mentioned that javelins and shields were used for game on Eid day. But that was after the Eid prayer gathering, and those wielding them were not mixed up with the spectators.

allowed weapons to enter the Sacred Precincts (of the Ka'bah), whereas weapons were not allowed to enter the Sacred Precincts."

967 Sa'īd ibn 'Amr ibn Sa'īd ibn al-'Āṣ reported: Ḥajjāj came to see Ibn 'Umar while I was with him. He said: "How are you?" He (Ibn 'Umar) said: "All right." He (Ḥajjāj) said: "Who caused you the injury?" He (Ibn 'Umar) said: "This has been caused to me by one who has ordered the carrying of weapons on a day in which their carrying is not lawful," meaning Ḥajjāj.[22]

Ch. 10:   **Going out early in the morning for Eid prayers**

'Abdullāh ibn Busr said: By this time we would be free (from the Eid prayers) and it would be time for the optional prayers (i.e., the mid-morning optional prayer known as *Ḍuḥā* or *Ishrāq*).

968 Al-Barā' (ibn 'Āzib) reported: The Prophet ﷺ delivered to us a sermon on the Day of Sacrifices. He said: "The first thing with which we begin this day of ours is that that we say our prayer ...". My maternal uncle Abū Burdah ibn Niyār stood up and said: I slaughtered before I said the prayer but I have a she-kid (*jadha'ah*) with me which is better than a two year old goat." He said: ...[23]

Ch. 11:   **Excellence of (good) deeds during days of *Tashrīq***

Ibn 'Abbās said: Remember the name of Allāh on the well-known days, the ten days, and the appointed days are the days of *Tashrīq*. Ibn 'Umar and Abū Hurairah used to go to the market during the ten days reciting aloud *Allāhu Akbar* and people used to recite the *takbīr* with them. And Muḥammad ibn 'Alī recited *takbīr* after optional prayers.[24]

969 Ibn 'Abbās reported from the Prophet ﷺ that he said: "No deed on other days is superior to those (deeds done) on these days (i.e., *Tashrīq*)." People asked: "Not even *jihād*?" He said: "Not even *jihād,* unless a person goes out endangering his life and property and returns with nothing" (i.e., loses his life and property).

---

[22] This is a repetition of h. 966.

[23] This is a repetition of h. 955 in words very similar to h. 965. The opening line is from h. 955. The omissions (...) in the translation can be read in h. 965.

[24] The Qur'ān says in connection with the Pilgrimage: "and (that they may) mention the name of Allāh on the well-known days (*ayyām ma'lūmāt*) over the cattle quadrupeds that He has given them" (22:28), and also: "And remember Allāh during the appointed days (*ayyām ma'dūdāt*)" (2:203). Ibn 'Abbās says here that the well-known days (*ayyām ma'lūmāt*) are the first ten days of the month of Dhul Ḥijjah, and the appointed days (*ayyām ma'dūdāt*) are the days of *Tashrīq*, i.e., the 11th, 12th and 13th of that month. Muḥammad ibn 'Alī is Imām Bāqir.

Ch. 12: **To say *Takbīr* (i.e., *Allāhu Akbar*) during the days at Minā and when going to ʿArafāt (on the 9th day of Dhul Ḥijjah)**

Ibn ʿUmar used to recite the *takbīr* in his own tent at Minā. People in the mosque used to hear him and they would join in. People in the market would recite the *takbīr* so much so that Minā would resound with *Allāhu Akbar*. Ibn ʿUmar recited *Allāhu Akbar* at Minā during those days (of *Tashrīq*), and after the prayers, and on his bed, and in his camp and place of sitting, and while walking about, throughout those days. Maimūnah used to recite *Allāhu Akbar* on the day of Sacrifice. Women used to recite *Allāhu Akbar* in the mosque after Abān ibn ʿUthmān and ʿUmar ibn ʿAbdul ʿAzīz during the days of *Tashrīq* along with the men.[25]

970 Muḥammad ibn Abū Bakr al-Thaqafī related: I asked Anas ibn Mālik, when we were going from Minā to ʿArafāt, about the saying of *Labbaika* ('Here I am in Your presence'): "How did you do it with the Prophet ﷺ?" He said: "Those who wanted to say *Labbaika* said that and there was no objection to it, while those who wanted to recite the *Takbīr* did so if they so wished and this was not objected to either."

971 Umm ʿAṭiyya reported: We were ordered to come out on the day of Eid, and even bring virgins from their houses and the menstruating women. They stood behind the men and said *Takbīr* as they did, and made supplication (*duʿāʾ*) when they made supplication, hoping to attain the blessings of this day and its purity.[26]

Ch. 13: **Praying on Eid day with lance in front**

972 Ibn ʿUmar reported that a spearhead used to be planted on the ground (as the *sutrah* or marker for prayer) before the Prophet ﷺ on the day of Eid-ul-Fiṭr and Eid-ul-Aḍḥā. Then he used to pray.[27]

---

[25] The days of Minā are four including the Eid day. The day of *ʿArafah* is the 9th day of Dhul Ḥijjah. Thus, the days of *Takbīr* are from the 9th to the 13th of Dhul Ḥijjah, five days in all. There is no saying of the Holy Prophet recorded in this connection, and as for the practice of the Companions, the most reliable reports are those from ʿAlī and ʿAbdullāh ibn Masʿūd, according to which the period of *Takbīr* starts from the morning of *ʿArafah* and ends with the *ʿAṣr* prayer on the 13th of Dhul Ḥijjah. During this period, men as well as women should say the *Takbīr* aloud after the congregational prayers in the mosque.

[26] This is a repetition of a part of h. 324 in which a statement by Umm ʿAṭiyya is reported. The chapter heading is related to the words: "and they (the women) said *Takbīr* as they (the men) did."

[27] This is a repetition of h. 494.

Ch. 14: Carrying of lance or short spear in front of the Imām on Eid day

973 Ibn 'Umar reported: The Prophet ﷺ would go out in the morning towards the prayer ground and a javelin used to be carried before him and planted in the prayer ground in front of him and he would pray facing it.[28]

Ch. 15: Going of women and those in menstruation to the place of prayer (for Eid)

974 Umm 'Aṭiyya reported: We were ordered to bring out the virgins and those in seclusion (to the Eid prayer-ground) — and it is added in the report from Ḥafṣah — (we should bring out) the virgins and those in seclusion, and the menstruating women should keep apart from the place of prayer (i.e., while being present in the prayer-ground).[29]

Ch. 16: Going of children to the place of prayer (for Eid)

975 Ibn 'Abbās said: I went out with the Prophet ﷺ on the day of Eid-ul-Fiṭr or Eid-ul-Aḍḥā. He said the prayer and then delivered the sermon. Then he went to the women and preached to them, reminded them (of their duties), and exhorted them to give in charity.[30]

Ch. 17: The Imām facing the people when delivering the Eid sermon

Abū Sa'īd said: The Prophet ﷺ stood facing the people.

976 Al-Barā' reported: The Prophet ﷺ went out on the day of Eid-ul-Aḍḥā towards al-Baqī' and he said two *rak'ahs* of prayer and then turned his face towards us. He said: "Our first act of worship on this day of ours is that we begin with prayer. Then we come back (home) and make sacrifices ..."[31]

Ch. 18: Marking (the boundaries of) the prayer ground

977 'Abdur Raḥmān ibn 'Ābis said: I heard from Ibn 'Abbās that he was asked: "Were you present in the company of the Prophet ﷺ at Eid prayers?" He said: "Yes, and if I had not been related to him, because of young age

---

[28] This, again, is a repetition of h. 494.

[29] This repetition of h. 324 is very brief.

[30] This is a repetition of h. 98. Further on, in h. 977 it is stated that at that time Ibn 'Abbās was a boy, which shows that even boys went to the Eid prayer-ground.

[31] This is a repetition of h. 955 with additional words at the beginning of the report. From this addition, the last words, "he turned his face towards us", give this chapter its heading. The remainder of the report is very much like h. 965 with slight variations. See h. 965 for the translation omitted here.

I could not have been present. When he came to the roadside mark near the house of Kathīr ibn aṣ-Ṣalt, he delivered a sermon, and then went towards the women, and Bilāl was with him. He preached to them and reminded them and exhorted them to give in charity. I saw them spreading out their hands and throwing (their ornaments) on the garment of Bilāl. Then he and Bilāl went towards his house.[32]

Ch. 19: Preaching of the Imām to women on Eid day

978 Jābir ibn 'Abdullāh reported that the Prophet ﷺ stood up on the day of Eid-ul-Fiṭr to say prayers. He started with the prayers and then delivered the sermon. When he finished, he descended (from the pulpit) and came to the women and preached to them. He was leaning on Bilāl's hand, who spread his garment on which women placed their charity. I said to 'Aṭā': "Was it the *Zakāt* of Eid-ul-Fiṭr?" He said: "No, but it was a voluntary charity which they were making at that time." I said: "Do you think it is incumbent on the Imām to preach to the women?" He said: "Surely it is incumbent on them and why should they not do it?"[33]

979 Ibn 'Abbās reported: I attended Eid-ul-Fiṭr prayers with the Prophet ﷺ and Abū Bakr and 'Umar and 'Uthmān (i.e., during the times of these Caliphs). They said the prayer before the sermon, then gave the sermon afterwards.[34]

The Prophet ﷺ came out, and it seems as if I am (even now) looking at him as he was making the people sit down by (pointing with) his hand. Then he advanced, making his way through the congregation until he came to the women, while Bilāl was with him. He then recited: "O Prophet, when believing women come to you giving you a pledge" (the Qur'ān, 60:12) till the end of the verse. As he finished it, he said: "Are you (women) adhering to it?" One woman among them said "Yes," and no one else replied. Ḥasan did not know who was this woman.[35] He said: "So you women should give in charity." Then Bilāl spread his garment and said: "Come along, O you women,

---

[32] This is a repetition of the subject of h. 98 in words very much like those of h. 863.

[33] This is a repetition of h. 961 with some differences. It contains the addition of the question to 'Aṭā': "Was it the *Zakāt* of Eid-ul-Fiṭr?" His reply shows that this was separate from the charity required to be given on Eid-ul-Fiṭr, known as *fiṭrānah*.

[34] This ḥadīth begins with a repetition of h. 962 up to this point. After that, it is a repetition of h. 98 in greater detail.

[35] In other words, this one woman spoke for all of them, saying that they were adhering to the pledge. Within that pledge it is also included that: "They shall not disobey you (the Prophet) in what is good" (60:12). Accordingly, he commanded them to perform the good deed of charity, as the report continues.

(give your charities), my father and mother be a sacrifice to you." Then they began to throw their big rings (*fatakh*) and smaller rings on Bilāl's garment. 'Abdur Razzāq said: *Fatakh* was the name of big rings used in the days of Ignorance.

Ch. 20:   When a woman does not have an over-garment on Eid day

980 Ḥafṣah, daughter of Sīrīn, reported: We used to prohibit our girls from going out on the day of Eid (for the prayer). Then a woman came and stayed at the palace of Banū Khalaf and I went to her. She narrated that her sister's husband fought alongside the Prophet ﷺ in twelve battles, and her sister was with him in six of them. ...[36]

Ch. 21:   Menstruating women to stand aside in the prayer ground

981 Umm 'Aṭiyyah said: We were ordered to go out (for Eid) and bring out the menstruating women and the virgin girls and the women in seclusion — Ibn 'Aun said: "or the virgin girls in seclusion." And as for the menstruating women, they should be present at the gathering of the Muslims and their supplication (*du'ā'* to Allāh), but should keep apart from their place of prayer.[37]

Ch. 22:   Sacrificing and slaughtering (of animals) on the day of Sacrifice at the prayer ground

982 Ibn 'Umar reported that the Prophet ﷺ used to sacrifice or slaughter animals at the prayer ground.[38]

Ch. 23:   The Imām and the people talking during the sermon and when the Imām is asked about anything while he is delivering the sermon

983 Al-Barā' ibn 'Āzib reported: The Messenger of Allāh ﷺ delivered to us a sermon on the Day of Sacrifices after the (Eid) prayers and he said: "Whoever says his prayers as we do and makes sacrifices as we do, he indeed has correctly sacrificed. Whoever makes sacrifice before the (congregational) prayers, that is only (non-sacrificial) meat." Abū Burdah ibn Niyār stood up and said: "O Messenger of Allāh, I have sacrificed before I went out for the

---

[36] This is a repetition of h. 324 with minor variation in wording. See there for the remainder of this report.

[37] The end part of h. 324 has been repeated here with a slight variation in wording.

[38] So there is nothing wrong if animal sacrifice is made right in the prayer ground or in a nearby place.

(Eid) prayer because I thought that today is the day for eating and drinking. So I made haste and ate, and I fed my family and my neighbours." The Messenger of Allāh ﷺ said: "That is only (non-sacrificial) meat." He said: "I have a young she-goat less than a year old which is better than two she-goats. Will that do on my behalf (as sacrifice)?" He said: "Yes, but it will never be considered sufficient for anyone else after you." [39]

984 Anas ibn Mālik said: The Messenger of Allāh ﷺ said the prayer on the Day of Sacrifices, then he delivered the sermon and ordered: Whoever slaughters before the (Eid) prayer should repeat his sacrifice. At this, a man from the Anṣār got up and said: "O Messenger of Allāh, I have some neighbours" — he either said "They passed their days in hunger" or "They are needy" — "and certainly I slaughtered my animal before the prayer but I have a she-goat which is dearer to me than the flesh of two she-goats." So he (the Holy Prophet) permitted him to do so.[40]

985 Jundab reported: The Prophet ﷺ said his prayer on the Day of Sacrifices, then delivered his sermon, and then he slaughtered (his animal) and said: "Whoever has slaughtered (his animal) before he has said his prayer, he should slaughter another in its place and whoever has not slaughtered he should slaughter (his animal) with the name of Allāh." [41]

Ch. 24: Taking a different route on returning from Eid

986 Jābir reported: The Prophet ﷺ used to take a different route on Eid day (while returning from the Eid prayer-ground).[42]

Ch. 25: When anyone misses Eid (prayers), he should say two *rak'ahs*

The same should be done by women, those at home and in villages in accordance with the saying the Prophet ﷺ: "This is our Eid,

---

[39] This is a repetition of h. 955 with minor variation in wording. Here the question and answer that took place in the course of the sermon was only in reference to a certain point of religion which the Holy Prophet was explaining. It does not mean that any kind of talk or conversation could take place during a sermon.

[40] This is a brief repetition of h. 955.

[41] This is a brief repetition of h. 955. The order of words in the statement "then he slaughtered (his animal) and said" has created the misconception that the Holy Prophet said this after slaughtering the animal. All that is meant by this report is that the Holy Prophet stated this in the course of the sermon. This is why Bukhārī has included it in this chapter, the heading of which refers to talking during the sermon.

[42] The change of route, it seems, was adopted in order to show the enemies of Islām living in Madīnah that Islām was growing in strength in spite of their opposition.

O followers of Islām." Anas ibn Mālik ordered his slave, Ibn Abū ʿUtbah, who was (living) in Zāwiyah, and the latter (accordingly) called together the people of his household as well as his sons and said prayers like the people in the city and called out the *Takbīr* like them. ʿIkrimah said: The people of the villages should assemble on Eid day and say two *rakʿahs* of prayers as the Imām does. ʿAṭāʾ said: When one misses Eid congregational prayer, one should say two *rakʿahs* of prayer.

987–988 ʿĀʾishah reported that Abū Bakr came to her (one day) and with her were two girls, in the days of Minā, beating drums and making music (thereby), while the Prophet ﷺ was lying, covering himself with his cloth. Abū Bakr scolded them. At this, the Prophet ﷺ took off the cloth from his face and said: "Leave them alone, O Abū Bakr, for surely these are the days of Eid." And those were the days of the Minā. [988] And ʿĀʾishah said: I saw the Prophet ﷺ acting as a screen for me and I was looking at the Abyssinians engaged in a game in the mosque; ʿUmar rebuked them, but the Prophet ﷺ said: "Leave them alone", (and said to them) "O Banī Arfidah, be at peace," meaning continue your game in peace.[43]

Ch. 26: Prayers before and after Eid

Abul Muʿalā said: I heard Saʿīd reporting on the authority of Ibn ʿAbbās that he disliked any prayers before the Eid congregational prayers.[44]

989 Ibn ʿAbbās reported that the Prophet ﷺ came out on the day of Eid-ul-Fiṭr and said two *rakʿahs* of prayer and did not say any prayer before it or after it and he was accompanied by Bilāl.[45]

---

[43] This is a repetition of h. 949; see also h. 454–455. In this report it is stated that those were the days of the Minā and the Holy Prophet called them as the days of Eid. This shows that if Eid prayers cannot be said on the very first day, they can be said on any of the other days collectively called the "days of Minā." Abū Bakr objected to the girls beating drums and singing, and ʿUmar objected to the game of the Abyssinians in the mosque. The Holy Prophet, however, prevented Abū Bakr and ʿUmar from stopping them. He thus left the law liberal in these matters because it is part of human nature to derive enjoyment by these means.

[44] There is difference of opinion on this question. There is a report in Ibn Mājah from Abū Saʿīd al-Khudrī (book: ʿEstablishing the Prayer and the *Sunnah* regarding them', h. 1351) that shows that the Holy Prophet used to say two optional *rakʿahs* of prayer on returning home after the Eid prayer, so there is no absolute prohibition in this regard. However, the Eid prayers consist only of two *rakʿahs* and not more.

[45] This report is like the beginning of h. 964, which itself is a repetition of h. 98 with additions. H. 98 mentions the Holy Prophet going out with Bilāl and his preaching to the women but it does not mention Eid or Eid prayers at all in this connection. However, it is the same incident.

Book 14: *Al-Witr*
Witr Prayer[1]

In the name of Allāh, the Beneficent, the Merciful

Ch. 1:   What is said regarding *Witr*

990–991 Ibn 'Umar reported that a man asked the Messenger of Allāh ﷺ about the prayer of the night. The Messenger of Allāh ﷺ said: "The prayer of the night is two *rak'ahs* followed by two *rak'ahs* (and so on), and when any of you fears (the approach of) dawn, he should say one *rak'ah* and it will make the prayer which he has said as *Witr*." [991] Nāfi' reported that 'Abdullāh ibn 'Umar used to say *Taslīm* between the (first) two *rak'ahs* and the (third) one *rak'ah* in *Witr*, and he even used to ask for something (in between) if he needed it.[2]

992 Ibn 'Abbās informed that he spent a night at the place of Maimūnah, his maternal aunt. ...[3]

993 'Abdullāh ibn 'Umar reported that the Prophet ﷺ said: "The prayer of the night is two *rak'ahs* followed by two *rak'ahs* (and so on), and if you want to finish it, say one *rak'ah*, making the prayer you have said as *Witr*. Al-Qāsim said: Since we attained the age of understanding we have seen some

---

[1] The word *witr* occurs with both *kasrah* (*witr*) and *fathah* (*watr*) and means 'an odd number'. Here it means the prayer of three *rak'ahs* which is said after the *'Ishā'* prayer. Bukhārī has a separate book dealing with *Tahajjud*, but in fact *Witr* is part of *Tahajjud*. Those who cannot rise up for *Tahajjud* say the three *rak'ah Witr* prayer immediately after the *'Ishā'* prayer.

[2] H. 990 is a repetition of h. 472 with slight differences. The closing statement of h. 472 made by Ibn 'Umar does not occur here. H. 991 is an addition to it, showing that Ibn 'Umar used to say a two *rak'ah* prayer, ending it with *Taslīm* (saying of *Salām*), and then the third *rak'ah* on its own, even speaking to someone in between.

[3] This is a repetition of h. 183 with very slight differences; see there for the full report. According to it, the Holy Prophet's *Tahajjud* prayer consisted of thirteen *rak'ahs*. However, as shown earlier in the note to h. 698, the repetitions of this ḥadīth mention different numbers of *rak'ahs* for *Tahajjud* prayers, which is definitely an error by some narrator. Despite these reports being authentic, some of them must be in error according to reason and knowledge. On the whole these reports tend to show that the Holy Prophet's *Tahajjud* prayers were usually of eleven *rak'ahs*, and in h. 994 'Ā'ishah too has mentioned eleven *rak'ahs*.

people saying three *rak'ahs* of *Witr* prayer, and all that is permissible. I hope there is no wrong in any of them.[4]

994 'Ā'ishah informed that the Messenger of Allāh ﷺ used to pray eleven *rak'ahs*[5] — that was his night prayer — and he used to prostrate in it for such a long time that one of you could recite fifty verses before he raised his head. He also used to pray two *rak'ahs* before the *Fajr* prayer. Then he would lie down on his right side till the caller to prayer came to him (to call him) for the prayer.

Ch. 2:   The times of *Witr*

Abū Hurairah said: "The Messenger of Allāh ﷺ ordered me to say *Witr* before going to sleep." [6]

995 Anas ibn Sīrīn related that he asked Ibn 'Umar: "What do you think as regards the two *rak'ahs* before the *Fajr* prayer, should I prolong the recitation (of the Qur'ān) in them?" He said: "The Prophet ﷺ used to pray at night two *rak'ahs* followed by two and so on, and then one *rak'ah Witr,* and he used to say two *rak'ahs* (of *sunnah*) before the *Fajr* prayer (almost) as if the *Adhān* was still sounding in his ears." Hammād said: This means immediately (after the *Adhān*).

996 'Ā'ishah reported: The Messenger of Allāh ﷺ said *Witr* prayer at all the various times of the night, and the latest time of *Witr* was at dawn.

Ch. 3:   The Prophet ﷺ waking up his wives for *Witr*

997 'Ā'ishah reported: The Prophet ﷺ used to say his prayers while I would be sleeping, lying across (the width of) his bed. When he wanted to say his *Witr* prayer, he would awake me, so I would say my *Witr* prayer.[7]

---

[4] This is a repetition of h. 472 with some differences in wording. As in h. 990, the closing statement of h. 472 made by Ibn 'Umar does not occur here. Instead of this, there is the statement by Al-Qāsim, which means that it is not wrong whether three *rak'ahs* are said as one prayer or *Taslīm* is said after the first two and then a single *rak'ah* is said on its own.

[5] Three of these *rak'ahs* were those of the *Witr* prayer, whether with one *Taslīm* or two. After this he would say the two *sunnah rak'ahs* of the *Fajr* prayer, making a total of thirteen. In the *Tahajjud* prayers the Holy Prophet used to make intense supplications (*du'ā'*), especially during prostration. This is why he was sometimes in prostration for a very long time.

[6] By this chapter Bukhārī intends to show that *Witr* can be said in any part of the night, whether the first, the middle or the last. It is best to say it in the last part, but this is for those who can wake up at that time. For those who cannot, it is better to say it before going to sleep, as the Holy Prophet instructed Abū Hurairah.

[7] This is a repetition of h. 512 with the same wording.

Ch. 4:   Making *Witr* the last prayer (of the night)

998 'Abdullāh ibn 'Umar reported from the Prophet ﷺ that he said: "Make *Witr* your last prayer of the night."

Ch. 5:   Saying *Witr* while riding on an animal.[8]

999 Sa'īd ibn Yasār reported: I was going towards Makkah with 'Abdullāh ibn 'Umar, and he added: When I apprehended the approaching dawn, I dismounted and said the *Witr* prayer and then joined him. 'Abdullah ibn 'Umar said: "Where were you?" I replied: "I apprehended the approaching dawn so I dismounted and said the *Witr* prayer." 'Abdullāh said: "Is there not a good example for you in the Messenger of Allāh ﷺ?" I replied: "Yes, by Allāh." He said: "The Messenger of Allāh ﷺ used to pray *Witr* while on the back of a camel."

Ch. 6:   Saying *Witr* when on a journey

1000 Ibn 'Umar reported: The Prophet ﷺ, while travelling, used to say the night prayer by gestures on his mount, in whichever direction it was facing, except the obligatory prayers (*farḍ*).[9] And he used to pray *Witr* on his mount.[10]

Ch. 7:   *Qunūt* before *Rukū'* (bowing down) and after it[11]

---

[8] According to the Ḥanafīs it is not permitted to say *Witr* while riding an animal. Bukhārī has contradicted this view in this chapter.

[9] By "gestures" is meant indicating a posture of prayer by a movement which is possible to make under the conditions of travel; for example, bowing the head to indicate prostration (*Sajdah*).

[10] Not saying the *farḍ* prayers on a transport is in the case when a person has control over starting and stopping the carriage wherein he is travelling. In a bus, railway train or aircraft, *farḍ* can also be performed in the same way as described here.

[11] By *Qunūt* is meant that supplication which is recited during prayer in the standing posture. It is sought to show in this chapter that the Holy Prophet usually said the *Qunūt* before bowing down for *Rukū'*, and it was only for a few days that he said it after *Rukū'* while he was cursing the persecutors. The chapter on *Qunūt* is brought under *Witr* because the saying of *Qunūt* in *Witr* is reported by Al-Ḥasan ibn 'Alī and accepted as authentic (*ṣaḥīḥ*) by Tirmidhī: "The Messenger of Allāh ﷺ taught me some prayers for *Witr*, as follows" (book: *Witr*, h. 464). This is the prayer:

اَللّٰهُمَّ اهْدِنِى فِيْمَنْ هَدَيْتَ وَعَافِنِى فِيْمَنْ عَافَيْتَ وَتَوَلَّنِى فِيْمَنْ تَوَلَّيْتَ وَبَارِكْ لِى فِيْمَا أَعْطَيْتَ وَقِنِى شَرَّ مَا قَضَيْتَ إِنَّكَ تَقْضِى وَلَا يُقْضَى عَلَيْكَ وَإِنَّهُ لَا يَذِلُّ مَنْ وَّالَيْتَ وَلَا يَعِزُّ مَنْ عَادَيْتَ تَبَارَكْتَ رَبَّنَا وَتَعَالَيْتَ نَسْتَغْفِرُكَ وَنَتُوْبُ اِلَيْكَ۔

"O Allāh! Guide me (to be) among those You have guided, and grant me security (to be) among those You have granted security, and befriend me (to be) among those of whom You have befriended, and make blessed for me what you have granted me, guard me from the evil of what You have decreed. Surely You it is Who decrees, and nothing can be decreed against You. He

1001 Muḥammad ibn Sīrīn reported that Anas ibn Mālik was asked: "Did the Prophet ﷺ say the *Qunūt* in the morning?" He replied: "Yes." He was asked: "Did he say the *Qunūt* before bowing down (*Rukū'*)?" He replied: "For some days it was after bowing down."

1002 ʿĀṣim related: I asked Anas ibn Mālik about the *Qunūt*. He said: "Definitely the *Qunūt* was recited." I asked: "Before *Rukū'* or after it?" He replied: "Before it." I said: "So and so has told me that you had said after *Rukū'*." He said: "He told wrongly. The Messenger of Allāh ﷺ said the *Qunūt* after bowing for one month — I think it was when he sent a group of about seventy men known as *qurrā'* (who knew the Qur'ān by heart) towards an idol worshipping people other than them, and there was a peace treaty between them and the Messenger of Allāh ﷺ. So the Messenger of Allāh ﷺ prayed against them for one month." [12]

1003 Anas reported: The Prophet ﷺ said the *Qunūt* for one month against Riʿl and Dhakwān. [13]

1004 Anas reported: The *Qunūt* used to be said in the *Maghrib* and the *Fajr* prayers. [14]

---

whom You befriend cannot be disgraced, and he whom You turn against cannot attain honour. Our Lord! You are blessed and the Highest. We seek Your protection and We turn to You."

Another well-known prayer recited in *Witr* is the following:

اَللّٰهُمَّ اِنَّا نَسْتَعِينُكَ وَنَسْتَغْفِرُكَ وَنُثْنِى عَلَيْكَ الْخَيْرَ وَلَا نَكْفُرُكَ وَنَخْلَعُ وَنَتْرُكُ مَنْ يَفْجُرُكَ ۔ اَللّٰهُمَّ اِيَّاكَ نَعْبُدُ وَلَكَ نُصَلِّى وَنَسْجُدُ وَاِلَيْكَ نَسْعٰى وَنَحْفِدُ نَرْجُو رَحْمَتَكَ وَنَخْشٰى عَذَابَكَ اِنَّ عَذَابَكَ بِالْكُفَّارِ مُلْحِقٌ ۔

"O Allāh! We ask for Your help and protection, and praise You best, and do not disbelieve in You, and separate ourselves from and leave those who disobey You. O Allāh! You it is Whom we serve, and to Whom we pray, and to Whom we submit, and to Whom we run and for Whom we strive. We hope for Your mercy and fear Your punishment. Surely Your punishment overtakes the disbelievers."

[12] Ibn Saʿd says that Abū Barāʾ ʿĀmir ibn Mālik ibn Jaʿfar Kalābī requested the Holy Prophet to send with him some of his Companions to the people of Najd for inviting them to Islam, saying he hoped they would accept Islam. So he sent seventy men who knew the Qur'ān by heart. In the way they passed the tribes of Riʿl and Dhakwān, who had a treaty with the Holy Prophet. These preachers stopped in Biʾr Maʿauna and sent to their leader, ʿĀmir ibn al-Ṭufail, a letter from the Holy Prophet. But he gathered these tribes and attacked them. The Holy Prophet prayed against them, for punishment to befall them, for one month after *Rukū'*. In this *ḥadīth* the word *kadhaba* is used (literally, "he lied"). As stated in *Fatḥ al-Bārī*, this word is used in the dialect of the Hijāz, not only for a deliberate lie but merely for an incorrect statement (hence translated above as "He told wrongly").

[13] This is a repetition in brief of a part of the last *ḥadīth*, h. 1002. See the footnote above.

[14] This is a repetition of h. 798. See the footnote to that *ḥadīth*.

Book 15: *Al-Istisqā'*
Prayer for Rain

In the name of Allāh, the Beneficent, the Merciful

Ch. 1:   Asking for rain and the Prophet ﷺ coming out to pray for rain[1]

1005 'Abbād ibn Tamīm reported that his uncle said: The Prophet ﷺ went out to pray for rain and he turned his cloak around.[2]

---

[1] The word *istisqā'* means asking for water or praying for rain. Just as all the people of an area go out to the Eid prayer ground to say the Eid prayer and make supplications before Allāh, in the same way when the country is suffering from drought due to lack of rain, the example set by the Holy Prophet is that people gather outside in the prayer ground and say a two *rak'ah* prayer, making heart-felt supplications with the utmost humility.

[2] The turning around of the cloak is described in a ḥadīth as follows: "He turned around his cloak, putting its right side upon his left shoulder, and its left side upon his right shoulder" (Abū Dāwūd, book: 'Prayer for Rain', ch. 1). This was either a coincidence or done on purpose. If he did it on purpose, the questions: was it specially for the prayer for rain or did he do it to prevent the cloak from slipping off when he raised his hands for supplication, and whether this was done before the supplication or after it, are difficult to answer with certainty. The majority opinion regards it as recommended for this prayer, but the question arises that since these days cloaks are not worn ordinarily, but only rarely, can the prayer for rain be said without a cloak or not? It is stated in *Fatḥ al-Bārī:* "Some say that the cloak was turned around so that when the hands were raised for prayer it would remain on the shoulders. Thus it is not a *Sunnah* in all conditions." It is further added that it is better to follow this practice instead of abandoning it. However, it can only be called *Sunnah* if, first of all, wearing a cloak is declared to be *Sunnah* which no one has ever done. Since the wearing of a cloak ordinarily and especially for the prayer for rain has not been considered by anyone as *Sunnah,* how can turning it around be *Sunnah?* Also, the wording of this ḥadīth does not show clearly whether the supplication was made first or the cloak was turned around first. But later, in the repetition of this ḥadīth in h. 1011, it is said clearly that he "prayed for rain and turned his cloak around". In h. 1012 it is stated that he "prayed for rain, then faced the *Qiblah,* and turned his cloak around and prayed two *rak'ah.*" In h. 1013 it says that the Holy Prophet prayed for rain during the Friday prayer, and there is no mention of turning his cloak around.

It is possible that this was given to him as a sign of the acceptance of prayer, that is, the turning around of the cloak was a sign that his prayer was accepted, and the condition of the people would be turned around, as the rain would bring an end to the drought. It is stated in *Fatḥ al-Bārī:* "And as to turning the cloak around, it was a sign between him and his Lord. It was said to him: Turn your cloak around so that your condition is turned around." In this case also, it cannot be *Sunnah.* According to Imām Abū Ḥanīfah and some followers of Imām Mālik it is not *Sunnah,* and that is the correct opinion. If it is considered to have been due to some unavoidable compulsion, even then to do it as a formal custom does not create any compulsion. Those who

389

Ch. 2: The prayer of the Prophet ﷺ: "Make their years for them like the years of Joseph (during the drought)" [3]

1006 Abū Hurairah reported that when the Prophet ﷺ used to raise his head from the last *rak'ah* he would say: "O Allāh, give salvation to 'Ayyāsh ibn Abū Rabī'ah, O Allāh, give salvation to Salamah ibn Hishām, O Allāh, give salvation to al-Walīd ibn al-Walīd, O Allāh, give salvation to the weak from among the believers! O Allāh, make your punishment severe for the Muḍar. O Allāh, bring (upon them) years (of famine) like the years of (the time of) Joseph!" And the Prophet ﷺ said: "May Allāh forgive the tribe of Ghifār, may Allāh keep safe the tribe of Aslam." [4]

The son of Abū az-Zinād reported from his father that this was in the morning prayer.

1007 Masrūq reported: We were with 'Abdullāh and he said, When the Prophet ﷺ saw the turning away of the people (from the truth) he said: "O Allāh! (send on them) seven (years) like the seven (years of drought) of Joseph." So a year of famine overtook them which destroyed every kind of life until they started eating hides, carcasses and dead animals. Whenever one of them looked towards the sky, he would see smoke because of hunger. So Abū Sufyān went to him and said: "O Muḥammad! You order people to obey Allāh and to do good to relatives; surely the people of your tribe are dying, so

---

consider it necessary differ among themselves as to whether only the Imām should turn his cloak around or those praying behind him should also do it. Laith and Abū Yūsuf hold that only the Imām should do it. Ibn al-Mājishūn has exempted women from it, which shows that women must also go out for the prayer for rain. Since the real object of the prayer for rain is that everyone should gather and turn to God in a state of humility and helplessness, for its acceptance much must depend on the size of the gathering and the feeling in the people's hearts.

[3] When a people become prey to worldly allurements beyond all limits, and run blindly after material gains and comforts, falling down far below the high moral level of humanity, Allāh afflicts them with suffering. The object is only to make them turn to God, and if their condition of ease and plenty has made them forget God then for the attainment of this high object tribulations are sent upon them. In the verse, "then We seized them with distress and affliction that they might humble themselves" (6:42), the Holy Qur'ān has clearly laid down this law. It was under this law that the Holy Prophet prayed for drought to befall the Quraish after they had exceeded all limits in wrong-doing. It was not a prayer for their destruction but suffering, so that upon being afflicted with it they might become humble. If a people will not reform without suffering being sent upon them, it is better that they should be struck with such affliction. It is a fact that those people, instead of accepting the message of truth, persecuted the Holy Prophet bitterly. It was in that condition of persecution that he had recourse to this prayer.

[4] This is a repetition of the last part of h. 804, which relates only to supplication, with some difference in wording. He prayed for these two tribes because the Ghifār had accepted Islam long ago, and the Aslam had made peace with him. At the end of the book of *Witr* in h. 1004 the report from Anas says: "The *Qunūt* used to be said in the *Maghrib* and the *Fajr* prayers."

pray to Allāh for them." [5] So Allāh, the Mighty, the Glorious revealed: "So wait for the day when the heaven brings a clear drought" (the Qur'ān, 44:10) to "(but) you will surely return (to evil). On the day when We seize (them) with the most violent seizing; surely We shall exact retribution." (44:15–16). The day of the most violent seizing was the day of Badr, and certainly the drought and the violent seizing and *al-lizām* and the signs mentioned in *Sūrah Rūm* (the Qur'ān, ch. 30) of the have come to pass.[6]

Ch. 3:   People asking the Imām to pray for water at time of drought

1008–1009 'Abdullāh ibn Dīnār reported: I heard Ibn 'Umar reciting the poetic verses of Abū Ṭālib: "And a white one (i.e., the Prophet who had a radiant countenance) who is requested to pray for rain, Who takes care of the orphans and is the guardian of widows." [1009] And 'Umar ibn Ḥamzah said: Sālim told that his father said: Sometimes this verse came to my mind when I looked at the face of the Prophet ﷺ while he was praying for rain. He did not get down till the rain water flowed profusely from every gutter: "And a white one (i.e., the Prophet who had a radiant countenance) who is requested to pray for rain, Who takes care of the orphans and is the guardian of widows." And this was said by Abū Ṭālib.[7]

---

[5] The prophecy of this famine is in the chapter *Al-Dukhān* of the Holy Qur'ān (ch. 44) as is clear from this ḥadīth. The *Ḥā Mīm* chapters, which include *Al-Dukhān*, were revealed in the middle Makkah period, i.e., the 6th, 7th and 8th years of the mission of the Holy Prophet. It seems that this famine began before the *Hijrah*, most probably in the 7th or 8th year, and its severity reached its peak towards the last period of the Holy Prophet's life in Makkah or at the beginning of his life at Madīnah, and thus Abū Sufyān came to him. His coming was, in any case, before the battle of Badr because it was after the end of the famine that the words were revealed: "On the day when We seize (them) with the most violent seizing" (44:16), which refer to the battle of Badr. It is not impossible that Abū Sufyān came to Madīnah before the battle of Badr, when war had not yet commenced. After the famine came to an end, the Makkans resumed their hostility towards the Muslims and sent an army against them. The result was that their chieftains were killed at Badr, and this was "the most violent seizing".

[6] Here four prophecies are mentioned as being fulfilled which were announced at a time when the Muslims were in a state of the utmost weakness: prophecy of the famine, prophecy of the battle of Badr, prophecy of the victory of the Romans (*al-Rūm*) over the Persians (the Qur'ān 30:2–6), and *lizām*. The word *lizām* occurs in the Holy Qur'ān twice: "And if a word had not gone forth from your Lord, and a term been fixed, it would surely have *come* upon them" (20:129) and "Now indeed you have rejected, so the punishment will (necessarily) *come*" (25:77). (In these verses, *lizām* is translated as "coming", and has the significance of *necessarily coming*). It is not made clear in Ḥadīth what is meant by *lizām*. Probably it refers to the conquest of Makkah because it brought about a state of subjugation which, so to speak, became a necessary part of their condition. It was the end of the power of the Quraish.

[7] There are two verses of poetry by Abū Ṭālib, one of which is quoted here, of the time when the unbelieving Quraish asked him to hand over the Holy Prophet to them. The narrator says that

1010 It is reported from Anas ibn Mālik that whenever drought came upon them ʿUmar ibn Al-Khaṭṭāb used to pray for rain by means of ʿAbbās ibn ʿAbdul Muṭṭalib. He used to say: "O Allāh! We used to invoke You for rain by the advocacy of our Prophet ﷺ, and You would grant us rain, and now we invoke You for rain by the advocacy of the paternal uncle of our Prophet. O Allāh! Bless us with rain." And it would rain on them.[8]

Ch. 4:   Turning the cloak around in the prayer for rain

1011 ʿAbdullāh ibn Zaid reported that the Prophet ﷺ prayed for rain and turned his cloak around.[9]

1012 ʿAbdullāh ibn Zaid reported that the Prophet ﷺ went out to the place of prayer, prayed for rain, faced the *Qiblah,* and turned his cloak around and prayed two *rakʿahs.*[10]

Ch. 5:   The retribution of the Lord, the Most High, Mighty and Glorious, for His creation by drought when they violate what Allāh has made sacred[11]

Ch. 6:   Praying for rain in the main mosque

1013 Anas ibn Mālik said that on a Friday a man entered (the Mosque of the Prophet) by the gate facing the pulpit while the Messenger of Allāh ﷺ

---

he recalled this verse whenever the Holy Prophet prayed for rain and the rain came, because it says that his face was so radiant that he was asked to pray for rain, i.e., his light dispelled and removed the suffering and distress of the people.

[8] It is clear that by "the advocacy of" (*wasīlah*) is only meant that the said person was made the Imām of the prayer. As the Imām is in a sense the representative of those praying behind him, he is called *wasīlah* or advocate of prayer here, i.e., during the life of the Holy Prophet he used to be our Imām in prayer, and now we make his paternal uncle the Imām in prayer. It is also obvious that along with the Imām the rest of the people were also praying. It was not the case that they believed that they had to appoint someone for prayer because their own prayers were not listened to by God. Their own participation in the prayer shows that the Companions, and ʿUmar in particular who was a zealous believer in the oneness of God, did not hold the view that is found among Muslims today, a view which amounts to making someone a partner with Allāh. Someone had to be made Imām, and ʿAbbās was made Imām due to his close kinship with the Holy Prophet.

[9] This is a repetition of h. 1005.

[10] This again is a repetition of h. 1005. He also said a prayer of two *rakʿahs* after praying for rain. At the end of this report Bukhārī has added that its narrator is not the ʿAbdullāh ibn Zaid who saw the dream relating to the *Adhān* but this was ʿAbdullāh ibn Zaid ibn ʿĀṣim al-Māzinī of the Māzin tribe of the Anṣār. In the case of the *Adhān,* it was ʿAbdullāh ibn Zaid ibn ʿAbd Rabih (see footnote to h. 604).

[11] This chapter occurs only in the version of Ḥamūwī. Under this title the ḥadīth by ʿAbdullāh ibn Masʿūd (h. 1007) would be most appropriate but for some reason it is not repeated here.

was standing delivering the sermon. He stood in front of the Messenger of Allāh and said: "O Messenger of Allāh! The livestock are dying and the roads are cut off, so pray to Allāh for rain." Anas added: The Messenger of Allāh ﷺ raised both his hands and said: "O Allāh! grant us rain! O Allāh! grant us rain! O Allāh! grant us rain!" Anas said: By Allāh, we could not see any trace of cloud in the sky and there was no building or a house between us and (the mountain of) Salʿ. He said: A heavy cloud like a shield appeared from behind it. When it came in the middle of the sky, it spread and then it rained. He said: By Allāh! We could not see the sun for a week. The following Friday a man entered by the same gate while the Messenger of Allāh ﷺ was delivering the sermon. He stood in front of him and said: "O Messenger of Allāh! The livestock are dying and the roads are cut off; so pray to Allāh to stop the rain." Anas added: The Messenger of Allāh ﷺ raised both his hands and said: "O Allāh! Around us and not upon us, O Allāh! On the plateaus, on the mountains, on the hills, in the valleys and on the places where trees grow." So the rain stopped and we came out walking in the sun. Sharīk said: I asked Anas, Was it the same man (who had asked for rain the Friday before)? Anas said: I do not know.[12]

Ch. 7: Praying for rain during the Friday sermon without facing the *Qiblah*

1014 Anas ibn Mālik reported that a man entered the Mosque on a Friday by the gate in the direction of Dār al-Qaḍā'…[13]

Ch. 8: Praying for rain on the pulpit

1015 Anas reported: While the Messenger of Allāh ﷺ was delivering the Friday sermon a man came and said: "O Messenger of Allāh! Rain is scarce; so pray to Allāh to grant us rain." So he made supplication, and it rained so much that we could hardly reach our homes and it continued raining till the next Friday. Anas further said: Then the same or some other man stood up and said: "O Messenger of Allāh! call on Allāh to withhold the rain." So the Messenger of Allāh ﷺ said: "O Allāh! Around us and not upon us." Anas

---

[12] This is a repetition of h. 933 with a difference in wording.

[13] This is a repetition of h. 933 in words very similar to those of the previous ḥadīth h. 1013. For the remainder, which we omit here, see h. 1013. Instead of "by the gate facing the pulpit" here it says: "by the gate in the direction of Dār al-Qaḍā'." Dār al-Qaḍā' was a house built by ʿUmar which was sold according to his will to pay his debts; hence its name. It is meant to show by this ḥadīth that in order to pray for rain it is not necessary to gather people and hold a special, separate prayer and make supplication (*duʿā'*). The supplication can be made in any conditions. In fact, any supplication can be made in any condition as a person may wish.

added: I saw the clouds dispersing right and left and it continued to rain but did not rain on the people of Madīnah.[14]

Ch. 9: He who considers it sufficient to pray for rain during the Friday Prayer

1016 Anas reported: A man came to the Prophet ﷺ and said: "Livestock are destroyed and the roads are cut off." So he prayed and it rained from that Friday till the next Friday. Then he came again and said: "Houses have collapsed, roads are cut off, and the livestock are destroyed, so pray to Allāh to withhold the rain." He ﷺ stood up and said: "O Allāh! (Let it rain) on the plateaus, on the hills, in the valleys and over the places where trees grow." So it (the cloud) was torn away from Madīnah as clothes are torn.[15]

Ch. 10: Prayer when roads are cut off due to excessive rain

1017 Anas ibn Mālik reported: A man came to the Messenger of Allāh ﷺ and said: "O Messenger of Allāh, livestock are destroyed and the roads are cut off. So pray to Allāh." …[16]

Ch. 11: It has been said that the Prophet ﷺ did not turn his cloak around for prayer for rain on Friday

1018 Anas ibn Mālik reported that a man complained to the Prophet ﷺ about the destruction of livestock and the hunger of the offspring. So he prayed to Allāh for rain. The narrator (Anas) did not mention that the Prophet ﷺ had turned his cloak around or faced the *Qibla*.[17]

Ch. 12: If people ask the Imām to pray for rain for them, he should not refuse

1019 Anas ibn Mālik reported: A man came to the Messenger of Allāh ﷺ and said: "O Messenger of Allāh, livestock are destroyed and the roads are cut off. So pray to Allāh." …[18]

---

[14] This is a repetition of h. 933 more briefly.

[15] This again is a repetition of h. 933 in different words.

[16] This repetition of h. 933 is very similar to h. 1016. For the remainder see h. 1016. The chapter heading indicates that just as prayer can be said for the coming of rain, a prayer can also be said if there is excessive rain causing damage.

[17] This repetition of h. 933 is very brief. It shows that it is not necessary to turn the cloak around for the prayer for rain.

[18] This repetition of h. 933 is very similar to h. 1016. For the remainder see h. 1016.

Ch. 13: When idol-worshippers ask Muslims for prayer at time of drought

1020 Masrūq reported: I went to Ibn Masʿūd who said: When the Quraish were slow in embracing Islam, the Prophet ﷺ prayed against them, so they were afflicted with a year (of drought) until many of them died and they ate carcasses and bones. So Abū Sufyān came to him and said: "O Muḥammad! You have come to order people to do good to relatives and the people of your tribe are dying, so call on Allāh (for them)." So he (the Prophet) recited: "So wait for the day when the heaven brings a clear drought" (the Qur'ān, 44:10). Then they returned to their (former) disbelief, and that is the word of Allāh (about it): "On the day when We seize (them) with the most violent seizing" (44:16) — this was the day of Badr.

Asbāṭ added on the authority of Mansūr: The Messenger of Allāh ﷺ prayed for them and it rained heavily and continued for seven days. The people complained of the excessive rain, so he (the Prophet) said: "O Allāh! (Let it rain) around us and not upon us." So the clouds dispersed over his head and it rained around the people.[19]

Ch. 14: Saying the prayer "around us and not upon us" when it rains excessively

1021 Anas reported: The Prophet ﷺ was delivering the sermon on a Friday when the people stood up, shouted and said: "O Messenger of Allāh! The rain has stopped, the trees have dried and the livestock are destroyed; so

---

[19] This ḥadīth is a brief repetition of h. 1007 with the addition at the end from Asbāṭ. It shows that the incident of the seven days' rain, mentioned in h. 933, relates to the seven years' drought faced by the Quraish. Objection has been raised to this on the basis that the incident of the seven days' rain took place in Madīnah since the Holy Prophet made the supplication in his Friday sermon. But this objection is not right because, most probably, the seven years of drought began when the Holy Prophet was still at Makkah and when it ended he was at Madīnah. It is possible that the man mentioned in h. 933 was sent by Abū Sufyān. In fact, there is a report in Baihaqī that Abū Sufyān along with several men from Makkah came to the Holy Prophet. Moreover, one should not be misled by the mention of just one man in h. 933. Its repetition in h. 1021 mentions that "people" stood up and shouted. It is therefore possible that different narrators mentioned different people. It is also possible that the reporter of this addition, Asbāṭ, confused the two events. Anyhow, the coming of the Quraish to request the Holy Prophet for prayer at a time of their utmost hostility towards him (he having been expelled from his native city) shows the great confidence people had in his kind behaviour. There is nothing strange in this, because when, after the conquest of Makkah, the opportunity arose to administer the severest punishment and the Holy Prophet asked these people what treatment they expected from him, they replied: "noble brother, son of a noble brother". The most bitter enemies approached him for their needs and he fulfilled their needs with an open heart. This example is not found in the life of any other prophet. Just as the enmity of his opponents had reached its height, so also did his mercy reach its height. As the Qur'ān says of him: "We have not sent you but as a mercy to the nations" (21:107).

pray to Allāh for rain." So he said twice: "O Allāh! grant us rain." By Allāh, we saw no trace of cloud in the sky and suddenly the sky became overcast with clouds and it started raining. He came down the pulpit and said the prayer. When he departed it was raining and it continued raining till the next Friday. When the Prophet ﷺ stood up to deliver the sermon, people started shouting to him: "The houses have collapsed and the roads are cut off; so pray to Allāh to withhold the rain." So the Prophet ﷺ smiled and said: "O Allāh! Around us and not upon us." And the sky became clear over Madīnah but it continued to rain around it and not a single drop of rain fell on Madīnah. I looked towards (the sky at) Madīnah and it was like a crown (*iklīl*).[20]

Ch. 15: To make supplication (*du ʻā'*) during prayer for rain while standing

1022 Abū Isḥāq reported that ʻAbdullāh ibn Yazīd al-Anṣārī went out with al-Barā' ibn ʻĀzib, and Zaid ibn Arqam and prayed for rain. He (ʻAbdullāh ibn Yazīd) stood up on his feet but not on a pulpit and made supplication for rain. Then he prayed two *rakʻahs* with loud recitation, and did not give the *Adhān* or *Iqāmah*.[21]

1023 ʻAbbād ibn Tamīm related that his uncle, who was one of the Companions of the Prophet ﷺ, informed him that the Prophet ﷺ went out with the people to pray for rain for them. He stood up and called on Allāh, then he faced the *Qiblah* and turned his cloak around and it rained.[22]

Ch. 16: Loud Recitation in Prayer for Rain

1024 ʻAbbād ibn Tamīm reported that his uncle said: The Prophet ﷺ went

---

[20] This is a repetition of the subject-matter of h. 933 which differs from the other versions. The word *iklīl* is applied to a crown, and it really means the thing which surrounds. The narrator means that the cloud surrounded the sky of Madīnah, which was clear over the city itself. The words of the prayer of the Holy Prophet are notable. He did not merely ask that Allāh stop the rain because the desire to bring the mercy of Allāh to an end can never arise in the heart of a prophet which is full of Divine knowledge. So he prayed that it should rain around them, where it was still required, and not upon them. The prayers of the Holy Prophet have wonderfully sublime aspects within them, which require a separate book to explain properly.

[21] This shows that ʻAbdullāh ibn Zubair, who was a Companion, said the regular prayers after the supplication. It is known that the Holy Prophet did the same; see h. 1012 and h. 1014. There is a report from ʻĀ'ishah in Abū Dāwūd (book: 'Prayer for rain', h. 1173) and from Ibn Abbās in Musnad Aḥmad about the Holy Prophet's prayer for rain which mentions him ascending the pulpit before the regular prayer. Other reports are to the contrary. It is probable that he prayed for rain on several occasions, sometimes making the *du ʻā'* before and sometimes after the regular prayer. The event reported here is from 64 A.H. when ʻAbdullāh ibn Yazīd was the governor of Kūfah, appointed by ʻAbdullāh ibn Zubair.

[22] This is a repetition of h. 1005 with more details. See footnote to h. 1005.

out to pray for rain and he faced the *Qiblah,* calling on Allāh, and he turned his cloak around. Then he prayed two *rak'ahs,* in both of which he recited (the Qur'ān) aloud.[23]

Ch. 17: How the Prophet ﷺ turned his back towards the people

1025 'Abbād ibn Tamīm reported that his uncle said: I saw the Prophet ﷺ on the day when he went out to pray for rain. He turned his back towards the people and faced the *Qiblah* and called on Allāh. Then he turned his cloak around, then led us in a two *rak'ah* prayer, in both of which he recited (the Qur'ān) aloud.[24]

Ch. 18: The Prayer for rain is two *Rak'ahs*

1026 'Abbād ibn Tamīm reported from his uncle that the Prophet ﷺ prayed for rain, then prayed two *rak'ahs* and turned his cloak around.[25]

Ch. 19: Prayer for rain at the Prayer Ground

1027 'Abbād ibn Tamīm said that his uncle reported: The Prophet ﷺ went out to the prayer ground to pray for rain, and faced the *Qiblah.* Then he prayed two *rak'ahs* and turned his cloak around.[26]

Abū Bakr reported: He put the right side (of his cloak) on the left.

Ch. 20: Facing the *Qiblah* during the prayer for rain

1028 'Abbād ibn Tamīm informed that 'Abdullāh ibn Zaid al-Anṣārī informed him that the Prophet ﷺ went out to the prayer ground to pray and when he called on Allāh, or intended to call on Allāh, he faced the *Qiblah* and turned his cloak around.[27]

---

[23] This repetition of h. 1005 is like h. 1012 with some addition. The chapter heading comes from its last words.

[24] This repetition of h. 1005 has more words than h. 1024, without any addition to the subject. H. 1024 does not contain the words "he turned his back towards the people." From both these reports it is clearly seen that the Holy Prophet led the two *rak'ah* prayer after he called on Allāh for rain.

[25] This again is a repetition of h. 1005.

[26] This again is a repetition of h. 1005. The words "to the prayer ground" are not found in the repetitions that have occurred before, and this chapter heading comes from them. Here, after facing the *Qiblah,* there is no mention of making the supplication (*du'ā'*) but only of saying the two *rak'ah* prayer, and turning the cloak around is after the prayer.

[27] This again is a repetition of h. 1005. The mention of a two *rak'ah* prayer is omitted here.

Ch. 21: **The people raising their hands with the Imām during the prayer for rain**

1029–1030 Anas ibn Mālik said: A man of the Bedouins came to the Messenger of Allāh ﷺ on a Friday and said: "O Messenger of Allāh! The livestock, the offspring, and the people have perished." So the Messenger of Allāh ﷺ raised both his hands, praying (for rain), and the people too raised their hands with him and they prayed. We had not left the mosque when it started raining. It rained till the next Friday when the same man came to the Prophet ﷺ and said: "O Messenger of Allāh! Travellers are inconvenienced and roads are unusable". [1030] Anas added that the Prophet ﷺ raised his hands so much that the whiteness of his armpits could be seen.[28]

Ch. 22: **The Imām raising his hands in the prayer for rain**

1031 Anas ibn Mālik reported: The Prophet ﷺ never raised his hands for any of his supplications except for that of the prayer for rain and he used to raise them so much that the whiteness of his armpits became visible.[29]

Ch. 23: **What should be said when it is raining**

Ibn Abbās said regarding *ka-ṣayyib-in* (the Qur'ān, 2:19), it is rain. Others said: *ṣāba yaṣūbu,* and (derived from it is) *aṣāba.*[30]

1032 'Ā'ishah reported that whenever the Messenger of Allāh ﷺ saw rain, he used to say: "O Allāh! Let it be a beneficial rain."

Ch. 24: **He who stays in the rain so long that water trickles down his beard**

1033 Anas ibn Mālik related: A famine visited the people in the time of the Messenger of Allāh ﷺ. When the Messenger of Allāh ﷺ was delivering his sermon on a Friday, a Bedouin got up and said: "O Messenger of Allāh,

---

[28] This is a repetition of h. 933. In h. 933 it is only mentioned that the Holy Prophet raised his hands and prayed. Here it is mentioned that the Companions also raised their hands, and therefore they all were making the supplication.

[29] The raising of the hands to make supplication will be discussed in detail later on. The meaning given to this statement, that he never raised his hands for supplications except for the supplication for rain, is that he raised his hands much more so in supplication for rain, and this was to make his beseeching more intense.

[30] *Ṣayyib* means rain, as Ibn Abbās said. Its perfect tense is *ṣāba,* meaning 'it came down', and imperfect is *yaṣūbu.* In the verbal form *af'āl,* its perfect tense is *aṣāba* which is the causative of the verb *ṣāba,* and the imperfect is *yuṣību.* The writers of this report have placed *aṣāba* between *ṣāba* and *yaṣūbu* while its correct position is after *yaṣūbu* (as in this translation). *Ṣayyib* is mentioned in the ḥadīth in this chapter, which is why the word occurring in the Qur'ān (2:19) required to be explained.

our wealth has perished and our families are starving, so pray to Allāh for us for rain." ...[31]

Ch. 25: When the wind blows[32]

1034 Anas ibn Mālik said: When the wind blew strongly its effect could be seen on the face of the Prophet ﷺ.[33]

Ch. 26: Saying of the Prophet ﷺ: "I was helped by (the wind of) Aṣ-Ṣabā"

1035 Ibn 'Abbās reported that the Prophet ﷺ said: "I was helped by (the wind of) Aṣ-Ṣabā and the people of 'Ād were destroyed by (the wind of) Ad-Dabūr." [34]

Ch. 27: What has been said about earthquakes and signs

1036 Abū Hurairah reported that the Prophet ﷺ said: "The Hour shall not come until knowledge is taken away, quakes are frequent, time passes quickly, afflictions appear, murder and slaughter will be widespread, and money will flow abundantly amongst you." [35]

---

[31] This is a repetition of h. 933. Its wording is very similar to h. 933 with only insignificant differences. For the remainder, omitted in this translation, see h. 933. The chapter heading seems to indicate that the Holy Prophet did not leave his place under the water dripping from the ceiling until he had completed his sermon.

[32] A gale and a stormy wind is meant, as the ḥadīth shows.

[33] It is not mentioned here what should be done at such time. It is only said that the Holy Prophet's face showed anxiety. Sometimes stormy wind has destroyed people and communities and it is possible that he was anxious in case his people be destroyed. In some other reports a prayer at this time is mentioned: "O Allāh, I ask of You any good that it (the wind) is commanded with (to bring), and I seek refuge in You from any evil that it (the wind) is commanded with (to bring)". Its Arabic text is as follows:

$$\text{اَللّٰهُمَّ إِنِّيْ أَسْأَلُكَ مِنْ خَيْرِ مَا أُمِرَتْ بِهِ وَأَعُوْذُ بِكَ مِنْ شَرِّ مَا أُمِرَتْ بِهِ}$$

[34] Aṣ-Ṣabā is the wind which comes from the east, while that from the west is known as Ad-Dabūr. The Holy Prophet was helped by the wind of Aṣ-Ṣabā in the battle of the Allies (*Aḥzāb*) which drove away his enemies in failure and defeat, but this wind did not kill even one man among them.

[35] This is a repetition of h. 85. If quakes (*al-zalāzil*) are taken to mean the agitation of the earth then its connection with lack of rain and blowing of storms is that these, too, are disasters, and to repel them it is necessary to turn to God. However, this may indicate tribulations of all kinds which arose later, and are still arising. By the taking away of knowledge is meant the knowledge of attaining to God, which these days has entirely disappeared. By time passing quickly is meant that people will be so engrossed in their worldly occupations, or there will be so many comforts of life, that they will not perceive the passage of time. This ḥadīth occurs in detail in the book of Tribulations (*Kitāb al-Fitan*), h. 7121.

1037 Ibn 'Umar reported, (the Prophet ﷺ) saying: "O Allāh, bless our Shām and our Yaman." People said: And our Najd? He said: "O Allāh, bless our Shām and our Yaman." They said: And our Najd? He said: "Quakes and tribulations are there, and from there the party of the devil will arise." [36]

Ch. 28:   Allāh the Most High's Saying: "And you make your denial your means of subsistence" (the Qur'ān, 56:82)

Ibn 'Abbās said: Your thankfulness. [37]

1038 Zaid ibn Khālid al-Juhanī reported: The Messenger of Allāh ﷺ led us in the morning prayer at Ḥudaibiyah after it had rained during the night. … [38]

Ch. 29:   None knows the time of the coming of rain except Allāh, the Most High

And Abū Hurairah reported from the Prophet ﷺ: "There are five things which none knows but Allāh."

1039 Ibn 'Umar reported that the Prophet ﷺ said: "Keys of the unseen are five, which none knows but Allāh — no one knows what will happen tomorrow, no one knows what is in the wombs, no one knows what he will gain tomorrow, no one knows in which land he will die, and no one knows when it will rain." [39]

---

[36] Apparently these statements were made by Ibn 'Umar but it has been said that the words "the Prophet ﷺ " have been omitted here in the manuscripts. Hence we have placed them in parentheses. Which tribulations will arise from Najd, only Allāh knows. Perhaps it is about the future. It may be that by Najd is meant the entire area which includes Yamama, from where Musailima the false prophet arose and this may be a reference to it.

[37] That is, by subsistence is meant thankfulness. The meaning is that you should have been thankful for the Divine blessings, but your thankfulness is that you belie the Divine message.

[38] This is a repetition of h. 846 in almost the same words, which describes it as an act of unbelief (*kufr*) to attribute the coming of rain to the fortune written in the stars instead of attributing it to Allāh. For the remainder of this ḥadīth see h. 846.

[39] Those five matters are mentioned regarding which fortune-tellers and astrologers mislead people by claiming that they can foretell them. Therefore, the Holy Prophet said that these are their conjectures, and the true knowledge is with Allāh. In chapter *Luqmān* of the Qur'ān five things are also mentioned (31:34) but there it says "knowledge of the hour" and here "what will happen tomorrow". The conjectures of fortune-tellers and astrologers are a hindrance to the real progress of man. For example, instead of trying to find out what will happen tomorrow a person should consider the consequences of his deeds. If his deeds are good, the consequences will be good. The words "knowledge of the hour" used in the Qur'ān indicate that the destruction of nations comes about due to their deeds. The conjectures as to whether the child to be born is male or female are also purposeless. Whichever offspring is bestowed by Allāh, one should bring it up

in the best possible way, whether it is a male or a female. To be over-joyed by the one and dismayed by the other is not right. As to what a person will gain tomorrow, this is mentioned to teach that a person should not postpone till tomorrow what he can do today. As to dying, no one knows when and where he will die, and therefore he must be prepared to face death at any time by being always in a state of obedience to God: "Do not die except as submitting ones" (the Qur'ān, 3:102). As to when it will rain, man does not know. Therefore, he must not rely on this for his business, but do whatever lies in his power.

Book 16: *Al-Kusūf*

Eclipses

In the name of Allāh, the Beneficent, the Merciful

Ch. 1: Prayer during an eclipse of the sun

1040 Abū Bakrah reported: We were with the Messenger of Allāh ﷺ when the sun eclipsed. The Messenger of Allāh ﷺ stood up, dragging his cloak till he entered the Mosque. So we (too) entered and he led us in a two *rak'ah* prayer till the sun appeared clearly. Then he said: "The sun and the moon do not become eclipsed because of the death of anyone. So whenever you see them, pray and call on Allāh until it becomes clear for you." [1]

1041 Abū Mas'ūd said that the Prophet ﷺ said: "The sun and the moon do not become eclipsed because of the death of any human being, but they are two signs from among the signs of Allāh. So whenever you see these two, stand up and pray." [2]

---

[1] This ḥadīth, which occurs in detail as h. 1044, occurs here in brief. As stated further on, this was the day of the death of the Holy Prophet's son Ibrāhīm, and people were saying that the sun was eclipsed due to his death. This was a miracle for the taking. But the Holy Prophet's religion was based on knowledge and wisdom, and he did not want to make his followers superstitious. Hence he told them that the eclipse of the sun is not caused by anyone's death, nor connected in any way with Ibrāhīm's death. However, he instructed them to pray at such a time, and a ḥadīth further on mentions the giving of charity. What is meant is that whenever an extraordinary event occurs, we must turn to Allāh, the Most High. Those persons who are charged with the Divine mission of turning people's minds towards God are not concerned with questions such as why, how or when does it rain, or why, how and when do eclipses occur. If it does not rain, or if an eclipse occurs, they ask people to bow before God. A Muslim is also commanded to pray every day when the sun starts to decline at mid-day, sets in the evening, or is about to rise at dawn. This is not worship of the sun but worship of God Who has full power to bring about these changes. Similarly, the eclipse of the sun is a change which occurs in normal circumstances, and it is taught that at such a time one must bow before God Who has caused this change with His total control over nature. This is not a prayer asking that the eclipse be brought to an end, nor is this mentioned in any ḥadīth. It is, of course, called a sign, which it is in the sense that just as light has been interrupted for a while from the world, similarly the light in the human heart can sometimes change to darkness for unknown reasons, or that the Divine light ceases to have any effect on man. The purpose of prayer is to try to create such a true link with Allāh which can never be broken even temporarily.

[2] This again is a repetition of h. 1044 with even briefer wording.

1042 Ibn ʿUmar reported, informing from the Prophet ﷺ: "The sun and the moon do not become eclipsed because of the death of anyone or his life, but they are two signs from among the signs of Allāh. So whenever you see them, pray." [3]

1043 Al-Mughīrah ibn Shuʿbah reported: The sun eclipsed in the time of the Messenger of Allāh ﷺ on the day Ibrāhīm died. People said: "The sun has eclipsed because of Ibrāhīm's death." So the Messenger of Allāh ﷺ said: "The sun and the moon do not become eclipsed because of the death of anyone or his life. So whenever you see (them), pray and call on Allāh." [4]

Ch. 2:　To give in charity for the eclipse

1044 ʿĀ'ishah reported: The sun eclipsed in the time of the Messenger of Allāh ﷺ, so he led the people in prayer. He stood up and remained for long in *Qiyām* (standing posture in prayer). Then he went into *Rukūʿ* and remained in it (the bowing posture) for long. Then he stood up and remained for long in *Qiyām,* but shorter than in the first *Qiyām.* Then he went into *Rukūʿ* and remained in it (the bowing posture) for long, but shorter than in the first *Rukūʿ.* Then he went into prostration and remained for long in *Sajdah* (prostration). Then he did the same in the second *rakʿah* which he had done in the first. He then finished and the sun became bright. He addressed the people, and after praising Allāh and extolling Him, he said: "The sun and the moon are two signs from among the signs of Allāh. They do not become eclipsed because of the death of anyone or his life. When you see this, call on Allāh, declare His greatness, pray and give in charity." Then he said: "O followers of Muḥammad! By Allāh! There is no one who has a greater sense of honour than Allāh that his servants, male or female, should commit illicit sexual intercourse. O followers of Muḥammad! By Allāh! If you knew what I know, you would laugh little and weep more." [5]

Ch. 3:　Making a loud announcement for prayer in congregation for eclipse

1045 ʿAbdullāh ibn ʿAmr reported: When the sun was eclipsed in the time of the Prophet ﷺ, it was announced that people should gather for prayer.

---

[3] This repetition of h. 1044 is like h. 1041. Here the words "or his life" are added to: "because of the death of anyone".

[4] In this repetition of h. 1044 it is further mentioned that this incident took place on the day of Ibrāhīm's death and people thought it was because of his death. The Holy Prophet dismissed this idea as wrong.

[5] A description of the Holy Prophet's eclipse prayer, with *Qiyām* and *Rukūʿ* etc., has already been given in h. 745. However, in that ḥadīth what he is reported as having said in his speech after the prayer is different from here. These two reports complement one another. Here moral reform has been emphasized in particular.

Ch. 4: A sermon (*khuṭbah*) delivered by the Imām at the time of the eclipse

'Ā'ishah and Asmā' said: The Prophet 🕌 gave a sermon (*khuṭbah*).[6]

1046 'Ā'ishah, wife of the Prophet 🕌, reported: The sun eclipsed during the life of the Prophet 🕌, so he went to the mosque and people formed rows behind him. He said the *Takbīr* and recited a long portion (of the Qur'ān). Then he said the *Takbīr* and went into *Rukū'* for long. Then he said *Sami' Allāhu li-man ḥamidah* ("Allāh hears him who praises Him"). He stood and did not go into prostration but recited a long portion (of the Qur'ān), which was shorter than the first one. Then he said the *Takbīr* and went into *Rukū'* for long, but shorter than the first one. Then he said *Sami' Allāhu li-man ḥamidah* ("Allāh hears him who praises Him"), *Rabba-nā wa la-ka-l-ḥamd* ("Our Lord! And Yours is the praise"). Then he went into prostration. He did the same in the second *rak'ah*. Thus he completed four *Rukū'* and four prostrations. The sun had cleared before he finished (the prayer). Then he stood up and eulogised Allāh as befits Him, and then he said: "These two are two signs from among the signs of Allāh. They do not become eclipsed because of the death of anyone or his life. When you see them, hasten to prayer." [7]

It is reported from Kathīr ibn 'Abbās that 'Abdullāh ibn 'Abbās used to report (the incident of) the day of the eclipse of the sun as it is in the ḥadīth narrated by 'Urwah from 'Ā'ishah. I (the narrator Az-Zuhrī) said to 'Urwah: "Your brother ('Abdullāh ibn Zubair), on the day there was an eclipse of the sun in Madīnah, prayed no more than two *rak'ahs* as in the morning prayer." He said: "Yes, because he made an error in (correctly knowing) the *Sunnah*." [8]

Ch. 5: Should one say *kasafat* or *khasafat* for the sun?

Allāh, the Most High, said: *Wa khasafa al-qamar* ("And the moon became dark", the Qur'ān, 75 : 8).

1047 'Ā'ishah, wife of the Prophet 🕌, informed that the Messenger of Allāh 🕌 prayed on the day the sun eclipsed. He stood up and said the *Takbīr*

---

[6] In h. 1044 reported by 'Ā'ishah the word *khuṭbah* occurs explicitly (*khaṭaba an-nās* — "he *addressed* the people"). In this chapter in h. 1046, and in h. 86, 745 and 1053 related by Asmā', although the word *khuṭbah* does not occur explicitly but the *khuṭbah* itself is found in all of them, and the incident these refer to is the same.

[7] This is a repetition of h. 1044. It has a more detailed description of the prayer. The words of his sermon differ somewhat from those in h. 1044. The last part of h. 1044, beginning, with "Then he said: O followers of Muḥammad", is not present here. The rest of the wording of this ḥadīth varies only slightly from h. 1044. It is followed by the addition from Kathīr ibn 'Abbās.

[8] See also h. 1066 in connection with this part.

and recited a long portion (of the Qur'ān). Then he went into *Rukū'* for long. Then he raised his head and said: *Sami' Allāhu li-man ḥamidah* ("Allāh hears him who praises Him"). He remained standing as he was, then recited a long portion (of the Qur'ān), which was shorter than the first one. Then he went into *Rukū'* for long, but shorter than the first one. Then he went into prostration for long. He did the same in the second *rak'ah*. Then he finished the prayer with *Salām* and the sun had cleared. He addressed the people and said about the eclipse of the sun and the moon: "These two are two signs from among the signs of Allāh. They do not become eclipsed because of the death of anyone or his life. When you see them, hasten to prayer." [9]

Ch. 6:   The saying of the Prophet ﷺ: "Allāh makes His servants fear by means of the eclipse."

Abū Mūsā reported it from the Prophet ﷺ.

1048 Abū Bakrah reported that the Messenger of Allāh ﷺ said: "The sun and the moon are two signs from among the signs of Allāh. They do not become eclipsed because of the death of anyone, but Allāh makes His servants fear by means of them." [10]

Ch. 7:   To seek refuge from punishment of the grave during eclipse

1049–1050 'Ā'ishah, wife of the Prophet ﷺ, reported that a Jewess came to ask her for something and said to her: "May Allāh grant you refuge from the punishment of the grave." So 'Ā'ishah asked the Messenger of Allāh ﷺ: "Will people be punished in their graves?" The Messenger of Allāh ﷺ said: "I seek refuge in Allāh from this." [1050] Then one morning the Messenger of Allāh ﷺ went riding but the sun was eclipsed. So he returned before noon[11] and passing between the rear of (his) dwellings (*ḥujur*) he (came to the Mosque and)[12] stood to pray and people stood behind him. ...[13]

---

[9] This repetition of h. 1044 is similar to h. 1046 but is briefer. The addition from Kathīr ibn 'Abbās found in h. 1046 is not here. In both these ḥadīth the word *khasafat* is used in connection with the sun, and this is what the chapter heading refers to.

[10] This is a repetition in brief of h. 1044. It then goes on to add that some reporters do not report the words: "but Allāh makes His servants fear by means of them."

[11] This was for the burial of his son Ibrāhīm who had died that day.

[12] The mosque is mentioned in the words "between the rear of (his) dwellings (*ḥujur*)" because these dwellings adjoined the mosque. In h. 1040, relating the same event, the mosque is explicitly mentioned.

[13] After this point, in this repetition of h. 1044, the two *rak'ahs* are described in detail individually, namely, that in each *rak'ah* he assumed the standing posture (*Qiyām*) twice and the bowing down posture (*Rukū'*) twice, and each posture was longer the first time than the second

He said whatever Allāh pleased that he should say, then he commanded them to seek refuge from the punishment of the grave.[14]

Ch. 8:　Prolonging the prostration (*Sajdah*) during the eclipse prayer

1051 'Abdullāh ibn 'Amr reported that when the sun was eclipsed in the time of the Messenger of Allāh ﷺ it was announced that people should gather for prayer. So the Prophet ﷺ bowed down for two *Rukū'* in one prostration (i.e., in one *rak'ah*), then he stood up and bowed down for two *Rukū'* in one prostration (i.e., *rak'ah*), then he sat (to finish the prayer), then the eclipse cleared. 'Ā'ishah said: I have never performed such a long prostration.[15]

Ch. 9:　Saying the eclipse prayer in congregation

Ibn 'Abbās led them in prayer in the porch of Zamzam. 'Alī ibn 'Abdullāh ibn 'Abbās gathered (people together) and Ibn 'Umar led (them) in prayer

1052 'Abdullāh ibn 'Abbās reported: The sun eclipsed during the life of the Messenger of Allāh ﷺ, so the Messenger of Allāh ﷺ prayed.[16] He stood for a long time, a time in which one could recite *Sūrah al-Baqarah*.[17] Then he went into *Rukū'* for long. ...[18]

Then he finished and the sun had cleared. He then said: "The sun and the moon are two signs from among the signs of Allāh. They do not become eclipsed because of the death of anyone or his life. When you see this, remember Allāh."

They said: "O Messenger of Allāh, we saw you going forward a little from your place and then we saw you retreating." He said: "I saw Paradise and tried

---

time. Here, while also mentioning the second *rak'ah*, the words are repeated: "but shorter than in the first *Qiyām* ... but shorter than in the first *Rukū'*." See h. 1044 for the translation omitted here.

[14] That is, after finishing the prayer he gave the sermon as stated in the other reports from 'Ā'ishah, but here its detail is not provided as it is in h. 1044, and he directed them to seek refuge from the punishment of the grave. By "grave" is meant the intermediate state between death and the rising to life, the *barzakh* between this world and the hereafter. See also the repetition of this ḥadīth in h. 1372.

[15] The first sentence is a repetition of h. 1045, and the rest is a brief version of h. 1044.

[16] In this ḥadīth, the accounts given in several preceding reports are repeated with some variation in wording. In its first part the details of the eclipse prayer are similar to those in h. 1046.

[17] It was not that *Sūrah al-Baqarah* was recited, but other chapters were recited.

[18] At this point, as in h. 1049–1050, the details of the second *rak'ah* are provided like those of the first. See h. 1049–1050 for the omitted translation.

to take a bunch (of fruit), and if I had taken it you would have eaten from it as long as the world remained.[19] I have been shown the fire (of hell), and I have never seen a sight more horrible than what I have seen today.[20] I saw that most of its inmates were women." People asked: "Why was it so, O Messenger of Allāh?" He said: "Because of their ungratefulness." It was said: "Were they ungrateful to Allāh?" He said: "They were ungrateful to their husbands and ungrateful for goodness (done to them). If you do good to one of them all life and she sees something from you (which she does not like), she says: I have never seen any good from you."

Ch. 10:   Women praying along with men during the eclipse

1053 Asmā', daughter of Abū Bakr, reported: I came to ʿĀ'ishah, wife of the Prophet ﷺ, when the sun was eclipsed and (saw that) people were standing praying, and she was also standing praying. ...[21]

Ch. 11:   He who likes to free a slave during the eclipse

1054 Asmā' reported: The Prophet ﷺ ordered the freeing of a slave during the eclipse.

Ch. 12:   Saying the eclipse prayer in the mosque

1055–1056 ʿĀ'ishah reported that a Jewess came to ask her for something ...[22]

Ch. 13:   The sun is not eclipsed because of the death of anyone or his life

This was reported by Abū Bakrah, Mughīrah, Abū Mūsā, Ibn ʿAbbās and Ibn ʿUmar.[23]

1057 Abū Masʿūd reported that the Messenger of Allāh ﷺ said: "The sun and the moon do not become eclipsed because of the death of anyone, but they

---

[19] Exactly these words are contained in h. 748. See the footnote to that ḥadīth.

[20] This sentence is found in exactly these words in h. 431. The part which follows, beginning "I saw that most of its inmates were women", is a repetition of h. 29 with a slight variation.

[21] Here h. 86 is repeated in words identical to its repetition in h. 184. For the omitted remainder see h. 184 and h. 86. H. 86 itself does not mention the eclipse. This ḥadīth states that ʿĀ'ishah and Asmā' both joined the congregation for the eclipse prayer. There are some reports to the effect that other women were also in the congregation. This shows that women joined men not only in the congregations for the five daily prayers but also for optional prayers.

[22] This repetition of h. 1044 consists of the same account as h. 1049–1050, using the same wording with slight variations. For the omitted remainder see h. 1049–1050.

[23] These reports occur as follows: Abū Bakrah, h. 1040; Ibn ʿUmar, h. 1042; Mughīrah, h. 1043; Ibn ʿAbbās, h. 1052; and Abū Mūsā, h. 1059.

are two signs from among the signs of Allāh. So whenever you see them, pray." [24]

1058 ʿĀʾishah reported: The sun eclipsed in the time of the Messenger of Allāh ﷺ, so the Prophet ﷺ stood up and led the people in prayer. He prolonged the recitation, then he went into *Rukūʿ* and remained in it for long. Then he raised his head and prolonged the recitation, but shorter than the first recitation. Then he went into *Rukūʿ* and remained in it for long, but shorter than in the first *Rukūʿ*. Then he raised his head and went into prostration, performing two prostrations. Then he stood up and did the same in the second *rakʿah*. Then he stood up and said: "The sun and the moon do not become eclipsed because of the death of anyone or his life, but they are two signs from among the signs of Allāh which He shows His servants. So whenever you see them, hasten to prayer."[25]

Ch. 14: Remembering Allāh during the eclipse

Ibn ʿAbbās related this.

1059 Abū Mūsā reported: The sun was eclipsed, so the Prophet ﷺ stood up quickly, fearing that the hour (of the Day of Judgment) had come. He came to the Mosque and prayed, taking the longest time in *Qiyām* (standing) and *Rukūʿ* and prostration that I had ever seen him doing. And he said: "These are signs sent by Allāh, not because of the death of anyone or his life but to make His servants fear by means of them. So when you see such a thing, hasten to the remembrance of Allāh, and to calling on Him, and to seeking His forgiveness." [26]

Ch. 15: Making supplication (*duʿāʾ*) during eclipse

Related by Abū Mūsā and ʿĀʾishah from the Prophet ﷺ.

1060 Mughīrah ibn Shuʿbah said: The sun eclipsed on the day Ibrāhīm died. People said: "It has eclipsed because of Ibrāhīm's death." So the Messenger of Allāh ﷺ said: "The sun and the moon are two signs from among the signs of Allāh. They do not become eclipsed because of the death

---

[24] This consists of only a part of the Holy Prophet's sermon from h. 1044 in words similar to those in h. 1041.

[25] This is a repetition of h. 1044 with the last part omitted, while the rest is repeated in different words.

[26] This is a repetition of h. 1044 in which the words are very different. This has also been related by others, but none of them said that the Holy Prophet feared that the Day of Judgment had arrived. Abū Mūsā only concluded this from the Holy Prophet's intense humility and pleading before Allāh and his lengthening of the prayer. Had the Holy Prophet mentioned the fear of the Day of Judgment, some other narrators would have recorded it as well.

of anyone or his life. So whenever you see them, call on Allāh and pray until it is clear." [27]

Ch. 16:   The Imām saying *Ammā ba'd* ("After this") in the sermon after the eclipse prayer

1061 Asmā' reported: When the Messenger of Allāh ﷺ finished, the sun had brightened. He then gave a sermon, praised Allāh as befits Him, and then said: "*Ammā ba'd*." [28]

Ch. 17:   To say prayer during an eclipse of the moon

1062 Abū Bakrah reported: The sun eclipsed in the time of the Messenger of Allāh ﷺ, so he prayed two *rak'ahs*. [29]

1063 Abū Bakrah reported: The sun eclipsed in the time of the Messenger of Allāh ﷺ. So he went out dragging his clothes until he reached the Mosque. People gathered around him and he led them in a prayer of two *rak'ahs*. The sun cleared (by this time) and he said: "The sun and the moon are two signs from among the signs of Allāh. They do not become eclipsed because of the death of anyone. When it is like this, pray and call on Allāh until it becomes clear for you." And this was because a son of the Prophet ﷺ, called Ibrāhīm, died and people said: It is because of that. [30]

Ch. 18:   A woman pouring water on her head when the Imām stays standing for long (in *Qiyām*) in the first *rak'ah* [31]

Ch. 19:   In the eclipse prayer the first *rak'ah* is longer

1064 'Ā'ishah reported that the Prophet ﷺ led them in the prayer of the eclipse of the sun, going into *Rukū'* four times in the two prostrations (i.e., in the two *rak'ahs*), the first being longer. [32]

---

[27] This is a repetition of h. 1043 with slight variation of wording. At the end there is the addition: "until it is clear".

[28] This is a repetition of a small part of h. 86

[29] This repetition of h. 1044 is very brief. From this it is inferred that a prayer should also be said during an eclipse of the moon.

[30] This repetition of h. 1044 is like h. 1040 with slight variation in wording. The meaning is that the Holy Prophet's saying that the sun and the moon "do not become eclipsed because of the death of anyone" was because his son Ibrāhīm died that day and people were attributing the eclipse to his death.

[31] This subject was covered in h. 86. Here Bukhārī does not repeat that ḥadīth.

[32] This repetition of h. 1044 is very brief. The meaning is that in the two-*rak'ah* prayer he performed *Rukū'* (bowing down) four times, and the first *rak'ah* took longer than the second.

Ch. 20:   To recite aloud in the eclipse prayer

1065 'Ā'ishah reported: The Prophet ﷺ did loud recitation (of the Qur'ān) in the eclipse prayer. When he finished his recitation he said the *Takbīr* (i.e., *Allāhu Akbar*) and went into *Rukū'*. When he raised up (his head) from *Rukū'* he said: *Sami' Allāhu li-man ḥamidah* ("Allāh hears him who praises Him"), *Rabba-nā wa la-ka-l-ḥamd* ("Our Lord! And Yours is the praise"). Then he again started recitation in the eclipse prayer, so that there were four *Rukū'* and four prostrations in the two *rak'ahs*.[33]

1066 And 'Urwah reported from 'Ā'ishah that the sun eclipsed in the time of the Messenger of Allāh ﷺ, so he sent an announcer (to proclaim) that people should gather for prayer. He stepped forward and performed four *Rukū'* and four prostrations in the two *rak'ahs*.[34]

Az-Zuhrī said:[35] I said (to 'Urwah): "What made your brother 'Abdullāh ibn Zubair do this, that he prayed only two *rak'ahs* like the morning prayer when he said the (eclipse) prayer in Madīnah?" He said: "Yes, he made an error in (correctly knowing) the *Sunnah*."

---

[33] The same incident described earlier in h. 1044 is repeated here briefly. However, loud recitation is mentioned here, which is not in h. 1044.

[34] This report includes the subject-matter of h. 1045 about the prayer announcement.

[35] This report from az-Zuhrī is the last part of h. 1046 which begins with the words "I said to 'Urwah", and here the name of 'Abdullāh ibn Zubair is mentioned.

Book 17: *Sujūd al-Qur'ān*

Prostrations (during the recitation) of the Qur'ān

In the name of Allāh, the Beneficent, the Merciful

Ch. 1: What is said concerning prostrations in the Qur'ān and the *Sunnah* about it[1]

1067 'Abdullāh (ibn Mas'ūd) reported: The Prophet ﷺ recited *An-Najm* (ch. 53 of the Qur'ān, 'The Star') in Makkah and went into prostration during it, and those with him also prostrated, except one old man who took a handful of small stones or dust, raised it to his forehead and said: "This is sufficient for me." I saw him later, killed as an unbeliever.[2]

Ch. 2: The prostration during (*Sūrah*) *Tanzīl*[3]

1068 Abū Hurairah reported: The Prophet ﷺ used to recite on Friday in the *Fajr* prayer *Alif, Lām, Mīm, Tanzīl* (ch. 32 of the Qur'ān) and *Hal atā 'ala-l-insān* (ch. 76).[4]

---

[1] What is meant are those places in the Qur'ān at which, during its recitation, a person must go into prostration (*Sajdah*). By requiring such prostrations, the Holy Prophet has taught that a Muslim must show immediate readiness to obey Divine commandments.

[2] In the commentary on *Sūrah An-Najm* in Bukhārī's book of 'Commentary on the Qur'ān', under ch. 'Make submission to Allāh and serve Him', it is stated: "The first chapter in which prostration was revealed was *Al-Najm*" (h. 4863). This shows, incidentally, that apart from the first five verses of chapter 96 of the Qur'ān (i.e., the very first revelation), the rest of that chapter was revealed later as there is a prostration at the end of it. The words "those with him" in this ḥadīth are also explained in the above commentary: "and Muslims and idolaters all prostrated with him" (h. 4862). It seems that the recitation of the Holy Qur'ān so overwhelmed the hearts that the unbelievers joined the Muslims in performing a prostration. The baseless reports which say that the Holy Prophet, after reciting the verses "Have you then considered Lāt and Uzzā, and another, the third, Manāt?" (53:19–20), then praised these idols, and for this reason the idolaters also prostrated, are all weak and inauthentic. The old man who did not prostrate was Umayya ibn Khalaf, as is mentioned in h. 4863 from 'Abdullāh ibn Mas'ūd. Had the reason why the idolaters prostrated been that their idols were praised, this old man, who was later killed while an un-believer, would also have prostrated.

[3] This is chapter 32 of the Qur'ān, also entitled *As-Sajdah*.

[4] This is a repetition of h. 891 in almost the same words. The name of this *Sūrah* itself, *As-Sajdah*, refers to the prostration which comes at 32:15.

Ch. 3:   The prostration during *(Sūrah) Ṣād*

1069 Ibn 'Abbās reported: The prostration during *(Sūrah) Ṣād* is not among the prostrations required, but I have seen the Prophet ﷺ prostrate during it.[5]

Ch. 4:   The prostration during *(Sūrah) An-Najm*

Ibn 'Abbās reported it from the Prophet ﷺ.

1070 'Abdullāh (ibn Mas'ūd) reported that the Prophet ﷺ recited *An-Najm* (ch. 53 of the Qur'ān, 'The Star') and went into prostration during it. There was not one of the people who did not go into prostration, but one man from among them took a handful of small stones or dust, raised it to his forehead and said: "This is sufficient for me." I saw him later, killed as an unbeliever.[6]

Ch. 5:   Muslims prostrating along with idolaters

An idolater is polluted and does not perform ablution (*Wuḍū'*). And Ibn 'Umar used to prostrate without *Wuḍū'*.[7]

1071 Ibn 'Abbās reported that the Prophet ﷺ went into prostration during (reciting) *Sūrah An-Najm,* and with him prostrated the Muslims, the idolaters, the *jinn* and the people.[8]

---

[5] In *Sūrah Ṣād* (38:24) there is no command to perform prostration but only a statement that David "fell down bowing and turned (to God)". However, as the Holy Prophet prostrated after reciting this verse, we do the same. In the commentary on *Sūrah Ṣād* in Bukhārī's book of 'Commentary on the Qur'ān' it is reported that Mujāhid asked Ibn 'Abbās why he prostrated at this verse, and he replied: "Do you not read: 'and of his descendants, David and Solomon... These are they whom Allāh guided, so follow their guidance' (the Qur'ān, 6:84, 6:90). So David was among those whom your Prophet ﷺ was commanded to follow" (see h. 4807). That is, as a prophet performed a prostration in these conditions, the Holy Prophet showed by his practice that Muslims must also prostrate.

[6] This is a repetition of h. 1067 with a slight variation in wording.

[7] As a person can recite the Holy Qur'ān without having performed *Wuḍū'*, he can also go into prostration without *Wuḍū'* while reciting it. Bukhārī has drawn an inference from two facts: firstly, the prostration performed by the idolaters, and secondly Ibn 'Umar prostrating without being in a state of *Wuḍū'*. The first inference is not strong, even though the Holy Prophet may not have forbidden it. As to an idolater being polluted, this is discussed elsewhere.

[8] This is a repetition of h. 1067. Ibn 'Abbās was not even born at the time, and the ethereal beings known as *jinn* cannot be seen by anyone. By "the *jinn* and the people" can only be meant the great and the small of the human population.

Ch. 6:   He who recites a verse of prostration and did not prostrate

1072 'Aṭā' ibn Yasār reported that he asked Zaid ibn Thābit, who said (in reply) that he recited *Sūrah An-Najm* to the Prophet ﷺ and he (the Prophet) did not prostrate in it.[9]

1073 Zaid ibn Thābit reported: I recited *Sūrah An-Najm* to the Prophet ﷺ and he (the Prophet) did not prostrate in it.[10]

Ch. 7:   The prostration during (the *Sūrah* beginning): "When the heaven bursts apart" (ch. 84)

1074 Abū Salamah reported: I saw Abū Hurairah reciting *Idha-s-samā'u-nshaqqat* (ch. 84 of the Qur'ān). He went into prostration during it. I asked him: "Abū Hurairah, am I not seeing you prostrate?" He said: "Had I not seen the Prophet ﷺ prostrating, I would not have prostrated." [11]

Ch. 8:   He who prostrates with the prostration of the reciter

Ibn Mas'ūd said to Tamīm ibn Ḥadhlam, and he was a boy who had recited a verse of prostration before him: "Prostrate, for you are our Imām in this." [12]

1075 Ibn 'Umar reported: When the Prophet ﷺ recited to us a *surah* in which there was a prostration, he would prostrate and we (too) would prostrate, and some of us could not even find a place for the forehead.

Ch. 9:   Crowding of people when the Imām recites a verse of prostration

1076 Ibn 'Umar reported: When the Prophet ﷺ recited (a *surah* in which there was) a prostration, and we were with him, he would prostrate and we

---

[9] Hence if the reciter on some occasion does not prostrate, it is not a sin. Here Zaid was the reciter. If he had prostrated, the Holy Prophet would also have done it. The Holy Prophet did not command him to do it, in order to establish that it need not always be done.

[10] This is a repetition of h. 1072 in the same words, but it is in the first person ("I recited", instead of "he recited").

[11] This is a repetition of h. 766. The wording is somewhat different but the meaning is the same. It appears from this that some people did not prostrate during this *Sūrah* (at 84:21). This may explain why Imām Mālik does not recognise a prostration at this point.

[12] The scholars are agreed that when the reciter performs a prostration, anyone who is listening to the recitation purposely and intentionally must also go into prostration. The reciter is regarded as the Imām in this situation, as Ibn Mas'ūd said to Tamīm ibn Ḥadhlam. The same appears from h. 1072, since Zaid, who was reciting, did not prostrate, the Holy Prophet also did not prostrate. In the ḥadīth of this chapter it is related that whenever the Holy Prophet prostrated, so did all those who were listening to him.

(too) would prostrate with him, and because of the crowding some of us could not even find a place for the forehead to prostrate at.[13]

Ch. 10: He who holds that Allāh, the Mighty, the Glorious, has not made prostration obligatory

'Imrān ibn Ḥusain was asked: What about a man who hears a verse of prostration although he is not sitting to hear it? He said: Even if he were sitting for this purpose. He meant it would not be obligatory for him. And Salmān said: We did not come for this purpose.

'Uthmān said: Prostration is only for the one who is intentionally listening. And az-Zuhrī said: Do not prostrate unless you are in a state of purity, and when you prostrate and you are not travelling, face the *Qiblah,* and if you are riding there is no sin on you whichever way you face.

As-Sā'ib ibn Yazīd did not prostrate at the prostration of story tellers.[14]

1077 Rabī'ah ibn 'Abdullāh ibn al-Hudair al-Taimī reported — Abū Bakr (ibn Abū Mulaikah) said: "Rabī'ah was one of the best people" — about what Rabī'ah saw of (the practice of) 'Umar ibn al-Khaṭṭāb: On a Friday he recited *Sūrah al-Naḥl* (ch. 16 of the Qur'ān) from the pulpit and when he reached the prostration (at 16:50), he descended and prostrated and people also prostrated. When the next Friday came, he recited the same and when he reached the (verse of) prostration, he said: "People! when we pass the verses of prostration, whoever prostrates does good, and whoever does not prostrate, there is no sin on him." And 'Umar did not prostrate.

---

[13] This is a repetition of h. 1075 with a slight variation in wording. It mentions crowding specifically. However, it does not say that such people did not prostrate, although that appears to be the case. It is possible that they prostrated one upon another.

[14] All these statements show two points: (1) If someone is present by co-incidence when a verse of prostration is recited, and is not there for the purpose of listening to the recitation, he is not obliged to prostrate; (2) even if he is there with that intention, it is not a sin if he does not prostrate. Az-Zuhrī has here expressed the following two opinions: (1) a person who is not in a state of *Wuḍū'* should not prostrate, but it has been said earlier (in heading of ch. 5) that even without being in a state of *Wuḍū'* prostration can be performed; (2) if a person is resident he must prostrate facing the *Qiblah.* It appears that in both these conclusions az-Zuhrī has treated the prostration during recitation like the prostration during prayer; hence he says that while travelling one can face any direction for this prostration. However, to draw the analogy of prayer is not correct. *Wuḍū'* and facing the *Qiblah* are essential only for prayer. Since *Wuḍū'* and facing the *Qiblah* are not requirements for reciting the Qur'ān, they cannot be requirements for the prostration during recitation.

Nāfi' added, from Ibn 'Umar, that Allāh has not made the prostration obligatory, except if we wish (to do it).

Ch. 11:   He who recited a verse of prostration during prayer and prostrated at it

1078 Abū Rāfi' reported: I said my *'Ishā'* prayer with Abū Hurairah and he recited *Idha-s-samā'u-nshaqqat* (ch. 84 of the Qur'ān) and went into prostration. So I said: "What is this?". He said: "I went into prostration at this (while saying prayer) behind Abul Qāsim ﷺ (the Holy Prophet), so I will continue to make this prostration in this (i.e., at 84:21) until I meet him (after death)." [15]

Ch. 12:   He who does not find a place for prostration because of crowding

1079 Ibn 'Umar reported: When the Prophet ﷺ recited to us a *sūrah* in which there was a prostration, he would prostrate and we (too) would prostrate, and some of us could not even find a spot as a place for the forehead.[16]

---

[15] This is a repetition of h. 766 in almost the same words.

[16] This is a repetition of h. 1075 in the same words, except that at the end the words are *makān-an li-mauḍi'i jabhati-hī* ("a spot as a place for the forehead") instead of *mauḍi'a jabhati-hī* ("a place for the forehead").

Book 18: *Taqṣīr aṣ-Ṣalāt*
Shortening the Prayers

In the name of Allāh, the Beneficent, the Merciful

Ch. 1: What is said regarding shortening (the prayers) and for what period of stay should they be shortened

1080 Ibn ʿAbbās reported: The Prophet ﷺ stayed for nineteen days and shortened the prayer. So when we were travelling for (up to) nineteen days we would shorten, but if it exceeded that we would say the complete prayers.[1]

1081 Yaḥyā ibn Abū Isḥāq related: I heard Anas say, "We went out from Madīnah for Makkah with the Prophet ﷺ. He prayed two *rakʿahs* for each prayer until we returned to Madīnah." I said (to Anas): "Did you stay in Makkah for a while?" He said: "We stayed there for ten days." [2]

Ch. 2: Prayer at Minā

1082 ʿAbdullāh (ibn ʿUmar) reported: I prayed with the Prophet ﷺ at

---

[1] This stay was at the time of the conquest of Makkah. There is much difference about its length in the reports. In Abū Dāwūd, according to the report by ʿIkramah from Ibn ʿAbbās it was 17, according to the report by ʿImrān ibn Ḥuṣain it was 18, and in the third report from Ibn ʿAbbās it was 15, and here in Bukhārī it is 19. According to Imām Mālik, Shafiʿī and Aḥmad, if the temporary stay is four days (or more) the prayers should be said complete. According to Imām Abū Ḥanīfah prayers can be shortened in a stay of less than 15 days, otherwise they must be said complete. He has followed the least of the lengths mentioned in these four reports and which is certain. Ibn ʿUmar also held the same view. However, there is no evidence that if the Holy Prophet had stayed for more than 19 days he would not have shortened the prayers. Also, the condition added by the jurists, that if the intention is to stay for four days or more then the prayers should be said complete, is not mentioned in Ḥadīth. The Holy Prophet stayed for 19 days and it cannot be said that his intention was to stay for less than four days. The next ḥadīth mentions that he stayed there for *Ḥajj* for ten days. It is obvious that he could not have returned in less time, and he knew beforehand that his return would be on the 14th of the month yet he still shortened his prayers. Hence, whether the intention existed or not, it is proved that he shortened prayers for 19 days. If a person is on a journey for longer, he can still shorten his prayers.

[2] This stay of ten days was for the Farewell Pilgrimage of the Holy Prophet. Those who have set the limit of four days for a journey say that he remained in Makkah itself for four days and then at Minā and ʿArafāt. This inference is not correct. Minā and ʿArafāt are included in Makkah; moreover, reports saying that he stayed for ten days or nineteen days do not establish a limit. What is meant is a state of journeying. However, if one takes up residence where one goes to, then that is not a state of journeying.

Minā two *rak'ah,* and (likewise) with Abū Bakr and 'Umar, and with 'Uthmān in the early part of his rule, and then he prayed it complete.[3]

1083 Ḥārithah ibn Wahb said: The Prophet ﷺ led us in prayer at Minā, when it was peace, in two *rak'ahs.*[4]

1084 'Abdur Raḥmān ibn Yazīd said: 'Uthmān ibn 'Affān led us in prayer at Minā in four *rak'ahs.* 'Abdullāh ibn Mas'ūd was asked about it and he said: "We belong to Allāh and to Him do we return." [5] Then he said: "I prayed with the Messenger of Allāh ﷺ at Minā two *rak'ahs,* and with Abū Bakr at Minā two *rak'ahs,* and with 'Umar at Minā two *rak'ahs.* May be my two *rak'ahs* will be accepted in place of four."

Ch. 3:   How many days did the Prophet ﷺ stay during his *Ḥajj?*

1085 Ibn 'Abbās reported: The Prophet ﷺ and his Companions came on the morning of the 4th, saying *Allāhumma Labbai-ka* for the *Ḥajj.* He ordered them to make it into an *'Umrah,* except for those who brought a sacrifice with them.[6]

Ch. 4:   For what length of journey is shortening of prayer allowed?

The Prophet ﷺ called one day and night (of travel) as a journey.[7] Ibn 'Umar and Ibn 'Abbās used to shorten prayers and stop fasting in a journey of four *burud* which is equal to 16 *farsakh.*[8]

---

[3] This action of 'Uthmān can be taken as meaning that he considered shortening the prayer as a concession and permission, and thought there was nothing wrong in saying it in full. See also h. 1102.

[4] Some people consider shortening of prayer to be allowed only in case of danger, and not under peaceful circumstances, because in the Qur'ān the shortening of prayer is conditional upon "if you fear" (4:101). However, the shortening mentioned here in the Qur'ān is in case of war. Shortening of prayer during a journey is established from the Holy Prophet's practice. By his example he showed that four *rak'ahs* when not on a journey become two *rak'ahs* when on a journey.

[5] These words from the Qur'ān (2:156) are sometimes used to express one's regret at someone else's action.

[6] The Holy Prophet arrived on the 4th of Dhul Ḥijjah. The 11th, 12th, and 13th are the *Tashrīq* days. He left for Madīnah on the morning of the 14th, which makes the stay 10 days.

[7] The report from Abū Hurairah referring to this length of journey, which takes one day and one night, occurs further down in this chapter. To set the limit by time rather than by distance is better since these days a car can cover more than forty miles in one hour's journey.

[8] A *barīd* (plural *burud*) is four *farsakh,* and one *farsakh* is equal to three miles. Thus the journey comes to 48 miles. 'Abdullāh ibn 'Umar and 'Abdullāh ibn 'Abbās must have appointed this limit in accordance with the practice of the time for the convenience of people, or it is the

1086 Ibn 'Umar reported that the Prophet ﷺ said: "A woman should not travel for three days without being accompanied by a *mahram*." [9]

1087 Ibn 'Umar reported from the Prophet ﷺ that he said: "A woman should not travel for three (days) without being accompanied by a *mahram*." [10]

1088 Abū Hurairah reported that the Prophet ﷺ said: "It is not allowed to a woman who believes in Allāh and the Last Day to travel for a day and a night without being accompanied by a *mahram*." [11]

Ch. 5: **Prayers can be shortened at the point of leaving the place of departure**

'Alī ibn Abū Ṭālib left (Kūfah) and started shortening his prayers even while he could see the houses. On his return (journey), it was said: "Here is Kūfah." He said: "No, until we enter it (we will continue shortening the prayers)." [12]

1089 Anas ibn Mālik reported: I prayed *Zuhr* with the Prophet ﷺ in Madīnah as four *rak'ah,* and two *rak'ah* (*'Aṣr*) at Dhul-Ḥulaifah. [13]

1090 'Ā'ishah reported: When prayers were first made obligatory, they were two *rak'ah*. Later, prayers on a journey remained like this but prayers when not on a journey were to be completed. [14]

Az-Zuhrī said: I asked 'Urwah, "What made 'Ā'ishah complete the prayer (to four *rak'ah*)?" He said: "She took the same view as 'Uthmān." [15]

---

distance estimated to be covered in one day and one night; otherwise there is no such limit mentioned by the Holy Prophet. The Ḥanafīs also hold that the limit of the journey is 48 miles.

[9] Here three days of travel is considered as a journey. To be accompanied by a *mahram*, i.e., her husband or a close male relative whom she cannot marry such as brother or father, is for a woman's protection,. But see also h. 1862 and its footnote.

[10] This is a repetition of h. 1086 with very slight variation in wording.

[11] Here travelling for a day and a night has been called a journey, although it does not prove that a journey cannot be shorter than this.

[12] After one has left the town of departure, prayers can be shortened and fasting stopped. The same applies when returning, as shown by the action of 'Alī.

[13] Dhul-Ḥulaifah is six miles from Madīnah, and the Holy Prophet was travelling to Makkah. When a person leaves his town of residence for a journey then prayers can be shortened whether he has gone one mile or six miles.

[14] This first part of h. 1090 is a repetition of h. 350. See the footnote to h. 350.

[15] This second part of h. 1090 is an addition here. It is reported in Baihaqī that 'Ā'ishah said: "It is no hardship on me." This shows that 'Uthmān, like her, considered the shortening as a concession, not a requirement.

Ch. 6:   *Maghrib* prayer to be said as three *rak'ah* during a journey

1091 'Abdullāh ibn 'Umar reported: I saw the Messenger of Allāh ﷺ, when he was in a hurry in a journey, delay the *Maghrib* prayer so much as to join it with the *'Ishā'* prayer. Sālim said: 'Abdullāh ibn 'Umar used to do the same when he was in a hurry in a journey.

1092 (And in another report) Sālim said: Ibn 'Umar used to join the *Maghrib* with the *'Ishā'* prayers at Muzdalifah. And Sālim said: Ibn 'Umar delayed the *Maghrib* prayer when he heard the news of the serious illness of his wife Ṣafiyyah, daughter of Abū 'Ubaid. I said to him: "Prayer (time)." He said: "Go on." I again said to him: "Prayer." He again said: "Go on." Until he went on two or three miles, then he came down and prayed. Then he said: "I saw the Prophet ﷺ pray like this whenever he was in a hurry in a journey." And 'Abdullāh (ibn 'Umar) also said: "I saw the Prophet ﷺ when he was in a hurry in a journey that he would have the *Maghrib* prayer announced by *Iqāmah* and pray it as three *rak'ah,* then close it with *Taslīm.* Then he would wait for a short while and have the *'Ishā'* prayer announced by *Iqāmah* and pray it as two *rak'ah,* then close it with *Taslīm.* He would not say any optional prayers after *'Ishā'* until he arose in the middle of the night." [16]

Ch. 7:   Optional prayers while riding animals whichever direction they face

1093 'Āmir ibn Rabī'ah reported: I saw the Prophet ﷺ praying on his mount, in whichever direction it was facing.[17]

1094 Jābir ibn 'Abdullāh informed that the Prophet ﷺ used to say optional prayers while riding, facing a direction other than the *Qiblah*.[18]

1095 Nāfi' reported: Ibn 'Umar used to pray upon his mount, and say *Witr* upon it, and inform (people) that the Prophet ﷺ did that.[19]

---

[16] This shows that the *Maghrib* prayer is not shortened, but said as three *rak'ah.* The *'Ishā'* and other four *rak'ah* prayers are shortened to two *rak'ah.* The optional (*sunnah*) prayers were also not said during a journey. However, the Holy Prophet continued to say *Tahajjud* and *Witr* prayers. See also h. 1109.

[17] This is a repetition of the first part of h. 1000. Here it is not mentioned that these were optional prayers (*nawāfil*), but in h. 1000, which is a repetition of the end of h. 999, the words are that he: "used to say the night prayer ... except the obligatory prayers (*farḍ*). And he used to pray *Witr* on his mount." The heading of this chapter is taken from this. See also h. 1104.

[18] This is a repetition of h. 400 in brief.

[19] This is a repetition of h. 999.

Ch. 8:   Praying by gestures while riding an animal

1096 ʿAbdullāh ibn Dīnār related: Ibn ʿUmar used to pray upon his mount by gestures, whichever direction it faced, and ʿAbdullāh mentioned that the Prophet ﷺ did that.[20]

Ch. 9:   To descend (from the mount) for obligatory prayer

1097 ʿĀmir ibn Rabīʿah informed: I saw the Messenger of Allāh ﷺ riding his mount, saying optional prayers by making gestures with his head, whichever way it (the animal) turned, but the Messenger of Allāh ﷺ did not do that in the obligatory prayers.[21]

1098 Sālim said: ʿAbdullāh (ibn ʿUmar) used to pray on his animal at night while travelling, without concern about which way it was facing. Ibn ʿUmar said: The Messenger of Allāh ﷺ used to pray on his mount facing whichever direction it was facing, and (also) said the *Witr* prayer on it, but he did not say the obligatory prayers on it.[22]

1099 Jābir ibn ʿAbdullāh related that the Prophet ﷺ used to say his prayers on his mount facing east, and when he intended to say the obligatory prayer he would alight and turn his face towards the *Qiblah*.[23]

Ch. 10:   Saying optional prayers while riding a donkey

1100 Anas ibn Sīrīn related: When Anas ibn Mālik returned from Syria we went to greet him and met him at ʿAin al-Tamr.[24] I saw him praying on a donkey which was facing this direction, that is, to the left of the *Qiblah*. I said: "I have seen you praying in a direction other than the *Qiblah*." He said: "Had I not seen the Messenger of Allāh ﷺ doing the same, I would not have done it." [25]

Ch. 11:   Not saying the optional prayers in a journey, after or before the obligatory prayers

1101 Ḥafṣ ibn ʿĀṣim related that he asked Ibn ʿUmar and he said: I used to accompany the Prophet ﷺ and I did not see him saying the optional prayers

---

[20] This is a repetition of h. 1000 and h. 999.

[21] This is a repetition of h. 1000 with different wording.

[22] This is a repetition of h. 999.

[23] This is a repetition of h. 400 in almost the same words. Instead of "in whichever direction it was facing", it says here: "facing east."

[24] This is a place on the border of Iraq with Syria where, near the end of the rule of Abū Bakr, there was a famous battle between Muslims, led by Khālid ibn Walīd, and the Persians.

[25] When praying while riding, one's face cannot remain in the direction of the *Qiblah*, because it is in the direction of travel. The same applies to travelling in a car, railway train, ship or aircraft.

while travelling, and Allāh says in His Word: "Certainly you have in the Messenger of Allāh an excellent exemplar" (the Qur'ān, 33:21).[26]

1102 Ibn 'Umar said: I accompanied the Messenger of Allāh ﷺ, and while travelling he did not pray more than two *rak'ahs*. And Abū Bakr and 'Umar and 'Uthmān did the same.[27]

Ch. 12:   **Saying the optional prayers in a journey at a time other than after the obligatory prayers and before them**

The Prophet ﷺ said two *rak'ahs* of *Fajr* prayer on a journey.

1103–1104 Ibn Abū Lailā reported: None but Umm Hānī informed us that they saw the Prophet ﷺ saying the mid-morning prayer (*Ḍuḥā*). She said: "The Prophet ﷺ, on the day of the conquest of Makkah, took bath in my house and then prayed eight *rak'ahs*. I have never seen him say such a quick prayer, but he did perform the bowing (*Rukū'*) and the prostration (*Sajdah*) fully."

[1104] 'Āmir ibn Rabī'ah informed that he saw the Prophet ﷺ saying optional prayers at night on a journey on the back of his mount in whichever direction it was facing.[28]

1105 Ibn 'Umar reported that the Messenger of Allāh ﷺ used to say optional prayers riding the back of his mount, whichever direction it faced, and would make gestures with his head, and Ibn 'Umar used to do the same.[29]

Ch. 13:   **Combining the *Maghrib* and *'Ishā'* prayers during a journey**

1106 Sālim reported from his father ('Abdullāh ibn 'Umar) that the Prophet ﷺ used to combine *Maghrib* and *'Ishā'* prayers when he had to hurry in a journey.[30]

---

[26] By optional prayers are here meant the *sunnahs* which are said before and after the *farḍ* prayers. It is known that the Holy Prophet did say the mid-morning and *Tahajjud* optional prayers while on a journey. As he shortened the *farḍ* part, he also omitted the *sunnah* part.

[27] This is a repetition of h. 1082. In that ḥadīth it is reported from Ibn 'Umar that 'Uthmān used to pray two *rak'ahs* at Minā in the beginning of his rule, and later prayed four *rak'ahs* there.

[28] H. 1103 is a repetition of h. 280. See also h. 1176. In h. 280 only the taking of bath by the Holy Prophet is mentioned, while here prayer is also mentioned. In h. 357 the prayer is described in more detail but there is no mention there of the quickness in prayer. This shows that the mid-morning prayers may be said during a journey, which is an optional prayer. Then h. 1093 is brought in again as h. 1104 but with the addition that these were optional prayers at night while travelling. This was the *Tahajjud* prayer, as is clear from the repetitions of this ḥadīth.

[29] This repetition is similar to h. 1000 which is a repetition of a part of h. 999.

[30] This is a repetition of h. 1091 in brief. Bringing this ḥadīth here seems to be for showing

1107 Ibn 'Abbās reported: The Messenger of Allāh ﷺ used to combine *Ẓuhr* and *'Aṣr* prayers when he was on a journey, and (also) combine the *Maghrib* and *'Ishā'* prayers.

1108 Anas ibn Mālik reported: The Prophet ﷺ used to combine *Maghrib* and *'Ishā'* prayers in a journey.[31]

Ch. 14: When *Maghrib* and *'Ishā'* prayers are combined, is *Adhān* or *Iqāmah* called out?

1109 'Abdullāh ibn 'Umar reported: I saw the Messenger of Allāh ﷺ, when he was in a hurry in a journey, delay the *Maghrib* prayer so much as to join it with the *'Ishā'* prayer. Sālim said: 'Abdullāh ibn 'Umar used to do the same when he was in a hurry in a journey.[32] He would have the *Maghrib* prayer announced by *Iqāmah* and pray it as three *rak'ah,* then close it with *Taslīm.* Then he would wait for a short while and have the *'Ishā'* prayer announced by *Iqāmah* and pray it as two *rak'ah,* then close it with *Taslīm.* He would not say any optional prayers between these, nor any prostration after *'Ishā',* until he arose in the middle of the night.[33]

1110 Anas related that the Messenger of Allāh ﷺ used to combine these two prayers in a journey, that is, the *Maghrib* and *'Ishā'* prayers.[34]

Ch. 15: Delaying *Ẓuhr* until *'Aṣr* when leaving on a journey before the declining of the sun

This contains a report from Ibn 'Abbās from the Prophet ﷺ.

1111 Anas ibn Mālik reported: When the Prophet ﷺ used to start a journey before the declining of the sun he would delay *Ẓuhr* until the time of

---

that in such a case he did not say the *sunnah* after the *farḍ* of *Maghrib* prayers, as the *farḍ* of *'Ishā'* were said immediately after the *farḍ* of *Maghrib.*

[31] This is a repetition of h. 1091 in brief, as is h. 1106. However, there is no mention of being in a hurry here as in h. 1106. So the prayers were combined whether or not he had to hurry for a journey.

[32] Up to this point, this is a repetition of the whole of h. 1091 in the same words.

[33] This is a repetition of the closing part of h. 1092. The *Iqāmah* is mentioned as having been called for each of the two prayers, but there is no mention of *Adhān.* This does not negate *Adhān* being called, but since the purpose of *Adhān* is to gather people, one *Adhān* can suffice for both prayers. But Bukhārī in his Book of Rites of the Pilgrimage (*Al-Manāsik*), in the chapter 'One who announces the *Adhān* and the *Iqāmah* for each one of them' (i.e., for the two prayers), in h. 1675, records the action of Ibn Mas'ūd in having *Adhān* called out for each of the two prayers.

[34] In this repetition of h. 1091 in brief, the words are like those in h. 1108.

'*Aṣr,* and then combine the two of them. If it (the sun) had declined, he would say *Ẓuhr* and then ride (to start the journey).[35]

Ch. 16:   When leaving on a journey after the declining of the sun, one should say the *Ẓuhr* prayer and then ride

1112 Anas ibn Mālik reported: When the Prophet ﷺ used to start a journey before the declining of the sun he would delay *Ẓuhr* until the time of '*Aṣr,* and then dismount and combine the two of them. If the sun had declined before he started the journey, he would say *Ẓuhr* and then ride.[36]

Ch. 17:   Prayer while sitting

1113 'Ā'ishah reported: The Messenger of Allāh ﷺ said his prayers in his house while he was ill. He said his prayers sitting and behind him a party of people said their prayers standing, so he made a sign to them to sit down. When he finished, he said: "The Imām is appointed to be followed: so when he bows (in *Rukū'*), you must bow, and when he rises up, you must rise up." [37]

1114 Anas reported: The Messenger of Allāh ﷺ fell from a horse and his right side got bruised or injured thereby, so we went to him to visit him in his illness. The time for prayer came, and he said his prayer sitting and we also said our prayers (behind him) sitting. He said: "The Imām is appointed to be followed: so when he says *Allāhu Akbar*, you must say *Allāhu Akbar,* and when he bows (*Rukū'*), you must bow, and when he rises up, you must rise up, and when he says, *Sami' Allāhu li-man ḥamidah* ('Allāh hears him who praises Him'), say: *Rabba-nā wa la-ka-l-ḥamd* ('Our Lord! And Yours is the praise')." [38]

1115 'Imrān ibn Ḥuṣain, who had haemorrhoids, reported: I asked the Messenger of Allāh ﷺ about the prayer of the man who sits down (to say prayers). He said: "It is best if he prays standing. If he prays sitting down, for

---

[35] When two prayers are combined at the time of the first, it is called *jam'i taqdīm* (combining earlier), and when they are combined at the time of the second, it is called *jam'i tākhīr* (combining later). Combining later is mentioned in many sound reports and all scholars, except a few from the generation after the Companions, acknowledge it. In this report also, combining later is mentioned. Some reports mention combining earlier. Although these are regarded as weak, it is known that the Holy Prophet combined prayers earlier at 'Arafāt. Therefore, both are permissible.

[36] This is a repetition of h. 1111 with minor variation in wording.

[37] This report is the same as the h. 688 repetition of h. 378, omitting a part at the end of h. 688. This ḥadīth mentions the Holy Prophet as praying while sitting due to illness. See also h. 1236.

[38] This report is much like the h. 805 repetition of h. 378, with minor difference in wording and the omission at the end of the prostration.

him is half of the reward of one who stands, and he who prays lying down, for him is half of the reward of one who sits down." [39]

Ch. 18:   Prayer while sitting by gestures

1116 'Imrān ibn Ḥuṣain, who had haemorrhoids, reported: ... [40]

Ch. 19:   He who has not the strength (to pray) while sitting down can pray lying

'Aṭā' said: When a man is unable to turn towards the *Qiblah,* he can pray facing any direction.

1117 'Imrān ibn Ḥuṣain reported: I suffered from haemorrhoids, so I asked the Prophet ﷺ about prayer. He said: "Pray standing (during *Qiyām*), but if you are unable (to do that), then sitting down, and if you are unable (to do that), then (lying) on your side." [41]

Ch. 20:   He who starts his prayer sitting down, then (during it) he recovers or feels better, should complete the rest standing

Ḥasan said: If the ill person wishes, he can pray two *rak'ahs* sitting down and two *rak'ahs* standing.

1118 'Ā'ishah, mother of the believers, reported that she never saw the Messenger of Allāh ﷺ praying at night sitting down until he was old. He would recite sitting down until, when he wanted to bow (in *Rukū'*), he would stand up. He would recite thirty or forty verses and then bow. [42]

---

[39] This is to encourage people to stand for prayer, since to pray sitting down shows laxity and laziness. Therefore, minor excuses should not be used to pray sitting down, and without valid reason prayer must not be said lying down. However, for good reason it is permitted to say prayers sitting down or lying.

[40] This is a repetition of the previous h. 1115 in almost the same words. It contains no mention of praying by gestures mentioned in the chapter heading. Bukhārī's argument appears to be that as it is allowed to pray sitting down, omitting to stand, it means that other postures of prayer can be omitted if there is good reason.

[41] H. 1115 is also a report from 'Imrān ibn Ḥuṣain but there the question and answer are general, and it is stated that to pray standing, during *Qiyām,* is better than sitting down. Here it is stated that he who is unable to stand can sit down, and he who cannot even sit can pray while lying down. When standing, a person is more alert and attentive, and the purpose of standing in prayer is that during the worship a person should be alert. Prayer does not make a person slow and lazy. The history of Islām testifies to the fact that the people of whom it was said that they "pass the night prostrating themselves before their Lord and standing" (the Qur'ān, 25:64) did not sleep during the day but carried on their work, and in addition, when necessary, fought battles in the way of God.

[42] As his recitation was very long, he would do most of it sitting down and the remaining thirty or forty verses standing. This ḥadīth is a briefer version of h. 1119.

1119 ʿĀʾishah reported: The Messenger of Allāh ﷺ used to pray sitting down (in old age). He would recite while sitting, and when there remained thirty or forty verses from his recitation he would stand up and recite them standing. Then he would bow (in *Rukūʿ*) and then go into prostration. He would do the same in the second *rakʿah*. When he completed his prayer he would look, and if I was awake he would talk to me, and if I was asleep he would lie down.

PART 5

Book 19: *At-Tahajjud*
The *Tahajjud* Prayer

In the name of Allāh, the Beneficent, the Merciful

Ch. 1: *Tahajjud*[1] at night

The word of Allah, the Mighty, the Glorious: "And during a part of the night, keep awake (*fa-tahajjad*) by it, beyond what is incumbent on you" (17:79).

1120 Ibn 'Abbās said: When the Prophet ﷺ used to get up at night to say the *Tahajjud* prayer, he used to say:[2] "O Allāh! All praise is for You, You are the Maintainer of the heavens and the earth and whatever is in them. And all praise is for You, You are the Light of the heavens and the earth and whatever is in them. And all praise is for You, You are the Master of the heavens and the earth and whatever is in them. And all praise is for You, You are the Truth and Your Promise is true and the meeting with You is true, and Your Word is

---

[1] *Tahajjud* is derived from *hujūd*, meaning 'sleep', and *tahajjud* means to come out of sleep. The prayer of the night is called *Tahajjud* because one has to make an effort to wake up from sleep. *Tahajjud* was made compulsory for the Holy Prophet in addition to the other prayers and he used to perform it with great care regularly, even during a journey. The person who, following the Holy Prophet, wishes to develop a closer relationship with Allāh, the Most High, must tread the same path. But this is an optional prayer and has not been made obligatory as it would impose hardship on Muslims in general. It has been mentioned in h. 1124 further on that the Holy Prophet missed *Tahajjud* prayer due to illness though he never missed any compulsory (*farḍ*) prayer.

[2] The Book on *Tahajjud* begins with a prayer to show that it is the most suitable time for making supplications. In those moments of solitude when there was no one else but Allāh, the Most High, to listen to the yearnings, the Holy Prophet's engagement in such intense prayers clearly indicates his strong faith in the grandeur and glory of Allāh, the Most High, His all-powerfulness, His ultimate authority, the truthfulness of His promises, His power of rewarding and punishing, and the truth of his own prophethood. During these prayers in solitude, the mentioning of the veracity of his prophethood, along with the truthfulness of other prophets, shows how his heart was ingrained with certainty about the truthfulness of his prophethood. What is prayer, after all? It is one's innermost desires that burst out as supplications in the presence of the August Master in the form of heartfelt outpourings. A person, while sitting among his friends or enemies, may say something about himself artificially. However, in such moments of solitude when the whole world around him is asleep, the spontaneous expression of the Holy Prophet's inner feelings shows his full confidence and faith in the truth of his prophethood. These utterings cannot be those of an imposter, nor can such ideas be nurtured by a lunatic.

the truth and Paradise is true and Hell is true and all the Prophets are true and Muhammad is true and the Day of Resurrection is true. O Allah! I submit to You, and I believe in You, and I rely on You, and to You I turn, and with Your help I contend (with the opponents), and You I take as a judge. So grant me protection from what I have already done and what I will do, and what I have concealed and what I have made known. You are the One Who brings (consequences) forward and You are the One Who defers. There is no God but You — or (he said), There is no God other than you."

(And in another report it is added:) "And there is no might nor power except with (the help of) Allāh."

Ch. 2:   Excellence of rising at night[3]

1121–1122 'Abdullāh ibn 'Umar reported: In the lifetime of the Prophet ﷺ whenever anyone saw a dream he would narrate it to the Messenger of Allāh ﷺ. I also wanted to see a dream and to narrate it to the Messenger of Allāh ﷺ. I was a young boy and used to sleep in the Mosque during the lifetime of the Messenger of Allāh ﷺ. I saw in a dream that two angels took hold of me and brought me to the Fire which was built all around like a well and it had two corners and there were people in it known to me. I started say-ing: "I seek refuge with Allāh from the Fire." — He (Ibn 'Umar) added: Then we met another angel who said to me: "Fear not."

[1122] So I narrated it (the dream) to Ḥafṣah, who related it to the Messen-ger of Allāh ﷺ. He said: " 'Abdullāh is a good man. He should say the night prayer." And after that he (Ibn 'Umar) used to sleep only a little at night.[4]

Ch. 3:   Lengthy prostration in the night prayer

1123 'Ā'ishah informed that the Messenger of Allāh ﷺ used to pray eleven *rak'ahs* — that was his (night) prayer — and he used to prostrate in it

---

[3] The Holy Qur'ān is replete with mention of the excellences of the *Tahajjud* prayer. Some characteristics of the servants of Allāh, the Most High, have been listed in the last section of *Sūrah Al-Furqān* in these words: "And they pass their night prostrating themselves before their Lord and standing (in prayer)" (25 : 64). In *Sūrah As-Sajdah*, *Tahajjud* prayer has been mentioned as a sign of perfect faith: "They forsake their beds, calling upon their Lord in fear and in hope" (32 : 16). In *Sūrah Adh-Dhāriyāt* the righteous ones have been praised in these words: "They used to sleep but little at night" (51 : 17).

[4] According to the Qur'ān, a true dream is a lower form of communication from Allāh. Sometimes through a dream Allāh warns a person. In the dream in which 'Abdullāh ibn 'Umar saw himself being dragged towards a fire, he was informed about a weakness in him. And that is why the Holy Prophet, after listening to the dream, advised him to start performing the *Tahajjud* prayer.

for such a long time that one of you could recite fifty verses before he raised his head. He also used to pray two *rak'ahs* before the *Fajr* prayer. Then he would lie down on his right side till the caller to prayer came to him (to call him) for the prayer.[5]

Ch. 4: Leaving off *Tahajjud* by a sick person

1124 Al-Aswad reported that he heard Jundab saying: The Prophet ﷺ became ill and did not get up (for *Tahajjud* prayer) for a night or two.

1125 Jundab ibn 'Abdullāh reported: Gabriel did not come to the Prophet ﷺ for some time. So one of the women of the Quraish said: "His Satan has delayed in coming to him." So it was revealed: "And by the brightness of the day! And the night when it is still! Your Lord has not forsaken you nor is He displeased" (93:1–3).[6]

Ch. 5: The Prophet's exhorting others to rise for prayer at night and *Nawāfil* without making them compulsory[7]

One night the Prophet ﷺ came to Fāṭimah and 'Alī (to wake them up) for the prayer.

1126 Umm Salamah reported that one night the Prophet ﷺ woke up and said: "Glory be to Allāh! What trials have descended tonight, and what treasures have been sent down! Is there anyone who can make the occupants of the (female) chambers wake up? For many women who are clothed in this world (physically) will be naked in the hereafter (spiritually)!"[8]

1127 'Alī ibn Abū Ṭālib informed that one night the Messenger of Allāh ﷺ came to him and Fāṭimah, daughter of the Prophet, and asked: "Do you two not pray (at night)?" ('Alī added:) I said: "O Messenger of Allāh, our

---

[5] This is an exact repetition of the words of h. 994. It mentions that in his *Tahajjud* prayer the Holy Prophet used to prolong his *Sajdah* so much so that one could recite fifty verses of the Qur'ān in that time. Besides glorification of Allāh during *Sajdah*, he used to make other supplications as well.

[6] This ḥadīth has apparently no relation to the chapter heading, but, in fact, it is a part of h. 1124. Tirmidhī has mentioned both parts together. Perhaps Bukhārī has considered the words of the Qur'ān, "And night when it is still" (93:2), as pointing towards his performing the *Tahajjud* prayer in the dead of night.

[7] In other words, the Holy Prophet wished that people should accomplish the *Tahajjud* prayer, but he did not make it compulsory.

[8] This is a repetition of h. 115 in almost the same words. By saying "for many women (physically) clothed in this world will be (spiritually) naked in the hereafter" the Holy Prophet has drawn attention to the fact that prayer serves as a garb, providing a safeguard against attractions of the material world.

souls are in the hands of Allāh, so if He wills that we wake up, He will wake us up." When I said that, he left us without replying to me. Later I heard that when returning he was striking his thigh and saying: "And man in most things is contentious" (the Qur'ān, 18:54).[9]

1128 'Ā'ishah reported: The Messenger of Allah ﷺ used to give up a deed, although he loved to do it, fearing that people might act on it and it might be made compulsory for them.[10] And the Messenger of Allah ﷺ never said the *Duḥā* (mid-morning) prayer, but I pray it." [11]

1129 'Ā'ishah, mother of the believers, reported that the Messenger of Allāh ﷺ one night said his prayer in the mosque and people followed him in his prayer. Then he said his prayer the next night and there were more people. Then more gathered on the third and the fourth nights but the Messenger of Allāh ﷺ did not come out to them. When it was morning, he said: "I saw what you did, and nothing prevented me from coming out to you except that I feared that it (the *Tahajjud* prayer) would be made compulsory for you (to say this night prayer)." And this was in Ramaḍān.[12]

---

[9] The Holy Prophet's striking of his hand on his thigh was an expression of his regret at the reply of 'Alī, as it was not correct. When a person resolves to get up in the night, he can do so. Today too, people make such excuses and ascribe their laxity and indifference to Allāh, and say about some duty or other that if Allāh had wished them to do it, they would have done it. The fact is that Allāh has endowed man with the ability to do what he firmly resolves to do. The wrong concept of *taqdīr* as being 'predestination' is based on the mistaken idea that whatever bad act one does, or whatever good one fails to do through neglect, is due to Allāh's will. Also, these sayings show the Holy Prophet's great strength of conviction that prayer is the only means to achieving success. This is why he always exhorted his wives, his daughter and his son-in-law to get up in the night to say *Tahajjud* prayer.

[10] By becoming "compulsory" for people is meant that they might take it as a mandatory duty and place themselves in difficulty beyond their capacity. This is in matters of worship. In optional prayers, as long as a person gains contentment, it leads to his progress and success. But if it becomes burdensome then it does not have this benefit. The Holy Prophet's giving it up sometimes was to make it clear that it was not obligatory.

[11] The mid-morning prayer was performed by the Holy Prophet (see h. 1103). It may be that he never said this prayer in the presence of 'Ā'ishah, but the fact that she herself said this prayer indicates that this practice of the Holy Prophet must have been reported to her.

[12] This is a repetition of h. 729 with different wording. There it has been mentioned that the Holy Prophet used to say his prayer in his house and the walls of the room were not very high so people saw him saying his prayer. Here it says that one night he said his prayer in the mosque, and in the repetition of h. 729 in h. 924 it is stated that he came out one night and said his prayers in the mosque. Here it has been added that it was during the month of Ramaḍān. It indicates, apparently, that the Holy Prophet had a small room constructed in the mosque for observing *I'tikāf,* and this is what is mentioned here. See also h. 2011–2012.

Ch. 6: **The Prophet's standing (for the *Tahajjud* prayer) till his feet would become swollen**

'Ā'ishah said: "Till his feet would become cracked (*tafaṭṭara*)." *Fuṭūr* means cracks, and *infaṭarat* means to get cracked.

1130 Al-Mughīrah said: The Prophet ﷺ would remain standing or prayed (for a long time) until his feet or calves would become swollen. When he was told about it, he said: "Why should I not be a thankful servant (of Allāh)?" [13]

Ch. 7: **Going to sleep at time of *saḥar***

1131 'Abdullāh ibn 'Amr ibn al-'Āṣ informed that the Messenger of Allah ﷺ said: "The most beloved prayer to Allāh is the prayer of David, and the most beloved fasting to Allāh is the fasting of David. He used to sleep for half of the night, rise up for prayer for one-third of it, and (again) sleep for one-sixth of it, and he used to fast one day and leave it off for one day (i.e., fast every other day)." [14]

1132 Masrūq said: I asked 'Ā'ishah: "Which deed was most loved by the Prophet ﷺ." She said: "A deed done constantly." [15] I asked: "When did he use to get up (in the night to pray)?" She said: "He used to get up when he heard the crowing of a cockerel." [16]

Al-Ash'ath reported: When he (the Holy Prophet) used to hear the crowing of the cockerel, he used to stand up and say his prayer.

---

[13] The Holy Prophet did not live the life of a hermit. In addition to his role as Head of State, he performed all sorts of work. But the real source of his happiness lay in his connection with Allāh. He used to feel so much happiness in worship that even bodily hardship could not reduce it. He did not even feel the pain of his feet becoming swollen or cracks resulting from standing for lengthy periods. Despite all worldly benefits potentially available to him as Head of State, and despite having the company of nine or ten wives, what gave him contentment to the extent of making him oblivious to bodily pain was connection with Allāh through prayer. This is why he used to say: "The coolness of my eyes lies in prayer." In the words, "Why should I not be a thankful servant (of Allāh)," he has explained the true nature of thankfulness for blessings. The more Allāh granted him blessings, the stronger his connection with Allāh became.

[14] In other words, two-thirds of the night should be for bodily rest, and one-third should be allocated for prayer. This is for him who wishes to pray at night. He must not deny himself sleep and bodily rest so much that his health suffers. Similarly, moderation has been advised in voluntary fasting. The last one-sixth of the night has been left for rest in order to recover from the exertions of the *Tahajjud* prayer and get ready for the *Fajr* prayer.

[15] An act, which may be small, if done with constancy, is bound to bring success and lasting results. But an act in which we alternate between overdoing it and not doing it at all, never brings good results nor does it leave any lasting effect.

[16] The first crowing of the cock after midnight is meant.

1133 ʿĀʾishah reported: I always found him — she meant the Prophet ﷺ — sleeping near me at the time of *saḥar*.[17]

Ch. 8: Taking of the pre-fast meal and not sleeping until the morning prayers

1134 Anas ibn Mālik reported that the Prophet of Allāh ﷺ and Zaid ibn Thābit took their pre-fast meals and when they had finished taking these meals, the Prophet of Allāh ﷺ stood up for prayer and both said the prayer. We said to Anas: "How much (time) was there between their finishing the pre-fast meal and their engaging in the prayer?" He said: "As much as (the time in which) a man can recite fifty verses (of the Qurʾān)."[18]

Ch. 9: To prolong standing in the night prayer

1135 ʿAbdullāh ibn Masʿūd reported: "One night I said the (*Tahajjud*) prayer with the Prophet ﷺ and he kept on standing till I intended to do a bad act." We asked: "What did you intend?" He said: "It was to sit down and leave the Prophet (standing)."[19]

1136 Ḥudhaifah reported that the Prophet ﷺ, when he used to get up for *Tahajjud* at night, would clean his mouth with the tooth-stick.[20]

Ch. 10: How is the prayer at night performed and how did the Prophet ﷺ pray at night?

1137 ʿAbdullāh ibn ʿUmar said that a man asked: "O Messenger of Allāh,

---

[17] It is mentioned in other reports that the Holy Prophet used to go to sleep after *Tahajjud* until the call for the *Fajr* prayer was made and then he used to get up. That is why it is said that at the time of *saḥar* he used to be asleep. However, as is found in the next ḥadīth, such was not the case in Ramaḍān because that was the time for the early morning meal before beginning the fast. The narration of ʿĀʾishah is about his general practice. If he went against it at some time, it makes no difference.

[18] This is a repetition of h. 576 in the same words except that, instead of "he (the Holy Prophet) said the prayer", the dual form is used here: "both said the prayer", that is, the Holy Prophet and Zaid ibn Thābit.

[19] This shows that the Companions of the Holy Prophet had developed such a deep sense of right and wrong that they would even regard it as a bad deed if, instead of keeping company with him, they sat down while he was standing. ʿAbdullāh ibn Masʿūd was a young man, yet he was not able to keep standing for that length of time which the Holy Prophet took in saying the *Tahajjud* prayer.

[20] This is a repetition of h. 245, with words "for *Tahajjud*" added. The prolonging of the prayer, as in the chapter heading, has not been mentioned. Bukhārī's inference may be that if the prolonging of the prayer had not been the purpose, then why should he have gone to the extent of brushing his teeth after rising in the night, or that preparation for prayer should be considered as part of the act of worship.

how is the night prayer (*Tahajjud*) performed?" He said: "Say two *rak'ahs* followed by two *rak'ahs* (and so on), and if you fear (the approach of) dawn, say one *rak'ah* to make them *Witr* (odd)." [21]

1138 Ibn 'Abbās reported: The night prayer (*Tahajjud*) of the Prophet ﷺ was of thirteen *rak'ahs*. [22]

1139 Masrūq reported: I asked 'Ā'ishah about the prayer of the Prophet ﷺ at night. She said: "It was seven, nine or eleven *(rak'ahs),* besides the two *rak'ahs* (*sunnah*) of the *Fajr* prayer." [23]

1140 'Ā'ishah reported: The Prophet ﷺ used to pray at night thirteen *rak'ahs,* which included *Witr* and two *rak'ahs* (*sunnah*) of the *Fajr* prayer. [24]

Ch. 11:   **The rising of the Prophet ﷺ at night, his sleeping, and what was abrogated of the rising at night**[25]

> The word of Allāh: "O you covering yourself up! Rise to pray by night except a little, half of it. … Truly you have by day prolonged occupation" (the Qur'ān, 73 : 1–7), and His word: "He knows that all of you are not able to do it, so He has turned to you (mercifully);

---

[21] This is a repetition of h. 472 in brief. That is, say two *rak'ah* prayers, and when the morning approaches, say one extra to make the number odd.

[22] This is again a repetition of h. 472 but very briefly. A detailed discussion about the number of *rak'ahs* of the *Tahajjud* prayer of the Holy Prophet is found in the footnote to h. 992.

[23] The Holy Prophet usually said eleven *rak'ahs* in *Tahajjud* prayer, as has been mentioned in h. 1140 and h. 1147. When he had less time, he may have said seven or nine *rak'ahs*. Reports from Ibn 'Abbās in which thirteen *rak'ahs* have been mentioned seem to be the result of a misunderstanding.

[24] See h. 1170 and foonote to it.

[25] Bukhārī has used the word *naskh* or 'abrogation' in the sense of explanation because, in fact, here there is nothing which abrogates nor anything which is abrogated. At the beginning of the *sūrah* of the Qur'ān mentioned in the chapter heading, the commandment is: "Rise to pray by night except a little, half of it or lessen it a little, or add to it, and recite the Qur'ān (distinctly) at a leisurely pace" (73 : 2–4). That is, stand for prayer for a little less than one-half of the night or a little more than it. In the second section of that *sūrah* (73 : 20) it is mentioned that the Holy Prophet and his Companions devoted to *Tahajjud* prayer two-thirds of the night, half the night, or one-third of it. But it is added that Allāh knew that they, all of them, could not always maintain it. The reason for it has also been given: that at times some may be ill, or some may have to undertake journeys to do business, and even go to fight in the way of Allāh. In such cases it is not possible to perform *Tahajjud* prayer regularly. In other words, the commandment "rise to pray" has been further explained to say that it is not always essential. Thus Bukhārī has clearly used the word *naskh* or 'abrogation' as meaning elucidation. The Companions also used this word in this sense to explain certain points.

so read of the Qur'ān whatever is easy for you. ... And ask forgiveness of Allāh. Surely Allāh is Forgiving, Merciful" (73:20).

Ibn 'Abbās said: *nasha'a* in *al-Ḥabashiyyah* (i.e., the Abyssinian language) means 'he stood up', and *waṭ'an* means to be in accord with the Qur'ān, that is, when the hearing, the sight and the heart of man are to the utmost in harmony with it (i.e., the recitation of the Qur'ān).[26] The word *li-yuwāṭi'ū* (related to *waṭ'an*) means *li-yuwāfiqū* ('to be in accord').[27]

1141 Anas said: Sometimes the Messenger of Allāh ﷺ would not fast in a month till we thought that he would not fast in that month, and sometimes he used to fast in a month till we thought he would not leave off fasting at all that month; and if you wanted to see him praying at night, you could see him praying, and if you wanted to see him sleeping, you could also see him sleeping.[28]

Ch. 12: Satan tying a knot at the nape of the neck of one who does not pray at night

1142 Abū Hurairah reported that the Messenger of Allah ﷺ said: "Satan puts three knots at the back of the head of anyone of you if he is asleep. He blows over every knot the following words: 'The night is long, so stay asleep.' If he wakes up and remembers Allāh, one knot is untied, if he then performs ablution (*Wuḍū'*), the second knot is untied, and if he then prays, the third knot is untied, and the next morning he finds himself happy, in good heart; otherwise, the next morning he gets up feeling bad and lazy." [29]

---

[26] It means that at that time a person's feelings, heart and mind are completely free from any extraneous thoughts or diversions, there is no disturbance from outside at that time, and the human mind is more receptive to the recitation of the Qur'ān.

[27] The explanation of Ibn 'Abbās is in connection with the following words of verse 73:6 of the Qur'ān: "The *rising (nāshi'at)* by night is surely *the firmest way to tread (ashaddu waṭ'an)*". He says that the "rising" means standing up for prayer. As regards *ashaddu waṭ'an*, there are different interpretations and translations of it, and Ibn 'Abbās here says it means that all the senses of man during the *Tahajjud* prayer are in full accord with what he is reciting from the Qur'ān.

[28] It means that the Holy Prophet prayed at night and also went to sleep. That is, he neither stayed awake throughout the night nor sleep during the whole night. It may also mean that on some nights he was awake for longer than on other nights. See also h. 1972 and h. 1973.

[29] In the Qur'ān and Ḥadīth generally, anything which prevents one from doing good has been attributed to Satan. During sleep, one naturally becomes lazy and careless and this prevents one from awakening. That is why it has been considered as a knot tied by Satan. The tying of three knots by Satan means excess of indifference and laxity. And Satan's blowing into the knot means casting bad thoughts that there is yet much time left in the night to be enjoyed in sleeping.

1143 Samurah ibn Jundab related from the Prophet ﷺ that he said of a dream: "He whose head was being crushed with a stone was one who had learnt the Qur'ān but then discarded it, and slept while ignoring the obligatory prayers." [30]

Ch. 13: He who sleeps and does not perform prayer, Satan urinates into his ears

1144 'Abdullāh (ibn Mas'ūd) reported: A man was mentioned before the Prophet ﷺ and someone said: "He kept on sleeping till morning and did not get up for the prayer." He (the Prophet) said: "Satan urinated into his ears." [31]

Ch. 14: Supplication and prayer in the last part of the night

Allāh said: "They used to sleep (*yahja'ūn*) but little at night" (51:17). *Yahja'ūn* means *yanāmūn* ('sleep').

But when one gets up, and invokes praise of Allāh, and performs ablution, and prays, the laziness is thereby entirely removed, and all the knots are, as it were, untied. Those who do not observe moderation in sleep and keep sleeping throughout long nights, rising late in the morning, become lazy and sluggish in the long run, and lose the motivation to work with devotion and concentration. On the other hand, those who maintain control over their sleep and are moderate in it remain fresh and active.

[30] This ḥadīth is a part of h. 1386. In that ḥadīth, a dream of the Holy Prophet has been narrated and it details what kinds of punishment he saw being inflicted on certain people. In this part, two things have been mentioned: to acquire knowledge of the Qur'ān but then forsake it, and to be indifferent to the obligatory prayers. In h. 1386, instead of this detail, the following words occur: "The one whose head you saw being broken is a man whom Allāh had given knowledge of the Qur'ān but he slept neglectful of it at night and did not act upon it by day." These words accord with the chapter heading as it refers to prayer at night. And in h. 1386 it is also mentioned that he does not recite the Qur'ān by getting up in the night, but in h. 1143 here the ignoring of obligatory prayers by sleeping is mentioned which has no connection with the chapter heading. It may be that *'Ishā'* and *Fajr* prayers have also been included in prayer at night. The other point which is explained in h. 1386 is that what has been considered as discarding or forsaking the Qur'ān here has been considered there as not acting upon it. In other words, not to act upon the Qur'ān after learning it amounts to discarding and forsaking it.

[31] The tying of knots by Satan has just been mentioned. Here, passing of urine (*bāla*) by Satan is mentioned. Both are in a metaphorical sense. Ibn Kathīr explains it as follows: "It is said that its meaning is to make a fool of the man and overwhelm him to such an extent that he slept becoming oblivious of obeying Allah, the Mighty, the Glorious. As a poet said: (The star) Suhail urinated (*bāla*) in the *faḍīkh* (a kind of wine made from raw dates) and it turned bad." The meaning is that when the star Suhail rose, the season of raw dates came to an end, and it was as if by its rising this wine turned bad. Similarly, the passing of urine by Satan also means to make things go wrong. Ibn Athīr, after quoting several other Ḥadīth reports about Satan urinating, writes that all this is by way of metaphor or simile. In *Tāj al-'Arūs*, the word *baul* or urine metaphorically means a son, and therefore if it is said about someone that "he has passed a noble urine" (*bāla baul-an sharīf-an*), it means that a noble son has been born to him. Similarly, the word *bāla* is also used for the sprouting of a thing or *infijār*. The words *bāla al-shaḥma* means 'the fat melted'. Therefore, to think that Satan urinates in the manner of a human being is not correct. It only means that Satan made him go wrong or that the charactersitics of Satan appeared in him.

1145 Abū Hurairah reported that the Messenger of Allah ﷺ said: "Our Lord, the Blessed, the Most High, comes down (*yanzilu*) every night to the nearest Heaven when the last one-third of the night remains, saying: 'Is there anyone who calls upon Me so that I may accept his call? Is there anyone who asks (something) from Me so that I may grant him (his request)? Is there any-one seeking My forgiveness so that I may forgive him?' " [32]

Ch. 15:   Going to sleep early at night and rising towards the last part of the night

> Salmān said to Abū al-Dardā': "Go to sleep." When it was the last part of the night he said: "Rise up." The Prophet ﷺ said: "Salmān spoke correctly." [33]

1146 Al-Aswad reported that he asked 'Ā'ishah: "How does the Prophet ﷺ perform the night prayer?" She replied: "He used to go to sleep early at night, and get up in its last part to pray, and then return to his bed. When the caller to prayer called the *Adhān*, he would get up. If he was in need of a bath he would take it; otherwise, he would perform *Wuḍū'* and go out (for the prayer)."

Ch. 16:   The keeping awake of the Prophet ﷺ at night in Ramaḍān and otherwise

1147 Abū Salamah ibn 'Abdur Raḥmān reported that he asked 'Ā'ishah: "How did the Messenger of Allāh ﷺ perform prayer during Ramaḍān?" She said: "The Messenger of Allāh ﷺ never exceeded eleven *rak'ahs* in Ramaḍān or in other months. He would say four *rak'ahs,* and do not ask me about their beauty and their length, then (again) four *rak'ahs,* and do not ask me about their beauty and their length, and then three *rak'ahs.*" 'Ā'ishah further said: "I asked, 'O Messenger of Allāh! Do you sleep before saying the *Witr* prayer?' He replied: 'O 'Ā'ishah! My eyes sleep but my heart does not!' " [34]

---

[32] Ibn Athīr has mentioned this ḥadīth under the word *nazala* (occurring above as *yanzilu,* "comes down") and writes that *nuzūl* (descent) and *su'ūd* (ascent), or movement and stillness, are characteristics of the human body and Allāh is above such actions. When used for Allāh the meaning here is mercy and bounties of Allāh and their nearness to human beings. The ḥadīth has itself explained what the *nuzūl* or "coming down" of Allāh means by adding that supplications made during that period are most likely to be accepted, and the suppliant is granted what he petitioned for, and also one seeking forgiveness is forgiven. In other words, the human heart at that time has such intense feelings of closeness to Allāh and His presence that there is greater acceptance by Allāh of supplications made at that time.

[33] This is a small portion of a lengthy ḥadīth in the Book of Manners (h. 6139).

[34] This shows that the Holy Prophet used to take some rest after saying four *rak'ahs*. At that

1148 ʿĀʾishah reported: I never saw the Prophet reciting anything (of the Qurʾān) in the night prayer sitting down until he was old, when he would recite sitting down. When there remained for him thirty or forty verses from the *sūrah,* he would stand up and recite them standing. Then he would bow (in *Rukūʿ*).[35]

Ch. 17: Excellence of being in a state of *Wuḍūʾ* day and night as well as of prayer after *Wuḍūʾ* day and night

1149 Abū Hurairah reported that the Prophet ﷺ asked Bilāl at the time of *Fajr:* "Bilāl, Tell me of the best deed you did after (embracing) Islām, for I heard your footsteps (*diffa naʿlai-ka*) ahead of me in Paradise." [36] Bilāl replied: "I did not do anything which I consider worth mentioning, except that whenever I perform ablution at any time during the day or night, I pray after that ablution as much as is destined for me."

Ch. 18: Excess in matters of worship is undesirable

1150 Anas ibn Mālik reported: Once the Prophet ﷺ entered the mosque and there was a rope tied between two of its pillars. He asked: "What is this rope for?" People said: "This rope is for Zainab. When she feels tired, she holds it (to keep standing for prayer)." The Prophet ﷺ said: "No (that should not be). Untie the rope. You should pray as long as you feel happy about it, and when you get tired, sit down." [37]

---

time his sleep was not so deep and the interval was to give some rest to the tired body. That is why when ʿĀʾishah asked him whether he used to take a little nap before saying *Witr*, which was probably referring to this interval, the Holy Prophet said: "My heart does not sleep." See also footnote to h. 1170, and h. 2013.

[35] This is a repetition of h. 1118 and h. 1119, with some words from both of them.

[36] It is evident that this was a dream. There are many arguments to show this. Firstly, it was said by the Holy Prophet after the *Fajr* prayer. It was his practice to ask the Companions about their dreams, and to relate to them his dreams, after the *Fajr* prayer. Secondly, in the book 'Merits of the Companions' under 'Virtues of ʿUmar' (book 62, ch. 6, h. 3679), somewhat similar remarks have been made about Bilāl, and it is stated: "I saw that I had entered Paradise." In a report in Ṣaḥīḥ Muslim the words are: "I heard last night" (book: 'Merits of the Companions', ch. 'Virtues of Bilāl'). This shows that it was a dream which he related to people. In it the Holy Prophet heard the sound of Bilāl walking ahead of him. It has been called *diffa naʿl-un,* that is, the sound which is produced by the shoes when one walks. He asked Bilāl as to which was the good deed which brought such a glad tiding. In his reply, by "I pray" Bilāl meant the optional prayer which is known as *taḥiyyat al-wuḍūʾ* ('greeting of ablution'). In other words, the Holy Prophet was shown in a dream that Bilāl was foremost in turning to Allāh. His spiritual condition was shown to the Holy Prophet in the form of his walking ahead in Paradise.

[37] The meaning of worship which was in vogue before him was changed by the Holy Prophet.

1151 ʿĀʾishah reported: There was a woman from the tribe of Banī Asad with me when the Prophet ﷺ came to me. He said: "Who is she?" I said: "She is so-and-so, she does not sleep at night", mentioning her prayers. He said: "Enough! Only those deeds are binding on you which you are able to do, for surely Allāh does not get tired (of accepting your prayers), but you get tired (of saying them)." [38]

Ch. 19: It is disliked for that person to give up the night prayer who used to get up for it[39]

1152 ʿAbdullāh ibn ʿAmr ibn al-ʿĀṣ related: The Messenger of Allāh ﷺ said to me: "O ʿAbdullāh! Be not like so and so, who used to get up at night (to pray) and then gave up getting up at night."

Ch. 20: Concerning the above

1153 ʿAbdullāh ibn ʿAmr said: Once the Prophet ﷺ said to me, "Have I not been informed that you pray during the (whole of the) night and fast during the day?" I said: "I do that." He said: "If you do so, your eyes will become sunken and you will become weak. Surely your body has a right over you, and your wife has a right over you. So keep fast (some days) and break it (on other days); and stand to pray and (also) sleep."

Ch. 21: Excellence of one who wakes up at night to pray

1154 ʿUbādah ibn aṣ-Ṣāmit reported from the Prophet ﷺ that he said: "Whoever gets up at night and says: 'There is none to be worshipped but Allāh, Who is One and has no partners; for Him is the Kingdom and all praise is for Him; He has power over all things; all praise is for Allāh, glory be to Allāh, and Allāh is the greatest; and there is no might nor power except with

---

He explained and showed by practice that worship is not hardship but a means of spiritual elevation. Obviously the only worship that can be a source of spiritual progress is the one which brings inner happiness and closer relationship with one's Creator. To glorify Allāh, or to say optional prayers, by some set number does not fulfil the true purpose of worship. The mention here of saying prayer while sitting may also mean that if one gets tired standing, one can sit down to continue the prayer, and it also may mean that one can end the prayer. This applies only to optional prayers.

[38] This is a repetition of h. 43 with difference in wording and omission of the concluding words about the religion dearest to Allāh..

[39] Just as coercion is not approved of in the matter of worship, as the real object of worship, i.e., the progress of the soul, is not attained in this manner, similarly it is disapproved that a person should adopt a certain way to make progress and then abandon it. One should always go forward and never retreat. If a person gets up in the night to pray, and then ceases to do it, he has taken a retrograde step and instead of progress he has followed the path of spiritual decline.

Allāh'; and then he says: 'O Allāh! Forgive me,' or makes supplication, his supplication will be responded to. And if he performs ablution and prays, his prayers will be accepted." [40]

1155 Al-Haitham ibn Abū Sinān informed that he heard Abū Hurairah in one of his preachings mention the Messenger of Allāh ﷺ as saying: "Your brother does not say inappropriate things", meaning thereby ʿAbdullāh ibn Rawāḥah (in these poetic verses):[41]

> "The Messenger of Allāh is among us who recites His Book / when the bright morning dawns.
>
> He showed us the guidance when we were blind, so our hearts / firmly believe that whatever he says will come to pass.
>
> At night his sides do not touch his bed / when the beds of the idolaters are heavy (with their weight)." [42]

1156–1158 Ibn ʿUmar reported: In the lifetime of the Prophet ﷺ I saw in a dream that a piece of silk cloth was in my hand and that it was flying me to whatever place in Paradise I wanted. I also saw two (angels) come to me who wanted to take me to Hell. Then an angel joined them and said (to me): "Be not afraid", (and to them): "Leave him." [43]

[1157] Ḥafṣah related one of my dreams to the Prophet ﷺ and he said: " ʿAbdullāh is a good man. He should say the night prayer." So (after that) ʿAbdullāh used to pray at night.

[1158] They (the Companions) used to relate their dreams to the Prophet ﷺ that it (*Lailat-ul-Qadr*) was on the seventh night of the last ten (i.e., 27th

---

[40] In other words, it is also a good deed if a person merely wakes up in the night and remembers Allāh, the Most High, and makes supplications. But it is much better if he performs ablution (*Wuḍūʾ*) and says his prayers.

[41] Abū Hurairah was preaching, and during it, referring to the Holy Prophet's worship, he said that the description given by ʿAbdullāh ibn Rawāḥah in his poetic verses was not mere poetry but accurately represented the Holy Prophet's worship.

[42] It means that the idolaters can never get up in the night for worship. Only a person who feels the highest pleasure in remembering Allāh can forsake sleep for it. He can sacrifice anything to achieve that state of bliss. The Companions of the Holy Prophet were much more convinced of his truth when they saw him passing nights in intense remembrance of Allāh, while he would not sleep during the day but would perform all his worldly duties. It is not possible for an imposter or a pleasure-seeker to spend his nights in this way in the worship of God. And if the Holy Qurʾān had been his own fabrication, he could not possibly have enjoyed its recitation so much that he would continue to recite it even after his feet had become swollen and stiff.

[43] The account of this dream has already occurred in h. 1121. But the details mentioned there and here are different.

Ramaḍān). The Prophet ﷺ said: "I notice that your dreams concur on the last ten (nights of Ramaḍān), so whoever wishes to search for it, let him search for it in the last ten." [44]

Ch. 22: Being regular in two *rak'ahs* (of *sunnah*) in *Fajr*

1159 'Ā'ishah reported: The Prophet ﷺ said the *'Ishā'* prayer. Then he said eight *rak'ahs,* and said two *rak'ahs* while sitting. He (then) said two *rak'ahs* between the two calls (i.e., between the *Adhān* and the *Iqāmah* for *Fajr*) and these two he never missed.[45]

Ch. 23: Lying down on the right side after two *rak'ahs* of the *Fajr* prayer

1160 'Ā'ishah reported: The Prophet ﷺ, after praying two *rak'ahs* (*sunnah*) of the *Fajr* prayer, used to lie down on his right side.

Ch. 24: He who talks after the two *rak'ahs* (*sunnah* of the *Fajr* prayer) and does not lie down

1161 'Ā'ishah reported: When the Prophet ﷺ used to finish his prayer and I was awake, he would talk to me; otherwise he would lie down till the call for prayer.[46]

Ch. 25: Concerning saying optional prayers in *rak'ahs* by twos

Muḥammad said: And this has been mentioned by 'Ammār and Abū Dharr and Anas and Jābir ibn Zaid and 'Ikrimah and az-Zuhrī. And Yaḥyā ibn Sa'īd al-Anṣārī said: I found the scholars of my time

---

[44] It is stated in a report from Ibn 'Umar: "Some Companions of the Prophet ﷺ were shown *Lailat-ul-Qadr* in their dreams in the last seven (nights of Ramaḍān). The Messenger of Allāh ﷺ said: I notice that your dreams concur on the last seven, so whoever wishes to search for it, let him search for it in the last seven" (h. 2015).

[45] This is a repetition of h. 1140. The two *rak'ahs* said between the *Adhān* and the *Iqāmah* are the two *sunnah* of the *Fajr* prayer. *Witr* prayer has not been mentioned here. 'Ā'ishah says in another ḥadīth that the Holy Prophet "used to say thirteen *rak'ahs,* nine while standing, one of which was *Witr,* and two while sitting" (Nasā'ī, book: 'Night Prayer and Optional Prayers during the Day', h. 1756). This shows that the ninth *rak'ah* was that of the *Witr,* and he said a further two *rak'ahs* while sitting. This was not the usual practice. Usually he said the *Witr* prayer towards the end.

[46] This is a repetition of the last part of h. 1119 with different wording. It is not mentioned here after which prayer he did this. In h. 1119, his talking and lying on his side to sleep have been mentioned after the night prayer. Both these have been explained in h. 1160, that his lying on his side to sleep was after saying the two *rak'ahs* of *sunnah,* before the *Iqāmah* for *Fajr* prayer. This has also been mentioned in h. 994 and h. 1123.

always ending the prayer with *Salām* after every two *rak'ahs* during the day.[47]

1162 Jābir ibn 'Abdullāh reported: The Messenger of Allāh ﷺ used to teach us to say the *Istikhārah*[48] prayer in (important) matters as he would teach us a chapter of the Qur'ān. He said: "If anyone of you intends to undertake a work he should pray two *rak'ahs* other than the obligatory ones and then say: O Allah! I seek goodness from You on account of Your knowledge, and seek power from You on account of Your might, and I ask You (to give me something) out of Your great grace. You have power and I do not. You know and I do not know, and You are the great Knower of the Unseen. O Allah! If You know that this work is good for me in my faith, in my livelihood and in the final end of my affairs — or he said: in the immediate and final result of my work — then ordain it for me and make it easy for me, and then make it blessed for me. And if You know that this work is harmful for me in my faith, in my livelihood and in the final end of my affairs — or he said: in the immediate and final result of my work — then keep it away from me and keep me away from it. And ordain for me good wherever it may be, and make me pleased with it."

He (then) said: "And he should name his need." [49]

1163 Abū Qatādah said that the Prophet ﷺ said: "When any of you enters a mosque, he should not sit down until he has said two *rak'ahs* of prayer." [50]

1164 Anas ibn Mālik reported: The Messenger of Allāh ﷺ led us in two *rak'ahs* of prayer, then he departed.[51]

1165 'Abdullāh ibn 'Umar reported: I prayed with the Messenger of Allāh ﷺ two *rak'ahs* before *Ẓuhr,* and two *rak'ahs* after *Ẓuhr*, and two *rak'ahs* after *Jumu'ah*, and two *rak'ahs* after *Maghrib*, and two *rak'ahs* after *'Ishā'*.[52]

---

[47] It is explicitly mentioned in h. 952 that the *Tahajjud* prayer is said in sets of two *rak'ahs*. Ending the prayer with *Salām* is the saying of *as-salāmu 'alai-kum wa raḥmatu-llāh*. This is known as the act of *Taslīm*.

[48] *Istikhārah* means to ask Allāh for guidance before making a decision.

[49] *Istikhārah* prayer, as is evident from its name, is to wish for good, asking that if what a person intends to do would prove to be good for him, which only Allāh knows, then Allāh should facilitate it by clearing the way for it and providing the necessary resources; but if Allāh knows that it would be harmful then He should disincline him from doing it. It does not mean that Allāh will necessarily indicate to him what to do.

[50] This is a repetition of h. 444 with a slight difference in wording.

[51] This is a repetition of only the last part of h. 380.

[52] In this repetition, the subject of h. 937 has been dealt with again. There the practice of the

1166 Jābir ibn ʿAbdullāh said that the Messenger of Allāh ﷺ, while he was delivering the sermon, said: "When any of you comes, and the Imām is delivering the sermon or has come forth (to deliver it), he should pray two *rak'ahs* (of *sunnah*)." [53]

1167 Mujāhid said: Someone came to Ibn ʿUmar in his house and told him: "This is the Messenger of Allāh ﷺ who has entered the Kaʿbah." He (Ibn ʿUmar) said: "So I reached there and found that the Messenger of Allāh ﷺ had gone out. I found Bilāl standing at the door and I said: 'Bilāl, Did the Messenger of Allāh ﷺ say his prayer inside the Kaʿbah?' He said: 'Yes.' I said: 'Where (did he pray)?' He said: 'Between those two pillars, then he came out and said two *rak'ahs* of prayer in front of the Kaʿbah'." [54]

Abū Hurairah said: The Prophet ﷺ advised me to pray two *rak'ahs* of *Ḍuḥā*. ʿItbān said: The next day the Messenger of Allāh ﷺ and Abū Bakr and ʿUmar came to me after sunrise and we made a row behind him (the Holy Prophet) and prayed two *rak'ahs*.[55]

Ch. 26: Talking after two *rak'ahs* (*sunnah*) of *Fajr*

1168 ʿĀ'ishah reported: The Prophet ﷺ, after saying two *rak'ahs*, would talk to me if I was awake; otherwise he would lie down.[56]

I said to Sufyān:[57] "Some people narrate that it was the two *rak'ahs* of *Fajr* prayer." Sufyān said: "Yes, That is so." [58]

Holy Prophet was mentioned, but here the narrator tells about his own practice. The words "with the Messenger of Allāh" should not be taken to mean that the Holy Prophet led him in prayer in these *rak'ahs*. What is meant is that both of them prayed individually. In h. 937 it is mentioned clearly that the Holy Prophet said two of these, i.e., those after *Maghrib* and those after *Jumu'ah* prayers, at home. And in h. 1172 it is mentioned that he used to say two *rak'ahs* at home after *Maghrib* and *'Ishā'*.

[53] This is a repetition of h. 930 in different words.

[54] Up to here this is a repetition of the subject of h. 397 with a slight difference of wording. After this ḥadīth, two separate reports have been added.

[55] The latter part of h. 1167 consists of these two extracts, each without continuous transmission. The second is a small part of a lengthy report by ʿItbān ibn Mālik in h. 425. There the name of ʿUmar has not been mentioned, and here it is mentioned in some, but not all, versions. The purpose of these reports in h. 1167 is to show that the Holy Prophet, after saying *sunnah* or other optional prayers in two *rak'ahs*, would finish the prayer, and this was his usual practice.

[56] This is a repetition of the last part of h. 1119.

[57] I.e., the last narrator in the chain said to Sufyān, from whom he was reporting.

[58] Thus the two *rak'ahs* mentioned by ʿĀ'ishah were the *sunnah* of the *Fajr* prayer.

Ch. 27: **Strictly observing the two (*sunnah*) *rak'ahs* of *Fajr* and the one who calls them as optional (*taṭawwu'*)[59]**

1169 'Ā'ishah reported: The Prophet ﷺ used to observe more strictly the two *rak'ahs* (*sunnah*) of the *Fajr* prayer, out of all the optional prayers (*nawā-fil,* plural of *nafl*).

Ch. 28: **What is to be recited in the two (*sunnah*) *rak'ahs* of *Fajr***

1170 'Ā'ishah reported: The Prophet ﷺ used to pray at night thirteen *rak'ahs,* then when he would hear the call for the morning prayer he would say two brief *ra'kahs.*[60]

1171 'Ā'ishah reported: The Prophet ﷺ used to say the two *rak'ahs* before the *Fajr* prayer so briefly that I could not say if he recited the *Fātiḥah* (or not).[61]

Ch. 29: **Optional prayers after obligatory ones**

1172–1173 Ibn 'Umar reported: I prayed with the Prophet ﷺ two *rak'ahs* before *Ẓuhr,* and two *rak'ahs* after *Ẓuhr,* and two *rak'ahs* after *Maghrib,* and two *rak'ahs* after *'Ishā',* and two *rak'ahs* after *Jumu'ah.* As to *Maghrib* and *'Ishā',* these were at his house.[62] [1173] (Ibn 'Umar added:) My sister Ḥafṣah told me that the Prophet ﷺ used to pray two *rak'ahs* briefly after the breaking of dawn and it was the time when I never went to the Prophet ﷺ.[63]

Ch. 30: **One who does not say optional prayers after the obligatory ones**

1174 'Amr (ibn Dīnār) reported: I heard Abū ash-Sha'thā' Jābir saying

---

[59] Besides the obligatory *(farḍ)* prayers, whatever extra is done optionally or voluntarily is known as *taṭawwu'* or *nafl,* whether it is *sunnah, Witr* or *nafl* prayers.

[60] This is a repetition of h. 1140 in which the latter half is different. There is a clear clash between these two reports, the former stating that the thirteen *rak'ahs* include the two *rak'ahs* of *Fajr,* while here the two *rak'ahs* of *Fajr* are in addition to the thirteen *rak'ahs.* In h. 1147 the report from 'Ā'ishah clearly states that in the month of Ramaḍān or in other months the Holy Prophet did not say more than eleven *rak'ahs* of *Tahajjud* prayer. Thus, there is an error in this repetition. From the mention of two brief *rak'ahs* here, it is inferred that in these two *sunnah rak'ahs* the recitation of the Qur'ān used to be short.

[61] What is meant is that he used to recite the shorter chapters of the Qur'ān. In Ṣaḥīḥ Muslim (book: 'Prayer of Travellers', ch. 14) it is mentioned that he used to recite ch. 109 (*Al-Kāfirūn*) and ch. 112 (*Al-Ikhlāṣ*).

[62] The wording of h. 1172 is similar to that of h. 1165, which is a repetition of the subject of h. 937. Here, instead of the word *rak'atain* (two *rak'ahs*), the word used for them is *sajdatain* (two prostrations), and the Friday prayer is mentioned towards the end. It has an addition at the end about the *Maghrib* and *'Ishā' sunnah rak'ahs.*

[63] See also h. 618 for a similar statement by Ḥafṣah.

that he heard Ibn 'Abbās saying, "I said eight *rak'ahs* together and seven *rak'ahs* together with the Messenger of Allāh ﷺ." I said: "O Abū ash-Sha'thā'! I think he must have delayed the *Ẓuhr* and brought forward the *'Aṣr,* and brought forward the *'Ishā'* and delayed the *Maghrib.*" He said: "I also think so." [64]

Ch. 31:   *Ḍuḥā* (mid-morning) prayer during a journey

1175 Muwarriq reported: I asked Ibn 'Umar, "Do you say the *Ḍuḥā* prayer?" He said: "No." I asked: "Did 'Umar (say it)?" He said: "No." I asked: "Did Abū Bakr?" He said: "No." I asked: "Did the Prophet ﷺ?" He said: "I do not think he did." [65]

1176 'Abdur Raḥmān ibn Abū Lailā said: None but Umm Hānī related to us that they saw the Prophet ﷺ saying the mid-morning prayer (*Ḍuḥā*). She said: "The Prophet ﷺ entered my house on the day of the conquest of Makkah, took bath and then prayed eight *rak'ahs.* I have never seen such a short prayer, but he did perform the bowing (*Rukū'*) and the prostration (*Sajdah*) fully." [66]

Ch. 32:   He who did not say *Ḍuḥā* prayer and thought there was flexibility in it

1177 'Ā'ishah reported: I did not see the Prophet ﷺ saying the *Ḍuḥā* prayer but I pray it.[67]

---

[64] This is a repetition of h. 543, where it is clearly mentioned that these were *Ẓuhr* and *'Aṣr* prayers together and *Maghrib* and *'Ishā'* prayers together. This shows that the Holy Prophet did not say the two *rak'ahs* of *sunnah* which are said after the *Ẓuhr* and the *Maghrib* prayers.

[65] Ibn 'Umar does not accept the *Ḍuḥā* (mid-morning) prayer. But in h. 1176 a report from Umm Hānī establishes that it used to be performed. Similarly, it has been reported on the authority of Anas by Aḥmad, Ibn Khuzaimah and Ḥākim that the Holy Prophet said eight *rak'ahs* of *Ḍuḥā* prayer during a journey. Of course, Ibn 'Umar did not know about it. It is mentioned in h. 1178 that Abū Hurairah said that the Holy Prophet advised him to say two *rak'ahs* of this prayer. The same has also been mentioned in one of the separate reports at the end of h. 1167. There is no condition mentioned about whether one is travelling or not. The fact remains that it is confirmed that Holy Prophet used to say the *Ḍuḥā* prayer. Bukhārī, by mentioning all sorts of reports in this connection, has shown the breadth of the matter, and that regarding certain questions there was a difference of opinion among the Companions also.

[66] In this repetition of h. 280, the report of 'Abdur Raḥmān ibn Abū Lailā occurs in almost the same words as h. 1103. In her narration in h. 280, the Holy Prophet's taking a bath has been mentioned but not that he said any prayer.

[67] This is a repetition of the last part of h. 1128. The chapter heading is related to the first part of h. 1128 where it is mentioned that sometimes when the Holy Prophet used to like a particular act he would not perform it regularly, fearing that it might be considered obligatory by people.

Ch. 33: The *Ḍuḥā* prayer when not travelling

'Itbān ibn Mālik reported it from the Prophet 🕌.

1178 Abū Hurairah reported: My friend 🕌 (i.e., the Holy Prophet) advised me to do three things and I shall not leave them till I die: To fast three days every month, to say the *Ḍuḥā* prayer, and to say the *Witr* prayer before sleeping.[68]

1179 Anas ibn Mālik said: A man of the Anṣār, who was very fat, said to the Prophet 🕌: "I am unable to join the prayer with you." He had a meal prepared for the Prophet 🕌 and invited him to his house. He washed one side of a mat for him with water and he (the Holy Prophet) prayed two *rak'ahs* on it. So and so, the son of so and so, the son of Jārūd asked Anas: "Did the Prophet 🕌 use to say the *Ḍuḥā* prayer?" He replied: "I never saw him praying it except on that day." [69]

Ch. 34: Two *rak'ahs* (*sunnah*) before *Ẓuhr*

1180–1181 Ibn 'Umar reported: I remembered ten *rak'ahs* from the Prophet 🕌: two *rak'ahs* before *Ẓuhr,* and two *rak'ahs* after it, and two *rak'ahs* after *Maghrib* in his house, and two *rak'ahs* after *'Ishā'* in his house, and two *rak'ahs* before the morning prayer, and that was a time when no one would enter to see the Prophet 🕌 in it.[70] [1181] (Ibn 'Umar added:) Ḥafṣah told me: When the caller to prayer would give the *Adhān,* and dawn broke, he (the Holy Prophet) would pray two *rak'ahs.*[71]

1182 'Ā'ishah reported that the Prophet 🕌 never omitted four *rak'ahs* (*sunnah*) before the *Ẓuhr* prayer and two *rak'ahs* (*sunnah*) before the *Fajr* prayer.[72]

---

[68] See also the repetition of this in h. 1981.

[69] This is a repetition of a small part of h. 425 in different words.

[70] H. 1180 is a repetition of h. 1172 with a different beginning. The Friday prayer is not mentioned here as in h. 1172. See also h. 937.

[71] See also h. 618. This is similar to h. 1173 but in addition it mentions the *Adhān.* It shows that the Holy Prophet used to say two *rak'ahs sunnah* after the call for *Fajr.*

[72] In h. 937, h. 1165, h. 1172 and h. 1180, which are all narrated by Ibn 'Umar, it is mentioned that the Holy Prophet used to say two *rak'ahs* of *sunnah* before *Ẓuhr.* Here 'Ā'ishah has said that the Holy Prophet never omitted four *rak'ahs* before *Ẓuhr* prayer. Her knowledge relates more to what was done at home, so it may be that he said four *rak'ahs* at home. This is confirmed by a report from 'Ā'ishah recorded in the collections of Aḥmad and Abū Dāwūd: "He (the Holy Prophet) used to pray in four *rak'ahs* before *Ẓuhr* prayer in my house" (Abū Dāwūd, book: 'Optional Prayers', h. 1251). The reports of Ibn 'Umar mentioning two *rak'ahs* relate to the practice in public. Or, it could be that sometimes he prayed four *rak'ahs* and sometimes two.

Ch. 35:　Prayer (*sunnah*) before *Maghrib*

1183 ʿAbdullāh al-Muzanī reported from the Prophet ﷺ that he said: "Pray (*sunnah*) before the *Maghrib* prayer." He said the third time: "Whoever wishes," not liking that people might take it as obligatory.[73]

1184 Marthad ibn ʿAbdullāh al-Yazanī said: I came to ʿUqbah ibn ʿĀmir al-Juhanī and said: "Should I not tell you something surprising about Abū Tamīm? He prays two *rakʿahs* (*Sunnah*) before *Maghrib*." ʿUqbah said: "We used to do it during the lifetime of the Messenger of Allāh ﷺ." I asked him: "What prevents you now?" He said: "Business."

Ch. 36:　Saying optional prayers (*nawāfil*) in congregation

Anas and ʿĀʾishah reported it from the Prophet ﷺ.[74]

1185–1186 Maḥmūd ibn ar-Rabīʿ al-Anṣārī informed[75] that he remembered the Messenger of Allāh ﷺ well and he remembered him drawing a mouthful of water (to rinse his mouth) and splashing it on his face, which was from a well in their house.[76] [1186] Maḥmūd said that he had heard ʿItbān ibn Mālik, who was among those who were in the Battle of Badr with the Messenger of Allāh ﷺ, saying:

I used to lead my people, the Banī Sālim,[77] in prayer, and there was a valley between me and them which, when it rained, became hard for me to cross to go to their mosque. So I went to the Messenger of Allāh ﷺ and said: "My eyesight has become weakened and the valley which is between me and my people flows with water when it rains, and it becomes hard for me to cross it. So I would like you to come and say your prayer in my house at a place which I could make a place of prayer." The Messenger of Allāh ﷺ said: "I shall do so."

So the next day the Messenger of Allāh ﷺ and Abū Bakr came to me after the sun had risen high, and the Messenger of Allāh ﷺ asked permission (to

---

[73] This prayer has been mentioned in h. 503 and h. 625. Two *rakʿahs* of *sunnah* before *Maghrib* are not confirmed by the practice of the Holy Prophet. It is also said here that it is optional and not obligatory.

[74] Regarding the saying of optional or voluntary (*nafl*) prayers in congregation, the report from Anas is in h. 380 and h. 727, and that from ʿĀʾishah is in h. 729.

[75] In h. 1185–1186 there is repetition of the subject of h. 425 with difference in wording and some addition.

[76] H. 1185 has occurred in h. 77, h. 189 and h. 839.

[77] The name of his tribe is an addition here. It is not given in h. 425.

enter) and I gave him permission. He did not sit but said: "Where do you like me to say my prayer in your house?" I pointed to him a place where I wanted him to pray. The Messenger of Allāh ﷺ stood up and proclaimed *Allāhu Akbar.* We lined up behind him and he said two *rak'ahs* of prayer, and then finished with *Salām.* We too did *Salām* when he did *Salām.* I detained him for some *khazīrah* (a meat pie) which had been prepared for him. People of the neighbourhood heard that the Messenger of Allāh ﷺ was in my house, so some men from among them gathered until there were many men in the house. One of them said: "What is the matter with Mālik that I do not see him?" One of them said: "He is a hypocrite who does not love Allāh and His Messenger." The Messenger of Allāh ﷺ said: "Do not say that. Have you not seen that he says 'There is no god but Allāh' (*Lā ilāha ill-Allāh*), seeking thereby the pleasure of Allāh?" He (that man) said: "Allāh and His Messenger know best. As for us, by Allāh we surely see his meeting and his talking with none but the hypocrites." The Messenger of Allāh ﷺ said: "Surely Allāh has forbidden the fire for the one who says: 'There is no god but Allāh', seeking thereby the pleasure of Allāh."

Maḥmūd (ibn Rabīʿ) said:[78] I told this to some people, among whom was Abū Ayyūb al-Anṣārī, a Companion of the Messenger of Allāh ﷺ, in the battle in which he died and Yazīd ibn Muʿāwiyah was their leader in the land of the Romans. He (Abū Ayyūb) refused to accept it before me and said: "By Allāh, I doubt that the Messenger of Allāh ﷺ ever said what you have said." I felt hurt very deeply, and I vowed to Allāh that if I remained alive in that battle, I would ask 'Itbān ibn Mālik if I found him still living in the mosque of his people. So when I returned, I put on the *Iḥrām* for *Ḥajj* or 'Umrah and then I proceeded until I reached Madīnah. I went to Banī Sālim, and 'Itbān was by then an old, blind man, and was leading his people in prayer. When he finished the prayer, I greeted him and told him who I was, and then asked him about that report. He repeated it (i.e., that report) in the same manner as he had narrated it the first time.[79]

---

[78] The relating of this incident by Maḥmūd ibn Rabīʿ is an addition here in h. 1186.

[79] Abū Ayyūb al-Anṣārī was killed during the siege of Constantinople in 50 A.H. during the rule of Muʿāwiyah. Most probably, he refused to accept the correctness of these words in the report from 'Itbān: "Surely Allāh has forbidden the fire for the one who says, 'There is no god but Allāh'." He must have been drawing attention to the need also of doing good deeds in order to save oneself from the fire of Hell. Maḥmūd thought that he may have made an error in preserving that ḥadīth, and that was why he went to have it confirmed again from 'Itbān. See also the discussion in the last footnote of h. 425.

Ch. 37: To say optional prayers at home

1187 Ibn 'Umar reported that the Prophet ﷺ said: "Say some of your prayers in your houses and do not make them graves." [80]

---

[80] This is a repetition of h. 432 in exactly the same words. The subject is that some of the prayers, i.e., the *nafl* prayers, should be said at home, and the home should not be made a spiritual graveyard.

Book 20: *Faḍl aṣ-Ṣalāt fī Masjid Makkah wa-l-Madīnah*

Excellence of Prayer in the Mosque of Makkah and of Madīnah

In the name of Allāh, the Beneficent, the Merciful

Ch. 1: Excellence of Prayer in the Mosque of Makkah and of Madīnah

1188 Qazaʻah reported: I heard four things from Abū Saʻīd.[1] He said: "I heard (these) from the Prophet ﷺ." He had taken part in twelve battles in the company of the Prophet ﷺ.

1189 Abū Hurairah reported from the Prophet ﷺ that he said: "There should be no journey except to three mosques: the Sacred Mosque, the Mosque of the Messenger of Allah ﷺ, and the Aqṣā Mosque." [2]

1190 Abū Hurairah reported that the Prophet ﷺ said: "One prayer in this

---

[1] All the four things of the Holy Prophet are mentioned in h. 1197 further on.

[2] Only one of the four things reported by Abū Saʻīd, which is reported by Abū Hurairah too, is mentioned here: to make a journey to visit three mosques. This is to show that these three enjoy great respect and honour. *Masjid al-Ḥarām* is the Sacred Mosque, the Kaʻbah in Makkah, which was the first house built for the worship of God and it is from here the last fountain of the Oneness of God gushed forth. *Masjid an-Nabawī* is the Prophet's Mosque in Madīnah, built by the Holy Prophet himself when he migrated to this city, and it is a symbol of the start of the glory of Islam. *Masjid al-Aqṣā* is the sacred place of worship of the Israelite prophets. When a person visits these three sacred places, but with spiritual zeal in his heart, he is sure to create a spiritual transformation in himself. The picture of the sacrifices of those prophets who rose from these sacred places, and their great exertions for the spiritual and social betterment of people, comes to mind and becomes a source of inspiration and motivation for the visitor. It should always be remembered that making something exclusive is often done to draw attention towards its greatness, and here it does not mean that these three mosques are to be visited exclusively, and that no other mosque on earth can be visited, nor can the grave of the Holy Prophet or any other sacred places be visited. The Qur'ān gives the general command: "Travel in the earth" (6 : 11). Here it is the grandeur of these three places that has been mentioned. In h. 1191 further on, it is mentioned that the Holy Prophet used to visit the Qubā' mosque every Saturday. This was the first mosque built where the Holy Prophet made his first stop before entering Madīnah. This shows that it is not prohibited to visit other mosques, but the purpose in this ḥadīth is to show special consideration for these three sacred places.

Mosque of mine is better than one thousand prayers in any other mosque except the Sacred Mosque." [3]

Ch. 2:   The Mosque of Qubā'

1191–1192 Nāfi' reported that Ibn 'Umar used to pray *Ḍuḥā* only on two days: the day he would come to Makkah, and he would reach it mid-morning, perform circuits round the House (i.e., Ka'bah), and then pray two *rak'ahs* at the rear of the Place (of Abraham, *Maqām Ibrāhīm*), and the day he would visit the Mosque of Qubā', for he used to visit it every Saturday, and when he entered the Mosque, he disliked leaving it until he had prayed in it. And he (Ibn 'Umar) used to relate that the Messenger of Allāh ﷺ used to visit it riding or walking. [1192] He (Nāfi') said: And he (Ibn 'Umar) used to say: "I only do what I saw my companions doing, and I do not forbid anybody to pray at any time of the night or day, except that one should not aim to pray at sunrise or sunset." [4]

Ch. 3   One who visited the Mosque of Qubā' every Saturday

1193 Ibn 'Umar reported: The Prophet ﷺ used to visit the Mosque of Qubā' every Saturday, walking or riding, and 'Abdullāh ibn 'Umar used to do the same.[5]

---

[3] It is evident that the intent of this ḥadīth cannot be that a person who says a prayer by way of hypocrisy or for show in the Prophet's Mosque has excellence over one who performs prayer with sincerity and humility in some other place. When it is stated in Ḥadīth that saying of prayer in congregation is superior to praying alone by twenty-five or twenty-seven degrees, commentators have given the reason as being that in congregation a person makes extra effort and finds the opportunity to create more humility in his prayer as compared to one who says his prayer at home. So the excellence of prayer in the Prophet's mosque must be on some such basis, especially since during the life of the Holy Prophet a person in that mosque would be praying behind the Holy Prophet himself. With such Godly people present in a congregation, by joining that congregation an intense humility would have been created which would have been impossible to achieve anywhere else. Even today, when a person undertakes a journey to go to the Prophet's Mosque, he experiences a deep sense of spirituality in his prayer which is not possible elsewhere. The mention of "journey" in h. 1189 refers to this.

[4] The mosque at Qubā' was owned by the Bani 'Amr ibn 'Auf, and was in the suburb of Madīnah some two or three miles away. There was a well there called Qubā', after which this mosque was named. This was the first mosque founded by the Holy Prophet. The Companions who migrated to Madīnah before the Holy Prophet used to pray in this mosque. This mosque was the first Islamic building and it was where a sizeable community of Muslims had settled down. That is why the Holy Prophet used to visit it once a week and say his prayers there. Ibn 'Umar used to adhere strictly to the practice of the Holy Prophet and loved to follow him. So he too used to go there regularly. The words of h. 1192, which is a continuation of h. 1191, have already occurred with a slight difference of wording in h. 589.

[5] This is a repetition of h. 1191.

Ch. 4:   To visit Mosque of Qubā' walking or riding

1194 Ibn 'Umar reported: The Prophet ﷺ used to visit (the Mosque of) Qubā', riding or walking. It is added (in another narration): Then he (the Holy Prophet) would say two *rak'ahs* in it.[6]

Ch. 5:   Excellence of the place between the grave and the pulpit (of the Holy Prophet)

1195 'Abdullāh ibn Zaid al-Māzinī reported that the Messenger of Allāh ﷺ said: "Between my house and my pulpit, there is a garden from among the gardens of Paradise."

1196 Abū Hurairah reported from the Prophet ﷺ that he said: "Between my house and my pulpit, there is a garden from among the gardens of Paradise and my pulpit is over my pond." [7]

Ch. 6:   The Mosque of *Bait al-Maqdis*

1197 Qaza'ah, freed slave of Ziyād, said: I heard Abū Sa'īd al-Khudrī relating four things from the Prophet ﷺ which I liked very much and considered them virtuous. He said: "A woman should not go on a two-day journey except with her husband or a permissible male relative (*maḥram*)."

---

[6] This again is a repetition of h. 1191 like h. 1193, with differences and an addition.

[7] This ḥadīth also occurs in the Book 'Excellences of Madīnah', h. 1888, at the end of the books on *Ḥajj*. The ḥadīth contains the word "house" but the chapter heading has the word "grave". Both words mean the same, as he was buried in his own house where he had died. Most probably by using the word "grave" instead of "house" Bukhārī wants to show that its excellence is permanent because the grave would remain there forever. Some have applied it in the physical sense, saying that this place will be moved to Paradise at the end of the world. But even this is not a physical interpretation because he says that this place is one of the gardens of Paradise, and to assert that it shall become so on the day of Resurrection is not a physical interpretation. Thus there is no doubt that this is metaphorically speaking. Some have taken it to mean that prayer in that area takes one to Paradise, but prayer anywhere, if said sincerely, takes one to Paradise. It has also been taken to mean that this place is like the garden of Paradise because Allāh's blessings are showered upon it and spiritual progress is attained in it since groups of people are engaged there in remembering Allāh, which happened especially during the life of the Holy Prophet.

The significance of "my pulpit is over my pond" evidently is that from his pulpit that deep knowledge and guidance was spread which can take one to the lake of Paradise. Likening the place from his house to his pulpit to Paradise may be due to the fact that the Holy Prophet walked in between these, and his arrival or the gathering of his Companions there was a source of spiritual pleasure to people which was truly like the atmosphere of Paradise itself, and the Companions enjoyed the delicious taste of faith in their hearts. This was the place where they most often encountered him, and even today when a person, after visiting the grave of the Holy Prophet, says prayers in the Mosque, he is sure to get some measure of the spiritual lustre and blessings which were diffused from that place during the life of the Holy Prophet.

"There is no fasting on two days, Eid-ul-Fiṭr and Eid-ul-Aḍhā." "There is no prayer after two prayers, (that is) after the *Fajr* prayer till the sun rises, and after the *'Aṣr* prayer till the sun sets." "There should be no journey except to three mosques: the Sacred Mosque, and the Aqṣā Mosque and my Mosque." [8]

---

[8] For a woman to undertake a journey, see h. 1086 to h. 1088, and h. 1862 and its footnote. For prayer after *Fajr* and *'Aṣr,* see h. 581, h. 582–583, h. 584 and h. 588. For journey to the three Mosques, see h. 1188. Discussion about fasting on the day of Eid-ul-Fiṭr and the day of Eid-ul-Aḍhā can be found in the Book on Fasting, chs. 65 and 66. In ch. 66 of that book, this ḥadīth has a repetition in h. 1995.

Book 21: *Al-'Amal fi-ṣ-Ṣalāt*
Actions during Prayer

In the name of Allāh, the Beneficent, the Merciful

Ch. 1: Taking help of hands during prayer in connection with prayer itself[1]

Ibn 'Abbās said: "A person can take the help of any part of his body that he wishes while praying. And Abū Isḥāq removed his cap during prayer and then put it on. 'Alī used to keep his (right) palm over his left hand except when he wanted to scratch his skin or to straighten his clothes."

1198 Ibn 'Abbās informed that he spent a night at the place of Maimūnah, mother of the believers, who was his maternal aunt. ...[2]

Ch. 2: What kind of talking is prohibited during prayer

1199 'Abdullāh (ibn Mas'ūd) reported: We used to greet the Prophet ﷺ while he was praying and he used to return our greetings. When we came back from (visiting) the Negus (the ruler of Abyssinia), we greeted him (during the prayer), but he did not answer our greetings and (after finishing the prayer) he said: "Surely in prayer there is engagement." [3]

---

[1] The real object of prayer is concentration on turning to God. If anything disturbs this concentration, it should be removed. The purpose of quoting Ibn 'Abbās and Abū Isḥāq is to explain what actions can be done during prayer to improve the performance of it. However, actions during prayer which are unrelated to its performance are not right.

[2] The wording of h. 1198 is almost the same as that of h. 183. For the remainder of this long ḥadīth, see h. 183. The connection with the chapter heading is that during prayer the Holy Prophet took Ibn 'Abbās by his ear and moved him from his (the Holy Prophet's) left to his right. See also h. 138 and h. 992.

[3] The Holy Prophet used to reply to the salutation of *As-salāmu 'alaikum*. But then he felt that it disturbed the serenity of the prayer, or it appears that some people extended this practice and started talking during prayer, as is mentioned in the next ḥadīth. So he gave up this habit. The Holy Prophet's saying, "Surely in prayer there is engagement", is to emphasise that during prayer all attention should be to Allāh, to the exclusion of all else, and to divert attention disturbs the deep engrossment in prayer. See also h. 1216.

1200 Zaid ibn Arqam said: In the lifetime of the Prophet ﷺ we used to talk to one another while praying, and one of us would speak about his needs to his companion, until the verse, "Guard the prayers and the most excellent (or middle) prayer, and stand up truly obedient to Allāh" (the Qur'ān, 2:238), was revealed. So we were ordered to remain silent (while praying).

Ch. 3: Permissibility for men of saying of *Subḥān Allāh* and *Al-ḥamdu li-llāh* during prayers

1201 Sahl ibn Saʿd reported that the Prophet ﷺ went out to effect reconciliation among the Banī 'Amr ibn 'Auf, and the time for prayer came, ...[4] and the Prophet ﷺ stepped forward and led the prayer.

Ch. 4: One who takes a people's name or greets them in prayer without facing them while he does not know

1202 'Abdullāh ibn Masʿūd reported: We used to say *at-taḥiyyah* during prayer and take a person's name, and send peace (*salām*) on one another. The Messenger of Allāh ﷺ heard it and said: "Say: 'All services (*At-taḥiyyāt*) rendered through words, actions and wealth are due to Allāh alone. Peace be on you, O Prophet, and the mercy of Allāh and His blessings. Peace be on us and on the righteous servants of Allāh. I bear witness that there is no god but Allāh and I bear witness that Muḥammad is His servant and Messenger.' If you do this, you have surely sent peace on every righteous servant of Allāh in heaven and earth." [5]

---

[4] In this ḥadīth the subject of h. 684 has been repeated with some difference in wording. From this point on, it is similar to h. 684, but the last part of h. 684 from the words "When he (the Holy Prophet) had finished, he said: O Abū Bakr, What prevented you from staying..." to the end is not present here. This ḥadīth says that on the occasion of the arranging of the truce between the tribes of the Banī 'Amr ibn 'Auf the Holy Prophet joined the congregation when the prayer had already started and he signalled to Abū Bakr to carry on leading the prayer, and when the latter raised his hands and praised Allāh and continued with the prayer, the Holy Prophet did not dislike it because prayer is also to praise and glorify Allāh. To talk during prayer is not the same as praising and glorifying Allāh. (As stated in these reports, Abū Bakr then retreated and the Holy Prophet went forward to lead the prayer.)

[5] This is a repetition of h. 831, which was also repeated in h. 835. See the footnotes under those reports. *Taḥiyyah* is a blessing for another person, and amounts to saying: "May Allāh give you life." This is the well-known prayer in the sitting posture, the beginning of which indicates that all the good that one does must be for Allāh's sake. Here the *Shahādah* is mentioned along with the prayer, whereas in h. 831 and h. 835 it is separated from it by the words beginning "If you say this". In h. 835 there are extra words at the end: "Then he should choose some supplication (*du'ā'*) which he likes best and pray accordingly". These are not found here. This ḥadīth shows that the kind of salutation found in *at-taḥiyyāt*, which is not addressed to someone actually present there, does not divert attention away from the prayer.

Ch. 5:   Clapping is (permissible) for women

1203 Abū Hurairah reported from the Prophet ﷺ that he said: "*At-tasbīḥ* (to say *Subḥān Allāh,* meaning 'Glory be to Allāh') is for the men and clapping (of hands) is for the women." [6]

1204 Sahl ibn Saʿd reported that the ﷺ Prophet said: "*At-tasbīḥ* (to say *Subḥān Allāh,* meaning 'Glory be to Allāh') is for the men and clapping (of hands) is for the women." [7]

Ch. 6:   Whoever retreated or went forward during his prayer for something he had to do

Sahl ibn Saʿd reported this from the Prophet ﷺ.

1205 Anas ibn Mālik informed that Muslims were saying *Fajr* prayer on Monday, and Abū Bakr was leading them in prayer, when the Prophet ﷺ suddenly removed the curtain of the chamber of ʿĀ'ishah. He looked at them while they were standing in rows (in prayer) and gave a broad smile. So Abū Bakr began to retreat and thought that the Messenger of Allāh ﷺ wanted to come out for the prayer. The Muslims were put to the test as regards their prayer (i.e., whether to break off) in the excitement of joy about the Prophet ﷺ when they saw him. But he made a sign with his hand as if to say "Complete your prayers." Then he went back into the chamber and pulled down the curtain. He expired that day.[8]

Ch. 7:   When a mother calls her son and he is praying

1206 Abū Hurairah said that the Messenger of Allāh ﷺ said: "A woman called her son while he was in his place of worship and she said: 'O Juraij!' He said: 'O Allāh, my mother (is calling me) and my prayer (is occupying me)!' She again said: 'O Juraij!' He said again: 'O Allāh, my mother and my prayer!' She again said: 'O Juraij!' He again said: 'O Allah, my mother and my prayer!' She said: 'O Allah! Let not Juraij die till he sees the faces of prostitutes.' A shepherdess used to come near to his place of worship to graze her sheep and she gave birth to a child. She was asked whose child it was.

---

[6] This is a repetition of the last words of h. 684. See the footnotes under it.

[7] This, like h. 1203, is a repetition of the last words of h. 684. See the footnotes under it.

[8] This is a repetition of h. 680 with differences in wording. The chapter heading is related to the point that one should keep facing the direction of the *Qiblah* while stepping back. Similarly, when the Imām and just one follower are praying and another person comes to join them, either the Imām should step forward or the follower should step back while continuing to face the *Qiblah* so that the two form a row behind the Imām.

She replied: 'It is from Juraij, and he had come out from his place of worship.' Juraij said: 'Where is she who claims that her child is from me?' Juraij asked the child: 'O Babūs, who is your father?' The child replied: 'The shepherd.' " [9]

Ch. 8: Removing pebbles during prayer

1207 Muʿaiqīb related that the Prophet ﷺ, talking about a man levelling the earth whereon he was prostrating, said: "If you must do so, then do it only once." [10]

Ch. 9: To spread a cloth for *Sajdah* while in prayer

1208 Anas ibn Mālik reported: We used to pray with the Messenger of Allāh ﷺ in excessive heat, and when one among us was unable to place his forehead on the ground, he would spread his cloth (across the place) and prostrate over it. [11]

Ch. 10: What kind of actions are allowed during prayer

1209 ʿĀ'ishah reported: I used to stretch my legs in front of the Prophet ﷺ while he was praying. When he would go into prostration, he would press me and I would fold my legs, and when he would stand up, I would stretch them again. [12]

1210 Abū Hurairah reported from the Prophet ﷺ that, once he said his prayers, and (then) said: "Satan came in front of me to distract me in prayer, but Allāh gave me power over him. I caught him and pushed him back. I intended to tie him to a pillar (of the mosque), so that you may have a look at him in the morning. Then I remembered the words of Solomon: 'My Lord, … grant me a kingdom which is not fit for anyone after me' (the Qur'ān, 38:35). So Allāh turned him back, humiliated." [13]

---

[9] This is a story taken from Jews or Christians. It serves little purpose in deciding the issue in the chapter heading. *Babūs* means an infant still being suckled.

[10] If there are some pebbles, dust or anything else at the place of prostration, which are causing inconvenience or disturbance in prayer, these should be removed. Doing it once is mentioned because done once it need not be repeated. To spread a piece of cloth over the place of prostration because of heat from the ground is allowed as it is for the purpose of avoiding discomfort and to maintain attention in prayer, as stated in the next chapter.

[11] This is a repetition of h. 385.

[12] This is a repetition of h. 382. It means that if needs be, there is nothing wrong with such an action as the Holy Prophet here did during praying.

[13] This is a repetition of h. 461 with a different opening. Here too the chapter heading shows

Ch. 11:   When an animal escapes while (you are) in prayer

Qatādah said: "If his clothes are taken he should follow the thief and leave the prayer."

1211 Al-Azraq ibn Qais related: We were at al-Ahwāz fighting with al-Ḥarūriyyah (a Khawārij tribe).[14] While I was at the bank of a river, a man came and started praying while the reins of his animal were in his hands. The animal was pulling it from him and he was following the animal — and Shu'bah said: "That man was Abū Barzah al-Aslamī." So a man from the Khawārij said: "O Allah! Deal with this old man." And when the old man finished his prayer, he said: "I heard what you said. I took part with the Messenger of Allāh ﷺ in six or seven or eight battles and saw his leniency, and I would rather return with my animal than let it go anywhere he wishes, and I should suffer." [15]

1212 'Ā'ishah said: Once the sun was eclipsed and the Messenger of Allāh ﷺ stood up (for prayer) and recited a long *surah*. Then he went into *Rukū'* for a long while and then raised his head and started reciting another *surah*. Then again he went into *Rukū'* and after completing it, he went into prostration. Then he did the same in the second *rak'ah*. Then he said: "These two (lunar and solar eclipses) are two signs from among the signs of Allāh. When you see them, pray till it (the eclipse) is cleared for you. While standing at this place I have surely seen everything which has been promised to me (by Allāh for the Hereafter), and when you saw me stepping forward I wanted to pluck a bunch (of grapes) from Paradise; and when you saw me stepping backward I surely saw Hell, different parts of which were destroying one another. And in it I saw 'Amr ibn Luḥayya who started the practice of freeing a bull in the name of idols." [16]

---

that Bukhārī is drawing the conclusion that this was a man whom the Holy Prophet caught and repelled, and thus if someone attacks you during prayer, you should guard yourself. See footnote on h. 461.

[14] Ahwāz is the name of a well-known city which lies between Basrah and Iran. It was conquered during the Caliphate of 'Umar. The Khawārij besieged the people of Basrah in 65 A.H. Azraq was the commander of the army which was fighting against the Khawārij.

[15] Abū Barzah was a Muslim soldier. He was saying his prayer while also holding the reins of his horse. When the horse got out of control he did not let it go but kept on holding it while it was running away, till he subdued it. This shows that the Holy Prophet and his Companions were quite flexible in such matters. If there is a dire need then there is no harm in doing what is required. However, without need it is not right to make any movement during prayer. The Khawārij went to a harsh extreme in enforcing religious matters. They would issue a verdict of *kufr* or unbelief on trivial issues. Most Muslim religious leaders of today are following more in the footsteps of the Khawārij than of the Companions of the Holy Prophet.

[16] This is a repetition of h. 1044. The sighting of Paradise and Hell has been mentioned in h.

Ch. 12:   Permissibility of spitting and blowing during prayer

It is reported from 'Abdullāh ibn 'Amr that the Prophet ﷺ blew out (*nafakha*) during prostrations while praying on the occasion of an eclipse.[17]

1213 Ibn 'Umar reported that the Prophet ﷺ saw some phlegm on the wall of the mosque facing the *Qiblah* and reprimanded the people of the mosque and said: "Surely Allāh is in front of every one of you during his prayer, so he should not spit (in that direction)." Or he said: "Do not expectorate." Then he got down and scratched it with his hand. Ibn 'Umar (after narrating it) said: "If anyone of you has to spit, let him spit towards his left."[18]

1214 Anas reported from the Prophet ﷺ that he said: "When a person is in prayer, he is privately communicating with his Lord. So he should not spit in front of him, nor towards his right, but towards his left underneath his left foot.[19]

Ch. 13:   If one of the men claps through ignorance, his prayer is not spoilt

In this (matter) Sahl ibn Sa'd reported from the Prophet.[20]

86, h. 536, h. 540, h. 1052 and h. 1053. The stepping forward and then stepping backward here during prayer does not amount to any distraction. The mention of 'Amr ibn Luḥayya is an addition here and it is stated that he started the tradition of freeing a bull in the name of idols. It is mentioned further in h. 3521.

[17] The coming of spit, saliva and sputum during prayer is not in one's control. *Nafakha* means to blow air, but this is not an involuntary action. The basis on which Bukhārī justifies blowing is a report accepted by Ibn Khuzaimah and others containing the words: "He (the Holy Prophet) blew on the earth and wept while in prostration." It seems that in this case the blowing out was by way of compulsion, which sometimes accompanies weeping. Or maybe blowing was due to nasal discharge, which flows when one is weeping profusely.

[18] This is a repetition of h. 405. In h. 405 the last words of Ibn 'Umar about spitting to the left are a part of what the Holy Prophet himself said.

[19] The wording of this repetition is similar to h. 405, but there is no mention of the incident of the Holy Prophet's seeing phlegm, etc., and there is only his instruction. The words of h. 405, "but towards his left or underneath his foot", are here: "but towards his left underneath his left foot." This shows that, where the words "towards his left" appear to be general, it also means that it should be squashed under the left foot, as the floor of the mosque was covered with pebbles.

[20] The report from Sahl ibn Sa'd has occurred in h. 684 and h. 1201, and occurs again in h. 1218, to the effect that when Abū Bakr was leading the congregational prayers and the Holy Prophet returned from his visit to the Banī 'Amr ibn 'Auf at Qubā', people started clapping in order to inform Abū Bakr about his arrival. The Holy Prophet did not consider that this spoiled their prayer.

Ch. 14: If a person praying is asked to start before (his companion) or to wait, and he waits, there is no harm

1215 Sahl ibn Saʻd reported: Men used to say their prayers with the Prophet ﷺ, tying their waist-wrappers, on account of short size, around their necks. So the women were told: Do not raise your heads until the men are sitting upright.[21]

Ch. 15: Greetings should not be returned during prayer

1216 ʻAbdullāh (ibn Masʻūd) reported: I used to greet the Prophet ﷺ while he was praying and he used to return my greeting. When we came back (from visiting the Negus, the ruler of Abyssinia), I greeted him (during the prayer), but he did not answer my greeting and (after finishing the prayer) he said: "Surely in prayer there is engagement." [22]

1217 Jābir ibn ʻAbdullāh reported: The Messenger of Allāh ﷺ sent me for some work of his. So I went, and when I returned after completing it and came to the Prophet ﷺ and greeted him, he did not return my greeting. A thought occurred to me, and Allāh best knows it, and I said to myself: "Perhaps the Messenger of Allāh ﷺ is displeased with me because I took a long time over it." Then, again, I greeted him but he did not return it. The same thought occurred to me again, even more strongly than the first time. Again I greeted him, and he returned the greeting and said: "I was only prevented from returning your greeting because I was praying." And he was riding, with his face in a direction other than the *Qiblah*.

Ch. 16: Raising hands to do something while in prayer

1218 Sahl ibn Saʻd reported: The news reached the Messenger of Allāh ﷺ that there were differences among the Banī ʻAmr ibn ʻAuf at Qubā'. So he went with some of his Companions to effect reconciliation between them. The Messenger of Allāh ﷺ was delayed and the time for prayer came. So Bilāl came to Abū Bakr and said: "O Abū Bakr, the Messenger of Allāh ﷺ has been delayed and the time for prayer has come. Will you lead the people (in

---

[21] This is a repetition of h. 362 but in exactly the words of its repetition in h. 814. As these garments were not long enough to cover the entire lower part, women were asked not to rise from prostration until the men had resumed their sitting position. By adding the words "on account of short size" (*min aṣ-ṣaghar*) it has been explained why women were asked to wait till men resumed the sitting position. The object of the chapter is to explain that this waiting was done because of an external reason. The instruction to women to wait necessarily implies the order that men should rise from prostration before women. See also footnote to h. 814.

[22] This is a repetition of h. 1199 with slightly different wording. Here the singular "I" is used about greeting, instead of the "we" as in h. 1199. See footnote to h. 1199.

prayer)?" He said: "Yes, if you wish." So Bilāl announced the prayer by the *Iqāmah* and Abū Bakr went forward and called out the *Takbīr* for the people. And the Messenger of Allāh ﷺ came, walking through the rows, cutting through them, till he stood in the first row. People started clapping, but Abū Bakr would not look around in his prayer. When people clapped more, he turned round and it was the Messenger of Allāh ﷺ, who made a sign to him ordering him to continue leading the prayer. Abū Bakr raised both his hands and praised Allāh. Then he retreated behind him till he stood in the (first) row and the Messenger of Allāh ﷺ stepped forward and led the people in prayer. When he had finished, he turned to the people and said: "O people, why is it that you start clapping when something happens to you in prayer? Clapping is only for the women. If something happens in one's prayer he should say *Subḥān Allāh.*" Then he looked towards Abū Bakr and said: "O Abū Bakr, what prevented you from leading the people in prayer when I made a sign to you (to continue)?" Abū Bakr said: "It did not befit Ibn Abū Quḥāfah that he should say his prayer ahead of the Messenger of Allāh ﷺ." [23]

Ch. 17: To place hands on the waist during prayer

1219 Abū Hurairah reported: It is prohibited to place hands on the waist (or the sides).

1220 Abū Hurairah reported: The Prophet ﷺ forbade that a man should pray with his hands on his waist.[24]

Ch. 18: Thinking about something during prayer

'Umar said: "I organize my army while I am praying.

1221 'Uqbah ibn al-Ḥārith reported: I prayed *'Aṣr* with the Prophet ﷺ and after finishing it with *Salām* he stood up in haste and entered the house of one of his wives and then came out. He noticed the signs of surprise on the faces of the people caused by his hurried departure. He then said: "I remembered while I was in prayer that a piece of gold was in my house and I disliked

---

[23] This is a repetition of h. 684. The first part is somewhat similar to the repetition of h. 684 in h. 1201. But in h. 1201 the last part of h. 684 has not been included in which the Holy Prophet spoke to Abū Bakr and the people. Here that part has been mentioned in reverse order. That is, the Holy Prophet's instruction to men regarding clapping comes first, and it is followed by his asking Abū Bakr why he did not continue with leading the prayer in spite of the signal given by Holy Prophet. See the footnotes to h. 684.

[24] The reason is that this is not a gesture of showing humility in prayer, and humility is the very object of performing prayer.

that it should remain with us till the evening — or the night — so I ordered its distribution." [25]

1222 Abū Hurairah said that the Messenger of Allāh ﷺ said: "When the *Adhān* is given for prayer, Satan turns back fleeing, making sounds of scoffing and denying, so that he may not hear the call to prayer. When the caller to prayer finishes, he (Satan) advances. When the call to *Iqāmah* is sounded, he turns back fleeing (again). When it is finished, he advances (again). He continues to say to a man, 'Remember (this and that)', about what he did not remember, till the man (is so distracted that he) does not know how much of the prayer he has said."

Abū Salamah ibn 'Abdur Raḥmān said: "If any of you has done this (i.e., forgetting the number of *rak'ahs*), he should perform two prostrations (of forgetfulness) while sitting." Abū Salamah heard and narrated this from Abū Hurairah.[26]

1223 Abū Hurairah said: People say (about me) that Abū Hurairah reports too much (from the Holy Prophet). I met a man and asked him: "What did the Messenger of Allāh ﷺ recite yesterday in the *'Ishā'* prayer?" He said: "I do

---

[25] This is a repetition of h. 851. There it is not mentioned that he said "I remembered while I was in prayer." But if, for the sake of argument, it is considered correct, even then there is no harm. He might have recited some portion of the Qur'ān which drew his attention towards it and he distributed that gold immediately after finishing the prayer. This shows that he had little inclination for worldly wealth and means of comfort, so much so that he did not wish to keep it any longer than necessary in his possession.

The object of prayer is to implant in one's heart complete attention towards Allāh and every effort should be made to achieve it completely. But it is also natural that a distracting thought may enter the heart of a human being. Such thoughts are of two kinds. Firstly, there are those which enter the mind of a righteousness person, such as the Holy Prophet's thought that a piece of gold was lying in his house and it should be given away in charity. Similarly, there was the thought in the mind of 'Umar to prepare the army to fight against the enemy. In some reports it is even mentioned that 'Umar forgot something while reciting the Qur'ān in *Maghrib* prayer for the same reason. It shows that his concern to save his people from the attacks of the enemy was uppermost in his mind. But such a thought does not arise from personal desires or insinuation of the devil, which is the second kind of thought. When such worldly thoughts come into the mind, it is due to a deficient spiritual state; and at the beginning of their spiritual progress this is the condition of most people. The real object of prayer is to remove this defect and to bring about complete absorption. It is done in this way, that when there is struggle in the mind between the worldly and the higher thoughts, one should repel the former and turn the mind towards Allāh, and do the same everytime a worldly thought occurs. Ultimately, the lower thoughts are overcome and attention gradually turns entirely towards Allāh only. In the next ḥadīth mention is made of the second kind of thoughts which arise from the devil's insinuations.

[26] This is a repetition of h. 608 with a slight difference in wording, and an addition by Abū Salamah at the end. See also h. 1231.

not know." I said: "Were you not present there?" He said: "Yes." I said: "But I know that he recited such and such *sūrah*." [27]

---

[27] It appears that Bukhārī has included this ḥadīth here to show that at that time the attention of that man must have strayed from his prayer, which is why he forgot the *sūrah*. But the object of Abū Hurairah seems to be only to indicate that if a person pays attention to what he is hearing, he can later recall it.

Book 22: *As-Sahw*
Forgetting during Prayer

In the name of Allāh, the Beneficent, the Merciful

Ch. 1: Concerning forgetting when one stands (instead of sitting) after two *rak'ahs* in obligatory prayer

1224 'Abdullāh ibn Buḥainah reported: The Messenger of Allāh ﷺ led us in one of the prayers in two *rak'ahs*. Then he stood up (immediately after the two *rak'ahs*) and did not sit down. The people stood up with him. When he was about to finish the prayer and we were waiting for his *Taslīm*, he said *Allāhu Akbar* before the *Taslīm* and performed two prostrations while he was sitting, and then he said the *Salām*.[1]

1225 'Abdullāh ibn Buḥainah reported that the Messenger of Allāh ﷺ stood up after the second *rak'ah* of the *Ẓuhr* prayer and did not sit down between them.[2] When he finished the prayer, he performed two prostrations, and then said the *Salām* after that.[3]

Ch. 2: When a person prays five *rak'ahs*

1226 'Abdullāh (ibn Mas'ūd) reported that the Messenger of Allāh ﷺ said the *Ẓuhr* prayer with five *rak'ahs*. He was asked: "Is there an increase in prayer?" He said: "What is that?" He (the questioner) said: "You prayed five *rak'ahs*." So he performed two prostrations after he had said the *Salām*.[4]

---

[1] This is a repetition of h. 829 with a slight difference in wording. There it was stated that it was during *Ẓuhr* prayer that the Holy Prophet stood up directly after completing two *rak'ahs*, instead of assuming the sitting position, and then before the *Taslīm* (i.e., saying *Salām*) he performed two *Sajdahs* as expiation. Here, instead of the *Ẓuhr* prayer, the words "one of the prayers" have been used.

[2] The words "between them" mean between the first two and the last two *rak'ahs*.

[3] This again is a repetition of h. 829 in brief. Here the *Ẓuhr* prayer has been mentioned.

[4] This is a repetition of h. 401. In h. 401 there are more details but neither *Ẓuhr* prayer nor the number of *rak'ahs* has been mentioned. Here the prostration of expiation for forgetting (*Sajdah Sahw*) was performed after the *Taslīm* or close of prayer. On the basis of this ḥadīth, Imām Mālik's view is that in case of praying more than the prescribed *rak'ahs*, two prostrations of

Ch. 3: **When a person finishes his prayer after two or three *rak'ahs* (by mistake), he should perform two prostrations like the prostrations of prayer, or longer**

1227 Abū Hurairah reported: The Prophet ﷺ led us in the *'Aṣr* or the *Ẓuhr* prayer and finished it with *Salām*. Dhu-l-Yadain said to him: "O Messenger of Allāh, Has the prayer been reduced?" The Prophet ﷺ asked his Companions: "Is it true what he is saying?" They answered: "Yes." Then he said two more *rak'ahs*, then performed two prostrations.

Sa'd said: I saw that 'Urwah ibn Az-Zubair had prayed two *rak'ahs* in *Maghrib* prayer when he finished it with *Salām* and engaged in conversation. Then (when he was informed about the omission) he prayed what remained (i.e., one *rak'ah*), and performed two prostrations, and said: "This is what the Prophet ﷺ did." [5]

Ch. 4: **He who does not say the *Tashahhud* after the two prostrations of forgetfulness (*Sajdah Sahw*)**

Anas and al-Ḥasan did *Taslīm* without *Tashahhud*. And Qatādah said: "There is no *Tashahhud*." [6]

Sajdah Sahw should be performed after the *Taslīm* and in case of missing any *rak'ah*, it should be performed before *Taslīm* as in h. 829. But in h. 482 and h. 1229, where the questioner's name is given as Dhu-l-Yadain, it is reported that in the latter case also he performed it after *Taslīm*, and then repeated the *Taslīm*. In the case of saying five *rak'ahs*, he did not realize this and he performed *Taslīm* to close the prayer before the *Sajdah Sahw*. According to the Ḥanafīs, *Sajdah Sahw* should always be after the *Taslīm*. According to Imām Aḥmad, the practice of the Holy Prophet should be followed exactly as it was done by him, and in cases where his practice is not to be found, *Sajdah Sahw* should be performed before the *Taslīm*.

The Holy Prophet performed it both ways in his practice and mentioned both ways in his instructions. At the end of h. 401 it is stated: "…I am only a mortal like you, I forget as you forget. So when I forget, remind me, and when anyone of you is in doubt about his prayer, he should seek what appears to be correct, and complete it (from that point). Then he should finish with *Salām*, and then perform prostration twice." In Ṣaḥīḥ Muslim there is a report from Abū Sa'īd al-Khudrī as follows: "When anyone of you has a doubt regarding his prayer, and does not know how much (i.e., how many *rak'ahs*) he has prayed, three or four, he should discard the doubt and act according to what is certain, and then perform two *Sajdahs* before the *Taslīm*" (book: 'Mosques and Places of Prayer', ch. 19, h. 571a).

Imām Baihaqi's view is that there is option and latitude, and it is permissible to perform *Sajdah Sahw* before or after the *Taslīm*. This is the correct view. The author of *Hidāyah* writes that the difference of opinion is only about whether the *Sajdah* is before or after the *Taslīm*; otherwise, all agree that it should be performed.

[5] This is a repetition of h. 482 in brief with an addition from Sa'd.

[6] The majority of jurists are of the opinion that there is no need to repeat the recitation of the *Tashahhud* if the *Sajdah Sahw* (the prostrations of forgetfulness) is performed before the *Taslīm*,

1228 Abū Hurairah reported that the Messenger of Allāh ﷺ left after saying two *rak'ahs*. Dhu-l-Yadain said to him: "Has the prayer been shortened or have you forgotten, O Messenger of Allāh?" The Messenger of Allāh ﷺ said: "Has Dhu-l-Yadain spoken the truth?" People said: "Yes." So the Messenger of Allāh ﷺ stood up and said two more *rak'ahs,* then he finished with *Salām.* Then he called out *Allāhu Akbar* and performed prostrations like his (usual) prostrations or for longer. Then he got up.[7]

Salamah ibn 'Alqamah reported: I said to Muḥammad (ibn Sīrīn): "Is there *Tashahhud* after the two prostrations of *Sahw?*" He said: "This is not in the ḥadīth of Abū Hurairah." [8]

Ch. 5: Saying the *Takbīr* in the two prostrations of forgetfulness (*Sajdah Sahw*)

1229 Abū Hurairah reported: The Messenger of Allāh ﷺ said one of the afternoon prayers — Muḥammad (ibn Sīrīn) said: I think most probably it was the '*Aṣr* prayer — in two *rak'ahs,* then finished it with *Salām.* He stood up near a piece of wood which was in front of the mosque and placed his hand over it. Among the people were Abū Bakr and 'Umar and these two were hesitant of talking to him, and those who were in a hurry went out and said: "Have the prayers been shortened?" A man whom the Prophet ﷺ called "the man with two hands" (*Dhul-Yadain*) said to him: "Have you forgotten or has it (the prayer) been shortened?" He (the Holy Prophet) said: "Neither have I forgotten nor has it been shortened." He (the man) said: "You certainly forgot." So he (the Holy Prophet) said two *rak'ahs* of prayer, then finished it with *Salām.* Then he called out *Allāhu Akbar* and prostrated like his (usual) prostrations or for longer. Then he raised his head and called out *Allāhu Akbar.* Then he put his head down and called out *Allāhu Akbar* and prostrated like his (usual) prostrations or for longer. Then he raised his head and called out *Allāhu Akbar.*[9]

---

but some consider it necessary. If the *Sajdah Sahw* is said after the *Taslīm,* according to Imām Aḥmad, Imām Isḥāq and Imām Abū Ḥanīfah, the *Tashahhud* should be repeated. But some are of the opinion that even in this case it is not essential. This chapter is about the latter case.

[7] This is again a repetition of h. 482 in brief, with a difference of wording. In these reports the repeating of the *Tashahhud* after the *Sajdah Sahw* has not been mentioned. This shows that the Holy Prophet did not repeat the *Tashahhud* after performing the prostrations of forgetfulness.

[8] H. 482, h. 1227 and h. 1229 have been reported by Abū Hurairah. There is no mention in them of the recitation of the *Tashahhud* after the *Sajdah Sahw.*

[9] This is again a repetition of h. 482 in wording like that of h. 482. While in h. 482 it is mentioned that Ibn Sīrīn said: "Abū Hurairah told the name of this prayer but I have forgotten", here it says: "Muḥammad (Ibn Sīrīn) said: I think most probably it was the '*Aṣr* prayer." Towards

1230 'Abdullāh ibn Buḥainah al-Asdī reported that the Messenger of Allāh ﷺ stood up in the *Ẓuhr* prayer when sitting is required. When he completed the prayer he performed two prostrations and called out *Allāhu Akbar* on each prostration while sitting, before saying the *Salām*. The people also performed the two prostrations with him on account of the sitting which he forgot.[10]

Ch. 6:   When a person does not remember whether he prayed three or four *rak'ahs*, he should perform two prostrations while sitting

1231 Abū Hurairah reported that the Messenger of Allāh ﷺ said: "When the call is made for prayer Satan turns back fleeing, making sounds of scoffing and denying, so that he may not hear the call to prayer. And when the call is finished, he advances. When the *Iqāmah* is sounded, he turns back fleeing (again). When the call of the *Iqāmah* is finished, he advances (again) till he casts evil suggestions between man and his self, saying, 'Remember this and remember that', about what he did not remember, till the man is in such a condition that he does not know how much of the prayer he has said. When any of you is uncertain as to how many *rak'ahs* he has prayed, whether three or four, he should perform two prostrations while sitting." [11]

Ch. 7:   Forgetting during obligatory and optional prayers

Ibn 'Abbās performed two prostrations after *Witr*.

1232 Abū Hurairah reported that the Messenger of Allāh ﷺ said: "When any of you stands up to say prayers, Satan comes and puts doubts in him till he does not know how much of the prayer he has said. If any of you finds himself in such a situation, he should perform two prostrations while sitting." [12]

Ch. 8:   When a person praying is spoken to and he points with his hand and listens

1233 Kuraib reported that Ibn 'Abbās and al-Miswar ibn Makhramah and 'Abdur Raḥmān ibn Azhar sent him to 'Ā'ishah and said: "Convey greetings to her from all of us and ask her about the two *rak'ahs* after the *'Aṣr* prayer and say to her: We were informed that you pray those two and we have (also)

---

the end of this report it is mentioned that *Takbīr* is to be said, i.e., before going into and while rising from the *Sajdah Sahw*.

[10] This is a repetition of h. 829 with difference in wording.

[11] This is a repetition of h. 608 with difference in wording, and an addition at the end ("When any of you is uncertain..."). In h. 1222 such an addition is attributed to Abū Salamah but here it is included in the saying of the Holy Prophet himself.

[12] This is a repetition of h. 608 consisting of the last part of h. 1231.

heard that the Prophet ﷺ forbade them".[13] And Ibn 'Abbās said: "I, along with 'Umar ibn al-Khaṭṭāb, used to hit people if they did it."

Kuraib said: I went in to see 'Ā'ishah and gave her the message they had sent me with. She said: "Ask Umm Salamah." So I came back to them and informed them of what she said. They then sent me to Umm Salamah with the same (question) with which they had sent me to 'Ā'ishah. Umm Salamah said: "I heard the Prophet ﷺ forbid them, and then I saw him saying them when he prayed *'Aṣr*. Then he came to my house and with me were some women of the Banū Ḥarām of the Anṣār. So I sent my girl servant to him and said to her: 'Stand besides him and say to him: Umm Salamah says to you: O Messenger of Allāh, I have heard from you that you forbid these but I have seen you praying them. If he points with his hand, then move back from him.' The girl servant did that, and he pointed with his hand and she moved back from him. When he had finished, he said: 'O daughter of Abū Umayyah, You have asked about the two *rak'ahs* after *'Aṣr*.[14] It is that the people of 'Abdul Qais came to me and they kept me busy from (being able to perform) the two *rak'ahs* after *Ẓuhr*, so these two were those'."

Ch. 9: To point during prayer

Kuraib reported it from Umm Salamah (who reported it) from the Prophet ﷺ.[15]

1234 Sahl ibn Sa'd reported: The news reached the Messenger of Allāh ﷺ that there were differences among the Banī 'Amr ibn 'Auf. So the Messenger of Allāh ﷺ went with some people to effect reconciliation between them. The Messenger of Allāh ﷺ was delayed and the time for prayer came. ...[16]

1235 Asmā' reported: I came upon 'Ā'ishah and she was praying, standing, and people were (also) standing (for prayer). I said (to her): "What

---

[13] The discussion about performing two *rak'ahs* of *sunnah* after the obligatory prayer of *'Aṣr* has occurred earlier.

[14] This shows that saying something to one who is praying, and his listening to it and pointing with the hand, is not objectionable if it is necessary. Abū Umayyah was the family name of the father of Umm Salamah, wife of the Holy Prophet.

[15] The previous ḥadīth, h. 1233, has been referred to here. To mention it under a separate chapter is to show that it is also permissible if the person praying takes the initiative in pointing to something (rather than as a response). The next ḥadīth supports the view.

[16] This is a repetition of h. 684 in words very similar to those of h. 1218. For the rest of the ḥadīth, see h. 1218. The Holy Prophet made a sign to Abū Bakr, ordering him to continue leading the prayer.

has happened to the people?" She pointed with her head towards (the eclipse in) the sky. I said: "A sign?" She indicated with her head to say "Yes." [17]

1236 'Ā'ishah, wife of the Prophet ﷺ, reported: The Messenger of Allāh ﷺ said his prayers in his house while he was ill, sitting, and behind him a party of people said their prayers standing, so he made a sign to them to sit down. When he finished, he said: "The Imām is appointed to be followed: so when he bows (in *Rukū'*), you must bow, and when he rises up, you must rise up." [18]

---

[17] This is a repetition of the opening of h. 86. It shows that 'Ā'ishah replied to Asmā' twice by means of indicating with her head or nodding during prayer.

[18] This is a repetition of h. 378 in words exactly the same as in h. 1113, with the minor difference of the omission of repeating "He said his prayers" before the word "sitting".

Book 23: *Al-Janā'iz*
Funerals[1]

In the name of Allāh, the Beneficent, the Merciful

Ch. 1: **Concerning funerals and one whose last words are:** *Lā ilāha ill-Allāh* **("There is no God but Allāh")**[2]

Wahb ibn Munabbih was asked: "Is not the formula 'There is no God but Allāh' the key to Paradise?" He said: "Yes, but there is no key without teeth. If you bring a key with teeth, it (the door to Paradise) will be opened for you, otherwise it will not be opened for you." [3]

1237 Abū Dharr reported that the Messenger of Allāh ﷺ said: "Someone came to me from my Lord and informed me" — or he said: "gave me good news" — "that if any of my followers dies not ascribing any partners to Allāh, he will enter Paradise." I asked: "Even if he had committed fornication and theft?" He replied: "Even if he had committed fornication and theft." [4]

---

[1] The word *janā'iz* is plural of *janāzah*. The word *janāzah* is used both with the vowel *fatḥah* after *j* (*a* in *janāzah*), and with the vowel *kasrah* after *j* (*i* in *jināzah*). Some hold that the second form, i.e., *jināzah*, is applied to the dead body when it has been placed on the body carrier (bier), while the former refers just to the corpse.

[2] This is part of a ḥadīth in Abū Dāwūd and Ḥākim from Muʿāz ibn Jabal, traced to the Holy Prophet. It runs thus: "The one whose last words are *Lā ilāha ill-Allāh* enters Paradise" (Abū Dāwūd, book: 'Funerals', ch. *at-Talqīn*, h. 3116).

[3] The meaning is that belief in the Oneness of God is the key to salvation. However, just as a key without teeth, a blank key, cannot open a door, likewise belief without good deeds does not benefit anyone.

[4] This ḥadīth means only that if a person is good at the end of his life, and he dies as a believer in the Oneness of God, he will enter Paradise, even if he had at some earlier stage committed sins such as fornication and theft, of which he had later repented and changed the course of his life. Not to ascribe partners to God, or adhering to the Oneness of God, means that one must try to obey Allāh's commands. As stated just above the ḥadīth, declaring the Oneness of God is the key to Paradise, and good deeds are its teeth. Declaring the Oneness of God is not merely to say in words that there is only One God, but really it is to not deviate from the commands of God in the face of temptation or attraction to do the opposite. Otherwise, he is making as a partner with God the person or the thing for whose sake he is violating the command of God. Sin and faith cannot go together, as is made clear in reports in Bukhārī itself: "A fornicator does not commit

1238 'Abdullāh (ibn Mas'ūd) related that the Messenger of Allāh ﷺ said: "Anyone who dies while ascribing partners to Allāh will enter the fire." And I say: "Anyone who dies not ascribing partners to Allāh will enter Paradise." [5]

Ch. 2: The command to follow funeral processions

1239 Al-Barā' ibn 'Āzib reported: The Prophet ﷺ commanded us to do seven things and forbade us to do seven others. He commanded us to follow a funeral procession, to visit the sick, to accept an invitation, to help the oppressed, to fulfil an oath, to return a greeting, and to pray for one who sneezes.[6] He forbade us to use silver utensils, to wear rings of gold, and to wear clothes of silk (*al-ḥarīr, ad-dībāj, al-qassī* and *al-istabraq*).[7]

1240 Abū Hurairah said that he heard the Messenger of Allāh ﷺ say: "There are five rights of a Muslim to be observed by another Muslim: to return (his) greeting, to visit the sick, to follow a funeral procession, to accept an invitation, and to pray for one who sneezes." [8]

Ch. 3: Going to see the body after death when it has been wrapped in its shroud

1241–1242 'Ā'ishah, wife of the Prophet ﷺ, informed that Abū Bakr

---

fornication while he is a believer" (h. 2475, h. 6772). The Qur'ān says: "Have you seen him who takes his desire as his god?" (25 : 43). Thus if a person ends his life acting on such a belief in the Oneness of God, even if he has committed fornication or theft earlier on, it means he had repented from it in practice, and led a good life till the end.

[5] These two sentences are found in Ṣaḥīḥ Muslim, in a report by Jābir, as one statement the whole of which is traced to the Holy Prophet (book: 'Faith', ch. 40). At the same place in Ṣaḥīḥ Muslim there is a report like the above (h. 1238) from Ibn Mas'ūd, which in some manuscripts is in the reverse form, so that the sentence mentioning "not ascribing partners" is attributed to the Holy Prophet, and the sentence mentioning "ascribing partners" is attributed to Ibn Mas'ūd. The sense in which both these sentences apply has been explained in the last footnote.

[6] To accompany a funeral is for the purpose of joining in carrying the bier and showing sympathy and love to the relatives of the deceased. The Holy Prophet used to lead funeral prayers of the poorest of people, accompany the funeral procession to the burial, and offer words of advice and consolation by the graveside. When a person sneezes and says *Al-ḥamdu li-llāh* ("Praise be to Allāh"), in reply one should say *Yarḥamu-ka-llāh* ("May Allāh bless you"). In this ḥadīth, seven things have been commanded which help to foster love and affection between people.

[7] The seven things which are forbidden to be used (one of which has not been included in this report) are by way of warning, as these are associated with a life of luxury, leading to moral laxity and spiritual weakness. However, these are permitted to women, such as gold and silver jewellery and silk clothing, as they are a means of their embellishment. Four kinds of clothes are mentioned, *al-ḥarīr, ad-dībāj, al-qassī* and *al-istabraq*, which may be summed up as clothes of silk.

[8] This is a repetition of the previous h. 1239.

came on his horse from his home in As-Sunḥ. He got down from it, entered the Mosque and did not speak to anyone until he came to ʿĀʾishah and went to the Prophet ﷺ with the intention to see him. He was covered with a striped blanket. Abū Bakr uncovered his face, he knelt down and kissed him. Then he started weeping and said: "My father be sacrificed for you, O Prophet of Allāh! Allāh will not combine two deaths on you. You have indeed died the death which Allāh decreed for you." [9]

[1242] Abū Salamah said: Ibn ʿAbbās informed me that Abū Bakr came out and ʿUmar was addressing the people. Abū Bakr said (to ʿUmar), "Sit down", but he refused. Abū Bakr again said, "Sit down", but he again refused. Then Abū Bakr recited the *Tashahhud* and the people turned to him and left ʿUmar. He said:

> "*Ammā baʿdu* (lit. meaning, 'After this'), whoever amongst you worshipped Muḥammad, then Muḥammad is indeed dead, but whoever worshipped Allāh, Allāh is alive and will never die. Allāh, the Most High, has said: 'And Muḥammad is only a messenger — messengers have already passed away before him. If then he dies or is killed, will you turn back upon your heels? And he who turns back upon his heels will do no harm at all to Allāh. And Allāh will reward the grateful' (the Qurʾān, 3:144)."

By Allāh! It was as if people never knew that Allāh had revealed it (i.e., 3:144) until Abū Bakr recited it. People then took it from him, and whoever was heard, he was reciting it. [10]

---

[9] The connection of the chapter heading with the ḥadīth is only that Abū Bakr removed the cloth from the Holy Prophet's face and looked at it. The heading refers to a shroud but the ḥadīth mentions that the Holy Prophet's body was covered with a sheet, and it was not yet wrapped in a shroud. Both mean that the face of the deceased should only be seen when it is properly covered, and generally it is when it is properly wrapped in the shroud. The words of Abū Bakr that God will never cause the Holy Prophet to die twice have been taken to mean that it cannot be that he would be brought back to life and then he would die because ʿUmar was saying in the mosque that the Holy Prophet would come back to life again. But it may also mean that the death which was destined for his body had taken place but death cannot come upon his soul. It may also mean that his physical death cannot cause death to his teachings and his religion as he is the Last of the Prophets and his religion will last till the day of Resurrection.

[10] Abū Bakr's inference from the verse of the Qurʾān, "And Muḥammad is only a messenger…" (3:144), that the Holy Prophet has died, clearly proves that all the Companions held the view that all the previous prophets had passed away. Otherwise, if the Companions had believed that Prophet Jesus was alive then they, and in particular ʿUmar, the one who was vehemently denying the Holy Prophet's death, would have certainly raised an objection against the view expressed by Abū Bakr. In fact, Abū Bakr's reciting of this verse on this occasion shows that the Companions unanimously agreed that all prophets before the Holy Prophet had died. This is

1243 Umm Al-ʿAlā', a woman of the Anṣār who took the pledge at the hands of the Prophet ﷺ, informed: The emigrants (*muhājir*) were distributed amongst us by drawing lots and in our share came ʿUthmān ibn Maẓʿūn. We accommodated him in our house. Then he suffered from a disease which led to his death. When he died, and was washed, and was shrouded in his clothes, the Messenger of Allāh ﷺ came[11] and I said: "May the mercy of Allāh be on you, O Abū Sā'ib! My evidence about you is that Allāh has honoured you." The Prophet ﷺ said: "How do you know that Allāh has honoured him?" I replied: "O Messenger of Allāh, may my father be sacrificed for you, to whom shall Allāh give honour?" He said: "No doubt death came to him. By Allāh! I too wish him well, but by Allāh! I do not know what will be done with me, and I am Messenger of Allāh." By Allāh! I shall never attribute purity to anyone after that.[12]

Nāfiʿ ibn Yazīd reported from ʿUqail (that the words of the Holy Prophet were): "…what will be done with him" (i.e., with ʿUthmān ibn Maẓʿūn).

1244 Jābir ibn ʿAbdullāh said: When my father was killed,[13] I lifted the sheet from his face, I wept and the people forbade me from it, but the Prophet ﷺ did not forbid me. Then my paternal aunt Fāṭimah began to weep. So the Prophet ﷺ said: "Weep or not weep, but the angels were keeping him under shade with their wings till you lifted him (from the field of battle)."

---

therefore a consensus or *Ijmā'* on the death of Jesus, a consensus on such a large scale that there is no other issue on which a similar consensus can be shown.

It is surprising that in spite of the verse of the Qur'ān mentioning Jesus's words to Allāh on the Day of Resurrection, "When You caused me to die" (5:117), and then the proof of this consensus in authentic ḥadīth, Muslims generally believe that Jesus is still alive. It also shows that before Abū Bakr drew attention to this verse, people's minds had not turned towards it. Similarly, the death of Jesus is established from thirty verses of the Qur'ān, but people did not think over them sufficiently until this issue was raised by Hazrat Mirza Ghulam Ahmad.

[11] In some reports it is stated that the Holy Prophet came, bowed close to him, wept and kissed him. This connects it with the chapter heading.

[12] In other reports, instead of *mā yuf'alu bī* ("what will be done with me"), the words are *mā yuf'alu bi-hi* ("what will be done with him"), as in the report from Nāfiʿ ibn Yāzid which follows. That is to say, "what will be done with ʿUthmān." The statement in the Qur'ān, "I do not know what will be done with me nor with you" (46:9), means I do not know what is going to happen in the future and in what state I will be, or you will be, because no one has knowledge of the details beforehand. However, knowledge about salvation is given to prophets for certainty. In fact, they are in the presence of Allāh in this world and so are in Paradise here. Thus, the correct wording here is "What will be done with him" and not "What will be done with me." The latter words, according to Imām Dāwūdi, are the narrator's own conjecture.

[13] The martyrdom of his father took place during the battle of Badr. See also h. 1293.

Ch. 4:   **A man who gives news of a death to the relatives by himself 14**

1245 Abū Hurairah reported that the Messenger of Allāh ﷺ gave (people) news of the death of the Negus (the King of Abyssinia) on the very day that he died. He went towards the prayer ground and made people form rows, and he pronounced four *Takbīrs* (during the funeral prayer).

1246 Anas ibn Mālik reported that the Prophet ﷺ said: "Zaid became the flag-bearer and was martyred. Then Ja'far took the flag and he was martyred. Then 'Abdullāh ibn Rawāḥah took it and he too was martyred". At that time the eyes of the Messenger of Allāh ﷺ were full of tears. (The Prophet added:) "Then Khālid ibn al-Walīd took the flag without being appointed (to the command) and was granted victory." 15

Ch. 5:   **To make an announcement about the funeral**

Abū Rāfi' reported this from Abū Hurairah that the Prophet ﷺ said: "Why did you not inform me?" 16

1247 Ibn 'Abbās reported: A person died and the Messenger of Allāh ﷺ used to visit him (while ill). He died at night and they buried him during the night. When morning came, they informed him (about the death). He said: "What prevented you from informing me?" They said: "It was night, and it was very dark, so we disliked to put you to trouble." He (the Prophet) went to his grave and said the (funeral) prayer for him.[17]

---

[14] Conveying news of someone's death is prohibited in certain ḥadīth reports. This does not mean that such news must not be given to people. The purpose is to discourage the loud proclamations that were made in pre-Islamic days, accompanied by the beating of drums and proudly announcing the horrific titles of the deceased. Otherwise, to inform relatives and friends is inevitable, and there cannot possibly be any harm in it.

[15] In this ḥadīth, mention has been made of the Battle of Mu'tah which was fought at the border of Syria. The commander of the army was Zaid ibn Ḥārithah, who was a freed slave. The Holy Prophet had said: "If he is killed, then Ja'far should be the commander; and if he also died then 'Abdullāh ibn Rawāḥah should be the commander." The army consisted of three thousand men and the enemy's strength was about a hundred thousand. All the three commanders were killed one after another, and the command was taken over by Khālid ibn Walīd who won the battle. The Holy Prophet was told about the news through revelation. The death of such dear and close friends brought tears to his eyes. See also h. 1299.

[16] When the *Janāzah* is ready, people should be informed about it so that they may join the congregation. This ḥadīth narrated by Abū Hurairah is mentioned in h. 458 to the effect that a woman who used to clean the mosque died and the Companions said her funeral prayer without informing the Holy Prophet. He asked: "Why did you not inform me?" and then he went to the graveyard and said the *Janāzah* prayer over the woman's grave.

[17] This person was Ṭalḥah ibn Barā'. This shows how much concerned was the Holy Prophet

Ch. 6:   Excellence of a person whose child dies and he shows patience

Allāh, the Mighty, the Glorious said: "And give good news to the patient ones" (the Qur'ān, 2:155).

1248 Anas reported that the Prophet ﷺ said: "There is no Muslim among the people, but if three of his (children) die before reaching maturity, Allāh will make him enter Paradise due to His immense mercy for them." [18]

1249–1250 Abū Sa'īd reported that women said to the Prophet ﷺ: "Appoint for us a day (to teach women only)." So he preached to them and said: "Any woman three of whose children die (during her life), these will be a screen (for her) from the fire (of Hell)." A woman said: "And (what about) two?" He replied: "Two also." [1250] Abū Hurairah reported from the Prophet ﷺ: "Those that have not attained maturity." [19]

1251 Abū Hurairah reported from the Prophet ﷺ that he said: "No Muslim three of whose children die will enter the fire (of Hell), though the vow will be fulfilled." [20]

Ch. 7:   A man saying to a woman besides a grave: "Be patient" [21]

1252 Anas ibn Mālik reported: The Prophet ﷺ passed by a woman who was sitting by a grave crying. So he said (to her): "Fear Allāh and be patient."

---

about the welfare of his Companions and always tried to be kept informed about them. See also h. 1319.

[18] Parents love the young among their children the most of all, and therefore their death is even more distressing than that of older offspring. If they show patience and submit to the will of Allāh they will enter Paradise. And in some ḥadīth reports it is mentioned that these young children will even intercede with Allāh for their parents.

[19] This is a briefer repetition of h. 101–102 with slight difference in wording.

[20] This is a repetition of h. 1248. The "vow" has been considered to be a reference to the verse of the Qur'ān: "And there is not one of you but shall come to it (i.e., hell)" (19:71). A person's coming to it does not mean entering it. Apparently it means that if such a person is sinful, even then he will not enter hell. In other words, these calamities suffered by him will atone for his other sins. The words referring to the fulfilment of the vow may also mean that the punishment of evil, which is absolutely and certainly hell, is like a vow, and the man will be taken out immediately after entering it, fulfilling the vow symbolically.

[21] In the previous chapter good news was given to those who show patience. Here it is exhorted to observe patience. The complete ḥadīth occurs later in h. 1283 in which it is said that a woman did not recognise the Holy Prophet and after listening to his exhortation she told him to go away and said that only the one who is faced with the distress knows what it is like. Later, realizing who he was, she went to his house and the Holy Prophet said to her that patience should be shown at the moment when the calamity strikes, meaning that later on no one has any choice but to show patience. See also h. 1302.

Ch. 8: **Bathing and ablution of the dead body with water and leaves of the lote-tree[22]**

Ibn 'Umar spread scent over the (body of) Sa'īd ibn Zaid's son and carried his body and said (the funeral) prayer for him but did not perform ablution. Ibn 'Abbās said: "A Muslim is not unclean whether alive or dead." Sa'd said: "If he had been unclean I would never have touched him." And the Prophet ﷺ said: "A believer is not unclean."[23]

1253 Umm 'Aṭiyyah al-Anṣāriyya reported: The Messenger of Allāh ﷺ came to us when his daughter died and said: "Wash her three or five times, or more than that if you see it necessary, with water and leaves of the lote-tree and at the end sprinkle camphor — or a little camphor — on her, and when you have finished, let me know." So when we finished, we informed him and he gave us his waist-sheet and said: "Shroud her in it."[24]

Ch. 9: **It is recommended to wash (the dead body) an odd number of times**

1254 Umm 'Aṭiyyah reported: The Messenger of Allāh ﷺ came to us when we were giving a bath to his (deceased) daughter[25] and said: "Wash her three or five times or more than that with water and leaves of the lote-tree and at the end sprinkle camphor on her, and when you have finished, let me know." So when we finished, we informed him and he threw his waist-sheet towards us and said: "Shroud her in it."[26]

---

[22] To perform ablution or *Wuḍū'* of the dead body means that the full bathing of the dead body should start first with the washing of those parts which are washed in *Wuḍū'*, as is mentioned in the next chapter in h. 1254. Bathing the dead body does not mean that the body of a person becomes unclean after death. The object is cleanliness and to make sure that any filth is removed.

[23] It means that by washing a dead body a person does not become unclean so that he needs to take a bath or perform *Wuḍū'*. The ḥadīth which is mentioned in Abū Dāwūd and Tirmidhī, that one who gives a bath to a dead body should also take a bath, is considered a weak ḥadīth. Or it may have been said when there is the possibility of dirt being splattered on the person who is washing the dead body.

[24] This is a repetition of h. 1254 with some differences. The words "if you see it necessary" have been added in this version. The additional part of h. 1254 starting "Ayyūb said" is not found here.

[25] In h. 1261 in the report from Ibn Sīrīn these words occur: "I do not know which of his daughters she was." In the report recorded in Ṣaḥīḥ Muslim (book: 'Funerals', ch. 12), her name is mentioned as Zainab, who was the mother of Umāmah and the wife of Abul-'Āṣ and had died in the beginning of 8 A.H. In some reports her name is given as Kalthūm.

[26] Regarding the act of shrouding (*al-ish'ār*), see h. 1261.

Ayyūb said: Ḥafṣah (bint Sīrīn) related to me a report similar to that of Muḥammad (ibn Sīrīn), and in that report of Ḥafṣah it was said: "Give her bath an odd number of times" and "three or five or seven times". It was also said in it that he (the Holy Prophet) said: "Start from the right side and with the parts washed in *Wuḍū'*" [27], and also that Umm 'Aṭiyyah said: "We combed her hair and divided them in three braids."

Ch. 10: Starting (washing) the dead body from its right side

1255 Umm 'Aṭiyyah reported that the Messenger of Allāh ﷺ said regarding the washing of (the body of) his (deceased) daughter: "Start from the right side and with the parts washed in *Wuḍū'*." [28]

Ch. 11: Parts of the body washed in *Wuḍū'*

1256 Umm 'Aṭiyyah reported: When we gave a bath to a (deceased) daughter of the Prophet ﷺ, while we were giving her the bath, he said to us: "Start from the right side and with the parts washed in *Wuḍū'*." [29]

Ch. 12: Can a woman be enshrouded in the waist-sheet of a man?

1257 Umm 'Aṭiyyah reported: The daughter of the Prophet ﷺ died and he said to us: "Wash her three or five times, or more than that if you see it necessary, and when you have finished, let me know." So when we finished, we informed him and he unfastened his waist-sheet and said: "Shroud her in it." [30]

Ch. 13: To sprinkle camphor at the end

1258–1259 Umm 'Aṭiyyah reported: One of the daughters of the Prophet ﷺ died, so he came out and said: "Wash her three or five times, or more than that if you see it necessary, with water and leaves of the lote-tree, and at the end sprinkle camphor — or a little camphor — on her, and when you have finished, let me know." So when we finished, we informed him and he threw his waist-sheet towards us and said: "Shroud her in it." [1259] Umm 'Aṭiyyah reported (in another narration) that he said: "Wash her three or five or seven times, or more than that if you see it necessary." [31] Ḥafṣah (bint Sīrīn) said that Umm 'Aṭiyyah said: We entwined her hair in three braids.

---

[27] This portion of the ḥadīth has already been mentioned in h. 167.

[28] This is an exact repetition of h. 167, and has also occurred at the end of h. 1254.

[29] Again, this is a repetition of h. 167 with a minor difference.

[30] This is a repetition of the portion of h. 1254 which is in h. 1253, but with omission of the mention of water, leaves of the lote-tree and camphor.

[31] This again is a repetition of h. 1254, but without the mention of "an odd number of times" or of starting "from the right and with the parts which are washed in *Wuḍū'*."

Ch. 14: To unravel the hair of a dead woman

Ibn Sīrīn said: There is no harm in undoing the hair of a dead woman.

1260 Umm ʿAṭiyyah related that they (the women) had entwined the hair of the daughter of the Messenger of Allāh ﷺ in three braids. They unravelled her hair, then washed it and then entwined it in three braids.[32]

Ch. 15: How to enshroud (*al-ishʿār*) a woman's dead body

Al-Ḥasan said: To wrap her thighs and buttocks with the fifth sheet under the shirt.[33]

1261 Ibn Sīrīn said: Umm ʿAṭiyyah, a woman of the Anṣār who had given the pledge to the Prophet ﷺ, came to Baṣrah to see her son but did not find him. She related to us (as follows):

The Prophet ﷺ came to us while we were giving the bath to his (deceased) daughter and said: "Wash her three or five times, or more than that if you see it necessary, with water and leaves of the lote-tree and at the end sprinkle camphor on her, and when you have finished, let me know." So when we finished, (we informed him and) he threw his waist-sheet towards us and said: "Shroud her in it." [34]

She (Umm ʿAṭiyyah) did not add to that (statement),[35] and I do not know which of his daughters she was. And *al-ishʿār* means to wrap the body in it.[36] And Ibn Sīrīn used to give similar instructions about women, saying that it should be wrapped around the body and not tied.[37]

Ch. 16: Should the hair of a woman be set in three braids?[38]

---

[32] This again is a repetition of the subject of h. 1254.

[33] This shows that according to Ḥasan five pieces of cloth are required for the shroud of a woman. In *Fatḥ al-Bārī* a report from Jauzqī adds the following words to the statement of Umm ʿAṭiyyah: "She said: We shrouded her in five pieces of cloth and wrapped a shawl over her (shoulders) as a living one is wrapped."

[34] This is a repetition of h. 1254, except that after "Wash her three or five times, or more than that", the words "if you see it necessary" are added as in many of the other repetitions of h. 1254.

[35] In some versions this is worded in the masculine, "He did not add to that", meaning that the Holy Prophet said no more than "Shroud her in it."

[36] The word *al-ishʿār* is in reference to the Holy Prophet's command "Shroud her (*ashʿirna-hā*) in it", in which this word is used.

[37] This whole paragraph is a statement by Ayyūb who was reporting from Ibn Sīrīn.

[38] The followers of Imām Abū Ḥanīfah are of the opinion that the hair of a woman should be entwined in two braids and placed on the chest. One should not attach much importance to such trifling matters.

1262 Umm 'Aṭiyyah reported: We entwined the hair of the daughter of the Prophet ﷺ in three braids. And Wakī' said that Sufyān said: One braid on the forehead and two on the sides of the head.[39]

Ch. 17: To set the hair of a woman in three braids and push them towards the back

1263 Umm 'Aṭiyyah reported: One of the daughters of the Prophet ﷺ died, so he came to us and said: "Wash her with leaves of the lote-tree an odd number of times, three or five times, or more than that if you see it necessary, and at the end sprinkle camphor — or a little camphor — on her, and when you have finished, let me know." So when we finished, we informed him and he threw his waist-sheet towards us. Then we entwined her hair in three braids and pushed them towards her back.[40]

Ch. 18: White cloth for the shroud[41]

1264 'Ā'ishah reported that the Messenger of Allāh ﷺ was shrouded in three Yemenite sheets of white washed cotton (*saḥūliyyah min kursuf-in*), and there was neither a shirt nor a turban.[42]

Ch. 19: To shroud the dead in two sheets

1265 Ibn 'Abbās reported: A man was stopping at 'Arafāt when (while riding) he fell down from his mount and broke his neck, or he was crushed by it (and died). The Prophet ﷺ said: "Wash him with water and leaves of the lote-tree and shroud him in two pieces of cloth, neither apply perfume to him, nor cover his head, for he will be raised on the Day of Resurrection saying *Labbaika* (i.e., like a pilgrim)." [43]

---

[39] This again is a repetition of h. 1254.

[40] This again is a repetition of h. 1254, in wording very similar to that of h. 1258. The last statement is different and the chapter heading is related to this.

[41] The ḥadīth in this chapter only mentions that the colour of the shroud of the Holy Prophet was white. In Tirmidhī (h. 994) and other collections it is stated that after mentioning white clothes the Holy Prophet said: "Shroud your dead in them."

[42] The most authentic report about the shroud of the Holy Prophet is that it was made of cotton (*kursuf*). The word *saḥūliyyah* is from *suhūl* which means 'washerman' and is also the name of a village.

[43] It is mentioned in the Book 'Penalty for Hunting (on Pilgrimage)' that the Holy Prophet said: "Shroud him in his two pieces of cloth" (h. 1851), i.e., what he was wearing for *Iḥrām*. The reason for burial in the *Iḥrām* sheets may be due to the reverence for the state of *Iḥrām*. It is also written in *Fatḥ al-Bārī*: "if there is no other cloth available", i.e., besides the *Iḥrām*. The fact is

Ch. 20: To apply perfume to the dead body

1266 Ibn 'Abbās reported: A man was stopping with the Messenger of Allāh ﷺ at 'Arafāt when (while riding) he fell down from his mount and broke his neck, or he was crushed by it (and died). The Messenger of Allāh ﷺ said: "Wash him with water and leaves of the lote-tree and shroud him in two pieces of cloth, neither apply perfume to him, nor cover his head, for Allāh will raise him on the Day of Resurrection saying *Labbaika* (i.e., like a pilgrim)." [44]

Ch. 21: How to shroud one in state of *iḥrām*

1267 Ibn 'Abbās reported: A man's neck was broken by his camel when we were with the Prophet ﷺ and the man was in the state of *Iḥrām*. The Prophet ﷺ said: "Wash him with water and leaves of the lote-tree and shroud him in two pieces of cloth, neither apply perfume to him, nor cover his head, for Allāh will raise him on the Day of Resurrection saying *Labbaika* (i.e., like a pilgrim)." [45]

1268 Ibn 'Abbās reported: A man was stopping with the Prophet ﷺ at 'Arafāt (riding), when he fell down from his mount — Ayyūb said: He broke his neck, 'Amr said: He was crushed by it — and he died. He (the Holy Prophet) said: "Wash him with water and leaves of the lote-tree and shroud him in two pieces of cloth, neither apply perfume to him, nor cover his head,

---

that as the garb for *Iḥrām* consists of two pieces of cloth, these can conveniently serve as the shroud. As to being raised on the Day of Resurrection reciting *Labbaika* ("Here I am in Your presence, O Allāh"), this indicates that a person is raised to life again in the same spiritual condition as that in which he was at the time of his death. For repetitions of h. 1265, see h. 1266 to h. 1268 below, and h. 1849 to h. 1851 later on.

[44] This is a repetition of h. 1265. The words "neither apply perfume to him, nor cover his head", which the Holy Prophet said about a person in the state of *Iḥrām*, who died after falling off from a camel, show that usually perfume was sprayed on the body and the head was washed. It was only regarding this deceased person that the Holy Prophet forbade the spraying of perfume and he also ordered that his head not be covered. This does not mean that the person remains in the state of *Iḥrām* even after his death. It is just to honour the state of *Iḥrām* because in that state a person forsakes everything in the world.

[45] This is again a repetition of h. 1265 with a slight difference in wording. Here, instead of the words *wa lā tuḥanniṭū-hu*, the words *wa lā tumissū-hu ṭīb-an* have been used, both having the meaning "do not apply perfume to him." Again, at the end, in some manuscripts, instead of the word *mulabbiy-an*, the word used is *mulabbad-an*. Apparently it is an error in the narration because *mulabbiy-an* means "while reciting *Labbaika*" while *mulabbad-an* means hair kept together with jell, which is done to prevent it from being scattered while in *Iḥrām*. In all other repetitions too, the word *mulabbiy-an* has been used. In h. 1268 we find the following: Ayyūb said: *Yulabbiy* ("He will recite *Labbaika*") and 'Amr said: *Mulabbiy-an* ("reciting *Labbaika*").

for he will be raised on the Day of Resurrection. Ayyūb said: He will recite *Labbaika*, and 'Amr said: reciting *Labbaika* (i.e., like a pilgrim)." [46]

Ch. 22:　To shroud (a dead body) in a stitched or unstitched shirt and one who is shrouded without a shirt

1269 'Abdullāh ibn 'Umar reported that when 'Abdullāh ibn Ubayy (the head of the hypocrites) died, his son came to the Prophet ﷺ and said: "(I request that you) grant me your shirt to shroud him in it, and say his funeral prayer, and ask for Allāh's forgiveness for him." So the Prophet ﷺ gave his shirt to him and said: "Let me know (when the funeral is ready) so that I may say the funeral prayer." So he informed him and when he (the Prophet) intended to offer the funeral prayer, 'Umar pulled him aside and said: "Has Allāh not forbidden you from saying funeral prayers for the hypocrites?" He (the Prophet) said: "I have been given discretion, as Allāh says: 'Ask forgiveness for them (i.e., hypocrites), or ask not forgiveness for them. Even if you ask forgiveness for them seventy times, Allāh will not forgive them' (the Qur'ān, 9:80)." So he said the funeral prayer for him. Then this revelation came: "And never offer prayer for any of them who dies nor stand by his grave" (the Qur'ān, 9:84).[47]

1270 Jābir said: The Prophet ﷺ came to (the grave of) 'Abdullāh ibn Ubayy after he was placed in the grave. He had the body brought out and then he put some of his saliva into his mouth and clothed him in his own (i.e., the Holy Prophet's) shirt.[48]

---

[46] This is again a repetition of h. 1265, but in words similar to those of h. 1266. See previous note for the closing statements by Ayyūb and 'Amr.

[47] 'Abdullāh ibn Ubayy was the well-known leader of the hypocrites and was secretly an inveterate enemy of the Muslims. He tried his best to cause great harm to them, but failed. His son, who was a Muslim, asked the Holy Prophet to gift him his shirt so that he could wrap his father's dead body in it as a blessing. He also requested the Holy Prophet to say the *Janāzah* prayer for him, to which he assented because, apparently, the deceased was a Muslim and had recited the *Kalimah*. 'Umar drew the Holy Prophet's attention to the verse of the Qur'ān: "Ask forgiveness for them or ask not forgiveness for them…" (9:80), whereupon the Holy Prophet said: "I have been given discretion." The Holy Prophet's deepest sympathy for such a bitter enemy shows that his kindness and mercy knew no bounds. It was after this incident that Allāh strictly forbade him from saying the *Janāzah* prayer for such hypocrites about whom he was informed by Allāh. This ḥadīth occurs in more detail in Bukhārī's book, *Commentary on the Qur'ān* (h. 4670–4672). It also occurs in more detail in h. 1350, particularly with further information about the shirt.

[48] In h. 1269 it was mentioned that his son came to the Holy Prophet and he gave his shirt to him (*fa-a'ṭāhu qamīsa-hu*), but here it is mentioned that his body was taken out from the grave and clothed with the Holy Prophet's shirt. Either h. 1269 means that the Holy Prophet promised

Ch. 23:   To shroud (the dead) without a shirt

1271 'Ā'ishah reported: The Prophet ﷺ was shrouded in three sheets of washed cotton (*saḥūl kursuf-in*), and there was neither a shirt nor a turban.[49]

1272 'Ā'ishah reported that the Messenger of Allāh ﷺ was shrouded in three sheets, and there was neither a shirt nor a turban.[50]

Ch. 24:   To shroud (the dead) without a turban

1273 'Ā'ishah reported that the Messenger of Allāh ﷺ was shrouded in three sheets of white washed (cotton), and there was neither a shirt nor a turban.[51]

Ch. 25:   Shroud (to be paid for) out of all wealth (of the deceased)[52]

This is also said by 'Aṭā', az-Zuhrī, 'Amr ibn Dīnār and Qatādah. 'Amr ibn Dīnār said: Perfume should be (paid for) out of his property. Ibrāhīm said: The first thing to be paid for is the shroud, then any debt and then the will. Sufyān said: The expenses for the grave and the washing (of the body) are a part of (what is known as expenses of) the shroud.

1274 Ibrāhīm (ibn 'Abdur Raḥmān) reported: One day his meal was brought to 'Abdur Raḥmān ibn 'Auf and he said: "Muṣ'ab ibn 'Umair was

---

to give his shirt, or in h. 1270 the correct order has not been maintained and all the events have been mentioned together in one place along with the mention of the shirt in which he had already been clothed. It may be that Holy Prophet reached late and the body had already been laid into the grave and then he had the body taken out in order to clothe him with the shirt, and the *Janāzah* prayer was also performed. While all this was done according to the wishes of his son 'Abdullāh, the Holy Prophet's putting his saliva into the mouth of the deceased was his own act which shows the Holy Prophet's deep love and sympathy which he had extended even to his enemies. As the Qur'ān says to him: "And We have not sent you but as a mercy to the nations" (21 : 107). See also h. 1350.

[49] This is a repetition of h. 1264 in the same wording except for the omission of the words *Yamāniyah* (Yemenite) and *bīḍ* (white). This chapter heading has also occurred at the end of the heading of the last chapter, and for this reason in some manuscripts this chapter does not exist. The meaning is that an ordinarily worn shirt is not usually used as a shroud and that is why such a shirt was not used as shroud for the Holy Prophet. In the next two reports the wording is almost the same as here except that in h. 1272 the words *saḥūl kursuf* do not occur and in h. 1273 the word *kursuf* does not occur.

[50] This is a repetition of h. 1264 in the words of h. 1271, without the words *saḥūl kursuf* (washed cotton).

[51] This is a repetition of h. 1264 in the words of h. 1271, without the word *kursuf* (cotton), but the word *bīḍ* (white) does occur here as in h. 1264.

[52] Out of the deceased person's estate, burial expenses are to be paid first of all.

killed and he was better than me. Nothing could be found to shroud him except one sheet. Ḥamzah, or another man, was killed and he was better than me. Nothing could be found to shroud him except one sheet. Indeed I fear that the rewards of our deeds have been given to us earlier in this world's life." Then he started weeping.[53]

Ch. 26: When only one sheet is available for the shroud

1275 Ibrāhīm (ibn 'Abdur Raḥmān) reported that a meal was brought to 'Abdur Raḥmān ibn 'Auf and he was fasting. He said: "Muṣ'ab ibn 'Umair was killed and he was better than me. He was shrouded in one sheet, (so short) that when his head was covered with it, his feet were bare, and when his feet were covered his head was bare." And I think he said: "Ḥamzah was killed and he was better than me. Now worldly wealth has been made abundant for us — or he said "we have been granted worldly wealth that we have". Indeed we fear that the rewards of our deeds have been given to us earlier (i.e., in this world)." Then he started weeping and left his food.[54]

Ch. 27: When only sufficient cloth for the shroud is available to cover either the head or the feet, then the head should be covered

1276 Khabbāb related: We emigrated with the Prophet ﷺ seeking Allāh's pleasure, and so it was Allāh Who was to grant us reward for it. Some of us died without taking anything from their rewards in this world, and among them was Muṣ'ab ibn 'Umair; and the others got it when their reward became due. He was killed in the Battle of Uḥud and we could get nothing except a sheet to shroud him in it. And when we covered his head, his feet were out, and when we covered his feet, his head was out. So the Prophet ﷺ ordered us to cover his head and to put some *idhkhir* (*idh-khir,* a kind of grass) over his feet.

Ch. 28: One who prepared his shroud in the time of the Prophet ﷺ and no objection was raised

1277 Sahl reported that a woman brought a woven sheet (*burdah*) with borders to the Prophet ﷺ. Then Sahl asked people: "Do you know what is *burdah*?" They said: "A cloak." He said: "Yes." (Sahl continued:) Then the

---

[53] This is a briefer repetition of the next ḥadīth, h. 1275. See next footnote.

[54] This incident relates to the time when Muslims became affluent. So 'Abdur Raḥmān ibn 'Auf, who was one of the ten Companions who were given the promise of Paradise by the Holy Prophet (the *'asharah mubashsharah*), reminded people of the time when even enough cloth was not available to cover the entire dead body.

woman said: "I have woven it with my own hands and I have brought it to put it on you." The Prophet ﷺ accepted it, and he was in need of it. So he came out to us, wearing it as his waist-sheet. A man praised it and said: "Will you give it to me? It is beautiful!" People said: "You have not done a good thing as the Prophet ﷺ is in need of it and you have asked for it when you know that he does not turn anyone down." [55] The man replied: "By Allāh! I have not asked for it to wear it, I only asked for it to make it my shroud." Sahl said: "Later it was his shroud."

Ch. 29: Women accompanying a funeral procession

1278 Umm ʿAṭiyyah reported: We (women) were prohibited from accompanying a funeral procession, but it was not an absolute prohibition.[56]

Ch. 30: Mourning of a woman for someone other than her husband

1279 Muḥammad ibn Sīrīn reported: One of the sons of Umm ʿAṭiyyah died, and when it was the third day she asked for some yellow perfume and rubbed it over her body, and said: "We (women) are forbidden to mourn for more than three days, except for our husbands." [57]

1280 Zainab, daughter of Abū Salamah, reported: When the news of the death of Abū Sufyān was received from Syria, Umm Ḥabībah, on the third day, asked for some yellow perfume and scented her cheeks and forearms, and she said: No doubt, I would not have used it, had I not heard the Prophet ﷺ saying: "It is not permissible for a woman who believes in Allāh and the Last Day to mourn for more than three days any dead person except her husband whom she should mourn for four months and ten days." [58]

1281–1282 Zainab, daughter of Abū Salamah, reported: I went to Umm Ḥabībah, wife of the Prophet ﷺ, and she said: I heard the Messenger of Allāh ﷺ saying: "It is not permissible for a woman who believes in Allāh and the

---

[55] This ḥadīth and so many others like it stand witness to the unique generosity practised by the Holy Prophet, who was one who never refused a person who asked him for something.

[56] For almost every act of worship, Bukhārī has allocated a separate chapter to the participation of women in it. It shows that in his view unnecessary imposition of restrictions on women is not only absent from the teachings of Islām but it is against Islām. Women tend to wail and cry excessively over the dead body. That was why they were prohibited from accompanying the funeral procession. Otherwise, as such there is no harm in their accompanying the dead body. In fact, it may at times be useful for them, so that if it happened that no men were available women could bury the dead body themselves. That is why Umm ʿAṭiyyah said that women had not been absolutely prohibited to join funeral processions.

[57] She applied perfume in case not using it may be considered as a sign of mourning.

[58] This is a repetition of h. 1281. Abū Sufyān was Umm Ḥabībah's father.

Last Day to mourn for more than three days any dead person except her husband (whom she should mourn) for four months and ten days." [1282] Later I went to Zainab, the daughter of Jaḥsh, when her brother died. She asked for some scent, and after applying it she said: I did not need any scent but I heard the Messenger of Allāh ﷺ saying: "It is not permissible for a woman who believes in Allāh and the Last Day to mourn for more than three days any dead person except her husband (whom she should mourn) for four months and ten days." [59]

Ch. 31: Visiting Graves

1283 Anas ibn Mālik reported: The Prophet ﷺ passed by a woman who was sitting by a grave crying. He said (to her): "Fear Allāh and be patient." She said to him: "Go away, for you have not been struck by a calamity like mine." And she did not recognise him. When she was informed that it was the Prophet ﷺ, she went to his house and there she did not find any guard at his door. She then said (to him): "I did not recognise you." He said: "Truly, patience is (what is shown) when the calamity first strikes." [60]

Ch. 32: Saying of the Prophet ﷺ: "The deceased is sometimes punished because of the crying of the people of his household, if wailing (*nauḥ*) was his custom."

Because of the word of Allāh, the Most High: "Save yourselves and your families from a fire" (66:6). And the Prophet ﷺ said: "Every one of you is a ruler and everyone will be asked about his subjects." But when it (i.e., wailing) is not a custom in his family, then his condition is as described by 'Ā'ishah: "No bearer of a burden bears the burden of another" (the Qur'ān, 6:164). And it is like the word of Allāh: "And if one weighed down by a burden calls on another

---

[59] The *'iddah* or "waiting period" for a widow is four months and ten days. During this period, she is not permitted to adorn herself.

[60] This is a repetition of h. 1252 in more detail. It shows that women used to go to graves. In Ṣaḥīḥ Muslim it is stated: "I had prohibited you from visiting graves, but now you can go" (book: 'Funerals', ch. 36). Perhaps in the beginning they were prohibited to prevent them from indulging in idolatrous practices which happened at graves, or perhaps because they wailed excessively. This ḥadīth also establishes that there was no doorman at the Holy Prophet's house. That did not mean that people could enter his house without permission, since the Qur'ān itself requires people to seek permission before entering any house. It is mentioned in some reports that people used to seek permission through a servant, as happened when 'Umar went to see the Holy Prophet at the place called Mashrabah when he vowed to keep away from his wives for one month. It means that there was no such doorman at the door of the Holy Prophet's house as government officials and important people keep at their doors, preventing needy persons from access to those in authority.

to carry his load, none of it will be carried" (35:18). And what is said about the permission of weeping without wailing. And the Prophet ﷺ said: "Nobody is killed unjustly but a part of the burden of (shedding) his blood is on the first son of Adam". That was because it was he who initiated the custom of killing (unjustly)." [61]

1284 Usāmah ibn Zaid related: A daughter of the Prophet ﷺ sent a message to him: "My child is dying (*qubiḍa*), come to us." [62] He returned the messenger with greetings and said (in reply): "To Allāh belongs whatever He takes and to Him belongs whatever He gives, and everything with Him has an appointed time. So be patient and seek His pleasure." She again sent for him, swearing that he should come. He rose, and with him were Saʻd ibn ʻUbādah, Muʻādh ibn Jabal, Ubayy ibn Kaʻb, Zaid ibn Thābit, and other men. The child was brought to the Messenger of Allāh ﷺ while yielding up to death — I think he (Usāmah) said: as if it was a leather water-skin. His (the Prophet's) eyes started shedding tears. Saʻd said: "O Messenger of Allāh! What is this?" He replied: "It is mercy which Allāh has placed in the hearts of His servants, and Allāh is merciful only to those of His servants who have mercy (on others)."

1285 Anas ibn Mālik reported: We were present at (the funeral of) one of the daughters of the Messenger of Allāh ﷺ, and he was sitting by the grave. I saw his eyes shedding tears. He said: "Is there any man among you who did

---

[61] If *nauḥ* or loud wailing by screaming at someone's death is the custom in a household, and the deceased participated in continuing that custom instead of trying to stop it, then when he dies and his relatives wail over his body he is held responsible for their wailing. Therefore, his being punished for their wailing is not contrary to the principle of the Qur'ān that "no bearer of a burden bears the burden of another" (6:164). This verse has been referred to in the saying of ʻĀ'ishah further on (h. 1288). It is mentioned therein that when this ḥadīth about a dead person being punished for the wailing of his family was narrated before her, she recited this verse of the Qur'ān, meaning that it cannot happen that the deceased is punished for the actions of his relatives who are wailing. However, the argument of ʻĀ'ishah only applies if the deceased did not participate in the continuation of the wrong custom of wailing. That is why Bukhārī, in the chapter heading, has added the word "sometimes", i.e. it is sometimes that the deceased is punished for the wailing of his relatives. This narration of ʻĀ'ishah occurs in detail in h. 1288. And further on in this chapter heading, people who innovate wrong customs are held responsible for evil of the people who follow those practices, just as we know that Cain, son of Adam, is held responsible for starting murders in mankind.

[62] There are several opinions about this. Some say it was ʻAlī ibn Abul-ʻĀṣ who was born to Zainab. Others consider it to be ʻAbdullāh ibn ʻUthmān who was born to Ruqayyah. Still others consider him to be Muḥsin ibn ʻAlī ibn Abū Ṭālib. But according to *Fatḥ al-Bārī* it is correct to say that it was not a boy but a girl whose name was Imāmah, and the word *qubiḍa* (literally, "has died") was used as the child was close to death since the words further on show that the child was still alive. It is also established that Imāmah remained alive and ʻAlī married her after Fāṭimah's death.

not go near to his wife last night?" Abū Ṭalḥah said: "I (did not)." He (the Prophet) said: "Get down (in her grave)." So he got down in her grave.[63]

1286 'Abdullāh ibn 'Ubaidullāh ibn Abū Mulaikah informed: One of the daughters of 'Uthmān died at Makkah, and we went to attend her funeral. Ibn 'Umar and Ibn 'Abbās were also present. I sat between them — or the reporter said: I sat next to one of them and the other came and sat besides me. 'Abdullāh ibn 'Umar said to 'Amr ibn 'Uthmān: "Will you not prohibit crying as the Messenger of Allāh ﷺ has said: 'The deceased is punished because of the crying of his relatives over him'?"[64]

1287 Ibn 'Abbās said: Sometimes 'Umar used to say it (that the deceased is punished because of the crying of his relatives over him). Then he added: I accompanied 'Umar on a journey from Makkah till we reached Al-Baidā'. There he saw some riders in the shade of a *samurah* tree. He said (to me): "Go and see who those riders are." So I saw that one of them was Ṣuhaib. I told this to him, and he asked me to call him. So I went back to Ṣuhaib and said: "Come and see the Chief of the Believers." Later, when 'Umar was stabbed, Ṣuhaib came in weeping and saying: "O my brother, O my friend!" So 'Umar said to him: "O Ṣuhaib! Are you weeping for me while the Messenger of Allāh ﷺ has said: 'The deceased is sometimes punished because of the crying of his relatives over him'? "[65]

---

[63] This daughter was Umm Kulthūm, who was 'Uthmān's wife. The purpose is to show that to weep or shed tears is part of human nature and is not reprehensible at all. The words *lam yuqārif al-lailah* ("who did not go near to his wife last night"), used in connection with Abū Ṭalḥah going down into the grave, have been the subject of discussion. The word *qārif* means 'to be near something'. Some took its meaning as 'not to be near a sin'. Others took it to mean that he did not go near *his wife*. But neither of these views has anything to do with taking the dead body into the grave. It is not found in the practice of the Holy Prophet that such a condition was ever laid down for taking the dead body, whether of a man or a woman, into the grave. That is why some say that it is an error on the part of the reporter and that the Holy Prophet must have said something else. It is possible that this was the case. Or maybe he said: "Anyone who has not gone near sleep"; that is, he was awake all night for worship, and this act of piety would make him a preferred person for this work. It is also a fact that Abū Ṭalḥah was well skilled in the work of taking a dead body down into the grave. See also h. 1342.

[64] See also h. 1290 and h. 1292.

[65] 'Umar has used the word "sometimes". It means that sometimes crying over the dead body may be the cause of punishment to the deceased, but this is not always the case. The reason for it can only be that which Bukhārī has given in the chapter heading, that the deceased himself allowed or promoted the wrong custom of wailing and shrieking in his family. However, 'Ā'ishah has taken a different view of the saying and specifically applied it to a disbeliever; that is, the punishment of a dead disbeliever is increased because of the crying of the people of his house, and the reason in her view may also have been that the disbeliever allowed this custom while a believer could never do so. Otherwise, whether it is an unbeliever or a believer, neither

1288 Ibn ʿAbbās said: When ʿUmar died I mentioned this to ʿĀʾishah and she said: "May Allāh have mercy on ʿUmar. By Allāh! The Messenger of Allāh ﷺ did not say that Allāh punishes a believer because of the crying of his relatives over him, but he said: 'Allāh increases the punishment of an unbeliever because of the crying of his relatives for him'." She further added: "The Qurʾān is sufficient for you: 'No bearer of a burden bears the burden of another' (the Qurʾān, 6:164, 35:18)." [66] Ibn ʿAbbās then said: "Only Allāh makes one laugh or cry."

Ibn Abū Mulaikah said: By Allāh, Ibn ʿUmar did not say anything.

1289 ʿĀʾishah, wife of the Prophet ﷺ, said: Once the Messenger of Allāh ﷺ passed by (the grave of) a Jewish woman whose relatives were crying over her. He said: "They are crying over her and she is being punished in her grave." [67]

1290 Abū Mūsā reported: When ʿUmar was stabbed, Ṣuhaib started crying: "O my brother!" ʿUmar said: "Do you not know that the Prophet ﷺ said: 'The deceased is punished because of the crying of the living'?" [68]

Ch. 33: Wailing over a deceased is disliked

ʿUmar said: "Leave the women to mourn over Abū Sulaiman as

---

of them can be punished for the misdeeds of someone else. In both cases it is equally against the clear principle of the Qurʾān: "No bearer of a burden can bear the burden of another" (6:164, 35:18), unless the former had led others to the wrong way. The incident of ʿUmar being injured in the murderous attack upon him, mentioned at the end of this ḥadīth, happened later.

[66] In Ṣaḥīḥ Muslim it is recorded that when the ḥadīth related by ʿUmar reached ʿĀʾishah, she said: "You have related to me from the two (ʿUmar and Ibn ʿUmar) who are neither liars nor do they speak untruths, but they must have heard it wrongly" (Muslim, book: 'Funerals', ch. 9). Here too ʿĀʾishah has contradicted the report from ʿUmar that the deceased is punished because some of the people of his house cry over his body. She has categorically stated that the Holy Prophet did not say this, and she quoted a verse of the Qurʾān in support of her stand. Thus it is established that it was the practice of the Companions that when they found any ḥadīth to be contrary to the Holy Qurʾān they immediately rejected it, even though its narrator might be of an exalted stature and reporting directly from the Holy Prophet. They had recourse to the Holy Qurʾān because it was preserved perfectly without error. On the other hand, ḥadīth reports were not preserved to this high standard and there was the strong possibility of error in hearing, narrating and understanding them. Thus any ḥadīth which has come down to us through several narrators, most of whom were not Companions, though the narration itself may be meaningful but it is not manifested in the practice of the Muslims, and is a description of history or events, if such a ḥadīth is against the Qurʾān then to reject it is perfectly in accord with the practice of the Companions.

[67] Here the Holy Prophet did not say that that deceased woman was being punished because of the crying of her relatives, but he stated a fact that they were crying while recounting her virtues but she was being punished for her sins.

[68] Here a portion of h. 1286 has been repeated.

long as they do not throw dust over their heads (*naq'-un*) or scream and cry (*laqlaqah*)." [69] *Naq'u* means to throw dust over the head, and *laqlaqah* means to scream.

1291 Al-Mughīrah reported: I heard the Prophet ﷺ saying, "Surely attributing (something) falsely to me is not like attributing falsely to anyone else. Whoever attributes falsely to me intentionally, let him take his place in the fire (of hell)." And I heard the Prophet ﷺ saying: "The deceased over whom people wail is punished on account of that wailing." [70]

1292 'Umar reported from the Prophet ﷺ that he said: "The deceased is punished in his grave for the wailing done over him." Shu'bah reported (the Holy Prophet as saying): "The deceased is punished for the crying of the living ones over him." [71]

Ch. 34:　Related to the above

1293 Jābir ibn 'Abdullāh said: On the day of the battle of Uḥud, my father's mutilated body was brought and placed in front of the Messenger of Allāh ﷺ and the body was covered with a sheet. I stepped forward in order to remove the sheet from over him but my people forbade me. Again, I went to uncover him but my people forbade me. So the Messenger of Allāh ﷺ gave an order and he was carried away. He heard the voice of a crying woman, and he asked: "Who is this?" They said: "It is the daughter or the sister of 'Amr." He said: "Why is she weeping? — or "Do not weep" — for the angels were keeping him under shade with their wings until he was carried away." [72]

Ch. 35:　He who tears off (the upper part of) his clothes (when grieving) is not one of us

1294 'Abdullāh (ibn Mas'ūd) reported that the Prophet ﷺ said: "He is not one of us who slaps his cheeks, tears off (the upper part of) his clothes, and calls out like the calling out in the days of Ignorance." [73]

---

[69] This shows that mere shedding of tears is not prohibited, but wailing and screaming is forbidden. In other words, to lament loudly and to cry while describing his virtues, or to throw dust over one's head or tear one's clothes, are acts contrary to the showing of patience.

[70] This may also mean that unrestrained lamentations cause pain to the deceased because the mourning is being shown in an improper way. Or it may refer to the deceased who himself was responsible for allowing and participating in that custom.

[71] This is a repetition of h. 1286, consisting of two reports.

[72] This is a repetition of h. 1244 with difference in wording.

[73] It has been prohibited to wail and scream over the body of the deceased, to beat oneself, to tear one's clothes, or (as mentioned later) to read lamentations because such acts artificially

Ch. 36: The Prophet's grieving over (*riṯẖā'*) the death of Saʿd ibn Khaulah[74]

1295 Saʿd ibn Abū Waqqāṣ reported: The Messenger of Allāh ﷺ used to visit me in the year of the last Pilgrimage to enquire after my health when I became seriously ill. I said (to him): "My illness has become very serious and I possess much wealth and have no one to inherit me except a daughter. Should I give two-thirds of my property in charity?" He said: "No." I asked: "Half?" He said: "No." Then he said: "One-third, and even one-third is much. It is better to leave your heirs wealthy rather than to leave them empty-handed, begging from people. And whatever you spend seeking the pleasure of Allāh you will be rewarded for it, even for the food you put in your wife's mouth." [75]

---

intensify the feelings of grief. It is natural to feel grief, and that is not in one's control. It is the result of love and mercy which have been implanted in the human heart by Allāh. But to intensify the grief by such outward acts weakens one's patience and removes the quality of courage and perseverance from one's morals. If a great person has died who has done good work in his life, it is better to inspire others by narrating his good works instead of making them mournful by repeating his qualities which will only result in others becoming discouraged and dejected and feel helpless to do the kind of work he had done. It is more worthy that people should be inspired and encouraged to inculcate in them the same noble qualities and devote everything, even their lives, to do their duties and accomplish good deeds as the deceased had done.

Mere mourning, beating oneself, lamenting and tearing of clothes creates fear of death in the heart and is not befitting of a Muslim. The Holy Prophet disliked this so much that he has described such a mourner in this ḥadīth as not being from among Muslims. It certainly does not mean that he is out of the pale of Islam, but such acts of his have been considered most unbecoming of a Muslim as they degrade him and render him bereft of courage and bravery. In such a situation, the Holy Prophet has taught us to pray thus: "O Allāh! I seek refuge in You from grief and distress."

[74] *Riṯẖā'* means to eulogise a deceased person in a gathering or in a group. Literally, it means to praise someone after his death. The term *marṯẖiyyah,* lamenting in verse, is derived from it. It also means to express sadness and grief at the time of someone's death. Here it has been used in this latter sense. Aḥmad ibn Ḥanbal, Ibn Mājah (book: 'Funerals', h. 1660) and Ḥākim have reported from ʿAbdullāh ibn Abū Aufā that the Holy Prophet has forbidden the practice of holding gatherings for mourning, or *marṯẖiyyah* readings, whose set purpose is to make people cry, mourn and grieve.

[75] The Holy Prophet advised Saʿd ibn Abū Waqqāṣ that when one spends in the way of Allāh, whether it is for one's wife or daughter or anyone else, it is considered as charity. He also said that it is better to leave wealth for the heirs than to leave them in poverty. How balanced are his teachings that give guidance both on valuing and safeguarding wealth and on spending it generously in the way of Allāh! It tells us to avoid excessive attachment to kith and kin, and yet also to take care of them. In another narration, instead of *a taṣaddaqu* ("should I give it in charity?") the words are: *ūṣī* ("should I make a will?"). It is clear from this that he was asking about making a will. And as this will pertained to charitable purposes, that is why the words *a taṣaddaqu* have been used. This incident happened at the time of the Farewell Pilgrimage in 10 A.H., many years after the verses in chapter 4 of the Qur'ān about the distribution of

I said: "O Messenger of Allāh! Will I be left behind after my companions (have gone)?" He said: "You will not be left behind, but whatever good deeds you do will raise you in rank and status.[76] You may perhaps live so that some people will benefit from you while others will be harmed by you.[77] O Allāh! Complete the emigration of my Companions and cause them not to turn back on their heels." But the Messenger of Allāh ﷺ felt sorry for poor Sa'd ibn Khaulah that he died in Makkah.[78]

Ch. 37:   Shaving the head at a calamity is forbidden[79]

1296 Abū Burdah ibn Abū Mūsā related: Abū Mūsā became seriously ill and fainted. His head was lying in the lap of a woman of his family and he could not reply to her at all. When he recovered he said: "I absolve myself from (the actions of) those from whom the Messenger of Allāh ﷺ absolved himself. The Messenger of Allāh ﷺ absolved himself from (the actions of) a woman who cries aloud, who shaves her head, and who tears off her clothes (in grief)." [80]

Ch. 38:   He who slaps his cheeks (in grief) is not one of us

1297 'Abdullāh (ibn Mas'ūd) reported from the Prophet ﷺ that he said: "He is not one of us who beats his cheeks, tears off (the upper part of) his clothes, and calls out like the calling out in the days of Ignorance."

---

inheritance had been revealed. Therefore, the verses about the distribution of inheritance have not abrogated the directive to make a will mentioned in chapter 2 in the words: "It is prescribed for you, when death approaches one of you, if he leaves behind wealth for parents and near relatives, to make a bequest in a kindly manner; it is incumbent upon the dutiful" (2:180), because such a bequest was to be made for charitable purposes and not for the heirs.

[76] Sa'd ibn Abū Waqqāṣ was from among the emigrants (*muhājirūn*) and had become ill in Makkah on the occasion of the Farewell Pilgrimage. He thought that if he breathed his last there and could not return to Madīnah then his emigration (*hijrah*) would not be considered accomplished as he would die at that very place from which he had migrated.

[77] Sa'd remained alive for a long time, according to the prophecy of the Holy Prophet, and at his hands Allāh brought about the conquest of Iraq and Iran. It was due to him that the Arabs benefitted and the Persians suffered harm.

[78] Sa'd ibn Khaulah was also a migrant (*muhājir*) and had migrated from Makkah to Madīnah and had died in Makkah. The Holy Prophet expressed his regrets over his death in Makkah. This fact relates it to the chapter heading.

[79] It was an absurd custom dating from the days of Ignorance, and which is still in vogue among Hindus, that when someone dies the near relatives shave their heads, beards and moustaches.

[80] This incident happened when Abū Mūsā was governor of Basrah appointed by 'Umar. He became unconscious and his wife came screaming. In another narration it is mentioned that when Abū Mūsā became conscious he absolved himself from all that his wife did, and said that the Holy Prophet also absolved himself from such foolish acts.

Ch. 39: **Prohibition of wailing and calling out at time of a calamity as in the days of Ignorance**

1298 'Abdullāh (ibn Mas'ūd) reported that the Prophet ﷺ said: ... [81]

Ch. 40: **Whoever sits with a mournful look in an affliction**

1299 'Ā'ishah said: When the Prophet ﷺ received the news of the killing of Ibn Ḥārithah, Ja'far and Ibn Rawāḥah[82] he sat down looking grieved, and I was looking through the chink of the door. A man came and said that the women of Ja'far were crying. The Prophet ﷺ ordered him to forbid them. He went and then came back again saying that they did not obey him. The Prophet said: "Forbid them." Again he came for the third time and said: "By Allāh! They prevailed over us. O Messenger of Allāh!" — 'Ā'ishah presumed he (the Holy Prophet) said: "Fill their mouths with dust." I ('Ā'ishah) said (to that man): "May Allāh stick your nose in the dust (i.e., humiliate you)! You could neither (make the women) carry out the order of Messenger of Allāh ﷺ nor did you refrain from causing distress to the Messenger of Allāh ﷺ."

1300 Anas reported: The Messenger of Allāh ﷺ said the *Qunūt* for one month when the *qurrā'* (men who had memorised the Qur'ān by heart) were killed. I never saw the Messenger of Allāh ﷺ so mournful as he was then.[83]

Ch. 41: **One who does not show his grief in affliction**

Muḥammad ibn Ka'b said: *Jaza'* is to say an evil word and to think an evil thought (about Allāh). And the Prophet Jacob said: "I complain of my grief and sorrow only to Allāh" (the Qur'ān, 12:86).[84]

---

[81] H. 1297 and h. 1298 have the same wording. They are both repetitions of h. 1294, and differ from it only in having the words "beats (*ḍaraba*) his cheeks" instead of "slaps (*laṭama*) his cheeks" as in h. 1294.

[82] This happened during the battle of Mu'tah (see also h. 1246). The Holy Prophet sent an army of three thousand men on this expedition and appointed Zaid ibn Ḥārithah as commander of the army and instructed that if he were killed, then Ja'far should be given the command, and if he, too, were killed then 'Abdullāh ibn Rawāḥah should take over the command. All these were martyred one after another. The Holy Prophet became very grieved over their deaths. 'Ā'ishah was very angry with the man who was unable to prevent women from wailing and lamenting in accordance with the order of the Holy Prophet. See also the end of h. 1304.

[83] This is a repetition of h. 1002 in different words; see also h. 1003. It shows that it is natural to look sad on the demise of friends.

[84] It is a commendable quality to bear grief silently and not to express it openly. It is evident that to mention the prophet Jacob's story here of bearing his grief, and to quote his statement that he complains about it to God alone, is meant to show that he did not openly display his grief on

1301 Anas ibn Mālik said: A son of Abū Ṭalḥah became sick and — he said — died and Abū Ṭalḥah was out of the house. When his wife saw that he was dead, she prepared some food and placed the dead body of the child in a corner of the house. When Abū Ṭalḥah came, he asked: "How is the boy?" She said: "He is taking rest and I hope he is at peace." Abū Ṭalḥah thought that she had spoken the truth.[85] He spent the night and when it was morning he took a bath. When he intended to go out, she informed him that his son had died. He said the (morning) prayer with the Prophet ﷺ and then informed the Prophet ﷺ of what his wife did. The Messenger of Allāh ﷺ said: "Perhaps Allāh will bless you in your night." [86]

Sufyān said that a man from among the Anṣār said: "I saw nine of their sons and all of them memorised the Qur'ān."

Ch. 42:   **Patience should be observed in the first instance when the calamity strikes**

'Umar said: "The burden on the two sides (*'idlān*) and the burden in the centre (*'ilāwah*) — what wonderful blessings are these." (And he recited these verses of the Qur'ān:) "Who, when a misfortune befalls them, say: Surely we are Allāh's and to Him we shall return. Those are they on whom are blessings and mercy from their Lord; and those are the followers of the right course" (2:156–157).[87] And the word of Allāh: "And seek assistance through

---

the disappearance of his son Joseph. The story that Jacob used to weep day and night till he lost his eyesight is not true.

[85] It is mentioned in another report that Umm Sulaim, the wife of Abū Ṭalḥah, asked her husband, after he had rested, that if someone lends something of his own to a family on their asking, and he then wants to take it back, can the family refuse? He replied: No. Then she told him of the son's death. (See Muslim, book: 'Virtues of the Companions', ch. 20: 'Virtues of Abū Talḥah'). She was a courageous, resolute and intelligent woman. Not only did she not display grief herself but she also, in a rational way, exhorted her husband to show patience. What she said at the beginning was not untrue but quite valid and deeply meaningful. Certainly death brings rest and peace and brings an end to all sorts of pains, but the words were couched in such a way that Abū Ṭalḥah did not realise what had actually happened.

[86] It means that Allāh will bless them with children.

[87] *'Idl* is from *'adl*, meaning 'equality'. Each of the weights on the two sides of an animal is called *'idl* because it equals the other in weight. The load which is put in between the two sides is called *'ilāwah*. 'Umar, by using the words *'idlān* ("two sides") and *'ilāwah*, has referred to the three rewards which Allāh grants to people who show forbearance. In other words, he has regarded "blessings and mercy" as *'idlān* and "the right course" as the *'ilawah*. Ṣalāwāt (blessings) here means forgiveness of sins and being guarded from their commission, and *raḥmat* (mercy) means further grace and favours. Thus these two are like *'idlān*. But the third reward, *'ilāwah*, is "true guidance" (*hidayat*), which, besides the two rewards — righteousness and mercy — helps

patience and prayer, and this is hard except for the humble ones"
(2:45).[88]

1302 Anas reported from the Prophet ﷺ that he said: "Patience is (what
is shown) when the calamity first strikes." [89]

Ch. 43:   The Prophet's saying: "We are grieving because of you."

Ibn 'Umar reported from the Prophet ﷺ: "Eyes shed tears and the
heart grieves."

1303 Anas ibn Mālik reported: We went with the Messenger of Allāh ﷺ
to see Abū Saif, a blacksmith, and he was the husband of the wet-nurse of
Ibrāhīm (son of the Holy Prophet). The Messenger of Allāh ﷺ took Ibrāhīm
and kissed him and smelt him. Then we entered Abū Saif's house after that
and Ibrāhīm was breathing his last and the eyes of the Messenger of Allāh ﷺ
started shedding tears. 'Abdur Raḥmān ibn 'Auf said to him: "And even you,
O Messenger of Allāh (are weeping)!" He said: "O Ibn 'Auf, this is mercy."
Then he wept again and said: "The eyes shed tears and the heart is grieved,
but we will not say except what pleases our Lord. Surely by your separation,
O Ibrāhīm, indeed we are grieved." [90]

Ch. 44:   Weeping besides a sick person

1304 'Abdullāh ibn 'Umar reported: Sa'd ibn 'Ubādah fell ill and the
Prophet ﷺ, along with 'Abdur Raḥmān ibn 'Auf, Sa'd ibn Abū Waqqāṣ, and
'Abdullāh ibn Mas'ūd, visited him to inquire after his health. When he came

---

in achieving the desired goal. To reach it is the completion of Divine favours and grace, just as
the *'ilāwah*, the central load, keeps the balance and helps the animal to continue its journey.

[88] In this verse, the method of facing difficulties has been explained. It consists of two things:
patience; that is, to exercise restraint and courage at the time of distress and difficulties and to be
steadfast and not to waver in determination; and, secondly, prayer; that is, to bow down before
Allāh and seek His help and make supplications, and this is what is done during the *ṣalāt* or
regular prayer.

[89] This is a repetition of h. 1252; see also h. 1283. It is true that to exhibit patience by not
wailing or making complaints at the very beginning is the most difficult part. Otherwise, later on,
time is the great healer and a calculated effort is not required then.

[90] Ibrāhīm, son of the Holy Prophet, was born to Maria the Copt. Abū Saif's wife was his
wet-nurse. It was during infancy that he died at the house of his wet-nurse. It was natural for the
Holy Prophet to be mournful and sad on the death of his young, innocent son. He himself was an
embodiment of mercy, as the Qur'ān says: "Certainly a Messenger has come to you from among
yourselves; very painful for him is your falling into distress, most concerned (he is) for you, to
the believers (he is) compassionate, merciful" (9:128). We have already read in h. 1299 how
grieved he was on the death of Ja'far, Ibn Rawāḥah, and others. Similarly, his shedding of tears
and showing grief on the death of his infant child were due to this natural tenderness.

to him he found him surrounded (*ghāshiyah*) by his family members.[91] He asked: "Has he died?" They said: "No, Messenger of Allāh." The Prophet ﷺ wept and when the people saw the Prophet ﷺ weeping, they also wept. He said: "Listen! Allāh does not punish for shedding tears nor for the grief of the heart, but He punishes because of this," and he pointed to his tongue and added: "or He has mercy, and the deceased is punished because of the crying of his relatives over him." [92]

(As to those who wailed) 'Umar used to beat with a stick and throw stones and put dust (over their faces).[93]

Ch. 45:   Prohibition of lamentation and wailing and remonstrating about it

1305 'Ā'ishah said: When the news of the killing of Zaid ibn Ḥārithah, Ja'far and 'Abdullāh ibn Rawāḥah came, the Prophet ﷺ sat down looking grieved, ...[94]

1306 Umm 'Aṭiyyah reported: At the time of the pledge (given by us) to the Prophet ﷺ, he took from us (the oath) that we would not wail, but it was not fulfilled except by five women: Umm Sulaim, Umm al-'Alā', the daughter

---

[91] *Ghāshiyah* is from *ghashiya*, which means 'to cover'. *Ghāshiyatu ahli-hi* means being surrounded by his family members who gathered around him. The words *jamā'at-un ghāshiyat-un* can also be used for this situation. In some reports the words *ahli-hi* ("his family members") are not found and in this case the meaning would be that he was unconscious, because the word *ghāshiyah* is also used for a tribulation which has spread all over.

[92] One is not held to account for shedding tears or for feeling grief in the heart. However, we are certainly held responsible in the eyes of Allāh for using improper words while lamenting in an inappropriate manner. But if some words are said expressing acceptance of the will of Allāh, they bring reward and mercy, as it is stated in the Qur'ān: "Those are they on whom are blessings and mercy from their Lord" (2 : 157). The Holy Prophet's crying on this occasion was in spite of the fact that he was told that Sa'd had not died. This shows that he had so much love for his Companions that extreme distress for them brought tears to his eyes. Sa'd recovered from this illness. Here his statement that the "deceased" is punished because of the crying of his relatives might refer to the dying person because their crying would be causing him distress, as he could not yet be called dead. On the other hand, as already discussed in the note to h. 1294, it may be meant that the deceased used to uphold the custom of wailing and the word *bukā'* as applied here to his relatives means wailing and screaming, not merely shedding tears.

[93] Such harshness is not traceable to the Holy Prophet, but only his prohibition is reported. In h. 1299 it is only mentioned that, when he was told repeatedly that the women relatives of Ja'far were not ceasing their wailing, he said: "Fill their mouths with dust." This was only a reprimand, meaning that they should be made to keep quiet. It is not established from this ḥadīth that their mouths were actually filled with dust, which shows that the Companions took it as a stronger reprimand. It may be that on some occasion 'Umar might have done all this literally, but the *Sunnah* is what the Holy Prophet did and he never resorted to such harshness in his practice.

[94] This is a repetition of h. 1299 with a slight difference in wording. See h. 1299.

of Abū Sabrah who was wife of Mu'ādh, and two others; or the daughter of Abū Sabrah, and the wife of Mu'ādh and another woman.[95]

Ch. 46: To stand for a funeral procession

1307 'Āmir ibn Rabī'ah reported from the Prophet ﷺ that he said: "Whenever you see a funeral procession, stand up till it passes you." Al-Ḥumaidī added (that the Holy Prophet said): "till it passes you or it (the coffin) is set down." [96]

Ch. 47: When to sit down after having stood for a funeral procession

1308 'Āmir ibn Rabī'ah reported from the Prophet ﷺ that he said: "If anyone of you sees a funeral procession and he is not accompanying it, he should stand until he passes it or it passes him, or it (the coffin) is set down before it passes him." [97]

Ch. 48: He who goes with the funeral procession should not sit down until the coffin is set down from people's shoulders, and if he sits down he is to be told to stand up

1309 Sa'īd al-Maqburī reported from his father that he said: While we were accompanying a funeral procession, Abū Hurairah took hold of the hand of Marwān and they both sat down before the coffin was set down. Then Abu Sa'īd came and took hold of Marwān's hand and said: "Get up. By Allāh! This one (i.e., Abū Hurairah) no doubt knows that the Prophet ﷺ forbade us from doing so." Abū Hurairah said: "He (Abū Sa'īd) has spoken the truth." [98]

---

[95] It does not mean that besides these five women all other Muslim women used to wail on such sad occasions, but that out of those who took the pledge not to wail, these five fulfilled their vow whereas others did not. It does not imply that the Holy Prophet used to take a pledge from all women that they should not wail or lament.

[96] This is a repetition of the next ḥadīth, h. 1308. To stand up is to pay respect to the dead and to express sympathy with the bereaved. Such a gesture is helpful to the close relations of the deceased. It is not generally practised among Muslims these days. The Holy Prophet stood up for the funeral procession of a Jew, which shows that this is enjoined for the funeral procession of a Muslim as well as a non-Muslim.

[97] In this ḥadīth it says: "until he passes it or it passes him". In Muslim (book: 'Funerals', ch. 24) and Nasā'ī (book: 'Funerals', h. 1915) the words are only "until it passes him" (ḥattā tukhallifa-hu). Undoubtedly, it means he should stand till the coffin leaves him behind or is set down. Muslims no longer practice this, going so far as to consider this command as abrogated. Christians, on the other hand, do observe this gesture of paying respect to the dead body by not only standing up but also taking off their hats. Unfortunately, Muslims do not show much concern on such occasions.

[98] In the report in Ḥākim it is mentioned that Marwān stood up. This shows that the Companions were courageous enough to tell the truth even to the rulers, and the rulers dared not

1310 Abū Sa'īd al-Khudrī reported from the Prophet ﷺ that he said: "Whenever you see a funeral procession, stand up. He who goes with it should not sit down until it (the coffin) is set down." [99]

Ch. 49:   One who stands for the funeral of a Jew

1311 Jābir ibn 'Abdullāh reported: A funeral procession passed by us and the Prophet ﷺ stood up, and we stood up too. We said: "O Messenger of Allāh! This is the funeral procession of a Jew." He said: "Whenever you see a funeral procession, stand up." [100]

1312 'Abdur Raḥmān ibn Abū Lailā said: Sahl ibn Ḥunaif and Qais ibn Sa'd were sitting in the city of Al-Qādisiyyah. A funeral procession passed by them and they stood up. They were told that funeral procession was of one of the local inhabitants, that is, from among unbelievers under the protection of the Muslims (*ahl adh-dhimmah*).[101] They said: "A funeral procession passed by the Prophet ﷺ and he stood up. When he was told that it was the funeral of a Jew, he said: 'Is it not of a human being?' " [102]

1313 Abū Lailā reported: I was with Qais and Sahl, and they said: "We were with the Prophet." And Zachariah, reporting from ash-Sha'bī who reported from Ibn Abū Lailā, said: Abū Mas'ūd and Qais used to stand up for the funeral procession.

Ch. 50:   Coffin should be carried by men and not women[103]

---

disobey commands of the Holy Prophet. Marwān's sitting prior to the coffin being set down was due only to his lack of knowledge.

[99] This again is a repetition of h. 1308.

[100] The Jews were bitterly hostile towards the Muslims and did not miss an opportunity to try to destroy them. But the Holy Prophet had such high moral qualities that he not only stood up for the passing coffin of a Jew but enjoined Muslims that they must not discriminate between the funeral procession of a Muslim and a non-Muslim: "Whenever you see a funeral procession, stand up," he ordered.

[101] This shows how meticulous the Companions were in following the instructions of the Holy Prophet. *Dhimmīs* or *ahl adh-dhimmah* were non-Muslim subjects living in a Muslim state. Here they have been called *ahl al-arḍ*, lit. 'inhabitants of the land' or local inhabitants, as the Muslims were there as conquerors. Qādisiyyah was situated in Iran.

[102] How immaculate is the teaching of Islam! Whether it is a Jew or a Christian, it is a human being. It is incumbent on every human being that he should pay respect to any dead fellow human being. Today Muslims even ridicule and laugh at the funerals of Muslims of other sects. How far removed are Muslims from what Islam teaches!

[103] Women are generally physically weaker. They should not carry the coffin except where circumstances make it necessary. During the time of the Holy Prophet women used to take part in battles, provide medical care and water to the wounded soldiers and move them from the battlefield to safe camps and even to their homes. Then why is the bearing of coffins prohibited?

1314 Abū Saʿīd al-Khudrī said that the Messenger of Allāh ﷺ said: "When the funeral bier is ready and the men carry it on their shoulders, if the deceased was a righteous person it will say, 'Take me ahead,' and if he was not a righteous person, it will say, 'Woe to it! Where are you taking it?' The voice is heard by everything except any human being, and if he were to hear it he would fall unconscious." [104]

Ch. 51: To make haste in carrying the coffin

> Anas said: "You are taking it (the coffin), so walk ahead of it and behind it and on its right and on its left side." And others said: "(And walk) near to it." [105]

1315 Abū Hurairah reported from the Prophet ﷺ that he said: "Hasten with the coffin, for if the deceased were righteous, you are taking it ahead towards goodness; and if he were otherwise, then you are getting rid of an evil from your necks." [106]

Ch. 52: The dead saying from the bier: "Take me ahead."

1316 Abū Saʿīd al-Khudrī said that the Prophet ﷺ used to say: "When the funeral bier is ready …[107]

What has been mentioned in h. 1314 here, as to men carrying the coffin, is the normal case, that men usually carried the coffin as it is physically laborious work. But it is not forbidden to women. There is a ḥadīth related by Abū Yaʿlā from Anas, which does not fulfil the conditions laid down by Bukhārī, in which it is mentioned that in a funeral procession there were some women as well, so the Holy Prophet asked them: "Do you carry the coffin?" They said: "No." Then he asked: "Do you bury it?" They replied: "No." He said: "Then go back." This does not imply that women were prohibited from performing any of those acts if there is a need. The Holy Prophet has tried to explain that when there is no need for their carrying the coffin or burying it, then there is no apparent benefit to them for accompanying the coffin. Religious scholars have prohibited their accompanying a funeral procession because in their view trouble may arise because of it.

[104] A human being cannot listen to such a voice. Thus, the voice does not come from the mouth of a living being. Either it is meant that it is the inner condition of the deceased which the living ones cannot know, or it may be meant that such a voice is heard by the angels and not by human beings. The comprehensive word *kullu shaiʾ-in* ("everything") has been used but it means only such a being which is related to the human soul because the voice comes from the soul or it is expressive of the spiritual condition of the deceased. See also h. 1338 and h. 1374.

[105] It means that people accompanying the coffin should not be close to one another. They should be in the front and at the back, or they should be on the right and the left, to help in carrying it.

[106] The words *asriʿū bi-l-jināzah* ("hasten with the coffin") includes two things: firstly, to make arrangements for burying the dead as early as possible, and, secondly, to carry it for burial as fast as possible. The purpose is to return to normality as soon as possible. In hot countries where there are no arrangements such as mortuaries, decomposition of the dead body is accelerated if the funeral is delayed.

[107] This is a repetition of h. 1314 in the same words, except that after the words, "if he was not a righteous person, it will say", the following is added: "to his relatives".

Ch. 53: To make two or three rows in a funeral prayer behind the Imām

1317 Jābir ibn 'Abdullāh reported that the Messenger of Allāh ﷺ said the funeral prayer for the Negus (the King of Abyssinia) and I was in the second or third row.[108]

Ch. 54: Rows in a funeral prayer

1318 Abū Hurairah reported: The Prophet ﷺ gave his Companions news of the death of the Negus. Then he went ahead (to lead the prayer) and the people formed themselves in rows behind him and he pronounced four *Takbīrs* (during the funeral prayer).[109]

1319 Ash-Sha'bī reported: One who had seen the Prophet ﷺ informed me that he (the Holy Prophet) came to a grave that was separate (from other graves) and he arranged the people in rows and pronounced four *Takbīrs*. I said: "Who related this to you?" He said: "Ibn 'Abbās." [110]

1320 Jābir ibn 'Abdullāh said that the Prophet ﷺ said: "Today a righteous man from Abyssinia (i.e., the Negus) has died. Let us say the funeral prayer for him." He (Jābir) said: We formed rows and the Prophet ﷺ led the prayer for him and we were in rows. He (Jābir) added: I was in the second row.[111]

Ch. 55: Boys joining men in making rows in a funeral prayer

1321 Ibn 'Abbās reported that the Messenger of Allāh ﷺ passed by a grave of one who had been buried during the night. He asked: "When was he buried?" People said: "At night." He said: "Why did you not inform me?" They said: "We buried him in the darkness of the night and we did not like to wake you up." He stood up and we formed rows behind him. Ibn 'Abbās said: I was one of them, and he (the Holy Prophet) said the funeral prayer for him." [112]

---

[108] This is a repetition of h. 1245. It is not clear whether there were two or three rows, only that the narrator was in the second or third row. But Ṣaḥīḥ Muslim records a report from Jābir that they made two rows (book: 'Funerals', ch. 22). This shows that two rows can be made in the *Janāzah* congregation.

[109] This again is a repetition of h. 1245.

[110] This is a repetition of the incident in h. 1247.

[111] This again is a repetition of h. 1245.

[112] This is a repetition of h. 1247. Ibn 'Abbās at the time was not an adult, and this fact relates it to the chapter heading.

Ch. 56: **Practice of the Holy Prophet (*Sunnah*) about prayer (*ṣalāt*) for funerals**[113]

The Prophet ﷺ said: "He who prays at a funeral" and he said: "Say the funeral prayers for your companion" and he said: "Say funeral prayers for the Negus." He called it *ṣalāt*, in which there is no bowing (*Ruku'*) nor prostration (*Sajdah*), nor any talking; but there is the saying of *Allāhu Akbar* (*Takbīr*) and *Taslīm*. Ibn 'Umar did not say *Janāzah* prayer without performing *Wuḍu'*, nor did he say it at the rising of the sun and at its setting.[114] And he used to raise his two hands (to say *Takbīr*). Al-Ḥasan said: "I found people regarding that person as most entitled to lead the funeral prayer whom they were happy with to lead them in obligatory prayers.[115] And when on Eid day or for funeral prayers a person happens to break wind, he should look for water and may not do *Taya-mmum*.[116] And when he reaches a funeral prayer and people are (already) praying, he should say *Takbīr* and join the congregation." Ibn al-Musayyab said: "One should proclaim four *Takbīrs* whether it is day or night or on a journey or not." Anas said: "One *Takbīr* is to start the funeral prayer." And the word of Allāh: "And never offer prayer for anyone of them (the hypocrites) who dies" (9:84). In a funeral congregation there are rows and an Imām.

1322 Ash-Sha'bī reported: One who passed along with your Prophet ﷺ by a grave that was separate (from other graves) informed me: "He (the Holy Prophet) led us in prayer and we formed rows behind him and prayed." We said: "O Abū 'Amr, who related this to you?" He said: "Ibn 'Abbās." [117]

---

[113] In the terminology of the *Sharī'ah*, the *Janāzah* prayer is called *ṣalāt*. So the conditions which are essential for prayer are also essential for *Janāzah*, such as purity of the body and the clothes, performance of *Wuḍū'*, facing the *Qiblah*, no talking, forming rows behind the Imām, etc. Fulfilling all these conditions clearly shows that in the funeral congregational prayers, besides special supplications, there are some more features distinguishing it from supplications of a general nature. Of course, there is only the standing posture, and neither *Rukū'* nor *Sajdah* is performed.

[114] According to followers of Imām Shāfi'ī, it is permissible to hold *janāzah* prayers at sunrise and sunset as well.

[115] According to followers of Imām Shāfi'ī and according to Imām Yūsuf, the closest relative to the deceased has the greatest right to be Imām.

[116] Some authorities consider that in case of the risk of missing the funeral prayers, a person can perform *tayammum*.

[117] This is a repetition of h. 1247 in words similar to those of h. 1319. The word *ṣallai-nā* ("we prayed") has occurred here and the leading of the prayer and the forming of rows is also mentioned. This is why it is called *ṣalāt* (regular prayer) in the chapter heading.

Ch. 57: Excellence of accompanying a funeral procession

Zaid ibn Thābit said: When you have said the (funeral) prayer, you have discharged the obligation due to you. Ḥumaid ibn Hilāl said: We do not think it necessary to seek permission (to leave) after performing the *Janāzah* prayer, but one who leaves after the prayer will get a reward equal to one *qīrāṭ*.[118]

1323–1324 Nāfiʿ said that Ibn ʿUmar was told that Abū Hurairah said: "Whoever accompanies a funeral will get a reward equal to one *qīrāṭ*." Ibn ʿUmar said: "Abū Hurairah reports a great many sayings for us." [119] [1324] ʿĀ'ishah confirmed Abū Hurairah and said: "I heard the Messenger of Allāh ﷺ saying this." Ibn ʿUmar said: "Then we have neglected (*farraṭ-nā*) to attain numerous *qīrāṭs*." [120]

Farraṭ-tu means "I neglected the command of Allāh." [121]

Ch. 58: To wait till the burial takes place

1325 Abū Hurairah said that he heard the Messenger of Allāh ﷺ say: "Whoever attends the funeral till he says the prayer (for the deceased) will get a reward equal to one *qīrāṭ*, and whoever accompanies it till burial, will get a reward equal to two *qīrāṭs*." Someone asked: "What are two *qīrāṭs*?" He said: "Like two great mountains."

Ch. 59: Boys joining other people in the funeral prayer

1326 Ibn ʿAbbās reported: The Messenger of Allāh ﷺ came to a grave and people said: "He or she was buried at night." Ibn ʿAbbās said: "We formed rows behind him and he prayed over it." [122]

---

[118] The general practice is that after the funeral prayer people ask permission to leave from the relatives who had custody of the body, or those relatives themselves announce that people can leave. It is reported by Ibrāhīm Nakhʿī and Mālik that permission should be sought after the funeral prayer. There are also some weak ḥadīth traceable to the Holy Prophet which are reported about this. Bukhārī has contradicted this by quoting Ḥumaid ibn Hilāl, and the majority also hold that it is not necessary to seek permission to leave. However, it has been stated in h. 1239 and h. 1240 that it is the duty of a Muslim to accompany a funeral, and this includes not only joining the funeral prayers but also helping to carry the coffin and burying the body. But he is given discretion to remain till the burial or leave after the prayer.

[119] This establishes that the Companions, in their time, used to investigate and scrutinise Ḥadīth reports before accepting them. Ibn ʿUmar expressed doubt about the correct reporting of this ḥadīth by Abū Hurairah.

[120] That is, by not accompanying funerals to the burial place, they lost much reward.

[121] *Farraṭ-tu* occurs in the Qur'ān, 39:56, meaning: "I fell short of my duty", or neglected it. Bukhārī, by this reference, explains the use of the same word by Ibn ʿUmar.

[122] This is a repetition of h. 1247. Ibn ʿAbbās was a child at the time.

Ch. 60:   To hold funeral prayer in an Eid prayer ground or mosque[123]

1327–1328 Abū Hurairah reported: The Messenger of Allāh ﷺ gave us news of the death of the Negus, ruler of Abyssinia, on the day he died. He said: "Ask forgiveness for your brother." [1328] Abū Hurairah (also) said: The Prophet ﷺ made them form rows at the prayer ground and he pronounced four *Takbīrs* (during the funeral prayer).[124]

1329 ʿAbdullāh ibn ʿUmar reported that the Jews brought to the Prophet ﷺ a man and a woman from among them who had committed adultery. He gave the order concerning both of them, so they were stoned (to death) near the place where funeral prayers were said besides the mosque.[125]

Ch. 61:   Dislike for the construction of a mosque over a grave

When Al-Ḥasan ibn al-Ḥasan ibn ʿAlī died, his wife put up a tent over his grave for a year and afterwards it was removed. They heard a caller saying: "Have they found what they had lost?" The other replied: "(No,) rather they returned dismayed."[126]

1330 ʿĀ'ishah reported from the Prophet ﷺ that, during his illness in which he died, he said: "Allāh cursed the Jews and the Christians because they took the graves of their prophets as places of worship." ʿĀ'ishah added: "If it were not for this, his (the Holy Prophet's) grave would have been in the open, nonetheless I fear that it might be taken as a mosque."[127]

---

[123] According to Bukhārī, it is permitted to hold funeral prayers in a mosque or Eid prayer ground. Some have disapproved of it but it is established that the funeral prayers for Abū Bakr and ʿUmar were said in the mosque.

[124] This is a repetition of h. 1245. He said the funeral prayers in the Eid prayer ground, but this was *in absentia,* the deceased's body not being there.

[125] This shows that there was a designated place for holding funeral prayers at which these prayers were usually held. It seems that the words "besides the mosque" refer to "near the place where funeral prayers were said", and by mosque is meant the Eid prayer ground. The meaning is that the place for holding funeral prayers was the Eid prayer ground. As it was permissible to hold funeral prayers in the Eid prayer ground, it would also be permissible to hold them in the mosque.

[126] It is not made clear here who the caller was. Perhaps it was a voice from the unseen which came as a revelation or a person who told the wife that she gained nothing by staying at the grave for a year. If she ultimately had to exercise patience and acceptance, she might as well have done so from the beginning. There is no mention in this ḥadīth of the undesirability of building a mosque over a grave but obviously she must have said prayers while living in the tent.

[127] This is a repetition of h. 435–436. The last part in this ḥadīth about what ʿĀ'ishah said does not occur there, but the condition of the Holy Prophet during his illness is mentioned at the opening. ʿĀ'ishah said that if it were not for the fear that his grave would have become a mosque

Ch. 62: Funeral prayer for a woman who died while giving birth

1331 Samurah (ibn Jundub) reported: I prayed behind the Prophet ﷺ for a woman who died during childbirth, and he stood by the central part of her body.[128]

Ch. 63: Where should the Imām stand during the *Janāzah* prayer of a male or a female?

1332 Samurah ibn Jundub related: ...[129]

Ch. 64: *Takbīr* in a funeral prayer (pronounced) four times

Ḥumaid said: "Anas led us in (a funeral) prayer and pronounced three *Takbīrs* and then said *Taslīm*. He was told (about the forgotten *Takbīr*), so he turned towards the *Qiblah* and pronounced the fourth *Takbīr* and then said *Taslīm*." [130]

1333 Abū Hurairah reported that the Messenger of Allāh ﷺ gave (people) news of the death of the Negus (the King of Abyssinia) on the very day that he died. He went with people towards the prayer ground and made them form rows, and he pronounced four *Takbīrs* (during the funeral prayer).[131]

1334 Jābir reported that the Prophet ﷺ prayed for Aṣhamah the Negus, pronouncing four *Takbīrs* (during the funeral prayer).[132]

---

it would have been left in the open, and that she fears it might be made a mosque. She said this at a time when the mosque had not been extended. When it was extended, her chamber was made triangular so that during prayer no one could face it. While such careful precautions were taken to ensure that the Holy Prophet's grave did not become a place of worship, Muslims today prostrate before their spiritual leaders and at their graves.

[128] This is a repetition of h. 332. See the footnote to that ḥadīth.

[129] This is a repetition of h. 1331. In Abū Dāwūd (book: 'Funerals', h. 3194) and Tirmidhī (book: 'Funerals', h. 1034) there is a report from Anas that he stood by the head of the deceased when leading the funeral of a man and stood by the middle for a woman, and said that the Holy Prophet used to do the same. Bukhārī has pointed to the inauthenticity of this report by saying that it is the same whether the deceased is a male or a female. In both cases the Imām stands by the middle of the dead body.

[130] The Companions differed in their practice in this respect. Zaid ibn Arqam and Ibn Mas'ūd reported that they pronounced five *Takbīrs*. 'Alī reported six, five and four *Takbīrs*, and Ibn 'Abbās reported three. It is stated in Musnad Aḥmad and Baihaqī that 'Umar united people on four *Takbīrs*. In Bukhārī the reports mention only four *Takbīrs* and this is in connection with the funeral prayer for the Negus. No greater number of *Takbīrs* is mentioned anywhere in Bukhārī.

[131] This is a repetition of h. 1245 almost exactly.

[132] This again is a repetition of h. 1245. Here the name of the Negus is given as Aṣhamah.

Ch. 65:   **To recite *Al-Fātiḥah* in the funeral prayer**

Al-Ḥasan said: The *Fātiḥah* should be recited (in the funeral prayer) for a child and then one should pray: "O Allāh! Make him what precedes us (to reach Allāh first) and what leads us and what brings us reward." [133]

1335 Ṭalḥah ibn 'Abdullāh ibn 'Auf reported: I said the funeral prayer behind Ibn 'Abbās and he recited the *Fātiḥah* and said: "You should know that it is *Sunnah* (practice of the Holy Prophet)."

Ch. 66:   **Prayer (for the deceased) at the grave after the burial**

1336 Ash-Sha'bī said: One who passed along with the Prophet ﷺ by a grave that was separate (from other graves) informed me that he (the Holy Prophet) led people in (the funeral) prayer and they prayed behind him. I said: "Who related this to you, O Abū 'Amr?" He said: "Ibn 'Abbās." [134]

1337 Abū Hurairah reported that there was a black man or a black woman who used to sweep the mosque and that person died. The Prophet ﷺ did not know about his death. One day he remembered him (or her) and said: "What happened to that person?" People said: "He (or she) has died, O Messenger of Allāh." He said: "Why did you not inform me?" They said: "His story was so and so," meaning, that they considered him to be unworthy of mention. He said: "Show me his grave." So he went to the grave and said prayers over it.[135]

---

[133] 'Abdur Razzāq has reported from Abū Umāmah ibn Sahl that the Holy Prophet's practice (*Sunnah*) for the funeral prayer was as follows: First pronounce *Allāhu Akbar* and then say the *umm-ul-Qur'ān*, i.e. *Sūrah Fātiḥah*, then blessings should be invoked for the Holy Prophet, and then pray earnestly for the deceased. (Nasā'ī in 'Funerals', h. 1989, mentions only the *Fātiḥah* and the *Takbīrs*.) Ḥakim has reported these actions from Ibn 'Abbās, and quoted the prayer for the deceased as said by Ibn 'Abbās as follows:

"O Allāh, your servant and the son of your servant are in need of Your mercy. You are above need of punishing him. If he were righteous, make him even more so, and if he were in error forgive him. O Allāh, deprive us not of his reward, nor let us go astray after this."

[134] This is a repetition of h. 1247 and has occurred several times in this form. Its wording resembles that of h. 857. See above h. 1319 and h. 1322.

[135] This is a repetition of h. 458 with difference in wording. It includes their reply to the Holy Prophet's question: "Why did you not inform me?", which is that they considered deceased to be unworthy of mention. By going to the grave and saying the funeral prayer for the deceased, he taught that none among Muslims is to be regarded as inferior, whatever kind of menial work he or she may do. This is also evidence of the high moral qualities of the Holy Prophet, that he accorded so much honour to an ordinary woman who had died. In both ḥadīth of this chapter it is stated that the Holy Prophet said the funeral prayer by the graveside. The majority believe in this and it is correct. Similarly, to say the funeral prayer more than once is also allowed.

Ch. 67: The dead hears the sound of footsteps

1338 Anas reported from the Prophet ﷺ that he said: "When a human being is placed in his grave and his companions return and go so that he even hears the sound of their footsteps, two angels come to him and make him sit and ask him: 'What did you use to say about this man, Muḥammad?'[136] He says: 'I bear witness that he is the servant of Allāh and His Messenger.' Then it is said (to him): 'Look at your place in the fire (of hell). Allāh has given you instead of it a place in Paradise.' " The Prophet ﷺ added: "So he will see both his places.[137] But an unbeliever or a hypocrite will say (to the angels): 'I had no knowledge, but I only said what people said!' It will be said to him: 'Neither did you (try to) get knowledge nor did you follow (those who had knowledge).' Then he will be hit once with an iron hammer between his two ears, and he will scream which will be heard by whoever will be near him, except people and *jinn*." [138]

Ch. 68: He who loves to be buried in the Holy Land or a place similar to it

1339 Abū Hurairah reported: The angel of death was sent to Moses, and when he went to him Moses slapped him very hard and put out one of his eyes. The angel went back to his Lord and said: "You sent me to a servant who does not want to die." Allāh restored his eye and said: "Go back and tell him to place his hand over the back of an ox, and he will be granted a year (of life) for every hair covered by his hand." Then Moses asked: "O my Lord! What

---

[136] As to whether the dead are able to hear, it is clearly stated in the Qur'ān: "You cannot make the dead to hear" (27:80), because they have departed from this world. The questioning of the deceased in the grave by the angels is done in case of everyone, whether Muslim, hypocrite or unbeliever, as stated in this ḥadīth. However, millions of unbelievers are cremated and their ashes remain on the ground, and there are many whose bodies are preserved but no one ever sees the deceased sitting. This shows that the deceased being made to sit and answer questions does not take place in this world but in the world of the hereafter. What is meant to convey here is that, after death, a human being is transported to another world, and that world is a reality in which one is conscious of life, and it is there that one receives reward or punishment to some extent for the deeds done in this world. H. 86 also mentions the questioning of believers and hypocrites, and their replies.

[137] This tells us that the believer in the grave is shown both hell and paradise, although these are not present in the cemetery. All these matters relate to the world of the hereafter.

[138] In h. 1314 the words are: "The voice is heard by everything except any human being". Here it is stated: "except people and *jinn*", thus excluding the *jinn* as well. This clearly shows that being hit with a hammer and screaming is not taking place in this physical world but in the next world. Being hit between the ears indicates that the person, when alive, did not listen to the call of truth and thus failed to make proper use of his ears, for which he had been granted the faculty of hearing. See also h. 1374.

will happen then?" He said: "Death." He said: "(Let it be) now." Then he asked Allāh to bring him near to the Holy Land to a distance of a stone's throw. And the Messenger of Allāh ﷺ said: "If I were there, I would have shown you his grave by the roadside near the red sand-hill." [139]

Ch. 69: To bury at night

Abū Bakr was buried at night.

1340 Ibn 'Abbās reported: The Prophet ﷺ said the funeral prayer of a man after he was buried at night, he (the Holy Prophet) and his Companions standing up (to do so). He had asked about him, saying: "Who is this?" They said: "He was so-and-so, who was buried during the night." So they said the funeral prayer for him.[140]

Ch. 70: Building a mosque over a grave

1341 'Ā'ishah reported: When the Prophet ﷺ fell ill, some of his wives mentioned a church they had seen in the land of Abyssinia which was called Māriya. Umm Salamah and Umm Ḥabībah had both been to the land of Abyssinia, and they mentioned the church's beauty and the pictures in it. He raised his head and said: "Those are a people who, when a righteous man among them dies, build a place of worship over his grave, then they make these pictures in it. They are the worst of creatures in the sight of Allāh." [141]

---

[139] At the most, this is a story told by Abū Hurairah. It is not a statement by the Holy Prophet, and the only words attributed to him are at the end: "If I were there, I would have shown you his grave…" This indicates that he was shown the grave of Moses in a vision, and he said that he was shown it so clearly that he could point it out if he were there. The reason is that it is stated in the Bible: "but no one knows his grave to this day" (Deuteronomy, 34:6). Moses' asking Allāh to bring him near to the Holy Land may be in reference to what is stated in the opening of ch. 34 of Deuteronomy, i.e., that God showed Moses all the land which the Israelites were promised to enter, but which did not happen in his lifetime. The rest of the story here, including his slapping the angel of death, putting out his eye, the angel returning to Allāh, etc., is either a reporter's own invention or taken by him from Jewish sources and attributed to Abū Hurairah. Or it may be that Abū Hurairah himself has recounted it from some Jewish sources and mixed it up with a vision of the Holy Prophet. This story is contrary to the principles taught in the Qur'ān and authentic ḥadīth reports. In this same report in Book of Prophets in h. 3407 it is stated at the very end that Abū Hurairah reported this from the Holy Prophet. This refers only to the statement of the Holy Prophet, "If I were there…", and not to the story.

[140] This is a repetition of h. 1247 with different wording.

[141] This is a repetition of h. 427. The meaning is that those people start worshipping the grave. This does not mean that the building of a mosque in a cemetery for the worship of Allāh is prohibited.

Ch. 71:   Who should get down into the grave of a woman?

1342 Anas (ibn Mālik) reported: We were present at (the funeral of) the daughter of the Messenger of Allāh ﷺ, and he was sitting by the grave. I saw his eyes shedding tears. He said: "Is there anyone among you who did not go near to his wife last night?" Abū Ṭalḥah said: "I (did not)." He (the Prophet) said: "Get down in her grave." So he got down in her grave and buried her.[142]

Ibn al-Mubārak said that Fulaiḥ said: I think it (i.e., *lam yuqārif* or "did not go near") means "has not committed sin". Abū 'Abdullāh (Bukhārī) says: *li-yaqtrifū* means "that they may commit sin".[143]

Ch. 72:   Funeral prayer for a martyr[144]

1343 Jābir ibn 'Abdullāh reported: The Prophet ﷺ placed together in pairs the men killed at Uḥud, (each pair) in one piece of cloth and then he would ask: "Which of them had learnt more of the Qur'ān?" When one of the two was pointed out to him, he would place that one first in the grave and say: "I shall be a witness for these on the Day of Resurrection." He ordered them to be buried with their blood (still on their bodies) and they were neither washed nor were funeral prayers said for them.[145]

1344 'Uqbah ibn 'Āmir reported: One day the Prophet ﷺ went out and said prayers for the men of Uḥud (i.e., those martyred) as prayers are said for

---

[142] Up to this point, this is a repetition of h. 1285 in almost the same words.

[143] The words *li-yaqtrifū* occur in the Qur'ān, 6:113. See footnote on h. 1285.

[144] In this chapter Bukhārī has included two reports, both relating to the martyrs of Uḥud. The first says that their bodies were not washed before burial nor were funeral prayers said for them. The second says that the Holy Prophet said the same prayer for them as is said in case of those who die. This in fact happened later. It is clear from this that there is no prohibition on holding funeral prayers for martyrs. Perhaps the funeral prayers were not said at the time of burial because the Holy Prophet himself was wounded, as were many of the Companions. Then there was the task of burying them. He gave priority to this task and left the prayers to be said later. By taking the two reports together we conclude that it is not obligatory to hold funeral prayers for martyrs, as it is for others who die, but it is permissible and perhaps the needs of the battle have to be taken into account.

[145] Under the circumstances, sufficient water would not have been available to wash the bodies, and even if it were available the act of washing bodies may have brought loss to the Muslims. For the same reasons, shrouding was not considered necessary and they were buried in their clothes. In addition, not washing off the blood of the wounds, nor saying the funeral prayer, was for the purpose of indicating their high spiritual status. They would meet God, as it were, in the state of martyrdom in which they left this world, and they would have created such strong grounds for being forgiven by Allāh that it became unnecessary for those left behind to pray for the forgiveness of these martyrs. All this was to draw attention to the greatness of the act of being killed in the way of God.

the dead. Then he ascended the pulpit and said: "I will be preceding you and will be a witness for you. By Allāh! I can see my *ḥauḍ* (pond of *Kauthar*) now and I have been given the keys of the treasures of the earth — or the keys of the earth.[146] By Allāh! I fear not that you will worship others besides Allāh after me, but I fear that you will make worldly things your goal."

Ch. 73:   To bury two or three men in one grave

1345 Jābir ibn ʿAbdullāh informed that the Prophet ﷺ placed together in pairs the men killed at Uḥud.[147]

Ch. 74:   Not considering the washing of a martyr as essential

1346 Jābir (ibn ʿAbdullāh) reported that the Prophet ﷺ said: "Bury them with their blood (still on their bodies)", that is, on the day of Uḥud, and they were not washed.[148]

Ch. 75:   Who is to be placed first in the *laḥd*

It is called *laḥd* because it is on the side. *Multaḥad-an* means a refuge. If it is straight (i.e., has no extension on the side), it is called *ḍarīḥ*.[149]

---

[146] According to one report this took place eight years after the battle of Uḥud. The Holy Prophet lived for a little less than seven and a half years after Uḥud but the words of this report show that this took place close to the death of the Holy Prophet. The seeing of the *ḥauḍ* of *Kauthar* ("abundance") refers not only to attaining it in the hereafter, where he and his Companions would receive abundant rewards, but also to the abundance of good that his followers were to receive in this world. He explained that both kinds of abundance are so certain to be bestowed that it is as if he could see it happening with his own eyes. After that, the mention of the keys of the earth indicates the conquests of the Muslims, and it is to this that his concluding words point, expressing his fear that Muslims would receive such abundance of worldly gains that they would become entirely engrossed in the world. This was a clear prophecy which was manifestly fulfilled, as his followers made unparalleled conquests and the whole known world came under their feet. However, they turned away from the religion to the world, and consequently rule on earth was taken away from them. Also fulfilled was the prophecy that idol-worship would never return to Arabia.

[147] This is a repetition of a small part of h. 1343. The Holy Prophet had each pair buried in one grave. In another report it is stated that on the day of Uḥud the Anṣār complained to the Holy Prophet about suffering from wounds and fatigue, and he said: "Dig wide graves and bury two or three in one grave" (Abū Dāwūd, book: 'Funerals', h. 3215). This is permissible at times of need.

[148] This is also repetition of a small part of h. 1343.

[149] *Ilḥād* means to deviate from something. One who deviates from religion is called a *mulḥid*. *Laḥd* is so-called because it deviates from the grave, being dug as an oblong extension or lateral hollow in the grave on the right side. The pit which is dug downwards into the ground is called

1347–1348 Jābir ibn 'Abdullāh reported that the Messenger of Allāh ﷺ placed together in pairs the men killed at Uḥud …[150] [1348] The Messenger of Allāh ﷺ would ask about those killed at Uḥud: "Which of these had learnt more of the Qur'ān?" When a man was pointed out to him, he would place that one first in the grave ahead of his companion. And Jābir said: My father and paternal uncle were shrouded in the same sheet (*namirah*).[151]

Ch. 76:   To spread *idhkhir* or some kind of grass in the grave

1349 Ibn 'Abbās reported from the Prophet ﷺ that he said: "Allāh made Makkah a sacred place. It (i.e., shedding blood therein) was not lawful for anyone before me nor for anyone after me. It was lawful for me for a few hours one day. None of its shrubs should be uprooted, none of its tree cut down, none of its game chased, and no fallen thing in it to be picked up except by one who makes announcement (to find the owner)." Al-'Abbās said: "Make an exception for *al-idhkhir* (*idh-khir,* a kind of grass), for (the use of) our goldsmiths and for our graves." So he (the Prophet) said: "Except *al-idhkhir.*"

Abū Hurairah reported from the Prophet ﷺ (the words): "for our graves and our houses." Ibn 'Abbās said: "for their blacksmiths and their houses." [152]

Ch. 77:   Can a dead body be taken out of the grave and *laḥd* for some reason?

1350 Jābir ibn 'Abdullāh said: The Messenger of Allāh ﷺ came to 'Abdullāh ibn Ubayy after he had been laid in his grave. He ordered regarding him (i.e., that he be taken out), so he was taken out. He placed him on his knees and put some of his saliva on him, and clothed him in his own (i.e., the Holy Prophet's) shirt — Allāh knows best (why he did it). He ('Abdullāh ibn Ubayy) had given his shirt to 'Abbās to wear (on some past occasion). The

---

ḍarīḥ and *shaqq*. The word *multaḥad-an* occurs in the Qur'ān, meaning a refuge (see 18:27 and 72:22).

[150] Up to this point, this is a repetition of the whole of h. 1343 with two minor differences: the words "on the Day of Resurrection" are omitted here after "I shall be a witness for these", and the words at the close of h. 1343 are reversed in their order so as to read: "neither were funeral prayers said for them nor were they washed". After repeating the whole of h. 1343, another version of the report has been added, numbered here as h. 1348.

[151] Of the two in the pair, the one having greater knowledge of the Qur'ān was buried first; hence the heading of the chapter. The man buried with Jābir's father was 'Amr ibn al-Jamūḥ. He was a friend of Jābir's father, 'Abdullāh ibn 'Amr, and was married to Hindah, sister of Jābir's father. In this report Jābir has called him paternal uncle out of respect. The word *namirah* means a striped sheet.

[152] This is a repetition of h. 112 with brevity and an additional part by Ibn 'Abbās.

Messenger of Allāh ﷺ was wearing two shirts at the time. The son of 'Abdullāh ibn Ubayy said to him: "O Messenger of Allāh, Make my father wear your shirt which has been touching your skin." Sufyān said: It is thought that the Prophet ﷺ made 'Abdullāh ibn Ubayy wear his shirt as recompense for what he had done.[153]

1351 Jābir reported: When the time of (the Battle of) Uḥud approached, my father called me at night and said: "I think I will be among the first of the Companions of the Prophet ﷺ to be killed and I do not leave after me anyone dearer to me than you, except the life of the Messenger of Allāh ﷺ.[154] I have some debt and you should repay it and I exhort you to treat your sisters well." So in the morning he was the first to be killed and was buried along with another (who was killed) in his grave. I did not like to leave him with the other, so I took him out (of the grave) after six months and he was just as he was on the day I buried him, except for his ear.[155]

1352 Jābir reported: A man was buried with my father (in the same grave) and I did not like it. So I took him out (i.e., his father) and buried him in a separate grave.[156]

Ch. 78:   The *laḥd* and the *shaqq* in the grave

1353 Jābir ibn 'Abdullāh reported: The Prophet ﷺ placed together in pairs the men killed at Uḥud and then he would ask: "Which of them had learnt more of the Qur'ān?" When one of the two was pointed out to him, he would place that one first in the grave and say: "I shall be a witness for these on the Day of Resurrection." He ordered them to be buried with their blood (still on their bodies) and they were not washed.[157]

---

[153] This is a repetition of h. 1270 in more detail. The recompense was for 'Abdullāh ibn Ubayy giving his shirt to 'Abbās when the latter was taken prisoner by the Muslims at the end of the battle of Badr. See also h. 1366.

[154] This gives an idea of the great love entertained by the Companions for the Holy Prophet, even though Jābir was his only son, the rest being daughters.

[155] It is reported in the Muwaṭṭa' of Imām Mālik that 'Amr ibn al-Jamūḥ and Jābir's father 'Abdullāh ibn 'Amr al-Anṣārī were buried in the same grave but flooding was removing the earth from the grave so it was dug up to bury the bodies elsewhere, and this was 46 years after the battle of Uḥud. It is possible that Jābir had re-buried his father in another grave nearby and due to this proximity the two graves seemed to be one. Or, a narrator of the report in Muwaṭṭa' made a mistake.

[156] This is a repetition of only the last part of h. 1351.

[157] This is a repetition of h. 1343 with two omissions: the mention of "one piece of cloth" and, at the end, their funeral prayers not being said. It is mentioned that the body of the man who

Ch. 79: **Can the funeral prayer be said for a boy who embraces Islām and then dies? Can Islām be presented to a boy?**

Al-Ḥasan, Shuraiḥ, Ibrāhīm, and Qatādah said: When one of the parents becomes a Muslim, the child will be with the Muslim (in religion). Ibn 'Abbās, with his mother, was considered among the weak and he was not with his father in following the religion of his people. He (the Holy Prophet) said: "Islam overcomes, and it is never overcome." [158]

1354–1355 Ibn 'Umar informed that 'Umar set out with the Prophet ﷺ in a group to Ibn Ṣayyād till they found him playing with the boys near the houses of Banī Mughālah. Ibn Ṣayyād was at that time approaching puberty and did not notice (us) until the Prophet ﷺ struck him with his hand and then he said to Ibn Ṣayyād: "Do you bear witness that I am the Messenger of Allāh?" Ibn Ṣayyād looked at him and said: "I bear witness that you are the Messenger of the unlettered people." [159] Then Ibn Ṣayyād said to the Prophet ﷺ: "Do you bear witness that I am Messenger of Allāh?" He (the Prophet) ignored it and said: "I believe in Allāh and in His Messengers." Then he said to him (i.e., to Ibn Ṣayyād): "What do you see (of the unseen)?" Ibn Ṣayyād said: "True and false news come to me." The Prophet ﷺ said: "Truth has become confused to you." Then the Prophet ﷺ said to him: "I have kept something in my mind for you (what is it?)" Ibn Ṣayyād said: "It is *Al-Dukh* (the smoke)." He (the Prophet) said: "Go away! You cannot go beyond your

---

knew more of the Qur'ān was placed into the *laḥd* (the extension dug to one side at the floor of the grave) ahead of the other body. In the chapter heading both words *laḥd* and *shaqq* (the pit which is dug straight downwards) have occurred. Perhaps Bukhārī is drawing the conclusion that the one who knew the Qur'ān more was placed in the *laḥd* and the other in the *shaqq,* and thus both spaces may be used. The meaning may also be that putting the body in the *shaqq* has not been disallowed, but as the *laḥd* is more spacious, it was given preference.

[158] In the chapter heading the word *ṣabbī* occurs and this is applicable to a child from its infancy till it attains adulthood. Here it means children who have reached the age of understanding though they have not yet become adults. Such boys can be presented with the teachings of Islām. The teachings of Islām are so simple to understand that a man of ordinary intellect too can follow them. Its basic principle, that God is one, is itself ingrained in human nature and therefore it is not difficult for even a child to understand it. And if one of the parents becomes a Muslim then the children are most likely to come into the fold of Islām. Ibn 'Abbās became a Muslim along with his mother when he was still a child.

[159] Ibn Ṣayyād was a Jewish boy who lived in Madīnah. The purpose of narrating his story is simply to show that although he had not attained adulthood, though he was near it, yet the Holy Prophet presented Islām to him. It is meant to show that Islām can be presented even to a boy who is not an adult but is intelligent enough to understand it. When the Holy Prophet asked him: "Do you bear witness that I am the Messenger of Allāh?", he replied: "I bear witness that you are the Messenger of the unlettered people" (i.e., of the Arabs). In other words, he did not believe him to be a messenger for the People of the Book (i.e., Jews). But later he became a Muslim.

level (of understanding)." [160] On that 'Umar said: "O Messenger of Allāh! Allow me to strike off his neck." The Prophet ﷺ said: "If he is him (i.e., Dajjāl), then you cannot overpower him, and if he is not, then it is no good killing him." [161]

[1355] Sālim said that he heard Ibn 'Umar saying: Then after that the Messenger of Allāh ﷺ went along with Ubayy ibn Ka'b to the date-palm trees where Ibn Ṣayyād was staying. He (the Prophet) wanted to hear something from Ibn Ṣayyād before Ibn Ṣayyād saw him. The Prophet ﷺ saw him lying under his sheet, murmuring inside it. Ibn Ṣayyād's mother saw the Messenger of Allāh ﷺ hiding behind the trunks of the date-palm trees. She said to Ibn Ṣayyād: "O Ṣāf!" — this was his pet name — "Here is Muḥammad." So Ibn Ṣayyād got up. The Prophet ﷺ said: "Had she left him (as he was), he would have disclosed (his reality)."

1356 Anas reported: A Jewish boy used to serve the Prophet ﷺ and he fell ill. So the Prophet ﷺ went to ask after him. He sat near his head and said to him: "Become a Muslim." The boy looked at his father, who was sitting by him, and he said: "Obey Abu-l-Qāsim" (i.e., the Holy Prophet). So the boy became a Muslim. The Prophet ﷺ came out and said: "Praise be to Allāh, Who saved him from hellfire." [162]

1357 Ibn 'Abbās said: My mother and I were among the weak (al-mustaḍ'afīn), I being from among the children, and my mother from among the women.[163]

---

[160] The story of Ibn Ṣayyād raises many difficulties. A detailed discussion about it will come later on. It appears that he used to make predictions like astrologers do, and also claimed to have knowledge about matters of the unseen. That is why when the Holy Prophet asked him about his predictions, he admitted that what he predicts turns out sometimes to be true and sometimes to be wrong. It also appears that he used to deceive people by claiming that he could read their minds. Perhaps the Holy Prophet questioned him just to prove that he was not true in what he claimed. However, it does appear that much of the details of the story are fabricated.

[161] Here the reference is taken to be to the Antichrist (ad-Dajjāl). Some of the Companions inferred that Ibn Ṣayyād was the Antichrist even though the sign of Dajjāl given by the Holy Prophet, that he would have the letters *k f r* (meaning disbelief) written on his forehead, was obviously not fulfilled in him. This shows that they did not take such signs literally. Also the Holy Prophet himself did not say here that Ibn Ṣayyād cannot be Dajjāl because he does not have the letters *k f r* written on his forehead, nor does he have an ass, nor does he possess God-like powers, these being the chief signs of Dajjāl as prophesied by the Holy Prophet.

[162] Such were the sublime moral qualities of the Holy Prophet which had won over the hearts of even the Jews. A servant who is a Jew falls ill and the Holy Prophet goes to see him to enquire about his health. The boy asks his father's permission to accept Islām and the father allows him. This shows that the father was also inwardly convinced of the truth of Islam.

[163] Ibn 'Abbās is here referring to the description in the Qur'ān of the weak left behind in Makkah after most Muslims emigrated from it: "...the weak (al-mustaḍ'afīn) among the men

1358 Ibn Shihāb said: The funeral prayer should be held for every deceased child even if he was of illegitimate birth, because he was born conforming to the nature of Islām.[164] If his parents claim to be followers of Islām, or only his father while his mother were not a follower of Islām, and the child cries at birth, then the funeral prayer must be held for him. And if the child does not cry at birth (i.e., is born dead) then his funeral prayer should not be held, as the pregnancy was incomplete. Abū Hurairah used to relate that the Prophet ﷺ said: "Every child is born conforming to (true human) nature. It is his parents who make him Jewish or Christian or Magian, just as an animal is born as a whole baby animal. Do you find it mutilated?" Then Abū Hurairah recited: "The nature made by Allāh in which He has created mankind" (the Qur'ān, 30:30).[165]

1359 Abū Hurairah said that the Messenger of Allāh ﷺ said: "Every child is born conforming to (true human) nature. It is his parents who make him Jewish or Christian or Magian, just as an animal is born as a whole baby animal. Do you find it mutilated?" Then Abū Hurairah recited: "The nature made by Allāh in which He has created mankind. There is no altering Allah's creation. That is the right religion" (the Qur'ān, 30:30).[166]

Ch. 80:   When an idolater (*mushrik*) recites "There is no god but Allāh" near his death

1360 Musayyib ibn Ḥuzn informed that when the time of the death of Abū

---

and the women and the children, who say: Our Lord, take us out of this town, whose people are oppressors…" (4:75).

[164] It is not the fault of the child if it was of illegitimate birth. Every child is born conforming to true human nature which is called the nature of Islām.

[165] Every child is said here to be born having true human nature (*fiṭrah*), and it is his parents who make him a Jew or a Christian. It shows that having true human nature means being inclined towards submission to the laws ordained by the Creator, which is what is Islām. The Qur'ān refers to it as "the nature (*fiṭrah*) made by Allāh in which He has created mankind" (30:30). The purpose of citing the example of the birth of quadrupeds is to show that Judaism and Christianity are deficient as compared to the perfection of Islam. See also h. 1359 and h. 1385 and the footnotes there.

[166] This is a repetition of the latter part of h. 1358, in which the verse of the Qur'ān recited by Abū Hurairah is given more completely. It has been inferred from this verse that since every child's nature is basically Islamic and it is according to it that Allāh has created everyone, and there is no alteration in the creation of Allāh, it implies that unbelief and *shirk* (worship of others than the One God) cannot efface the nature with which the child was born, but rather that it continues to exist. Unbelief, *shirk* and bad deeds cast a dark curtain of sin upon man. This is treated by a process of correction in Hell. When the dirt of polytheism and disbelief is removed, the original pure nature is cleansed and the person ultimately enters the state of Paradise. This is a very reasonable interpretation. See also the repetition of this ḥadīth in h. 1385 and the footnote under that ḥadīth.

Ṭālib approached, the Messenger of Allāh ﷺ went to him and found Abū Jahl ibn Hishām and ʿAbdullāh ibn Abū Umayya ibn al-Mughīrah by his side. The Messenger of Allāh ﷺ said to Abū Ṭālib: "Uncle! Say the words: 'There is no god but Allāh', and I shall bear witness of it for you before Allāh." [167] Abū Jahl and ʿAbdullāh ibn Abū Umayya said: "Abu Talib! Are you going to renounce the religion of ʿAbdul-Muṭṭalib?" The Messenger of Allāh ﷺ continued to put it (i.e., the *Kalimah*) to him while those two kept on repeating what they said till Abū Ṭālib said the last thing to them, that he was a follower of the religion of ʿAbdul-Muṭṭalib and he refused to say: "There is no god but Allāh." Then the Messenger of Allāh ﷺ said: "By Allāh! I will keep on asking Allāh's forgiveness for you unless I am forbidden (by Allāh) to do so." So Allāh, the Most High, revealed in this regard: "It is not for the Prophet and those who believe to ask forgiveness for those who set up partners (with Allāh), even though they should be near relatives, after it has become clear to them that they are companions of the flaming fire" (the Qur'ān, 9:113).[168]

Ch. 81:   To plant a twig of a palm tree on a grave

Buraidah al-Aslamī made a dying wish that two twigs be planted on his grave. And Ibn ʿUmar saw a tent over the grave of ʿAbdur

---

[167] The Qur'ān says: "But their faith could not profit them when they saw Our punishment" (40:85). Apparently it means that the punishment which is the result of deeds done earlier cannot be withdrawn at that time. How people will be dealt with on the Day of Judgment, only Allāh knows. The Holy Prophet's asking Abū Ṭālib at the time of his death to say *Lā ilāha ill-Allāh* ('There is no god but Allāh'), and his promising that if he did so even at that time, he would testify to his acceptance of Islām before Allāh, shows that the person who recites the *Kalimah* becomes a Muslim. Therefore, if a non-believer recites the *Kalimah* at the time of his death he still becomes a Muslim. What will be done with him in the Hereafter, we do not know. Apparently, he did not get the opportunity in this life to correct his wrong beliefs and actions. It is also a fact that all Muslims will not be treated equally; everyone will be dealt with according to his deeds. Furthermore, there are no limits to the vast forgiveness and mercy of Allāh. A person who recites the *Kalimah* only as words of his mouth will be considered a Muslim for all purposes in this world, if he does it in full consciousness, no matter how close he may be to his death.

[168] There are not less than twelve years between the death of Abū Ṭālib and the revelation of this verse of the Qur'ān. According to this verse, the Holy Prophet was prevented from seeking forgiveness for idol-worshippers when it became clear that they were doomed to enter Hell. The next verse mentions Abraham asking forgiveness for his sire and says: "When it became clear to him that he was an enemy of Allāh, he disassociated himself from him" (9:114). In other words, when it became clear to Abraham that his sire was an enemy of Allāh and wanted to destroy the truth, he cut off relations from him. Thus this verse of the Qur'ān, "It is not for the Prophet and those who believe to ask forgiveness…" (9:113), is only about those who surpassed all limits in stoking the fires of enmity towards the Truth. Ordinary unbelievers are not included among them. Abū Ṭālib showed such tremendous steadfastness in providing protection to the Holy Prophet against his enemies that he cannot possibly fall under the purview of this verse.

Raḥmān and said: "O boy! Take down this. His (good) deeds will provide shade for him." [169]

Khārijah ibn Zaid said: We were young in the time of 'Uthmān and I saw that he who could jump over the grave of 'Uthmān ibn Maz'ūn was considered the longest jumper. And 'Uthmān ibn Ḥakīm said: Khārijah ibn Zaid took hold of my hand and made me sit on a grave and told me what was narrated by his uncle, Yazīd ibn Thābit: "It is forbidden to him who passes urine or excrement over it." [170] And Nāfi' said: 'Abdullāh ibn 'Umar used to sit on graves.

1361 Ibn 'Abbās reported from the Prophet ﷺ that he passed by two graves, the occupants of which were being punished. He said: "These two are being punished, but they are not being punished for a major sin. One of these two did not protect himself from urine and the other used to go about spreading falsehood about others." Then he took a green branch of a date-tree and split it into two, then he planted one on each grave. People said: "O Messenger of Allāh, Why did you do this?" He said: "May be their punishment will be lightened until these two (pieces of date branch) dry up." [171]

Ch. 82:   **Exhortation delivered by a scholar at a grave with his companions sitting around him**

"They will go forth from their *ajdāth*" (the Qur'ān, 54:7; see also 70:43) — *ajdāth* means 'graves'. "And when the graves are *bu'thirat*" (82:4) — *bu'thirat* means 'to be laid open'. *Ba'thar-tu ḥauḍī* means 'I made its lower part to become its upper'. *Al-īfāḍ* means 'to be quick'. And al-A'mash read: "They run to their goal (*nuṣub*)", that is, they vie with one another to reach an appointed point. *An-nuṣb* is singular and *an-naṣb* is its verbal noun. "The day of coming forth" (50:42) means (the dead coming forth) from the graves. "They will hasten (*yansilūn*)" (36:51) means they will come forth.[172]

---

[169] Most are of the view that it is of no benefit to the deceased if fresh branches are put on the grave. Bukhārī also seems to be of the same view. Ibn 'Umar saying, "his good deeds will provide shade for him", is the argument of this chapter that it is only one's good deeds which can bring blessings to the deceased and not fresh branches. See also note to h. 216.

[170] If someone sits on a grave, it does not make any difference to the deceased buried in it. But bearing in mind the decorum and etiquette which the Holy Prophet has taught in regard to funerals, to sit on a grave is disrespectful to the deceased.

[171] This is a repetition of h. 216. See the footnotes to that ḥadīth.

[172] When someone passes on to the other world, those who witness this sad phenomenon naturally experience pain and an inner change is produced in their hearts which turns them away

1362 'Alī reported: We were in a funeral procession at Baqī' al-Gharqad when the Prophet ﷺ came to us and sat down and we sat around him. He had a stick and he bent his head and started scratching the ground with it. He then said: "There is none among you, nor a created soul, but has his place written down in Paradise or in Hell, and it is also written down for him whether he will be one of the wretched or one of the blessed." [173] A man said: "O Messenger of Allāh! Then should we not (just) rely on what has been written for us and give up (doing good) deeds? Whoever of us is from among the blessed people will be inclined to do the deeds of a blessed one, and whoever of us is from among the wretched people will be inclined to do the deeds of a wretched one." He replied: "As for the blessed people, deeds of the blessed ones are facilitated for them, and as for the wretched people, deeds of the wretched ones are facilitated for them." Then he recited: "As for him who gives (in charity) and keeps his duty, and accepts what is good..." (92:5–6). [174]

---

from worldly pleasures. In such grim circumstances, it become more effective to give them exhortations about morality and the need to prepare for the journey to the next world. Bukhārī has, in the chapter heading, explained words which occur in the Qur'ān about the grave and the raising of the dead from the graves. He has brought together the following verses of the Qur'ān: "They will go forth from their graves" (54:7), "And when the graves are laid open" (82:4), and "when lo! from their graves they will hasten on to their Lord" (36:51). By this he points to this chapter to indicate that these verses all refer to the rising to life on the Day of Judgment, and that the preacher by the graveside should draw people's attention to the life after death and the accountability of deeds that will take place in it.

[173] The writing down of Allāh means that everything is in His knowledge. In other words, He knows whether a person is wretched or blessed, and if he will go to Hell or to Paradise.

[174] The question was based on the questioner's own conception that whether a person is spiritually blessed (*sa'īd*) or is wretched and unfortunate (*shaqiyy*), i.e., whether he will enter paradise or go to hell, is determined by Allāh's pre-knowledge of it, and not determined by that person's deeds. The Holy Prophet corrected this misconception by saying that it is deeds which determine whether he is spiritually blessed or is wretched, and not the knowledge of Allāh. Therefore, he told him that the blessed ones have their way facilitated to the doing of good and the wretched ones have their way facilitated to the doing of evil, so that a person becomes good or evil because of the deeds he chooses to do. Even though Allāh has prior knowledge, that does not make a person blessed or wretched. It is his deeds which make him so. This is also what is stated in the Qur'ān as follows: "Then as for him who gives (in charity) and keeps his duty, and accepts what is good — We facilitate for him the way to ease. And as for him who is miserly and considers himself self-sufficient, and rejects what is good — We facilitate for him the way to distress" (92:5–10). This says that "ease" or blessing is the consequence of good deeds and "distress" or wretchedness is the consequence of evil deeds. In the system of this universe, the knowledge of all things that exist was possessed by Allāh before these things came into existence, but each of them actually came into existence due to a cause. The knowledge of Allāh is not the cause of their existence, otherwise as His knowledge has always been there from the most ancient times, anything which is caused by that knowledge would also have always been there.

Ch. 83:   What is said about one who kills himself (*qātil-un-nafs*)?[175]

1363 Thābit ibn aḍ-Ḍaḥḥāk reported that the Prophet ﷺ said: "Whoever intentionally swears falsely by a religion other than Islām, then he is just what he has said.[176] And whoever kills himself with (a piece of) iron will be punished with the same in the fire of hell."

1364 Al-Ḥasan reported: Jundub narrated to us in this mosque and we have neither forgotten it nor do we believe that Jundub would falsely attribute anything to the Messenger of Allāh ﷺ. He said: "A man suffered wounds and he killed himself. So Allāh said: My servant has preceded Me in taking his own life, so I have forbidden Paradise for him." [177]

1365 Abū Hurairah reported that the Prophet ﷺ said: "One who strangles himself to death will keep on strangling himself in the fire (of Hell), and one who stabs himself to death will keep on stabbing himself in the fire (of Hell)." [178]

Ch. 84:   About the dislike of saying funeral prayers for hypocrites and praying for forgiveness for idolaters

Ibn 'Umar reported this from the Prophet ﷺ.

1366 'Umar ibn al-Khaṭṭāb reported: When 'Abdullāh ibn Ubayy ibn Salūl died, the Messenger of Allāh ﷺ was called upon to lead his funeral prayer. When the Messenger of Allāh ﷺ stood up (to lead the prayer), I went to him and said: "O Messenger of Allāh! Are you going to pray for Ibn Ubayy and

---

[175] *Qātil-un-nafs* has been taken to mean in particular *qātala nafsa-hu,* i.e. 'one who kills himself', although this expression in a general sense includes both a person who kills someone else and a person who kills himself, i.e., commits suicide. There is no ḥadīth that the funeral of one who commits suicide is disallowed, nor has Bukhārī included any such ḥadīth. However, strong warnings have been given regarding one who commits suicide. There is a ḥadīth that the Holy Prophet did not lead the funeral prayers of a man who committed suicide, but there is no mention that he prohibited others from holding his funeral prayers. According to the report in Nasā'ī he said: "*As for me,* I will not say the prayer for him" (book: 'Funerals', h. 1964). Therefore there is no proof that it is disallowed.

[176] For instance, a man says: "If I have done such and such, then I am a Jew". If he has done that thing then he has himself described himself as a Jew. This ḥadīth has also occurred in the Book of Manners (h. 6047 and h. 6105).

[177] Islām has taught man to value the blessings God has given him, and regarded it as an act extreme of ingratitude to waste them. Among these, life is the greatest bounty. Anyone who takes his own life is the most ungrateful person. It is God Who takes away life and it is He who grants it. Moreover, a person generally commits suicide when he is unable to face suffering and tribulations and he gets rid of this unbearable situation by killing himself. But the Qur'ān says: "Despair not of Allāh's mercy. Surely none despairs of Allāh's mercy except the disbelieving people" (12:87). That is why committing suicide has been regarded as a grave sin.

[178] In Islām, all punishments have been based on the principle that punishment corresponds to the sin committed, as the Qur'ān says: "Recompense corresponding" (78:26).

he said so and so at such and such times?" I started recounting all that he had said. The Messenger of Allāh ﷺ smiled and said: " 'Umar! Leave me and go back." When I insisted with him too much, he said: "I have been given the discretion, so I have chosen (to say the prayer). Had I had known that if I asked forgiveness for him more than seventy times he would be forgiven, I would have done so." 'Umar added: The Messenger of Allāh ﷺ said his funeral prayer and returned, and after a short while the two verses of *Al-Barā'ah* (ch. 9 of the Qur'ān) were revealed: "And never offer (*Janāzah*) prayer for anyone of them who dies, nor stand by his grave. Surely they disbelieved in Allāh and His Messenger and they died in transgression" (9:84). And 'Umar said: Afterwards, I was surprised at my boldness before the Messenger of Allāh ﷺ on that day. And Allāh and His Messenger know it well.[179]

Ch. 85: People recounting the good deeds of the deceased[180]

1367 Anas ibn Mālik said: They (the Companions) passed by a funeral procession and the people praised the deceased. The Prophet ﷺ said: "It has become obligatory (for him)." Then they passed by another funeral procession and the people spoke badly of the deceased. The Prophet ﷺ said: "It has become obligatory (for him)." 'Umar ibn al-Khaṭṭāb asked: "What has become obligatory?" He replied: "You people praised this one, so Paradise became obligatory for him, and you spoke badly of that one, so the fire became obligatory for him. You are Allāh's witnesses on earth." [181]

1368 Abū al-Aswad reported: I came to Madīnah and there an epidemic had broken out. While I was sitting with 'Umar ibn al-Khaṭṭāb a funeral procession passed by and the people praised the deceased. 'Umar said: "It has become obligatory (for him)." Then another funeral procession passed by and

---

[179] See the note on h. 1269. Here details are given which are not found in h. 1269. See also h. 1350.

[180] To recount the good qualities of the deceased endears him to the people and encourages and reminds them to seek Allāh's mercy for him. But, according to Ḥadīth, such praising of a living person is disliked because it may make him proud and consider others as inferior to him.

[181] Paradise and hell are attained according to one's deeds. Here the Holy Prophet, referring to one person being praised and the other despised, said that the former will be granted Paradise and the latter will be granted Hell. It means that when righteous and good people are praising someone, he must be a person with a record of good deeds. Similarly, righteous and good people would never speak ill of a person unless he had committed bad deeds excessively. The Holy Prophet has here called the Companions as "bearers of witness" and this was according to the verse of the Qur'ān: "… that you may be bearers of witness to the people" (2:143). This provides clear testimony of the righteousness and truthfulness of the Companions, and it was entirely due to the Holy Prophet's spiritual power that a great community of such righteous and noble people came into existence in the world.

the people praised the deceased. 'Umar said: "It has become obligatory (for him)." A third (funeral procession) passed by and the people spoke badly of the deceased. 'Umar said: "It has become obligatory (for him)." I asked: "O Chief of the Believers: What has become obligatory?" He replied: "I said the same as the Prophet ﷺ had said, that is: 'If four persons testify to the goodness of a Muslim, Allāh will grant him Paradise.' We asked (the Prophet): 'What if three persons do so?' He (the Prophet) replied: 'Even three.' Then we asked: 'If two?' He replied: 'Even two.' We did not ask him about one witness." [182]

Ch. 86: About punishment in the grave[183]

The word of Allāh, the Most High: "If you could see when the wrongdoers are in the agonies of death and the angels stretch forth their hands, (saying): Yield up your souls. This day you are awarded a punishment of disgrace (*hūn*)" (6:93). Abū 'Abdullāh (Bukhārī) said: *Hūn* means disgrace and *hawn* means gentleness. And the word of Allāh: "We will punish them twice, then they will be turned back to a severe punishment" (9:101). And the word of Allāh: "… and evil punishment befell Pharaoh's people — the Fire. They are brought before it (every) morning and evening, and on the day when the Hour comes to pass: Make Pharaoh's people enter the most severe punishment" (40:45–46).

---

[182] For later generations to praise the departed ones is also mentioned with approval in the Qur'ān: "And We left for him (i.e., Noah) praise among the later generations" (37:78). The more good a person has done, the more people there are who recall his works after his demise.

[183] It has been stated in h. 1338 that punishment in the grave is given only to disbelievers and hypocrites. It means that the punishment is because of their evil deeds. The verses of the Qur'ān quoted in this chapter heading in support of the concept of punishment in the grave refer to punishment after death for the wicked. The first verse may also mean punishment at the time of death itself. In the second verse the punishments given twice apparently mean punishments given twice in this world. However, in the third verse it has been clearly mentioned that followers of Pharaoh will be punished before the Day of Judgment. These verses, and the Ḥadīth reports which occurred earlier and those which follow, establish that some sort of reward or punishment does begin just after the death. The Qur'ān has named this state as *barzakh* (interval between death and Resurrection). So *qabr* or grave means the state of *barzakh*, whether the body of the deceased has been buried in a grave under the earth or cremated or been devoured by an animal. The soul is the real substance and it is given a new "body" according to the deeds of the deceased, and the reward or punishment is given to this new body. *Fatḥ al-Bārī* says that there is difference of opinion about whether the punishment is given to the soul or the body. But one thing is certain: the physical body is not always buried in a grave. Therefore, the punishment of the grave does not mean the punishment of the physical body. Otherwise, what will be the case with bodies which are preserved? Pharaoh's body was preserved as a mummy but the Qur'ān says that he and his followers "are brought before the fire morning and evening" (40:46). Thus punishment of the grave means that state of *barzakh* where some sort of punishment is given for evil deeds.

1369 Al-Barā' ibn ʿĀzib reported from the Prophet ﷺ that he said: "When a believer is made to sit in his grave, then (the angels) come and then he bears witness that there is no god but Allāh and Muḥammad is the Messenger of Allāh." This is as the word of Allāh: "Allāh confirms those who believe with the sure word in this world's life and in the Hereafter" (14:27).

And in another report it is said that the verse "Allāh confirms those who believe" was revealed about punishment in the grave.[184]

1370 Ibn ʿUmar informed: The Prophet ﷺ looked at the (dead) people in the well (i.e., where bodies of the unbelievers killed at Badr were placed) and said: "Have you found true what your Lord promised you?" Someone said to him: "You are calling the dead." He replied: "You do not hear any more than they, but they cannot reply."[185]

1371 ʿĀ'ishah reported: The Prophet ﷺ only said: "They now know that what I used to tell them was true." And Allāh has indeed said: "Certainly you cannot make the dead to hear" (27:80).

1372 ʿĀ'ishah reported that a Jewish woman came to her and mentioned the punishment of the grave and said to her: "May Allāh grant you refuge from the punishment of the grave." So ʿĀ'ishah asked the Messenger of Allāh ﷺ about the punishment of the grave. He said: "Yes, punishment of the grave (is true)." ʿĀ'ishah said: After that I never saw the Messenger of Allāh ﷺ saying any prayer in which he did not seek refuge with Allāh from the punishment of the grave. Ghundar added: Punishment of the grave is true.[186]

---

[184] The Holy Prophet has himself explained this verse of the Qur'ān by saying that the "sure word" means bearing witness to the Unity of Allāh and to the prophethood of the Holy Prophet; and to continue believing in it in the next life means to give the right reply to the angels in the grave. This ḥadīth shows that a true believer is not given any punishment in the grave; rather, he is granted a sort of "peace" by Allāh. To make the dead sit in the grave is also in the state of *barzakh*, as has been mentioned earlier, and it is not a physical posture of the dead body.

[185] By their hearing is not meant that they hear with their physical ears; rather, it means that they are transformed into a state like that of one who can hear. If they could hear with their physical ears, then they would also be able to reply with their tongues. This explanation has also been attributed to the Holy Prophet by ʿĀ'ishah in the next ḥadīth because she plainly rejects the hearing by the dead and in this connection she refers to this verse of the Qur'ān: "Certainly you cannot make the dead to hear" (27:80). ʿĀ'ishah reported that the Holy Prophet said: "They now know that what I used to tell them was true." In other words, this realisation on their part was their "hearing". It did not mean that they were hearing now. And even if it is taken to mean that they could hear what was being said now, then it was Allāh Who conveyed the message of His Prophet to them. Even this does not establish in general that the dead can hear. The object is to convey that with death their lives do not come to an end; instead, they have entered a new life.

[186] A part of this subject has already been discussed in the beginning of h. 1049–1050, which is a repetition of h. 1044. But in h. 1044 this subject has not been discussed.

1373 Asmā', daughter of Abū Bakr, said: The Messenger of Allāh ﷺ stood up delivering a sermon and mentioned the trial of the grave by which a man is tried. When he mentioned that, the Muslims started crying loudly.[187]

1374 Anas ibn Mālik reported (to Qatādah) that the Messenger of Allāh ﷺ said: "When a human being is placed in his grave and his companions return and he even hears the sound of their footsteps, two angels come to him and make him sit and ask him: 'What did you use to say about the man, Muḥammad?' As for the believer, he says: 'I bear witness that he is the servant of Allāh and His Messenger.' Then it is said to him: 'Look at your place in the fire (of hell). Allāh has indeed given you instead of it a place in Paradise.' So he will see both his places."

Qatādah said: We were told that for him (i.e., the believer) his grave will be widened. Then he (Qatādah) returned to the report from Anas (as below).

"And as for the hypocrite and the unbeliever, he will be asked: 'What did you use to say about this man?' He will say: 'I had no knowledge, but I only said what people said!' It will be said to him: 'Neither did you (try to) get knowledge nor did you follow (those who had knowledge).' Then he will be hit once with an iron hammer, and he will scream which will be heard by whoever will be near him, other than people and *jinn*." [188]

Ch. 87:   To seek refuge with Allāh from punishment of the grave

1375 Abū Ayyūb reported: The Prophet ﷺ went out after sunset and he heard a sound, and said: "The Jews are being punished in their graves." [189]

---

[187] They had full faith in the hereafter and that deeds will have consequences in the life hereafter, and that is why they were overwhelmed by the fear of Allāh's judgment. In fact, a deep realisation of accountability for one's deeds is the only evidence of having faith.

[188] This is a repetition of h. 1338 with slight difference in wording and an addition by Qatādah, who was reporting from Anas. The widening or expansion of the grave does not mean the physical grave. Such widening is against what is observed, and no meaning can be based on something which against observation. In fact, it means that in the state of *barzakh* the deceased is shown a scene of happiness which instills peace and comfort in it. The deceased receives some measure of reward for his good deeds in that state of *barzakh* and will find its full reward on the Day of Judgement.

[189] He heard this sound in a state of vision, that is, through the special senses granted by Allāh to His devotees. It could not be heard by others, as also happens in the case of Divine revelation. It has been clearly mentioned in h. 1370, just above, that the dead "cannot reply". Thus the hue and cry of the dead mentioned here is made in the realm of *barzakh*. Seeking protection of Allāh has not been explicitly mentioned in this ḥadīth. Some are of the opinion that it was the sound of the angels which was heard.

1376 The daughter of Khālid ibn Saʿīd ibn al-ʿĀṣ related that she had heard the Prophet ﷺ seeking refuge with Allāh from the punishment of the grave.

1377 Abū Hurairah reported: The Messenger of Allāh ﷺ used to make the supplication: "O Allāh! I seek refuge in You from the punishment of the grave, and from the punishment of the fire (of hell), and from the trials of life and death, and from the tribulation of the Antichrist (*al-Masīḥ ad-Dajjāl*)." [190]

Ch. 88: Punishment of the grave because of backbiting and passing urine

1378 Ibn ʿAbbās said: The Prophet ﷺ passed by two graves and said: "These two are being punished, but they are not being punished for a major sin. Then he said: "Yes (these are also major), one of these two used to go about spreading falsehood about others and the other did not protect himself from his own urine." Then he took a green branch of a date-tree and broke it into two, then he planted one on each grave. Then he said: "May be their punishment will be lightened until these two (pieces of date branch) dry up." [191]

Ch. 89: The deceased is shown his abode morning and evening

1379 ʿAbdullāh ibn ʿUmar reported that the Messenger of Allāh ﷺ said: "When anyone of you dies, his abode is shown to him in the morning and in the evening.[192] If he is one of the people of Paradise, it is among them; and if he is one of the people of the fire, it is among them. Then it is said to him: This is your abode till Allāh raises you on the Day of Resurrection."

Ch. 90: The deceased speaking at the funeral

1380 Abū Saʿīd al-Khudrī said that the Messenger of Allāh ﷺ said: "When the funeral bier is ready and the men carry it on their shoulders, ..." [193]

Ch. 91: What has been said about children of Muslims[194]

---

[190] This is a repetition of the first part of h. 832 in brief and with a slight difference in wording.

[191] This is a repetition of h. 216 and h. 1361 with a slight difference in wording.

[192] It is possible that being shown his abode morning and evening is itself the reward or punishment which is given in the state of *barzakh*. By "morning and evening" may be meant all the time. It may also be that this showing is in addition to the reward or punishment given in the state of *barzakh*.

[193] This is a repetition of h. 1314 with a very slight difference of wording. For the remainder, see h. 1314. In the note to that ḥadīth the talking of the deceased at his funeral has been explained.

[194] As has been stated in the note on h. 1358, according to the teachings of Islām every child

Abū Hurairah, reporting from the Prophet ﷺ, said: "One whose three offspring die before reaching adulthood, they will screen him from the fire (of hell)" or "he will enter Paradise".

1381 Anas ibn Mālik reported that the Messenger of Allāh ﷺ said: "There is no Muslim among the people, but if three of his children die before reaching maturity, Allāh will make him enter Paradise due to His immense mercy for them." [195]

1382 Al-Barā' ibn 'Āzib said: When Ibrāhīm died, the Messenger of Allāh ﷺ said: "He has a wet-nurse in Paradise." [196]

Ch. 92: What has been said about children of idolaters[197]

1383 Ibn 'Abbās reported: The Messenger of Allāh ﷺ was asked about the children of the idolaters. He said: "When Allāh created them, He knew well what they would have done (if they had lived to adulthood)." [198]

---

is born conforming to true human nature, known as the "nature of Islām", and if he dies while at the stage of innocence, he is considered to have died in Islām and will enter Paradise. And as he becomes a source of intercession for his parents, screening them from hell, he must necessarily be an inmate of Paradise.

[195] This is a repetition of h. 1248 with minor difference in wording.

[196] As soon as a person departs from this world he progresses to another world, and there is no limit to progress after that. Ibrāhīm, the infant child of the Holy Prophet, died while still a suckling. From this the Holy Prophet said that his physical progress has stopped with his death but his spiritual progress did not, and means of his progress exist in Paradise. This shows that those who die in childhood find that in the next world Allāh has made available to them the means of their development.

[197] By children of the idolaters are meant their under-aged children, just as in the previous chapter by "children of Muslims" are meant under-aged children of Muslims. Three reports — h. 1383, h. 1385 and h. 1386 — have been included which contain whatever has been said about these children. The substance of h. 1383 is that Allāh knows about their deeds. H. 1385 tells us that all children, whether they are of Muslims, or idolaters or Jews or Christians, are born with true human nature, the nature of Islām. H. 1385 is a long ḥadīth in which a vision of the Holy Prophet has been mentioned. One part of it is that he saw the prophet Abraham near a tree and around him were infants of Muslims and non-Muslims. The last two reports tell us clearly that all infants will get salvation and will be in Paradise. Therefore, the first ḥadīth, h. 1383, cannot be given a meaning which is contrary to these two.

[198] There are many explanations recorded of this ḥadīth, but as stated in the last footnote none of the interpretations is acceptable which contradicts the two ḥadīth reports occurring after it. If this ḥadīth is taken to mean that Allāh knew what they would have done if they had grown to adulthood, and they are rewarded or punished accordingly, then it should be the same in the case of Muslim children because a Muslim too would go to Paradise or Hell according to his deeds. Thus it is not possible that because a child is born to a Muslim he will enter Paradise merely on the basis of his birth. Since an adult Muslim goes to Paradise or Hell according to his deeds, what

1384 Abū Hurairah said: The Prophet ﷺ was asked about the offspring of the idolaters. He said: "Allāh knew well what they would have done (if they had lived to adulthood)." [199]

1385 Abū Hurairah reported that the Prophet ﷺ said: "Every child is born conforming to (true human) nature. It is his parents who make him Jewish or Christian or Magian, just as an animal is born as a whole baby animal. Do you find it mutilated?" [200]

---

would apply to deceased Muslim children is the same as that which would apply to non-Muslim children. But it has been stated in the previous chapter that deceased children of Muslim parents will act as intercessors for them and thus save them from Hell. This means they must necessarily go to Paradise, whereas it is possible that if they had grown up some of them would have committed evil deeds and would have certainly gone to Hell accordingly.

Moreover, the interpretation that, because Allāh knows what evil deeds someone would have committed as an adult, He would punish him accordingly, even if he dies before committing those deeds, is against the principles of the Qur'ān. According to the Qur'ān, reward or punishment is determined by the good or bad deeds committed, and not by God's knowledge of the future. Thus it will have one of two meanings. It may mean, as is stated in *Fath al-Bārī*, that God knew that they would not commit any misdeeds of unbelief or idolatery because they would die while in infancy, and therefore they cannot be punished and they will be dealt with according to their pure human nature. And as they conform to the nature of Islām, which has been mentioned in the next ḥadīth, they will be in Paradise where they will make progress, each according to his nature. The other meaning is that the words "what they would have done" indicate that God knew that they would die while in infancy, and again the meaning of the ḥadīth would be the same as what has just been explained. A ḥadīth is reported from the Holy Prophet that "the children of idolaters will go to Hell." This has been considered as an extremely "weak" ḥadīth (*Fath al-Bārī*).

It should be remembered that Ibn 'Abbās did not hear this ḥadīth from the Holy Prophet. It is mentioned in *Fath al-Bārī* that Aḥmad has reported from Ibn 'Abbās that he used to hold the opinion that the children of idolaters would be inmates of Hell until he heard this ḥadīth from one of the Companions of the Holy Prophet, and then he stopped holding this opinion. This shows that the object of this ḥadīth was the same, and Ibn 'Abbās himself understood this ḥadīth to mean, that the deceased children of idolaters do not enter Hell.

[199] This is a repetition of h. 1383.

[200] This is a repetition of the part of h. 1358 given in h. 1359, omitting the verse from the Qur'ān. See the footnotes there. What is meant by a child being born conforming to true human nature (*fiṭrah*)? Abū Hurairah used to recite this verse of the Qur'ān in order to explain it: "the nature (*fiṭrah*) made by Allāh in which He has created mankind" (30:30). Here, Islām has been regarded as the religion of human nature. Also, in *Fath al-Bārī*, the opinion of Ibn 'Abdul Birr has been mentioned to the effect that earlier commentators are of the same opinion and all scholars are unanimous that this interpretation, that in this verse, by the word "nature" is meant Islām, is correct, and in support of this opinion the narration of 'Ayyāḍ has been quoted wherein the Holy Prophet reported Allāh as saying: "I have created all My servants in an upright state (*ḥunafā'*, plural of *ḥanīf*)." Jews, Christians, idolaters, etc. are included in "all". In another report it has been stated that all have been created as "upright, submitting to God (*ḥunafā' muslimīn*)." And thinking over the wording of this ḥadīth itself, it is realized that here by being "born

Ch. 93:   Concerning the above

1386 Samurah ibn Jundab reported:[201] Whenever the Prophet ﷺ finished the (morning) prayer, he would turn to us and ask: "Which of you had a dream last night?" So if anyone had experienced a dream he would narrate it, and he (the Prophet) would say (in interpreting it) whatever Allāh wished. One day he asked us: "Did any of you see a dream?" We said: "No." He said: "But I saw last night (in a dream) that two men[202] came to me, took hold of my hands, and brought me to the Sacred Land (i.e., Jerusalem). There, I saw a man sitting and another one standing and in his hand was — some of our companions report from Mūsā — an iron hook. He was pushing it in the mouth of the first man (on one side) till it reached the back of the neck (tearing off one jaw), and then did the same with the other side. In the meantime, the first jaw returned (to its normal position). Then he repeated the same again. I said: 'What is this?' The two men said: 'Proceed on.'

"So we went on till we came to a man lying flat on his back, and another man standing at his head carrying a stone or a piece of rock[203] and breaking his head with it. Whenever he struck him, the stone rolled away. So he went to bring it, but before he returned, the head was back to its normal condition, as it was before. So he returned and struck him again. I said: 'Who is this?' The two men said: 'Proceed on.'

---

conforming to nature" means Islām, as other religions, Judaism, Christianity and Magianism, have been mentioned in contrast to "nature". In particular, the Christian doctrine that every child is born sinful and, as such, doomed to Hell has been refuted and it has been emphasised, as against this, that every child is born in the state of Islām, a state of submission to the laws of nature, and as such he is destined for Paradise. In Ṣaḥīḥ Muslim there are several narrations of this ḥadīth which bear witness to the fact that by "nature" or *fiṭrah* is meant Islām, as is stated in a report: "No child is born but he is in religion (*millah*)", and in another version: "No child is born but he is in this religion" (Muslim, book: *Qadr,* ch. 6). Further, in his Book on 'Commentary on the Qur'ān', in the chapter heading above h. 4775, Bukhārī has added the word "Islām" after *fiṭrah,* to show that it means being born in Islām, i.e., in a state of submission to God.

[201] This ḥadīth has occurred in somewhat different words and in more detail at the end of the Book of 'Interpretation of Dreams' (h. 7047). The Holy Prophet was shown in a dream the state of the sinful people in the hereafter along with the place of the righteous and the infant children. It was just a scene showing the consequences of evil deeds in the next life as well as the position of the righteous and the innocent. Apparently the punishments mentioned relate to the realm of *barzakh,* because some are said to continue till the Day of Resurrection. However, they cannot be taken as being physical and bodily. It is some spiritual state.

[202] At the end of this ḥadīth it is stated that these two men were Jibrīl and Mīkā'īl, but in the dream they were shown to the Holy Prophet as two men. This shows that in whatever form a thing is shown in a dream, it is not necessarily its form in reality.

[203] Two words for 'stone' are used here: *fihr* and *ṣakhrah. Fihr* is that stone which can be held by hand.

"So we went on till we passed by a hole in the ground like a clay oven, narrow at the top and wide at the bottom. Fire was burning at the bottom, and whenever it raged upwards the people in it were raised till they almost came out, and whenever the fire died down the people went down with it, and there were naked men and women in it. I said: 'What is this?' The two men said: 'Proceed on.'

"So we went on till we reached a river of blood and a man was standing in the middle of it, and — said Yazīd ibn Hārūn and Wahb ibn Jarīr, from Jarīr ibn Ḥāzim — on its bank another man with stones in front of him. The man in the river came forward, and when he wanted to come out the other man threw a stone at his mouth and turned him back to where he was. Whenever he wanted to come out the other would throw a stone at his mouth, and he would return to where he was. I asked: 'What is this?' The two men said: 'Proceed on.'

"So we went on till we reached a green orchard in which there was a huge tree and near its base was an old man with some children. There was another man near the tree, with fire in front of him which he was kindling. The two men took me up the tree and made me enter a house, more beautiful and better than any I had ever seen. In it were old and young men, and women and children. Then they took me out of this house and further up the tree and made me enter another house that was even more beautiful and better (than the first). In it were old and young people.

"I said: 'You two have taken me around all night. So inform me about what I have seen.' The two men said:

'Yes. As for the one whose jaw you saw being torn away, he was a liar and he used to tell lies. Those lies from him were circulated till they spread to the distant horizons. So he will suffer punishment like that till the Day of Resurrection. The one whose head you saw being broken is a man whom Allāh had given knowledge of the Qur'ān but he slept neglectful of it by night[204] and did not act upon it by day. So he will suffer punishment like that till the Day of Resurrection. Those you saw in the oven were adulterers. Those you saw in the river of blood were devourers of usury. The old man sitting at the base of the tree was Abraham, peace be upon him, and the children around him were children of the people (in general).[205] The one who was kindling the fire was Mālik, the guard of

---

[204] The meaning is that he neglected the obligatory prayers. See footnote on h. 1143.

[205] In the Book on 'Interpretation of Dreams' where this ḥadīth is repeated (h. 7047), the

hell-fire. The first house which you entered was the house of ordinary believers, and the second house was the house of martyrs.[206] And I am Gabriel (*Jibrīl*) and this is Michael (*Mīkā'īl*). Raise your head.'

"I raised my head and there was a thing like a cloud above me. They said: 'That is your place.' I said: 'Leave me that I may enter my place.' They said: 'There still remains some of your life which you have not yet completed. Had you completed it, you would have entered your place.' "

Ch. 94:   Death on a Monday[207]

1387 Hishām's father reported from 'Ā'ishah that she said: "I went to Abū Bakr (in his last illness) and he asked me: 'In how many garments was the Prophet ﷺ shrouded?' " She replied: "In three pieces of washed, white cloth, in which there was neither a shirt nor a turban." He (Abū Bakr) asked her: "On which day did the Messenger of Allāh ﷺ die?" She replied: "On a Monday." He asked: "Which day is it today?" She replied: "Monday." He said: "I hope I may die sometime between now and the night." Then he looked at a garment that he was wearing during his illness and it had a saffron stain upon it. He said: "Wash this garment of mine and add to it two more garments and shroud me in them." I said: "This is old." He said: "The living has more right to wear new clothes than the dead one. This is only for the blood and pus (of the dead body)." He did not die until Tuesday night[208] and was buried before the morning.

---

wording is as follows: "The children who were around him (i.e., Prophet Abraham) were all of those who died conforming to nature (*fiṭrah*). It is said that some Muslims said: 'O Messenger of Allāh! the children of idolaters also?' He said: 'Also the children of idolaters'." These words clearly show that deceased children of idolaters are with the Prophet Abraham in Paradise, and that would apply even more so to the children of Jews and Christians. As compared to this broad-minded teaching of Islām, there is the doctrine of Christianity that all non-Christians, young and old, will enter Hell. Even Christians who die before being baptised are believed to go to eternal Hell and be accursed forever. And according to a Christian elder, they will crawl over the surface of Hell.

[206] This ḥadīth shows that, besides during the Night of Ascension (*Mi'rāj*), the Holy Prophet was shown Paradise and Hell several other times. In h. 86 it occurs that he was shown Paradise and Hell in a vision during a prayer. Thus, when he was shown such scenes in a vision several times, it is reasonable to hold that the experience of the *Mi'rāj* was in a state of dream or vision.

[207] In the ḥadīth in this chapter only the wish of Abū Bakr is mentioned that his death might be on the same day of the week as when the Holy Prophet had died, and that day was Monday.

[208] The death of Abū Bakr, may Allāh be pleased with him, took place in Jamādī-uth-Thānī, 13 A.H., eight days before the end of the month.

Ch. 95: Unexpected death[209]

1388 'Ā'ishah reported that a man said to the Prophet ﷺ: "My mother has died suddenly and I think if she could talk now she would give in charity. If I give in charity on her behalf, will she get the reward?" The Prophet said: "Yes." [210]

Ch. 96: What is said about the graves of the Prophet ﷺ, Abū Bakr and 'Umar

Fa aqbara-hū ("then He assigns to him a grave" — the Qur'ān, 80:21). *Aqbartu ar-rajula uqbiru-hū* means "I made a grave for him". And *qabartu-hū* means "I buried him."

Kifāt-an ("draw to itself" — 77:25) means that they (human beings) exist in it (i.e., in the earth) when living, and are buried in it when dead.

1389 'Ā'ishah reported: The Messenger of Allāh ﷺ during his illness felt discomfort (in moving from the house of one wife to that of another) and said: "Where am I today and where will I be tomorrow?" He would think that the day of being in the house of 'Ā'ishah was far off.[211] When my turn came,

---

[209] In some ḥadīth reports sudden and unexpected death has been mentioned as if the Holy Prophet considered it to be a bad death. In this connection, it is stated in Abū Dāwūd that sudden death is like being caught by the punishment of Divine wrath (book: 'Funerals', ch. 14). According to a report in the Musnad of Aḥmad, the Holy Prophet was passing by a leaning wall, so he passed by it hurriedly and said: "I dislike sudden death." This report is very clear that the wall appeared to be likely to fall down so the Holy Prophet said that he disliked sudden death, meaning that the wall could have fallen on him and killed him. Here the question is not of the occurrence of death in a particular manner. In the case of the first ḥadīth, in Abū Dāwūd, we could limit it to Divine punishment for a sinner because by sudden death he could not get the opportunity to repent. This is further corroborated by a ḥadīth reported by Ibn Shaibah attributed to 'Ā'ishah, and also mentioned in *'Ainī* and *Fatḥ al-Bārī*: "Sudden death for a true believer is a blessing and for a sinful one it is a Divine punishment." Otherwise the ḥadīth in Abū Dāwūd will have to be discarded in view of the ḥadīth in this chapter of Bukhārī. In fact, the occurrence of death in one manner or another is not under anyone's control so that it could be considered as good or bad. In the ḥadīth in this chapter the Holy Prophet, on hearing the news of a sudden death, did not declare it as bad.

[210] This shows that if charity is given on behalf of a deceased, its reward reaches the dead person. An objection is raised that when the deed has not been done by the person himself, how can he be rewarded? Accordingly, it is mentioned in the ḥadīth that the questioner told the Holy Prophet that if his mother could talk she would have given the charity. That was her intention but she did not get the opportunity. And in fact every true believer always intends to spend in the way of Allāh. However, in the matter of reward for the dead for deeds done on their behalf, we cannot generalize and must restrict ourselves to whatever the Holy Prophet has stated.

[211] The meaning of *yata'aḏh-ḏhar* ("felt discomfort") is given by Ibn Athīr as "prevented by

Allāh took his soul while he was (in my lap) between my arms and my chest and he was buried in my house.

1390 (1) 'Ā'ishah reported that the Messenger of Allāh ﷺ, during his illness from which he did not recover, said: "Allāh cursed the Jews and the Christians because they took the graves of their prophets as places of worship." 'Ā'ishah said: "If it were not for this, his grave would have been in the open, nonetheless it is feared that it might be taken as a mosque." [212]

1390 (2) Sufyān, a date-seller, reported that he saw the grave of the Prophet ﷺ (in a convex shape) like the hump of a camel.[213]

1390 (3) 'Urwah reported that when, during the time of the Caliphate of Walīd ibn 'Abdul Malik, the wall (of the room of 'Ā'ishah) fell down, people started repairing it,[214] and a foot appeared to them. The people were afraid and thought that it was the foot of the Prophet ﷺ. They could not find anyone who would know about it, until 'Urwah said to them: "By Allāh! This is not the foot of the Prophet ﷺ, but it is certainly that of 'Umar." [215]

---

difficulty", probably meaning experiencing hardship in going from one house to another. And in the chapter 'Illness of the Prophet and his death', 'Ā'ishah has reported that when his illness became serious, he asked his wives for their approval for him to stay with 'Ā'ishah during his illness and they agreed to his request (h. 4450). Ibn Sa'd has a report that Fāṭimah also told his wives that the Holy Prophet was finding difficulty in moving from one house to another and he would prefer to be looked after by 'Ā'ishah. It was because the Holy Prophet loved 'Ā'ishah more than the others and also because he considered her understanding of religion to be greater than that of the others. This ḥadīth also shows that the grave of the Holy Prophet is in 'Ā'ishah's apartment.

[212] This part of h. 1390 is a repetition of h. 1330 in almost the same wording. See the footnote to h. 1330. This shows that a structure was built over the grave and it was sealed.

[213] The shape of the grave is described here as resembling the hump of a camel.

[214] During the caliphate of Walīd ibn 'Abdul Malik, 'Umar ibn 'Abdul 'Azīz was governor of Madīnah and he ordered him to pull down the apartments of the wives of the Holy Prophet and extend the mosque.

[215] By "foot" (*qadam*) is meant the lower leg, up to the knee. From ḥadīth reports it is seen that the graves of Abū Bakr and 'Umar were on either side of the grave of the Holy Prophet in such a way that the head of Abū Bakr was near the shoulder of the Holy Prophet and the head of 'Umar was near the feet of the Holy Prophet. It appears that 'Umar was a tall person, and this was why when he was buried in the grave his legs went under the wall. So when the wall fell, his legs became visible. 'Umar ibn 'Abdul 'Azīz was present on that occasion. When the building was constructed over the graves, the old structure of the apartments from inside was dismantled and it was then that all three graves were seen, and from the base of one of the walls sand came out and the legs of 'Umar became visible. 'Umar ibn 'Abdul 'Azīz was so moved by this that he started crying. The object of Bukhārī in mentioning this ḥadīth was most probably to tell that the graves of Abū Bakr and 'Umar were on either side of the grave of the Holy Prophet.

1391 Hishām reported from his father who reported from 'Ā'ishah that she made a will instructing 'Abdullāh ibn Zubair thus: "Do not bury me with them (i.e., the Holy Prophet and Abū Bakr and 'Umar) but bury me with my companions (*ṣawāḥibī*, referring to wives of the Prophet) in the cemetery of al-Baqī', as I do not wish thereby to be considered more praiseworthy (by being buried near the Prophet)." [216]

1392 'Amr ibn Maimūn al-Audī reported: I saw 'Umar ibn al-Khaṭṭāb (after he was stabbed) saying (to his son): "O 'Abdullāh ibn 'Umar! Go to the Mother of the Believers, 'Ā'ishah, and say, 'Umar ibn Al-Khaṭṭāb sends his greetings to you, and ask her permission that I may be buried with my two companions." 'Ā'ishah said: "I intended to have that place for myself but today I prefer him ('Umar) over me." When he returned, 'Umar asked him: "What reply have you brought?" He replied: "O Chief of the Believers! She has given you permission." 'Umar said: "There was nothing more important to me than (to be buried in) that resting place. So, when I die, carry me there and then give greetings and say: 'Umar ibn al-Khaṭṭāb asks permission. If she gives permission, then bury me (there), otherwise take me to the graveyard of the Muslims." [217]

---

[216] 'Ā'ishah showed the utmost selflessness on this occasion. By *ṣawāḥibī* are meant other wives of the Holy Prophet. 'Ā'ishah said that she did not like to be given preference such that while she would be buried alongside the grave of the Messenger of Allāh, all others are buried elsewhere. This is what is meant when she said: "I do not wish thereby to be considered more praiseworthy." She did not wish to be praised above the other wives or to have superiority over them. How selfless was she, that she did not even like to be given preference over the other wives in a visible way by being buried along with the Holy Prophet, and wished to remain equal to them. But, undoubtedly, she gained distinction because of her personal excellences. It is probable that 'Ā'ishah took this decision when 'Umar asked her to allow him to be buried alongside the Holy Prophet, as is mentioned in the next ḥadīth (h. 1392), and that it was at that time (or even prior to it) that she made the will instructing 'Abdullāh ibn Zubair which is mentioned here in this ḥadīth. The words "she made a will" do not establish that it was made at the time when she was on her deathbed because there was no space left in the apartment after 'Umar was buried there, who took the only remaining space.

[217] This ḥadīth is part of a long report which Bukhārī has included in his book on 'Virtues of the Companions' as h. 3700. Here, the first part is related to the chapter heading and gives more details about the grave of 'Umar being alongside the graves of the Holy Prophet and Abū Bakr.

When 'Umar was wounded and was near death, he sought permission from 'Ā'ishah that he might be allowed to be buried in her apartment beside the graves of the Holy Prophet and Abū Bakr. When 'Abdullāh, son of 'Umar, went to 'Ā'ishah with his request, she said that she had kept that space for herself but would give preference to 'Umar over herself. This shows that in the apartment there was space for one more grave only and it was 'Ā'ishah's original wish that she should be buried alongside the graves of her husband and her father. But now, having regard for the high stature and honour of 'Umar, and keeping in view the thought mentioned in the previous ḥadīth (h. 1391) that she did not like to be given more honour than the other wives, she

"I do not know of anyone who has more right in the matter of the caliphate than those with whom the Messenger of Allāh ﷺ was pleased till his death. So after me whoever is made Caliph by them will be the Caliph, and you people must listen to him and obey him." He then mentioned the names of 'Uthmān, 'Alī, Ṭalḥah, Zubair, 'Abdur Raḥmān ibn 'Auf, and Sa'd ibn Abī Waqqāṣ.[218]

Now a young man of the Anṣār came and said: "O Chief of the Believers! Be glad with good news from Allāh. The high place you have in Islām is known to you, then you were made Caliph and you ruled with justice, then after all that you have been granted martyrdom." 'Umar replied: "O nephew! If only all these (achievements) would leave me level, so that (in sum total) there is nothing against me and nothing in my favour.[219] I advise the Caliph after me to be good to the early emigrants, to give full recognition to their rights, and to protect their honour. And I also advise him to be good to the Anṣār who had homes (in Madīnah) and remained on the Faith, that he should value the good ones among them and overlook the wrongdoers among them.[220] I advise him regarding the compacts made by Allāh and His Messenger [221]

---

gave this space to 'Umar. 'Umar too was a very conscientious and cautious person and said to his son that after his death permission should be sought again from 'Ā'ishah and only when she granted permission he should be buried there. He knew that 'Ā'ishah desired to be buried alongside the graves of her husband and her father. Both 'Umar and 'Ā'ishah were highly righteous and selfless persons. Where this ḥadīth occurs again (h. 3700), in the chapter 'Qualities of 'Uthmān', it is stated that 'Umar told his son to go to 'Ā'ishah and "not say the Chief of the Believers … but say 'Umar requests your permission", so that it does not sound like a command.

[218] 'Umar named six men out of the ten Companions who were given the promise of Paradise by the Holy Prophet (the *'ashrah mubash-sharah*) to select, by majority opinion, one of them to be the *khalīfah*. In this nomination, he kept in view public opinion, as these were the six persons who were considered most suitable for this position.

[219] This shows that 'Umar considered *khilāfat* or governance as a very responsible and important institution for serving the people. In spite of the fact that during his time the Islamic state was vastly extended, and he excelled in dispensing fair justice, and he accepted the barest minimum as salary from the government treasury, and wore patched clothes, ate simple food, slept on the floor, and worked like an ordinary labourer, but still he considered governance such a great responsibility that he felt that, even if by an unintentional error, he had not fulfilled his duty in some trifling matter he would be held accountable for it before God. That is why he said that if his humble services could counter-balance his omissions in discharging governmental responsibilities, that would be sufficient satisfaction for him. No worldly person can be so highly conscientious with such a sense of responsibility.

[220] It is also in the Qur'ān: "These are they from whom We accept the best of what they do and overlook their evil deeds — among the owners of the Garden" (46 : 16).

[221] Some commentators of Ḥadīth consider *dhimmat-ullāh wa dhimmat rasūli-hī*, the "compacts made by Allāh and His Messenger", as applying to the Muslim masses, but some have taken it to mean the responsibility towards non-Muslim subjects in a Muslim state. Where this ḥadīth has been repeated under 'Qualities of 'Uthmān' (h. 3700) with more details, it shows

(with non-Muslims for their protection) that he must fulfil the agreements with them completely, and fight for them, and not to burden them (with tax) beyond their capacity."

Ch. 97:   What is forbidden as regards speaking ill of the dead

1393 'Ā'ishah reported that the Prophet ﷺ said: "Do not speak ill of the dead, because they have reached (the consequences of) what they sent on ahead (i.e., the deeds they did)." [222]

---

categorically that it means non-Muslim subjects in a Muslim state, because we find separate instructions for various groups. After saying "I advise the Caliph after me", he gives instructions about the early emigrants. Then, each time saying "I advise", he gives instructions about other groups: the Helpers (Anṣār), people of the towns, dwellers of the desert, and then those under the compact of Allāh and His Messenger. This last group can only be non-Muslim subjects of the Muslim state since all Muslims have been covered by the groups mentioned before. The words "he must fulfil the agreements with them completely", which occur both here and in h. 3700, show that non-Muslims are meant because agreements were made with them specifically. By calling these as compacts made by Allāh and His Messenger, it shows how the non-Muslim subjects of a Muslim state have been honoured, and how much importance is given to their rights.

The words of parting advice bequeathed by 'Umar need to be written in letters of gold, especially those uttered in relation to non-Muslim subjects in a Muslim state, who are known in Islamic terminology as _dhimmī_ or _ahl adh-dhimmah_, i.e., those with whom a compact has been made. His instructions were: (1) That the agreement which has been entered into, or will be entered into, with them must be fulfilled. The agreement covers the responsibility of protecting various kinds of rights of the people. It means that the rights of non-Muslim subjects should be fully protected and there should be no negligence in discharging this responsibility. (2) That their lives and properties should be protected at all costs, even if war needs to be waged for their protection against their enemies. (3) That no such demand should be made of them which they do not have the capacity to comply with. It means that the government should not impose any responsibility on them which they have difficulty in carrying out. These were the reasons why non-Muslims preferred to live under Muslim rule rather than the rule of their own co-religionists. Once 'Umar saw an old non-Muslim begging. As a result, he not only instructed that _jizyah_ should not be imposed on people who cannot pay it, but even that that man and other disabled or old people should be paid a regular stipend from the government treasury.

[222] Just as it is forbidden to speak ill of the dead, it is also forbidden in case of a living person. But there is a difference between the two. Sometimes the faults of a living person are mentioned with the aim to correct him so that he may turn away from his wrong-doing and adopt the right way. But this object cannot be achieved in the case of a dead person, as he is already facing the consequences of the deeds he did in this world, as has been made clear in this ḥadīth. Thus, by speaking ill is meant speaking badly of him regarding his personal matters which affect only him. But where his misdeeds affect others or the community as a whole, then it is allowed to the wronged party to criticise him, whether he is alive or dead, as the Qur'ān says: "Allāh does not love the public utterance of hurtful speech, except by one who has been wronged" (4:148). For example, to scrutinise the narrators of Ḥadīth, and to expose their carelessness or fabrication, or in any matters which affect other people's rights, it is allowed to mention the faults of the dead.

Ch. 98:　Mentioning the evil ones among the dead[223]

1394 Ibn 'Abbās reported that Abū Lahab once said to the Prophet ﷺ: "May you always be doomed to destruction!" Then it was revealed: "Abū Lahab's hands will perish and he will perish!" (the Quran, 111:1).

Thus, the prohibition in the ḥadīth applies only to matters which affect just the deceased personally. That is why Bukhārī has used the words "What is forbidden" in the chapter heading, which implies that in certain cases talking ill of a dead person is allowed, and this has been further explained in the next chapter.

[223] Here by "the evil ones among the dead" are not meant such dead persons who have committed evil that is merely harmful to their own selves, but those who spread wickedness, as has been explained by mentioning the name of Abū Lahab. His name is mentioned in the Qur'ān not because he was wicked in his person but because he spread wickedness and persecuted people. Wherever the Holy Prophet went to preach, Abū Lahab followed him and told people that he was a liar and that they should not listen to him, and sometimes he even threw stones at the Holy Prophet and injured him. Talking about the evil deeds and wickedness of such people is not prohibited because the intention is to warn or admonish others.

PART 6

Book 24: *Az-Zakāt*

Zakāt — Obligatory Charity

In the name of Allāh, the Beneficent, the Merciful

Ch. 1: *Zakāt* enjoined and the word of Allāh: "Keep up prayer and pay the *Zakāt*"[1]

Ibn 'Abbās said: Abū Sufyān narrated to me, mentioning the ḥadīth of the Prophet ﷺ, and said: "He (the Prophet) enjoins on us prayer and *Zakāt* and regard for ties of relationship and chastity."[2]

1395 Ibn 'Abbās reported that the Prophet ﷺ sent Mu'ādh to Yaman and said: "Invite them to bear witness that there is no god but Allāh and that I am the Messenger of Allāh. If they follow this, let them know that Allāh has made

---

[1] *Zakāt,* i.e., to give away a fixed portion of your wealth for the poor and needy, is the second fundamental principle of Islām. The Qur'ān also generally mentions it after *Ṣalāt* or Prayer or both together: "And keep up prayer and pay the *Zakāt*" (2:43, etc.). The word *zakāt* is derived from *zakā,* which means growth of the crop. It has been applied to the giving away of a fixed portion of wealth for the upkeep of the poor because in reality the wealth increases thereby. If we ponder over it, we will see that increase in wealth does not depend on one individual but is related to the collective effort of the whole community. Thus the purpose of paying *Zakāt* is to help the poor to work and earn money, which increases the wealth of the community and enables all its members to progress financially. The way Muslims generally pay *Zakāt* these days, it goes mostly to a few idle and indolent people who consume it while doing nothing. This does not fulfil the real purpose of *Zakāt. Zakāt* is a means of increasing the wealth of the community and that is the Divine reward for it in this world because the payer himself benefits from the material development of the community as a whole. Its reward in the hereafter is that, since money is what a man loves most, he indulges in many wrongful ways of acquiring it, so when he gives away a share of his wealth in obedience to the Divine command two things happen. Firstly, in his heart love for wealth is reduced and, as a consequence, love for God is increased which is the source of all good deeds. Secondly, when he acquires the habit of giving his wealth in obedience to God, it will restrain him from unjustly taking the wealth of others which is also forbidden by the command of God. Thus the paying of *Zakāt* leads to reward in the hereafter.

[2] Bukhārī has started the Book on *Zakāt* with a verse of the Qur'ān, as all commandments are based on the Qur'ān while their details are found in the Ḥadīth. Here a portion of a report about *Zakāt* by Ibn 'Abbās has been mentioned which occurs in h. 7. But there the word *zakāt* is not found and it says: "…he enjoins on us prayer and truthfulness and chastity and regard for the ties of relationship." Here the commandments regarding prayer, *Zakāt,* ties of relationship and moral purity have been mentioned.

obligatory for them five prayers during the day and night. If they follow this, let them know that Allāh has made obligatory for them to pay charity (*ṣada-qah*) on their wealth, which is taken from their wealthy ones and given to their needy ones." [3]

1396 Abū Ayyūb reported that a man asked the Prophet ﷺ: "Inform me of an act which may make me enter Paradise." Somebody asked: "What is the matter with him, what is the matter with him?" The Prophet ﷺ said: "He wants to know; nothing is the matter with him. Serve Allāh and do not set up any partner with Him, and keep up prayer, and pay the *Zakāt*, and show regard for the ties of relationship."

1397 Abū Hurairah reported that a Bedouin came to the Prophet ﷺ and said: "Tell me of an act which if I do I will enter Paradise." He (the Prophet) said: "Serve Allāh and do not set up any partner with Him, and keep up the prescribed prayer, and pay the obligatory *Zakāt*, and keep fast in the month of Ramaḍān." The Bedouin said: "By Him in Whose Hand is my life, I shall not add to this." When he left, the Prophet ﷺ said: "Whoever likes to see an inhabitant of Paradise, let him see this (person)." [4]

1398 Ibn ʿAbbās said that a delegation of the tribe of ʿAbdul Qais came to the Prophet ﷺ and said: "O Messenger of Allāh, we are from the tribe of Rabīʿah and the unbelievers of the tribe of Muḍar stand between us and you, so we cannot come to you except during the sacred months. So order us to do things which we may carry out and also invite to them our people whom we have left behind." He (the Prophet) said: "I order you to do four things and forbid you four things. To believe in Allāh and bear witness that there is no god but Allāh" — and he clenched his hand like this — "and to keep up prayer,

---

[3] This is a gradual process of inviting to Islām, which is the right way of preaching. First, people were enjoined to believe in the Oneness of God and the Messengership of Muḥammad, then prayer, followed by *Zakāt*. The definition of *Zakāt* mentioned at the end states its real objec-tive: to take from the wealthy and give to the needy. In this way both sections of society become active partners in economic progress, and thus a source of strength for the entire community.

[4] The statement "I shall not add to this" implies also that he would not detract from this because when one side is mentioned the other side is generally also implied. That is why in Ṣaḥīḥ Muslim in the same report the words "nor shall I detract from this" have been added in his statement (book: 'Faith', ch. 4). See also h. 46 and h. 1891. The Holy Prophet's saying that he is an inhabitant of Paradise means that a person who is so committed and enthusiastic as to act on these commandments with full understanding shows signs of one who earns Paradise. As to the question that several other commandments have not been mentioned, we can reasonably presume that such a dedicated person will not refuse to act upon any commandment of Allāh or His Messenger which will come to him. It is meant that entry into Paradise is dependent on the inner state of a person and he who meets Allāh after obeying Him with a sincere and true heart will not be deprived of Paradise.

and pay the *Zakāt*, and to give (in Allāh's way) one-fifth of what you acquire in war. And I forbid you to use *dubbā', ḥantam, naqīr* and *muzaffat*.".[5]

1399–1400 Abū Hurairah said: When the Messenger of Allāh ﷺ died and Abū Bakr became the Caliph, some from among the Arabs became disbelievers. 'Umar said (to him): "How are you going to fight with the people, whereas the Messenger of Allāh ﷺ said: 'I have been commanded to fight with people until they say that there is no god but Allāh, so whoever affirms it he will save his property and his life from me, except if there is some duty upon him (to fulfil), and he shall be accountable before Allāh'."

[1400] So he (Abū Bakr) said: "By Allāh! I shall fight with him who differentiates between prayer and *Zakāt*, because *Zakāt* is a charge over wealth. By Allāh! if they withhold from me even a kid of a she-goat which they used to give to the Messenger of Allāh ﷺ, I shall fight them for their withholding of it." 'Umar said: "By Allāh! The fact was that Allāh had opened Abū Bakr's heart (in understanding), so I realised that it was right." [6]

Ch. 2: To pledge to pay the *Zakāt*

"But if they repent and keep up prayer and give the due charity, they are your brethren in faith" (the Qur'ān, 9:11).[7]

---

[5] This is a repetition of h. 53 in brief. The four things in the closing words are names of utensils used for preparing alcoholic drinks, being respectively: vessels made of gourd, green jars, troughs of hollowed palm-trunk, and vessels smeared with pitch.

In h. 53, fasting in Ramaḍān has also been mentioned which is missing here as well as in the repetition of h. 53 in h. 523.

[6] The words attributed to the Holy Prophet in this report have already occurred in h. 25 and h. 392, and have been fully discussed in the footnotes under those reports. It has been shown there that this refers to *ceasing* to fight those people against whom fighting had *already* been undertaken by the Muslims according to the verse of the Qur'ān: "And fight in the way of Allāh against those who fight against you" (2 : 190). If they should become Muslims, then fighting with them should be stopped. As regards the waging of war by Abū Bakr against the people who refused to pay *Zakāt* on the death of the Holy Prophet, it was because this was a movement against paying tax to the government. *Zakāt* was a tax levied on Muslims, just as *jizyah* was a tax on non-Muslims. Refusal by a community to pay government taxes is rebellion, and there is no option but to fight it. However, the words of Abū Bakr to fight against the one who differentiates between prayer and *Zakāt* have given rise to a misconception that fighting must also be undertaken against those who do not say prayers. There is no evidence in the law or in the history of Islām that the Holy Prophet ever gave any such order or taken any such action, or that any of the Righteous Caliphs had done so. The statement only means that if people who believe in prayer, that is, they are Muslims, but do not accept the commandment to pay *Zakāt* and thus do not pay this tax to the government, he will fight them to take what is due from them. This is what happened at that time. To "differentiate" (*farraqa*) means to accept one belief but not the other. See also h. 1456–1457.

[7] This verse refers to those who were already fighting against the Muslims. Muslims are told

1401 Jarīr ibn ʿAbdullāh (al-Bajalī) said: I swore allegiance to the Prophet ﷺ to keep up prayer, pay the *Zakāt* and have goodwill for every Muslim.[8]

Ch. 3:   The sin of him who does not pay the *Zakāt*

The word of Allāh: "And those who hoard up gold and silver and do not spend it in Allāh's way … so taste what you used to hoard" (the Qur'ān, 9:34–35).[9]

1402 Abū Hurairah said that the Prophet ﷺ said: "(On the Day of Judgment) camels healthier than before will come upon their owner if he has not paid the due *(Zakāt)* for them and trample him under their feet; and she-goats healthier than before will come upon their owner if he has not paid the due *(Zakāt)* for them and tread upon him with their hooves and gore him with their horns." And he (the Holy Prophet further) said: "And among the dues for them is that they should be milked near the water." [10] And he (the Prophet further) said: "Let not anyone from among you come to me carrying a sheep upon his neck, while she would be moaning, and say: 'O Muḥammad (save me)!' for I will say: 'I can do nothing for you. I had conveyed to you the

---

that if such people embrace Islām then Muslims must stop fighting them as they are now their brothers, and forgive their previous animosities.

[8] This is a repetition of h. 57 in the same words. Jarīr swore allegiance (referred to as taking a pledge or *baiʿat*) with the Holy Prophet to do these things.

[9] In these verses, those people are mentioned who amass wealth and do not spend it in the way of Allāh; that is, they do not pay the *Zakāt* which is obligatory. So as a punishment, on the Day of Judgment their foreheads etc. will be branded with that same wealth. Bukhārī has quoted this verse here to show that the punishment for people who refuse to pay the *Zakāt* is of the same form in the Ḥadīth as it is in this verse of the Qur'ān. There is no doubt that punishment for any evil act is in accordance with the nature of the act and bears resemblance to it. But as the punishment spoken of is spiritual, it is mentioned in the same terms as the evil in order only to show the similarity. Also, it cannot be that a person who amasses wealth in the form of cash or in bank accounts, instead of as gold and silver, will escape God's punishment. The real purpose is to show that as the wealth was amassed to satisfy his physical desires and earn worldly glory, the same wealth will become the source of his humiliation and suffering. Further on in h. 1403 it is mentioned that the same wealth will become like a snake around his neck, as the Qur'ān says: "They shall have a collar of their miserliness on their necks on the day of Resurrection" (3:180). The real purpose is to mention the punishment, the nature of which in the life after death is known only to Allāh. Similarly, in this ḥadīth various punishments are described in words related to the sin. Camels and goats will not be physically resurrected on the Day of Judgment. These have been mentioned as symbolic of the punishment.

[10] In some reports the following words occur: "Certainly in (your) wealth there are other dues in addition to *Zakāt*" (Tirmidhī, book: *Zakāt*, h. 659, 660). One example is to milk a cow at the pasture. Because water is available at such places, travellers take a break there, and milk can be given away to the needy among them. This shows how strongly the Holy Prophet felt about the need to relieve every kind of human suffering.

message.' [11] Nor let anyone from among you come to me carrying a camel upon his neck, while it would be grunting, and say: 'O Muḥammad (save me)!' for I will say: 'I can do nothing for you. I had conveyed to you the message.' "

1403 Abū Hurairah reported that the Messenger of Allāh ﷺ said: "To Whomever Allāh gives wealth and he does not pay *Zakāt* on it, that wealth on the Day of Judgment will be like a bald snake on whose eyes will be two black spots. On the Day of Judgment it will be around his neck and it will hold the two corners of his mouth and say: 'I am your wealth, I am your treasure'." Then he recited (the verse): "And those who are miserly in spending what Allah has granted them out of His grace should not think that it is good for them. Rather, it is evil for them. They shall have a collar of their miserliness on their necks on the day of Resurrection" (3:180).

Ch. 4: Wealth on which *Zakāt* has been paid is not considered hoarded[12]

As the Prophet ﷺ said: "On anything less than five *auqiyah* there is no *Zakāt*."

1404 Khālid ibn Aslam reported: We went out with 'Abdullāh ibn 'Umar, and a Bedouin said: "Explain to me the word of Allāh: 'And those who hoard up gold and silver and do not spend it in Allāh's way' (the Qur'ān, 9:34)." Ibn 'Umar said: "Anyone who hoarded wealth and did not pay *Zakāt* on it, woe to him! This was before the command of *Zakāt* had been revealed; when that was revealed, Allāh purified the wealth through it." [13]

---

[11] People who neglect doing good deeds because they think they can depend entirely on the intercession of the Holy Prophet on the day of Judgment should seriously ponder over his words in this ḥadīth.

[12] The word *kanz* means amassing or hoarding wealth. It occurs in the Qur'ān: "Those who hoard up gold and silver" (9:34), and the hoarders have been warned about the punishment for them in the Hereafter. The heading means that when *Zakāt* has been paid on wealth, it no longer is regarded as *kanz* or "hoarded". The verse itself says: "and they do not spend it in Allāh's way" (9:34), where spending in the way of Allāh means paying *Zakāt* out of it.

[13] Ibn 'Umar, commenting on 9:34 of the Qur'ān, said that this commandment was revealed before *Zakāt* was promulgated and he has understood it as meaning the spending of all the wealth one has accumulated. Then he added that when the commandment of *Zakāt* was revealed, it declared that wealth was purified after *Zakāt* was paid on it. In other words, the accumulation of wealth is allowed subject to the condition that *Zakāt* is paid out of it. However, chapter 9 of the Qur'ān was revealed in 9 A.H. and *Zakāt* was made obligatory long before it. It is possible that full details about *Zakāt* were given afterwards, but that cannot be called the time when *Zakāt* was promulgated. That, however, is a separate discussion.

1405 Abū Saʿīd (al-Khudrī) said that the Prophet ﷺ said: "On anything less than five *auqiyah* there is no *Zakāt,* on camels fewer than five there is no *Zakāt,* and on anything less than five *wasq* there is no *Zakāt.*" [14]

1406 Zaid ibn Wahb reported: I passed by ar-Rabadhah[15] and chanced to meet Abū Dharr.[16] I asked him: "Why have you settled here?" He said: "I was in Syria and I had a difference with Muʿāwiyah[17] as to people who were hoarding gold and silver and not spending it in the way of Allāh. Muʿāwiyah said: 'This (i.e., 9:34) has been revealed about the People of the Book.' I said: 'It is about us as well as them.' So there was a discussion between Muʿāwiyah and me about it. He wrote to (the Caliph) ʿUthmān, complaining about me. ʿUthmān then wrote to me to come to Madīnah. I came and people started asking me (about my stay) so much as if they had not seen me before. I mentioned this to ʿUthmān and he said to me: 'If you wish you can go elsewhere to live and be near.' That is why I am living at this place. And even if a black African had been made leader over me I would listen (to him) and obey." [18]

1407–1408 Abul-ʿAlā' ibn ash-Shikhkhīr reported from al-Aḥnaf ibn Qais that he said: I was sitting among a group of Quraish when a man came, who had very rough hair, clothes and appearance. He stood by them and greeted them. Then he said: "Inform those who hoard wealth that (in the Hereafter) there will be a stone which will be heated in the fire of Hell and then placed on the nipples of their breasts till it pierces through the bones of their shoulders, and it will be put on the bones of their shoulders till it pierces through their nipples and it will be moving from one side to the other." Then he went and sat near a pillar and I followed him and sat besides him. I did not know

---

[14] One *auqiyah* is 40 dirhams (said to be about 128 grams). Its plural, used in this ḥadīth, is *awāq* (and this is for reckoning *Zakāt* on silver). One *wasq* is 60 *ṣāʿ* (one *ṣāʿ* said to be about 3 kgs). Its plural, used in this ḥadīth, is *ausuq* (and this is for grain). Anyone who has less wealth than this does not have to pay *Zakāt.* See also h. 1447, h. 1459 and h. 1484.

[15] Ar-Rabadhah was a village at a distance of three days' journey from Madīnah.

[16] Abū Dharr was a Companion of the Holy Prophet with an ascetic bent of mind. His view was that the keeping of any wealth was a sin, and it should all be given in the way of Allāh as charity. On this point he differed with all the other Companions.

[17] At that time Muʿāwiyah was Governor of Syria appointed by the Caliph ʿUthmān.

[18] In regard to *Ijtihād,* or exercise of personal judgment and reasoning, the Companions enjoyed such complete freedom that in the matter of the accumulation of wealth, Abū Dharr held one view and all other Companions held the opposite view. But no one condemned Abū Dharr for holding such an extreme view. Today, anyone who differs with the majority view is declared as doomed to Hell. In this case, as far as is known, one Companion is opposing all other Companions, but no stricture or edict is passed against him. However, as his extreme view was spreading dissension, ʿUthmān advised him privately to live away from people but nearby, and he agreed to the suggestion.

who he was. I said to him: "I think the group did not like what you said." He replied: "They do not know anything. [1408] My friend said this to me." I said: "Who do you mean by your friend?" He said: "The Prophet ﷺ said: 'O Abū Dharr! Do you see the Mount of Uḥud?' So I started looking towards the sun to see how much time of the day was left as I thought that the Messenger of Allāh ﷺ wanted to send me to do something he required. I said: 'Yes.' He (the Prophet) then said: 'I do not like that I should have gold as much as the Mount of Uḥud but that I would distribute it all except three dinārs.' [19] And these people do not know anything and hoard worldly wealth. And by Allāh! I will not ask them anything about this world nor anything relating to religion until I meet my Lord."

Ch. 5:   Spending of wealth rightly

1409 Ibn Mas'ūd reported that he heard the Prophet ﷺ say: "There shall be no envy except in (case of) two: a man to whom Allāh has given wealth and the power to spend it in the way of truth, and a man to whom Allāh has given wisdom and he judges according to it and teaches it." [20]

Ch. 6:   Giving charity for show

Because of the word of Allāh: "O you who believe, do not make your charity worthless by reproach and injury, like him who spends his wealth to be seen by people and does not believe in Allāh and the Last Day. So his parable is as the parable of a smooth rock with earth upon it, then heavy rain (*wābil-un*) falls upon it, so it leaves it bare (*ṣald-an*)! They are not able to gain anything of what they earn. And Allāh does not guide the disbelieving people" (2:264).

Ibn 'Abbās said: "*Ṣald-an* means there is nothing on it." 'Ikrimah said: "*Wābil-un* means heavy rain, and *aṭ-ṭall-un* means dew."

Ch. 7:   Allāh does not accept charity from wealth dishonestly earned and only accepts charity from wealth earned by lawful means

Because of the word of Allāh: "A kind word with forgiveness is better than charity followed by injury. And Allāh is Self-sufficient, Forbearing" (2:263).

---

[19] The error made by Abū Dharr was to believe that every Muslim could reach the high standard on which the Holy Prophet or his great Companions were established. To spend all wealth in the way of Allāh is the highest degree of charity but to keep wealth after paying due *Zakāt* on it is not a sin.

[20] This is a repetition of h. 73. See the footnotes to that ḥadīth.

Ch. 8: Charity from wealth honestly earned

Because of the word of Allāh: "Allāh will blot out usury, and He causes charity to prosper. And Allāh does not love any ungrateful sinner. Those who believe and do good deeds and keep up prayer and give the *Zakāt* — their reward is with their Lord; and they have no fear, nor shall they grieve" (2:276–77).

1410 Abū Hurairah reported that the Messenger of Allāh ﷺ said: "Whoever gives charity even to the extent of one date out of wealth earned honestly — for Allāh only accepts charity earned honestly — surely Allāh accepts it with His right hand and then increases it for its giver just as anyone of you who brings up a calf till it becomes (big in size) like a mountain."

Ch. 9: To give charity before (the time comes when) there is no one to accept it

1411 Ḥārithah ibn Wahb said: I heard the Prophet ﷺ saying: "Give charity because surely a time will come on you when a man will go about with charity and he will find no one to accept it. Someone will say: If you had come with it yesterday I would have accepted it, but today I have no need of it." [21]

1412 Abū Hurairah reported that the Prophet ﷺ said: "The (promised) hour will not come till you will have abundance of wealth as if it were flowing (like water). A wealthy one will become worried as to who will accept his charity and at that time he will offer it and to whomsoever he will present it he will say: I do not need it."

1413 ʿAdiyy ibn Ḥātim said: I was with the Messenger of Allāh ﷺ when two men came to him. One of them complained about his poverty and the other complained about insecurity (during travelling) on the highways. The Messenger of Allāh ﷺ said: "As to insecurity on the highways, you will shortly see a time when a caravan will leave Makkah without any guard. And as to poverty, the (promised) hour will not come until one of you will go around with his charity but will not find anyone to accept it. Then one of you will stand before Allāh and there will be no veil between him and Allāh, nor an interpreter to interpret for him. Then Allāh will say to him: 'Had I not given you wealth?' He will say: 'Certainly.' Then Allāh will say: 'Did I not send a Messenger to you?' He will say: 'Certainly.' Then he will look to his right and

---

[21] As is evident from h. 1413 this prophecy was made at a time when Muslims were going through very difficult times. During the reign of ʿUmar, and afterwards, because of the extension of the Muslim state, immense wealth came to Madīnah, which was beyond the imagination of the Arabs. It was not concentrated in the hands of a few individuals but the whole Muslim nation benefitted from the affluence. The prophecy intends to convey that Muslims will not only get immense wealth but even the poorest of them will also benefit from it.

he will see nothing but fire, and then he will look to his left see nothing but fire. So every one of you should guard himself against the fire (of hell) even by (giving in charity) a piece of date. And if you do not find even that, then (at least say) a good word." [22]

1414 Abū Mūsā reported from the Prophet ﷺ that he said: "A time will come over the people when a man will walk around with gold as charity but will not find anyone to accept it. And one man will be seen followed by forty women seeking his protection because of scarcity of men and abundance of women." [23]

Ch. 10: **And guard yourselves against the fire (of hell) even by a piece of date**

And with a little charity: "And the parable of those who spend their wealth to seek Allah's pleasure and for the strengthening of their souls is as the parable of a garden on elevated ground" (the Qur'ān, 2:265) to the word of Allāh: "he has in it all kinds of fruits" (2:266).

1415 Abū Mas'ūd reported: When the verse of charity was revealed, at that time they used to work as porters. A man came and donated a great quantity of goods in charity. They (the hypocrites) said: "He is doing it for show." A man came and gave one *ṣā'* in charity. They said: "Allāh does not need this (small amount of) one *ṣā'*." So this was revealed: "Those who taunt the free-givers of charity among the believers as well as those who cannot find anything to give but with hard labour..." (the Qur'ān, 9:79).[24]

1416 Abū Mas'ūd al-Anṣārī reported: When the Messenger of Allāh ﷺ used to command us to give charity, one of us would go to the market and work as a porter and would earn one *mudd* (and give charity out of it). And today some of them own one hundred thousand.[25]

---

[22] Here even speaking a good and kind word to someone has been regarded as a charity (*ṣadaqah*), thus broadening the concept of charity. To see nothing but fire is an indication that the person is extremely miserly. Let alone the punishment in the hereafter, in this world also when a nation is miserly in spending on good works it sees nothing but disappointment and failure. The condition of Muslims today is that they are suffering punishment for not sacrificing wealth in the way of Allāh.

[23] The preponderance of women in the population generally happens during wars when men are killed in great numbers. The prophecy about the abudance of women indicates that Muslims will have to face wars, and the increase in wealth predicts their victory.

[24] The rest of this verse is as follows: "— they scoff at them. Allāh will pay them back their mockery; and for them is a painful punishment."

[25] *Mudd* is a weight equal to about 700 grams. Muslims were so enthusiastic for the cause of

1417 ʿAdiyy ibn Ḥātim said that he heard the Messenger of Allāh ﷺ say: "Guard yourselves against the fire (of hell) even by (giving in charity) a piece of date." [26]

1418 ʿĀ'ishah reported: A woman came with her two daughters and asked for some charity. I did not have anything except a date, so I gave it to her. She divided it among her two daughters and did not eat of it herself. Then she got up and left. The Prophet ﷺ came to us and I informed him about it. He said: "Anyone who is tried because of daughters, it will act as a shield for him against the fire (of hell)." [27]

Ch. 11: Excellence of giving of charity while one desires wealth (*shaḥīḥ*) [28] and is in good health

> Because of the word of Allāh: "And spend out of what We have given you before death comes to one of you..." (the Qur'ān, 63:10). And His word: "O you who believe, spend out of what We have given you before the day comes in which there is no bargaining, nor friendship, nor intercession..." (2:254).

1419 Abū Hurairah related: A man came to the Prophet ﷺ and asked: "O Messenger of Allāh, Which charity is more rewarding?" He (the Prophet) said: "That you give charity when you are healthy, desiring of wealth (through greed and miserliness), afraid of poverty and hope to be wealthy, and that you do not

---

religion that when they were commanded to give in charity — and this was for the service of the faith — they would not hesitate to do even the lowly work of lifting loads in the market to earn and give in charity.

[26] This is a repetition, in a slightly different form, of the words occurring just before the end of h. 1413.

[27] The Holy Prophet Muhammad was the ruler of the country, the spiritual teacher, and prophet. Yet he had nothing in his home but a date. It is taught here that if someone can only give a meagre amount in charity he should give even that much, without feeling embarrassed. This ḥadīth also shows that to bring up daughters and to educate them are highly commendable and worthy tasks, and if somebody faces difficulties while bringing them up, these should be accepted cheerfully, because bearing hardship for their sake will save one from the punishment of the fire in the hereafter.

The Holy Prophet has enjoined Muslims to honour women. They hold the position of mother, wife and daughter. Service to the mother is mentioned by him in the words: "Paradise lies at the feet of mothers"; regarding good treatment of the wife he said: "The best of you is he who treats his wife the best" (Ibn Majah, book: 'Marriage', ḥadīth 1977, 1978); and for bearing difficulties and hardship in bringing up a daughter, he said it saves that parent from the punishment of the fire.

[28] The word *shaḥīḥ* is from *shaḥḥ* which means miserliness combined with greed. Thus *shaḥīḥ* is one who desires to earn wealth but his own requirements are so much that he is disinclined to spend anything in the way of Allāh.

delay it until death approaches and then you say: 'Give so much to this person and so much to that person,' while it already belongs to such and such." [29]

Ch. 12:   Regarding the above

1420 'Ā'ishah reported that some of the wives of the Prophet ﷺ asked him: "Which one of us will be the first to meet you (after death)?" He replied: "Whoever of you has the longest hand." So they started measuring their hands with a stick, and Saudah had the longest hand. Later (when Zainab died),[30] we came to know that by the length of her hand was meant giving in charity, and she was the first to die after him, and she had great love for giving in charity.

Ch. 13:   To give charity publicly

The word of Allāh: "Those who spend their wealth by night and day, privately and publicly, their reward is with their Lord. And they have no fear, nor shall they grieve" (the Qur'ān, 2:274).

Ch. 14:   To give charity privately (or secretly)

Abū Hurairah reported from the Prophet ﷺ: "And a person gives charity hiding it, so much so that his left hand does not know what his right hand gives."

---

[29] The real object of charity is to reduce one's love of wealth. Thus the Holy Prophet said that the right time of giving wealth in charity is when there is no fear of approaching death, and there is desire to earn more and become wealthier. Giving in charity in such a state helps in perfecting one's moral character. Then the Holy Prophet mentions the condition of people generally, that during life they love wealth so much so that they never think of giving anything in charity, but when death stares them in the face they then start distributing charity, when in fact their wealth now belongs to others who are about to inherit it.

[30] This is apparently referring to Saudah, and it is written in *Fath al-Bārī*, the famous commentary on Ṣaḥīḥ Bukhārī, that Bukhārī, in his book *Tarīkh al-Ṣaghīr*, has explicitly written that "Saudah was the first to die" from among the wives of the Holy Prophet. But historically it is wrong. In the report in Ṣaḥīḥ Muslim it is clearly stated by 'Ā'ishah that Zainab was the first to die: "Zainab was the most generous (lit., one with the longest hands) among us because she used to work with her own hands and give (out of that) in charity" (book: 'Virtues of the Companions', ch. 17: 'Virtues of Zainab'). *Fath al-Bārī* mentions a report from Ḥākim in *Mustadrak* that 'Ā'ishah said: "When we (wives of the Prophet) would get together in a house of one of us after the death of the Prophet ﷺ, we would measure our hands on the wall. We continued doing so till Zainab ibn Jaḥsh died. She was short in height and did not have the longest hand. Then we realised that by length of hand the Prophet meant charity. Zainab used to work with the hands and do tanning of leather and used to give (what she made) in charity." That is why in translating this ḥadīth, Zainab has been indicated. She died in 20 A.H. This ḥadīth also tells us that the wives of the Holy Prophet measured their hands in front of him but he did not forbid them. The ḥadīth has been included here to show the excellence of acts of charity.

The word of Allāh: "If you manifest charity, how excellent it is! And if you hide it and give it to the poor, it is good for you. And it will do away with some of your evil deeds; and Allāh is aware of what you do" (2:271).[31]

Ch. 15:   When charity is given to a wealthy one unknowingly

1421 Abū Hurairah reported that the Messenger of Allah ﷺ said: "A man said: 'I will certainly give in charity.' So he set out with his charity and gave it to a thief. People started talking, that a thief has been given charity. He said: 'O Allāh, praise be to You! I will certainly give (even) more charity.' Again he set out with his charity and gave it to a prostitute. People started talking, saying this night a prostitute was given charity. He said: 'O Allāh, praise be to You for (my giving charity to) a prostitute! I will certainly give (even) more charity.' Again he set out with his charity and gave it to a wealthy person. People started talking, that a wealthy person has been given charity. He said: 'O Allāh, praise be to You for (my giving charity to) a thief and a prostitute and a wealthy person.' Then someone came to him and said: 'As to your giving charity to a thief, it may prevent him from his stealing, and as to the prostitute, it may prevent her from her whoredom, and as to the wealthy person, he may learn a lesson and start giving out of what Allāh has given him'." [32]

Ch. 16:   When one gives charity to one's own son unknowingly

1422 Ma'n ibn Yazīd related: I took the pledge at the hand of the Messenger of Allāh ﷺ, I as well as my father and my grandfather. He (the Holy Prophet) proposed a marriage for me and conducted my *nikāḥ* (marriage solemnisation). I brought to him a dispute (to settle). My father Yazīd took out some gold coins for charity and kept them with a man in a mosque. I came and took them (from the man) and brought them to my father. He said: "By Allāh! I did not intend to give them to you." So I brought this dispute to the Messenger of Allāh ﷺ. He said: "O Yazīd, for you is what you intended, and Ma'n, for you is what you took." [33]

---

[31] By having two chapters, one about giving in charity publicly and openly (ch. 13), and one about giving in charity privately and secretly (ch. 14), Bukhārī shows that the teachings of Islām are perfect. It does not advocate that you should give charity only in secrecy but also encourages people to give charity openly because for national projects public acts of charity are essential. Where charity is meant for needy individuals, it should be done in secrecy, as he has made clear by quoting the Qur'ān (2:271). Just as this verse mentions public charity first, Bukhārī has adopted the same order in placing the chapter on public charity before the one on secret charity.

[32] The giver of charity is consoled that he would not be deprived of reward if his charity goes to one not deserving it.

[33] The Holy Prophet allowed the giving of charity by the father to his son, by saying "for you

Ch. 17: Giving charity with the right hand

1423 Abū Hurairah reported from the Prophet ﷺ that he said: "There are seven persons whom Allāh, the Most High, will give His protection ..." [34]

1424 Ḥārithah ibn Wahb said: I heard the Prophet ﷺ saying: "Give charity because a time will come on you when a man will go about with charity and someone will say: If you had come with it yesterday I would have accepted it from you, but today I have no need of it." [35]

Ch. 18: One who orders his servant to give in charity and does not give it in person himself

Abū Mūsā reported from the Prophet ﷺ: "He (the servant) is one of the two who give in charity." [36]

1425 ʿĀ'ishah reported that the Prophet ﷺ said: "When a woman gives in charity from the meal of her house without causing any loss, she will get the reward for what she gave, and her husband will get the reward for what he earned (i.e., the money spent on the food). And a guardian of (someone's) money will get similar reward. No one will decrease the reward for anyone else at all." [37]

---

is what you intended", i.e., you intended to give to a deserving person and such a one has received it. He did not ask him to return it. It appears that the son was earning an income because he was married, but as he was not wealthy he was not considered ineligible for charity due merely to being the son. Still, it is not clear from this ḥadīth, nor the previous one, whether the charity mentioned came under the head of *Zakāt* or general charity. But the finally established system for *Zakāt* in those days was that it all went to the public treasury and it was disbursed from there. Therefore, if someone is entitled to receive *Zakāt* he cannot be deprived because his father is wealthy. A father cannot be considered responsible for the whole of his life for providing financial support to his son.

[34] This is a repetition of h. 660 with very slight difference in wording. For the remainder see h. 660, and see also the footnotes under it. Seven persons are mentioned as being kept under His protection by Allāh. One of these is "a man who gives charity in secret so much so that his left hand does not know what his right hand spends." The chapter heading is related to these words.

[35] This is a repetition of h. 1411 in almost the same wording, except that it does not include the words: "and he will find no one to accept it." The mention of giving charity with the right hand in the chapter heading does not occur in this ḥadīth.

[36] It means that one giver of charity is the master, by whose instructions and from whose wealth charity is being given, and the other giver of charity is the servant who is distributing charity in compliance with the instructions of the master. Often it is servants who become a hindrance for their masters in the distribution of charity.

[37] The relationship between husband and wife is obvious: he earns and entrusts his earning to the wife as to how to spend it. That is why it is said that as long as she does not cause financial problems thereby, she is allowed to give something out of it in charity. A guardian of someone's

Ch. 19:   Charity is only when one has sufficient wealth

And as to one who gives in charity while he or his family are poor, or he is under debt, paying off the debt has priority over giving in charity or freeing a slave or making a gift. Such charity will be returned to him; it is not right for him to waste the wealth of people (who are more entitled to it). The Prophet ﷺ said: "One who takes the wealth of (other) people wishing to destroy it, Allāh will destroy him." Except when he is known for his patience, he can prefer a needy person over his own hardship as was done by Abū Bakr when he gave away all his wealth in charity, and likewise, the *Anṣār* ('Helpers of Madīnah') preferred (to give for) the needs of the *Muhājirīn* ('Refugees from Makkah'). The Prophet ﷺ forbade the squandering of wealth; so no one has the right to waste the wealth of people in charity. And Ka'b ibn Mālik said: "I said: 'O Messenger of Allāh ﷺ, it is a part of my repentance to give my wealth in charity to Allāh and His Messenger ﷺ and be free of it.' He (the Holy Prophet) said: 'Keep some of your property for yourself; that will be better for you.' So I said: 'I will keep to myself what I acquired at Khaibar'." [38]

1426 Abū Hurairah reported that the Prophet ﷺ said: "A good charity is that which is given while one is well-off. And pay him first for whom you are responsible." [39]

1427–1428 Ḥakīm ibn Ḥizām reported from the Prophet ﷺ that he said: "The upper hand is better than the lower hand. And pay him first for whom you are responsible. And a good charity is that which is given while one is well-off. And he who wishes to save himself (from asking for charity), Allāh

---

money is in a similar position. However, as he is only entrusted with the money, he cannot give any of it in charity without order or permission of the owner, as indicated in the heading of the chapter. See also h. 1437.

[38] The perfection of the teachings of Islām is shown by the fact that on the one hand it emphasises so much the giving away of wealth in charity as to declare it as one of the fundamentals of the religion, but on the other hand it exhorts that you should not give away everything and become penniless and start begging, or that you should give in charity while your family are in need, or that you give charitable gifts and donations when you are in debt since your property belongs to those to whom you owe money. If, however, a person can cheerfully bear hardship in the way of Allāh, and feels no difficulty in imposing burden on himself, then he may give away even all his wealth, as Abū Bakr did, or if he, despite his own needs, can give preference to relieving the hardship of others, he can do so, as did the Helpers of Madīnah.

[39] This ḥadīth consists of two parts of h. 1427, which occur here in reverse order.

saves him. And he who wishes sufficiency in wealth, Allāh makes him self-sufficient." [40] [1428] Abū Hurairah reported the same.

1429 Ibn ʿUmar reported that the Messenger of Allāh ﷺ, while he was on the pulpit, mentioned charity, saving oneself from asking others, and begging, and said: "The upper hand is better than the lower hand. The upper hand is the giver and the lower hand is the one who asks." [41]

Ch. 20:   **To follow charity with reproach**

> Because of the word of Allāh: "Those who spend their wealth in the way of Allāh, then do not follow up what they spent with reproach or injury…" (2:262).[42]

Ch. 21:   **One who wishes to give in charity at the earliest the same day**

1430 ʿUqbah ibn al-Ḥārith related: The Prophet ﷺ led us in *ʿAṣr* prayer, then he quickly went to his house and returned without delay. I asked — or he was asked — (about it). He said: "I had left behind at home a piece of gold

---

[40] By the "upper hand" (*al-yad al-ʿulyā*) is meant the hand of the giver and by the "lower hand" is meant the hand of the recipient, as is clearly evident from h. 1429. According to some, h. 1429 is the explanation given by the Holy Prophet himself, but others consider it to be a statement of Ibn ʿUmar. It means that only such a person can give away wealth in charity if he owns some wealth. If a person makes himself poor by giving away what he owns, then he will later on beg from others and be dependent on them. In other words, you should not give away so much as to become needy yourself. That is why it has been mentioned here that charity should begin with those for whom you are responsible to look after them financially. In other words, if someone has wealth, it must first be spent on his wife, children, parents and brothers and sisters, etc. who need his support. Thus Nasāʾī records a ḥadīth in which a person said to the Holy Prophet that he had one dīnār to give in charity. The Prophet replied: "Spend it on yourself." The man said: "I have another dīnār." The Prophet said: "Spend it on your wife." He said: "I have another dīnār." The Prophet said: "Spend it on your children." He said: "I have another dīnār." The Prophet said: "Spend it on your servant." He said: "I have another dīnār." The Prophet said: "You know best (how to spend it)" (Nasāʾī, book: *Zakāt*, h. 2535). This is an excellent practical teaching which one can adopt as a guideline of living.

The words "he who wishes to save himself" *(man yastaʿfif)* here mean to save yourself from asking help of others. The only way to do that is to put away some savings for hard times. The meaning of wishing for self-sufficiency in wealth is the same, i.e., the desire not to be dependent on others. The Holy Prophet has exhorted us to maintain our dignity, so that one should not spend so much in the way of Allāh as to become destitute. Unfortunately, among Muslims today begging, indebtedness and dependence on others is widely prevalent, so much so that they are like slaves to others. But this is not due to spending in the way of Allāh but to wastefulness and excessive spending in pursuance of social customs and practices. At the same time it should be remembered that spending on the family should not be made an excuse for not spending in charity, as this sort of miserliness is the worst of all social ills.

[41] This is a repetition of a part of h. 1427–1428. See the last footnote.

[42] There is no ḥadīth in this chapter, and a verse of the Qurʾān is considered sufficient.

from charity, and I disliked to keep it in my house during the night, so I ordered it to be distributed." [43]

Ch. 22:   To urge (others) to give charity and recommend it

1431 Ibn ʿAbbās reported: The Prophet ﷺ came out on the day of Eid and prayed two *rak'ahs* (in congregation). He did not perform any *rak'ah* before or after it. Then he came to the women and Bilāl was with him. He preached to them and exhorted them to give in charity. The women started putting their bangles and earrings (into the sheet spread by Bilāl).[44]

1432 Abū Mūsā reported: Whenever a person came to the Messenger of Allāh ﷺ to ask (for something), or a need was put to him, he used to say (to people): "Recommend (to someone that he should help him); you will be rewarded for it. And Allāh enjoins whatever He wishes through the tongue of His Prophet." [45]

1433 Asmā' reported: The Prophet ﷺ said to me: "Do not withhold (charity), for it will be withheld from you."

(And in another report:) "Do not count (while giving charity), for Allāh will count out for you (when giving you anything)." [46]

Ch. 23:   Give charity as much as you can afford

1434 Asmā', daughter of Abū Bakr, reported that she went to the Prophet ﷺ and he said: "Do not keep wealth locked up (in a box), or Allāh will lock upon you (what He would give you). Spend (in Allāh's way) whatever you can." [47]

---

[43] This is a repetition of h. 851 with some brevity and difference in wording. See footnote to h. 851.

[44] See h. 98 and h. 964. H. 98 has been repeated here with a slight difference.

[45] Even if someone only requests another person to do a charitable act, he gets reward for it. In other words, if you cannot help a needy person, you should at least recommend to others to do it.

[46] The word *īkā'* (withholding) means to tie the opening of a water-skin. It implies that if you withhold charity, then Allāh will withhold sustenance from you. Today, history has proven that nations that have abstained from charitable works have suffered poverty. In the second report, the words *lā tuḥṣī* ("do not count") mean that while performing charity a person should not take into account what he had given before and let it reduce what he is giving now. Allāh gives to humans without measure. When giving in charity, if a person starts counting out of what Allāh has given him, it is tantamount to restricting Allāh in what He gives him.

[47] This is a repetition of h. 1433 with variations. The word *ī'ā'* (from which the word "locked" in this ḥadīth is derived) means to keep wealth locked in a box.

Ch. 24: Charity is an expiation for sins

1435 Ḥudhaifah reported that ʿUmar said: "Who among you has preserved the saying of the Messenger of Allāh ﷺ relating to the Trial *(fitnah)*?" I said: "I remember it as he (the Holy Prophet) said it." He said: "You are surely bold about it. How was it?" I said: "The trial of a man in connection with his family and his children and his neighbour is expiated by (his) prayer and charity and goodness *(al-maʿrūf)*." — Sulaimān (al-Aʿmash) said that he (the narrator before him) used to say: "prayer and charity and enjoining what is good and forbidding what is evil." [48] — He (ʿUmar) said: "I do not mean this but I mean that which surges like the surging waves of the ocean." I said: "You have nothing to fear from it, O Chief of the Believers, for between you and it there is a closed door." He (ʿUmar) said: "Will the door be broken or opened?" I said: "No, it will certainly be broken." He (ʿUmar) said: "Then if it is broken it will never be closed." I said: "Yes."

We feared to ask him (Ḥudhaifah) about the door, so we said to Masrūq: "Ask him." He asked him and he said: "It (the door) was ʿUmar." We asked: "Did ʿUmar know who was meant (by the door)?" He (Ḥudhaifah) said: "Yes, just as (it is known that) there is night after the next day. And this ḥadīth I have narrated is not wrong." [49]

Ch. 25: One who gave charity in the state of *shirk* (worship of others besides God) and then became a Muslim

1436 Ḥakīm ibn Ḥizām reported: I said: "O Messenger of Allāh! Is there any reward for deeds which I performed during the time before Islām, such as charity, freeing slaves and having regard for ties of relationship?" The Prophet ﷺ said: "You became Muslim because of the good done before *(salf)*." [50]

---

[48] Here a narrator further down in the chain, al-Aʿmash, says that, instead of just the word *al-maʿrūf* (goodness), sometimes the full expression was used: *al-amr bi-l-maʿrūf wa-n-nahyu ʿani-l-munkar* (enjoining what is good and forbidding what is evil).

[49] This is a repetition of h. 525 with a slight difference in wording but with no difference in significance. It also contains the explanation by al-Aʿmash mentioned in the last footnote. The only words in it relating to the chapter heading are: "The trial of a man in connection with his family and his children and his neighbour is expiated by (his) prayer and charity and goodness *(al-maʿrūf)*." See also h. 1895.

[50] According to Ibn Athīr, *salf* (what has gone before) relates to mutual dealings and the Arabs refer to debt as *salf*. In Ḥadīth the words in a prayer for the dead are: "Make it for us a *salf*", that is, it is a thing which was given before, the reward for which is to come. So by saying "the good done before" it means that the good done in the days of unbelief will also be rewarded. In *Fatḥ al-Bārī* Māzari is reported as saying: "Apparently it means that any good which he had done in the past has been recorded for him." Although some scholars have denied that a disbeliever will

Ch. 26: Reward of the servant when he gives in charity on the instructions of his master without causing any loss

1437 ʿĀ'ishah reported that the Messenger of Allāh ﷺ said: "When a woman gives in charity from the meal of her husband's house without causing any loss, she will get the reward for it, and her husband will get the reward for what he earned. And a guardian of (someone's) money will get similar reward." [51]

1438 Abū Mūsā reported from the Prophet ﷺ that he said: "An honest Muslim treasurer who carries out the orders (of the owner)" — and sometimes he said: "who gives" — whatever is commanded to him in full, being pleased with it, and pays to whom he was commanded to give, he is one of the two persons who have given in charity."

Ch. 27: Reward of a woman when she gives in charity or feeds (a needy person) from her husband's house without causing any loss[52]

1439–1440 ʿĀ'ishah reported from the Prophet ﷺ, meaning: "When a woman gives in charity from her husband's house" [1440] ʿĀ'ishah reported that the Prophet ﷺ said: "When a woman gives in charity from her husband's house without causing any loss, she will get the reward for it, and he will get a like reward. And a guardian of (someone's) money will get similar reward. He (the husband) gets it because of earning (the money) and she will get it because of giving in charity."

1441 ʿĀ'ishah reported from the Prophet ﷺ that he said: "When a woman gives in charity from the meal of her house without causing any loss, she will

---

have reward for good done by him, nevertheless the Qur'ān clearly accepts in principle that any good done will be rewarded: "So he who does an atom's weight of good will see it. And he who does an atom's weight of evil will see it" (99:7–8). In this entire *sūrah* (ch. 99), it is human beings in general, and not only Muslims, who are referred to. The previous verse says: "On that day people will come forth, in diverse bodies, that they may be shown their works." (99:6). This ḥadīth tells us that even the good work of a disbeliever is recorded and he gets a reward for it. As it cannot happen that a Muslim is not punished for an evil deed he commits, similarly it cannot happen that a disbeliever is not rewarded for a good deed that he has done. In the heading of the chapter, apparently the reward of a good deed of a disbeliever has been made conditional on his becoming a Muslim, but this condition is not mentioned in the ḥadīth itself or in the Qur'ān.

[51] H. 1425 has been repeated with a slight difference in wording, which does not affect the meaning. The concluding sentence of h. 1425 is not found here. See also h. 1439 to h. 1441.

[52] The subject of h. 1425 as expressed in h. 1437 has been repeated in the three reports of this chapter with slight differences in wording. The word used for "gives in charity" is different in h. 1440 (*aṭ'amat*), and yet again different in h. 1441 (*anfaqat*), from what it is in h. 1437 and h. 1439 (*taṣaddqat*). H. 1441 refers to "her house", whereas h. 1439 and h. 1440 refer to "her husband's house".

get the reward for it, and the husband will get the reward for what he earned (i.e., the money spent on the food). And a guardian of (someone's) money will get similar reward."

Ch. 28:   The word of Allāh:

"Then as for him who gives (charitably) and keeps his duty, and accepts what is good — We facilitate for him (the way to) ease. And as for him who is miserly and considers himself self-sufficient..." (the Qur'ān, 92:5-8).

"O Allāh, Recompense the one who gives wealth (in charity)."

1442 Abū Hurairah reported that the Prophet ﷺ said: "Every day when it dawns and people get up, two angels descend. One of them says: 'O Allāh, Recompense the one who gives charity,' and the other says: 'Destroy the wealth of the one who withholds (it).' "

Ch. 29:   Parable of one who gives in charity and a miser

1443–1444 Abū Hurairah reported that the Prophet ﷺ said: "The parable of a miser and a charitable one" — or in another narration that he heard the Messenger of Allāh ﷺ say: "The parable of a miser and one who spends" — "is like two men who have two iron shirts (*jubbatān*) which cover them from their chests to their collar bones. Then as to the charitable one, when he spends, the shirt expands over his body or lengthens in size till it hides his fingers and erases his foot impressions. And as to the miser, whenever he wishes to spend anything, every ring of it sticks to its place, and when he tries to widen it, it does not widen." [1444] Abū Hurairah heard from the Prophet ﷺ: "two shields (*junnatān*)".[53]

Ch. 30:   To give charity from earning and trading

The word of Allāh: "O you who believe, spend (on good works) out of the good things that you earn and out of what We bring forth for you from the earth... And know that Allāh is Self-sufficient, Praise-worthy" (2:267).[54]

---

[53] It has been explained through an example that when a person intends to give in charity, Allāh opens his heart for it. By the breadth of his shirt is meant his generosity of heart. The extension of the shirt up to the fingers may refer to his act of giving, and the erasing of the impression of his feet may mean the effacing of his faults. The sticking of the rings to the miser indicates his narrowness of heart. H. 1444 reports the variation that the Holy Prophet had said "two shields" (*junnatān*), and not "two shirts" (*jubbatān*).

[54] There is no ḥadīth in this chapter, only an inference drawn from this verse. From Mujāhid

Ch. 31:   Charity is incumbent on every Muslim. One who can find nothing (to give) should do good deeds

1445 Abū Mūsā reported from the Prophet ﷺ that he said: "Charity is incumbent on every Muslim." People asked: "O Prophet of Allāh, what about one who can find nothing (to give)?" He said: "He should work with his hands, so that he benefits himself and gives in charity." People said: "But if he still cannot find anything?" He replied: "He should help a needy person in distress." Again, people asked: "If he cannot even do that?" He said: "Let him do some good and keep away from evil. This will be an act of charity by him." [55]

Ch. 32:   How much *Zakāt* or charity (*ṣadaqah*) should be given and one who gives a she-goat in charity[56]

1446 Umm 'Aṭiyyah reported: A she-goat was sent to Nusaibah al-Anṣāriyya (as charity) and she sent some of it to 'Ā'ishah. The Prophet ﷺ asked: "Do you have something (to eat)?" 'Ā'ishah replied: "Nothing but what Nusaibah has sent of this she-goat." He said: "Bring it. It has reached its destined place." [57]

---

the meaning has been reported that "good things that you earn" refer to trading, and from 'Alī that "out of what We bring forth for you from the earth" refers to grain and fruits, etc. Bukhārī has given the chapter the heading of earning (*kasb*) and trading (*tijārah*). It is possible that by "earning" or *kasb* he is referring to agricultural work, while in the verse "earn" or *kasb* refers to trading. The word *kasb* is broad, although trading is considered as the best kind of earning.

[55] Here charity has been made obligatory for every Muslim, whether rich or poor. At the same time, its scope has been widened so that everybody can act upon it. One of its forms is that a person should save some time from his daily duties and do some manual work to give charity out of its income. Zainab, wife of the Holy Prophet, used to do tanning of animal skins and gave charity out of its income. If somebody cannot do any such work, he should help some needy person; for instance, to help an unemployed to find work, or to help in relieving someone's hardship. Failing all else, he should do a good deed and avoid doing wrong. This is also a kind of charity because someone else might benefit by his example.

[56] According to Arabic lexicons, the words *zakāt* and *ṣadaqah* may both indicate obligatory or voluntary charity. However, most frequently the word *zakāt* is used in the sense of obligatory charity, while the word *ṣadaqah* is used in a broader sense. The object of this chapter is to show how much is to be given out of *Zakāt* or charity to its deserving recipients.

[57] Nusaibah al-Anṣāriyya is Umm 'Aṭiyyah herself, the reporter of this ḥadīth. In the report in Ṣaḥīḥ Muslim it is stated that the Holy Prophet sent one she-goat to her out of charity (of *Zakāt*) and it was out of this that she sent a portion as a gift to 'Ā'ishah (book: *Zakāt*, ch. 52). Charity in the form of *Zakāt* is not permissible for the Holy Prophet and his family, but when *Zakāt* is given to a deserving person, he can give a portion of it as a gift to others, as it is no longer being given as *Zakāt*. It has also been stated here that the recipient of charity should not be looked down upon, but rather if the recipient gives a gift out of the charity that he or she received, it should be accepted just as any other gift. There is no rule specified here as to how much charity is to be given. What is meant is that there is no limitation on the amount of charity, as here a whole she-goat has been given in charity.

Ch. 33:   *Zakāt* on silver

1447 Abū Saʿīd al-Khudrī said that the Messenger of Allāh ﷺ said: "On camels fewer than five there is no *Zakāt,* on anything less than five *auqiyah* there is no *Zakāt,* and on anything less than five *wasq* there is no *Zakāt.*" [58]

Ch. 34:   To receive goods as *Zakāt* [59]

Ṭā'us said that Muʿādh said to the people of Yaman: "Give as *Zakāt* goods or stripped sheets or any cloth, instead of barley and corn. It will be easier for you, and better for the Companions of the Prophet in Madīnah." The Prophet ﷺ said: "And Khālid has given his coat of arms and other weapons (as charity) in the way of Allāh." The Prophet ﷺ also said: "Give in charity even if it is from your ornaments." He did not make any distinction between charity in the form of goods from other things. So women started giving out their earrings and necklaces. He (the Prophet) did not specify gold and silver (for *Zakāt*) out of goods.

1448 Anas related that Abū Bakr wrote to him what Allāh commanded His Messenger ﷺ (about *Zakāt*): "One whose *Zakāt* amounts to a one-year old she-camel, and he does not have it, but he does have a two-year old she-camel, it shall be accepted from him and the collector (of *Zakāt*) shall pay him 20 dirhems or two she-goats.[60] If he does not have a one-year old she-camel but he has a two-year old he-camel, that shall be accepted from him and nothing shall be paid to him."

1449 Ibn ʿAbbās said: I was witness when the Messenger of Allāh ﷺ said (Eid) prayers before delivering the sermon, and then he realized that the women had not heard it. So he went to them and with him was Bilāl who was spreading his garment. He preached to them and exhorted them that they should give in charity. The women began to throw — and Ayyūb pointed towards his ears and his neck.[61]

---

[58] This is a repetition of h. 1405, with only the difference that its first two sentences have been interchanged.

[59] It means that *Zakāt* of one kind can be taken in lieu of another kind. Thus it is not essential that *Zakāt* should be taken in the form of gold and silver.

[60] The object is to prove that whatever property is to be received in *Zakāt* it is permitted to take something else of the same value.

[61] This is a repetition of h. 98 with a different opening. At the end, after the words "they began to throw" (*tulqī*), it is added that Ayyūb, a narrator further down the chain, pointed towards his ears and neck, meaning that the women threw the ornaments which are worn on these parts.

Ch. 35:   **Do not put together different properties nor separate what is together**

And the like of this is related from Sālim on the authority of Ibn ʿUmar from the Prophet ﷺ.

1450 Anas related that Abū Bakr wrote to him what was prescribed by the Messenger of Allāh ﷺ (about *Zakāt*): "Do not put together different properties nor separate what is together out of fear of *Zakāt*." [62]

Ch. 36:   **If goods belong to two partners, they should share the *Zakāt* (due on the whole) equally between them**

Ṭāʾus and ʿAṭāʾ say: When each of the two partners recognise their properties, these should not be combined. Sufyān said: *Zakāt* is not liable unless the number of she-goats for one partner is forty and similarly forty for the other.

1451 Anas related that Abū Bakr wrote to him what was prescribed by the Messenger of Allāh ﷺ (about *Zakāt*): "If goods belong to two partners, they should share the *Zakāt* (due on the whole) equally between themselves."

Ch. 37:   ***Zakāt* on camels**

Abū Bakr, Abū Dharr and Abū Hurairah reported it on the authority of the Prophet ﷺ.

1452 Abū Saʿīd al-Khudrī reported that a Bedouin asked the Messenger of Allāh ﷺ about emigration (*hijrah*). He said: "Pity be on you! It entails much difficulties. Do you have camels and do you pay *Zakāt* on them?" He said: "Yes." He (the Prophet) said: "Work on this side of the seas. Allāh will not waste any of your deeds." [63]

---

[62] If a person's own property is below the limit (*nisāb*) for liability to *Zakāt*, then *Zakāt* is not chargeable on it, whether he shares his property with another or not. If the property of two persons, when taken jointly, is above the limit, then neither of them is liable to pay *Zakāt*. On this basis Imām Abū Ḥanīfah has explained this ḥadīth by saying that if two persons jointly own twenty she-goats each, it should not be considered as forty she-goats so that one she-goat is taken as *Zakāt*, because the properties cannot be combined for the purpose of determining if the limit is reached. This is the meaning of the words: "Do not put together different properties". The meaning of "nor separate what is together" is that if, for example, a person has 120 she-goats, they should not be considered as three separate groups of forty, so that *Zakāt* of one she-goat is charged for each group, but rather that a *Zākat* of only one she-goat should be charged if their total number is from forty to 120.

[63] Another meaning of the word *biḥār* ('seas') is 'a city'. The ḥadīth means that wherever you are, you should follow the Divine commandments. Allāh does not waste one's good deeds

Ch. 38: One whose *Zakāt* is a one-year-old she-camel and he does not have it

1453 Anas related that Abū Bakr wrote to him what Allāh commanded His Messenger ﷺ about the obligation of *Zakāt*: "One whose *Zakāt* from camels amounts to a four-year old she-camel, and he does not have a four-year old one, but he does have a three-year old one, the three-year old shall be accepted from him; and with it he should give two she-goats if available to him, or twenty dirhams. One whose *Zakāt* amounts to a three-year old she-camel, and he does not have a three-year old one, but he does have a four-year old one, the four-year old shall be accepted from him, and the collector (of *Zakāt*) shall pay him twenty dirhams or two she-goats. And one whose *Zakāt* amounts to a two-year old she-camel, and he has a three-year old one, the three-year old shall be accepted from him and the collector (of *Zakāt*) shall pay him twenty dirhams or two she-goats. And one whose *Zakāt* amounts to a two-year old she-camel, and he does not have it, but he does have a one-year old one, the one-year old shall be accepted from him and he shall pay the collector along with it twenty dirhams or two she-goats.

Ch. 39: *Zakāt* on she-goats

1454 Anas related that when Abū Bakr sent him (as governor) to Bahrain, he gave him this written order:

"In the name of Allāh, the Beneficent, the Merciful. This is the obligatory charity which the Messenger of Allāh ﷺ made compulsory for Muslims, having been enjoined by Allāh through His Messenger. From whoever among Muslims it (*Zakāt*) is demanded, at the prescribed rate, he must pay it, and from whoever more than it is demanded, he should not pay it.[64]

For twenty-four or fewer camels, she-goats are payable (as *Zakāt*), one for every five camels.[65] When the number of camels reaches twenty-five to thirty-five, a one-year old she-camel is payable. When the number reaches thirty-six to forty-five, a two-year old she-camel is payable. When the number reaches forty-six to sixty, a three-year old she-camel, capable of bearing offspring, is

---

even if done while one is living outside Madīnah. This incident relates to a time when Islām had spread and there was no need for people to emigrate. It is also meant to indicate that, after emigrating to a new place, one is bound to face all sorts of unforeseen difficulties.

[64] It is taught here that Muslims must safeguard their rights themselves. Those in authority should not demand from them more than what is prescribed, and Muslims must resist injustice in order to guard their legitimate rights.

[65] On camels numbering from 5 to 24, one she-goat per five camels is payable. As a she-goat is different in kind from a camel, this shows *Zakāt* may be taken in the form of something different from that on which *Zakāt* is being charged.

payable. When the number reaches sixty-one to seventy-five, a four-year-old camel is payable. When the number reaches seventy-six to ninety, two two-year old she-camels are payable. When the number reaches ninety-one to one hundred and twenty, two three-year old she-camels, capable of bearing off-spring, are payable. When the number exceeds one hundred and twenty, a two-year old she-camel is payable for every forty, and a three-year old for every fifty camels. If anyone has only four camels, there is no *Zakāt* owing on them, unless their owner wishes (to pay it). When there are five camels, one she-goat is payable.

When she-goats are able to graze in the fields and the number is from forty to one hundred and twenty, then one she-goat is payable. When the number exceeds one hundred and twenty, till it reaches two hundred, two she-goats are payable. When the number exceeds two hundred, till it reaches three hund-red, three she-goats are payable. When the number exceeds three hundred, then for every one hundred, one she-goat is payable. And if someone has even one fewer than forty, there is no *Zakāt* on them, unless their owner wishes (to pay it).

In the case of silver, it is one-fortieth. But if its value is only one hundred and ninety (dirhems), there is no *Zakāt* on it, unless its owner wishes (to pay it)."

Ch. 40: No old or defective animal should be taken as *Zakāt*, nor a male animal, unless the payer of charity so wishes

1455 Anas related that Abū Bakr gave him a written order as Allāh had commanded His Messenger ﷺ: "In *Zakāt* no old or defective animal should be given, nor any male animal (*tais*) unless the payer (*muṣaddiq*) so wishes." [66]

Ch. 41: To take kid of a she-goat in *Zakāt*

1456–1457 Abū Hurairah said that Abū Bakr said: "By Allāh! if they withhold from me even a kid of a she-goat which they used to give to the Messenger of Allāh ﷺ, I shall fight them for their withholding of it." [1457] 'Umar said: "The fact was that Allāh had opened Abū Bakr's heart for fighting, so I realised that it was right." [67]

---

[66] A male kept for breeding is called *tais*. The word *muṣaddiq* has been reported by most as *muṣṣaddiq*. It is from *mutaṣaddiq,* meaning one who gives charity. The words "unless the payer so wishes" relate only to "male animal", meaning that the owner may give the male animal if he so wishes, and only then should the collector accept it. Such an animal is of great value and is kept by the owner out of need.

[67] This is a repetition of h. 1400, in which, after the words "Allāh had opened Abū Bakr's

Ch. 42:   Valuables should not be taken as *Zakāt*

1458 Ibn ʿAbbās reported that when the Messenger of Allāh ﷺ sent Muʿādh to Yaman he said: "You are going to a people who are People of the Book (i.e., Jews and Christians). Firstly, you should invite them to the worship of Allāh; when they recognize (the need to obey) Allāh, then inform them that Allāh has made obligatory for them five prayers during the day and the night; when they do this, then inform them that Allāh has made obligatory for them (the paying of) *Zakāt*, which is taken from their wealth and is given to the needy among them. When they follow this, then take it from them, and desist from taking valuable goods from the wealth of people." [68]

Ch. 43:   No *Zakāt* on fewer than five camels

1459 Abū Saʿīd al-Khudrī reported that the Messenger of Allāh ﷺ said: "On anything less than five *wasq* of dates there is no *Zakāt*, on anything less than five *auqiyah* of silver there is no *Zakāt*, and on camels fewer than five there is no *Zakāt*." [69]

Ch. 44:   *Zakāt* of cow and oxen

Abū Ḥumaid reported that the Prophet ﷺ said: "I will certainly recognise a person who will come before Allāh with a cow who will be bleating (*khuwār*)." [70]

It is also said *Juʾār* (instead of *khuwār*). *Yajʾaruna* means 'they raised their voices like the bleating of a cow'.[71]

---

heart", it is added: "for fighting". From the mention of "a kid of a she-goat" (*ʾanāq*) it has been inferred that even a kid of a she-goat used to be taken as *Zakāt*. *ʿAnāq* is a kid of a she-goat that is four months old and is a female.

[68] This is a repetition of h. 1395 with extra text at the beginning and the end. The closing words mean that he should refrain from specifically selecting their most valuable possessions to be taken in *Zakāt*. See also h. 1496.

[69] Apart from h. 1405, this ḥadīth has also occurred in h. 1447. The subject of all the three reports is the same. Here, after five *wasq* (plural: *ausuq*) the word *tamr* (dates) has been added, after five *auqiyah* the word *wariq* (silver) has been added, and the three sentences are in a different order.

[70] This report by Abū Ḥumaid occurs in the Book *Al-Ḥiyal* (Contrivances) in chapter 15 in more detail (see h. 6979). It is mentioned there that if a revenue collector steals a camel, cow or a she-goat from the *Zakāt* property, he will carry it on the day of Judgment. From this ḥadīth it can be inferred that an ox or a cow can be accepted as *Zakāt*.

[71] Both words *khuwār* and *juʾār* are used for the bleating of a cow or ox. These have been used in the Qurʾān: "Then he brought forth for them a calf, a body, having a lowing sound (*khuwār*)" (20:88); and "Until, when We seize those who lead easy lives among them with punishment, then they cry (*yajʾaruna*) for help" (23:64).

1460 Abū Dharr reported: I came to the Prophet ﷺ, who said: "I swear by the One in Whose hand is my life" or "I swear by Him besides Whom there is no god," or however he swore, (he then said): "Whoever has camels, oxen or goats and he does not pay what is due on them,[72] then on the Day of Judgment these will be brought to him more plump and fat than before. They will trample him with their hoofs and gore him with their horns. When the last of them passes over him, the first one will return to him until the matter will be decided between the people."

Ch. 45:   Giving *Zakāt* to relatives

The Prophet ﷺ said: "It has two rewards — reward for giving to relatives and for paying the *Zakāt*." [73]

1461 Anas ibn Mālik said that among the Anṣār in Madīnah Abū Ṭalḥah owned more (gardens of) dates than anyone else. From among his gardens he most liked the date gardens of Bairuḥā', which was in front of the mosque. The Messenger of Allāh ﷺ used to go there and drink its pure water. Anas said: When this verse was revealed, "You cannot attain to righteousness unless you spend out of what you love" (3:92), Abū Ṭalḥah went to the Messenger of Allāh ﷺ and said: "O Messenger of Allāh! Allāh, the Blessed and the Most High, says: 'You cannot attain to righteousness unless you spend out of what you love,' and out of my wealth I like the Bairuḥā' the most, so I give it as charity in the way of Allāh, hoping for abundant good and reward for it from Allāh. Spend it, O Messenger of Allāh, as Allāh shows you." Anas said that the Messenger of Allāh ﷺ said: "Well done! This is a profitable deal! A profitable deal indeed! I have heard what you have said and I deem it more proper that it should be distributed among your relatives." Abū Ṭalḥah replied: "I will do so, O Messenger of Allāh". So he distributed it among his relatives and paternal cousins.

1462 Abū Saʿīd al-Khudrī reported: The Messenger of Allāh ﷺ went out on the day of (Eid-ul-) Aḍḥā or (Eid-ul-) Fiṭr towards the place of prayer. Then he turned and addressed the people, exhorting them to give in charity, and said: "O people, give in charity". He passed by the women and said: "You women! Give in charity because I have been shown you as being most of the people of Hell." At this they said: "And why, O Messenger of Allāh?" He

---

[72] Bukhārī takes the words "paying what is due" to mean *Zakāt* which is due, or has included this in it. Hence the word *Zakāt* occurs in the heading of the chapter.

[73] The reward for giving to relatives is the strengthening of the bonds of unity and love with them. The reward for giving in charity is the purification of one's inner self. This isolated ḥadīth, without the chain of narrators, consists of the words at the end of h. 1466, which contains more details.

said: "You curse too much and are ungrateful to your husbands and I have not seen anyone more defective in understanding and in religion who take away the wisdom of a resolute man more than you, O you women!" [74]

Then he returned and when he reached his house, Zainab, the wife of Ibn Mas'ūd, came and sought permission to see him. He was informed: "Messenger of Allāh, this is Zainab." He asked: "Which of the two Zainabs?" He was told: "Wife of Ibn Mas'ūd." He replied: "Yes, let her come in." She was allowed in. She said: "O Prophet of Allāh! Today you have commanded us to give in charity. I have some jewellery which I wish to give in charity. Ibn Mas'ūd said that he and his children deserve it more than those to whom it will be given in charity." The Prophet ﷺ said: "Ibn Mas'ūd has spoken the truth. Your husband and your children deserve it more than those to whom you will give in charity." [75]

Ch. 46:   There is no *Zakāt* upon a Muslim for his horse

1463 Abū Hurairah reported that the Prophet ﷺ said: "There is no *Zakāt* upon a Muslim for his horse or his slave." [76]

Ch. 47:   There is no *Zakāt* upon a Muslim for his slave

1464 Abū Hurairah reported from the Prophet ﷺ that he said: "There is no *Zakāt* upon a Muslim for his slave or his horse." [77]

Ch. 48:   Giving of charity to orphans

1465 Abū Sa'īd al-Khudrī related that the Prophet ﷺ was one day sitting on the pulpit and we were sitting around him, and he said: "Among the matters which I fear for you after me is the opening of the door of the charms and attractions of the world for you." A man said: "O Messenger of Allāh, Can good bring forth evil?" The Prophet ﷺ kept quiet. Someone said to the man:

---

[74] Up to here this is a repetition of the first part of h. 304 with a little difference at the beginning. (The proper transliteration of Eid is 'Īd. Eid is the common spelling.)

[75] See also h. 1466 and its footnote. This ḥadīth shows that a wife can spend charity on her husband as well. Apparently, this was not *Zakāt* but general charity. However, Bukhārī has used the word *ṣadaqah* in a wider sense which includes both obligatory and voluntary charity. Thus the same can be applied to the *Zakāt* charity, except that *Zakāt* was usually paid into the public treasury. Nonetheless, in certain cases a part of it was allowed to be spent according to the discretion of the payer. Here the children of Zainab have also been considered as more deserving than others to receive the *Zakāt*.

[76] Obviously by "horse" here is meant the horse which is kept for one's own riding. *Zakāt* on horses kept for trading can be accepted in the form of camels and she-goats.

[77] This is a repetition of h. 1463 with difference of wording but no difference in meaning.

"What is the matter with you that you are talking to the Prophet ﷺ while he is not talking to you?" Then we realised that revelation was descending on him. He (the narrator) said: He (the Prophet) wiped off his perspiration and then said: "Where is the questioner?", as if praising him. Then he said: "Good does not bring forth evil. It is like that (grass) which grows during the spring, sometimes it causes death or almost causes death. But the animal that eats green grass eats until its belly is filled and faces the sun to pass faeces and urine, and it starts grazing again. Similarly, this wealth is also green and sweet. It is a good companion of a Muslim as long as he gives out of it to the needy, orphan and traveller — or as commanded by the Prophet ﷺ — and whoever keeps wealth without paying the due on it, he is like the one who eats but is not satisfied and such wealth will stand as witness against him on the Day of Resurrection." [78]

Ch. 49:   Giving of *Zakāt* to the husband and orphans for whom one is caring

Abū Saʿīd (al-Khudrī) reported it from the Prophet ﷺ.

1466 Zainab, wife of ʿAbdullāh (ibn Masʿūd), reported: I was in the mosque and I saw the Messenger of Allāh ﷺ, who said: "Give charity (O women) even if it is out of your jewellery." And Zainab used to spend on ʿAbdullāh and the orphans for whom she was caring. She said to ʿAbdullāh: "Ask the Messenger of Allāh ﷺ if it is right for me to spend on you and on the orphans in my care from out of *Zakāt?*". He said: "You ask the Messenger of Allāh ﷺ yourself." So (Zainab said) I went to the Messenger of Allāh ﷺ and found a woman of the Anṣār at the door whose problem was similar to mine. Bilāl passed by us and we said (to him): "Ask the Prophet ﷺ if it is right for me to spend (from out of *Zakāt*) on my husband and on the orphans in my care?" And we said to him: "Do not mention our names." He went inside and asked him, at which he (the Prophet) said: "Who are these two?" He said: "She is Zainab." He said: "Which Zainab?" He said: "Wife of ʿAbdullāh."

---

[78] The question was that, since the coming of wealth is good and by doing good a person receives blessings from Allāh, can good deeds produce evil? In reply, the Holy Prophet said that good cannot produce evil but a power endowed for doing good can be used for a bad purpose. Then he gave the example of cattle. When it goes on eating grass, then the very grass can be the cause of its death. But if eats and whatever it eats is excreted after digestion, that grass will never be harmful for it. Similarly, wealth is a good companion of a Muslim as long as he takes something out of it and gives it to the poor, the orphans, etc. However, he who acquires wealth but does not pay the due out of it (or he earns it by unfair means and takes what belongs to others), then such wealth will ultimately bring distress and destruction to him.

He answered: "Yes. For her there is double reward: one reward for giving it to the near relation and the other for giving charity." [79]

1467 Zainab, daughter of Umm Salamah, reported (her mother as saying): I said: "O Messenger of Allāh: Will I have a reward for spending on the children of Abū Salamah and they are my sons?" He replied: "Do spend on them, for there is reward for you for what you spend on them." [80]

Ch. 50:   **The word of Allāh: "Charity (*Zakāt*) is for … (freeing) the captives, those in debt, and in the way of Allāh …" (the Qur'ān, 9:60).**

It is related from Ibn 'Abbās that *Zakāt* can be paid from one's wealth for freeing a slave and to perform *Hajj*. Al-Ḥasan said: "It is permissible to spend *Zakāt* to buy (freedom for) one's father, and *Zakāt* can also be given to those engaged in *jihād,* and to one who has not performed *Hajj*." Then he recited the verse: "Charity (*Zakāt*) is only for the poor…" (9:60). It is permissible to spend on any one of them. And the Prophet ﷺ said: "Khālid has dedicated his coat of iron in the way of Allāh."

It is also related from Abū Lās: "The Prophet ﷺ mounted us upon camels which were of *Zakāt* for performing *Hajj*." [81]

---

[79] This ḥadīth has already occurred briefly in h. 1462, where it is mentioned towards the end. Here we find more details and some differences. For example, there the question is of spending the *ṣadaqah* on Ibn Mas'ūd and his children and it is Zainab herself who went to the Holy Prophet to ask the question, but here the question is about spending the *ṣadaqah* on her husband Ibn Mas'ūd and some orphans and the person who is asking is said to be Bilāl. The explanation of the first difference may be that Zainab may have been spending *ṣadaqah* on the children of Ibn Mas'ūd from his first wife and also on orphans, the orphans being the children of her brother and her sister, as has been said. As to the second difference, it can only be that the reporter of h. 1462 either did not consider it necessary to mention Bilāl's name or he forgot to mention it. It is established from these two reports that *Zakāt* can be spent, if need be, on the payer's husband, her close relatives, and on the other children of her husband. See h. 1422 where the spending of *Zakāt* is allowed on one's own children who have grown up and they need such help. This report also shows that Muslim women were so active and enterprising that they earned money and spent it for the upkeep of others.

[80] Umm Salamah was married to Abū Salamah, and after she became a widow she was married to the Holy Prophet. She asked about spending wealth on her children from Abū Salamah, but spending out of charity is not explicitly mentioned.

[81] Eight heads of expenditure of *Zakāt* have been mentioned in the Qur'ān in 9:60 (in which it is called *ṣadaqāt*). Out of these, three have been mentioned by Bukhārī in this chapter heading. By the first one, the freeing of slaves, some take it to mean helping in getting freedom for those slaves who had an agreement with their masters to purchase their own freedom for money. But Bukhārī has taken it generally, that *Zakāt* can be spent in buying a slave and setting him free. By

1468 Abū Hurairah reported: The Messenger of Allāh ﷺ ordered the collection of *Zakāt*. At this, someone said: "Ibn Jamīl, Khālid ibn Walīd and ʿAbbās ibn ʿAbdul Muṭṭalib do not pay *Zakāt*." The Prophet ﷺ said: "Ibn Jamīl is not thankful that he was poor, and Allāh and His Messenger made him wealthy.[82] As to Khālid, you are unjust to him. He has dedicated his coat of iron and other weapons in the way of Allāh.[83] And ʿAbbās ibn ʿAbdul Muṭṭalib is paternal uncle of the Messenger of Allāh. *Zakāt* is binding on him, and the same amount in addition to it." [84]

Ch. 51:   To avoid begging

1469 Abū Saʿīd al-Khudrī reported that some men of the Anṣār begged something from the Messenger of Allāh ﷺ, and he gave them. They again begged from him and again he gave to them until nothing was left with him. He said: "Whatever good I may have I will never refuse to give it to you. And whoever wishes to avoid begging, Allāh will save him, and whoever wishes to be self-sufficient, Allāh will make him self-sufficient, and whoever has recourse to patience, Allah will make him patient. And no one is granted a blessing better and greater than patience." [85]

1470 Abū Hurairah reported that the Messenger of Allāh ﷺ said: "By Allāh in Whose hand is my life, if one of you takes his rope, collects wood,

---

"in the way of Allāh" is meant people who are engaged in *jihād*. Some are of the view that such a person should be lacking in means, but in that case he would fall in the category of a poor or a needy person. A person engaged in *jihād* does not need money for himself but for *jihād* in the way of Allāh, which is for the defence or the propagation of Islām. That need can never end, and today the best object for *Zakāt* under this heading is the propagation of Islam. *Zakāt* can also be spent on the care of orphans if they come in the category of the poor and needy. They have not been mentioned specifically in this verse because sometimes they possess wealth. Help for those performing *Ḥajj* comes under the category of spending *Zakāt* on travellers (*ibn as-sabīl*).

[82] The Holy Prophet expressed his annoyance that Ibn Jamīl did not pay *Zakāt*, saying that previously he was very poor, but because of Islām and its victories in battle, he had become wealthy and should be thankful and pay *Zakāt*. According to commentators of Ḥadīth he was not a sincere Muslim at that time.

[83] The Holy Prophet said that Khalid was always ready to fight for the cause of Islām, and other fighters benefitted from his property and weapons. This itself constitutes giving *Zakāt*.

[84] That is to say, double shall be taken from him. In the report in Muslim, the Holy Prophet's words are: "I shall be responsible for it and an equal amount along with it" book: *Zakāt*, ch. 3). Some hold that ʿAbbās had already paid in advance to the Holy Prophet the amount of *Zakāt* due for two years, and thus he did not pay the collector.

[85] The Holy Prophet stated in a subtle way how to avoid asking money of others. An even better way is mentioned in the next ḥadīth. It is distressing that there is such a large number of beggars among Muslims, many of them having adopted it as a profession.

and carries it on his back, this is better than he should beg from another, who may give him or refuse to give him." [86]

1471 Az-Zubair ibn al-ʿAwwām reported from the Prophet ﷺ that he said: "If one of you takes his rope and brings (with it from the forest) a bundle of wood (carrying it) on his back and sells it, and Allāh saves his honour (by means of it), this is better for him than that he should beg from people, who may give him or refuse to give him." [87]

1472 Ḥakīm ibn Ḥizām said: I begged from the Messenger of Allāh ﷺ, and he gave me. I again begged from him, and again he gave me. Then he said: "O Ḥakīm! Wealth is luxuriant and sweet; if one takes it with a generous heart, there will be blessing in it for him; but for the one who takes it with greed (*ishrāf*) of heart, there is no blessing for him in it, and he will be like one who goes on eating but is never satisfied. The upper hand is better than the lower hand." Ḥakim said, I said: "O Messenger of Allāh ﷺ! By Him Who has sent you with the truth, I will never beg from anyone after you till I depart from this world." [88]

Afterwards, whenever Abū Bakr called Ḥakim to give him his share, he would refuse to take anything from it. Then ʿUmar called him to give him, but

---

[86] See also the next ḥadīth, h. 1471.

[87] On the one hand, the Holy Prophet was so generous that he never refused anyone who asked for something and he would give away whatever he had. On the other hand, he was a teacher also and taught that people should avoid begging, saying that better than begging is to bring wood from the forest on your back and sell it in the market. In this way he taught his followers to honour and value the doing of work. He even said that if a man does work Allāh will guard his honour. But the one who begs loses all honour. In other words, even the most menial of labour is honourable in the sight of Allāh while begging in any form is an act of disgrace.

[88] Ḥakīm ibn Ḥizām was one of the close friends of the Holy Prophet since before the time of his prophethood and accepted Islām after the conquest of Makkah. This incident most probably happened after the Battle of Ḥunain, the wealth being from the booty of the battle. As is mentioned in *Fatḥ al-Bārī*, the Holy Prophet gave less to Ḥakim than to the others who were with him, so he said to the Holy Prophet that he thought he would be given less than his companions, and the Holy Prophet gave him more. Worldly wealth had no value in the eyes of the Holy Prophet. He distributed it according to people's needs. When he said that in whatever form you beg, it makes you inferior, and you must try to be the giver rather than the recipient, as you will have the upper hand, and thus that man becomes honourable because of his moral qualities and help for others, and not because of wealth, Ḥakim was very moved and he promised never again to ask from anyone except the Holy Prophet, nor even to take any share of the booty. He kept his promise until his death. This shows that the Companions of the Holy Prophet also did not attach any importance to material wealth.

The word *ishrāf* in relation to wealth, used in this ḥadīth as well as the next, means to raise oneself up and glance towards something which one wants to attain. In case of wealth, it means the greed of the heart for it, as one keeps on looking towards it, desiring to get a share of it.

he refused to take anything from him. 'Umar said: "O community of Muslims, I make you witness that I am calling him to give him his share of this war gain but he is refusing to take it." So after the Messenger of Allāh ﷺ, Hakīm never took anything from anyone till he died.

Ch. 52: **One whom Allāh grants something without (his) asking or being greedy (*ishrāf*): "And in their wealth there was a due share for one who asks and one who is deprived" (the Qur'ān, 51:19)**

1473 'Abdullāh ibn 'Umar said that he heard 'Umar say: The Messenger of Allāh ﷺ used to give me something, so I said: "Give it to him who needs it more than me." He (the Holy Prophet) said: "Take it. When something of this property comes to you, and you are neither greedy (*ishrāf*) nor asking for it, then take it. And if it does not come, do not let your mind pursue it." [89]

Ch. 53: **One who asks people to increase his wealth**

1474–1475 'Abdullāh ibn 'Umar said that the Prophet ﷺ said: "A man who constantly begs from people will come to the Day of Judgment with no flesh on his face at all." [90] [1475] And he (the Holy Prophet) said: "On the Day of Resurrection the sun will come so near (to people) that perspiration will reach halfway along the ear. When people will be in that state, they will appeal for help to Adam, then to Moses and then to Muḥammad." [91]

And it is added to another narration: He (the Holy Prophet) will intercede so that judgment may be given between the people. Then he will walk till he takes hold of the chain of the door (of Paradise). On that Day Allāh will bestow on him a position of great glory (*maqām-an maḥmūd-an*). All the people gathered there will praise him.

---

[89] It is evident that this wealth was not from *ṣadaqah*. Some say it was given in lieu of working as a tax collector. It may be that it came to the Holy Prophet for distribution as was the case of wealth from Bahrain. As 'Umar was a prosperous man, he said this should be given to a needy person. The Holy Prophet said that if some wealth comes without a person yearning for it, he should not refuse it. This was to teach that wealth is also a blessing from Allāh and one should be thankful for it.

[90] It is pointed out here that begging is a degrading act. To express this degradation, it is said that it takes away all flesh from the face, leaving only bones. In fact, this state is reached meta-phorically during life on earth due to disgrace. On the day of Resurrection, this spiritual condition of such a person will acquire an outward form visible to everyone. The chapter heading relates to this part.

[91] This ḥadīth occurs later in more detail in the book *ar-Riqāq* in h. 6565.

Ch. 54:   **The word of Allāh: "they do not beg of people insistingly" (2:273). And what is the limit of wealth?**

And the saying of the Prophet ﷺ: "And he does not find (enough) wealth to free him from need".[92] (As the Word of Allāh says): "(Charity is) for the poor who are confined in the way of Allah, they cannot go about in the land; the ignorant man thinks them to be rich on account of (their) abstaining (from begging).[93] ... And whatever good thing you spend, surely Allah is Knower of it." (the Qur'ān, 2:273).

1476 Abū Hurairah reported from the Prophet ﷺ that he said: "A needy person (*miskīn*) is not the one who goes from door to door asking for a morsel or two of food, but he is the one who has no wealth and yet he does not beg from people insistently." [94]

1477 Warrād, a scribe of al-Mughīrah ibn Shuʿbah, related: Muʿāwiyah wrote to al-Mughīrah ibn Shuʿbah: "Write to me what you heard from the Prophet ﷺ." He (al-Mughīrah) wrote to him: "I heard the Messenger of Allāh ﷺ saying: 'Allāh does not like three things from you (people): talking uselessly, squandering money, and excessive begging'." [95]

1478 Saʿd (ibn Abī Waqqāṣ) reported: The Messenger of Allāh ﷺ gave some gifts (to a party of men), while I was sitting among them. But he omitted a man among them, not giving him (anything), whom I admired the most. So I went up to the Messenger of Allāh ﷺ and whispered to him: "What is your reason in his case, for, by Allāh, I consider him to be a believer?" He replied:

---

[92] This is a part of h. 1479 where the definition of *miskīn* or a needy person is given.

[93] Those in real need are the people restricted from going about in the land to do work or conduct trade due to their support for the cause of Islām. Three kinds of people fall in this category: (a) Those who have devoted their lives in the service of the religion or students who have devoted their lives to acquiring knowledge of religion, for example, the *Aṣḥāb al-Ṣuffah*, who stayed in the courtyard of the Holy Prophet's Mosque; (b) Those who, because of facing persecution from disbelievers or due to lack of security because of war, cannot carry on business; (c) Those who are not able to work, such as injured persons, but they should be such that "they do not beg of people insistently" (2:273). Some people have adopted it as a profession to go about preaching and asking people for money in return, or by pretending to be students, or asking falsely in the name of the propagation of Islām, etc. All these are beggars who call out in the streets asking for money.

[94] See h. 1479.

[95] Attention is drawn here to the value of time, money and the natural faculties granted by Allāh. One should not waste time in useless talk, waste money by squandering it, or waste one's own faculties by remaining idle and asking from others. In "excessive begging" the asking of needless and useless questions is included, as it is a waste of time of both the questioner and the one whom he asks.

"No, a Muslim." I was silent for a while, but I was overcome by what I knew of him, so I said: "Messenger of Allāh, What is your reason in his case, for, by Allāh, I consider him to be a believer?" He replied: "No, a Muslim." I was silent for a while, but I was overcome by what I knew of him, so I said: "Messenger of Allāh, What is your reason in his case, for, by Allāh, I consider him to be a believer?" He replied: "No, a Muslim." Then he said: "I give to a man while another is dearer to me than him, out of fear that he may be thrown (*yukabba*) into the fire (of hell) on his face." [96]

Then the Messenger of Allāh ﷺ placed his hand between my neck and shoulder and said: "Sa'd! Listen, I give to a man." [97]

Abū 'Abdullāh (Bukhārī) said: *Kubkibū* (the Qur'ān, 26:94) means they will be hanged upside down. *Mukibb-an* (67:22) …[98]

1479 Abū Hurairah reported that the Messenger of Allāh ﷺ said: "A needy person (*miskīn*) is not one who goes around people (begging), and one or two morsels or a date or two are enough to make him return. But a needy person is one who does not find (enough) wealth to free him from need, and his condition is not known (to people) that he may be given charity, nor does he go and ask from people."

1480 Abū Hurairah reported from the Prophet ﷺ that he said: "If one of you should take his rope, then go in the morning", and I think he said, "to the mountains and collect wood, sell it and eat (from the income) and give charity out of it, this is better for him than that he should beg from people." [99]

Ch. 55:   Assessing the value of dates on palm trees (for *Zakāt*)[100]

---

[96] This is a repetition of h. 27 with difference in wording. See the footnote there for further details. What the Holy Prophet meant was that the one who was left out was strong in faith, and not being given would not weaken his faith nor would he ask to be given.

[97] This addition is an alternative version of what the Holy Prophet did. Although it ends at the words "I give to a man", it is implied that the Holy Prophet continued with the rest of his statement as given just above ("while another is dearer…").

[98] Here Bukhārī explains the word "thrown" (*yukabba*) and says that *kubkibū* in the Qur'ān means *qulibū* or they will be hanged upside down. Then he goes on to refer to *mukibb-an* in the Qur'ān, saying that it is from *akabba* indicating falling or being thrown on your face. We have omitted his full explanation in the translation above.

[99] See h. 1470 and 1471. It is said here that instead of begging it is better to earn by doing work and give in charity. Even from such a small income, something should be given in the way of Allāh.

[100] *Kharṣ-un* means to estimate the value of fruit or crop before it is ripe or ready, so that *Zakāt* is based on this assessment. There are reports in Tirmidhī and Abū Dāwūd directly showing that the Holy Prophet allowed such estimation and indeed ordered it (Tirmidhī, book: *Zakāt*, h. 643–644, Abū Dāwūd, book: *Zakāt*, h. 1605).

1481–1482 Abū Ḥumaid as-Sāʿidī reported: We joined the Prophet ﷺ for the expedition of Tabūk. When he reached the valley of Qurā', there was a woman in her garden. The Prophet ﷺ said to his Companions: "Assess (the value of the fruit of the garden)." The Messenger of Allāh ﷺ assessed its value to be ten *wasq*. He said to her: "Keep account of what it yields." When we reached Tabūk, he said: "Tonight will be very stormy, so no one should stand, and whoever has a camel, he should tie it securely." So we tied the camels. A strong wind blew and one man stood up and he was blown away to the mountain of Ṭayy.

And the king of Ailah sent a gift of a white mule and a cotton shawl to the Prophet ﷺ and he granted him rulership of the country.[101] When he (the Holy Prophet) returned to the valley of Qurā', he asked the woman: "How much was the yield of your garden?" She said: "Ten *wasq*", as the assessment of the Messenger of Allāh ﷺ. The Prophet ﷺ said: "I want to hurry to Madīnah. Whoever among you wants to hurry along with me, let him come quickly." Ibn Bakkār (a narrator) said something which meant: When he (the Holy Prophet) saw Madīnah, he said: "This is Ṭābah." And when he saw Uḥud, he said: "This mountain loves us and we love it.[102] Should I inform you of the best houses of the Anṣār?" They said: "Yes." He said: "First, are the houses of the Banī an-Najjār, then come the houses of Banī ʿAbdul Ashhal, then the houses of Banī Sāʿidah or Banī al-Ḥārith ibn al-Khazraj and there is goodness in all the houses of the Anṣār." Abū ʿAbdullāh said: "A garden which has a wall around it is called a *ḥadīqah* and one which has no wall around it is not a *ḥadīqah*." [103]

[1482] (In another version the words are:) "Then the houses of Banī al-Ḥārith ibn al-Khazraj, then Banī Sāʿidah". ʿAbbās reported from his father,

---

[101] Ailah is a city on the border between the Hijaz and Syria. Here there was a king called Yūḥannah ibn Rūbah. According to a report in Ṣaḥīḥ Muslim, his emissary brought a letter from the king along with a mule as a gift for the Holy Prophet (book: ʿVirtues, ch. 3). In the *Maghāzī* of *Ibn Isḥāq* it is mentioned that when the Holy Prophet reached Tabūk, the king of Ailah came to meet him and entered into a peace treaty, accepting to pay the *jizyah* tax. It is possible that his emissary came first, and after some discussions the king himself came. As the city was on the coast, the income from the sea of his area and the governance of the whole area was entrusted to him. The words "he granted him rulership of the country" (*kataba la-hu bi-baḥri-him*) may include the sea. *Baḥr* also means a city.

[102] Mount Uḥud is situated at a distance of three miles from Madīnah. It means the surrounding area of Madīnah or the city of Madīnah itself. The reference may be to the events of the Battle of Uḥud, as it was from there that the enemy went back unsuccessful.

[103] Because they were helpers in the cause of Islām.

who reported that the Prophet ﷺ said: "Uḥud is the mountain which loves us and we love it." [104]

Ch. 56: One-tenth tax (*'ushr*) on (produce of) land irrigated by rain or running water

'Umar ibn 'Abdul 'Azīz did not levy any *Zakāt* on honey.

1483 'Abdullāh ibn 'Umar reported from the Prophet ﷺ that he said: "Land which is irrigated by rain or water from a stream or a ditch is liable to one-tenth in *Zakāt*, and that which is irrigated from a well, it is one-twentieth." [105]

Abū 'Abdullāh (Bukhārī) said:[106] This ḥadīth explains the preceding one because no quantity was mentioned in it, that is the ḥadīth of Ibn 'Umar where it is mentioned that in case of land irrigated by rainwater it is one-tenth (of the produce) and the quantity has been mentioned and made clear, and the addition (in this report) must be accepted. An explanation is decisive over an ambiguous statement if its reporters are sound, as al-Faḍl ibn 'Abbās reported that the Prophet ﷺ did not pray within the Ka'bah and Bilāl said that he did pray, so Bilāl's statement was accepted and that of al-Faḍl was rejected.[107]

Ch. 57: There is no *Zakāt* on (property worth) less than five *wasq*

1484 Abū Sa'īd al-Khudrī reported from the Prophet ﷺ that he said: "On anything less than five *wasq* there is no *Zakāt*, on camels fewer than five there is no *Zakāt*, and on anything less than five *auqiyah* of silver there is no *Zakāt*." [108]

Ch. 58: To charge *Zakāt* on dates when they are being picked

And can a child be allowed to touch dates taken in *Zakāt*?

---

[104] This report mentions some alternative wordings of statements of the Holy Prophet in the last part of h. 1481.

[105] The tax or land revenue is one-tenth (*'ushr*) on land where the owner needs to make no effort (or to spend anything) for getting water for irrigating it, but where he makes effort for getting water, the tax is one-twentieth (5%). The lower rate is to compensate for that effort.

[106] Commentators of Ḥadīth say that this statement of Bukhārī is misplaced here by the scribes and should be placed after the next ḥadīth, h. 1484. By "this ḥadīth" he means h. 1484 of Abū Sa'īd al-Khudrī and by "the preceding one" he means h. 1483 of Ibn 'Umar.

[107] Bukhārī added this comment (which should really occur after h. 1484) because the Ḥanafīs are of the view that there is no minimum limit (*nisāb*) for levying *Zakāt* on food grain, so that *Zakāt* is levied on the entire amount of grain, no matter how small that amount may be. Bukhārī contradicts this by saying that, although the report from Ibn 'Umar (h. 1483) does not mention any *nisāb*, but as a *nisāb* is mentioned in h. 1484 (a repetition of h. 1405), that must be followed.

[108] This is a repetition of h. 1405 with a slight difference of wording.

1485 Abū Hurairah reported: Dates after being picked from the trees used to be brought to the Messenger of Allāh ﷺ. One person after another would bring his dates until he (the Holy Prophet) had a heap of dates. Al-Ḥasan and al-Ḥusain were playing with these dates. One of them took a date and put it into his mouth. The Messenger of Allāh ﷺ looked towards him and took it out from his mouth and said: "Do you not know that the offspring of Muḥammad do not eat from *Zakāt*?" [109]

Ch. 59: **One who sells his fruit or date trees or land or field which is liable for *Zakāt* or *'ushr* (one-tenth tax) and he pays the *Zakāt* from other property or sells his fruit which is not liable for *Zakāt***

The saying of the Prophet ﷺ: "Do not sell fruit until these are ripe," and he did not forbid anyone from selling them after they were ripe, nor did he distinguish between that on which *Zakāt* was payable and that on which it was not payable.

1486 Ibn 'Umar said: The Prophet ﷺ forbade the selling of dates until they are ripe. And when he (Ibn 'Umar) was asked when they were ripe, he said: "Until the time has passed when it could be ruined." [110]

1487 Jābir ibn 'Abdullāh reported: The Prophet ﷺ forbade the selling of fruit until it is ripe." [111]

1488 Anas ibn Mālik reported that the Messenger of Allāh ﷺ forbade the selling of fruit until it is ripe. He said (in explanation): "Until it is red."

Ch. 60: **Can a person buy what he has given in *Zakāt*?**

There is no harm if he wants to buy what another gave in *Zakāt* because the Prophet ﷺ has only specifically forbidden the giver of *Zakāt* from buying, and not forbidden anyone else.

1489 'Abdullāh ibn 'Umar related that 'Umar ibn al-Khaṭṭāb gave a horse in charity in the way of Allāh and then saw it being sold and wanted to buy it.

---

[109] As the Holy Prophet did not allow *Zakāt* to be used for himself and his family, he was so cautious that he did not allow his grandsons, Ḥasan and Ḥusain, even to eat a single date from the *Zakāt* property. He wanted to impress on their minds that *Zakāt* is not allowed to them at all. Otherwise, there is no harm in children touching *Zakāt* property.

[110] Bukhārī has inferred from this ḥadīth that when the time has passed during which the fruit could be ruined, then it can be sold, whether *Zakāt* has been paid on it or not, because the Holy Prophet has not placed the restriction that *Zakāt* should have been paid on it. In the words "And when he was asked", Ibn 'Umar is meant.

[111] In this repetition of h. 1486, instead of the word *thamar* (date), the plural word *thamār* has been used, indicating fruit.

Then he came to the Prophet ﷺ to seek his permission. The Prophet ﷺ said: "Do not take back your charity." [112] Thus if Ibn 'Umar ever bought anything he had given in charity, he would never leave it without giving it in charity.

1490 'Umar said: I gave away my horse in the way of Allāh (to someone for riding), but he who had it made it useless (i.e., did not look after it). I intended to buy it and thought he would sell it cheaply. I asked the Prophet ﷺ about it and he said: "You cannot buy or take back your charity even if he sells it to you for one *dirham,* because he who takes back his charity is like one who swallows his own vomit." [113]

Ch. 61:   What is mentioned about giving charity to the Prophet ﷺ and his family[114]

1491 Abū Hurairah said: Ḥasan ibn 'Alī took a date from the dates of *Zakāt* and put it into his mouth. The Prophet ﷺ said: "Throw it out of your mouth." Then he said: "Do you not know that we do not eat of charity?" [115]

Ch. 62:   Giving of *Zakāt* to the slaves (*mawālī*) of the wives of the Prophet ﷺ [116]

1492 Ibn 'Abbās reported: The Prophet ﷺ saw a dead she-goat which was given as *Zakāt* to the slave-girl of Maimūnah. The Prophet ﷺ asked: "Why did you not derive benefit from its skin?" They said: "It was a dead animal." He said: "It is only prohibited to eat it." [117]

1493 'Ā'ishah reported that she wanted to buy Barīrah and free her, but her masters wanted to continue *walā'* with her. 'Ā'ishah mentioned it to the

---

[112] It appears that by "taking back" the Holy Prophet meant buying back what has been given in *Zakāt* from the person to whom it was given. This is because, feeling obliged, the recipient will sell it back to the giver at a cheaper price than its real value. Some people devised it as a way of avoiding parting with the *Zakāt* property.

[113] This is a repetition of h. 1489 with more detail.

[114] The Holy Prophet did not allow charity, whether it was obligatory or voluntary, for himself or his family (*Āl*). According to Imām Abū Ḥanīfah and Imām Mālik, by *Āl* here is meant the tribe of Banū Hāshim.

[115] This is a repetition of h. 1485 where the last words were: "Do you not know that the offspring of Muḥammad do not eat from *Zakāt*?" The two reports together show that the Holy Prophet and his family were not allowed to take charity of any kind.

[116] The same applies to the wives of the Holy Prophet as to him. They also were not allowed to take charity. By *mawālī* here seems to be meant freed slaves.

[117] This shows that a prohibition is limited only to the specific act which is forbidden. Eating meat of certain animals has been forbidden, but it is not forbidden to to use their skin, bones, etc., for other purposes. This *ḥadīth* again comes in h. 2221.

Prophet ﷺ, who said to her: "Buy her, for surely the *walā'* is with the one who frees (the slave)." She then said: Once meat was brought to the Prophet ﷺ and I said: "This is what was given in charity to Barīrah." He said: "It was a charity (*ṣadaqah*) for her but a gift for us." [118]

Ch. 63: When (ownership of) charity is transferred

1494 Umm 'Aṭiyyah al-Anṣāriyya reported that the Prophet ﷺ came to 'Ā'ishah and inquired: "Do you have anything (to eat)?" She said: "Nothing but the meat which Nusaibah (i.e., Umm 'Aṭiyyah) sent to us from the she-goat which you sent to her as charity." He said: "It has reached its destined place." [119]

1495 Anas reported that meat sent as charity (*ṣadaqah*) to Barīrah was brought to the Prophet ﷺ. He said: "It was a charity (*ṣadaqah*) for her but a gift for us." [120]

Ch. 64: To take *Zakāt* from the wealthy and give it to the needy wherever they may be[121]

1496 Ibn 'Abbās reported that the Messenger of Allāh ﷺ said to Mu'ādh ibn Jabal when he sent him to Yaman (as governor): "You are going to a country whose people are People of the Book. When you go to them, invite them to bear witness that there is no god but Allāh and that Muḥammad is the Messenger of Allāh. If they follow you in this, inform them that Allāh has made obligatory for them five prayers during the day and night. If they follow you in this, inform them that Allāh has made obligatory for them to pay charity (*ṣadaqah*), which is taken from their wealthy ones and given to their needy ones. If they follow you in this, then avoid taking their valuable properties (in tax), and beware of the curse of the oppressed because there is no barrier between it and Allāh." [122]

---

[118] See h. 456. *Walā'* were guardianship rights which the former owner of a slave retained even after the slave was freed. See the footnotes under h. 456. Barīrah was a slave-girl who was freed by 'Ā'ishah. The chapter heading relates to this. When *Zakāt* reaches the deserving person, it no longer remains a charity and it can be given as a gift to those who are not entitled to receive *Zakāt*. This has been proved in the next chapter dealing with change of ownership. See also the note on h. 1446.

[119] See h. 1446.

[120] The last part of h. 1493 has been repeated here.

[121] That is, it is not essential that the *Zakāt* collected in a particular city should he distributed among the poor of that very city. It may be spent for the welfare of deserving Muslims wherever they reside.

[122] This is a repetition of h. 1395 with some difference in wording. As in h. 1395, it is stated

Ch. 65: **Prayers (*ṣalāt*) of the Imām and his supplication (*du ʿāʾ*) for the giver of *Zakāt***

The word of Allāh: "Take charity (*ṣadaqah*) out of their property — you would cleanse them and purify them thereby — and pray (*ṣalli*) for them" (9:103). [123]

1497 ʿAbdullāh ibn Abū Aufā reported: Whenever a tribe brought its *Zakāt* to the Prophet ﷺ, he would say: "O Allāh! Bless (*ṣalli alā*) such and such people." My father came to him with his *Zakāt* and he (the Holy Prophet) said: "O Allāh! Bless (*ṣalli alā*) the family of Abū Aufā."

Ch. 66: **Wealth which is taken out of the sea**

Ibn ʿAbbās said: Ambergris is not included in treasure-trove (*rikāz*); it is a thing which the sea throws out. And al-Ḥasan (al-Baṣrī) said: In case of ambergris and pearl, (*Zakāt* is) one-fifth of its value. The Prophet ﷺ has only fixed one-fifth on treasure-trove, but not on what is found in the seawater. [124]

1498 Abū Hurairah reported from the Prophet ﷺ that a man of the Israelites asked another Isrealite to lend him one thousand *dinār* and he lent it to him. He (the debtor) went to the seaside (to take a ship to go and pay the debt in person) but did not find any ship to ride. So he took a piece of wood and hollowed it out and filled it with a thousand *dinār* and threw it into the sea. The man who lent the money came out, saw the wood and took it to use

---

here that *Zakāt* "is taken from their wealthy ones and given to their needy ones", and the chapter heading is related to this definition. See previous note. See also h. 1458. At the close there is an addition in which Muʿādh has been cautioned by the Holy Prophet to avoid doing injustice, whether to Muslims or non-Muslims, because an oppressed, helpless and weak person will seek justice only from Allāh, and as his supplications arise from the depth of his heart they immediately attract acceptance from Allāh Who punishes the oppressor.

[123] In the chapter heading the word *du ʿāʾ* has been added after "*ṣalāt* of the Imām" to show that here the word *ṣalāt* refers to prayer in general and not funeral prayers said by the Imām for a deceased. The words "prayers of the Imām" also indicate that it is the right of the ruler or government to collect *Zakāt*, and in the words "take charity out of their property" the command is also addressed to a Muslim ruler as he deputises for the Holy Prophet in this respect. In Nasāʾī there is a report from Wāʾil ibn Ḥajar that a person presented a beautiful she-camel as *Zakāt* and the Holy Prophet prayed for him thus: "O Allāh, bless it and bless his camels" (book: *Zakāt*, ch. 12, h. 2458). When the head of state prays for the payer of *Zakāt*, it pleases the latter and encourages him.

[124] The people of the Ḥijāz called a treasure-trove discovered from beneath the earth, buried during the *Jāhilīyah* period, as *rikāz*, and the people of Iraq call it also as *maʿādin* (plural, meaning 'mines'). According to Ibn Athīr, the word includes both meanings. Bukhārī does not consider ambergris and pearls from the sea as treasure-trove, but some scholars do. I prefer the opinion of Bukhārī.

as firewood for his family. He (the Holy Prophet) narrated the story, (adding that) when he cut it, he found his property.[125]

Ch. 67: In treasure-trove (*ar-rikāz*) one-fifth (is *Zakāt*)

Imām Mālik and Ibn Idrīs (Imām Shāfiʿī) said: *Ar-rikāz* is the treasure of the days of Ignorance; whether it is little or much, it is one-fifth (as *Zakāt*). And a mine (*maʿdin*) is not considered as treasure-trove (*rikāz*). And the Prophet ﷺ said about the mine: "It is exempted (from *Zakāt*) and on the treasure-trove it is one-fifth." [126]

ʿUmar ibn ʿAbdul ʿAzīz took from mines (as *Zakāt*) five on every two hundred (i.e., one-fortieth). And al-Ḥasan said: Whatever treasure-trove is found in the land at war, on it is one-fifth (as *Zakāt*), and whatever is found in the land at peace, it is (the usual) *Zakāt*. And if you find anything on enemy land, let it be identified. If it belongs to the enemy, then it is one-fifth.

Some are of the opinion that a mine is also treasure-trove like the treasure of the days of Ignorance because it is said (by the Arabs): *Arkaza al-maʿdin* when something comes out of it. The reply is that if something is given to a person as a gift, or he obtains a great profit, or has much fruit produce, then it is said: *Arkazta* (while these are not *ar-rikāz*). Then they contradict their own opinion because they say: There is nothing wrong if the person conceals it and does not pay one-fifth (as *Zakāt*).[127]

1499 Abū Hurairah reported that the Messenger of Allāh ﷺ said: "In case of (harm or injury caused by) an animal it is excused, and in case of a well, it

---

[125] In my opinion, it is difficult to infer anything from this story. Bukhārī most likely seems to imply that as the person who found that piece of wood from the sea became owner of what he found within it, similarly whoever finds ambergris, pearls etc. from the sea, these belong to him.

[126] The view of Ibn Athīr about *rikāz* has been mentioned earlier, that he includes both mines and treasure-troves in it. The same view is expressed in *Lisān al-ʿArab*. Bukhārī's inference that the Holy Prophet exempted mines from *Zakāt* is not correct, as explained in the note to the following ḥadīth, h. 1499. According to Imām Abū Ḥanīfah, both treasure-trove and mines come under the purview of taxation.

[127] The words "some are of the opinion" are generally considered to refer to Imām Abū Ḥanīfah. Commentators of Ḥadīth say that it is wrong to raise the objection against Imām Abū Ḥanīfah mentioned in the words: "Then they contradict their own opinion." His view is that if someone does not receive his entitlement from the public treasury, it is right for him, in lieu of that, not to pay one-fifth of his property as tax to the public treasury and adjust it against what is due to him. This does not contradict his view that one-fifth is to be levied as *Zakāt* on a mine. Imām Abū Ḥanīfah has not inferred that *rikāz* includes mines. It is lexicologists who have included both treasure-troves and mines in the meaning of *rikāz*.

is excused, and in case of a mine, it is excused. And on treasure-trove there is one-fifth (tax)." [128]

Ch. 68: The word of Allāh, the Most High: "And those employed to administer it" (the Qur'ān, 9:60), and the accountability of the collectors to the Imām

1500 Abū Ḥumaid as-Sā'idī reported: The Messenger of Allāh ﷺ appointed a man of al-Asd called Ibn al-Lutbiyyah to collect *Zakāt* from the tribe of the Banī Sulaim. When he came back, he (the Holy Prophet) took account from him.[129]

Ch. 69: To use camels taken in *Zakāt* and their milk for travellers

1501 Anas reported that some people of the 'Urainah tribe came to Madīnah, but the climate did not suit them. The Messenger of Allāh ﷺ ordered that they should be moved to (the open and better place) where the camels that had been given as charity were kept, and that they should drink the milk and urine of the camels (for their health). But (after gaining their health) they killed the herdsmen and drove away the camels. So the Messenger of Allāh ﷺ sent some men after them, who caught and brought them. He had their hands and feet cut off and their eyes pricked with heated spokes and their bodies thrown in the open sun where they were biting on stones.[130]

---

[128] In the Book *Ad-diyyāt* (Blood-Money or Compensation), ch. 29, the ḥadīth says that for "loss caused by an animal" payment of compensation is excused (h. 6913). In ch. 28 it is stated in a ḥadīth that for "injury caused by an animal" payment of compensation is excused (h. 6912). The same reports also go on to indicate that if a person is killed or injured by accident due to a well dug by someone, the latter is excused from paying compensation. The same applies to death or injury by accident in a mine. The issue here is not about paying *Zakāt*. It is mentioned in *Fatḥ al-Bārī* that the "excusing" here is not being excused from paying *Zakāt* but from paying the compensation known as *diyat* or blood-money.

If it is taken to mean that tax is excused on the property obtained from a mine, then for what reason could one-fortieth (the normal rate for *Zakāt*) be charged? If one-fifth is not chargeable, then there is also no basis for one-fortieth. It is agreed that to take one-fifth from treasure-trove or mine, it is not a condition that the property must have been in possession for one year. There is no doubt that the words "And on treasure-trove there is one-fifth" seem to be irrelevant, but sometimes this happens in reports. It is possible that two separate statements have been put together by Abū Hurairah or another reporter.

[129] This shows that accounts must be taken from everyone who is responsible for the management of public money.

[130] This is a repetition of h. 233 with some brevity and difference of wording.

Ch. 70: The Imām marking with his own hands the camels taken in *Zakāt* [131]

1502 Anas ibn Mālik related: I brought 'Abdullāh ibn Abū Ṭalḥah to the Messenger of Allāh ﷺ in the morning for *taḥnīk* (placing something sweet on the palate of a newly-born baby). I saw him with an instrument for marking camels in his hand, with which he was marking the camels of *Zakāt*.

Ch. 71: Obligation of the charity of (Eid-ul-) Fiṭr

Abū al-'Āliyah, 'Aṭā' and Ibn Sīrīn considered the charity of (Eid-ul-) Fiṭr as obligatory. [132]

1503 Ibn 'Umar reported: The Messenger of Allāh ﷺ prescribed one *ṣā'* of dates or one *ṣā'* of barley as charity of Fiṭr on the slave or free, male or female, young or old, among Muslims, and he commanded that it should be given before people go out for prayer.

Ch. 72: Charity of (Eid ul-) Fiṭr for a slave and other Muslims

1504 Ibn 'Umar reported that the Messenger of Allāh ﷺ prescribed one *ṣā'* of dates or one *ṣā'* of barley as charity of Fiṭr on every free person or slave, male or female, among Muslims.

Ch. 73: One *ṣā'* of barley (as charity of Eid-ul- Fiṭr)

1505 Abū Sa'īd (al-Khudrī) reported: We used to give one *ṣā'* of barley as charity. [133]

Ch. 74: One *ṣā'* of grain as charity of Fiṭr

1506 Abū Sa'īd al-Khudrī said: We used to give out, as charity of Fiṭr, one *ṣā'* of grain (*ṭa'ām*), [134] or one *ṣā'* of barley, or one *ṣā'* of dates, or one *ṣā'* of cheese (*'aqiṭ*), or one *ṣā'* of raisins (*zabīb*).

---

[131] The Imām or head of state is the guardian and trustee of the public treasury. The Holy Prophet used to mark the camels with his own hands, and this marking distinguished them from other camels. Some say that the Companions are unanimous that the marking should be with the word *Zakāt* or *Ṣadaqah*. This does not support the view that cattle in general can be branded.

[132] All Muslims except followers of Imām Abū Ḥanīfah believe that the charity of Eid-ul-Fiṭr is obligatory, i.e., a *farīḍah*. The Ḥanafīs regard it as essential (*wājib*). The obligatory nature of this charity is only established from Ḥadīth reports which are *ẓannī*, i.e., below the level of being conclusive.

[133] See h. 1508 below.

[134] *Ṭa'ām* means any kind of grain. See also h. 1508.

Ch. 75:   One *ṣā'* of dates as charity of Fiṭr

1507 'Abdullāh ibn 'Umar said: The Prophet ﷺ commanded, to be given as charity of Fiṭr, one *ṣā'* of dates or one *ṣā'* of barley. He added: But (later on) people started giving two *mudd* of wheat as equal to it.[135]

Ch. 76:   One *ṣā'* of raisons as charity of Fiṭr

1508 Abū Sa'īd al-Khudrī reported: During the time of the Prophet ﷺ we used to give one *ṣā'* of grain, or one *ṣā'* of dates, or one *ṣā'* of barley, or one *ṣā'* of raisins (as charity of Fiṭr). When Mu'āwiyah came (to the caliphate) and wheat became available, he said: "I think one *mudd* of this is equal to two *mudd* (of the above-mentioned things)."

Ch. 77:   Charity of Fiṭr to be given before the Eid prayer

1509 Ibn 'Umar reported that the Prophet ﷺ commanded the giving of the charity of Fiṭr before people go out for the prayer.[136]

1510 Abū Sa'īd al-Khudrī reported: During the time of the Prophet ﷺ we used to give, on the day of (Eid-ul-) Fiṭr, one *ṣā'* of grain. And Abū Sa'īd said: Our meal used to be barley, raisins, cheese, and dates.[137]

Ch. 78:   Charity of Fiṭr (is obligatory) on the free and the slaves

> And az-Zuhrī said regarding slaves kept for trade that *Zakāt* should be paid for them, and charity of Fiṭr should also be paid for them.

---

[135] See h. 1511. The next ḥadīth says that this was started by Mu'āwiyah. There is no doubt that wheat was scarcely available during the time of the Holy Prophet, and Ibn Mandhir says that there is no ḥadīth of the Holy Prophet about wheat in this connection. The Holy Prophet has prescribed one *ṣā'* of barley, dates, cheese or raisins, even though all of these could not have been the same price. At least cheese and raisins must be more costly than barley and dates. However, the Companions gave half a *ṣā'* of wheat as the equivalent, and this is stated to be the view of 'Uthmān, 'Alī, Abū Hurairah, Ibn 'Abbās, and others. It appears that they fixed Eid-ul-Fiṭr charity on the basis of its monetary value. Today also, the amount should be fixed on the basis of money. At present the cost of one *ṣā'* of barley is the least of these, then wheat, raisins and dates in increasing order. However, wheat is not twice as expensive as barley. It is safer to fix the amount according to the price of one *ṣā'* of wheat.

[136] There should be an organised system of collecting Eid charity among Muslims which, if benefit is derived from it today, would be a great source of financial strength for the whole Muslim community. The Holy Prophet commanded that it should be paid before the congregational prayers so that the needy section of society can be assisted by it and they too can enjoy good food and fine clothes on this day. Today, if Eid charity were to be collected in an organised manner and distributed in a planned way, it would provide permanent help for thousands of needy Muslims.

[137] It is mentioned here that this was the practice on the day of Eid. Probably it is from this that it has been concluded that it was done before the Eid prayers because on Eid day the foremost act was to hold the Eid congregational prayers.

1511 Nāfiʿ reported that Ibn ʿUmar said: "The Prophet ﷺ made obligatory the charity of Fiṭr" — or he said Ramaḍān — "on males and females, free and slaves, one ṣāʿ of dates or one ṣāʿ of barley." Then people made half a ṣāʿ of wheat equal to this. Ibn ʿUmar used to give dates. When there was shortage of dates for the people of Madīnah, he gave barley. And Ibn ʿUmar used to give it on behalf of young and old, and even for my sons.[138] Ibn ʿUmar used to give it to those who would accept it. And people used to give it a day or two before (Eid-ul-) Fiṭr.

Abū ʿAbdullāh (Bukhārī) said: "My sons" means sons of Nāfiʿ. He also said: They used to give it to be collected, not to beggars.[139]

Ch. 79: Eid charity is obligatory on young and old

Abū Maʿmar said: In the opinion of ʿUmar, ʿAlī, Ibn ʿUmar, Jābir, ʿĀʾishah, Ṭaʾus, ʿAṭāʾ and Ibn Sīrīn, *Zakāt* should be paid on the wealth of an orphan. Az-Zuhrī said: *Zakāt* should be charged on the wealth of an insane person.[140]

1512 Ibn ʿUmar reported: The Messenger of Allāh ﷺ made obligatory the charity of Fiṭr as one ṣāʿ of dates or one ṣāʿ of barley on young and old, and free and slaves.[141]

---

[138] Nāfiʿ, son of ʿAbdullāh ibn ʿUmar, is reporting from his father. In other words, Ibn ʿUmar used to pay the Eid charity on behalf of his grandsons as well.

[139] In other words, when a person is appointed by the Imām to collect the Eid charity, people used to give only to him and not to the needy ones directly. In the Ḥadīth collection *Muwaṭṭaʾ*, there is a report from Nāfiʿ stating that Ibn ʿUmar used to send the Eid charity to the man who was appointed to collect it. In Bukhārī, in the Book of *Wakālah*, there is a report from Abū Hurairah beginning with the words: "The Messenger of Allāh ﷺ deputed me to keep the charity of Ramadan" (h. 2311). This shows that during the time of the Holy Prophet, and even afterwards, there was an organised arrangement for collecting Eid charity, like that for the collection of *Zakāt*, and it was distributed among the needy according to that system. There is a need to re-introduce the same type of system today.

[140] Orphans and mentally ill people derive benefit from the government or the administrators of charity, just as other deserving people do. Therefore, the wealthy among them must also contribute to the expenses required to maintain these institutions.

[141] This is a repetition of the last ḥadīth, h. 1511.

Book 25: *Al-Manāsik*
Rites of the Pilgrimage[1]

In the name of Allāh, the Beneficent, the Merciful

Ch. 1: The obligation of *Ḥajj* and its excellence

The word of Allāh: "And pilgrimage (*Ḥajj*) to the House is a duty which people owe to Allāh — whoever can find a way to it. And whoever disbelieves, surely Allāh is above the need of the worlds" (the Qur'ān, 3:97).[2]

1513 'Abdullāh ibn 'Abbās reported: Al-Faḍl was riding behind the Messenger of Allāh ﷺ when a woman of the tribe of Kha<u>th</u>'am came. Al-Faḍl started to look at her and she also looked at him. The Prophet ﷺ kept on turning al-Faḍl's face to the other side. The woman said: "O Messenger of Allāh! The obligation from Allāh on His servants to perform the *Ḥajj* has come but my father is very old and cannot keep himself steady on a mount. May I perform *Ḥajj* on his behalf?" He said: "Yes." This happened during the Farewell Pilgrimage.[3]

---

[1] According to the list in h. 8, "Islām is based on five (pillars)", of which *Ḥajj* is the fourth and occurs after *Zakāt*. Bukhārī has kept the same sequence in his collection, and thus the book of *Ḥajj* occurs following the book of *Zakāt*.

Manāsik is the plural of *mansak* and means worship or forms of worship. It is applied particularly to the rites of *Ḥajj*. The Pilgrimage was performed even before Islām, but all its rites were performed for idols and some practices had also been added to its original form by the idol-worshippers. Islām retained the performance of *Ḥajj* but cleared it of all the polytheistic rituals and concepts.

[2] *Ḥajj* means, in fact, the 'intention of a visit'. In the terminology of the Islamic *Sharī'ah*, it is reserved for the intention of visiting the House of Allāh, the Ka'bah. Bukhārī has based its obligation on the Qur'ān and has inferred its duty from the words *'al-an-nās* (lit. "upon people", translated above as "a duty which people owe" to Allāh).

[3] The object here is only to show that *Ḥajj* is obligatory. This incident took place at the time of the Farewell Pilgrimage, but the words here do not mean the *Ḥajj* was made obligatory just then. The woman was only making the point that while *Ḥajj* was obligatory for her father he was old and unable to perform it.

Ch. 2:   The word of Allāh: "…they will come to you on foot and on every lean camel, coming from every remote path (*fajj-in*) that they may witness benefits provided for them…" (the Qur'ān, 22:27–28).[4]

Fijāj-an means wide roads.

1514 Ibn 'Umar said: I saw the Messenger of Allāh ﷺ riding on his she-camel at Dhul Ḥulaifah. When it would stand up, he would recite the *Talbiyah*.[5]

1515 Jābir reported that the Messenger of Allāh ﷺ would start reciting the *Talbiyah* from Dhul Ḥulaifah when his she-camel stood up.

Ch. 3:   To perform *Ḥajj* sitting on a saddle

1516 'Ā'ishah reported that the Prophet ﷺ sent her brother 'Abdur Raḥmān with her to perform *'Umrah* from Tan'īm and he made her to sit at the back of the pack saddle. And 'Umar said: Fasten saddles over (camels) for *Ḥajj* as it is one of the two *jihāds*.[6]

1517 Thumāmah ibn 'Abdullāh ibn Anas reported: Anas performed *Ḥajj* while sitting on the saddle (of a camel), and he was not a miserly person. He also reported that the Prophet ﷺ performed *Ḥajj* while sitting on the saddle (of a camel) with his luggage loaded on it.[7]

1518 Al-Qāsim ibn Muḥammad reported from 'Ā'ishah that she said: "O Messenger of Allāh, you all have performed *'Umrah* but I have not." He said: "O 'Abdur Raḥmān, go with your sister, and let her perform the *'Umrah* from Tan'īm." So he made her sit behind him on the she-camel and she performed the *'Umrah*.[8]

---

[4] It means that one should try to come for the *Ḥajj* in any way possible. There is no harm in coming by riding or by means of a conveyance. By mentioning "lean" camels (22:27) the travelling of long distances is indicated.

[5] For the words of the *Talbiyah* and its translation, see h. 1549 and h. 1550.

[6] *Ḥajj* is called "one of the two *jihāds*" because it is a struggle against one's inner self. This shows that the Companions of the Holy Prophet did not consider *jihād* only as fighting by the sword. They considered every good act as an act of *jihād* and, in accordance with the Word of Allāh, they regarded *jihād* with the Qur'ān, or efforts to spread the teachings of the Qur'ān, as the greater *jihād*: "… and strive against them (i.e., do *jihād* against the unbelievers) a mighty *jihād* with it" (25:52).

[7] The object is to observe frugality and simplicity as far as possible, as was the life of the Holy Prophet and as he liked simplicity in whatever he did. He never forbade means of adornment and comfort, but preferred to bear difficulties and hardship. While travelling for the *Ḥajj* he would sit on the saddle without placing any cushions or bedding on it. Even though women are delicate, 'Ā'ishah sat on the wood of the saddle while performing *'Umrah*.

[8] See h. 316.

Ch. 4:   Excellence of the *Ḥajj Mabrūr* (the "righteous" *Ḥajj*)[9]

1519 Abū Hurairah reported: The Prophet ﷺ was asked, "Which is the best deed?" He said: "Belief in Allāh and His Messenger." It was said: "Then which one?" He said: "*Jihād* in the way of Allāh". Again, it was asked: "Then which one?" He said: "*Ḥajj Mabrūr.*" [10]

1520 ʿĀ'ishah, mother of the faithful, reported that she said: "O Messenger of Allāh! We consider *jihād* the best deed, then why should we not do *jihād?*" He said: "The better *jihād* is to perform *Ḥajj Mabrūr.*" [11]

1521 Abū Hurairah said: I heard the Prophet ﷺ saying: "One who performed *Ḥajj* for (seeking the pleasure of) Allāh without uttering immodest (or lustful) speech or committing sin, he will return as he was on the day when his mother gave him birth (i.e., in a state of innocence)."

Ch. 5:   Fixing of points (*mawāqīt*) for entering into *Iḥrām* for *Ḥajj* and ʿUmrah[12]

1522 Zaid ibn Jubair related: I went to the home of ʿAbdullāh ibn ʿUmar and saw that tents and side-screens had been fixed. I asked him: "Which is the correct place for me to start the *'Umrah?*" He said: "The Messenger of Allāh ﷺ has appointed Qarn for the people of Najd, Dhul Ḥulaifah for the people of Madīnah, and al-Juḥfah for the people of Syria.[13]

Ch. 6:   The word of Allāh: "And make provision for yourselves, the best provision being to keep one's duty" (the Qur'ān, 2:197)[14]

---

[9] The definition of *Ḥajj Mabrūr,* a righteous or virtuous *Ḥajj* that is accepted by Allāh, is as follows: "Nothing of sin should be mixed with it."

[10] This is a repetition of h. 26.

[11] This shows that women also had the heart-felt desire to do *jihād*. The Holy Prophet said that *Ḥajj Mabrūr* is the best *jihād* of all because it is a permanent duty while *jihād* by the sword is only required if certain circumstances arise. The direction here is given particularly to women because, due to lack of physical strength and the need to look after their children, they were unable to take part in fighting the *jihād* of the sword equally with men. Nonetheless, they did assist in the battles in other ways.

[12] The word *mīqāt*, singular of *mawāqīt*, is from *waqt* (time), meaning the time which is fixed for doing something. It is used both for time and place. Here it has been used for a place, i.e., the place at which a person enters into the state of *Iḥrām* for *'Umrah* or *Ḥajj*.

[13] Compare h. 1524. The people of Yaman are not mentioned here, nor is the last part of h. 1524 included here.

[14] The keeping of one's duty or guarding oneself (*taqwā*) mentioned in 2:197 is applied here in the sense of guarding oneself from begging while on the Pilgrimage.

1523 Ibn 'Abbās reported: People of Yaman used to perform *Ḥajj* and did not take any provisions (for the journey with them). They used to say: "We trust in Allāh." When they would reach Makkah, they would beg from people. So Allāh revealed: "And make provision for yourselves, the best provision being to keep one's duty" (2:197).

Ch. 7:   Place for entering into *Iḥrām* for *Ḥajj* or *'Umrah* for the people of Makkah

1524 Ibn 'Abbās reported: The Prophet ﷺ fixed Dhul Ḥulaifah as the *mīqāt* for the people of Madīnah, al-Juḥfah for the people of Syria, Qarn al-Manāzil for the people of Najd, and Yalamlam for the people of Yaman. These are for them and for others who come there (from other countries) for *Ḥajj* and *'Umrah*. And whoever lives nearer (to Makkah) than these places, it is from where he starts, so that for the people of Makkah it is Makkah itself.[15]

Ch. 8:   The *mīqāt* for the people of Madīnah and they should not enter into *Iḥrām* before Dhul Ḥulaifah

1525 'Abdullāh ibn 'Umar reported that the Messenger of Allāh ﷺ said: "The people of Madīnah should enter into *Iḥrām* from Dhul Ḥulaifah, the people of Syria from al-Juḥfah, and the people of Najd from Qarn." 'Abdullāh also said: And the report reached me that the Messenger of Allāh ﷺ also said: "and the people of Yaman from Yalamlam." [16]

Ch. 9:   The place for entering into *Iḥrām* for the people of Syria

1526 Ibn 'Abbās reported: The Messenger of Allāh ﷺ fixed Dhul Ḥulaifah as the *mīqāt* for the people of Madīnah, ... And whoever lives nearer (to Makkah) than these places, he should enter into *Iḥrām* from his place of dwelling, so that the people of Makkah enter into *Iḥrām* from Makkah itself.[17]

Ch. 10:   The place for entering into *Iḥrām* for people of Najd

1527 'Abdullāh (ibn 'Umar) reported that the Prophet ﷺ had fixed the *mīqāt* (places for entering into *Iḥrām*).

---

[15] The word *Iḥrām* is from *ḥaram*, meaning to prohibit or to prevent. *Iḥrām* is to desist from doing all such acts which have been forbidden to do during *Ḥajj*. This is why the pilgrim removes his ordinary clothing and puts on a special garb. This will be mentioned later and is also mentioned in h. 134. People coming from the Indian subcontinent enter into *Iḥrām* after their vessel passes the mountain of Yalamlam.

[16] H. 133 has been briefly repeated here. Ibn 'Umar adds that "the report reached me", i.e., he did not himself hear the words about the people of Yaman from the Holy Prophet.

[17] This is a repetition of h. 1524 with slight difference in wording. See h. 1524 for the translation omitted here, as indicated by (...).

1528 'Abdullāh (ibn 'Umar) reported: I heard the the Messenger of Allāh ﷺ saying: "The place for entering into *Iḥrām* for the people of Madīnah is Dhul Ḥulaifah, for the people of Syria it is Mahya'ah, which is al-Juḥfah, and for the people of Najd it is Qarn." Ibn 'Umar added: They claim that the Prophet ﷺ also said, but I did not hear it, "and the place for entering into *Iḥrām* for the people of Yaman is Yalamlam." [18]

Ch. 11:   **The place for entering into *Iḥrām* for people living within the *mīqāt* (i.e., nearer to Makkah)**

1529 Ibn 'Abbās reported: The Prophet ﷺ fixed Dhul Ḥulaifah as the *mīqāt* for the people of Madīnah, …[19]

Ch. 12:   **The place for entering into *Iḥrām* for people of Najd**

1530 Ibn 'Abbās reported: The Prophet ﷺ fixed Dhul Ḥulaifah as the *mīqāt* for the people of Madīnah, …[20]

Ch. 13:   **Dhāt 'Irq is the place for entering into *Iḥrām* for the people of Iraq ('Irāq)**

1531 'Abdullāh ibn 'Umar reported: When these two cities were conquered,[21] people came to 'Umar and said: "O Chief of the Believers, the Messenger of Allāh ﷺ appointed Qarn as the place for entering into *Iḥrām* for the people of Najd, but that does not fall in our way, and if we come through Qarn, then we have to bear hardship." He said: "Find some other place which is parallel to Qarn on your way." So he appointed Dhāt 'Irq for them.[22]

Ch. 14:   **Offering of prayer at Dhul Ḥulaifah**

1532 'Abdullāh ibn 'Umar reported that the Messenger of Allāh ﷺ made his she-camel to sit down at al-Baṭḥā' in Dhul Ḥulaifah and prayed there. And 'Abdullāh ibn 'Umar used to do the same.[23]

---

[18] This is a repetition of h. 133 similar to h. 1525, with slight variation of wording.

[19] This is a repetition of h. 1524 with slight difference in wording.

[20] This is also a repetition of h. 1524 with slight difference in wording.

[21] By the "two cities" are meant Baṣrah and Kūfah. These two were established after the conquest of Iraq. Hence the reference here is to the conquest of Iraq.

[22] The same rule applies to people coming from other such countries, from which the route to Makkah does not pass any of the appointed places mentioned in Ḥadīth. They should enter into *Iḥrām* from a place lying parallel to any appointed place.

[23] See h. 484, which is a long report in which stops of the Holy Prophet on his way from Madīnah to Makkah have been mentioned.

Ch. 15:   The setting out of the Prophet ﷺ through the way of ash-Shajarah

1533 ʿAbdullāh ibn ʿUmar reported that the Messenger of Allāh ﷺ used to leave (Madīnah) by the way of ash-Shajarah and used to enter (Madīnah on his return) by the way of al-Muʿarras, and that whenever the Messenger of Allāh ﷺ used to travel towards Makkah, he would pray at the mosque of ash-Shajarah, and when he returned he would pray in the middle of the valley of Dhul Ḥulaifah and spend the night there till morning.[24]

Ch. 16:   The saying of the Prophet ﷺ: "Al-ʿAqīq is a blessed valley"

1534 ʿUmar said: I heard the Prophet ﷺ saying about the valley of al-ʿAqīq: "Tonight a comer came to me from my Lord and said, Pray in this blessed valley and tell them that *'Umrah* has been included in the *Ḥajj*." [25]

1535 Mūsā ibn ʿUqbah related: Sālim, son of ʿAbdullāh (ibn ʿUmar), related to me from his father, who reported from Prophet ﷺ that he saw a dream while he was staying in the middle of the valley of Dhul Ḥulaifah in the latter part of the night[26] in which he was told: "You are in the blessed valley". Sālim also made us halt at that point, where ʿAbdullāh would halt his camel to find the place where the Messenger of Allāh ﷺ had halted in the latter part of the night. It is further down from the mosque that is in the valley, and is in between them (i.e., people who halt) and the road.

Ch. 17:   To wash perfume off clothes three times

1536 Ṣafwān ibn Yaʿlā informed that Yaʿlā said to ʿUmar: Show me when the Prophet ﷺ is receiving revelation. He added:

When the Prophet ﷺ was at al-Jiʿrānah,[27] along with a group of his Companions, a man came and said: "O Messenger of Allāh! What do you say about a man who enters into the state of *Iḥrām* for *'Umrah* and he is

---

[24] See h. 484. The word *mu'arras* means a place to stop for the night (see note on h. 1535). The "way (*ṭarīq*) of ash-Shajarah" and the "way (*ṭarīq*) of al-Muʿarras" are two roads. The Holy Prophet took the former for going to Makkah and the latter for returning to Madīnah.

[25] The valley of ʿAqīq is four miles away from Madīnah and is near Baqīʿ. The Holy Prophet used to stay for the night there after leaving Madīnah so that all those people who desired to accompany him could join him. This incident is a dream, as is evident from the next ḥadīth.

[26] The word translated here and later in this ḥadīth as "the latter part of the night" is *mu'arras*. See also note on h. 1533.

[27] Jiʿrānah is a place between Makkah and Ṭāʾif, closer to Makkah. Here the Holy Prophet distributed the war acquisitions and it was from here that he went to perform the *'Umrah*. See Book of *'Umrah,* ch. 3, h. 1778.

besmeared with perfume?" The Prophet ﷺ kept silent for a moment, and then a revelation came down on him. 'Umar pointed towards Ya'lā. He came and there was a cloth covering the Messenger of Allāh ﷺ. Ya'lā entered his head into it and saw that the face of the Messenger of Allāh ﷺ was red and he was snoring. Then this condition was removed.[28] So he asked: "Where is the one who asked about the *'Umrah*?" The man was called and he (the Prophet) said: "The perfume you have applied should be washed off three times, and take off the robe, and do for your *'Umrah* as you do for your *Hajj*."

I said to 'Aṭā (who reported from Ṣafwān): "Did he (the Prophet) mean cleanliness when he ordered him to wash three times?" He said: "Yes."

Ch. 18: Applying perfume when entering into *Iḥrām*, and what to wear in that state, and combing hair and applying oil[29]

Ibn 'Abbās said: A person in the state of *Iḥrām* can smell a flower, look into a mirror and use as medicine edible things such as olive oil and butter oil. 'Aṭā said: He can wear a ring and a waist-band. Ibn 'Umar did circuits (of the Ka'bah) in a state of *Iḥrām* while he had tied a cloth around his belly. 'Ā'ishah did not see any harm as regards wearing of shorts. Abū 'Abdullāh (Bukhārī) says: She meant those who fastened her saddle on camels.[30]

1537–1538 Sa'īd ibn Jubair reported: Ibn 'Umar used oil in his hair (while in *Iḥrām*) so I mentioned this to Ibrāhīm Nakh'ī. He said: "What will you do by his statement? [1538] Al-Aswad related to me from 'Ā'ishah: 'As if I were now observing the shine of the perfume in the parting of the hair of the Messenger of Allāh ﷺ while he used to be in *Iḥrām*'." [31]

---

[28] For a description of the condition of the Holy Prophet while he was receiving revelation, see h. 2 and the last two footnotes under it. This ḥadīth shows that the same also used to be the condition of the Holy Prophet while he was receiving "inner revelation" (*waḥy khafiyy*, revelation of a lower kind, different from the higher kind which became part of the Qur'ān). This incident is repeated in h. 1789.

[29] It is permissible to apply perfume and oil and to comb one's hair before the state of *Iḥrām*. There is no harm if its smell remains even after taking a bath or washing it. But the use of these things while being in the state of *Iḥrām* is not permissible.

[30] The majority opinion is that the wearing of shorts while in the state of *Iḥrām* for servants and labourers is not allowed because it is considered like trousers. 'Ā'ishah considered it permissible in case of necessity.

[31] See h. 271. Ibn 'Umar used only oil and refrained from applying perfume. So Ibrāhīm Nakh'ī cited the words of 'Ā'ishah showing that perfume was applied to the Holy Prophet's hair.

1539 ʻĀʼishah, wife of the Prophet ﷺ, reported: I used to apply perfume to the Messenger of Allāh ﷺ for his *Iḥrām* when he entered into this state, and also when he left this state before making the circuits of the Kaʻbah (i.e., the *Ṭawāf az-ziyārah*).[32]

Ch. 19:　Who puts on *Iḥrām* after matting his hair?

1540 ʻAbdullāh (ibn ʻUmar) reported: I heard the Messenger of Allāh ﷺ reciting the *Talbiyah* with his hair matted.

Ch. 20:　To recite the *Talbiyah* near the Mosque of Dhul Ḥulaifah

1541 ʻAbdullāh ibn ʻUmar said: The Messenger of Allāh ﷺ never entered into the state of *Iḥrām* but at the Mosque, meaning the Mosque of Dhul Ḥulaifah.[33]

Ch. 21:　Which clothes a person in *Iḥrām* should not wear?

1542 ʻAbdullāh ibn ʻUmar reported that a man asked: "O Messenger of Allāh, what kind of clothes should a person in *Iḥrām* wear?" The Messenger of Allāh ﷺ said: "He should not wear a shirt, or a turban, or trousers, or headgear, or socks unless he cannot find shoes so he may wear socks, cutting them off (so they are) below the ankles. And he should not wear any clothes perfumed with saffron or *wars* (a kind of scent)."

Abū ʻAbdullāh (Bukhārī) said: The person in *Iḥrām* can wash his head but should not comb his hair. He should not scratch his body, and he can brush lice from his head and body to the ground.[34]

---

[32] See h. 267. For *Ṭawāf az-ziyārah* see footnote to the heading of ch. 130.

[33] The knowledge that the Holy Prophet had entered into the state of *Iḥrām* came from his reciting of *Labbaika* loudly. In h.1545 it is stated that he entered into *Iḥrām* at al-Baidāʼ which is further on from Dhul Ḥulaifah. According to h. 1514 and h. 1515, he entered into *Iḥrām* at Dhul Ḥulaifah when he mounted his camel. This report has it that he entered into *Iḥrām* at the mosque of Dhul Ḥulaifah. The report of Ibn ʻAbbās given in Abū Dāwūd and Ḥākim can be made consistent with this by the explanation that he entered into *Iḥrām* at the mosque of Dhul Ḥulaifah after finishing his prayer while he was still sitting there and loudly proclaimed *Labbaika* for *Ḥajj,* and then he proclaimed it again after mounting the camel, and still again after reaching al-Baidāʼ. So whoever heard him proclaiming this at a certain place, he reported it accordingly. The *Labbaika* of entering into *Iḥrām* was called out by him as soon as he finished his prayer while he was still sitting in the mosque.

[34] H. 134 has been repeated here with difference in wording. The word for "headgear" here, *barānis,* is plural, while it is the singular *burnus* in h. 134, and the words "and no socks" have been added (meaning socks of leather). In short, this ḥadīth tells us that one in the state of *Iḥrām* should not wear a sewn cloth, or cover his head, or cover his ankles, or wear perfumed clothing. However, it is agreed that for women, except perfumed clothes, no other kind of clothing is

Ch. 22:   Riding or sitting behind someone during *Ḥajj*

1543–1544 Ibn ʿAbbās reported that Usāmah rode behind the Prophet ﷺ from ʿArafāt to Muzdalifah, then al-Faḍl rode behind him from Muzdalifah to Minā. He (Ibn ʿAbbās) added: Both of them said that the Prophet ﷺ did not cease reciting the *Talbiyah* till he cast pebbles at Jamrat al-ʿAqabah.

Ch. 23:   Which of clothes or sheets or waste-cloth should a person in *Iḥrām* wear?

‘Āʾishah wore a dress coloured in safflower while she was in *Iḥrām*. She said: A woman should not cover her lips, nor cover her face,[35] and nor wear a cloth dyed in *wars* or saffron. Jābir said: I do not consider safflower a perfume. ‘Āʾishah saw no harm in women wearing ornaments, black and pink clothes, or socks. Ibrāhīm said: There is no harm if she changes her clothes (during *Iḥrām*).

1545 ‘Abdullāh ibn ʿAbbās reported: The Prophet ﷺ went from Madīnah after combing his hair, applying oil (to hair), and wearing his waist-cloth and his upper sheet, he as well as his Companions (doing so). He did not forbid any upper sheet or waist-cloth to be worn except that they should not be coloured so much with saffron that it stains the skin. He stayed at Dhul Ḥulaifah till it was morning. Then he mounted his she-camel until he reached al-Baidā’. He and his Companions entered into the state of *Iḥrām* and garlanded their sacrificial camels. And still five days were left of the month of Dhul Qaʿdah. When he reached Makkah on the 4th of Dhul Ḥajjah, he made circuits of the Kaʿbah and ran between the Ṣafā and the Marwah. He could not leave the state of *Iḥrām* because of the sacrificial camel which he had already garlanded. Then he alighted at the upper side of Makkah near al-Ḥajūn, still in *Iḥrām* for the *Ḥajj*. He did not go near the Kaʿbah after making circuits of it until he returned from ʿArafāt. Then he ordered his Companions to make circuits of the Kaʿbah, and (run) between the Ṣafā and the Marwah, cut short the hair of their heads, and leave the state of *Iḥrām*. And this was only for anyone who did not have with him a sacrificial camel which he had garlanded.

---

disallowed, and every part of her body should be covered except for the face. In the additional comment of Bukhārī, the prohibition of scratching the body is not the real purpose but it seems to be prohibited to avoid killing lice. Thus the principle of complete non-violence is to be observed during these few days of the *Ḥajj*. See also h. 1838.

[35] During the Pilgrimage, a woman should not cover her face while she wears her usual clothes, as opposed to men who cover their bodies with just two unsewn sheets. This shows conclusively that the Qurʾān does not command women to cover their faces, otherwise it would have been in contradiction to the injunction of the Qurʾān to order them to keep their faces uncovered during the Pilgrimage.

And anyone who had his wife with him, she was (now) permissible for him, and (permissible) also was use of perfume and (usual) clothes.

Ch. 24:　Staying the night at Dhul Ḥulaifah till morning

This was reported by Ibn 'Umar from the Prophet ﷺ.

1546 Anas ibn Mālik reported: The Prophet ﷺ said four *rak'ahs* of prayer in Madīnah and two *rak'ahs* in Dhul Ḥulaifah. Then he spent the night till it was morning at Dhul Ḥulaifah. When he mounted his animal and it stood up, he recited the *Talbiyah*.[36]

1547 Anas ibn Mālik reported that the Prophet ﷺ said four *rak'ahs* of *Ẓuhr* prayer in Madīnah, and he said two *rak'ahs* of *'Aṣr* prayer in Dhul Ḥulaifah. He added: I think he spent the night there till it was morning.

Ch. 25:　To recite the *Talbiyah* loudly

1548 Anas reported: The Prophet ﷺ said four *rak'ahs* of *Ẓuhr* prayer in Madīnah, and two *rak'ahs* of *'Aṣr* prayer in Dhul Ḥulaifah, and I heard people reciting the *Talbiyah* together loudly.

Ch. 26:　The *Talbiyah*

1549 'Abdullāh ibn 'Umar reported that the *Talbiyah* of the Messenger of Allāh ﷺ was: "I am here, O Allāh, I am here. I am here, no one is Your partner, I am here. To You is surely all praise and (from You are) all favours. And Yours is the Kingdom, no one is Your partner." [37]

1550 'Ā'ishah reported: I surely know how the Prophet ﷺ used to recite the *Talbiyah*. It was: "I am here, O Allāh, I am here. I am here, no one is Your partner, I am here. To You is surely all praise and (from You are) all favours." [38]

Ch. 27:　Praising Allāh and glorifying Him and proclaiming His greatness before entering into *Iḥrām* while mounting an animal

1551 Anas reported: We were with the Messenger of Allāh ﷺ when he said four *rak'ahs* of the *Ẓuhr* prayer at Madīnah and two *rak'ahs* of *'Aṣr* at Dhul Ḥulaifah. Then he spent the night there till the morning. Then he rode

---

[36] This is a part of h. 1551.

[37] The words in Arabic are: *Labbaika Allāhuma labbaik. Labbaika lā sharīka laka, labbaik. Inna-l-ḥamda wa-n-ni'matah laka. Wa-l-mulka laka. Lā sharīka laka.*

[38] In this report from 'Ā'ishah, the words of the *Talbiyah* are as in h. 1549, except that the closing words, "And Yours is the Kingdom, no one is Your partner", are not present here.

till the she-camel reached al-Baidā', and he praised Allāh and glorified Him and proclaimed His greatness.[39] Then he entered into the state of *Iḥrām* for *Ḥajj* and *'Umrah*,[40] and the people also entered into *Iḥrām* for both. When we arrived (at Makkah), he ordered people to leave the state of *Iḥrām*, till the 8th when they entered into *Iḥrām* for *Ḥajj*.[41] He (Anas) said: The Prophet ﷺ sacrificed camels himself while standing. And the Messenger of Allāh ﷺ slaughtered at Madīnah two striped (*amlaḥain*) sheep.[42]

Ch. 28:   He who enters into *Iḥrām* when he has mounted his she-camel

1552 Ibn 'Umar reported: The Prophet ﷺ entered into *Iḥrām* when he mounted his she-camel and it stood up.

Ch. 29:   Entering into *Iḥrām* facing the Ka'bah

1553 Nāfi' reported: Ibn 'Umar, after saying his morning prayers at Dhul Ḥulaifah, would order his mount (to be ready). Then the pack-saddle would be fixed on it and he would mount it. When it would stand up straight with him, he would face the Qiblah on it. Then he would recite the *Talbiyah* until he reached the *Ḥaram* (Makkah). Then he would stop reciting it until he reached Dhu Ṭuwā. He would stay the night there till next morning. After saying the morning prayers, he would take a bath. He asserted that the Messenger of Allāh ﷺ did that.

1554 Nafi' reported: Whenever Ibn 'Umar decided to go to Makkah, he applied oil (to himself) which had no fragrance. Then he would go to the mosque at Dhul Ḥulaifah and say his prayer. Then he would mount and when the she-camel would stand up straight with him, he would enter into *Iḥrām*. Then he would say: I saw the Prophet ﷺ doing the same.

---

[39] Saying *Al-ḥamdu li-llāh, Subḥān Allāh* and *Allāhu Akbar.*

[40] From these words, and the words of h. 1534 "and tell them that *'Umrah* has been included in the *Ḥajj*", and the statement in h. 1548 "and I heard people reciting the *Talbiyah* together loudly", it appears that the Holy Prophet combined the *'Umrah* and the *Ḥajj*, and entered into *Iḥrām* for both. It is stated in h. 1545: "he alighted at the upper side of Makkah near al-Ḥajūn, still in *Iḥrām* for the *Ḥajj*". This means that he entered into *Iḥrām* for the *'Umrah* and the *Ḥajj* and remained in that state after making the circuits of the Ka'bah and between the Ṣafā and Marwah, and unlike his Companions he did not re-enter the state of *Iḥrām* at Makkah for *Ḥajj*.

[41] The people mentioned here are those who did not have animals for sacrifice, and therefore after performing *'Umrah* they left the state of *Iḥrām*. The 8th of Dhul Ḥajjah is referred to here as the day of *Tarwiyah* because this word means 'to water', and on that day pilgrims watered the camels that they rode upon.

[42] *Amlaḥain* is the dual form of *amlaḥ*, which means mixed white and black. The sacrifice of these two sheep does not relate to the *Ḥajj*, but was a sacrifice done in Madīnah.

Ch. 30:   Recitation of *Talbiyah* while descending in the stream

1555 Mujāhid reported: We were with Ibn ʿAbbās, and people mentioned Dajjāl (the Anti-Christ), that he (the Prophet) had said: "Between his eyes is written the word *kāfir*." Ibn ʿAbbās said: I have not heard this, but he (the Prophet) said: "As if I am seeing Moses descending into the stream, reciting the *Talbiyah*." [43]

Ch. 31:   How should a menstruating woman and one suffering from child-birth bleeding enter into *Iḥrām?*

Ahallah means to say a thing, and *istahlal-nā* and *ahlal-na-l-hilāl* all mean that which is manifest. *Istahalla-l-maṭar* means the rain came out of the clouds. In (the verse) "that on which a name other than that of Allāh has been invoked (*uhilla*)" (the Qur'ān, 5:3), it comes from *istihlāl aṣ-ṣabiyy* (crying of a child).

1556 ʿĀ'ishah, wife of the Prophet ﷺ, reported: We set out with the Prophet ﷺ on the Farewell Pilgrimage. So we entered into the state of *Iḥrām* for *'Umrah.* Then the Prophet ﷺ said: "Anyone who has an animal for sacrifice with him should enter into *Iḥrām* for *Ḥajj* with *'Umrah* (i.e., *qirān*). He then should not leave the state of *Iḥrām* until he has performed both (*'Umrah* and *Ḥajj*)."

When I reached Makkah, I was menstruating and I could not make circuits of the Kaʿbah nor (run) between the Ṣafā and the Marwah. I complained about this to the Prophet ﷺ, and he said: "Undo your hair, comb it, enter into *Iḥrām* for *Ḥajj,* and disregard the *'Umrah.*" I did so. When we had performed the *Ḥajj,* the Prophet ﷺ sent me with ʿAbdur Raḥmān ibn Abū Bakr to Tanʿīm and I performed the *'Umrah.* Then he (the Prophet) said: "This is in place of your *'Umrah.*" [44]

She (ʿĀ'ishah) said: Those who had entered into the state of *Iḥrām* for *'Umrah* made circuits of the Kaʿbah and (ran) between the Ṣafā and the Marwah, and then left the state of *Iḥrām.* Then, on their return from Minā, they performed another *Ṭawāf.* But those who combined the *Ḥajj* and the *'Umrah* performed only one *Ṭawāf.*

---

[43] The words "As if I" (*ka-annī*) show that he saw Moses in a dream or vision. At that time Dajjāl or the Anti-Christ was not dominating the world with his acts of deception (*dajl*), but it was a prophecy by the Holy Prophet about his arising and dominance in later times. The Holy Prophet had described him as having the word *kāfir* (unbeliever) written between his eyes. This knowledge was given to him in a dream or vision, and in that state what is shown is meant metaphorically, not physically.

[44] See h. 316 and h. 1561.

Ch. 32: **He who entered into the state of *Iḥrām* in the time of the Prophet ﷺ as the Prophet ﷺ did**

This was reported by Ibn 'Umar from the Prophet ﷺ.

1557 Jābir said: The Prophet ﷺ commanded 'Alī always to enter *Iḥrām* as he did. He then mentioned the incident of Surāqah.[45]

Muḥammad ibn Bakr added from Ibn Juraiḥ as follows. The Prophet ﷺ said to him: "O Ali! For what purpose have you entered into the state of *Iḥrām*?" He said: "For the same purpose that the Prophet ﷺ has entered into *Iḥrām*." He said: "Make the sacrifice and remain in *Iḥrām* as you are."

1558 Anas ibn Malik reported: 'Alī came to the Prophet ﷺ from Yaman. He (the Prophet) asked him: "For what purpose have you entered into the state of *Iḥrām*?" He replied: "For the same purpose that the Prophet ﷺ has entered into *Iḥrām*." He (the Prophet) said: "If I did not have a sacrificial animal with me, I would have left the state of *Iḥrām*." [46]

1559 Abū Mūsā reported: The Prophet ﷺ sent me to some people of Yaman. When I came back, he was at al-Baṭḥā', and he asked: "For what purpose have you entered into the state of *Iḥrām*?" I said: "I have entered into the state of *Iḥrām* like the entering of the Prophet ﷺ into *Iḥrām*." He said: "Do you have a sacrificial animal with you?" I said: "No." So he commanded me to make circuits of the Ka'bah. I made circuits of the Ka'bah and (ran) between the Ṣafā and the Marwah. Then he commanded me to leave the state of *Iḥrām*.[47] Then I came to a woman of my tribe. She combed my hair or washed my head.[48]

---

[45] The statement of Surāqah has been mentioned at the end of h. 1785 in these words: "Surāqah ibn Mālik ibn Ju'shum met the Prophet ﷺ at al-'Aqabah while he was casting pebbles and he asked: Is it specially for you, O Messenger of Allāh? He said: No, it is for all time to come." In other words, he wanted to know whether the performance of *'Umrah* during the time of the *Ḥajj* was only for the Holy Prophet or for the whole of the Muslim *Ummah*. The Holy Prophet said it was for all time.

[46] The same incident has been mentioned here as in h. 1557. But here it is a report by Anas and is part of the lengthy ḥadīth, h. 1651.

[47] 'Alī and Abū Mūsā al-Ash'arī had both entered into the state of *Iḥrām* without a clear intent but had merely followed what the Holy Prophet had done. As 'Alī had a sacrificial animal with him, the Holy Prophet did not tell him to leave the state of *Iḥrām*. Abū Mūsā al-Ash'arī did not have a sacrificial animal with him, so the Holy Prophet commanded him to emerge from *Iḥrām* after performing the *'Umrah*.

[48] Here it is only mentioned that he came to a woman of his people and she washed his hair and combed it. Some commentators say that she must be someone who would have been a *maḥram*, a closely-related woman with whom marriage is prohibited (like a mother or sister, for

Then (the caliphate of) 'Umar came and he said: "If we act upon the Book of Allāh, it commands us to complete it, as Allāh says: 'And accomplish the *Ḥajj* and the *'Umrah* for Allāh' (2:196). If we act according to the practice of the Prophet ﷺ, he did not leave the state of *Iḥrām* until making the sacrifice."[49]

Ch. 33: **The word of Allāh: "The months of the Pilgrimage (*Ḥajj*) are well known;[50] so whoever determines to perform the Pilgrimage therein, there shall be no immodest speech, nor abusing, nor altercation during the Pilgrimage" (the Qur'ān, 2:197). "They ask you about the new moons. Say: These are times appointed for people, and for the Pilgrimage" (2:189).**

Ibn 'Umar said: Months of the Pilgrimage are Shawwāl, Dhul Qaʻdah, and ten days of Dhul Ḥajjah. Ibn 'Abbās said: It is *Sunnah* that one can only enter into *Iḥrām* for *Ḥajj* during the months of *Ḥajj*. And 'Uthmān considered it undesirable to enter into *Iḥrām* from Khurāsān or Karmān.[51]

1560 'Ā'ishah reported: We set out with the Messenger of Allāh ﷺ during the months of *Ḥajj*, in the nights of *Ḥajj*, and in the *Ḥajj* season. We alighted at Sarif.[52] He came out to his Companions and said: "Anyone of you who has no sacrificial animal with him and wishes to perform *'Umrah*, he can do so.[53]

---

example). If that had been the case, the inference (*qiyās*) would be that the relationship itself should have been specified.

[49] In a report from Abū Mūsā in Ṣaḥīḥ Muslim (book: *Pilgrimage*, ch. 22) he says that he used to give the verdict to people allowing *'Umrah* in the days of *Ḥajj* during the rule of Abū Bakr and 'Umar. Then a man came to him and said: "Don't you know that the Chief of the Believers has instituted a new thing in the rites of *Ḥajj*?" 'Umar did not consider it right to emerge from *Iḥrām* after performing *'Umrah* in the days of *Ḥajj* and then enter into *Iḥrām* for the *Ḥajj* (i.e., *Tamattuʻ*), and he considered the Holy Prophet's command to emerge from *Iḥrām* (after performing the *'Umrah*) only to apply in that year of the Farewell Pilgrimage.

[50] This shows that there is no particular time for performing *'Umrah*. *'Umrah* is like optional prayers for which there is no fixed time or system, while *Ḥajj* is like the obligatory prayers.

[51] As there are appointed times for the obligatory prayers, similarly there is a particular time for the *Ḥajj*. It is against the *Sunnah* to enter into the state of *Iḥrām* earlier than the months of the *Ḥajj* or before arriving at the *mīqāt*, the appointed places for starting it, and thereby subject oneself to hardship. If it had been allowed to enter into the state of *Iḥrām* whenever and from wherever one wished to do, then it would be useless to fix the months of the Pilgrimage and appoint places for entering into *Iḥrām*.

[52] Sarif is the name of a place located at a distance of ten miles from Makkah. It is now known as the Valley of Fāṭimah.

[53] The Holy Prophet ordered on two occasions the cancelling of the state of *Iḥrām* for *Ḥajj* and emerging from this state after performing the *'Umrah*. Once it was in Sarif, as appears from

And anyone who has a sacrificial animal with him, he should not." So, some of his Companions did accordingly and some did not. As to the Messenger of Allāh ﷺ and some of his Companions who were strong and had sacrificial animals with them, they could not perform (only) the *'Umrah*.

She added: The Messenger of Allāh ﷺ came to me and I was crying. He said: "Why are you crying, O *hanatāh* (simple woman)?" I said: "I heard what you said to your Companions. I cannot perform the *'Umrah*." He said: "What is the matter with you?" I said: "I cannot say my prayers (due to menstruation)." He said: "There is no harm[54] for you. You are a woman among the daughters of Adam. Allāh has ordained for you what He ordained for them (i.e., menstruation). Remain in your *Ḥajj*. May be Allāh will grant you the opportunity to perform *'Umrah*."

She added: So we set out for *Ḥajj* till we reached Minā. I became clean of menstruation and left Minā and made circuits of the Ka'bah.[55] She added: Then I set out with him (i.e., the Holy Prophet) in the last departing group till he alighted at al-Muḥaṣṣab[56] and we alighted with him. He called 'Abdur Raḥmān ibn Abū Bakr and said to him: "Take your sister out of the Sacred Precincts (*al-Ḥaram*) and let her enter into the state of *Iḥrām* for *'Umrah*. Then after finishing, both of you should come back here. I will wait for you two, until you come to me." She added: We set out until I, and he ('Abdur Raḥmān), finished the *Ṭawāf*, and then came back to him (the Holy Prophet) at dawn. He asked: "Have you done it?" I said: "Yes." So he announced to his Companions to leave and the people set off. He started travelling towards Madīnah.

---

this ḥadīth. But on this occasion it was also left to the individual's discretion as seen from the words: "wishes to perform *'Umrah*". That is why some cancelled the *Ḥajj* and some did not. The second occasion was at Makkah after the *Ṭawāf* as mentioned in h. 1561. This was a definite order but some Companions took this also as discretionary. However, when the Holy Prophet made it clear, then they cancelled their state of *Iḥrām* for *Ḥajj*, as is mentioned in h. 1568.

[54] Bukhārī explains the derivation of the word *yaḍurru* ("harm") at the end of this ḥadīth.

[55] The conditions for making circuits of the Ka'bah are almost the same as those for performing the regular prayers. Just as a menstruating woman cannot perform the regular prayer, she cannot make circuits of the Ka'bah. That was why 'Ā'ishah could not perform the *'Umrah* as it is essential to perform *Ṭawāf* of the Ka'bah during the *'Umrah*. All other rites of the *Ḥajj* can be performed while in the state of menstruation, as she performed them in that state. When she became cleansed of it at Minā, she then made circuits of the Ka'bah on the 10th of Dhul Ḥajjah after proceeding from Minā.

[56] The first departure starts on the 12th of Dhul Ḥajjah and the last one on the 13th. Al-Muḥaṣṣab is an open plain between Makkah and Minā where there are pebbles because of frequent floods. It is also called Abṭaḥ or al-Baṭḥā'.

Abū 'Abdullāh (Bukhārī) says about *yaḍīru* that it has the forms: *ḍāra, yaḍīru, ḍair-an.* And it is said: *ḍāra, yaḍūru, ḍaur-an* and *ḍarra, yaḍurru, ḍarr-an.*

Ch. 34: *Tamattu', Qirān* and *Ifrād* in *Ḥajj*, and the cancelling of *Ḥajj* by one who has no sacrificial animal with him[57]

1561 'Ā'ishah reported: We set out with the Prophet ﷺ, intending only to perform the *Ḥajj*. When we reached Makkah, we made circuits of the Ka'bah. The Prophet ﷺ ordered those who did not take sacrificial animals to leave the state of *Iḥrām*, so those who did not take sacrificial animals left this state. His wives did not take sacrificial animals, so they also left the state of *Iḥrām*.

'Ā'ishah said: My menstruation started and I could not make circuits of the Ka'bah. When it was the night of Ḥaṣbah,[58] I said: "O Messenger of Allāh! People will return after performing both *'Umrah* and *Ḥajj*, and I will return after performing only *Ḥajj*. He said: "Did you not make circuits of the Ka'bah at night when we were Makkah?" I said: "No." He said: "Go with your brother to Tan'īm and enter into *Iḥrām* for *'Umrah*. Then the meeting point (for us) will be such and such a place." Ṣafiyyah said: "I only see that I am delaying you (from proceeding)." He said: "How strange (*'Aqrā ḥalqā*)![59] Did you not make circuits on the day of Sacrifices?" She said: "Yes." He said: "There is no harm — depart!"

'Ā'ishah said: So the Prophet ﷺ met me (as decided) while he was ascending from Makkah and I was descending to it, or I was ascending and he was descending from it.

---

[57] *Tamattu'* is the performance of both *'Umrah* and *Ḥajj* in one visit, while entering into *Iḥrām* separately for each of them. *Qirān* is to perform both in the same state of *Iḥrām*. *Ifrād* is to perform only the *Ḥajj*, entering into *Iḥrām* only for *Ḥajj*. In *Tamattu'*, the state of *Iḥrām* is entered into for *'Umrah* at one of the appointed places (*mīqāt*). Then after reaching Makkah, making circuits of the Ka'bah and between the Ṣafā and the Marwah — known as *'Umrah* — the state of *Iḥrām* is left and all things prohibited in the state of *Iḥrām* become allowed. Then on 8th Dhul Ḥajjah, the day of *Tarwiyah*, the state of *Iḥrām* is entered into at Makkah for the *Ḥajj*.

[58] Ḥaṣbah and Muḥaṣṣab are names of the same place. The Holy Prophet stopped here on the night of the 13th.

[59] *'Aqrā* and *ḥalqā* both are infinitive nouns (like *da'wā*), the former meaning 'to cut' and 'to destroy', and the latter meaning 'to shave' (the head) or 'to have a throat complaint'. According to Aṣma'ī (famous philologist), these words are used to express surprise. According to the Nihāyah, anything which arouses surprise and wonder is expressed by the words *'aqrā ḥalqā*, and also a wretched woman who creates difficulties is accosted with these words. Obviously here Ṣafiyyah had not committed a fault, but she simply wanted to say that she also was menstruating and was prevented from performing the last *Ṭawāf*, as was the case with 'Ā'ishah. The Holy Prophet expressed his surprise in these words. Ṣafiyyah had not said anything to deserve being condemned with this expression. Some commentators of Ḥadīth have misunderstood these words as being addressed to Ṣafiyyah.

1562 'Ā'ishah reported: We set out with the Messenger of Allāh ﷺ in the year of the Farewell Pilgrimage. Some of us entered into *Iḥrām* for *'Umrah,* and some for both *Ḥajj* and *'Umrah*, and some for *Ḥajj* only. The Messenger of Allāh ﷺ entered into *Iḥrām* for for *Ḥajj* only.[60] Those who entered into *Iḥrām* for *Ḥajj* or for both *Ḥajj* and *'Umrah* left the state of *Iḥrām* only on the day of Sacrifices.

1563 Marwān ibn al-Ḥakam reported: I was with 'Uthmān and 'Alī. 'Uthmān forbade *al-mut'ah,* and that these two be combined.[61] When 'Alī saw this, he entered into *Iḥrām* for both, saying *Labbaika* for *'Umrah* and *Ḥajj*. He said: "I cannot leave the *Sunnah* of the Prophet ﷺ on the basis of someone's saying." [62]

1564 Ibn 'Abbās reported: People used to consider performing *'Umrah* during the months of *Ḥajj* as the worst sin on earth and used to consider month of Muḥarram as Ṣafar. They used to say: "When the back of the camel heals and signs of injuries disappear and the month of Ṣafar passes, *'Umrah* is then for the one who wishes to perform it." [63] The Prophet ﷺ and his Companions reached Makkah on the morning of the 4th in the state of *Iḥrām* for *Ḥajj*. He ordered them to convert it into *'Umrah*. They felt it against their inclination and said: "O Messenger of Allāh, Which things will be permissible?" He said: "Everything of it (i.e., disallowed during *Iḥrām*) is permissible."

---

[60] Anas reports in h. 1551 that the Holy Prophet entered into *Iḥrām* for both the *Ḥajj* and the *'Umrah*. The same appears to be the case from h. 1534. In reports about *Ḥajj* from 'Ā'ishah, narrators have shown much unease. Imām Mālik says: "We do not consider it right to act upon the ḥadīth of 'Urwah from 'Ā'ishah." Similarly, Abū 'Amr says: "Reports from her (about *Ḥajj*) her are unsatisfactory." Therefore, the report from Anas about *qirān* has been given preference.

[61] *Al-mut'ah* usually means *Tamattu',* but it has sometimes been used in the sense of *qirān*. It is therefore possible that here only *qirān* is meant in this prohibition, and the words "these two be combined" are an explanation of the previous word *al-mut'ah*. The discussion with 'Alī also related to the same question. The proclaiming of *Labbaika* by 'Alī for both the *Ḥajj* and the *'Umrah*, i.e., entering into *Iḥrām* for *qirān* and his declaring it as the *Sunnah* of the Holy Prophet, also shows that 'Uthmān used to prevent people from observing *qirān*. Alterrnatively, by the word *al-mut'ah* may be meant *Tamattu',* and 'Uthmān may have forbidden the observation of both. There is no detail here as to why he used to forbid these. Either he misunderstood the issue or there was some expediency for it.

[62] A great characteristic of the Companions of the Holy Prophet was that they never followed any person, however great he may be, if he went against the *Sunnah* of the Holy Prophet and they always stood up for the truth.

[63] By "Ṣafar" in "the month of Ṣafar passes" they meant Muḥarram. The three consecutive months of Dhul Qa'dah, Dhul Ḥajjah and Muḥarram were "sacred", during which the Arabs had to refrain from murder, looting and highway robbery. This being too long a stretch for them, they used to treat the last month, Muḥarram, as being Ṣafar, and thus not sacred. The Qur'ān refers to this practice in the words: "Postponing (of the sacred month) is only an addition in disbelief" (9:37).

1565 Abū Mūsā reported: I came to the Prophet ﷺ and he ordered me to leave the state of *Iḥrām*.[64]

1566 Ḥafṣah, wife of the Prophet ﷺ, reported that she said: "O Messenger of Allāh, what is the matter with people that they have left the state of *Iḥrām* after *'Umrah* but you have not left *Iḥrām* after your *'Umrah*?" He said: "I have matted my hair and garlanded my sacrificial animal, so I will not leave the state of *Iḥrām* until I perform the sacrifice."

1567 Abū Jamrah Naṣr ibn 'Imrān aḍ-Ḍuba'ī informed: I performed *Tamattu'* and people forbade me. I asked Ibn 'Abbās and he ordered me (to perform it). I saw in a dream that a man said to me: "A righteous (*mabrūr*) *Ḥajj* and an accepted (*mutaqabbalah*) *'Umrah*." I informed Ibn 'Abbās, who said: "This is the *Sunnah* of the Prophet ﷺ." Then he said to me: "Stay with me and I will give you a share of my property."

Shu'bah (reporting from Abū Jamrah) said: I asked him, "How is that?" He (Abū Jamrah) said: "Because of the dream I saw." [65]

1568 Abū Shihāb related: I came to Makkah for performing *Tamattu'* in the state of *Iḥrām,* and we reached there three days before the *Tarwiyah* (8th of Dhul Ḥajjah). Some people of Makkah said to me: "Your *Ḥajj* now would be (like) the *Ḥajj* of (the people of) Makkah." So I went to 'Aṭā to ask his opinion. He said: Jābir ibn 'Abdullāh told me that he had performed *Ḥajj* along with the Prophet ﷺ on the day he had taken sacrificial animals with him and people had entered into the state of *Iḥrām* only for the *Ḥajj*. He (the Prophet) told them: "Leave the state of *Iḥrām* after making circuits of the Ka'bah and (running) between the Ṣafā and the Marwah, get your hair cut and then stay on without *Iḥrām* until it is the day of *Tarwiyah,* and then enter into *Iḥrām* for *Ḥajj;* and make the intention with which you came into one for *'Umrah.*" They asked: "How can we make it into *'Umrah,* for we had intended to perform *Ḥajj*?" He said: "Do as I have commanded you. If I had not brought sacrificial animals I would have done what I have told you (to do), but it is not permissible for me to leave the state of *Iḥrām* until the sacrifice is performed." So they complied with his orders.[66]

---

[64] For details, see h. 1559.

[65] Because his dream corroborated the view of Ibn 'Abbās.

[66] The fact is that, as has been mentioned in h. 1560, at Sarif the Holy Prophet allowed people the discretion to do whatever they wanted. It is possible that the Companions on this occasion wrongly thought that that discretion was still allowed. When the Holy Prophet explained that the discretion was only for that occasion, the people complied with the commandment.

1569 Saʿīd ibn al-Musayyab reported: ʿAlī and ʿUthmān had a disagreement while they were at ʿUsfān about *Ḥajj at-Tamattuʿ*. ʿAlī said: "You only wish to forbid people from something which the Messenger of Allāh ﷺ did himself?" ʿUthmān replied: "Leave me to be as I am." When ʿAlī saw this, he entered into *Iḥrām* for both (*'Umrah* and *Ḥajj*).[67]

Ch. 35:   One who calls *Labbaika* for *Ḥajj* by name

1570 Jābir ibn ʿAbdullāh related: We came with the Messenger of Allāh ﷺ while we were calling out the *Talbiyah* for *Ḥajj*. The Messenger of Allāh ﷺ commanded us, so we made it into *'Umrah*.

Ch. 36:   *Tamattuʿ* during the time of the Prophet ﷺ

1571 ʿImrān ibn Ḥusain reported: We performed *Tamattuʿ* during the time of the Messenger of Allāh ﷺ. It was also revealed in the Qur'ān. A man said according to his opinion whatever he wished.[68]

Ch. 37:   The word of Allāh: "This is for him whose family is not present in the Sacred Mosque" (2:196)

1572 Ibn ʿAbbās reported that he was asked about the *Ḥajj* of *Tamattuʿ* and he said: The Emigrants (*Muhājirūn*), the Helpers (*Anṣār*), and wives of the Prophet ﷺ, all of us, entered into the state of *Iḥrām* at the Farewell Pilgrimage. When we reached Makkah, the Messenger of Allāh ﷺ said: "Make your *Iḥrām* for *Ḥajj* into one for *'Umrah,* except those who have garlanded their sacrificial animals." We made circuits of the Kaʿbah and (ran) between the Ṣafā and the Marwah, came back to our wives[69] and put on our usual clothes. He (the Prophet) said: "Whoever has garlanded his sacrificial animal cannot leave the state of *Iḥrām* until the sacrifice is performed." Then he ordered us on the evening of the *Tarwiyah* (the 8th) to enter into *Iḥrām* for *Ḥajj*. When we had completed the rites of *Ḥajj*, we came and made circuits of the Kaʿbah and (ran) between the Ṣafā and the Marwah, and our *Ḥajj* was complete. The sacrifice became obligatory on us as Allāh has said (in the Qur'ān): "(he should take) whatever offering is easy to obtain. But he who cannot find (an offering) should fast for three days during the pilgrimage and

---

[67] See h. 1563.

[68] The reference here is to the words of the verse: "… whoever profits by combining the visit (*'Umrah*) with the Pilgrimage (*Ḥajj*)" (2:196). The words "A man said according to his opinion" refer to ʿUmar.

[69] The meaning is that sexual relations were allowed.

for seven days when you return" (2:196) to your home. One goat is sufficient (for sacrifice).

So they joined the two rites, *Ḥajj* and *'Umrah,* in one year, for Allāh, the Most High, revealed this in His Book and through the *Sunnah* of His Prophet ﷺ, and allowed it for all people who do not live in Makkah. Allāh, the Most High, said: "This is for him whose family is not present in the Sacred Mosque" (2:196). The months of *Ḥajj* which Allāh has mentioned in His Book are: Shawwāl, Dhul Qaʻdah and Dhul Ḥajjah. Whoever performs *Tamattuʻ* in these months, sacrifice or fasting is obligatory on him.

Rafath means sexual relations, *fusūq* means sin, and *jidāl* means altercation.[70]

Ch. 38:　Taking a bath on entering Makkah

1573 Nāfiʻ reported that Ibn ʻUmar, when entering the *Ḥaram* (Makkah), used to stop reciting the *Talbiyah.* Then he would pass the night at Dhu Ṭuwā. Then he would say the morning prayers there and take a bath. He used to relate that the Prophet of Allāh ﷺ used to do the same.[71]

Ch. 39:　To enter Makkah during the day or night

1574 Ibn ʻUmar reported: The Prophet ﷺ passed the night at Dhu Ṭuwā till it was morning and then he entered Makkah. And Ibn ʻUmar used to do the same.

Ch. 40:　From where to enter Makkah?

1575 Ibn ʻUmar reported: The Messenger of Allāh ﷺ used to enter Makkah from the upper part of the valley (Thaniyya) and used to leave it through its lower part.[72]

Ch. 41:　Which way to leave Makkah?

1576 Ibn ʻUmar reported that the Messenger of Allāh ﷺ entered Makkah from Kadā', the upper part of the valley (Thaniyya) which is in Baṭḥā', and left from its lower side.

---

[70] The reference here is to the words of the verse: "The months of the pilgrimage are well known; so whoever determines to perform pilgrimage in them, there shall be no *rafath,* nor *fusūq,* nor *jidāl* in the Pilgrimage" (2:197).

[71] See h. 1553.

[72] See h. 1576. Some facts have been preserved as mere events, but it is neither possible to act accordingly nor did the Holy Prophet issue any command about them.

1577 ʿĀʾishah reported that when the Prophet ﷺ came to Makkah he entered it from its upper side and left from its lower side.

1578 ʿĀʾishah reported that, in the year Makkah was conquered, the Prophet ﷺ entered from Kadāʾ and left from Kudā, the upper side of Makkah.

1579 ʿĀʾishah reported that, in the year Makkah was conquered, the Prophet ﷺ entered from Kadāʾ, the upper side of Makkah. Hishām said:[73] And ʿUrwah used to enter (Makkah) from both Kadāʾ and Kudā, most often from Kadāʾ, as it was nearer to his home.

1580 ʿUrwah reported: In the year Makkah was conquered, the Prophet ﷺ entered from Kadāʾ, the upper side of Makkah, and ʿUrwah used to enter (Makkah) most often from Kadāʾ, as it was nearer to his home.

1581 ʿUrwah reported: In the year Makkah was conquered, the Prophet ﷺ entered from Kadāʾ. And ʿUrwah used to enter (Makkah) from both of them (Kadāʾ and Kudā), most often from Kadāʾ, as it was nearer to his home. Abū ʿAbdullāh (Bukhārī) said: Kadāʾ and Kudā are two places.[74]

Ch. 42:   The excellence of Makkah and construction of the Kaʿbah

> The word of Allāh: "And when We made the House a resort for people and a (place of) security, and (said): Take the Place of Abraham for a place of prayer. And We commanded Abraham and Ishmael, saying: Purify My House for those who visit (it) and those who abide (in it) for devotion and those who bow down (and) those who prostrate themselves. And when Abraham said: My Lord, make this a secure town and provide its people with fruits, such of them as believe in Allāh and the Last Day. He said: And whoever disbelieves, I shall grant him enjoyment for a short while, then I shall drive him to the punishment of the Fire. And it is an evil destination. And when Abraham and Ishmael raised the foundations of the House: Our Lord, accept from us; surely You are the Hearing, the Knowing. Our Lord, and make us both submissive to You, and (raise) from our offspring, a nation submissive to You,

---

[73] Hishām was son of ʿUrwah. He is the reporter from ʿUrwah in the five reports h. 1577–h. 1581, while in h. 1577–h. 1579 ʿUrwah in turn reports from ʿĀʾishah.

[74] The four reports h. 1578–h. 1581 mention "the year Makkah was conquered", while h. 1581 does not contain the words "the upper side of Makkah". Three of these (h. 1579–h. 1581) mention what ʿUrwah used to do. According to Nihāyah (the dictionary of Ḥadīth) Kadāʾ is a mound of Makkah adjacent to the graves, and Kudā is a lower mound adjacent to Bab al-ʿUmrah. H. 1578 says that he "left from Kudā, the upper side of Makkah", which is contrary to the other reports here which state that Kadāʾ is on the upper side.

and show us our ways of devotion and turn to us (mercifully); surely You are the Oft-returning (to mercy), the Merciful" (the Qur'ān, 2:125–128).[75]

1582 Jābir ibn 'Abdullāh said: When the Ka'bah was being built (i.e., reconstructed), the Prophet ﷺ and 'Abbās (his uncle) were carrying stones, 'Abbās said to the Prophet ﷺ: "Put your waist-cloth on your shoulders." He fell to the ground (due to modesty) and his eyes were staring at the sky. He said: "Give me my waist-cloth." And then he tied his waist-cloth (around his lower part).[76]

1583 'Ā'ishah, wife of the Prophet ﷺ, reported that the Messenger of Allāh ﷺ said to her: "Do you not know that when your tribe (the Quraish) built the Ka'bah they left it short of (some of) the foundations laid by Abraham?" (She added:) I asked: "O Messenger of Allāh, will you not rebuild it on the foundations of Abraham?" [77] He said: "If your tribe had not come out of disbelief so newly, I would have done it."

'Abdullāh (ibn 'Umar, who reported from 'Ā'ishah) said: If 'Ā'ishah heard this from the Messenger of Allāh ﷺ, then I think the Messenger of Allāh ﷺ left out kissing the two corners (of the Ka'bah) opposite the *Hijr* (adjoining the *Hatīm*) because the House was not rebuilt on the foundations laid down by Abraham.[78]

---

[75] Bukhārī has deduced the excellence of Makkah from these verses of the Holy Qur'ān in which the supplications of Prophet Abraham for this city have been mentioned, and wherein it is called the place of Pilgrimage and the place of peace. It is remarkable that in these two respects Makkah enjoys a distinction which no other city in the world has. Firstly, there is no city which attracts people in such large numbers: "a resort for people and a (place of) security" (2:125), as Makkah really is. Secondly, no other city in the world enjoys so much security as Makkah, to the extent that no conflict takes place within its boundaries, and even its animals and its very vegetation are safe.

[76] See also h. 364 which ends with the words: "and he was never seen exposed after that." See the footnote to h. 364. Raising the waist-cloth may have exposed his upper thighs. Hadīth reports show that the Holy Prophet was as modest as a bashful young girl. The purpose of this hadīth is to show that just as the prophets Abraham and Ishmael worked like labourers in the construction of the Ka'bah, the Holy Prophet worked in the same way in its construction. No other house of worship ever had labourers of such high spiritual rank working for its construction.

[77] This hadīth and reports occurring later in this chapter support the verse of the Qur'ān: "And when Abraham raised the foundations of the House, and Ishmael" (2:127). An almost identical topic is in h. 126 (see footnote on h. 126).

[78] The Ka'bah has four corners as follows: The Black Stone and the Yamani corner, these two being called the two Yamani corners which the Holy Prophet used to kiss, the *Shāmī* or Syrian corner facing Syria, and the Iraqi corner facing Iraq, these latter two being called the two Syrian corners which the Holy Prophet did not kiss. It is regarding these two latter corners that

1584 ʿĀʾishah reported: I asked the Prophet ﷺ about the *Ḥaṭīm,* if it was a part of the House (Kaʿbah)? He said: "Yes." I then asked: "Then why did they not include it in the House?" He said: "Your tribe did not have sufficient money for it." I then asked: "Why is its door on a height?" He said: "Your tribe did it so that they could allow to enter whom they wish and prevent whom they wish. And if your tribe had not come out of the era of Ignorance so newly that I feared they would have disliked it, I would have included the *Ḥaṭīm* in the Kaʿbah and lowered its door to the level of the ground."

1585 ʿĀʾishah reported: The Messenger of Allāh ﷺ said to me: "If your tribe had not come out of disbelief so newly, I would have demolished the House and rebuilt it on the foundations of Abraham because the Quraish had decreased (the area of) its building, and I would have constructed for it a door opposite (the existing one)."

Abū Muʿāwiyah said: Hishām related to us that *khalf-an* means a door.[79]

1586 ʿĀʾishah reported that the Prophet ﷺ told her: "O ʿĀʾishah, if your tribe had not come out of the era of Ignorance so newly, I would have ordered the House (Kaʿbah) to be demolised and I would have included in it the portion which has been left out and brought its door to the level of the ground; and I would have inserted two doors, one eastern and one western, and made it reach the foundations laid down by Abraham."

This was what encouraged Ibn az-Zubair to demolish it. Yazīd (a narrator) said: I saw Ibn az-Zubair when he demolished it and rebuilt it[80] and included the *Ḥaṭīm* in it. And I saw the foundations of Abraham, which were of stones like the humps of a camel. Jarīr (reporting from Yazīd) said: I asked Yazīd where the place of the original foundations was. He said: "I will show it to you just now." I entered the *Ḥaṭīm* with him and he pointed to a place and said: "It is here." Jarīr said: "I assessed (the area of) the *Ḥaṭīm* as being approximately the measure of six hands or thereabouts."

ʿAbdullāh ibn ʿUmar used to say that perhaps the Holy Prophet did not kiss them because they are not on the foundations laid by the Prophet Abraham. The *Ḥijr* or *Ḥaṭīm* is that part of the Kaʿbah which was not included in it when the Quraish rebuilt the Kaʿbah, but it is included while making circuits of the Kaʿbah. A question about this has been raised in the next ḥadīth.

[79] The word translated as "a door opposite" is *khalf-an.* Bukhārī has explained this word from a disconnected report of Hishām as meaning a door, so that what the Holy Prophet meant was that he would have constructed another door for the Kaʿbah directly opposite to the present door.

[80] ʿAbdullāh ibn az-Zubair reconstructed the Kaʿbah during 64–65 A.H. as the building was damaged during Yazīd ibn Muʿāwiyah's attack on Makkah.

Ch. 43: Excellence of the Sacred City (*Ḥaram*)[81]

The word of Allāh: "I am commanded only to serve the Lord of this city, Who has made it sacred, and to Him belong all things, and I am commanded to be of those who submit" (the Qur'ān, 27:91). And His word: "Have We not settled them in a safe, sacred territory to which fruits of every kind are drawn? A sustenance from Us — but most of them do not know" (28:57).

1587 Ibn 'Abbās reported that the Messenger of Allāh ﷺ said on the day of the conquest of Makkah: "Allāh has granted this city sanctity; no thorn of it should be cut, nor should its game be chased, nor anything fallen in it should be picked up except by one who announces it (as lost property)."

Ch. 44: Inheritance of buildings in Makkah and their sale and purchase

All people in the Sacred Mosque are equal, in particular, because of the word of Allāh: "Those who disbelieve and hinder (people) from Allāh's way and from the Sacred Mosque, which We have made for all people equally, (for) the dweller (*'ākif*) in it and the visitor (*bād*). And whoever inclines to wrong in it, unjustly, We shall make him taste of painful punishment" (22:25). Abū 'Abdullāh (Bukhārī) says: *bādī* means one from outside, and *ma'kūf* (passive of *'ākif)* means one who remains.[82]

1588 Usāmah ibn Zaid reported that he asked: "O Messenger of Allāh, where in your house in Makkah will you be staying?" He said: "Has 'Aqīl left any property or house?" 'Aqīl and Ṭālib inherited from Abū Ṭālib, but Ja'far and 'Alī did not inherit anything as they were Muslims and 'Aqīl and Ṭālib were unbelievers. And 'Umar ibn al-Khaṭṭāb used to say: "A believer cannot inherit from an unbeliever."

---

[81] *Ḥaram* means the sanctified area of Makkah, and includes the land which comprises Makkah. In order to maintain the sanctity of Makkah and the House of God, the surrounding area has also been included in the sanctified area and all those acts which are not allowed in Makkah are also prohibited in the sacred territory. According to Azraqī, the sacred area extends three miles up to the Tan'īm Pass towards Madīnah, seven miles towards Yaman, eleven miles towards Ṭā'if, ten miles towards Iraq and five miles towards the Jawāfah path.

[82] According to some authorities, the houses and buildings of Makkah are considered as private properties and can be sold, but others consider them to be within the sanctified area and infer from the words "equally for the dweller" of 22:25 of the Qur'ān that no one owns them. However, the words of the Qur'ān "who were driven from their homes and their possessions" (59:8) are clear evidence that these were properties in ownership. Bukhārī has drawn the same inference from the ḥadīth in this chapter, that the houses are owned by people and their sale and purchase is permissible. See the heading of the next chapter.

Ibn Shihāb (a narrator in the line) said: They made this inference from the word of Allāh: "Surely those who believed and fled (their homes) and struggled hard in Allāh's way with their wealth and their lives, and those who gave shelter and helped — these are friends one of another…" (the Qur'ān, 8:72).[83]

Ch. 45:   Arrival of the Prophet ﷺ at Makkah

Abū 'Abdullāh (Bukhārī) said: The houses were associated with 'Aqīl, and the houses could be inherited, sold or purchased.[84]

1589 Abū Hurairah said: When the Messenger of Allāh ﷺ intended to visit Makkah, he said: "Tomorrow, God willing, our stay will be in the valley (*khaif*)[85] of Banū Kinānah where they took oaths for mutual agreement on (supporting the cause of) unbelief."

1590 Abū Hurairah reported: The Prophet ﷺ said on the day after the day of Sacrifices (*nahr*) while he was at Minā: "Tomorrow we will stay in the *khaif* of Banū Kinānah where they took oaths for mutual agreement on (supporting the cause of) unbelief," meaning by this (the place called) Al-Muhassab.[86] This was where the Quraish and the Kinānah had taken oaths to agree against the Banī Hāshim and the Banī 'Abdul Muttalib or the Banī al-Muttalib that they would not have any marital or trade relationship with them till they handed over the Prophet ﷺ to them.[87]

---

[83] Up to this point in this verse there is no mention that a believer cannot inherit from a disbeliever. Even further on, it is only the believers who have been mentioned: "And those who believed and did not flee, you are not responsible for their protection until they flee" (8:72).

[84] The text from "Abu 'Abdullāh said" up to this point does not exist in the Egyptian manuscript. This seems to be right because this subject is connected with the heading of the last chapter, not with the heading of the present chapter, and therefore it should be part of the previous chapter's heading.

[85] *Khaif* means a place at the foot of a mountain above a stream.

[86] The Holy Prophet said this while he was coming from Minā to Makkah on the 11th Dhul Hajjah. On the 12th, he stopped at Muhassab and it was from here that he sent 'Ā'ishah with her brother 'Abdur Rahmān for the *'Umrah*. See h. 1561. It was here that the idolaters of Makkah made an agreement to impose a social boycott against the Banī Hāshim and the Banī Muttalib. The Holy Prophet stopped there in thankfulness to Allāh and to show that the promises Allāh made to the Muslims when they were utterly weak and helpless, in particular in the following verses of the Qur'ān addressed to the Holy Prophet, "He will surely bring you back to the Place of Return" (28:85) and "you will be made free from obligation in this City" (90:2), were fulfilled word for word.

[87] This agreement, as a result of which the Banī Hāshim and the Banī Muttalib underwent

And (according to another report the words are): Banī Hāshim and Banī al-Muṭṭalib. Abū ʿAbdullāh (Bukhārī) says that the Banī al-Muṭṭalib is more correct.[88]

Ch. 46:   The word of Allāh

"And when Abraham said: O my Lord, make this city secure, and save me and my sons from worshipping idols. My Lord, surely they have led many people astray" to His word "perhaps they may be grateful" (14:35 to 38).

Ch. 47:   The word of Allāh

"Allāh has made the Kaʿbah, the Sacred House, a means of support for the people, and the sacred month" to His word "Allāh is the Knower of all things" (5:97).

1591 Abū Hurairah reported from the Prophet ﷺ that he said: "The Kaʿbah will be ruined by one with two lean legs[89] from Africa."

1592 ʿĀ'ishah reported: People used to fast on the day of *'Āshūrā'* (10th Muḥarram) before it was made obligatory in Ramaḍān and this was the day that the Kaʿbah used to be covered (with a covering).[90] When Allāh made (fasting in) Ramaḍān obligatory, the Messenger of Allāh ﷺ said: "Whoever wants to fast (on *'Āshūrā'*) he may fast, and whoever wants to leave it, he may leave it."

1593 Abū Saʿīd al-Khudrī reported from the Prophet ﷺ that he said: "The *Ḥajj* and the *'Umrah* will continue even after the appearance of Gog and Magog."

---

untold hardship and persecution for three years for supporting the Holy Prophet, was entered into at the beginning of the month of Muḥarram in the 7th year of the Holy Prophet's mission. The paper on which it was written was hung inside the Kaʿbah. Gradually it was eaten by worms and Allāh informed the Holy Prophet of its destruction. He told his uncle Abū Ṭālib who passed on the news to the Quraish. The news turned out to be true and they were deeply embarrassed. Some Quraish chiefs put on their arms and went to the Banī Hāshim and Banī Muṭṭalib and asked them to come back to their homes. So they came out of the valley of Shiʿb Abī Ṭālib and returned to their homes in the 10th year of the Holy Prophet's mission.

[88] The designation Banī al-Muṭṭalib is more correct as Muṭṭalib was the brother of Hāshim and offsprings of both were treated equally according to the agreement. As ʿAbdul Muṭṭalib was the son of Hāshim, he was included among the Banī Hāshim.

[89] The term used for this man is *dhu-us-suwaiqatain,* having two slim calves or lean legs. More details are found below in ch. 49: "Demolishing of the Kaʿbah".

[90] Covering the building of the Kaʿbah is for its respect and protection. There is no question of worshipping it.

(And in another report:) "The Hour (Day of Resurrection) will not come until the *Ḥajj* is abandoned." The first report occurs more frequently.[91]

Ch. 48:   Cover of the Ka'bah

1594 Abū Wā'il reported: I was sitting with Shaibah on a chair in the Ka'bah, and he said:

'Umar was sitting at this place and he said: "I had intended that I should not leave anything of yellow (gold) or white (silver) in it but distribute it." I said to him: "Your two companions (i.e., the Holy Prophet and Abū Bakr) did not do this." He said: "They are the two men both of whom I follow." [92]

Ch. 49:   Demolishing of the Ka'bah

'Ā'ishah reported that the Prophet ﷺ said: "An army will attack the Ka'bah, but it will be disgraced."

1595 Ibn 'Abbās reported from the Prophet ﷺ that he said: "It is as if I am seeing (in a vision) a black man with two thin legs dismantling each stone of the Ka'bah." [93]

---

[91] Bukhārī has here placed two reports together. The first is that the *Ḥajj* of the Ka'bah will continue even after the appearance of Gog and Magog, and as the coming of Gog and Magog is considered as one of the signs of the Day of Judgment, this shows that the *Ḥajj* will continue to be performed till that Day. The second report indicates that the *Ḥajj* be stopped before the "Hour" comes. Bukhārī, considering that the two reports are contrary to each other, has added that the first report occurs more frequently, i.e., it is narrated by more people than the second, and therefore it is more reliable. The first report confirms that Gog and Magog will be dominant everywhere but this does not mean that they will conquer even the Ka'bah. Their being dominant everywhere, as mentioned in the Qur'ān in the words "and they sally forth from every elevated place" (21:96), points towards their extensive control as is mentioned in the ḥadīth: "No one in the world will have the power to fight them." The two reports can be reconciled in this way that the cessation of the *Ḥajj* spoken of in the second report will be temporary as a sign of the "Hour" (of their appearance) and it will not be abandoned permanently.

[92] Shaibah was son of 'Uthmān ibn Ṭalḥah who was guardian of the Ka'bah and used to keep its key. Ibn Mājah and Ṭabarānī have more details. Abū Wā'il says that someone sent some money through him as a gift for the Ka'bah, so he went into the Ka'bah and Shaibah was sitting on a chair. He gave him the money, but Shaibah told him to take it back. He replied: If I could have taken it, I would not have come to you. After that he narrated a saying of 'Umar which has been mentioned here. Shaibah inferred from it that spending the money donated to the Ka'bah is permissible. It is recorded that people used to come to the Ka'bah and donate money. Bukhārī has inferred from it that distribution or sale of the cover of the Ka'bah is also permissible because it also comes in the category of treasure of the Ka'bah.

[93] On the one hand there is a Divine promise that the Ka'bah will be safeguarded and the *Ḥajj* will be performed till the Day of Resurrection, and on the other hand we have the prophecies

1596 Abū Hurairah said that the Messenger of Allāh ﷺ said: "The Kaʿbah will be ruined by one with two lean legs from Africa." [94]

Ch. 50: What has been said regarding the Black Stone

1597 ʿĀbis ibn Rabīʿah reported that ʿUmar came to the Black Stone and kissed it, and then said: "I know for certain that you are a stone which can neither cause any harm nor bring any benefit, and if I had not seen the Prophet ﷺ kissing you, I would not have kissed you." [95]

Ch. 51: Closing the door of the Kaʿbah (from inside) and offering prayer in any of its corners as one wishes

1598 Sālim reported from his father (ʿAbdullāh ibn ʿUmar): The Messenger of Allāh ﷺ entered the Kaʿbah with Usāmah ibn Zaid, Bilāl and ʿUthmān ibn Abū Ṭalḥah and closed the door after them. When they opened it I was the first to enter. I met Bilāl and asked him: "Did the Messenger of Allāh ﷺ pray?" He said: "Yes, between the two right pillars." [96]

Ch. 52: Saying prayer inside the Kaʿbah

1599 Nāfiʿ reported from Ibn ʿUmar that whenever he entered the Kaʿbah he would walk straight ahead on entering, keeping the door at his back. He would proceed until there were about three arm-lengths between him and the

---

which show that damage to the Kaʿbah and cessation of the *Ḥajj* will be a temporary phase of tribulation or this will happen when evil becomes widespread in the world and the Hour of Judgment is near.

[94] This is a repetition of h. 1591.

[95] See also h. 1605. Some critics of Islām allege that the Holy Prophet retained the pre-Islamic traditions relating to the Black Stone and the Kaʿbah because otherwise the Arabs would have refused to obey his commands. But the fact is just what ʿUmar said: If the Messenger of Allāh had not kissed it then I would not have kissed it. Regarding the Black Stone it is mentioned in some reports that it is one of the jewels of Paradise whose light was removed by Allāh. Other reports say that the Black Stone was brought down from Paradise and it was whiter than milk but it became black because of the sins of the progeny of Adam. There are other similar reports which fall below the standard of authenticity both as regards their transmission and their contents. Bukhārī found only the report of ʿUmar as meeting both standards, which is perfectly in accordance with the principles of Islām as well as a sufficient reply to the critics. It is merely a stone which can, by itself, neither harm anyone nor bestow benefit on anyone. It is kissed only because it is a memorial of the Unity of God taught by the Prophet Abraham and a blessed spiritual remnant of the most chosen devotees of the One True God. Islām came to abolish idolatry and absolutely not to reinforce it in any manner.

[96] The subject of h. 504 occurs here with some difference in wording, but h. 504 does not contain the words about closing the door which give rise to the heading of this chapter. However, these words occur in this ḥadīth, and also in h. 505.

wall in front of him. There he would pray aiming at the place where Bilāl had informed him that the Messenger of Allāh ﷺ prayed. There is no harm for anyone to pray at any place where he wishes inside the Ka'bah.[97]

Ch. 53:   One who does not enter the Ka'bah

Ibn 'Umar used to perform the *Ḥajj* frequently but he did not enter (the Ka'bah).

1600 'Abdullāh ibn Abī Aufā reported: The Messenger of Allāh ﷺ performed the *'Umrah*. He went round the Ka'bah and said two *rak'ahs* behind the place of Abraham. With him were some (Companions) who were shielding him from the people. A man asked him: "Did the Messenger of Allāh ﷺ enter the Ka'bah?" He replied: "No." [98]

Ch. 54:   One who proclaims *Allāhu Akbar* at the corners of the Ka'bah

1601 Ibn 'Abbās reported: When the Messenger of Allāh ﷺ came (to Makkah), he refused to enter the Ka'bah as there were idols in it. So he ordered concerning them, and they were removed. People also removed the images of Abraham and Ishmael which had divining arrows in their hands. The Messenger of Allāh ﷺ said: "May Allāh destroy them! By Allāh, they know that the two of them never practised divining (i.e., fortune-telling)." Then he entered the Ka'bah and proclaimed *Allāhu Akbar* at its corners[99] but did not say prayers in it.[100]

---

[97] This is a repetition of h. 506 with a slight change of wording. It is mentioned here that prayer can be offered in any direction within the Ka'bah. The narrator of this ḥadīth and of h. 1598 is Ibn 'Umar and this statement is made by him.

[98] This *'Umrah* was performed the next year after the Truce of Ḥudaibiyah was made. It is called *'Umrat-ul-Qaḍā'* (the belated *'Umrah*). At that time idols were still present within the Ka'bah, and Makkah was ruled by the idolaters, the Ka'bah being under their control. Further explanation about the shielding or guarding of the Holy Prophet is given in h. 1791 where the words are: "We were shielding him from the people of Makkah in case someone shoot an arrow at him."

[99] This happened at the conquest of Makkah. The Holy Prophet did not enter the Ka'bah until all the idols were removed from it. Raising the cry of *Allāhu Akbar* at the four corners of the Ka'bah indicates that Muslims worship only Allāh and nothing besides Him.

[100] Ibn 'Abbās did not enter the Ka'bah with the Holy Prophet, but Bilāl did. Therefore, the statement of Bilal mentioned in h. 397 and h. 1599 that the Holy Prophet said two *rak'ahs* of prayer inside the Ka'bah is correct. Ibn 'Abbās was not aware of this, and that is why in this ḥadīth and in h. 398 he says that the Holy Prophet did not say any prayer inside the Ka'bah. The report of Ibn 'Abbās is clearly related to the conquest of Makkah, and thus to apply it to the Farewell *Ḥajj* is not correct.

Ch. 55:   How (the practice of) walking briskly round the Ka'bah (ramal) began

1602 Ibn 'Abbās reported: The Messenger of Allāh ﷺ came (to Makkah) with his Companions (for the *'Umrah)*, and the idolaters said (to people): "They are coming to you and are weak because of the fever of Madīnah." So the Prophet ﷺ ordered the Companions to make three circuits walking briskly and walk at normal pace between the two corners. He refrained from ordering them to walk fast during all the circuits only to make it easy for them.[101]

Ch. 56:   The kissing of the Black Stone first of all in making the circuits *(Ṭawāf)* when one comes to Makkah, and walking briskly *(ramal)* in the first three circuits

1603 Sālim reported that his father ('Abdullāh ibn 'Umar) said: I saw the Messenger of Allāh ﷺ coming to Makkah; he kissed the Black Stone in the first circuit and walked briskly *(yakhubbu)* for the first three of the seven circuits.[102]

Ch. 57:   To walk briskly *(ramal)* in *Ḥajj* and *'Umrah* (while making circuits)

1604 'Abdullāh ibn 'Umar reported: The Prophet ﷺ walked briskly in the (first) three circuits and walked at normal pace in the (remaining) four in *Ḥajj* and *'Umrah*.[103]

1605 Zaid ibn Aslam reported from his father that 'Umar ibn al-Khaṭṭāb said concerning the Black Stone: "By Allāh! I know for certain that you are a stone which can neither cause any harm nor bring any benefit, and if I had not seen the Messenger of Allāh ﷺ kissing you, I would not have kissed you."

---

[101] This happened in 7 A.H. when the Holy Prophet performed the *'Umrah.* This was his first *'Umrah* after coming to Madīnah. While making circuits, he ordered his Companions to make the first three circuits walking fast. Ibn 'Abbās thinks that the Holy Prophet ordered them to walk briskly to dispel the rumour spread by the disbelievers of Makkah that the Muslims had become weak due to fever at Madīnah. If this were the only reason, then why did the Holy Prophet perform it the same way in the Farewell *Ḥajj* when there were no disbelievers of Makkah to make such remarks, nor was it required to demonstrate the physical strength of the Muslims to people? The fact is that the *Ḥajj* is a demonstration of the feeling of extreme love and devotion. Therefore, brisk walking is a sign of that passion. It is also meant to emphasise that Muslims should always be active and energetic in all their works. *Ramal* means to walk fast moving one's shoulders.

[102] See h. 1616. The word *khubbu* means to walk fast as if running. The same word is used for walking behind a funeral procession. It has also been ordered that one should walk fast in the funeral procession.

[103] This shows that during the Farewell Pilgrimage also the Holy Prophet walked briskly in the first three circuits. Thus it is a permanent commandment. See h. 1616.

Then he kissed it and said: "What was the reason for us walking briskly (during the circuits)? Only that we wanted to show it to the idolaters and Allāh has now destroyed them." Then he said: "It was something which the Messenger of Allāh ﷺ did, and we do not like to give it up." [104]

1606 Nāfi' reported from Ibn 'Umar that he said: I did not leave kissing the two corners whether in times of difficulty or ease since I saw the Messenger of Allāh ﷺ kissing them.

I ('Ubaidullāh who was reporting from Nāfi') asked Nāfi': "Did Ibn 'Umar walk (at normal pace) between the two corners?" He said: "He used to walk (at normal pace between them) so that he could easily kiss it (i.e., the Black Stone)."

Ch. 58: Kissing the Black Stone by means of a stick

1607 Ibn 'Abbās reported: The Prophet ﷺ made the circuits during the Farewell Pilgrimage while riding a camel, kissing the Black Stone with his stick. [105]

---

[104] The reason for *ramal*, i.e., walking briskly and fast during the first three circuits of the *Ṭawāf*, given by 'Umar is the same as that given by Ibn 'Abbās (see note on h. 1602). Perhaps it was a case of one Companion copying the view of another. The *Ḥajj* is an act of worship and all its rites and etiquette were established by either revelation in the Qur'ān or by revelation of ideas into the mind of the Holy Prophet (known as *waḥy khafī*). Thus it was a proper commandment to walk briskly in the first three circuits. Despite 'Umar giving his own opinion about its origin, nonetheless he said: We cannot give up the practice of the Messenger of Allāh.

Kissing the Black Stone was in fact an act of memoriam pointing to the prophecy in the Psalms, "The stone which the builders rejected has become the chief cornerstone" (Psalms 22:118), which was repeated by Jesus (Matthew 21:42). The prophecy of this stone referred to the Prophet Ishmael whose progeny was rejected by the Children of Israel as being deprived of the blessings of God. By calling them the "chief cornerstone", the reference is to the appearance from among them of the Holy Prophet Muḥammad who was from the progeny of Ishmael; and his being the *Khātam an-nabiyyīn* made him the corner stone of the edifice of Prophethood.

[105] Riding a camel and kissing the Black Stone by touching it with a stick clearly shows that in the Holy Prophet's mind there was no thought of worshipping it or even giving it any special reverence. Critics who, without applying any thought, say that the kissing of the Black Stone is a remanant of ancient Arab idolatry, should ponder whether riding on a camel and pointing towards it with a stick has the slightest element of idolatry in it. The fact is that this act is just a symbolic gesture. No Muslim has ever even had the least inkling that he was worshipping it, nor will anyone ever think that. Generally, when a person reaches in front of it, he points towards it as the Holy Prophet did, as described in h. 1612. In the very next ḥadīth, h. 1608, the kissing of the two or all four of the corners of the Ka'bah has also been mentioned, whereas there is no particular stone there. This further clarifies that the worshipping of the Black Stone is furthest from the minds of Muslims. Here, kissing it with a stick means pointing towards it with a stick instead of actually kissing it, as mentioned clearly in the repetition of this ḥadīth in h. 1612. Taking the pointing with the stick to stand for kissing it, this action has been called "kissing with a stick".

Ch. 59:   One who kisses only the two Yamani corners (of the Ka'bah)

1608 Abū Ash-sha'thā' was reported as saying: "Who avoids kissing a part of the Ka'bah?" And Mu'āwiyah used to kiss all the corners. Ibn 'Abbās said to him: "We do not kiss the two Yamani corners." He (Mu'āwiyah) said: "No part of the Ka'bah is forsaken." And Ibn az-Zubair (also) used to kiss all the corners.[106]

1609 'Abdullāh Ibn 'Umar reported: I saw the Prophet ﷺ kissing nothing but the Yamani corners.

Ch. 60:   Kissing of the Black Stone

1610 Zaid ibn Aslam reported that his father said: I saw 'Umar ibn al-Khaṭṭāb kissing the Black stone, and then saying: "If I had not seen the Messenger of Allāh ﷺ kissing you, I would not have kissed you." [107]

1611 Az-Zubair ibn 'Arabiyy reported: A man asked Ibn 'Umar about the kissing of the Black Stone, and he replied: "I saw the Messenger of Allāh ﷺ kissing it, while touching it with his hands." He further asked: "Tell me, if I cannot do it because it is too crowded?" He replied: "Keep your excuses to yourself. I saw the Messenger of Allāh ﷺ kissing it, while touching it with his hands." [108]

Ch. 61:   He who points towards the Black Stone when he reaches in front of it

1612 Ibn 'Abbās reported: The Prophet ﷺ made circuits of the Ka'bah while riding on a camel. Whenever he came to the Corner (i.e., the Black Stone) he pointed towards it.[109]

---

[106] In the next ḥadīth and also in h. 166 it is mentioned that the Holy Prophet used to kiss only the two Yamani corners of the Ka'bah. The reason was, as is explained by 'Abdullāh ibn 'Umar in h. 1583, that the Ka'bah was not rebuilt on the foundations of Prophet Abraham. In other words, the Syrian and Iraqi corners are not on the foundations raised by Prophet Abraham. Most of the Companions followed the practice of the Holy Prophet and used to kiss only the Black Stone and the other Yamani corner, but some Companions, for example Mu'āwiyah and Ibn az-Zubair used to kiss all the four corners. But according to Azraqī it was when Ibn az-Zubair rebuilt the Ka'bah on the foundations of Prophet Abraham that he kissed all the four corners.

[107] See h. 1597 and h. 1605.

[108] It seems from the reply of Ibn 'Umar that the questioner wanted to avoid kissing or touching it. If he was enquiring about the case where he was unable to do it, then the reply, which is *aj'al ara'ai-ta bil-Yaman*, literally "keep your 'ifs and buts' in Yaman", amounts to saying: Try not to find excuses; it is the practice of the Prophet, do it if you can, otherwise it is not essential. It is made clear in the next chapter that mere pointing with a stick towards it is enough.

[109] It is stated in h. 1607: "kissing the Black Stone with his stick". Pointing here has been considered as the equivalent of kissing it.

Ch. 62:   To proclaim *Allāhu Akbar* near the Black Stone

1613 Ibn ʿAbbās reported: The Prophet ﷺ made circuits of the Kaʿbah while riding on a camel. Whenever he came to the Corner (i.e., the Black Stone) he pointed towards it with a thing he had with him and proclaimed *Allāhu Akbar.*[110]

Ch. 63:   Making circuits of the Kaʿbah when coming to Makkah before returning home, then saying two *rakʿahs* of prayer and then proceeding to the Ṣafā

1614–1615 Muḥammad ibn ʿAbdur Raḥmān reported: I mentioned it to ʿUrwah who said:

ʿĀʾishah informed me[111] that when the Prophet ﷺ came to Makkah the first thing he did was to perform *Wuḍūʾ*, then he made circuits and the *ʿUmrah* had not yet been performed. Then Abū Bakr and ʿUmar did the same. [1615] Then I performed the *Ḥajj* with my father Az-Zubair, and the first thing he did was to make circuits of the Kaʿbah. Then I saw the *Muhājirīn* and the *Anṣār* doing the same. My mother (Asmāʾ) told me that her sister (ʿĀʾishah), Az-Zubair, and some others entered into the state of *Iḥrām* for *ʿUmrah* and when they had stroked the Black Stone, they left the state of *Iḥrām*.[112]

---

[110] This has the same wording as h. 1612 followed by an addition at the end. See also h. 1607. The proclaiming of *Allāhu Akbar* clearly signified that real glory and worship are due to Almighty Allāh.

[111] The words: "I mentioned it to ʿUrwah who said: ʿĀʾishah informed me" will be explained in h. 1641.

[112] From this ḥadīth Bukhārī has inferred that, during the time of the Holy Prophet, Abū Bakr and ʿUmar, only making circuits of the Kaʿbah was not considered as constituting *ʿUmrah*, nor did anyone intending to perform just the *Ḥajj* leave his *Iḥrām*. The same was the practice of the *Muhājirīn* and the *Anṣār*. The statement of ʿUrwah, that his mother (Asmāʾ) and her sister (ʿĀʾishah) and az-Zubair and others went out of *Iḥrām* for *ʿUmrah* after kissing the Black Stone, was apparently contrary to the practice of the Holy Prophet, Abū Bakr, and the *Muhājirīn* and the *Anṣār* because in their time the mere making of circuits of the Kaʿbah was not considered as constituting *ʿUmrah* so that after kissing the Black Stone, leaving *Iḥrām* was allowed. In fact, it was essential to perform the running between the Ṣafā and the Marwah in order to complete the *ʿUmrah*. Commentators of Ḥadīth have interpreted the words: "When they had stroked the Black Stone, they left the state of *Iḥrām*" as meaning that after both making circuits and running between the Ṣafā and the Marwah, leaving the state of *Iḥrām* was allowed. As can be seen in the explanation given in h. 1641, ʿUrwah has related this ḥadīth to refute the idea that only making circuits of the Kaʿbah allows a person performing the *ʿUmrah*, or the *Ḥajj* only, to leave the state of *Iḥrām*, so there is no reason why ʿUrwah should contradict his view by putting forward the action of ʿĀʾishah, Asmāʾ and az-Zubair etc. as being against the unanimous practice followed during the time of the Holy Prophet, Abū Bakr and ʿUmar.

1616 ʿAbdullāh ibn ʿUmar reported that the Messenger of Allāh ﷺ, in the *Ḥajj* and the *ʿUmrah,* used first to make circuits of the Kaʿbah, walking briskly in the first three circuits and walking at a normal pace in the remaining four circuits, then he would say two *rakʿahs* of prayer and then go between the Ṣafā and the Marwah.

1617 ʿAbdullāh ibn ʿUmar reported that the Prophet ﷺ used first to make circuits of the Kaʿbah, walking briskly in the first three circuits and walking at a normal pace in the remaining four circuits, and he used to run in the valley of Masīl when he went between the Ṣafā and the Marwah.[113]

Ch. 64: Women making circuits along with men

1618 Ibn Juraij reported: ʿAṭā' informed me that when Ibn Hishām prohibited women from making circuits along with men, he asked him: "How do you prohibit them while the wives of the Prophet ﷺ made circuits along with men?" I (Ibn Juraij) asked him: "Was it after (the revelation of the verse of) the *ḥijāb* or before?" He said: "Yes, I swear I saw them after the injunction of the *ḥijāb.*" Then I (Ibn Juraij) asked: "How did they mix with the men?" He said:

"They did not mix (with the men). ʿĀ'ishah made circuits separately from men and did not mix with them. A woman requested: 'O Mother of the Faithful, let us kiss the Black Stone.' She said: 'You go on.' She refused to do so herself. Those women used to go out in the night when they could not be recognised and used to make circuits of the Kaʿbah with men, but when they wanted to go into the Kaʿbah, they would remain standing before entering until the men came out. ʿUbaid ibn ʿUmair and I used to go to ʿĀ'ishah and she was staying at the Mount Thabīr."

I (Ibn Juraij) said: "What was her *ḥijāb*?" He said: "She was staying in a Turkish tent and it had a curtain and there was nothing between us and her except that curtain and I saw her wearing a long pink shirt." [114]

---

[113] This is a repetition of h. 1616 with some differences. There is a valley between the Ṣafā and the Marwah which is meant by "the valley of Masīl" or *Baṭn al-Masīl.*

[114] This happened during the rule of Hishām ibn ʿAbdul Malik. Ibn Hishām (Muḥammad), his maternal uncle, was the *Amīr* of Makkah. He prohibited women from making circuits of the Kaʿbah along with men. ʿAṭā' objected to it by saying that during the time of the Holy Prophet women used to make circuits of the Kaʿbah along with men while he (the *Amīr*) was preventing women from making circuits along with men. Ibn Juraij, who reported from ʿAṭā', thought that it was allowed only before the verse of "veiling" was revealed. In reply, ʿAṭā' not only refuted it but reported that he used to go to ʿĀ'ishah and, on one occasion, she was wearing a pink shirt. It shows that as Muslims became affluent, and distant from the time of the Holy Prophet, the

1619 Umm Salamah, wife of the Prophet ﷺ, reported: I complained to the Messenger of Allāh ﷺ that I was ill. He said: "Make the circuits behind the people, while riding (on an animal)." So I made circuits (in that way), and the Messenger of Allāh ﷺ was saying his prayers at the side of the House (of Ka'bah), and he was reciting: "By the Mountain, and a Book written" (the Qur'ān, 52:1–2).[115]

Ch. 65: Talking during making circuits

1620 Ibn 'Abbās reported that the Prophet ﷺ, while making circuits of the Ka'bah, passed by a man who had tied his hand with another man with a string or lace or something else. So the Prophet ﷺ cut it with his own hands and said: "Take him by his hand."[116]

Ch. 66: Seeing a string or anything disliked while making circuits and cutting if off

1621 Ibn 'Abbās reported that the Prophet ﷺ saw a man making circuits of the Ka'bah tied with a rope or something like it, so he cut it off.[117]

Ch. 67: No naked person to make circuits of the Ka'bah nor an idolater to perform the *Ḥajj*

1622 Abū Hurairah informed that in the *Ḥajj* before the Farewell Pilgrimage, in which the Messenger of Allāh ﷺ appointed Abū Bakr as leader (of the Pilgrims), he (Abū Bakr) sent me on the day of Sacrifices to announce to

---

concept of the veil started to change. A time came when practices which were usual for people during the time of the Holy Prophet became disliked, and some measures were taken to curb them. According to the Islamic concept of the veil or *purdah* it was never forbidden that women and men should get together in one venue while offering prayers in a mosque, making circuits during the *Ḥajj*, attending religious lectures, in battles, or in conducting business transactions. Nor did they wear complete coverings during these gatherings, but of course they remained separate. In mosques they had their own rows at the back, and during making circuits of the Ka'bah, men and women were together but not intermingling. Even during the lifetime of 'Ā'ishah, which was until about 50 A.H., it was not essential for women to put on an extra covering over their normal clothes. (Note that the usual dress of men and women in Arabia, even now, is a long cloak which covers a person from the neck to the ankles.)

[115] This is a repetition of h. 464 in almost the same words. The Holy Prophet allowed Umm Salamah, due to her physical weakness, to make circuits of the Ka'bah riding an animal while keeping herself behind the people. Both here and in h. 464 it is mentioned that people were praying at the time. So she passed through them.

[116] Although making circuits is a form of worship, talking during it is allowed if necessary.

[117] This is a briefer repetition of h. 1620. In other words, it is permissible to talk or to do any such act while making circuits.

the people: "After this year, no idolater is to perform the *Ḥajj*, nor a naked person to make circuits of the Ka'bah." [118]

Ch. 68:   Stopping while making circuits

'Aṭā' said: As to the one who was making circuits and the prayer was called, or he was moved from his place, when he says the *Salām* (i.e., completes his prayer) he should return to the place where he was interrupted and resume circuits from there. And similar is reported from Ibn 'Umar and 'Abdur Raḥmān ibn Abū Bakr. [119]

Ch. 69:   The Prophet ﷺ made circuits and prayed two *rak'ahs* after the seven circuits

Nāfiʿ said: Ibn 'Umar used to say two *rak'ahs* of prayer after every seven circuits. Ismā'īl ibn Umayyah said: I told az-Zuhrī that 'Aṭā' said that the obligatory prayer accomplishes the two *rak'ahs* of prayer after the circuits, and he said: It is better to follow the *Sunnah* — the Prophet ﷺ, whenever he made the seven circuits, said two *rak'ahs* of prayer.

1623–1624 'Amr reported: We asked Ibn 'Umar whether a man can have intercourse with his wife during the *'Umrah* before going between the Ṣafā and the Marwah? He said: The Messenger of Allāh ﷺ came (to Makkah) and made circuits of the Ka'bah seven times, then he said two *rak'ahs* of prayer behind the place of Abraham and went between the Ṣafā and the Marwah. He added: "Certainly you have in the Messenger of Allāh an excellent exemplar" (the Qur'ān, 33:21). [1624] He ('Amr) said: I asked Jābir ibn 'Abdullāh and he said: He should not approach his wife (for sexual intercourse) before going between the Ṣafā and the Marwah. [120]

Ch. 70:   One who does not go near the Ka'bah after making the first *Ṭawāf* nor makes circuits so much so that he goes to 'Arafat and returns

1625 'Abdullāh ibn 'Abbās reported: The Prophet ﷺ came to Makkah and made the circuits and he ran between the Ṣafā and the Marwah and he did not go near the Ka'bah after his *Ṭawāf* until he returned from 'Arafat.

---

[118] The first part of h. 369 is repeated here with slight change in wording.

[119] If due to some reason a person could not complete *Ṭawāf* of the Ka'bah, then he can resume it from the place where he stopped and complete the remainder.

[120] This shows that running between the Ṣafā and the Marwah is obligatory in the *'Umrah* and without it the *'Umrah* is not complete. See also h. 1645–1646.

Ch. 71:   **Saying two *rak'ahs* of the *Ṭawāf* outside the (Sacred) Mosque**

'Umar prayed outside the Sacred Mosque (*Ḥaram*).

1626 Umm Salamah reported: I complained to the Messenger of Allāh ﷺ (that I was ill).

Umm Salamah, wife of the Prophet ﷺ, reported (in another narration) that the Messenger of Allāh ﷺ was in Makkah and intended to leave, but she had not yet made the circuits of the Ka'bah and she (also) intended to leave (with him), so the Messenger of Allāh ﷺ said to her: "When the morning (*Fajr*) prayer is ready to start, go and perform the circuits on your camel while people are saying their prayer." So she did that and did not say the prayer until leaving.[121]

Ch. 72:   **Saying two *rak'ahs* of the *Ṭawāf* behind the place of Abraham**

1627 Ibn 'Umar said: The Prophet ﷺ came (to Makkah) and made seven circuits of the Ka'bah, and he said two *rak'ahs* of prayer behind the place of Abraham. Then he left for Ṣafā. And Allāh indeed said: "Certainly you have in the Messenger of Allāh an excellent exemplar" (the Qur'ān, 33:21).[122]

Ch. 73:   **Making circuits after the morning and *'Aṣr* prayers**

Ibn 'Umar used to say two *rak'ahs* of prayer after the circuits when the sun had not risen. 'Umar performed circuits after the *Fajr* prayer, and then he rode, and said two *rak'ahs* of prayer at Dhu Ṭuwā.[123]

1628 'Ā'ishah reported that people made circuits of the Ka'bah after the morning prayer and then sat to listen to the talk of a preacher, and when the sun was about to rise, they stood up and started to pray. 'Ā'ishah added: They kept sitting until the time came when prayer is disapproved and they started praying.[124]

1629 'Abdullāh (ibn 'Umar) reported: I heard the Prophet ﷺ forbidding prayers at the rising of the sun and at its setting.[125]

---

[121] The heading of the chapter is proved by the concluding words, that Umm Salamah said two *rak'ahs* of prayer only after leaving the Mosque. See also h. 464.

[122] This is a repetition of h. 1623, with omission of the question and reply.

[123] Dhu Ṭuwā is at a distance of approximately a mile from Makkah.

[124] It is meant that two *rak'ahs* should have been said after making the circuits.

[125] See h. 582 and h. 585. See also the whole range h. 581–h. 588.

1630–1631 'Abdul 'Azīz ibn Rufai' related: I saw 'Abdullāh ibn az-Zubair making circuits after the *Fajr* prayer and saying two *rak'ahs* of *(Ṭawāf)* prayer. [1631] And 'Abdul 'Azīz said: And I saw 'Abdullāh ibn az-Zubair saying two *rak'ahs* of prayer after the *'Aṣr* prayer. He also used to inform that 'Ā'ishah told him that whenever the Prophet ﷺ entered her house (at that time), he used to say these two *rak'ahs*.[126]

Ch. 74:   An ill person making circuits on an animal

1632 Ibn 'Abbās reported that the Messenger of Allāh ﷺ made circuits of the Ka'bah while riding on a camel. Whenever he came to the Corner (i.e., the Black Stone) he pointed towards it with a thing he had in his hand and proclaimed *Allāhu Akbar*." [127]

1633 Umm Salamah reported: I complained to the Messenger of Allāh ﷺ that I was ill. He said: "Make the circuits behind the people, while riding." I made circuits (in that way), and the Messenger of Allāh ﷺ was praying at the side of the Ka'bah, reciting *Sūrah aṭ-Ṭūr*.[128]

Ch. 75:   To give drink of water to the pilgrims

1634 Ibn 'Umar reported: Al-'Abbās ibn 'Abdul Muṭṭalib sought permission from the Messenger of Allāh ﷺ to stay at Makkah during the nights of Minā, as he used to supply water to the people, so he allowed him.[129]

1635 Ibn 'Abbās reported that the Messenger of Allāh ﷺ came to the place where water was served and asked for water. Al-'Abbās said: "O Faḍl, go to your mother and bring water for the Messenger of Allāh ﷺ from her." He (the Prophet) said: "Give me water to drink." He said: "O Messenger of Allāh, people put their hands into it (to take out the water)." He repeated: "Give me water to drink," so he drank from it.[130] Then he went to the spring

---

[126] See h. 590–593.

[127] This is a repetition of h. 1613; see also h. 1607 and h. 1612. Here it is mentioned that the Messenger of Allāh made circuits of the Ka'bah while riding, but it is not mentioned if he was unwell. If it is allowed even in a state of health, then it follows it must also be allowed for a sick person. But it is not proper to do it without reason when there is a big crowd, nor can the Mosque remain clean if too many people are riding on animals. (But nowadays circumstances have entirely changed.)

[128] This is a repetition of h. 464; see also h. 1619. The Holy Prophet allowed Umm Salamah to make circuits while riding as she was sick.

[129] It means that people who were managing the supply of drinking water to the pilgrims were allowed to stay in Makkah instead of going to Minā. This did not affect their *Ḥajj*. Evidently, they did not stay in Makkah for any personal reason. See also h. 1743, h. 1744 and h. 1745.

[130] According to a report in Ṭabarānī, on the Holy Prophet's request for water, al-'Abbās

of Zamzam and people were serving water and were also working (bringing the water out of it). He said: "Continue doing it, for you are doing a good deed." He added: "If it were not to become burdensome for you (as a *Sunnah*), I would have gone down and placed the rope on this", meaning his shoulders, and he pointed towards his shoulders.[131]

Ch. 76:   What has been related about the Zamzam[132]

1636 Anas ibn Mālik said that Abū Dharr used to relate that the Messenger of Allāh ﷺ said: "The roof of my house was opened while I was at Makkah and Gabriel descended. He opened my breast, then washed it with the water of Zamzam. Then he brought a golden trough filled with wisdom and faith and poured it in my breast, and then closed it. Then he took hold of my hand and ascended to the nearest heaven. Gabriel said to the gatekeeper of the nearest heaven: "Open." He asked: "Who is it?" He replied: "Gabriel." [133]

---

said: "This water has become distasteful. If you wish I can bring water for you from my home." The Holy Prophet said: "Give me the water which the people are drinking." It teaches two lessons: firstly, to treat people equally, and in fact the *Hajj* is based on the principle of equality; secondly, that water should be drinkable for everyone, low or high, so that clean water is available for every one without distinction.

[131] According to Azraqī, ʿAbd Manāf used to bring water in water bags and pour it into the leather ponds built in the courtyard of the Kaʿbah and serve it to the pilgrims. After him, the service passed on to his son Hāshim, and subsequently to the latter's son ʿAbdul Muṭṭalib. ʿAbdul Muttalib, who was father of al-ʿAbbās, dug the Zamzam spring and it was from there that water was supplied to the pilgrims. After him, his son al-ʿAbbās took over its management. The Holy Prophet allowed this service to remain with him and it remained with the descendants of al-ʿAbbās for a long time. As for the Holy Prophet's saying that if he had not feared that it would have been burdensome for them, he would have put a rope over his shoulders and drawn the water himself, he feared that it would have been taken as a *Sunnah* and caused people unnecessary hardship. Otherwise, the Holy Prophet was ever ready to do the most menial labour and work without being embarrassed about it.

[132] *Zamzamat-un* means abundance and gathering. That is why *mā'-un zamzūm-un wa zamzām-un* means abundance of water. There are some reports about the water of Zamzam in Ṣaḥīḥ Muslim, in which some of its excellences and qualities have been mentioned. In this connection, Bukhārī could find only this one ḥadīth meeting his criteria of authenticity, stating that the chest of the Holy Prophet was washed with its water on the Night of the *Miʿrāj,* as mentioned in the report under the chapter heading.

[133] This is a repetition of the opening part of h. 349 with slight difference in wording. The chapter heading relates to the following words: "He opened my chest, then washed it with the water of Zamzam." This was a vision, as is attested by these words of the report that "a golden trough filled with wisdom and faith" was poured into the Holy Prophet's breast. Washing his breast with the water of Zamzam metaphorically means that it was cleansed to the highest degree. In Makkah Zamzam is the only source of sweet water.

1637 Ibn 'Abbās related: I served Zamzam water to the Messenger of Allāh ﷺ and he drank it while standing. 'Āṣim said: 'Ikrimah swore that he (the Holy Prophet) was surely on a camel that day.

Ch. 77:   A *Qārin* (one who performs *Hajj* and *'Umrah* in one *Iḥrām*) making circuits of the Ka'bah[134]

1638 'Ā'ishah reported: We set out with the Messenger of Allāh ﷺ on the Farewell Pilgrimage. So we entered into the state of *Iḥrām* for *'Umrah*. Then he said: "Anyone who has an animal for sacrifice with him should enter into *Iḥrām* for *Hajj* with *'Umrah* (i.e., *qirān*). He then should not leave the state of *Iḥrām* until he has performed both (*'Umrah* and *Hajj*)."

When I reached Makkah, I was menstruating. When we had performed our *Hajj*, he sent me with 'Abdur Raḥmān to Tan'īm and I performed the *'Umrah*. Then he (the Holy Prophet) said: "This is in place of your *'Umrah*." Those who had entered into the state of *Iḥrām* for *'Umrah* made circuits (of the Ka'bah), then left the state of *Iḥrām*. Then, on their return from Minā, they performed another *Tawāf*. But those who combined the *Hajj* and the *'Umrah* performed only one *Tawāf*.[135]

1639 Nāfi' reported that 'Abdullāh, son of 'Abdullāh ibn 'Umar, entered his father's house, at a time when the mount (for riding) was ready (for the *Hajj*). He (the son) said: "I fear this year there will be a battle between the people (i.e., the Muslims) and they will prevent you from going to the Ka'bah; so stay here." He (Ibn 'Umar) said: "The Messenger of Allāh ﷺ set out for

---

[134] *Tawāf* (circuits of the Ka'bah) is of four kinds: *Tawāf al-qudūm*, performed upon arrival in Makkah and is like the prayer said upon entering a mosque; *Tawāf al-'umrah*, for performing the *'Umrah*; *Tawāf al-ifāḍah*, circuits which are obligatory for the *Hajj* and performed on returning from 'Arafāt and before making the sacrifice; and *Tawāf al-widā'*, performed before leaving Makkah. *Qārin* refers to a person who performs both the *'Umrah* and the *Hajj* remaining in the same *Iḥrām*. According to Bukhārī and most opinion, he performs just one set of circuits, the *Tawāf al-ifāḍah*, and this inference is based on the saying of 'Ā'ishah which is mentioned in the ḥadīth in this chapter and in h. 1556: "But those who combined the *Hajj* and the *'Umrah* performed only one *Tawāf*." According to the Hanafī view, a *qārin* will perform *Tawāf* twice: one for the *'Umrah* and another for the *Hajj*. In both h. 1623 from Ibn 'Umar and in h. 1625 from Ibn 'Abbās it is reported that the Holy Prophet made circuits of the Ka'bah and ran between the Ṣafā and the Marwah before performing the *Hajj*. Bukhārī and most authorities consider this *Tawāf* as *Tawāf al-qudūm*, not as the *Tawāf* for the *'Umrah*. But as the Holy Prophet also ran between the Ṣafā and the Marwah, and because making circuits and running between the Ṣafā and the Marwah constitute an *'Umrah*, therefore, it is apparently *Tawāf* for the *'Umrah* and not *Tawāf al-qudūm*.

[135] This is a repetition of h. 1556 in almost the same words with omissions in two places. See also h. 1560. The chapter heading is derived from the closing words: "But those who combined the *Hajj* and the *'Umrah* performed only one *Tawāf*."

(the *Ḥajj*), and the unbelievers of the Quraish intervened between him and the Ka'bah. If anything should intervene between me and the Ka'bah, I will do the same as the Messenger of Allāh ﷺ — 'Certainly you have in the Messenger of Allāh an excellent exemplar' (the Qur'ān, 33:21)." Then he said: "I make you witness that I have made obligatory on me the *Ḥajj* with my *'Umrah*." He then went to Makkah and performed one set of circuits for both the *Ḥajj* and the *'Umrah*.

1640 Nāfi' reported that the year al-Ḥajjāj went to fight with Ibn az-Zubair, Ibn 'Umar intended to perform the *Ḥajj*. So he was told: "There is going to be a battle between the people (i.e., the Muslims) and we fear that they will prevent you." He said: " 'Certainly you have in the Messenger of Allāh an excellent exemplar' (the Qur'ān, 33:21). At this time, I will do what the Messenger of Allāh ﷺ did.[136] I make you witness that I have made the *'Umrah* obligatory on me." Then he set off and when he reached al-Baidā', he said: "The *Ḥajj* and the *'Umrah* are similar. I make you witness that I have made obligatory on me the *Ḥajj* with my *'Umrah*." He took with him a sacrificial animal which he had bought at Qudaid and did nothing more than that. He did not make any sacrifice, nor make anything permissible for him which was forbidden (due to *Iḥrām*), nor had his hair shaved or trimmed until the day of Sacrifices. Then he made sacrifice and shaved his head and considered that his initial *Ṭawāf* was sufficient for the *Ḥajj* and the *'Umrah*. Ibn 'Umar said: "The Messenger of Allāh ﷺ had done it like that."

Ch. 78:   To make circuits in a state of *Wuḍū'*

1641–1642 Muḥammad ibn 'Abdur Raḥmān ibn Naufal al-Qurashiyy reported that he inquired of 'Urwah ibn az-Zubair and he replied: "The Prophet ﷺ performed the *Ḥajj* and 'Ā'ishah told me that the first thing he did when he came (to Makkah) was to perform *Wuḍū'*.[137] Then he made circuits of the Ka'bah and it was not an *'Umrah*. Then Abū Bakr performed the *Ḥajj* and the first thing he did was to make circuits of the Ka'bah and that was not an *'Umrah*. Then 'Umar did likewise. Then 'Uthmān performed the *Ḥajj* and I saw that the first thing he did was to make circuits of the Ka'bah and that was not an *'Umrah*. Then Mu'āwiyah and 'Abdullāh ibn 'Umar (did the same). Then I, with my father az-Zubair ibn al-'Awwām, performed the *Ḥajj*, and the first thing he did was to make circuits of the Ka'bah and that was not

---

[136] He meant that as the Holy Prophet performed the sacrifice at the point where he was prevented from proceeding to the *Ḥajj* and returned from there, he would do the same.

[137] The inference from this, in the chapter heading, is that *Wuḍū'* should be performed before making the circuits.

an *'Umrah*. Then I saw the *Muhājarīn* and the *Anṣār* doing the same and that was not an *'Umrah*. Then the last of those whom I saw do it was Ibn 'Umar, who did it in the same way. He did not break the *Hajj* to convert it into an *'Umrah*. Now Ibn 'Umar is with them but they do not ask him nor the earlier ones. And they, on entering (Makkah), would not start with anything until they made circuits of the Ka'bah and would not leave the state of *Iḥrām*. And I saw my mother (Asmā') and my maternal aunt ('Ā'ishah), whenever they came, they would not begin with anything before they made circuits of the Ka'bah, and they did not leave the state of *Iḥrām*."

[1642] (He added:) "And my mother informed me that she and her sister ('Ā'ishah) and az-Zubair, and such and such persons, entered into the state of *Iḥrām* for the *'Umrah* and when they had passed their hands over the Black Stone they left the state of *Iḥrām*."

Ch. 79: The obligation of (going between) the Ṣafā and the Marwah, and it being made one of the signs (*sha'ā'ir*) of Allāh[138]

1643 'Urwah said: I asked 'Ā'ishah how she interpreted the word of Allāh: "The Ṣafā and the Marwah are truly among the signs of Allāh; so whoever makes a pilgrimage (*Hajj*) to the House or pays a visit (*'Umrah*), there is no blame on him if he goes round[139] them" (the Qur'ān, 2:158). So, by Allāh! there is no blame on anyone who does not go round the Ṣafā and the Marwah. She said: "My nephew, what you have said is wrong. If it had been what you have said, then it (the verse) would have been this: 'There is no blame on him if he does not go round them.' But it was revealed for the Anṣār who, before they embraced Islām, used to enter into the state of *Iḥrām* to worship the idol Manāt which was placed at al-Mushallal. Whoever (of them) was in the state of *Iḥrām*, he considered it wrong to go round the Ṣafā and the Marwah. When they became Muslims they asked the Messenger of Allāh ﷺ about it, saying: 'O Messenger of Allāh, we used to consider it wrong to go around the Ṣafā and the Marwah,' so Allāh revealed: 'Surely the Ṣafā and the Marwah are among the signs of Allāh.' "

'Ā'ishah said: "The Messenger of Allāh ﷺ established the practice of going round them and no one has the discretion to abandon it." Then I informed Abū Bakr ibn 'Abdur Raḥmān and he said:

---

[138] The word *sha'ā'ir* is plural of *sha'īrah*, meaning a thing which has been designated as a symbol to show one's obedience to Allāh. This is why the devotional acts of the *Hajj* have been called *sha'ā'ir Allāh* or the signs of Allāh.

[139] The word for "going round" them used here in the Qur'ān is also *ṭawāf*.

"This is a matter relating to knowledge but I had not heard it. And I have heard from several learned men that everyone except those whom ʿĀʾishah has mentioned used to enter into the state of *Iḥrām* to worship Manāt and all of them went around the Ṣafā and the Marwah. So when Allāh mentioned making circuits of the Kaʿbah and did not mention the Ṣafā and the Marwah in the Qurʾān, they asked: 'O Messenger of Allāh, we used to go round the Ṣafā and the Marwah, and Allāh has revealed (the commandment of) making circuits of the Kaʿbah but not mentioned the Ṣafā. Is it then a sin for us to go round the Ṣafā and the Marwah?' Then Allāh revealed: 'The Ṣafā and the Marwah are truly among the signs of Allāh'."

Abū Bakr said: "I hear that this verse has been revealed regarding both groups: those who, during the days of Ignorance, considered it wrong to go round the Ṣafā and the Marwah, and those who used to do it but after they became Muslims they considered it wrong as Allāh commanded the making of circuits of the Kaʿbah but did not mention Ṣafā, till He mentioned it later after mentioning making circuits of the Kaʿbah." [140]

Ch. 80:   About running (*saʿy*) between the Ṣafā and the Marwah

> Ibn ʿUmar said: The running was from the houses of Banī ʿAbbād to the street of Banī Abī Ḥusain.[141]

1644 Ibn ʿUmar reported: The Messenger of Allāh ﷺ used first to make circuits of the Kaʿbah, walking briskly in the first three circuits and walking at a normal pace in the remaining four circuits, and he used to run in the valley of Masīl when he went between the Ṣafā and the Marwah. I asked Nāfiʿ:[142] "When ʿAbdullāh (ibn ʿUmar) used to reach near the Yamani corner, did he walk at a normal pace?" He said: "No, except if there was a large crowd of

---

[140] ʿĀʾishah said that if not going round the Ṣafā and the Marwah was not a sin, then the verse should have been: There is no blame on him if he does not go round them. Then she gave as the reason for the revelation of the verse that the Anṣār used to enter into the state of *Iḥrām* to worship the idol Manāt which was placed on al-Mushallal, a mound at Qadīd. And there were two idols, Asāf and Nāʾilah, that were not worshipped by the Anṣār, so they never went there. Gradually they started regarded it as wrong to go to the Ṣafā and the Marwah. So God revealed this verse, saying that there was no harm in it. It was already included in the rites of the *Ḥajj* and this verse was revealed only to remove the misunderstanding of the Anṣār. Another explanation is mentioned further on, that when the verse to do *Ṭawāf* of the Kaʿbah was revealed, and it did not mention *Ṭawāf* of the Ṣafā and the Marwah, some people thought that they should give up this running (which is known as *saʿy*), so this verse was revealed to correct them. But the explanation of ʿĀʾishah is better.

[141] There is now a minaret at each of these two places to mark the limits of the run.

[142] ʿUbaidullāh ibn ʿUmar asked Nāfiʿ, as he was reporting from Nāfiʿ what Ibn ʿUmar said and did.

people near the corner, then he would walk at a slow pace so that he did not pass the Black Stone without kissing it." [143]

1645–1646 'Amr ibn Dinār reported: We asked Ibn 'Umar whether a man who has performed circuits of the Ka'bah for *'Umrah* but not gone between the Ṣafā and the Marwah, if he can come to his wife (for sexual intercourse)? He said: The Messenger of Allāh ﷺ came (to Makkah) and made circuits of the Ka'bah seven times, then he said two *rak'ahs* of prayer behind the place of Abraham and went between the Ṣafā and the Marwah seven times. "Certainly you have in the Messenger of Allah an excellent exemplar" (the Qur'ān, 33:21). [1646] And we asked Jābir ibn 'Abdullāh and he said: "He should not approach her (for sexual intercourse) before going between the Ṣafā and the Marwah." [144]

1647 Ibn 'Umar said: The Prophet ﷺ came to Makkah and made circuits of the Ka'bah, and then he said two *rak'ahs* of prayer. Then he ran between the Ṣafā and the Marwah. Then he (Ibn 'Umar) recited: "Certainly you have in the Messenger of Allah an excellent exemplar" (the Qur'ān, 33:21).[145]

1648 'Āṣim informed that he asked Anas ibn Mālik: "Did you use to dislike running between the Ṣafā and the Marwah?". He said: "Yes, because it was one of the traditions of the days of Ignorance, until Allāh revealed: 'The Ṣafā and the Marwah are truly among the signs of Allāh; so whoever makes a pilgrimage (*Hajj*) to the House or pays a visit (*'Umrah*), there is no blame on him if he goes round them' (the Qur'ān, 2:158)."

1649 Ibn 'Abbās reported: The Messenger of Allāh ﷺ ran when making circuits of the Ka'bah and (ran) between the Ṣafā and the Marwah so that he could show his strength to the idolaters.

Ch. 81:　A menstruating woman can perform all the rites of the *Ḥajj* except making circuits of the Ka'bah, and when she runs between the Ṣafā and the Marwah without *Wuḍū'*

1650 'Ā'ishah reported: When I reached Makkah I had menstruation. I did not make circuits of the Ka'bah nor (run) between the Ṣafā and the Marwah.

---

[143] This is a repetition of h. 1616, and is like h. 1617. At the end of h. 1606, this question and answer are in the following words: 'I asked Nāfi': "Did Ibn 'Umar walk (at normal pace) between the two corners?" He said: "He used to walk (at normal pace between them) so that he could easily kiss it (i.e., the Black Stone)".'

[144] This is a repetition of h. 1623–1624. Here after the words "and went between the Ṣafā and the Marwah," the word *sab'an* (seven) is added for further explanation. It means that running between the Ṣafā and the Marwah is also seven times.

[145] This is a repetition of that part of h. 1623 which is in h. 1627.

She further said: Then I asked the Messenger of Allāh ﷺ about it and he said: "Do as the pilgrims do, but do not make circuits of the Ka'bah till you are clean." [146]

1651 Jābir ibn 'Abdullāh reported: The Prophet ﷺ and his Companions entered into the state of *Iḥrām* for the *Ḥajj* and none had sacrificial animals with him except the Prophet ﷺ and Ṭalḥah. 'Alī came from Yaman and he had a sacrificial animal with him. He said: "I have entered into *Iḥrām* for what the Prophet ﷺ has entered into it." The Prophet ﷺ commanded his Companions to make it (i.e., the *Ḥajj*) into *'Umrah* and to make circuits, then to get their hair trimmed and leave the state of *Iḥrām* except anyone who had a sacrificial animal with him. They said: "Should we proceed to Minā while we have been to our wives?" [147] When the news reached the Prophet ﷺ, he said: "If I had known before what I came to know later, I would not have brought the sacrificial animal; and if I did not have the sacrificial animal with me I would have left the state of *Iḥrām*." And 'Ā'ishah got menstruation so she performed all the acts of the *Ḥajj* except making circuits of the Ka'bah. When she became clean, she did the circuits of the Ka'bah. Then she said: "O Messenger of Allāh, all of you will return having performed the *Ḥajj* and the *'Umrah* and I will return having performed only the *Ḥajj*." So he ordered 'Abdur Raḥmān ibn Abū Bakr to take her to Tan'īm, and thus she performed the *'Umrah* after the *Ḥajj*.

1652 Ḥafṣah reported: We used to prohibit our virgin girls from going out (for the two Eid gatherings).[148] Then a woman came and stayed at the palace of Banī Khalaf. She told that her sister was married to a man from among the Companions of the Messenger of Allāh ﷺ who had fought alongside the

---

[146] A part of h. 1560 occurs here with differences. The chapter heading is established from just the words: "Do as the pilgrims do, but do not make circuits of the Ka'bah till you are clean." As the Holy Prophet did not prevent 'Ā'ishah from running between the Ṣafā and the Marwah because of her menstruation, it is permissible to do it in a state of menstruation. Thus a woman who has made circuits of the Ka'bah, and experiences menstruation after that, can run between the Ṣafā and the Marwah.

[147] The words "while we have been to our wives" refer to the fact that after leaving the state of *Iḥrām*, all those acts which are prohibited during the *Ḥajj* are permissible, including sexual relations. During the days of Ignorance, doing the *'Umrah* in the period of the *Ḥajj* was considered highly undesirable. Those who had not left the state of *Iḥrām* thought that the Holy Prophet had given them the discretion to leave it or remain in it, as has been mentioned earlier. However, when they came to know that it is obligatory, they all left the state of *Iḥrām*. The matters dealt with in this ḥadīth have already occurred in various reports in previous chapters.

[148] This ḥadīth is a repetition of h. 324, in which the words "for the two Eid gatherings" occur here. The closing words of this ḥadīth are related to the chapter heading.

Messenger of Allāh ﷺ in twelve battles, and (she said) "my sister was with him in six of the battles". She said:

> "We used to treat the wounded and look after the sick. My sister asked the Messenger of Allāh ﷺ: 'Is it a sin for any of us not to go out when she does not possess any over-garment?' He said: 'Her companion should cover her with her own over-garment as well, and she should be present at the doing of good works and at the prayers of the believers'.'"

So when Umm 'Aṭiyyah came, I asked her — or she said, we asked her — "Did you hear the Messenger of Allāh ﷺ saying such a thing?" She said: "Yes, may my father be sacrificed (for him)" — and she used to mention the Messenger of Allāh ﷺ but by saying: May my father be sacrificed (for him) — "and he said: 'Virgins in seclusion — or virgins and those in seclusion — and menstruating women should come out and be present at the doing of good works and at the prayers of the Muslims, and the menstruating women should keep apart from the place of prayer'." I asked her: "The menstruating women (are they to go out)?" She said: "Are they not present at 'Arafāt and at such and such places?"

Ch. 82:   Entering into the state of *Iḥrām* from al-Baṭḥā' and other places when residents of Makkah and the pilgrims (who remained in Makkah) set out for Minā[149]

'Aṭā' was asked about one who is a resident of Makkah, if he should recite *Labbaika* for *Ḥajj*? He said: When Ibn 'Umar had said *Ẓuhr* prayer on the 8th of Dhul Ḥajjah (*Yaum at-Tarwiyah*) and had mounted his she-camel, he would recite *Labbaika*. Jābir reported: We came with the Prophet ﷺ and we were out of *Iḥrām* till the 8th, and we recited *Labbaika* while Makkah was at our backs. And Abū az-Zubair reported from Jābir: We entered into the state of *Iḥrām* from al-Baṭḥā'.

'Ubaid ibn Juraij said to Ibn 'Umar: I see you, that when you are in Makkah and the people enter into *Iḥrām* when they see the new moon, you do not enter into the state of *Iḥrām* till the 8th. He said: I did not see the Prophet ﷺ entering into the state of *Iḥrām* till his she-camel stood up while he was on it.[150]

---

[149] Baṭḥā' is the plain of Makkah as mentioned in h. 1653. For the people of Makkah, it is Makkah which is the point for them to enter into the state of *Iḥrām*. As Jābir entered into *Iḥrām* at Baṭḥā', that is why it has been specifically mentioned.

[150] He means to say: The Holy Prophet did not allow any interval between entering into the state of *Iḥrām* and performing acts of the *Ḥajj*, wherever he may have entered into *Iḥrām*, and I also act in the same manner.

Ch. 83:   **Where *Ẓuhr* prayer is to be said on the day of *Tarwiyah* (8th of Dhul Ḥajjah)?**

1653 'Abdul 'Azīz ibn Rufai' reported: I asked Anas bin Mālik: "Tell me something which you had remembered from the Prophet ﷺ as to where he said his *Ẓuhr* and *'Aṣr* prayers on the day of *Tarwiyah*." He said: "At Minā." [151] I asked: "Where did he say his *'Aṣr* prayer on the day of departure?" He said: "At al-Abṭaḥ." [152] Then he said: "Do as your leaders do." [153]

1654 'Abdul 'Azīz reported: I went to Minā on the day of *Tarwiyah* and met Anas who was going on a donkey. I asked him: "Where did the Prophet ﷺ say his *Ẓuhr* prayer on this day?" He said: "See where your leaders pray, and pray (as they do)."

Ch. 84:   **Prayer at Minā[154]**

1655 'Abdullāh bin 'Umar reported: The Messenger of Allāh ﷺ prayed two *rak'ahs* at Minā, and so did Abū Bakr and 'Umar, and 'Uthmān (also) during the first years of his rule.

1656 Ḥārithah ibn Wahb al-Khuzā'iyy reported: The Prophet ﷺ led us in prayer of two *rak'ahs* at Minā, and this was when we were more numerous and secure than ever.

1657 'Abdullāh (ibn Mas'ūd) reported: I prayed with the Prophet ﷺ (at Minā) two *rak'ahs,* and with Abū Bakr two *rak'ahs,* and with 'Umar two *rak'ahs*. Then you differed in opinion. May be my two *rak'ahs* will be accepted in place of four.

Ch. 85:   **Fasting on the Day of *'Arafah*[155]**

---

[151] There is a report in Ṣaḥīḥ Muslim (book: *Pilgrimage*, ch. 19) that the Holy Prophet offered his *Ẓuhr* and *'Aṣr*, *Maghrib* and *'Ishā'*, and *Fajr* prayers at Minā. After saying the *Fajr* prayer, he used to leave for 'Arafāt.

[152] Al-Abṭaḥ is al-Muḥaṣṣab where the Holy Prophet had to set up his camp, and it was from there that he left for Madīnah. See h. 1560.

[153] It means that no particular place has any significance for saying prayer. It depends on the leader of the *Ḥajj* and one should pray with him. There is no particular place we should select in order for supplications to be accepted.

[154] The three reports in this chapter have occurred in the book *Shortening the Prayers*, ch. 2. See h. 1082, h. 1083 and h. 1084.

[155] There are many reports in Ḥadīth regarding the excellence of fasting on the day of *'Arafah*. Bukhārī has not accepted them. Even the ḥadīth mentioned in Ṣaḥīḥ Muslim (book: 'Fasting', ch. 36), which says "It expiates sins of the previous and the following year", does not seem to be genuine. Scholars of Ḥadīth have given a characteristic of a weak ḥadīth as being that it promises for a deed an abundant reward which is out of proportion to the deed.

1658 Umm al-Faḍl reported: People were in doubt as to whether the Prophet ﷺ was fasting on the day of *'Arafah*. So I sent him something to drink, and he drank it.[156]

Ch. 86: Recitation of *Labbaika* and *Allāhu Akbar* while going from Minā to 'Arafāt in the morning

1659 Muḥammad ibn Abū Bakr al-Thaqafiyy reported that he asked Anas ibn Mālik, when the two of them were going from Minā to 'Arafāt: "How did you do it on this day with the Prophet ﷺ?" He said: "Those of us who wanted to recite *Labbaika* did that and there was no objection to it, while those of us who wanted to recite *Allāhu Akbar* did so and there was no objection to it."[157]

Ch. 87: To proceed at noon on the day of *'Arafah*[158]

1660 Sālim (son of Ibn 'Umar) reported: 'Abdul Malik wrote to al-Ḥajjāj (asking him) not to oppose Ibn 'Umar regarding the rites of the *Ḥajj*. Ibn 'Umar came and I was with him on the day of *'Arafah* when the sun declined, and he called loudly by the tent of al-Ḥajjāj. He came out and he had covered himself with a yellow sheet and said: "O 'Abdur Raḥmān, what is the matter?" Ibn 'Umar said: "If you wish to follow the *Sunnah*,[159] then proceed." He said: "At this time?" He said: "Yes." He replied: "Give me some time so that I may pour some water on my head (to take bath), then I will come out." Then Ibn 'Umar dismounted till al-Ḥajjāj came out. He was walking between me and my father. I said to him: "If you wish to follow the *Sunnah*, then make your sermon brief and hasten for your stay (at 'Arafāt)." He looked at 'Abdullāh (ibn 'Umar). When 'Abdullāh saw this, he said: "He speaks the truth."

---

[156] See h. 1661. Thus it is clear that the Holy Prophet did not keep fast on the day of *'Arafah*.

[157] In this repetition of h. 970, the words "on that day" have been added after "How did you do it", which throws light on the chapter heading. In h. 1543–1544 it has already been mentioned that the Holy Prophet continued reciting *Labbaika* until throwing stones at the Jamrah. The same is mentioned in h. 1670.

[158] There is a place called Namirah outside the Sacred Mosque near 'Arafāt. According to a ḥadīth in Ṣaḥīḥ Muslim, the Holy Prophet encamped at this place while coming from Minā and as soon as the sun declined he set off for 'Arafāt on his she-camel, al-Qaṣwah (see Ṣaḥīḥ Muslim, book: *Pilgrimage*, ch. 19: *Ḥajj* of the Prophet). Afterwards the leaders of *Ḥajj* also used to stay at this place. The chapter heading is referring to proceeding from Namirah to the valley of 'Arafāt.

[159] If an act is called *Sunnah* by the Companions it means the *Sunnah* (practice) of the Holy Prophet; and if in any ḥadīth they call an act as *Sunnah*, then Ḥadīth scholars categorize that ḥadīth as *marfū'* (traceable to the Holy Prophet), even though that act may not have been explicitly ascribed to the Holy Prophet.

Ch. 88:   Staying at ʿArafāt while riding

1661 Umm al-Faḍl, daughter of al-Ḥārith, reported that people with her differed on the day of *ʿArafah* about the Prophet ﷺ fasting (on that day). Some people said that he was fasting (on the day of *ʿArafah*) and others said he was not. So she sent a cup of milk to him while he was staying, riding on his camel, and he drank it.[160]

Ch. 89:   Combining of two prayers at ʿArafāt

Ibn ʿUmar used to combine two prayers even when he missed (congregational) prayer with the Imām.[161]

1662 Ibn Shihāb reported: Sālim told me that the year al-Ḥajjāj ibn Yūsuf attacked ʿAbdullāh ibn az-Zubair, he asked ʿAbdullāh (ibn ʿUmar): "What did you use to do during your stay on the day of *ʿArafah?*" Sālim said: "If you wish to follow the *Sunnah*, then pray at the declining of the sun on the day of *ʿArafah*." ʿAbdullāh ibn ʿUmar said: "He (Sālim) speaks the truth. They (the Companions) used to combine the *Ẓuhr* and the *ʿAṣr* prayers according to the *Sunnah*." I (Ibn Shihāb) asked Sālim: "Did the Messenger of Allāh ﷺ do it?" Sālim replied: "What do you follow in this matter but the *Sunnah?*" [162]

Ch. 90:   Shortening the sermon (*khuṭbah*) at ʿArafāt

1663 Sālim, son of ʿAbdullāh (ibn ʿUmar), reported that ʿAbdul Malik ibn Marwān wrote to al-Ḥajjāj (asking him) to follow ʿAbdullāh ibn ʿUmar regarding the rites of the *Ḥajj*. When it was the day of *ʿArafah,* Ibn ʿUmar came and I was with him when the sun descended or declined. He called loudly by his (al-Ḥajjāj's) encampment: "Where is he?" So he came out to him and Ibn ʿUmar said: "Proceed." He said: "Now?" He replied: "Yes." He said: "Give me some time so that I may pour some water on myself." Then Ibn ʿUmar dismounted till he (al-Ḥajjāj) came out. He was walking between me and my father. I said: "If you wish to follow the *Sunnah* today, then make your sermon brief and hasten for your stay (at ʿArafāt)." Ibn ʿUmar said: "He (Sālim) speaks the truth." [163]

---

[160] This ḥadīth has repetitions in h. 1988 and h. 1989.

[161] The *Ẓuhr* and the *ʿAṣr* prayers are combined at ʿArafāt, whether performed individually or in congregation.

[162] See h. 1660. The heading of this chapter is related to the words "They (the Companions) used to combine the *Ẓuhr* and the *ʿAṣr* prayers according to the *Sunnah*." But these words do not occur in h. 1660.

[163] This is a repetition of h. 1660 with minor difference in wording.

Ch. 91:　To make haste for staying at 'Arafāt[164]

Ch. 92:　To stay at 'Arafāt

1664 Jubair ibn Muṭ'im reported: I lost my camel so I started searching for it on the day of *'Arafah* and I saw the Messenger of Allāh ﷺ staying at 'Arafāt, so I said to him: "By Allāh! He is from among the Ḥums. Why is he here?" [165]

1665 Hishām ibn 'Urwah reported that 'Urwah said: During the time of Ignorance people used to make circuits naked, except the Ḥums, and the Ḥums are the Quraish and their offspring. The Ḥums used to give out clothes to people as a good deed. Men would give clothes to men to make circuits wearing them, and women would give clothes to women to make circuits wearing them. As for those to whom the Ḥums did not give clothes, they made circuits naked. All other people used to return from 'Arafāt, but the Ḥums used to return from Muzdalifah. Hishām said: My father ('Urwah) informed me from 'Ā'ishah that this verse was revealed about the Ḥums: "Then hasten on from where the people hasten on" (the Qur'ān, 2:199). He said: They used to return from Muzdalifah (to Minā), so they were commanded to go to 'Arafāt before returning.

Ch. 93:　At what pace to start when leaving 'Arafāt?

1666 'Urwah reported: Someone asked Usāmah, and I was sitting with him: "How (i.e., at what pace) did the Messenger of Allāh ﷺ start off from 'Arafāt during the Farewell Pilgrimage?" He said: "He used to walk briskly (*'anaq*) but when he found space (*fajwah*) he walked faster (*naṣṣa*)." [166]

Hishām said: *Naṣṣa* is faster than *'anaq*. *Fajwah* means 'wide space' and

---

[164] This point has already been established in the previous h. 1660.

[165] *Ḥums* is the plural of *aḥmas,* and *ḥimāsah* means bravery. The Quraish, Kinānah and Jadīlah Qais were called *Ḥums* because they were very stern in the matter of their religion and they did not go to the place in 'Arafāt where the pilgrims used to stay as it was outside the area of the Sacred Mosque. This happened before the *Hijrah* when Jubair had not yet embraced Islām. Here the words *aḍlal-tu ba'īr-an* ("I lost my camel") throw light on the use of the word *iḍlāl* in the Arabic idiom. Literally *iḍlāl* means leading astray and when it is used in the Qur'ān (as in 2:26) with reference to Allāh the meaning is wrongly taken to be that *Allāh leads certain people astray.* Its use in this ḥadīth shows that it is also used in Arabic to mean *finding* that something has gone astray. Thus the meaning of this expression in the Qur'ān with reference to Allāh is that Allāh *pronounces* a people to be astray and in error, or that He *leaves them* in error, not that He *leads them astray.*

[166] According to a ḥadīth by Jābir in Ṣaḥīḥ Muslim (book: *Pilgrimage,* ch. 19), the Holy Prophet stayed on at 'Arafāt till sunset and then left for Muzdalifah, and as he wanted to combine the *Maghrib* and the *'Ishā'* prayers at Muzdalifah, he therefore walked very briskly.

its plural is *fajawāt-un* and *fijā'-un,* just as there is (the word) *rakwah* the plural of which is *rikā'-un.* *Manāṣ* is used in 'no time for escape' (in the Qur'ān, 38:3).[167]

Ch. 94:   Stopping between 'Arafāt and Muzdalifah

1667 Usāmah ibn Zaid reported: When the Prophet ﷺ was returning from 'Arafāt, he went towards a ravine. He answered the call of nature and performed *Wuḍū'.* I asked: "Messenger of Allāh, Will you pray (here)?" He said: "Prayer will be further on from where you are." [168]

1668 Nāfi' reported: 'Abdullāh ibn 'Umar used to combine *Maghrib* and *'Ishā'* prayers at Muzdalifah but with the difference that he would pass by the ravine through which the Messenger of Allāh ﷺ passed and enter it, and after completing the call of nature he would perform *Wuḍū'.*[169] He would not pray there, but pray at Muzdalifah.

1669–1670 Usāmah ibn Zaid reported: I rode behind the Messenger of Allāh ﷺ from 'Arafāt. When the Messenger of Allāh ﷺ came to the left side of the ravine near Muzdalifah, he sat his she-camel down and urinated. When he came back, I poured water for his *Wuḍū'* and he performed a light *Wuḍū'.* Then I asked: "Prayer, O Messenger of Allāh?" He said: "Prayer will be further on from where you are." Then the Messenger of Allāh ﷺ rode until he reached Muzdalifah and prayed (there). Then on the morning at Muzdalifah, al-Faḍl rode behind him. [1670] Kuraib said: 'Abdullāh ibn 'Abbās informed me from al-Faḍl that the Messenger of Allāh ﷺ did not cease reciting *Labbaika* till he reached the Jamrah.[170]

Ch. 95:   The Prophet ﷺ ordered calmness in returning from 'Arafāt and he pointed towards people with his whip

1671 Ibn 'Abbās related that he returned with Prophet ﷺ on the day of *'Arafah.* The Prophet ﷺ heard behind him much noise and beating and

---

[167] *Naṣṣa* is a "doubled verb" (root: *n, ṣ, ṣ*) and means to walk very fast. On the other hand, *nāṣ* is a "hollow verb" (root: *n, w, ṣ*) and from it comes the noun of time *manāṣ,* meaning time for escape. Bukhārī has given their meaning separately because the words *naṣṣa* and *manāṣ* come from different roots.

[168] This is a brief repetition of h. 139. This stopping was to answer the call of nature, and was not a rite of the *Ḥajj.*

[169] It was only because of his deep love for following the Holy Prophet that Ibn 'Umar copied him even in small matters which are not part of worship.

[170] See h. 139 and h. 1543–1544. The report from al-Faḍl in h. 1670 has already been mentioned in h. 1543–1544.

screaming of camels. So he pointed towards them with his whip and said: "O people, be calm, because rushing (*īḍā'*) is not a virtuous act." [171]

Auḍa'ū means to run around fast. *Khilāla-kum* is from *takhallul* and means "among you", and *fajjar-nā khilāla-humā* means "between the two of them".[172]

Ch. 96:   Combining two prayers at Muzdalifah

1672 Usāmah ibn Zaid reported: The Messenger of Allāh ﷺ returned from 'Arafāt and stopped at the ravine (near Muzdalifah). He urinated and then performed *Wuḍū'* but a light *Wuḍū'*. I said to him: "Prayer?" He said: "Prayer will be further on from where you are." When he came to Muzdalifah, he performed *Wuḍū'* completely. Then prayer was called by *Iqāmah* and he prayed *Maghrib*. Then every man made his camel sit at his place, and then (the *'Ishā'*) prayer was called by *Iqāmah*, and he prayed. He did not say any prayer between them.[173]

Ch. 97:   One who combines the two prayers but does not say the optional prayers

1673 Ibn 'Umar reported: The Prophet ﷺ combined the *Maghrib* and the *'Ishā'* prayers at Muzdalifah, each prayer being called by (a separate) *Iqāmah*. He did not say any optional prayer between the two (prayers) nor after either of them.

1674 Abū Ayyub al-Anṣārī related that during the Farewell Pilgrimage the Messenger of Allāh ﷺ combined the *Maghrib* and the *'Ishā'* prayers at Muzdalifah.

Ch. 98:   One who announces the Call to prayer (*Adhān*) and the *Iqāmah* for each one of them (i.e., the two prayers)

1675 'Abdur Raḥmān ibn Yazīd said: 'Abdullāh (ibn Mas'ūd) performed

---

[171] The Holy Prophet forbade driving animals at a fast pace because it could be dangerous due to the size of the crowd. And as he had commanded walking briskly during the circuits of the Ka'bah, he also reminded people that mere running or driving animals fast is not a virtuous deed in itself.

[172] The word *īḍā'* for "rushing" occurs as *auḍa'ū* in the Qur'ān, and Bukhārī here refers to the words in the Qur'ān *auḍa'ū khilāla-kum* (9:47) which mean "hurrying to and fro among you" to spread dissension. He then goes on to explain the words *khilāla-kum* ("among you") in this verse by referring to the words *fajjar-nā khilāla-humā* in the Qur'ān: "We caused to gush forth in their midst…" (18:33), where *khilāla-humā* means "in between the two of them".

[173] This is a repetition of h. 139 with slight differences. He did not say any optional prayers between the *Maghrib* and the *'Ishā'* obligatory congregational prayers.

the *Ḥajj* and we reached Muzdalifah at or near the time of the Call for prayer for the *'Ishā'* prayer. He ordered a man to announce the Call to prayer and then to recite the *Iqāmah*. Then he said the *Maghrib* prayer and after it he prayed two *rak'ahs*.[174] Then he called for his evening meal and ate it. Then — I think, and 'Amr said the doubt was only raised by Zuhair[175] — he again ordered the Call to prayer and the *Iqāmah*. Then he said two *rak'ahs* of *'Ishā'* prayer. When it was morning, he said: "The Prophet ﷺ never prayed at this hour except this prayer at this place on this day." 'Abdullāh added: "These are two prayers which have been shifted from their time — the *Maghrib* prayer after people reach Muzdalifah, and the *Fajr* prayer when the morning dawns. He said: "I saw the Prophet ﷺ doing it." [176]

Ch. 99: **One who sends the weak among his family members early (to Minā) before night falls, so that they stay at Muzdalifah, make supplications and proceed on when the moon sets[177]**

1676 Ibn Shihāb reported Sālim as saying: 'Abdullāh ibn 'Umar used to send the weak among his family members earlier. They would stay at night by al-Mash'ar al-Ḥarām at Muzdalifah and used to remember Allāh as long as they wished. Then they would return (to Minā) before the Imām completed his stay (at Muzdalifah) and returned. Some of them would reach Minā at the time of the *Fajr* prayer and others would reach there afterwards. When they reached, they would throw pebbles on the Jamrah. Ibn 'Umar used to say that the Messenger of Allāh ﷺ had allowed this.

1677 Ibn 'Abbās reported: The Messenger of Allāh ﷺ sent me from Muzdalifah at night.

---

[174] In other versions, it is reported that *sunnah rak'ahs* were not said, and this seems to be correct.

[175] 'Amr ibn Khālid, the latest narrator in the chain, was reporting from Zuhair, and he says that the words "I think", which raise the doubt, were said by Zuhair. These words were not said by the original reporter, 'Abdur Raḥmān ibn Yazīd.

[176] Some views are particular to certain Companions. Or it may be that the reporters made an error in understanding what was said.

[177] Going to Muzdalifah, staying there for the night, and remaining with the leader of the *Ḥajj*, are all parts of the rites of the *Ḥajj*. Weak persons such as children, women, the old and the sick are allowed to leave late in the night for Minā without staying overnight at Muzdalifah. The Holy Prophet's allowing weak persons, and Saudah's seeking permission to leave Muzdalifah in the night (see h. 1680 and 1681), show that exemption and allowance are only for handicapped people because it would be hard for them to move in a crowd.

1678 Ibn 'Abbās said: I was among those weak members of his family whom the Prophet ﷺ sent ahead (to Minā) on the night of Muzdalifah.[178]

1679 'Abdullāh, slave of Asmā', reported from her that she got down at Muzdalifah at night, and stood for prayer, and prayed for some time. Then she asked: "My son, has the moon set?" I said: "No." She continued praying for some time and then asked: "Has the moon set?" I said: "Yes." She said: "Let us go (to Minā)." We set off and went on until she threw pebbles at the Jamrah and then returned and said her *Fajr* prayer at her home. I asked: "O lady, we have thrown pebbles while it was still dark." She said: "My son, the Messenger of Allāh ﷺ has allowed women to do so."

1680 'Ā'ishah reported: Saudah asked permission of the Prophet ﷺ at the night of Muzdalifah (to depart from it). She was heavy and slow in moving. So he permitted her.

1681 'Ā'ishah reported: We arrived at Muzdalifah and Saudah asked permission of the Prophet ﷺ to depart earlier than the crowd of people, and she was a woman who moved at slow pace. So he permitted her. She departed before the crowd of people. We stayed there till morning broke, and then we departed with him (i.e., the Holy Prophet). If I had also asked permission from the Messenger of Allāh ﷺ as Saudah had done, I would have liked it more than anything else which could please me.

Ch. 100: Saying *Fajr* prayer at Muzdalifah

1682 'Abdullāh (ibn Mas'ūd) reported: I never saw the Prophet ﷺ saying a prayer (i.e., obligatory prayer) out of its time except that he combined the two prayers of *Maghrib* and *'Ishā'* and said the *Fajr* prayer before its time.[179]

1683 'Abdur Raḥmān ibn Yazīd reported: We went to Makkah with 'Abdullāh (ibn Mas'ūd) and came to Muzdalifah. He combined the two prayers with (separate) *Adhān* and *Iqāmah* for each one, and food was taken between the two (prayers). Then he said the *Fajr* prayer when the dawn had appeared. Some were saying that it was dawn and some were saying that it was not yet dawn. Then he said that the Messenger of Allāh ﷺ said: "The two prayers of *Maghrib* and *'Ishā'* have been shifted from their appointed time

---

[178] According to a report in the collection of Ṭaḥāwī, the Holy Prophet said to 'Abbās: "Go with our weak people and women and say the *Fajr* prayer at Minā, and they should throw the pebbles at the Jamrat-ul-'Aqabah before it becomes crowded." (See *Ṭaḥāwī Sharīf*, with Urdu translation, published by Ḥāmid & Company, Lahore, 1993, v. 2, p. 554–555.) Note that h. 1677 is a brief repetition of h. 1678.

[179] See h. 1675. As he was to leave for Minā after stopping at Muzdalifah, he would say the *Fajr* prayer as soon as the dawn appeared.

for this place. People should not enter Muzdalifah before dark, and the *Fajr* prayer should be said at this time." He (ʿAbdullāh ibn Masʿūd) remained there till it was quite bright and then said: "If the Commander of the Faithful starts now, he would be following the *Sunnah*." I (says the narrator) do not know whether his words came first or the departure of ʿUthmān. On the day of the Sacrifice, ʿAbdullāh did not cease reciting *Labbaika* till he threw pebbles at the Jamrat-ul-ʿAqabah.[180]

Ch. 101: When to depart from Muzdalifah

1684 ʿAmr ibn Maimūn said: I was with ʿUmar and he said the *Fajr* prayer at Muzdalifah, then he stayed and said: "The idolaters would not depart (from Muzdalifah) till the rising of the sun and they used to say: Shine, O Thabīr,[181] but the Prophet ﷺ opposed them and departed before the rising of the sun."

Ch. 102: Reciting *Labbaika* and *Allāhu Akbar* on the morning of the day of Sacrifices, until throwing pebbles at the Jamrah and having someone ride behind (on one's mount)

1685 Ibn ʿAbbās reported that the Prophet ﷺ had al-Faḍl ride behind him. Al-Faḍl informed that he (the Holy Prophet) did not cease reciting *Labbaika* till he threw pebbles at the Jamrah.[182]

1686–1687 Ibn ʿAbbās reported that Usāmah ibn Zaid rode behind the Prophet ﷺ from ʿArafāt to Muzdalifah, then al-Faḍl rode behind him from Muzdalifah to Minā. He (Ibn ʿAbbās) added: Both of them said that the Prophet ﷺ did not cease reciting *Labbaika* till he cast pebbles at the Jamrat-ul-ʿAqabah.[183]

Ch. 103: "… whoever profits by combining the *ʿUmrah* with the *Ḥajj* should take whatever offering is easy to obtain. But he who cannot find (an offering) should fast for three days during the

---

[180] See h. 1675. The statement which begins by referring to the shifting of the times of the two prayers was made by ʿAbdullāh ibn Masʿūd according to h. 1675, but here it has been given as a command of the Holy Prophet, thus making it clear here. The words, "he (ʿAbdullāh) remained there till it was quite bright" show that staying at Muzdalifah is till after the *Fajr* prayer as is also seen from the action of ʿUmar mentioned in h. 1684 that he remained there after saying the *Fajr* prayer but departed before the sun had risen.

[181] *Thabīr* is the name of a mound in Muzdalifah which is to the left while going to Minā. The expression "Shine, O Thabīr" means that the rays of sun should make it brighten.

[182] This is a repetition of a part of h. 1543. In neither h. 1543 nor in this report is *Allāhu Akbar* mentioned, but it is deduced from the reciting of *Labbaika*.

[183] H. 1543 is repeated here with a very slight variation in wording. See also h. 1670.

***Ḥajj* and for seven days when you return. These are ten (days) complete. This is for him whose family is not present in the Sacred Mosque" (the Qur'ān, 2:196).**

1688 Abū Jamrah related: I asked Ibn 'Abbās about *Tamattu'*, so he commanded me to perform it. And I asked him about the sacrifice (*al-hady*) and he said: "It is of a camel, cow, she-goat or share in a sacrifice." Abū Jamrah said: It appears that people did not like doing *Tamattu'*. I went to sleep and had a dream as if a man was announcing: a righteous (*mabrūr*) *Ḥajj* and an accepted (*mutaqabbalah*) *Tamattu'*. I went to Ibn 'Abbās and related it to him. He said: "*Allāhu Akbar,* this was the *Sunnah* of Abul Qāsim ﷺ.

Shu'bah reported (that the words in the dream were): an accepted (*mutaqabbalah*) *'Umrah* and a righteous (*mabrūr*) *Ḥajj*.[184]

Ch. 104: To ride sacrificial animals (*budn*)

The word of Allāh: "And the camels (*budn*), We have made them from among the signs (*sha'ā'ir*) appointed by Allah for you — in them there is much good for you.[185] So mention the name of Allah on them standing in a row. Then when they fall down (*wajabat*) on their sides, eat of them and feed the contented one (*qāni'*) and the beggar (*mu'tar*). Thus have We made them subservient to you that you may be grateful. Not their flesh, nor their blood, reaches Allah, but to Him is acceptable the observance of duty on your part. Thus has He made them subservient to you, that you may magnify Allah for guiding you aright. And give good news to those who do good to others" (the Qur'ān, 22:36–37).

Mujāhid said: They are called *budn* (singular: *badanah*) because of their bulky size. *Qāni'* means a beggar and *mu'tar* is he who roams about for the meat of a sacrificial animal, whether he is wealthy or poor.[186] *Sha'ā'ir* refers to honouring the sacrificial animals and beautifying them. *'Atīq* (name of the Ka'bah in the Qur'ān, 22:33) means it is safe (*'itquh*) from tyrants. And what is called *wajabat* is

---

[184] This is a repetition of the first part of h. 1567 in more detail. Ibn 'Abbās has taken *al-hadyi* to mean the sacrifice of a camel, cow or she-goat. The words "share in a sacrifice" mean that up to seven people can share in the sacrifice of a cow or camel.

[185] It has been inferred from the words "in them there is much good for you" (22:36) that it is permissible to derive benefit from the camel and this includes riding it.

[186] In the verse of the Qur'ān as quoted above, the words *qāni'* and *mu'tar* are translated as "the contented one and the beggar". By "contented one" is meant one who is content to receive a little, and this is not in conflict with the meaning of *qāni'* given here by Mujāhid.

to fall on the ground, from which comes the expression *wajabat al-shams* ("the sun has set").

1689 Abū Hurairah reported that the Messenger of Allāh ﷺ saw a man driving his sacrificial animal (*badanah*). He said: "Ride it." The man said: "It is a sacrificial animal." He said (again): "Ride it." He said: "It is a sacrificial animal." He said (yet again): "Ride it, woe to you!" It was on the third or the second time (that the Holy Prophet added: "woe to you!").[187]

1690 Anas reported that the Prophet ﷺ saw a man driving his sacrificial animal (*badanah*). He said: "Ride it." The man said: "It is a sacrificial animal." He said (again): "Ride it." He said: "It is a sacrificial animal." He said (yet again): "Ride it". It was three times (that the Holy Prophet said this).[188]

Ch. 105: One who takes sacrificial animals (*budn*) with him

1691–1692 Sālim ibn 'Abdullāh reported that ('Abdullāh) Ibn 'Umar said: In the Farewell Pilgrimage, the Messenger of Allāh ﷺ joined *'Umrah* with *Ḥajj* (i.e., *Tamattu'*). He made sacrifice, taking the sacrificial animal (*al-hady*) with him from Dhul Ḥulaifah. The Messenger of Allāh ﷺ started by entering into the state of *Iḥrām* for the *'Umrah,* and then for the *Ḥajj*. People also joined *'Umrah* with *Ḥajj* along with the Prophet ﷺ. Some people brought sacrificial animals, driving them along with them, and some did not have sacrificial animals. When the Prophet ﷺ reached Makkah, he said to the people: "Whoever among you has brought a sacrificial animal, let him know that whatever is prohibited for him (in *Iḥrām*) is not permissible for him until he completes the *Ḥajj*. But whoever among you has not brought a sacrificial animal, he should make circuits of the Ka'bah, and (run between) the Ṣafā and the Marwah, get his hair trimmed, and leave his state of *Iḥrām*. Then he should enter into the state of *Iḥrām* for the *Ḥajj*. And he who cannot find any sacrificial animal, he should fast for three days at the place of the *Ḥajj* and for seven days when he reaches his home."

When he (the Holy Prophet) reached Makkah, first he made circuits of the Ka'bah and kissed Black Stone. In the first three circuits of Ka'bah he walked at fast pace *(ramal),* and walked (at normal pace) during the other four circuits. When he had completed his circuits of the Ka'bah, he said two *rak'ahs* of prayer near the Place of Abraham and ended it with *Taslīm.* After finishing it

---

[187] Obviously, riding the animal will only be done when there is need for it. The object of mentioning it is to point out that if there is need, riding it is not forbidden. It appears that this man did not want to ride the animal because he considered it sacred for sacrifice. A report in Nasā'ī mentions that "he was exhausted because of walking" (book: *Ḥajj*, ch. 75, h. 2801).

[188] This is a repetition of h. 1689. There is no mention of "woe to you" here. See also h. 1706.

he went to the Ṣafā and went between the Ṣafā and the Marwah seven times; and whatever was prohibited for him (in *Iḥrām*) did not become permissible until he completed the *Ḥajj*, sacrificed the animal on the day of Sacrifices, and returned and made circuits of the Kaʿbah. Then everything which was prohibited for him became permissible. Those who brought sacrificial animals with them, driving them along with them, did the same as what the Messenger of Allāh ﷺ did.

[1692] And ʿUrwah reported that ʿĀ'ishah informed him regarding the Prophet ﷺ joining *'Umrah* with *Ḥajj* (*Tamattuʿ*), and people joining *'Umrah* with *Ḥajj* along with him, similarly to what Sālim informed me from Ibn ʿUmar from the Messenger of Allāh ﷺ.

Ch. 106: He who buys a sacrificial animal on the way (to *Ḥajj*)

1693 Nāfiʿ reported: ʿAbdullāh ibn ʿAbdullāh ibn ʿUmar said to his father (i.e., to ʿAbdullāh ibn ʿUmar): "Stay here (i.e., do not go for the *Ḥajj*) as I do not consider it safe as you will be prevented from reaching the Kaʿbah. He said: "At this time, I will do what the Messenger of Allāh ﷺ did. And Allāh has indeed said: 'Certainly you have in the Messenger of Allāh an excellent exemplar' (the Qur'ān, 33:21). I make you witness that I have made the *'Umrah* obligatory on me." So he entered into the state of *Iḥrām* for *'Umrah*. Then he set off and when he reached al-Baidā', he entered into *Iḥrām* for *Ḥajj* and *'Umrah* and said: "The *Ḥajj* and the *'Umrah* are similar." Then he bought a sacrificial animal (*hady*) at Qudaid. Then he came (to Makkah) and performed *Ṭawāf* for both (the *'Umrah* and the *Ḥajj*) once, and he did not leave the state of *Iḥrām* until he had performed both (the *Ḥajj* and the *'Umrah*).[189]

Ch. 107: Marking and garlanding a sacrificial animal at Dhul Ḥulaifah, then entering into the state of *Iḥrām*

Nāfiʿ said: When Ibn ʿUmar used to bring a sacrificial animal from Madīnah, he used to garland (*qallada*) it and mark (*ashʿara*) it at Dhul Ḥulaifah when it was sitting facing towards the Kaʿbah, and make a slight cut with his spear on the right side of its hump.[190]

---

[189] This is a repetition of h. 1640 with some differences.

[190] *Shiʿār* (the act referred to in *ashʿara*) means to mark with a knife on the hump, as has been explained in the text. *Taqlīd* (the act referred to in *qallada*) means to garland an animal of sacrifice. The purpose of both acts was to distinguish the sacrificial animals from other animals so that they could be identified if they were lost. Another reason was that people may not cause any harm to them. The marking of the hump of a camel with a knife causes no distress to the animal as the cut is very slight, intended only to bring out a few drops of blood which mark the body at that point.

1694–1695 Al-Miswar ibn Makhramah and Marwān both reported: The Prophet ﷺ set out from Madīnah with more than one thousand of his Companions. When they reached Dhul Ḥulaifah the Prophet ﷺ put a garland around his sacrificial animal, marked it and entered into the state of *Iḥrām* for the *'Umrah*.

1696 'Ā'ishah reported: I stringed garlands with my own hands for the sacrificial animals of the Prophet ﷺ. Then he garlanded them, marked them and despatched them to Makkah. Even then nothing was forbidden for him out of what is allowed.[191]

Ch. 108: Stringing of garlands for sacrificial camels and cows

1697 Ḥafṣah reported that she said: "O Messenger of Allāh, what is the matter with people that they have left the state of *Iḥrām* but you have not?" He said: "I have matted my hair and garlanded my sacrificial animal, so I will not leave the state of *Iḥrām* until I am free from the *Ḥajj*." [192]

1698 'Ā'ishah said: The Messenger of Allāh ﷺ used to send the sacrificial animal from Madīnah, and I would string the garlands for his sacrificial animals. Then he did not refrain from anything which a pilgrim must avoid.[193]

Ch. 109: Marking of sacrificial animals

'Urwah reported from al-Miswar: The Prophet ﷺ garlanded the sacrificial animal, marked it and entered into the state of the *Iḥrām* for *'Umrah*.

1699 'Ā'ishah reported: I stringed the garlands for the sacrificial animals of the Prophet ﷺ. Then he marked them and garlanded them — or (she said) I garlanded them. Then he despatched them to the Ka'bah but remained himself in Madīnah. And nothing was forbidden for him out of what is allowed.[194]

Ch. 110: Placing garland by own hands

1700 'Amrah, daughter of 'Abdur Raḥmān, reported that Ziyād ibn Abū Sufyān wrote a letter to 'Ā'ishah stating that 'Abdullāh ibn 'Abbās said:

---

[191] This is a brief version of h. 1700. The garlanding and marking of animals was done even when he was not in the state of *Iḥrām*. The chapter derives its heading from this.

[192] This is a repetition of h. 1566 with a small difference of wording. It closes with "until I am free from the *Ḥajj*" instead of "until I perform the sacrifice".

[193] This is a repetition of h. 1700 in its form as in h. 1696. The sacrificial animal (*Hady*) includes both a camel and a cow.

[194] This repetition of h. 1700 is also much like h. 1696, with a little addition.

"Whoever sends his sacrificial animal (to the Kaʿbah), whatever is forbidden for a pilgrim becomes forbidden for him until his sacrificial animal is slaughtered." ʿAmrah reported that ʿĀʾishah said: "It is not like what Ibn ʿAbbās said. I strung the garlands for the sacrificial animals of the Messenger of Allāh ﷺ with my own hands, and then the Messenger of Allāh ﷺ garlanded them with his own hands. Then he sent them with my father (to Makkah). And nothing was forbidden for the Messenger of Allāh ﷺ which was allowed by Allāh until the animals were sacrificed." [195]

Ch. 111: Garlanding of she-goats[196]

1701 ʿĀʾishah reported: Once the Prophet ﷺ sent a she-goat for sacrifice.[197]

1702 ʿĀʾishah reported: I used to string garlands for (the sacrificial animals of) the Prophet ﷺ. He used to garland the she-goats and stay in his house with everything allowed (i.e., as one not in *Iḥrām*).

1703 ʿĀʾishah reported: I used to string garlands for the she-goats of the Prophet ﷺ. He would send them (to the Kaʿbah) and then he would remain with everything allowed (i.e., as one not in the state of *Iḥrām*).

1704 ʿĀʾishah reported: I stringed garlands for the sacrificial animals of the Prophet ﷺ before he entered into the state of *Iḥrām*.

Ch. 112: Garlands of wool

1705 ʿĀʾishah reported: I stringed garlands (for the sacrificial animals) from the wool which I had with me.

Ch. 113: Garlanding with shoes

1706 Abū Hurairah reported that the Prophet of Allāh ﷺ saw a man driving his sacrificial animal (*badanah*). He said: "Ride it." The man said: "It is a sacrificial animal." He (the Holy Prophet) again said: "Ride it." Abū Hurairah added: Then I saw him riding it, walking alongside the Prophet ﷺ and the shoe was hanging from its neck.[198]

---

[195] It is a powerful testimony to the depth of knowledge possessed by ʿĀʾishah, and to her efforts to preserve the example of the Holy Prophet, that she had no hesitation in correcting the errors of the greatest Companions of the Holy Prophet.

[196] The reports in this chapter and the next are repetitions in brief of h. 1700.

[197] The repetition of h. 1700 here is very brief but it deals with a different subject from the chapter heading. In h. 1702 and h. 1703 the garlanding of she-goats is mentioned.

[198] This is a repetition of h. 1689; see also h. 1690. The object was to mark the animal by the shoe. There is no harm if a shoe is hung from the neck of a sacrificial animal in order to remove the idea of its sacredness.

Ch. 114: Pack-saddles of sacrificial camels

Ibn 'Umar used to cut open the pack-saddles only near the hump of the camels and when he sacrificed them he removed the pack-saddles in case these might be be sploit with blood. Then these were given in charity.

1707 'Alī reported: The Messenger of Allāh ﷺ commanded me to give in charity the pack-saddles of the animals which I sacrificed and also their skins.

Ch. 115: He who buys his sacrificial animal on the way (to *Ḥajj*) and garlands it[199]

1708 Nāfi' reported: Ibn 'Umar intended to perform the *Ḥajj* in the year of the *Ḥajj* of al-Ḥarūriyyah during the rule of Ibn az-Zubair.[200] So he was told[201] … He took with him a sacrificial animal, garlanded, which he bought,[202] so that he came and performed circuits of the Ka'bah and (ran between) the Ṣafā (and the Marwah), and did nothing more than that. He did not make anything permissible for him which was forbidden (due to *Iḥrām*) until the day of Sacrifices. Then he shaved his head and made sacrifice and considered that his initial *Ṭawāf* was sufficient for the *Ḥajj* and the *'Umrah*. Then he said: "The Prophet ﷺ had done it like that." [203]

Ch. 116: Slaughtering (*dhabḥ*) a cow by a man on behalf of his wives without them asking for it

1709 'Ā'ishah said: We set off with the Messenger of Allāh ﷺ when five days remained in the month of Dhul Qa'dah with no intention except to perform the *Ḥajj*. When we were near Makkah, the Messenger of Allāh ﷺ commanded that whoever had no sacrificial animal should make circuits (of the Ka'bah) and run between the Ṣafā and the Marwah, and leave the state of *Iḥrām*. She said: Some meat of a cow was brought to us on the day of the

---

[199] See heading of ch. 106, to which "garlanding it" is added here.

[200] By al-Ḥarūriyyah are meant the Khawārij, the people who initially revolted against the central authority in Madīnah and were responsible for the assassination of 'Uthmān. Their *Ḥajj* was in 64 A.H. In that year Yazīd ibn Mu'āwiyah had died and Ibn az-Zubair was not yet the Caliph. Al-Ḥajjāj attacked Makkah in 73 A.H. in order to kill Ibn az-Zubair. Apparently, the opening of this ḥadīth conflicts with h. 1640 which begins as follows: "the year al-Ḥajjāj went to fight with Ibn az-Zubair, Ibn 'Umar intended to perform the *Ḥajj*."

[201] From this point on, this ḥadīth is almost the same as h. 1640 until reaching the words "He took with him a sacrificial animal". It then continues as above.

[202] The chapter heading is based on these words.

[203] This is a repetition of h. 1640 with differences.

Sacrifice. I asked: "What is this?" I was told: "The Messenger of Allāh ﷺ has sacrificed (*naḥara*) on behalf of his wives." [204]

Ch. 117: Sacrificing where the Prophet ﷺ sacrificed at Minā

1710 Nāfiʿ reported that ʿAbdullāh (ibn ʿUmar) used to sacrifice at the place of sacrifice. ʿUbaidullāh said: The place where the Messenger of Allāh ﷺ used to sacrifice (is meant).

1711 Nāfiʿ reported that Ibn ʿUmar used to send his sacrificial animal from Muzdalifah late in the night so that it could reach the place of sacrifice of the Prophet ﷺ with the pilgrims, who included the free and the slaves.

Ch. 118: He who sacrifices (*naḥara*) with his own hands[205]

1712 Anas reported: And the Prophet ﷺ sacrificed with his own hands seven camels (while they were) standing. He also sacrificed two spotted rams with two horns in Madīnah.[206]

Ch. 119: Sacrificing camels by tying them

1713 Ziyād ibn Jubair reported: I saw Ibn ʿUmar come to a man who had made his camel sit for sacrificing it. He told him: "Make it stand up and tie it (for sacrificing). This is the *Sunnah* of Muḥammad ﷺ."

Ch. 120: Sacrificing sacrificial camels standing

> Ibn ʿUmar said: It is the *Sunnah* of Muḥammad ﷺ. Ibn ʿAbbās said: *Ṣawāff* means standing.

1714 Anas reported: The Prophet ﷺ said four *rakʿahs* of the *Ẓuhr* prayer at Madīnah and two *rakʿahs* of the *ʿAṣr* prayer at Dhul Ḥulaifah, and spent the night there. When it was morning, he rode his animal and started saying: "There is no God but Allāh" and "Glory be to Allāh". When he reached al-Baidā' he said *Labbaika* together (for both *Ḥajj* and *'Umrah*). When he entered Makkah, he ordered people to leave their state of *Iḥrām*. The Prophet

---

[204] See h. 1561. The chapter heading is related to the words: "Some meat of a cow was brought to us on the day of the Sacrifice". From her question, "What is this?" it has been inferred that ʿĀʾishah did not know that the Holy Prophet had sacrificed on behalf of his wives. *Naḥara* ("has sacrificed") here means slaughtering, *dhabḥ*. See also h. 1720.

[205] *Naḥr* literally means chest and this word is used in particular for slaughtering a camel because it is slaughtered by piercing his chest with a spear. But it can be used also in the broader sense of *dhabḥ*, or slaughtering in general. Some scholars are of the view that a cow can also be slaughtered in the same manner as a camel.

[206] This is a repetition of the closing words of h. 1551. See also h. 1714 and h. 1715.

🕮 sacrificed seven camels with his own hands (while they were) standing. He also sacrificed two spotted rams with two horns in Madīnah.[207]

1715 Anas reported: The Prophet 🕮 said four *rak'ahs* of the *Ẓuhr* prayer at Madīnah and two *rak'ahs* of the *'Aṣr* prayer at Dhul Ḥulaifah. Ayyūb reported from someone who reported from Anas: Then he spent the night (there) until morning, and said the morning prayer. Then he rode his animal until arriving at al-Baidā', and there he entered into the state of *Iḥrām* for *'Umrah* and *Ḥajj*.[208]

Ch. 121: Nothing from the sacrifice should be given to a butcher[209]

1716 'Alī reported: The Prophet 🕮 sent me and I supervised the sacrifices. He commanded me to distribute the meat, and then he commanded me to distribute their pack-saddles and skins.

(And it is reported in another narration:) The Prophet 🕮 commanded me to supervise the sacrifices and that I should not give anything from it to the butcher as wages.

Ch. 122: Skins of the sacrificial animals should be given in charity

1717 'Alī informed that the Prophet 🕮 commanded him to supervise the sacrifices, and to distribute all the sacrifices — the meat and the skins and the pack-saddles — and to give nothing from it as wages to the butcher.[210]

Ch. 123: Pack-saddles of sacrificial animals should be given in charity

1718 'Alī reported: The Prophet 🕮 sacrificed one hundred camels and commanded me to distribute the meat, so I distributed it. Then he commanded me to distribute the saddle-packs, so I distributed them, then to distribute the skins, so I distributed them.

Ch. 124:

> "And when We pointed to Abraham the place of the House, saying: Do not set up any partner with Me, and purify My House for those who make circuits and stand to pray and bow and prostrate themselves. And proclaim to mankind the Pilgrimage: they will come to you on foot and on every lean camel, coming from every remote path, that they may witness benefits (provided) for them, and

---

[207] This is a repetition of h. 1551 with some omissions and difference of wording.

[208] This again is a repetition of h. 1551 with differences, and the end part omitted.

[209] It means that nothing should be given as wages.

[210] H. 1717 and h. 1718 are repetitions of h. 1716 with differences.

mention the name of Allah on appointed days over the cattle quadrupeds that He has given them; then eat of them and feed the distressed one, the needy. Then let them accomplish their needful acts of cleansing, and let them fulfil their vows and make circuits of the Ancient House. That (shall be so). And whoever respects the sacred ordinances of Allah, it is good for him with his Lord" (the Qur'ān, 22:26–30).

Ch. 125: What to eat from the sacrifices and what to give in charity

'Ubaidullāh said: Nāfi' informed me from Ibn 'Umar that one should not eat out of what is given as compensation[211] nor out of an offering, and one can eat out of what is besides that. And 'Aṭā' said: Eat and feed (others) from the meat of the sacrifice for *Hajj* which is *Tamattu'*.

1719 Jābir ibn 'Abdullāh said: We did not eat from the meat of our sacrifices after three days of Minā. So the Prophet ﷺ permitted us and said: "Eat and keep it as provision for travelling." So we ate it and also kept it as provision for travelling. I (Ibn Juraij) said to 'Aṭā':[212] "Did he (Jābir) also say: Till we reached Madīnah?" He said: "No."[213]

1720 'Ā'ishah said: We set off with the Messenger of Allāh ﷺ when five days remained in the month of Dhul Qa'dah with no intention except to perform the *Hajj*. When we were near Makkah, the Messenger of Allāh ﷺ commanded that whoever had no sacrificial animal should make circuits of the Ka'bah, then leave the state of *Ihrām*. She said: Some meat of a cow was brought to us on the day of the Sacrifice. I asked: "What is this?" I was told: "The Prophet ﷺ has slaughtered (*dhabaha*) on behalf of his wives."[214]

Ch. 126: To slaughter before shaving the head

1721 Ibn 'Abbās reported: The Prophet ﷺ was asked about one who

---

[211] That is to say, the compensation given for the offence of killing game during the Pilgrimage, as stated in the Qur'ān: "O you who believe, do not kill game while you are on pilgrimage. And whoever among you kills it intentionally, the compensation of it is the like of what he killed..." (5:95). See further Bukhārī's Book 28: 'Penalty for hunting'.

[212] Ibn Juraij was reporting from 'Aṭā', who in turn was reporting from Jābir ibn 'Abdullāh.

[213] According to some reports, the Holy Prophet forbade the eating of the sacrificial meat beyond three days. This contradicts those reports. It is possible that the misconception may have arisen from a temporary command or from what people did on their own, and the Holy Prophet cleared this misunderstanding.

[214] This is a repetition of h. 1709. The significant differences are that the words "and run between the Ṣafā and the Marwah" do not occur here, and that the closing statement is: "The Prophet ﷺ has slaughtered (*dhabaha*) on behalf of his wives."

shaved his head before slaughtering. He said: "There is no harm! There is no harm!"

1722 Ibn ʿAbbās reported: A man asked the Prophet ﷺ: "I made circuits of the Kaʿbah before throwing the pebbles." He (the Holy Prophet) said: "There is no harm." The man then said: "I shaved my head before slaughtering." He (the Holy Prophet) said: "There is no harm." The man said: "I slaughtered before throwing pebbles." He (the Holy Prophet) said: "There is no harm."

1723 Ibn ʿAbbās reported: The Prophet ﷺ was asked by a man who said: "I threw pebbles in the evening." He said: "There is no harm." Someone asked: "I shaved my head before making the sacrifice." He (the Holy Prophet) said: There is no harm." [215]

1724 Abū Mūsā reported: I went to the Messenger of Allāh ﷺ when he was at al-Baṭḥāʾ. He asked: "Have you performed the *Ḥajj*?" I said: "Yes." He asked: "For what purpose did you enter into the state of *Iḥrām*?" I said: "I entered into *Iḥrām* for the same purpose as the Prophet ﷺ." He said: "You have done well. Now go and make circuits of the Kaʿbah and (run between) the Ṣafā and the Marwah." Then I went to a woman of the Banū Qais, and she took out lice from my hair. Then I entered into *Iḥrām* for *Ḥajj*. I used to give this ruling to people till the Caliphate of ʿUmar. When I mentioned it to him, he said: "If we act upon the Book of Allāh, it orders us to complete it, but if we act upon the *Sunnah* of the Messenger of Allāh ﷺ, then he did not leave his *Iḥrām* until the sacrifice was completed." [216]

Ch. 127: Matting hair of the head when entering into the state of *Iḥrām* and shaving it off when leaving the *Iḥrām*

1725 Ḥafṣah reported that she said: "O Messenger of Allāh, what is the matter with people that they have left the state of *Iḥrām* after *ʿUmrah* but you have not left *Iḥrām* after your *ʿUmrah*?" He said: "I have matted my hair and

---

[215] H. 1721 to h. 1723 are repetitions of h. 83 and h. 84 in different words and with some changes. In these reports, four things have been mentioned: shaving the head before the sacrifice, making circuits before throwing of pebbles at the Jimār, making the sacrifice before the throwing of pebbles, and throwing pebbles after the setting of the sun. In all these cases, the Holy Prophet replied that there was no harm. According to the *Sunnah*, the sequence should be: throwing of pebbles, making the sacrifice, getting the head shaved or the hair trimmed, and finally making circuits of the Kaʿbah. But if there is a slight deviation from this sequence, even then the *Ḥajj* is considered as performed. See also h. 1734 to h. 1738.

[216] This is a repetition of h. 1559 with differences and changes. The chapter heading is related to the last words, that he made the sacrifice, then left the state of *Iḥrām* and shaved his head.

garlanded my sacrificial animal, so I will not leave the state of *Iḥrām* until I perform the sacrifice." [217]

Ch. 128: Shaving of head or trimming of hair when leaving the state of *Iḥrām*

1726 Ibn 'Umar said: The Messenger of Allāh ﷺ shaved his head in the *Ḥajj*.

1727 'Abdullāh bin 'Umar reported that the Messenger of Allāh ﷺ said: "O Allāh, have mercy on those who shave their heads." People asked: "And what about those who get their hair trimmed, O Messenger of Allāh?" He (again) said: "O Allāh, have mercy on those who shave their heads." People (again) asked: "And what about those who get their hair trimmed, O Messenger of Allāh?" He said: "And (have mercy also) on those who get their hair trimmed."

Nāfi' related (that the Holy Prophet said): "May Allāh have mercy on those who shave their heads" once or twice. He also related: The fourth time he said: "And on those who get their hair trimmed."

1728 Abū Hurairah reported that the Messenger of Allāh ﷺ said: "O Allāh, forgive those who shave their heads." People asked: "And what about those who get their hair trimmed?" He (again) said: "O Allāh, forgive hose who shave their heads." People (again) asked: "And what about those who get their hair trimmed?" He said (the same) for the third time. He (then) said: "And (forgive also) those who get their hair trimmed." [218]

1729 'Abdullāh (ibn 'Umar) said: The Messenger of Allāh ﷺ and a group from among his Companions shaved their heads and some of them got their hair trimmed.

1730 Mu'āwiyah reported: I cut the hair of the Messenger of Allāh ﷺ with scissors.[219]

---

[217] This is a repetition of h. 1566. See also h. 1697.

[218] There is a difference in the reports as to whether the Holy Prophet made this supplication at the Farewell Pilgrimage or during the *'Umrah* of Ḥudaibiyah. The Qur'ān says: "You shall certainly enter the Sacred Mosque if Allah please, in security, your *heads shaved* and *hair cut short*, not fearing" (48:27). There is no difference between the two.

[219] Mu'āwiyah had not embraced Islām by the time of the Truce of Ḥudaibiyah and the Holy Prophet had his head shaved at the Farewell Pilgrimage. Thus, the trimming of the hair of the Holy Prophet by Mu'āwiyah might have been on the eve of performing the *'Umrah* Ja'rānah, which was done at night after the distribution of the booty of the battle of Ḥunain, or it might have been when the Holy Prophet performed the *'Umrat-ul-Qaḍā'* after the Treaty of Ḥudaibiyah.

Ch. 129: Trimming of hair at *Tamattu' Ḥajj* after the *'Umrah*

1731 Ibn 'Abbās reported: When the Prophet ﷺ came to Makkah, he commanded his Companions to make circuits of the Ka'bah, and (run between) the Ṣafā and the Marwah, and then to leave the state of *Iḥrām* and get their heads shaved or hair trimmed.[220]

Ch. 130: To make circuits (*Ṭawāf az-ziyārah*) on the day of Sacrifices

> Abū az-Zubair reported from 'Ā'ishah and Ibn 'Abbās that the Prophet ﷺ delayed performing *Ṭawāf az-ziyārah* till the night. And it is reported from Abū Ḥassān, who heard it from Ibn 'Abbās, that the Prophet ﷺ performed *Ṭawāf az-ziyārah* in the days of Minā.[221]

1732 Ibn 'Umar reported that he performed *Ṭawāf* once, then he took some rest (at noon), then he came to Minā, that is, on the day of Sacrifices. And 'Abdur Razzāq considered this (report) as *marfū'* (traceable to the Holy Prophet).

1733 'Ā'ishah said: We performed the *Ḥajj* along with the Prophet ﷺ and we performed *Ṭawāf al-ifāḍah* on the day of Sacrifices. Ṣafiyyah had menstruation and when the Prophet ﷺ intended from her what a man intends from his wife, I said: "Messenger of Allāh, she is in menses." He said: "Is she going to delay us?" He was told: "Messenger of Allāh, she has already performed *Ṭawāf al-ifāḍah* on the day of Sacrifices." He said: "Then proceed." [222]

It is reported from al-Qāsim, 'Urwah and al-Aswad from 'Ā'ishah: "Ṣafiyyah has already performed *Ṭawāf al-ifāḍah* on the day of Sacrifices." [223]

Ch. 131: Throwing pebbles after sunset, or shaving one's head before slaughtering the sacrificial animal, by mistake or in ignorance

1734 Ibn 'Abbās reported that the Prophet ﷺ was asked about making the

---

[220] This is a repetition of a small part of h. 1545.

[221] Jābir and Ibn 'Umar have reported that the Holy Prophet made circuits of the Ka'bah during the day on the day of the Sacrifice. Thus delaying the circuits of the Ka'bah till the night, mentioned in the comment under the chapter heading, refers to the visit in the days of Minā after the day of the Sacrifice. *Ṭawāf al-ziyārah* is also known as *Ṭawāf al-ifāḍah*, *Ṭawāf aṣ-ṣadr* and *Ṭawāf ar-rukn*, as it is part of the rites of the *Ḥajj* since the Holy Prophet said that if Ṣafiyyah has not performed *Ṭawāf al-ifāḍah*, she would prevent us from departing (see h. 1733). In h. 1732, reported by Ibn 'Umar, this same *Ṭawāf* is meant.

[222] This is a repetition of the part of h. 1561 relating to Ṣafiyyah with more detail.

[223] In this report the name "Ṣafiyyah" occurs instead of "she" as in the report above.

Sacrifice, shaving of the head, and the throwing of pebbles, as to which comes before and which comes after. He said: "There is no harm."

1735 Ibn 'Abbās reported: When the Prophet ﷺ used to be asked about the day of Sacrifices at Minā, he would say: "There is no harm (in the order in which you perform the rites)." A man asked him, saying: "I got my head shaved before I slaughtered (the sacrificial animal)." He (the Holy Prophet) said: "Slaughter (now), and there is no harm." Another man said: "I threw pebbles after the evening." He (Holy Prophet) said: "There is no harm (in what you have done)." [224]

Ch. 132: Giving a verdict while riding an animal near the Jamrah

1736 'Abdullāh ibn 'Amr reported that the Messenger of Allāh ﷺ stopped during the Farewell Pilgrimage and people asked him questions. A man said: "I did not know, and I got my head shaved before slaughtering." He said: "Slaughter (now), and there is no harm." Another man came and said: "I did not know, and I made the sacrifice before throwing pebbles." He said: "Throw (the pebbles now), and there is no harm." So, on that day, whenever he was asked about anything, as to which comes before and which comes after, he said: "Do it (now), and there is no harm." [225]

1737 'Abdullāh ibn 'Amr ibn al-'Āṣ reported that he witnessed the Prophet ﷺ on the day of Sacrifices delivering the sermon, a man stood up and said: "I thought this act was to be done before that act." Then another one stood up and said: "I thought that act was to be done before this act. I shaved my head before making the sacrifice, and I made the sacrifice before throwing the pebbles." People asked similar questions. The Prophet ﷺ said: "Do it (now), and there is no harm" for all of the questions. So, on that day, whenever he was asked about anything, he said: "Do it (now), and there is no harm." [226]

1738 'Abdullāh ibn 'Amr ibn al-'Āṣ said: The Messenger of Allāh ﷺ stopped while on his she-camel. Then he (the reporter reporting from 'Abdullāh) completed the narration (as given above).

Ch. 133: Delivering a *khuṭbah* during the days at Minā

1739 Ibn 'Abbās reported that the Messenger of Allāh ﷺ addressed people on the day of Sacrifices and said: "O people, Which day is this?" They

---

[224] H. 1734 and h. 1735 are both repetitions of h. 84. See also h. 1721 to h. 1723.

[225] This is a repetition of h. 83 with slight differences. Whereas in h. 83 it says that the Holy Prophet stopped during the Farewell Pilgrimage "at Minā for people who had something to ask him", here it only says: "and people asked him questions."

[226] This again is a repetition of h. 83, but with much difference in wording.

said: "The Sacred Day." He asked: "Which city is this?" They said: "The Sacred City." He asked: "Which month is this?" They said: "The Sacred Month." He said:

> "Then remember, your blood and your wealth and your honour are sacred to one another as this day of yours is sacred, in this (sacred) city of yours, in this (sacred) month of yours."

He repeated this several times. Then he raised his head and said:

> "O Allāh! Have I conveyed (Your message)? O Allāh! Have I conveyed (Your message)?"

Ibn ʿAbbās said: I swear by Allāh, in Whose hand is my life, this is his will for his *Ummah*. Those who are present must convey it to those who are absent — (the Holy Prophet said:) "Do not return to unbelief after me by striking off necks of one another." [227]

1740 Ibn ʿAbbās said: I heard the Prophet ﷺ delivering the sermon at ʿArafāt.[228]

1741 Abī Bakrah reported: The Prophet ﷺ addressed us on the day of Sacrifices and said: "Do you know which day is this?" We said: "Allāh and His Messenger know best." He remained silent so much so that we thought he might give it another name. He said: "Is this not the day of Sacrifices?" We said: "Yes, it is." He asked: "Which month is this?" We said: "Allāh and His Messenger know best." He remained silent so much so that we thought he might give it another name. He said: "Is this not Dhul Ḥajjah?" We said: "Yes, it is." He asked: "Which city is this?" We said: "Allāh and His Messenger know best." He remained silent so much so that we thought he might give it another name. He said: "Is this not the Sacred City?" We said: "Yes, it is." He said: "Then remember, your blood and your wealth are sacred to one another as this day of yours is sacred, in this (sacred) month of yours, in this (sacred) city of yours, till the day you meet your Lord. Beware: Have I conveyed (the message to you)?" They said: Yes." Then he said: "O Allāh! Be witness. Those who are present must convey it to those who are absent.

---

[227] See h. 67 and the note on it. The Holy Prophet delivered this sermon on the day of Sacrifices. This day is also one of the days at Minā. The last words of this sermon, "Do not return to unbelief after me by striking off necks of one another", are a note of warning because it is an act of disbelief that a Muslim should kill another Muslim. Some of the commentators of Ḥadīth have explained it thus: Do not make fighting among yourselves permissible by declaring one another as disbelievers.

[228] This ḥadīth is not related to the chapter heading because the day of ʿArafāt is not one of the days at Minā.

Some of those to whom it is conveyed might remember it better than those who listened to it. Do not become disbelievers after me by striking off necks of one another." [229]

1742 Ibn 'Umar reported that the Prophet ﷺ said at Minā: "Do you know which day is this?" They said: "Allāh and His Messenger know best." He said: "It is the sacred day. Do you know which city is this?" They said: "Allāh and His Messenger know best." He said: "The Sacred city. Do you know which month is this?" They said: "Allāh and His Messenger know best." He said: "The Sacred month." He then said: "Allāh has made your blood and your wealth and your honour sacred to one another as this day of yours is sacred, in this (sacred) month of yours, in this (sacred) city of yours."

Ibn 'Umar reported: The Prophet ﷺ stopped between the two Jamrahs on the day of Sacrifices during the Pilgrimage which he performed and said: "Today is the day of *al-Ḥajj al-Akbar* (the greatest day of the Pilgrimage)." Then the Prophet ﷺ started saying repeatedly: "O Allāh! Be witness." He said farewell to the people and they said: "This is the Farewell Pilgrimage (*Ḥajjat al-wadā'*)." [230]

Ch. 134: May those who supply water etc. stay at Makkah during the nights at Minā?

1743 Ibn 'Umar reported: The Prophet ﷺ permitted.[231]

1744 Ibn 'Umar reported that the Prophet ﷺ allowed.[232]

1745 Ibn 'Umar reported that Al-'Abbās sought permission from the Prophet ﷺ to stay at Makkah during the nights of Minā, as he used to supply water to the people, so he allowed him.[233]

Ch. 135: Throwing of pebbles at the Jimār[234]

---

[229] This, like h. 1739, is a repetition of h. 67. It contains additional matter.

[230] This is also a repetition of h. 67. It shows that the Holy Prophet bade farewell to people in a manner which indicated that he would not be meeting them here again. Therefore people called it the Farewell Pilgrimage.

[231] See h. 1745 below for the complete report. Here Bukhārī is only showing a different chain of narrators for the report.

[232] See the last footnote, which also applies here.

[233] This is a repetition of h. 1634 with almost the same wording. The Holy Prophet allowed 'Abbās to remain in Makkah to supply water to the people, athough it was the day for staying in Minā.

[234] In each of the rites of the *Ḥajj* there is a physical act which expresses feelings of the heart. For instance, the state of of *Iḥrām*, that is, wearing a special garb which establishes equality of

Jābir said: The Prophet ﷺ threw pebbles on the day of Sacrifices at forenoon and after that (day) he threw pebbles in the afternoon.

1746 Wabarah reported: I asked Ibn 'Umar: "When should I throw pebbles at the Jimār?" He said: "When your imām throws, you also throw." I asked him the question again, and he said: "We used to wait and when the sun declined, we then threw." [235]

Ch. 136: Throwing of pebbles at the Jimār from the midst of the valley

1747 'Abdur Raḥmān ibn Yazīd reported: 'Abdullāh (ibn 'Umar) threw pebbles from the midst of the valley, so I said: "Abū 'Abdur Raḥmān, people throw pebbles from above it." He said: "By Him besides Whom there is no god, this is the place (of throwing) of the one to whom *Sūrah al-Baqarah* (chapter 2, *The Cow,* of the Qur'ān) was revealed." [236]

Ch. 137: Throwing of seven pebbles at the Jimār

Ibn 'Umar reported it from Holy Prophet ﷺ.

1748 'Abdur Raḥmān ibn Yazīd reported from 'Abdullāh (ibn Mas'ūd) that when he reached the big Jamrah (*al-Jamrat al-Kubrā*), he kept the Ka'bah on his left and Minā on his right and threw seven pebbles and said: "The is how he threw, the one to whom *Sūrah al-Baqarah* was revealed." [237]

Ch. 138: One who keeps the Ka'bah on his left side while throwing pebbles at the Jamrat-ul-'Aqabah

1749 'Abdur Raḥmān ibn Yazīd reported that he performed the *Ḥajj* with

---

all, and abstaining from beautifying the body, is expressive of the state of love. Amorous relations between husband and wife are not allowed so that love is shown entirely for God. Making circuits around the Ka'bah, which is known as *Ṭawāf,* expresses the condition of a lover who goes round and round the house of his beloved, looking for the beloved only, and is madly in the greatest anxiety to find him. The running between the Ṣafā and the Marwah manifests the pilgrim's belief that hardships and trials borne in the way of Allāh bring everlasting rewards and blessings, as happened with prophet Ishmael (Ismā'īl) and his mother Hagar (Hājarah). The gathering in the plain of 'Arafāt is symbolic of the unity and equality of all mankind before their Maker. The throwing of pebbles at the Jimār is to indicate keeping a distance from the devil and all evil that he represents. Finally, the animal sacrifice is to show the resolve to sacrifice one's own animal passions.

[235] As in the statement under the chapter heading, to throw pebbles after the sun begins to decline is particular to the remaining days of Minā, except the day of Sacrifices. On that day pebbles are usually thrown in the forenoon before the sacrifice takes place.

[236] 'Abdullāh ibn 'Umar is distinguished for closely following the *Sunnah* of the Holy Prophet. Otherwise, one has discretion in such minor observances, and can throw pebbles from below or above, from the left or the right, or the front.

[237] This is repetition of the end part of h. 1750. 'Abdullāh is 'Abdullāh ibn Mas'ūd.

Ibn Mas'ūd and he saw him throwing seven pebbles at the big Jamrah, keeping the Ka'bah on his left and Minā on his right. Then he said: "This is the place (of throwing) of the one to whom *Sūrah al-Baqarah* was revealed." [238]

Ch. 139: Proclaiming *Allāhu Akbar* while throwing each pebble

Ibn 'Umar reported it from the Prophet 🕮.

1750 Al-A'mash related: I heard al-Ḥajjāj saying at the pulpit: "The *Sūrah* in which the cow has been mentioned (ch. 2 of the Qur'ān), and the *Sūrah* in which the Family of 'Imrān is mentioned (ch. 3), and the *Sūrah* in which women are mentioned (ch. 4)." So I mentioned this to Ibrāhīm, who said: [239]

'Abdur Raḥmān ibn Yazīd told me that he was with Ibn Mas'ūd when he threw pebbles at Jamrat-ul-'Aqabah.[240] He went to the midst of the valley till he reached the tree, he stood in front of it and threw seven pebbles and he proclaimed *Allāhu Akbar* while throwing each pebble. Then he said: "By Him besides Whom there is no god, it is here where stood the one to whom *Sūrah al-Baqarah* was revealed."

Ch. 140: He who throws pebbles at the Jamrat-ul-'Aqabah and then does not stop there

Ibn 'Umar reported it from the Prophet 🕮.[241]

Ch. 141: Having thrown pebbles at the (first) two Jamrahs, to stand on soft level ground facing the Ka'bah[242]

1751 Sālim reported from Ibn 'Umar that he used to throw seven pebbles at the first Jamrah, proclaiming *Allāhu Akbar* while throwing each pebble. Then he would move forward till he reached soft level ground and stand facing the Ka'bah for a long time, and pray with his hands raised. Then he would throw pebbles at the middle Jamrah. Then he would go to the left to the soft

---

[238] This is a repetition of the same part of h. 1750 as in h. 1748.

[239] Al-Ḥajjāj did not mention the names of the chapters, but called each as the chapter in which such and such is mentioned. Ibrāhīm Nakh'ī, when asked by al-A'mash, presented the saying of Ibn Ma'sūd showing that the Companions of the Holy Prophet used the names of these chapters.

[240] *Jamrah* is a place where the pebbles are piled up together and it is the same place towards which these are thrown. Jamrat-ul-'Aqabah is a place towards Makkah at the border of Minā. It was here that the group of Anṣār took the pledge (*bai'at*) of the Holy Prophet during the *Hajj*, which is called the *Bai'at* of 'Aqabah.

[241] This report of Ibn 'Umar occurs in h. 1751 in the next chapter and also in h. 1753.

[242] On the first day, pebbles are thrown at the Jamrat-ul-'Aqabah first of all, and afterwards it is the last of all.

level ground and stand facing the Ka'bah for a long time, and pray with his hands raised. Then he would throw pebbles at the Jamrat-ul-'Aqabah from the midst of the valley. He would not stay there and depart and say: "This is how I saw the Prophet ﷺ doing it." [243]

Ch. 142: To raise hands (for supplication) near the first and the middle Jamrah

1752 Sālim reported that Ibn 'Umar used to throw seven pebbles at the first Jamrah, ...[244]

Ch. 143: To make supplication near the two Jamrahs

1753 Az-Zuhrī reported that when the Messenger of Allāh ﷺ used to throw pebbles at the Jamrah which was near the Minā Mosque, he would throw at it seven pebbles and proclaim *Allāhu Akbar* whenever he threw a pebble. Then he would go ahead, stand facing the Ka'bah, raise his two hands and make supplications, staying there for a long time. Then he would come to the second (middle) Jamrah, throw seven pebbles at it, proclaim *Allāhu Akbar* whenever he threw a pebble. Then he would go down to the left near the stream, and stand facing the Ka'bah, raise his two hands and make supplications. Then he would come to the Jamrah near al-'Aqabah, throw seven pebbles at it, proclaiming *Allāhu Akbar* with each pebble. Then he would leave and did not stay by it.

Az-Zuhrī said: I heard Sālim ibn 'Abdullāh relating similarly from his father, who reported it from the Prophet ﷺ. And Ibn 'Umar used to do the same.[245]

Ch. 144: To apply perfume after throwing pebbles at the Jimār and shaving head, before performing *Ṭawāf al-ifāḍah*

1754 'Ā'ishah said: I perfumed the Messenger of Allāh ﷺ with my own hands when he entered into the state of *Iḥrām* and when he left *Iḥrām* before making the circuits, and she spread her hands.[246]

---

[243] This report describes what Ibn 'Umar used to do, and ends with his statement that this was how he saw the Holy Prophet doing it. See h. 1753, which describes what the Holy Prophet used to do and ends with the statement that Ibn 'Umar used to do the same.

[244] This is a repetition of h. 1751 in almost the same words. From this point onwards, read h. 1751.

[245] Zuhrī belonged to the generation after the Companions (the *Tābi'īn*) and could not report the actions of the Holy Prophet as an eye-witness. Thus it has been explained at the end that Zuhrī's report came via Sālim from his father Ibn 'Umar.

[246] This is a repetition of h. 267 in words like those of h. 1539. Her spreading her hands was to show the position of the hands while the perfume was being applied. Thus applying perfume before performing the *Ṭawāf al-ifāḍah* is allowed.

Ch. 145: Performing farewell circuits of the Ka'bah

1755 Ibn 'Abbās reported: People were ordered that their last act should be to make circuits of the Ka'bah, but a menstruating woman is exempt.[247]

1756 Anas ibn Mālik related that the Prophet ﷺ said *Ẓuhr, 'Aṣr, Maghrib* and *'Ishā'* prayers, then he had a short sleep at al-Muḥaṣṣab. Then he went to the Ka'bah riding and made circuits around it.[248]

Ch. 146: When a woman gets menstruation after making *Ṭawāf al-ifāḍah*

1757 'Ā'ishah reported that Ṣafiyyah bint Ḥuyayy, wife of the Prophet ﷺ, had menstruation. I mentioned it to the Messenger of Allāh ﷺ. He said: "Is she going to delay us?" He was told: "She has already performed *Ṭawāf al-ifāḍah.*" He said: "Then there is no problem." [249]

1758–1759 'Ikrimah reported that people of Madīnah asked Ibn 'Abbās about a woman who has menstruation after performing *Ṭawāf al-ifāḍah.* He said to them: "She can go (from Makkah)." They said: "We cannot accept your word and forsake the word of Zaid." He said: "When you reach Madīnah, you may ask about it." When they came to Madīnah, they enquired about it. Among the people from whom they asked was Umm Sulaim, who told them the report of Ṣafiyyah.[250]

1760–1761 Ibn 'Abbās reported: A menstruating woman is permitted to leave (Makkah) if she has performed the *Ṭawāf al-ifāḍah.*[251] [1761] And

---

[247] See book 6, ch. 27. This report occurs in Muslim as follows: "No one of you should return unless his last act was to make circuits of the Ka'bah" (book: *Pilgrimage,* ch. 67: 'The farewell *Ṭawāf* is obligatory but dropped for one menstruating').

[248] This incident happened on the 13th of the month. Muḥaṣṣab is an open plain between Makkah and Minā. This name is derived from *ḥaṣbah,* which means pebbles. The other name of this plain is al-Abṭaḥ. On the morning of the 14th, the Holy Prophet left for Madīnah after performing *Ṭawāf.*

[249] Here that part of h. 1561 has been repeated which relates to Ṣafiyyah.

[250] Ibn al-Mundhir says that Zaid ibn Thābit and Ibn 'Umar hold the same view as that of 'Umar, that a woman who experiences menses before performing the farewell *Ṭawāf* can perform it after becoming clean and then leave. But it is established from Ibn 'Umar and Zaid that they abandoned this view and only 'Umar retained it. In other words, the view of 'Umar was different from the view of all other Companions together. People who pass a verdict of condemnation against anyone who opposes a generally-held view should ponder over this case.

[251] This is a repetition of h. 329 in almost the same words.

I heard Ibn 'Umar say: "She should not leave." Then I heard him say afterwards: "Surely the Prophet ﷺ has permitted them." [252]

1762 'Ā'ishah reported: We set out with the Prophet ﷺ, intending only to perform the *Ḥajj*. When the Prophet ﷺ reached Makkah, he made circuits of the Ka'bah and (ran between) the Ṣafā and the Marwah. He did not leave the state of *Iḥrām* as he had a sacrificial animal with him. Those of his wives and his Companions who were with him also made circuits, and anyone among them who did not have a sacrificial animal with him left the state of *Iḥrām*.

I had menstruation and we had performed all the rites of our *Ḥajj*. When it was the night of Ḥaṣbah, the night of departure, I said: "O Messenger of Allāh! All your Companions will return after performing both *Ḥajj* and *'Umrah* except me (being deprived of *'Umrah*)." He said: "Did you not make circuits of the Ka'bah at night when we were Makkah?" I said: "No." He said: "Go with your brother to Tan'īm and enter into *Iḥrām* for *'Umrah*, and your meeting point (for joining me) will be such and such a place." So I went with 'Abdur Raḥmān to Tan'īm and entered into *Iḥrām* for *'Umrah*.

Ṣafiyyah bint Ḥuyayy had menstruation. The Prophet ﷺ said: "How strange (*'Aqrā ḥalqā*)! You will delay us. Did you not make circuits on the day of Sacrifices?" She said: "Yes." He said: "There is no harm — depart!"

So I met him (the Holy Prophet) while he was ascending the heights of Makkah and I was descending, or I was ascending and he was descending.[253]

Ch. 147: One who offers *'Aṣr* prayer on the day of departure at al-Abṭaḥ (Muḥaṣṣab)[254]

1763 'Abdul 'Azīz ibn Rufai' reported: I asked Anas bin Mālik: "Tell me something which you had remembered from the Prophet ﷺ as to where he said his *Zuhr* prayers on the day of *Tarwiyah*." He said: "At Minā." I asked: "Where did he say his *'Aṣr* prayer on the day of departure?" He said: "At al-Abṭaḥ." (He added:) "Do as your leaders do." [255]

---

[252] This is a repetition of h. 330 in similar words. This shows that Ibn 'Umar turned away from his first view.

[253] This is a repetition of h. 1561 with difference in wording at some places. See also the footnotes under h. 1561.

[254] A wide plain in a valley is called Abṭaḥ or Baṭḥā'. Here it means that plain which lies between Makkah and Minā. In the next chapter, it has been called Muḥaṣṣab.

[255] This is a repetition of h. 1653 with the same wording, except that in the first question only the *Zuhr* prayer is mentioned. See the footnotes under h. 1653.

1764 Anas ibn Mālik related, relating from the Prophet ﷺ, that he said *Ẓuhr*, *'Aṣr*, *Maghrib* and *'Ishā'* prayers and he had a short sleep at al-Muḥaṣ-ṣab. Then he went to the Ka'bah riding and made circuits around it.[256]

Ch. 148: Al-Muḥaṣṣab (stopping there)

1765 'Ā'ishah reported: It was only a place where Prophet ﷺ stopped because it was convenient for his departure (for Madīnah), meaning al-Abṭaḥ.[257]

1766 Ibn 'Abbās reported: It is not an obligation to get down at al-Muḥaṣ-ṣab. It is only a place where the Messenger of Allāh ﷺ stopped.

Ch. 149: To camp at Dhī Ṭuwā before entering Makkah, and at the stony plain in Dhul Ḥulaifah when returning from Makkah

1767 Nāfi' reported that Ibn 'Umar used to spend the night at Dhī Ṭuwā between the two hills. Then he used to enter (Makkah) from the mount which is at its upper side. And when he used to come to Makkah for *'Umrah* or *Ḥajj*, he would not let his she-camel set down except at the door of the (Sacred) Mosque. Then he would enter it, go to the Black Stone and start (the circuits) from there. Then he would complete seven circuits: three while running and four while walking. When he finished he would pray two *rak'ahs,* and before returning home he would go between the Ṣafā and the Marwah. And when he used to return from the *Ḥajj* or *'Umrah*, he would make his she-camel sit down in that stony plain (al-Baṭḥā') which is at Dhul Ḥulaifah, where the Prophet ﷺ used to set down his she-camel also.

1768 Nāfi' reported: The Messenger of Allāh ﷺ, 'Umar and Ibn 'Umar stayed in al-Muḥaṣṣab. And Nāfi' reported that Ibn 'Umar used to pray *Ẓuhr* and *'Aṣr* in al-Muḥaṣṣab — I (the narrator) think he also mentioned *Maghrib*. Khālid said: I have no doubt about *'Ishā',* and then he had a short sleep, and the same practice is mentioned of the Prophet ﷺ.[258]

Ch. 150: One who camps at Dhī Ṭuwā when returning from Makkah

1769 Nāfi' reported from Ibn 'Umar that when he used to come (to Makkah) he used to stay for the night at Dhī Ṭuwā, and when it was morning he would enter (Makkah). And when he would return, he would pass by Dhī

---

[256] This is a repetition of h. 1756.

[257] It means that stopping at this place was not a rite of the *Ḥajj*.

[258] This is a repetition of h. 1756 with differences and additions.

Ṭuwā and spend the night till morning came. He used to say that the Prophet ﷺ used to do the same.[259]

Ch. 151: Trading during the days of *Ḥajj* and doing business in the markets of the days of Ignorance

1770 Ibn ʿAbbās said: Dhul Majāz and ʿUkāẓ were public markets during the days of Ignorance. When Islām came, people disliked doing business there until the verse was revealed, "It is no sin for you to seek the bounty of your Lord" (the Qurʾān, 2:198), in the days of *Ḥajj*.[260]

Ch. 152: To set off from al-Muḥaṣṣab in the later part of night

1771 ʿĀʾishah reported: Ṣafiyyah had menstruation on the night of departure (from *Ḥajj*), so she said: "I only see that I am delaying you (from proceeding)?" The Prophet ﷺ said: "How strange! Did she perform circuits on the day of Sacrifices?" He was told: "Yes." He said: "So let us depart."[261]

1772 ʿĀʾishah reported: We set out with the Messenger of Allāh ﷺ intending only to perform the *Ḥajj*. When we reached (Makkah and performed the rites of the *Ḥajj*), he ordered us to leave the state of *Iḥrām*. When the night for departure came, Ṣafiyyah bint Ḥuyayy had menstruation. The Prophet ﷺ said: "How strange! I only see that she is going to delay you!" Then he asked: "Did you make circuits on the day of Sacrifices?" She said: "Yes." He said: "Then go."

I (ʿĀʾishah) said: "Messenger of Allāh! I have not yet left the state of *Iḥrām*." He said: "Perform the *'Umrah* from Tanʿīm." So my brother took me to perform the *'Umrah* and we met him (the Holy Prophet) in the darkness of

---

[259] This is a repetition of the last part of h. 1553. According to *Fatḥ al-Bārī*, Dhī Ṭuwā is a place near Makkah.

[260] Dhul Majāz was on one side of ʿArafāt, and ʿUkāẓ was between Nakhlah and Ṭāʾif. The market of ʿUkāẓ used to be held from the 1st to the 20th of Dhul Qaʿdah and then at Majnah till the end of that month. Then from the 1st to the 8th Dhul Ḥajjah it was held at Dhul Majāz. These markets continued to be held under Islām also. The market at ʿUkāẓ was closed in 129 A.H. during the time of the Khawārij and the market of Ḥabāshah was closed in 197 A.H. during the Abbasid period. According to a report in Musnad Aḥmad, the Holy Prophet preached the message of Allāh to gatherings of people at Majnah and ʿUkāẓ for ten years continuously. The Qurʾān has explicitly allowed trading during the *Ḥajj* period, and in fact emphasised its necessity by calling it the "seeking of the bounty of your Lord" (2:198). If, on the one hand, the purpose of the grand gathering of the *Ḥajj* is for spiritual benefits and religious blessings, on the other hand, people are also encouraged to seek worldly benefits from it. In Islām, spiritual and material progress have been placed side by side as is clear from the prayer: "Our Lord! Grant us good in this world and good in the Hereafter" (2:201).

[261] Here that part of h. 1561 has been repeated which relates to Ṣafiyyah.

night.[262] He said: "Your meeting point (for joining me) will be such and such a place."[263]

---

[262] That is, the Holy Prophet was going to perform the *Ṭawāf al-widā'* on the last night and after finishing it he set off for Madīnah early in the morning. This relates to the chapter heading.

[263] This is a briefer repetition of h. 1561. See also h. 1762.

PART 7

Book 26: *Al-ʿUmrah*
The Minor Pilgrimage

In the name of Allāh, the Beneficent, the Merciful

Ch. 1:   The obligation of *ʿUmrah* and its excellence

Ibn ʿUmar said: *ʿUmrah* and *Ḥajj* is an obligation for everyone. And Ibn ʿAbbās said: It (*ʿUmrah*) is in the Book of Allāh with its companion (*Ḥajj*): "And accomplish the *Ḥajj* and the *ʿUmrah* for Allāh" (the Qur'ān, 2 : 196).[1]

1773 Abū Hurairah reported that the Messenger of Allāh ﷺ said: "The *ʿUmrah* after an (earlier) *ʿUmrah* is an expiation of the sins committed (during the time) between the two, and the reward of a *Ḥajj Mabrūr* (Pilgrimage performed with righteousness) is nothing but Paradise." [2]

---

[1] Followers of Imām Mālik and Imām Abū Ḥanīfah consider *ʿUmrah* as an additional virtue but not obligatory. (This is the *ʿUmrah* consisting of entering into the state of *Iḥrām*, making circuits of the Kaʿbah and running between the Ṣafā and the Marwah). However, Imām Shāfiʿī and Imām Aḥmad ibn Ḥanbal consider it obligatory and in support of this view Bukhārī has given this chapter the title: 'The obligation of *ʿUmrah* and its excellence'. Ibn ʿAbbās, supporting this view, quotes the words of the Qur'ān: "And accomplish the *Ḥajj* and the *ʿUmrah* for Allāh" (2 : 196). But the verse in which *Ḥajj* has been made a duty and obligatory, "And pilgrimage to the House is a duty which people owe to Allāh" (3 : 97), does not mention *ʿUmrah* along with *Ḥajj*. Nonetheless, *ʿUmrah* is *Sunnah* and was practised by the Holy Prophet Muḥammad.

[2] Some of the highest acts of virtue expiate sins in the sense that they outweigh the wrongful deeds. This law applies also in this world where we judge a person, who has good qualities as well as some weaknesses, by taking account of them collectively and seeing which are the dominant. However, the true expiation of sins is as described in the Qur'ān in the words: "Surely good deeds take away evil deeds" (11 : 114). When a person does good deeds, his ability to do good is strengthened, and it is natural that when a human faculty is exercised, it develops and becomes strong and at the same time the tendency to do the opposite becomes weaker. In other words, the stronger becomes the power to do good, the weaker will become the power to do wrong. A person who is ready to bear the hardships in the way of Allāh, of forsaking his home, comforts and ease, and does so more than once, as indicated by the words "the *ʿUmrah* after an (earlier) *ʿUmrah*", his inclination towards committing wrong deeds will become weaker and weaker. This is the true expiation or atonement for sins.

Ch. 2: Performing *'Umrah* before *Ḥajj*

1774 Ibn Juraij informed that 'Ikrimah ibn Khālid asked Ibn 'Umar about performing *'Umrah* before *Ḥajj*, and he said: "There is no harm." 'Ikrimah said that Ibn 'Umar said: "The Prophet ﷺ performed *'Umrah* before the *Ḥajj*." [3]

Ch. 3: How many times did the Prophet ﷺ perform *'Umrah*?

1775 Mujāhid reported: I and 'Urwah ibn az-Zubair entered the Mosque (of the Prophet in Madīnah), and there 'Abdullāh ibn 'Umar was sitting near 'Ā'ishah's room, and some people were saying *Ḍuḥā* (forenoon) prayers in the Mosque. So we asked him about their prayer. He said: "It is an innovation." [4] Then we asked him: "How many times did the Messenger of Allāh ﷺ perform *'Umrah*?" He said: "Four times, and one of them was performed in the month of Rajab." We did not like to contradict him.

1776 (Mujāhid continued:) We heard the sound of chewing of *miswāk* by 'Ā'ishah, Mother of the Faithful, coming from her room. 'Urwah said: "O mother, O Mother of the Faithful! Did you not hear what Abū 'Abdur Raḥmān was saying?" She asked: "What was he saying?" We told her that he said that the Messenger of Allāh ﷺ performed *'Umrah* four times, and one of them was in the month of Rajab. She replied: "May Allāh have mercy on Abū 'Abdur Raḥmān! Whenever he (the Prophet) performed *'Umrah*, he (Ibn 'Umar) was with him, and he never performed *'Umrah* in the month of Rajab." [5]

1777 'Urwah ibn az-Zubair reported: I asked 'Ā'ishah. She said: "The Messenger of Allāh ﷺ never performed *'Umrah* in the month of Rajab." [6]

1778 Qatādah reported: I asked Anas: "How many times did the Prophet ﷺ perform *'Umrah*?" He said: "Four — *'Umrah* at Ḥudaibiyah in the month

---

[3] *'Umrah* can be performed at any time of the year. If *Ḥajj* has become obligatory for a person, it is still right for him to perform *'Umrah* before it. According to the ḥadīth in this chapter, it appears that *Ḥajj* had been made obligatory on the Holy Prophet, but he performed *'Umrah* and then the *Ḥajj* in the year 10 A.H. This shows that it is not necessary that *Ḥajj* should be performed immediately after it becomes obligatory, as there is no time limit fixed for it like that for prayer and fasting.

[4] Saying of the forenoon prayer (known as *Ḍuḥā*, or in Urdu as *Chāsht*) is established from the practice of the Holy Prophet. It appears that Ibn 'Umar did not know about it. See h. 1175–1176.

[5] All these four *'Umrahs* are mentioned in h. 1778. Even a man as cautious as Ibn 'Umar made a clear mistake. 'Ā'ishah corrected him, though with due respect.

[6] This is a repetition in brief of h. 1776 just above.

of Dhul Qaʻdah where the idol-worshippers prevented him (from performing *'Umrah*), the *'Umrah* next year in the month of Dhul Qaʻdah according to the peace treaty (of Ḥudaibiyah), the *'Umrah* from al-Jiʻrānah when he distributed the gains, I think from the battle of Ḥunain". I asked: "How many *Ḥajj* (did he perform)?" He said: "One." [7]

1779 Qatādah reported: I asked Anas, and he replied: "The Prophet ﷺ performed *'Umrah* where they (the unbelievers) forced him to return, and the next year the *'Umrah* of Ḥudaibiyah (i.e., according to the terms of the treaty), and another *'Umrah* in the month of Dhul Qaʻdah, and an *'Umrah* with the *Ḥajj*."

1780 Hammām related: He (the Holy Prophet) performed four *'Umrahs,* (and these were) in the month of Dhul Qaʻdah except the *'Umrah* which he performed with his *Ḥajj* — his *'Umrah* of Ḥudaibiyah, the one next year, and the one from al-Jiʻrānah where he distributed the gains from Ḥunain, and the *'Umrah* with his *Ḥajj*.[8]

1781 Abū Isḥaq reported: I asked Masrūq, ʻAṭā' and Mujāhid, and they said: "The Messenger of Allāh ﷺ performed *'Umrah* in the month of Dhul Qaʻdah before he performed *Ḥajj*." And he further said: I heard al-Barā' ibn ʻĀzib saying: "The Messenger of Allāh ﷺ performed *'Umrah* in the month of Dhul Qaʻdah on two occasions before performing *Ḥajj*." [9]

Ch. 4: Performing of *'Umrah* in the month of Ramaḍān

1782 ʻAṭā' reported: I heard Ibn ʻAbbās informing us, saying: The Messenger of Allāh ﷺ asked a woman of the Anṣār — Ibn ʻAbbās did mention her name but I have forgotten it — "What prevents you from performing *Ḥajj* with us?" She said: "We had a camel for fetching water. The father of so-and-so and his son rode it away — meaning her husband and her son — and left one camel to fetch water for us." He said: "When it is Ramaḍān, perform *'Umrah* in it because *'Umrah* in Ramaḍān is equal to *Ḥajj*." Or he (the Holy Prophet) said some words to that effect.

---

[7] The fourth *'Umrah,* which the Holy Prophet performed at the time of the Farewell Pilgrimage, has not been mentioned here, but it has been made clear in the repetitions of this ḥadīth. In h. 1781 it is stated that before performing the *Ḥajj*, he performed *'Umrah* twice in the month of Dhul Qaʻdah. The first *'Umrah* was performed at the occasion of Ḥudaibiyah in 6 A.H., when he was prevented by the unbelievers, but as he had entered into the state of *Iḥrām* it is considered as having been performed. Thus he performed *'Umrah* three times, in 6 A.H., 7 A.H. and 8 A.H., in the month of Dhul Qaʻdah, and the last *'Umrah* along with *Ḥajj* in 10 A.H.

[8] H. 1779 to h. 1781 are repetitions of h. 1778. The repetition in h. 1780 is clearer.

[9] See footnote to h. 1778 above.

Ch. 5: To perform *'Umrah* on the night at al-Muḥaṣṣab or any other day

1783 'Ā'ishah reported: We set out with the Messenger of Allāh ﷺ as the new moon of Dhul Ḥajjah was about to appear, and he said to us: "Whoever of you wishes to enter into the state of *Iḥrām* for *Ḥajj* may do so, and whoever wishes to enter into the state of *Iḥrām* for *'Umrah* may do so for *'Umrah*. If I had not brought the sacrificial animal with me, I would have entered into the state of *Iḥrām* for *'Umrah*." So there were those of us who entered into *Iḥrām* for *'Umrah* and those who entered into it for *Ḥajj*. I was among those who who entered into it for *'Umrah*.

When the day of *'Arafah* came, I was having menstruation. So I complained to the Prophet ﷺ and he said: "Leave your *'Umrah,* undo your hair, comb it and enter into *Iḥrām* for *Ḥajj*." When the night of (stopping at) al-Muḥaṣṣab came, he sent 'Abdur Raḥmān with me to Tan'īm, and I entered into the state of *Iḥrām* for *'Umrah* in place of my (earlier missed) *'Umrah*.[10]

Ch. 6: To perform *'Umrah* from Tan'īm

1784 'Amr ibn Aus said that 'Abdur Raḥmān ibn Abū Bakr informed him that the Prophet ﷺ commanded him to let 'Ā'ishah ride behind him and take her from Tan'īm to perform *'Umrah*.[11]

1785 Jābir ibn 'Abdullāh related that the Prophet ﷺ and his Companions entered into the state of *Iḥrām* for the *Ḥajj* … … and thus she performed the *'Umrah* after the *Ḥajj* in the month of Dhul Ḥajjah.[12]

Surāqah ibn Mālik ibn Ju'shum met the Prophet ﷺ at (Jamrat) al-'Aqabah while he was casting pebbles and he asked: "Is it (the throwing of pebbles) specially for you, O Messenger of Allāh?" He said: "No, it is for all time to come." [13]

Ch. 7: To perform *'Umrah* after *Ḥajj* without a sacrifice[14]

---

[10] The wording here is almost the same as that of h. 317, except that the statement by Hishām at the end in h. 317 does not occur here. See also h. 1560.

[11] See also h. 1560.

[12] Up to this point, this ḥadīth is a repetition of h. 1651 with very slight differences in wording. See h. 1651 for the part of the translation omitted here. It then has the addition referring to Surāqah ibn Mālik ibn Ju'shum and the question he asked the Holy Prophet.

[13] There is a reference to this question of Surāqah in h. 1557: "He (Jābir) then mentioned the incident of Surāqah." See the footnote there.

[14] It means that if *'Umrah* is performed after *Ḥajj* in the same month of Dhul Ḥajjah, then it

1786 'Ā'ishah informed: We set out with the Messenger of Allāh ﷺ as the new moon of Dhul Ḥajjah was about to appear, and the Messenger of Allāh ﷺ said: "Whoever of you wishes to enter into the state of *Iḥrām* for *'Umrah* may do so, and whoever wishes to enter into the state of *Iḥrām* for *Ḥajj* may do so. If I had not brought the sacrificial animal with me, I would have entered into the state of *Iḥrām* for *'Umrah*." So there were those of them who entered into *Iḥrām* for *'Umrah* and those who entered into it for *Ḥajj*.

I had menstruation before entering Makkah. When the day of *'Arafah* came, I was still having menstruation. So I complained to the Messenger of Allāh ﷺ and he said: "Leave your *'Umrah,* undo your hair, comb it and enter into *Iḥrām* for *Ḥajj*." I did so. When the night of (stopping at) al-Muḥaṣṣab came, he sent 'Abdur Raḥmān with me to Tan'īm.

He let her ('Ā'ishah) ride behind him and she entered into the state of *Iḥrām* for *'Umrah* in place of her (earlier missed) *'Umrah*. Thus Allāh made her *Ḥajj* and her *'Umrah* complete. And in none of these was there was any sacrifice, charity or fasting.[15]

Ch. 8: The reward of *'Umrah* is according to hardship borne[16]

1787 Al-Aswad reported that 'Ā'ishah said: "O Messenger of Allāh! People are returning after performing two rites (*'Umrah* and *Ḥajj*), but I am returning with one." She was told (by the Holy Prophet): "Wait till you are clear (of menstruation), then go to Tan'īm, enter into *Iḥrām* and then meet us at such and such place. It (the reward for performing *'Umrah*) is according to what you spend (of effort or money) or your hardship." [17]

Ch. 9: If one leaves after performing *Ṭawāf* for *'Umrah*, can it replace *Ṭawāf al-widā'* (farewell *Ṭawāf*)?

1788 'Ā'ishah reported: We set out in the state of *Iḥrām* during the months of *Ḥajj* towards the sacred precincts of *Ḥajj*. We alighted at Sarif. The Prophet

---

is not essential to sacrifice an animal. Sacrificing an animal is essential only if it is a *tamattu'* (performing *Ḥajj* and *'Umrah* together in different *Iḥrāms*). In a *tamattu'* the *'Umrah* is performed before *Ḥajj*. After performing *'Umrah* the pilgrim leaves the state of *Iḥrām*. If *'Umrah* is performed after *Ḥajj,* it is not *tamattu'*.

[15] Like h. 1783, the wording here is almost the same as in h. 317. There the closing statement ("And in none of these…") is ascribed to Hishām, while here his name is not indicated. The chapter heading is related to this statement. See also h. 1561.

[16] There is no separate rule of reward for the *'Umrah* different from that for other good deeds. The reward for every deed is according to the hardship and devotion undertaken in doing it.

[17] This is repetition of a part of h. 1561 with brevity. The closing statement about reward for doing *'Umrah,* which is related to the chapter heading, is not in h. 1561.

said to his Companions: "Anyone of you who has no sacrificial animal with him and wishes to perform *'Umrah,* he can do so. And anyone who has a sacrificial animal with him, he should not." The Prophet and some of his Companions who could afford it had sacrificial animals with them, so they could not perform (only) the *'Umrah.*

The Prophet came to me and I was crying. He said: "Why are you crying?" I said: "I heard what you said to your Companions. I cannot perform the *'Umrah.*" He said: "What is the matter with you?" I said: "I cannot say my prayers (due to menstruation)." He said: "There is no harm for you. You are from among the daughters of Adam. What is ordained for you is what is ordained for them (i.e., menstruation). Remain in your *Ḥajj.* May be Allāh will grant you the opportunity to perform *'Umrah.*" [18]

She said: I carried on until we came back from Minā and alighted at al-Muḥaṣṣab. He called 'Abdur Raḥmān and said: "Take your sister out of the sacred precincts (to Tan'īm), let her enter into *Iḥrām* for *'Umrah,* then when you both have made circuits of the Ka'bah I will be waiting for you two here." So we came back very late in the night. He asked: "Have you both finished it?" I said: "Yes". Then he ordered his Companions to set off. So people departed, and any who had made circuits of the Ka'bah set off before the morning prayer and proceeded towards Madīnah. [19]

Ch. 10:   To do in *'Umrah* the same as what is done in *Ḥajj*

1789 Ṣafwān ibn Ya'lā ibn Umayyah related from his father: A man came to the Prophet when he was in Ji'rānah. He was wearing a robe with stains of perfume on it or there were yellow stains, and he asked: "What do you order me to do in the *'Umrah?*" So Allāh sent a revelation to the Prophet. He was covered with a cloth and I wished to see (the condition of) the Prophet when revelation was coming to him. Then 'Umar said: "Do you want to see the Prophet when Allāh is sending revelation"? I said: "Yes". He raised

---

[18] Up to this point, this ḥadīth is a repetition of h. 1560 in similar words.

[19] There is some difference in the ḥadīth reports as to where 'Ā'ishah met the Holy Prophet after performing the *'Umrah.* In h. 1561 it is mentioned that 'Ā'ishah was returning after performing *'Umrah* and the Holy Prophet was on his way to perform *Ṭawāf al-widā'* and both met on the way. But here it is mentioned that the Holy Prophet was still at al-Muḥaṣṣab when 'Ā'ishah returned. Now the question is, as also the title suggests, whether 'Ā'ishah performed *Ṭawāf al-widā'* after the *'Umrah* or not? In this repetition where these words occur "So people departed, and any who had made circuits of the Ka'bah set off", Ibn Ḥajar says that correctly it should be: "So people departed, then he made circuits of the Ka'bah and then set off", meaning that the Holy Prophet made *Ṭawāf al-widā'* after 'Ā'ishah had returned. It is clear that 'Ā'ishah should also have returned with the Holy Prophet. Anyhow, the matter is not clear from the way it has been narrated in ḥadīth reports.

a corner of the cloth and I looked at him. He was snoring — and I think he said — like the snoring of a young camel. When he came out of that state, he said: "Where is the one who asked a question about *'Umrah*? Take off your robe, wash off the stains of perfume from you, clean the yellow colour, and do in your *'Umrah* the same as what you do in your *Ḥajj*." [20]

1790 Hishām ibn 'Urwah reported from his father: When I was a boy I asked 'Ā'ishah, wife of the Prophet ﷺ: "What is your view in regard to the word of Allāh, the Blessed, the Most High: 'The Ṣafā and the Marwah are truly among the signs of Allāh; so whoever makes a pilgrimage (*Ḥajj*) to the House or pays a visit (*'Umrah*), there is no blame on him if he goes round them' (2:158)? I see no blame on anyone who does not go round them." 'Ā'ishah said: "No. If it had been what you are saying, then it (the verse) would have been this: 'There is no blame on him if he does not go round them.' This verse was revealed for the Anṣār who used to enter into the state of *Iḥrām* in the name of the idol Manāt which was installed at Qudaid, and they did not consider it right to go between the Ṣafā and the Marwah. When Islām came, they asked the Messenger of Allāh ﷺ about it, so Allāh revealed: 'The Ṣafā and the Marwah are truly among the signs of Allāh; so whoever makes a pilgrimage (*Ḥajj*) to the House or pays a visit (*'Umrah*), there is no blame on him if he goes round them' (2:158)." [21]

Sufyān and Abū Mu'āwiyah added this from Hishām: Allāh does not consider the *Ḥajj* of anyone or his *'Umrah* to be complete without going between the Ṣafā and the Marwah.

Ch. 11: When should the one performing *'Umrah* leave the state of *Iḥrām*?

'Aṭā' reported from Jābir: The Prophet ﷺ commanded his Compa-

---

[20] This is a somewhat different version of h. 1536. The question asked in that ḥadīth was: "O Messenger of Allāh! What do you say about a man who enters into the state of *Iḥrām* for *'Umrah* and he is besmeared with perfume?" Here, it is said before the question: "He was wearing a robe with stains of perfume on it". So the question was relating to that very robe, and the Holy Prophet's answer was that what is required for *Iḥrām* for performing *Ḥajj* is exactly what is required for *Iḥrām* for performing *'Umrah*. Hence he said: "Take off your robe, wash off the stains of perfume." Ṭabarānī in his *al-Mu'jam al-Awsaṭ* has a report that the revelation which came down at that time was: "And accomplish the *Ḥajj* and the *'Umrah* for Allāh" (2:196), and from this the Holy Prophet inferred the command that *Iḥrām* for *Ḥajj* and *'Umrah* should be the same. However, it is also possible that when the question was asked it simply co-incided with the coming of a revelation which need not have been about this question.

[21] This is a briefer repetition of h. 1643 in different words. The chapter heading is derived from the fact that the running between the Ṣafā and the Marwah is a part of both the *Ḥajj* and the *'Umrah*.

nions that they should perform it as *'Umrah* and make circuits, then have their hair trimmed and leave the state of *Iḥrām*.

1791–1792 'Abdullāh ibn Abū Aufā reported: The Messenger of Allāh ﷺ performed *'Umrah*, and we performed *'Umrah* along with him. When he entered Makkah, he made circuits of the Ka'bah, and we made circuits with him. Then he came to the Ṣafā and the Marwah, and we came there with him.[22] We were shielding him from the people of Makkah in case someone shoot an arrow at him.

[1792] A friend of mine (i.e., of the reporter) asked him ('Abdullāh ibn Abū Aufā): "Did he (the Holy Prophet) enter the Ka'bah"? He replied: "No." He then said: "Tell us what he said about Khadījah?" He replied: "He said: Give Khadījah the good news of a house of pearls in Paradise, wherein there will be no noise or distress." [23]

1793–1794 'Amr ibn Dīnār reported: We asked Ibn 'Umar whether a man who has made circuits of the Ka'bah in *'Umrah* but has not gone between the Ṣafā and the Marwah, can have intercourse with his wife. He said: "The Prophet ﷺ came (to Makkah) and made circuits of the Ka'bah seven times, then he said two *rak'ahs* of prayer behind the place of Abraham and went between the Ṣafā and the Marwah seven times" and (he added:) "Certainly you have in the Messenger of Allāh an excellent exemplar" (the Qur'ān, 33:21). [1794] He ('Amr) said: We asked Jābir ibn 'Abdullāh and he said: "He should not approach her (for sexual intercourse) before going between the Ṣafā and the Marwah." [24]

1795 Abū Mūsā al-Ash'arī reported: I went to the Prophet ﷺ when he was at al-Baṭḥā' where he was staying. He asked: "Have you performed the *Ḥajj*?" I said: "Yes." He asked: "For what purpose did you enter into the state of *Iḥrām*?" I said: "I entered into *Iḥrām* for the same purpose as the Prophet ﷺ." He said: "You have done well. Make circuits of the Ka'bah and (run between) the Ṣafā and the Marwah. Then exit the state of *Iḥrām*." So I made circuits of the Ka'bah and (ran between) the Ṣafā and the Marwah. Then I went to a woman of the Banū Qais, and she took out lice from my hair. Then I entered into *Iḥrām* for *Ḥajj*. I used to give this ruling till it came to the Caliphate of 'Umar. He ('Umar) said: "If we act upon the Book of Allāh, it

---

[22] The chapter heading is taken from this. This is a repetition of h. 1600 in more detail.

[23] This ḥadīth occurs in the book 'Merits of the Anṣār', ch. 'Marriage of the Prophet ﷺ with Khadījah and her excellence', h. 3819.

[24] This is a repetition of h. 1623 in slightly different words.

orders us to complete it, but if we act upon the word of the Prophet ﷺ, then he did not leave his *Iḥrām* until the sacrifice was completed." [25]

1796 'Abdullāh, slave of Asmā', daughter of Abū Bakr, related that he used to hear Asmā', whenever she used to pass by al-Ḥajūn, saying: "May Allāh bless Muḥammad. We alighted here with him and in those days we used to have light luggage, few animals for us to ride upon, and little provisions. I, my sister 'Ā'ishah, az-Zubair, and such and such other persons performed *'Umrah*. When we touched the Ka'bah, we left the state of *Iḥrām*. Then we entered into *Iḥrām* for the *Ḥajj* in the evening." [26]

Ch. 12: What to proclaim when returning from *Ḥajj* or *'Umrah* or military expedition?

1797 'Abdullāh ibn 'Umar reported that when the Messenger of Allāh ﷺ used to return from a military expedition or *Ḥajj* or *'Umrah*, he used to proclaim *Allāhu Akbar* (Allāh is the Greatest) three times on any high ground (which would come on the way). Then he would recite: "There is none worthy of worship except Allāh. He is the One. He has no partner. His is the Kingdom and all praise is due to Him, and He has power over all things. We are returning, repenting, worshipping, prostrating before our Lord, praising Him. Allāh made true His promise and helped His servant, and it was Allāh alone Who made the armies (of the opponents) to be routed."

Ch. 13: To welcome the pilgrims coming to Makkah and three people riding one animal

1798 Ibn 'Abbās reported: When the Prophet ﷺ came to Makkah, some young boys of the Banī 'Abdul Muṭṭalib accorded welcome to Him. He carried one of them in front of him (on the animal) and the other behind him.

Ch. 14: Arriving in the morning

1799 Ibn 'Umar reported that whenever the Messenger of Allāh ﷺ used to travel towards Makkah, he would pray at the mosque of ash-Shajarah, and

---

[25] This is a repetition of h. 1559 in words very similar to its version in h. 1724.

[26] Ḥajūn is the name of a famous mountain in Makkah. This report is either too brief or some confusion has crept into it. Apparently this happened during the Farewell Pilgrimage, but on that occasion 'Ā'ishah, for reason of menstruation, performed *'Umrah* after the *Ḥajj*. In mentioning leaving the state of *Iḥrām* after making circuits of the Ka'bah, there seems to be brevity because there is no mention of running between the Ṣafā and the Marwah.

when he returned he would pray in the middle of the valley of Dhul Ḥulaifah and spend the night there till morning.[27]

Ch. 15:   Returning home in the evening

1800 Anas reported: The Prophet ﷺ never returned home late at night (from a journey). He would return home either in the morning or after the sun declined (i.e., afternoon up to sunset).

Ch. 16:   When reaching one's city, not to arrive home at night

1801 Jābir reported: The Prophet ﷺ forbade returning home at night (from a journey).[28]

Ch. 17:   Making the she-camel run faster on approaching Madīnah

1802 Ḥumaid informed that he heard Anas saying: Whenever the Messenger of Allāh ﷺ returned from a journey and he saw the heights of Madīnah, he would make his she-camel run faster, and if it were another animal, he would spur it on.[29]

It is added from Ḥumaid (in another report): He would spur it on (to run faster) because of his love for Madīnah.

Anas said (through other reporters): Walls of Madīnah (instead of heights of Madīnah).

Ch. 18:   The word of Allāh, the Most High: "And go into houses by their doors" (the Qur'ān, 2:189)

1803 Abū Isḥāq reported that he heard al-Barā' saying: This verse has been revealed regarding us. When the Anṣār used to return from *Hajj*, they never entered their houses through their front doors but from their backs. A man of

---

[27] This is a repetition of the latter half of h. 1533; see also h. 484. Dhul Ḥulaifah was a halting place where travellers would spend the night and leave for Madīnah in the morning. They would usually reach Madīnah in day time.

[28] The details given in these short chapters are not meant to put people to hardship but are instructions according to the needs of the time. Forbidding people from returning home at night from a journey was most probably to avoid inconvenience to those at home who would have to stay awake till late. In those times people could start their journeys whenever they wanted, so they could plan their arrival time at the destination. In modern times, however, one often has to follow the timetables of public transport such as railway trains or planes. It may be noted, though, that in big cities train arrivals are not allowed during the night, due to the same considerations of convenience as indicated by these ḥadīth reports.

[29] It is natural near the end of a journey to be excited to reach home as quickly as possible.

the Anṣār came and entered through its front door, and he was reviled for it. So this verse was revealed: "And it is not righteousness that you enter the houses by their backs, but he is righteous who keeps his duty. And go into houses by their doors" (2:189).[30]

Ch. 19:   Journey is a kind of torment (*'adhāb*)

1804 Abū Hurairah reported from the Prophet ﷺ that he said: "Journey is a kind of torment. It deprives you of eating, drinking and sleeping. When a (journeying) person completes his work, he should make haste in returning to his home." [31]

Ch. 20:   When a traveller is hastening in his journey to return to his home as soon as possible

1805 Zaid ibn Aslam reported that his father said: I was with 'Abdullāh ibn 'Umar on the way to Makkah when the news reached him that Ṣafiyyah bint Abū 'Ubaid was very ill. So he speeded up his journey until it was after the disappearance of evening twilight, and then he camped, and said the *Maghrib* and *'Ishā'* prayers, combining the two. Then he said: "I have seen that when the Prophet ﷺ had to hasten in a journey, he would delay the *Maghrib* prayer, combining the two (i.e., the *Maghrib* with the *'Ishā'* prayer)." [32]

---

[30] It was a custom not only among the Anṣār but also other Arabs that they would enter their homes by the back door when they returned from *Ḥajj* or a journey. All such superstitious traditions and customs were abolished by Islām.

[31] Considering the difficulties and inconveniences which are borne during travelling, it has been regarded as a kind of punishment, but travelling has never been prohibited. Of course, it has been advised that there should be a purpose for undertaking a journey, and when it is accomplished, one should return at the earliest.

[32] In this report, only that part of h. 1092 has been repeated, in different wording, which mentions that Ibn 'Umar received news about his wife's illness.

Book 27: *Al-Muḥṣar*
One prevented from Pilgrimage

In the name of Allāh, the Beneficent, the Merciful

Ch. 1: Pilgrim who is prevented from Pilgrimage, and compensation for hunting (during *Ḥajj*)

The word of Allāh: "But if you are prevented (*uḥṣir-tum*), (send) whatever offering is easy to obtain; and do not shave your heads until the offering reaches its destination" (2:196). And ʿAṭāʾ said: Anything which prevents is called *iḥṣār*.[1]

Ch. 2: When one going for *ʿUmrah* is prevented

1806 Nāfiʿ reported that when ʿAbdullāh Ibn ʿUmar set out for Makkah to perform *ʿUmrah* during the (days of the) conflict, he said: "If I am prevented from reaching the Kaʿbah, I will do what we did when we were with the Messenger of Allāh ﷺ." So he entered into the state of *Iḥrām* for *ʿUmrah* because the Messenger of Allāh ﷺ had entered into the state of *Iḥrām* for *ʿUmrah* in the year of (the Truce of) Ḥudaibiyah.[2]

1807–1808 Nāfiʿ reported that ʿUbaidullāh ibn ʿAbdullāh and Sālim ibn ʿAbdullāh both informed him that they talked to ʿAbdullāh ibn ʿUmar during the days when the (opposing) army had attacked Ibn Zubair, and said: "There is no harm for you if you do not perform *Ḥajj* this year. We fear that some obstacle may intervene between you and the Kaʿbah." He (ʿAbdullāh ibn ʿUmar) said: "We set out with the Messenger of Allāh ﷺ and the disbelievers of the Quraish became an obstacle for (us to reach) the Kaʿbah. So the Prophet ﷺ sacrificed his sacrificial animal and had his head shaved. I make you my witnesses that I have made *ʿUmrah* obligatory on me. If Allāh wills, I will go. If the way is clear between me and the Kaʿbah, I will make circuits, but if

---

[1] What is meant is that the term *iḥṣār* is applied to anything, whether an enemy or an illness or some other strong reason, which prevents a person from reaching the sacred precincts of Makkah. According to the lexicon too, *iḥṣār* has a wide meaning. It occurs in the verse quoted in the form *uḥṣir-tum,* "you are prevented". The word *muḥṣar* is its passive participle ('one who is prevented').

[2] This is a very brief repetition of h. 1640.

there is an obstacle between me and the Ka'bah, then I shall do as the Prophet ﷺ did and I was with him."

So he entered into the state of *Iḥrām* for *'Umrah* from Dhul Ḥulaifah. Then he went on for a while and said: "The matter of both (the *'Umrah* and the *Ḥajj*) is the same. I make you my witnesses that I have made the *Ḥajj* along with my *'Umrah* obligatory for me." So he did not leave the state of *Iḥrām* till the day of Sacrifices and made the sacrifice. And he used to say: "One should not leave the state of *Iḥrām* until making the circuits once on the day of entering Makkah."

[1808] Nāfi' reported that some sons of 'Abdullāh (ibn 'Umar) said to him: "If you stay (at home) this year." [3]

1809 'Ikrimah reported that Ibn 'Abbās said: The Messenger of Allāh ﷺ was prevented (from *'Umrah*). So he had his head shaved, and had sexual relations with his wives, and sacrificed his sacrificial animal, and next year he performed *'Umrah*.

Ch. 3:   Being prevented from performing *Ḥajj* [4]

1810 Sālim informed that Ibn 'Umar used to say: "Is the *Sunnah* of the Messenger of Allāh ﷺ not sufficient for you? If one of you is prevented from performing *Ḥajj*, he should make circuits of the Ka'bah and (run) between the Ṣafā and the Marwah. After that everything (which is not allowed during *Ḥajj*) will become permissible. He should perform *Ḥajj* next year and make sacrifice or fast if he cannot find (i.e., afford) a sacrificial animal." [5]

Ch. 4:   Making the sacrifice before shaving the head when prevented

1811 Al-Miswar reported that the Messenger of Allāh ﷺ made the sacrifice before having his head shaved and commanded his Companions to do the same.[6]

---

[3] By "some sons" are meant 'Ubaidullāh and Sālim as mentioned at the beginning of h. 1807 above. The sons may also have used these words in their advice to him.

[4] The command as to what to do in case of *iḥṣār*, or being prevented, is the same whether for *Ḥajj* or for *'Umrah*, and is clear from the Qur'ān, which Imām Bukhārī has quoted at the very start of this Book.

[5] 'Abdullāh ibn 'Abbās gave the verdict that one can leave the state of *Iḥrām* if it was entered on condition that in case of being prevented one would leave this state. Ibn 'Umar has here, by presenting the practice of the Holy Prophet, contradicted this view as he did not stipulate such a condition before going to Ḥudaibiyah.

[6] This is a small part of a long ḥadīth, h. 2731–2732, which occurs in Book 54, *Ash-shurūt* ('Conditions'), where details of the Truce of Ḥudaibiyah have been mentioned.

1812 Nāfi' related that 'Ubaidullāh and Sālim talked to Ibn 'Umar and he said: "We set out for *'Umrah* with the Prophet ﷺ, but disbelievers of the Quraish became an obstacle for (us to reach) the Ka'bah. So the Messenger of Allāh ﷺ sacrificed his sacrificial animal and had his head shaved." [7]

Ch. 5: Those who say: The one prevented is not required to do substitution (i.e., perform another in place of it)[8]

Ibn 'Abbās reported that substitution is only necessary for him who invalidates his *Hajj* by indulging in some sensual pleasure. As to the one who is prevented by a valid excuse, or other reason, he must leave the state of *Ihrām* and there is no substitution (to perform later on). If he has a sacrificial animal with him and he is prevented, he should sacrifice it if he cannot send it. But if he can send it, he should not leave the state of *Ihrām* until the sacrifice reaches its destination.

Imām Mālik and others say: He should sacrifice his sacrificial animal and have his head shaved head wherever he is, and there is no substitution required of him, because the Prophet ﷺ and his Companions sacrificed at Hudaibiyah, had their heads shaved and emerged from the state of *Ihrām* in all things without performing *Tawāf* and without the sacrifice reaching the Ka'bah. Again, it has not been mentioned that the Prophet ﷺ ordered anyone to do anything in substitution nor to perform it again. And Hudaibiyah was outside the sacred precincts.

1813 Nāfi' reported that when 'Abdullāh Ibn 'Umar set out for Makkah to perform *'Umrah* during the (days of the) conflict, he said: "If I am prevented from reaching the Ka'bah, I will do what we did when we were with the Messenger of Allāh ﷺ." So he entered into the state of *Ihrām* for *'Umrah* because the Prophet ﷺ had entered into the state of *Ihrām* for *'Umrah* in the year of (the Truce of) Hudaibiyah.[9]

Then 'Abdullāh ibn 'Umar considered his affair and said: "The case of both (*'Umrah* and *Hajj*) is nothing but the same." He then turned towards his companions and said: "The case of both is nothing but the same. So I make

---

[7] This is a very brief repetition of h. 1640, as in cases of h. 1806 and h. 1807–1808.

[8] In other words, if one has been prevented from performing *Hajj,* it is not essential to perform it again. It is a different case if a person can afford it. In case of *'Umrah,* as it is not obligatory, if one is prevented there is no requirement to perform it later. The *'Umrah* performed in 7 A.H., and which is called the delayed *'Umrah* (*'Umrat-ul-Qadā'*), was according to the agreement entered into at Hudaibiyah in 6 A.H. that the Muslims, prevented from *'Umrah* on that occasion, would be allowed to perform *'Umrah* the next year. Many of the people who had gone in 6 A.H. did not go for *'Umrah* in 7 A.H. when it was allowed.

[9] In this repetition of h. 1640, up to this point the words are as in h. 1806.

you witnesses that I have made *Ḥajj* obligatory for me with the *'Umrah.*" Then he made one *Ṭawāf* for both, and considered that to be sufficient, and he made the sacrifice.

Ch. 6:   The word of Allāh: "Then whoever among you is sick or has an ailment of the head, (he may effect) a compensation by fasting or charity or sacrificing" (the Qur'ān, 2:196). He has discretion (to do any one of these) and as regards fasting, it is for three days.

1814 Ka'b ibn 'Ujrah reported that the Messenger of Allāh ﷺ said to him: "Perhaps your lice are troubling you." He said: "Yes, O Messenger of Allāh." The Messenger of Allāh ﷺ said: "Have your head shaved, and fast for three days or feed six needy persons or sacrifice a she-goat." [10]

Ch. 7:   The word of Allāh: "...or charity..." (the Qur'ān, 2:196). It means feeding six needy persons.

1815 Ka'b ibn 'Ujrah related: The Messenger of Allāh ﷺ was standing with me at Ḥudaibiyah and lice were falling off my head. He said: "The lice are troubling you." I said: "Yes." He said: "Have your head shaved" or he said: "Have (it) shaved." He (Ka'b) added: This verse was revealed about my case: "Then whoever among you is sick or has an ailment of the head", to the end. So the Prophet ﷺ said: "Fast for three days or give charity of one *faraq* (weight of grain) between six persons, or make a sacrifice of whatever you can." [11]

Ch. 8:   To give half a *ṣā'* of food as compensation (*fidyah*)

1816 'Abdullāh ibn Ma'qil reported: I was sitting with Ka'b ibn 'Ujrah and I asked him about *fidyah*. He said:

It was revealed for my case specially, and it is for you a general rule. I was taken to the Messenger of Allāh ﷺ and lice were falling from my head over my face. He (the Prophet): "I did not think that your affliction has reached the stage that I see" or he said: "I did not think that your hardship has reached the stage that I see". "Do you have a she-goat (for sacrifice)?" I said: "No." He said: "Fast for three days or feed six needy persons, each person to be given half a *ṣā'* (of grain)." [12]

---

[10] See h. 1815 for further details. This is an explanation of the words of the Qur'ān: "fasting or charity or sacrificing".

[11] One *faraq,* a measure of weight, is equal three *ṣā'.* One *ṣā'* is 3 kilograms.

[12] This repetition of h. 1815 is in somewhat different words. The subject is the same. Here, instead of one *faraq* between six needy persons, half a *ṣā'* per needy person has been mentioned,

Ch. 9:   Sacrificial animal here means a she-goat

1817 Ka'b ibn 'Ujrah reported that the Messenger of Allāh ﷺ saw him while lice were dropping on his face. He asked: "Are the lice troubling you?" He said: "Yes." So he ordered him to shave his head while he was at Ḥudaibiyah. It was not yet clear to them that they would leave the state of *Iḥrām* as they were hoping to enter Makkah.[13] So Allāh revealed (the verse of) the *fidyah*. Then the Messenger of Allāh ﷺ ordered him to feed one *faraq* (of food) between six needy persons or sacrifice a she-goat or fast for three days.[14]

1818 Ka'b ibn 'Ujrah reported that the Messenger of Allāh ﷺ saw him while lice were dropping on his face. Then it is as above.

Ch. 10:   The word of Allāh: "...there shall be no immodest speech... in the Pilgrimage" (the Qur'ān, 2:197)

1819 Abū Hurairah reported that the Messenger of Allāh ﷺ said: "One who performed *Ḥajj* to this House (Ka'bah) without uttering immodest (or lustful) speech or committing sin, he will return as he was when his mother gave him birth (i.e., in a state of innocence)." [15]

Ch. 11:   The word of Allāh: "...nor abusing, nor altercation in the Pilgrimage" (the Qur'ān, 2:197)

1820 Abū Hurairah reported that the Messenger of Allāh ﷺ said: "One who performed *Ḥajj* to this House (Ka'bah) without uttering immodest (or lustful) speech or committing sin, he will return as he was on the day when his mother gave him birth (i.e., in a state of innocence)." [16]

---

which is the same amount as in h. 1815. Whatever is available for sacrifice, it can be given. Here the sacrifice of a she-goat has been mentioned.

[13] This shaving of the head was not because they were leaving the state of *Iḥrām* due to being prevented from entering Makkah, but because of the problem with his head lice. They were still hoping to reach Makkah to perform the *'Umrah*. Thus the order to Ka'b ibn 'Ujrah to fast or give in charity and sacrifice was not due to *iḥṣār* or prevention from entering Makkah.

[14] This again is a repetition of h. 1815.

[15] This is a repetition of h. 1521 in almost the same words.

[16] This again is a repetition of h. 1521 in almost the same words.

Book 28: *Jazā' aṣ-Ṣaid*
Penalty for hunting (in *Iḥrām*)

In the name of Allāh, the Beneficent, the Merciful

Ch. 1: The Word of Allāh:

"O you who believe, do not kill game while you are on pilgrimage (*ḥurum,* or in the state of *Iḥrām*). And whoever among you kills it intentionally, the compensation *(jazā'* or penalty) of it is the like of what he killed, from the cattle, as two just persons among you judge, as an offering to be brought to the Ka'bah, or the expiation of it is the feeding of the poor or equivalent of it in fasting, that he may taste the unwholesome result of his deed. Allāh pardons what happened in the past. And whoever returns (to it), Allāh will punish him. And Allāh is Mighty, Lord of retribution. Lawful to you is the game of the sea and its food, a provision for you and for the travellers, and the game of the land is forbidden to you so long as you are in *Iḥrām,* and keep your duty to Allāh, to Whom you shall be gathered" (the Qur'ān, 5:95–96).[1]

Ch. 2: When a person not in *Iḥrām* hunts and gives it as gift to one in the state of *Iḥrām,* the latter should eat it

Ibn 'Abbās, Anas and others did not consider slaughtering of such an animal to be wrong which is not killed in hunting, like a camel, she-

---

[1] To kill game on land while one is in the state of *Iḥrām* has been prohibited. Firstly, it is because the Pilgrimage is a spiritual exercise during which a person tries to moderate and control his physical desires. The desire to eat and drink is the strongest of all, and hunting is one of the most attractive sources of eating meat. Its prohibition aims at bringing this desire within bounds. Secondly, on this occasion people come to Makkah in large numbers from all over the world, and there is an apprehension that hunting may result in human death. Thirdly, the object is to maintain the sanctity of the Ka'bah. By game *(ṣaid)* is meant any kind of wild animal whose meat is lawful to eat. The killing of a dangerous and harmful animal is allowed during the state of *Iḥrām,* nor is there any punishment for killing an animal by mistake or forgetfulness. The "game of the sea" *(ṣaid-ul-baḥr),* mentioned in 5:96, generally meaning fishing, is exempt from restriction because it would take place far from the Ka'bah, at locations where there is no gathering of human beings.

goat, cow, hen, horse etc. It is said: *'adl dhālika* ("equivalent of it" in 5:95) means "similar to it". With the *kasrah* vowel, *'idl* means "equal in weight". *Qiyām-an* means "means of support" (*qiwām-an*).[2] The word *ya'dilūn* means "to make similar".[3]

1821 'Abdullāh ibn Abū Qatādah reported: My father (Abū Qatādah) set out in the year of Ḥudaibiyah and his companions entered the state of *Iḥrām* but he did not. The Prophet ﷺ was informed that an enemy wanted to attack him. So the Prophet ﷺ proceeded.[4] Meanwhile I was with my companions when they started laughing among themselves. ...[5]

Ch. 3:   When those in the state of *Iḥrām* on seeing a game start laughing and those not in *Iḥrām* get the meaning

1822 'Abdullāh ibn Abū Qatādah reported that his father related to him: We proceeded with the Prophet ﷺ in the year of Ḥudaibiyah, and his Companions entered into the state of *Iḥrām* while I did not. We received news that the enemy was at Ghaiqah, so we started marching towards them.[6] Then (on the way) some of my companions saw a wild ass and they started laughing among themselves. I looked and I also saw it. I pursued it on my horse and stabbed it and caught it. I asked others to help me but they refused to help me. We then ate from it.

Then I went to join the Messenger of Allāh ﷺ and we were afraid of being left behind. I would make my horse run fast and then slow. Towards midnight I happened to meet a man from the tribe of Banī Ghifār. I asked him: "Where did you leave the Messenger of Allāh ﷺ?" He said: "I left him at Ta'hin and he was to take afternoon rest at as-Suqyā."[7] So I joined the Messenger of

---

[2] The reference here is to the word *qiyām-an* in the Qur'ān, 5:97: "Allāh has made the Ka'bah, the Sacred House, a means of support (*qiyām-an*) for the people."

[3] The word *ya'dilūn*, in this sense, occurs in the Qur'ān in 6:1 and 6:150. Using this word, polytheists are mentioned in these verses as those who "make (others) equal to their Lord".

[4] Up to this point, the report is from 'Abdullāh, the son of Abū Qatādah, and then it continues in the words of his father. In h. 1822 the entire report is from Abū Qatādah himself. Although h. 1821 has the form of a *mursal* report, a report by someone from the generation after the Companions (i.e., not a contemporary of the Holy Prophet), it is reported absolutely from his father, as can be seen from its other versions.

[5] This report is a repetition of h. 1822, but has a different opening which is shown here. After the words "laughing among themselves", it gives the same account as h. 1822 does after the same point, with only verbal differences. It is omitted here.

[6] The Holy Prophet instructed a group to proceed along the coast because he received information that the enemy was present in the valley of Ghaiqah.

[7] Ta'hin and as-Suqyā are names of two places between Makkah and Madīnah. The word

Allāh ﷺ and, coming to him, I said: "O Messenger of Allāh, your Companions have sent me and they send you their greetings, and (call for) the mercy of Allāh and His blessings upon you, and they were afraid that the enemy might cut them off from you, so wait for them." So he did that. Then I said: "O Messenger of Allāh, we hunted a wild ass and we have some of its meat left over." The Messenger of Allāh ﷺ said to his Companions: "Eat", while they were in the state of *Iḥrām*.

Ch. 4: One in the state of *Iḥrām* should not help one not in *Iḥrām* to hunt game

1823 Abū Qatādah said: We were with the Prophet ﷺ at al-Qāḥah,[8] which is at three stages of journey from Madīnah. (In another report) We were with the Prophet ﷺ at al-Qāḥah, and some of us were in the state of *Iḥrām* and others were not. Suddenly I saw my companions showing something to one another. So I looked and it was a wild ass — he meant his whip fell down (and he asked them to help him). They said: "We cannot help you at all as we are in the state of *Iḥrām*." [9] So I got down and picked it up. Then I went to the ass from behind a hillock and slaughtered it and took it to my companions. Some of them said: "Eat it", but some said: "Do not eat it." I went to the Prophet ﷺ who was ahead of us and I asked him. He said: "Eat it, it is lawful." [10]

Ch. 5: One in the state of *Iḥrām* should not point towards game so that one not in the state of *Iḥrām* should hunt it

1824 'Abdullāh ibn Abū Qatādah informed that his father informed him that the Messenger of Allāh ﷺ set off for *Ḥajj* and they (his Companions) went with him. He sent a group of them, including Abū Qatādah, saying: "Take the route by the coast of the sea until we meet again." So they took the route by the coast of the sea. When they returned, they entered into the state of *Iḥrām* but Abū Qatādah did not. While they were proceeding, they saw wild asses. Abū Qatādah attacked the wild asses and killed a female one. They all got down and ate from its meat, but (then) they said: "How can we eat the meat of game while we are in the state of *Iḥrām?*" So we carried what remained of its meat. When they came to the Messenger of Allāh ﷺ, they said:

---

qā 'il here ("take rest") is from *qailūlah* (afternoon nap) and the meaning is that he would take rest in the afternoon at as-Suqyā.

[8] Qāḥah is one mile from as-Suqyā.

[9] The heading of the chapter is taken from these words that they did not even help him in picking up his whip.

[10] This is a briefer repetition of h. 1822, with difference in wording.

"O Messenger of Allāh, we were in the state of *Iḥrām* and Abū Qatādah was not. We saw wild asses and Abū Qatādah attacked them and killed a female one. We got down and ate from its meat. Then we said: How can we eat the meat of game while we are in the state of *Iḥrām?* So we carried what remained of its meat." He (the Messenger of Allāh) said: "Did anyone of you tell him to attack it or (did anyone even) point at it?" They said: "No." He said: "Then eat what remains of its meat." [11]

Ch. 6: When one in the state of *Iḥrām* is given a gift of a living wild ass he should not accept it

1825 Aṣ-Ṣaʿb ibn Jath-thāmah al-Laithī reported that he gave to the Messenger of Allāh ﷺ a gift of a wild ass while he was at al-Abwā' or Waddān, but he returned it to him. And when he (the Holy Prophet) saw signs of disappointment over his face, he said: "We have only returned it to you because we are in *Iḥrām*." [12]

Ch. 7: The kind of animals that can be killed by one in the state of *Iḥrām*[13]

1826 ʿAbdullāh ibn ʿUmar reported that the Messenger of Allāh ﷺ said: "There are five animals the killing of which is not a sin for one in the state of *Iḥrām*." [14]

1827 ʿAbdullāh ibn ʿUmar said that one of the wives of the Prophet ﷺ related to him from the Prophet ﷺ: "One in the state of *Iḥrām* can kill (some animals)."

---

[11] This again is a repetition of h. 1822. The opening statement, that the Holy Prophet "set off for *Ḥajj*", is due to carelessness because the incident relates to setting off for the *'Umrah* of Ḥudaibiyah. The mention at the end, that the Holy Prophet asked them if they told a person not in the state of *Iḥrām* to attack it or even pointed him towards it, and they said they did not, is what gives the heading to this chapter.

[12] Abwā' is the name of a mountain and Waddān is the name of a place. It seems that Ṣaʿb hunted the game to present it to the Holy Prophet, or that it being sent alive to him at least created the impression that it was hunted for him, as it is mentioned in some reports that Ṣaʿb sent a portion of its meat to the Holy Prophet and he and his Companions ate it. It seems most likely that after it was sent alive and returned, Ṣaʿb slaughtered it himself, ate from it, and sent a part to the Holy Prophet which he ate.

[13] It is evident that the prohibition, "Do not kill game while you are on pilgrimage" (5 : 95), is only regarding those animals whose meat is lawful. The prohibition does not extend to animals whose meat is not lawful and who can be harmful.

[14] This and h. 1827 are brief repetitions of h. 1829. The names of the five animals are not mentioned here.

1828 'Abdullāh ibn 'Umar said that Ḥafṣah said that the Messenger of Allāh ﷺ: said: "There are five animals that it is not a sin for one (in the state of *Iḥrām*) to kill: the crow, the kite, the mouse, the scorpion and the rabid dog."[15]

1829 'Ā'ishah reported that the Messenger of Allāh ﷺ said: "There are five animals all of which are dangerous (*fāsiq*)[16] and should be killed even in the sacred precincts (*Ḥaram*): the crow, the kite, the scorpion, the mouse and the rabid dog."

1830 'Abdullāh (ibn Mas'ūd) reported: We were with the Prophet in a cave at Minā when *Al-Mursalāt* (ch. 77 of the Qur'ān) was revealed to him. He was reciting it and I was learning it from his mouth and his mouth was fresh with it, when suddenly a snake appeared in front of us. The Prophet ﷺ said: "Kill it." We hastened to kill it but it escaped. Then the Prophet ﷺ said: "It escaped harm from you just as you escaped harm from it."

Abū 'Abdullāh (Bukhārī) said: We inferred from it that although Minā is in the *Ḥaram* (sacred precincts) they saw nothing wrong in killing the snake.[17]

1831 'Ā'ishah, wife of the Prophet ﷺ, reported that the Messenger of Allāh ﷺ called the lizard *fawaisiq* (harmful) but I have not heard him ordering its killing.[18]

Ch. 8: No tree should be cut down in the Sacred Precincts

Ibn 'Abbās reported from the Prophet ﷺ: "Not a thorn of it should be cut down."

1832 Abū Shuraiḥ al-'Adawī reported that he said to 'Amr ibn Sa'īd when he was sending armies to Makkah (to fight 'Abdullāh ibn Zubair): "Permit me, O chief, I will relate to you a saying which came from the Messenger of Allāh ﷺ the day after the conquest of Makkah. My ears heard it, my heart preserved it and my eyes saw him when he said it. He praised Allāh and eulogised Him, and then said:

---

[15] This is again a repetition of h. 1829, with some difference in wording.

[16] According to Ibn Athīr they have been called *fāsiq*, or deviators from the right path, because of their evil. He says that in Ḥadīth a mouse (*fa'rat-un*) has been called *fawaisiqah* (diminutive noun *of fāsiqī*) because of its spoiling things and causing harm. The real meaning of *fisq* (wickedness) shows that these animals have been called *fāsiq* because of their harmfulness.

[17] In the report from Ismā'īl it is stated: "This was the night of 'Arafāt." Thus this incident took place in the sacred precincts while they were in the state of *Iḥrām*.

[18] This ḥadīth also occurs as h. 3306 in the book 'Beginning of Creation', ch. 'The best property of a Muslim', but there, after the above words of h. 1831, the following is added: "Sa'd ibn Abī Waqqāṣ asserted that the Prophet ordered its killing."

'Surely it is Allāh Who has made Makkah sacred, it is not people who have made it sacred. So it is not lawful for a man who believes in Allāh and the Last Day to shed blood in it, nor to cut down any tree. If anyone wants leave (to fight in it) on the basis of the Messenger of Allāh ﷺ fighting in it, tell him: Allāh has certainly permitted His Messenger ﷺ and not permitted you. He permitted me only for a few hours one day, and today its sacredness has returned as it was sacred yesterday. So those who are present must convey this to those who are absent.' "

Abū Shuraiḥ was asked: "What did 'Amr say to you (in reply)?" He said: "('Amr replied) O Abū Shuraiḥ, I know better about it than you. Surely the sacred city does not give protection to a sinner, nor to a fugitive who has murdered or committed a crime (*kharbah*)." *Kharbah* means to create disorder or commit theft.[19]

Ch. 9:   Game in the Sacred Precincts should not be chased

1833 Ibn 'Abbās reported that the Prophet ﷺ said: "Surely Allāh made Makkah a sacred place. It (i.e., shedding blood therein) was not lawful for anyone before me and is not lawful for anyone after me. It was lawful for me only for a few hours one day. None of its shrubs should be uprooted, none of its tree cut down, none of its game chased, and no fallen thing in it to be picked up except by one who makes announcement (to find the owner)." Al-'Abbās said: "O Messenger of Allāh, make an exception for *al-idhkhir* (*idh-khir*, a kind of grass) for (the use of) our goldsmiths and for our graves." So he (the Prophet) said: "Except *al-idhkhir*."

Khālid reported that 'Ikrimah said: "Do you know what is meant by its game not to be chased? It means chasing it out of the shade (where it is taking rest) to occupy its place (yourself)." [20]

Ch. 10   Fighting in Makkah is not permitted

Abū Shuraiḥ reported from the Prophet ﷺ: "Blood must not be shed in it." [21]

---

[19] This is a repetition of h. 104 with only slight variation of wording. At the end the meaning of *kharbah* has been added in the words: *Kharbah* means *baliyyah*, i.e., to create disorder or commit theft. However, it is clearly wrong to use this as justification for invading Makkah.

[20] This ḥadīth is in almost the same words as h. 1349, after which the report from Khālid of what 'Ikrimah said is added. In this addition the meaning of chasing game is explained as driving it away from under shade to take its place yourself. However, the words "none of its game (should be) chased" are general and the chapter heading is derived from them.

[21] This ḥadīth relates to the prohibition of fighting in Makkah, meaning that those who follow

1834 Ibn 'Abbās reported that on the day Makkah was conquered the Prophet ﷺ said: "There is no *hijrah* (after this) but there is *jihād* and intention (of doing good), and when you are called upon to go forth, then go forth. Surely Allāh has made this city sacred from the day He created the heavens and the earth, and it will remain sacred till the Day of Resurrection due to Allāh making it sacred. Fighting in it was never made lawful for anyone before me, and (even) for me it was not lawful except for a few hours of one day. Again (I say), it will remain sacred till the Day of Resurrection due to Allāh making it sacred. Not a thorn of it should be cut down, none of its game chased, no fallen thing in it to be picked up except by one who makes announcement (to find the owner), and none of its shrubs should be uprooted." Al-'Abbās said: "O Messenger of Allāh, make an exception for *al-idhkhir* (*idh-khir*, a kind of grass) for (the use of) our blacksmiths and in our homes." It is reported that he (the Prophet then) said: "Except *al-idhkhir*." [22]

Ch. 11: Cupping for one in the state of *Iḥrām*

Ibn 'Umar cauterized his son and he (the son) was in the state of *Iḥrām*.[23] And such a one can use a medicine which does not contain perfume.

1835 Ibn 'Abbās said: The Messenger of Allāh ﷺ had cupping while he was in the state of *Iḥrām*.

1836 Ibn Buḥainah reported: The Messenger of Allāh ﷺ had cupping in the middle of his head while he was in the state of *Iḥrām* at (the place) Laḥi Jamal.

Ch. 12: Getting married (*tazwīj*) in the state of *Iḥrām*

1837 Ibn 'Abbās reported that the Prophet ﷺ married Maimūnah while he was in the state of *Iḥrām*.[24]

---

the Holy Prophet Muḥammad must not wage war in it. Al-Ṭaḥāwī (the great scholar of Ḥadīth, d. 933 C.E.) has written that if idolaters hold sway over Makkah then Muslims are permitted to fight against them in Makkah and kill them. The report from Abū Shuraiḥ, in h. 104 and just above in h. 1832, clearly states: "…it is not lawful for a man who believes in Allāh and the Last Day to shed blood in it…". However, there are exceptions to this rule for the maintenance of law and peace. The Holy Prophet himself allowed Ibn Khaṭal to be killed on the day of the conquest of Makkah when he was holding on to the cover of the Ka'bah, as stated in h. 1846.

[22] This ḥadīth from the words "Fighting in it was never made lawful for anyone before me", which are related to the chapter heading, is similar to h. 1349. However, the words "and is not lawful for anyone after me" of h. 1349 do not occur in this report.

[23] That is to say, for medical treatment such actions are allowed in the state of *Iḥrām*.

[24] This report by Ibn 'Abbās also occurs in the Book of Expeditions, ch. *'Umrat-ul-Qaḍā'* (h.

Ch. 13:   Prohibition of perfume for a man or a woman in the state of *Iḥrām*

> 'Ā'ishah said: A woman in *Iḥrām* should not wear any clothes dyed in *wars* (a kind of scent) or saffron.

1838 'Abdullāh ibn 'Umar reported that a man came and said: "O Messenger of Allāh, what kind of clothes do you order us to wear in the state of *Iḥrām?*" The Prophet ﷺ said: "Do not wear a shirt, or trousers, or turban, or headgear, except if one does not have shoes he can wear socks (of leather), cutting them off (so they are) below the ankles. And do not wear anything perfumed with saffron or *wars*. And the woman in the state of *Iḥrām* should not cover her face or wear gloves." [25]

1839 Ibn 'Abbās reported: The she-camel of a man, who was in the state of *Iḥrām,* crushed him. His body was brought to the Messenger of Allāh ﷺ,

---

4258) and in the Book of Marriage, ch. '*Nikāḥ* of one in the state of *Iḥrām*' (h. 5114), the latter not mentioning the name Maimūnah. The word used for getting married in these reports is *tazwīj*. This state of *Iḥrām* was for that *'Umrah* which could not be performed. There is a report in Ṣaḥīḥ Muslim that a person while in the state of *Iḥrām* cannot enter into *nikāḥ* (book: 'Marriage', ch. 5). Either this report has to be discarded or the word *nikāḥ* in it has to be taken in its literal sense of sexual relations between husband and wife, and not contracting a marriage.

[25] This report has already occurred in h. 1542. Here the opening is slightly different, after which there is repetition of the contents of h. 134 with variation of wording and word order. The last statement, "And the woman in the state of *Iḥrām* should not cover her face or wear gloves", is an addition here. In some reports it is traced to the Holy Prophet and in others it is attributed to Ibn 'Umar.

Just as it is agreed unanimously that a woman can keep her hands uncovered, which has been allowed in the Qur'ān in the words "except what appears thereof" (24:31), but it is not prohibited to wear gloves in case of need, similarly in this verse of the Qur'ān a woman is allowed to keep her face uncovered, but in case of need she has not been prohibited from covering her face. However, in the state of *Iḥrām* gloves and face covering (*niqāb*) have both been prohibited. Thus Islamic teachings applying to the covering of a woman's hands and her face are the same: both may be kept uncovered or in case of need they may be covered, but neither may be covered in the state of *Iḥrām*. To infer from this ḥadīth that, when not in the state of *Iḥrām*, a woman must cover her face is the same as saying that a woman must wear gloves when she is not in the state of *Iḥrām*. Again, if it is argued that it was because women ordinarily had to cover their faces that they had to be told not to cover the face in *Iḥrām,* this is also like saying the same about the wearing of gloves. This order clearly shows that the Qur'ān never required women to cover their faces or their hands, because if that had been so, the Holy Prophet could not have ordered to the contrary for the Pilgrimage, that on such an occasion where men and women are gathered in great numbers, women should not cover their faces or hands. The reason for the prohibition at the Pilgrimage could only be that a mark of superiority has been forbidden in order to make everyone equal and remove social distinctions, as only the wealthy and affluent among women covered their faces and hands. There were two kinds of face covering, as mentioned in *Fatḥ al-Bārī:* that which covered the lips and chin below the nose and that which covered everything below the eyes. In Arabia the face covering was worn to guard against dusty wind as well as to show a superior social rank.

who said: "Wash him and shroud him but do not cover his head nor bring near him any perfume, for he will be raised (on the Day of Resurrection) in the state of *Iḥrām*." [26]

Ch. 14: Taking of bath by one in the state of *Iḥrām*

Ibn ʿAbbās said: One in the state of *Iḥrām* can go to a public bath. Ibn ʿUmar and ʿĀ'ishah did not see any wrong in scratching the body.[27]

1840 ʿAbdullāh ibn Ḥunain reported: There was a difference of opinion between ʿAbdullāh ibn ʿAbbās and al-Miswar ibn Makhramah at (the place of) al-Abwā'. ʿAbdullāh ibn ʿAbbās said: "A person in the state of *Iḥrām* can wash his head" while al-Miswar said: "A person in the state of *Iḥrām* cannot wash his head." So ʿAbdullāh ibn ʿAbbās sent me to Abū Ayyūb al-Anṣārī. I found him taking bath between two wooden posts while he was screened with a sheet of cloth. I greeted him and he said: "Who is it?" I said: "I am ʿAbdullāh ibn Ḥunain. ʿAbdullāh ibn ʿAbbās has sent me to ask you, how the Messenger of Allāh ﷺ used to wash his head while in the state of *Iḥrām*?" Abū Ayyūb put his hand on the sheet of cloth, and lowered it till his head appeared before me. Then he said to a man who was pouring water on him: "Pour". So he poured water over his head. Then he (Abū Ayyūb) rubbed his head with his hands, bringing them forwards and backwards, and said: "This is how I saw him ﷺ doing it."

Ch. 15: Wearing of socks by one in *Iḥrām* when he does not find shoes

1841 Ibn ʿAbbās said: I heard the Prophet ﷺ delivering a sermon at ʿArafāt (saying) about one in the state of *Iḥrām*: "He who cannot find shoes should wear socks (of leather) and he who cannot find a waist-wrapper (*izār*) should wear trousers." [28]

1842 ʿAbdullāh (ibn ʿUmar) reported: The Messenger of Allāh ﷺ was asked: "What kind of clothes should one in the state of *Iḥrām* wear?" He said: "He should not wear a shirt, or turban, or trousers, or headgear, or clothes

---

[26] This is a repetition of h. 1265. See also h. 1849 and h. 1850.

[27] To take a bath while in the state of *Iḥrām*, whether because of nocturnal emission or to clean or to cool down the body, is in any case perfectly proper. According to Baihaqī, Ibn ʿAbbās was in the state of *Iḥrām* at a place called Juḥfah and he went to a public bath (*hamām*) saying: "Allāh has no need of your dirt and filth."

[28] This is a brief repetition of h. 134.

perfumed with saffron or *wars,* and if he cannot find shoes he can wear socks (of leather), cutting them off until they are below the ankles." [29]

Ch. 16: When one cannot find a waist-wrapper (*izār*), he can wear trousers

1843 Ibn 'Abbās reported: The Prophet ﷺ delivered to us a sermon at 'Arafāt saying: "He who cannot find a waist-wrapper (*izār*) should wear trousers and he who cannot find shoes should wear socks (of leather)." [30]

Ch. 17: Wearing of weapons by one in the state of *Iḥrām* [31]

'Ikrimah said: When there is fear of an enemy, one should wear weapons and give charity (as penance). But none agreed with him regarding giving of charity. [32]

1844 Al-Barā' reported: The Prophet ﷺ wanted to perform *Umrah* in the month of Dhul Qa'dah but the people of Makkah refused to allow him to enter Makkah until he agreed not to bring weapons to Makkah except in their sheaths. [33]

Ch. 18: Entering the Sacred Precincts (*Ḥaram*) and Makkah without *Iḥrām*

Ibn 'Umar entered it while not in the state of *Iḥrām*. And the Prophet ﷺ ordered the state of *Iḥrām* only for those who intend to perform *Ḥajj* or *'Umrah* and he did not mention it for woodcutters etc.

---

[29] This is another brief repetition of h. 134.

[30] This is a variation of h. 1841, omitting reference to "one in the state of *Iḥrām*".

[31] There is a report in Ṣaḥīḥ Muslim from Jābir that he heard the Holy Prophet say: "It is not allowed to any of you to carry weapons in Makkah" (book: Pilgrimage, ch. 'Prohibition of carrying weapons in Makkah without need'). According to h. 966 Ibn 'Umar told Ḥajjāj: "You allowed weapons to enter the Sacred Precincts (of the Ka'bah), whereas weapons were not allowed to enter the Sacred Precincts."

[32] Most probably Bukhārī has considered these reports to relate to times of peace, which is why he has quoted this statement of 'Ikrimah according to which, when there is apprehension of attack by the enemy, the carrying of weapons is allowed. The permissibility of carrying weapons during the *'Umrat-ul-Qaḍā'* (the *'Umrah* allowed to Muslims under the Treaty of Ḥudaibiyah) is shown by the condition that the Muslims were required keep their swords in their sheaths. This *'Umrah* was performed when there was peace due to the Treaty of Ḥudaibiyah, but in spite of the peace agreement the idolaters of Makkah could not be trusted.

[33] This ḥadīth occurs in more detail in the Book of Conditions in h. 2731–2732.

1845 Ibn 'Abbās reported that the Prophet ﷺ fixed Dhul Ḥulaifah as the *mīqāt* for the people of Madīnah, Qarn al-Manāzil for the people of Najd, and Yalamlam for the people of Yaman. These are for them and for all others who come there (from other countries) for *Ḥajj* and *'Umrah*. And whoever lives nearer (to Makkah) than these places, it is from where he starts, so that for the people of Makkah it is Makkah itself.[34]

1846 Anas ibn Mālik reported that the Messenger of Allāh ﷺ entered (Makkah) in the year of victory wearing a helmet on his head. When he took it off, a man came and said: "Ibn Khaṭal is holding on to the cover of the Ka'bah (for refuge)." He said: "Kill him." [35]

Ch. 19:   To enter into the state of *Iḥrām* ignorantly while wearing a shirt

'Aṭā' said: If someone applies perfume or wears a sewn cloth through ignorance or forgetfulness, there is no expiation (i.e., penalty) for him.

1847–1848 Ya'lā reported: I was with the Messenger of Allāh ﷺ when a man came to him wearing a cloak which had spots of yellow colour or something like it. 'Umar used to ask me: "Would you like to see him (the Holy Prophet) when revelation comes to him?" Just then, revelation started coming to him and then this state passed. So he (the Holy Prophet) said: "Do for your *'Umrah* what you do for your *Ḥajj*." [1848] A man bit another man's hand but the latter pulled back his hand and the former's front tooth came off. The Prophet ﷺ disallowed any compensation (for this damage).[36]

---

[34] This is a repetition of h. 1524 with a slight difference in wording, and it has been inferred from it that the Holy Prophet appointed fixed points only for those who intended to perform *Ḥajj* or *'Umrah*. Those not intending to do so enter Makkah without being in the state of *Iḥrām*.

[35] The title of chapter is entering Makkah without being in the state of *Iḥrām* while this ḥadīth says that the Holy Prophet entered Makkah wearing a helmet. This shows that he was not in the state of *Iḥrām* otherwise he would have been wearing the clothing for *Iḥrām*. As to Ibn Khaṭal, there is a report in Ibn Isḥāq that the Holy Prophet appointed him incharge of a district and sent him there along with an Anṣārī and a Muslim slave. He killed the slave for not preparing food on time and became an apostate. A report in Fākihī mentions the Anṣārī being murdered. Perhaps Ibn Khaṭal killed both of them. Anyhow, he was executed in Makkah for committing murder and could not save himself by holding on to the covering of the Ka'bah.

[36] H. 1847 is a brief repetition of h. 1536. In the original report (h. 1536) it is stated that the Holy Prophet asked him to take off the cloak and wash the stains of yellow perfume, but did not order him to pay any compensation or penalty. H. 1848 mentions another incident and that is related to blood-whit. In that incident, compensation for the broken tooth was refused because the man who was bitten was forced to pull back his hand.

Ch. 20:   If one in the state of *Iḥrām* dies at ʿArafāt

The Prophet ﷺ did not order that the remaining (parts of the) *Hajj* should be completed on his behalf.

1849 Ibn ʿAbbās reported: A man was stopping with the Prophet ﷺ at ʿArafāt when he fell down from his mount and broke his neck, or he was crushed by it (and died). The Prophet ﷺ said: "Wash him with water and leaves of the lote-tree and shroud him in two pieces of cloth — or he said, his two pieces of cloth — neither apply perfume to him, nor cover his head, for Allāh will raise him on the Day of Resurrection saying *Labbaika* (i.e., like a pilgrim)." [37]

1850 Ibn ʿAbbās reported: ... and shroud him in two pieces of cloth, do not put fragrance on him, nor cover his head, nor apply perfume to him, for Allāh will raise him ... [38]

Ch. 21:   The *Sunnah* regarding one in the state of *Iḥrām* if he dies

1851 Ibn ʿAbbās reported that a man was with the Prophet ﷺ when his she-camel broke his neck while he was in the state of *Iḥrām* and he died. The Messenger of Allāh ﷺ said: "Wash him with water and leaves of the lote-tree and shroud him in his two pieces of cloth, do not put fragrance on him, nor cover his head, for for he will be raised on the Day of Resurrection saying *Labbaika* (i.e., like a pilgrim)." [39]

Ch. 22:   To perform *Hajj* or fulfil vow on behalf of a deceased, and a man performing *Hajj* on behalf of a woman[40]

---

[37] This is a repetition of h. 1265 in almost the same words, although after the words, "in two pieces of cloth", it is added: "or he said, his two pieces of cloth". It meant that he should be wrapped and buried in the two sheets he was wearing in *Iḥrām*.

[38] This is also a repetition of h. 1265. It begins and ends with the same words as the last ḥadīth h. 1849, but between the words "shroud him in two pieces of cloth" and the ending "for Allāh will raise him ...", there is a difference as shown above.

[39] Again, this is a repetition of h. 1265 with some differences shown above.

[40] There is a difference of opinion on the issue of nominating someone to perform a religious obligation on one's behalf. These obligations are of two kinds: monetary and bodily. *Hajj* is comprised of both kinds. For monetary obligations, the Qurʾān allows nomination. It has enjoined making a will, and in a will the testator can nominate someone as an executor to spend a portion of his property after his death as directed by the testator. Even while alive, a person can depute someone else to spend his wealth for him in charity. It is also possible to spend from the deceased's property according to his wishes even without the existence of a will. Thus, whether the deceased or a handicapped person had made a vow for *Hajj* or not, if that was his intention then *Hajj* can be performed on behalf of that person, and is in fact an excellent deed for which

1852 Ibn 'Abbās reported that a woman from Juhainah came to the Prophet ﷺ and said: "My mother made a vow that she would perform *Ḥajj* but she could not perform it and she died. Can I perform *Ḥajj* on her behalf?" He said: "Yes. Perform *Ḥajj* on her behalf. If your mother had a debt to pay, would you have paid it? So pay the debt which is due to Allāh. He has a greater right that a duty to Him be fulfilled."

Ch. 23:   To perform *Ḥajj* for one who is unable to sit on a mount

1853–1854 Al-Faḍl ibn 'Abbās reported that a woman...[41] [1854] Ibn 'Abbās reported: A woman of the tribe of Khath'am came (to the Holy Prophet) in the year of the Farewell Pilgrimage and said: "O Messenger of Allāh! The obligation from Allāh on His servants to perform the *Ḥajj* has come but my father is very old and is unable to sit on his mount. May I perform *Ḥajj* on his behalf?" He said: "Yes."

Ch. 24:   A woman performing of *Ḥajj* on behalf of a man

1855 'Abdullāh ibn 'Abbās reported: Al-Faḍl was riding behind the Prophet ﷺ when a woman of the tribe of Khath'am came. Al-Faḍl started to look at her and she also looked at him. The Prophet ﷺ kept on turning al-Faḍl's face to the other side. The woman said: "O Messenger of Allāh! The obligation from Allāh has come but my father is very old and cannot keep himself steady on a mount. May I perform *Ḥajj* on his behalf?" He said: "Yes." This happened during the Farewell Pilgrimage.[42]

Ch. 25:   Young boys performing *Ḥajj*

1856 'Abdullāh ibn 'Abbās said: The Prophet ﷺ sent me — or (he said) sent me ahead — with luggage from Muzdalifah (*Jam '-in*) at night.[43]

---

there is reward for both of them. The one performing the *Ḥajj* spent the other's property according to the latter's intentions and by doing so he was enabled to perform the *Ḥajj* himself. According to Ibn 'Umar and Laith, such nomination in the case of *Ḥajj* is not correct. Imam Mālik considers it permissible only if the deceased had made a will for it. The chapter heading refers to a man performing *Ḥajj* on behalf of a woman but the ḥadīth under it mentions a woman performing *Ḥajj* on behalf of a woman. The heading may be inferring that if a woman can perform *Ḥajj* on behalf of a woman, so can a man perform *Ḥajj* on behalf of a woman. See h. 1855 for a woman performing *Ḥajj* on a man's behalf.

[41] H. 1853 is terminated at this point and continues in h. 1854 through a different line of reporting. It is a repetition of h. 1513 without any mention of Al-Faḍl riding.

[42] This is a repetition of h. 1513 without the words "on His servants to perform the *Ḥajj*" after "The obligation from Allāh has come".

[43] This is a repetition of h. 1678. Ibn 'Abbās was not yet an adult at the time.

1857 ʿAbdullāh ibn ʿAbbās said: I was nearly an adult when I came (for *Hajj*) riding on a she-ass, and the Messenger of Allāh ﷺ was leading prayers at Minā. I passed somewhat ahead of the first row and then dismounted, leaving the animal to graze, and joined the people (praying) behind the Messenger of Allāh ﷺ.[44]

In another narration: "…at Minā during the Farewell Pilgrimage."

1858 As-Sāʾib ibn Yazīd reported: I was sent to perform *Hajj* with the Messenger of Allāh ﷺ when I was seven years old.

1859 Al-Juʿaid ibn ʿAbdur Rahmān reported: I heard ʿUmar ibn ʿAbdul ʿAzīz saying to As-Sāʾib ibn Yazīd, and he was sent to perform *Hajj* with the luggage of the Prophet ﷺ.[45]

Ch. 26:   Women performing *Hajj*

1860 Ibrāhīm ibn ʿAbdur Rahmān (ibn ʿAuf) related: ʿUmar in his last *Hajj* allowed wives of the Prophet ﷺ to perform *Hajj* and he sent with them ʿUthmān ibn ʿAffān and ʿAbdur Rahmān ibn ʿAuf (to accompany them).[46]

1861 ʿĀʾishah, Mother of the Faithful, reported that she asked: "O Messenger of Allāh, Should we not join you all in (military) expeditions and *jihād*?" He said: "For you the best and most approved *jihād* is *Hajj*, a *Hajj Mabrūr* (a Pilgrimage of righteousness)." ʿĀʾishah said: "I never missed *Hajj* after I heard this from the Messenger of Allāh ﷺ." [47]

1862 Ibn ʿAbbās reported that the Prophet ﷺ said: "A woman should not travel except with a permissible male relative (*mahram*), nor should a man come to see her unless a *mahram* is present." A man said: "O Messenger of Allāh, I wish to go out with such and such an army and my wife wishes to go for *Hajj*." He said: "Go with her." [48]

---

[44] This is a repetition of h. 76.

[45] It is not mentioned here what ʿUmar ibn ʿAbdul ʿAzīz was saying. In another report it is stated that this was about the age limit for performing *Hajj*. Children were kept with the luggage to avoid inconvenience.

[46] ʿUthmān ibn ʿAffān and ʿAbdur Rahmān ibn ʿAuf were not *mahram* (i.e., permissible male relatives, such as husband, brother or son) for the wives of the Holy Prophet. This shows that a woman can perform *Hajj* with a man who is not *mahram*, even though in this case the women's Pilgrimage was voluntary.

[47] This is a more detailed repetition of h. 1520. It shows that after the death of the Holy Prophet ʿĀʾishah always performed *Hajj*, but it is not mentioned that she was always accompanied by a *mahram*. For *Hajj Mabrūr*, a righteous or virtuous *Hajj* that is accepted by Allāh, see h. 1519 and h. 1520.

[48] It is stated here that a woman should not travel without a permissible male relative (a

1863 Ibn 'Abbās reported: When the Prophet ﷺ returned from his *Ḥajj*, he asked Umm Sinān the Anṣārī: "What prevented you from performing *Ḥajj?*" She said: "Father of so-and-so — meaning her husband — had only two camels. On one he performed *Ḥajj* and the other is used for watering our land." He (the Holy Prophet) said: "'*Umrah* during the month of Ramaḍān is equivalent to *Ḥajj*" or "(is equivalent to) a *Ḥajj* performed with me." [49]

1864 Qaza'ah, slave of Ziyād, reported that he heard Abū Sa'īd, who was in twelve expeditions with the Prophet ﷺ, saying: "There are four things I heard from the Messenger of Allāh ﷺ — or he said: (four things) were related from the Prophet ﷺ — which I liked very much and considered them virtuous:

"A woman should not go on a two-day journey when she does not have her husband or a permissible male relative (*maḥram*) with her." "There is no fasting on two days, Eid-ul-Fiṭr and Eid-ul-Aḍḥā." "There is no prayer after two prayers, (that is) after the '*Aṣr* prayer till the sun sets and after the *Fajr* prayer till the sun rises." "There should be no journey except to three mosques: the Sacred Mosque, and my Mosque and the Aqṣā Mosque." [50]

Ch. 27:   One who makes a vow to go to Ka'bah on foot

1865 Anas reported that the Prophet ﷺ saw an old man walking with the support of his two sons. He asked: "What has happened to him?" People said: "He took a vow to go on foot (to the Ka'bah)." He (the Prophet) said: "Allāh does not need this man to put himself to hardship", and he ordered him to ride.[51]

---

maḥram), nor should a stranger visit her in the absence of a permissible male relative. In h. 1860, just above, it has been reported that 'Umar allowed the wives of the Holy Prophet to travel for *Ḥajj* accompanied by men who were not *maḥram* to them. No one objected to this action by 'Umar nor did the wives of the Holy Prophet refuse to go with them. This shows that a woman can travel even a long distance without a *maḥram*. All that it amounts to is that if there is safety for a woman she can travel on her own. Again, it depends on the nature of the journey. Different ḥadīth reports mention different lengths of journeys which a woman should not undertake without a *maḥram:* it is one day in h. 1088, two days in h. 1864, and three days in h. 1086. A journey shorter than this can be undertaken without a *maḥram*. It is also agreed that a woman can travel with other women. All this shows that if there is safety in a journey for a woman, she can travel without a *maḥram*. Otherwise a *maḥram* is required.

[49] This is a repetition of h. 1782.

[50] This is a repetition of h. 1197. It mentions that a woman should not travel for two days without a *maḥram*.

[51] It means that it is not the purpose of an act of worship that a person should put himself to extreme hardship. Before Islām, it was believed that the more hardship a person undertook for

1866 'Uqbah ibn 'Āmir reported: My sister made a vow to go to the Ka'bah on foot and told me to ask the Prophet ﷺ to give a decision on it. I asked him for his decision and he said: "She should go on foot and also should ride."

---

an act of worship, the more he was excelling in performing that act. The Holy Prophet removed and corrected this concept.

Book 29: *Faḍā'il al-Madīnah*
Excellences of Madīnah

In the name of Allāh, the Beneficent, the Merciful

Ch. 1:   Sacredness of Madīnah

1867 Anas reported from the Prophet ﷺ that he said: "From such place to such place Madīnah is sacred. None of its trees should be cut down nor should any innovation be made in it. Whoever makes an innovation, upon him is the curse of Allāh, of the angels and of people altogether." [1]

1868 Anas reported: The Prophet ﷺ came to Madīnah and ordered the construction of a mosque, saying: "O Banī an-Najjār! Agree a price with me." They said: "We ask its price only from Allāh". So he gave an order regarding the graves of the idolaters and they were dug up, then (he gave an order) regarding the ruins and they were levelled, and (he gave an order) regarding the date trees and they were cut down. The date trees were laid in lines in the direction of the *qiblah* of the mosque.[2]

---

[1] In this ḥadīth the limits of the area are not specified by name, just "from such place to such place". In h. 1870 it is mentioned: "from 'Ā'ir to such place", without naming the other place. 'Ā'ir or 'Anīr is name of a mountain near Madīnah. In a report in Ṣaḥīḥ Muslim the other end is said to be Thaur, and Thaur is in Makkah. It is possible that a place of this name also existed in Madīnah. In some versions of the report in Muslim it is added: "He (the Holy Prophet) declared twelve miles around Madīnah as a preserved area" (book: Pilgrimage, ch. 85: 'Excellence of Madīnah and Prayer of the Prophet for it…'). In a report in Abū Dāwūd, it is stated that the Messenger of Allāh "declared twelve miles (*barīd-an, barīd-an*) in every direction around Madīnah as preserved. Leaves of its trees are not to be shaken off, nor a tree cut down, except what is used to drive camels" (book: Rites of the Pilgrimage, ch. 'About the Sacredness of Madī-nah', h. 2036). It appears from all these reports that the Holy Prophet declared the land around Madīnah as preserved temporarily. Ṭaḥāwī says that what is meant may be that the beauty of Madīnah should not be spoilt, and Mahlab says that the conclusion to be drawn from the report of Anas is that the cutting of trees is only forbidden if it would cause harm and damage, but if it is meant to bring about some improvement such as clearing an area to plant a garden, then that is not prohibited. The next ḥadīth supports this conclusion.

[2] This is a brief repetition of h. 428. This shows that the Holy Prophet had the trees cut, etc., to clear the area and for further improvement. It is generally said in explanation that this incident took place shortly after the *Hijrah* and that afterwards the area of Madīnah was declared as sacred.

1869 Abū Hurairah reported that the Prophet ﷺ said: "The sacredness of what is between the two stony ends (*lābatain*)[3] of Madīnah was declared by me." He (Abū Hurairah further) said: Then the Prophet ﷺ came to Banī Ḥārithah and said: "O Banī Ḥārithah! You have come out of the sacred territory." Then, looking around, he said: "No, you are within it."

1870 ʿAlī reported: We have nothing except the Book of Allāh and this paper from the Prophet ﷺ stating: "Madīnah is sacred from (mount) ʿĀʾir to such place. Whoever makes an innovation in it or gave shelter to one who made an innovation, upon him is the curse of Allāh, of the angels and of people altogether. No plea will be accepted from him nor recompense (for wrong-doing)." He (the Holy Prophet further) said: "The covenant of the Muslims is one (i.e., a covenant made with any Muslim is made with all Muslims). So whoever (among the Muslims) breaks the trust of a Muslim, upon him is the curse of Allāh, of the angels and of people altogether. No plea will be accepted from him nor recompense. And whoever makes another his master without the permission of his master, upon him is the curse of Allāh, of the angels and of people altogether. No plea will be accepted from him nor recompense." [4]

Ch. 2:   Excellence of Madīnah and that it drives away (evil) people

1871 Abū Hurairah reported that the Messenger of Allāh ﷺ said: "I was commanded about (migrating to) a town which will swallow all other towns. They call it Yathrib and that is Madīnah. It drives away (evil) people just as a furnace removes impurities from iron.[5]

---

[3] *Lābat-ain* is the dual of *lābat-un,* which means a land of black stones.

[4] The paper in possession of ʿAlī has already been referred to in h. 111, and there three things are mentioned in it: blood-money, freeing of prisoners and not killing a Muslim for killing a disbeliever in battle. Here also, three things have been mentioned: making innovations, breaking a pledge made with a Muslim, and a freed slave making another his master. Regarding "plea" *(sarf)* and "recompense" (*ʿadl*), there are ten opinions. The commentator of the Qurʾān Baiḍāwī explains the word *sarf* as *shafāʿat,* which is intercession, and *ʿadl* as *fidyah* which is recompense or expiation (*Fatḥ al-Bārī*), and these meanings are appropriate here. Some have explained the word *sarf* as repentance and *ʿadl* as *fidyah,* but it is meaningless to say that repentance will not be accepted. Similarly, the interpretation that *sarf* means the obligatory acts of worship and *ʿadl* means voluntary acts, neither of which will be accepted, is also meaningless. The word curse (*laʿnat*) in "upon him is the curse of …" means estrangement, i.e., due to their wrongdoing they will be far removed from Allāh, from the angels, who inspire people to good, and from righteous people. For ʿĀʾir see note on h. 1867.

[5] In other words, in Madīnah Islamic rule will be established and knowledge of Islām will progress, and from there the Muslim regime and religion will expand to prevail over other regimes and religions. This was a prophecy which came true manifestly, and the religion of Islām and Muslim rule spread in all directions. Before Islām, the name of Madīnah was Yathrib which

Ch. 3:   Madīnah is (called) Ṭābah

1872 Abū Ḥumaid reported: We returned from (the expedition to) Tabūk with the Prophet ﷺ and when we reached near Madīnah he said: "This is Ṭābah." [6]

Ch. 4:   Two stony plains of Madīnah

1873 Abū Hurairah said: If I see deer grazing in Madīnah, I would not disturb them, (for) the Messenger of Allāh ﷺ said: "What is between its two stony plains is sacred." [7]

Ch. 5:   One who turns away from Madīnah

1874 Abū Hurairah reported that he heard the Messenger of Allāh ﷺ say: "They will leave Madīnah while it is in the best condition, and (then) only wild animals and birds of prey will remain to live there. Last of all, there will be two shepherds from Muzainah wanting to go to Madīnah, calling out to their she-goats (driving them towards it), but they will find it a desolate place and when they reach Thaniyyat-ul-Wadā' they will fall down on their faces." [8]

1875 Sufyān ibn Abū Zuhair reported that he heard the Messenger of Allāh ﷺ say: "Yaman will be conquered, and some people will come driving (their mounts) fast,[9] carrying with them their families and any who obey them, but (remaining in) Madīnah would have been better for them if they only knew. Syria will also be conquered, and some people will come driving (their mounts) fast, carrying with them their families and any who obey them, but (remaining in) Madīnah would have been better for them if they only knew. And Iraq will be conquered, and some people will come driving (their mounts) fast, carrying with them their families and any who obey them, but (remaining in) Madīnah would have been better for them if they only knew." [10]

---

comes from *tathrīb* meaning blame, and the word *tharb* means disorder. The Holy Prophet did not like such names, so he named it as *Madīnah,* and also *Ṭābah Ṭayyibah* which simply meant a pleasant city. By driving people away is meant driving away of those who used to hatch evil schemes and plans against the Muslims.

[6] This is a very brief repetition of h. 1481.

[7] This is repetition of a part of h. 1869, with some addition.

[8] To desert Madīnah has been declared here as a sign of approach of the Day of Judgment. Deserting Madīnah may also be in the sense of loss of importance by moving the seat of government to another city.

[9] *Bassa* means to drive the ride with great speed.

[10] There are six prophecies in this ḥadīth: conquest of Yaman, conquest of Syria, conquest of

Ch. 6: Faith (*īmān*) retreats to Madīnah

1876 Abū Hurairah reported that the Messenger of Allāh ﷺ said: "Faith retreats to Madīnah as a snake retreats into its hole." [11]

Ch. 7: The sin of him who plans against the people of Madīnah

1877 Sa'd said that he heard the Prophet ﷺ saying: "Whoever plans against the people of Madīnah will melt as salt melts into water." [12]

Ch. 8: High buildings (or forts)[13] of Madīnah

1878 Usāmah said: The Prophet ﷺ ascended a high building (*uṭum*) from among the high buildings (*āṭām*) of Madīnah and said: "Do you see what I see? Surely I see places of trouble among your houses like places where raindrops fall." [14]

Iraq, and in each case people of Madīnah going over to these places. All these six prophecies were fulfilled. Yaman was conquered during the time of the Holy Prophet, and again after its revolt at the beginning of the caliphate of Abū Bakr. Syria and Iraq were conquered during the time of 'Umar. As Madīnah was the fountainhead of the worldly and spiritual blessings of Islām and its victories, and the centre of Islām and the Muslims, the Holy Prophet did not approve of Muslims migrating from there, and declared such migration to be dangerous for Islām and the Muslims, and it did prove disastrous for them. That was why some people objected to 'Alī making Kūfah the capital and leaving Madīnah to go to Iraq.

[11] Some have interpreted the retreating of faith to Madīnah as taking place by the Day of Judgment while others consider it as happening by the end of the third generation of Muslims. But it appears to relate to the conquest of Makkah, because before that Muslims could not practise Islām openly in Arabia and they were forced to leave Makkah and take refuge in Madīnah. To take this to mean that the people of Madīnah will adhere correctly to the true faith till the time of Resurrection is not a valid conclusion. It is people who are judged on the basis of principles as to whether they are right or wrong, and it is not principles that become right or wrong depending on whether certain people living in a certain place accept them or not. It is also possible that by the retreating of the faith to Madīnah is meant its becoming the centre of knowledge and learning which it remained for a long time.

[12] This prophecy was made at a time when the enemies were bent upon destroying the people of Madīnah. It says that however great the power may be which seeks to destroy the Holy Prophet and his Companions, they will meet their own destruction. Not only is the failure of the Arab opponents of Islām, and the Jews and Christians of Arabia, an evidence of the truth of this prophecy, but when the great powers of the Byzantine and Persian empires sought to destroy the people of Madīnah, i.e., the Muslims whose capital city it was, they melted away despite their mighty strength. This prophecy will always prove true.

[13] According to the *Nihāyah,* the word *uṭum* (which occurs here in the plural, *āṭām*) means a high building. It is also applied to a fort.

[14] The Holy Prophet saw future events in this vision. These troubles began with the assassination of 'Uthmān in Madīnah and after that great tribulations befell the people of Madīnah during the Umayyad period.

Ch. 9: Dajjāl shall not enter Madīnah

1879 Abū Bakrah reported from the Prophet ﷺ that he said: "The terror of *al-Masīḥ ad-Dajjāl* (the Antichrist) shall not enter Madīnah. It will have that day seven doors, each door guarded by two angels." [15]

1880 Abū Hurairah reported that the Messenger of Allah ﷺ said: "On the roads to Madīnah angels have been stationed. Neither plague nor Dajjāl (the Antichrist) shall enter it." [16]

1881 Anas ibn Mālik related from the Prophet ﷺ that he said: "There is no town but Dajjāl will destroy it except Makkah and Madīnah. There is no road leading to them but has angels standing in rows guarding it. Then Madīnah will shake with its inhabitants three times and Allāh will expel every disbeliever and hypocrite." [17]

1882 Abū Saʿīd al-Khudrī said: The Messenger of Allāh ﷺ related to us a lengthy narrative about Dajjāl. Among what he related to us about him was that he said: "Dajjāl will come, and it is prohibited for him to enter the doors of Madīnah. He will descend on a marshy land by Madīnah. A man will come to him that day who will be the best of the people, or from among the best of the people, and say: 'I bear witness that you are the Dajjāl about whom the Messenger of Allāh ﷺ related to us his narrative.' Dajjāl will say (to people): 'If I kill this man and then raise him to life again, will you doubt about the matter?' They will say: 'No.' Then he will kill him and raise him to life again. When raised to life, that man will say: 'By Allāh! I have never had so much

---

[15] See longer version in h. 1881 below. This shows that influence of the Antichrist (*al-Masīḥ ad-Dajjāl*) will not be able to penetrate Madīnah and Makkah while its influence will dominate in other places.

[16] See longer version in h. 1882 below.

[17] This prophecy was clearly fulfilled as the disbelievers attacked Madīnah three times to destroy it and its people: at Badr, then Uḥud and again at the battle of Aḥzāb. The word *rajf,* used here meaning shaking or earthquake, has also been used for battles. The word *zalzalah,* meaning earthquake, has been used in the Qur'ān itself (33:11) for the battle of Aḥzāb: "There the believers were tried and they were shaken with a severe shaking (*zilzāl-an shadīd-an)*", and the banishment of the hypocrites from Madīnah has also been mentioned in the same chapter: "and they shall not be your neighbours in it but for a short while" (33:60). So the disbelievers and the hypocrites both were turned out. As regards Dajjāl not entering Makkah and Madīnah, it has been explained in the previous ḥadīth that its terror or influence will not reach there. The guarding by angels standing in rows was evidenced by everyone in the lifetime of the Holy Prophet when the Quraish kept on attacking Madīnah with powerful forces but they could not enter it. The same angelic forces will prevent Dajjāl from entering Madīnah. As regards Dajjāl destroying every other town, Ibn Ḥazm says that those sent by him and his armies will reach every town. In fact it means that Dajjāl will be dominant and prevail everywhere.

insight (into the matter) as now.' Dajjāl will say, 'I will kill him', but he will not be able to overpower him." [18]

Ch. 10:   Madīnah drives away the impure

1883 Jābir reported: A dweller of the desert came to the Prophet ﷺ and took the pledge to embrace Islām. Next day he came with fever and said: "Cancel my pledge." He (the Holy Prophet) refused this, (and this happened) three times. Then he said: "Madīnah is like a furnace which drives away the impure and retains what is pure." [19]

1884 Zaid ibn Thābit said: When the Prophet ﷺ set out for Uḥud, some among those with him turned back.[20] One party (of the believers) said: "We will kill them." Another party said: "We will not kill them." Then this verse was revealed: "Why should you, then, be two parties in relation to the hypocrites?" (the Qur'ān, 4:88).[21] The Prophet ﷺ said: "Surely it (i.e., Madīnah) drives away some people as fire drives away impurities out of iron."

Ch. 11:   Relating to the above

1885 Anas reported from the Prophet ﷺ that he said: "O Allāh! Grant Madīnah twice the blessing that You have granted blessed Makkah." [22]

1886 Anas reported that whenever the Prophet ﷺ returned from a journey and he saw the walls of Madīnah, he would make his mount run faster, and if

---

[18] Reports about the Dajjāl occur later in the Book of Tribulations (*Fitan*).

[19] This ḥadīth occurs in more explicit terms in the Book of Judgments (*Aḥkām*), ch. 'He who takes the pledge, then demands it back', h. 7211. There the words are *"Aqilnī bai'atī"*, where the words "my pledge" (*bai'atī*) occur explicitly, while here he says only *"Aqilnī"*, and the words "my pledge" are understood. This ḥadīth shows that his pledge was of embracing Islām, and for no other reason, and his asking to rescind the pledge means that he was leaving Islām, which in other words is apostasy. This is a very strong evidence against the belief that in Islām apostasy must be punished by killing the apostate. In h. 7211 it is said that "he left", which means he left Madīnah, showing that he was not executed. To regard his pledge as a pledge of *hijrah* is against the words of the ḥadīth here which are that he took the pledge "to embrace Islām" (*'ala-l-Islām*).

[20] The hypocrites led by 'Abdullāh ibn Ubayy are meant.

[21] The meaning of the verse of the Qur'ān was that they cannot be executed, which was why 'Abdullāh ibn Ubayy and his companions were not killed by the Muslims. The words of the Holy Prophet further on show that evil-minded people would leave by themselves. Ultimately all such people either left of their own accord or they were expelled due to the wrongs they had committed, and thus Madīnah was cleared of the hypocrites.

[22] Here blessing (*barakah*) means progress of Islam, and "twice" indicates that while in Makkah Islām possessed only spiritual power, in Madīnah along with this spiritual power the foundations of worldly rule were laid.

he was on another animal, he would spur it on because of his love for Madīnah.[23]

Ch. 12:　The Prophet ﷺ disliked that Madīnah be vacated

1887 Anas reported: Banū Salimah intended to move closer to the (Prophet's) Mosque, but the Messenger of Allāh ﷺ disliked it because (a part of) Madīnah would be vacated. He said: "O Banū Salimah! Do you not want the reward for your footsteps (in coming to the Mosque)?" So they remained (at their original residence).[24]

Ch. 13:　Relating to the above

1888 Abū Hurairah reported from the Prophet ﷺ that he said: "Between my house and my pulpit, there is a garden from among the gardens of Paradise and my pulpit is over my pond." [25]

1889 ʿĀʾishah reported: When the Messenger of Allāh ﷺ came to Madīnah, Abū Bakr and Bilāl fell ill with fever. When Abū Bakr's fever increased, he would recite (the poetic verse):

> "Everyone receives the blessing of long life from his family,[26]
> And yet death is nearer to him than the lace of his shoe."

And when Bilāl's fever would subside, he would raise his voice and recite:

> "I wish I could know that I would spend a night,
> in a valley (i.e., Makkah) again, and around me would be *idhkhir* and *jalīl.* [27]

And one day I would be at (*aridan*) the water of Majannah,[28]

---

[23] In this repetition of h. 1802 there is a slight difference of wording, and an addition at the end.

[24] Banū Salimah wished to reside nearer to the Holy Prophet's Mosque but he did not like this as it would have made Madīnah exposed and unsafe from its defence point of view. This shows that the Holy Prophet was not only a spiritual leader but was well aware of minor details of the responsibilities of the state. See also h. 655–6.

[25] This is a repetition of h. 1196. See the footnote to that ḥadīth.

[26] The "blessing of long life" is mentioned here by the word *muṣabbaḥ*. There is a well-wish based on this word in vogue till today among the Arabs: *Ṣabbaḥak-Allāhu bi-l-khair*, which conveys the significance of "May you have a long life". One who receives this greeting is called *muṣabbaḥ* as here.

[27] *Idhkhir* (*idh-khir*) and *jalīl* are two kinds of grass found in Makkah.

[28] *Aridan* is derived from *warūd*, meaning arriving or coming. Majannah is the name of a place some miles away from Makkah.

And I would be seeing Shāmah and Ṭafīl!"[29]

He said: "O Allāh! Curse Shaibah ibn Rabī'ah and 'Utbah ibn Rabī'ah and Umayyah ibn Khalf, for they have expelled us from our land to an epidemic-stricken land." Then the Messenger of Allāh ﷺ said: "O Allāh! Endear Madīnah to us as we loved Makkah, or even more. O Allāh! Bless for us our measure of *ṣā'* and of *mudd*,[30] and make it (Madīnah) salubrious for us, and drive away its fever towards al-Juḥfah."[31] 'Ā'ishah said: We came to Madīnah and it was the most epidemic-stricken place of Allāh's earth. She further said: The stream of Buṭḥān flowed only a little, meaning its water had a bad taste and smell.

1890 'Umar is reported as saying: O Allāh! Grant me martyrdom in Your way and let my death be in the city of Your Messenger![32]

---

[29] Shāmah and Ṭafīl are two mountains about thirty miles from Makkah.

[30] *Ṣā'* and *mudd* are measures of weight; see footnote to h. 201. Here they symbolize food.

[31] The climate of Makkah was dry, healthy and good for digestion. On the other hand, the climate of Madīnah was damp and sanitation was not satisfactory. In the beginning, the climate of Madīnah did not suit the emigrants (*muhājirūn*) from Makkah and many fell ill. Later on, they became acclimatized and with better sanitation the incidence of illness declined. Juḥfah is the place from where pilgrims from Egypt enter into the state of *Iḥrām*. It is said that the Holy Prophet prayed that the illness of fever may be driven towards Juḥfah because it was inhabited by idolaters. However, at that time all towns were inhabited by idolaters. The purpose of this prayer does not seem to be that the illness of fever should be transferred to Juḥfah, but rather that whatever was causing the climate of Madīnah to be spoilt and creating the epidemic should retreat in that direction.

[32] This is to show how beloved Madīnah had become to the emigrants from Makkah.

Book 30: *Aṣ-Ṣaum*

Fasting

In the name of Allāh, the Beneficent, the Merciful

Ch. 1: Obligation of fasting in Ramaḍān

The word of Allāh, the Most High: "O you who believe, fasting is prescribed for you, as it was prescribed for those before you, so that you may guard against evil" (the Qur'ān, 2:183).[1]

1891 Ṭalḥah ibn 'Ubaidullāh reported that a desert Arab with unkempt hair came to the Messenger of Allāh ﷺ and said: "O Messenger of Allāh, inform me as to what Allāh has made obligatory for me of prayer." He replied: "Five prayers (a day), but any (voluntary prayers you may add) of your own accord." Then he asked: "Inform me as to what Allāh has made obligatory for me of fasting." He replied: "The month of Ramaḍān, but any (voluntary fasts you may add) of your own accord." Then he asked: "Inform me as to what Allāh has made obligatory for me of *Zakāt*." So the Messenger of Allāh ﷺ informed him of the rules of Islām. He said: "By Him Who has honoured you, I will neither add anything of my own accord nor will I fall short in any way of what Allāh has made obligatory for me." The Messenger of Allāh ﷺ said: "He will be successful if he has spoken the truth." Or he said: "He will enter Paradise if he has spoken the truth." [2]

1892 Ibn 'Umar reported: The Prophet ﷺ fasted on *'Āshūrā'* (the 10th day of the month of Muḥarram) and ordered fasting on that day. When (fasting

---

[1] Two things have been stated in this verse of the Qur'ān. Firstly, that fasting is found in all the previous religions of the world. Although the Christian religion has rejected any such worship, it is proved from the Gospels that Jesus kept fast himself and commanded his disciples also to do the same. Secondly, the object and purpose of fasting has been stated here. It is to make a person righteous by weakening the inclination to do evil deeds and to nourish and strengthen the power to do good deeds. Undoubtedly during fasting man gains the ability to control his lower, animal desires. He forsakes permissible acts merely in obedience to the commandments of Allāh, and thus gains the strength to abstain from his lower desires in order to seek the pleasure of Allāh. When a person can forsake his permissible desires, why will he not refrain from wrongful and evil desires? This is what it is to be righteous.

[2] This is a repetition of h. 46. See also h. 63.

in) the month of Ramaḍān was made obligatory, this was given up. And ʿAbdullāh (ibn ʿUmar) did not fast on that day unless it coincided with his (day of voluntary) fast.[3]

1893 ʿĀ'ishah reported that the Quraish used to fast on the day of *'Āshūrā'* in the days of Ignorance. Then the Messenger of Allāh ﷺ ordered fasting on that day until (fasting in) the month of Ramaḍān was made obligatory, and the Messenger of Allāh ﷺ said: "Anyone who so wishes may fast (on the day of *'Āshūrā'*) and anyone who so wishes may not fast." [4]

Ch. 2:　Excellence of fasting

1894 Abū Hurairah reported that the Messenger of Allāh ﷺ said: "Fasting is a shield (with which you protect yourself); so let not him (who fasts) utter immodest (or foul) speech, nor let him act in an ignorant manner; and if a man quarrels with him or abuses him, he should say twice, 'I am fasting'.[5] And by Him in Whose hand is my soul, the odour of the mouth of one fasting is sweeter in the estimation of Allāh than the odour of musk. (Allāh says:) 'He gives up his food and his drink and his (sexual) desire for My sake; fasting is for Me and I will grant its reward; and a virtue brings reward ten times like it'."

Ch. 3:　Fasting is an expiation

1895 Ḥuzaifah reported that ʿUmar said: "Who has preserved the saying from the Prophet ﷺ about the Trial (*fitnah*)?" Ḥuzaifah replied: "I heard him saying: 'The trial of a man in connection with his family and his property and his neighbour is expiated by (his) prayer, fasting and charity'." ʿUmar said: "I do not ask about that, but I ask about that which surges like the surging

---

[3] The meaning is that if, for example, he fasted on a certain day of the week and such a day happened to fall on the 10th of Muḥarram, he would fast on that day.

[4] All the good practices found in the previously revealed religions were adopted by the Holy Prophet until he was informed by revelation of a better way. Following this principle, the Holy Prophet fasted on the day of *'Āshūrā'* and enjoined his followers to do the same. It seems the Quraish took fasting on the day of *'Āshūrā'* from the Jews. It is mentioned in h. 2004 that when the Holy Prophet went to Madīnah and saw the Jews fasting on the day of *'Āshūrā'*, he enquired about it and they told him that it was an auspicious day because on this day Allāh liberated the Children of Israel from their enemies, and for this reason this Moses fasted on that day. So the Holy Prophet told them: "I have more right to (commemorate) Moses than you have." But when fasting in the month of Ramaḍān was prescribed, the fast of *'Āshūrā'* was declared optional. See also h. 2001 and h. 2002.

[5] As the purpose of fasting is to control physical desires and the lower urges, and to acquire mastery over them, this is why the Holy Prophet said that if during fasting circumstances arise which could lead the fasting person away from the high objective he is seeking to attain, he should control his emotions and refrain from following them.

waves of the ocean." Ḥuzaifah replied: "There is a closed door before it." 'Umar asked: "Will it be opened or broken?" He replied: "It will be broken." 'Umar said: "Then that door will not be closed till the Day of Resurrection."

We asked Masrūq: "Ask him (i.e., Ḥuzaifah) if 'Umar knew this door?" So he asked him, and he said: "Yes, he knew it as he knew there is night after the next day." [6]

Ch. 4: *Ar-Rayyān* for those who fast

1896 Sahl reported from the Prophet ﷺ that he said: "There is a door in Paradise which is called *ar-Rayyān* through which those who fast will enter on the Day of Resurrection. None will enter through it except them. It will be said: Where are those who fasted? They will stand up, and none will enter through it except them. When they have entered, it will be closed and none will enter through it." [7]

1897 Abū Hurairah reported that the Messenger of Allāh ﷺ said: "Whoever gives a pair of things in charity in the way of Allāh will be called from the doors of Paradise (and told): 'O servant of Allāh, This is a good door!' He who was among those who said prayers will be called from the door of prayer; and he who was among those who took part in *Jihād* will be called from the door of *Jihād;* and he who was from among those who kept fast will be called from the door of *ar-Rayyān;* and he who was among those who gave in charity will be called from the door of charity."

Abū Bakr asked: "My parents may be sacrificed for you, O Messenger of Allāh! It is not required that a person be called from all these doors. So, is

---

[6] This is a repetition of h. 525 with brevity and difference in wording but subject is the same. The heading of the chapter is related to the words: "The tribulation of a man in connection with his family, and his property, and his neighbour is expiated by prayer, fasting and charity." These actions suppress the capacity to do evil and develop the powers of doing good in a person, and expiation of misdeeds is nothing other than the development of strength in man to refrain from them. See the note on h. 525. See also h. 1435.

[7] One of the doors of Paradise has here been called *ar-Rayyān*. In *Nihāyah,* while discussing fundamentals of religion, it is said that this word is derived from *rawā'* which is the water used for irrigation and is the lowest layer of a stream. It is the abundant or sweet water which refreshes those who drink it. Here, mentioning *ar-Rayyān* as being reserved exclusively for the one who fasts, bearing pang of thirst, is according to the principle that the reward for any deed corresponds to the nature of that deed. He who withstands thirst for the sake of attaining pleasure of Allāh — and in fasting thirst is what is the hardest to bear — he is granted in reward an exclusive kind of refreshment of drink to the full, symbolised as sweet and refreshing water.

This ḥadīth also appears to show that those who have not been able to fast will enter Paradise through other doors due to their other virtuous deeds. This sheds light on the true nature of Paradise and its bounties. The next ḥadīth also makes this nature clear.

there anyone who will be called from all these doors?" He said: "Yes. I hope you will be one of them." [8]

Ch. 5: Should it be called Ramaḍān or the month of Ramaḍān, and he who thinks either is correct

The Prophet ﷺ said: "He who fasts in Ramaḍān", and he said: "Do not fast ahead of Ramaḍān".[9]

1898 Abū Hurairah reported that the Messenger of Allāh ﷺ said: "When Ramaḍān comes, the doors of Paradise are opened."

1899 Abū Hurairah said that the Messenger of Allāh ﷺ said: "When the month of Ramaḍān starts, the doors of heaven are opened and the doors of hell are closed, and the Satans are shackled in chains." [10]

1900 Ibn ʿUmar said that he heard the Messenger of Allāh ﷺ say: "When you see it (the new moon of Ramaḍān), start fasting, and when you see it (the new moon of the next month), break the fasting. And if it is cloudy, then calculate it."

(And in another report:) "The new moon of Ramaḍān (is meant)." [11]

---

[8] This shows that every kind of good deed opens a door of Paradise for the doer. The question raised by Abū Bakr is that if a person has already entered Paradise through one door, it would appear that it is not required for him to be called to enter from other doors. However, what is made clear here is that every person has his own individual Paradise, some of these being superior to those of others. If the person who is called from all the doors of Paradise enters the same Paradise as that which is entered by those who are called from only one door, it would mean that a person who did only one good deed and he who did all the good deeds are equal, and this cannot happen. Thus the conclusion is that every good deed done by a person opens a door of his own Paradise.

[9] These are discussions of those times. There is a weak report that the Holy Prophet said: "Say not Ramaḍān, but say month of Ramaḍān." Bukhārī in this chapter indicates its weakness.

[10] The opening of the doors of Paradise and the closing of the doors of hell are for those who benefit from the fasts of Ramaḍān, inculcating in themselves the true spirit of Ramaḍān in their lives. Fasting strengthens the nobler powers in a person and weakens the lower desires. The former opens the doors of Paradise and the latter closes the doors of hell, and due to the suppression of the lower desires Satan is unable to exploit them, and thus Satan is chained. H. 1898 is a briefer version of this.

[11] The Arabic *ra'aitumū-hu* ("when you see it") refers to the moon, i.e., when you see the new moon start the daily fasting, and when you see the next month's moon, break the fast, meaning end the daily fasting. If the weather is not clear, it has been enjoined: "then calculate it (*fa-qdurū la-hū*)". H. 1907 says: "And if it is cloudy, then complete the period of thirty days", and h. 1909 says: "And if it is cloudy, then complete the period of thirty days of Shaʿbān." The interpretation of *fa-qdurū lahū* (calculate, measure, determine, or estimate it) is generally that thirty days should be completed. The interpretation of several authorities (Abul ʿAbbās ibn Suraij

Ch. 6:   One who fasts in Ramaḍān with faith and seeking the pleasure of Allāh and having a purpose (*niyyah*)

'Ā'ishah reported from the Prophet ﷺ: "People will be raised (on the Last Day) according to their intentions." [12]

1901 Abū Hurairah reported from the Prophet ﷺ that he said: "Whoever keeps up (the optional night) prayers on *Lailat-ul-Qadr* with faith and seeking the pleasure of Allāh, he is forgiven the sins he committed before, and whoever fasts in Ramaḍān with faith and seeking the pleasure of Allāh, he is forgiven the sins he committed before." [13]

Shāfi'ī, Muṭrif ibn 'Abdullāh *Tābi'i*, Ibn Qutaibah *Muḥaddith*, Ibn Khuwaiz Mandād *al-Māliki* and Imam Shāfi'ī) is as follows: "Calculate it according to the reckoning of the stages of the moon." It is recorded from Ibn Suraij that the words "then calculate it" are addressed to "those who have been blessed with this knowledge (of the stages of the moon) specially by Allāh", and the words "complete the period of thirty days" are addressed to the general public. Thus in case the weather is cloudy those who are expert in calculating stages of moon should fix the date of the first of Ramaḍān and the first of Shawwāl and the public should start the month of fasting and end it accordingly. In those places where there are no such experts or knowledge available, people should act on the instruction to "complete the period of thirty days".

The above explanation of "then calculate it (*fa-qdurū la-hū*)", in case the weather is cloudy, does not negate h. 1913 wherein it is stated: "We are an illiterate people, who neither write nor keep account". Its explanation in *Fatḥ al-Bārī* is as follows: "What is meant are those Muslims who were present with the Holy Prophet at this conversation, or it applies to the masses, or it may refer to his own self".

In my opinion it meant only the Arabs of that time. It does not mean that Muslims will never be able to write or keep account. In our day and age, when the knowledge of the stages of the moon is widely available, I see no reason why calculation should not be used to fix one date in every country, so that all Muslims there should start fasting on the same day and celebrate Eid on the same day. It does happen that in many places, due to cloud or dust in the air, the observation of the new moon by eye is not possible. The sending of telegraphic messages at the last moment also does not serve this purpose. The result is that in neighbouring villages Eid is on two different days, and the same disruption is found even in cities. If the date is fixed in advance by computation and announced, this too would be in accordance with the instructtion of the Holy Prophet to "calculate it (*fa-qdurū la-hū*)", which meant that where the weather is not clear the calculated date will serve the purpose, and where it is clear the new moon will be seen. See the note on h. 1913.

[12] Similar words also occur in regard to other acts. The meaning is that those who carry them out, for example, prayer or fasting, merely as a ritual, cannot benefit from them. Only those can benefit who understand their aim and purpose and try to achieve it. For them, the fasts can bring such spiritual progress that it protects them from committing sin. The word *niyyah* means purpose, intention or aim.

[13] This repetition is combination of h. 35 and 38, the first part about *Lailat-ul-Qadr* being a repetition of h. 35, and the second part about the month of Ramaḍān being a repetition of h. 38. See the note on h. 35.

Ch. 7:   The Prophet ﷺ used to be most generous during Ramaḍān

1902 Ibn ʿAbbās said: The Prophet ﷺ was the most generous of all people in doing good, and he would be at his most generous in Ramaḍān when Gabriel met him, and Gabriel met him in every night in Ramaḍān till it ended. The Prophet ﷺ read to him the Qurʾān. When Gabriel met him, he was more generous in the doing of good than the wind which is sent forth (on every-one).[14]

Ch. 8:   One who does not give up falsehood and acting according to it while fasting

1903 Abū Hurairah reported that the Messenger of Allāh ﷺ said: "He who does not give up uttering falsehood and acting according to it, Allāh has no need of his giving up his food and his drink." [15]

Ch. 9:   When abused, should one say: I am fasting

1904 Abū Hurairah said that the Messenger of Allāh ﷺ said: "Allāh says: 'Every act done by the son of Adam is for himself, except fasting which is for Me and I will grant its reward.' Fasting is a shield (with which you protect yourself); so when one of you is fasting, let not him utter immodest (or foul) speech, nor quarrel. If someone should abuse him or fight with him, he should say: 'I am fasting'. And by Him in Whose hand is the soul of Muḥammad, the odour of the mouth of one fasting is sweeter in the estimation of Allāh than the odour of musk. The person who fasts has two pleasures which he enjoys: when he breaks the fast he is pleased, and when he will meet His Lord (in the hereafter) he will be pleased because of his fasting." [16]

Ch. 10:   Fasting for him who fears for himself (illicit) sexual desire

1905 ʿAlqamah reported: Once I was walking with ʿAbdullāh (ibn

---

[14] This is a repetition of h. 6 with somewhat different wording. This ḥadīth shows that the Holy Prophet did not have any written manuscript of the Qurʾān, to which he could compare what he had learnt by heart. This checking was done by him with the angel Gabriel. Other people possessed written manuscripts, and there was never any difference of even a single word between them and the one learnt by the Holy Prophet by heart which was regularly compared by him while reciting with the angel Gabriel. This shows conclusively that bringing down of the Holy Qurʾān by the angel Gabriel by means of revelation and his repeating and reciting it with the Holy Prophet, specially during the month of Ramaḍān, was a proven fact.

[15] It means it is of no benefit for a person to fast if he cannot resist indulging in falsehood, dishonesty and deceit.

[16] This is a repetition of h. 1894 with some differences. The closing words about the two pleasures do not occur there. The pleasure at breaking the fast is because the hunger creates a real desire to eat, and the true enjoyment of food comes from that real desire to eat.

Mas'ūd) and he said: We were in the company of the Prophet ﷺ and he said: "He who is able to marry should marry, for it keeps the eye cast down and keeps a man chaste; and he who cannot, should take to fasting, for it will restrain sexual desire for him." [17]

Ch. 11:   The saying of the Prophet ﷺ: "When you see the new moon, start fasting, and when you see it (the new moon of the next month) break the fasting."

Ṣilah reported from 'Ammār: One who fasts on a doubtful day has indeed disobeyed Abul Qāsim ﷺ (i.e., the Holy Prophet).[18]

1906 'Abdullāh ibn 'Umar reported that the Messenger of Allāh ﷺ mentioned Ramaḍān and said: "Do not start fasting until you see the new moon, nor break the fasting until you see it (again). And if it is cloudy, then calculate it." [19]

1907 'Abdullāh ibn 'Umar reported that the Messenger of Allāh ﷺ said: "The (lunar) month is (sometimes) 29 nights, but do not start fasting until you see it (the new moon). And if it is cloudy, then complete the period of thirty days." [20]

1908 Ibn 'Umar said that the Prophet ﷺ said: "A month is this and this", and he folded his thumb on the third time.[21]

1909 Abū Hurairah said: The Prophet ﷺ — or he said Abul Qāsim ﷺ — said: "Start fasting on seeing it and break fasting on seeing it. And if it is cloudy, then complete the period of thirty days of Sha'bān."

---

[17] *Wijā-un* means castration, the object of which is eradication of sexual urges. Here fasting is advised in order to suppress or decrease sexual urges.

[18] In other words, if the new moon has not been sighted, nor is it known through computation that it has appeared, fasting must not be started in such doubtful cases.

[19] This is a repetition of h. 1900.

[20] This is a repetition of h. 1900. It means to say that if on the 29th of Sha'bān (the month preceding Ramaḍān) the new moon is not visible, then thirty days should be completed and fasting started the next day, as the lunar month can never be more than thirty days. For the general public, and particularly in those days, that was the only satisfactory method. In other reports, the words *fa-qdurū lahū* ("then calculate it") occur. Today there are more advanced methods available and we can pre-determine the first day of every month so that the start of fasting, as well as its ending, can be on the same day in any country.

[21] By showing the ten fingers of the two hands three times, and then repeating this action but on the third time folding a thumb, the Holy Prophet wanted to explain to people that the lunar month is either thirty days or twenty-nine days.

1910 Umm Salamah reported that the Prophet ﷺ took a vow to keep aloof from his wives for a month. When twenty-nine days had passed, he came down in the morning or in the afternoon. It was said to him: "You took a vow not to come for a month." He said: "A month is also of twenty-nine days."

1911 Anas reported: The Messenger of Allāh ﷺ took a vow to keep aloof from his wives (for a month) and he had sprained his foot. He stayed in the upper room (of his house) for twenty-nine days and then came down. People said: "O Messenger of Allāh! You vowed to keep aloof for a month." He said: "A month is also twenty-nine." [22]

Ch. 12: The two months of Eid are never both short

Abū ʿAbdullāh (Bukhārī) said that Isḥāq (ibn Rāhuwiya) said: Even when they are short, they are full (in reward). Muḥammad (ibn Sīrīn) says both cannot be short.[23]

1912 Abū Bakrah reported from the Prophet ﷺ that he said: "There are two months which are never both short, the two months of Eid — Ramaḍān and Dhul Ḥajjah."

Ch. 13: The saying of the Prophet ﷺ: "We neither write nor keep account."

1913 Ibn ʿUmar reported from the Messenger of Allāh ﷺ that he said: "We are an illiterate people, who neither write nor keep account. A month is this and this." He meant it is sometimes of twenty-nine days and sometimes of thirty days.[24]

---

[22] This is a repetition of h. 1910. This report also occurs in the Book of Divorce (h. 5289) in explanation of the verse of the Qur'ān: "Those who swear that they will not have sexual relations with their wives should wait four months..." (2:226). It is mentioned there that he had sprained his foot and during that period he stayed in the upper room of his house. See also h. 378.

[23] By the two months of Eid are meant Ramaḍān and Dhul Ḥajjah. Isḥāq ibn Rāhuwiya has explained the ḥadīth, "The two months of Eid are never short", as meaning that even when Ramaḍān and Dhul Ḥajjah are 29 days in length they are equal in reward to when they are 30 days in length. However, the performance of the *Ḥajj* does not take the entire month of Dhul Ḥajjah, and it makes no difference to the exertions of the pilgrim whether that month is 29 days or 30 days long. Bukhārī has given it the meaning that both of these months cannot be of 29 days as months alternate between 29 days and 30 days in length (and Ramaḍān is the 9th month while Dhul Ḥajjah is the 12th month). However, Bukhārī's statement is contrary to actual experience because sometimes both these months are 29 days long. The meaning of this ḥadīth could be that if human error is made in sighting the new moon, or despite all possible efforts the correct date could not be established, and as a result Ramaḍān or Dhul Ḥajjah was started on the wrong day, it would make no difference to the reward for fasting or to the correctness of the dates of the *Ḥajj*.

[24] In all probability, by the words, *innā ummat-un ummiyyat-un* ("We are an illiterate people")

Ch. 14:   Not to fast a day or two before the month of Ramaḍān

1914 Abū Hurairah reported from the Prophet ﷺ that he said: "None of you should fast a day or two before the month of Ramaḍān, except for him who is used to fasting (voluntarily on certain days), so let him fast on that day." [25]

Ch. 15:   The word of Allāh mentioning this:

"It is made lawful for you to have intercourse with your wives on the night of the fast. They are an apparel for you and you are an apparel for them. Allāh knows that you acted unjustly to your-selves, so He turned to you in mercy and removed (the burden) from you. So now be in contact with them and seek what Allah has ordained for you…" (the Qur'ān, 2:187).

1915 Al-Barā' reported: When any man from among the Companions of Muḥammad ﷺ was fasting, and the time of breaking the fast came but he was sleeping before that time, he would not eat that night nor the next day till it was evening. Qais ibn Ṣirmah al-Anṣārī was fasting, and when the time for breaking the fast came, he went to his wife and asked her: "Do you have anything for eating?" She said: "No, but I will go and find it for you." He used to work during the day, so he fell asleep. When his wife came to him and saw him, she said: "How bad for you!" When it was mid-day (the next day) he became unconscious. This was mentioned to the Prophet ﷺ, so this verse was revealed:[26] "It is made lawful for you to have intercourse with your wives on

---

the reference is to the Arab nation among whom writing and calculation were not in vogue. It cannot possibly mean that no Muslims in the world will ever be able to write or be numerate. After that the Holy Prophet said that sometimes a month is of 29 days and sometimes of 30 days. For an illiterate people not familiar with doing calculations he has taught a simple method: if the new moon is seen on the evening of the 29th, the month will be of 29 days, and if it is not visible then it will be of 30 days. Of course, if the weather is cloudy on the 29th and it cannot be deter-mined if the new moon has appeared or not, the month should be considered as of 30 days. But the Holy Prophet's statement does not mean that keeping records or making calculations is against Islam. That is why it is stated in h. 1900: *fa-qdurū la-hū* (calculate or estimate it). While a simple and easy method was prescribed for the unlettered Arabs, when there are methods of calculation readily and widely available to find out the visibility of the new moon, to use these methods is not against Islamic law in any way.

[25] If someone routinely keeps a voluntary fast on a certain day of the week, and that day happens to fall one or two days before Ramaḍān, he may fast on that day.

[26] The practice of the Companions of the Holy Prophet, that if they went to sleep before the time of the breaking of the fast in the evening, and were asleep at that time, they would not eat in the night or the next day, was not due to any commandment of the Holy Prophet. In some of the reports it is stated that Muslims used to do it and so did the People of the Book. This verse

the night of the fast." The people rejoiced greatly, and it was revealed: "and eat and drink until the whiteness of the day becomes distinct from the blackness of the night" (the Qur'ān, 2:187).

Ch. 16: **The word of Allāh:**

"…and eat and drink until the whiteness of the day becomes distinct from the blackness of the night at dawn, then complete the fast till nightfall…" (the Qur'ān, 2:187). Al-Barā' has reported about it from the Prophet ﷺ.

1916 'Adiyy ibn Ḥātim reported: When this was revealed, "until the whiteness of the day becomes distinct from the blackness of the night", I took a black thread and a white thread and kept the two under my pillow. I kept on checking them during the night, but I could not find the difference. So in the morning I went to the Messenger of Allāh ﷺ and told him about it. He said: "It means the blackness of the night and the whiteness of the day."

1917 Sahl ibn Sa'd reported: It was revealed, "and eat and drink until the whiteness of the day becomes distinct from the blackness of the night", and the words "at dawn" (*min al-fajr*) were not yet revealed. When men intended to fast, one of them would tie a white thread and a black thread around his leg and continue to eat until both threads became clearly distinguishable to him. So Allāh then revealed "at dawn". They then realised that it meant the night and the day.[27]

Ch. 17: **The saying of the Prophet ﷺ: "The *Adhān* (call to prayer) of Bilāl should not prevent you from eating the pre-fast meal."**

1918–1919 Nāfi' reported from Ibn 'Umar, and al-Qāsim ibn Muḥammad reported from 'Ā'ishah, that Bilāl used to call the (*Fajr*) *Adhān* while it was still night. So the Messenger of Allāh ﷺ said: "Eat and drink until Ibn Umm Maktūm calls out the *Adhān* because he does not give the call until it is dawn."

---

may have been revealed on that occasion or it could be that it was revealed before that time but the particular person mentioned here did not know. The word *nuzūl* for "revealed", according to Shāh Walī-ullāh, is sometimes used in this latter way, meaning that the verse was already revealed but not known to some people.

[27] In this repetition of h. 1916, the mention of "men" observing the white and black threads seems to refer to just 'Adiyy himself, whose report is given earlier in h. 1916. However, in h. 1916 'Adiyy himself does not say what Sahl ibn Sa'd says here, that the words "at dawn" (*min al-fajr*) were not yet revealed. The statement of 'Adiyy is more reliable. It seems that Sahl ibn Sa'd has simply assumed from the action of 'Adiyy that these words were not yet revealed. Perhaps 'Adiyy did not pay attention to these words, or it is possible that he took them to mean that the white and the black threads should become distinct at dawn.

Al-Qāsim said: There was only this much difference that one would be going up (to call out the *Adhān*) while the other would be coming down (after (calling it out).[28]

Ch. 18:   Delaying the pre-fast meal (*saḥūr*)

1920 Sahl ibn Sa'd reported: I used to take my pre-fast meal at home. Then I would hurry to catch the prostration with the Messenger of Allāh ﷺ.[29]

Ch. 19:   How much interval was there between taking the pre-fast meal and the *Fajr* prayer

1921 Anas reported that Zaid ibn Thābit said: "We took the pre-fast meal with the Prophet ﷺ, then he stood up for the prayer." I asked: "How much (time) was there between the *Adhān* and the pre-fast meal?" He said: "As much as (for reciting) fifty verses." [30]

Ch. 20:   The pre-fast meal is a blessing, but is not obligatory

Because the Prophet ﷺ and his Companions combined fasts and did not mention the pre-fast meal.[31]

1922 'Abdullāh reported that the Prophet ﷺ combined fasts,[32] and people also combined them but it was hard for them. So the Prophet forbade them. They said (to him): "But you combine them." He said: "I am not like you, for I am given (spiritual) food and drink all along." [33]

---

[28] This is a repetition of h. 617, with some difference and addition. The comment at the end by al-Qāsim shows that there was not much interval of time between the two *Adhāns*.

[29] This is a repetition of h. 577, the difference being that here it says "to catch the prostration" while in h. 577 it says "to catch the *Fajr* prayer". The subject is that Sahl, after eating his pre-fast meal, would quickly go to the Mosque so that he could join the *Fajr* prayer with the Holy Prophet. In other words, the ending of this meal came very close to the *Fajr* prayer.

[30] This is a repetition of h. 576.

[31] The purpose of this chapter is to explain that if someone has not taken the pre-fast meal, even then his fasting is acceptable, even though the taking of this meal is a *Sunnah* of the Holy Prophet, both according to his sayings and his actions. The argument here is that the Holy Prophet and his Companions combined fasts without taking the pre-fast meal, i.e., a fast after the last day's fast was not started by a meal. Discussion on the combining of fasts comes later on. See the note under ch. 47.

[32] Combining means not taking a break from fasting in the night between two fasts. See chs. 47–49 for details.

[33] The meaning is that he receives spiritual nourishment, but they do not possess the spiritual power to enable them to overcome the physical hardship.

1923 Anas ibn Mālik said that the Prophet ﷺ said: "Do take food before the fast as there is blessing in the pre-fast meal (*suḥūr*)." [34]

Ch. 21: When during the day someone makes the intention to fast

Umm ad-Dardā' said: Abū ad-Dardā' used to ask, "Do you have something for eating?" If we said "No", he would say: "I will fast this day." And Abū Ṭalḥah, Abū Hurairah, Ibn ʿAbbās and Ḥuzaifah used to do the same.[35]

1924 Salamah ibn al-Akwaʿ reported that the Prophet ﷺ sent a man to announce among the people on the day of *'Āshūrah*: "Whoever has eaten something, he should complete (the rest of the day as a fast) — or (the Prophet said) he should fast — and whoever has not eaten anything, he should not eat."

Ch. 22: When a fasting person rises in the morning under obligation to have bath *(junub)*

1925–1926 ʿĀ'ishah and Umm Salamah informed that the Messenger of Allāh ﷺ used to get up in the morning under obligation to have a bath because of (having sexual relations with) his wife, and he would then take bath and start the fast. Marwān said to ʿAbdur Raḥmān ibn al-Ḥārith: "I adjure you in the name of Allāh that you should relate this clearly to Abū Hurairah." Marwān was at that time governor of Madīnah. Abū Bakr (ibn ʿAbdur Raḥmān) said:

" ʿAbdur Raḥmān did not like it. Once it so happened that we were all together in Dhul Ḥulaifah, where Abū Hurairah had some land. ʿAbdur Raḥmān said to Abū Hurairah: 'I am going to relate to you a matter, and if Marwān had not placed me under oath in this regard I would not have mentioned it to you.' Then he mentioned the statement of ʿĀ'ishah and Umm Salamah."

Abū Hurairah said: "This is what was related to me by al-Faḍl ibn ʿAbbās, and he knows it better." And Hammām and the son of ʿAbdullāh ibn ʿUmar

---

[34] This maintains a person's strength and he can do his normal work.

[35] This practice of the Companions was in the case of voluntary fasts, and the ḥadīth reported by Salamah, which follows, mentions only the fasting on the 10th of Muḥarram which was voluntary. However, the conditions relating to obligatory and voluntary fasts are the same. Thus, if a voluntary fast is valid even if the intention to fast was made during the day, the same applies to an obligatory fast. In the *Sunan* books of Ḥadīth there is a report from Ḥafṣah: "Whoever has not made the intention to fast during the night (preceding the fast), his fast is not valid" (Nasā'ī, book: 'Fasting', h. 2334; see also Tirmidhī, book: 'Fasting', h. 730). However, this report is not considered to be *marfūʿ* (continuously traceable to the Holy Prophet).

reported from Abū Hurairah that "the Prophet ﷺ (in such cases) would order the breaking of the fast" but the former (report) is more authoritative.[36]

Ch. 23:   Embracing (*mubāsharah*) during fasting[37]

'Ā'ishah said: It is forbidden for him to have sexual intercourse with her (while fasting).

1927 'Ā'ishah reported: The Prophet ﷺ used to kiss and embrace (his wives) while he was fasting and he had more control than any of you over his desires (*irbah*).

He (a narrator) said that Ibn 'Abbās said: *Ma'ārib* means 'need'. Ṭā'ūs said: *Ghaira ūl-il-irbah* means 'an imbecile who has no (sexual) need of woman'.[38]

Ch. 24:   Kissing by one who is fasting

Jābir ibn Zaid said: If he looks (at his wife with sexual desire) and has seminal discharge, he should complete his fast.

1928 'Ā'ishah reported: "The Messenger of Allāh ﷺ sometimes used to kiss a wife of his while he was fasting". Then she laughed.[39]

1929 Zainab, daughter of Umm Salamah, reported that her mother said: Once while I was (lying) with the Messenger of Allāh ﷺ under a sheet, I had menstruation, so I moved away and took my cloth of menstruation (to put it on). He said: "What is the matter with you? Have you got menstruation?" I said: "Yes." Then I entered under the sheet with him (again). She and the

---

[36] If someone during the night becomes *junub*, or under obligation to have a bath due to having sexual relations, and does not take bath till morning, this does not prevent him from fasting the next day. Abū Hurairah has reported to the contrary, as mentioned above at the end. When a report from 'Ā'ishah and Umm Salamah was related before him, he said that he had heard the same from al-Faḍl ibn 'Abbās. In other words, he recanted from his previous view. In some reports, instead of the words "he knows it better" (*huwa a'lamu*), the words are *hunna a'lamu* or *humā a'lamu*, meaning that the wives of the Prophet, or his two wives, "know it better".

[37] *Mubāsharah* means "the body (*basharah*) of a man being in contact with the body of a woman" (from *Nihāyah*). *Basharah* is the upper layer of the skin. Thus *mubāsharah* means a man's body and a woman's body touching each other. It also indicates the sexual act. Here and in the ḥadīth in the chapter it is obvious that the sexual act is not meant, but touching affectionately in a general sense.

[38] The word *ma'ārib*, related to *irbah*, occurs in the Qur'ān, 20:18, where Moses says regarding his staff that he has other "uses", or needs, for it. The expression *ghaira ūl-il-irbah* occurs in the Qur'ān, 24:31, meaning those male servants who have no desire for sex. These statements are added here to show the meaning of the word *irbah* from the Qur'ān.

[39] This is a repetition of h. 1927.

Messenger of Allāh ﷺ used to take bath from the same vessel (of water) and he used to kiss her while he was fasting.[40]

Ch. 25:　Taking of bath by one who is fasting

Ibn ʿUmar moistened his cloth and placed it over him while he was fasting. Ash-Shaʿbiyy entered a bath while he was fasting. Ibn ʿAbbās said: There is no harm if one tastes the food in the cooking-pot or anything else. Al-Ḥasan said: There is no harm for the fasting person to rinse his mouth and getting cooled. Ibn Masʿūd said: When one of you is fasting, he can get up in the morning, apply oil to his head and comb his hair. Anas said: I have a pond, I dive into it while I am fasting. It has been reported about the Prophet ﷺ that he brushed his teeth (with *miswāk*) while he was fasting. Ibn ʿUmar said: One can brush teeth early in the day and at the end of the day, and should not swallow the spittle. ʿAṭāʾ said: If he swallows his spittle I cannot say that his fast is nullified. Ibn Sīrīn said: There is no harm in brushing teeth with fresh *miswāk*. Somebody said to him that it has a taste. He said: Water has a taste and you rinse with it. And Anas, al-Ḥasan and Ibrāhīm did not see any harm in applying collyrium (to the eyes).

1930 ʿĀʾishah said: The Prophet ﷺ used to get up in the morning in Ramaḍān, without nocturnal discharge, and take a bath and keep fast.[41]

1931–1932 Abū Bakr ibn ʿAbdur Raḥmān said: I went with my father till we came upon ʿĀʾishah. She said: "I bear witness that the Messenger of Allāh ﷺ used to get up in the morning being under obligation to take a bath (due to having sexual relations with his wife), not due to nocturnal discharge (during sleep), and then keep fast." [1932] Then we went to Umm Salamah and she made a similar statement.[42]

Ch. 26:　When a fasting person eats or drinks by forgetfulness

ʿAṭāʾ said: If he takes water into his nose and it goes into the throat unintentionally, there is no harm. Al-Ḥasan said: If a fly goes into the throat, there is nothing for him to do about it. And Al-Ḥasan

---

[40] This is a repetition of h. 298 with the addition of the last sentence. The chapter heading, about kissing, is taken from this last sentence. This addition is also found in h. 322.

[41] This is a repetition of the opening of h. 1925. The chapter heading relates to his having a bath. H. 1931 shows that "without nocturnal discharge" here means that his taking bath was not due to nocturnal discharge but to having sexual relations.

[42] This is a repetition of the opening part of h. 1925–1926.

and Mujāhid said: If he has sexual relations by forgetfulness, there is nothing for him to do about it.[43]

1933 Abū Hurairah reported from the Prophet ﷺ that he said: "If he (the fasting person) forgets and eats or drinks, he should complete his fast, for Allāh fed him and made him drink."

Ch. 27: **Brushing of teeth with fresh or dried *miswāk* by one who is fasting**

It is reported about ʿĀmir ibn Rabīʿah that he said: I saw the Prophet ﷺ brushing his teeth while he was fasting so many times that I cannot count. Abū Hurairah reported the Prophet ﷺ as saying: "If I had not apprehended that it would be hard for my followers, I would have ordered them to brush teeth with *miswāk* at every *Wuḍū'*." And the same has been reported from the Prophet ﷺ by Jābir and Zaid ibn Khālid, and he (the Holy Prophet) did not make any distinction between the one fasting and anyone else. ʿĀ'ishah reported the Prophet ﷺ as saying: "It (*miswāk*) cleans the mouth and is a way of pleasing the Lord." [44] ʿAṭā' and Qatādah said: One can swallow the spittle.

1934 Ḥumrān reported: I saw ʿUthmān performing *Wuḍū'*. He poured water on his hands three times and rinsed his mouth and drew water into his nose and washed it. Then he washed his face three times. Then he washed his right arm up to the elbow three times, and his left arm up to the elbow three times. Then he wiped his head. Then he washed his right foot three times, and the left three times. Then he said: I saw the Messenger of Allāh ﷺ performing *Wuḍū'* like this *Wuḍū'* of mine, and then he (the Prophet) said: "Whoever performs *Wuḍū'* like this *Wuḍū'* of mine, and says two *rak'ahs* of prayer during which no thought (of other things) enters his mind, his previous sins are forgiven." [45]

---

[43] That is, he is not required to fast again to make up for the spoiled fast. This is unlike the opinion of Imām Mālik about eating and drinking through forgetfulness, and unlike the opinion of Ḥanafī scholars about the case if water goes inside unintentionally while gargling or taking it in the nose.

[44] Some people consider it wrong to use fresh *miswāk*, but there is no argument for it and Ḥadīth reports contradict it clearly.

[45] This is a repetition of h. 159 with difference of wording, and the addition "I saw the Messenger of Allāh performing *Wuḍū'* like this *Wuḍū'* of mine". The part of h. 159 which comes there after the statement about previous sins being forgiven does not occur here.

Ch. 28: **The saying of the Prophet ﷺ: "When performing *Wuḍū'*, he should put water into the nostrils" and he did not make any distinction between the person fasting and anyone else.**

Al-Ḥasan said: There is no harm if the person fasting puts water into the nostrils provided it does not reach his throat and he can apply collyrium (to the eye lids). 'Aṭā' said: If after rinsing the mouth, he spits out all the water from it, there is no harm provided he does not swallow spittle and what remains in his mouth. He should not chew mastic gum (*'ilk*)[46] and if (while chewing) he swallows its liquid, I do not say that his fast is broken, but it is prohibited. There is no harm if he puts water into the nose and some of it goes down his throat, because he cannot help it.[47]

Ch. 29: **When one has sexual relations in Ramaḍān (during fasting hours)**

It is reported from Abū Hurairah and it is *marfū'* (traceable to the Holy Prophet): "Whoever fails to fast even for one day in Ramaḍān without any reason or illness, he cannot make up for it even by fasting all his life."[48] Ibn Mas'ūd said the same. Sa'īd ibn al-Musayyab, al-Sha'bī, Ibn Jubair, Ibrāhīm, Qatādah and Ḥammād said: He should keep fast for one day in place of the missed one.

1935 'Ā'ishah said that a man came to the Prophet ﷺ and said that he was burning[49] (in hell). He asked: "What has happened to you?" He said: "I had sexual relations with my wife in Ramaḍān." Shortly later a bag full of dates was brought to the Prophet ﷺ known as *'araq*. He (the Prophet) said: "Where is the man who was burning (in hell)?" He said: "I am here." He (the Prophet) said: "Give it in charity."[50]

---

[46] In Persian and Urdu, *'ilk* is called *maṣṭagī*, which in English is mastic. It is chewed for dental hygiene.

[47] All these sayings tell us that if a medicine is put into the nose or mouth or eyes, the fast does not become void provided nothing is swallowed. Similarly, there is no harm if some medicine is applied to the throat, as it is not swallowed. There is no harm even if some water goes down into the stomach inadvertently.

[48] There is no unanimity on this statement from Abū Hurairah being *marfū'* and it has been criticised as well. It is contrary to the great broadmindedness in the teachings of the Holy Prophet.

[49] The word used here, *iḥtaraqa*, means he burnt in hell. In other words, he says he committed a great sin.

[50] See the next ḥadīth for details.

Ch. 30: **When one has sexual relations in Ramaḍān (during fasting hours), but has nothing to give (in charity), and is given charity, one should give expiation from it**

1936 Abū Hurairah said: We were sitting with the Prophet ﷺ, when a man came and said: "O Messenger of Allāh! I am ruined." He asked: "What has happened to you?" He said: "I had sexual relations with my wife while I was fasting." The Messenger of Allāh ﷺ said: "Can you afford to (buy and) set a slave free?" He said: "No." He said: "Can you fast for two successive months?" He said: "No." He said: "Can you afford to feed sixty needy poor people?" He said: "No."

Abū Hurairah added: The Prophet ﷺ kept quiet for a while. We were still like that when an *'araq* containing dates was brought to him — *'araq* is a bag. He (the Holy Prophet) said: "Where is the questioner?" He said: "I am here." He said: "Take this and give it in charity." The man asked: "O Messenger of Allāh! Should I give it to someone poorer than me? By Allāh! There is no family between the two stony ends (of Madīnah) poorer than my family." The Prophet ﷺ laughed until his teeth showed and then said: "Feed your family with it." [51]

Ch. 31: **Can one who has sexual relations in Ramaḍān (during fasting hours) feed his family with the expiatory charity when they are needy?**

1937 Abū Hurairah reported that a man came to the Prophet ﷺ and said: "This wretch has had sexual relations with his wife during the month of Ramaḍān." He (the Holy Prophet) said: "Can you afford to (buy and) set a slave free?" He said: "No." He said: "Can you fast for two successive months?" He said: "No." He said: "Can you afford to feed sixty needy poor people?" He said: "No."

Abū Hurairah added: A bag (*'araq*) containing dates was brought to the Prophet ﷺ — it was a *zabīl* (kind of bag). He (the Prophet) said: "Feed this

---

[51] What great mercy is there in the teachings of the Holy Prophet! No doubt, his teachings impose hardships and difficulties by requiring prayer and fasting. Moreover, for infringing a rule of fasting a penalty has to be imposed: freeing a slave, or failing that, keeping sixty consecutive fasts, or failing that, feeding sixty poor people. All this is prescribed in order to show the importance of this commandment. However, if a person acknowledges that he has disobeyed some commandment of Allāh, and is sincerely repentant, this incident shows how great the sympathy and mercy is with which he is treated. When something came to the Holy Prophet as a gift, he gave it to the sinner to give it in charity to expiate for his sin, and when he said that he and his family are the poorest of all, the Holy Prophet allowed him to give it to himself and his family as charity. This clearly shows that the real purpose was to inculcate the spirit to abide by the Divine commandments, and it was not to impose difficulty and hardship.

(as charity to the poor) on your behalf." He said: "To someone more needy than us? There is no family between the two stony ends (of Madīnah) more needy than my family." He (the Prophet) said: "So feed your family with it." [52]

Ch. 32: Cupping and vomiting while fasting

Abū Hurairah reported that vomiting does not break the fast because he expels (something), not takes in (something). It is (also) reported from Abū Hurairah that his fast is broken, but the former version is more likely to be correct. Ibn ʿAbbās and ʿIkrimah said: A fast is broken by something entering, not by something being expelled. Ibn ʿUmar used to have cupping while fasting, then he gave it up and started having cupping in the night. And Abū Mūsā (al-Ashʿarī) had cupping in the night. It is reported about Saʿd (ibn Abī Waqāṣ), Zaid ibn Arqam and Umm Salamah that they had cupping while fasting. Bukair reported from Umm ʿAlqamah: We used to have cupping at ʿĀʾishah's house and she did not stop us. It is reported from al-Ḥasan, who reported it from many Companions as *marfūʿ* (traced to the Prophet): The one who applies cupping and the one to whom it is applied both break their fasts. The same was reported from al-Ḥasan (via another line). He was asked: Is this from the Prophet ﷺ? He said: Yes. Then he said: Allāh knows best.

1938 Ibn ʿAbbās reported that the Prophet ﷺ had cupping while he was in the state of *Iḥrām,* and he had cupping while he was fasting. [53]

1939 Ibn ʿAbbās reported: The Prophet ﷺ had cupping while he was fasting.

---

[52] This is a repetition of h. 1936 above, with some differences.

[53] This ḥadīth provides clear evidence that cupping does not nullify a fast. It has been recorded in reports without a chain of transmission (*taʿlīqāt*) that "the one who applies cupping and the one to whom it is applied both break their fasts", while according to h. 1940 the treatment of cupping for a person who is fasting is disapproved because it causes weakness in the person being treated and the one who applies the cupping sucks blood, raising the possibility that some blood may go into him. In principle it is correct that a fast is not nullified by something coming out of the body but by something going into the body. This is why vomiting does not nullify a fast. However, there is a difference of opinion about vomiting when it is not involuntary but under a person's control. Keeping in view the basic principle, it would seem that in this case also the fast is not nullified. The report according to which the Holy Prophet "vomited and then broke the fast" does not state that he broke the fast because of vomiting. It could have been that he needed to take some medicine, or it may be due to weakness or some other illness, that he broke his fast.

1940 Shuʿbah related that he heard from Thābit al-Bunānī that he used to ask Anas ibn Mālik: "Did you disapprove of cupping for a person fasting?" He said: "No, except if it caused weakness."

It has been added (in another narration): During the time of the Prophet ﷺ (we did this).

Ch. 33: Fasting during a journey and breaking it

1941 Ibn Abī Aufā said: We were on a journey with the Messenger of Allāh ﷺ and he asked a man: "Get down and mix ground-barley for me." He said: "O Messenger of Allāh, the sun (is still out)!" He (the Holy Prophet) asked again: "Get down and mix ground-barley for me." He said: "O Messenger of Allāh, the sun (is still out)!" He (the Holy Prophet) asked yet again: "Get down and mix ground-barley for me." He got down and mixed it for him. He drank it and then pointed his hand (towards the east) and said: "When you see the night advancing from this side, a person fasting should break the fast." 54

1942–1943 ʿĀ'ishah reported that Ḥamzah ibn ʿAmr al-Aslamī said: "O Messenger of Allāh, I fast continuously." [1943] He (further) asked the Prophet ﷺ: "Should I fast on a journey"? He used to fast frequently. He (the Holy Prophet) said: "If you wish you can fast and if you wish can break it."

---

54 This ḥadīth shows that, despite being on a journey, the Holy Prophet was fasting. In the next ḥadīth the Holy Prophet clearly said about fasting during a journey: "If you wish you can fast and if you wish you can break it." All the reports which follow, except h. 1946, clearly establish that fasting during a journey is valid and the Holy Prophet himself kept fast while on a journey, and that the command in the Qur'ān "whoever among you is sick or on a journey, (he shall fast) a (like) number of other days" (2:184) is a permission. Only in h. 1946 the Holy Prophet said: "It is not a virtuous act to fast on a journey." But this was said regarding the man who was fainting during his fast and people gathered around him to provide shade. So the Holy Prophet contradicted the notion that this man had performed an act of great virtue by fasting while on a journey even though it reduced him to this state. From other reports it is clear that the Companions of the Holy Prophet used to fast on a journey and also to give up fasting on a journey. This is the correct standpoint. The view is not correct that, since Allāh has given permission not to fast on a journey, it is therefore obligatory to benefit from this permission, because this leave is only for those days when travelling, and it is obligatory afterwards to make up those fasts which have been missed. As regards the shortening of prayers during a journey, because the shortfall does not have to be made up later on, it is essential to take advantage of this permission. However, since fasts missed on a journey must be observed later on, it means that this permission is only to save the traveller from hardship. If a person experiences no hardship on a journey, he can perform the obligation of fasting during Ramaḍān. The Qur'ān clearly states: "Allāh desires ease for you" (2:185), so when there is ease on a journey, there is no harm in fasting, and the fast is valid.

Ch. 34:   When fasting for some days in Ramaḍān and then travelling

1944 Ibn 'Abbās reported that the Messenger of Allāh ﷺ set out towards Makkah in Ramaḍān and he fasted. When he reached al-Kadīd he broke the fast, so people also broke the fast. Abū 'Abdullāh (Bukhārī) says: Al-Kadīd is the water between 'Usfān and Qudaid.[55]

1945 Abū al-Dardā' reported: We set out with the Prophet ﷺ on one of his journeys on a day so hot that a man would put his hand over his head due to the extreme heat, and no one among us was fasting except the Prophet ﷺ and Ibn Rawāḥah.[56]

Ch. 35:   The saying of the Prophet ﷺ regarding a person on whom shade was made and it was extremely hot: "It is not a virtuous act to fast on a journey."

1946 Jābir ibn 'Abdullāh reported: The Messenger of Allāh ﷺ was on a journey and he saw a crowd and a man over whom shade was made. He said: "What is this?" People said: "He is fasting." He (the Holy Prophet) said: "It is not a virtuous act to fast on a journey." [57]

Ch. 36:   The Companions of the Prophet ﷺ would never find fault with one another for fasting or not fasting (during a journey)

1947 Anas ibn Mālik reported: We used to be on a journey with the Prophet ﷺ and a person who was fasting would not find fault with anyone

---

[55] This journey was for the conquest of Makkah. The Holy Prophet set out from Madīnah with ten thousand fighting men during the month of Ramaḍān and he kept on fasting till he reached Kadīd which is two stages of journey from Makkah. During this journey some Companions fasted and some did not. Ṭaḥāwī reports that when the Holy Prophet reached Kadīd, he came to know that fasting was difficult for people. So he asked for a cup of milk and broke his fast in front of the people. There is a report in Ṣaḥīḥ Muslim that it was at the time of 'Aṣr, and in the report just before this it has been mentioned that even after that some people kept on fasting and the Holy Prophet said that these people were disobedient (Muslim, book: 'Fasting', ch. 15).

[56] The fact that the Holy Prophet was fasting in spite of extremely hot weather, whereas none of the Companions except Rawāḥah was fasting, clearly shows that in this regard there was a free choice for the people. A person who can bear the hardship of fasting because of his greater stamina is allowed to fast during a journey.

[57] The man had imposed unnecessary hardship on himself in performing a religious observance, which is in fact against the teachings of Islam, as the Qur'ān says in connection with fasting: "Allāh desires ease for you, and He does not desire hardship for you" (2:185). The Holy Prophet dispelled the idea that it is a great virtue to bear unnecessary hardship by fasting during a journey.

who was not fasting, nor would a person who was not fasting find fault with anyone who was fasting.[58]

Ch. 37:   One who breaks fast during travelling to show people

1948 Ibn 'Abbās reported: The Messenger of Allāh ﷺ set out from Madīnah towards Makkah and he fasted till he reached 'Usfān. Then he asked for water and raised it in his hand to show it to people and broke the fast, until he reached Makkah.[59] This happened in Ramaḍān. Ibn 'Abbās used to say: The Messenger of Allāh ﷺ used to fast as well as break the fast (in a journey), so whoever wishes may fast and whoever wishes may break it.[60]

Ch. 38:   "And those who find it extremely hard may effect redemption..." (the Qur'ān, 2:184)

Ibn 'Umar and Salamah ibn al-Akwa' said: This (verse) has been abrogated by the following:[61] "The month of Ramaḍān is that in which the Qur'ān was revealed, a guidance to people and clear proofs of the guidance and the Criterion. So whoever of you is present in the month, he shall fast in it, and whoever is sick or on a journey, (he shall fast) a (like) number of other days. Allāh desires ease for you, and He does not desire hardship for you, and (He desires) that you should complete the number and that you should exalt the greatness of Allāh for having guided you and that you may give thanks" (2:185).

Ibn Abū Lailā reported that the Companions of Muḥammad ﷺ told us: When (the command to fast in) Ramaḍān was revealed, it was hard for them. So whoever could feed a poor person every day, he would give up fasting while he was one of those who were able to fast, and this was allowed to them. This was abrogated by the following verse: "And that you fast is better for you..." (2:184).[62]

---

[58] This is the teaching of moderation. Islam has allowed much freedom of choice in the details of the observance of its teachings.

[59] The meaning is that he did not then resume fasting until he reached Makkah.

[60] This is a repetition of h. 1944. According to some reports he discontinued fasting at al-Kadīd and according to others at Kurā' al-ghamīm. Here it is 'Usfān and in h. 1944 it is al-Kadīd. These places are very near to each other.

[61] See the next footnote for this statement about abrogation.

[62] There is disagreement between the earlier statement of Ibn 'Umar and Salamah ibn al-Akwa', given without a chain of reporters, and the ḥadīth reported here by Ibn Abū Lailā in the same chapter heading. Ibn 'Umar says that the verse beginning "The month of Ramaḍān is..."

Thus they were commanded to fast.[63]

1949 It is reported of Ibn 'Umar that he read (the words of 2:184) "may effect redemption by feeding a poor one," and said: "This is abrogated."

Ch. 39:   When to make up for fasts missed in Ramaḍān?[64]

(2:185) has abrogated the words of 2:184 which say: "those who find it extremely hard may effect redemption". But according to this ḥadīth, this was abrogated by the last words of 2:184 itself which say: "and that you fast is better for you." There is a report from Ibn 'Abbās in the Book of Commentary of the Qur'ān (h. 4505) that the words of 2:184, "those who find it extremely hard may effect redemption by feeding a poor person", are not abrogated. In this disagreement, the view of Ibn 'Abbās is acceptable because those who consider these words as abrogated do so due to the fact that they cannot reconcile these words with the verse 2:185, but Ibn 'Abbās says they can be reconciled. The standpoint that there are some commands in the Qur'ān which cannot be reconciled with certain other commands is contrary to an argument which the Qur'ān itself puts forward to support that it is a Divine revelation: "And if it were from any other than Allāh, they would have found in it many a discrepancy" (4:82). This statement in the verse 2:184, that "those who find it extremely hard", does not contradict the command to fast because preceding it there is mention of people who are ill or are on a journey. The word "those" here refers to such people, included among whom are those who are too old, and pregnant and breast-feeding women. The word *yuṭīqūna-hu* means those who find it extremely hard to make up missed fasts in other days as well. Such people can effect redemption by feeding poor people and thus there is no abrogation.

[63] It seems to be the personal view of the narrator that this verse contained the permission to allow people to feed a poor person instead of fasting. So when the words of the next verse made the position clear, he concluded that they abrogated the earlier permission. In fact, it was not any words of the Qur'ān which were abrogated, but rather it was the misconception about their meaning which was in someone's mind which was removed, and it is this removal which is referred to as *naskh,* which also means abrogation.

[64] 'Alī and 'Ā'ishah are of the view that there should be no interval between the fasts of Ramaḍān and the making up of any fasts missed during Ramaḍān, and it is necessary that the latter follow the former connectedly, without a break. Those who take religious matters in the literal sense also hold this view. Apparently, Bukhārī intends to say that it is not necessary for them to follow immediately and in support of his view he has quoted a saying of Ibn 'Abbās who, in his support, quoted the words from the Qur'ān "he shall fast a like number of other days" (2:184) because these contain no condition of making up the missed fasts immediately. This seems to be the correct position. According to the majority opinion, if the missed fasts have not been performed before the start of the next Ramaḍān, without valid cause, then in addition to completing the missing fasts, the redemption (*fidyah*) of feeding a poor person has to be made for each such fast, as reported by Abū Hurairah and Ibn 'Abbās. According to Ibrāhīm Nakh'ī and Imām Abū Ḥanīfah the missed fasts have only to be made up and there is no requirement for *fidyah*. Bukhārī has also supported this by the argument that there is no *fidyah* mentioned along with the words "he shall fast a like number of other days" (2:184), nor is it established by any saying of the Holy Prophet. There is a report from Ibn 'Umar with sound transmission that if, due to illness, the missed fasts could not be made up by the time of the next Ramaḍān, then only the *fidyah* is required for them, while if fasts are missed again in that Ramaḍān also, then they should be made up. This is the correct view in the light of the words: "and those who find it extremely hard may effect redemption by feeding a poor man" (2:184).

Ibn ʿAbbās said: There is nothing wrong in completing the missed fasts on non-successive days, because of the Word of Allāh, the Most High: "He shall fast a like number of other days" (2:184). Saʿīd ibn al-Musayyab has said about fasting for the ten days (of Dhul Ḥajjah): It is not right before completing (the missed fasts of) Ramaḍān. Ibrāhīm said: In case of negligence (in completing the missed fasts) till the next month of Ramaḍān comes, the fasts of both of the months must be completed, and the feeding (of the poor as *fidyah*) is not necessary. It is reported *mursal* from Abū Hurairah,[65] and reported from Ibn ʿAbbās, that he should feed (the poor as *fidyah*), but Allāh has not mentioned the feeding and only said: "he shall fast a like number of other days".

1950 Abū Salamah reported that he heard ʿĀ'ishah say: "It used to happen to me that I had to make up missed fasts from Ramaḍān and I could not make them up but in the month of Shaʿbān." Yaḥyā said: "Because of being busy in service of the Prophet ﷺ." [66]

Ch. 40: **A menstruating woman should leave fast and prayer**

Abū az-Zinād said: Many a time the path of religion and truth are in conflict with one's opinion, and Muslims have no option but to follow the religion. One of these cases is that a menstruating woman must make up (her missed) fasting later but needs not to make up (her missed) ritual prayers.

1951 Abū Saʿīd (al-Khudrī) reported that the Prophet ﷺ said: "Is it not the case that when she is having menstruation, she neither prays nor fasts? Then this is the defect in her (observance of) religion." [67]

Ch. 41: **One who died and fasts are due on him**

Al-Ḥasan said: If thirty men fast on his behalf for one day, it is allowed.[68]

---

[65] A ḥadīth is *mursal* if it is reported by someone from the generation after the Companions, who does not report from a Companion.

[66] This shows that it is permissible to delay the making up of missed fasts. It is stated in h. 1969 that the Holy Prophet used to fast frequently in the month of Shaʿbān. That might be the reason why ʿĀ'ishah used to delay the missing fasts till Shaʿbān. The reason which she herself has given is that this was due to her preoccupation in serving the Holy Prophet. Although the Holy Prophet used to visit his wives by turns, it is a fact that he spent most of his time with ʿĀ'ishah. Spending nights with the wives by turns is a different matter.

[67] This is a repetition of a small part of h. 304.

[68] If a person dies and he had yet to make up some missed fasts, apparently Bukhārī holds the

1952 'Ā'ishah reported that the Messenger of Allāh ﷺ said: "One who dies and fasts are due on him, his guardian can keep fasts on his behalf."

1953 Ibn 'Abbās reported: A man came to the Prophet ﷺ and said: "O Messenger of Allāh, my mother has died, and fasts of one month are due on her. Can I complete them on her behalf?" He said: "Yes. The obligation due to Allāh has the greatest right that it should be fulfilled."

(In another version) Ibn 'Abbās reported: A woman said to the Prophet ﷺ: "My sister has died."

(In another version) Ibn 'Abbās reported: A woman said to the Prophet ﷺ: "My mother has died and she had a vow of fasting to be fulfilled."

(In another version) Ibn 'Abbās reported: A woman said to the Prophet ﷺ: "My mother has died and fifteen days of fasting is due on her." [69]

Ch. 42: When should the fast be broken?

Abū Saʿīd al-Khudrī broke the fast when the disc of the sun disappeared.

1954 'Umar ibn al-Khaṭṭāb reported that the Messenger of Allāh ﷺ said: "When the night advances from this side and the day departs from that side, and the sun sets, a person fasting should break the fast."

---

view that his representative or one in charge of his affairs can complete the fasts on his behalf. The Ahl Ḥadīth and followers of Imam Shāfiʿī are also of the same view and the two reports in this chapter appear to support the same. The view of Imām Abū Ḥanīfah and Imām Mālik, as well as the later view of Imām Shāfiʿī, is that no one can fast on anyone else's behalf. The principle is that in performing any bodily act of worship, no one can be deputized or made representative to do so on someone's behalf. The purpose of such acts of worship is self-purification and spiritual progress, and this cannot be achieved by someone else performing the act. Also, in the case of an old person who cannot fast, redemption is only effected by feeding poor people, while no one holds that fasting can be performed on his behalf by another person, and in lacking capacity the old person and a deceased person are in the same position. Again, in the case of prayers, deputizing someone else or appointing a representative to perform prayers is not regarded as correct by anyone. On this basis, the reports in which it is mentioned that fasts can be kept on behalf of a deceased person have been interpreted to mean the redemption of feeding a poor person for every fast missed. The same view is recorded from 'Ā'ishah and Ibn 'Abbās, who are also the narrators of the two reports in this chapter.

[69] There is much disagreement among the reporters of this ḥadīth. In h. 1513 it is said that the questioner was a woman, who in that case asked about performing *Ḥajj* for her father. Here in h. 1953 too, except in the first report where the questioner was a man, in all other reports a woman has been mentioned. Again, some reports say "My sister has died" while in others the wording is: "My mother has died." According to some reports, one month's fasting is due on the deceased, according to others the deceased had made a vow of fasting, and still others say that fifteen fasts are due on the deceased. That is why some Ḥadīth scholars have regarded this ḥadīth as unsatisfactory and thus declared it as unreliable.

1955 ʿAbdullāh ibn Abī Aufā reported: We were on a journey with the Messenger of Allāh ﷺ and he was fasting. When the sun set, he asked someone: "O you, get up and mix ground-barley for us." He said: "O Messenger of Allāh, should you not wait for a while?" He (the Holy Prophet) asked again: "Get down and mix ground-barley for us." He said: "O Messenger of Allāh, should you not wait for a while?" He (the Holy Prophet) asked yet again: "Get down and mix ground-barley for us." He said: "You are yet in daytime." He (the Holy Prophet) asked again: "Get down and mix ground-barley for us." He got down and mixed it for them. The Prophet ﷺ drank it and then said: "When you see the night has advanced from this side, a person fasting should break the fast." [70]

Ch. 43:   To break fast with whatever is available, water etc.

1956 ʿAbdullāh ibn Abī Aufā said: We were travelling with the Messenger of Allāh ﷺ and he was fasting. When the sun set... [71]

He got down and mixed it. Then he (the Holy Prophet) said: "When you see the night advancing from this side, a person fasting should break the fast." And he pointed with his finger towards the east.

Ch. 44:   To make haste in breaking the fast

1957 Sahl ibn Saʿd reported that the Messenger of Allāh ﷺ said: "People will continue to benefit as long as they hasten in breaking the fast." [72]

1958 Ibn Abī Aufā reported: I was on a journey with the Prophet ﷺ. He fasted till the evening and said to a man: "Get down and mix ground-barley for me." He said: "Should you not wait till (later in) the evening?" He (the Holy Prophet) asked again: "Get down and mix ground-barley for me. When you see the night has advanced from this side, a person fasting should break the fast." [73]

---

[70] This is a repetition of h. 1941.

[71] This ḥadīth is a repetition of h. 1941, in words similar to h. 1955. At this point occurs the exchange between the Holy Prophet and the man as in h. 1955, but here it is only once, and not twice, that the man says: "O Messenger of Allāh, should you not wait for a while?" After this exchange, h. 1956 differs somewhat from h. 1955.

[72] One benefit is that they will save themselves from unnecessary hardship, as not breaking the fast after sunset is to subject oneself to hardship for no reason. Moreover, they will be acting in a balanced way, avoiding both extremes.

[73] This is a briefer repetition of h. 1941. See also h. 1955 and h. 1956 above.

Ch. 45: If the fast was broken in Ramaḍān and then the sun appears (again)

1959 Asmā', daughter of Abū Bakr, reported: During the time of the Prophet ﷺ we broke the fast on a cloudy day and then the sun appeared.

Hishām was asked: "Were they commanded to make up the fast (by another fast)?" He said: "There is no other way but to make it up." Ma'mar said: "I heard Hishām saying: I do not know whether they made up the fast or not." [74]

Ch. 46: Fasting by children

'Umar said to a drunken man in Ramaḍān: "Woe on you! Even our children are fasting." Then he beat him.[75]

1960 Ar-Rubayyi', daughter of Mu'awwadh, reported: The Prophet ﷺ sent (a messenger) to the localities of the Anṣār on the morning of *'Āshūrah* (saying): "Whoever has eaten in the morning, he should fast for the rest of the day, and whoever is fasting since the morning, he should complete the fast." [76]

She added: After that we would fast on the day of *'Āshūrah,* and make our children fast. We used to make toys of wool for them, and if one of them cried for food we would give him the toy, until the time of breaking the fast.[77]

---

[74] Asmā' did not say that they were commanded to make up for that fast, which they broke before sunset, by another fast. In fact, her statement clearly shows that it was considered a properly completed fast. Had that not been so, they would have been commanded to make up for it by another fast. When Hishām, who transmitted this report from Fāṭimah, who had reported it from Asmā', was asked whether it was commanded to make up the fast by another fast, he gave his opinion that there was no other option but to make it up, but added that he did not know as a matter of fact whether they fasted again to make up for it. The majority opinion is that in such a case it is obligatory to make up for the fast. However, since in case of eating by forgetfulness or by mistake, it is not required to repeat the whole fast, the same should apply when it was erroneously decided that the sun had set.

[75] Followers of Imām Mālik hold that non-adults should not fast. Bukhārī has quoted this saying of 'Umar that "even our children are fasting". And there is the statement in h. 1960 that children had to fast on the day of *'Āshūrah,* even though it was an optional fast. Thus there is no harm if children are asked to keep a few fasts in order to get them accustomed to it, provided there is no great hardship involved. However, the teachings of Islām do not require non-adults to fast.

[76] Up to here this is a repetition of h. 1924. The following part is an addition to it.

[77] It appears that the Holy Prophet was unaware that children were being made to fast and, when asking for food, were placated with toys. It is far from the kind and affectionate man that the Holy Prophet Muḥammad was, that he would have asked children to fast or approved of such

Ch. 47: **Combining fasts (i.e., joining fasts together without a break at night) and one who said: There is no fast at night**

As (Allāh) the Most High said: "Then complete the fast till night-fall" (2:187). The Prophet ﷺ forbade this out of mercy for them, and that their energy may remain, and because severity in religion is disapproved.[78]

1961 Anas reported from the Prophet ﷺ that he said: "Do not combine fasts." People said: "But you combine them." He said: "I am not like any of you, for I am given (spiritual) food and drink", or he said "for I spend the night being given food and drink." [79]

1962 ʿAbdullāh ibn ʿUmar reported: The Messenger of Allāh ﷺ forbade combining fasts. People said: "But you combine them." He said: "I am not like you, for I am given (spiritual) food and drink."

1963 Abū Saʿīd reported that he heard the Prophet ﷺ saying: "Do not combine fasts. If you want to combine them, do so as far as *saḥar* (the starting time of the next fast)." People said: "But you combine them, O Messenger of Allāh." He said: "I am not like you, for while I spend the night, the One Who feeds gives me food and the One Who provides drink gives me drink."

1964 ʿĀ'ishah reported: The Messenger of Allāh ﷺ forbade combining fasts out of mercy for them. So people said: "But you combine them." He said: "I am not like you, for my Lord gives me food and drink."

Ch. 48: **Warning the one who combines fasts frequently**

Anas reported it from the Prophet ﷺ.

1965 Abū Hurairah said: The Messenger of Allāh ﷺ forbade the combining of fasts. A man from among Muslims said to him: "But you combine them, O Messenger of Allāh." He said: "Which of you is like me? While

---

fasting. There is another report that he would ask mothers of infants not to breastfeed their children till the fast ended, implying that he even made infants to fast. It is absurd to attribute this to the Holy Prophet.

[78] The term *wiṣāl* (lit., 'joining', meaning joining fasts together without breaking the fast at night) denotes abstaining intentionally throughout the night, or in any part of the night, from those actions which infringe the fast. It is acknowledged by all that *wiṣāl* brings severity in religion and that the Holy Prophet did not permit it to his Companions. It is also against the commandment of the Qur'ān, as it requires the fast to be ended at night. Some Ḥadīth reports show that the Holy Prophet himself combined fasts and allowed the Companions to fast till the next morning's fast starting meal. He may have allowed this in exceptional cases where the person fasting might have had the necessary stamina and strength.

[79] H. 1961 to h. 1967 are repetitions of h. 1922 in different forms.

I spend the night, my Lord gives me food and drink." When people refused to refrain from combining fasts, he joined with them in combining one day's fast with the next day's fast. Then they saw the new moon (for Eid). He said: "If it had been delayed, I would have continued (the combining of fasting) for you." This was a warning for them when they refused to refrain from combining fasts.[80]

1966 Abū Hurairah reported from the Prophet ﷺ that he said twice: "Be cautious of combining fasts." It was said: "But you combine them." He said: "While I spend the night, my Lord gives me food and drink. So undertake deeds of only the hardship for which you have the strength."

Ch. 49:　Combining the fast till the next morning meal time

1967 Abū Saʿīd al-Khudrī reported that he heard the Messenger of Allāh ﷺ saying: "Do not combine fasts. If you want to combine them, do so as far as *saḥar* (the start time of the next fast). People said: "But you combine them, O Messenger of Allāh." He said: "I am not like you, for while I spend the night, the One Who feeds gives me food and the One Who provides drink gives me drink." [81]

Ch. 50:　One who adjures his brother to break his voluntary fast, to make up the fast later is not required for him when it is appropriate for him (to break it)

1968 Abū Juḥaifah reported: The Prophet ﷺ established brotherhood between Salmān and Abū ad-Dardā'.[82] Salmān came to meet Abū ad-Dardā' and found Umm ad-Dardā' (his wife) was dressed poorly. He asked her: "Why are you in this state?" She said: "Your brother Abū ad-Dardā' feels no need of worldly things." Meanwhile Abū ad-Dardā' came in and prepared food for Salmān. He asked Abū ad-Dardā': "Eat with me." Abū ad-Dardā' said: "I am fasting." Salmān said: "I will not eat unless you eat." So Abū ad-Dardā' ate (with him).

---

[80] See h. 1922. It appears that the Holy Prophet's act was in protest and also to make them realise that it entails unnecessary hardship which most people do not have the strength to bear. Considering the obedience of the Companions to the commands of the Holy Prophet, it is difficult to believe that they could have refused to refrain from combining fasts in spite of his repeated instructions.

[81] This is a repetition of h. 1922 with words similar to those of h. 1963.

[82] After the migration to Madīnah, the Holy Prophet established strong bonds of brotherhood between individuals from among the emigrants from Makkah and individuals from among the helpers at Madīnah. Salmān came to Madīnah after 3 A.H. This bond of brotherhood must have been established after his arrival.

When it was night, Abū ad-Dardā' rose to stand up (for prayer), but Salmān said: "Go to sleep". So he went to sleep. Again (after a while) he rose to stand up (for prayer), but Salmān said: "Go to sleep." So he went to sleep. When it was the last part of the night, Salmān said to him: "Now you can get up", and they both said the prayer. Salmān told him: "Allāh has a right over you, and your own self has a right over you, and your family has a right over you. So fulfil the rights of everyone who has a right over you." Abū ad-Dardā' came to the Prophet ﷺ and mentioned this incident to him. The Prophet ﷺ said: "Salmān spoke the truth." [83]

Ch. 51:   Fasting in the month of Sha‘bān

1969 ‘Ā’ishah reported: The Messenger of Allāh ﷺ would carry on fasting till we said that he would not stop fasting. And he would cease fasting till we said that he would not fast (again). I did not see the Messenger of Allāh ﷺ fasting for a whole month except Ramaḍān, and I did not see him fasting in any other month more than in the month of Sha‘bān.

1970 ‘Ā’ishah related: The Prophet ﷺ did not keep more fasts in any other month than in the month of Sha‘bān. He used to fast throughout Sha‘bān[84] and used to say: "Undertake only those deeds for which you have the strength, as Allāh does not get tired but you get tired." [85] And the prayer dearest to the Prophet ﷺ was that which was performed with regularity, although it may be little. And whenever he said any (voluntary) prayer, he did it regularly.

Ch. 52:   What is mentioned regarding the fasting of the Prophet ﷺ and his breaking the fast

1971 Ibn ‘Abbās reported: The Prophet ﷺ never fasted for a whole month except Ramaḍān. And (in other months) he would carry on fasting until someone could say: "By Allāh, he will not stop fasting." And he would cease fasting until someone could say: "By Allāh, he will not fast (again)." [86]

---

[83] Moderation is the most excellent teaching. Acts of worship of Allāh should be performed within the limitation which allows a person to discharge his obligations and responsibilities to himself and to other people.

[84] According to h. 1969 and h. 1971, the Holy Prophet never fasted for the whole month except in Ramaḍān. Therefore, by "throughout" here is meant during much of Sha‘bān. It was also his practice to fast on the 13th, 14th and 15th of every month.

[85] This statement has occurred in h. 43. Ibn Athīr says that it means "Surely Allāh never gets tired but you get tired or you cannot bear it", or "Allāh does not abandon you but you get tired of the act", or "Allāh does not withdraw His blessings from you but you get tired of asking Him" (*Jāmi‘ al-Uṣūl*, vol. 1, pp. 88, 303.).

[86] This is a repetition of h. 1969 with differences.

1972 Anas said: Sometimes the Messenger of Allāh ﷺ would not fast in a month till we thought that he would not fast in that month, and sometimes he used to fast in a month till we thought he would not leave off fasting at all that month; and if you wanted to see him praying at night, you could see him praying, and if you wanted to see him sleeping, you could also see him sleeping.[87]

1973 Ḥumaid informed that he asked Anas about the fasting of the Prophet ﷺ. He said: Whenever I desired to see him fasting in a month, I could see him (fasting), and whenever not fasting I could see him (not fasting), and whenever (I desired to see him) praying at night I could see him (praying), and whenever sleeping I could see him (sleeping). I never touched velvet or silk which was softer than the hand of the Messenger of Allāh ﷺ and never smelled musk or perfume more pleasant than the smell of Messenger of Allāh ﷺ.[88]

Ch. 53:   Right of the guest while the host is fasting

1974 ʿAbdullāh ibn Amr ibn al-ʿĀṣ related: "The Messenger of Allāh ﷺ came to me." Then he mentioned this ḥadīth, that is: "Your guest has a right over you and your wife has a right over you." So I asked him: "How was the fast of (the prophet) David?" He said: "Half of the time (i.e., fasting every other day)." [89]

Ch. 54:   Right of the body while (one is) fasting

1975 ʿAbdullāh ibn Amr ibn al-ʿĀṣ related: The Messenger of Allāh ﷺ said to me: "O ʿAbdullāh, have I not been informed that you fast during the day and pray during the (whole) night?" I said: "Indeed (I do), O Messenger of Allāh!" He said: "Do not do it (like that). Fast, but also leave off fasting. Pray (during the night), but also sleep. For, your body has a right over you, your eyes have a right over you, your wife has a right over you and your guest has a right over you. It is sufficient for you to fast three days a month, for each good deed brings you ten times the reward (for the deed), so this would be like fasting all the time."

ʿAbdullāh said: I insisted on hardship, so hardship was imposed on me. I said: "O Messenger of Allāh, I have more strength (to fast)." He said: "Then fast like the prophet of Allāh, David, peace be upon him, and no more than

---

[87] This is a repetition of h. 1141 in the same words.

[88] This is a repetition of h. 1141 with the addition at the end: "I never touched ..."

[89] This is a brief repetition of h. 1976.

that." I asked him: "How was the fast of the prophet David, peace be upon him?" He said: "Half of the time (i.e., fasting every other day)."

'Abdullāh used to say afterwards when he became old: "I wish I had accepted the relief given by the Prophet ﷺ (to fast three days a month)." [90]

Ch. 55:   Fasting every day all the time

1976 'Abdullāh ibn 'Amr said: The Messenger of Allāh ﷺ was informed that I had said: "By God! I will most certainly fast every day and pray all night as long as I live." I said to him: "May my parents may be sacrificed for your sake, I have said so." He said: "You are not able to do that. So fast (for a few days) and then leave it off (for a few days), pray and also sleep. And fast three days a month, for each good deed brings ten times the reward (for the deed), so this would be like fasting all the time." I said: "I have strength to do more than that." He said: "Fast one day and leave it off for two days." I said: "I have strength to do more than that." He said: "Fast one day and leave it off for one day. That was the fasting of David, peace be upon him, and it is the best fasting." I said: "I have strength to do more than that." The Prophet ﷺ said: "There is no fasting better than that."

Ch. 56:   Right of the family while (one is) fasting

Abū Juḥaifah reported it from the Prophet ﷺ.

1977 'Abdullāh ibn 'Amr said: "The news reached the Prophet ﷺ that I fast every day and pray all through the night. He sent for me — or (the wording is) I met him."

So he (the Holy Prophet) said: "Have I not been informed that you fast but do not leave it off (at all) and pray but do not sleep? Fast but also leave off fasting. Pray (during the night) but also sleep. For, your eyes have a right over you, and your own self and your family have a right over you." He ('Abdullāh) said: "I am stronger than that." He said: "Then fast like David, peace be upon him." He ('Abdullāh) said: "How?" He said: "He used to fast one day and leave it off for one day (i.e., fast every other day), and he did not flee when he met (the enemy)." He ('Abdullāh) said: "Who can guarantee that on my behalf?" [91]

'Aṭā' said: I do not know how fasting permanently was mentioned (in this ḥadīth); however, the Prophet ﷺ said: "That person has not fasted who fasts permanently (i.e., every day)."

---

[90] This is a repetition of h. 1976, with the last comment by 'Abdullāh as additional.

[91] This is a repetition of h. 1975 with difference of wording, and omissions and additions.

Ch. 57:   Fasting every other day

1978 ʿAbdullāh ibn ʿAmr reported from the Prophet ﷺ that he said (to him): "Fast three days a month." He replied: "I have strength to do more than that." This (exchange between them) continued till he (the Holy Prophet) said: "Fast one day and leave it off for one day", and "Complete the recitation of the Qurʾān in one month". He (ʿAbdullāh) said: "I have strength to do more." This (exchange between them) continued till he (the Holy Prophet) said: "In three days." [92]

Ch. 58:   The fasting of David, peace be upon him

1979 ʿAbdullāh ibn ʿAmr ibn al-ʿĀṣ said: The Prophet ﷺ said to me: "You fast every day and say prayers during the night." I said: "Yes." He said: "If you do so, you will have sunken eyes and become weak. That person has not fasted who fasts all the time i.e., every day). Fasting three days (a month) is like fasting all the time." I said: "I have strength to do more than that." He said: "Then fast like David, peace be upon him. He used to fast one day and leave it off for one day (i.e., fast every other day), and he did not flee when he met (the enemy)." [93]

1980 ʿAbdullāh ibn ʿAmr related: The Messenger of Allāh ﷺ was informed about my fasts. So he came to see me and I offered him to sit on a pillow which was stuffed with the bark of a palm tree. But he sat on the ground and the pillow remained between me and him. He said: "Are three days a month (for fasting) not enough for you?" I said: "O Messenger of Allāh (I can do more)!" He said: "Five." I said: "O Messenger of Allāh (I can do more)!" He said: "Seven." I said: "O Messenger of Allāh (I can do more)!" He said: "Nine." I said: "O Messenger of Allāh (I can do more)!" He said: "Eleven." Then the Prophet ﷺ said: "There is no fasting better than the fasting of David, peace be upon him. It was for half of the time. Fast one day and leave it off for one day." [94]

Ch. 59:   Fasting on the 13th, 14th and 15th (*ayyām al-bīḍ*)[95]

1981 Abū Hurairah reported: My friend ﷺ (i.e., the Holy Prophet) advised me to do three things: To fast three days every month, to say two

---

[92] This is a repetition of h. 1976 more briefly with an addition at the end.

[93] This is a repetition of h. 1976 with difference in wording. See also h. 1977.

[94] This is a repetition of h. 1976 with difference in wording, and omissions and additions.

[95] These three days of the lunar month are known as *ayyām al-bīḍ*, or the white days, as these nights are bright due to the full moon.

rak'ahs of the *Ḍuḥā* prayer, and that I say the *Witr* prayer before I go to sleep.[96]

Ch. 60:　He who visits a people and does not break the (voluntary) fast at theirs

1982 Anas reported: The Prophet ﷺ came to visit Umm Sulaim and she brought dates and butter-oil for him. He said: "Put your butter-oil in its cup and your dates in their bag as I am fasting." Then he stood in a corner of the house and said prayers other than the obligatory prayers and prayed for Umm Sulaim and the people of her house. Umm Sulaim said: "O Messenger of Allāh, I have a dear one." He asked: "Who is that?" She said: "Your servant Anas." He (the Holy Prophet) did not omit anything of good in the hereafter and the world in praying for me to be granted it. He (also) said: "O Allāh, Grant him wealth and children, and bless him." I am now one of the wealthiest people among the Anṣār. My daughter Umainah told me that when Ḥajjāj came to Baṣrah, more than 120 of my descendants had been buried.[97]

Ch. 61:　Fasting towards the end of the month

1983 'Imrān ibn Ḥusain reported from the Prophet ﷺ that he asked him — or he asked a man and 'Imrān was listening —"O father of so and so, have you not fasted at the end (*sarar*) of this month." [98] The narrator said: I think he said "it means the month of Ramaḍān." The man replied: "No, O Messenger of Allāh." He (the Holy Prophet) said: "When you finish fasting (in Ramaḍān), fast for two days." Aṣ-Ṣalt did not say: I think it means the month of Ramaḍān.

---

[96] This is a repetition of h. 1178 with a slight difference of wording and a little omission. In the fasting for three days every month, there is no mention here of *ayyām al-bīḍ* or the dates 13th, 14th and 15th.

[97] Ḥajjāj ibn Yūsuf came to Baṣrah in 75 A.H. At that time Anas was more than eighty years old.

[98] According to some, *sarar* means 'middle', that is the 13th, 14th and 15th of the month, while some have taken it to mean the beginning of the month. The majority of lexicologists take it to mean from the 28th to the end of the month (i.e., the last two days if the month is of 29 days, and the last three days if the month is of 30 days). Bukhārī has preferred this view, as according to h. 1914 the Holy Prophet has prohibited fasting on the last two days before the month of Ramaḍān, except if they happen to coincide with such days on which a person habitually fasted (for example, if he always fasted on certain days of the week). It seems that the man whom the Holy Prophet asked, "have you not fasted at the end (*sarar*) of this month", was one who used to fast on those days. However, in view of Holy Prophet's prohibition on fasting before the month of Ramaḍān, he had not fasted before Ramaḍān. Since constancy is considered a good quality, the Holy Prophet told him to make up those fasts after the month of Ramaḍān.

(According to another version) 'Imrān reported from the Prophet ﷺ the words: "At the end (*sarar*) of Sha'bān." [99]

Ch. 62: Fasting on Friday: One who fasts on Friday has the duty to break it

1984 Muḥammad ibn 'Abbād reported: I asked Jābir whether the Prophet ﷺ forbade fasting on Friday? He said: "Yes." It is added (by other narrators): "This is for only Friday by itself." [100]

1985 Abū Hurairah reported: I heard the Prophet ﷺ saying: "None of you should fast on a Friday, unless (he also fasts) the day before it or the day after it." [101]

1986 Juwairiyah, daughter of al-Ḥārith, reported that the Prophet ﷺ came to see her on a Friday while she was fasting. He said: "Did you fast yesterday?" She said: "No." He said: "Do you intend to fast tomorrow?" She said: "No." He said: "Then break it."

In another narration, Juwairiyah said that he ordered her and she broke the fast.

Ch. 63: Can a day be specially set aside (for fasting)

1987 'Alqamah reported that he asked 'Ā'ishah: "Did the Messenger of Allāh ﷺ set aside some days specially (for fasting)?" She said: "No. Whatever he would do, he would persist in it. And who among you has as much strength as the strength that the Messenger of Allāh ﷺ had?" [102]

---

[99] The words in the report itself are: *sarara hādha ash-shahr* ("the end of this month"). The narrator thought this meant the month of Ramaḍān. Apparently, this is senseless because fasts are obligatory throughout Ramaḍān, and there is no point in mentioning the end of Ramaḍān. The correct position is that "this month" means the month of Sha'bān as mentioned in this version, and the same is in the report in Ṣaḥīḥ Muslim (book: 'Fasting', ch. 37). However, it does not show that it is recommended to fast at the end of every month, as is the suggestion in the chapter heading.

[100] This is a repetition of h. 1985.

[101] The Holy Prophet did not, as a rule, like to fix a particular day for fasting outside Ramaḍān. See h. 1987. But he forbade fasting on Friday in particular because it is a day of a gathering when people meet each other and have the opportunity to eat together, which strengthens mutual bonds of love. This is also the reason that fasting is prohibited on the Eid days as stated later on.

[102] In some reports in Ḥadīth the excellence of fasting on certain days of the week has been mentioned, such as Monday or Thursday. Bukhārī has not accepted them. As regards Friday, the day of the notable gathering of the Muslims, the Holy Prophet has forbidden setting that day aside for fasting. However, certain days of the month, such as the 13th, 14th and 15th, have been mentioned in Bukhārī as these were the days when the Holy Prophet used to fast.

Ch. 64: Fasting on the day of *'Arafah*

1988 Umm al-Faḍl, daughter of al-Ḥārith, reported that people with her disagreed on the day of *'Arafah* about the Prophet ﷺ fasting (on that day). Some people said that he was fasting (on the day of *'Arafah*) and others said he was not. So she sent a cup of milk to him while he was staying, riding on his camel, and he drank it.[103]

1989 Maimūnah reported that people were doubtful whether the Prophet ﷺ was fasting or not on the day of *'Arafah*. So she sent a bowl of milk while he had stopped at one stopping place, and he drank from it while people were watching.[104]

Ch. 65: Fasting on the day of Eid-ul-Fiṭr (*'Īd-ul-Fiṭr*)

1990 Abū 'Ubaid, slave of Ibn Azhar, reported: I was present at Eid along with 'Umar ibn al-Khaṭṭāb, who said: "These are two days on which the Messenger of Allāh ﷺ has forbidden fasting: the day on which you break from your fasting, and the other day on which you eat out of your sacrifice." [105]

1991–1992 Abū Sa'īd (al-Khudrī) reported: The Prophet ﷺ forbade fasting on the day of *Fiṭr* and of Sacrifice, and wrapping one's body with a cloth so that the hands are shut up within, and a man's sitting on his buttocks with his knees raised up while wearing only one piece of cloth,[106] [1992] and praying after *Fajr* and *'Aṣr* prayers.

Ch. 66: Fasting on the day of Sacrifice

1993 Abū Hurairah reported: Two fasts and two kinds of sale are forbidden: fasting on the day of *Fiṭr* and (on the day of) Sacrifice, and *mulāmasah* and *munābadhah*.[107]

---

[103] This is a repetition of h. 1661. To settle the disagreement whether the Holy Prophet was fasting or not, she sent him a cup of milk which he drank. This shows that the Holy Prophet did not fast on the day of *'Arafah*. In some reports in Ḥadīth fasting on the day of *'Arafah* has been considered so meritorious that it is said that it eradicates the sins of the past year as well as of the coming year. Bukhārī has contradicted these reports by quoting this ḥadīth.

[104] This is a repetition of h. 1661. According to h. 1661 (and h. 1988) Umm Faḍl was the one who sent the milk, but in this ḥadīth it was Maimūnah. Umm Faḍl and Maimūnah were sisters, so perhaps they both agreed to send it.

[105] On the days of gathering for Eid-ul-Fiṭr and Eid-ul-Aḍḥā, the socialising and the eating together intensify love and cordial relations. That is why on both Eids fasting has been prohibited by the Holy Prophet.

[106] This is a repetition of h. 367. For explanation, see the note on that ḥadīth.

[107] This is a briefer repetition of h. 584, but with some addition. See the note on h. 584. See

1994 Ziyād ibn Jubair reported: A man came to Ibn 'Umar and said: "A man made a vow to fast one day" — I think he said on Monday — "and it turned out to be the day of Eid." Ibn 'Umar said: "Allāh has enjoined to fulfil the vow and the Prophet ﷺ has forbidden fasting on that day." [108]

1995 Abū Sa'īd al-Khudrī, who had taken part in twelve battles in the company of the Prophet ﷺ, reported: I heard four things from the Prophet ﷺ which I liked very much. He said: "A woman should not go on a journey of two days except with her husband or a permissible male relative (*mahram*)." "There is no fasting on two days: Eid-ul-Fiṭr and Eid-ul-Aḍḥā." "There is no prayer after the *Fajr* prayer till the sun rises, nor after the *'Aṣr* prayer till the sun sets." "There should be no journey except to three mosques: the Sacred Mosque, and the Aqṣā Mosque and this Mosque of mine."[109]

Ch. 67:   Fasting during the *Tashrīq* days[110]

1996 Hishām reported: My father informed me that 'Ā'ishah used to fast on the days of Minā. And his father (Hishām's father 'Urwah) also fasted on those days.

1997–1998 'Ā'ishah and Ibn 'Umar reported: It is not permitted to fast during the days of *Tashrīq* except for him who does not have the sacrificial animal with him.

1999 Ibn 'Umar reported: Fasting is for the one who performs *tamattu'* between *'Umrah* and *Ḥajj*,[111] (who may fast) up to the day of *'Arafah*. But if he could not find a sacrificial animal, nor has he fasted, he should fast during the days of *Tashriq*.

---

also h. 368. *Mulāmasah* and *munābadhah* were two kinds of sales in pre-Islamic times. *Mulāmasah* was that if a buyer touched an item which was for sale, this confirmed the transaction and he was obliged to buy it. *Munābadhah* was that the same happened if the seller threw an item for sale towards the buyer; it committed the buyer to buy it.

[108] Even if someone has made a vow to fast on a certain day and it happens to fall on an Eid day, he is not allowed to fulfil the vow.

[109] This is a repetition of h. 1197 with an addition at the beginning and minor difference of wording.

[110] The *Tashrīq* days are the day of Eid-ul-Aḍḥā and the two or the three days after it. *Sharq* means the brightening of the sun. These days are so-called because the sacrifice is made on these days after the sun has risen. The Companions of the Holy Prophet differed in regard to fasting on these days, as is evident from Ḥadīth reports.

[111] *Tamattu'* is the performance of both *'Umrah* and *Ḥajj* in one visit, while entering into *Iḥrām* separately for each of them.

Ch. 68: Fasting on the day of *'Āshūrā'*

2000 'Abdullāh ibn 'Umar reported that the Prophet ﷺ, regarding the day of *'Āshūrā'*, said: "Whoever wishes may fast (on this day)."

2001 'Ā'ishah said: The Messenger of Allāh ﷺ ordered fasting on the day of *'Āshūrā'*. When (fasting in) the month of Ramaḍān was made obligatory, anyone who so wished fasted (on the day of *'Āshūrā'*) and anyone who so wished did not fast." [112]

2002 'Ā'ishah reported: On the day of *'Āshūrā'* the Quraish used to fast in the days of Ignorance. The Messenger of Allāh ﷺ also used to observe fasting on it. When he came to Madīnah, he continued to observe fasting on it and ordered (Muslims) to fast on it. When (fasting in) the month of Ramaḍān was made obligatory, he gave up fasting on the day of *'Āshūrā'*. Then anyone who so wished fasted on that day and anyone who so wished gave it up." [113]

2003 Ḥumaid ibn 'Abdur Raḥmān reported that he heard Mu'āwiyah ibn Abū Sufyān, on the day of *'Āshūrā'*, in the year he performed *Ḥajj*, saying on the pulpit: "O people of Madīnah, Where are your religious scholars? I have heard the Messenger of Allāh ﷺ saying: 'This is the day of *'Āshūrā'*. It is not obligatory for you to observe fasting on it, but I am fasting. So anyone who so wishes may fast and anyone who so wishes may not fast'."

2004 Ibn 'Abbās reported: The Messenger of Allāh ﷺ came to Madīnah and saw the Jews fasting on the day of *'Āshūrā'*. He asked: "What is this?" They replied: "This is an auspicious day. This is the day on which Allāh delivered the Children of Israel from their enemies. Moses observed fasting on it." He (the Prophet) said: "I have more right to (commemorate) Moses than you have." So he fasted on that day and ordered (Muslims) to observe fasting on it.

2005 Abū Mūsā reported: The Jews took the day of *'Āshūrā'* as a day of celebration (Eid). So the Prophet ﷺ said (to the Muslims): "You should also observe fasting on it." [114]

2006 Ibn 'Abbās reported: I did not see the Prophet ﷺ intending to fast on a day which was special over other days (for fasting), except the day of *'Āshūrā'* and this month, that is, the month of Ramaḍān.

---

[112] This is a briefer repetition of h. 1893.

[113] This is also a repetition of h. 1893, with additions.

[114] This is a brief repetition of h. 2004. The Jews celebrated on that day as they believed that it was on that day that Moses and the Israelites were saved from the Pharaoh. By way of thanks giving, they fasted on that day.

2007 Salamah ibn al-Akwaʿ reported: The Prophet ﷺ ordered a man of the Banū Aslam to announce among the people: "Whoever has eaten something, he should fast for the rest of the day; and whoever has not eaten anything, he should fast; for it is the day of *ʿĀshūrāʾ*." [115]

---

[115] This is a repetition of h. 1924.

Book 31: *Ṣalāt al-Tarāwīḥ*

Tarāwīḥ Prayers

In the name of Allāh, the Beneficent, the Merciful

Ch. 1: Excellence of one who keeps up optional prayers in Ramaḍān[1]

2008 Abū Hurairah said: I heard the Messenger of Allāh ﷺ say of Ramaḍān: "Whoever keeps it up (i.e., optional night prayers) with faith and seeking the pleasure of Allāh, he is forgiven the sins he committed before."[2]

2009 Abū Hurairah reported that the Messenger of Allāh ﷺ said: "Whoever keeps up (the optional night) prayers in Ramaḍān with faith and seeking the pleasure of Allāh, he is forgiven the sins he committed before."

Ibn Shihāb said: "The Messenger of Allāh ﷺ died and it continued like that. Then it continued like that during the Caliphate of Abū Bakr and the early period of the Caliphate of ʿUmar."[3]

2010 ʿAbdur Raḥmān ibn ʿAbdul Qārī reported: I went out with ʿUmar ibn al-Khaṭṭāb one night in Ramaḍān towards the mosque and found that people were in separate groups. One man would be praying alone, and another one praying while a group is following him in his prayer. Then ʿUmar said: "I think it is better that I should gather them behind one *qārī* (to lead them all in prayer)." Then he resolved (to do it) and gathered them under the lead of Ubayy ibn Kaʿb.

Then I went out with him another night and the people were praying behind their *qārī*. So ʿUmar said: "What an excellent innovation this is! But the part of night during which they will be sleeping is better than that in which

---

[1] The word used here and in h. 2008 and 2009 is *qāma*, meaning "keeps up (prayer)". Here the post-midnight prayer *Tahajjud* is referred to. Just as the daytime during the month of Ramaḍān is distinguished by fasting, the nighttime during this month is distinguished by the particular attention that is paid to *Tahajjud* prayers.

[2] H. 37 is repeated here in almost the same words. See also second part of h. 2014.

[3] H. 37 is repeated here in almost the same words, with this addition of Ibn Shihāb. The words of the addition mean that during the time of the Holy Prophet, the rule of Abū Bakr, and the early period of the rule of ʿUmar, people said *Tahajjud* prayers individually without forming a congregation. It was later on in his Caliphate that ʿUmar organized it as a congregational prayer, as mentioned in the next ḥadīth.

they are praying." He meant the latter part of the night, while people were praying in its first part.[4]

2011–2012 'Urwah reported from 'Ā'ishah, wife of the Prophet ﷺ, that the Messenger of Allāh ﷺ prayed (at night in congregation) and this was in Ramaḍān. [2012] 'Urwah informed that 'Ā'ishah informed him that the Messenger of Allāh ﷺ came out one night in the middle of the night (from his apartment) and said his prayer (i.e., *Tahajjud*) in the mosque and some people said the same prayer with him. Then in the morning people talked about it and (the next night) more of them gathered (in the mosque) and said their prayer with him. Then again in the morning people talked about it and the people in the mosque increased in number on the third night. So the Messenger of Allāh ﷺ came out and prayed and they said their prayer with him. And when it was the fourth night the mosque proved too small for the people who came, (but the Holy Prophet did not come out) till he came out for his morning prayer. When he had finished the *Fajr* prayer, he turned his face towards the people and after reciting the *shahādah* he said: "*Ammā ba'du,* surely it was not that I feared your attendance but I feared lest it (the *Tahajjud* prayer) should be made obligatory on you and you are unable to observe it." Thus did it remain till the Messenger of Allāh ﷺ died.[5]

2013 Abū Salamah ibn 'Abdur Raḥmān reported that he asked 'Ā'ishah: "How did the Messenger of Allāh ﷺ perform prayer during Ramaḍān?" She said: "He never exceeded eleven *rak'ahs* in Ramaḍān or in other months. He would say four *rak'ahs,* and do not ask me about their beauty and their length, then (again) four *rak'ahs,* and do not ask me about their beauty and their length, and then three *rak'ahs.* I asked, 'O Messenger of Allāh! Do you sleep before saying the *Witr* prayer?' He replied: 'O 'Ā'ishah! My eyes sleep but my heart does not!' "[6]

---

[4] 'Umar referred to the congregational prayer at night as an innovation (*bid'ah*) because such prayers were not done in an organised manner before he made these arrangements. It was never prohibited to say these prayers in congregation as the Holy Prophet himself had on one occasion led *Tahajjud* prayer in congregation for three nights successively, discontinuing it for fear that people might take it as being obligatory, as has already been mentioned in h. 729 and also in h. 2011–2012 which follows.

According to Arabic lexicons, *bid'ah* means any new act or new way of doing things. However, in Islamic terminology this term is reserved for unlawful or deplorable actions. Here it has been used in its literal sense. The best time for the prayer at night is the latter part of the night, the time for the *Tahajjud* prayer. Those who cannot get up at that time because they need to go to work in the morning can say this prayer at the start of the night. The optional prayers at the start of the night during the month of Ramaḍān are called *Tarawīḥ*.

[5] See h. 729, h. 924 and h. 1129.

[6] This is a repetition of h. 1147 in almost the same words.

Book 32: *Faḍl Lailat al-Qadr*
Excellence of *Lailat-ul-Qadr*

In the name of Allāh, the Beneficent, the Merciful

Ch. 1:   Excellence of *Lailat-ul-Qadr*

The word of Allāh: "Surely We revealed it on the Night of Majesty — and what will make you comprehend what the Night of Majesty is? The Night of Majesty is better than a thousand months. The angels and the Spirit descend in it by the permission of their Lord for every affair. Peace it is, till the rising of the morning" (the Qur'ān, ch. 97). [1]

Ibn 'Uyainah said: Where it occurs in the Qur'ān *mā adrā-ka* (i.e., "what will make you comprehend", in 97:2 quoted above), it means that Allāh has taught him (the Prophet). Where Allāh says *wa mā yudrī-ka,* it means He has not taught him.[2]

---

[1] *Lailat-ul-Qadr* means the Night of Majesty or Power. Allāh says: "Surely We revealed it on the Night of Majesty" (97:1), that is to say, its revelation started on that night. According to Ḥadīth reports, the first revelation came to the Holy Prophet on the 25th of Ramaḍān. In *Fatḥ al-Bārī* forty-six views are recorded regarding *Lailat-ul-Qadr*. In Ḥadīth reports it is mentioned that the Holy Prophet instructed that one should seek it during the last seven nights of Ramaḍān, or more specifically on the 25th, 27th and 29th nights. However, a believer can only find it after intense devotion and worship. The last ten days or the last week of Ramaḍān have been selected for it because, due to fasting, it is the most effective time to undertake spiritual exertions. Again, as it is not night everywhere in the world at the same time, it means that *Lailat-ul-Qadr* occurs at different times for those seeking it in different places.

The descent of the angels and the Spirit is mentioned in 97:4 as taking place during the *Lailat-ul-Qadr*. Their descent is related to the advent of a prophet because angels impel the hearts of human beings towards righteousness and assist his mission of giving birth to spiritual life. So the period of the mission of a prophet can also be called as a *Lailat-ul-Qadr,* as human souls achieve great spiritual heights during that time. In this regard the Qur'ān also says: "We revealed it on a blessed night — truly We are ever warning. Therein is made clear every affair full of wisdom" (44:3–4). Just as this spiritual awakening is related to the life of a prophet, it is also related to the appointment of a *Mujaddid* (or Divinely-appointed Reformer). And as, according to a ḥadīth, it is promised that a *Mujaddid* shall appear at the head of every century, *Lailat-ul-Qadr* may also refer to the time during which a *Mujaddid* carries out his mission.

[2] A distinction is drawn here between the perfect tense in *mā adrā-ka,* which occurs in 97:2, and the same expression when used with the imperfect tense as *mā yudrī-ka.* The words *mā yudrī-*

2014 Abū Hurairah reported from the Prophet ﷺ that he said: "Whoever fasts during Ramaḍān with faith and seeking the pleasure of Allāh, he is forgiven the sins he committed before,[3] and whoever keeps up (the optional night) prayers in *Lailat-ul-Qadr* with faith and seeking the pleasure of Allāh, he is forgiven the sins he committed before." [4]

Ch. 2:   Seeking *Lailat-ul-Qadr* in the last seven (nights of Ramaḍān)

2015 Ibn 'Umar reported that some Companions of the Prophet ﷺ were shown *Lailat-ul-Qadr* in their dreams in the last seven (nights of Ramaḍān). The Messenger of Allāh ﷺ said: "I notice that your dreams concur on (*Lailat-ul-Qadr* being in) the last seven (nights of Ramaḍān), so whoever wishes to search for it, let him search for it in the last seven." [5]

2016 Abū Salamah reported: I asked Abū Sa'īd (al-Khudrī), who was a friend of mine, and he said: We were observing *I'tikāf* with the Prophet ﷺ in the middle ten days of Ramaḍān. He came out on the morning of the 20th and addressed us saying:

> "I have been shown (the date of) *Lailat-ul-Qadr*, but then I was made to forget it, or I have forgotten it. So search for it in the last ten of the odd (nights). And I saw (in a dream) that I am performing *Sajdah* in mud. So whoever has been observing *I'tikāf* with me, he should return."

So we returned (to observing *I'tikāf*) and we did not see any patch of cloud in the sky. Then a cloud appeared and it rained until the roof of the mosque started leaking, and it was made of branches of palm trees. Prayer was called by *Iqāmah* and I saw the Messenger of Allāh ﷺ performing *Sajdah* in mud so much so that I saw patches of mud on his forehead.[6]

Ch. 3:   Searching for *Lailat-ul-Qadr* in odd (nights) of the last ten
This contains a report from 'Ubādah.

---

ka occur, for example, in the following verse of the Qur'ān: "And what will make you comprehend that the Hour may be near?" (33 : 63); the meaning being that the Holy Prophet has not been given the knowledge whether or not the Hour is near. See also the same expression in 80 : 3.

[3] Up to here, h. 2014 is a repeat of h. 38.

[4] The second part of h. 2014 is a repeat of h. 37 with the difference that, while h. 37 speaks of keeping up the optional night prayers "during Ramaḍān", here it mentions the same "in *Lailat-ul-Qadr*" and the chapter heading is taken from this.

[5] This shows that *Lailat-ul-Qadr* can only be found and experienced by means of conducting a spiritual search, which means performance of hard spiritual exertion.

[6] This is a briefer repetition of h. 813. That ḥadīth first mentions the Holy Prophet and those with him being in *I'tikāf* in the first ten days of Ramaḍān, which is omitted here. See also the repetition in h. 2018.

2017 ʿĀʾishah reported that the Messenger of Allāh ﷺ said: "Search for *Lailat-ul-Qadr* in the odd (nights of the) last ten (nights) of Ramaḍān." [7]

2018 Abū Saʿīd al-Khudrī reported: The Messenger of Allāh ﷺ used to observe *Iʿtikāf* in the ten days of Ramaḍān which are in the middle of the month. He would continue till the 20th night, and when it was the 21st he would return to his house and whoever was observing *Iʿtikāf* with him would also return. One Ramaḍān he continued in *Iʿtikāf* in the night in which he used to return (home). He addressed the people and ordered them whatever Allah wished and then said:

> "I used to observe *Iʿtikāf* in these (middle) ten days, but now it has been disclosed to me that I should observe *Iʿtikāf* in these last ten days. So whoever is observing *Iʿtikāf* with me should remain in his place of *Iʿtikāf*. And I have been shown (the date of) this night (*Lailat-ul-Qadr*), but then I was made to forget it. Search for it, therefore, in the last ten in every odd night. I saw myself (in a dream) performing *Sajdah* in mud."

Then that night the sky became overcast and it rained. The roof of the mosque started leaking at the place where the Prophet ﷺ was praying. This was the night of the 21st. I saw with my own eyes, and I looked at him, departing after the morning prayer with his face covered with mud.[8]

2019 ʿĀʾishah reported from the Prophet ﷺ that he said: "Seek it (i.e., *Lailat-ul-Qadr*)." [9]

2020 ʿĀʾishah reported: The Messenger of Allāh ﷺ used to observe *Iʿtikāf* in the last ten (days) of Ramaḍān, and he used to say: "Search for *Lailat-ul-Qadr* in the last ten (nights) of Ramaḍān."

2021 Ibn ʿAbbās reported that the Prophet ﷺ said: "Seek *Lailat-ul-Qadr* in the last ten (nights) of Ramaḍān. It is when nine nights remain, or seven nights remain, or five nights remain." [10]

2022 Ibn ʿAbbās said that the Messenger of Allāh ﷺ said: "It is in the (last) ten (nights), when nine have passed or seven remain." That is to say,

---

[7] This is a repetition of the second of the two parts of h. 2020.

[8] This is a repetition of h. 813 with some omissions and additions. This ḥadīth makes it clear that it was the night of the 21st when it rained, and it was *Lailat-ul-Qadr*.

[9] H. 2019–2022 cover the same subject in different ways.

[10] These would be the 21st, 23rd, or 25th nights of Ramaḍān. In some reports it is the 25th, 27th, or 29th.

Lailat-ul-Qadr. Ibn ʿAbbās also reported (through other narrators): Seek it on the 24th.[11]

Ch. 4: Knowledge about *Lailat-ul-Qadr* was taken away due to the quarrelling of people

2023 ʿUbādah ibn aṣ-Ṣāmit reported: The Prophet ﷺ came out to inform us about *Lailat-ul-Qadr,* but two men from among the Muslims were quarrelling with one another. So he said: "I came out to inform you about *Lailat-ul-Qadr* but so-and-so were quarrelling with one another, and it (i.e., news about it) was taken away. It may be that this is better for you. So seek it on the 29th, 27th, and the 25th." [12]

Ch. 5: Greater devotion during the last ten days of Ramaḍān

2024 ʿĀʾishah reported: When the last ten days (of Ramaḍān) would come, the Prophet ﷺ used to gird up his loins,[13] keep wake at night (for prayer), and awaken his family (for prayer).

---

[11] What the different statements about which night is *Lailat-ul-Qadr* have in common is that it is an odd night of the last ten nights, i.e., the 21st, 23rd, 25th, 27th, or the 29th. But here the 24th is mentioned. It may be an error in reporting or what is meant may be the night which comes after the 24th fast has been completed.

[12] This is a repetition of h. 49 with slight difference of wording.

[13] The expression used is literally: *tighten his waist belt.* The meaning is to be ready and prepared for the exertion required.

Book 33: *Al-I'tikāf*

I'tikāf (Retiring to the Mosque)

In the name of Allāh, the Beneficent, the Merciful

Ch. 1: **To observe *I'tikāf* in the last ten (days of Ramaḍān) and to observe it in all the mosques[1]**

The word of Allāh: "…and do not touch them while you keep to the mosques. These are the limits of Allah, so do not go near them. Thus does Allāh make clear His messages for people that they may keep their duty." (2:187).

2025 'Abdullāh ibn 'Umar informed: The Messenger of Allāh ﷺ used to observe *I'tikāf* during the last ten days of Ramaḍān.[2]

2026 'Ā'ishah, wife of the Prophet ﷺ, reported that the Prophet ﷺ used to observe *I'tikāf* during the last ten days of Ramaḍān until Allāh caused him to die. Then his wives observed *I'tikāf* after him.[3]

2027 Abū Sa'īd al-Khudrī reported that the Messenger of Allāh ﷺ used to observe *I'tikāf* in the middle ten days of Ramaḍān. One year he observed *I'tikāf* (during these days) until it was the twenty-first night, and this used to be the night on the morning of which he came out of *I'tikāf*. He said: "Whoever was observing *I'tikāf* with me should remain in *I'tikāf* for the last ten days, as I have been shown (the date of) this night (*Lailat-ul-Qadr*) but then I was made to forget it. I saw myself (in a dream) performing *Sajdah* in mud in the morning of that night. So search for it in the last ten (nights), in every odd one."

---

[1] The word *i'tikāf* is from *'ukūf,* meaning to adhere, cling, reside or stay, but in Islamic terminology *I'tikāf* means to stay in a mosque, isolated from worldly affairs. There is every form of devotion in Islām. This devotion of ten days in the year consists of relinquishing all worldly affairs during this period of seclusion, and the last ten days of the month of Ramaḍān are specially set aside for its observance.

[2] This is a repetition of the first part of h. 2020.

[3] This repetition of h. 2020, as in h. 2025, does not mention *Lailat-ul-Qadr,* but it mentions additionally the *I'tikāf* of the wives of the Holy Prophet.

It rained that night, and the roof of the mosque, made of branches of palm trees, was leaking. I saw with my own eyes the Messenger of Allāh ﷺ with signs of mud on his forehead, on the morning of the twenty-first.[4]

Ch. 2: A menstruating woman may comb the hair of one who is observing *I'tikāf*

2028 'Ā'ishah reported: The Prophet ﷺ, while observing *I'tikāf* in the Mosque, used to lean out his head towards me and I would comb it while I had menstruation.[5]

Ch. 3: One observing *I'tikāf* cannot go home except out of necessity

2029 'Ā'ishah, wife of the Prophet ﷺ, said: The Messenger of Allāh ﷺ used to pass his head (into the house) while he was in the Mosque, and I would comb his hair. While observing *I'tikāf* he never used to enter the house except out of necessity.

Ch. 4: Taking of bath by a person observing *I'tikāf*

2030–2031 'Ā'ishah reported: The Prophet ﷺ used to embrace me while I was having menstruation, and he used to extend his head out of the Mosque while observing *I'tikāf* and I would wash it while I was having menstruation.[6]

Ch. 5: To observe *I'tikāf* only for a night

2032 Ibn 'Umar reported that 'Umar asked the Prophet ﷺ: "I made a vow during the time of Ignorance that I would observe *I'tikāf* for one night in the Sacred Mosque." He (the Holy Prophet) said: "Fulfil your vow." [7]

Ch. 6: Women observing *I'tikāf*

2033 'Amrah reported from 'Ā'ishah: "The Prophet ﷺ used to observe *I'tikāf* during the last ten days of Ramaḍān. I used to pitch a tent for him, and he would enter it after saying the morning prayer." Ḥafṣah (a wife of the Holy

---

[4] From the statement of the Holy Prophet till the end of this ḥadīth, it is a repetition of h. 813 with difference of wording, but here also it is made clear that this was the night of 21st Ramaḍān. See also h. 2016 and h. 2018.

[5] This is a briefer repetition of h. 2029. See also h. 2046.

[6] This is a repetition of h. 301.

[7] This *I'tikāf* was not that which is observed during the last ten days of Ramaḍān, but it was a vow which 'Umar made before he was a Muslim. Bukhārī has inferred from it that *I'tikāf* can be observed more generally, so that it can also be observed outside the month of Ramaḍān as well as for any length of time that one wishes.

Prophet) sought permission from ʿĀʾishah to pitch a tent for herself, and she gave her the permission. When Zainab, daughter of Jaḥsh, (a wife of the Holy Prophet) saw this, she pitched another tent (for herself). When it was morning, the Prophet ﷺ saw the tents and he said: "What is all this?" He was informed. So the Prophet ﷺ said: "Do you think righteousness was intended by this?" He abandoned *I'tikāf* in that month, and then he observed it for ten days in the month of Shawwāl.[8]

Ch. 7:   Tents in the mosque

2034 ʿĀʾishah reported that the Prophet ﷺ intended to observe *I'tikāf*. When he went to the place where he intended to observe *I'tikāf*, he saw some tents: the tent of ʿĀʾishah, the tent of Ḥafṣah, and the tent of Zainab. He said: "Do you say righteousness was intended by this?" Then he went away and did not observe *I'tikāf* until he observed it for ten days in the month of Shawwāl.[9]

Ch. 8:   Can a person observing *I'tikāf* go for his needs to the door of the mosque?

2035 Ṣafiyyah, wife of the Prophet ﷺ, informed that she came to visit the Messenger of Allāh ﷺ while he was observing *I'tikāf* in the Mosque during the last ten days of Ramaḍān. She talked to him for a while and then stood up to go back. The Prophet ﷺ also stood up with her to escort her back. When she reached the gate of the Mosque near the door of Umm Salamah, two men of the Anṣār passed by and greeted the Messenger of Allāh ﷺ. The Prophet ﷺ said to them: "Wait, this is Ṣafiyyah, daughter of Ḥuyai." They said: "Glory be to Allāh, O Messenger of Allāh!" (i.e., how could we think evil of you). And this (statement of the Holy Prophet) weighed upon them. The Prophet ﷺ said: "Surely Satan reaches all through man just as blood reaches (all through man) and I feared that he might put an evil thought in your minds." [10]

---

[8] This report shows that women can also observe *I'tikāf,* and the chapter heading is related to this. The Holy Prophet abandoned his *I'tikāf,* and as stated later in h. 2041 he gave instructions to remove the tents, for the reason that there should not be any competition in observing acts of worship, as might be the impression created. It may also be because too many tents might reduce the space in the Mosque for people.

[9] This is a briefer repetition of h. 2033. The pitching of tents in the Mosque was for devotional purposes. Besides this, according to h. 463 when Saʿd ibn Muʿādh was wounded in a battle, a tent was also put up for him in the Mosque.

[10] It means that just as blood flows in the body of a human being so do evil suggestions cast by Satan and his promptings invisibly cast their influence on the human mind. Here the Holy Prophet has tried to show people how to avoid a situation which may lead to suspicion and false allegation. Although everyone was fully convinced of the Holy Prophet's unblemished life and

Ch. 9:   Observance of *I'tikāf*

The Prophet ﷺ came out (of *I'tikāf*) on the morning of the twentieth (of Ramaḍān).

2036 Abū Salamah ibn ʿAbdur Raḥmān said: I asked Abū Saʿīd al-Khudrī, Did you hear the Messenger of Allāh ﷺ mentioning *Lailat-ul-Qadr*? He said: Yes, we were observing *I'tikāf* with the Messenger of Allāh ﷺ in the middle ten days of Ramaḍān. We came out on the morning of the 20th, and the Messenger of Allāh ﷺ addressed us that morning saying:

> "I have been shown (the date of) *Lailat-ul-Qadr*, but I have forgotten it. So search for it in the last ten of the odd (nights). And I saw (in a dream) that I am performing *Sajdah* in mud. So whoever has been observing *I'tikāf* with me, he should return."

So people returned to the Mosque, and we did not see any patch of cloud in the sky. Then a cloud appeared and it rained. Prayer was called by *Iqāmah* and the Messenger of Allāh ﷺ performed *Sajdah* in mud so much so that I saw mud on his nose and forehead.[11]

Ch. 10:   Observance of *I'tikāf* by a woman suffering from metrorrhagia (bleeding outside of periods)

2037 ʿĀʾishah reported: One of the wives of the Messenger of Allāh ﷺ observed *I'tikāf* with him while she suffering from metrorrhagia (bleeding outside of periods). She used to see red and yellow discharge. Often we would place a tray beneath her when she was praying.[12]

Ch. 11:   A woman visiting her husband during his *I'tikāf*

2038 ʿAlī ibn al-Ḥusain reported that Ṣafiyyah, wife of the Prophet ﷺ, informed him that the Prophet ﷺ was in the Mosque and with him were his wives. Then they departed and he said to Ṣafiyyah, daughter of Ḥuyai: "Do not be in a hurry, for I will accompany you." Her house was in Dar Usāmah. So the Prophet ﷺ went out with her. Two men of the Anṣār came across him. They looked at the Prophet ﷺ and made to pass by quickly. The Prophet ﷺ said to them: "Come here. She is Ṣafiyyah, daughter of Ḥuyai." They said: "Glory be to Allāh, O Messenger of Allāh ﷺ." He said: "Surely Satan runs

---

character, nonetheless he was open and above board so that no suspicion or doubt about him could arise.

[11] This is a repetition of h. 813 in almost the words of h. 2016, with only slight differences.

[12] See h. 309–311. This is not menstruation during the normal monthly cycle but menstrual discharge even at other times.

around inside man as blood runs (inside man), and I feared that he might cast an evil thought in your minds." [13]

Ch. 12:　Can one observing *I'tikāf* remove a misconception about himself?

2039 'Alī ibn al-Ḥusain reported that Ṣafiyyah informed him that she came to the Prophet ﷺ while he was observing *I'tikāf*. When she returned, he accompanied her. A man of the Anṣār saw him. When he (the Holy Prophet) saw him, he called him and said: "Come here. She is Ṣafiyyah" — a narrator adds he perhaps said: "This is Ṣafiyyah." (The Holy Prophet went on:) "Surely Satan runs around inside the offspring of Adam as blood runs (inside him)."

I (a narrator) said to Ṣufyān: "Did she come at night?" He replied: "How could it be other than at night?" [14]

Ch. 13:　One who emerges from his *I'tikāf* in the morning[15]

2040 Abū Sa'īd reported: We were observing *I'tikāf* with the Messenger of Allāh ﷺ in the middle ten days (of Ramaḍān). When it was the morning of the 20th, we moved our baggage. The Messenger of Allāh ﷺ came to us and said:

"Whoever has been observing *I'tikāf*, he should return to his place of *I'tikāf*, for I have seen (the date of) this night (*Lailat-ul-Qadr*), and I saw myself (in a dream) performing *Sajdah* in mud."

When he returned to his place of *I'tikāf*, the sky became overcast and it rained. By Him Who sent him (the Holy Prophet) with the Truth, the sky was covered with clouds from the end of that day, and (the roof of) the Mosque was made of branches of palm trees (which started leaking). And I saw signs of mud on his forehead and nose.[16]

Ch. 14:　*I'tikāf* in the month of Shawwāl

2041 'Amrah, daughter of 'Abdur Raḥmān, reported from 'Ā'ishah: The Messenger of Allāh ﷺ used to observe *I'tikāf* in every Ramaḍān. After saying

---

[13] This is a repetition of h. 2035 with some variation of wording.

[14] This again is a repetition of h. 2035, more briefly. The last statement is not part of the original ḥadīth. It was because it was night-time that the Holy Prophet had to say that it was his wife who was with him.

[15] The permissibility of emerging from *I'tikāf* in the morning is shown here, while it is generally believed that one must emerge from *I'tikāf* after sunset. There is thus flexibility in this.

[16] This is a repetition of h. 813 with some brevity and addition. See footnote there.

the morning prayer, he would enter the place where he used to observe *I'tikāf.* 'Ā'ishah asked him permission to observe *I'tikāf,* and he permitted her. So she pitched a tent for herself in the Mosque. When Ḥafṣah heard of it, she pitched a tent, and when Zainab heard of it, she pitched a tent. When the Messenger of Allāh ﷺ left the next day (after the morning prayer), he saw four tents. He asked: "What is all this?" He was informed about them. He said: "What made them do this? Was it the thought of righteousness? Pull them down. I do not see any good in it." So they were removed. He did not observe *I'tikāf* that Ramaḍān, but observed it in the last ten days of Shawwāl.[17]

Ch. 15:   One who does not consider fasting necessary for himself while observing *I'tikāf*

2042 'Abdullāh ibn 'Umar reported from 'Umar ibn al-Khaṭṭāb that he said: "O Messenger of Allāh ﷺ, I made a vow during the time of Ignorance that I would observe *I'tikāf* for one night in the Sacred Mosque." The Prophet ﷺ said to him: "Fulfil your vow." So he observed *I'tikāf* for one night.[18]

Ch. 16:   Making a vow during the time of Ignorance to observe *I'tikāf,* then embracing Islam[19]

2043 Ibn 'Umar reported that 'Umar made a vow during the time of Ignorance that he would observe *I'tikāf* in the Sacred Mosque. A narrator added: I think he said for one night. The Messenger of Allāh ﷺ said to him: "Fulfil your vow." [20]

Ch. 17:   *I'tikāf* in the middle ten days of Ramaḍān

2044 Abū Hurairah reported: The Prophet ﷺ used to observe *I'tikāf* for ten days in every Ramaḍān. When it was the year of his death, he observed *I'tikāf* for twenty days.[21]

---

[17] This is a repetition of h. 2033 with more detail.

[18] This is a repetition of h. 2032 with slight difference of wording and an addition at the end. As the *I'tikāf* was for one night, there could be no fasting in it. From this it is concluded that *I'tikāf* can also be observed without fasting.

[19] *Nazar* is a vow made with God for an intended objective. To fulfil a vow made with God is in any case obligatory. The Qur'ān says: "And fulfil the covenant of Allāh, when you make a covenant" (16:91). Islām strictly requires all oaths and covenants to be fulfilled, even if made during the time of Ignorance before Islām.

[20] This is a repetition of h. 2032 with slight difference of wording.

[21] That is to say, he added the middle ten days to the last ten days.

Ch. 18: He who intends to observe *I'tikāf* but then changes his mind and leaves it

2045 'Amrah, daughter of 'Abdur Raḥmān, reported from 'Ā'ishah that the Messenger of Allāh ﷺ mentioned that he would observe *I'tikāf* in the last ten days of Ramaḍān. 'Ā'ishah asked him permission and he permitted her. Ḥafṣah asked 'Ā'ishah to obtain permission for her, and she did so. When Zainab, daughter of Jaḥsh, saw this, she ordered a tent to be pitched, and it was pitched for her. The Messenger of Allāh ﷺ used to leave for his tent after the (morning) prayer. He saw the tents and asked: "What is all this?" People said: "Tents of 'Ā'ishah, and Ḥafṣah and Zainab." The Messenger of Allāh ﷺ said: "Is it righteousness they intended by this? I am not going to observe *I'tikāf*." He returned back. When the fasting ended, he observed *I'tikāf* for ten days in the month of Shawwāl.[22]

Ch. 19: One observing *I'tikāf* may pass his head into the house for washing

2046 'Ā'ishah reported that she used to comb the hair of the Prophet ﷺ while she was having menstruation and he was observing *I'tikāf* in the Mosque. She would be in her apartment and he would stretch his head towards her.[23]

---

[22] This is a repetition of h. 2033 with some more details. This shows that even while observing *I'tikāf*, it is permitted to cancel it.

[23] This is a repetition of h. 2029. It shows a wife, out of love for her husband, doing something for him.